BAR REVIEW

Practice Questions

MULTISTATE TESTING

celebrating over
35 YEARS
of preparing
law studen
for the b

THOMSON
™
BAR/BRI

SUMMARY OF CONTENTS

Test yourself through the Internet

You can now do the questions in this book with StudySmart® Bar Review Software.

BAR/BRI students with Internet access who are registered for the current bar review course can download the StudySmart® Bar Review software from the BAR/BRI website at **www.barbri.com** once their course begins by doing the following:

1. Select your state and then go to the My BAR/BRI page and select StudySmart® Software to get to the Bar Review software download.
2. Enter your BAR/BRI identification number and your last name.
3. Once you are at the file selection screen, you can click on the file you want to download.
4. Once the download is complete, go to the directory on your computer where the file was stored and double click on the file to begin the installation process.

For StudySmart® technical support call 1-877-385-6238

Get it from the BAR/BRI website at www.barbri.com

barbri®

BAR REVIEW

HOW TO USE THE MULTISTATE TESTING BOOKS

The Practice Questions Book *("Practice Book" or "MPQ")* is one of three volumes comprising BAR/BRI Multistate Testing. The other two volumes are the Drills and Released Questions Book *("Drills Book" or "MDR")* and the Simulated Exam Book *("Exam Book" or "MSE")*. Altogether, BAR/BRI Multistate Testing contains over 2,000 MBE-type multiple choice questions. We do *NOT* recommend that you do all of the questions that are offered, *especially at the expense of reading through the outlines and working on essay questions.* Your course will probably provide a "Paced Program" with specific assignments from these books, or you can follow the suggested approach below to focus your MBE preparation.

The *Practice Book* (this book) is divided into three component parts:

(i) *Introductory Problems* arranged by subject. These questions have relatively straightforward fact patterns.

(ii) *Intermediate Questions* arranged by subject. These questions are of average degree of difficulty.

(iii) *Advanced Drills* arranged by subject. Most of these questions are *more difficult than average* so they should be worked after you have completed other practice questions in that subject. *NOTE:* This *concentration* of difficult questions would not occur on the actual exam, where you will find a mix of easy, medium, and difficult questions. Therefore, you should use the drills as learning tools but don't be too concerned if you find yourself not keeping on pace for a subject or not scoring as well as you have on other practice questions.

SUGGESTED STUDY APPROACH

Step 1: Do the *Workshop Testing Drills* (in the Drills Book) for a subject soon after you have completed the substantive lecture on that subject, and review the questions using the corresponding Workshop Testing Drills audio lecture from the BAR/BRI website.

Step 2: Do questions in the *Practice Book* (this book) *or* by using the BAR/BRI *Study Smart®* *Software* (available from the BAR/BRI website). These questions are arranged by subject and grouped into three levels of difficulty. Unless your course instructs otherwise, you should do some of the Introductory Problems in a subject before moving on to Intermediate Questions in that subject. You generally do not need to do all of the questions at these levels before moving on unless that subject is giving you difficulty. Finally, do *all* of the Advanced Drills questions in each subject. Working through the questions by subject will perform two valuable functions for you: (i) familiarize you with MBE-type questions; and (ii) provide a diagnostic measurement of your strengths and weaknesses (thus, if you did poorly in a subject area, it may indicate that you should devote more study time to that subject). If you wish to obtain a more detailed diagnostic analysis of your performance, *including a ranking of your performance against other students*, you can do these questions using the BAR/BRI StudySmart® Software.

Step 3: Once you have completed all of the substantive lectures for the MBE subjects, your course will administer the *Simulated Exam* (in the Exam Book) under timed conditions similar to the actual MBE. BAR/BRI strongly recommends that you take this exam when it is scheduled by your course. There is no substitute for experiencing the time pressures imposed by a pace of 1.8 minutes per question along with the inevitable distractions of a group setting.

Step 4: If you want exposure to additional questions in a mixed subject format, you can do some of the *Mixed Subject questions* in the Drills Book.

Some final comments: The MBE is not an easy exam. You need to start preparing early—don't try to do all of the practice questions the week before your exam; you'll be overwhelmed—but, on the other hand, don't wear yourself out trying to go through every question from every source. Use our suggested approach and work through enough questions to make yourself feel comfortable with the topics tested and the format of the exam.

Don't become distressed if, even after studying a subject, you still miss some of the questions. A student achieving an average score on the MBE will miss about 70 to 80 questions (out of 200).

Good luck, and start studying!

BAR REVIEW

*Introductory Problems
and Analytical Answers*

CONSTITUTIONAL LAW QUESTIONS

Question 1

The State Occupational Health and Safety Board of East Virginia recently issued regulations valid under its statutory mandate requiring that all employers in the state provide ionizing air purification systems for all employee work areas. These regulations replaced previous guidelines for employee air quality that were generally not mandatory and did not specify the method of air purification used.

The requirements regarding air purification systems are *least* likely to be constitutional as applied to which of the following employers?

(A) CompuMart, a wholly owned subsidiary of Taksuki Electronics, a Japanese corporation, which provides personalized instruction for private citizens in the use of home computers and has seven outlets all within the state.

(B) The state supreme court, which recently completed construction of its new courthouse complete with non-ionizing air purification systems that are to be serviced by the installing contractor for three years under the terms of an installation and service contract signed prior to enactment of the new regulations.

(C) The United States Armed Forces Recruiting Center on the mall in Capitol City, East Virginia.

(D) The Double V Recreation Center, a privately operated community service center funded by donations and constructed through use of a loan provided by the Veterans Administration and repayable to that agency.

Question 2

Felonious Punk committed a particularly brutal series of crimes that, because of their interstate character, were violations of a federal criminal statute. Punk was convicted in federal court and sentenced to life imprisonment. Six months after Punk was incarcerated, the President pardoned him. There was a great public outcry, amid charges that the President issued the pardon because Punk's uncle had made a large contribution to the President's reelection campaign fund. Responding to public opinion, Congress passed a bill limiting the President's power to pardon persons convicted under the specific statute that Punk had violated. The President vetoed the bill, but three-quarters of the members of each house voted to override the veto.

The legislation is:

(A) Unconstitutional, because the power to pardon is expressly granted to the President in the Constitution and is an unqualified power (except as to impeachment).

(B) Unconstitutional, because the President has the duty to enforce the laws, and therefore has plenary powers.

(C) Constitutional, under Article I, Section 1.

(D) Constitutional, because Congress wrote the federal criminal statutes and has the right to determine who should be convicted under such statutes.

Question 3

Samantha Scoop was an investigative reporter for the *Daily Defamer*, the leading newspaper in Sleazy City. Samantha told her editor that she had uncovered evidence that the mayor and several city council members had accepted bribes to rezone several parcels of land in which local organized crime leaders had substantial interests. Samantha was excited about a story on the bribes because it could make her reputation as an investigative reporter and open up lucrative opportunities for her in television. The editor was also interested in the story, but he told Samantha that he would not print her exposé unless she told him the sources of her information.

Samantha refused to reveal her sources. The editor refused to print the story because he was afraid that the *Defamer* might be sued by the mayor and the council members named by Samantha.

Does Samantha have a First Amendment right to a court order compelling the *Defamer* to publish the story?

(A) Yes, under the Free Speech Clause.

(B) Yes, because the First Amendment allows a newspaper reporter to protect her sources.

(C) No, because the newspaper is a private entity and can publish what it likes.

(D) No, because the freedom of the press is more wide-ranging than freedom of speech.

Question 4

The federal government recently constructed a huge radio telescope facility at Punta Gorda, Puerto Rico. Among the scientific marvels at the facility was a powerful transmitter that could beam radio waves far out into space. As part of the bill providing for operational funding for the facility, Congress provided for a program to "inform any aliens who might be listening in outer space of the 'American Way of Religion.'" A $10 million appropriation was provided; any religious group whose membership exceeded 500 members in the United States might prepare a five-minute presentation, and the federal government would pay for the recording of the presentations and broadcast them into space using the transmitter in Puerto Rico. The President signed the bill and it became law. A religious group with a large following in Europe, but only 100 members in the United States, protested and filed suit.

Will the court find the religious broadcasts to be constitutional?

(A) Yes, because the power to regulate commerce with foreign nations and among the several states implies that commerce with outer space is included as well.

(B) Yes, because the commerce power is not limited by First Amendment prohibitions.

(C) No, because the First Amendment prohibits state involvement with religion without a compelling state interest.

(D) No, because the broadcasts are a waste of money and exceed the spending powers of Congress.

Question 5

Luis operated a one-person field station of the United States Department of Agriculture in East Rabbit's Foot, Wyoming. Pursuant to directives from his superiors at the Department of Agriculture office in Casper, Luis began selling surplus government cheese and butter to the low income residents of East Rabbit's Foot at 10% of market value. All sales were conducted at the USDA warehouse next to Luis's field station.

Wyoming statutes authorized city governments to establish reasonable regulations governing the retail sale of foodstuffs. East Rabbit's Foot city ordinances required that any establishment for the retail sale of food must pass a health and sanitation inspection and meet other specified criteria for obtaining a city license. Since Luis did not obtain a city license, he was prosecuted under the enforcement provisions of the city ordinance.

Which of the following will provide the best defense for Luis in this prosecution?

(A) The ordinance under which he is being prosecuted is invalid as an undue burden upon interstate commerce.

(B) The ordinance violates the Equal Protection Clause of the Fourteenth Amendment.

(C) The ordinance deprives Luis of property without due process of law.

(D) The ordinance violates the principles of intergovernmental immunity as applied to Luis.

Question 6

Congress has enacted a law providing that all disagreements between the United States and a state over federal grant-in-aid funds shall be settled by the filing of a suit in the federal district court in the affected state. The law further provides: "The judgment of the federal court shall be transmitted to the head of the federal agency dispensing such funds, who, if satisfied that the judgment is fair and lawful, shall execute the judgment according to its terms."

This law is:

(A) Constitutional, because disagreements over federal grant-in-aid funds necessarily involve federal questions within the judicial power of the United States.

(B) Constitutional, because the spending of federal monies necessarily includes the authority to provide for the effective settlement of disputes involving them.

(C) Unconstitutional, because it vests authority in the federal court to determine a matter prohibited to it by the Eleventh Amendment.

(D) Unconstitutional, because it vests authority in a federal court to render an advisory opinion.

Question 7

The city council of Tooleville passed an ordinance reading: "No person may contribute more than $100 annually to any group organized for the specific purpose of supporting or opposing referenda to be voted on by the Tooleville electorate or regularly engaging in such activities."

If the ordinance is challenged in federal court, how should the court rule on the constitutionality of this ordinance?

(A) Strike it down, because it violates First Amendment rights of free speech and freedom of association.

(B) Strike it down as a violation of due process, because no hearing mechanism has been provided for.

(C) Uphold it, because the city council has a legitimate interest in controlling such contributions.

(D) Dismiss the case, because it involves a political question and is thus a nonjusticiable matter.

Questions 8-9 are based on the following fact situation:

East Dakota is a state in the Upper Midwest subject to severe winters. Therefore, many drivers in the state find it useful to install snow tires with metal studs to improve traction. However, the use of these tires is controversial because highway experts assert that use of these tires tears up the pavement, requiring repairs more frequently than if only standard snow tires were used. Therefore, no other state allows use of studded snow tires. Because of the general popularity of studded tires among the voters of East Dakota, the legislature was reluctant to pass an outright ban on the use of the tires in the state. It did ban their use between April 1 and October 1 on state highways by passing a law to that effect. The law gave each county in the state an option whether to ban use of the tires during the snowy months between October 1 and April 1. The law contains one exception: it excludes "doctors" from any county ban on the use of snow tires. The reasoning behind this provision, of which there is a record in the debates of the state legislature, was that in rural areas of the state, physicians might have to cross county lines, and it would be unfortunate if a doctor had to stop at a county line to change tires when rushing to an emergency. After the passage of the legislation, only one county in the state, Fillmore County, was concerned enough about the costs of repairing roads that its county board invoked its right to ban the use of studded snow tires in Fillmore County throughout the year.

8. Lisa lives in Millard County, which borders Fillmore County. She was not aware that Fillmore County had enacted regulations banning the use of studded snow tires. On a snowy January night, she left her home in Millard County to attend the birthday party

of her father, who lived 20 miles away, but still in Millard County. Lisa had studded tires on her car. She drove on the road that was the shortest distance between her house and her father's house. Unbeknownst to Lisa, because there were no county line signs on this road, four miles of the road passed through Fillmore County. When she was on that stretch of road, a police officer from the Fillmore County Sheriff's Office heard the clicking sound of Lisa's tires striking the road, giving him probable cause to believe that she had studded snow tires. He pulled Lisa over, inspected her car, and ticketed her for driving through Fillmore County with studded snow tires. She was convicted in county court, but was angry enough to appeal her case to the federal courts.

What is Fillmore County's most appropriate argument for upholding the constitutionality of the Fillmore County regulation?

(A)   The regulation has a rational relationship to the purpose of saving county taxpayers the expense of additional road repairs.

(B)   The county has a compelling interest in saving its taxpayers the money that would have to be expended on extra road repairs.

(C)   There is no less restrictive means of preventing damage to Fillmore County roads.

(D)   Ignorance of the law is no excuse.

9.   Assume for purposes of this question only that Lloyd is a lawyer in East Dakota. He read about the state legislature's studded tire law and became furious. He was angered that the legislature had given privileges to the medical profession, but had failed to extend the same privileges to lawyers. Therefore, one January day, with studded tires on his car, he drove from his home in Chilblain County to Fillmore County, where he knew that studded tires had been declared illegal. He deliberately drove several times around the block where the Fillmore County Sheriff's Office is located. Finally, one of the sheriff's police noticed Lloyd's studded tires and cited him. After being convicted and fined in Fillmore County Court, Lloyd appealed.

Lloyd's best argument for getting the ban invalidated is:

(A)   The statute interferes with his fundamental right to practice his profession in violation of the Privileges and Immunities Clause of Article IV.

(B)   The statute violates his right to travel.

(C)   The statute violates the Commerce Clause by placing an unreasonable restraint on interstate commerce.

(D)   The ban on studded snow tires results in loss of life, because more fatal accidents occur when cars lack the traction that the studded tires provide, and therefore the statute is not rationally related to a legitimate state interest.

Questions 10-11 are based on the following fact situation:

A religious group, the Sons And Daughters of Salvation ("SADS"), that believes in the power of prayer to restore the sick to good health, has taken to distributing leaflets on the grounds of hospitals in the Dunston area. The Dunston City Council, upon the urging of local hospital administrators concerned that many patients may be adversely affected by the leaflets, passed an ordinance forbidding the passing out of leaflets by any group on hospital grounds or on the sidewalks within five feet of the hospital entrances during visiting hours. It is customary for Dunston hospitals to have relatively short visiting periods—two hours in the morning and two hours in the early evening. The ordinance goes on to provide that anyone violating the ordinance will be fined $100, with the proceeds of the fine to go to the building fund of Dunston Memorial Hospital. Sister Clarabelle, a member of SADS, distributed leaflets on the sidewalk within five feet of an entrance to Dunston Memorial during visiting hours. She was arrested by police and fined $100 by the municipal court. Sister Clarabelle appealed, claiming that her constitutional rights were violated.

The case was heard by the state supreme court, which ruled that while the ordinance was permissible under the United States Constitution, it was unconstitutional under the state constitution because the fine money was designated to go to Dunston Memorial Hospital rather than to the city of Dunston. The city decided not to try to appeal the case to the federal courts, but instead amended the ordinance so that the fine money was received by the city. Dunston Memorial Hospital now seeks to intervene in the case and bring it before the United States Supreme Court.

10. Should the United States Supreme Court grant certiorari?

   (A) No, because the case was decided on independent state grounds.

   (B) No, because the case is moot.

   (C) No, because this is a political question.

   (D) Yes, the Supreme Court should hear the case on its merits, because it involves an important federal question.

11. Assume for purposes of this question only that the *amended* ordinance comes before the United States Supreme Court. How should the Court rule on the constitutionality of the law?

   (A) Unconstitutional, because it violates the Free Exercise Clause.

   (B) Unconstitutional, because it infringes freedom of speech.

   (C) Constitutional, because the regulation is reasonable as to time, place, and manner.

   (D) Constitutional, because patients' and visitors' freedom of association right to be let alone is being infringed by the leaflet distributors.

Questions 12-13 are based on the following fact situation:

The town of LeMaize, Iowa, faced financial difficulties and its city council sought new ways to raise revenue. In addition to its usual resort to "sin taxes" on alcohol and tobacco, the council passed a new sin tax, aimed at electronic game arcades frequented by local juveniles. The tax is a one-cent per game tax imposed on the manufacturers of the games based on the estimated number of plays over a machine's lifetime. There are no electronic game manufacturers in Iowa.

12. Which of the following constitutional provisions would support the best argument *against* enforcement of the tax?

   (A) The Equal Protection Clause.

   (B) Substantive due process.

   (C) The Privileges and Immunities Clause of Article IV.

   (D) The Commerce Clause.

13. Which of the following would most likely be found to have standing to challenge the tax?

   (A) The Taxbite Federation, a civic watchdog and good government group.

   (B) Tommy P. Wizard, owner of "Gunga's Den," a game arcade located in LeMaize.

   (C) The Rally Manufacturing Company of Chicago, Illinois, a manufacturer of electronic games that sells its games in LeMaize.

(D) Judie DeLinquente, a 16-year-old girl who regularly plays electronic games at Gunga's Den and other LeMaize arcades.

Question 14

The town of Madison has two high schools. Madison High is the public school, and St. Anne's High is a parochial school. Shortly before the school year began, Yvette Poulet, the French teacher at Madison High, died suddenly. Although the Board of Education made an honest effort, they could find no one in the area qualified and willing to teach French at Madison High. Faced with the prospect of canceling all French classes at Madison High, the board agreed to a friendly proposal offered by Father Finegan, the principal of St. Anne's. Paula Renard, a qualified French teacher and a layperson, was a full-time employee of St. Anne's. Finegan proposed that Renard could spend half her time teaching French at Madison High, if the Board of Education reimbursed St. Anne's for half of Renard's salary and half of her benefits package (including health insurance premiums and retirement fund payments). Ms. Renard began the school year teaching two French classes at St. Anne's in the morning and two French classes at Madison High in the afternoon. The Board of Education began forwarding monthly checks to St. Anne's to cover 50% of Renard's salary and benefits.

Assuming that there are no problems with jurisdiction or standing, if Atheists and Other Americans Against Religious Education, a group favoring complete separation of church and state, files suit in federal district court to block the payment of funds to St. Anne's, they will:

(A) Lose, because the arrangement is for a secular purpose, has a primary effect of neither advancing nor inhibiting religion, and does not unduly entangle a governmental body with religion.

(B) Lose, because the arrangement has a secular purpose.

(C) Win, because the arrangement violates the Establishment Clause of the First Amendment.

(D) Win, because it is unconstitutional to transfer public funds to a parochial school.

Question 15

Which of the following acts would be improper for the United States Senate to perform?

(A) Adjudicating a border dispute between states.

(B) Defining certain qualifications for being a member in good standing of the United States Senate.

(C) Sitting in joint session with the House of Representatives.

(D) Passing a resolution directing the President to pursue a particular course of foreign policy.

Question 16

The International Wildlife Welfare Federation, a highly respected conservation organization, placed the pfu bird on its endangered species list. Congress responded to this by passing legislation banning the hunting of pfu birds within the United States. The range of the pfu bird is quite limited, and Montoming is one of a few states in which the pfu bird can be found. Hunters from many other states have traditionally traveled to Montoming during its pfu bird hunting season, bringing considerable revenue into the state. A Montoming statute allows hunting of the pfu bird during a two-week period in November and charges a $50 license fee for Montoming residents and a $250 fee for hunters from other states. The bag limit is one pfu bird per licensed hunter.

The Montoming statute allowing pfu bird hunting is:

(A) Valid, because states have the right to control their own natural resources and wildlife.

(B) Valid, because the power exercised is reserved to the states by the Tenth Amendment.

(C) Invalid, because of the Supremacy Clause.

(D) Invalid, because of the Commerce Clause.

Question 17

The legislature of State Green was concerned about the problems caused by overpopulation. Therefore, it enacted a statute providing for criminal penalties for any person who is the biological parent of more than two children. The stated purpose of the statute is to preserve the state's natural resources and improve the quality of life for the state's residents. Jane and John Doe, a married couple, have just had their third child. They have been arrested and convicted under the statute.

Which of the following is the strongest argument for voiding the convictions of Mr. and Mrs. Doe?

(A) The statute is an invalid exercise of the state's police power because there is no rational basis for concluding that the challenged statute would further the government's stated interests.

(B) The statute places an unconstitutional burden on the fundamental privacy interests of married persons.

(C) The statute places too great a discretion in state officials to determine who will be permitted to bear children.

(D) The statute denies married persons equal protection of law.

Question 18

The town of Equinox, a medium-sized industrial municipality in the northeast, occasionally suffered from air pollution problems due to the typical sources of urban air pollution. The Equinox town council passed the "Equinox Anti-Air Pollution Ordinance," to be effective October 1. The ordinance contained many exhortations to "voluntary compliance," but the only section of the law with any "teeth" read: "Anyone who burns trash, garbage, leaves, or similar matter in the open within the confines of the town of Equinox shall be subject to arrest, and may be jailed for up to a maximum of 15 days or fined up to a maximum of $500, or both; however, nothing in this ordinance shall prevent the use of outdoor barbecue grills for the preparation of food."

On the night of October 31, Jezebel, self-proclaimed "Priestess of the Mother Goddess," and three of her "acolytes" raked large quantities of leaves into a big pile in the center of Jezebel's backyard. At the stroke of midnight, they ignited the leaves and danced around the flaming pyre, chanting invocations to the Mother Goddess. Although Jezebel and her followers were careful in building the fire, so that there was no danger that it could spread to any structure in the neighborhood, Gantry, a neighbor, reported the fire to the police and fire departments. The firefighters doused the fire and Jezebel and her followers were charged under the antipollution ordinance. At trial, Jezebel told the court that she was merely observing one of the important tenets of her faith. The trial judge summarily fined her $250 and fined her three followers $50 each. Jezebel appealed to the federal courts, asserting that her freedom to practice her religion has been infringed by Equinox.

Will the fines be upheld?

(A) Yes, because Jezebel does not belong to a traditional established religion.

(B) Yes, because the ordinance was adopted to reduce air pollution and not to prohibit religious practices.

(C) No, because the town could accomplish its goal through less restrictive means.

(D) No, because the ordinance is not necessary to promote a compelling interest.

Question 19

Although relations between the United States and the Despotate of Ruritania were tense, and a number of "incidents" over the past few years had on occasion brought the two nations to the brink of war, the United States continued to maintain diplomatic relations with Ruritania. The most recent incident occurred when the state of Michisota tried and convicted Jacques Plastique, a subject of Ruritania, of crimes arising from the bombing of a crowded theater frequented by personnel of a nearby United States Air Force base. Several persons were killed and many more wounded in the bombing. Plastique received the death penalty, but none of his appeals had yet been heard when agents of the Ruritanian secret police seized the American ambassador on the streets of the capital city and imprisoned him in a jail notorious for its inhumane conditions. The United States complained vigorously to the Ruritanian government and also brought its case before the United Nations. However, the Despot of Ruritania steadfastly refused to release the ambassador, whom he claimed was guilty of spying and endangering the security of Ruritania. The President determined that the only way he could ensure the safety of the ambassador was to enter into a distasteful executive agreement with the Despot. Under the terms of the executive agreement, signed by both the President and the Despot, the ambassador would be flown to a neutral country and released to United States authorities on condition that Plastique was likewise released from prison and flown to a neutral country for release to Ruritanian officials. The President asked Bombast, the Governor of Michisota, to order Plastique's release from the state penitentiary so that State Department officers could fly him to a neutral country. The Governor felt it would be politically damaging to release Plastique, and she refused to do so.

Which of the following is the best argument that the President can use to compel Governor Bombast to release Plastique?

(A) Under the President's foreign policy power, the President may negotiate executive agreements with foreign governments that have priority over inconsistent state laws.

(B) The power of the President to appoint ambassadors implies that he has the right to do anything in his power to protect them.

(C) The requirement in the Constitution that the President "faithfully execute" the laws means that the President is the final arbiter on questions of division of authority between federal and state governments.

(D) Under the President's plenary power over foreign affairs, ambassadors are agents of the President and he has the power to protect them.

Question 20

A Camptown city ordinance states that anyone who wishes to speak in a public park must have a permit to do so issued by the city. The ordinance grants the mayor the discretion to issue or deny such permits based upon the mayor's judgment of whether the speech would be "in the public interest." The mayor has never denied a permit to anybody desiring to speak on a political topic.

Dermot, a person with something to say, went to a public park in Camptown, where he made a 10-minute speech accusing the mayor and the city council of gross incompetence and urging voters to "throw the rascals out" at the next election. Dermot had not applied for a permit. After Dermot completed his oration, the police arrested Dermot and charged him with violating the permit ordinance.

Would a conviction of Dermot be constitutional?

(A) Yes, because Dermot did not have a permit to speak, and a municipality has the right to regulate the time, place, and manner of speech.

(B) Yes, because the mayor would have issued the permit, because Dermot's speech was on a political topic.

(C) No, because the ordinance is void on its face.

(D) No, but only if Dermot could prove that the mayor would not have issued him a permit to speak.

Question 21

The state of Sunny has a climate that is unusually pleasant and mild, with only a few days of really chilly weather in the winter. The federal government owned a building in Solar, Sunny's second city in terms of population but its first in terms of history and commerce. The federal building in Solar housed the regional offices of some federal agencies, as well as a federal records archive. The building was old, but functional, and a typical example of National Recovery Act architecture from the 1930s. The furnace heating the building in winter was quite outmoded, but because the weather in Sunny was so mild there was never a strong drive to ask Congress or the General Services Administration to allocate money for a new heating plant when other needs seemed far more pressing. However, on the approximately two or three days each winter that it was necessary to operate the furnace at full blast, it emitted a noticeable quantity of smoke and particulate matter. The amount of pollutants exuded into Sunny's air on those days was far in excess of the state's stringent environmental regulations.

If the state attempts to enforce its environmental standards and compel the federal building to comply, the likely result of any litigation of the question in federal court is:

(A) Sunny wins, because under the state's police powers it has the right to regulate the quality of its own air.

(B) Sunny wins, because the states and the federal government have joint responsibility for clean air and the federal government should give full faith and credit to Sunny's laws and regulations in the area.

(C) The United States wins, because the Supremacy Clause of Article VI prevents the state from imposing its regulations on the federal government.

(D) The United States wins, because the emissions from the building occur so seldom as to be minimal and the state cannot assert sufficient harm to the health of its citizens as a basis for interference.

Questions 22-23 are based on the following fact situation:

A statute of the state of Yonder makes it unlawful to sell milk for home consumption in containers less than one quart in size. Violation of the statute is a misdemeanor, punishable by a $500 fine and loss of the retail business license.

22. Which of the following grounds would a court most likely use for striking down the statute?

(A) It violates the Equal Protection Clause of the Fourteenth Amendment.

(B) It violates substantive due process.

(C) It violates the clause forbidding states to impair the obligation of contracts.

(D) It violates the Privileges and Immunities Clause of the Fourteenth Amendment.

23. LeAnn Smith operates a convenience market in a downtown location that specializes in sales of pints of milk to walk-in lunchtime buyers. Shortly after an inspection of Smith's market, the state agency responsible for enforcing the milk statute notifies Smith that her sales license has been revoked. Smith's best argument in a suit to defeat the revocation is that the action of the state agency:

(A) Impaired her contract with wholesale distributors of pint cartons of milk.

(B) Was a denial of equal protection.

(C) Was a denial of procedural due process.

(D) Was a denial of substantive due process.

Question 24

Pandora is a student activist at University, a state supported institution of higher learning. University's administrators have grown sick and tired of reading Pandora's tirades against their actions and her frequent rousing of other students to acts of disobedience, including sit-ins and picketing. Several officials of University have made statements to the local press about Pandora, falsely accusing her of both bizarre sexual activities and former felonious crimes. In addition, Pandora has found herself generally harassed on campus. Pandora has filed suit against University in federal district court, asking the court for an order to compel University's officials to cease and desist defaming and otherwise harassing her. Within a week after the suit was filed, the defamations and harassments ceased. When the case came before the district court four months later, both sides stipulated that the defamations and harassments had ceased.

What action should the district court take?

(A) Dismiss the suit for lack of standing.

(B) Dismiss the suit for mootness.

(C) Dismiss the suit, because the case is not ripe.

(D) Hear the case on the merits.

Questions 25-27 are based on the following fact situation:

At 5 o'clock in the evening, Roger entered the Tonto County Fairgrounds where the annual Tonto County Fair was in progress. Roger began to hand out leaflets advertising a commercial country and western music concert scheduled at the fairgrounds two weeks after the Tonto County Fair was due to end. The fair manager, Milan, approached Roger and politely asked him to stop distributing the leaflets since it was in contravention of the fair's rules, but Roger told the manager, "Bug off, Shorty. These folks want to know about this big country concert," and he continued to pass out the leaflets. Milan ran to fetch the police and returned with a police officer to the place where Roger was distributing the leaflets. In the officer's presence, Milan again told Roger to stop handing out the leaflets. Roger ignored Milan and continued to hand out leaflets, at which point he was arrested for criminal trespass and charged in municipal court. Roger posted bond and filed suit in federal district court to enjoin the pending prosecution and for a declaratory judgment that the criminal trespass ordinance was unconstitutional as applied.

25. Which of the following if true is most damaging to Roger's First Amendment claims?

(A) The place where he distributed leaflets was private property leased to the county for holding the fair.

(B) The rules of the county fair clearly prohibit all leafleting or other solicitations on fair property, except at designated hours other than the time Roger was engaged in distributing leaflets.

(C) The means of communication was printed leaflets rather than oral speech.

(D) The message on the leaflets promoted a commercial event.

26. Which of the following variations of fact would be most helpful to Roger's First Amendment claim?

(A) The manager did not repeat his "cease and desist" request in the police officer's presence.

(B) The county fairgrounds is completely surrounded by public sidewalks.

(C) Milan has permitted some people to distribute leaflets at all hours.

(D) The proceeds of the country and western concert were to be used to support the campaign fund of a political candidate.

27. Will the federal court hear Roger's case?

   (A) No, unless he argues that the trespass ordinance is invalid on its face.

   (B) No, unless he argues that the state prosecutor had no hope of conviction, but was proceeding to harass Roger.

   (C) Yes, unless the county argues that Roger lacks standing.

   (D) Yes, unless the county argues that the prosecution involves a political question.

Question 28

The state of Kanbraska passes a statute requiring all employers in the state to provide a medical insurance plan for full-time employees. The Kanbraska Employers Association ("KEA"), a trade organization to which many employers belong, brings suit in federal court, asking the court to strike down the statute as unconstitutional.

The burden is on:

(A) KEA, to prove no rational relationship.

(B) KEA, to prove no compelling state interest.

(C) The state, to prove a rational relationship.

(D) The state, to prove a compelling state interest.

Question 29

Congress was concerned at the decline of the American Merchant Marine and at the unfortunate fact that over 80% of the lucrative Caribbean cruise trade, the bulk of whose passengers were American, was conducted in liners of foreign registry and ownership. To remedy the situation, Congress passed a bill providing that six outmoded United States Navy vessels would be sold to Popeye The Sailor Lines ("PTSL") for $1 each, on condition that the cruise company refurbish the ships at its own expense and operate the ships as cruise ships for at least four years. The conditions for the refurbishing were highly specific, and it would cost PTSL at least $3 million to refit each ship as a modern cruise liner. PTSL agreed to the conditions, but a competitor, Bluto Cruises, filed suit in federal court to block the sale.

Which of the following statements is most valid?

(A) The federal court should treat the sale as presumptively valid, because the Constitution expressly gives Congress the power to dispose of property of the United States.

(B) The federal court should treat the sale as presumptively invalid, because the Constitution expressly denies Congress the right to deprive persons of property without due process of law.

(C) The federal court should rule the statute constitutional only if the President or the Secretary of Defense has certified that the Navy ships are obsolete for defense purposes.

(D) The federal court should rule the statute unconstitutional, because it denies other cruise ship operators the equal protection of the laws.

Question 30

Congress passed a law forbidding the United States mails to be used for the distribution of unsolicited advertising for contraceptives. Although the legislation was cheered by some religious groups and organizations fearful of a "birth dearth" among the American middle class, the legislation was strongly opposed by a number of family planning and civil liberties groups. This eventually led to litigation in the federal courts regarding the constitutionality of the statute.

The best argument against the constitutionality of the statute is that:

(A) The statute offends certain rights that give rise to a constitutional right of privacy.

(B) The statute constitutes a taking without due process of law.

(C) The statute improperly infringes on the commercial speech protection of the First Amendment.

(D) The statute unduly burdens interstate commerce.

Question 31

Dottie Sue always wanted to own and operate her own business. After many years of hard work and saving, Dottie Sue accumulated enough capital assets to apply for a "Burger Heaven" fast food franchise. The Burger Heaven national office in Illinois granted Dottie Sue a franchise to operate a Burger Heaven restaurant in her hometown, Fescue, the second largest city in the state of Greengrass. To operate a restaurant in Fescue, a permit from the Division of Public Health ("DPH") was required. Dottie Sue carefully made sure that every aspect of her Burger Heaven operation complied with all public health regulations, and then she applied to the DPH for a permit. One week later, Dottie Sue received a letter from the DPH denying her a permit to operate her restaurant. No reasons were given for the denial, and Dottie Sue's queries to the DPH were no more enlightening. She was merely told, "You can reapply for a permit at any time." Dottie Sue promptly reapplied, and was once again denied a permit without any reasons being given. Dottie Sue reapplied three more times with identical results. In the meantime, four other fast food restaurants had been granted permits by the DPH. Dottie Sue demanded a hearing on her case, but DPH officials summarily refused, again telling Dottie Sue, "You can reapply for a permit at any time."

If Dottie Sue brings suit in federal court, asserting that the DPH is violating her constitutional rights, her best argument would be based on which of the following?

(A) The DPH has denied Dottie Sue due process of law.

(B) The DPH's actions impair contractual obligations in violation of the Contracts Clause.

(C) The DPH's actions deny Dottie Sue the privileges and immunities of citizenship.

(D) The DPH's actions violate the Commerce Clause of the United States Constitution.

Question 32

Concerned about the number of households headed by single teenage mothers, and the deleterious effects of overpopulation, the state of Northwest enacts legislation requiring that any person under the age of 25 must obtain a certificate of responsibility before having children. Any child born whose parents do not have a certificate of responsibility will be placed up for adoption. Sarah, a pregnant 21-year-old resident of Northwest, challenges the legislation.

If Sarah's action proceeds to substantive determination, which of the following is most accurate?

(A) The state bears the burden of proving that its law is necessary to achieve a compelling government purpose, because it has a substantial impact upon a fundamental right.

(B) The state bears the burden of proving that its law is necessary to achieve a compelling government purpose, because it creates a suspect classification.

(C) Sarah bears the burden of proving that the law is not necessary to achieve a compelling government purpose, because it is presumed valid.

(D) Sarah bears the burden of proving that the law is not necessary to achieve a compelling government purpose, because it is an exercise of the state's police power.

Question 33

Competition from foreign automobiles had taken so much of the domestic auto market away from the manufacturers located in the state of Great Lakes that it was experiencing a recession. To ease the desperate plight of the thousands of auto workers suffering layoffs, plant closures, and pay cuts, the state legislature enacted an excise tax on any auto sold in the state that had not been manufactured in the state; the tax was graduated from 10% of sales price for the cheapest cars up to 1% for the most expensive. Watanabi of America, Inc., a corporation that manufactured cars in a neighboring state and sold cars in Great Lakes, brought an appropriate action in federal court to enjoin enforcement of the auto tax statute as to its products.

Which of the following is the strongest constitutional argument supporting the invalidity of the special tax?

(A) It is an undue burden upon interstate commerce.

(B) It violates the Equal Protection Clause of the Fourteenth Amendment.

(C) It violates the Fourteenth Amendment's protection of the privileges and immunities of national citizenship.

(D) It violates the Due Process Clause of the Fourteenth Amendment.

Question 34

When the brutal and oppressive dictatorship of the Caribbean Island of Tropicana was overthrown by a vaguely Marxist group of patriots, the President of the United States, bowing to overwhelming public pressure, reluctantly extended official recognition to the new Tropicana government. However, in selecting the first United States ambassador to the People's Republic of Tropicana, the President nominated an aging industrialist who was a close personal friend of the deposed dictator.

Unable to muster enough votes to block approval of the new ambassador, the President's political opponents in the Senate caused a resolution to be passed requiring that all consular staff below the rank of ambassador be selected from a list of "approved" candidates who have been certified as acceptable by the new government of Tropicana. The President refused to consider any of the Senate's list of approved candidates.

Which of the following is the President's strongest constitutional basis for refusing to obey the Senate resolution?

(A) The Senate could have effectuated its policies by a less intrusive method, such as refusing to appropriate funds to staff the new embassy if the President's selections were inappropriate.

(B) The President has the authority to nominate and appoint the diplomatic representatives of the United States.

(C) The President has exclusive authority, as commander in chief, to protect American interests abroad.

(D) The President's control over the foreign policy of the United States may not be limited by other branches of government.

Question 35

The Denneky family had been prominent in the politics of the state of Codfish for more than three generations, and the current head of the clan was rumored to have plans to run for the presidency. Through reliable informants in the state police, Kirby, an investigative reporter for *The World,* the largest circulation newspaper in Codfish, learned that a 16-year-old member of the Denneky family, Bugsy, was caught burglarizing a luxury condominium apartment and that a large quantity of cocaine was found on his person. Kirby went to the clerk of the local juvenile court and demanded access to the records concerning Bugsy Denneky. The clerk refused, citing a state statute that required that all court and police records relating to juveniles be sealed. After exhausting all remedies in the Codfish courts, Kirby filed suit in federal court demanding access to documents relating to Bugsy Denneky's criminal activities.

The court should rule that, as applied to this case, the Codfish statute requiring the sealing of juvenile records is:

(A) Unconstitutional, because it limits freedom of the press as guaranteed by the First Amendment.

(B) Unconstitutional, because the press has a right of access to all public documents.

(C) Constitutional, because the state has a compelling interest in rehabilitating juvenile offenders and this is furthered by protecting them from embarrassment in later life through revelation of juvenile offenses.

(D) Constitutional, unless Kirby can establish that Bugsy Denneky qualifies as a public figure.

Question 36

Furtwangler, a candidate for the state legislature, brought an action under the Fourteenth Amendment against Stepside Cabs to compel Stepside to accept his political advertisements on its vehicles. Stepside is a privately owned and operated company. It has been licensed to operate by the city of East Rabbit's Foot. As part of its taxi business, Stepside uses pickup trucks to ferry its largely rurally based customers and the agriculturally related items they often carry around the East Rabbit's Foot metropolitan area. Stepside sells space on the wooden slats surrounding the bed of each pickup truck to commercial advertisers, but it refuses to carry any political advertising.

Which of the following is the strongest justification for the trial court's denying Furtwangler any relief?

(A) The sides of Stepside Cabs are not a public forum.

(B) Furtwangler has reasonable alternative methods of getting his message to the public.

(C) The Fourteenth Amendment provides no basis upon which to compel Stepside to accept Furtwangler's ads.

(D) The right of Stepside to choose what messages to display outweighes Furtwangler's right to insist that Stepside accept his advertising.

Question 37

In compliance with a federal statute that permits government agencies to sell or give away surplus government property, the Secretary of State directed that one of the State Department's surplus airplanes be given to the International Evangelical Church. The Secretary knew that the church planned to use the plane to fly medical supplies to its missions in Third World countries. These missions provide medical assistance, but they also attempt to evangelize residents of the countries in question, and the Secretary was aware that, in addition to medical supplies, the plane might transport Bibles and religious tracts translated into local languages. Had the Secretary not ordered the plane to be given to the International Evangelical Church, it would have been sold at a very reasonable cost to the Future Flyers of America, a nonprofit organization that helps teach young people the fundamentals of piloting and maintaining aircraft.

Which of the following parties would be most likely to have standing to sue to prevent the Secretary of State from making the gift to the church?

(A) A taxpayer.

(B) A citizen of the United States.

(C) Future Flyers of America.

(D) The attorney general of the state in which the airplane is located.

Question 38

The state of Ohio enacted legislation providing for a program of testing the skills of all high school students to perform tasks considered necessary to effective functioning in the adult world, such as following instructions on a form, balancing a checkbook, preparing a shopping list, and similar items. The test was given annually to all public school students by government employees on campus, and both religious and secular private schools were reimbursed for the costs of administering the tests and reporting the results to the state using their own personnel. The state office of education regularly audited the reimbursement program to make sure that the private schools were paid for no more than the reasonable costs, in terms of what government employees would be paid for similar services, of giving the test and recording and reporting the results.

Citizens for Religious Freedom filed suit seeking to enjoin the reimbursement to the religious schools, claiming that the legislation violates the Establishment Clause of the First Amendment to the United States Constitution.

The trial court should:

(A) Grant the injunction, because direct state payment to religious schools violates the Establishment Clause.

(B) Grant the injunction, because the state may not require the religious schools to conduct tests that violate their religious principles.

(C) Deny the injunction, because the legislation has a secular purpose which neither advances nor inhibits religion and which will not entangle the state in religion.

(D) Deny the injunction, because the tests do not involve matters of religion.

Question 39

Davis City decided that it wanted to limit to the extent possible the proliferation of unsightly commercial advertising, and so it amended its zoning ordinance so that billboards were permitted only within 100 yards of the interstate highway that passed through town, and on no other streets within the city limits. A year after the amended zoning ordinance took effect, the state converted the old two-lane road connecting the nearby town of Woodland to the interstate into a divided, four-lane freeway. The new freeway intersected the interstate within the city limits of Davis City and remained therein for about five miles of its northward course to Woodland. Design Concepts, a firm whose business includes renting billboard space to advertising agencies, has contracted with the landowners adjacent to the new freeway and obtained permission to erect 10 billboards, all of which would be within the city limits. You are an attorney consulted by Design Concepts about the likelihood of success of an action to challenge the constitutionality of the Davis City zoning ordinance.

You should advise your client that a court would most likely rule that the zoning ordinance is:

(A) Unconstitutional, because it is "spot zoning."

(B) Unconstitutional, because it restricts freedom of expression.

(C) Valid, because commercial speech is not entitled to protection by the First Amendment.

(D) Valid, because freedom of expression is subject to reasonable time, place, and manner restrictions.

Questions 40-41 are based on the following fact situation:

When the President was unable to convince the Federal Reserve to lower the interest rate it charged financial institutions for money, so that the prime rate would drop and stimulate the national economy, he succeeded in having Congress pass a federal usury law, which proscribed loans at interest higher than 10% per annum or 2% above the rate set by the Federal Reserve, whichever was higher at the time the loan was made. The Conference Committee report on the usury statute stated that it was an emergency measure designed to alleviate the destructive effect of high interest rates on businesses of all sizes throughout the United States.

The Commercial Bank of West Rabbit's Foot, Texas, a statewide bank with several billion dollars in assets, operates primarily as a factor for wholesalers and retailers in Texas, lending money to cover inventory which is repaid when the inventory is sold. It is currently charging its customers between 14% and 15% interest per annum, and the rate charged by the Federal Reserve is 8%. Commercial Bank determines that if it is forced to loan money at 10%, its profits will be reduced by 80%. The Texas usury statute prohibits loans made for more than 7% over the rate charged by the Federal Reserve.

40. If Commercial Bank attempts to challenge the federal usury statute on the grounds that it is not within the enumerated powers of the federal government, it will most likely:

(A) Win, because the federal government may not regulate the interest charged by private lenders who do not lend in interstate markets.

(B) Lose, because the commerce power permits Congress to regulate commerce in money, and Commercial Bank's activities have a substantial effect on that commerce.

(C) Lose, because the general welfare power permits Congress to aid the national economy, and any measure which in the opinion of Congress will aid that economy is necessary and proper.

(D) Win, because interest rates are a particularly local problem not amenable to treatment on a national level.

41. If the state of Texas seeks to enjoin enforcement of the federal usury statute within its boundaries on the grounds that no financial institution in the state can make an adequate profit at a 10% or lower interest rate, and that all lending will cease, the federal court should rule that:

(A) The issue should be certified to the court of appeals immediately because of the importance of the issue.

(B) The issue is a peculiarly local one that is better addressed on a state level, and should enjoin enforcement of the federal law.

(C) The federal statute preempts the state usury law, and the latter is invalid pursuant to the Supremacy Clause.

(D) It has no jurisdiction to hear the case, since a state is a party and original jurisdiction lies with the United States Supreme Court.

Questions 42-43 are based on the following fact situation:

Roger was hired as a registered nurse by Watsonville Community Hospital and given an information booklet explaining that during the first nine months of employment he would be on probationary status and could be dismissed for any reason and without an explanation. After six months, Roger was notified by hospital administrators that he was dismissed. If he had been employed for over nine months, hospital regulations required that he could be dismissed only for cause and after notice and a hearing.

42. Which of the following, if true, most strongly supports Roger's dismissal without notice or hearing?

(A) He could be replaced with a more competent nurse.

(B) His performance as a nurse had been unsatisfactory.

(C) He had not been employed for at least nine months.

(D) He had violated hospital regulations by talking with a newspaper reporter about the hospital's policy of allowing registered nurses to dispense medication without doctor authorization.

43. Which of the following, if true, most strongly supports Roger's argument that he should have been afforded notice and a hearing before dismissal?

   (A) He was the only newly hired nurse not to have survived the probationary period for the past three years.

   (B) There is no evidence that nurses with permanent status are any more competent than Roger.

   (C) He moved his household from out of state to Watsonville in reliance upon an oral promise by the hospital chief administrator that the job would be permanent and that he could be dismissed only for cause.

   (D) He purchased a home with a large mortgage in Watsonville in the expectation that he would become a permanent employee of the hospital.

Questions 44-45 are based on the following fact situation:

Pursuant to statute, the department of education of the state of North Washabama provides model lesson plans complete with sample examinations, suggested class activities, and additional reading lists for any subject taught in the elementary schools of North Washabama to any school or school district in the state requesting such plans. The state has never officially sanctioned segregation in its public schools, but in its large cities, housing patterns have resulted in a de facto concentration of nonwhites in certain inner city schools and of whites in suburban schools and school districts. During the 1970s, as the consequence of litigation in the federal courts, most of the state's school districts adopted voluntary busing plans to more evenly distribute students according to ethnicity. At the same time, there was a renaissance of private secular and religious schools, located mostly in the suburbs near the state's main cities.

The Jefferson Davis Academy is a private school that has the stated policy of admitting only white students. Its administration applied for and received model lesson plans from the department of education on subjects taught at the Academy.

The Tenfold Path is a Zen-Baptist school that admits students without regard to race but whose curriculum is more than 50% religious matters. The Path applied for and received model lesson plans for the nonreligious subjects taught in its classrooms.

44. Which of the following is the best argument supporting the constitutionality of the state of North Washabama's statutory policy of providing model lesson plans to The Tenfold Path?

   (A) The teaching of religious matters in private schools is not constitutionally prohibited.

   (B) The purpose and effect of the lesson plan program is secular and does not entangle government and religion.

   (C) Private religious schools fulfill an important educational function.

   (D) The state's refusal to provide lesson plans to private religious schools would violate the Free Exercise Clause of the First Amendment by discriminating against their students in favor of students in secular private and public schools.

45. Which of the following is the best argument supporting the unconstitutionality of the state's statutory policy of providing model lesson plans to the Jefferson Davis Academy?

   (A) The Constitution prohibits private discrimination.

(B) The state may not aid private schools.

(C) Segregation is furthered by the provision of lesson plans.

(D) No legitimate educational function is served by the giving of model lesson plans to private schools.

Questions 46-47 are based on the following fact situation:

Bradley is subpoenaed to appear before the House of Representatives Armed Services Committee and answer certain questions. When he appears, he refuses to answer, and is cited for contempt of Congress. The entire House later votes to order the United States Attorney General to prosecute Bradley pursuant to a federal statute that establishes criminal penalties for contempt of Congress.

46. Assume for the purposes of this question only that Bradley is prosecuted. Which of the following is his best defense to the charge of contempt of Congress:

(A) He demonstrates that the questions asked him did not relate to any matters upon which Congress could legislate.

(B) He establishes that he is an employee of the Department of Defense and may not be questioned relating to his duties as an officer of the executive branch of the federal government.

(C) He establishes that he holds an office by appointment of the President and may not be questioned as to his duties except by the Senate.

(D) He demonstrates that the questions asked him did not relate to any matter as to which funds appropriated by the House were expended.

47. If the Attorney General refused to prosecute Bradley, would his refusal be constitutional?

(A) Yes, if Bradley were an appointive official of the executive branch, since he would then be immune from prosecution for acts performed in the course of his duties.

(B) Yes, because the decision to prosecute is exclusively within the discretion of the executive branch.

(C) No, because the Attorney General may not lawfully disobey a directive from Congress to punish a contempt.

(D) No, because the Attorney General may not refuse to prosecute one who has violated federal law.

Question 48

Which of the following would provide the best constitutional underpinning for federal legislation requiring that state and local police departments receiving financial assistance from the Federal Law Enforcement Assistance Agency devote a specified amount of those resources to combatting "white-collar" crimes?

(A) The power to enforce the penal statutes of the United States.

(B) The police power.

(C) The war and defense power.

(D) The power to tax and spend for the general welfare.

Questions 49-52 are based on the following fact situation:

In certain parts of the state of Pacifica, a single-family residence had become so expensive that the vast majority of families could no longer afford to buy a home of any kind, even with both husband and wife working. To alleviate this problem, the legislature enacted statutes creating a State Housing Development Corporation. This agency, organized along the lines of a private corporation, was authorized to act as general contractor and build homes in counties where the average cost of a new home exceeded by 50% the national average cost of a new home, then to sell the homes at the cost of materials and labor to first-time homebuyers. The national average cost of a new home at all relevant times was $74,000. In Midvalleyville, a medium-sized city in the middle of Pacifica, the average cost of a new home was $84,000. In Metropolis, a large city on the coast of Pacifica, the average cost of a new home was $135,000. The State Housing Development Corporation began building and selling homes in Metropolis, but did not operate in Midvalleyville.

49. About 35% of the population of Midvalleyville is of Armenian ethnicity. Sassoonian, of Armenian heritage, brings a class action against the state seeking to have the Housing Development Corporation's failure to operate in Midvalleyville declared a violation of the right to equal protection of the Armenian citizens of that city. What fact would be most helpful for Sassoonian in challenging the statute?

(A) The state could have permitted the housing corporation to build and sell homes in all areas of the state.

(B) Armenian citizens experience difficulty in affording single-family residences.

(C) The legislation setting up the housing corporation was intended to discriminate against Armenian citizens.

(D) The percentage of Armenian citizens is much higher in Midvalleyville than in Metropolis.

50. Rocky, a general contractor who builds and sells homes in Metropolis, discovers that his business has fallen off about 30% since the state housing corporation started doing business in Metropolis. He brings an action seeking to enjoin the operation of the state housing corporation. What will be the probable outcome of this litigation?

(A) Rocky will win, because operation of a state agency in competition with a private business violates the Due Process Clause of the Fourteenth Amendment.

(B) Rocky will win, because permitting some citizens to purchase from a state corporation while others purchase from private businesses violates the Equal Protection Clause of the Fourteenth Amendment.

(C) Rocky will lose, because he lacks standing to challenge the legislation, having suffered no direct injury.

(D) Rocky will lose, because the state housing corporation is a valid exercise of the state's powers.

51. Citizens for Fair Housing, a group of Midvalleyville residents, brings an action in federal court seeking to compel the State Housing Corporation to begin operations in Midvalleyville. What will be the probable outcome of this litigation?

(A) The action will be dismissed, because the state is immune from litigation under the Eleventh Amendment.

(B) The action will be dismissed, because the housing corporation is organized as a private business and thus does not engage in any state action.

(C) The state will prevail, because it has a rational basis for not operating in Midvalleyville.

(D) The citizens will prevail, because the state cannot show a compelling state interest in not operating in Midvalleyville.

52. Assume for the purposes of this question only that the federal government has enacted legislation operative for the relevant period that regulates the manner in

which building contractors conduct business. Is the State Housing Development Corporation subject to these federal regulations?

(A) No, because its activities take place entirely within the state.

(B) No, because as an agency of state government, it is immune from federal regulation.

(C) No, because the federal government is not empowered to enact legislation regulating state governments or their agencies.

(D) Yes.

Question 53

The economy of the state of Michiconsin relies heavily on the automobile business, which in recent years has suffered due to the success of automobile imports. Feeling the pressure of a growing unemployment problem, and becoming impatient with federal efforts to deal with the problem, Michiconsin enacts a statute calling for a $100 per car tax on all foreign cars sold in Michiconsin. The money is to be placed into a state fund to be used to retrain the state's unemployed automobile workers.

The Toyobishi Corporation, a major automobile importer and dealership owner, brings suit in federal district court seeking to halt the enforcement of the statute on constitutional grounds.

The court should find the statute:

(A) Constitutional, because it is a proper exercise of a state's rights under the Import-Export Clause.

(B) Constitutional, if consented to by Congress.

(C) Unconstitutional, because the statute violates the Privileges and Immunities Clause of Article IV.

(D) Unconstitutional, unless the state can show that the statute is necessary to promote a compelling state interest.

Question 54

Congress created by statute the Small Business Administration Appeals Tribunal, which was empowered to review claims made by clients of the SBA and make recommendations to the agency regarding their merits. Agnew was properly appointed to the Tribunal. Six years later, the Tribunal was abolished by repeal of the authorizing legislation, and Agnew was offered an administrative position in the Department of Transportation at a lower salary. Agnew has now brought an action against the federal government on the grounds that Congress may not remove a federal judge from office during good behavior nor decrease his salary during continuance in office. Counsel for the government has made a motion to dismiss.

The trial court should rule:

(A) For the government, because Agnew was not an Article III judge and is not entitled to life tenure.

(B) For the government, because Agnew lacked standing to raise the question.

(C) For Agnew, because he has established a property right to his position on the Tribunal.

(D) For Agnew, because of the independence of the federal judiciary constitutionally guaranteed by Article III.

Question 55

The state of New Calexico requires all businesses engaged in any form of retail sales to be licensed. The state legislature amended the statutes governing licensing so that any business seeking a license to engage in retail sales must establish that at least 40% of the items sold will be manufactured or produced within the state.

Which of the following constitutional provisions will provide the best basis upon which to attack the validity of the state licensing provision requiring a minimum percentage of local goods?

(A) The Privileges and Immunities Clause of the Fourteenth Amendment.

(B) The Commerce Clause.

(C) The Equal Protection Clause.

(D) The Due Process Clause of the Fourteenth Amendment.

Questions 56-57 are based on the following fact situation:

Bev and Nate had lived together for several years, but had never married because Nate was still married to another woman. During this time, Bev was not employed, but she took care of their home, did housekeeping and other chores, and acted as Nate's companion. Nate, however, informed her one day that he did not want to live with her anymore and told her to move out of the residence.

During the time Nate and Bev lived together, they had accumulated property. The state in which they lived recognized in general the validity of property agreements entered into by nonmarried couples who lived together, but there was a statute that provided that such agreements were void as being against public policy when one of the parties living together was married to another. Bev brought suit against Nate, alleging that they had an agreement to share equally all property accumulated by them during the time they lived together, and challenging the constitutionality of the statute. The state intervened to defend the statute.

56. Will Bev prevail in her challenge to the statute?

(A) Yes, if the state fails to prove that the statute is rationally related to a legitimate state purpose.

(B) Yes, if Bev can prove that the statute is not necessary to effectuate a compelling state interest.

(C) No, if Bev fails to prove that the statute is not rationally related to a legitimate government purpose.

(D) No, if the government proves that the statute was necessary and proper.

57. The state's strongest defense of the statute would be that:

(A) The Constitution of the United States does not affect the state's authority over marital and quasi-marital relationships.

(B) The state's interest in the promotion of family life and the preservation of marital property rights gives the law a rational basis.

(C) The statute does not proscribe all suits of this nature; thus there is no showing of invidious discrimination.

(D) The Constitution does not affect a state's inherent police powers.

Question 58

A federal statute was enacted that provided federal funds to open child health care centers in inner-city areas. The strongest constitutional basis for this enactment is the:

(A) Commerce Clause.

(B) Equal Protection Clause.

(C) Taxing and Spending Clause.

(D) General federal police powers.

Question 59

In which of the following cases does the United States Supreme Court *not* have original jurisdiction?

(A) A case involving an ambassador.

(B) A case involving a dispute between two states.

(C) A case involving maritime jurisdiction.

(D) A case involving a state and the federal government.

Question 60

Congress determined that there should be a uniform law for handgun registration throughout the United States, and enacted the Federal Firearms Act.

Which of the following constitutional provisions could most easily be considered the basis of such enactment?

(A) The Equal Protection Clause of the Fourteenth Amendment.

(B) The Second Amendment.

(C) The Commerce Clause.

(D) The Necessary and Proper Clause.

Questions 61-63 are based on the following fact situation:

Congress enacted legislation that was intended to open up federal lands to private industry to explore for, and extract, oil and coal deposits. The act established the Federal Lands Exploitation Commission to supervise the exploration and extraction of fossil fuels from federal lands, and empowered the Commission to enter into contracts on behalf of the federal government with the private companies that wish to mine for coal and drill for oil. The Commission members were also required to investigate safe and sound methods of exploiting the oil and coal deposits without doing unnecessary harm to the environment and to make recommendations to Congress for new laws that would govern the exploitation of federal lands. Further, the commissioners were given the power to make the rules and regulations concerning the contracts with the companies and to appoint administrative law judges to conduct hearings regarding violation of the Commission's rules and disputes concerning the contracts.

The Commission's chairperson was designated as an Undersecretary of the Interior; the President appointed two commissioners from environmental groups; and the oil and coal companies selected one commissioner each, who were then appointed by Congress to the Commission.

61. The authority for the establishment of the Federal Lands Exploitation Commission is most likely:

(A) The Commerce Clause.

(B) The taxing and spending power.

(C) Congress's authority to regulate federal land.

(D) The war and defense power.

62. For its violation of the Commission's rules with regard to pollution of water resulting from drilling operations, AmOil was fined $5,000. AmOil files suit in the federal court to enjoin the Commission's enforcement of this rule. AmOil's best argument in support of its contention that the rule was illegal is:

(A) Regulations concerning criminal conduct cannot be made by agency rules, but must be made by federal statute.

(B) The appointment of the commissioners was illegal; therefore, the rules promulgated by the Commission are invalid.

(C) Since the fine was potentially $5,000 for violation of the rule, AmOil had a right to a trial by jury, which was denied when the matter was heard by the administrative law judge.

(D) The proceeding before the administrative law judge violated AmOil's rights of equal protection as guaranteed by the Fourteenth Amendment.

63. Administrative Law Judge May had been appointed to his position by a former Undersecretary of the Interior who was the Commission chairperson. When the new administration came into office, the new Commission chairperson removed May from his position as the ALJ, but offered May a position as an attorney in the enforcement division. May brought suit in the federal court to enjoin the Commission chairperson from removing him from his position. May should:

(A) Prevail, because a judge cannot be removed from office after appointment.

(B) Prevail, if it is shown that at all times he maintained good behavior.

(C) Not prevail, because he was not a judge within the meaning of Article III.

(D) Not prevail, because the appointing authority had changed.

Questions 64-65 are based on the following fact situation:

The President of the United States and the Prime Minister of Canada, recognizing a growing problem involving the killing of baby harp seals, agreed that each should appoint three members to a special commission to look into the problem. The commission was instructed to make a comprehensive study of the baby harp seal problem and to draft regulations that would provide for the preservation of the seal population while still allowing fur traders to take a certain number of furs each year. After studying the problem, the commission drafted proposed regulations and submitted them to the President and the Prime Minister. The President of the United States, acting in concert with the Prime Minister of Canada, named the commission as a permanent enforcement agency for the regulations that were adopted by both nations. The President, acting with prior congressional authorization, then entered into an executive agreement with the Prime Minister whereby the joint commission was granted adjudicative as well as enforcement powers with respect to the regulation of baby harp seals.

64. The executive agreement by the President is:

(A) Valid, because the President has unlimited powers in entering into executive agreements.

(B) Valid, because the President has plenary powers in the area of foreign affairs.

(C) Invalid, unless the Senate ratified the executive agreement by a two-thirds vote.

(D) Invalid, because conservation of wildlife is not an area left solely to Presidential discretion.

65. Assume that the joint commission adopted a regulation whereby all baby harp seal hunters were restricted to taking furs between December 1 and April 30 of each year, and that each hunter could take no more than one baby harp seal fur per day. Assume further that the state of Maine adopted a statute requiring baby harp seal hunters to register with the state and obtain a special hunting license that allowed year-round hunting of baby harp seals, for the price of $5,000. The joint commission filed an action in federal district court seeking to enjoin Maine from enforcing the statute. The district court most likely would declare the state statute to be:

(A) Constitutional, because the conservation of wildlife is an issue best left to the states in which the wildlife are located.

(B) Constitutional, because a state statute takes precedence over any executive agreement.

(C) Unconstitutional, because an executive agreement is the law of the land, and any acts by a state inconsistent therewith are null and void.

(D) Unconstitutional, because the state statute discriminates against baby harp seal hunters from the state of Maine.

Question 66

In an effort to protect the dwindling California condor population, Congress enacted the Condor Preservation Act, which made it illegal to take, possess, or sell any part of a California condor. The constitutionality of the Act is challenged by Zephyr, a seller of gifts and artifacts, including artifacts made out of California condor feathers.

Is the Act valid?

(A) No, the statute violates due process because the absolute prohibition on sale is an effective taking under the Fifth Amendment Due Process Clause without just compensation.

(B) No, because the statute is discriminatory as applied.

(C) Yes, because the regulation is rationally related to interstate commerce.

(D) Yes, because the statute is designed to protect a dwindling national resource.

Question 67

Broad Acres is a housing development of one-, two-, and three-bedroom units. All units are suitable for occupancy, and the developers of the project have filed the appropriate documents and deeds, including a Declaration of Restrictions that limits ownership and occupancy of the units to families or to groups of unrelated adults of not more than three in

number. Each deed to the individual units contains the following statement:

> As shown on recorded plat (page and plat book reference) and subject to the restrictions stated therein.

One of the two-bedroom units was purchased by Dora and her boyfriend Greg. They immediately moved into the unit with another unmarried couple who were friends of theirs. Other unit owners brought suit against Dora and Greg to enjoin the occupancy by the other couple.

If judgment is in favor of Dora and Greg, the issue that most likely would determine this result is whether:

(A) The restriction constitutes an unlawful restraint against alienation.

(B) Enforcement of the restriction would violate the Equal Protection Clause of the Fourteenth Amendment.

(C) Notice was given by Dora and Greg to the sellers of the unit that they intended to occupy the residence with another couple.

(D) A two-bedroom unit can comfortably contain a group of four adults.

Question 68

Foley was a permanent resident alien of the United States who was awaiting an opportunity to become a citizen. Foley filed an application to become an instructor in the local public high school but was denied the position solely on the ground that he was not a citizen. Foley now brings suit, alleging that his status as a resident alien was not a proper ground for denying him a position as an instructor.

May the state deny a permanent resident alien employment as an instructor in the public high school?

(A) Yes, because employment by the state is a privilege, not a right.

(B) Yes, because citizenship bears some rational relationship to the interest that is being protected.

(C) No, to do so would be a denial of equal protection.

(D) No, because the evidence presented was uncontroverted that he was awaiting the opportunity to become a citizen.

Question 69

City passed a municipal ordinance that prohibited door-to-door solicitation of contributions by charitable organizations that did not use at least 75% of their receipts for "charitable purposes." The ordinance further provided that anyone wishing to solicit for purposes of charity must obtain a permit and present satisfactory proof that at least 75% of the proceeds of such solicitation shall be used directly for the charitable purposes of the organization. The Citizens for an Easier Passing, a corporation organized to promote "the knowledge and the use of accepted methods of euthanasia among terminally ill people," brought this action after City refused to issue it a permit to solicit because it did not meet the 75% requirement.

The case is before the Supreme Court. The Court should declare the ordinance:

(A) Constitutional, because the 75% rule serves a legitimate state interest in preserving the integrity of charities.

(B) Constitutional, because the right to solicit for a charity is balanced against the interest of the state in preventing fraud and crime.

(C) Unconstitutional, because the ordinance violates the protections afforded by the First Amendment.

(D) Constitutional, because the ordinance has as a purpose the protection from undue annoyance and the preservation of residential privacy.

Question 70

The city of Kingco amended its ordinance to require that "adult theaters" (defined in the ordinance) could not be located either within 100 feet of each other or within 500 feet of any residential area. This zoning requirement was passed to protect the residential character of neighborhoods from destruction. American Red-White-and-Blue Movies, Inc., is the owner of two adult theaters. One is a regular theater building located about 1,000 feet from another adult theater. The second theater is a converted gas station which is near another adult theater and adjacent to a residential area, in violation of the zoning ordinance. American has filed this action to have the zoning requirement declared unconstitutional.

The court should hold that:

(A) The zoning ordinance is in violation of the protections afforded by the First Amendment of the Constitution.

(B) The zoning ordinance is invalid because it is a form of spot zoning.

(C) The zoning ordinance is valid in that it covers the whole city of Kingco.

(D) The zoning ordinance is valid because material protected by the First Amendment is subject to zoning and licensing requirements.

Questions 71-73 are based on the following fact situation:

The state of Aricaltex was suffering a dual problem—that is, an influx of illegal immigrants and high unemployment as a result of a near-depression caused by layoffs in the tourist-service industry. In an attempt to alleviate both problems, the state of Aricaltex enacted a statute providing for the immediate hiring of 100,000 employees to repair, maintain, and otherwise work at the discretion of the Director of Highways. The statute further stated that preference would be given to persons who had worked in the tourist-service industry for five years and had been laid off. Section 2 of the statute provided that resident aliens would be employed only if no employees were available from the tourist-service industry as provided for above.

71. In a challenge to the constitutionality of that part of the statute providing for the hiring of resident aliens only on a second-priority basis, which of the following would be most helpful?

   (A) The Privileges and Immunities Clause of the Fourteenth Amendment.

   (B) The reserved powers of the state under the Tenth Amendment.

   (C) The Equal Protection Clause of the Fourteenth Amendment.

   (D) The Fourteenth Amendment Due Process Clause.

72. In a challenge to the first part of the statute providing for the employment of persons who worked five years for the tourist-service industry and were laid off, which of the following is most relevant?

   (A) The Privileges and Immunities Clause of Article IV.

   (B) The Equal Protection Clause of the Fourteenth Amendment.

   (C) The reserved powers of the state under the Tenth Amendment.

   (D) The Privileges and Immunities Clause of the Fourteenth Amendment.

73. Assume, for the purpose of this question only, that the state supreme court of Aricaltex declared the statute to be unconstitutional on the ground that it was in conflict with the Supremacy Clause of the Constitution as well as the Equal Protection Clause of the state constitution. Will the decision be reviewed by the United States Supreme Court?

   (A) No, because it does not meet the requirements of certiorari.

   (B) Yes, because it meets the requirements of appeal.

   (C) Yes, because the Supreme Court has original jurisdiction of all cases to which the state is a party.

   (D) No, because of the "adequate and independent state ground" theory.

Question 74

The state of New York passed a statute that provided for direct reimbursement from public funds to nonpublic schools of the cost of performing various testing and reporting services required of all schools by state law. The three state-prepared tests involved consisted of a student evaluation test, a comprehensive achievement test, and scholarship and college qualification tests. The law also provided for payment to the nonpublic schools for the grading of the tests.

On review by the Supreme Court, the statute should be held:

(A) Constitutional, if objective grading standards are used and reimbursement covers only secular services.

(B) Constitutional, if the state interest is great enough to justify the burden on religion, and no alternative means are available.

(C) Unconstitutional, because direct payment to nonpublic schools is a violation of the Establishment Clause of the First Amendment.

(D) Unconstitutional, because the statewide administration of the test for nonpublic as well as public schools entangles the state with religious schools.

Questions 75-77 are based on the following fact situation:

Horseshoe Lake, located in Laketree County, is known throughout the country for its beautiful scenery and clean beaches. Since Horseshoe Lake is the only one of its kind in Laketree County, the county has always limited commercial access to the beachfront property. There is one marina, one swimming area, two restaurants, and one hotel. The remainder of the property is uninhabited and owned by the county.

To improve facilities around the lake, the county leased the land adjacent to the public facilities to a privately owned corporation, Lakeco. The lease required Lakeco to design, build, operate, and maintain a restaurant, marina, and swimming area, and to pay 10% of the net profits as rent. Lakeco submitted its bylaws to the county for review. The bylaws provided that its facilities would be open to members only, and that its membership committee would set "standards" for membership, including membership fees and dues. The county approved Lakeco's bylaws.

Shortly after the facilities were completed, the State Liquor Licensing Board granted Lakeco a license to sell alcoholic beverages at the restaurant. Lakeco's membership committee decided on a $1,000 initial application fee and monthly dues of $100. The committee has also decided that no applications for membership would be accepted from atheists or persons of Asian descent.

75. A citizen of Korea, who now legally resides in the United States, was denied membership in Lakeco. He brought suit against Lakeco on the ground that the membership standards violated his constitutional rights to equal protection. Who will prevail?

(A) Plaintiff, because the standards are not necessary to promote a compelling state interest.

(B) Plaintiff, unless Lakeco can prove some rational basis for the denial of Asian-Americans.

(C) Lakeco, because plaintiff lacks standing to raise an equal protection claim because he is not a citizen.

(D) Lakeco, because its bylaws make no mention of race or national origin.

76. A resident of Laketree County who could not afford the application fee and the monthly dues brought suit against Lakeco on the ground that the fees discriminate against the poor in violation of the Equal Protection Clause. Who will prevail?

(A) Plaintiff, because a person cannot be deprived of a public right or benefit on the basis of inability to pay.

(B) Plaintiff, because the poor qualify as a protected class.

(C) Lakeco, because only de jure discrimination against the poor has been held to violate the Equal Protection Clause.

(D) Lakeco, because the membership privilege is not an important enough deprivation.

77. An avowed atheist who was denied membership brought suit against Lakeco on the ground that the membership standards violated his freedom of religion. Who will prevail?

(A) Plaintiff, because denial of membership to atheists has been held to hinder the free exercise of religion.

(B) Plaintiff, because the purpose and effect of Lakeco's policy results in a violation of the Establishment Clause.

(C) Lakeco, because freedom of religion is not protected against acts of private individuals or groups or a privately owned corporation.

(D) Lakeco, because plaintiff has no standing to challenge the membership standards on religious grounds because he is an atheist.

CONSTITUTIONAL LAW ANSWERS

Answer to Question 1

(C) The armed forces recruiting center is least likely to be required to comply with the new state law. A state has no power to regulate activities of the federal government unless Congress consents to the regulation. Accordingly, agents and instrumentalities of the federal government, such as the armed forces recruiting center, are immune from state regulations relating to performance of their federal functions. (D) is incorrect because, although the recreation center's construction was funded by a loan from the Veterans Administration, the center itself is privately operated and funded by donations. As a result, the center has only a tenuous connection with the federal government, so that it cannot claim the immunity afforded to a federal agency or instrumentality. Accordingly, in the same sense as is employed in the federal tax immunity cases, the agency does not "stand in the shoes" of the federal government. Thus, the application of the state regulations to the recreation center would not present constitutional problems. (A) apparently refers to the principle that the power to regulate foreign commerce lies exclusively with Congress. However, the mere fact that CompuMart is a wholly owned subsidiary of a Japanese corporation does not mean that the state regulations affect foreign commerce. CompuMart's activities are conducted entirely within the state, and do not touch upon foreign commerce in any way. Therefore, application of the regulations so as to require CompuMart to provide an ionizing air purification system for its employee work areas will not constitute a proscribed state regulation of foreign commerce. Thus, (A) is incorrect. (B) is more troubling, but does not offer as compelling an argument as (C). The Contract Clause prohibits states from acting to **substantially** impair contract rights (*i.e.,* destroy most or all of a party's rights under an existing contract). Under the Clause, the Supreme Court will subject state actions that impair their own contracts to strict scrutiny. In any case, even if state action substantially impairs rights under an existing contract, the action still may be upheld if it: (i) serves an important and legitimate public interest; and (ii) is a reasonable and narrowly tailored means of promoting that interest. Here, the state supreme court, as an instrumentality of the state, would probably not have grounds for complaining that its rights under the contract have been impaired, but the vendor might have grounds (*e.g.,* the vendor might have future economic interests during the three-year service period that will be substantially impaired if the court is required to install an ionizing system). Nevertheless, the regulation still may be valid if the state can prove that it truly serves the important public interest of protecting the health and safety of workers in the state and is narrowly tailored to promoting that interest. In any case, since it is uncertain whether the vendor's rights have been substantially impaired and, if so, whether the state can prove the worth of the regulation, (C) is a better choice.

Answer to Question 2

(A) The legislation is unconstitutional because the President has exclusive power to pardon. Article II, Section 2 of the United States Constitution grants the President the power to grant reprieves and pardons for offenses against the United States, except in cases of impeachment. This pardon power is not subject to control by Congress and it includes the power to commute a sentence on any conditions the President chooses (as long as the conditions do not offend some other constitutional provision). As applied to the facts here, Congress quite simply lacks the authority to circumscribe the President's power to pardon persons convicted under the statute at issue. (B) is incorrect because it is too broad. It is true that the President has the duty to enforce the laws, and that certain powers are part of and emanate from this duty. However, the call of this question clearly points toward the need to address the pardon power specifically, as well as any possible congressional limitations on that power. (C) is incorrect because Article I, Section 1 of the

Constitution simply vests all legislative powers in the Congress. As explained above, this legislative power does not include the authority to set limitations on the President's pardon power. Consequently, the congressional action undertaken here is unconstitutional. (D) is incorrect because it also concludes that Congress is empowered to limit the pardon power. In addition, the language of (D) amounts to a bill of attainder if applied to Punk. A bill of attainder is a legislative act that inflicts punishment without a judicial trial upon individuals who are designated either by name or in terms of past conduct. Both the federal and state governments are prohibited from passing bills of attainder. The assertion by Congress of the right to determine who should be convicted under a statute would amount to an attempt to pass a bill of attainder, because conviction would be imposed without a judicial trial.

Answer to Question 3

(C) The *Defamer* cannot be compelled to print the story because it is a private entity and may refuse to print what it likes. Pursuant to the First Amendment, Congress can make no law abridging freedom of speech or of the press. This provision is applicable to the states through the Fourteenth Amendment Due Process Clause. Freedoms of speech and press include not only the rights to speak and publish freely but also the right to refrain from speaking or publishing. A court order compelling a newspaper to publish a particular story would violate the freedom of the press just as much as would a court order or other governmental action preventing the publication of a particular story. The government cannot dictate the content of a newspaper or require it to disseminate a message with which it disagrees. (A) relies on an inaccurate interpretation of the Free Speech Clause. Samantha's First Amendment right to free speech means that her own freedom of speech is protected from government infringement. This freedom is not being abridged simply because a court refuses to order a newspaper to print her story. Samantha remains perfectly free to disseminate her story by speaking or writing about it, but she may not force the *Defamer* (or any other newspaper) to publish the story. (B) is incorrect because the sources of a reporter's information have not been held to be entitled to protection under the Constitution. Also, even if sources were entitled to such protection, this still would not authorize the state to compel a newspaper to publish a particular story. (D) is incorrect because the First Amendment rights of the press generally are no greater than the First Amendment freedom of speech afforded to other members of the public. (D) incorrectly implies that this question involves a competition between the relative merits of freedom of the press and general First Amendment free speech. However, as noted previously, Samantha's freedom of speech is not at issue, because that freedom is not violated by a refusal to order the *Defamer* to print Samantha's story. Governmental compulsion to print the story would, however, infringe upon the freedom of the press.

Answer to Question 4

(C) The legislation, which is not narrowly tailored to promote a compelling state interest, violates the Establishment Clause. The Establishment Clause of the First Amendment prohibits any law "respecting an establishment of religion." While usually a three-part test based on *Lemon v. Kurtzman* is used to determine whether legislation creates improper government involvement with religion, the "compelling state interest" test is used if a law or government program discriminates among religions. Here, the law differentiates among different religious groups, allowing only those with larger memberships to record presentations. There is no compelling state interest for discriminating among the religious groups in this way; thus the legislation is unconstitutional. (A) is incorrect despite the fact that the federal commerce power could be interpreted as extending to commerce with outer space should the occasion arise. Nevertheless, the commerce power does not override independent constitutional restrictions (the Establishment Clause) on the conduct in question here. (B) is an incorrect statement of law. The federal commerce power cannot be used to abrogate freedom of speech or discriminate in favor of religious groups. (D) is incorrect. Regardless of merit, almost all expenditures made by Congress are permissible under its spending power. [U.S. Const. art. I, §8] Rather than limit the power only to spending for accomplishment of other enumerated powers, this provision grants Congress broad power to spend for the "general welfare" (*i.e.,* any public purpose). As long as the expenditure is not conditioned on requiring a recipient to forgo an individual constitutional right, it is within the spending power of Congress.

Answer to Question 5

(D) The city ordinance unconstitutionally impinges upon a duly authorized federal program. The United States government, as well as its agencies and instrumentalities, is immune from state regulation that interferes with federal activities, functions, and programs. To the extent that state regulations substantially interfere with an authorized federal program, the state laws must yield. Here, Luis, as an agent of the federal government, was carrying out a duly authorized program of the Department of Agriculture by conducting sales of surplus government food at a federally owned warehouse. To sustain the power of the city to prosecute Luis for not having a retail food sale license would give the city overriding authority over the selection of personnel to administer a federal program, as well as over the means by which this program is to be implemented. Thus, the ordinance would substantially interfere with the proper functioning of this federal program by directly interfering with a federal employee in the carrying out of his orders. (A) is incorrect because the facts do not indicate that the licensing ordinance is in any way a measurable burden upon interstate commerce, much less an ***undue*** burden. The ordinance appears to affect, almost exclusively, the peculiarly local concerns of health and sanitation. (B) is incorrect because an equal protection violation exists where a law limits the liberty of some persons but not others, *i.e.,* where a law treats similar persons in a dissimilar manner. The ordinance at issue here is apparently being applied in an evenhanded fashion, and Luis is not being treated differently from anyone else who does not have the required license. Thus, there is no equal protection problem. (C) is incorrect because Luis is not being deprived of any property or interest to which he has a legitimate claim; *e.g.,* he is not being deprived of employment to which he is entitled. Because there is no deprivation of property, there is no due process issue.

Answer to Question 6

(D) The law is unconstitutional because it gives the federal district courts authority to render advisory opinions. The Supreme Court has interpreted the constitutional power of the federal courts to hear "cases and controversies" to mean that federal courts may not render advisory opinions. Under the law here, the district court's decision is not binding on an agency dispensing funds, since the agency head is given discretion to decide whether the court's judgment is fair. Therefore, the judgment is merely advisory and so is not within the jurisdiction of the federal courts. (A) is incorrect because while it is true that the cases would present a federal question, it is not enough merely that a federal question exists; there must be a case or controversy. (B) is incorrect for the same reason. Congress certainly has authority to provide for the settlement of disputes under federal grant programs, but that authority does not permit Congress to violate the case or controversy requirement. (C) is incorrect because the Eleventh Amendment only prohibits the federal courts from hearing an action by a citizen of a state against his state; actions between the federal government and a state are not barred.

Answer to Question 7

(A) The federal court should strike the ordinance for violating the First Amendment. While the government may limit the amount of contributions that an individual can contribute to a candidate's campaign (to avoid corruption or the appearance of corruption), the government may not limit the contributions to a political committee that supports or opposes a ballot referendum, because such a law does not serve a sufficiently important interest to outweigh the restraints that it puts on the First Amendment freedoms of speech and association. (B) is incorrect because the Due Process Clause does not require that every law provide for a hearing, but only those laws involving the deprivation of life, liberty, or property of an *individual*. The law here does not involve a deprivation of life or property, and liberty is not being denied to individuals on a judicial basis (*i.e.*, according to the facts of each case), but rather is being denied to all persons on a legislative basis. In such a case, individual hearings are not required to satisfy due process; as long as the law was lawfully adopted (*e.g.*, with notice to all interested parties), the Due Process Clause has been satisfied. (C) is incorrect because a legitimate interest in controlling contributions to a political committee for ballot referendum is not enough. The statute must be "closely drawn" to match a "sufficiently important interest," which is an intermediate scrutiny standard, and the Supreme Court has invalidated limitations on contributions to influence referendum elections. (D) is incorrect because political questions, which are nonjusticiable, arise when the issue is committed to another branch of the government by the Constitution or is incapable of resolution and enforcement by the judiciary. Determining whether a law is valid is within the realm of the judiciary and certainly is capable of resolution (*i.e.*, the law could be invalidated). Thus, there is no political question here.

Answer to Question 8

(A) The county's most appropriate argument for upholding the constitutionality of the ban is that the regulation is rationally related to saving the taxpayers money. Whether the law here is examined under the substantive provisions of the Due Process Clause or the Equal Protection Clause, the analysis will be the same: If no fundamental right or suspect or quasi-suspect class is involved, the law will be assessed under the rational basis standard. Under that standard, government action will be upheld as long as it is rationally related to a legitimate government interest. Here, the right involved (driving with studded snow tires) is not fundamental, and no suspect or quasi-suspect class is involved. Thus, the regulation will be assessed under the rational basis standard. Saving taxpayers money is a legitimate (although often ignored) government interest, and prohibiting studded snow tires is rationally related to that interest. Therefore, the regulation will be valid under this argument. (B) is incorrect because under the appropriate standard for the case here, the government need not show a *compelling* interest to justify its action; a rational relationship is sufficient. Moreover, it is doubtful that saving money would be considered to be a compelling interest in any case. (C) is incorrect because under the rational basis standard, the government need not choose the least restrictive means available to accomplish its goal; indeed, there need not be a very close fit at all between the legislative goal and the means used to achieve that goal, as long as there is some rational relationship. (D) is incorrect because while it may be true in many cases that ignorance of the law is no excuse, it is irrelevant to determining whether government action is constitutional.

Answer to Question 9

(D) The best argument for getting the law invalidated is that it is not rationally related to a legitimate state interest. Lloyd would argue that the statute violates equal protection because it singles out one class of citizens for special treatment. Since neither a fundamental right nor a suspect nor quasi-suspect class is involved here, the case would be decided under the rational basis standard. For a law to be held invalid under the rational basis standard, the plaintiff must show that the law is not rationally related to a legitimate state interest. Toward this end, Lloyd might argue that the law will really cost more money than it will save, perhaps because the resulting number of injuries due to the absence of studded tires will more than offset the money saved in road repair. (This argument will likely fail, however, because courts give legislatures broad discretion in making such determinations, and the statute does appear to be rational. Nevertheless, this is Lloyd's best argument.) (A) is incorrect because the Privileges and Immunities Clause of Article IV applies only to discrimination by a state against nonresidents, and here Lloyd is a resident of East Dakota. (B) is incorrect because nothing in the facts indicates the right to travel is involved. The right to travel involves *interstate* travel, and here, all travel concerns are wholly intrastate. (C) is incorrect because there is no unreasonable restraint on interstate commerce. If Congress has not allowed or prohibited state regulation in the area, a nondiscriminatory state regulation will be upheld only if its burden on commerce does not outweigh a legitimate local interest. Here, since no other state allows studded snow tires, the ban does not discriminate against out-of-state vehicles and does not burden commerce. (If other states allowed these snow tires, there might be a viable Commerce Clause issue.)

Answer to Question 10

(A) The Court should refuse to grant certiorari because the case was decided on independent state grounds. The Supreme Court will not hear a case from state court, even though it has jurisdiction over the parties and the subject matter, if there are adequate and independent state grounds to support the decision. Here, the state court held the law invalid on state, rather than federal, constitutional grounds. Therefore, the Supreme Court should refuse to grant certiorari. (B) is incorrect because mootness goes to whether there is a real, live controversy at this stage of the proceeding. The case here is not moot because the hospital wants to challenge the ruling that the law was unconstitutional under the state constitution. If the hospital wins, the city will not have to amend its law and Dunston Hospital may continue to receive fine money. (C) is incorrect because no political question is involved here. A political question, which is nonjusticiable, is one involving an issue that the Constitution has committed to another branch of the government or that is inherently incapable of judicial resolution and enforcement. Whether a law is constitutional—a determination of law—is certainly capable of judicial resolution and is properly within the judiciary branch's powers. Thus, a political question is not involved. (D) is incorrect because, as explained above, the basis for the decision was a state, not federal, violation. Therefore, there is no federal question.

Answer to Question 11

(C) The Court should uphold the statute as a valid time, place, and manner restriction on the exercise of First Amendment rights. The First Amendment protects the freedoms of speech and assembly; however, the protection is not absolute. The government is allowed to adopt regulations concerning the time, place, and manner of the exercise of speech and assembly in public forums and designated public forums to facilitate order and to protect other important government interests. To be valid, such a law must: (i) be content neutral; (ii) be narrowly tailored to serve a significant government interest; and (iii) leave open alternative channels of communication. The law here, although it restricts speech on public sidewalks, serves a significant government interest—the health and welfare of hospital patients. It is content neutral since it prohibits all leafleting around the hospital, not just leafleting concerning a particular message. It is narrowly tailored because it does not prohibit a broad range of speech, merely leafleting at a particular time and place (during visiting hours, within five feet of hospital entrances). Finally, the law leaves open alternative channels of communication, since people are allowed to distribute leaflets at all times other than the brief visiting hours, and during visiting hours may adopt other forms of expression. Thus, the statute is valid. (A) is incorrect because the Free Exercise Clause does not protect the leafleters' conduct here. The Free Exercise Clause provides that the government may not prohibit the free exercise of religion. However, the Clause does not provide an absolute right, and the Supreme Court has held that the government may regulate general conduct without violating the Constitution, even if the regulation happens to interfere with a person's or group's religious practices. The Clause merely prohibits the regulation of conduct because it is religious. Since the statute here is a broad regulation and is not specifically aimed at religious conduct, it does not violate the Constitution. (B) is incorrect because it is too broad. As explained above, some infringement of speech is constitutionally allowed (*i.e.*, reasonable time, place, and manner restrictions on speech in public forums are allowed). (D) is incorrect because, as a general rule, the Constitution does not protect people from the acts of other people, but rather from the acts of the government. Thus, the rationale of (D) does not make sense—a law will not be held "constitutional" because it prevents persons from violating others' constitutional rights.

Answer to Question 12

(D) The best argument against enforcement of the tax is that it violates the Commerce Clause. If Congress has not adopted laws regarding a subject, local governments are free to tax or regulate local aspects of the subject area as long as the tax or regulation does not discriminate against interstate commerce or unduly burden it. Here, the tax does not discriminate against interstate commerce, since it does not single out interstate commerce for taxation in order to benefit the local economy. However, it could be argued that the tax unduly burdens interstate commerce. A local tax will be held to unduly burden interstate commerce if the locality's need for the revenue does not outweigh the burden on interstate commerce. The Supreme Court will consider whether there is a substantial nexus between the activity or property taxed and the taxing state, whether the tax is fairly apportioned, and whether there is a fair relationship between the tax and the benefit the taxed party receives from the state. Here, there is little nexus between the manufacturer and LeMaize. The facts indicate that out-of-state manufacturers' machines are used in LeMaize, but do not indicate whether the manufacturers conduct any selling activity in LeMaize. Similarly, nothing indicates that there is a relationship between the tax and any benefit that the manufacturers derive from LeMaize. Thus, the tax would probably be unconstitutional under the Commerce Clause. (A) is not as good an argument as (D) because the Equal Protection Clause prohibits the states from treating similarly situated persons differently without sufficient justification. Where a classification does not involve a suspect or quasi-suspect class or a fundamental right, the classification will be upheld as long as it is rationally related to a legitimate government interest. While the tax here singles out arcade game manufacturers for special tax treatment, no suspect or quasi-suspect class is involved, nor is a fundamental right affected. Thus, the tax will be valid under the Equal Protection Clause because it is rationally related to the legitimate government interest of raising revenue. (B) is not a good argument because substantive due process requires that laws not be arbitrary. When laws do not involve a fundamental right, they will be held valid under the Due Process Clause as long as they are rationally related to a legitimate government interest. As established above, no fundamental right is involved and the tax is rationally related to a legitimate government interest. Thus, under the Due Process Clause the tax may be enforced. (C) is not a good argument because the Privileges and Immunities Clause of Article IV prohibits states from discriminating against out-of-state residents when a fundamental right is involved, and the tax here does not differentiate between residents and nonresidents.

Answer to Question 13

(C)   The Rally Manufacturing Company is most likely to have standing to challenge the tax. To have standing, a plaintiff must show that it has a concrete stake in the outcome of the litigation sufficient to ensure its zealous participation. On a constitutional issue, the plaintiff must be able to show that it is or will be injured by the government action involved and that its injury can be remedied by a decision in its favor. Rally meets both requirements. Under the tax law, it will either have to pay the tax or bear the expense of modifying its machines, which amounts to a direct injury to it. If Rally prevails, it will have the tax overturned, which will remedy the problem. Thus, it has standing. (Note that the prohibition against taxpayer standing to challenge federal taxes on the basis of how they are spent is not relevant here, because the challenge here regards whether the tax can constitutionally be imposed on Rally; not how the tax is spent.) (D) is the next best choice. A person who regularly plays arcade games might have to pay the one cent tax if the manufacturer decides to modify the machines to accept the tax from the player. However, if the manufacturer decides to pay the tax, a player such as Judie would have little claim. Thus, she is not in as good a position as Rally to challenge the tax. (B) is not a good choice because the way the tax is structured, it is not likely to injure Wizard, the arcade owner, in any significant way. The tax is levied against the manufacturers or the players, not the arcades themselves. The only injury that Wizard might claim is that his business will decline because of the extra cost added to playing arcade games, but this seems too indirect and uncertain a ground on which to base standing. Note that a third party, such as Wizard, who had some injury himself might be able to represent the parties who have a more substantial injury if it would be difficult for them to raise their own rights. It might be argued that most arcade game players are minors and would have a difficult time asserting their own rights here, so that Wizard would have standing. However, this claim to standing is less direct than the players' own claim. (A) is the worst choice because the Taxbite Federation has no concrete stake in the outcome. It has not shown that it will be injured by the tax in any manner other than the way everyone is injured by unlawful governmental conduct, and that is not a sufficient injury to sustain standing. (Note that an organization may have standing to represent its members if there is a sufficient injury to the members that is related to the organization's purpose, and the nature of the claim and the relief sought does not require participation of the members; but since this organization is not limited to arcade owners or customers, its injury is not sufficient to allow standing.)

Answer to Question 14

(A)   The group will lose because the action does not violate the Establishment Clause. Where government aid is given to a religious body and no sect preference is involved (the case here, since the school board did not require that the teacher be from a particular religious sect), the aid will be upheld if: (i) it has a secular purpose; (ii) its primary effect neither advances nor inhibits religion; and (iii) it does not produce excessive government entanglement with religion. Here, the payments made to St. Anne's constitute government aid, since the government is sending money to the school. However, all three requisites to constitutional validity are met: the program serves the secular purpose of providing the public school with a French teacher; the primary effect of the program does not promote religion, rather it promotes the learning of French; and no excessive government entanglement is involved because all the school board is required to do is to send the parochial school a check for half of the teacher's compensation. Thus, the program is valid. (B) is incorrect because all three requisites must be met; it is not enough that the program has a secular purpose. (C) is incorrect because, as explained above, the Establishment Clause is not violated. (D) is incorrect because it is too broad; while usually a transfer of public funds to a parochial school would violate the Establishment Clause, such transfers are permissible where the three-part test (above) is satisfied.

Answer to Question 15

(A) It would be improper for the Senate to adjudicate a border dispute between states. The Constitution divides the power of the federal government among the three branches. The power to adjudicate actions where two or more states are involved, which would include actions to adjudicate border disputes, is vested in the judicial branch by Article III of the Constitution. Thus, it would be improper for the Senate to adjudicate such a border dispute. (B) is incorrect because it would be proper for the Senate to define certain qualifications for being a member in good standing of the Senate. The Constitution lists certain minimal requirements for Senators, but grants each House of Congress the power to be the judge of member qualifications and allows each to determine rules for proceedings. [U.S. Const. art. I, §5] (C) is incorrect because the Constitution contains no prohibition against joint sessions of Congress and, as mentioned above, it grants both Houses the power to regulate their proceedings, which would include the manner of their meetings. (D) is incorrect because Congress has some power over foreign affairs—through its war power, its treaty power, and its power to regulate foreign commerce—and a resolution would probably be proper pursuant to such power. Moreover, while the President's power over foreign affairs is paramount, a resolution such as the one here amounts to nothing more than a suggestion to the President, and so would not be a usurpation of the executive.

Answer to Question 16

(C) The Montoming statute is invalid because of the Supremacy Clause. Under the Supremacy Clause, if the federal government adopts legislation that it has the power to adopt, the federal legislation is supreme, and a conflicting state law is rendered invalid. The federal law here, banning the hunting of pfus, is within the federal government's power under the Commerce Clause, which gives the government power to regulate anything that might affect interstate commerce. Since the birds themselves are found in a few states, they probably cross state lines. Also, hunters come from out of state and generate revenue in Montoming, so interstate commerce is involved. The Montoming law directly conflicts with the federal law since it allows hunting of pfus. Therefore, the state law will be held invalid under the Supremacy Clause. (A) is incorrect because while states do have a limited right to control their natural resources, the right is concurrent with the federal government's power, and cannot be exercised to conflict with federal regulation in the area. Note also that a state's power to control its natural resources is also limited even if Congress does not act: a state may not adopt a law discriminating against interstate commerce or excessively burdening interstate commerce, even absent federal legislation. Regarding (B), the Tenth Amendment reserves all powers not granted to the federal government to the states. (B) is incorrect because the Court will not likely strike down on Tenth Amendment grounds a federal regulation that subjects state governments to the same regulations as apply to the private sector. In such cases, the states' interests are best protected by the states' representation in Congress. (D) is incorrect because the Commerce Clause does not render the state's action invalid; it merely gives Congress the power to act. It is the Supremacy Clause that makes the interfering state law invalid.

Answer to Question 17

(B) Mr. and Mrs. Doe's strongest argument is that the law burdens their fundamental right of privacy. The right of privacy is not specifically mentioned in the Constitution, but the Supreme Court has recognized the right on a number of occasions. The right is strong when it involves acts of procreation by married couples. When the government restricts a fundamental right such as the right here, the government must show a *compelling interest* in the regulation and that the regulation is *necessary* to achieve that purpose. This is a difficult standard to meet, and thus the statute will probably be struck down. Here, the stated purposes for the law (improving the quality of life and preserving natural resources) are compelling; even if the Court would find them compelling, the limitation on the number of children that couples may have certainly is not *necessary* to these purposes. Thus, this is Mr. and Mrs. Doe's best argument. (A) is not a good argument for two reasons: (i) since a fundamental right is involved, the rational basis standard (suggested by this choice) is improper because strict scrutiny is the appropriate standard; and (ii) the statute here in fact is *rationally* related to its stated purpose since this standard is a very easy one to meet. (C) is not a good argument because the facts do not indicate that any official discretion is involved. The statute is violated when anyone is the biological parent of more than two children. (D) is incorrect because the Equal Protection Clause merely prohibits treating classes of persons differently without adequate justification, and here, the statute applies equally to all persons; it does not classify.

Answer to Question 18

(B) The fines will be upheld because the ordinance was enacted to reduce air pollution. The First Amendment provides that government may not make a law prohibiting the free exercise of religion. This prohibition, however, is not absolute, and the Supreme Court has held that a law of general applicability will not be struck down on free exercise grounds unless it was enacted for the purpose of burdening religion. [Employment Division v. Smith (1990)] The ordinance here was clearly enacted to reduce air pollution, and thus, is valid as applied to Jezebel. The Court will not force Equinox to carve out an exception to this prohibition on religious grounds. (A) is incorrect because it is irrelevant what religious group Jezebel belongs to; the result would be the same even if she belonged to a traditional religion. Moreover, the fact that Jezebel's religion is not traditional cannot even be considered by the court, because a court is not allowed to assess the validity of religious belief; it may only assess whether a person sincerely holds the religious belief that she claims. (C) is incorrect because it goes to the balancing test formerly used by the Supreme Court to assess whether a law was valid under the Free Exercise Clause. Since *Employment Division v. Smith,* factors such as less restrictive means are irrelevant. (D) is incorrect because the compelling interest test is no longer important in judging laws affecting religious *conduct*. (This was also a factor under the old balancing test.) As stated above, a law of general application not enacted to burden religion is valid, and the Court does not consider whether the state's interest is compelling.

Answer to Question 19

(A) The best argument for compelling the governor to release Plastique is that the President may negotiate executive agreements with foreign nations that take precedence over inconsistent state laws. While the President's power to enter into executive agreements with foreign nations is not explicitly granted in the Constitution, the Supreme Court has long recognized the power as an incident to the President's power over foreign relations. Since executive agreements are part of the federal law, they take precedence over conflicting state law under the Supremacy Clause. A governor's power to pardon or release state prisoners can be considered state law, and thus an executive agreement could override a governor's decision not to release a state prisoner. Choice (A) best reflects these concepts. (D) is the next best choice since it is based on the President's power over foreign affairs. However, it is not as good an answer as (A) because it gives no rationale for why the federal power should override the state power. (A)'s implicit invocation of the Supremacy Clause makes (A) the better choice. (B) is incorrect because the power to appoint ambassadors creates no implied power to enter into executive agreements to protect them. The power to protect ambassadors arises from the President's power over foreign relations. (C) is incorrect because the President's power "to faithfully execute" the laws does not empower the President to resolve conflicts between federal and state governments. Instead, the Supreme Court has assumed the role of final arbiter of these conflicts under its power of judicial review.

Answer to Question 20

(C) A conviction of Dermot would not be constitutional because the ordinance is void on its face. Although a municipality can place reasonable time, place, and manner restrictions on certain aspects of speech, it may not adopt a regulation that gives officials broad discretion over speech issues. If a statute gives licensing officials unbridled discretion, it is void on its face, and speakers need not even apply for a permit. They may exercise their First Amendment rights even if they could have been denied a permit under a valid law, and they may not be punished for violating the licensing statute. Here, the law allows the mayor to grant or deny permits based on his assessment of public interest. This is too much discretion to be valid. Therefore, the ordinance is void. (A) is wrong because, as explained above, the ordinance was void on its face and thus need not be obeyed. Therefore, Dermot did not need to apply for the permit. Also, although it is true that the municipality has a right to reasonable restrictions, this ordinance is not reasonable since it gives too much discretion to the mayor. (B) is wrong because even if the mayor has not abused his discretion, the ordinance is void on its face and thus need not be obeyed. (D) is wrong because, as stated, Dermot's case does not depend on whether the mayor would grant or deny the permit.

Answer to Question 21

(C) The United States will win because of the Supremacy Clause. Where the federal government and the state government share power to regulate a particular subject matter, the Supremacy Clause provides that federal law is the supreme law of the land, and consequently a conflicting state law will be superseded by a federal law. A corollary of this rule is that the states have no power to regulate the legitimate activities of the federal government unless Congress consents. Running a government building is a legitimate governmental activity, and so the Supremacy Clause prevents the state regulation here. (A) is incorrect because although regulation of air quality is certainly within the scope of a state's police power (the power to legislate for the health, safety, and morals of the community), it does not allow the state to regulate the legitimate activities of the federal government. An immunity is afforded the federal government by the Supremacy Clause, and the state's police power cannot overcome that immunity. (B) is incorrect because while it is true that the power to regulate air quality is shared, this means that when the federal government acts, conflicting state law will be superseded by virtue of the Supremacy Clause. The federal government does not have to defer to the state. (D) is incorrect because if the state clean air law were not superseded here, it would be no defense that the federal government was only breaking the law minimally. It is for the states to choose what effluents are harmful.

Answer to Question 22

(B) Of the choices presented, the only likely basis to strike down the statute is that it would violate substantive due process. Substantive due process tests the reasonableness of a statute; it prohibits arbitrary governmental action. Under substantive due process, where the government action limits a fundamental right, the government must prove that the action is necessary to promote a compelling interest. If a fundamental right is not involved, the challenging party must prove that the act is not rationally related to any legitimate government interest. The retail sale of milk is not a fundamental right, and so a challenger must prove that there is no rational basis for the statute. Although no basis is stated in the facts, almost any law can be justified under the rational basis standard, and so this argument will probably not actually succeed. Nevertheless, none of the other choices states a viable ground for invalidating the statute, and so (B) is the best choice. (A) is wrong because equal protection applies where a statute or governmental action treats similar people in a dissimilar manner (*i.e.,* classifies people), and here there is no classification—under the statute *no one* can sell milk for home consumption in containers smaller than one quart. Thus, an equal protection argument is not applicable. (C) is wrong because the Impairment of Contracts Clause prohibits only the *substantial* impairment of existing contracts (and there are exceptions even where there is substantial impairment), and forbidding the retail sale of milk in small containers probably does not substantially impair any existing contract. Even assuming that dairies have supply contracts with retailers, it is doubtful that the size restriction would have any substantial effect. (D) is wrong because the privileges and immunities covered by the Fourteenth Amendment are those attributes peculiar to United States citizenship (*e.g.,* the right to petition Congress for redress or the right to vote for federal officers). The statute here does not affect such rights.

Answer to Question 23

(C) The lack of notice and hearing prior to termination of Smith's license points to procedural due process as being the strongest argument. Procedural due process requires that fair procedure be used before a government agency takes away a person's life, liberty, or property. At the very least, this requires notice of the government's proposed action and an opportunity to present objections to an unbiased decisionmaker. A person has a protectable property interest whenever she has a legitimate claim to a benefit under state law. Smith has a protectable property interest in her business license because presumably the license cannot be terminated without cause. Thus, revocation of Smith's license violates procedural due process since she was not given notice or an opportunity to respond. (A) is incorrect because it is not the strongest argument; it is not clear that there is any substantial impairment of any contract between Smith and her wholesale distributors. The Impairment of Contracts Clause prohibits only *some* government action substantially impairing existing contracts. Nothing here indicates that a contract with wholesalers will be substantially impaired by Smith's no longer ordering pints. Even if there would be substantial impairment, the law may be valid if it serves an important state interest and is a narrowly tailored means of promoting that interest. Here, an important state interest will likely be found (*e.g.,* reduction of litter on the streets and highways or reduction of trash in state landfills), and this law could be seen as narrowly tailored to that interest. Thus, the law would probably be valid despite its impairment of the contract. Therefore, this is not Smith's best argument. (B) is incorrect because the state agency's action does not indicate that Smith has been subjected to a governmental classification in which similar people are treated in a dissimilar manner. Smith was apparently not singled out for a license revocation while certain other retailers were not obliged to comply with the statute. As far as can be known, all sellers of milk for home consumption are required to comply with the statute. (D) is incorrect because violation of substantive due process is not a very strong argument in this case. As discussed in the previous answer, the rational basis standard would be applied (since no fundamental right was involved). Most statutes tested under this standard are upheld since the statute need be rational in light of *any* legitimate government interest. The law here, for example, could be said to reduce litter or trash and this is a legitimate government interest, and so the government would probably win on this basis. Therefore, this is not Smith's best argument.

Answer to Question 24

(D) The court should hear the case on the merits. This question is best answered by eliminating the incorrect choices. (A) is incorrect because Pandora has standing. To have standing, one must have a concrete stake in the outcome of the controversy. To have such a stake, the person must be suffering an injury in fact caused by governmental action that is greater than the injury that all persons suffer when the government acts improperly, and her injury must be able to be remedied by a decision in her favor. Pandora is suffering an injury to her reputation, and more importantly from a constitutional law point of view, a governmental body (the University officials) is attempting to suppress her First Amendment speech and assembly rights. A cease and desist order will remedy her harm. Thus, she has standing. (B) is incorrect because the case is not moot, even though the officials are currently not harassing Pandora. Under the mootness doctrine, a federal court will not hear a case unless there is a real, live controversy at all stages of the proceedings. However, there is an exception to this rule: Controversies capable of repetition but evading review will be heard even though the controversy might not continue for the entire case. The exception applies where the controversy involves issues of short duration (*e.g.,* pregnancy) or where, as here, the defendant voluntarily stops the offending practice (since the defendant could resume the offending practice as soon as the case is dismissed). (C) is incorrect because the case here is ripe. Ripeness is a bar to hearing actions ***before*** a controversy arises, and here the controversy has already arisen, since the officials have already harassed Pandora. Therefore, the case is ripe. Thus, because there are no grounds presented on which to refuse jurisdiction, the court should hear the case on the merits.

Answer to Question 25

(B)   The most damaging fact to Roger's First Amendment claims is that the fair's rules clearly prohibit leafleting except at designated hours other than the time Roger was distributing his leaflets. The First Amendment freedom of speech is not absolute. To avoid chaos and to protect other governmental interests, government is allowed to adopt reasonable time, place, and manner regulations on speech in public forums and designated public forums. To be valid, such regulations must be content neutral, narrowly tailored to serve a significant government interest, and leave open alternative channels of communication. The fact that the rule here allows solicitation at specified times indicates that it is narrowly tailored and leaves open alternative channels of communication. The rule also seems to be content neutral and it serves the government's significant interest of keeping the fair orderly. Therefore, the rule would probably be valid if (B) is true. (A) would not be damaging to Roger because the First Amendment protects against government infringement on speech, regardless of whether the speech is on private or public property; the fact that the fairgrounds are private property does not preclude the property from being a public forum during the time that the county was leasing it and conducting a fair on it. Hence, the fairgrounds would be considered to be government property for purposes of application of the public forum rule. (C) is not damaging because the First Amendment protections extend to most forms of speech, including certain symbolic acts and the right not to speak. It certainly also extends to leafleting. (D) is not very damaging because the First Amendment protects commercial speech, although the standard for regulation differs from other speech—the government may ban false or misleading commercial speech and may regulate (including content regulation) other commercial speech with narrowly tailored regulations that directly advance a substantial government interest. The regulation here appears to meet this standard.

Answer to Question 26

(C)   The most helpful additional fact for Roger is that Milan allowed other people to distribute leaflets at all hours. Although the government may adopt reasonable time, place, and manner restrictions in public forums and designated public forums, such restrictions must be content neutral. Milan's allowing some people to distribute leaflets at all hours shows that the restriction here is probably being used as a content regulation, which would be prohibited under these facts. Additionally, if Milan is allowing others to distribute leaflets at all hours, his discriminatory application of the rule might also violate the Equal Protection Clause. (A) is not very helpful because the fact that Roger was informed once of the rule would be sufficient to give him notice that he was violating the law. There is no requirement that persons be warned twice that they are violating speech regulations. (B) might help Roger because he could claim that since the fairgrounds are surrounded by a public forum (sidewalks), the grounds themselves are also a public forum. This argument will probably not prevail, however, since the Court has never made such a holding (and indeed has held that although the sidewalks around the Supreme Court building are public forums, the Supreme Court building itself is not a public forum). This fact might even hurt Roger, since it indicates that alternative public forums were readily available to him. (D) is not very helpful because while political speech might receive a little more First Amendment protection than commercial speech, it is still subject to time, place, and manner regulations, and so could be regulated by rules such as the one here.

Answer to Question 27

(B) The federal court will hear Roger's case if he argues that the prosecutor was merely trying to harass him. The federal courts generally will abstain from enjoining pending state criminal proceedings such as the one here, even if they have jurisdiction over the case. For purposes of this rule, a case is deemed to be pending as soon as it is filed. Thus, the federal court would ordinarily not hear Roger's claim here until after the state prosecution has ended. However, there is an exception to the general rule—a federal court will hear an action to enjoin a pending state court prosecution if it is being conducted in bad faith; *e.g.,* merely to harass the defendant. Thus, (B) is correct. (A) is incorrect because the abstention rule does not distinguish between claims that ordinances are invalid on their face and claims that they are invalid as applied. (C) is incorrect because Roger clearly has standing. A person has standing to challenge a governmental action if he can show an injury in fact from the action that is greater than the injury everyone suffers when the government acts unlawfully, and that a decision in his favor will remedy the injury. If the ordinance here is being applied unconstitutionally, Roger has suffered a sufficient injury, and a decision in his favor will remedy his injury. (D) is incorrect because whether an ordinance is being applied in an unconstitutional manner is not a political question. Political questions are those committed by the Constitution to another branch of the government or that are inherently incapable of resolution and enforcement by the judicial process. This case is properly within the judiciary branch and the courts can resolve it.

Answer to Question 28

(A) KEA will have to prove that there is no rational basis for the statute. Whether the statute is treated as a due process challenge (because the law affects all employees), or as an equal protection problem (because employers are singled out for special treatment), the same standard will apply. Since there is no fundamental right involved and employers are neither a suspect nor quasi-suspect class, the rational basis standard will apply. Under the rational basis standard, the party challenging the government action has the burden of proving that the action is not rationally related to any legitimate state interest—a very difficult burden to meet. Thus, the burden will be on KEA and (A) is correct. (B) is incorrect because it states the wrong standard. (C) and (D) are incorrect because they place the burden on the wrong party.

Answer to Question 29

(A) The court should hold the sale presumptively valid pursuant to Congress's property power. Article IV, Section 3 of the Constitution gives Congress the power to dispose of all property belonging to the federal government. There are no express limits placed on this power, and a disposal has never been invalidated on the ground that it places a competitor of the purchaser at a disadvantage. (B) is incorrect because the Due Process Clause would not prevent the sale here. The Due Process Clause prohibits the government from denying persons life, liberty, or property without due process of law. For the restrictions of the Clause to apply, a person must have a legitimate property interest in the property taken. "Property" includes more than personal belongings, but a mere expectation or desire for the benefit is not enough. One must have a legitimate claim or entitlement to the benefit before one may make a procedural due process challenge, and here Bluto has no claim to a right to be offered the ships that were sold to Popeye. (C) is incorrect because, as indicated above, there is no express limit on Congress's power to dispose of government property; nothing in the Constitution requires Congress to get the President's (or any other executive officer's) permission to exercise the power. (D) is incorrect because there is no denial of equal protection here. While the Equal Protection Clause is not applicable to the federal government, equal protection guarantees are applicable through the Fifth Amendment Due Process Clause. Nevertheless, there is no equal protection violation here: Since no suspect class or fundamental right is involved, the action would be tested under the rational basis standard (discriminatory government action is valid as long as it is rationally related to any legitimate government interest) and would be upheld since the sale is rationally related to the government's interest in reviving the cruise ship industry. It does not matter that the government is not doing all that it can; a first step is permissible.

Answer to Question 30

(C) The statute here unconstitutionally infringes upon the commercial speech protections of the First Amendment since it forbids truthful advertisement of a lawful product. Commercial speech is protected by the First Amendment, but it can be subject to significantly more regulation than noncommercial speech. In determining whether a restriction on commercial speech is valid, a court first asks whether the speech concerns lawful activity and is not misleading or fraudulent. The activity here is lawful, and nothing indicates fraud or falsity. Next, the court will determine whether: (i) the government interest in the regulation is substantial; (ii) the regulation directly advances that interest; and (iii) the regulation is narrowly tailored to the substantial interest. The facts do not indicate what interest the government seeks to promote with this regulation. The "birth dearth" might be one purpose; however, even assuming that the "birth dearth" is a significant government interest, the regulation still will not stand because it does not directly advance that interest; *i.e.,* it does not directly encourage having babies, but rather only limits one method of advertisement of contraceptives. Thus, the restriction on commercial speech is invalid. (A) is not the best argument against the statute because it is not as direct as (C). It is true that the right to privacy is protected by the Constitution and the right to contraceptives is probably included within that right, but the regulation here does not make contraceptives illegal (it merely bans one form of advertisement) and limits can be placed on advertisements. Since advertisement is commercial speech, the appropriate place to look for constitutional protection is the First Amendment. (B) is incorrect because regulation will amount to a taking only when it unjustly reduces the economic value of property, so that there cannot be a fair return on investment. Nothing here indicates that the ban is unjust, but more importantly nothing indicates that makers of contraceptives will not be able to obtain a fair return if they are prohibited from soliciting through the mail. (D) is incorrect because while the statute indeed burdens interstate commerce, Congress has the power to control interstate commerce in nearly any manner it desires (as long as it does not violate some other constitutional provision). Only the states are prohibited from unduly burdening interstate commerce.

Answer to Question 31

(A) Before a government agency can deprive a person of liberty or property, the Due Process Clause requires that fair procedures be used, including the opportunity to present objections to an agency's action to a fair, neutral decisionmaker. Clearly, it is procedurally unfair to refuse to inform a person of why a license is being denied. However, it is not equally clear that Dottie Sue has a liberty or property interest at stake. Liberty interests have been held to include the right to engage in gainful employment in a broad sense, but here Dottie Sue is being denied only a very specific employment, this fast food restaurant. Similarly, property rights include interests already acquired in specific benefits—there must be a "legitimate claim of entitlement" to the benefit—but do not include interests not yet acquired and for which there is only a unilateral expectation, not a legitimate claim. Nevertheless, it is at least arguable that the DPH's establishment of specific regulations for granting the permit and its grant of permits to other fast food restaurants created for Dottie Sue a "legitimate claim of entitlement" to the same treatment. Thus, denial of due process of law is Dottie Sue's best argument. (B) is incorrect because the Contracts Clause only prohibits states from adopting laws that invalidate, release, or extinguish contractual obligations. The failure to act on the part of DPH did nothing to change the contractual obligations of the parties. (C) is incorrect regardless of which privileges and immunities provision is being considered. The Article IV privileges and immunities provision prohibits a state from discriminating against out-of-state residents when a "fundamental" right is involved. Dottie Sue is a citizen of the state in which she is seeking approval of the permit, so this provision does not apply. The Fourteenth Amendment Privileges and Immunities Clause, which states that "no state shall enforce any law which shall abridge the privileges and immunities of citizens of the United States," has been judicially interpreted to apply only to attributes peculiar to United States citizenship, such as the right to petition Congress. (D) is incorrect because, even assuming the denial of the license affects interstate commerce, the state may regulate local aspects of interstate commerce (such as public health) as long as the legislation does not conflict with federal regulations, the subject matter does not require national uniformity, the regulation does not discriminate against out-of-state competition, and the incidental burden on interstate commerce does not outweigh the local benefits. There is nothing to suggest that these criteria could not be established in this case.

Answer to Question 32

(A) If the case goes to trial, the state will have the burden of proving that the statute is necessary to achieve a compelling government purpose because it has a substantial impact on a fundamental right. The right to have children involves the fundamental right of privacy, and when a statute imposes on a fundamental right, it will violate due process unless the state can show that it is necessary to promote a compelling interest. (B) is incorrect because no suspect class is involved here. It is true that if a law impacts a suspect class, it is unconstitutional unless the state can prove that the law is necessary to achieve a compelling interest, but age—the only classification involved in the question—is not a suspect class. (C) is incorrect because statutes are presumed to have a sufficient relationship to a government interest only if they are tested under the rational basis test (*i.e.,* where neither a suspect class nor a fundamental right is involved), and the statute here will be tested under strict scrutiny since a fundamental right is involved. (D) is incorrect because it is an incorrect statement of law—the burden of persuasion is not placed on the challenger merely because the law is within the state's police power.

Answer to Question 33

(A) The strongest argument against the tax is that it burdens interstate commerce. The Commerce Clause of the Constitution gives Congress plenary power to authorize or forbid state taxation that affects interstate commerce. Unless approved by Congress, state taxes that discriminate against interstate commerce are invalid. The special tax here does not pass muster because it directly discriminates against out-of-state competition. Thus, the tax violates the Commerce Clause and (A) is correct. (B) is not a good argument because the Equal Protection Clause is not violated here. The Equal Protection Clause prohibits government from treating similarly situated people differently without good reason. What constitutes a good reason depends on the classification and the right involved. If the class is suspect or the right is fundamental, a compelling reason is required. Otherwise, the reason need only be rational. For most state or local government taxes, equal protection requires only that the tax classifications have a rational relationship to a legitimate government interest. Here, there is a rational reason for the regulation—protection of local jobs. Thus, the tax does not violate the Equal Protection Clause. (C) is incorrect because the Fourteenth Amendment clause protecting the privileges and immunities of national citizenship does not apply here. The clause protects only those rights attributable to being a United States citizen, *e.g.,* the right to petition Congress. The clause is inapplicable here. (D) is incorrect because the Due Process Clause is not violated here. For state taxation of interstate commerce to be valid under the Due Process Clause, the benefits and protection afforded by the taxing state must have a sufficient relationship to the subject matter taxed such that it is reasonable for the taxed party to expect to be subject to the taxing state's jurisdiction. Here, the tax is imposed on autos sold in the taxing state; this is a sufficient relationship to satisfy the Due Process Clause.

Answer to Question 34

(B) Article II, Section 2 provides that the President shall nominate, and with the advice and consent of the Senate shall appoint, ambassadors and other officers of the United States. The section also provides that Congress may vest the appointment of inferior officers in the President alone, in the courts of law, or in the heads of departments. Under separation of powers principles, however, Congress may not vest in itself any broader appointment powers than what is provided for by the Constitution. Where Congress has not vested the appointment power in courts of law or the heads of departments, it is not permitted to restrict the candidates that the President may nominate for appointment. Thus, the Senate's attempt here to exert some control over the President's choice of lower-level diplomatic representatives is an unconstitutional violation of separation of powers. (A) is incorrect for two reasons. First, if the Senate's action had been constitutionally permissible, there would be no requirement of using a "less intrusive method" to effectuate such action. The President would simply be required to seek the approval of the Senate. Second, if the Senate refused to appropriate funds to staff the embassy because it deemed the President's selections inappropriate, this would simply be another way of exerting control over the President's selection of lower-level diplomatic personnel, and would be as unconstitutional as the resolution passed by the Senate. (C) is incorrect because the President's status as commander in chief is not at issue here. The President does have rather extensive military powers as commander in chief of the armed forces. However, the appointment of a consular staff involves the President's power in foreign relations, not his power as commander in chief. In addition, (C) incorrectly states that the President has *exclusive* authority to protect American interests abroad. Although the President has broad authority to protect American interests abroad, Congress also has some authority in this field. For example, Congress has the power to declare war, to raise and support armies, and to give its advice and consent in the making of treaties. Similarly, (D) incorrectly asserts a limitless presidential control over foreign policy. While the President's authority in foreign policy is quite broad, it has some limits; *e.g.,* the requirement of senatorial advice and consent in the making of treaties.

Answer to Question 35

(C) The state interest in rehabilitating juvenile offenders outweighs the First Amendment interests of the press in obtaining access to the juvenile court records. The press and the public have a broad

First Amendment right of access to criminal proceedings which can only be outweighed by a compelling government interest. Juvenile proceedings are different from criminal proceedings, however. The juvenile justice system was established as an alternative to the criminal justice system in order to rehabilitate juvenile offenders before they become adult criminals. The goal of giving juveniles a clean slate when they become adults is accomplished in part by sealing all court records relating to juveniles. Even in criminal proceedings, a state's compelling interest in protecting minors allows a court to close portions of a criminal trial to protect children who are victims of sex offenses. [Globe Newspaper Co. v. Superior Court (1982)] In juvenile proceedings, the press's right of access is not as strong and the state's interest is equally compelling, justifying the statute in this case. (A) is incorrect because freedom of the press is not absolute. Here it is outweighed by the state's interest in rehabilitating juvenile offenders. (B) is incorrect because the juvenile records are not public documents. The press is free to publish information about juveniles found in public documents or obtained through legal means, even where the juvenile's court and police records are otherwise sealed. [Smith v. Daily Mail Publishing Co. (1979)] However, the records that are sealed are not themselves public documents, even if some of the information in the records has been disclosed to the public. The records themselves need not be disclosed to the press or public. (D) is incorrect because even if it is assumed that Bugsy is a public figure, while it might afford Kirby a defense if Bugsy brought an invasion of privacy action for disclosing the information, Bugsy's status would not override the state's interest in the confidentiality of its juvenile court records.

Answer to Question 36

(C) The strongest basis for denying Furtwangler relief is that there is no state action upon which the Fourteenth Amendment can operate. Stepside is privately owned and operated. For state action to be present, the government must be significantly involved in the private entity; mere city licensing does not convert the private company's operations into state action. (A), (B), and (D) are incorrect because they ignore this critical factor. If state action were involved, these justifications would tend to support Stepside's position, but there is no need to apply First Amendment doctrines because the government is not involved.

Answer to Question 37

(C) The entity most likely to have standing to challenge the gift is Future Flyers. To have standing to challenge government action on constitutional grounds, a person must show that he has a concrete stake in the outcome of the litigation. This is to ensure adequate presentation of the issues. To have such a stake, the potential litigant must show that he has an injury in fact caused by the government that is more than the theoretical injury that all persons suffer when the government engages in unconstitutional acts, and that a decision in his favor will eliminate his harm. Future Flyers can show both components here: If the gift is unconstitutional, Future Flyers has suffered more than a theoretical injury—it has lost the opportunity to purchase the airplane from the federal government at a good price, and a decision in the club's favor will eliminate the injury since it will then be able to purchase the plane. Thus, Future Flyers has standing. (B) is incorrect because the only injury that a citizen would suffer here is the theoretical injury that we all suffer by the government's unconstitutional acts. People have no standing merely as "citizens" to claim that government action violates federal law or the Constitution. (A) is incorrect because a person's injury as a taxpayer is generally held to be insufficient to establish standing. There is an exception where the federal government acts under the taxing and spending power and that action allegedly violates the Establishment Clause, but the government action here falls under the Property Clause and not the Spending Clause; thus, the exception does not apply. (D) is incorrect because the state attorney general has no stake in the outcome of the litigation, and it is not sufficient even if he is deemed to represent the interests of all the citizens in the state.

Answer to Question 38

(C) In *Committee for Public Education and Religious Liberty v. Regan* (1980), the United States Supreme Court held that a similar statute passed by the state of New York did not violate the Establishment Clause because it had a secular legislative purpose. Its principal effect did not advance or inhibit religion, and it did not foster an excessive government entanglement with religion. (A) is therefore incorrect; aid can be given to religious schools that pass this test. (B) is wrong. It misstates the facts given, which make no mention of a specific religious group. Rather, the suit is filed by an association challenging the reimbursement. (D) is irrelevant. The question is not whether the tests involve "matters of religion," but whether the reimbursement program impermissibly advances religion.

Answer to Question 39

(D) The city may ban billboards in a particular area for purposes of traffic safety or aesthetics if the ordinance constitutes a valid time, place, and manner regulation; *i.e.*, it must be content neutral, it must be narrowly tailored to further a significant government interest, and there must be alternative media available for the protected expression. (A) is wrong because this is not "spot zoning," which describes zoning actions that burden a single or limited number of properties in ways inconsistent with the general scheme. This ordinance simply enacts a general rule. (B) is wrong because it is overbroad. As indicated, expression may be subjected to reasonable time, place, and manner regulations. (C) is a misstatement of law; commercial speech is protected by the First Amendment, but it is subject to greater regulation than other forms of speech.

Answer to Question 40

(B) Congress may regulate, under the commerce power, anything that has a substantial economic effect upon interstate commerce. Since the lending of money within Texas has a substantial economic effect on the interstate traffic in money, Commercial Bank would not prevail. (A) is wrong because the commerce power is broad enough to regulate intrastate activities that have a substantial economic effect on interstate commerce. (C) is wrong because the General Welfare Clause is a limitation on Congress's power, not a source of its power. (D) is wrong because interest rates can be and are regulated on a national basis.

Answer to Question 41

(C) The court should rule that the federal statute preempts the state law. Even if Congress had not preempted the subject of interest rates, the state would not be permitted to establish a standard less strict than the federal rule. (A) is wrong because there is no basis for certification under the facts presented. While (B) might state an alluring policy choice, it is both outside the purview of the court and inappropriate in the face of the express determination by Congress to preempt local control. (D) is incorrect because while the Constitution gives the Supreme Court original jurisidction over cases in which a state is a party, that jurisdiction is not exclusive. Congress has given the lower federal courts concurrent jurisdiction over all cases in which the Supreme Court has original jurisdiction except those between states. This is a case between the United States and a state. Therefore, the Supreme Court's jurisidiction is not exclusive and the case can be heard in a lower federal court.

Answer to Question 42

(C) Since Roger is an at-will employee, the hospital is not required to provide any justification. Absent this fact, Roger would have been entitled to notice and a hearing, regardless of the substantive merit in his dismissal. (C) is, accordingly, the hospital's strongest defense. (A) and (B) state grounds the hospital could conceivably raise, but since it is not required to, it should not. (D), in turn, raises the possibility of a First Amendment defense to the firing (assuming "community" equals "public," giving rise to state action), since the allegation regarding dispensing medicine would fall within the public policy comment privilege recognized by the Court.

Answer to Question 43

(C) Breaching the oral contract between Roger and the chief administrator deprived Roger of a property right created as a result of the voluntary promise made by the chief administrator, and such deprivation may not be accomplished without due process, meaning notice and an opportunity to respond. None of the other answers raises any constitutional issues or alters his status as a terminable-at-will employee. Thus, (A), (B), and (D) are wrong.

Answer to Question 44

(B) Government is not involved in the establishment of religion if its acts have neither a religious purpose nor an effect on religion, and if the measure does not foster an excessive government entanglement with religion. While religious schools may fulfill an important educational function and the teaching of religious matters is not prohibited, neither statement is material as to the constitutionality of state action. Thus, (A) and (C) are incorrect. (D) is incorrect because the state is compelled by the Establishment Clause not to provide certain types of aid to religious schools; in such cases, the Free Exercise Clause is not violated.

Answer to Question 45

(C) The state's policy is a significant involvement in the segregated educational activities of the Academy, and thus violates the Equal Protection Clause. The Constitution forbids discriminatory state action, not private bias (federal legislation that prohibits private discrimination is not constitutionally mandated), and a state may aid anyone as long as it does not violate a specific constitutional restriction. Thus, (A) and (B) are incorrect. (D) is also incorrect. Distribution of the model lesson plans does serve a "legitimate" state interest. A state may not, however, escape the express constitutional prohibition against invidious discrimination by asserting that its support of the education programs in a school like Jefferson Davis is somehow "legitimate" in spite of the discriminatory character of the overall program.

Answer to Question 46

(A) Congress may investigate only matters upon which it can legislate, but it is not limited to matters as to which it has made appropriations of money. Thus, (D) is incorrect. Executive privilege is not absolute, and both branches of Congress have investigatory powers. Thus, (B) and (C) are incorrect.

Answer to Question 47

(B) The doctrine of separation of powers prohibits legislative interference with the executive discretion as to whether to prosecute. Thus, (C) and (D) are incorrect. (A) is incorrect because officials of the executive branch are not immune from prosecution relating to their duties.

Answer to Question 48

(D) Prior to disbursement, the federal government may attach any reasonable condition to expenditures under the general welfare power. (A) is not a power of Congress enumerated in the Constitution. There is no general federal police power, the federal government being one of limited, enumerated powers. Thus, (B) is incorrect. (C) is incorrect because the war and defense power does not apply to the facts presented.

Answer to Question 49

(C) State action that is facially neutral will nevertheless be struck down if it can be shown that it was intended to discriminate on the basis of race or national origin and does in fact have that effect. Sassoonian must show that the legislature selected the specific cost guidelines with full knowledge of the population characteristics in Midvalleyville and with the specific intent to disqualify that city from participation in the program because of its high concentration of Armenians. If he proves that intent, he will prevail, and (C) is accordingly his best argument. (A) would not be as helpful because the state could show a rational basis for not operating in Midvalleyville—that housing costs were not high enough to warrant state intervention—which would suffice to justify different treatment not based upon purposeful discrimination. (B) is not a good answer because the difficulty experienced by Armenian citizens in obtaining housing may have nothing to do with state action and may be experienced by other groups as well. (D) is not the best answer because, while it is arguably some evidence of purposeful discrimination, it does not state it as clearly as (C).

Answer to Question 50

(D) Providing housing for its citizens is clearly within the reserved police powers of the state. Since this is facially neutral economic and social legislation, the state simply needs a rational basis for its actions, and that is present. (A) and (B) are, accordingly, wrong. A state may undertake traditionally private business activities, and the analysis for both due process and equal protection purposes is rational basis review, under which the state will prevail. (C) is not a good answer because Rocky has suffered a direct injury (lost business) caused by the state government action. He has standing to challenge the legislation, but standing has nothing to do with the merits of his claim and he will lose.

Answer to Question 51

(C) Because this is economic legislation not involving fundamental rights or suspect classifications, it will be upheld if it has a rational basis. The higher housing costs justify intervention in areas like Metropolis rather than in Midvalleyville, and so the legislation would probably be valid. (A) is wrong because while the Eleventh Amendment immunizes states from suit in federal courts, that immunity does not authorize a state to violate the Constitution; a suit alleging such a violation may be filed against the responsible officials. (B) is an incorrect statement of law; as an agency of the state, the corporation's operations are state action. (D) is wrong because it applies the wrong standard of review.

Answer to Question 52

(D) In theory, the Tenth Amendment prohibits federal regulation of state activities if the regulation would virtually eliminate the state's local functions. As a practical matter, the Court's holding in *Garcia v. San Antonio Metropolitan Transit Authority* (1985) gives Congress broad authority when it acts pursuant to its enumerated powers. Accordingly, a federal regulation that controls the states as well as private persons is valid. Thus, the housing corporation would have to follow the federal regulations which control due to the Supremacy Clause. Thus, (D) is correct, and (B) and (C) are wrong. (A) is wrong because even intrastate activities are subject to Federal Commerce Clause regulation if they substantially affect interstate commerce.

Answer to Question 53

(B) Under Article I of the Constitution, a state cannot lay any imposts or duties on imports or exports without the consent of Congress unless it is necessary to execute the state inspection laws. Thus, (A) is incorrect. (C) is wrong because the Privileges and Immunities Clause does not apply to corporations or aliens. (D) is wrong because without congressional consent, the statute is unconstitutional despite the compelling nature of the state's interest.

Answer to Question 54

(A) Only Article III judges enjoy the constitutional grant of life tenure, and Agnew is not an Article III judge. The Tribunal is an administrative agency with limited jurisdiction, and while Agnew exercises some adjudicatory powers, all persons with some adjudicatory functions are not judges within the meaning of Article III. (A) is thus correct and (D) is wrong. (C) is also wrong, since the Constitution does not recognize property rights in employment. Agnew could show some kind of wrongful discharge only if he could claim that he was deprived of something "in the nature of a property right." (B) is incorrect because Agnew clearly has standing; he alleges a specific injury to himself and brings the claim in his own right, alleging the violation of a constitutional right.

Answer to Question 55

(B) The statute burdens interstate commerce by diverting purchase of items from interstate to intrastate commerce, discriminating against the former. (A) is incorrect because the Privileges and Immunities Clause does not apply: the sale of products does not fall within the limited number of "privileges" the Court has recognized under the Fourteenth Amendment. Since the statute applies to all businesses, it does not create the sort of classification that triggers equal protection analysis and so (C) is incorrect. Since the license requirement is well within the traditional state police powers, and would be reasonable except for the Commerce Clause problems, (D) is incorrect.

Answer to Question 56

(C) Since the statute neither burdens a fundamental right nor creates a suspect or quasi-suspect classification, the rationality test is proper. Thus, (B) is wrong because it uses the wrong standard. Furthermore, the burden is on the challenger to show that a statute passes constitutional muster under the rational basis test. Thus, (A) is incorrect because it misallocates the burden. (D) is incorrect; the Necessary and Proper Clause has nothing to do with state statutes.

Answer to Question 57

(B) The right to enter into agreements is not a fundamental right; therefore, the state need only show that there is a rational basis for the statute. (A) is wrong because there are many instances when the Constitution may affect the state's authority over marital and quasi-marital relationships. Hence, (D) is also wrong. (C) makes no sense; if anything, the fact that other persons similarly situated can bring suits in this circumstance, but Bev cannot, tends to show some kind of discrimination, albeit not invidious.

Answer to Question 58

(C) The federal government has the power to tax and spend funds for the general welfare of the citizens of the United States. (A) is arguable since, under the Commerce Clause, Congress has enacted a wide variety of social legislation. However, since this legislation is strictly dealing with welfare, the act would most probably be based on the Taxing and Spending Clause. (B) is incorrect because the facts do not indicate that any citizen is being deprived of any federal right. There is no general federal police power, so (D) is wrong.

Answer to Question 59

(C) The Supreme Court has original jurisdiction in all cases affecting ambassadors, other public ministers and consuls, and those in which a state shall be a party. In all other cases, such as maritime disputes, the Supreme Court has only appellate jurisdiction. Thus, (A), (B), and (D) are wrong.

Answer to Question 60

(C) This statute deals with activities that have an effect on interstate commerce and, therefore, is within the commerce power. (B) is wrong because the Second Amendment is prohibitory; therefore, it could not be the basis of enactment, but could only prohibit some types of enactments. (A) is wrong because the Fourteenth Amendment Equal Protection Clause, which applies only to the states, cannot be the basis for federal powers by itself. Congress must rather invoke its powers pursuant to Section 5 of the Fourteenth Amendment when it acts to guarantee the equal protection of the laws. (D) is wrong because the Necessary and Proper Clause only broadens congressional power authorized under some other provision; it does not itself create the power to act.

Answer to Question 61

(C) Congress is specifically given the power to regulate federal lands in Article IV. Since there is no other authority that can regulate the use of federal lands but Congress, this is all the authority Congress would need to enact this type of statute. Thus, (B) and (D) are wrong. (A) is wrong because although Congress has broad powers under the Commerce Clause, this is not a matter falling under that clause.

Answer to Question 62

(B) The Appointment Clause of the Constitution permits Congress to vest appointments of inferior officers only in the President, the courts, or the heads of departments. Enforcement is an executive act; therefore, Congress cannot appoint its own members to the Commission to exercise enforcement powers. A duly appointed commission does have the power to make rules and regulations governing the subject matter for which it is appointed. Those rules are not "criminal" statutes in this case. Thus, (A) is wrong. (C) is wrong because Congress may establish new public rights and actions that may be adjudicated by agencies, without juries. (D) is wrong because there is no discrimination.

Answer to Question 63

(C) May is not a judge within the sense of Article III, and only such judges are protected by the provisions of that article. Thus, (A) and (B) are incorrect. (D) makes no sense. The statutory authority for appointments remains the same, and only the person holding the office has changed.

Answer to Question 64

(B) The Supreme Court has stated that in the field of foreign affairs, the President has "plenary" powers. Coupled with the President's power to enter into executive agreements, his power is almost unlimited in the area of foreign affairs. (A) is wrong because there are some limits on the President's powers to enter into executive agreements. (C) is wrong because a two-thirds vote is not required for an executive agreement. (D) is a correct statement, since Congress has authority to act to preserve wildlife. That authority does not, however, deprive the President of the power to enter agreements of this sort.

Answer to Question 65

(C) The Supreme Court has held that executive agreements are the law of the land until Congress enacts a statute that is inconsistent with the executive agreement. Since this is a state statute, it must be declared unconstitutional because it is in conflict with the executive agreement. Thus, (B) is incorrect. (A) is incorrect. The issue is not whether the question is "best" left to the states, but rather whether the President has the authority to enter into the agreement. (D) states the right conclusion, but the logic is not as good as in alternative (C).

Answer to Question 66

(C) Regulating the possession or sale of an item made from a California condor clearly affects commerce. Thus, Congress can act under its broad commerce power. Since the regulations do not compel surrender of the artifacts, and there is no physical invasion or restraint upon them, there is no taking of a property right without just compensation. Therefore, Congress's power to regulate is proper, even though it diminishes the opportunity to make a profit. Thus, (A) is incorrect. (B) is not supported by the facts. (D) states the right conclusion, but for the wrong reason.

Answer to Question 67

(B) The restrictions involve action by the court in discriminating against unmarried adults. In the case of *Shelley v. Kramer* (1948), the United States Supreme Court held that restrictions in deeds based on race are not enforceable, and several state courts have used similar reasoning in striking down other discriminatory provisions in zoning laws and the like. Hence this argument might also be made under the facts of this case. (A) is not the best answer, because under the facts of the case, the problem is not alienation to groups of more than two unrelated adults, but occupancy. (C) and (D) are really irrelevant facts to the determination of the enforceability of this restriction.

Answer to Question 68

(B) Although state classifications based on alienage are generally suspect, a state may reserve a government position for citizens if it is related to self-governance, involves policymaking, or requires exercise of important discretionary power over citizens. In these cases, only a rationality test is used. A public school teacher performs an important governmental function (*e.g.*, he influences students' attitudes about government, the political process, citizenship, etc.), and therefore the exclusion of aliens is rationally related to the state's interest in furthering educational goals. [Ambach v. Norwick (1979)] (C) is, accordingly, incorrect. The principle articulated in (A) is correct, but has no bearing here, where the question is whether a distinction based on alienage is permissible. (D) is true, but irrelevant; the state may deny Foley's application regardless of his ultimate intentions, so long as he remains an alien.

Answer to Question 69

(C) The Court should declare the ordinance unconstitutional, because charitable solicitations for funds in residential areas are within the protection of the First Amendment. In *Village of Schaumburg v. Citizens for a Better Environment* (1980), the Supreme Court held unconstitutional a municipal ordinance that prohibited the door-to-door solicitation of contributions by charitable organizations that did not use at least 75% of their receipts for charitable purposes. After review, the Court stated that the precedent of earlier decisions established clearly that the charitable appeal for funds involves a variety of speech interests that are within the protection of the First Amendment. The Court concluded that the ordinance unduly intruded upon the rights to free speech because the justifications for the restriction were not sufficiently compelling. (A) is wrong because the state's "legitimate interest" is not enough to justify violation of First Amendment rights. Similarly, (B) and (D) are wrong because the First Amendment rights outweigh the state's purposes and there is a less intrusive way of accomplishing the state's goals.

Answer to Question 70

(D) In *Young v. American Mini Theaters* (1986), the Court held that the mere fact that the commercial exploitation of certain material was protected by the First Amendment does not prevent the city from zoning or imposing other licensing requirements, as long as the businesses are not totally banned. The Court has upheld zoning ordinances such as the one here as reasonable regulations of the secondary effects of the speech involved. [*See* City of Renton v. Playtime Theaters (1986)]

Answer to Question 71

(C) State classifications based on alienage that do not involve alien participation in the self-government process are suspect under the Equal Protection Clause and are subject to strict judicial scrutiny. (A) is wrong because the Privileges and Immunities Clause of the Fourteenth Amendment protects the privileges and immunities of United States citizens, not aliens. (B) is wrong because, even if applicable, the Tenth Amendment could only help the state; it does not carry any prohibitions. (D) is wrong because the classification makes equal protection the better analysis, and it is a stretch to find a burden on a fundamental right.

Answer to Question 72

(B) The Equal Protection Clause of the Fourteenth Amendment is the most relevant because the classification scheme makes a series of distinctions between residents and aliens, individuals who worked in tourism and those who did not, and those who worked for five years versus those with a lesser period of employment. (A) is wrong, since the Privileges and Immunities Clause of Article IV has no bearing: the state is not treating residents of other *states* differently. (C) is not the best answer, since the reserved powers doctrine again helps, rather than hinders, the state. (D) is wrong because employment is not within the category of privileges protected by the Fourteenth Amendment.

Answer to Question 73

(D) The Supreme Court probably would not review the state decision because it is, in part, based on a violation of the Equal Protection Clause of the state constitution, an adequate and independent state ground upon which the decision would rest even if the federal issue were resolved (assuming that the state court's disposition of the state constitutional issue did not depend on federal doctrines). (A) is wrong because if it were not for the adequate and independent state ground, this type of challenge could be heard by the Court in its discretion. (B) is wrong because this type of case would not meet the very narrow requirements of appeal. (C) is wrong because this is a question of appellate jurisdiction, not original jurisdiction.

Answer to Question 74

(A) The nature of the aid provided by the statute has a secular purpose, is of legitimate interest to the state, and does not present any risk of being used to aid the transmission of religious views. (B) misstates the test; this is a test that was used for the Free Exercise Clause, and this is an Establishment Clause case. (C) is incorrect because not all aid to religious schools violates the Establishment Clause. (D) has no basis in the facts given.

Answer to Question 75

(A) State action can often be found when the state has affirmatively encouraged or facilitated discriminatory acts by private groups. Since Laketree County leased land to Lakeco, approved its members-only policy, and stands to profit by Lakeco's operations, state action can be found. Generally, state discrimination against lawful aliens is suspect and will be upheld only if it is necessary to promote a compelling state interest. (B) is incorrect because discrimination based on national origin cannot be justified by a mere "rational" basis. (C) is incorrect because resident aliens are "persons" within the meaning of the Fourteenth Amendment. (D) is incorrect because even though the bylaws are nondiscriminatory on their face, the facts show that they are being applied in a discriminatory manner.

Answer to Question 76

(D) Only the denial of particularly important rights to those unable to pay for them has been held to violate equal protection. Therefore, (A) is wrong. (C) is wrong because a number of de facto discriminations against the poor have been held to violate equal protection. (B) is an incorrect statement of the law.

Answer to Question 77

(B) This policy does not have a secular purpose and it arguably advances religion; hence, it violates the Establishment Clause. (A) is not as strong an answer as (B) because the Supreme Court has never specifically held that atheism is a religion protected by the Free Exercise Clause. (C) is wrong because, as was pointed out above, state action can be found in Laketree County's dealings with Lakeco. (D) is wrong because a person asserting a violation of the Establishment Clause does not have to allege infringement of a particular religious freedom in order to have standing; it is enough that he is directly affected by the government action challenged.

CONTRACTS QUESTIONS

Questions 1-2 are based on the following fact situation:

Tinker Builders learned of a bid being let by the local school board for a new high school. Anxious to get the job, Tinker quickly estimated the cost of a general bid. Tinker then began receiving sub-bids. The lowest such sub-bid came from Slam-Dunk, Inc. It was for $160,000, which was $40,000 less than the next lowest sub-bid.

After receiving Slam-Dunk's sub-bid, Tinker submitted its general bid to the school board. Based on the relatively low sub-bid, Tinker's general bid was $30,000 lower than the school board had originally anticipated.

Pleasantly surprised by the low bid, the school board accepted. After the acceptance, Slam-Dunk informed Tinker that there had been a mistake in computing the sub-bid. The correct sub-bid was $210,000. Tinker had been unaware of this mistake.

1. In a suit for rescission of its contract with Tinker, Slam-Dunk should:

    (A) Not succeed, because the mistake in the figures was made before the bid was accepted.

    (B) Not succeed, unless Tinker actually knew or should have known of the mistake involved.

    (C) Succeed, because the mistake was part of the basis of the bargain.

    (D) Succeed, because this was a unilateral, not a bilateral, mistake.

2. If the dispatching of Slam-Dunk's sub-bid of $160,000 were by telegraph and the error was due to the telegraph company's faulty transmission of a $60,000 bid instead of a $160,000 bid, Slam-Dunk's best argument to successfully refuse to perform the resulting contract is:

    (A) The contract would be unconscionable.

    (B) The great difference between the $60,000 figure and the next lowest bid should have alerted Tinker to the existence of a mistake in the telegram bid.

    (C) Slam-Dunk would not be responsible for the negligence of the telegraph company.

    (D) Tinker's own negligence in not checking out all bids precludes enforcement of the contract.

Question 3

In March, Larry contracted to sell his house to Cindy for $80,000, the purchase price to be paid and deed to be delivered on July 1. On May 1, Cindy wrote Larry, "I've had second thoughts about buying your home. I won't pay that amount of money, unless you repaint the house and fix up the yard."

If Larry wishes to treat the contract as breached:

(A) Larry may sue Cindy upon receipt of the letter.

(B) Larry may sue Cindy only on or after July 1, when the purchase price was to be paid.

(C) Larry may sue Cindy only if Larry expressly refuses in writing to comply with Cindy's requests.

(D) Larry cannot sue Cindy since the parties' promises are executory at this stage.

Question 4

In answer to a radio advertisement, Andrew Howard, age 16, contracted to buy a late model Albatross from Bumble Motors. The agreement required a $1,500 down payment with the remainder of the $7,200 price to be paid in monthly installments to the Albatross Finance Company. Andrew's first six payments were made regularly until his driver's license was suspended. He then informed the company that no further payments would be forthcoming. The finance company must sue for the remaining payments.

If the age of majority in Andrew's state is 18 years, the court would, in all likelihood, rule that:

(A) Andrew is totally liable for the balance of the payments.

(B) Andrew's disaffirmance discharges any liability he might have, if he returns the car.

(C) Andrew's liability is limited to the reasonable market value of the car.

(D) Andrew's minority at the time of contracting allows him to avoid all liability for the remaining payments.

Question 5

On January 1, Shaftum and Howe Realty Corp. mailed a written offer to Martin Enterprises for the sale of a large tract of land. The offer included the following terms:

This offer expires on February 1, if the offeree has not caused an acceptance to be received by the offeror on or before that date.

The first thing in the morning, on February 1, M. in sent a telegram of acceptance but the tel aph company negligently withheld delivery Shaftum until February 2. On February 4, Sh: entered into a contract for sale of the trac other buyer but did not inform Martin of th action. As a result, Martin contacted Shaf hone on February 10 and was told that n between Shaftum and Martin would

Which is the most correct statemen

(A) No contract between Shaftum and Martin arose on February 2.

(B) A contract would have arisen if a letter of acceptance were mailed on February 1.

(C) Shaftum's silence constituted an acceptance of Martin's telegram on February 2.

(D) A voidable contract arose on February 1.

Question 6

Builder contracted to build a house for Owen. Terms of the contract provided that Builder would receive the contract price when the building was fully completed. Just when Builder was within a day or two of completing one-half of the structure, a tornado struck the area and demolished the building.

What is Builder entitled to recover from Owen under the contract?

(A) Nothing.

(B) One-half of the contract price.

(C) One-half of the fair market value of what remains of the house.

(D) Cost of materials and reasonable labor costs.

Questions 7-8 are based on the following fact situation:

Wholesaler sent a telegram to Jobber "Send 500 'Madewell' chairs at your usual price." Jobber responded, also by telegram, "Will ship our last 500 'Madewell' chairs at $75 per chair, our usual price. 'Madewell' line is being discontinued." Jobber's staff immediately began the paperwork for processing the order and started preparing and packing the chairs for shipment. Wholesaler wired back to Jobber, "Cancel order for 'Madewell' chairs; your price is too high." Wholesaler tried to find an alternate source for "Madewell" chairs and found that Rebboj was the only other dealer in the chairs. Rebboj's price was also $75 per chair, and Wholesaler bought 500 "Madewell" chairs from Rebboj at the $75 price. The day after receiving Wholesaler's cancellation, Jobber was able to sell the 500 "Madewell" chairs in Jobber's stock to Relaselohw for $75 each.

7. If Jobber sues Wholesaler for damages, how much should Jobber recover?

   (A) Nothing, because this was a contract between merchants and Wholesaler canceled within a reasonable time.

   (B) Nothing, because Jobber was able to cover by selling the chairs at the same price she would have received from Wholesaler.

   (C) $37,500, the full contract price, because Wholesaler breached the contract and $75 per chair was a fair price.

   (D) Jobber's incidental costs of preparing the paperwork and other office costs connected with preparing and packing the chairs for shipment to Wholesaler.

8. Assume for purposes of this question only that Jobber is unable to find an alternate buyer for the chairs, and that she is forced to sell them at a "salvage" price of $10,000. If Jobber sues Wholesaler for damages, how much should Jobber recover?

   (A) Nothing, because this was a contract between merchants and Wholesaler canceled within a reasonable time.

   (B) The full contract price (because Wholesaler breached the contract and the price was fair) plus Jobber's incidental expenses.

   (C) The full contract price plus incidentals less $10,000 salvage.

   (D) The full contract price less $10,000 salvage.

Questions 9-10 are based on the following fact situation:

HotelCorp planned to build a new hotel in Stateville. HotelCorp is a major chain that owns and operates more than 80 hotels around the world. HotelCorp advertised for bids to build the hotel in Stateville. Four bids were received. Three of them were, respectively, $17 million, $17.2 million, and $17.4 million. The lowest bid was submitted by Skabco Construction. Skabco's bid was $15 million. Beancounter, the chief financial officer of HotelCorp, went over the bids. Beancounter told Plush, the chief executive officer of HotelCorp, "I expected a low bid from Skabco, because he uses a lot of non-union labor, but there's no way he can possibly make an honest cent on this project for $15 million, and Skabco always does honest work."

In fact, Joe Skab, the president of Skabco, had stayed up for 72 hours without sleep preparing the bid for the Stateville project and had neglected to include the plumbing expenses in the bid. With Skabco's normal method of doing things, the cost of plumbing, including Skabco's profit, would have been about $2 million. Skab discovered his mistake before he signed a contract with HotelCorp to build the hotel for $15 million.

HotelCorp was very anxious for the hotel to be built before the end of the year. Although HotelCorp was optimistic about the new hotel's success, there was no certainty as to the amount of money it would bring in. Beancounter's staff estimated that first year profits would be about $10,000 per day. To encourage Skabco to work in a timely manner, the contract included a liquidated damages clause, providing that Skabco would be liable to pay HotelCorp $100,000 per day for each day that Skabco is late in completion of the project.

9. Assume for purposes of this question only that shortly after the contract is signed by both parties, Skab discovers his mistake. Skab telephones Plush and tells him that he'd forgotten to include the cost of plumbing.

Skab says, "I'd normally charge $2 million for plumbing." Plush agrees to pay the additional $2 million, but this arrangement is never reduced to writing. If Skab completes the project on time and HotelCorp sends Skabco a check for only $15 million, may Skabco compel HotelCorp to tender the additional $2 million?

(A) Yes, because HotelCorp was on notice of Skab's mistake.

(B) Yes, but only if there was additional consideration for the agreement to pay the additional $2 million.

(C) No, because Skabco had a preexisting legal duty to complete the project for $15 million.

(D) No, because evidence of the agreement to pay the additional $2 million is barred by the parol evidence rule.

10. Assume for purposes of this question only that Skabco fails to place an order for the hotel's elevators in a timely manner. As a result of Skabco's oversight, the elevators are installed late and the hotel consequently opens 30 days later than scheduled. Assume that an expert witness can testify that the hotel would have received $300,000 in income during that 30-day period and would have expended $200,000, leaving a profit of $100,000. How much should Skabco be required to pay to HotelCorp in damages?

(A) $100,000, representing HotelCorp's lost profits.

(B) $300,000, representing HotelCorp's lost income.

(C) $3 million, representing damages provided in the contract.

(D) $3.1 million, representing damages provided in the contract plus lost profits.

Questions 11-12 are based on the following fact situation:

Oboe owned a large apartment complex. She contracted with Piper to paint the porches for $5,000. The contract was specifically made subject to Oboe's good faith approval of the work. Piper finished painting the porches. Oboe inspected the job and believed in good faith that Piper had done a bad job. Piper demanded payment, but Oboe told Piper that the paint job was poor and refused to pay. Piper pleaded that he was desperately in need of money. Oboe told Piper, "Okay, I've got a soft heart; I'll give you a check for $4,500, provided that you repaint the porches." Piper reluctantly agreed, and Oboe gave Piper a check in the amount of $4,500. Piper went to his bank, indorsed the check "under protest, Piper," and deposited the check in his account. Piper never returned to repaint the porches.

Oboe sues Piper for specific performance, demanding that Piper repaint the porches. Piper counterclaims for $500, which Piper believes he is still owed on his contract to paint the porches.

11. Will Piper prevail in his claim for $500 against Oboe?

(A) Yes, because he indorsed the check "under protest."

(B) Yes, but only if he repaints the porches.

(C) Yes, because he performed the contract by painting the porches the first time.

(D) No, even if he repaints the porches.

12. Will Oboe prevail in her action for specific performance?

(A) Yes, because there has been a novation.

(B) Yes, because she honestly believed Piper did a poor job.

(C) No, because Oboe had a preexisting legal duty to pay Piper.

(D) No, because Piper's services are not unique.

Question 13

On September 4, the *Metropolis Sentinel-Herald-Examiner* printed an advertisement paid for by Mortimer's Mechanics, an auto repair business, that included the following statement: "Special! Wednesday, September 5 only! Anyone ordering our regular complete four-cylinder engine tune-up, at the regular price of $249.95 (plus parts and lubricants), will receive in addition to the tune-up, at absolutely no additional cost, his or her choice of either (1) an all expenses paid bus trip to Fresno, California, complete with motel accommodations for three days and two nights, or (2) a set of Singu knives, with a knife and scissors sharpener, plus a fruit and vegetable peeler!" The next day, Mortimer's was inundated with tune-up customers, and by 3:15 p.m. it had exhausted its entire supply of Singu knives and accessories. At 3:17 p.m., Nancy pulled her import sedan into Mortimer's service bays, jumped out, and said to the mechanic on duty, "Give me your complete four-cylinder engine tune-up plus a set of those wonderful Singu knives, plus accessories!" The mechanic, knowing that no Singu knives were available, briefly tried to talk Nancy into a trip to Fresno, which proved unavailing. He then looked quickly under Nancy's hood and pronounced her engine "in tip top condition—no tune-up needed here." Finally, when Nancy insisted that her car had been burning a quart of oil a week and frequently lost power going downhill, the mechanic stated that there was not enough time left before closing to complete the tune-up, and that Nancy should try Mike's Motors down the street. In fact, it would have taken about four hours to complete a tune-up on Nancy's car, and Mortimer's closed at 5 p.m. that day, its regular closing time. Nancy drove home without a tune-up and without any Singu knives.

What is Mortimer's strongest defense against a breach of contract action brought by Nancy?

(A) A tune-up of Nancy's car could not have been completed in the time available before the shop closed.

(B) The advertisement in the newspaper was merely an invitation to offer, and Mortimer's had the right to refuse to accept any offer made.

(C) Since Nancy never expressly tendered payment of the $249.95, there was no acceptance of Mortimer's offer.

(D) Nancy's unwillingness to travel to Fresno indicated lack of good faith on her part.

Question 14

XYZ Corp., a general contractor, wished to bid on a construction project and solicited bids from a variety of subcontractors. Four electrical subcontractors, Alpha, Beta, Gamma, and Delta, submitted bids to XYZ. The bids were as follows: Alpha—$75,000; Beta—$85,000; Gamma—$90,000; and Delta—$95,000.

As XYZ was making out its bid on the construction project based upon the low bid submitted by Alpha, XYZ's president called Alpha and told him, "We won't be able to do it with your present bid, but if you can shave off $5,000, I'm sure that the numbers will be there for us to get that project." Alpha responded, "No way! In fact, that bid we submitted was based on a $15,000 error; we can't do it for a cent less than $90,000." XYZ lost the construction job and subsequently sued Alpha.

Alpha is liable for:

(A) Breach of contract, because the mistake was not so unreasonably obvious as to make acceptance of Alpha's bid unconscionable.

(B) Breach of contract, because the mistake was unilateral.

(C) Nothing, because Alpha rejected XYZ's counteroffer.

(D) Nothing, because even though Alpha lacked authority to renege on its bid, XYZ suffered no damages since no bidder was willing to do the work for $70,000.

Questions 15-16 are based on the following fact situation:

Osman, a homeowner, wanted Khaled, a contractor, to make some improvements on Osman's house. They made a written contract whereby Khaled would do the improvement for $5,000. Shortly after the contract was signed, Khaled told Osman, "When the job is finished, give the money to my daughter, Nadja. Nadja is getting married soon and I want her to have a nice wedding present from me." Nadja was aware that Khaled made this statement to Osman. Nadja married, but soon thereafter Khaled told Osman, "Pay me the $5,000 for the home improvement job. I think my son-in-law may have a gambling problem and that the money would probably just be used to play the ponies."

15. Against whom, if anyone, may Nadja enforce the agreement to pay her $5,000?

    (A) Osman.

    (B) Khaled.

    (C) Either Osman or Khaled.

    (D) Neither Osman nor Khaled.

16. What is the best argument in favor of Nadja's being able to enforce a contract for $5,000 in her favor?

    (A) Statute of Frauds.

    (B) Parol evidence rule.

    (C) Nadja was an intended third-party beneficiary.

    (D) Nadja married in reliance on a promise.

Question 17

Phlo was looking for an apartment to rent, and she was interested in a particular apartment because of its very distinctive features in a building managed by Deeds' Real Estate Company, but she was also interested in a number of other apartments in town. Because she wanted some time to make up her mind, she contacted Deeds, president of Deeds' Real Estate, and asked him to reserve her right to rent the particular apartment. After some discussion they made the following agreement:

> Phlo is to pay Deeds $200 on June 1. Upon timely receipt by Deeds of Phlo's payment, Phlo shall have the right to inform Deeds that she wishes to rent the apartment any time on or before July 1. If Phlo fails to notify Deeds that she wants the apartment on or before July 1, Deeds shall keep the $200. However, if Phlo does notify Deeds that she desires the apartment, Deeds has 15 days in which to accept or reject Phlo's application. If the application is accepted, Deeds will apply the $200 to the first month's rent. If the application is rejected, Deeds will refund the $200 to Phlo.

Phlo paid Deeds $200.

On June 9, Deeds rented the apartment to Tony. On July 1, Phlo told Deeds that she wanted the apartment. Deeds told Phlo, "The apartment has been rented; here's your $200 back."

Assuming that Phlo wants the court to compel Deeds to rent her the apartment, and that the court determines that Deeds has breached his agreement with Phlo, would it be appropriate for the court to order Deeds to rent the apartment to Phlo?

(A) Yes, but only because Deeds should not have rented the apartment to Tony before July 2.

(B) Yes, but only because Deeds should not have rented the apartment to Tony before July 16.

(C) No, because the contract was unconscionable.

(D) No, because Phlo has not suffered irreparable harm.

Question 18

Bernaise, the sole proprietor of Bernaise Distributors, a food service and food brokerage concern, entered into oral negotiations with Hollandaise, president and chief executive officer of Holsauce, a corporation that manufactured gourmet food products for restaurants and select retail outlets. Bernaise wished to secure an exclusive distributorship for Holsauce products in the six New England states. At the end of the first stage of oral negotiations between Bernaise and Hollandaise, both parties agreed on the major points of their arrangement, but a few points of disagreement remained. Both, however, were anxious to begin distribution of Holsauce products in New England and so Hollandaise assured Bernaise, "Don't worry about it; we'll work these things out." Assuming from this that he would be the New England distributor for Holsauce, Bernaise went out and leased larger facilities, bought a number of trucks, hired 30 new workers, and expanded his management staff by hiring, among others, an experienced distribution manager who was given a two-year contract with a high salary. Shortly after Bernaise had done these things, Hollandaise informed him that Bechamel Distributors, and not Bernaise, would receive the New England distributorship.

If Bernaise prevails in a suit against Holsauce and Hollandaise, it will most likely be because the court applies which of the following theories?

(A) Implied-in-fact contract.

(B) Promissory estoppel.

(C) Unjust enrichment.

(D) Quasi-contract.

Questions 19-23 are based on the following fact situation:

Richelle owns and operates an electronic equipment store. On December 6, Richelle sent a letter to Morris, a manufacturer of small computers, asking for the price on a specific type of computer, the Morristronic 606. Morris replied by letter, enclosing a catalog giving the prices and describing all of his available computers, along with various accessories. Morris's letter stated that the terms of sale were cash within 30 days of delivery. On December 14, Richelle ordered the Morristronic 606. She enclosed a check for the amount of the listed price of the Morristronic 606, which was $4,000.

Immediately upon receipt of Richelle's order and check, Morris sent Richelle a letter indicating that there had been a mistake in the catalog as to the price of the Morristronic 606, which should have quoted the price as $4,300. Morris went on to state that he would ship the computer to Richelle if Richelle would pay the additional $300 upon receipt of the machine.

On December 31, Richelle replied: "Ship me the Morristronic 606 and I'll pay the additional $300, but it must be delivered on or before January 19 as it's promised to a customer for January 20."

Morris shipped the Morristronic 606, but made no specific reply to Richelle's December 31 letter.

The machine did not actually arrive to Richelle until February 14. Richelle accepted the computer from the carrier, but promptly wrote a letter to Morris, stating: "Since you didn't deliver the computer on time, I'm not going to pay the extra $300. I'm also putting you on notice that if I lose any money because of your late shipment, I am going to hold you liable for that amount."

Richelle delivered the computer to her customer on February 15. The customer accepted the Morristronic 606 and paid for it.

19. Richelle's letter of December 14 in which the $4,000 check was enclosed can be characterized as:

    (A) Not an acceptance, because Morris's first communication stated terms calling for cash within 30 days after delivery.

    (B) Not an acceptance, because of the mistake as to price.

    (C) Not an acceptance, because Morris's first communication did not constitute an offer.

    (D) An acceptance.

20. Assume for purposes of this question and the questions following that a contract arose on December 14. Is Richelle's promise to pay $300 more than the price listed in the catalog enforceable?

    (A) No, because Morris did not ship the computer so that it would arrive at Richelle's store by January 19.

    (B) No, because it was only a counteroffer, which Morris did not accept.

    (C) No, because Morris had a preexisting legal obligation to ship the computer to Richelle.

    (D) Yes, it is enforceable.

21. Is the provision in Richelle's letter of December 31 requiring delivery by January 19 an enforceable additional term?

    (A) Yes.

    (B) No, because it is not supported by sufficient consideration.

    (C) No, because it contradicts an implied term of shipment within a reasonable period of time.

    (D) No, because Morris did not reply to Richelle's December 31 letter.

22. Assume for purposes of this question and the following question that Morris's delivery of the computer by January 19 and Richelle's payment of $300 upon delivery are enforceable terms. When Richelle accepted the computer on February 14, did her duty to pay the $300 arise?

    (A) No, but she retained the right to sue for damages.

    (B) No, and she lost the right to sue for any damage incurred because of the delay.

    (C) Yes, but she retained the right to sue for any damages she incurred because of the delay in delivery.

    (D) Yes, and she lost the right to sue for any damage incurred because of the delay in delivery.

23. In an action by Richelle's customer against Morris for damages he sustained as a result of Morris's delay in shipment, will the customer prevail?

    (A) Yes, because Morris's tardiness caused his damages.

    (B) No, because Richelle refused to pay the extra $300.

    (C) No, because the customer accepted the computer.

    (D) No, because the customer was only an incidental beneficiary.

Questions 24-25 are based on the following fact situation:

Fox mailed the following offer to Sack, a designated offeree: "I hereby offer to sell my property consisting of a house and lot at 337 Green Street for $100,000. Terms $30,000 cash, the balance secured by a first mortgage. Advise immediately if you accept." This offer was mailed on February 3, and reached Sack on February 5. On February 8, Sack replied: "Your offer received and under advisement. I would much prefer a straight cash deal. Would you consider an immediate purchase for $90,000 cash?" On February 10, this reply was received by Fox, who responded with a one-word telegram: "No." Receiving this telegram on February 11, Sack wired: "Telegram received. I accept your offer of February 3. Tender the deed c/o my agent, The First National Bank of Commerce."

24. If Fox now refuses to sell and Sack sues, the court would probably hold:

    (A) A valid contract exists.

    (B) No contract exists because Sack's response of February 8 operated to terminate Fox's offer.

    (C) No contract exists because Sack's communications to Fox both contained alterations of the terms of the offer.

    (D) No contract exists because the offer relates to real estate, and the communications fail to establish the terms of the proposed agreement with sufficient definiteness.

25. Assume that the day after Fox mailed his offer to Sack, Fox mailed a revocation which arrived one day after the offer. As the mail carrier handed the letter of revocation to Sack, Sack simultaneously handed his letter of unqualified acceptance to the mail carrier. What result?

    (A) The revocation was effective upon mailing, and the acceptance would be treated as a counteroffer.

    (B) The acceptance was effective, as long as Sack had no knowledge of the contents of Fox's letter when he handed his letter to the mail carrier.

    (C) The outcome would turn upon the court's determination as to whether Fox's letter had been received by Sack before he had entrusted the letter of acceptance to the mail carrier.

    (D) Handing a letter to a mail carrier is not a proper posting of the acceptance, and hence Sack's purported acceptance is not timely.

Questions 26-27 are based on the following fact situation:

Aerial Advertisers signed a contract with Zenith Film Productions to advertise Zenith's new film, *Battle Zone,* by flying over Central City towing a giant streamer belonging to Zenith which read "See the Blood and Guts of War in BATTLE ZONE." This contract specified that the flights were to be conducted each Saturday morning at noon, for two weeks (the time in which the film was showing locally) and Zenith was to pay Aerial $500 per flight.

The first Saturday, Aerial was unable to fly because of a defective fuel pump. The defective condition was entirely unforeseeable and did not occur through any negligence or fault of Aerial.

The second Saturday, Aerial was ready, but the Zenith streamer was suddenly destroyed by fire, through the fault of neither party, and could not be replaced in time.

Each of the parties has sued the other for damages.

26. Which of the following best states the rights and liabilities of the parties following the first Saturday?

    (A) Zenith is entitled to recover damages from Aerial on account of Aerial's failure to fly.

    (B) Aerial is entitled to recover from Zenith the $500 contract price, as the incapacity of the airplane was not Aerial's fault.

(C) Neither party is entitled to recover against the other, because Aerial's duty to fly was discharged by impossibility, and Zenith's duty to pay was contingent on Aerial's flight.

(D) Neither party is entitled to recover against the other, because Zenith's offer to pay $500 per flight was in effect an offer for an act, and since the act was not performed, there was no valid acceptance.

27. Which of the following best states the rights and liabilities of the parties following the second Saturday?

(A) Aerial is entitled to recover from Zenith $500, less the costs and expenses (gasoline, etc.) it would have incurred in performing.

(B) Zenith is entitled to at least nominal damages against Aerial, because destruction of the streamer was not Zenith's fault, and therefore Aerial was in technical breach of contract in failing to fly.

(C) Neither party is entitled to recover against the other because destruction of the contemplated subject matter of the contract (the streamer) terminated Zenith's offer by operation of law.

(D) Neither party is entitled to recover against the other because destruction of the streamer excused Aerial's duty to fly, which was a condition precedent to Zenith's duty to pay.

Questions 28-29 are based on the following fact situation:

Emma owns a high-style ladies' fashion store in Richville. Freddie is the designer and manufacturer of a world-famous line of original gowns.

On April 1, Emma and Freddie signed a written agreement wherein Emma was appointed the "sole and exclusive" retail distributor for Freddie's clothes in Richville.

On May 1, Emma handed Freddie a written order for $50,000 worth of his original gowns, to be delivered to Emma on September 1. Freddie did not sign an acknowledgment of Emma's order, but in her presence he set aside the originals designated in her order by putting her name on them.

To publicize her new line of merchandise, Emma conducted a large advertising campaign announcing to the Richville public that she would have a wide selection of Freddie's originals on display on September 1. She also made substantial improvements to the store to display these clothes in lush and expensive settings.

On August 15, Freddie wired Emma, "Sorry, darling, your competitor in Richville, Beulah, has made an offer for the clothes you ordered that I simply couldn't pass up. I know you'll understand. Best wishes, Freddie."

Upon receipt of the message, Emma files suit against Freddie.

28. Assume that there was an enforceable contract between Emma and Freddie. What legal effect would his telegram of August 15 have?

(A) It is a breach of contract by anticipatory repudiation, entitling Emma to bring an immediate action to enforce the contract without waiting until September 1.

(B) It is a breach of contract by anticipatory repudiation allowing Emma to sue, but only if Emma first demands adequate assurances of performance from Freddie, and he fails to provide these within a reasonable time.

(C) It is an anticipatory breach, requiring Emma to tender the purchase price on September 1, and sue after that date.

(D) Its legal effect depends on whether Freddie was acting in good faith in refusing to perform; if he was, there is no breach until after September 1.

29. Assume for purposes of this question only that there was an enforceable contract, and that Freddie is in breach thereof. Which of the following remedies is a court most likely to grant?

   (A) An award of damages for the difference between the $50,000 and costs of "covering" with other goods.

   (B) A decree of specific performance directing Freddie to sell the gowns to Emma in exchange for $50,000.

   (C) An award of damages based on a theory of reimbursement so that Emma may collect her reliance losses.

   (D) All consequential damages proximately caused by the breach.

Questions 30-32 are based on the following fact situation:

Archie's Typewriter Exchange advertised used Regal Typewriters for sale at its store, for $100 each. Barney, whose business is 250 miles away, mailed Archie a check for $500 with a note stating, "Send me five of the used Regal Typewriters you advertised."

Upon checking his stock, Archie found that he had only two Regals left, but he had plenty of Overwoods, and therefore he sent Barney two Regals and three Overwoods by common carrier. En route, the two Regals were stolen, so that the carrier ended up delivering only three Overwoods.

Because he was short of typewriters, Barney started using these machines. One week later, however, his secretaries complained about the Overwoods, and therefore Barney wrote to Archie: "I'm rejecting the three Overwoods you sent me. Return my $500." Archie refused to do so.

30. The legal effect of Archie's shipment of the two Regals and three Overwoods in response to Barney's order for five Regals was:

   (A) An acceptance of Barney's offer with respect to the two Regals, and a counteroffer as to the three Overwoods.

   (B) An acceptance of Barney's offer to purchase five Regals, and a breach of the contract formed thereby.

   (C) Neither an acceptance nor a counteroffer, because a mere shipment of goods is not a manifestation of assent to any particular terms.

   (D) A mere offer to furnish substituted goods as an accommodation.

31. With respect to the theft of the two Regals in the course of shipment:

   (A) The loss falls on Archie because it was he who selected the carrier and made the arrangements for shipment.

   (B) The loss falls on Archie because under the facts here, the seller bears the risk of loss.

   (C) The loss falls on Barney because the typewriters were advertised as being available for sale only at Archie's store, and therefore the risk of loss passed there.

   (D) The loss falls on Barney because title to the goods passed to Barney upon shipment, and he therefore bears the risk of loss.

32. The legal effect of Barney's retention and use of the Overwoods for one week before notifying Archie was:

   (A) An acceptance of the three machines as long as Barney was aware that the machines were not Regals.

   (B) An acceptance of the three machines if Barney's use thereof was more than reasonably required to test whether the Overwoods were acceptable substitutes for the Regals.

(C) Not an acceptance, because the goods shipped were nonconforming.

(D) A waiver of any claim for damage against Archie on account of nondelivery of the Regals.

Question 33

Paddy is a county fair promoter who arranges publicity and signs up attractions for various county fairs throughout the central states. Drumm is the owner of "Maxipig," a champion hog that has been trained to do a number of entertaining tricks. Paddy and Drumm contracted that Maxipig would perform at the Hayseed County Fair next month for a fee of $500, payable to Drumm. Shortly before the Hayseed County Fair was scheduled to open, Maxipig contracted an epizootic disease, and the pig was too sick to appear at the fair. Paddy demanded that Drumm either bring Maxipig to perform as scheduled or pay damages.

Drumm's best argument for not performing the contract would be based upon which of the following?

(A) Statute of Frauds.

(B) Parol evidence rule.

(C) Impossibility of performance.

(D) Failure of consideration.

Question 34

Warren lived in City and Joshua lived in the small town of Hamlet, about 25 miles away. Both had attended college together in City; Warren had studied accounting and went to work for a large corporation; Joshua studied agronomy and went to work for a large corporate farm. On March 15, Warren wrote the following letter to Joshua:

> Dear Joshua,
>
> Remember that 1966 Mustang you were always pestering me to sell to you? I have decided to part with it and

will let you have it for $15,000, if you buy it before April 15. After that, the deal's off.

Your pal,

Warren

Joshua did some research into the current market value of the automobile and discovered that comparable vehicles were being sold by used car dealers for $18,000. On April 1, Joshua was just leaving his home to drive to City and give Warren a check for $15,000 when he received a telegram from Warren stating: "Forget about sale of Mustang. Have decided not to sell as indicated in letter of March 15." Joshua drove into City anyway, and went to Warren's residence. The Mustang was parked out front with a "for sale" sign in its window. Joshua stopped, knocked at the door, and when Warren answered, tendered the $15,000 check and demanded the Mustang. Warren refused.

Joshua brings an action for damages for breach of contract against Warren. What should be the outcome of this litigation?

(A) Joshua will recover nothing, because the offer to sell the Mustang was withdrawn before he accepted.

(B) Joshua will recover $15,000, because Warren has failed to perform under the contract of sale.

(C) Joshua will recover $3,000, because his tender of the purchase price was an acceptance of Warren's offer.

(D) Joshua will recover $3,000, because Warren's letter created an enforceable option.

Questions 35-36 are based on the following fact situation:

Argon, a merchant, telephoned Bismuth, also a merchant, and said, "I've got 5,000 pounds of thingamabobs ready for delivery [at a stated price]." Bismuth agreed to purchase the thingamabobs, but stated that he would appreciate it if Argon would deliver 2,000 pounds now and 3,000 pounds next month. No further communications ensued between the parties.

35. The most likely result of the conversation between Argon and Bismuth is:

   (A) A contract was formed to deliver 2,000 pounds now and 3,000 pounds next month.

   (B) A contract was formed to deliver 5,000 pounds now.

   (C) No contract was formed, because Bismuth's response was merely a counteroffer and a rejection.

   (D) No contract was formed, unless Argon notified Bismuth within a reasonable time of his assent to the proposed schedule of delivery.

36. Assume for purposes of this question only that Argon answered Bismuth's request for separate deliveries by saying he would only ship the entire 5,000 pounds now. If Argon then tenders the 5,000 pounds, Bismuth:

   (A) May reject the entire delivery.

   (B) Must accept the entire delivery.

   (C) May demand that Argon deliver only 2,000 pounds now and 3,000 pounds next month.

   (D) Must accept or reject the entire delivery.

Question 37

Meagan entered into a written agreement with Larry, whereby Meagan agreed to rent some commercial space in Larry's shopping center and Larry agreed to fix the premises to suit Meagan's purpose. The contract between Meagan and Larry provided that the store premises would be ready by June 1 or July 1 at the outside. Larry immediately contracted with Raoul to do the construction in accordance with Meagan's requirements. When the premises were not

ready by July 1, Meagan notified Larry that she had decided to rent store space elsewhere. Three days later, on July 8, Larry sent Meagan a letter by certified mail that the construction had been delayed because Raoul had breached his contract, and Larry had to employ another contractor. However, Larry stated, the premises would be completed no later than July 15, and that under the circumstances, he believed he was entitled to this short period of time to complete the agreement since the renovations, done especially for Meagan, had already cost him $15,000. On July 15, Larry tendered performance to Meagan, but she refused to accept the lease. Larry brought suit against Meagan for breach of contract.

The most likely fact that will decide who prevails in this suit is:

   (A) Whether someone else will rent the premises with the renovations done especially for Meagan.

   (B) Whether Larry should have foreseen that Raoul would not complete the construction.

   (C) Whether Meagan can show that she would have suffered "undue hardship" if she waited until July 15 to see if the construction would be completed.

   (D) Whether the contract provision that the store premises will be ready by July 1 "at the outside" would be considered to be a time of the essence provision.

Questions 38-39 are based on the following fact situation:

Alfred is in the business of selling industrial tools. He entered into an agreement with Meta-Cut's salesperson to purchase 500 of their Series B saw blades. The agreement required Alfred to pay for the blades when he placed the order, and Alfred gave Meta-Cut's salesperson $5,000 in full payment for this order. When the blades arrived the following week, Alfred inspected them and found that they were Meta-Cut's Series A saw blades. Alfred immediately contacted

Meta-Cut and demanded the return of his payment. Meta-Cut refused to accept the return of the blades or to return Alfred's payment because they claimed that there was no significant difference between the Series B and Series A blades.

38. Which of the following statements is most accurate with regard to the consequence of Alfred's paying for the saw blades in advance of his inspecting them?

(A) Paying for goods is an acceptance, and therefore Alfred waived his right to reject the goods.

(B) Paying for goods in advance does not act to waive a buyer's right to object to a total breach of contract, but it does act as an acceptance if the goods shipped substantially conform to the buyer's requirements.

(C) Paying for goods in advance impairs neither the buyer's right to inspect nor his right to assert his remedies for any breach of contract.

(D) Goods are never deemed accepted until the buyer notifies the seller in writing that the goods are acceptable, and therefore, paying for goods in advance has no effect.

39. If the Series A saw blades are nonconforming, what are Alfred's remedies?

(A) None, because he waived his rights by paying for the blades in advance.

(B) He may demand that Meta-Cut deliver the Series B blades immediately, but he does not have to return the nonconforming blades.

(C) He is entitled to damages based on the difference between the contract price and the price to buy conforming goods.

(D) He is entitled to damages based on the difference between the contract price and the value of the saw blades he received.

Questions 40-41 are based on the following fact situation:

Sherwood and Thurman owned summer homes adjacent to each other on the lake. One summer, after Sherwood's 20-year-old son, Wesley, had spent a few weeks at the summer home, Sherwood received a telephone call from Thurman. Thurman told Sherwood that he had just gone up to his own home and found that his boat dock had been badly damaged. Another neighbor told him that Wesley and some friends had gotten drunk and accidentally crashed their boat into Thurman's dock. Sherwood was very surprised at the accusation because he was sure that if Wesley had caused the damages, Wesley would have told him. However, Thurman wanted Sherwood to give him Wesley's address at college, and since Sherwood was in the middle of some important business negotiations and did not want to become distracted by a dispute with his neighbor, he told Thurman that if he agreed not to bring a claim against Wesley for the damage to the dock, he would arrange to have it repaired and pay for the repairs.

Thurman agreed, and Sherwood had one of the local carpenters, Kerry, repair the dock. However, Kerry was not really a good carpenter and the job he did on the dock was very poor.

40. Thurman was forced to hire another to do the repairs on the dock and he had to sue Sherwood for reimbursement of the money he had to pay on the repairs. Sherwood was able to show at trial that, in fact, the damages were done to Thurman's dock after Wesley had returned to college and that the neighbor was mistaken when he identified Wesley as one of the persons involved in the accident. Is Sherwood obligated to pay Thurman for the repairs?

(A) No, because Sherwood never really believed that Wesley caused the damage.

(B) No, because Wesley in fact did not cause the damage.

(C) No, because Thurman was wrong when he accused Wesley of causing the damage, and it would be unfair to enforce an agreement when there was a mutual mistake of fact.

(D) Yes.

41. Assuming that there is an enforceable agreement between Thurman and Sherwood, would Thurman have an action against Kerry?

(A) No, because there was no agreement between Kerry and Thurman with regard to the repairs on the dock.

(B) No, because Thurman was only an incidental beneficiary of the contract between Kerry and Sherwood.

(C) Yes, because Thurman was a creditor beneficiary of the contract between Kerry and Sherwood.

(D) Yes, because Thurman was a donee beneficiary of the contract between Kerry and Sherwood.

Question 42

Marvin, a stockboy at a local hardware store, was dating Linda, who was very much in love with him, but reluctant to marry him because of his meager income and his job potential. Marvin told his father, Tony, about his desire to marry Linda and about her reservations. Tony, who was anxious to see his son married, told Linda that if she married Marvin, Tony would support them for six months and send Marvin to a six-month computer technology training school. This was sufficient to dispel Linda's reservations, and Marvin and Linda married the very next day. When Marvin and Linda returned from their honeymoon, Tony refused to go through with his offer.

If Linda sues Tony for damages and Tony prevails, it will be because:

(A) Linda's promise was not supported by valid consideration.

(B) The contract is against public policy.

(C) The contract was oral.

(D) Linda is happy and therefore has incurred no detriment.

Questions 43-44 are based on the following fact situation:

AeroFlyte was given the opportunity to enter into contract negotiations with a foreign country to sell military aircraft and parts. Accordingly, it entered into a written agreement with Rudy for her to act as its agent in what were expected to be lengthy negotiations. Rudy was a highly respected salesperson in the industry and one of the most qualified to act as an agent in these types of negotiations.

Rudy was required by the contract to begin meetings with the representatives of the foreign country on August 1. However, on July 19, Rudy accepted a job with Bowing, a large aircraft manufacturer, and could not thereafter represent AeroFlyte. To fulfill her contractual obligations with AeroFlyte, Rudy called her friend Cliff, who was reputed to be "the best in the business," and orally assigned the AeroFlyte contract to him, paying him $600.

43. Assume for this question only that Aero-Flyte does not want Cliff to represent it and sues Rudy for damages for breach. What result?

(A) AeroFlyte will prevail, because the assignment was oral.

(B) AeroFlyte will prevail, because Rudy's performance was personal.

(C) Rudy will prevail, because Cliff is a better negotiator than Rudy and so AeroFlyte was not damaged.

(D) Rudy will prevail, because damages are speculative.

44. Assume for this question only that Aero-Flyte agrees to allow Cliff to represent it, but before the negotiations have begun, Cliff informs AeroFlyte that he will not represent it. AeroFlyte sues Cliff for breach. What result?

    (A) Cliff will prevail, because AeroFlyte's only remedy is against Rudy.

    (B) Cliff will prevail, because $600 is grossly inadequate consideration.

    (C) AeroFlyte will prevail, because there has been a novation.

    (D) AeroFlyte will prevail, because it is an intended third-party beneficiary of the Rudy-Cliff contract.

Questions 45-46 are based on the following fact situation:

Alex wanted to have his driveway resurfaced. He called a number of commercial establishments that do such work and received bids ranging from $4,500 to $5,000. Bart submitted a bid to do the work for $4,000, and Alex entered into a contract with him to have the driveway resurfaced.

Shortly before Bart was scheduled to begin work, he called Alex and said, "I just found out my secretary made a mistake in adding figures. I couldn't possibly do the work for less than $4,600 or I'd lose money."

45. If Alex sues Bart for breach of contract, who will prevail?

    (A) Alex, but only if it is too late for Alex to accept the bid of the next lowest bidder.

    (B) Alex, but only if Alex did not have reason to know of Bart's erroneous bid.

    (C) Bart, because he had not yet commenced performance under the contract.

    (D) Bart, because he can successfully assert the defense of mistake.

46. Assume that Alex responded to Bart's statement by saying, "O.K., I'll pay you the extra $600, but I think you're being unfair." After Bart finished the driveway, he asked Alex for his money. Alex handed Bart $4,000 in cash and said, "This is all I'm going to pay you because you had no right to up the price on me." If Bart sues Alex for the additional $600, who will prevail?

    (A) Alex, because Bart was already under a preexisting duty to resurface the driveway for $4,000.

    (B) Alex, because the promise to pay the additional money was not in writing.

    (C) Bart, because he relied on Alex's promise to pay the additional money to his detriment.

    (D) Bart, because the promise to pay the additional money was the settlement of a good faith dispute.

Questions 47-49 are based on the following fact situation:

At the start of the academic year, September 1, Professor announced to his class that he would pay the tuition of the bar review course of the student's choice for the student who receives the highest grade in Professor's Constitutional Law class. Professor reduced his offer to writing and posted it on the student bulletin board the next day, stating the same essential terms with the added statement, "Maximum award, $1,000."

Stillwell, a student in Professor's class, told Professor prior to the September 8 class that: "I'm really going to give my best effort to get the highest grade in your class and win that prize. I started studying three days ago and yesterday I purchased every substantive constitutional law outline on the market just so I can win the prize."

Shortly thereafter, the Dean of the law school told Professor that she had been receiving complaints from many of the other law professors about the lack of study on the part of the students because the students were concentrating their efforts on constitutional law only. The Dean also stated that she felt that Professor's offer could be interpreted as an improper school policy. Professor stated that, although he still wished to perform on his agreement, he would post a notice announcing the withdrawal of his offer. Professor posted the withdrawal notice on October 1 and stated the reasons why he was forced to withdraw his offer to his class. He apologized, but said that in the interest of the school, he had no choice.

Later that day, Stillwell told Professor that the offer could not be withdrawn after he, Stillwell, had started to perform by purchasing the outlines and devoting his studying exclusively to Constitutional Law for the past month. Professor again stated that he had no choice. Stillwell received the highest grade in Professor's class and now requests performance by Professor.

47. Professor's offer to his class on September 1 and the announcement posted on the bulletin board the next day would be interpreted as:

    (A) Preliminary negotiations.

    (B) A promise to make a conditional gift.

    (C) A contractual offer, creating a power of acceptance.

    (D) A mere statement designed to induce the students to study harder and achieve higher grades.

48. If the Professor's announcement to his class was held to be an offer, it would be an offer for:

    (A) A bilateral contract.

    (B) A unilateral contract.

    (C) A bilateral contract or a unilateral contract, according to the offeree's intentions.

    (D) A unilateral contract that became a bilateral contract when Stillwell began to perform.

49. Professor's announcement of withdrawal of the offer to his class and the posting of the withdrawal notice on the bulletin board would most likely be interpreted as:

    (A) Having no legal effect, because no offer had been made.

    (B) An effective revocation of the offer.

    (C) An ineffective revocation as to any student who failed to hear Professor's announcement or read the notice on the bulletin board.

    (D) An ineffective revocation as to Stillwell because Stillwell relied on the promise.

Questions 50-53 are based on the following fact situation:

Accucomp, a manufacturer of home computers, decided to introduce a new commercial product line at the winter trade show in December. After much research, it decided to purchase Fastprint's series 40X printers to include with its keyboards and computers to sell as a system.

Although a major consideration for purchasing the 40X printer was that it came with a wide selection of different printing options, printing speed was equally important. Therefore, the written agreement between Fastprint and Accucomp provided that the 40X printers must be able to print 300 characters per second or more. Fastprint was to provide, during the term of the agreement, 150 printers for Accucomp at $300 each. The printers were to be delivered at the rate of 10 per month, commencing March 15, and Accucomp was to pay for the printers as they were delivered.

When the first shipment arrived, Accucomp paid the shipper for Fastprint's account a cashier's check for $2,000. However, when Accucomp put one of the printers on line with its system, it found that the printer was printing at a rate of only 200 characters per second. Accucomp then tested the entire shipment and found that none of the printers met the contract specifications. The cost of the test, including overtime, was $1,500.

Although the printers did not meet the specifications, Accucomp was under special contract with its own lawyers, Law Firm, to deliver two systems by April 1. Accucomp negotiated with them, and it was agreed that Accucomp would install the two systems with the Fastprint 40X printers, but that Accucomp would have to deliver two high speed printers at no extra cost to Law Firm by December to replace these two printers. Immediately upon making this agreement, Accucomp sent a telegram to Fastprint telling them that the shipment did not conform to the contract and that no further shipments would be accepted.

50. With regard to Accucomp's right to inspect the printers:

(A) It retained the right to inspect despite the prior payment.

(B) It forfeited the right to inspect by paying for them without inspection.

(C) It forfeited the right to inspect by accepting them without inspection.

(D) It had no right to inspect because there was no such provision in the contract.

51. Because of the sale of the systems with the printers to Law Firm, Accucomp has accepted:

(A) None of the printers, because it has to replace the two within six months.

(B) The two printers sold to Law Firm.

(C) The entire first shipment of 10.

(D) The entire order because it has shown it is capable of selling the systems with the slower printer.

52. How much could Accucomp recover from Fastprint for the printers delivered to Law Firm?

(A) Nothing, because they were resold to another.

(B) Nothing, because it accepted them knowing they were defective.

(C) The difference between the contract price and the printers' actual value.

(D) The difference between their actual value and the cost of the printers that Accucomp must provide Law Firm within the next six months.

53. With respect to the eight delivered printers that were not acceptable, Accucomp may recover:

(A) Nothing.

(B) The money it has already paid for them, and it gets to keep the printers.

(C) The difference between the value of the printers, and the price it could have sold them for on the market.

(D) The money it paid for the printers, but it may sell the printers for Fastprint's account.

Questions 54-56 are based on the following fact situation:

Futsworth, a lawyer, and Green, a carpenter, entered into an oral contract in which Green agreed to build a redwood deck in Futsworth's backyard for $1,500 plus the cost of materials. Futsworth intended to have a hot tub installed and wanted everything ready for the upcoming summer, and so he told Green that "time is of the essence" and that the deck must be completed by May 15. Futsworth also made Green promise that he would complete the deck "in a good and workmanlike manner."

Green completed work on the deck on May 14, and asked Futsworth for immediate payment of the $1,500 because Green needed the money to finish another project for which he was also on a deadline. Futsworth refused to pay, asserting that Green had not built the deck as agreed and that inferior materials and workmanship prevented installation of the hot tub Futsworth had purchased. The next day, Green mailed to Futsworth via registered mail an invoice demanding payment for all the materials used to construct the redwood deck, listing them, and for the agreed contract price for services of $1,500. The total amount demanded by Green is $2,300.

Futsworth consulted with another carpenter who stated that he could modify the deck at a cost of $300 in additional materials and $150 in labor costs so that the hot tub Futsworth had purchased could be installed. Futsworth purchased the necessary additional materials, then mailed Green a letter offering to pay him $2,150 if he would make the modifications, using Futsworth's materials, to enable installation of the hot tub. When Futsworth received no reply within a week, Futsworth mailed Green a check for $2,150 on which he had written, "Payment in full for construction of redwood deck." Upon receipt of the check from Futsworth, Green cashed it and used the proceeds to complete another project he was working on.

54. Green brings an action against Futsworth for $150, the difference between the agreed contract price and the amount paid. Futsworth defends on the basis of an accord and satisfaction. The trial court should rule for:

(A) Green, because he cashed the check from Futsworth under economic duress.

(B) Futsworth, because Green cashed the check without objection.

(C) Green, if he can establish that the deck was completed in a good and workmanlike manner.

(D) Futsworth, because Green is entitled to only the reasonable value of his services, or $1,500.

55. If the trial court is called upon to determine whether Futsworth has breached his contract with Green, it should conclude that:

(A) Futsworth totally breached the agreement only if Green completed the deck in a good and workmanlike manner.

(B) Futsworth totally breached the agreement regardless of the nature of Green's performance.

(C) Futsworth partially breached the agreement only if Green completed the deck in a good and workmanlike manner.

(D) Futsworth partially breached the agreement regardless of the nature of Green's performance.

56. Futsworth files a cross-complaint seeking to recover the $150 he was forced to pay another carpenter to complete the modifications necessary to permit installation of the hot tub. As to the cross-complaint, the trial court should probably rule for:

(A) Futsworth, because Green accepted Futsworth's offer by not replying to the latter's letter.

(B) Futsworth, because Green accepted Futsworth's offer by cashing the latter's check.

(C) Green, because there was no consideration to support a promise by Green to make the modifications.

(D) Green, because he never accepted the offer contained in Futsworth's letter.

Questions 57-59 are based on the following fact situation:

Steven was the owner in fee simple of Gold Acre, an undivided tract of land. On January 1, Steven decided to sell Gold Acre. On January 10, Steven orally agreed to sell Gold Acre to Barny for $79,000 to be paid on February 28. As a condition of the sale, Barny orally agreed to pay $30,000 of the purchase price to Terry in satisfaction of a debt that Steven had promised to pay to Terry. On February 1, Barny told his secretary of his agreement to buy Gold Acre from Steven and asked her to prepare a formal, typewritten copy of the contract. In so doing, Barny's secretary accidentally typed $74,000 rather than $79,000 as the purchase price. Both Barny and Steven read the document before signing, but neither noticed the mistake in the purchase price. The signed document made no reference of the payment of $30,000 to Terry.

57. Terry files suit against Barny for $30,000. Which of the following is a correct statement?

  I.   Barny could successfully raise the Statute of Frauds as a defense because the Barny/Steven agreement was to answer to the debt of another.

  II. Barny could successfully raise the Statute of Frauds as a defense because the Barny/Steven agreement was for the sale of an interest in land.

  (A) I. only.

  (B) II. only.

  (C) Both I. and II.

  (D) Neither I. nor II.

58. Which of the following would be most important in deciding an action by Terry against Barny for $30,000?

  (A) Whether Barny was negligent in not having carefully read the written agreement.

  (B) Whether the Barny/Steven agreement was completely integrated.

  (C) Whether Steven was negligent in not having carefully read the agreement.

  (D) Whether the omission of Terry from the written document was intentional or accidental.

59. Assume for this question only that Barny refuses to pay more than $74,000 for Gold Acre. If Steven brings suit against Barny to recover the additional $5,000, which of the following, if proved, would be of the most help to Steven?

  (A) There was a mistake in integration.

  (B) There was a misunderstanding between Steven and Barny concerning the purchase price.

  (C) The writing was only a memorialization.

  (D) The writing was only a partial integration.

Questions 60-62 are based on the following fact situation:

Duncan, the owner of a large chain of small doughnut shops, decided to add fresh-baked cookies to his menus. To that end, Duncan developed a line of cookies. Since each of his doughnut shops is small, Duncan decided that it would be most cost-efficient and would ensure the highest quality if he created cookie mixes at a central location and shipped the mixes to each shop. One of Duncan's better-tasting cookies was his chocolate chip. Duncan decided to make that his flagship cookie, and sought out the very best ingredients for this mix. After a little research, Duncan found out what the rest of the country already knew: the best semisweet chocolate chips in the country were made by Chipco. Although Chipco's chocolate chips were more expensive than any other on the market, Duncan thought they were well worth the cost because he would be able to benefit from the chips' reputation as "the best." Duncan met with Chipco and impressed them with the quality of his products. They offered to supply him with whatever amount of chocolate chips he needed. Duncan entered into a written contract with Chipco whereby Chipco agreed to send Duncan 5,000 pounds of chips on the first day of each month. Duncan was to pay $12,500 for each shipment by the 10th day of each month. The contract was to expire at the end of one year.

60. Assume for this question only that when Duncan opened the first shipment of chips, he found that 60% of them were tainted with rat hairs. He immediately called Chipco and informed them of the breach. Chipco offered to send replacements, but Duncan, having become uncertain of the probable success of the cookie venture, refused the offer and told Chipco that he was canceling the contract. Will Chipco prevail in an action to enforce the contract?

   (A) No, because Chipco breached the contract and Duncan was entitled to a perfect tender.

   (B) No, because damages are speculative.

   (C) Yes, because Duncan's notice of breach had to be in writing.

   (D) Yes, because Chipco had a right to cure.

61. Assume for this question only that Chipco and Duncan properly fulfilled their contractual obligations for two months. The day after Chipco made the third delivery, Chipco's president ventured into one of Duncan's shops and tasted a chocolate chip cookie made with Chipco chips. Finding the cookie to be the worst he ever tasted, the president called Duncan and told him that to protect Chipco's reputation, Chipco will absolutely not send Duncan any more chips. Duncan immediately files an action for breach. What result?

   (A) Chipco will prevail because it was not in breach when the action was filed.

   (B) Chipco will prevail if it can show that Duncan's cookies tasted bad.

   (C) Duncan will prevail because the president's action amounts to an anticipatory repudiation.

   (D) Duncan will prevail because the president's action amounts to a prospective inability to perform.

62. Assume for this question only that after three months of proper performance, Chipco refuses to send Duncan any more chips because of Chipco's president's perception that Duncan's cookies taste bad and thus will harm Chipco's reputation. If Duncan sues to force Chipco to ship the chips, will he prevail?

   (A) Yes, if Chipco's chips really are the best, and no other chip would be sufficient.

   (B) Yes, because Duncan relied to his detriment.

   (C) No, because specific performance is not available for a contract for the sale of goods.

   (D) No, if Duncan's cookies will harm Chipco's reputation since that would be inequitable and specific performance is an equitable remedy.

Questions 63-65 are based on the following fact situation:

Lucy needed a new television set. She went from store to store looking for the perfect set but always was disappointed. Finally, when she was just about to give up, she walked by the local Azimuth Television Co. store and saw the television of her dreams: the Azimuth 360. Lucy walked right into the store and up to the nearest salesperson and asked, "How much for that black 360 in the window?" The salesperson replied, "$500," and Lucy said, "Fine, I'll take one." The salesperson happily complied, and within minutes Lucy was on her way home with the new television set.

When Lucy got home, she opened the box containing the television. Inside, she found an owner's manual that contained instructions on how to operate the set, warnings regarding the danger of electricity, and a warranty that stated:

Azimuth expressly warrants that this set shall be free of manufacturing defects for five days. If a set is defective, Azimuth's liability shall be limited to the cost of repair or replacement of defective parts. **AZIMUTH HEREBY DISCLAIMS ANY AND ALL OTHER WARRANTIES, EXPRESS OR IMPLIED, INCLUDING THE WARRANTY OF FITNESS FOR PARTICULAR PURPOSE AND THE WARRANTY OF MERCHANTABILITY.**

63. Assume for this question only that when Lucy takes the set out of the box, she discovers that it is not black, but green. She takes it back to Azimuth and demands an exchange or refund. Azimuth refuses, on the ground that the set is not defective. If Lucy sues for a refund, who will prevail?

   (A) Lucy, because in consumer transactions a consumer has an absolute right to return goods within 24 hours under the "buyer's remorse" laws.

   (B) Lucy, because an express warranty that the television would be black arose and was breached.

   (C) Azimuth, because the television is not defective in that color does not affect the television's operation.

   (D) Azimuth, because the express warranty has not been breached.

64. Assume now that 10 days later, after the set was properly installed and Lucy had read the owner's manual, she turned on the set, heard a crackling noise, and watched as her television exploded. The television was destroyed. Under which of the following theories will Lucy most likely recover?

   (A) Breach of express warranty.

   (B) Breach of the implied warranty of merchantability.

   (C) Breach of the implied warranty of fitness for a particular purpose.

   (D) None of the above.

65. If in addition to destroying the television, the explosion injured Lucy and caused damage to her house, in a breach of warranty action, what damages may Lucy recover?

   I.   The cost of the television.

   II. Her personal injuries.

   III. The damage to her house.

   (A) I. and II., but not III.

   (B) I. and III., but not II.

   (C) I., II., and III.

   (D) None of the above.

Questions 66-67 are based on the following fact situation:

Debbie owns a sporting goods store. On April 1, she noticed that her tent stock was running low. After consulting her manufacturers' catalogues, she decided to order from Oilman, a large manufacturer of camping equipment. The Oilman catalogue listed the 9×12 tent that Debbie wanted, at a cost of $70. Debbie phoned Oilman and placed her order for 10 tents. The next day, Oilman mailed Debbie a letter informing her that the tents were now $72 and that they would be shipped to her on April 16. Debbie received the letter on April 4, but never responded. On April 15, Debbie received a catalogue from another tent company showing tents similar to the ones that she ordered, but for a cost of $50. She immediately called Oilman to cancel her order. Nevertheless, Oilman shipped the tents to Debbie on April 16.

66. If Oilman sues Debbie to enforce the contract, who will prevail?

    (A) Debbie, because there was no meeting of the minds regarding the price term.

    (B) Debbie, because her promise was not in writing.

    (C) Oilman, because its April 2 letter was sufficient to bind Debbie.

    (D) Oilman, because Debbie's phone call on April 15 to cancel is proof that there was a contract.

67. Assume for this question only that the parties' communications were sufficient to form a contract. On what day was the contract formed?

    (A) April 1, the day Debbie placed her order.

    (B) April 2, the day Oilman sent its letter.

    (C) April 4, the day Debbie received the letter.

    (D) April 16, the day the tents were shipped.

Question 68

John's acquaintance Kevin offered to sell John a piano for $400. John had been to Kevin's house and knew that Kevin owned a Steinberg piano, so he accepted. Unbeknownst to John, Kevin also owned a Hairwin piano, and that was the piano that Kevin intended to sell, although he was aware that John had only seen the Steinberg.

If John sues Kevin to obtain the Steinberg, who will prevail?

(A) John, because Kevin knew of the ambiguity.

(B) John, because that was his objective intent.

(C) Kevin, because there was a mutual mistake.

(D) Kevin, because he subjectively intended to sell the Hairwin instead of the Steinberg.

Question 69

On December 10, Painter agreed to paint Owner's home for $8,000, to be paid on completion of the work. On December 20, before the work was completed, Painter sent a letter to Owner telling Owner to pay the $8,000 to Curtis, who was one of Painter's creditors. Painter sent a copy of the letter to Curtis. Painter then completed the work.

If Curtis sues Owner for the $8,000, which of the following, if true, will act as Owner's best defense?

(A) Curtis was not the intended beneficiary of the Painter-Owner contract.

(B) Curtis was incapable of performing Painter's work.

(C) Painter had not performed his work in a workmanlike manner.

(D) On December 10, Painter had promised Owner that he would not assign the contract.

Question 70

Owner and Purchaser orally agreed that Owner would convey 20 acres of his 160-acre farm to Purchaser. At the time of their agreement, Owner wrote on the back of an envelope, "I hereby promise to convey the 20 acres of the northeast corner of my farm to Purchaser for $10,000." One month later, Purchaser tendered $10,000 to Owner, but Owner refused to convey the 20 acres.

If Purchaser sues Owner to convey the land and Owner prevails, it will most likely be because the writing:

(A) Was not signed by Owner.

(B) Was not signed by Purchaser.

(C) Did not describe the property with specificity.

(D) Was on the back of an envelope.

Question 71

Ted owned bowling lanes and needed to buy some new bowling balls. On February 1, he read an ad from FMA, a major manufacturer of bowling balls, that they were having a special on balls: 40 balls in various weights and drilled in various sizes for $10 per ball. Ted immediately filled out the order form for the 40 balls and deposited it, properly stamped and addressed, into the mail. The very next day, Ted received in the mail a letter from FMA, sent out as part of their advertising campaign, stating in relevant part that they will sell Ted 40 bowling balls at $10 per ball. On February 3, FMA received Ted's order. On February 4, the balls were shipped.

On what day did an enforceable contract arise?

(A) February 1, the day Ted deposited his order in the mail.

(B) February 2, the day Ted received the letter from FMA.

(C) February 3, the day FMA received Ted's letter.

(D) February 4, the day the balls were shipped.

Questions 72-74 are based on the following fact situation:

Mary, 17 years old, was an unemployed disappointment to her parents. To teach Mary to be more self-sufficient, Mary's parents took a one-month trip to Europe, leaving Mary at home to take care of the house. They left Mary $400, which she promptly spent on her first weekend party. By the end of the next week, Mary ran out of food and became hungry. She walked to the local grocery store (the family car was out of gas) and explained her predicament to the manager. He told Mary that if she agreed to work at the store for 20 hours a week for three weeks, she could have $75 worth of groceries. Although it seemed like a lot of work for $75 worth of groceries, Mary needed to eat, and so she accepted, picked up her groceries, promised to report for work the next day, and left.

While on the way home, Mary decided that the idea of credit was not so bad—for a mere promise she obtained $75 worth of groceries. Just then, she passed Buddy's Budget Autos and decided that she would really impress her parents if she had her own car when they returned. She negotiated with Buddy, the owner of Buddy's, to obtain an $800 car in exchange for her promise to work for Buddy 20 hours a week for eight weeks. When Buddy agreed, they drew up a written contract.

While driving home from Buddy's, Mary lost control of the car and crashed into a tree. Both the car and the groceries were completely destroyed. Mary suffered minor injuries. Mary's parents immediately flew home to care for their injured daughter.

72. If the grocery store sues Mary for the cost of the groceries and **wins**, it will be because:

(A) Mary promised to pay for them.

(B) Mary cannot return the groceries so she cannot return the store to the status quo ante.

(C) Mary needed the food.

(D) The contract was not within the Statute of Frauds.

73. If the grocery store sues Mary for the cost of the groceries and **loses**, it will be because:

(A) Mary was a minor.

(B) The groceries were destroyed and thus there was a failure of consideration.

(C) The contract was unconscionable.

(D) It was impossible for Mary to perform.

74. If Buddy sues Mary for the price of the car and *loses*, it will be because:

(A) The contract was unconscionable.

(B) Mary did not need the car.

(C) Since the car was destroyed, there is no consideration to support the bargain.

(D) The purpose of the contract has been frustrated.

Question 75

On June 15, Homeowner and Carpenter formed a valid oral contract in which Carpenter agreed to construct an extension to Homeowner's home, using materials supplied by Homeowner, in exchange for $2,000. After the work had been completed but before Homeowner had made any payment, Carpenter called Homeowner and instructed him to pay the $2,000 due on the extension work to Woodshop, a creditor of Carpenter's.

If Woodshop thereafter brings an action against Homeowner for $2,000, will Woodshop prevail?

(A) Yes, because Woodshop was the intended beneficiary of the original Homeowner-Carpenter contract.

(B) Yes, because there has been a proper assignment.

(C) No, because personal service contracts are not assignable.

(D) No, because Woodshop could not perform the construction work done by Carpenter.

Question 76

Lana was a prominent socialite, noted for her lavish entertainments and her attractiveness. Although Lana was "fortyish," she regularly worked out at her health club and was proud of her mature but youthful figure. She decided to have a nude painting done of herself, and she looked forward to watching people's reactions seeing the painting prominently displayed in her living room. She contracted in writing with artist Pierre. He agreed to paint Lana nude for $10,000. The fee was payable upon completion of the painting, provided that the painting was to Lana's "complete and utter satisfaction." On the same afternoon that Pierre entered into the contract with Lana he assigned the contract to Taylor. Pierre then painted Lana's picture. After the job was done, Lana told him, "That's a very good likeness of me, but it shows my defects, so I'm not satisfied." Lana refused to accept the painting or to pay Pierre or Taylor.

Can Taylor recover from Lana?

(A) Yes, because the condition in the agreement between Lana and Pierre did not apply to Taylor.

(B) Yes, because otherwise an unjust enrichment will occur.

(C) No, because rights arising under personal services contracts are not assignable.

(D) No, because Lana was not satisfied with the painting.

Question 77

Joni met Jasper in "Singleton's," a tavern catering to young, unattached urban professionals. After exchanging about a half an hour of small talk, Joni told Jasper that she greatly admired the diamond stickpin he had in his lapel. "Oh this," Jasper laughed. "It's no diamond; it's only a piece of glass." Joni acknowledged Jasper's statement, but kept commenting on how nice it looked, and that it would go perfectly with her favorite designer business suit. After about a half hour of further conversation, Jasper orally agreed to sell the stickpin to her for $510. It was agreed that on Friday, two days hence, at 6 p.m., Jasper would bring the stickpin to Singleton's and Joni would bring the $510 in cash. Jasper duly appeared with the pin, but Joni failed to appear. Jasper filed suit against Joni for $510.

Joni's best defense is:

(A) $510 was an unconscionable amount to pay for a piece of glass.

(B) The agreement was not supported by consideration.

(C) The agreement violated the Statute of Frauds.

(D) Neither Joni nor Jasper was a merchant.

CONTRACTS ANSWERS

Answer to Question 1

(B) Slam-Dunk should not succeed because its computation error was a unilateral mistake. Where only one of the parties entering into a contract is mistaken about facts relating to the agreement, this unilateral mistake will not prevent formation of a contract unless the nonmistaken party is or had reason to be aware of the mistake made by the other party. Here, the computation error was Slam-Dunk's mistake alone, and the contract may not be rescinded unless Tinker actually knew or should have known of the mistake. While such errors may be canceled in equity if the non-mistaken party has not relied on the contract, Tinker clearly relied upon the contract with Slam-Dunk by submitting the bid to the school board. (A) is incorrect because the fact that the mistake was made before the bid was accepted by the school board is irrelevant by itself. What *is* crucial to Slam-Dunk's suit is whether Tinker knew or should have known of the mistake before submitting the bid to the school board. If so, as discussed above, grounds for rescission exist. (C) is incorrect because Slam-Dunk's error was not a mutual mistake that was part of the basis of the bargain. When both parties entering into a contract are mistaken about facts relating to the agreement, the contract may be voidable by the adversely affected party if, among other things, the mutual mistake concerns a basic assumption on which the contract is made. Here, the computation error was a unilateral, not a mutual mistake, and did not concern an assumption on which the agreement of both parties is based. While there is modern authority indicating that a unilateral mistake that is so extreme that it outweighs the other party's expectations under the agreement will be a ground for cancellation of the contract in equity, the error here probably is not sufficiently extreme to justify cancellation. (D) is incorrect because a unilateral mistake is generally ***not*** a defense to the formation of a contract. As discussed above, where only one of the parties is mistaken about facts relating to the agreement, the mistake will not prevent formation or enforcement of the contract unless the other party knew or had reason to know of the mistake. Therefore, Slam-Dunk will not succeed simply because the error was a unilateral mistake.

Answer to Question 2

(B) If Tinker had reason to be aware of the mistake, it will not be permitted to snap up Slam-Dunk's offer. Where only one of the parties entering into a contract is mistaken about facts relating to the agreement, that unilateral mistake will not prevent formation of a contract. However, if the nonmistaken party is or had reason to be aware of the mistake made by the other party, the contract is voidable. Therefore, if the difference between the $60,000 figure and the next lowest bid alerted or should have alerted Tinker to the existence of a mistake, Slam-Dunk should be able to refuse to perform the contract. (A) is incorrect because the concept of unconscionability concerns clauses in a contract that are so one-sided as to be unconscionable under the circumstances existing at the time the contract was formed, not unilateral mistakes. The unconscionability concept is often applied to one-sided bargains where one of the parties has substantially superior bargaining power. Slam-Dunk's error did not cause the contract to be so one-sided when formed. (C) is incorrect because Slam-Dunk will be held to the amount stated in the message unless Tinker should have been aware of the error. Where there is a mistake in the transmission of an offer by an intermediary, the prevailing view is that the message as transmitted is operative unless the other party knew or should have known of the mistake. Thus, Slam-Dunk will have to perform the contract with Tinker unless Tinker knew or should have known of the mistake. (D) is incorrect because Tinker's negligence in not checking out the bids alone would not result in grounds for rescission. There is no duty to check out all bids. As discussed above, a contract may be rescinded because of unilateral mistake only if the nonmistaken party knew or should have known of the mistake.

Answer to Question 3

(A) Larry may sue Cindy when he receives the letter because an anticipatory breach situation exists. Anticipatory repudiation occurs where a promisor, prior to the time set for performance of her promise, indicates that she will not perform when the time comes. Anticipatory repudiation serves to excuse conditions if: (i) there is an executory bilateral contract with *executory duties on both sides*; and (ii) the words or conduct of the promisor *unequivocally* indicates that she cannot or will not perform when the time comes. The requirements for anticipatory repudiation are met here because Larry's duty to deliver the deed and Cindy's duty to pay have yet to be performed, and Cindy's writing unequivocally states that she will not pay unless Larry performs extra tasks. In the case of anticipatory repudiation, the nonrepudiating party has the option to treat the contract as being breached and sue immediately. Therefore, Larry may sue Cindy upon receipt of the letter. (B) is incorrect. As stated above, Larry may sue upon receipt of the letter because of Cindy's anticipatory repudiation. The doctrine of anticipatory repudiation would not apply if both sides did not have executory duties to perform. In such a case, the nonrepudiator must wait to sue until the time originally set for performance by the repudiating party. However, as discussed above, Larry's duty was still executory at the moment of Cindy's repudiation. Therefore, he does not have to wait until July 1 to sue Cindy for breach. (C) is incorrect because Larry is not required to expressly refuse Cindy's requests before he may sue. Larry is not obligated to perform the additional duties that Cindy has requested since the duties were not in the original contract and the parties have not agreed to any modification. Therefore, Cindy's unequivocal repudiation is a breach. The doctrine of anticipatory repudiation does not require the nonrepudiating party to notify the repudiating party that he is refusing to comply with her unenforceable demands. (D) is incorrect because Larry can sue Cindy immediately *because* their promises are still executory. As discussed above, the doctrine of anticipatory repudiation is applicable only if there are executory duties on both sides. Here, Larry's duty to deliver a deed and Cindy's duty to pay are both executory, so the doctrine applies and Larry can sue Cindy now.

Answer to Question 4

(B) The court will rule that disaffirmance by Andrew, a minor, discharges any liability. Minors generally lack capacity to enter into a contract binding on themselves. Therefore, minors may plead lack of capacity and disaffirm most contracts, even though such contracts are binding on the adult party. Disaffirmance discharges the minor's liability under the contract. Here, Andrew's refusal to make any more payments is a disaffirmance of the contract. Because Andrew is a minor, the disaffirmance discharges any liability he might have. (A) is incorrect because, as discussed above, the contract entered into by Andrew, a minor, was *voidable* at his election, and Andrew has disaffirmed the contract by refusing to make any more car payments. Therefore, any liability he might have is discharged. (C) is incorrect because the Albatross was not a necessity. While a contract entered into between a minor and an adult is generally voidable by the minor, a minor is bound to pay the reasonable value of "*necessities*." However, while what constitutes a necessity depends on the minor's station in life, there is nothing here to indicate that the car was a necessity to Andrew. Therefore, Andrew is not liable for the reasonable market value of the car. (D) is incorrect because it fails to address the necessity of a disaffirmance, which discharges all liability. As discussed above, a contract entered into by a minor is voidable by the minor. However, such a contract is binding on both parties unless and until it is avoided by the minor through disaffirmance. Thus, Andrew's mere minority at the time of contracting would not release him from liability. He must disaffirm the contract to avoid liability.

Answer to Question 5

(A) No contract arose on February 2 because Shaftum's offer expired on February 1, when Shaftum did not receive Martin's acceptance. If a period of acceptance is stated in an offer, the offeree must accept within that period to create a contract. Failure to timely accept terminates the power of acceptance in the offeree (*i.e.*, a late acceptance will not be effective and will not create a contract). Under the mailbox rule, an acceptance generally is effective upon dispatch (*i.e.*, the acceptance creates a contract at the moment it is mailed or given to the telegraph company). However, the mailbox rule does not apply where the offer states that acceptance will not be effective until received. In the latter case, acceptance is effective only upon receipt. Here, Shaftum's offer specifically stated that the acceptance must be received by February 1 to be effective. Thus, Shaftum opted-out of the mailbox rule and no contract was created by delivery of the telegram on February 2. Note that Martin will not be able to successfully argue that the acceptance was valid since the late delivery was the telegraph company's fault. This would be a valid argument if the mailbox rule applied here, because the acceptance would have been effective on February 1, when the message was given to the telegraph company. However, by opting-out of the mailbox rule, Shaftum put the burden of any negligence in delivery on Martin. Thus, there was no valid acceptance. (B) is incorrect because of the requirement that acceptance be *received* by February 1. This requirement obviates the general "mailbox rule," so that the mere mailing of a letter (or sending of a telegram) does not operate as an effective acceptance. (C) is incorrect because Shaftum was not obligated to respond in any way to the telegram received on February 2. Once the specified time passed without receipt of acceptance, the offer (as well as Martin's power of acceptance) was terminated. Thus, receipt of the telegram on February 2 created neither a contract nor an obligation on the part of Shaftum to respond to the telegram. (D) is incorrect because no contract, voidable or otherwise, arose on February 1. As explained above, there could be no contract because acceptance of the offer was not received as specified by the offer. Also, the facts do not indicate circumstances under which a contract is usually held to be voidable. A voidable contract is a contract that one or both parties may elect to avoid or to ratify (*e.g.*, contracts of infants). The facts of this question provide no basis for concluding that any contract that might have arisen between these parties would be voidable.

Answer to Question 6

(A) Builder will not be able to recover anything from Owen because he has not performed his duty. Under the parties' contract, Builder's completion of the house was a condition precedent to Owen's duty to pay. The condition precedent was not discharged by the destruction of the work in progress since construction has not been made impossible, but rather merely more costly—Builder can rebuild. Thus, Builder is not entitled to any recovery. Note, however, that a number of courts will excuse *timely* performance since the destruction was not Builder's fault. (B) is incorrect because the contract is not divisible (*i.e.*, it is not divided into an equal number of parts for each side, each part being the quid pro quo of the other); thus completion on one-half of the house did not entitle Builder to one-half of the price. (C) is incorrect because it is not a correct measure of recovery. As stated above, Builder cannot recover under the contract; however, he may be able to recover under a quasi-contract theory. Quasi-contract is a remedy that prevents unjust enrichment by imposing on a recipient of requested goods or services a duty to pay for the benefit received when there is a failed contract or no contractual relationship between the parties. Here, if Builder decides not to perform under the contract by rebuilding, he may still be able to obtain a quasi-contract remedy. The measure of recovery here would be the fair market value of what remains of the house since that is the benefit conferred—it would not be cut in half merely because the house was only half completed. (D) is an incorrect contract recovery since Builder has not fulfilled the condition precedent to Owen's duty to pay, and it is an incorrect quasi-contract recovery where the claimant has breached his duty to perform because such a recovery is measured by the benefit conferred and not by the costs of conferring the benefit.

Answer to Question 7

(D) Jobber will recover only its incidental damages, *i.e.,* the costs of preparing to ship the chairs. An offer calling for shipment of goods, such as the offer here, may be accepted by prompt shipment with notice or by a promise to ship. Acceptance forms a contract. Here, Jobber accepted Wholesaler's offer by promising to ship (the warning that Jobber had no more chairs was unimportant surplus-age since it could fill Wholesaler's order), and a contract was formed. Wholesaler breached the contract by canceling its order. When a buyer breaches by repudiating its offer, as Wholesaler did here, the seller has a right to recover its incidental damages plus either the difference between the contract price and the market price or the difference between the contract price and the resale price of the goods. If neither measure is adequate to put the seller in as good a position as perfor-mance would have, she may recover lost profits. Here, the contract price was the same as both the resale price and the market price; thus, that measure of damages is not useful. Lost profits are not possible here because Jobber sold the chairs and they were the last ones she had and would have since she discontinued the line. Therefore, Jobber lost no profits. She made what she would have if the sale with Wholesaler had gone through. Thus, Jobber would be limited to her inciden-tal damages under the first two measures of damages. (A) is incorrect because there is no rule under the U.C.C., which governs the contract here, that makes contracts between merchants cancelable within a reasonable time. (B) is incorrect because, as indicated above, the U.C.C. allows the seller to recover incidental damages. (C) is incorrect because the U.C.C. seeks only to put the nonbreaching party in as good a position as she would have been had the other party performed, and here, awarding Jobber lost profits would put her in a better position than perfor-mance would have, since it would give Jobber a double recovery for selling the same goods. (The result would be different, however, if Jobber had had more chairs to sell, because in that case, the breach would have cost Jobber additional sales—*i.e.,* Jobber could have sold to Whole-saler *and* Relaselohw.)

Answer to Question 8

(C) Jobber is entitled to recover the incidental damages plus the difference between the contract price and the resale price. As explained in the previous answer, when a buyer breaches a contract to purchase by repudiating his offer, the seller is entitled to recover her incidental damages plus either the difference between the contract price and the market price or the difference between the contract price and the resale price. Since Jobber chose to resell the chairs here, her damages would be the difference between the resale price and the contract price, plus incidental damages. Thus, Jobber can recover $37,500 less $10,000, plus incidental damages. (A) is incorrect because there is nothing in the U.C.C., which governs the contract here, that makes contracts between merchants cancelable within a reasonable time. (B) is incorrect because the U.C.C. remedy gives the seller the *difference* between the contract price and the resale price, not just the contract price. (D) is incorrect because it fails to account for Jobber's incidental damages; Jobber has a right to resale price *plus* her incidental damages.

Answer to Question 9

(A) Skabco will be able to force HotelCorp to pay the additional $2 million because HotelCorp was on notice of the mistake. Skabco has the defense of unilateral mistake. Although the general rule

exception to unilateral mistake

is that a contract will not be avoided by a unilateral mistake, there is an exception where the nonmistaken party either knew or should have known of the mistake. Here the facts clearly indicate that HotelCorp knew that Skabco's bid could not be correct, yet they relied on it anyway. Thus, Skabco had grounds to avoid the contract. Rather than completely avoid the contract here, the parties agreed to reform it, but they failed to record the reformation in writing. Nevertheless, the court will allow the parties to show the reformed terms here, because of the mistake. (B) is incorrect because although consideration is usually required to modify a contract, it is not required where the parties are modifying **merely to correct an error** in the original contract. Also, it is not even clear that the parties here are modifying their contract; since the mistake would have served to discharge Skabco from the contract completely, the reformed contract can be viewed as a new contract, which is enforceable even though it is not in writing because it is not within the Statute of Frauds (a contract to build a building is not within the Statute). (C) is incorrect because the unilateral mistake here was sufficient to discharge Skabco from its duties under the contract, so there was no preexisting duty. (If the mistake had not been sufficient to discharge Skabco, (C) would be correct because where one is under a preexisting legal duty to perform, performance of that same duty will not be sufficient consideration to support a promise to pay additional sums for the performance.) (D) is incorrect because the parol evidence rule only prevents introduction of oral statements made prior to or contemporaneously with a written contract. Here, the $2 million term, although oral, was agreed upon after the original contract was made; thus, the parol evidence rule would not be a bar.

Answer to Question 10

(A) HotelCorp will be able to recover $100,000, its lost profits. The purpose of contract damages is to put the nonbreaching party into as good a position as it would have been had the breaching party fully performed. This would be represented here by HotelCorp's lost profits, which is its income ($300,000) minus its expenses ($200,000), or $100,000. The liquidated damages provision will not apply because it is unreasonable (*see* below). (B) is incorrect because giving HotelCorp its $300,000 income would put it in a better position than it would have been in if Skabco had performed, because such an award does not take into account the expenses that HotelCorp avoided by not being in operation. (C) is incorrect because a court would not uphold the liquidated damages clause here. Liquidated damages clauses are enforceable only if damages were difficult to estimate at the time the contract was formed, and the amount agreed upon is a reasonable forecast of the damages that would result from a breach. Here, the damages may have been difficult to predict when the contract was formed because it is not known just how well a new hotel will do; however, the amount agreed upon seems to be too high. The facts indicate that a reasonable estimate at the time of the contract was about $10,000 per day, but since the liquidated damages amount ($100,000 per day) is 10 times that amount, it seems that this amount was unreasonable. (D) is incorrect because it seeks to combine the actual damages with the liquidated damages. Regardless of whether the liquidated damages clause will be enforced here, this measure is improper because a party may recover either liquidated damages, or if not available, the actual damages, but not both.

Answer to Question 11

(D) Piper will be unable to recover the $500 because he did not satisfy the condition precedent to payment under the contract. A party does not have a duty to perform if a condition precedent to that performance has not been met. Here, the parties made Oboe's satisfaction with Piper's paint job a condition precedent to Oboe's duty to pay the $5,000. Since Oboe was not satisfied with the paint job, her duty to pay Piper never arose. The fact that Oboe offered to give Piper $4,500 if he repainted the porches has no effect on this analysis, since the offer constituted a **new contract**, Oboe having been excused from the old one. (A) is wrong because it does not matter whether Piper indorsed under protest. The indorsement will not change the result here because the new contract did not seek to **discharge** any contractual duty—Oboe was already excused from her duties since the condition precedent was never met. (B) is wrong because the old contract is considered to be at an end due to Piper's breach (a material breach discharges the other party's duty to perform), and under the terms of the new contract, Piper is entitled only to $4,500. The terms of the old contract would have allowed payment of the $500, but the new contract was for $4,500 for repainting. Thus, if Piper repainted, all he is entitled to is $4,500. (C) is wrong because Piper did not perform his contractual duties. It was Piper's duty to paint to Oboe's satisfaction, and Oboe was under a duty of good faith. The courts have held such conditions to be valid—not illusory promises—because of the promisor's duty to exercise good faith in assessing satisfaction. Here, Oboe acted in good faith, and Piper did not perform his contractual duties. Thus, he is not entitled to the $500.

Answer to Question 12

(D) Oboe will not prevail in her suit for specific performance because Piper's services are not unique. Specific performance is only available where the legal remedy (*i.e.,* money damages) is inadequate. Money damages can be inadequate for a number of reasons, such as where the goods or services sought are unique. Here, although personal services are involved, they are not the type of services that are considered to be unique (the facts do not indicate that Piper was hired because he painted differently from any other painter). Thus, Oboe could hire someone else to repaint the porches and sue Piper for damages. Moreover, the courts generally will not grant a decree of specific performance in personal services contracts to force someone to work (although they will sometimes enjoin someone from working for anyone else in violation of contract). (A) is wrong because a novation is a substitution of a third party for one of the parties to a contract by agreement of all the parties involved, and nothing in the facts indicates that such a substitution was involved here. Moreover, if a novation were involved, Oboe would not be able to force Piper to work because Piper would have been the party released. (B) is wrong because while Oboe's good faith dissatisfaction with Piper's paint job was sufficient to establish a breach (*see* previous answer), it is not enough for specific performance. The fact that there was a breach is not enough; the legal remedy must also be inadequate, and here it is adequate. (C) is wrong because Oboe's duty to pay Piper never arose, since Piper did not satisfy the condition precedent to Oboe's duty to pay (painting to Oboe's satisfaction).

Answer to Question 13

(B) Mortimer's strongest defense is that the advertisement was not an offer, but merely an invitation for offers. Statements of promise, undertaking, or commitment (*i.e.,* offers) must be distinguished from statements of future intent or preliminary negotiations. Advertisements are generally construed to be mere invitations to make offers, although some advertisements may be construed as offers, especially if they are very definite as to terms. Here, the advertisement is fairly specific in its terms and thus it is not easy to tell whether it is an offer or mere invitation for offers. Following the general rule that advertisements are mere invitations, and since all of the other choices do not provide Mortimer's with a defense, this is the best answer. (A) is wrong because the advertisement, if it is construed as an offer, did not say anything about when the tune-up had to be performed or completed; it merely stated that the tune-up had to be ordered on that day. (C) is wrong because the "offer" called for acceptance by "ordering" the tune-up, not by actual payment or any other performance. (D) is wrong because Nancy's refusal to take the trip is irrelevant. The "offer" gave her a choice of the trip or the knife set; she did not have to take the trip.

Answer to Question 14

(C) Alpha is liable for nothing because no contract was formed between Alpha and XYZ. Formation of a contract requires mutual agreement between the parties (offer and acceptance) and consideration. There was no contract here because there was no acceptance. Alpha's bid constituted an offer—a certain and definite promise, undertaking, or commitment to enter into a contract communicated to the offeree. An offer gives the offeree the power to accept and create a contract until the offer is terminated. An offer can be terminated in a number of ways, including through a counteroffer from the offeree. A counteroffer serves as both a rejection terminating the original offer and a new offer from the original offeree, thus reversing the former roles of the parties and giving the original offeror the right to accept or reject the new offer. Here, XYZ's president's call constituted a rejection and a counteroffer that Alpha rejected, and so no contract was formed. Therefore, Alpha cannot be held liable. (A) and (B) are incorrect because, as stated above, a contract was never formed between XYZ and Alpha. Thus, it is irrelevant whether the mistake was unilateral or obvious. (Note that the general rule is that a contract will not be set aside for a unilateral mistake unless the nonmistaken party either knew or should have known of the mistake. Thus if XYZ had accepted Alpha's bid, Alpha would be liable on the contract despite its mistake because (B) the mistake was unilateral and (A) it was not obvious.) (D) is incorrect for several reasons. First, it relies on the existence of a contract, and as stated above, there is no contract here. Second, the premise that Alpha could not renege on its offer is untrue. The general rule is that offers are revocable until accepted. In a subcontractor bid situation, a bid is treated as irrevocable for a reasonable amount of time because of detrimental reliance (*i.e.,* the general contractor will rely on the mistaken bid in preparing his bid). However, here XYZ learned of Alpha's mistake before any reliance on Alpha's bid. Moreover, it is unclear whether XYZ is complaining about Alpha's reneging on its bid; XYZ appears to be complaining that Alpha refused to lower the mistaken bid. Alpha would have no duty to lower its bid in any case. The final premise in (D) is irrelevant. If Alpha lacked the power to renege, the lack of power goes to the $75,000 bid; the fact that no one would do the job for $70,000 has no bearing on the issue.

Answer to Question 15

(D) Nadja cannot enforce the contract because the assignment of rights to her has properly been revoked. Nadja gave no consideration for the right to receive the $5,000 that was assigned to her. A gratuitous assignment generally is revocable unless the obligor has already performed or the assignee has relied on the promise to her detriment. Revocation of the assignment can be accomplished in a number of ways, including by giving notice to the obligor or assignee. Here, the obligor (Osman) had not yet performed (paid the money), and Nadja did not rely on the promise. Nadja's marriage will not be considered to be detrimental reliance because Nadja was already engaged to be married and even had a wedding date planned (Khaled said that Nadja was to be married soon). Khaled revoked the assignment by giving notice to Osman. Thus, the revocation was proper, and Nadja cannot enforce the assignment against either party. Therefore, (D) is correct and (A), (B), and (C) are incorrect.

Answer to Question 16

(D) Nadja's best argument to enforce the contract in her favor is that she married in reliance on the contract (detrimental reliance), although she will probably be unsuccessful. As established in the previous answer, Nadja was a gratuitous assignee and her rights under the contract were revoked. Thus, her strongest argument will be one that nullifies the revocation. The only possible choice here is (D), since under the doctrine of detrimental reliance, a promise will be enforced to the extent necessary to prevent injustice if it was made with a reasonable expectation that it would induce reliance, and such reliance was in fact induced. The problem with this argument here is that it is not clear that Nadja relied on the promise to give her $5,000, since she already had planned to get married. However, none of the other choices is a possible argument so (D) is Nadja's best choice. (A) would not help her because the Statute of Frauds is a defense to enforcement of certain contracts when there is no writing, including contracts where the consideration is marriage, but here Nadja is seeking to *enforce the contract*, not prevent its enforcement. (B) is incorrect because the parol evidence rule only prevents the introduction of prior or contemporaneous oral statements to contradict the terms of an integrated written contract, and here, the clause that gave Nadja her rights and the one that took them away were both *subsequent* oral statements. (C) does not help Nadja because she was not an intended third-party beneficiary. If a contract between two parties contemplates performance to a third party, that third party may have rights to enforce the contract. To do so, the third party must be an intended beneficiary (*e.g.,* designated in the contract). An assignment, on the other hand, is a contract that does *not* contemplate performance to a third party when the contract is made, but later, one of the parties transfers his rights to another. Here, Khaled and Osman signed their contract and *later*, Khaled assigned his rights to his daughter. Thus, Nadja was not an intended third-party beneficiary who could enforce the agreement, but merely an assignee who gave no consideration for the assignment. As such, Nadja cannot recover the $5,000.

Answer to Question 17

(A) The court should order Deeds to rent the apartment to Phlo because he rented it to Tony before July 2. Phlo and Deeds created an option contract, the terms of which required Deeds to consider accepting Phlo's application to rent the apartment if she applied on or before July 1. Deeds breached the contract by renting the apartment to Tony on June 9, since renting the apartment before July 2 prevented Deeds from considering Phlo's application (it is breach by anticipatory repudiation). Since the apartment was apparently unique (it had some very distinctive features), specific performance would be the proper remedy here, because the remedy at law (money damages) would not be adequate. (B) is wrong because the option required Deeds to keep the apartment open only until the end of July 1. If Phlo submitted her application by then, the contract gave Deeds up to 15 days to decide whether to accept, but it did not require him to use all 15 days—he could have decided immediately. Thus, he could refuse Phlo's application and rent to Tony before July 16. (C) is wrong because nothing in the facts shows the contract to be unconscionable. Unconscionability prevents oppression and unfair surprise. The basic test is whether at the time the contract was formed the clauses involved were extremely one-sided. Here, while the contract did not require Deeds to rent the apartment to Phlo, it cannot be said that it is one-sided because it requires Deeds to hold open the apartment until July 2. (D) is wrong because Phlo has suffered irreparable harm since she apparently cannot rent another apartment exactly like the one on which she had the option.

Answer to Question 18

(B) The doctrine of promissory estoppel under section 90 of the Restatement (Second) of Contracts provides that a promise that the promisor should reasonably expect to induce action or forbearance on the part of the promisee, and which does induce such action or forbearance, is binding if injustice can be avoided only by enforcement of the promise. When Hollandaise promised Bernaise that "we'll work these things out," he should have reasonably expected Bernaise to take exactly the sort of action he did to prepare for the distributorship, since the parties had already agreed on the major points of their arrangement. Hollandaise will therefore be liable for Bernaise's detrimental reliance on a theory of promissory estoppel. (A) is incorrect because an implied-in-fact contract arises when assent is manifested by conduct, as opposed to assent by oral or written language, which gives rise to an express contract. A typical example of an implied-in-fact contract is where a customer enters a barbershop and receives a haircut from the barber. The circumstances imply that the customer has agreed to pay for the haircut, even though this was not discussed beforehand. Hollandaise and Bernaise had specifically negotiated the major points of their agreement and were still working on the minor ones; thus, there was nothing expected to be implied. (C) is incorrect because unjust enrichment arises in situations where there is no enforceable contract, yet one person has for some reason conferred a benefit on another with the expectation of being compensated. If the second person retains the benefit without paying for it, he will be unjustly enriched. Bernaise's expenditures did not serve to enrich Hollandaise, so the concept of unjust enrichment does not apply. (D) is incorrect because quasi-contract is a legal fiction used to avoid injustice and provide a remedy in situations of unjust enrichment. It is based on equitable principles and is not really a contract at all. In some cases, courts will allow a plaintiff in a quasi-contract action to recover the market value of his services even if they do not directly benefit the defendant, as long as they were done with the expectation of being compensated or they benefit a third party at the request of defendant. The costs incurred by Bernaise, on the other hand, were expenditures to enable Bernaise to perform the contract that he had been promised; hence, promissory estoppel is the appropriate theory for Bernaise to use.

Answer to Question 19

(D) Richelle's December 14 letter was an acceptance. Whether the letter was an acceptance depends on whether Morris's letter was an offer, since an acceptance is a manifestation of assent to an offer. For a communication to be an offer, it must create a reasonable expectation in the offeree that the offeror is willing to enter into a contract on the basis of the offered terms. There must be a promise, undertaking, or commitment to enter into a contract with certain and definite terms. Courts usually hold that if a statement is made broadly, such as in an advertisement or catalog, it will not constitute an offer because it is not reasonable to expect that the sender intended to make offers to all who received the advertisement; rather, the courts usually find such advertisements to be invitations seeking offers. However, the courts will look to the surrounding circumstances, and here a court would probably determine that the catalog that Morris sent *was* an offer because it was sent in response to Richelle's specific inquiries about prices on specific computers and it included delivery terms and conditions of sale. (A) is incorrect because although the letter called for payment in cash, tender by check is sufficient unless the seller demands legal tender and gives the buyer time to obtain cash. Moreover, since the contract called for payment within 30 days of delivery, even if the check was not sufficient, Richelle still had time under the contract to obtain cash. (B) is incorrect because the mistake was unilateral. Generally, a unilateral mistake will not be grounds to rescind a contract unless the nonmistaken party either knew or should have known of the mistake. Here, nothing in the facts indicates that Richelle knew of the mistake, and the mistake was not so large that it could be said that she should have known of it. (C) is incorrect because, as explained above, Morris's catalog was sent in response to Richelle's request for information and his terms for sale did constitute an offer.

Answer to Question 20

(D) Richelle's promise to pay $300 is enforceable under the U.C.C. The contract here is governed by the U.C.C., since it is for the sale of goods. Under the U.C.C., a promise to modify an existing contract is enforceable even without consideration. The only requirement is that the proposal to modify be made in good faith. Here, the proposal was made in good faith, because it was to correct an error in the catalog. Thus, the promise to pay the $300 is enforceable. (Note that this modification would be enforceable even in a non-U.C.C. case because the new shipping date would be consideration for the additional $300.) (A) is incorrect because even if shipping late was a breach of contract (and it probably was, since the shipment date was part of the modification sought in good faith), it would not give Richelle the right to unilaterally decide not to pay a portion of the price. The breach would only give her the right to reject the computer and cancel or "cover," or accept it and sue for damages. (B) is incorrect because even if Richelle's promise is a counteroffer, it was also an acceptance of Morris's offer to modify. Under the U.C.C., unlike under common law, if a merchant accepts another merchant's offer and proposes additional or different terms, there is an effective acceptance and a contract is formed. Therefore, Richelle's promise is enforceable. (C) is incorrect because the common law preexisting legal duty rule does not apply to modifications under the U.C.C. The common law enforces promises only if they are supported by consideration, and a promise to perform a preexisting duty is not valid consideration. But, as stated above, the U.C.C. allows good faith modifications even without consideration. [U.C.C. §2-209]

Answer to Question 21

(A) The additional delivery term became part of the contract under the U.C.C. rules for accepting offers. Under the U.C.C., an acceptance is valid even if it contains additional or different terms, unless acceptance is made conditional on assent to those terms. (*Compare:* Under the common law, an acceptance with additional terms is a rejection and a counteroffer.) Whether the additional terms become part of the contract depends on the nature of the parties. If both parties are merchants, the additional terms become part of the contract unless (i) the additional terms materially alter the original terms of the offer, (ii) the offer expressly limits acceptance to the terms of the offer, or (iii) the offeror rejects the additional terms within a reasonable time. Here, the contract was between merchants (ones who deal in goods of that kind sold). Morris proposed a modification and Richelle accepted the modification, but added a new delivery term. The acceptance was not conditional upon assent to the delivery term (since it did not state that it was conditional— e.g., "I accept but only if . . . "), but merely said that delivery had to be by January 20. The delivery term does not seem to be materially different from the offered terms, since it gave Morris 20 days to deliver. Morris did not object to the delivery term or limit acceptance to the terms of the offer. Thus, the contract included the new delivery term. (B) is incorrect because under the U.C.C. a modification need not be supported by consideration; it need only be made in good faith, and here the customer's needs were a good faith reason for the modification. (C) is incorrect because while it is true that the contract had an implied term calling for delivery at a reasonable time, the parties were free to modify the term, as they did here. (D) is incorrect because, under the U.C.C., Morris became bound by the additional term since he did not object to it. As indicated above, between merchants the additional terms are included unless the offeror objects.

Answer to Question 22

(C) When Richelle accepted the computer, her duty to pay the $300 arose, but she retained the right to sue for damages because of the late delivery. When nonconforming goods are delivered, the buyer may: (i) reject them and cancel the contract or sue for damages; or (ii) accept any commercial units, reject the rest, and sue for damages. Once the goods are accepted, the buyer generally is bound on the contract and it is too late to cancel; however, the buyer retains the right to sue for damages for any nonconformity. Acceptance occurs when the buyer: (i) indicates that she will accept the goods after a reasonable opportunity to inspect them; (ii) fails to reject within a proper time; or (iii) does any act inconsistent with the seller's ownership. Here, Richelle indicated that she would accept the computer even though she knew that it did not conform to the contract (because of the late delivery); thus, the time for rejection had passed. Since she accepted the computer, she became bound on the contract, and since the contract included a term for the extra $300, she was bound to pay it. Nevertheless, she can sue for damages that arose from the late delivery. Therefore, (C) is correct, and (A), (B), and (D) are incorrect.

Answer to Question 23

(D) The customer will not prevail because he was only an incidental beneficiary of the contract between Morris and Richelle. Generally, one must be a party to a contract to sue for breach under it. However, there are exceptions for certain intended third-party beneficiaries. Incidental third-party beneficiaries have no right to enforce the contract. The best way to determine whether a person is an intended third-party beneficiary is to ask "to whom is performance to be rendered under the contract?" If the language of the contract indicates that the promisee intended someone other than himself as the primary beneficiary of the contract, that person is an intended third-party beneficiary. In determining the promisee's intentions, the courts will consider: whether the third party was designated in the contract; whether performance was to be made directly to the third party; whether the third party was specifically given any rights under the contract; and whether the third party had such a relationship with the promisee as would indicate that the promisee wanted to benefit him. Here, the only factor indicating that the customer may have been an intended third-party beneficiary was the fact that in the modified contract, Richelle mentioned that her customer needed the computer by January 20. However, that fact alone is not enough to make the customer an intended third-party beneficiary; the purchase was clearly for Richelle's benefit (a purchase of merchandise for her store to sell). Thus, the customer is only an incidental beneficiary. (A) is incorrect because while it may be true that the customer's damages were caused by Morris's late delivery, Morris owed the customer no duty. (B) is incorrect because even if Richelle had paid the $300, the customer would not be able to recover, since he is only an incidental beneficiary. (C) is incorrect because if the contract were otherwise enforceable by the customer, his acceptance would not have cut off his right to sue for damages. The goods were nonconforming because of the late delivery, and a buyer can sue to recover for a nonconformity even if he accepts the goods.

Answer to Question 24

(A) A contract was formed here because there was mutual assent and valid consideration. For there to be mutual assent, there must be a valid offer and an unequivocal acceptance before the offer is either rejected by the offeree or revoked by the offeror. Here, Fox offered to sell his house and lot at 337 Green Street for $100,000. This was clearly an offer to Sack. The issue here is whether either of Sack's replies constitutes an unequivocal acceptance of this offer. A counteroffer serves as a rejection of the original offer as well as a new offer. However, a mere inquiry about additional terms or matters is not a counteroffer. The test of whether the reply is a counteroffer or inquiry is whether a reasonable person would believe that the offer was being rejected. Here, Sack's February 8 communication was a mere inquiry, rather than a counteroffer. His statements do not show an outright rejection unless his terms are agreed to; he merely states what he would prefer, and then asks Fox to consider his proposal. Most likely this would be considered to be an inquiry. The February 11 communication is an acceptance. Sack clearly states that he accepts the "offer of February 3" (showing that he is agreeing to Fox's original terms). The additional language in Sack's telegram (about the deed and his agent) is not an alteration of the original terms because implicit in a sale of land contract is that a deed will be conveyed, and the use of an agent is immaterial. Statements by the offeree that make implicit terms explicit do not prevent acceptance of the offer. Thus, Sack's second communication unequivocally accepts Fox's offer. Since promises were exchanged (a promise to sell the property for a promise to pay $100,000), valid consideration existed, and a contract was formed. (B) is wrong because, as explained above, Sack's February 8 communication did not constitute a counteroffer, which would act as a rejection of the offer. Since the communication was a mere inquiry, the offer was still viable and Sack could accept it. (C) is wrong because the first communication only inquired about altering the deal and the second merely expressed terms already implicit to the offer. Neither contained alterations of the offer's terms. (D) is wrong because a contract for the sale of land need only identify the land and contain a price term. Here, the offer adequately described the property and stated the price. It was a sufficiently definite offer.

Answer to Question 25

(C) At common law, an acceptance is effective upon dispatch (*e.g.,* upon mailing a properly addressed and stamped letter) under the "mailbox rule." There is no mailbox rule, however, for revocations—revocations are effective only upon receipt. Receipt does not require knowledge of the revocation, but merely possession of it. [*See* Restatement (Second) of Contracts §68] The facts here present a close question as to whether there has been a dispatch of the acceptance before the receipt of the revocation. The outcome of this question will depend on the court's determination as to what came first (the posting of the acceptance or receipt of the revocation). This will decide the existence or nonexistence of the contract. (A) is incorrect because, as indicated above, revocation is effective only upon receipt, not mailing. (B) is incorrect because whether the acceptance is effective depends on whether the revocation was received before the acceptance was dispatched, and whether the revocation was received first is not dependent on whether Sack had knowledge of its contents, but rather it depends on whether Sack had possession of it. (D) is incorrect because the mailbox rule makes acceptances effective upon posting, and there is no reason to hold that handing a properly addressed, stamped letter to a mail carrier is not a valid posting.

Answer to Question 26

(A) Zenith will be able to recover damages from Aerial since Aerial's failure to fly constituted a breach of contract. The parties entered into a bilateral contract—Aerial promised to fly with the streamer and Zenith promised to pay for the flights. Aerial breached the contract by failing to fly on the first Saturday. Aerial's duty to fly was not discharged by impossibility. A contractual duty to perform may be discharged by objective impossibility (*i.e., no one* could have performed), but subjective impossibility (*defendant* could not perform) is insufficient. Here, the defect in the plane constituted only subjective impossibility (if it amounted to impossibility at all) since Aerial could have obtained another plane to pull the streamer. If Aerial had been unable to fly the plane because of weather (*e.g.,* a severe ice storm), it would have been objective impossibility and Aerial would be discharged. However, under the facts, Zenith is entitled to damages for Aerial's breach. (B) is incorrect because Zenith's duty to perform (pay $500) was subject to the condition precedent of Aerial's performance (flying), and, as discussed above, Aerial breached the contract by failing to fly. Therefore, Zenith's duty to pay never arose. The fact that the engine problem was not Aerial's fault does not change things. His inability to perform, even if it could be considered impossibility, would merely discharge the contract, and each party would be excused from performance. Thus, Zenith would not have to pay the $500. (C) is incorrect because, as determined above, Aerial's duty was not discharged since performance was only subjectively impossible. (If there had been objective impossibility, (C) would have been the correct choice.) (D) is incorrect because it suggests that the contract was a unilateral one (the offer to pay could only be accepted by completion of performance). This interpretation is clearly contrary to the facts. Although Zenith offered to pay $500 for each flight, Aerial accepted that offer by signing the contract. A promise to pay was given in exchange for a promise to fly. Thus, there was a contract to which both parties were bound.

Answer to Question 27

(D) Neither party is entitled to recover from the other because destruction of the streamer without the fault of either party discharged Aerial since it made performance impossible. Contractual duties will be discharged if it has become impossible to perform them. To result in discharge of the contract, the impossibility must be objective; *i.e., no one* would be able to perform. Here, performance was objectively impossible because the subject matter of the contract (the streamer) was destroyed without the fault of either party and could not be replaced in time. Thus, Aerial's duty to fly was discharged because of destruction of the thing necessary to fulfill the contract. Under the terms of the contract, Aerial's flying was a condition precedent to Zenith's duty to pay. Therefore, Zenith's duty to pay never arose. In this case, then, neither party may recover. (A) is incorrect because when a party is excused from performing by impossibility, the excuse is not a substitute for performance. Rather, the contract is discharged and each party is excused from contractual duties yet to be fulfilled. Therefore, Zenith does not have to pay Aerial on the contract. (B) is incorrect because when the destruction of the subject matter of the contract is not the fault of either party, the parties are discharged from their duties to perform. It is not a breach of the contract—technical or otherwise. (C) is incorrect because it incorrectly states the effect of the destruction of the streamer. It is true that neither party may recover (*see* above), but the reason is that the *contract* between Aerial and Zenith was discharged by impossibility. The offer was not terminated by the impossibility; it had already been accepted when the parties signed the contract.

Answer to Question 28

(A) Freddie's telegram constitutes anticipatory repudiation, which entitles Emma to sue immediately. Anticipatory repudiation occurs where a promisor, prior to the time set for performance of his promise, indicates that he will not perform when the time comes. The contract must be executory on both sides and the repudiation must be unequivocal. Upon anticipatory repudiation, the nonrepudiating party has several options, including suing immediately for breach. Here, Freddie unequivocally indicated that he would breach before the agreed-upon delivery date, and the contract was executory on both sides since Emma had not paid for the gowns and Freddie had not delivered them. Thus, Emma could sue for damages immediately. (B) is incorrect because Emma need not demand assurances before suing on the contract. As explained above, if there has been a repudiation of the contract, the other party may sue immediately. [U.C.C. §2-610] This choice would be correct if Freddie's actions had not been so clearly a repudiation. U.C.C. section 2-609 provides that when actions or circumstances increase the risk of nonperformance, but do not clearly indicate that performance will not be forthcoming, there is no breach. Rather, the party has a right to demand assurances. If proper assurances are not given within a reasonable time, then the contract may be seen as having been breached. Here, Freddie's statements were clear indications that he would not perform, and so section 2-609 does not apply. (C) is incorrect because anticipatory breach is the same as anticipatory repudiation. Although the nonbreaching party has a number of options—including waiting for the performance date—she is not obliged to choose any particular option and, as indicated above, she may sue immediately. (D) is incorrect because whether a breach was made in good faith or bad faith is irrelevant. If there is a breach, the nonbreaching party is entitled to her U.C.C. remedies, and as stated above, Emma may sue before September 1. The motive for Freddie's breach does not alter her right to sue.

Answer to Question 29

(B) Emma is entitled to specific performance of the contract since the gowns are unique. When one party breaches a contract, the nonbreaching party may obtain specific performance of the contract when the legal remedy (*e.g.,* damages) is inadequate. Legal remedies are generally considered to be inadequate when the subject matter of the contract is unique. Also, this contract falls under the U.C.C. since it involves goods. U.C.C. section 2-716 allows a buyer to get specific performance if the goods are unique even when the goods have not been identified to the contract. Here, the goods (gowns) are unique; they are designer originals, part of a "world-famous line." (Arguably they were identified by Freddie's placing them aside for Emma.) Thus, the court will order specific performance. (A) is incorrect because "cover" requires purchasing substitute goods. Since the gowns here are unique, adequate substitutions are not available (even if Emma could find similar-looking gowns, they would not have Freddie's designer label, and that is part of what makes Freddie's gowns valuable). If the dresses were fungible, (A) would be an adequate remedy. (C) is incorrect because contractual remedies are generally designed to put the nonbreaching party in as good a position as she would have been had the promise been performed, and merely refunding Emma's expenses will not achieve this result—she will have lost the entire benefit of her bargain. (D) is incorrect because a nonbreaching party is not entitled to *all* consequential damages, but rather only foreseeable consequential damages proximately caused by the breach.

Answer to Question 30

(B) Archie's shipment constituted both an acceptance of Barney's offer and a breach of the resulting contract. The U.C.C. applies here because goods are involved. Under the U.C.C., an offer to buy goods can be accepted by the seller by either a promise to ship or by prompt shipment of conforming *or* nonconforming goods. Shipment of nonconforming goods will constitute an acceptance *and a breach* unless the seller notifies the buyer that the goods are offered only as an accommodation. Here, Archie shipped nonconforming goods without a notice of accommodation; thus, the shipment was both an acceptance and a breach. (A) is incorrect because the shipment was not an acceptance of the conforming goods and a counteroffer as to the nonconforming goods. Barney ordered five Regal typewriters. He did not receive what he ordered. Instead, he received three Overwoods. Since he did not receive what he ordered, the whole shipment is nonconforming. As mentioned above, under the U.C.C., shipment of nonconforming goods is an acceptance (and breach), not a counteroffer, unless notice of accommodation is given. Since Archie gave no notice of accommodation, the shipment of the Regals and Overwoods is an acceptance. (C) is incorrect because under the U.C.C. shipment of requested goods, even nonconforming goods, is an acceptance [U.C.C. §2-206], and it could be a counteroffer if notice of accommodation is given. (D) is incorrect because under the U.C.C. the result of the shipment is more than a mere offer to furnish substituted goods. (*See* above.) For the shipment to function as an offer to furnish substituted goods, notice must be given that the goods are intended as an accommodation. Here, no such notice was given, so the shipment was an acceptance.

Answer to Question 31

(B) Archie suffers the loss because the risk of loss was still with him when the Regal typewriters were stolen. Under the U.C.C., when the contract authorizes or requires the seller to ship the goods by carrier but does not explicitly require him to deliver them at a particular location, risk of loss passes to the buyer when the goods are duly delivered to the carrier. [U.C.C. §2-509] However, if the goods are so defective that the buyer has a right to reject them, the risk of loss does not pass until the defects are cured or the buyer accepts the goods. [U.C.C. §2-510(1)] Here, the shipment of nonconforming goods constituted a breach, and Barney had a right to reject them. Thus, the loss falls on Archie with respect to the theft. (A) is incorrect because risk of loss here is determined by the fact that the shipment was a breach of contract; it is not determined by who selected the carrier and made the arrangements. (C) is incorrect because it is irrelevant what Archie's advertisements say, since they are not part of the contract but rather are solicitations for offers. (D) is incorrect because, as stated above, risk of loss does not pass to the buyer if the goods are so defective that the buyer has a right to reject them. (D) would be correct if not for the breach, because this is probably a shipment contract (requiring Archie to put the goods in the hands of a carrier, but not requiring delivery at a particular destination).

Answer to Question 32

(B) Barney's use of the typewriters is an acceptance only if the use was more than reasonably necessary to determine whether they were suitable, since they did not conform to the contract. The U.C.C. gives a buyer the right to reject goods that do not conform to the contract until he has accepted the goods. Acceptance occurs when the buyer: (i) indicates that he will keep the goods, after reasonable inspection, even though they are nonconforming; (ii) fails to reject within a reasonable time after tender or delivery of the goods or fails to seasonably notify the seller of his rejection; or (iii) does an act inconsistent with the seller's ownership. Thus, the buyer is allowed a reasonable time to inspect the goods before accepting or rejecting them. Here, Barney used the typewriters for a week and then found them to be unacceptable substitutes for the Regals. If this trial period was reasonable, he did not accept the goods and therefore may reject them. If the period is more than what reasonably would be required to test them, Barney will be seen as having accepted them and can no longer reject them. (A) is wrong because it does not provide for Barney's right to reasonably inspect. It is not enough that Barney simply knew that the typewriters were nonconforming; he is entitled to inspect them to determine whether he will keep them even though they are not what he ordered. (C) is wrong because even nonconforming goods can be accepted. After reasonable inspection a buyer may decide to keep the goods despite the nonconformity, and this is an acceptance. (D) is wrong because under the U.C.C. if a buyer accepts nonconforming goods, he may still sue for damages. [U.C.C. §2-714] Here, as explained above, it is unclear whether Barney accepted the typewriters (he did so only if the week trial period was unreasonable). But even if there was an acceptance, Barney could still recover damages due to the nonconforming shipment. Thus, he has not waived a claim for damages due to the nondelivery of the two Regals.

Answer to Question 33

(C) Drumm's best defense is impossibility. Contractual duties will be discharged where it has become impossible to perform them. For impossibility to operate, the duty must be objectively impossible (*i.e., no one* would be able to perform). One common situation where impossibility is applied is where either the means for carrying out the contract or the subject matter of the contract is destroyed or damaged. Here, the pig's illness can be seen as damaging the means of performing under the contract. Note that impossibility is also often applied where the person to perform is sick or injured, and the pig's illness here is analogous. In any case, the pig cannot perform, and apparently no other pig could take his place, so performance is impossible and Drumm can avoid the contract. (A) is not a good defense because the Statute of Frauds is not applicable to the contract here because it is a contract to perform, which will by its terms be completed within a year. Such a contract is not covered by the Statute and may be enforced without a writing. (B) is not a good defense because the parol evidence rule merely prohibits introduction of prior or contemporaneous oral statements to contradict a written contract, and here the facts do not indicate whether there was a written contract, and even if there was, Drumm is not trying to contradict it. (D) is incorrect because failure of consideration does not apply to Drumm. Failure of consideration is not a claim that the contract lacked consideration when made, but rather that some element of the promised consideration cannot now be given. Failure of consideration is a ground for breach. Here, Paddy is apparently able to pay (perform under the contract), so failure of consideration does not excuse Drumm. (Paddy, on the other hand, could use this as a claim for not paying Drumm.)

Answer to Question 34

(A) Joshua will not recover because no contract was formed. To create a contract, there must be an effective offer and acceptance. To be effective, an acceptance must be made before the offer is terminated. An offer may be terminated in a number of ways, including directly informing the offeree that the offer is being revoked. Here, Joshua received a revocation of the offer from Warren before he accepted the offer. Thus, his acceptance was not effective if Warren's revocation was effective. An offeror has the power to revoke an offer any time before an acceptance has occurred, even if the offeror has promised to keep the offer open, unless (i) consideration has been paid to keep the offer open (thus forming an option contract), (ii) the offeree reasonably relies on the offer to his detriment, or (iii) the offer is a merchant's firm offer. Here, Joshua did not pay Warren to keep the offer open, there was no reasonable detrimental reliance on the offer before the revocation (Joshua did not drive to City until after receiving the revocation), and Warren could not make a merchant's firm offer with respect to the car since he is not a car merchant. Thus, Warren had the power to revoke, his revocation was effective, and Joshua's acceptance was therefore ineffective. (B) is wrong for two reasons: (i) there was no contract between the parties (*see* above), and (ii) even if there were a contract, Joshua would not recover $15,000. In a contract for the sale of goods, the basic remedy for nondelivery is the difference between the contract price and either the market price or the cost of cover, plus consequential and incidental damages. Here, there is a $3,000 difference between the contract price and the market price (and cover price), and so $3,000 is the appropriate amount. (C) is incorrect because, as indicated above, Joshua's power of acceptance was terminated by Warren's prior revocation of the offer. (D) is incorrect because, as indicated above, no option contract was created since Joshua did not pay to keep the offer open.

Answer to Question 35

(A) The conversation created a contract for 2,000 pounds of thingamabobs now and 3,000 pounds next month. Since the contract here is for the sale of goods, the U.C.C. governs. Under the U.C.C., a contract is formed whenever it appears from the parties' communications that they intended to enter into a contract. Here, it is clear that the parties intended to enter into a contract, but the acceptance contained terms additional to the offer terms. When this occurs, the U.C.C. provides for which terms govern: If the contract is between merchants, the additional terms in the acceptance are included in the contract, unless (i) the additional terms materially alter the contract, (ii) the offer expressly limits acceptance to the terms of the offer, or (iii) the offeror objects within a reasonable time. Here, the facts state that both parties are merchants, and it does not appear that the delivery terms materially alter the contract. There is no indication that the offer limited acceptance to the terms of the offer or that Argon objected to the terms; thus, there is a contract containing the additional terms. (B) would be correct if one of the parties were not a merchant, because under the U.C.C., when an acceptance proposes additional terms, a contract would be formed under the offer terms unless both parties are merchants. (C) would be correct if the U.C.C. did not apply, because under the common law, an acceptance must mirror the offer (the "mirror image" rule); if new terms are added in the acceptance, it is treated as a counteroffer. (D) is incorrect because under the U.C.C., no notice was necessary to form the contract. Notice would be required, however, if Argon did not want to be bound by the additional terms.

Answer to Question 36

(B) If Argon objected to Bismuth's new delivery term, Bismuth must accept the entire 5,000-pound delivery because Bismuth's delivery term did not become part of the contract. Under the U.C.C., which applies here because the contract is for the sale of goods, additional terms in a contract between merchants usually become part of the contract when the acceptance does not mirror the offer; however, there are several exceptions to this general rule, and one applies here: If the offeror notifies the offeree within a reasonable time after receiving the acceptance that he objects to the new terms, the contract is formed according to the terms of the offer. Thus, the contract was formed under Argon's terms and a single delivery of 5,000 pounds is a proper delivery; so Bismuth must accept all 5,000 pounds. (A), (C), and (D) might be correct if Bismuth's additional terms were part of the contract, but since the contract was formed under the offer terms, these three choices constitute breach.

Answer to Question 37

(D) In general, it is a condition of each party's duty to perform that there is no uncured *material* failure by the other party to render any performance due under the contract at an earlier time. The issue posed by this question is whether Larry's failure to complete his promised performance by July 1 is a material breach. The factor most likely to have an impact on the resolution of this case is whether Meagan can show that the provision requiring the premises to be ready on July 1 "at the outside" was a "time of the essence" provision. If she can prove this, then she had the absolute right to cancel the contract when the premises were not ready by that date. Absent this, the 15-day delay would not be considered to be a material breach. (A), (B), and (C) are incorrect because none of them bears on whether Larry's failure to perform on time is a "material breach."

Answer to Question 38

(C) Under U.C.C. section 2-512(2), paying for goods in advance neither impairs the buyer's right to inspect nor his right to assert his remedies. (A) and (B) are wrong, since paying for goods in advance does not constitute an acceptance. (D) is wrong, since there is no requirement that goods be accepted by a written notice.

Answer to Question 39

(C) Alfred is entitled to damages based on the difference between the contract price and the price to buy conforming goods, plus any incidental and consequential damages. (This is the rule of U.C.C. section 2-712(2).) (A) is incorrect, as indicated by the answer to the previous question. (B) is incorrect because there is nothing in the facts that indicates that these saw blades are so unique that Alfred cannot buy them elsewhere and even if that were the case, Alfred would have to hold the nonconforming goods at Meta-Cut's disposition. (D) is an incorrect measure of damages.

Answer to Question 40

(D) Modern courts would hold that a promise to forbear suit on a claim that the promisor *honestly and reasonably* believes to be valid is good consideration to support an agreement, even if the claim ultimately turns out not to be valid. Hence, (A) and (B) are wrong. (C) is wrong because the mutual mistake was only as to the reason for entering the contract, not the terms of the contract. There is no reason why a contract should not be enforced when the parties were mistaken as to the need for the contract if the contract is otherwise valid. Additionally, it is not "unfair" to enforce it because Sherwood always had the right to investigate the truth of the facts before he agreed to pay for the dock.

Answer to Question 41

(C) Sherwood bargained with Kerry to discharge an obligation Sherwood had to Thurman, therefore Thurman was the third-party creditor beneficiary of the agreement to repair the dock, and could sue on this agreement. Hence, (A) and (D) are wrong. (B) is wrong because performance of Sherwood's duty is clearly *intended* to benefit Thurman alone.

Answer to Question 42

(C) A contract in consideration of marriage must be evidenced by a writing to be enforceable. (A) is wrong because a promise to marry is a sufficient detriment to constitute valid consideration. (B) is wrong because there is no public policy against *encouraging* marriage. (D) is wrong because a person's pleasure or displeasure from performing a contractual duty is irrelevant as to whether performance constitutes consideration.

Answer to Question 43

(B) The general rule is that all contracts can be assigned. However, where a contract is assigned in total, such as the contract here, the assignment includes a delegation of duties. A duty that calls for personal service is nondelegable, and a contract calling for service of a skilled negotiator is personal. (A) is wrong because assignments can be oral. (C) is wrong because the damage lies in taking away the negotiator that AeroFlyte has chosen. (D) is wrong because the damage could be measured by the cost of hiring another negotiator of AeroFlyte's choosing.

Answer to Question 44

(D) Ordinarily, when a duty is delegated, the obligee (here AeroFlyte) cannot force the delegate (Cliff) to perform because the delegate has made no promise to the obligee. However, where the delegate's promise is supported by consideration, a contract arises and the obligee is a third-party beneficiary of that contract. As such, the obligee can enforce the contract. Thus, (A) is wrong. (B) is wrong because a court would probably not even inquire into adequacy. (C) is wrong because nothing in the facts indicates that there has been a novation (*i.e.*, release).

Answer to Question 45

(B) Bart's only defense is unilateral mistake. A contract generally cannot be rescinded for a unilateral mistake. One exception to this rule is where the other party knew of the mistake. However, if the facts are as stated in (B), Bart has no defense, and Alex will win. Therefore, (B) is correct, and (D) is wrong. (A) is wrong because it is irrelevant whether the nonmistaken party can make an alternative contract. (C) is incorrect because it is irrelevant that the contract is still executory.

Answer to Question 46

(A) Bart was already under contract to resurface a driveway for $4,000. Therefore, Alex's promise to pay Bart an additional $600 to do the same work was not supported by consideration. (B) is wrong because contracts for services do not come within the Statute of Frauds unless they cannot be performed within one year of their making. (C) is wrong, because reliance would not cure the lack of consideration. (D) is wrong, because there was no dispute between the parties.

Answer to Question 47

(C) Since Professor had stated the nature of the performance he was requesting, and had specified the terms, Professor would be held to have made an offer, creating a power of acceptance in the student who received the highest grade. Thus, (A) and (D) are incorrect. (B) is incorrect because Professor's motive was to induce a detriment (intensive study), and gratification from influencing the mind of another may be sufficient to establish bargained-for consideration. Thus, this was not to be a gift.

Answer to Question 48

(B) Since Professor's offer could be accepted only by completion of performance (that is, obtaining the highest grade in his class), when Stillwell received the highest grade a unilateral contract was formed. (A), (C), and (D) are therefore incorrect.

Answer to Question 49

(D) A unilateral contract is revocable until performance is begun. Here, Stillwell's purchase of every substantive Constitutional Law outline, while it may be preparation to perform rather than the beginning of performance, was in reliance on Professor's promise. Furthermore, his devoting his studying exclusively to Constitutional Law at the expense of other subjects probably did constitute beginning performance, making the offer irrevocable. Even if his studying were deemed only preparation to perform, it was sufficently substantial and foreseeable to make the promise binding on Professor. Thus, the offer is irrevocable as to Stillwell. (A) is wrong, because the offer was valid. (B) is wrong as to Stillwell, although it would be correct as to anyone who had not detrimentally relied on the offer. (C) is wrong because a revocation need only be published in the same manner as the offer; it need not actually reach everyone who knew of the offer.

Answer to Question 50

(A) The contract called for payment on delivery. Under U.C.C. section 2-512(2), such provision means that payment does not constitute "acceptance" and does not affect the right to inspect. Inspection can be made within a reasonable time after delivery. Thus, all other answers are misstatements of law.

Answer to Question 51

(B) Upon receiving nonconforming goods, a buyer may accept all, reject all, or accept any commercial unit and reject the rest. The sale of the two nonconforming printers, even for temporary use only, is acceptance by Accucomp. Thus, (A) is wrong. There is no showing that the 10 constitute a commercial unit, and so (C) is wrong. (D) is a misstatement of the law.

Answer to Question 52

(C) Accucomp's acceptance of the two printers *does not* waive its right to collect damages for the defect in printing speed. Thus, (A) and (B) are wrong. Having accepted the nonconforming printers, Accucomp's damages would be the difference between the value of the printers as received and what they would have been worth if they had been as warranted, plus foreseeable incidental and consequential damages. (D) is wrong, because the agreement with Law Firm was to accommodate Accucomp only and was not foreseeable by Fastprint.

Answer to Question 53

(D) A buyer who has rejected goods as nonconforming is entitled to any prepayment, *or*, if the seller refuses to refund, to resell the goods and apply the proceeds to what is owed him from the seller. The buyer is not entitled to both. Hence, (B) and (A) are wrong. (C) is a misstatement of the law.

Answer to Question 54

(B) Cashing a check offered as payment in full, where there is a bona fide dispute as to the amount owed, will establish an accord and satisfaction. (A) is incorrect because mere economic duress is insufficient to avoid a contract. (C) is incorrect because the accord and satisfaction would release the parties from their obligations on the original contract. (D) is incorrect because Green, if entitled to recover under the contract, would be entitled to recover the contract price not limited by the reasonable value of his services.

Answer to Question 55

(C) Since Futsworth's performance is to pay money, a total refusal to pay would be a total breach; since he has paid some (in fact most) of the amount he was obligated to pay, he can be only in partial breach. Thus, (A) and (B) are incorrect. The condition that Green perform in a workman-like manner is not too vague to be enforceable (in fact, such a condition would be implied if not expressly included); thus, Futsworth would be bound only if Green fulfilled this condition. Thus, (D) is incorrect.

Answer to Question 56

(B) Communications concerning a contract must be interpreted in context and in proper sequence. When Green cashed Futsworth's check shortly after receiving a letter offering the check as part of an agreement to do additional work, he is considered to have accepted the offer. Thus, (B) is correct, and (D) is incorrect. (A) is incorrect since an offer cannot be accepted by silence except in the most unusual circumstances. (C) is incorrect since consideration would be found in Green's promise to perform additional work and Futsworth's forbearance to sue for any breach of contract claim that he believed he had.

Answer to Question 57

(D) I. is wrong because Barny is not promising to act as a guarantor when he promises to pay some of the money to Terry. II. is wrong because Barny's oral promise to pay part of the purchase price to Terry would most likely be interpreted as collateral to the land transaction itself, all the terms of which must be in writing to be enforceable. Therefore, (D) is the correct answer.

Answer to Question 58

(D) (B) is wrong because even if the Barny/Steven agreement was completely integrated, the contract could still be reformed for mutual mistake if the omission of Terry was accidental. However, if it was intentional, the valid modification would invalidate Terry's rights because they had not vested. (A) and (C) are wrong because the negligence of either Barny or Steven should not adversely affect Terry's claim.

Answer to Question 59

(A) Where the parties have actually made a mistake in integrating their agreement into a writing, then the court will grant relief from the drafting error. (B) is wrong because the presence of a misunderstanding between the parties would not necessarily entitle one of them to relief. (C) is immaterial. (D) is wrong because one does not need to show that the writing was only partially integrated to prove a mistake in drafting. In the case of an actual mistake by both parties, parol evidence would be admissible to show the mistake.

Answer to Question 60

(D) The contract here is an installment contract and the U.C.C. provides that a buyer cannot cancel the entire contract because of a defect in one installment if the defect can be cured. (A) is wrong because "perfect tender" is not the rule for installment contracts. (B) is wrong because damages could be measured by lost profits or by standard contract measure. (C) is wrong because a notification of rejection need not be in writing.

Answer to Question 61

(C) An anticipatory repudiation arises where a promisor expressly and unequivocally indicates, prior to the time of performance, that he will not perform. In such a case, the other party has several options, including treating the repudiation as an immediate breach and suing for damages. Thus, (A) is wrong. (B) is wrong because the poor quality of the cookies would not be a defense under the contract since the contract made no provision regarding the quality of Duncan's product. (D) is wrong because prospective inability to perform involves *conduct* rather than expression, indicating an intent not to perform.

Answer to Question 62

(A) The buyer of goods may obtain specific performance where the seller refuses to deliver goods if the goods are unique or circumstances are otherwise proper. Thus, (C) is wrong. (B) is wrong because if the chips are not unique, damages could be measured by the cost of buying substitute goods or by other U.C.C. measures. (D) is a misstatement of the law.

Answer to Question 63

(B) An express warranty will arise from any affirmation of fact or promise or from any model or description if the statement, promise, model, or description is part of the basis of the bargain. Here, Lucy based her decision to buy on the model in the window; thus, an express warranty arose that the television she purchased would conform to the model. This warranty was not negated by the attempted disclaimer since that came too late to be part of the parties' contract. (A) is a misstatement of the law. (C) and (D) both go to the warranty included in the box, which came too late to be part of the bargain.

Answer to Question 64

(B) In every sale of goods, unless expressly disclaimed, there arises a warranty that the goods shall be merchantable, which means that the goods shall be fit for ordinary purposes. A television that explodes after 10 days of use breaches this warranty. Furthermore, the warranty here was not effectively disclaimed since the disclaimer came too late to be included in the parties' contract. Thus, (D) is wrong. (A) is wrong because no express warranty was made as to quality at a time sufficient to become part of the bargain. (C) is wrong because such a warranty arises only where the buyer relies on the seller's expertise to pick suitable goods, and here Lucy picked the television herself.

Answer to Question 65

(C) A buyer of defective goods may recover as damages "loss resulting in the normal course of events from the breach," which includes damages to the goods themselves plus all foreseeable incidental and consequential damages, including injuries to persons and property. Thus, Lucy may recover damages for all of these injuries, and so (C) is correct, and (A), (B), and (D) are wrong.

Answer to Question 66

(C) This fact situation is governed by U.C.C. section 2-207, since it involves an acceptance or written confirmation that varies the original offer. Under common law, no contract would have been formed, because of the difference in the price term ($72 vs. $70 in the original offer). However, under section 2-207, a contract was formed when the seller mailed its letter; thus, (A) is wrong. (B) is wrong because, under U.C.C. section 2-201, a writing in confirmation of the contract (even if it varies the original offer) that is sufficient to bind the sender will also satisfy the Statute of Frauds against the recipient unless a written objection is made within 10 days, which was not done by Debbie here.

Answer to Question 67

(B) An offer to buy goods for shipment is generally construed as inviting acceptance either by a promise to ship or by shipment. Here, the letter constitutes a promise to ship and thus is an acceptance. The rule for acceptances is that they are effective as soon as they are dispatched, which was April 2. Thus, (B) is correct, and (C) is wrong. (A) is wrong because the order was an offer, not an acceptance to the catalogue. (D) is wrong because acceptance occurred before shipment when Oilman sent its *promise to ship*.

Answer to Question 68

(A) Where the parties' contract seems clear, but because of subsequently discovered facts it can be interpreted in more than one way, there is a latent ambiguity. If one party is aware of the latent ambiguity but the other party is not, a contract will be enforced in favor of the unaware party. (B) is wrong because John did not objectively indicate which piano he wanted. (C) is wrong because even though where there is a latent ambiguity it can be said there is a mutual mistake, in this situation the unaware party's intent controls. (D) is a misstatement of the law.

Answer to Question 69

(C) Painter apparently has assigned his claim against Owner to Curtis. In the absence of an enforceable agreement to the contrary, an assignee would take subject to defenses good against his assignor. Therefore, if Painter has not properly performed the work, Owner could use this as a defense in a suit brought by Curtis. (A) is wrong because Curtis is not claiming he is a third-party beneficiary, but rather is an assignee of the rights of Painter. (B) is wrong because the fact that Curtis is incapable of performing Painter's work is immaterial. (D) is wrong because a contract term prohibiting assignment of "the contract" bars only the delegation of the assignor's duty, not the assignment of the assignor's right to payment. [Restatement (Second) of Contracts §322]

Answer to Question 70

(A) Under the Statute of Frauds, to be enforceable a contract for the sale of land must be evidenced by a writing signed by the party sought to be charged. Here, Owner is the party that Purchaser is seeking to charge, so his signature is required on the writing. (B) is wrong because Purchaser's signature is not required to bind Owner. (C) is wrong because the contract need only reasonably describe the subject matter; great specificity, such as a legal description, is not required. (D) is wrong because it does not matter on what substance the writing is made.

Answer to Question 71

(D) The general rule is that an offer can be accepted by performance or a promise to perform unless the offer clearly limits the method of acceptance. Here, the offer would be Ted's order since a magazine ad is usually held to be merely solicitation to accept offers rather than an offer. Thus, FMA accepted and the contract was formed when FMA shipped the balls. (A) is wrong because Ted's order was an offer to buy, and no contract could be formed until that offer was accepted. (B) is wrong because this is a case of crossing offers; even though both offers contain the same terms, they do not form a contract. (C) is wrong because no contract will be formed until there has been an acceptance, and, as stated, Ted's letter was merely an offer.

Answer to Question 72

(C) Generally, a contract by a minor is not enforceable against the minor, and persons under age 18 are considered minors. However, minors are bound for the reasonable value of necessities for which they contract. (A) is wrong because a mere promise to pay by a minor is not sufficient to bind the minor. (B) is irrelevant. (D) is wrong because it does not address the issue of Mary's minority.

Answer to Question 73

(C) U.C.C. section 2-302 allows a court to refuse to enforce a contract that it finds unconscionable. Unconscionability usually arises where bargaining power is unequal and one party dictates unfair terms to the other party. Here, Mary told the manager that she needed food and he forced her to agree to work for, in essence, $1.25 per hour. (A) is not a defense because the contract was for necessaries. (B) is wrong since Mary did in fact receive the groceries. (D) is wrong because nothing in the facts indicates that performance is impossible.

Answer to Question 74

(B) Since Mary is a minor, she will not be bound to her contract unless some exception to the general rule applies. No exception applies here. The car is not a necessity. (A) is wrong since the terms seem fair. (C) is wrong since a minor does not need to return the goods in the same condition as received. (D) is wrong because no basic assumption on the part of both parties has been frustrated.

Answer to Question 75

(B) The general rule is that all contractual rights can be assigned and all Carpenter assigned here was his right to payment. (A) is wrong because it is contrary to the facts; nothing indicates that payment to Woodshop was contemplated in the original contract. (C) is a misstatement of the law. (D) is irrelevant.

Answer to Question 76

(D) Taylor will not recover from Lana because Lana has a defense inherent in the contract. When one of the original parties to a valid contract assigns his rights under the contract to a third party, the assignee may enforce his rights against the obligor directly but is generally subject to any defenses that the obligor had against the assignor. As long as the defense is inherent in the contract, such as failure of a condition, it is always available against an assignee because it was in existence when the contract was made (even if whether the obligor would be able to utilize it was uncertain). Here, Pierre (the assignor) and Lana (the obligor) had a valid contract—her promise to purchase the painting only if she was satisfied with it is not illusory because she has to exercise her right of rejection in good faith. When Pierre assigned his rights under the contract to Taylor (the assignee), Taylor became subject to the condition in the contract that Lana be satisfied with the painting. Lana's dissatisfaction with the painting excuses her duty to pay for it; this is a defense inherent in the contract that precludes Taylor's recovering from Lana. (A) is incorrect because the assignee always takes subject to conditions in the original agreement between the obligor and the obligee. The only defenses that the obligor could not raise against the assignee are setoffs and counterclaims unrelated to the assigned contract that came into existence after the obligor learned that the contract was assigned. (B) is incorrect because Lana has not been enriched by Pierre's services. She has justifiably refused to accept the painting and has received no benefit from the transaction that would constitute unjust enrichment. (C) is incorrect because the only right that Pierre has assigned is the right to receive payment from Lana if she accepted the painting. Lana's duty is the same regardless of to whom she has to pay the money; therefore, Pierre could validly assign his right to Taylor. Note that the analysis would be different if Pierre had also attempted to delegate his duty of painting Lana to Taylor: duties involving personal judgment and skill may not be delegated. When an assignor assigns "the contract," the words are interpreted as including a delegation of the duties unless a contrary intention appears. Here, the contrary intention is indicated by the fact that Pierre did the painting rather than Taylor; hence, there was no attempt by Pierre to delegate a nondelegable duty.

Answer to Question 77

(C) A promise for the sale of goods for $500 or more is not enforceable under the Statute of Frauds unless evidenced by a writing signed by the party to be charged. Uniform Commercial Code section 2-201(1) applies to the agreement between Jasper and Joni because the stickpin is a tangible, movable item of property, which is the definition of goods under the Code. The Statute of Frauds provision applies regardless of the fact that neither Jasper nor Joni is a merchant. Joni's promise, therefore, cannot be enforced by Jasper because it was an oral promise to purchase goods that cost more than $500. (A) is incorrect because the concept of unconscionability allows avoidance of a contract only where the terms are so one-sided as to indicate unfair surprise or a contract of adhesion. Here, neither party had superior bargaining power and Joni knew exactly what she was buying when she made the agreement. (B) is incorrect because the agreement was a bargained-for exchange in which both parties would suffer detriments by giving something up. Regardless of whether the pin was objectively worth much less than $510, its appearance gave it a higher value in this transaction; and a court will not evaluate the adequacy of the consideration. (D) is incorrect because the parties' status as nonmerchants is irrelevant. While the Code relaxes the Statute of Frauds rule in the case of a written confirmation between merchants [U.C.C. §2-201(2)], that exception does not apply here. Thus, even if Joni and Jasper were merchants, the agreement would be unenforceable.

CRIMINAL LAW QUESTIONS

Question 1

Justin and Jennifer were a married couple. Shortly after they awoke one morning, Jennifer berated Justin about spending too much of his paycheck on alcohol and gambling. Justin lost his temper and slapped Jennifer several times. He then went off to work.

After work, he visited a local tavern, had a few drinks, and then took a bus to the local dog-racing track. He owed a local loan shark $800, which was overdue, and hoped to win enough at the track to pay off the debt. After the first four races, however, Justin had lost all the money he took with him, except for enough to pay for the bus ride home. When Justin got off the bus, Ricky, the loan shark's enforcer, was waiting for him. Justin told Ricky, "I just lost all my cash at the dog track, but I've got $400 in the sugar bowl at my house. It's only a block away. I'll give you the money if you'll give me a break." Ricky replied, "O.K., but this better not be a trick or you're a dead man!" Justin walked quickly to his house as Ricky followed in his car. Justin climbed the porch steps as Ricky waited in the car. Justin pounded on the door. Jennifer, still angry about being slapped that morning, refused to let Justin in. Justin became more desperate and told her, "Look, there's someone in that car who is going to shoot me if I don't give him the $400 in the sugar bowl. If you don't want to open the door, slip the money through the mail slot. Or at least call the police before I get killed!" Jennifer saw Ricky in the car, and knowing about Justin's debts, figured that Justin was probably telling the truth. Nevertheless, she told Justin, "You can go to blazes for all I care, Justin." She then pulled down the shades and closed the curtains. Justin began to yell, "Please, please, let me in or I'll be killed!" Jennifer continued to ignore Justin's pleas. Justin started to run down the block, pursued by Ricky. Ricky drove his car onto the sidewalk ran Justin over, killing him.

Can Jennifer be found guilty of criminal homicide?

(A) Yes, because she was Justin's wife and had a duty to aid him.

(B) Yes, because she acted in the heat of passion because Justin had slapped her.

(C) Yes, but only if she intended that Justin be harmed.

(D) No, because she was not the cause in fact of Justin's death.

Question 2

The Calivada State Legislature passed a statute that reads in pertinent part as follows: "Any licensed medical doctor who willfully neglects to assist anyone with a life-threatening injury shall be guilty of a crime, subject to punishment of up to two years' imprisonment in the state penitentiary or a fine of $15,000, or both." This statute had been in effect for one week when Dr. Doofus, a licensed physician, while jogging in City Park, heard the sounds of a man moaning in the bushes next to the jogging path. Dr. Doofus stopped to investigate and found Blodgett bleeding in the bushes. Blodgett was lying flat on his back, but when Dr. Doofus asked him, "Are you O.K.?" Blodgett sat up and told Dr. Doofus, "Yes, I'll be fine." Not having seen any indications of a serious condition, Dr. Doofus returned to her morning jog. Blodgett subsequently bled to death an hour later. The coroner's report made clear that Blodgett could have been saved if he had received medical attention as late as 15 minutes before his eventual death, and that medical help of a "first aid" variety would have been sufficient to keep Blodgett alive until an ambulance arrived. Tattletale, another jogger, had observed the incident involving Dr. Doofus and Blodgett. Tattletale reported this to the police, and Dr. Doofus was arrested and charged under the new statute.

Should Dr. Doofus be convicted?

(A) Yes, because she neglected someone whose life was in danger.

(B) No, because the statute is too vague and raises mere negligence to criminal status.

(C) No, if Dr. Doofus was unaware of the new statute.

(D) No, if Dr. Doofus reasonably believed that Blodgett's condition was not life-threatening.

Question 3

The city of Morality Springs has its own ordinance against prostitution. The Morality Springs law states in pertinent part that "Anyone who engages in sexual intercourse where money is exchanged therefor shall be guilty of the crime of Illicit Sex."

Mona, a prostitute, regularly worked the streets of the Morality Springs business district during the evening hours. Mona left her apartment in the early evening, dressed in her usual autumn "uniform," consisting of very high heels, very brief shorts, and a halter top. When she got to the business district, she realized that an early cold snap had hit the city. Rather than take the time necessary to go home (and thus lose some possible business), Mona went directly to a women's clothing store and told Leslee, a salesclerk, "It's gotten really cold out there; I'm a prostitute, so I've got to be out on the streets until around 3 a.m., and I don't want to freeze to death in the process. Have you got a warm coat that's not too frumpy and not too expensive?" Leslee picked out a coat and asked, "Will this one do? It's on sale for only $95." Mona took the coat and paid $95 to Leslee, who rang up the sale.

In the meantime, Rurik was in a state of depression, because he had just lost his job and was completely broke. Rurik visited his older brother, Sven, and told Sven his sad story, adding, "I'm so depressed; I'd like to go out and get drunk or pick up a woman, but I'm too broke to do either." Sven replied, "Here's $150; party tonight and come talk to me tomorrow about getting a new start." Rurik headed downtown, undecided as to whether he should head for a singles' bar or a bar frequented by

prostitutes. Before Rurik came to the intersection at which he had to make his decision, he was accosted by Mona, who asked him, "Want a date tonight, 'Good lookin'?" Rurik felt that fate had intervened, and he arranged to pay Mona $100 for an hour of sex. The couple went to the Sleazy Arms Hotel, where on reaching the room, he paid Mona $100, and they began to engage in an act of sexual intercourse. During the course of the act, the police, acting with probable cause, entered the room and arrested Rurik and Mona. Mona was duly convicted of "Illicit Sex."

Under the ordinance, what parties other than Rurik could be successfully prosecuted for "Illicit Sex"?

(A) Leslee.

(B) Sven.

(C) Sven and Leslee.

(D) None of the above.

Question 4

Which of the following most clearly violates Defendant's Fifth Amendment self-incrimination rights?

(A) Defendant testifies before a grand jury. The prosecution wishes to introduce the grand jury testimony at Defendant's trial.

(B) Defendant is arrested and taken to a police station, where he is interrogated without first being given *Miranda* warnings. The prosecution wishes to introduce Defendant's statements at his trial.

(C) Defendant is charged with murdering Victim. Prosecutor wishes to get a sample of Defendant's handwriting to compare with a note found on Victim's body.

(D) Police officers enter Defendant's office with a valid search warrant. They seize Defendant's desk calendar, which has information written on it relating to appointments, which may be incriminating.

Questions 5-6 are based on the following fact situation:

Fenster lived with his wife and three children. Fenster had an erratic temper and sometimes beat his wife and/or children. Lately, Fenster had been having problems at work and had taken to stopping at the neighborhood bar before coming home. On many of these nights, Fenster had attacked his family members. Three days after a particularly savage beating of his 17-year-old son, Samson, Fenster came home late from work in a drunken state. Fenster's wife was not home, and Samson was taking care of his younger siblings. Fenster asked where his dinner was, knowing that his wife usually left him a plate of food if he missed the family meal. Samson told Fenster that he had given the food to the dog. Angered by his son's statement, Fenster said, "I'll teach you to have some respect for your father," but feeling a little unsteady, he added, "after a little nap." Fenster then collapsed on the couch. Samson knew that there would be trouble when his father came to, and so he took the children to a next-door neighbor's house, asking the neighbor to keep them for a while. Samson returned home and looked for his father's handgun but could not find it. After thinking for a while, he got a large knife from the kitchen drawer, and waited near the couch for his father to awaken. When Fenster awoke a short time later, he saw his son holding the knife. Worried, he asked, "Samson? Son?" Samson replied, "You won't hurt us anymore," and jabbed the knife into his father's chest. Fenster died instantly. Samson is brought to trial as an adult. The jurisdiction generally follows the common law definitions of crimes.

5. The court is most likely to find that:

    (A) Samson is guilty of murder, because he intended to kill Fenster.

    (B) Samson is guilty of voluntary manslaughter, because Fenster provoked him.

    (C) Samson is guilty of voluntary manslaughter, because his beatings by his

father constituted a continuing provocation.

    (D) Samson was justified in killing Fenster, because he acted in self-defense.

6. Assume for purposes of this question only that Samson's lawyer introduced an insanity defense. If the jurisdiction follows the Model Penal Code test, and psychiatric testimony is introduced indicating that Samson suffered from a mental illness, he will most likely be relieved of criminal responsibility if the defense can prove that:

    (A) Samson's actions were a product of his mental illness.

    (B) Samson could not appreciate the criminality of stabbing Fenster, or he could not conform his conduct to the requirements of the law.

    (C) Samson did not know that killing Fenster was wrong, or he could not understand the nature and quality of his actions.

    (D) Samson was unable to control himself or conform his conduct to the law.

Question 7

Able was in the habit of carrying a lot of cash with him as he walked home from work. His good friend Baker was worried that someday Able might get robbed. To teach Able to be more careful, and intending only to frighten him, Baker purchased a realistic-looking toy gun and a face mask and hid in the bushes one night, waiting for Able to come home from work. As Able passed by, Baker jumped out of the bushes, pointed the toy gun at Able, and took all of his money. Able was badly frightened by the incident. Shortly thereafter, Baker returned the money to Able and explained why he had staged the holdup.

Of what crime could Baker be convicted?

(A) Robbery.

(B)   Armed robbery.

(C)   Assault.

(D)   None of the above.

Question 8

Late one spring evening, Marju heard a knock on the door of her apartment. Looking through the peephole in the door, she recognized her boyfriend, Skipper, and she let him into the apartment. In Skipper's arms was a full-length ranch mink coat. He handed it to Marju, saying, "It's yours." Marju asked, "Where did you get it?" Skipper responded, "From the Easter Bunny." She tried on the coat and admired how good it looked on her, spending almost an hour looking into the mirror. Skipper told her, "I still have some other things to do tonight. I'll see you for dinner on Friday."

The next day, Marju read in the newspaper that Za Sue Gabber, a prominent socialite, had had her home burglarized the night before. Among the missing items, according to the paper, was a full-length ranch mink coat. Marju took the coat from the closet and rifled through the pockets. She found a handkerchief with the monogram "Z.S.G." on it. Marju hugged the fur coat to her bosom and said aloud to herself, "This coat is mine! If that socialite wants another fur coat she can easily afford to buy one, and she's probably insured to the hilt." Marju kept the coat.

Which of the following best describes the crime or crimes, if any, Marju has committed?

(A)   Accessory after the fact to burglary.

(B)   Larceny and accessory after the fact to burglary.

(C)   Receipt of stolen property.

(D)   None of the above.

Questions 9-10 are based on the following fact situation:

An underworld informer advised police officer Andy that Harry Hood was running an illegal bookmaking operation in his apartment, and that the informer had placed bets with Hood at this location.

Andy obtained a search warrant, based upon his affidavit reciting the foregoing facts, and further stating that the underworld informer was a person who had given him accurate information in previous cases, but whose identity could not be revealed because it might jeopardize other criminal investigations being carried on by the police.

Armed with the search warrant, police officers Barb and Charlie came to Hood's apartment and, finding the door unlocked, opened it and saw Hood in the midst of conducting an illegal bookmaking transaction. They seized various wagering slips and bookmaking apparatus (described in the search warrant) and placed Hood under arrest.

Based upon the evidence obtained by Barb and Charlie, Hood is now being prosecuted for illegal bookmaking.

How should the trial court rule on each of the following issues? (Assume that all defenses and objections are properly before the court.)

9.   Was the search warrant valid?

(A)   No, because it was based on hearsay information.

(B)   No, because Andy failed to disclose the identity of the informer, so that the accuracy of his information could not be verified.

(C)   No, because the reason given by Andy for the failure to disclose the informer's identity was not constitutionally sufficient.

(D)   Yes.

10.   Are the wagering slips and bookmaking apparatus seized from Hood admissible in evidence?

(A) Yes, because regardless of whether the search warrant itself was valid, the evidence was in "plain view" upon entry.

(B) No, because Barb and Charlie failed to state their authority and purpose in obtaining admission to Hood's betting parlor.

(C) Yes, because regardless of the unannounced entry, the door was unlocked.

(D) No, because the wagering slips and apparatus were "mere evidence" of a crime (rather than contraband, fruits, or instrumentalities of the crime).

Question 11

A series of jewel robberies occurred in Swankton, an upper-crust resort town where many celebrities go to enjoy the sun, golf, tennis, and the famous Swankton Mineral Hot Springs. The method of operations had all the hallmarks of "Kate the Cat Burglar," a former circus acrobat who had done time for daring jewel robberies. The Swankton police discovered that Kate was currently living in Swankton under an assumed name and working in a local health spa as an aerobics instructor. After finishing a day's work, Kate was approached by George, an undercover Swankton police officer. George told Kate, "I know who you are and what you can do, and I've got a plan that can make us both lots of money. Countess LaBonza is staying in Swankton for the winter, and she's got a stash of jewels you wouldn't believe, but it'll take someone with your particular skills to pull off the heist." Kate assured George that she'd been trying very hard to "go straight" and did not want to get involved. However, after an hour's cajoling by George, Kate agreed to the plan.

Kate thought all of this over, and called George the next day, telling him, "I just don't want to do it." George, however, was very stubborn and persistent, telling Kate, "You've got to do this. There's no security in what you

are doing and Countess LaBonza's jewels will set you up for life. You know those people you work for would fire you in a minute if they knew who you were." Kate again reluctantly agreed to assist George in the jewel theft. However, the more Kate thought about it, the more unnerved she became.

Three hours before the theft was scheduled to take place, Kate called the Swankton police and told them, "I'm Kate the Cat Burglar, and I'm trying to go straight, but this guy George keeps trying to talk me into stealing Countess LaBonza's jewels. The theft is supposed to take place at 11 p.m. tonight at the Swankton Inn. I'm not going to show up, but George is a tall guy with red hair, thick glasses, and a beard. He's supposed to be parked outside the Inn at 11 p.m. in a purple roadster. I suggest that you lock him up." Kate did not appear at the scheduled meeting with George.

Is Kate guilty of conspiracy at common law?

(A) Yes, because she made an agreement with George to commit the theft.

(B) No, because there was no agreement.

(C) No, because the intended crime was never completed.

(D) No, because she effectively withdrew.

Question 12

Verbena called the police to report that she had been raped. She gave the police a detailed description of her attacker, and they picked up Dross, who matched Verbena's description and was discovered lurking in an alley near the site of the attack. The police took Dross to the police station and read him his *Miranda* warnings. Dross asked for a public defender to be appointed. Before the public defender arrived, Verbena came to the police station. She was told there would be a lineup as soon as the suspect's lawyer arrived. On the way to the viewing room, Verbena passed a holding cell where Dross was being held. She pointed at him and said loudly,

"That's the man who attacked me!" Dross did not respond in any way. Verbena later picked Dross out of a lineup.

At the trial the prosecutor wishes to introduce evidence that Dross said nothing when Verbena confronted him. Would such evidence be admissible?

(A) Yes, because it is the truth.

(B) Yes, because Dross had been read his *Miranda* warnings and knew that any behavior could be used against him.

(C) No, because Dross's right against self-incrimination would be violated if he were required to speak.

(D) No, because counsel was not present at the time of the incident.

Question 13

Prof, a high school teacher of many years, shot and killed Learner, a student in his class, on the spur of the moment. Psychiatric examinations have indicated that Prof believed Learner was trying to ridicule him in front of other students in the class and that he had to do something to stop him. The examinations have also indicated that Prof did not know killing was condemned by society when he shot Learner. If Prof pleads not guilty by reason of insanity in a jurisdiction that applies the "*M'Naghten* test," his best argument would be that:

(A) He did not know that the act of shooting Learner was wrong.

(B) He lacked the substantial capacity to appreciate the criminality of his act.

(C) He did not know the nature and quality of his act.

(D) His act was the result of an irresistible impulse.

Question 14

Stagehand decided to play a practical joke on his friend, Actor. Stagehand went to the storage room where stage props were stored and took what he believed to be a stage gun from the locker where such guns were kept. In fact, a week before, Constance had put her real pistol in the stage gun locker and borrowed the stage gun for an amateur theatrical her church group was putting on.

Constance had forgotten to remove the bullets that her husband always kept in the gun. Stagehand went into Actor's dressing room and yelled, "You've stolen the part that I always wanted to play, now die for it!" Actor knew that Stagehand was an incorrigible practical joker, and after an initial frightened reaction, Actor broke out laughing. Stagehand laughed too, shouted, "Bang, you're dead!" and pulled the trigger. A bullet hit Actor in the heart, killing him.

Of which, if any, of the following crimes may Stagehand be convicted?

(A) Second degree murder.

(B) Voluntary manslaughter.

(C) Involuntary manslaughter.

(D) None of the above.

Question 15

While out walking one evening, Phoebe was stopped at gunpoint by a robber who demanded all of her money. Phoebe hesitated in going for her wallet, and so the robber hit her over the head. In doing so, the robber accidentally dropped the gun, panicked, and started to run. Phoebe was stunned for a second by the blow to the head, but she recovered quickly, grabbed the gun from the ground, and shot at the fleeing robber. The bullet missed the robber but hit a bystander, killing him instantly. Phoebe was arrested and charged with murder.

At trial, her attorney contends that Phoebe should be charged with voluntary manslaughter rather than murder. This statement is:

(A)   Correct, because Phoebe had no intent to kill the bystander.

(B)   Correct, because there was adequate provocation for Phoebe's actions.

(C)   Incorrect, because she intended to kill the robber.

(D)   Incorrect, because she was in no danger when she shot at the fleeing robber.

Question 16

The police suspected that Dunston, a convicted cat burglar out of prison on parole, had stolen the "Faith Diamond," a rare gem previously on display at a local museum. Thus, the police went to Dunston's home, where he lived with his mother, Mom, the owner of the house. Dunston was not at home, but the police asked Mom if they might enter and search the house for the diamond. Mom allowed the police to enter, and she also consented to show them the room where Dunston slept and kept his personal belongings. There was a locked trunk in the room, and the police asked Mom to open it for them. Mom told the police that Dunston had the only key to the trunk, which he always kept locked. Mom also told them that, as far as she was concerned, the police could go ahead and open the trunk if they were unable to do so without a key. The police pried the trunk open and found the missing diamond in the trunk.

Did this constitute a valid search?

(A)   No, because the police did not inform Mom that she could refuse permission to allow the search.

(B)   No, because Mom did not have the authority to consent to the search of the trunk.

(C)   Yes, unless Dunston told Mom that he did not want anyone to touch his trunk.

(D)   Yes, because Mom owned the house and thus could consent to the search of the entire premises.

Question 17

Sonya was a busy commodities trader on the Central Commodities Exchange. After a particularly harrowing week when markets were highly volatile, Sonya lost much sleep tracking prices on exchanges in Tokyo, Sydney, and London, as well as the great exchanges in the United States. At the close of business on Friday, Sonya felt she had earned a weekend of complete rest. She drove six hours to her cabin in the Northwoods, built a fire in the fireplace, propped up her feet, and began reading a detective novel. Late that night, a cold polar air mass swept into the American Midwest, bringing with it blizzard conditions and freezing temperatures. At about 11 p.m., snow was swirling outside Sonya's cabin and the temperature had dropped to 18 degrees below zero.

At 10 p.m., Ollie's car broke down on an isolated road three miles from Sonya's cabin. Because the terrible weather had come suddenly, Ollie was not adequately dressed to brave the elements. Nevertheless, he trudged off into the deepening snow. After a while, Ollie became disoriented, and he staggered lost through the woods. Finally, at 11:15 p.m., through the swirling white flakes he spotted the light from Sonya's cabin. At the limits of his endurance, Ollie made his way to Sonya's cabin and began pounding on the door. An irritated Sonya got up and looked out the window and saw the haggard Ollie at the door. Sonya pulled the curtain shut, yelled, "Get lost, I'm here because I don't want to see ANYONE," and went back to reading her book. Ollie trudged off 30 yards from Sonya's cabin and then dropped in his tracks into the deepening snow. Ollie froze to death that night, and Sonya has been charged with his death.

The most serious crime of which Sonya can be charged is:

(A)   Murder.

(B)   Voluntary manslaughter.

(C) Involuntary manslaughter.

(D) No crime.

Question 18

Lisa was late for an appointment across town. Because of this, she was driving recklessly through traffic at a high speed. While driving across town, Lisa ran through a red light. There were a number of people crossing the street at the time and Lisa hit one of them. The person she hit was seriously injured and was rushed to the hospital. Lisa was arrested and charged with attempted murder.

Lisa should be:

(A) Acquitted, if she did not intend to kill the pedestrian.

(B) Acquitted, because she had not gone far enough in her actions to constitute attempt.

(C) Convicted, because a person is presumed to intend the natural and probable consequences of her act.

(D) Convicted, because from her recklessness an intent to inflict serious bodily harm will be presumed.

Question 19

Donald was arrested for burglarizing Raymond's apartment. He was duly given *Miranda* warnings, and Donald invoked his right to remain silent. When Donald was put into the lockup, the police took from him his wallet, watch, and other personal possessions. Cyndy, a police officer, immediately began to make an inventory of Donald's personal effects. During the course of the inventory, Cyndy noticed that Donald's watch bore the inscription, "To Victor Victim with love." Two days earlier, Cyndy had taken the complaint of Victor Victim when Victim reported a burglary. Cyndy concluded that Donald had probably burglarized Victim's dwelling. She reported the inscription on the watch to Dorothy, the detective who had

arrested Donald. Donald was subsequently charged with the Victim burglary.

Did Cyndy violate Donald's constitutional rights?

(A) Yes, because items to be inventoried may be listed, but they may not be closely examined.

(B) Yes, because no search warrant was obtained.

(C) No, if the inventory was a routine procedure of the kind the police normally conduct when an incarceration takes place.

(D) No, but only if the police had probable cause to believe that Donald had burglarized Victim based on a source other than the watch.

Question 20

To crack down on prostitution in its business district, especially that involving minors, City decided to aggressively use the state's statutory rape laws. Thus, several people purchasing the services of underage prostitutes had been arrested and convicted of statutory rape. Sally is 15 years old and worked as a prostitute in City. On the night in question, Sally approached John and offered her services. John readily agreed and the two retired to the backseat of John's car, where they engaged in sexual intercourse. These events were noticed by an undercover police officer, who arrested John and Sally. John admitted to having sex with Sally, and he was charged with statutory rape. Sally was charged with being an accomplice to statutory rape.

At Sally's trial, her best defense is that:

(A) Since John has not yet been convicted, she may not be convicted as an accomplice.

(B) The statute is designed to protect minors and therefore she cannot be convicted as an accomplice.

(C) As a minor, she does not have the capacity to be an accomplice.

(D) Since Sally is a prostitute and consented to the sexual acts, John cannot be convicted of statutory rape; therefore, Sally cannot be an accomplice.

Question 21

Horus and his wife, Winkie, were charged with stealing credit cards and charging expensive items on the misappropriated cards. Alan was appointed by the court to represent Horus and Winkie. At the preliminary hearing, the judge found that Alan would have no conflict representing both defendants in the joint trial. Halfway through the trial, however, a conflict arose between the defenses of Horus and Winkie. At Winkie's request, Alan moved that another attorney be appointed to represent Winkie and that a mistrial be declared. The trial judge moved favorably on Alan's motion.

Linda was appointed to represent Winkie. As soon as Winkie's trial began, Linda moved to have the case against Winkie dismissed on the grounds that jeopardy had attached during Winkie's first trial and that she was being retried in violation of the United States Constitution.

Should the judge grant Linda's motion?

(A) Yes, because jeopardy attached when the jury began to hear evidence in the first trial.

(B) Yes, because the judge incorrectly ruled that there would be no conflict of interest for Alan to represent Winkie.

(C) No, because Winkie requested the mistrial.

(D) No, because it is premature to move for a dismissal based on double jeopardy until the defendant is convicted.

Question 22

Radical despised every aspect of the "consumer society." He particularly loathed luxury goods, such as deluxe sedans, yachts, and any product tagged with a "designer" name. One afternoon, during the busy Christmas shopping season, Radical entered Moochi's, a fashionable designer boutique. He screamed, "Your products stink, and anyone who'd buy them stinks too!" He set off a device that filled the store with malodorous fumes, and then swiftly ran out the store's main entrance. Just as he exited the store, wealthy socialite Phoebe T. Wallingford was walking down the street with the intention of purchasing at Moochi's a number of gifts for family, servants, and friends. As Radical exited the store, he rushed past Mrs. Wallingford, passing about six inches in front of her. She was taken aback, which caused her to trip and strike her head on the pavement. Radical was promptly apprehended and charged with the misdemeanor of breach of the peace for his conduct in the store and charged with assault against Mrs. Wallingford.

Which of the following represents Radical's best defense to the charge of assault?

(A) The underlying offense was a misdemeanor rather than a felony.

(B) Radical made no physical contact with Mrs. Wallingford.

(C) Mrs. Wallingford's injury was not a foreseeable consequence of Radical's criminal activity at Moochi's.

(D) Radical lacked the requisite mens rea.

Question 23

Ralph, an employee of the state government, always received his state paycheck on the last day of the month, or the latest work day of the month if the last day fell on a weekend or holiday. Ralph was not a good money manager, and just barely managed to make it from paycheck to paycheck each month. On August 28, a Friday, Ralph had $45 in his checking account, and needed to purchase a birthday gift for his sister, who was turning 21 the next day. Ralph had decided to purchase a lead crystal decanter for $85 and fill it with an expensive cognac that cost $50. Since he knew he would be receiving his paycheck on Monday, and could immediately deposit it before any checks written on Friday would clear, Ralph bought the decanter and the cognac, writing checks to each store.

Ralph had not been paying attention to the news, and was not aware that the state legislature was having another of its annual budget impasses. Because the state constitution prohibited any deficit spending, if a new state budget was not approved as of August 31 for the next fiscal year beginning September 1, the state controller would not issue any state payments of any kind. Despite midnight legislative sessions, no state budget was passed, and Ralph did not receive his paycheck on Monday, August 31. The two checks written on the previous Friday were returned for insufficient funds, and the merchants filed complaints against Ralph under a statute that prohibited "issuing a check knowing that it is drawn against insufficient funds, with intent to defraud the payee of the check."

What should be the outcome of Ralph's prosecution?

(A) Not guilty, if the jury believes that Ralph intended to deposit his paycheck on Monday so that the two checks would be honored.

(B) Not guilty, if the jury finds that it was reasonable for Ralph to expect that he would receive his paycheck as usual on Monday.

(C) Guilty, because Ralph knew when he wrote both checks that he did not have sufficient funds in his account to honor them.

(D) Guilty, because reliance upon a future source of income does not vitiate Ralph's violation of the statute when he wrote the two checks.

Question 24

Louie, stopped while driving his car by a police officer in a patrol car, believed that the officer had stopped him solely because a large sign painted on the side of his vehicle proclaimed him a member of KAPP—Kill All Police Pigs—a leftist political organization dedicated to the eradication of all police forces. When additional police units arrived at the scene, Louie was convinced it was a setup. Although unarmed and slightly built, he swung his fist at the original officer. Another officer, seeing this, drew his revolver and shot Louie in the stomach. Louie then seized the revolver of the officer he had slugged and shot at the second officer, missing him and killing an onlooker.

Assume that the trier of fact at Louie's trial for murder of the onlooker accepts the testimony of Louie's expert that Louie was rendered unconscious by being shot in the stomach. In the absence of a felony murder or misdemeanor manslaughter rule, the most that Louie can be convicted of is:

(A) Murder, because Louie started the fight in which he eventually shot the bystander.

(B) Murder, because although the killing might have been mitigated as to the second officer, no mitigating circumstances would apply to the innocent bystander.

(C) Manslaughter, because Louie did not intend to kill the onlooker.

(D) Neither murder nor manslaughter, because Louie was unconscious when he shot the onlooker.

Question 25

Winthrop's wife suffered from a particularly virulent form of cancer, and had degenerated to a nearly comatose state where she spent most of her time lying in bed semiconscious. Since the doctors had indicated that any treatment they could prescribe would be of little value, Winthrop decided to administer various poisons to his wife, thinking that they might stimulate her natural body defenses, or kill the cancer cells, resulting in her recovery. He tried doses of cyanide, perchloric acid, strychnine, dioxin, and DBCP. Despite his ministrations, his wife died three days later. An autopsy performed by the county coroner established the cause of death as cancer.

If Winthrop is prosecuted for the murder of his wife, the best reason why he would be acquitted is that:

(A) He was trying to save her life.

(B) He did not have the necessary malice for his actions to constitute murder.

(C) Medical science had given her up for dead.

(D) He did not cause her death.

Question 26

At Terry's prosecution for robbery of a drug-store, the main prosecution witness was Cathy, who testified that Terry had asked her to drive him to the town where the drugstore was located. Cathy testified that Terry did not explain his purpose for going to the town, and that he had stopped at a relative's house along the way to pick up a bundle that could have been the sawed-off shotgun used by the robber.

On cross-examination, Terry's attorney asked a number of pointed questions of Cathy, implying that Terry had asked her to drive to the town so that he could visit relatives there and suggesting that Cathy had obtained a sawed-off shotgun for use by a confederate. Terry did not testify on his own behalf.

In final argument, the prosecutor calls the jury's attention to the two versions of events suggested by Cathy's testimony on direct examination and the defense attorney's questions on cross-examination, and then said, "Remember, you only heard one of the two people testify who know what really happened that day."

If Terry is convicted of robbery, his conviction will probably be:

(A) Overturned, because the prosecutor's comment referred to Terry's failure to testify, a violation of his Fifth Amendment privilege of silence.

(B) Overturned, because under the circumstances the attack on Cathy's credibility was not strong enough to permit the prosecutor to mention Terry's failure to testify in rebuttal.

(C) Upheld, because the prosecutor is entitled to comment upon the state of the evidence.

(D) Upheld, because even if it was error to comment upon Terry's failure to testify, the error was harmless beyond a reasonable doubt.

Questions 27-29 are based on the following fact situation:

Smarts, a plainclothes police officer, frequently ate lunch at Nick's Deli in downtown Manhattan. Smarts had heard rumors that Nick placed bets on sporting events, and Smarts peeked into an envelope next to the register and saw betting slips. In response to Smarts's questioning, Lola the cashier said that Nick had given her the envelope and that someone was to pick it up. Smarts passed the word to his superiors, who in turn informed the F.B.I.

Several weeks later, based on the information provided to them, the F.B.I. agents obtained a search warrant for Nick's home, a condominium in a large building. The agents went to the condo in the early evening, while Nick was at the deli. After announcing their purpose to Nick's wife, they searched the condo and found betting slips and other materials related to illegal gambling. The agents then went to the deli. Nick had left for the night. The agents searched the deli, one agent finding a large black leather bag on a table in the back room. The bag contained more betting slips.

Nick was indicted for conspiracy to violate federal gambling laws, a federal statute prohibiting the use of interstate phone lines to conduct gambling, and for the possession of betting slips. Each offense was punishable by sentences of no more than 20 years.

27. At Nick's trial, Lola is called to testify as to what she knew about Nick's gambling activities. Lola's testimony will most likely be:

   (A) Inadmissible, because it is the fruit of the poisonous tree.

   (B) Inadmissible, because she is an un-indicted co-conspirator.

   (C) Inadmissible, because Lola's privilege against compelled self-incrimination permits her to refuse to even take the stand.

   (D) Admissible.

28. If the evidence obtained from Nick's home is excluded, the best reason for the exclusion will be:

   (A) Nick was not home.

   (B) The search was conducted at night.

   (C) The warrant failed to specify which condominium was to be searched.

   (D) Lola had never been used before as an informant.

29. As to the search and seizure at Nick's deli following the search of his home:

   (A) This is a valid warrantless plain view search and seizure.

   (B) The validity of the search and seizure depends on the validity of the search warrant for Nick's home.

   (C) This is a valid warrantless search and seizure in hot pursuit.

   (D) The search and seizure without a warrant are invalid.

Questions 30-31 are based on the following fact situation:

Vic Tumm owned a summer cottage in an ocean resort area. He stayed there only during the summer months, and left the cottage unoccupied during the balance of the year. His neighbor, Doyle, was aware of this practice.

Recently, Vic underwent hospitalization as a result of a cardiac problem that first manifested itself during the Christmas holidays. Upon his discharge from the hospital in February, he followed the doctor's suggestion to spend a few weeks in seclusion at the cottage.

Unaware that Vic was occupying the cottage, Doyle decided to remove from it a portable color television set that he knew Vic kept in the cottage. To avoid being seen, he entered the cottage late at night through an unlatched window. He found the television set, disconnected it, and headed for the rear of the house to leave. He opened the kitchen door and found Vic seated there in the dark, having a late night snack. Both men were startled. Because the kitchen was dark, neither man recognized the other. Doyle assumed that Vic was a burglar, and was concerned that he might be armed. Doyle therefore decided to flee. While trying to get out of the kitchen as rapidly as possible, Doyle dropped the television set in the middle of the kitchen floor. As the set hit the floor, the picture tube exploded with a loud noise. The noise so frightened Vic that he had an immediate heart attack and died.

30. If Doyle is charged with burglary, which of the following facts, if proved, would enable him to avoid conviction?

   (A) The cottage was not Vic's principal residence and he intended to return home as soon as he had recuperated.

   (B) Doyle genuinely and reasonably believed that the cottage was unoccupied, and would not have entered had he known Vic was there.

   (C) Doyle entered the cottage by raising a window that Vic had carelessly left unlocked.

   (D) Doyle intended only to keep the television set for a few days while his own set was in the shop for repairs.

31. If Doyle is charged with felony murder as the result of Vic's death, his best hope of avoiding conviction would be to establish that:

(A) He had no reason to know that Vic was in the cottage and so he cannot be regarded as having intended to kill Vic.

(B) His only intent was to borrow the television set for a few days.

(C) Larceny is not an inherently dangerous crime, and it was not being committed in an inherently dangerous manner.

(D) Vic's heart attack was an unforeseeable consequence of Doyle's acts.

Question 32

Amos and Bob were drinking at a local bar. Bob was a burly athlete, while Amos was anemic and weak. After several hours and many drinks, an argument ensued between them. Bob insulted Amos's religion and national origin, whereupon Amos spat on Bob, and Bob responded by pouring a glass of beer over Amos's head. Then, Amos punched Bob in the nose, catching him off guard and knocking him to the floor. Bob got to his feet, pulled out a knife, and advanced toward Amos. Amos reached inside his boot top and drew out a small zip gun and shot Bob in the face, killing him instantly. Amos is charged with murder.

If Amos claims the killing was in self-defense, which of the following facts, if proven, would be the most helpful to the prosecution in overcoming Amos's claim?

(A) Amos actually initiated the violence by spitting on Bob; and his punching Bob in the nose is what caused Bob to threaten Amos with the knife.

(B) Amos was standing very close to the door and could have broken off the affray if he had chosen to do so.

(C) The use or possession of a zip gun is a crime under state law, and carrying any concealed weapon is a separate crime.

(D) Before any violence erupted, Amos was aware that Bob was becoming increasingly quarrelsome and belligerent and continued to drink and argue with him notwithstanding.

Question 33

Amos had a dream one night, in which God spoke to him and told him that because God helps those who help themselves, he should go where poor people live and preach to them that they were poor because they were not devout enough, and that hard work and earnest prayer would raise them from their poverty. The next morning, Amos put on his finest clothes and took his well-thumbed Bible to the poorest ghetto area of the city in which he lived. He stood on a street corner and shouted to all who would listen that their poverty and squalor were the product of their own laziness and lack of piety, and entreated them to praise God for sending them the messenger of their salvation. Hector, who had just been fired from his job cleaning toilets in one of the downtown high-rise office buildings because he had been seen conversing with a union organizer, picked up Amos, threw him against the wall of a building, and clubbed him over the head with a tire iron, shouting, "That should shut you up, you Bible-thumping son of a bleep!" Amos, lying on the sidewalk and bleeding profusely from a severe laceration of his skull, looked up and saw Mort, who had observed Amos since he started preaching. "Help me," croaked Amos. "God helps those who help themselves," replied Mort, and walked away. When an ambulance arrived 35 minutes later, Amos had died. An autopsy established that Amos would have survived if he had received prompt medical attention.

Hector is prosecuted for murder and Mort for manslaughter. Who, if anyone, should be convicted?

(A) Both Hector and Mort are guilty as charged.

(B) Hector is guilty but Mort is innocent.

(C) Mort is guilty but Hector is innocent.

(D) Both Hector and Mort are innocent of the charges.

Question 34

Dolan rented a room for two nights at the Quality Inn Motor Hotel. This room, like all others in the motor hotel, was equipped with a large color television set. Dolan decided to steal the set, pawn it, and keep the proceeds. To conceal his identity as the thief, he contrived to make his room look as if it had been burglarized. However, he was traced through the pawnbroker and arrested.

On these facts, Dolan is guilty of:

(A) Embezzlement.

(B) False pretenses.

(C) Larceny.

(D) Larceny by trick.

Question 35

Digby was the owner of a furnished cottage, which she leased to Tanner for one year. While this lease was in effect, Digby found herself in immediate need of cash, and decided to burn down the house to collect the insurance on it. She waited until one evening when Tanner was away at the theater, and then used her own key to gain access to the house. To make it appear that the fire was caused accidentally by Tanner, she soaked one end of the mattress on the bed in the bedroom with gasoline and then left a lighted cigarette burning at the other end of the mattress. She planned that the cigarette would ignite the mattress and that when the fire smoldered to the area soaked in gasoline, the entire bed would burst into flames, and the resulting fire would destroy the house. However, Tanner

returned home earlier than expected and discovered the fire just as the mattress burst into flames. He immediately put it out with a fire extinguisher. A police investigation revealed Digby's activities.

Digby is guilty of:

(A) Burglary as to the house and arson as to the mattress.

(B) Neither burglary nor arson because Digby owned the structure and its contents.

(C) Burglary and attempted arson.

(D) Attempted arson but not burglary because Digby entered with her own key.

Questions 36-37 are based on the following fact situation:

Coe had long been suspected by the police of illegal drug dealing throughout the state. The police, after gathering a sufficient amount of evidence, obtained a search warrant and went to Coe's home. They arrested Coe and conducted a thorough search of his home. The police found and confiscated large amounts of cocaine.

36. Coe brought a motion to suppress the evidence against him. At the suppression hearing, the prosecution informed the court that a warrant had been issued on the basis of information provided by a police informant. Coe then requested the prosecution to produce the informant for questioning. When the prosecution refused to do so, Coe made a further motion to suppress on the basis that he was denied the right of confrontation of his accuser because of the state's refusal to produce the informant. Coe's motion to suppress based on his right of confrontation should be:

(A) Granted, because the denial of the right of cross-examination effectively prevents a fair trial.

(B) Granted, because the rights of a defendant override any right of the police to keep an informant anonymous.

(C) Granted, because the Confrontation Clause is the basis of the American adversary system.

(D) Denied, because the prosecution is not required to either name or produce the informant.

37. Assume for the purpose of this question only that the state has extracted a confession from Coe in violation of the *Miranda* warnings. At the time of trial, Coe took the witness stand and testified on his own behalf, declaring his innocence. The prosecution, on cross-examination, produced the confession extracted from Coe concerning his illegal drug sales. Coe objected to the admission of the confession. Coe's objection should be:

(A) Sustained, because all evidence obtained in violation of *Miranda* rights is inadmissible.

(B) Sustained, because the prosecution did not get permission from the court in advance to use the confession for any purpose.

(C) Overruled, because the prosecution may question Coe on cross-examination concerning any issue that was brought out in his defense.

(D) Overruled, but the confession should be admitted only for the limited purpose of impeachment.

Question 38

Which of the following defendants is guilty as an accomplice, and punishable for the charged offense?

(A) Dirk received a letter stating that if he did not place $50,000 in a locker at the bus

terminal by the following Friday, his house would be burned to the ground. He showed the letter to the police, who recommended that Dirk not pay the money. Ignoring this advice, Dirk withdrew the money from the bank and placed it in the appropriate locker at the bus terminal. Dirk was charged as an accomplice to extortion.

(B) After a violent argument with his wife, Dunston left his home in a rage. He drove to a local bar, where he met Xavier. After a brief conversation Dunston agreed to give Xavier $10,000 if Xavier would rape Dunston's wife that evening. After the rape, Dunston was charged as an accomplice to forcible rape.

(C) Drago, though only 14 years old, worked as a prostitute on weekends. She accepted money from a 45-year-old man to have intercourse with him. The next day, she was arrested and charged as an accomplice to statutory rape.

(D) DuBonnet discovered that his brother had hit and killed a pedestrian while driving that afternoon, and that he had fled from the scene of the crime before the police arrived. To prevent the discovery that his brother had committed the crime, he fixed all the dents in the car caused by the collision and had the vehicle painted a different color. DuBonnet was charged as an accomplice to vehicular manslaughter.

Question 39

As he entered the United States, Dave was instructed by the customs agent to open his suitcase. When he did, the customs agent found heroin wrapped in a package covered with transparent paper. Dave claimed that a stranger had paid him to bring the package into the country and had assured him that there was nothing in it that was illegal.

Dave is charged with knowingly and intentionally importing illegal narcotics. The jury should be instructed that Dave is:

(A) Guilty, no matter what he thought was in the package, because there is strict liability for border crossing offenses.

(B) Guilty, if he knew or believed that the package contained illegal narcotics.

(C) Guilty, if he knew that the package contained contraband, not necessarily illegal narcotics.

(D) Guilty, because he should have known that the package contained some kind of illegal substance.

Question 40

Dave was working at a liquor store one evening when a young girl came in and put a bottle of wine on the counter to purchase. Dave thought that she looked too young to buy wine, so he asked her for her driver's license. The young girl reached into her purse as if to get her license. As Dave reached under the counter to get a bag, she grabbed the bottle of wine, threw $5 on the counter, and ran out.

In this state it is a misdemeanor to sell wine or liquor to a person under the age of 21. If Dave is prosecuted for violation of this statute, his best defense is that:

(A) He asked for a driver's license.

(B) He did not know that the girl was actually a minor.

(C) He did not sell her the wine.

(D) He was only a salaried employee rather than the owner and benefits in no way from the transaction.

Question 41

Vickie was walking out of the store when she saw Arnold suddenly fall to the street with an apparent heart attack. Momentarily diverted because of this, Vickie was unaware that as she was staring at Arnold, his accomplice, Drew, was removing her wallet from her purse. Another passerby shouted to Vickie to watch out. Vickie turned and caught Drew by his sleeve. Drew pushed her hand away and started to run but tripped over a newspaper vending machine that he had not noticed. In the ensuing fall, Drew dropped the wallet, and Vickie was able to grab it before Drew escaped with Arnold.

The most serious crime that Drew could be charged with is:

(A) Attempted larceny.

(B) Larceny.

(C) Larceny by trick.

(D) Robbery.

Question 42

Even though the gambling laws of the state prohibit gambling on professional sports games, Jim bet Rudy $500 on the outcome of Sunday's football game. There was a disputed call near the end of the game which resulted in Jim's team winning. However, later films showed that in fact Rudy's team won. Jim refused to pay the $500 to Rudy. Later that night, Rudy broke into Jim's home and took $500 from his wallet.

Rudy's best defense to a charge of common law burglary is that:

(A) He was so enraged that he had an irresistible impulse to take the money.

(B) Since the original gambling agreement was illegal, he and Jim are in pari delicto and the court should not interfere.

(C) He lacked the specific intent necessary for burglary because he believed that Jim owed him the money.

(D) He had a mistaken belief that the definition of burglary would not apply to a dispute over gambling winnings.

Question 43

Horvath was tried in state court for sale and possession of heroin. The prosecution offered in evidence five rolled-up toy balloons containing heroin, which police officers had found lying on the living room cocktail table of Horvath's apartment. At the hearing on the defense motion to suppress, testimony was presented that established that the police had put the apartment under surveillance, and had watched their police informant go to the door of the apartment, hand four balloons of heroin to Horvath, and leave. The police had then knocked on the door of the apartment, identified themselves as police officers, and demanded entrance. Having heard nothing for 30 seconds, the police had then broken down the door and entered the apartment, discovering the heroin. The police had intended to arrest Horvath for purchase of heroin, a felony. When they had gotten inside the apartment, they discovered that Horvath had left by a back exit. He was later arrested at the nearby newsstand.

The trial court denied the motion to suppress, and the case is on appeal following Horvath's conviction for possession of heroin. The appellate court should:

(A) Affirm the conviction on the ground that the error, if any, in admitting the heroin was harmless error.

(B) Affirm the conviction on the ground that the police complied with "knock-notice" even though no one was there to admit them.

(C) Reverse the conviction on the ground that Horvath's Fourth Amendment rights (as applied to the state by the Fourteenth Amendment) have been violated.

(D) Reverse the conviction on the ground that "knock-notice" is not complied with when the police announce their presence and identity to an empty residence.

Question 44

After being arrested on suspicion of murder, Tim was taken to the police station and informed of his constitutional rights as required by the *Miranda* decision. He immediately requested that a lawyer be provided since he had no money to hire one. The arresting officer said that he would get his lawyer after being booked, and proceeded to book him. During the booking search, Tim said to the arresting officer, "I only killed the bastard because he made a pass at me."

If Tim attempts to prevent introduction of the statement made by him to the officer during booking, he will most likely:

(A) Fail, because booking is not a critical stage of criminal proceedings requiring the assistance of counsel.

(B) Fail, because the statement was not the result of a custodial interrogation.

(C) Succeed, because the statement was the product of illegal police conduct.

(D) Succeed, because the request for an attorney should have been honored immediately.

Questions 45-46 are based on the following fact situation:

Zack and Rhonda recently split up, and Rhonda kicked Zack out of the apartment they were sharing. A major reason for the breakup was that Rhonda felt that Zack was not paying his fair share of the expenses. To ensure that he made up for past arrearages she claimed were owing, Rhonda would not let Zack back in to remove his clothing, books, and stereo equipment.

Zack found a temporary place to stay with his sister's boyfriend, Sonny, president of the local Deathriders Motorcycle Club. Sonny finances his lifestyle by dealing in various narcotics and wholesaling stolen property, a fact known to Zack.

When Sonny learned of Zack's predicament, he suggested that the two of them go to Rhonda's apartment, kick the door in, and take Zack's possessions. Zack declined, but, remembering that Rhonda was going to be out of town the upcoming weekend, suggested to Sonny that he help Zack get into the apartment when Rhonda is out and obtain Zack's property. Sonny agreed. They drove Zack's pickup to Rhonda's apartment, and Sonny entered through an unlocked window. Sonny let Zack inside, and the two men collected Zack's clothing, books, and stereo equipment and loaded it into the pickup. While Zack was getting ready to drive away, Sonny returned to the apartment and carried Rhonda's video recorder and color television to the pickup. At this point, police officers alerted by neighbors arrived and arrested Zack and Sonny.

45. Zack is charged with burglary. His best defense is that:

  (A) There was no "entry," since as an occupant of the apartment, he consented to the entry.

  (B) There was no breaking, since the window was unlocked.

  (C) There was no intent to commit a felony.

  (D) He only took his own property.

46. Zack and Sonny are charged with conspiracy to commit burglary. Their best defense is that:

  (A) There was no overt act.

  (B) There was no agreement.

  (C) There was no intent to commit burglary.

  (D) Zack did not actually commit a burglary.

Question 47

Boss operated his own consulting firm from an office in his home. Dexter was one of several people Boss employed at his office. Dexter asked if he could stay late one night and type on Boss's computer a short story he had written. Boss replied, "Sure. I hate that machine. Consider it yours. I am getting a new one tomorrow." Dexter mistakenly believed that Boss was giving Dexter the computer. Dexter waited to take it home until he could borrow a car because it was too unwieldy to carry on the bus.

The next week, Boss's business took a dramatic turn for the worse, and Boss was forced to lay off all of his employees, effective immediately.

Since he no longer had a job, Dexter spent all of his time finishing his novel. He finished the novel late one night and thought he would get started typing it up right away. He borrowed his roommate's car and went to Boss's house to pick up the computer. Not wishing to wake anyone up at the late hour, Dexter went to the door leading directly to the office. It was unlocked, so he let himself in and took the computer.

The next day, Boss reported the computer as stolen, and the police arrested Dexter. Dexter can be convicted of:

(A) Burglary.

(B) Attempted burglary.

(C) Larceny.

(D) None of the above.

Question 48

State A's penal statutes contain the following: "Any person who commits a battery upon a state official knowing that the victim is a state official shall be punished by imprisonment in the county jail for not more than one year or fined not more than $5,000, or both." While picking up his unemployment check at the state office building, Rod got into an argument with a man wearing a brown suit and angrily shoved the man against the wall, causing him no injuries. The man Rod shoved was the director of the state department of unemployment, and Rod is prosecuted under the penal statute quoted.

Rod admits that he shoved the victim intentionally, but denies that he knew the man was a state official. The jury should return a verdict of:

(A) Not guilty, if they find that the state should have warned Rod that the victim was an official, even though they do not believe Rod's testimony.

(B) Guilty, even if they believe Rod, because this is a public welfare offense.

(C) Not guilty, if they believe Rod's testimony.

(D) Guilty, regardless of whether they believe Rod or not, because he admitted that he intentionally shoved the victim.

Question 49

Edgar owned and operated a used car dealership in the City of Oakridge. For several months, Philmont, an agent for the Internal Revenue Service, has been investigating Edgar and his car dealership because of suspected fraudulent tax returns Edgar had been filing. In addition, Oscar, a detective for State, which had been investigating a stolen car ring, uncovered evidence indicating that Edgar might be a part of the ring. Oscar went to Edgar's car lot and found evidence indicating that the ring was operating through Edgar's used car sales lot. Oscar asked Edgar to go with him to the police station to make a statement regarding the evidence Oscar had just uncovered, and Edgar agreed. While in the police car on the way to the station, Edgar voluntarily informed Oscar about the fraudulently filed tax returns, because he believed that by revealing these facts he might receive a lighter sentence for his involvement in the stolen car ring.

Edgar was tried for filing false tax returns. At the trial, Edgar's attorney moved to exclude the statements made to Oscar in the police car. The prosecuting attorney argued strongly against granting the motion. The best argument for admitting the statement is that:

(A) Oscar was not an agent of the Internal Revenue Service.

(B) Edgar had not been formally charged at the time that the statement was made.

(C) The statement was volunteered by Edgar.

(D) The statement was made prior to the arrest of Edgar.

Questions 50-52 are based on the following fact situation:

Xavier, Yancy, and Zack agreed to break into Alice's house and steal two paintings hanging in Alice's den. They were arrested shortly after they pried open Alice's back door and charged with conspiracy to commit larceny. Xavier testified that he suspected Yancy and Zack of being thieves and agreed to go with them in order to catch them, and that he had made an anonymous telephone call to the police alerting them to the crime, enabling the police to arrest Xavier, Yancy, and Zack "in the act." Yancy testified that he thought the paintings belonged to Zack, that they had been stolen from Zack by Alice, and that he was helping Zack to retrieve his own property. Zack did not testify. The jurisdiction follows common law conspiracy rules.

50. If the jury believes Xavier, it should find him:

(A) Not guilty, because he did not intend to steal.

(B) Not guilty, because he prevented the theft from occurring.

(C) Guilty, because there was an agreement, and the prying open of the back door was sufficient for the overt act.

(D) Guilty, because he is not a police officer, and thus cannot claim any privilege of apprehending criminals.

51. If the jury believes Yancy, it should find him:

(A) Not guilty, because he did not intend to steal.

(B) Not guilty, because he did not have a corrupt motive.

(C) Guilty, because there was an agreement, and the prying open of the back door was sufficient for the overt act.

(D) Guilty, because good motives are not a defense to criminal liability.

52. If the jury believes both Xavier and Yancy, it should find Zack:

(A) Not guilty, because a conviction would penalize him for exercising his right not to be a witness.

(B) Not guilty, because Xavier and Yancy did not intend to steal.

(C) Guilty, because there was an agreement, and the prying open of the back door was sufficient for the overt act.

(D) Guilty, because he intended to steal.

Question 53

As Velma was walking home on a dark cloudy night, a man came upon her from behind and stole her purse. Dirk was arrested nearby shortly thereafter. After Dirk had been booked, the police took his photograph. They then showed Dirk's photograph, along with the photographs of four people who had the same general features as Dirk, to Velma. Velma identified Dirk as the culprit. At trial, after Velma had identified Dirk as the person who stole her purse, Dirk's attorney objects to the prosecution's introduction into evidence of the photograph identification.

The objection will most likely be:

(A) Denied.

(B) Sustained, because Dirk's right to counsel was violated at the showing of the photograph to Velma.

(C) Sustained, because Velma did not have a good opportunity to observe the culprit.

(D) Sustained, because a photograph identification must be considered a critical stage of the proceeding.

Question 54

While on routine patrol late one night, Officer Heart noticed that a car, driven by Daniels, was weaving recklessly across several lanes of traffic. Officer Heart stopped Daniels, believing that he was driving while intoxicated. By state law, Officer Heart was empowered to arrest Daniels and take him to the nearest police station for booking. Officer Heart arrested Daniels and then searched Daniels's vehicle looking for evidence of alcohol consumption. In the glove compartment, Officer Heart discovered a vial containing a small amount of cocaine. Daniels was charged with possession of cocaine. At trial, Daniels's attorney moves to prevent introduction of the cocaine into evidence on the grounds that the search violated his client's federal constitutional rights.

This motion will most likely be:

(A) Denied, because Officer Heart was acting under a fear for his own personal safety.

(B) Denied, because the search was incident to a valid custodial arrest.

(C) Granted, because Officer Heart needed a warrant to search the glove compartment.

(D) Granted, because there was no reasonable or proper basis on which to justify conducting the search.

Question 55

Art had been hospitalized for several weeks suffering from a very rare blood disorder, which had proven to be fatal in most cases. It was determined that Art's life could be saved only by undergoing a new treatment developed by Doctor. However, Doctor was the only person capable of administering the treatment. It was, therefore, arranged that Art would fly to the city where Doctor would perform the treatment. The day before Art was to leave, Sarah, who was Art's sole heir and stood to inherit from him, poisoned him. The poison produced a reaction that required postponement of the journey. The plane on which Art was to have flown crashed and all aboard were killed. The next day Art died from the combined effects of the poison and the blood disorder. Sarah was arrested and charged with criminal homicide.

Sarah should be found:

(A) Not guilty, because the poison was not the sole cause of death.

(B) Not guilty, because Art would have died anyway if Sarah had not poisoned him.

(C) Not guilty, because her actions resulted in postponing Art's death by one day.

(D) Guilty.

Question 56

The police noticed that there had been an increase in reported drug activity in a certain neighborhood in recent months. One night police officers entered the neighborhood accompanied by a dog trained to sniff out cocaine. The first house that police approached was occupied by Dopson. The police entered Dopson's backyard and brought the dog to an area immediately outside Dopson's back door. The dog acted as if he smelled cocaine. Police officers knocked on the back door. Dopson answered the door and let them in. Dopson was immediately placed under arrest. After a brief search, police officers found and confiscated a small quantity of cocaine from the bedroom closet. Dopson is charged with possession of cocaine. At trial, Dopson moves to prevent introduction of the cocaine into evidence.

This motion will most probably be:

(A) Granted, because, under the circumstances, the police activity violated Dopson's reasonable expectation of privacy.

(B) Granted, because this kind of detection by a trained dog has not been scientifically verified and cannot be the basis for probable cause.

(C) Denied, because Dopson allowed the police officers to enter his home.

(D) Denied, because the search was incident to a valid arrest.

Question 57

Ken, John, and Sally were good friends. Ken knew that John and Sally cared deeply for each other and encouraged John to ask Sally to marry him. Unbeknownst to Ken, John was already married to a woman who lived in another state. Finally, after continued encouragement by Ken, John went through a marriage ceremony with Sally, and Ken was John's best man at the ceremony.

If Ken is charged with being an accessory to bigamy, he should be found:

(A) Guilty, because he encouraged John, and his mistake as to the existence of a prior marriage is no defense to a charge of bigamy.

(B) Guilty, because he was present when the crime occurred and is thus a principal in the second degree.

(C) Not guilty, because he did not have the mental state required for aiding and abetting.

(D) Not guilty, because his encouragement and assistance was not the legal cause of the crime.

Question 58

Acting on an anonymous telephone call, police went to Della's apartment, pounded on the door, and demanded to search it for possible stolen property. Della refused. The police then kicked open the door and placed Della under arrest. As they were escorting Della out of her home, she offered to give the officers some inside information in exchange for her release. Before she could say anything else, Della was given *Miranda* warnings by the police. Thereafter, she told the police that she knew of a large supply of stolen property stored at a nearby warehouse leased by a friend of hers, and said that she and her friend had been selling the stolen property out of the warehouse for years. The police raided the warehouse and recovered the stolen property. Della was charged with conspiracy to sell stolen property and for possession of stolen property. At her trial, Della moved to suppress the statements.

Which of the following is Della's best argument in support of the motion to suppress?

(A) Della was intimidated by the forced entry into her home and since her statements were involuntary and coerced, their use against her would violate due process of law.

(B) Della is entitled to know the identity of her accuser, and the state cannot supply this information.

(C) The statements were fruits of an unlawful arrest, and though the *Miranda* warnings may have been sufficient to protect her right against self-incrimination, they were not sufficient to purge the taint of the illegal arrest.

(D) The police should have given Della *Miranda* warnings prior to entry into her home and the warnings were ineffectual once Della offered to give the police information.

Question 59

Gordon was weaving all over the road and driving very erratically when stopped by state troopers and arrested for drunk driving. He was advised of his constitutional rights and elected to remain silent. At trial for his drunk driving charge, Gordon testified in his own defense, stating that he had just left his doctor's office and had been administered medication without being told that it would seriously and immediately hamper his coordination. On cross-examination, the prosecutor asks, "Didn't you just make up this medication story after the fact to evade legitimate liability for driving while intoxicated?" When Gordon replied that he had not, the prosecutor asked, "Then why didn't you tell the arresting officer about the medication?" Defense counsel objects.

The trial court should rule that the question is:

(A) Improper, because to require the defense to inform the prosecution of defendant's testimony prior to trial would be unconstitutional pretrial discovery.

(B) Improper, because use of defendant's post-arrest silence violates his right to due process of law.

(C) Proper, since defendant's silence was not used as direct evidence but only for impeachment on cross-examination.

(D) Proper, because defendant's post-arrest silence is a prior inconsistent statement which is admissible to show recent fabrication.

Questions 60-61 are based on the following fact situation:

Randall was trimming his sidewalk-bordering high hedge, wearing garden gloves, when a wasp took offense to his presence and began various dive-bombing attacks. Randall, allergic to wasp toxin, frantically attempted to bat or smash the wasp with his gloved hands. During one of his grabs, Randall struck Bill, a jogger running past on his morning exercise jaunt, in the face. Bill, reacting to the unexpected blow to his head, pulled out a knife and stabbed Randall, seriously injuring him.

60. If Bill is prosecuted for aggravated battery, he will probably be found:

   (A) Not guilty, because he believed Randall was attacking him.

   (B) Not guilty, because his acts constituted an assault, not a battery.

   (C) Guilty, because he used a deadly weapon.

   (D) Guilty, because he actually injured Randall.

61. If Randall is prosecuted for criminal battery, he will probably be found:

   (A) Not guilty, because his act did not cause serious bodily injury.

   (B) Not guilty, because he did not have the mental state required for criminal battery.

   (C) Guilty, because he failed to exercise due care in flailing his arms about near a public sidewalk.

   (D) Guilty, because he caused an offensive touching.

Question 62

In which of the following circumstances is the defendant most likely to be convicted of common law murder?

(A) While at a bar, a patron throws a drink in the defendant's face, and the defendant, in a rage, stabs and kills the patron.

(B) Defendant is hunting deer and shoots and kills another hunter.

(C) Defendant drives his car up onto and along a crowded city sidewalk, killing a pedestrian.

(D) During an argument, Defendant shoves his opponent, who stumbles backward several feet and falls through a large retail display window. Glass shards penetrate the opponent's heart, killing him.

Question 63

Officer Taylor saw Elmer grab a coat off the rack of a store and run. As Taylor gave chase, Elmer ducked into an alley. When Taylor came to the alley, she saw movement behind some boxes. She yelled for Elmer to come out or she would shoot. When Elmer did not, Taylor shot at the boxes. Polly, a bag lady, had been asleep behind them, and she was killed. Taylor is charged with homicide.

A jury should find Taylor:

(A) Not guilty of homicide, because she was attempting to catch Elmer, who was fleeing from a crime, and Taylor had the right to use deadly force.

(B) Not guilty of homicide, because she saw Elmer commit a misdemeanor, and therefore she had the right to use deadly force if necessary to arrest him.

(C) Guilty of homicide, unless she had reason to believe that Elmer was a felon.

(D) Guilty of homicide, because she was not entitled to use deadly force.

Questions 64-65 are based on the following fact situation:

Bob and his employer, Don, had a dispute over how much money Bob was due for work done at the garage. Don alleged that he had paid Bob $300 that month for work on cars that Bob did not do, and Bob contended that he had done the work. At the conclusion, Bob said he was going to quit, and Don said it was fine with him but he was going to keep Bob's tools until Bob repaid him the money he had been overpaid.

Bob, still very angry, went down the street to a bar where he saw a friend of his, Greg, a small-time thief. They had a few drinks together, and Bob told Greg what happened. Greg suggested to Bob that he could go to the garage and get an estimate of how much it would cost to replace the transmission in his car. Then, while Don was writing the estimate, Greg would take Bob's tool box and put it in the trunk of his car. Bob thought this was a great idea and described the location of his tool box and gave its description to Greg.

Greg went to the garage as planned, and when Don went into the office to write up an estimate, Greg grabbed what he believed to be Bob's tool kit and put it in his car. But Don had locked Bob's tool kit in the storage room, and another mechanic who worked in the garage had taken over Bob's station, so the kit taken by Greg was the other mechanic's.

After Greg left, Don realized that Greg must have stolen the tool kit. He took the license number he had on the work sheet and gave it to the police. Several minutes later, the police spotted Greg's car outside the bar, and, as Bob and Greg came out to go to the car, arrested them both.

64. If Greg and Bob are charged with conspiracy to steal, of the following, their best defense is:

    (A) There was no agreement.

    (B) Bob disputed Don's claim.

    (C) They would have returned the tool box they took by accident.

    (D) They had not intended to commit a crime.

65. Of the following, which is the best argument for Greg as a defense to a charge of larceny?

    (A) He had the consent of the owner to take the tool box.

    (B) He thought the tool box belonged to Bob.

    (C) He was not intending to keep the tool box, but to give it to Bob.

    (D) He was apprehended by the police before Bob could inspect the tool box.

Question 66

Alan was arrested by a police officer when he was found carrying an ice pick concealed in his pants. Alan stated that he carried the ice pick only for protection. Alan was convicted of violating a state statute prohibiting the carrying of a concealed "knife or dagger." Alan appeals his conviction on the basis that an ice pick does not fall within the purview of the statute under which he was convicted.

The appellate court will hold that:

(A) Alan's conviction should be upheld if the appellate court finds that the statute sought to outlaw the classic instruments of violence and their homemade equivalents, such as an ice pick.

(B) Alan's conviction should be upheld, because an ice pick is a weapon, by Alan's own admission.

(C) Alan's conviction should be overturned, because he was carrying the ice pick for protection only.

(D) Alan's conviction should be overturned, because he harbored no malicious intent.

Question 67

While in a department store, Defendant picked up a $400 imported cashmere sweater and slipped it under his shirt. Defendant then started for the door. Customer, who also was shopping in the store, saw Defendant take the sweater. Customer grabbed a baseball bat from the sporting goods aisle and chased Defendant into the parking lot. Customer began swinging the bat at Defendant's head, hoping to knock him out and thus prevent the theft. Defendant pulled a knife from his pocket and stabbed Customer, killing him. Defendant was arrested and charged with murder.

At trial, Defendant will most likely be found:

(A) Guilty, because the evidence shows that Defendant provoked the assault on himself by his criminal misconduct.

(B) Guilty, because the evidence shows that Defendant intended to kill or cause serious bodily harm.

(C) Not guilty, because the jury could find that Defendant acted recklessly and not with the intent to cause death or serious bodily harm.

(D) Not guilty, because Defendant was acting in self-defense.

Question 68

Fred did not like Joe, his daughter Lisa's boyfriend. In spite of the fact that Fred had told Lisa never to see Joe, Lisa continued to do so. One night when Lisa's parents went to a movie, Joe came over to the house. Lisa and he were in the den with the lights out when Fred and his wife came home unexpectedly. When Fred found Lisa and Joe together, he grabbed Joe and told him to get out of the house. Joe tried to explain to Fred why he was there, but Fred would not listen, and he threatened to beat Joe up if he did not leave immediately. When Joe attempted again to protest, Fred grabbed a poker from the den fireplace and raised it above his head in a threatening manner. Joe threw a heavy ashtray at Fred, hitting him in the side of the head and killing him. Joe was charged with murder.

The jury should find Joe:

(A) Guilty, because he had refused to immediately leave the house.

(B) Guilty, because his presence in Fred's home with Lisa provoked Fred to attack him.

(C) Not guilty, because a poker is a dangerous weapon.

(D) Not guilty, because it was Lisa's home also, and she invited Joe into it.

Question 69

As Bob walked out of a store, he saw his friend Rick under the hood of a car trying to get it started. When Bob asked what was wrong, Rick told him that he had lost the keys to his car and was trying to "hot wire" it. Bob told Rick to get behind the steering wheel, and when Rick was ready, Bob started the car by "hot wiring" it. In fact, Rick did not own the car, and Bob is charged with being an accessory to larceny.

Bob should be found:

(A) Guilty, because his actions enabled Rick to steal the car.

(B) Guilty, because he had no reason to believe that the car was really Rick's.

(C) Not guilty, because he did not intend to aid Rick in stealing a car.

(D) Not guilty, because Rick would have probably stolen the car without his help.

Question 70

Joe, who had been Bubba's roommate and lover for several years, decided to leave Bubba and move in with Roger. On the day that Joe was to move into Roger's condominium, Bubba shot Joe in the neck, intending to kill him. Joe was not severely wounded, but he was hospitalized for several days. During his stay at the hospital, it was discovered that Joe had developed a form of cancer that was invariably fatal. Three weeks after being shot, Joe died of pneumonia caused by an infection resulting from the bullet wound in his neck. Roger had been killed when his condo burned down as he slept. The fire occurred two days after Bubba shot Joe.

Is Bubba guilty of a criminal homicide?

(A) No, because his actions merely constituted attempt.

(B) No, because Joe was already suffering from an incurable disease.

(C) No, because Bubba actually prolonged Joe's life because he prevented his probable death in the fire that destroyed Roger's condo.

(D) Yes, because Bubba's act was the proximate cause of Joe's death.

Question 71

Joseph, angered because a rival gang member had twice beaten him up after school, obtained a heavy length of lead pipe and waited in a deserted alleyway which he knew the rival took as a route home every day after school. When his enemy came walking down the alley, Joseph leapt out behind him and smashed the pipe into the victim's head, knocking him to the ground. Joseph then rolled the victim over and pounded his face with 15 to 20 heavy blows with the lead pipe, killing him. The jurisdiction defines first degree murder as murder committed with premeditation and deliberation. All other murders are defined as second degree murders.

If Joseph is convicted of first degree murder (as opposed to second degree murder), it will be because:

(A) The nature of the acts causing death distinguishes Joseph's action as first degree murder.

(B) The degree of causative relationship between Joseph's acts and the death of the victim renders it murder of the first degree.

(C) The relationship between Joseph and the victim requires that a finding of first degree murder be made.

(D) Joseph's mental state up to and including the moment of the attack determines that the act is first degree murder.

Question 72

Doppler wanted to steal some papers from Compton's office safe, and so he arranged to have a meeting with Compton at the office. When Compton left the room, Doppler put a knock-out drug that he had prepared in Compton's coffee. Doppler stole the papers. Unfortunately, Doppler miscalculated the dosage, and Compton died.

What is the most serious offense of which Doppler can be convicted?

(A) Murder.

(B) Voluntary manslaughter.

(C) Involuntary manslaughter.

(D) None of the above.

Question 73

Defendant was at a bar with a couple of friends when he spotted Tony. For several weeks, Defendant had been calling Tony a "sissy" and other such names because Tony had reported that Defendant's best friend was stealing goods from the loading dock where they all worked. As a result, Defendant's friend was arrested. This particular night, Tony came into the bar with his girlfriend, and Defendant went over to their table and asked her to dance. When she politely refused, Defendant said, "Come on, honey, you don't want to spend an evening with a sissy like that. Why don't you come home with a real man?" Tony, infuriated after taking Defendant's abuse for so long, jumped up and attacked Defendant with a broken beer bottle. Defendant could have easily run away, but instead ducked under Tony's swing with the bottle, and with his shoulder slammed Tony backwards. Tony went crashing through the front window, and was severely cut on a shard of glass. He died before he could be taken to the hospital.

At common law, Defendant would most likely be guilty of:

(A) Murder.

(B) Voluntary manslaughter.

(C) Involuntary manslaughter.

(D) None of the above.

Question 74

Deanna purchased a wardrobe closet at an antique auction. The sale of all merchandise was specifically designated "as is." Three days later, while cleaning the inside of the closet, Deanna discovered a small quantity of a white powder inside a box. She showed the box to her boyfriend, a paralegal. He identified the powder as driscamine, a controlled substance. He told her that it was illegal to buy driscamine, but that since she did not know that it was in the closet when she purchased it, it was okay to keep it, which she did. A state statute prohibits "willful and unlawful possession of a controlled substance."

If Deanna is charged with violating this statute, she should be found:

(A) Guilty, because she knowingly possessed the driscamine.

(B) Guilty, because she acquired the driscamine when she intentionally purchased the wardrobe closet and, in doing so, committed the requisite unlawful act.

(C) Not guilty, because she thought she was acting lawfully.

(D) Not guilty, because she did not willfully acquire the driscamine and, hence, committed no unlawful act.

Questions 75-76 are based on the following fact situation:

Two days before the junior prom, Brenda was horrified to discover that her cat had clawed the back of her taffeta prom dress. She hurried to Zelda's Tailoring Shop where she explained her predicament to Zelda. Zelda assured her she could make the gown as good as new for $175. Brenda knew she could not pay Zelda $175 but asked her to do the work anyway. Zelda worked furiously and phoned Brenda at 4:30 the following afternoon to let her know the dress was ready. Brenda told Zelda she would be by the next morning to pick the dress up and pay for the work. After talking to Zelda, Brenda telephoned her best friend Cheryl and promised Cheryl that if she would stop by Zelda's shop after 5 p.m. and pick up Brenda's gown, Cheryl could dance with Brenda's boyfriend Newt at the prom. (Brenda knew that Zelda would be gone by that time and that Milt, the always intoxicated janitor, would hand the gown over with no questions asked.) Brenda forged a claim ticket and gave it to Cheryl to show to Milt. Cheryl did as Brenda asked and picked up the gown from Milt and gave it to Brenda.

75. Zelda makes a criminal complaint against Brenda for larceny. Brenda will most likely be found:

(A) Not guilty, because it was Brenda's gown to begin with.

(B) Not guilty, because Cheryl took the gown.

(C) Guilty, because Cheryl took the gown from Milt without Zelda's knowledge or permission.

(D) Guilty, because Brenda promised to pay Zelda for her work when she came to get her gown.

76. Cheryl will be found not guilty of taking the gown from Zelda's shop because:

(A) Brenda was the principal in the conspiracy to obtain the gown without payment.

(B) She was acting under Brenda's direction.

(C) Milt, whom Cheryl knew was intoxicated, handed over the gown without asking questions.

(D) She sincerely believed that Zelda was expecting the gown to be picked up without money changing hands.

Question 77

Chuck recently moved to Hangtown and discovered an old friend, Roy, was living there. Chuck asked Roy to introduce him to the town's banker so that Chuck could apply for a loan to set up a hardware business. Roy, also a friend of the banker, arranged a meeting and later gave Chuck a glowing recommendation based upon their long and deep friendship. When the banker approved a $25,000 loan, Roy was present at the signing of the loan papers and co-signed on Chuck's behalf. Unknown to Roy, Chuck intentionally misrepresented his intentions as to the proceeds of the loan and his financial status, forging some documents used to verify his solvency. Chuck has been tried and convicted of obtaining money by false pretenses (a felony) and sentenced to state prison.

If Roy is charged as an accessory to obtaining money by false pretenses, he should be found:

(A) Guilty, because he was present when the crime was committed and was thus a principal in the second degree.

(B) Guilty, because he encouraged and aided Chuck, and his ignorance of Chuck's insolvency is no defense to the charged crime.

(C) Not guilty, because he lacked the requisite mental state to be an aider and abettor.

(D) Not guilty, because his encouragement and aid was not the legal cause of the offense.

CRIMINAL LAW ANSWERS

Answer to Question 1

(A) As Justin's wife, Jennifer has a duty to aid Justin. Criminal liability requires that the defendant have either performed a voluntary physical act or failed to act under circumstances imposing a legal duty to act. Such a duty to act can arise from the relationship between the defendant and the victim, if it is sufficiently close to create the duty. For example, a person has a duty to prevent harm to her spouse. Existence of the duty to act also requires that the defendant be aware of the facts creating the duty (*e.g.,* a person must know of the danger to her spouse before her failure to rescue the spouse will render her liable), and it must be reasonably possible for the defendant to perform the duty or to obtain the help of others in performing it. Here, Jennifer was aware that Justin, her husband, was confronted with a life-threatening situation. Thus, Jennifer had a duty to assist Justin in preventing the harm threatened. It was reasonably possible for Jennifer to do so, as she simply had to slip the money through the mail slot, or she could have called the police for help. Having failed to fulfill her duty to aid Justin, Jennifer is criminally liable for Justin's death, which resulted from her failure to act. (B) incorrectly applies the term "acting in the heat of passion." An intentional killing can be reduced from murder to voluntary manslaughter if the defendant acted under sudden and intense provocation, with insufficient time between the provocation and the killing for the passions of a reasonable person to cool. Because Justin had slapped Jennifer in the morning, it cannot be said that Jennifer was acting under the heat of passion in the evening, when the incident with Ricky occurred. More than enough time had elapsed for the passions of a reasonable person to cool. Note also that, even if Jennifer were acting in the heat of passion, this would be a *mitigating* factor, rather than one tending to establish Jennifer's guilt, as (B) states. (C) is incorrect because one can be guilty of criminal homicide even without intending harm. For example, Jennifer could be guilty if she was aware of an unjustifiably high risk to human life, or she could be guilty of involuntary manslaughter if her failure to act constituted criminal negligence. (D) is incorrect because Justin's death would not have occurred but for Jennifer's inaction; *i.e.,* if Jennifer had provided Justin with the $400, it is highly unlikely that Ricky would have hit Justin. Although Ricky actually hit Justin, Jennifer's failure to respond to the danger confronting Justin may also be considered a cause of Justin's death.

Answer to Question 2

(D) If Dr. Doofus reasonably believed that Blodgett's condition was not life-threatening, then Dr. Doofus should not be convicted because she lacked the requisite intent for the crime. The statute here makes it a crime for a licensed physician to *willfully* neglect someone with a life-threatening injury. A requirement of willful action means that the person must have acted *knowing* that her conduct would necessarily cause such a result. Thus, she must be aware of the circumstances and act with the awareness of what the results of her conduct will be. To be convicted under this statute, Dr. Doofus must have been aware that Blodgett's condition was life-threatening and that leaving him there without any assistance could cost him his life. If, as choice (D) states, Dr. Doofus reasonably believed that Blodgett was not in a life-threatening situation, she did not violate the statute by leaving Blodgett unattended. She did not "willfully" neglect him, because she was not aware of the status of his situation. (A) is wrong because it fails to account for the required mental state (*i.e.,* willfulness). Choice (A) would impose a strict liability; a doctor would be liable whether or not she knew of the life-threatening situation. The statute here does not impose strict liability; only willful neglect is punishable. (B) is wrong because the statute is not too vague. The statute gives a person of ordinary intelligence fair notice of what sort of action or inaction is punishable (*i.e.,* the willful failure of a licensed medical doctor to assist someone with a life-threatening injury). (B) is also wrong because the statute requires more than mere negligence. Mere negligence requires a failure to be aware of a **substantial and unjustifiable** risk and thus failure to act as a reasonable person would under the circumstances. Criminal negligence requires a **very unreasonable** risk on the part of the defendant, in light of the utility of her conduct, knowledge of the facts, and extent of harm possible. Here the statute punishes more than mere negligence; it punishes a medical doctor's willful neglect of a person in a **life-threatening** situation. The willfulness requirement makes this statute punish more than mere negligence. (C) is wrong because ignorance of the law is no excuse. It is not a defense to a crime that the defendant did not know that her acts were prohibited by criminal law. This is true regardless of whether her ignorance was reasonable. Thus, despite the fact that the statute was in effect for only one week, Dr. Doofus may be convicted whether she was aware of it or not.

Answer to Question 3

(D) Neither Leslee nor Sven had the requisite intent to aid or encourage Mona in the commission of "Illicit Sex." Thus, neither is subject to liability for this crime. The statute in question provides for criminal liability for anyone who engages in sex for money. Here that would be Mona and Rurik. However, persons other than the principals to a crime (*i.e.,* accomplices) may be convicted. An accomplice is one who aids, counsels, or encourages the principal, before or during the commission of the crime, with the intent to aid or encourage the principal in the commission of that crime. Absent a statute providing otherwise, mere knowledge that a crime will result from the aid is insufficient for accomplice liability. However, selling something at a higher price because of the buyer's purpose may constitute a sufficient stake in the venture for a court to find intent to aid. Here, the only basis on which either Sven or Leslee can be found guilty of this crime is as an accomplice. In giving the money to Rurik, Sven probably had a good idea that the money would be used to purchase the services of a prostitute. However, "party" is a fairly broad term, encompassing a wide range of activities. And even if Sven knew that Rurik would use the money to patronize a prostitute, this knowledge alone would not be enough to make Sven an accomplice. Therefore, Sven cannot be convicted of this crime, so (B) and (C) are wrong. Leslee knew that her sale of the coat would better enable Mona to engage in prostitution on the night in question. However, the coat was not an illegal item, nor did Leslee sell it at a higher price because of Mona's purpose in buying it. Consequently, Leslee's mere knowledge that selling the coat to Mona would aid her in engaging in prostitution will not subject Leslee to accomplice liability. Leslee intended simply to make a sale as was her job as a salesclerk, not to aid or encourage the commission of "Illicit Sex." Thus, Leslee cannot be successfully prosecuted as an accomplice to "Illicit Sex," and so (A) is wrong.

Answer to Question 4

(B) This is the only situation in which Defendant's Fifth Amendment self-incrimination rights have clearly been violated. The Fifth Amendment privilege against compelled self-incrimination forms the basis for ruling upon the admissibility of a statement obtained while a defendant is in custody. A person in custody must, prior to interrogation (except for standard booking questions), be clearly informed that: he has the right to remain silent, anything he says can be used against him in court, he has the right to an attorney, and if he cannot afford an attorney, one will be appointed for him if he so desires. These *Miranda* warnings are a prerequisite to the admissibility of any statement made by the defendant during a custodial interrogation. The defendant in (B) was arrested and taken to the police station. He was in custody while he was interrogated. Because this interrogation took place prior to the giving of the *Miranda* warnings, there has been a direct violation of the Fifth Amendment privilege against compelled self-incrimination. (A) is wrong because use of Defendant's grand jury testimony does not violate his Fifth Amendment rights because Defendant waived those rights. Pursuant to the Fifth Amendment, a criminal defendant may invoke the privilege against self-incrimination by refusing to answer questions on the grounds that it may incriminate him. If he testifies, he has waived his privilege. Here, Defendant testified at the grand jury proceeding and thus waived the privilege. (C) is wrong because the Fifth Amendment protects only testimonial or communicative evidence, not real or physical evidence. Thus, the state may compel a person to give a handwriting sample without violating the Fifth Amendment, even if the evidence may be incriminating. Here, the prosecution may get Defendant's handwriting sample without violating his Fifth Amendment rights. (D) is wrong because the Fifth Amendment protects against being compelled to communicate information, not against disclosure of communications made in the past. Thus, the police may search for and seize documents tending to incriminate a person. Here, Defendant is not being compelled to give any information. Rather, the police, pursuant to a valid search warrant, seized the calendar with the appointments marked on it. Thus, Defendant's Fifth Amendment rights have not been violated.

Answer to Question 5

(A) Samson is guilty of murder. Murder is the unlawful killing of a human being with malice afore-thought. Malice aforethought (which may be either express or implied) exists if the defendant has any of the following states of mind: (i) intent to kill; (ii) intent to inflict great bodily injury; (iii) awareness of an unjustifiably high risk to human life; or (iv) intent to commit a felony. An intentional killing can be reduced from murder to voluntary manslaughter if the killing occurs while the defendant is acting under a provocation that would arouse sudden and intense passion in the mind of an ordinary person so as to cause him to lose self-control, with insufficient time between the provocation and the killing for the passions of a reasonable person to cool. One type of adequate provocation is exposure to a threat of deadly force. Here, Samson's stabbing his father in the chest with a large knife, while saying "You won't hurt us anymore," indicates an intent to kill Fenster. The question arises as to whether circumstances exist to reduce this killing to voluntary manslaughter. Because of the previous violence that Fenster had inflicted on Samson, Samson most likely found himself exposed to a threat of deadly force at the moment that Fenster uttered his angry words. Thus, there may have been adequate provocation *at that time.* However, Samson did not kill until some time later. The issues then are whether there was sufficient time for a reasonable person's passions to have cooled and whether Samson did cool off. If the time period was sufficient for a reasonable person's passions to cool *or* if Samson did in fact cool off, there can be no reduction of this killing to manslaughter. Here it is debatable whether the time period was sufficient for a reasonable person to have calmed down; the facts are not very helpful as to how much time has passed. However, they state that Samson went to a neighbor's house, talked to the neighbor, returned home, looked for a gun, contemplated his options when he could not find a gun, and finally got a knife and waited a short time more for his father to awaken. These actions tend to indicate that probably more than a few minutes passed, but it is difficult to tell whether this period would be sufficient time for a reasonable person to cool off. They do indicate that Samson was not acting under the heat of passion caused by his father's angry and threatening words; based on his actions, Samson seems to have calmly made his plans to kill his father. Thus, the killing does not constitute voluntary manslaughter because Samson was no longer acting under sufficient provocation. Therefore, (B) is wrong. (C) is wrong because the consistent beatings by Fenster do not provide a basis for reducing this crime to manslaughter if, at the time of the killing, Samson's passions had cooled. There is no rule of "continuing provocation" that will result in a finding of manslaughter without regard for whether that particular killing was committed under adequate provocation, before a sufficient time for cooling off. (D) is wrong because Samson did not have a right to use deadly force here. The use of deadly force in self-defense requires that the defendant reasonably believe that he is faced with *imminent* death or great bodily harm. There is no right to use deadly force if harm is merely threatened at a future time. Since Fenster had collapsed and Samson had already left the house, Samson faced no threat of imminent death or great bodily harm, and thus had no right to use deadly force in self-defense.

Answer to Question 6

(B) This choice states the Model Penal Code test. Pursuant to the Model Penal Code, a defendant is entitled to acquittal if he suffered from a mental disease or defect and as a result lacked substantial capacity to either: (i) appreciate the criminality of his conduct; or (ii) conform his conduct to the requirements of law. (A) is wrong because it would be helpful to Samson only if the jurisdiction followed the *Durham* insanity test, pursuant to which a defendant is entitled to acquittal if his crime was the product of mental disease or defect. (C) is wrong because it presents a valid defense under the *M'Naghten* rule, which provides for acquittal if a disease of the mind caused a defect of reason, such that the defendant lacked the ability at the time of his actions to either: (i) know the wrongfulness of his actions; or (ii) understand the nature and quality of his actions. (D) is wrong because it presents the irresistible impulse test, which provides for acquittal if, because of mental illness, the defendant was unable to control his actions or to conform his conduct to the law. Note that the Model Penal Code test combines the *M'Naghten* and irresistible impulse tests. Thus, choices (C) and (D) contain elements of the Model Penal Code test, but are not as good as (B) because the question asks for the set of facts that gives Samson the greatest likelihood of being relieved of criminal liability. Therefore, (B), which sets forth the complete test used in the jurisdiction, is the best choice.

Answer to Question 7

(C) Baker can be convicted of assault. There are two actions covered by the crime of assault: (i) an attempted battery, and (ii) the intentional creation of a reasonable apprehension in the mind of the victim of imminent bodily harm. Baker's conduct fits within the second type of assault. He intended to create an apprehension of an imminent bodily harm in Able's mind, since he used a realistic toy gun and a mask and pretended to rob Able. Thus, despite the fact that it was only to teach his friend a lesson, Baker committed an assault. (A) is wrong because Baker did not have the requisite intent for robbery. Robbery is a taking of another's personal property from the other's person by force or intimidation with the intent to permanently deprive him of his property. Here Baker never intended to keep the money; thus, he did not have the intent necessary for robbery. (B) is wrong for the same reason. "Armed robbery" is robbery with a weapon; it also requires the intent to permanently deprive the owner of his property. (D) is wrong because, as explained above, Baker can be convicted of assault.

Answer to Question 8

(D) Marju is not an accessory after the fact to burglary, and has committed neither larceny nor receipt of stolen property by keeping the coat. (A) is incorrect because, assuming that Skipper committed burglary to obtain the coat, Marju would be liable as an accessory after the fact only if she assisted him to avoid apprehension knowing that he had committed a felony. Here, even if Marju's acceptance of the fur coat helped Skipper by getting the stolen property out of his possession, it is clear that she had no knowledge at that time that he had committed burglary. (B) is incorrect both as to accessory after the fact to burglary (discussed above) and as to larceny. Larceny at common law requires a taking and carrying away of the tangible personal property of another by trespass, with intent to permanently deprive the other of the property. In this case, there was neither a taking and carrying away by Marju nor, at the time she accepted the coat, an intent to deprive the owner of it. Thus, Marju is not guilty of larceny. (C) is incorrect because, again, Marju's criminal intent was not formulated at the time she accepted the coat. Receipt of stolen property requires that defendant receive possession and control of stolen personal property knowing it to have been stolen by another person and with the intent to permanently deprive the owner of it. Marju accepted the coat not knowing it to be stolen and not having an intent at that time to deprive the true owner of it. Her later decision to keep the coat does not relate back to her earlier conduct; there must be a concurrence of the mental state and the physical act for the crime to be committed.

Answer to Question 9

(D) The search warrant is valid because the affidavit accompanying it is sufficiently detailed to allow a determination of probable cause. A warrant must be based on a showing of probable cause. Along with a request for a warrant, a police officer must submit to a magistrate an affidavit setting forth sufficient underlying circumstances to enable the magistrate to make a determination of probable cause independent of the officer's conclusions. The affidavit may be based on an informer's statements. The sufficiency of the affidavit is evaluated according to the "totality of the circumstances." There must be sufficient information for the magistrate to be able to make a common sense evaluation of probable cause. Among the factors determinative of probable cause are the informer's reliability, credibility, and basis of knowledge. Here, Andy's affidavit indicates that the informer has previously proved to be reliable by providing accurate information in other cases. This, in turn, enhances the credibility of the informer. Also, the informant's knowledge is based on his having personally placed bets with Hood at Hood's apartment. Thus, Andy's affidavit is supported by sufficient underlying circumstances to allow a magistrate's finding that there was a showing of probable cause. (A) is incorrect because probable cause for issuance of a search warrant may be based on hearsay, if the information comes from a reliable informer. (B) is incorrect because the failure to disclose the identity of the informer does not necessarily invalidate the search warrant. The identity of an informer does not have to be revealed to allow the magistrate to make a determination of probable cause. The magistrate may make this determination based on the police officer's information about the informer showing reliability, credibility, and knowledge. The magistrate need not personally question the informer. (C) is incorrect because, at this point in the proceedings, the informer's identity need not be revealed. If the informer is a witness to the crime and his testimony may be material to a determination of the defendant's guilt or innocence, the identity of the informer may have to be revealed at or before trial. However, at this time, it is not crucial that the identity be disclosed.

Answer to Question 10

(B) In executing the search warrant, Barb and Charlie violated the requirement to knock and announce their identity and purpose. In executing a search warrant, the police officers must knock and announce their authority and purpose except where there is a reasonable suspicion, based on facts, that their announcement will be dangerous or futile or will inhibit the investigation (*e.g.,* lead to destruction of evidence). [Richards v. Wisconsin (1997)] The facts here do not indicate that Barb and Charlie were faced with such circumstances. Thus, the requirement to "knock and announce" is applicable to these facts, and the failure of Barb and Charlie to do so renders inadmissible the evidence seized from Hood. (C) is incorrect because the fact that the door was unlocked does not mean that Barb and Charlie were justified in entering without announcing their authority and purpose. The "knock and announce" requirement still applies. (A) is incorrect because the plain view exception to the warrant requirement applies only when police: (i) are legitimately on the premises; (ii) discover evidence, fruits or instrumentalities of crime, or contraband; (iii) see such evidence in plain view; and (iv) have probable cause to believe that the item is evidence, contraband, or a fruit or instrumentality of crime. Because of the failure of Barb and Charlie to knock and announce under the circumstances, they were not legitimately on Hood's premises. Thus, the seizure of the wagering slips and bookmaking apparatus cannot be justified under the plain view exception. (D) incorrectly implies that mere evidence of a crime cannot be the legitimate subject of a police seizure. Although this was formerly the law, such is no longer the case. Now, police may seize an item that is mere evidence of a crime, as long as there is some nexus between the item seized and the commission of a crime.

Answer to Question 11

(B) There was an insufficient agreement for conspiracy liability. Conspiracy consists of: (i) an agreement between two or more persons; (ii) an intent to enter into an agreement; and (iii) an intent to achieve the objective of the agreement. In addition, most states require an act in further-ance of the conspiracy, although an act of mere preparation will usually suffice. The agreement requirement means that the parties must agree to accomplish the same objective by mutual action. There must be a meeting of at least two "guilty minds"; *i.e.,* between two or more persons who are actually committing themselves to the scheme. If one person in a two-party conspiracy is only feigning agreement, the other person cannot be convicted of conspiracy at common law. Here, George, in his capacity as an undercover police officer, was simply trying to set up a situation in which Kate would be caught in the act of stealing jewels. Thus, George merely pretended to reach an agreement with Kate to steal the jewels. At no time did George actually commit himself to a scheme of jewel theft, nor did he otherwise agree to accomplish the objec-tive of stealing the jewels by mutual action with Kate. Therefore, there could have been no agreement of two "guilty minds." Absent the requisite agreement, Kate cannot be guilty of conspiracy. (A) is incorrect because, as explained above, there was no agreement sufficient for a conspiracy conviction since George never intended to commit the theft. (C) is incorrect because completion of the substantive crime is not necessary for a conviction of conspiracy. Conse-quently, although the actual theft of the jewels was not consummated, this would not preclude a conviction of conspiracy. (D) is incorrect because withdrawal is not a defense to a charge of conspiracy. Note that, by withdrawing, a person may *limit her liability* for subsequent acts of the other members of the conspiracy. However, this question pertains to Kate's potential guilt for conspiracy. As applied to the conspiracy charge, withdrawal will not afford a defense to Kate.

Answer to Question 12

(C) Introduction of the proffered evidence would in effect penalize Dross for exercising his right to be free from compulsory self-incrimination. *Miranda* warnings are given to safeguard the Fifth Amendment right to be free from compelled self-incrimination. Prior to interrogation, a person in custody must be clearly informed that he has the right to remain silent and anything he says can be used against him in court. These warnings implicitly assure that silence will carry no penalty. Thus, a prosecutor may not comment on a defendant's silence after defendant is arrested and has received the *Miranda* warnings. To allow the prosecutor to introduce evidence of Dross's silence in the face of Verbena's accusation would run counter to the very purpose of the *Miranda* warn-ings, which is to allow the defendant to remain silent without fear of being prejudiced by such silence. Dross was no more required to respond to Verbena's accusation than he would have been to an accusation or question coming from the police. Dross's privilege against compelled self-incrimination would be meaningless if he were required to either respond to Verbena or have his failure to respond introduced against him. (A) is wrong because the mere fact that evidence is true does not render such evidence admissible. Evidence that runs afoul of some rule of evidentiary exclusion (*e.g.,* a statement that is hearsay not subject to any of the exclusions to the hearsay rule) or that would violate a right of constitutional magnitude is not admissible, regardless of whether it is true. Because evidence of Dross's silence would violate his Fifth Amendment right to be free of compelled self-incrimination, this evidence is not admissible, even though it is true. (B) is wrong because it turns the *Miranda* warnings on their head. The warnings are to apprise the suspect that he has a right to remain silent, and that if he chooses to say something, this statement can be used against him. The warnings do not, as (B) suggests, apprise the suspect that he *must* respond to questions or accusations, and that a failure to respond can be used against him. As has been explained above, the crux of the *Miranda* warnings is the right to remain silent, and to be free of coercion to speak at all. (D) is wrong for two reasons. (D) implies that the evidence would be admissible if Dross's lawyer was present at the time of the incident. Regardless of the presence of counsel, admission of evidence as to Dross's silence in the face of Verbena's accusation would violate Dross's privilege against compelled self-incrimination. Also, events had not yet reached a stage at which Dross was entitled to counsel. At the time of this incident, Dross was waiting to take part in a lineup. The facts indicate that Dross had not been charged with a crime. The right to counsel applies to post-charge lineups, but not to pre-charge lineups. Note also that Verbena's accusation did not even occur in a lineup setting, but during an inadvertent viewing of Dross. Thus, the right to counsel had not yet attached.

Answer to Question 13

(A)   If the jurisdiction uses the *M'Naghten* test, Prof's best argument is that he did not know that his act was wrong. The *M'Naghten* test provides for a defendant's acquittal if he has a disease of the mind causing a defect of reason so that at the time of his actions he lacked the ability to know the wrongfulness of his actions or understand the nature and quality of his actions. (A) states one branch of this test and is consistent with the facts (which state that Prof did not know that the killing was wrongful), and so it is Prof's best argument. (C) is wrong because it is contrary to the facts. Although (C) also states part of the *M'Naghten* test, Prof's illness has not left him so irrational that he is unable to comprehend that his acts will result in Learner's death. He seemed to have known that he was killing Learner; he just did not know that killing was wrong. (B) is wrong because although Prof did lack the substantial capacity to appreciate the criminality of his act, this is not a criterion for insanity in a state that follows the *M'Naghten* test; rather, (B) states the Model Penal Code standard. (D) is wrong because it states conduct outside the scope of the *M'Naghten* test. Also, the facts do not show that Prof's mental illness had deprived him of his volitional controls.

Answer to Question 14

(D)   Stagehand cannot be convicted of any of these crimes. Murder is the unlawful killing of a human being with malice aforethought. Malice aforethought exists if the defendant has any of the following states of mind: (i) intent to kill; (ii) intent to inflict great bodily injury; (iii) awareness of an unjustifiably high risk to human life; or (iv) intent to commit a felony. Modern statutes often divide murder into degrees. For instance, a deliberate and premeditated killing (*i.e.,* one in which the defendant made the decision to kill in a cool and dispassionate manner, and actually reflected on the idea of killing) may be designated first degree murder. Second degree murder is generally a killing with malice aforethought that is not specifically made first degree murder. Here, Stagehand did not even realize that he was pointing a real gun at Actor. Thus, Stagehand did not possess any of the states of mind that would constitute malice aforethought (*i.e.,* he did not intend to kill or to inflict great bodily injury, nor was he aware of a high risk to human life). Consequently, Stagehand cannot be convicted of murder, either first or second degree. Thus, (A) is incorrect. Voluntary manslaughter is an intentional killing distinguishable from murder by the existence of adequate provocation. At the time of the killing, the defendant must have been acting under a provocation that would arouse sudden and intense passion in the mind of an ordinary person so as to cause him to lose self-control, with an insufficient time between the provocation and the killing for the passions of a reasonable person to cool. Stagehand cannot be convicted of voluntary manslaughter because: (i) his killing of Actor was accidental, rather than intentional; and (ii) in shooting Actor, he was not acting under any type of provocation. Therefore, (B) is incorrect. Involuntary manslaughter occurs when a death is caused by criminal negligence. There is negligence when a person fails to be aware of a substantial and unjustifiable risk that circumstances exist or that a result will follow, and such failure constitutes a substantial deviation from the standard of care that a reasonable person would exercise under the circumstances. Criminal negligence requires a greater deviation from the "reasonable person" standard than is required for civil liability. Stagehand's firing the gun at Actor was probably negligent. However, Stagehand's conduct did not rise to the level of criminal negligence, because he had insufficient knowledge of the true risk posed by his actions. If Stagehand knew he was using a real gun, it would probably have been criminally negligent to have pointed it at Actor and pulled the trigger. However, Stagehand actually believed that he was using a *stage gun*. Thus, Stagehand cannot be said to have taken the type of very unreasonable risk that would constitute criminal negligence. Therefore, (C) is incorrect.

Answer to Question 15

(B) Phoebe's actions were motivated by adequate provocation and therefore manslaughter is the more appropriate crime. Voluntary manslaughter is an intentional killing distinguishable from murder by adequate provocation. Provocation is sufficient to reduce the killing from murder to manslaughter if it would arouse sudden and intense passion in an ordinary person, and there has been insufficient time for the passions of a reasonable person to cool. Also, the defendant must actually be provoked and have acted under that provocation (*i.e.,* did not cool off). Here, Phoebe's use of a deadly weapon under these circumstances shows that she intended to kill the robber or at least inflict great bodily harm. However, the commission of a violent felony (especially one that included a staggering blow) is provocation that would arouse a reasonable person and apparently did arouse Phoebe. She acted very quickly after her attack, and thus a reasonable person would not have cooled off nor, apparently, had Phoebe. Thus, she had the intent and provocation for manslaughter. However, she did not intend to kill the bystander. Under the transferred intent doctrine, if a defendant intended injury to a person, and in trying to carry out that intent caused similar injury to another, her intent is transferred from the intended person to the one harmed. In addition, any mitigating circumstances that the defendant could have asserted against the intended victim (such as provocation) will also usually be transferred. Therefore, Phoebe can be guilty of voluntary manslaughter for the death of the bystander. (*Note:* It is possible that Phoebe could escape conviction altogether by claiming that the intent she formed was "justified" as an effort to prevent the escape of a fleeing felon. However, the question does not ask for an actual assessment of Phoebe's probable criminal liability, but only whether she has committed murder or manslaughter.) (A) is wrong because it overlooks the transferred intent doctrine. If Phoebe intended to kill the robber, this intent will be transferred to the bystander and she cannot escape criminal liability simply because she hit the wrong person. (C) is wrong because, as explained above, her intent was mitigated by adequate provocation, and thus manslaughter is the more appropriate crime. (D) is wrong because even though Phoebe was in no danger when she shot at the robber, she was at least acting under adequate provocation so that she should be convicted of voluntary manslaughter rather than murder.

Answer to Question 16

(B) Although Mom, as the owner of the house, had the authority to consent to a search of the house, she had no right to consent to the search of the trunk. A warrantless search by the police is valid if they have a voluntary and intelligent consent to the search. Any person with equal right to use or occupation of the property may consent to a search, and any evidence found may be used against the other owners or occupants. The search is valid as long as the police reasonably believed that the consenting party had a right to use or occupy the premises, even if she in fact lacked such right. Here, Mom owns the house. As the owner, Mom clearly had the right to the use and occupation of the house and could thus consent to the warrantless police search. However, the fact that Dunston kept the trunk locked, with the only key in his possession, indicates that Dunston had the exclusive right of use and access to the trunk. Because Mom told the police that the trunk was always locked and that Dunston had the only key, they could not have reasonably believed that Mom had a right of use or access to the trunk. Therefore, consent to search the trunk was not given by a person with a right to give such consent. Absent proper consent, the warrantless search of the trunk was invalid. (D) is incorrect because Mom's ownership of the house does not confer on her a right to use or gain access to the trunk. Without such a right, Mom could not validly consent to a search of the trunk. (A) is incorrect because knowledge of the right to withhold consent is not a prerequisite to establishing a voluntary and intelligent consent (although it is a factor to be considered). Thus, the failure of the police to inform Mom that she could refuse permission for the search does not automatically invalidate her consent (and the subsequent search). (C) is incorrect. There is no requirement that the owner of property must declare in advance that it is off-limits. The circumstances of Dunston's possession and use of the trunk make it clear that his consent was needed to search it.

Answer to Question 17

(D) Sonya is not guilty of any crime because she had no legal duty to help Ollie. For virtually all crimes, including homicides, one element that must be proved is a physical act or an unlawful failure to act by the defendant. Failure to act will constitute a crime only where there is a legal duty to act and it is reasonably possible to perform the act. Here, it would have been very easy for Sonya to save Ollie by allowing him into her cabin. However, she had no legal duty to do so. A legal duty can arise by statute, contract, a close relationship between the victim and the defendant, the voluntary assumption of care by the defendant, or the creation of the peril by the defendant. None of these conditions is indicated in the facts here. Thus, Sonya can be convicted of no crime. Note that if Sonya had allowed Ollie into her cabin but subsequently kicked him out, the result might be different because she would then have voluntarily assumed the care of Ollie. (A), (B), and (C) are all incorrect because each of these homicide crimes requires the element of a physical act or unlawful failure to act.

Answer to Question 18

(A) Although Lisa would have been guilty of murder had the pedestrian been killed, it does not necessarily follow that she is guilty of attempted murder when she almost killed the pedestrian. Murder does not require an intent to kill; an awareness of an unjustifiably high risk to human life will suffice. *Attempted* murder, however, is a specific intent crime and requires an intent to kill. If Lisa did not intend to kill the pedestrian, she cannot be convicted of attempted murder. (B) is wrong because although Lisa can avoid guilt for attempted murder, she cannot do so for the reason given here. Attempt requires an act beyond mere preparation for the offense. If Lisa had the required intent to kill, her act of running down the pedestrian would be sufficient for attempted murder. (C) is wrong. It is often loosely said that one is presumed to intend the natural and probable consequences of her act. This is not to be taken literally. It means that if a particular result is a natural and probable consequence of what a defendant does, the fact finder **may** draw the inference from such circumstance that the defendant intended that result. Here, however, it is likely that the jury would infer that Lisa, who wanted to keep a crosstown appointment, never intended to kill a pedestrian. (D) is wrong for the same reason. It is simply another phrasing of (C). But, as explained above, attempted murder requires an actual intent to kill, not a fictitious, imputed, or constructive one.

Answer to Question 19

(C) If this was an inventory incident to incarceration, Donald's rights were not violated. After a valid arrest, the police may make a warrantless search of a defendant's personal effects as part of an established procedure incident to incarceration. This type of search is valid under the Fourth Amendment. Here, it appears that Donald was validly arrested and incarcerated. Therefore, Cyndy could inventory his possessions. Her discovery of the inscription on the watch, as she examined it to inventory it, is within the scope of a valid inventory. (A) is wrong because a valid inventory allows an examination of the items so that they can be properly identified in the inventory. As mentioned, Cyndy's examination of the watch was within the scope of a valid inventory. (B) is wrong because, as mentioned, a warrant is not required for an inventory incident to incarceration. (D) is wrong because the police do not need an independent source for charging Donald with the second burglary. The police have probable cause to charge Donald with Victim's burglary based on the watch. The police did not violate Donald's rights by inventorying the watch and noticing the inscription. Thus, they did not violate his rights by charging him with this crime. If there had been a taint on the evidence (*e.g.,* if the watch had been discovered during an invalid search or incident to an invalid arrest), then an independent source would be required, but the facts here show no taint and no reason for an independent source of probable cause.

Answer to Question 20

(B) Sally's best defense is that she cannot be convicted under the statute because it was designed to protect minors. Statutory rape is the crime of carnal knowledge of a female under the age of consent (generally under age 16 or 18). This crime, by definition, limits criminal liability to the male; a female cannot be convicted. However, one who may not be convicted as a principal may be convicted as an accomplice. Therefore, a woman acting as an accomplice to the crime could be convicted. If, however, the legislative intent is to protect members of a class from exploitation or overbearing, members of that class are presumed to be immune from liability, even if they participate in the crime. Here, Sally can argue that the crime of statutory rape was intended to protect minors from exploitation and therefore, the legislative intent is that she, as a minor, be immune from prosecution. (A) is wrong because an accomplice may be convicted before the principal. Although the common law rule required that the principal's guilt be determined first, or at least at a joint trial, this rule has been abandoned by most jurisdictions. (C) is wrong because it is too broad; a minor may be an accomplice to a crime. To be convicted as an accomplice, a person must have acted with the intent to aid or encourage the principal in the commission of the crime. As long as a child is old enough to be able to form this intent, she could be convicted as an accomplice. A 15-year-old is certainly capable of forming that intent. (Even under the common law presumptions, children over age 14 are treated as adults.) (D) is wrong because John could be convicted despite Sally's consent. Consent is not a defense to statutory rape; even if the female willingly participates in the sexual acts, the male may be convicted. Thus, Sally's consent, or her status as a prostitute, is not the reason she may not be convicted as an accomplice.

Answer to Question 21

(C)   Although jeopardy attached in Winkie's first trial, her retrial is not barred because she initiated the grant of the mistrial in her first trial. As a general rule, the right to be free of double jeopardy for the same offense bars a retrial for the same offense once jeopardy has attached in the first trial. However, one of the exceptions permitting retrial even if jeopardy has attached is when a mistrial is granted in the first trial at the request of the defendant on any grounds not constituting an acquittal on the merits. Here, Winkie requested the mistrial because a conflict arose between the defenses of her and her co-defendant in the joint trial, and the judge granted the mistrial solely to allow Winkie to obtain another attorney. Thus, no acquittal on the merits occurred and the double jeopardy rule does not apply. (A) is incorrect for several reasons. Merely because jeopardy attaches does not mean that the double jeopardy rule will apply; retrial will be permitted under certain exceptions, one of which is applicable here. Furthermore, (A) is not a correct statement of law. Jeopardy attaches in a jury trial when the jury is impaneled and sworn in, even if it has not yet heard any evidence. (B) is incorrect because the judge's finding at the preliminary hearing stage appears to be an honest error rather than bad faith conduct. In the absence of bad faith conduct by the judge or prosecutor designed to force the defendant to seek a mistrial, the defendant's securing of a mistrial does not preclude a retrial. (D) is incorrect because the right to be free of double jeopardy creates a bar as soon as the defendant is retried for the same offense, rather than on her conviction.

Answer to Question 22

(D)   Radical evidently did not have the mens rea for assault. An assault is either: (i) an attempt to commit a battery; or (ii) the intentional creation (other than by mere words) of a reasonable apprehension in the mind of the victim of imminent bodily harm. An attempt to commit a battery would require a specific intent to unlawfully apply force to the person of another, resulting in either bodily injury or an offensive touching. In this question, Radical was simply fleeing from the boutique at the time he darted past Mrs. Wallingford, who happened to be in his path. There apparently was no intent on the part of Radical to bring about any sort of bodily injury or offensive touching to Mrs. Wallingford. Thus, Radical did not possess the requisite mens rea (*i.e.,* specific intent) for an attempt to commit a battery. Likewise, the facts indicate that Radical did not intend to create in the mind of Mrs. Wallingford a fear of imminent bodily harm. Thus, Radical also lacked the requisite mens rea for the second of the two types of assault. (A) states a factor that is totally irrelevant to a charge of criminal assault. In determining possible criminal liability for assault, there is no such thing as an "underlying offense," as in felony murder, where a killing occurring during the course of a felony (the underlying offense) is deemed to be murder. Whether Radical is guilty of assault on these facts does not depend on any other offense that he committed or was in the process of committing. Thus, it is of no significance that Radical's conduct in the boutique constituted a misdemeanor rather than a felony. (B) does not state a defense to assault because, where there is an assault, there is no actual touching of the victim (a touching would constitute a battery, not an assault). Consequently, the absence of contact between Radical and Mrs. Wallingford is of no help to Radical's defense. (C) is not helpful to the defense because foreseeability of Mrs. Wallingford's injury as a consequence of Radical's criminal activity at Moochi's is irrelevant to a charge of assault. As detailed above, assault requires an *intent* to either commit battery or to create fear of imminent bodily harm. "Foreseeability" speaks to negligence rather than intent, and is not applicable to assault. Even if Mrs. Wallingford's injury *were* a foreseeable consequence of Radical's criminal activity at Moochi's (and it may well have been foreseeable that a passerby would be injured as Radical fled the scene), Radical would not be guilty of assault based on mere foreseeability of injury, absent the presence of the requisite intent on his part.

Answer to Question 23

(A) If Ralph intended to deposit his paycheck before the checks cleared, he lacked the intent to defraud required by the statute. The statute under which Ralph is being prosecuted is a variation of the offense of false pretenses. As with false pretenses, the statute requires a specific intent, *i.e.,* an intent to defraud. If Ralph intended to deposit sufficient funds to honor both checks before they reached his bank, then Ralph did not intend to defraud the two stores that were payees of the checks. Thus, Ralph lacked the specific intent that is a necessary element of the crime charged. (B) is incorrect because Ralph's expectation that he would receive his paycheck as usual need not have been reasonable. Even if such an expectation were unreasonable, Ralph would not be guilty if he did not intend to defraud the payees, as required by the statute. (C) is incorrect because it would result in a verdict of guilty without requiring intent to defraud. Knowledge that the checks were drawn against insufficient funds is just one element of the statute. The intent to defraud is also required to convict under the applicable statute. (D) also incorrectly assumes that Ralph violated the statute merely by knowingly writing checks on insufficient funds. As explained above, the requisite intent to defraud is absent. Thus, there is no "violation" to be vitiated.

Answer to Question 24

(D) Louie cannot be convicted of either murder or manslaughter in the death of the onlooker because he did not commit a voluntary act. Virtually all crimes, including homicide, require either a voluntary physical act or a failure to act under circumstances imposing a legal duty to act. An act performed while the defendant is unconscious is not voluntary because it does not stem from a conscious exercise of the will. Thus, if the trier of fact accepts the expert testimony, Louie cannot be convicted of the onlooker's homicide. (A) is wrong because the death of the bystander was not proximately caused by Louie's initial conduct in swinging at the first officer. A crime such as homicide that requires not merely conduct but also a specified result of that conduct imposes liability on the defendant only for results that occur as a "natural and probable" consequence of the conduct. Even if the jurisdiction did apply the felony murder doctrine or misdemeanor man-slaughter doctrine to the initial battery of the officer, it would require that the death be a foresee-able result of the felony or misdemeanor, and here it could be argued that it was not foreseeable that other officers would respond to the battery with deadly force and that a gun battle would ensue, causing the death of a bystander; in any event, the battery does not suffice for homicide in the absence of these doctrines. (B) is incorrect because, under the transferred intent doctrine, any mitigating circumstances excusing or justifying the killing of the second officer would generally be transferred to the bystander; if mitigated as to the former, it would be mitigated as to the latter. The same reasoning applies to (C); if Louie had the requisite intent for murder as to the officer, this intent would be transferred to the onlooker, making Louie liable for murder. Nor would Louie's battery suffice for involuntary manslaughter based on criminal negligence, because the proximate cause requirement cannot be established.

Answer to Question 25

(D) Winthrop cannot be convicted because he did not cause his wife's death. Murder is defined as the unlawful killing of another human being with malice aforethought. To be guilty of murder, the defendant's action must be both the cause in fact and the proximate cause of the victim's death. The defendant's act will be a cause in fact of death if, but for the defendant's action, the victim would not have died as and when she did. Here, the victim would have died when she did even if Winthrop had not administered the poison, since she died not from the poison, but only from her cancer. Thus, Winthrop's actions were not the cause in fact of death, and (D) is correct. (A) and

(B) are incorrect because if the other elements of murder are established, administering poison might be sufficient to establish malice aforethought. Malice aforethought for murder can be established by conduct done with the awareness of an unjustifiably high risk to human life, and Winthrop knew that the poisons were dangerous and could kill. (C) is incorrect because the law forbids shortening a life even for one second, so it is not a defense that medical science had given the victim up for dead. If the defendant's action in any way shortened the victim's life, he can be held liable for murder.

Answer to Question 26

(A) The prosecutor's comment improperly burdened Terry's assertion of his privilege against self-incrimination. The prosecution is not allowed to comment upon the defendant's failure to testify at trial, since the latter is privileged under the Fifth Amendment to remain silent. (B) is incorrect because no amount of attacks upon the credibility of prosecution witnesses will justify such a comment as a rebuttal. (C) is incorrect because the Fifth Amendment privilege outweighs the prosecutor's right to comment upon the state of the evidence. (D) is not the best answer even though the harmless error test does apply to improper comments by the prosecution (*i.e.,* the conviction will not be overturned if the prosecution can show beyond a reasonable doubt that the comments did not affect the outcome of the case). Because there is no real indication as to the strength of the case against Terry, it is impossible to conclude that the error was harmless beyond a reasonable doubt.

Answer to Question 27

(D) Although the betting slips discovered by Smarts as a result of an illegal search may be said to have led to Lola's testimony, such testimony will not be excluded as the product of illegal police activity. Under the exclusionary rule, not only must illegally obtained evidence be excluded, but also all evidence obtained or derived from exploitation of that evidence must be excluded. Such derived evidence is called the fruit of the poisonous tree. Despite this general rule, it is difficult for a defendant to have live witness testimony excluded as the fruit of the poisonous tree, because a more direct link between the taint and the evidence is required than for exclusion of other evidence. Among the factors that a court considers in determining the existence of a sufficiently direct link is the extent to which the witness is freely willing to testify. Here, Smarts did not have a search warrant when he looked into the envelope. Of all the exceptions to the warrant requirement, the only one that might be applicable here is plain view. The facts are not clear as to whether the betting slips were in plain view, but the fact that we are told that Smarts peeked into the envelope indicates that the slips were not in plain view. Thus, the search that disclosed the presence of the betting slips was illegal. Nick will argue that, because Smarts's questioning of Lola followed the illegal search of the envelope, the testimony of Lola is derived from exploitation of the evidence found in the envelope. However, there is no indication from the facts of such a direct link between the illegal conduct of Smarts and the testimony as would be required to exclude the testimony. Even prior to seeing the betting slips, Smarts was aware of rumors regarding Nick's gambling. Thus, it is entirely possible that at some point the police would have questioned Lola as to her knowledge of this matter and obtained from her the same information that now forms the basis of her testimony. Consequently, the link between the proffered testimony and the illegal police conduct is insufficiently direct to render the testimony inadmissible. Because Nick will be unable to have Lola's testimony excluded as the fruit of the poisonous tree, (A) is incorrect. (B) is incorrect for two reasons. First, there is no indication that Lola is a co-conspirator with Nick. The mere fact that Nick gave Lola the envelope to hold for someone, and that Lola might have some knowledge of Nick's gambling activities, does not mean that Lola and

Nick agreed to achieve some common objective by means of mutual action. Second, even if Lola is a co-conspirator, there is no principle of law that prohibits an unindicted co-conspirator from testifying. (C) is incorrect because Lola is not a defendant. The Fifth Amendment privilege against compulsory self-incrimination affords a criminal defendant the right to refuse to take the stand at trial. A nondefendant witness, however, may not use the privilege to avoid being sworn as a witness or to avoid being asked questions. Such a witness must listen to the questions and specifically invoke the privilege rather than answer the questions. Because Lola is a nondefendant witness, it is inaccurate to state, as does (C), that she has the right to refuse to take the stand.

Answer to Question 28

(C) If the warrant was invalid, any evidence obtained thereunder will be excluded. A warrant must be based upon a showing of probable cause. When requesting a warrant, officers must submit to a magistrate an affidavit setting forth sufficient underlying circumstances to enable the magistrate to make a determination of probable cause independent of the officers' conclusions. Also, a warrant must describe with reasonable precision the place to be searched and any items to be seized. A finding that a warrant was invalid because it was not supported by probable cause will not entitle the defendant to exclude evidence obtained under the warrant if the police have acted in good faith and reasonable reliance on a facially valid warrant. However, a police officer cannot in good faith rely on a defective search warrant if: (i) the affidavit underlying the warrant is so lacking in probable cause that no reasonable police officer would have relied on it; (ii) the warrant is defective on its face (e.g., it fails to state with particularity the place to be searched or the things to be seized); (iii) the affiant lied to or misled the magistrate; or (iv) the magistrate has wholly abandoned his judicial role. Because Nick lives in a condominium, the warrant should have specified which unit in the multi-unit dwelling was to be searched. If the warrant did not so specify, then it failed to describe with sufficient particularity the place to be searched. Such an absence of precision renders the warrant defective on its face, so that the F.B.I. agents cannot be said to have relied in good faith on a facially valid warrant. Thus, the evidence obtained pursuant to this facially defective warrant will be excluded. (A) and (B) each incorrectly imply that there was something wrong with the execution of the warrant. A warrant must be executed by the police without unreasonable delay, with the police knocking and announcing their purpose (unless they reasonably believe that such notice will endanger them or lead to the destruction of evidence). The F.B.I. agents conducted themselves in accordance with these standards. The fact that a warrant is executed at night or at a time when a particular person is not on the premises will not invalidate a search conducted pursuant to the warrant. Here, the agents announced themselves to Nick's wife, and they were not required to wait until Nick returned in order to conduct their search. (D) is incorrect because it states a fact that will not, in and of itself, invalidate a warrant and a search pursuant thereto. The sufficiency of a search warrant affidavit based on an informer's hearsay is evaluated under the totality of the circumstances. The informer's reliability and credibility, as well as her basis of knowledge, are all elements that may illuminate the issue of probable cause, but they are not strictly separate requirements. Had Lola been used before as an informant, and been previously found to be reliable, this would have been one factor in determining her present reliability. However, the fact that Lola has not previously served as an informer does not invalidate the warrant. Lola may well have enough of a basis for her information and have sufficient credibility to permit a magistrate to make a determination of probable cause.

Answer to Question 29

(D) The search and seizure of the betting slips by the F.B.I. agents at the deli are invalid because they were executed without a warrant and no exception to the warrant requirement is applicable. All warrantless searches are unconstitutional unless they fit into one of the six recognized exceptions to the warrant requirement. To be valid, a warrantless search must meet all the requirements of at least one exception. These exceptions are: (i) search incident to a lawful arrest; (ii) the automobile exception; (iii) plain view; (iv) consent; (v) stop and frisk and other limited intrusions; and (vi) hot pursuit, evanescent evidence, and similar emergencies. When the agents conducted the search of the deli, they had no warrant for the search. Thus, the validity of the search and seizure depends on whether an exception to the warrant requirement is applicable. Clearly, the automobile exception does not apply, as there was no search involving a vehicle. The police activity cannot be classified as a stop and frisk or other limited intrusion because the facts state that a search took place and because the activity described—searching the restaurant and looking inside the leather bag—would not be considered a limited intrusion. No person with authority to use the bag gave consent to the search of the bag, so the search and seizure are not justified under the consent exception. The agents were not engaged in arresting someone, which would have permitted them to search the arrestee and areas into which he might reach to obtain weapons or destroy evidence. Pursuant to the plain view exception, the police may make a warrantless seizure when they: (i) are legitimately on the premises; (ii) discover evidence, fruits, or instrumentalities of crime, or contraband; (iii) see such evidence in plain view; and (iv) have probable cause to believe that the item is evidence, contraband, or a fruit or instrumentality of crime. Here, because the agents lacked a search warrant for the deli, the agent in the back room was not there legitimately (as opposed to being in the part of the deli that is open to the public). Also, the betting slips, which were in the bag, were hardly in plain view of the agent who seized them. Therefore, the plain view exception is inapplicable, and (A) is incorrect. The final exception to the warrant requirement, the hot pursuit exception, provides that officers in hot pursuit of a fleeing felon may make a warrantless search and seizure. The scope of such a search may be as broad as is reasonably necessary to prevent the suspect from resisting or escaping. Here, the F.B.I. agents were not hotly pursuing a fleeing felon. In fact, the agents had not even come into contact with Nick at the time they conducted the search and seizure of the deli. Consequently, the hot pursuit exception does not apply, and (C) is incorrect. Thus, none of the exceptions to the warrant requirement applies to these facts. As a result, the warrantless search and seizure at the deli are invalid, as stated in (D). (B) is incorrect because the validity of the search and seizure at the deli is unrelated to the validity of the search warrant for Nick's condominium. Even if valid, the warrant to search Nick's condominium only confers a right to search the condominium, and it does not carry with it a right to also search Nick's place of business. Conversely, if the warrant is invalid, the search and seizure at the deli will be valid if they fall within one of the exceptions to the warrant requirement. Thus, the search and seizure at the deli must stand or fall on its own merits, regardless of the validity of the search warrant for the condominium.

Answer to Question 30

(D) If Doyle intended merely to borrow the television set for a while, he lacked the intent to commit larceny, and thus would not be guilty of burglary. Common law burglary consists of: (i) a breaking; (ii) and entry; (iii) of the dwelling; (iv) of another; (v) at nighttime; (vi) with the intent of committing a felony therein. Doyle entered the cottage intending to remove the television set. Thus, the facts indicate that the only felony Doyle could have intended to commit at the time of entry would be larceny. Larceny, which is the only potential felony applicable here, consists of: (i) a taking; (ii) and carrying away; (iii) of tangible personal property; (iv) of another; (v) by trespass; (vi) with intent to permanently (or for an unreasonable time) deprive the person of his interest in the property. If the defendant intended to return the property within a reasonable time and at the time of the taking had a substantial ability to do so, such an unauthorized borrowing does not constitute larceny. Consequently, if Doyle intended to keep the television set only for the short time required to have his own set repaired, then Doyle did not intend to permanently deprive Vic of his interest in the set. Because Doyle thus lacked the intent to commit a felony in Vic's cottage at the time he entered, Doyle would not be guilty of burglary. (A) is incorrect because, for purposes of the crime of burglary, a structure is deemed to be a dwelling simply if it is used regularly for sleeping purposes. The temporary absence of the occupants will not deprive a structure of its character as a dwelling. Although the cottage is not Vic's principal residence, and he intended to return home upon his recuperation, the fact remains that Vic used the cottage regularly every summer for sleeping purposes, and he intended to return the following summer. Therefore, the cottage constitutes a dwelling for purposes of burglary. (B) is incorrect because a mistake of fact affects criminal guilt only if it shows that the defendant did not have the state of mind required for the crime. As noted above, the state of mind required for burglary is an intent to commit a felony. Any mistake by Doyle as to whether the cottage was occupied does not relate to whether he had the intent to commit a felony in the cottage. The crime of burglary would have been complete if Doyle had broken and entered the cottage with the intent of committing a felony therein, regardless of whether the cottage was occupied. Consequently, Doyle's good faith belief that the cottage was unoccupied would provide him with no defense to a charge of burglary. (C) is incorrect because the breaking needed for burglary requires only minimal force to gain entry. Therefore, raising an unlatched window would be a sufficient use of force to constitute a breaking.

Answer to Question 31

(B) By establishing that he only intended to borrow the television set for a few days, Doyle will show that he did not have the intent to commit a felony. Absent such intent, Doyle cannot be guilty of any underlying felony, which guilt is necessary for a conviction of felony murder. A killing (even if accidental) committed during the course of a felony is murder. Malice is implied from the intent to commit the underlying felony. To be guilty of felony murder, a defendant must be guilty of the underlying felony. Here, the possible felonies being committed by Doyle, during which the death of Vic occurred, would be larceny and burglary. As noted in the answer to the previous question, burglary requires an intent to commit a felony within the dwelling, and larceny requires an intent to permanently deprive a person of his interest in property. If Doyle's only intent was to borrow Vic's television set for a few days, then Doyle lacked the intent to permanently deprive Vic of his interest in the set; *i.e.,* the requisite intent for larceny is missing. Likewise, the absence of intent to steal the set would mean that, at the time of breaking and entering the cottage, Doyle did not intend to commit a felony therein. Consequently, Doyle is not guilty of burglary. Because under these circumstances no felony would have been committed, it cannot be said that the death of Vic occurred during the commission of a felony. Therefore, Doyle would not be guilty of felony murder. (D) is tempting, because generally a conviction of felony murder requires that the death must have been a foreseeable result of commission of the felony. However, some courts do not apply a foreseeability requirement and require only that the underlying felony be malum in se. Furthermore, even those courts applying a foreseeability requirement have been willing to find most deaths occurring during the commission of a felony to be foreseeable. Here, Doyle believed that the cottage was unoccupied for the winter. Thus, it was arguably unforeseeable that Doyle's entering the cottage and taking a television set would result in the death of an occupant, but it is by no means certain that a court would agree. Furthermore, in those jurisdictions that do not require foreseeability of death, Doyle could be convicted of felony murder if the death occurred during the commission of a burglary, because burglary is always classified as a mala in se felony. Because the circumstances in choice (B) would assure Doyle of avoiding conviction in all jurisdictions, (B) is a better answer than (D). (A) incorrectly focuses on intent to kill. Intent to kill is one of the states of mind by which a defendant is deemed to have malice aforethought, which is necessary for a killing to constitute murder. However, this question refers to felony murder, wherein malice aforethought exists in the form of intent to commit a felony. Thus, it is irrelevant whether Doyle intended to kill Vic. If Doyle intended to commit a felony, and Vic's death was a foreseeable result of the commission of that felony, then Doyle will be guilty of felony murder. Regarding (C), it is true that most courts limit the felony murder doctrine to felonies that are inherently dangerous, and that larceny is not considered to be inherently dangerous. However, assuming the existence of the requisite intent, Doyle may have committed burglary, which is deemed to be inherently dangerous. Thus, (C) might provide no defense at all to a charge of felony murder.

Answer to Question 32

(B) The most helpful fact for the prosecution would be that Amos had an opportunity to retreat safely. The general rule is that one may use deadly force in self-defense even if the use of force could be avoided by retreating safely. This rule, however, does not apply to one who is the initial aggressor. Generally, one who begins a fight has no right to use force in his own defense during the fight. But the aggressor can regain his right to use self-defense either (i) by withdrawing and communicating the withdrawal to the other person or (ii) when the other person suddenly escalates a minor fight into one involving deadly force without giving the aggressor the chance to withdraw. Here, Amos was the initial aggressor because he spat on Bob and struck the first blow when he punched Bob in the nose. Bob then escalated the fight into one involving deadly force by pulling a knife. However, Amos would not regain his right to self-defense unless "his back was to the wall"; *i.e.,* if he had a chance to withdraw rather than respond to Bob's deadly force, he had a duty to do so. Thus, the prosecution could overcome Amos's claim of self-defense by establishing that he was very close to the door and could have withdrawn from the confrontation. (A) is incorrect because the fact that Amos initiated the violence does not necessarily extinguish his right of self-defense here, because Bob escalated the fight into one involving deadly force. To rebut Amos's claim under these circumstances, the prosecution must show that Amos had an opportunity to withdraw that he did not use. (C) is incorrect because it is irrelevant to Amos's right to use deadly force in self-defense. The fact that Amos is guilty of weapons violations could be used in a separate prosecution against Amos, but it would have no bearing on his right of self-defense. (D) is also irrelevant to Amos's right of self-defense. Amos was under no duty to retreat or to refrain from arguing with Bob despite Bob's belligerence. The only basis for Amos's losing his right to defend himself was his initiation of the physical contact.

Answer to Question 33

(B) Hector should be convicted of murder and Mort should be found innocent of manslaughter. Murder is the unlawful killing of another human being with malice aforethought, which includes an intent to inflict great bodily injury or an awareness of an unjustifiably high risk to human life. Here, Hector is guilty of murder because his attack was unlawful and resulted in Amos's death, and it was committed with malice aforethought. It does not matter that the death would not have occurred had Mort intervened to aid Amos, because failure of another to provide assistance is not a superseding intervening cause that will relieve a defendant from liability. If Mort had done something more, such as hiding Amos from rescuers, that would probably be a superseding intervening act that would have relieved Hector from liability. Manslaughter can arise from establishing a provocation defense to a murder charge or from a killing resulting from criminal negligence or an unlawful act. Mort has not committed manslaughter here because there is no law that requires citizens to aid others in distress, even if their lives are in peril. Such a duty can be imposed under certain circumstances, such as where the defendant is the victim's parent or the defendant has contracted to aid the victim, but not under the circumstances here. Therefore, (B) is correct and (A), (C), and (D) are incorrect.

Answer to Question 34

(C) Dolan is guilty of larceny because, while having mere custody of the television set, he carried it away from the hotel intending to permanently deprive the hotel owner of his interest in the set. Larceny consists of the taking and carrying away of tangible personal property of another by trespass, with intent to permanently (or for an unreasonable time) deprive the person of his interest in the property. Property must be taken from someone who has a possessory interest superior to that of the defendant. If the defendant has custody of the property, rather than possession, his misappropriation of the property is larceny. Possession involves a much greater scope of authority to deal with the property than does custody. Here, Dolan only had the authority to use the television set for viewing purposes while he was staying at the hotel. Thus, Dolan had only enough authority to deal with the set as to indicate that he had custody of it rather than possession. Consequently, the hotel owner had a possessory interest in the set superior to that of Dolan. Dolan took the set by trespass (without the consent of the owner) and carried it away with the intent to permanently deprive the owner of his interest in the set. Thus, Dolan is guilty of larceny. (D) is incorrect because larceny by trick occurs when the victim consents to the defendant's taking possession of the property but such consent has been induced by a misrepresentation. Here, the hotel owner never consented to give Dolan possession of the television set, through misrepresentation or otherwise. Instead, Dolan simply took the set without the consent of the owner. Therefore, this is not larceny by trick. (B) is incorrect for a similar reason. The offense of false pretenses consists of obtaining title to the property of another by an intentional or knowing false statement of past or existing fact, with intent to defraud the other. Dolan made no misrepresentations to the hotel owner, nor did the owner convey title to the television set to Dolan. Thus, Dolan is not guilty of false pretenses. (A) is incorrect because embezzlement requires the fraudulent conversion of property of another by a person in lawful possession of that property. Dolan never had lawful possession of the television set. The taking of the set without the consent of the hotel owner was trespassory. Thus, Dolan has not committed embezzlement.

Answer to Question 35

(C) Digby is guilty of burglary because the right of occupancy belonged to Tanner. However, the fact that there was no burning of the structure means that Digby is guilty of attempted arson, rather than arson. Burglary is a breaking and entering of the dwelling of another at nighttime, with the intent of committing a felony therein. A breaking requires some use of force to gain entry, but minimal force is sufficient. In determining whether the dwelling is that of another, occupancy rather than ownership is material. Thus, an owner can commit burglary of her own structure if it is rented and used as a dwelling by someone else. Here, although Digby owned the cottage, Tanner had the right to occupy it pursuant to a lease. Thus, for purposes of the crime of burglary, Digby is deemed to have entered the dwelling of another. Although Digby used her own key to gain access to the cottage, this was still an unconsented use of force to effectuate entry, thereby constituting a breaking. This breaking and entering of Tanner's dwelling occurred in the evening. At the time of the entry, Digby intended to commit the felony of arson. Consequently, all the elements of burglary are in place, making Digby guilty of this crime.

Arson consists of the malicious burning of the dwelling of another. There is a requirement of some damage to the fiber of the wood or other combustible material. As with burglary, ownership of the structure is not material for determining whether the dwelling is that of another; rather, the right to occupancy is material. Digby left a lighted cigarette on the mattress, intending to burn down the entire cottage. However, Tanner extinguished the fire before any damage was done to the structure of the cottage, even mere charring. Absent such damage, arson cannot have been committed. Digby did commit attempted arson. A criminal attempt is an act which, although done with the intention of committing a crime, falls short of completing the crime. The defendant must intend to perform an act and obtain a result that, if achieved, would constitute a crime. Also, the defendant must have committed an act beyond mere preparation for the offense. Digby intended to perform an act that would have culminated in the crime of arson. By soaking the mattress with gasoline and leaving a lighted cigarette on it, Digby committed an act that came dangerously close to successfully burning the cottage. This act in combination with the intent to commit arson means that Digby is guilty of attempted arson. (A) is incorrect because there can be no arson as to the mattress. Arson requires a burning of a dwelling. Because the cottage was not burned, Digby is not guilty of arson. (B) is incorrect because the key element in determining whether a dwelling is that of another, for both arson and burglary, is the right of occupancy. Under the terms of his lease, Tanner had the right to occupy the cottage for one year. Therefore, Digby's ownership of the cottage will not be a defense to either arson or burglary. (D) is incorrect because, as explained above, Digby's use of a key to gain access to the cottage without the consent of the person who had the right of occupancy is deemed to be a use of force to gain entry, in the same way as if a person who did not own the cottage were to gain entry by means of a skeleton key.

Answer to Question 36

(D) Coe's motion should be denied. The United States Supreme Court has held that when the only issue is that of probable cause for issuance of a warrant, the name of the informer is a type of privileged information. (Only if the informer were a material witness to the crime might his identity have to be revealed at or before trial.) The validity of a warrant based on information obtained from informers is based on the totality of the circumstances. (A) and (C) are incorrect because the Confrontation Clause and the right of cross-examination of one's accusers have been deemed to be fundamental rights, but they do not apply when the issue is only that of probable cause for issuance of a warrant, as compared to guilt or innocence. (B) is incorrect because, as noted above, unless the informer were also a material witness to the crime, his identity need not be revealed. Here, the facts do not indicate that the informer was a material witness to the crime.

Answer to Question 37

(D) Coe's objection should be overruled. A confession obtained in violation of *Miranda,* but otherwise voluntary, can be used for the limited purpose of impeaching a defendant who testifies at trial. In contrast, an involuntary confession cannot be used to impeach. (A) is too broad a statement. Although a confession obtained in violation of *Miranda* is inadmissible in the state's case in chief as evidence of guilt, as discussed above, such evidence is admissible for limited purposes. (B) is wrong. Advance permission from the court is not a requirement if the confession is used to impeach. (C) is a correct statement but it does not speak directly to the issue of whether the confession is admissible and to what extent.

Answer to Question 38

(B) Dunston conspired with Xavier to have Xavier rape Dunston's wife. Dunston would therefore be vicariously liable for Xavier's crime. While at common law a man could not rape his own wife, he could be found guilty under principles of accomplice liability on these facts. (A) is incorrect because there are no grounds for holding Dirk vicariously liable. (C) is incorrect because a young woman cannot be convicted of aiding and abetting her own statutory rape even if she solicits a man to have sexual relations with her. (D) is incorrect because the modern trend is not to treat an accessory after the fact as a party to the felony, but rather to find him guilty of obstruction of justice.

Answer to Question 39

(B) The crime with which Dave is charged is both a specific intent crime and one that requires knowledge. Thus, the jury instructions should touch on both these elements. (A) is wrong because it touches on neither the element of intent nor knowledge. (C) is wrong because it fails to include the element of intent. It is not sufficient that Dave merely know that he is carrying contraband; he must also have the specific intent of smuggling in illegal narcotics. (D) is not the best answer. Although a defendant may be deemed to possess the requisite knowledge if he deliberately avoids discovering the facts when he can readily do so, this instruction fails to touch on the element of intent. Thus, (B) is the best answer because it includes both elements of the crime.

Answer to Question 40

(C) In most states, this would be a strict liability crime. Therefore, Dave's best defense is that he did not sell the young girl the wine. (A) is not a valid defense, because under a strict liability statute it is illegal to sell to a minor even if she presented a false I.D. Thus, if Dave had actually made a sale to the young girl, he would have violated the statute even if he had asked for her driver's license. Similarly, (B) is a wrong answer because under a strict liability statute it is illegal to sell to a minor even if the defendant did not know that the purchaser was a minor. Even if the statute were not a strict liability crime, (C) would be his best defense. (B) would only be a defense if the statute required knowledge of age. (D) ignores the stated facts that the seller of the liquor is the guilty party, not the seller's employer.

Answer to Question 41

(D) Robbery is larceny from the person or presence of the victim by means of violence or intimidation. The use of force constituting a battery is sufficient, and if the defendant uses force to overcome the victim's resistance to the taking, there is sufficient force to constitute a robbery. All that is required for taking is that the defendant have possession of the item, and the slightest movement will suffice for the carrying away. Hence, Drew could be charged with robbery, which is the most serious crime of these four.

Answer to Question 42

(C) (C) is Rudy's best defense because the definition of common law burglary requires that the defendant break into the dwelling place with the intent to commit a *felony*. If Rudy actually believed that Jim owed him the money, he could not have been committing larceny because there was no intent to deprive another of his property. Absent the intent to commit a felony, Rudy would not have had the specific intent necessary to be found guilty of burglary. (A) is incorrect because the "irresistible impulse" must be a product of some mental disease as opposed to anger. (B) is incorrect because the theory of pari delicto is a tort theory, not a criminal defense. (D) is wrong because a mistake as to the *law* is not an excuse for an act otherwise criminal.

Answer to Question 43

(C) In *Payton v. New York* (1980), the United States Supreme Court held that, absent an emergency, a forcible, warrantless entry into a residence for the purpose of making a felony arrest is an unconstitutional violation of the Fourth Amendment as made applicable to the states by the Fourteenth Amendment. No exigent circumstances justified the warrantless arrest, and searches of a home without a warrant are presumptively unreasonable.

Answer to Question 44

(B) If, after being given his *Miranda* warnings, the accused invokes his right to counsel, all interrogation must stop until counsel is present. "Interrogation" includes any words or actions by the police that the police should know are likely to produce an incriminating response. The defendant may volunteer information to the police at any time. (A) is not the best answer. While it is true that booking is not a critical stage for purposes of the right to counsel, that is not the reason the statement will be allowed. The statement would be excluded if it had been the result of interrogation during the booking. (C) is wrong; there is no illegal police conduct set forth in the facts. (D) is an incorrect statement of the law.

Answer to Question 45

(C) Zack intended merely to retrieve his property. Therefore, he had no intent to commit a felony when he entered the apartment. (A) is wrong because Zack was no longer an occupant of the apartment and so could not consent to the entry. (B) is wrong because opening the closed but unlocked window was a breaking. (D) is not his best defense. While it is true that he took only his property, he would have been guilty if he entered the apartment with the intent to commit a felony inside.

Answer to Question 46

(C) Conspiracy to commit burglary requires an intent to commit a burglary. Since the intent was only to retrieve Zack's property and not to commit a felony, they did not have the necessary intent. (A) is wrong; there was an overt act. (B) is wrong; there was an agreement. (D) is wrong; even if an actual burglary was not committed, they could be found guilty of conspiracy.

Answer to Question 47

(D) To be guilty of burglary, a person must have the intent to commit a felony in the structure at the time of entry. Attempted burglary requires the same specific intent. Since Dexter merely intended to retrieve what he believed was his own property, he did not intend to commit a felony. Thus, (A) and (B) are wrong. Likewise, (C) is wrong because, since Dexter believed the computer was his own, he lacked the intent to permanently deprive Boss of his interest, which would be necessary for his act to constitute larceny. Thus, (D) is correct.

Answer to Question 48

(C) The statute punishes a battery committed against a victim the defendant *knows* is a state official. Therefore, if the jury believes Rod's testimony that he did not know the man was a state official, they must find him not guilty of the charged violation. This is not a public welfare offense, but a particular form of battery. Thus, (B) is incorrect. (D) is incorrect because the statute requires knowledge of the status of the victim. (A) is wrong. There is no duty on the part of the state to warn Rod. If Rod knew, he will be guilty; if Rod did not know, he will not be guilty.

Answer to Question 49

(C) Even though Edgar may have been in custody and may not yet have received his *Miranda* warnings, no violation of Edgar's constitutional rights occurs if he volunteers revelations of his criminal conduct, especially when they are unrelated to the crime for which he is under arrest. (A) is wrong. The fact that a confession offered in a federal prosecution was made to a state police officer will not automatically allow it into evidence. It will be suppressed if it is the product of some violation of the accused's constitutional rights by the state officer. (B) is wrong; if Edgar had not been formally charged, his Sixth Amendment right to counsel would not be implicated by his confession to Oscar. However, this would not prevent suppression of the confession if his Fifth Amendment *Miranda* rights were violated. (D) is not the best answer because *Miranda* violations can occur before a formal arrest.

Answer to Question 50

(A) The crime of conspiracy requires that each conspirator intends to achieve an unlawful goal. If the jury believes Xavier, he must be found innocent since he did not intend to achieve an unlawful goal. (C) is therefore incorrect. (B) is incorrect because his act of prevention would not have excused the conspiracy if he had the proper mental state. (D) is incorrect because the privilege to apprehend criminals is not in issue here.

Answer to Question 51

(A) This choice is correct because it reflects the fact that Yancy did not intend to achieve the objective of the conspiracy—to permanently deprive the owner of his property—since Yancy thought Zack was the owner. It follows that (C) and (D) are incorrect. (B) is incorrect because he could be guilty even if he did not have a corrupt motive.

Answer to Question 52

(B) If the jury believes both Xavier and Yancy, neither could be guilty of conspiracy for the reasons stated above. Therefore, Zack could not be guilty of conspiracy because, at common law, conspiracy requires at least two guilty parties. (C) and (D) are therefore incorrect. (A) is a nonsensical statement.

Answer to Question 53

(A) Under Federal Rule of Evidence 801, after a witness has testified, statements of prior identification are admissible to prove their truth unless the defendant can show that the circumstances of the identification were unnecessarily suggestive and likely to result in irreparable misidentification. There is no evidence of that in the facts. (B) is wrong since there is no right to counsel at a photo display. (C) is wrong because it goes to the weight to be given the evidence rather than its admissibility. (D) is wrong because the photograph identification would not be considered a critical stage.

Answer to Question 54

(B) A search incident to a full custodial arrest can be made without a warrant or probable cause to believe that evidence or weapons will be found. Thus, (B) is correct and (D) is wrong. (A) is wrong because the police officer need not fear for his safety to make a valid search incident to a lawful arrest. (C) is wrong because, incident to a lawful arrest, the police may conduct a warrantless search of the area within the defendant's "wingspan." This includes the glove compartment.

Answer to Question 55

(D) Sarah's act was not only the "but for" cause, but also, since the death was the natural foreseeable result, the "proximate" cause. The fact that other preexisting conditions contributed to the death does not absolve Sarah. (A) is wrong; there is no requirement that the defendant's acts be the sole cause of the result. Most results have more than one cause. (B) is wrong; we all will die at some point.

Answer to Question 56

(A) Dopson had a reasonable expectation of privacy in his bedroom closet. The search of the closet was not based on a valid warrant or circumstances justifying an exception to the warrant requirement. (B) is wrong. There is no such rule of law. (C) is wrong; allowing the police to enter the house is no "consent" to search the bedroom closet. (D) is wrong; a search of the closet would be outside the area of the immediate control of the defendant and could not be justified as a search incident to an arrest.

Answer to Question 57

(C) To hold Ken liable as an accessory, the state must show that his assistance or encouragement was given with intent that the crime be committed or knowing that he was aiding a crime. The facts indicate neither state of mind was present on Ken's part. (A) is wrong because it involves a mistaken legal premise insofar as liability as an accessory is concerned. (B) is accurate in part, but ignores the requirement of a mental state. (D) is wrong because the accessory can be liable even if he did not "cause" the crime.

Answer to Question 58

(C) The entry in Della's apartment and her arrest without a warrant, probable cause, or circumstances permitting an exception from these requirements were illegal. The statements she made thereafter were fruits of the original illegality and are to be suppressed unless the taint is purged. The giving of *Miranda* warnings is not sufficient. (A) is wrong because the facts indicate that the statements were voluntarily made. (B) is an incorrect statement of law. (D) is wrong because *Miranda* warnings are only required prior to custodial interrogation.

Answer to Question 59

(B) After arrest a defendant has a right to remain silent, and his silence cannot be used against him. (A) is wrong; the question is improper but not for the reason set forth in (A). (C) and (D) are incorrect. Statements made without proper *Miranda* warnings can sometimes be used to impeach, but the defendant's silence would not be classified as a prior statement.

Answer to Question 60

(C) Bill's act constituted an unlawful application of force to the person of another and is, thus, a battery. Use of a deadly weapon in the commission of a battery elevates the crime to aggravated battery. (A) is incorrect because a person must *reasonably* believe that he is faced with imminent death or great bodily harm in order to use deadly force. The accidental blow struck by Randall would not rise to that level. (B) is wrong because this is clearly battery, not assault. (D) is wrong because battery requires only an offensive touching, not an injury; in any case, this answer does not address the element of aggravation.

Answer to Question 61

(B) The mental state necessary for criminal battery is either intentional or reckless conduct. Clearly Randall did not intend to have bodily contact with Bill, and in light of the circumstances it will be unlikely that his conduct will be considered such an extreme deviation from ordinary behavior as to establish recklessness. (A) is wrong; a serious injury is not required for battery. (C) is wrong because recklessness requires a much greater deviation from ordinary behavior than simply a "failure to exercise due care." (D) is not as accurate as (B). It does not address the critical issue in the case—the mental state of Randall.

Answer to Question 62

(C) Driving onto and along a crowded sidewalk is the kind of reckless conduct likely to cause serious bodily injury, which justifies a "depraved heart" theory of common law murder. In (A), the battery on the defendant will be considered a provoking event, which would mitigate the homicide to voluntary manslaughter. (B) has no indication of intent or the reckless disregard of life that might be sufficient for murder. (D) suggests an accidental death lacking intent to kill, cause serious bodily harm, or reckless disregard of life.

Answer to Question 63

(D) The Supreme Court has held that it is unconstitutional for an officer to use deadly force to effectuate an arrest of an unarmed escaping felon unless the officer has probable cause to believe that the suspect poses a significant threat of death or serious physical injury to the officer or others. In jurisdictions following this approach, the use of deadly force to apprehend a fleeing felon is reasonable only where it is necessary to prevent the felon's escape *and* where the felon threatens death or serious bodily harm. Other jurisdictions allow use of deadly force whenever necessary to prevent a fleeing felon's escape. Regardless of the approach used, here it does not appear that shooting at Elmer was necessary to prevent his escape or that Elmer threatened serious bodily injury. Thus, (A), (B), and (C) are incorrect. (D) is a correct statement of the law because Taylor had the requisite intent for homicide.

Answer to Question 64

(D) Since Greg and Bob were charged with conspiracy to steal, it must be established that they intended to commit the crime of larceny or some other theft offense. Bob and Greg intended only to recover the tool box that Bob believed to have been wrongfully withheld by Don. Thus, there was no intention to commit a crime. (A) is wrong because there was an agreement. (B) is wrong because regardless of the fact that Bob disputed Don's claim, if Bob knew that Don had the right to hold the tool box until the dispute was resolved, Bob would have been committing a crime by taking the tool box. (C) is wrong because it refers to facts that occurred after the alleged conspiracy was entered into and has no relevance to whether a conspiracy existed in the first place.

Answer to Question 65

(B) Larceny is a specific intent crime, and the defendant must have had the intent to take the property of another. If Greg, as Bob's agent, was intending to take only Bob's tool box, he had no intent to take the property of another. (A) is wrong, of course, because he did not have the consent of the owner of the tool box he took. (C) is incorrect because it is not a defense to a charge of larceny that the defendant was not intending to keep the item taken for his own use. (D) is incorrect because, although once he found out his mistake, he may have intended to return the tool box, he could have just as easily decided to keep it.

Answer to Question 66

(A)   The question here is one of statutory interpretation. The status of Alan's conviction will rest on how the appellate court interprets the statute. If the court interprets the statute to include the ice pick, Alan's conviction is proper. Thus, (A) is correct. (B) is wrong because it does not reach the issue of statutory interpretation; the statute prohibits a concealed "knife or dagger," not merely a concealed "weapon." Thus, Alan's "admission" is not enough to convict him under this statute. (C) and (D) are wrong because Alan's motive or intent is irrelevant; the statute makes carrying a concealed knife or dagger a crime regardless of the intent.

Answer to Question 67

(D)   A person is privileged to use deadly force to prevent a crime only if it is a *dangerous* felony. Shoplifting is not a dangerous felony; thus, Customer's use of deadly force was not privileged. Therefore, Defendant was entitled to defend himself against Customer's improper use of deadly force by using deadly force himself. (A) is wrong because Defendant did not initiate an assault. (B) is wrong because even if Defendant intended to kill Customer, his action was justified. (C) is a misstatement of the law and of the facts.

Answer to Question 68

(C)   Clearly Joe was acting in self-defense, and even if throwing a heavy ashtray could be deemed to be deadly force, Joe had the right to defend himself against the unprivileged attack with the use of deadly force. (A) and (B) are incorrect because Joe's presence in the house and failure to leave immediately did not give Fred a privilege to use deadly force against him. (D) is irrelevant.

Answer to Question 69

(C)   To hold a person liable under the theory of accessory or accomplice liability, the prosecution must show that the defendant helped with the crime with the intent to see the crime committed. Unless the prosecution can establish the unlawful mental state, there can be no criminal liability. Since Bob did not have the intent to see a larceny committed, he cannot be guilty. (A) is wrong because he did not have the necessary mental state. (B) is wrong; the issue is not whether he had reason to believe the car was Rick's, but whether he intended a larceny to take place. (D) is wrong because the fact that Rick would probably have stolen the car anyway will not relieve the defendant from liability if he helped with the necessary intent.

Answer to Question 70

(D)   Bubba shot Joe, intending to kill him, and Joe died. The only issue is whether Bubba's act was the proximate cause of Joe's death. Proximate cause is found when the results are the natural and foreseeable results of the defendant's acts. Infections and negligent medical treatment are deemed to be a foreseeable risk in homicide cases; since Joe died of pneumonia that resulted from the bullet, most courts would conclude that proximate cause has been established. (A) would be correct if proximate cause could not be established. (B) and (C) are wrong. The fact that Joe already had an incurable disease or would likely have died from another cause will not negate proximate cause.

Answer to Question 71

(D)   The degree of murder under the statute is determined by the defendant's mental state—whether the killing was intentional and accomplished after premeditation and deliberation. The defendant's relationship with the victim and the manner of killing may have evidentiary significance with regard to the defendant's mental state, but do not themselves distinguish first from second degree murder. Thus, (A) and (C) are incorrect. The causal relationship between the defendant's act and the death of the victim may determine whether the act is murder, but once that analytical hurdle has been passed, it has no further significance as to the degree of murder. Therefore, (B) is incorrect.

Answer to Question 72

(A) Doppler could properly be convicted of murder. Doppler intended to, and in fact did, commit a dangerous felony (*i.e.*, robbery). This intent to commit a felony constitutes malice aforethought for common law murder purposes. Moreover, depending on the nature and dosage of the drug, Doppler may have been acting in the face of such high risk that his actions evidenced a wanton and malignant heart. Thus, murder is the most serious crime that Doppler can be convicted of, and thus (B), (C), and (D) are necessarily wrong.

Answer to Question 73

(D) Defendant's use of force was privileged because it was reasonably necessary to defend him from Tony's unlawful attack. Defendant had no duty to retreat. Furthermore, Defendant did not lose the privilege of self-defense because he started the fight. He would not be considered the aggressor by provoking the fight with mere words. Thus, since Defendant's use of force was privileged, he can be convicted of none of the listed crimes. Therefore, (D) is correct, and (A), (B), and (C) are incorrect.

Answer to Question 74

(A) As soon as Deanna's boyfriend informed her that driscamine was a controlled substance and she decided to keep it, she violated the statute, since she willfully possessed a controlled substance. (B) is incorrect because the statute does not punish mere possession; the possession must be "willful." (C) is incorrect because ignorance of the law is generally no excuse. It clearly does not negate the mental state required for this statutory crime. (D) is incorrect because the statute does not punish willful acquisition but willful possession.

Answer to Question 75

(C) Larceny is the taking and carrying away of the personal property in the possession of another with the intent to permanently deprive the other of the property. It is possible to commit larceny of your own property if another person, such as a bailee, has a superior right to possession of the property at that time. Since Zelda had a right to possession of the gown until she was paid, Brenda committed larceny when she had Cheryl take the gown without Zelda's consent. (B) is wrong. A person can be guilty even though she did not personally engage in the behavior if she acts through an innocent agent. (D) is slightly off center. Brenda is guilty but not for the reason stated in (D). She would be guilty even if she had not made the promise to pay.

Answer to Question 76

(D) The crime of larceny requires an intent to steal. Cheryl was operating under an honest mistake of fact. (A) is incorrect because there was no conspiracy; if there were a conspiracy, Cheryl would be guilty. (B) is incorrect because a person can be guilty of a crime even though someone else directs her to do it. (B) does not state the reason why Cheryl would not be guilty. (C) is incorrect because the fact that Milt handed it over would not absolve Cheryl of liability.

Answer to Question 77

(C)   To be liable as an aider and abettor (*i.e.*, an accomplice), the defendant must encourage or aid in commission of the underlying crime with intent that the crime be committed or, in certain cases, with knowledge that it was to be committed. Since Roy had no knowledge of the crime, he could not be an aider and abettor. (A) is wrong because mere presence at the scene of the crime is not enough to make Roy a principal in the second degree. (B) is wrong because, as stated, there must be intent or knowledge to be an aider and abettor. (D) is wrong because if the requisite intent is present, the defendant can be liable even though he did not "cause" the crime.

EVIDENCE QUESTIONS

Question 1

In a personal injury case involving a two-car collision, Plaintiff wishes to introduce a sworn deposition taken from Witt, a witness who died two weeks before the case came to trial. In the deposition, taken in Plaintiff's attorney's office, Witt stated that she saw Defendant run a red light at the time of the collision with Plaintiff's car. Both Plaintiff and Defendant's attorneys were present at the deposition. Defendant objects in the appropriate manner to the introduction of Witt's statement.

How should the court rule on the admissibility of the deposition?

(A) Admissible, because Defendant had an opportunity to cross-examine Witt at the time the deposition was taken.

(B) Admissible, as a dying declaration.

(C) Inadmissible, because the statement was not made while Witt was testifying in court.

(D) Inadmissible, because Defendant has no opportunity to cross-examine Witt at trial.

Questions 2-5 are based on the following fact situation:

Winston owned and operated an exclusive jewelry store, and employed Abigail and Charles as clerks in his store. One day, Charles reported to Winston that he saw Abigail stealing pieces of less expensive jewelry from the store.

Winston thereupon discharged Abigail and brought a civil action against her for the value of various pieces of jewelry missing from the store.

2. At the trial of the action, Winston calls Charles as his first witness. Charles testifies that he "does not remember" either having seen Abigail take anything from the store or having told Winston that she had done so. Winston then takes the witness stand and proposes to testify to what Charles had told him about seeing Abigail stealing pieces of less expensive jewelry from the store. Assuming appropriate objection by Abigail, such testimony by Winston would be:

(A) Admissible as a statement against interest by Charles.

(B) Admissible as proper impeachment of Charles's testimony.

(C) Inadmissible as irrelevant.

(D) Inadmissible hearsay if offered to prove thefts by Abigail.

3. Winston then calls Abigail as an adverse witness, and asks her one question—if it is not true that she has stolen jewelry from his store. She refuses to answer, claiming a privilege against self-incrimination. The trial court should:

(A) Order her to disclose to the court in camera the circumstances of her removing the jewelry from the store, so that the court can determine whether she reasonably fears prosecution for a crime.

(B) Order her to answer because the privilege against self-incrimination does not apply in civil proceedings.

(C) Sustain her claim of privilege, as no witness can be compelled to answer questions that may tend to incriminate.

(D) Sustain her claim of privilege only if it appears from other evidence that she in fact is a likely subject of criminal prosecution by either federal or state authorities.

4. Winston then offers in evidence a certified copy of a court record that indicates Abigail

had been convicted of grand larceny (a felony) six years previously. The trial court should:

(A) Admit the record as relevant character evidence if the larceny involved dishonest acts toward an employer.

(B) Admit the record as impeachment evidence.

(C) Exclude the record as irrelevant because as yet Abigail has given no testimony to be impeached.

(D) Exclude the record because the conviction is too remote and does not necessarily reflect on her credibility as a witness in the present proceedings.

5. Winston then offers in evidence a letter, addressed to him at the store, which reads:

> Dear Winston: I'm sorry that I took some jewelry pieces from the store, but I needed to raise some money quickly for emergency medical care. I'll try to repay you as soon as I can. Please give me another chance.
>
> /s/ Abigail.

Winston also testifies that he is familiar with Abigail's handwriting, and recognizes the signature on the letter as being hers.

Assuming appropriate objection by Abigail, who claims that she did not sign the letter, the trial court should:

(A) Exclude the letter for lack of foundation because lay opinion testimony regarding handwriting identification is not admissible.

(B) Admit the letter but instruct the jury that it is up to them to decide whether the letter is authentic.

(C) Admit the letter as authentic and instruct the jury accordingly.

(D) Exclude the letter unless its authenticity is established by a preponderance of the evidence.

Question 6

Donald was on trial for a criminal offense. The prosecutor had a tape recording of Donald's voice and called Wanda to the stand to authenticate the voice as Donald's. The only time Wanda had heard Donald's voice before was after Donald's arrest.

Assuming a proper foundation has been laid, may Wanda properly authenticate Donald's voice?

(A) Yes, if Wanda is now familiar with Donald's voice.

(B) Yes, but only if Wanda is an expert on voices.

(C) No, because Wanda's testimony would be inadmissible hearsay.

(D) No, because Wanda heard Donald's voice after Donald was arrested.

Question 7

Who, among the following, would **not** be permitted to verify writing as the handwriting of Darrin, a criminal defendant charged with forgery?

(A) An expert witness who examined it and compared it with a genuine specimen of Darrin's handwriting.

(B) The jury, when offered a comparison known to be Darrin's, obtained after Darrin's arrest.

(C) A police officer who had a copy of Darrin's true handwriting.

(D) A secretary who had worked for Darrin for five years.

Question 8

Beatrix wanted to buy an antique chair that she had seen at a local antique dealer's display show. Beatrix tried to make an offer for the chair and to ask other questions of Simonson, the owner, but was unable to do so successfully because Beatrix spoke only the Dutch language and Simonson spoke only English.

The day after Beatrix saw the chair, she asked her brother Henrik if he would speak to Simonson about the chair on her behalf and generally act as a go-between. Henrik agreed to do so. Henrik went to see Simonson and they reached an agreement that Beatrix would pay Simonson $15,000 for the chair. The agreement was not reduced to writing. That very afternoon, Henrik told Beatrix of the agreement with Simonson. Two days later, Henrik died.

On the day following Henrik's death, Beatrix brought Simonson a certified check for $15,000. She showed the check to Simonson and pointed at the chair. Simonson shook his head vigorously and made various hand gestures indicating that he would not accept $15,000 for the chair. Beatrix sued Simonson on a contract theory.

At the trial, Beatrix, through an interpreter, wished to testify to a conversation she had with Henrik, where Henrik said, "Simonson has agreed to sell you the chair for $15,000."

If the jurisdiction has a typical "Dead Man Act," what effect will the Act have upon the admissibility of the conversation with Henrik?

(A) It will render the conversation inadmissible because a civil action is involved.

(B) It will render the conversation inadmissible because Beatrix is an interested party.

(C) None, because Simonson is not a protected party.

(D) None, because a civil action is involved.

Question 9

Jim and Emma were driving in their motor home from their residence in Florida to see their grandchildren in New York. It was late at night; Jim was driving and Emma was asleep in a bed at the rear of the motor home. Suddenly, there was a collision and Emma was jolted awake. She rushed to the front of the vehicle and saw that it had struck a small foreign car. Jim said, "I just ran a red light and hit that car." Emma got out of her vehicle and began to inspect the damage to both the motor home and the foreign car. A woman said, "What happened?" Not knowing that the woman was a passenger in and owner of the car that had been struck, Emma said, "My husband ran a red light."

At trial of a negligence action against Jim and Emma filed by the occupants of the car that was struck, the plaintiff's first witness is the woman, a plaintiff, who will testify as to Emma's statement. Should the trial court admit this evidence?

(A) Yes, because it will impeach Emma if she denies having said it in her case-in-chief.

(B) Yes, because it is an admission by a party-opponent.

(C) No, because Emma had no foundational knowledge when she made the statement.

(D) No, because Emma did not know she was talking to an occupant of the car when she spoke.

Questions 10-13 are based on the following fact situation:

Kathy was employed as an auto mechanic by the Arrow Body Shop. She often test-drove cars she repaired. During one routine test-drive, Kathy was exceeding the posted speed limit when she collided with Elmer's vehicle at an intersection. Elmer had failed to stop at the stop sign preceding the intersection. Elmer was thrown out of his car into a ditch and his car was totaled. When she saw that Elmer had been seriously injured, Kathy ran to the ditch to help him. She told him, "I'm really sorry. I guess I didn't fix the brakes as well as I thought." Later, Kathy readjusted the brakes of the vehicle she had been driving at the time of the accident. Elmer brought an action against Arrow Body Shop for personal injuries and property damage.

10. At trial, Elmer called Bystander to testify to Kathy's statement about the brakes after the accident. Arrow's objection to Bystander's testimony should be:

    (A) Sustained, because Kathy's statement is inadmissible against Arrow.

    (B) Sustained, because Elmer did not stop at the stop sign.

    (C) Overruled, because it is a declaration against interest.

    (D) Overruled, because it is an admission of a party-opponent.

11. Elmer offered evidence proving that Kathy had readjusted the brakes of her vehicle after the accident. Arrow's objection to the evidence should be:

    (A) Overruled, because it tends to prove Kathy's negligence.

    (B) Overruled, because it is relevant to Kathy's state of mind.

    (C) Sustained, because it constitutes assertive conduct.

    (D) Sustained, for public policy reasons.

12. Kathy sought to introduce evidence proving that she had a good driving record. The evidence is:

    (A) Inadmissible, because it is character evidence.

    (B) Inadmissible, because it is self-serving.

    (C) Admissible, because it is character evidence.

    (D) Admissible, because it is habit evidence.

13. Kathy brought a counterclaim against Elmer, contending that his negligence

caused the accident. She calls Allen, Elmer's friend, to testify to the fact that Elmer never stops at the stop sign at the accident intersection and invariably "runs" every stop sign. Elmer's objection to Allen's testimony should be:

    (A) Sustained, because it is not the best evidence.

    (B) Sustained, because character evidence is inadmissible in a civil case.

    (C) Overruled, because it is evidence of habit.

    (D) Overruled, because it is self-serving.

Question 14

Violet, a pedestrian, was struck by a car in a hit-and-run accident. Pamela, a police officer, arrived half an hour after the accident. Violet was in shock and came in and out of consciousness. As Pamela applied first aid, Violet muttered, "I know I'm going to die. Oh God, he ran the light!" Violet fell back into unconsciousness, but revived again and muttered, "Why didn't he stop?" Pamela heard Violet's comments clearly and made a note of them. Good police work by Pamela and others led to the discovery that Daft was driving the car that struck Violet. Almost miraculously, Violet survived, although her injuries would leave her with some severe disabilities. Violet filed a tort action against Daft. Before the case came to trial, Violet died of a heart attack. The causes of the heart attack were totally unrelated to the accident. The laws of the jurisdiction allow for survival of personal injury actions. Thus, Violet's estate is substituted for Violet as plaintiff.

Plaintiff's attorney seeks to have Pamela testify to Violet's statements at the time of the accident. How will the court rule?

(A) Inadmissible, because Violet did not die as a result of the accident.

(B) Inadmissible, because this is a civil case and not a criminal matter.

(C) Admissible, because Violet's statements were present sense impressions.

(D) Admissible, because the statements were made at a time when Violet feared impending death.

Question 15

Pye's and Delta's cars collided at an intersection. The impact of the collision was sufficient to cause both cars to overturn. Immediately after the accident occurred, Wrench came upon the scene. Wrench noted that the wheels of both cars were still spinning, and that the wheels of Delta's car were spinning faster than the wheels of Pye's car.

At the trial that arises out of the collision, Pye's attorney calls Wrench to the stand. Wrench testifies that he is an automobile mechanic with 12 years' experience. Wrench also testifies that he arrived at the scene immediately after the accident and saw the wheels on both cars still spinning. Pye's attorney asks Wrench to testify as to what speed the respective cars were traveling at the time of the accident based upon his observations of the spinning wheels. Delta's attorney objects.

Should Wrench's testimony regarding the speed of the cars be admitted?

(A) Yes, as Wrench's personal opinion.

(B) Yes, as a matter based upon personal observation.

(C) No, unless Wrench has been qualified as an expert in accident reconstruction.

(D) No, unless there is another witness to corroborate Wrench's presence at the accident scene.

Question 16

Laura, a pedestrian, heard a horn sounding. She looked up and saw two cars (driven by Porter and Davidson) enter an intersection and collide. Porter sued Davidson, and Porter's attorney calls Laura to the stand as a witness. On direct examination, she is asked to describe the accident scene, position of the cars in the intersection, etc. On cross-examination, Davidson's attorney goes over the same ground with the witness. He asks her whether there was any broken glass on the pavement, to which she responds, "Yes, lots of it," and before Davidson's lawyer can ask his next question, Laura blurts out, "They had to be going over 50!" Davidson's attorney moves to strike the statement.

How should the court rule?

(A) Strike it, as unresponsive to any question asked.

(B) Strike it, because Laura had no way of knowing how fast the cars were traveling.

(C) Not to strike, because Davidson's attorney "opened the door" to anything Laura might say about the accident.

(D) Not to strike, because the statement accuses both cars of going over 50, and is not prejudicial to only one side.

Question 17

A state court is *least* likely to take judicial notice of which of the following?

(A) The blood type that occurs with greatest frequency in the population is O-positive.

(B) Main Street, upon which the courthouse is situated, runs north and south.

(C) The sun rose at 6:52 a.m. on Friday, December 12, of last year.

(D) In Australian law, there is no private action for environmental issues.

Question 18

In its lead editorial in the Sunday edition, *The Daily Bugle,* a suburban daily newspaper, printed the following: "There is only one expression that accurately describes the activities of businessman-real estate developer Rodney Richman in our community. That expression is 'common thief,' and Richman knows it." Rodney Richman promptly filed suit against *The Daily Bugle* for defamation.

During the course of the presentation of Richman's case, Richman sought to put Sarge on the stand. Sarge is prepared to testify that Richman once saved the life of a fellow soldier in Vietnam.

If the newspaper's lawyer objects, the court should rule that Sarge's testimony is:

(A) Admissible, because the plaintiff has a right to introduce evidence of his good character.

(B) Admissible, because Richman's character has been brought into question by the editorial.

(C) Inadmissible, because Sarge's testimony is not probative of any material issue.

(D) Inadmissible, because specific instances of conduct are not admissible to prove character.

Question 19

Pat filed suit against Don, asserting that "Goering," a German shepherd dog belonging to Don, had bitten her without provocation. Don denied that his dog bit Pat. At the trial, Porter, Pat's attorney, called Pat to the stand. After asking Pat's name and address, he asked only one further question, namely: "Were you bitten by a German shepherd dog with a white forepaw?" Pat replied in the affirmative and was dismissed from the stand.

Porter then called Don to the stand as an adverse witness. After ascertaining Don's name and address, Porter asked Don only one question: "Do you own a German shepherd dog with a white forepaw?" Upon receiving Don's affirmative answer, Porter said, "No further questions, Your Honor."

Don's attorney, Debra, rose to cross-examine Don. Her first question to Don was, "Has your German shepherd dog ever displayed anything other than a gentle disposition?" Porter immediately objected to the question.

What would be the most likely ruling of the court on Porter's objection?

(A) Sustained, because Debra is improperly attempting to introduce character evidence when character has not been called into question.

(B) Sustained, because Debra's question goes beyond the proper scope of cross-examination.

(C) Overruled, because the plaintiff brought up the dog in direct examination.

(D) Overruled, because the testimony sought is relevant and is otherwise admissible.

Question 20

Pontius, a pedestrian, was struck by a car driven by Driver. Pontius was taken to the emergency room of Hacksaw Hospital immediately after the accident, treated by Dr. Diaz, and released 30 minutes later. Pontius later went to his own physician, Dr. Duckspeak.

Pontius filed suit in municipal court against Driver. At trial, Pontius testified that he suffered from lower back pains and sought damages from Driver therefor. Driver's attorney subpoenaed Dr. Diaz and put Dr. Diaz on the witness stand. After a line of questioning establishing who Dr. Diaz is and where he is employed, Driver's attorney asked Diaz to describe Pontius's condition when Diaz examined Pontius immediately after the accident. Pontius's attorney objected on the grounds that his client wished to invoke the physician-patient privilege.

How should the court rule on the objection?

(A) Sustained, because the patient has the right to invoke the privilege.

(B) Sustained, because Dr. Diaz's testimony is irrelevant to Pontius's present condition.

(C) Overruled, because Pontius is suing for personal injuries.

(D) Overruled, because Dr. Diaz was not Pontius's physician prior to the accident.

Question 21

The police arrested Doohan and charged him with the murder of Vespasian. After Doohan's arrest, two police officers went to Doohan's home, where they found his wife, Winniehaha. Vespasian had been killed on the night of March 13, and the officers asked Winniehaha to give them the jacket that Doohan wore on the evening of March 13. Without saying a word, Winniehaha handed the officers an imitation leather jacket that was covered with bloodstains. Crime lab tests established that the blood on the jacket matched Vespasian's blood characteristics. At Doohan's trial for murder, the prosecution seeks to introduce Doohan's jacket into evidence.

If the defense objects, the court should rule that the jacket is:

(A) Admissible, as relevant evidence linking Doohan to the crime.

(B) Inadmissible, because of the marital privilege.

(C) Inadmissible, as hearsay not within any exception.

(D) Inadmissible, because of the privilege against self-incrimination.

Question 22

Arabella sues Belinda in a contract dispute. Arabella calls Quincy to testify as to his personal knowledge of the agreement. Arabella now wants Zelda to testify as to her knowledge of Quincy's honesty. Belinda objects and the court sustains the objection.

Arabella may not bring Zelda to testify, because:

(A) Quincy's credibility has not been questioned.

(B) It would be inadmissible under the hearsay rule.

(C) Zelda may not testify as to an opinion.

(D) Reputation evidence is generally inadmissible in civil cases.

Question 23

Flight 982, a regularly scheduled flight of Chaptereleven Airlines, crashed in the state of Illiana. The entire flight crew and most of the passengers, including passenger Adam, were killed. Eve, the executor of Adam's estate, brought suit in Illiana against Chaptereleven Airlines and Crates, Inc., the manufacturer of the aircraft in which Adam was killed. The Federal Aviation Administration ("FAA") is required by law to investigate the causes of all commercial airline crashes. The FAA prepared a report that indicated that the crash of Flight 982 was caused by the pilot's negligence. Eve seeks to introduce the FAA report into evidence.

Should the judge admit the report into evidence?

(A) Yes, because it is a public record.

(B) Yes, but only for impeachment purposes.

(C) No, because it is hearsay, and the pilot is unavailable to testify.

(D) No, because of the best evidence rule.

Question 24

Arlo was driving north on Main Street, when his car went out of control, crossed the center line, and struck the vehicle that Barlow was driving south on Main Street. Immediately after the accident, Paulette came by, and seeing an interesting possibility for a good photograph, took out her camera and photographed the accident scene. Barlow sues Arlo for damages and seeks to introduce the photograph taken by Paulette.

Is the photograph of the scene of the accident admissible?

(A) Yes, but only if Paulette was a police officer who took the photo for an official report.

(B) Yes, but only if Paulette is available to testify at trial.

(C) No, unless a proper foundation is laid.

(D) No, because of the best evidence rule.

Question 25

Dennoyer was charged with the January 12 armed robbery of a "U-Bag-Em" grocery store in Gainesville, Texas. Dennoyer's defense is that he was not in Texas on the date of the armed robbery and thus he could not have committed the crime. To show that he was not in the area on January 12, Dennoyer wishes to introduce into evidence a letter he wrote to his sister, Sara, stating, "I will see you in Stowe, Vermont, on January 12." The prosecution objects.

The letter is:

(A) Admissible, as evidence of Dennoyer's intent to go to Vermont on the date in question.

(B) Admissible, as a present sense impression.

(C) Inadmissible, because the statement in the letter is irrelevant.

(D) Inadmissible, because it is hearsay not within any recognized exception to the hearsay rule.

Question 26

The state of New Hades has a modern arson statute with the common law requirement that the intentional burning be of "the dwelling of another" removed. Under this statute Dolph was charged with first degree felony arson. The indictment alleged that Dolph burned down his own building, which housed Dolph's failing business, to avoid bankruptcy and to collect the insurance on the building and the business. At Dolph's trial, the defense called Wiener as a witness. On direct examination, Wiener testified that he was with Dolph at the place of business when the fire started and that some cleaning solvent caught fire and spread out of control. Wiener testified that the ignition of the fire was purely accidental. On cross-examination, the prosecutor asks Wiener, "Isn't it true, Mr. Wiener, that you are being prosecuted for first degree felony arson in a separate trial for the burning of the same building?" Dolph's lawyer objects.

Should the court allow the prosecutor's question?

(A) Yes, but only if Dolph's attorney has introduced evidence tending to establish that Wiener is a person of good character.

(B) Yes, because the question is appropriate to show bias or interest on the part of the witness.

(C) No, because Wiener has not been convicted of the crime.

(D) No, because the question violates Wiener's Fifth Amendment right to be protected from self-incrimination.

Question 27

In a tort case involving personal injury, Hugo, a hospital orderly, is called to the stand. There is some dispute as to whether Plaintiff ever lost consciousness. Plaintiff's attorney wishes to have Hugo, who was working in the hospital emergency room when Plaintiff was brought in, testify that Plaintiff was unconscious at the time she entered the emergency room.

Would such testimony be admissible over Defendant's objection?

(A) Yes, because it is proper opinion testimony by a lay witness.

(B) No, because Hugo is not an expert witness.

(C) No, because it impermissibly intrudes upon the province of the jury.

(D) No, because it is not the best evidence.

Question 28

Parker is suing Dillon for injuries arising out of a collision between vehicles driven by the parties. Parker alleges that Dillon ran a red light when he struck Parker's vehicle in an intersection. Parker wishes to call Weiss to the stand. Weiss was near the intersection at the time of the accident. Weiss is prepared to testify that Dillon offered to pay Weiss $500 to testify falsely in Dillon's favor.

Such testimony should be:

(A) Admitted, as substantive evidence of the weakness of Dillon's case.

(B) Admitted, for the limited purpose of impeachment by specific bad conduct.

(C) Excluded, because it is irrelevant to the case.

(D) Excluded, because although relevant, such evidence is misleading and prejudicial.

Questions 29-30 are based on the following fact situation:

Daffy's car struck Porky's car, and Porky suffered physical injuries. The police arrived on the scene and required Daffy to take a breathalyzer test. Daffy was cited for driving while intoxicated, tried in traffic court, and duly convicted. He received the maximum sentence for driving while intoxicated, which is 90 days' imprisonment in the county correctional facility.

Porky brings a civil action against Daffy, seeking compensation for his personal injuries.

29. At the trial of Porky's suit, Porky's attorney offers a properly authenticated photocopy of the court judgment showing that Daffy was convicted of driving while intoxicated. The evidence is:

(A) Admissible as a public record.

(B) Admissible as a final judgment offered to prove a fact essential to a point in controversy.

(C) Inadmissible, because the crime was punishable by imprisonment of at most 90 days.

(D) Inadmissible, because it is not the best evidence of Daffy's conviction.

30. Porky's attorney calls Wanda, a witness to the accident. The attorney asks Wanda to describe Daffy's condition at the time of the accident. She describes Daffy's condition and concludes by saying that he appeared to be intoxicated. Daffy's attorney objects. How should the court rule?

(A) Sustained, because this is an opinion.

(B) Sustained, unless Wanda is qualified as an expert.

(C) Overruled, because this is proper opinion testimony.

(D) Overruled, because this is a present sense impression.

Question 31

Phil is being prosecuted for the rape of Andrea. He testifies in his own defense that for two weeks prior to the date of the alleged rape, he was working on his uncle's ranch several hundred miles from the city, and so could not have been the rapist of Andrea. On rebuttal, the prosecutor offers the testimony of Trinette, who states that she was picked up by Phil in a bar near Andrea's apartment on the day before the rape, and that Phil subsequently paid her to perform a sex act with him.

Should Trinette's testimony be admitted over Phil's objection?

(A) No, because Phil has not put his character at issue in the case.

(B) No, because the evidence offered pertains to a prior uncharged offense.

(C) Yes, because it is offered to show that Phil was present in the city near the time of the charged rape.

(D) Yes, because it demonstrates that Phil was seeking sexual gratification near the time of the charged rape.

Question 32

Robert is charged with having been one of two men who robbed the Roundup Bar and its patrons at gunpoint at 5:30 p.m. on December 16. Robert calls June as a witness in his defense. She testifies that she drove to Robert's home at 10 a.m. on December 16 and picked up Robert and his wife, then took them to a birthday party for Robert's mother-in-law at the latter's home that lasted until 7 p.m. The prosecutor asks on cross-examination, "What is your relationship to Robert's wife?" Defense counsel objects.

How should the court rule?

(A) Overruled, because the question attacks the witness's truth and veracity.

(B) Overruled, because the question is directed at discovering possible bias in the witness.

(C) Sustained, because the question seeks to elicit irrelevant information.

(D) Sustained, because the answer to the question would create prejudice that would outweigh its probative value.

Question 33

Louise is on trial for arson of the restaurant owned by her sister. Chemical tests by the fire department indicate that gasoline was used as the igniting agent of the fire. The prosecution calls to the stand Shari, a waitress who works at an all-night diner near the burned restaurant. She will testify that on the night of the fire, Louise came into the diner and ordered a cup of coffee, and that Louise smelled like gasoline.

Should the court admit this testimony over Louise's objection?

(A) No, it is inadmissible as the opinion of a nonexpert witness.

(B) No, it is inadmissible because the best evidence is the result of the chemical tests.

(C) Yes, it is admissible lay opinion testimony.

(D) Yes, it is admissible expert testimony because everyone who drives a car is an expert as to the smell of gasoline.

Question 34

In a civil action for personal injuries, Paul asserts that he was injured when Dawn negligently operated her motor vehicle and caused it to strike Paul's vehicle when both cars were being driven along Main Street, the principal north-south arterial street in Humberton. The accident occurred the previous July 15.

Concerning the following facts that arise during the trial, to which is it most appropriate for the judge trying the case to apply the doctrine of judicial notice?

(A) On July 15, the pavement on Main Street was wet, based on the judge's recollection that he had to cancel a golfing engagement on July 15 because it was raining heavily.

(B) Main Street runs in a north-south direction, based on information generally known by residents of Humberton.

(C) The brakes on Dawn's car were faulty, based on the uncontroverted testimony of Dawn's auto mechanic and an automotive engineer testifying as an expert for the plaintiff.

(D) Dawn was exceeding the speed limit when the accident occurred, based upon the testimony of Paul, two credible eyewitnesses, and the police officer who examined the skid marks, controverted by the testimony of Dawn and the nervous and rather unsure testimony of Walt, who was a passenger in Dawn's car.

Question 35

In Amy's civil suit for personal injuries against her stepfather, arising from acts of sexual abuse allegedly committed by him against her when she was a minor, Amy calls as a witness a police officer who will testify that, 11 years ago, the stepfather confessed to the witness that he had committed the acts complained of by Amy.

Should the trial court admit the police officer's testimony over the stepfather's objection?

(A) Yes, because past instances of misconduct may be used to impeach a witness.

(B) Yes, because the stepfather's confession is an admission of a party-opponent.

(C) No, because the best evidence of a conviction is the judgment of the court that convicted him.

(D) No, because the sexual assault that is the subject of the evidence is more than 10 years old.

Question 36

Jack has brought an action for personal injuries against Store, in connection with an incident in which Jack slipped and fell after Store's linoleum floors had been mopped. A major issue at trial is the degree of moisture that remained on the floor, since it had been mopped 45 minutes before Jack walked on it. Store offers the testimony of Edgar, who will tell about an experiment he conducted measuring the amount of time necessary for a linoleum floor to dry completely after having been mopped.

Should the court admit this testimony?

(A) Yes, if a representative of Jack was present when the experiment was conducted.

(B) Yes, if it is shown that the conditions of Edgar's experiment were substantially similar to the conditions of Store's floor when Jack slipped.

(C) Yes, if Jack was given an opportunity to conduct his own experiment with the same type of linoleum used by Edgar.

(D) Yes, if it is shown that Edgar is not an employee or otherwise related in interest to Store.

Question 37

Office Building, Inc. contracted to build a large, multistory building for a client and began, through various subcontractors, construction. Mid-State Excavators, Inc. dug the excavation for the foundation and basement levels as called for by the plans, and Acme Engineering, a partnership, began work on the foundation. Just after the foundation was completed, Jed, an employee of the subcontractor doing structural work, was killed when one of the walls of the excavation collapsed, burying him under tons of soil.

Jed's survivors brought an appropriate action against all of the involved parties, and each defendant cross-complained for indemnity against each of the other defendants. At trial, Acme Engineering calls Willis, a civil engineer licensed by the state, who is prepared to testify that he examined the geologist's reports of the soil conditions surrounding the construction site, plus a report by the engineer who retrieved Jed's body and examined the site of the collapse, and that it is his (Willis's) opinion that the collapse of the wall of the excavation was caused by Mid-State Excavators' failure to take into consideration the composition of the soil being excavated, rather than any defects in the shoring constructed by Acme.

Is Willis's testimony admissible?

(A) Yes, if civil engineers in his field rely upon such materials as plans and reports by geologists and others in reaching conclusions such as his.

(B) Yes, if he was not professionally negligent in his analysis.

(C) No, because his opinion relates to an ultimate issue that must be determined in the case.

(D) No, because his opinion was based upon facts not personally within his knowledge.

Question 38

Deft drove his automobile into the intersection and struck Plain, a pedestrian. Deft immediately left his car and ran to Plain. Deft made two statements to Plain before the ambulance arrived.

Statement 1: "It was all my fault; I'm sorry I ran the red light."

Statement 2: "I'll pay for all your medical expenses."

Plain sued Deft for his injuries and, at the resulting trial, Plain wished to testify to the two statements made by Deft. The defense objected.

The court should rule:

(A) Both Statement 1 and Statement 2 are admissible.

(B) Statement 1 is admissible; Statement 2 is inadmissible.

(C) Statement 1 is inadmissible; Statement 2 is admissible.

(D) Neither Statement 1 nor Statement 2 is admissible.

Question 39

Harry is charged with the federal crime of conspiracy to embezzle $50,000 from his employer, a bank. At trial, the prosecutor calls Harry's wife, Wilma, and asks her to testify about a meeting between Harry and Sybil that Wilma observed three weeks prior to her marriage to Harry.

Which of the following is the most accurate statement of the applicable rule concerning whether Wilma may testify?

(A) The choice is Wilma's.

(B) The choice is Harry's.

(C) Wilma is permitted to testify only if both Wilma and Harry agree.

(D) Wilma may be compelled to testify, even if both Wilma and Harry object.

Question 40

Warren is on trial for assault with a deadly weapon. The sole prosecution witness is the victim, who testifies as to his version of the events leading up to and including the charged assault. Warren's first witness is Leon, who contradicts the victim's testimony that Warren engaged in an unprovoked attack. Leon testifies that the victim pulled a knife on Warren and that Warren, in defending himself, wrested the knife away and accidentally stabbed the victim. Warren's next and final witness is Salvadore, who intends to testify that Warren's reputation in the community for honesty and veracity is very good. Aware of the intended testimony, the prosecutor moves in limine to exclude it.

How should the court rule?

(A) For the state, because Warren may not introduce evidence of his character to prove that he acted in conformity therewith.

(B) For the state, because Salvadore's testimony is irrelevant.

(C) For Warren, because a criminal defendant may put his character in issue.

(D) For Warren, because the reputation for honesty and veracity of a criminal defendant is always at issue.

Questions 41-42 are based on the following fact situation:

Carla was injured when the car she was driving was struck by a truck driven by Elwood and owned by Art's Freight Lines. Carla brings an action for personal injuries against Art's. The complaint alleges that Elwood was drunk at the time of the accident and that Art's was negligent in hiring him and permitting him to drive knowing that he had a drinking problem and convictions for drunk driving.

41. Elwood is called as a witness by Art's and is expected to testify that he was not drunk at the time of the accident. Instead, Elwood states on direct examination that he had had several beers as he drove his truck that evening and was "really high" when his truck struck Carla's car. The counsel for Art's wants to confront Elwood with his deposition testimony that he was "stone cold sober" at the time of the accident. Will this be permitted?

(A) No, the statement is hearsay not within any recognized exception.

(B) No, Art's cannot impeach its own witness.

(C) Yes, but it may be used only to refresh Elwood's recollection.

(D) Yes, it can be used to impeach and as substantive evidence that Elwood was sober.

42. Carla calls Art, the owner of Art's, as a hostile witness and attempts to elicit testimony that after the accident, Art hired a consultant to screen potential employees for alcohol related problems and to institute a program to help current employees with alcohol abuse. Will this be permitted?

(A) Yes, to establish that Art was negligent in hiring Elwood and permitting him to drive a truck.

(B) Yes, to show that Art was aware of the need for better screening of employees.

(C) No, because its admission would discourage other tortfeasors from taking remedial measures.

(D) No, because it is not a proper form of impeachment.

Question 43

At Oglethorpe's trial for rape, he calls Tad as a defense witness. Tad testifies that he was on his patio barbecuing some hamburgers at the time of the charged rape and saw the assailant run from the victim's apartment. He further testifies that the person who ran from the victim's apartment was not Oglethorpe.

On cross-examination by the prosecutor, as to which of the following questions would a defense objection most likely be sustained?

(A) "Weren't you convicted of perjury 11 years ago?"

(B) "Weren't you under the influence of heroin at the time you were barbecuing those hamburgers?"

(C) "Haven't you and Oglethorpe known each other since grammar school?"

(D) "Weren't you fired from your job last week because they discovered you were embezzling funds?"

Question 44

The police in Metropolis set up an undercover "sting" operation in which they posed as fences of stolen property and bought and sold such property to anyone who came into their downtown warehouse. Mike is being prosecuted for receiving stolen property in connection with his arrest by the undercover operatives, and the prosecution attempts to introduce a videotape showing Mike offering to sell a television set to one of the police officers.

If this evidence is held to be inadmissible, the most likely reason is that:

(A) It is hearsay not within any exception.

(B) It violates Mike's privilege against self-incrimination.

(C) A proper foundation was not established for its introduction into evidence.

(D) Criminality may not be proven by specific instances of misconduct.

Questions 45-47 are based on the following fact situation:

Donald was arrested and charged with the September 15 murder of Wilma.

45. At trial, Donald called as his first witness Able, to testify to Donald's reputation in the community as "a peace-loving man." Able's testimony will most likely be held to be:

(A) Admissible as tending to prove Donald is innocent.

(B) Admissible as tending to prove Donald is believable.

(C) Inadmissible, because reputation is not a proper way to prove character.

(D) Inadmissible, because Donald has not testified.

46. Donald then called his next-door neighbor, Baker, to testify that on September 12 Donald said that he was about to leave that day for a one-week visit with his brother, who lived in another state. Baker's testimony is most likely to be held to be:

(A) Admissible, because it is not hearsay.

(B) Admissible, because it is a declaration of present mental state.

(C) Inadmissible, because it is hearsay not within any exception.

(D) Inadmissible, because it is irrelevant.

47. Donald then called Daniel to testify as to Donald's alibi. On cross-examination, the prosecutor asked Daniel, "Weren't you on a jury that acquitted Donald of another criminal charge?" If the judge sustained an objection to this question, the most likely reason will be that:

(A) The question is leading.

(B) The question goes beyond the scope of direct examination.

(C) The probative value of the answer would be substantially outweighed by its tendency to mislead.

(D) A proper foundation was not laid.

Questions 48-49 are based on the following fact situation:

Alex and his son, Benji, were driving home from an evening of bowling when their car, which Alex was driving, was struck broadside by a van driven by McKenzie at an intersection controlled in all directions by stop signs. A personal injury action was initiated by Alex and Benji against McKenzie.

48. At trial, Alex calls Benji as a witness to testify that he was looking directly at McKenzie's van from his place in the front passenger seat of his father's car as Alex drove into the intersection, and that McKenzie never slowed down as she drove past the stop sign and collided with Alex's car. Should this testimony be admitted over McKenzie's objection that Benji is not competent to testify?

(A) No, as a close relative of a party, Benji may not testify on that party's behalf.

(B) No, since he is a party-plaintiff, Benji may not testify as to the facts of the accident.

(C) Yes, but only if Benji is age 12 or over.

(D) Yes, there is nothing to indicate that Benji is incompetent to testify.

49. Alex calls Bob as a witness, who testifies that he was standing on the sidewalk at the intersection at which the accident occurred and ran to see if McKenzie was injured after the collision. He further testifies that as the ambulance was leaving with Alex and Benji, McKenzie offered him $500 in cash to testify falsely that McKenzie had stopped at the stop sign before proceeding into the intersection. Should this last statement have been admitted into evidence?

(A) No, it is hearsay not within an exception.

(B) No, it is not relevant to the issue of negligence.

(C) Yes, it is relevant and not hearsay.

(D) Yes, it is a declaration against interest by McKenzie.

Question 50

Parker has brought an action against Davidson for breach of contract. The existence and terms of the contract are in dispute. Parker's counsel calls him to the witness stand and seeks to elicit testimony that Parker and Davidson met in a restaurant on a certain date and reached an agreement that was reduced to a writing. Parker then intends to testify, "The writing, which was subsequently inadvertently destroyed, provided that Davidson would purchase 300 widgets from me at a price of $1,000."

The quoted testimony is admissible only if:

(A) The judge finds that the writing is unavailable.

(B) The judge finds that Parker is accurately relating the contents of the writing.

(C) The jury finds that the writing is unavailable.

(D) The jury finds that Parker is accurately relating the contents of the writing.

Questions 51-52 are based on the following fact situation:

Lucy was seriously injured when the bus in which she was riding ran a red light and was hit broadside by a cement mixer. She has brought an action against the bus company for damages from personal injuries on theories of respondeat superior and negligent hiring.

51. Winston, a passenger on the same bus that Lucy was riding on when injured, is called as a witness by Lucy to testify that, just after the bus came to a stop after Lucy was injured, he said to another passenger, "We must have been going at least 50 miles per hour!" Is this testimony admissible?

(A) Yes, if it is offered as a prior consistent statement as to Winston's trial testimony.

(B) Yes, because the statement was an excited utterance.

(C) No, because the statement is hearsay not within an exception.

(D) No, because the testimony is improper opinion evidence.

52. Lucy's counsel offers evidence that one year before the accident, but four years after the driver of the bus that injured her was hired, the bus company instituted a requirement that prospective bus driver employees pass a thorough driving test and background check before being hired. The driver of Lucy's bus was required only to pass a written test and possess a driver's license. In fact, he had an extensive record of traffic offenses at the time he was hired. Is the evidence regarding the new employment requirements admissible?

(A) No, because it is irrelevant.

(B) No, because it is evidence of remedial measures.

(C) Yes, because it is evidence of the bus company's negligence.

(D) Yes, because it is evidence that the bus driver was incompetent.

Question 53

Which of the following questions is most likely to be subject to the objection that it is leading?

(A) On direct examination, counsel asks his own client: "You live at 555 Northward Avenue, don't you?"

(B) On cross-examination of an expert witness, counsel asks: "Isn't it true that most family practice attorneys routinely asserted a community interest in military pensions at that time?"

(C) On direct examination of the victim, a four-year-old child, the prosecutor asks: "Did the defendant touch you there?"

(D) On direct examination of an eyewitness to an accident, plaintiff's counsel asks: "Was the light red when the defendant drove through the intersection?"

Question 54

During trial of her personal injury action against ChemCo, Darlene testifies in response to a question by her own counsel that shortly after she and her family were forced to leave their home because of the fumes, the president of ChemCo telephoned her motel room and said, "If you or any member of your family requires medical treatment, ChemCo will pay all medical expenses in full. We will not have it said that ChemCo's negligence resulted in the illness of a local family." ChemCo's counsel makes a motion to strike all of Darlene's testimony, and the court does so.

Was the court's action correct?

(A) Yes, because the testimony relates to inadmissible hearsay.

(B) Yes, because the statement was made in connection with an offer to pay medical expenses.

(C) No, because the statement includes an admission by a party-opponent that it was negligent.

(D) No, because the statement is a factual admission made in connection with an offer to compromise.

Questions 55-57 are based on the following fact situation:

Rob and his parents sued Gary for $75,000 for injuries they claim were caused when Gary's car hit Rob one night when Rob was out delivering papers. Rob was knocked unconscious in the accident, and Gary claims it was not his car that hit Rob. Except for damages, the main issue in the suit is whether it was Gary's car that hit Rob.

55. Rob's attorney asked Gary, "Is it true you spent $500 to put speed equipment on your car?" The court should rule this question:

(A) Objectionable, because it is leading.

(B) Objectionable, because it is irrelevant.

(C) Unobjectionable, because it shows Gary is irresponsible.

(D) Unobjectionable, because Gary can testify as to what he spent even though a receipt may exist.

56. Gary's own attorney asked him, "Could Rob have mistaken your car for another?" This question is:

(A) Objectionable, because the answer would be hearsay.

(B) Objectionable, because the answer would be an opinion.

(C) Unobjectionable, because the answer would be relevant to the issue of whose car hit Rob.

(D) Unobjectionable, if a proper foundation has been laid.

57. Gary seeks to testify that he always takes a specific road when he goes home from work at night, and that road was different from the one on which Rob was hit. The judge should find the offer to testify:

(A) Objectionable as calling for a self-serving declaration.

(B) Objectionable, because it is not relevant.

(C) Unobjectionable, as calling for evidence of habit.

(D) Unobjectionable, if it is offered as impeachment evidence.

Questions 58-59 are based on the following fact situation:

Ron's father, Ed, died without a will. Ron was his only heir. During the probate of Ed's estate, Leslie, Ed's former nurse, made a claim for the family residence and offered a deed to show that the house had been transferred to her two months before Ed's death. Ron disputed Leslie's claim and alleged that his father's signature on the deed was forged. Assume a jury trial.

58. Leslie testified at trial that she and Ed had entered into a written agreement when she first became employed by him which stated that if she accepted a lower monthly salary and worked with him for the rest of his life, he would leave the house to her in his will. Ron objects to this evidence, and the best reason for a judge to rule the evidence inadmissible is that:

(A) It is hearsay.

(B) The contract is not a proper will.

(C) The agreement violates the Statute of Frauds.

(D) The evidence violates the best evidence rule.

59. Ron testified that he was familiar with his father's signature and the signature on the deed was not his. The judge should rule this testimony:

(A) Inadmissible, because Ron is not a handwriting expert.

(B) Inadmissible, because Ron has a stake in the outcome and his opinion is unreliable.

(C) Admissible, because Ron knows his father's signature.

(D) Admissible, because he is disputing the genuineness of the document, not seeking to establish it.

Questions 60-62 are based on the following fact situation:

Tammy is on trial for the murder of her husband. She is accused of pushing him from the window of their 12th-floor apartment; she claims he committed suicide.

60. Tammy took the stand to testify on her own behalf. The prosecutor on cross-examination asked her, "Isn't it true that you were convicted of forgery six years ago?" The judge should rule this question:

(A) Proper, because Tammy has waived the privilege against self-incrimination by taking the stand to testify.

(B) Proper, because the prosecutor may inquire into matters bearing on a witness's credibility.

(C) Improper, because the purpose of the question was to elicit prejudicial evidence.

(D) Improper, because on cross-examination, the prosecutor is limited to matters testified to on direct examination.

61. Tammy called Jerry to testify that Tammy had a reputation of being a "good and loving person who would never hurt anyone." The trial judge should rule the testimony:

    (A) Admissible, because it is not hearsay.

    (B) Admissible, because this is a criminal matter, and it tends to show relevant good character.

    (C) Inadmissible, because the prosecution has not introduced evidence concerning Tammy's reputation.

    (D) Inadmissible, because character evidence is not permissible to show that an accused has acted in conformity with the character.

62. Tammy called Barbara, an operator for a suicide-prevention clinic, to testify that Tammy's husband had called the clinic on more than one occasion threatening to "end it all." The judge should rule the testimony:

    (A) Admissible, because the statement was made in "contemplation" of death.

    (B) Admissible, because it tends to show Tammy's husband intended to commit suicide.

    (C) Inadmissible, because it violates the psychiatrist-patient privilege.

    (D) Inadmissible, because no phone calls were made to the clinic by Tammy's husband on the day he died.

Questions 63-64 are based on the following fact situation:

Bob was helping his neighbor Ray clean out his garage. As he and Ray were moving some boards out of the garage, Ray ran into the overhead door's hinge, causing it to fall and hit Bob on his head. Bob's wife, Linda, sued Ray for the wrongful death of her husband, seeking damages of $100,000.

63. Linda, who was present when the accident occurred, is called to testify that at the time of the accident, Bob was carrying the boards on his shoulder, and he therefore was unable to see that Ray had hit the door hinges. As a witness, Linda is:

    (A) Competent, if she is testifying as the personal representative of her husband's estate.

    (B) Competent, in spite of the fact she is the plaintiff.

    (C) Incompetent, because she is unqualified to give opinion evidence.

    (D) Incompetent, because she cannot testify for her husband in a civil case.

64. Ray sought to testify that Linda told him that if he paid for all of Bob's hospital costs and gave her $25,000, she would not bring suit. Linda's attorney objected to the testimony, and the judge should rule that the testimony is:

    (A) Inadmissible, because it is hearsay.

    (B) Inadmissible, because it was an offer of compromise.

    (C) Admissible, because it is a statement against interest, and thus, an exception to the hearsay rule.

    (D) Admissible, because it is relevant to show that Linda tried to "blackmail" Ray, and does not really have a claim.

Questions 65-66 are based on the following fact situation:

Able, Baker, Charlie, and Dick were on their way to Pasadena to the Rose Bowl when they were injured as their car was sideswiped and driven off the road by a large truck belonging to D-Liver-Co. Dick was driving the car at the time. Rev and Relief were the alternate drivers of the truck. Rev was driving and Relief was asleep in the sleeping cab portion of the truck at the time of the accident. Able, Baker, Charlie, and Dick brought an action against Rev and D-Liver-Co., alleging negligence by Rev in driving too fast. D-Liver-Co. answered and asserted the affirmative defense that Dick had been on quaaludes and cocaine and was intoxicated at the time of the accident.

65. D-Liver-Co.'s counsel seeks to have the highway patrolman who investigated the accident state that he overheard Dick tell Able, Baker, and Charlie, "This was probably all our fault; we shouldn't have been on 'ludes and snow." Assuming the trial judge takes judicial notice that "'ludes" means "quaaludes" and "snow" means "cocaine," the judge should rule that the tender of evidence is:

(A) Admissible, as an admission of a party.

(B) Admissible, to save time because the same statement could be admitted by way of the accident report.

(C) Inadmissible, because if he had been intoxicated he would not be capable of making a rational decision as to fault.

(D) Inadmissible, because it is hearsay not within any exception.

66. Counsel for the plaintiffs seeks to introduce the statement of Relief, no longer in the employ of D-Liver-Co., that just before the accident he had stated to Rev, "You had better slow down. You have been warned by D-Liver-Co. many times not to go this fast." The judge should rule the statement admissible only if:

(A) The statement was made immediately after the accident, and was made under oath.

(B) Relief is unavailable to testify to the matters in the statement.

(C) Plaintiffs' attorney produces a record of three citations that Rev received in the last year for speeding, driving the same truck.

(D) Plaintiffs' attorney first proves as a preliminary question of fact that during the trip Relief was an agent of D-Liver-Co. and that the statement concerned the scope of his employment.

Questions 67-69 are based on the following fact situation:

Don was tried for the aggravated assault of Victor. He is alleged to have stabbed Victor. After the prosecution rested, Don called Susan. Don asked Susan if she was familiar with Don's reputation in the community, to which Susan answered, "Yes." There was no objection. Don then asked, over objection, what Don's reputation in the community was for the trait of peaceableness.

67. The testimony is:

(A) Inadmissible, because reputation must be proven by generalities and not by specific items of character.

(B) Inadmissible, because Don did not take the witness stand.

(C) Admissible, as tending to prove that the reputation of Don is inconsistent with the criminal charge.

(D) Admissible, under the general rule that the defendant is given the benefit of the doubt when testimony is questionable.

68. Don called Xact to the witness stand. Xact was to testify that the night before the alleged crime, Don stated to Xact that he was going to visit his mother in a distant city some 1,000 miles away. The testimony is:

(A) Admissible, because it is a declaration of intent to do a future act.

(B) Admissible, because of the verbal acts exception.

(C) Inadmissible, because it is not relevant.

(D) Inadmissible, because it is hearsay not within any exception.

69. Don called Zeke to testify on his behalf as an alibi witness. Zeke stated, over objection, that Don was visiting his mother 1,000 miles away on the day of the alleged crime. On cross-examination of Zeke, the prosecutor asked, "Is Don related to you?" The court should rule that the question is:

(A) Proper, because it relates to bias.

(B) Proper, because relatives are not competent witnesses.

(C) Improper, because the question goes beyond the scope of direct examination.

(D) Improper, because it involves a collateral matter.

Questions 70-72 are based on the following fact situation:

Midtown Bank was robbed on Thursday afternoon. The perpetrator was short (under 5' 5") and was wearing a purple jumpsuit with a red hood and green gloves. On Friday, the police received a tip from Katrina that her neighbor, Digby, treated the entire apartment complex to breakfast, boasted about coming into some money, and flashed a huge roll of bills. The police went to Digby's apartment. Digby, a man no taller than 5' 2", answered the door. Digby explained that a friend had paid off an old debt that Digby had long ago written off. After a few more questions, the police left. Late Friday afternoon, the police were summoned back to the building by sanitation workers who had found a purple jumpsuit and green gloves in the building's dumpster. The police arrested Digby and executed a search warrant for his apartment, which turned up nothing.

70. At Digby's trial for bank robbery, the prosecution seeks to introduce into evidence the clothing recovered from the dumpster. The clothing is:

(A) Admissible, as circumstantial evidence that Digby committed the robbery.

(B) Admissible, as direct evidence that Digby committed the robbery.

(C) Inadmissible, because it is irrelevant.

(D) Inadmissible, unless the prosecution proves beyond a reasonable doubt that it is the same clothing the robber wore.

71. The prosecution calls Katrina to the stand. She testifies that, one month prior to the robbery, Katrina's Aunt Minnie was visiting from Australia. Upon Katrina's return from work one day, Aunt Minnie commented, "You Yanks sure have some strange get-ups. Today I saw that short fellow across the hall wearing a one-piece purple outfit." Digby's lawyer objects. The objection should be:

(A) Overruled, because the statement is a present sense impression.

(B) Overruled, because the statement is relevant and Aunt Minnie is unavailable, having gone back to Australia.

(C) Sustained, because this is circumstantial evidence within circumstantial evidence.

(D) Sustained, because the statement is hearsay not within any exception.

72. On cross-examination, Digby's attorney asks Katrina, "Isn't it true that Digby's ex-wife paid you $500 to make the call to the police and that she is paying you another $500 for your testimony today?" The prosecutor objects. The objection should be:

(A) Overruled, because the question gives Katrina an opportunity to explain or deny the allegation.

(B) Overruled, because the question is a proper form of impeachment.

(C) Sustained, because the question addresses a collateral issue.

(D) Sustained, because it is a leading question.

Questions 73-74 are based on the following fact situation:

Parker brought suit against his employer, the Douglas Grain Co., for injuries that he suffered in a fire and explosion in a grain elevator. Douglas Grain Co. filed a cross-complaint against Parker for damages and alleged that Parker was contributorily negligent in that he cut through some electrical wires while working in the elevator, and the sparks from these wires caused the explosion. Parker denies these allegations.

73. Douglas Grain Co. calls Walt, who was also working in the elevator, and he testifies that he pulled Parker and Tod, Parker's assistant, out of the elevator just after the explosion. At that time, Walt intends to testify, Tod said to him, "We should have been able to tell that that wire was hot." Parker's attorney objects to Walt's testimony concerning this conversation. The trial judge should rule that the testimony is:

(A) Inadmissible, because it is hearsay not within any exception.

(B) Inadmissible, because it is improper opinion evidence.

(C) Admissible, as an admission.

(D) Admissible, as being a prior inconsistent statement.

74. Douglas Grain Co. calls Wilmont to testify that he was in the grain elevator just before the explosion and he heard Vance, an employee who was killed in the elevator, say just before the explosion, "Don't cut that wire. It's hot!" The judge should rule that Wilmont's testimony on this point is:

(A) Inadmissible, because it is hearsay not within any exceptions.

(B) Inadmissible, because it violates the Dead Man Statute.

(C) Admissible, because it is an excited utterance.

(D) Admissible, because it is a dying declaration.

Question 75

Gustave brought a lawsuit against BD&F Laboratories. He alleges that he was prescribed some medicine manufactured by them, and that after he took the medicine, a blood clot formed in his left leg, resulting in its having to be amputated. BD&F Laboratories denies liability, claiming that there is nothing in the medicine that could cause clotting of the blood. Gustave offered to have Dr. Hamilton, the chief surgeon of White Chapel Hospital, testify that in the past 15 months, she has treated four persons (who are otherwise proved to have taken the same medicine as Gustave) who suffered from complications caused by blood clotting in their lower extremities. BD&F Laboratories strongly objected to this testimony.

The trial judge should find the testimony:

(A) Inadmissible, because the testimony of the other patients' condition is hearsay not within any exception.

(B) Inadmissible, because it violates the best evidence rule for the doctor to testify concerning her patients' physical condition when there is no showing that the patients are unavailable to testify.

(C) Admissible, if there is shown to be a connection between these patients' ailments and the medicine manufactured by BD&F Laboratories.

(D) Admissible, but only if the doctor is qualified to testify as an expert.

Questions 76-77 are based on the following fact situation:

Sam brought suit against Bill for breach of a contract involving the sale of 100 imported, handcarved coffee tables. The basis of Sam's suit was that Bill failed to pay as was required in the contract. Bill defends against Sam's action by introducing evidence that the shipment delivered to his place of business was only 68 handcarved coffee tables, which he rejected. Sam introduced a bill of lading showing that import taxes were paid on 100 handcarved coffee tables.

76. Bill then offers evidence that a clause in the Sam-Bill contract stated, "Bill has no obligation to receive any coffee tables from Sam unless they are delivered in one lot of 100 tables." Sam objected. The most likely result is:

(A) Bill is entitled to introduce evidence of any part of the transaction necessary to make it understood.

(B) By not objecting to the contract, Bill has waived any right to introduce any part of it.

(C) Bill's evidence is inadmissible as irrelevant.

(D) Bill's evidence is inadmissible as hearsay.

77. Assume that Sam introduced a Fast Freight record showing that Fast Freight attempted delivery to Bill on the date specified. May Bill now compel Sam to introduce the remainder of the record, showing that Fast Freight had only 68 coffee tables on its truck?

(A) Yes, but only if a proper foundation is laid.

(B) Yes, because in all fairness it should be considered contemporaneously with what Sam is offering.

(C) No, unless Bill can prove that the information would be relevant to the case.

(D) No, because the record would constitute inadmissible hearsay.

EVIDENCE ANSWERS

Answer to Question 1

(A)   The deposition testimony of Witt, who is now unavailable, is admissible under the former testimony exception to the hearsay rule. Witt's statement is hearsay because it is a statement, other than one made by the declarant while testifying at the trial or hearing, offered in evidence to prove the truth of the matter asserted. Unless such a statement falls within a recognized exception to the hearsay rule, it must be excluded upon appropriate objection to its admission. [Fed. R. Evid. 802] Pursuant to the former testimony exception to the hearsay rule, the testimony of a now unavailable witness given at another hearing or in a deposition taken in accordance with law is admissible in a subsequent trial as long as there is a sufficient similarity of parties and issues so that the opportunity to develop testimony or cross-examine at the prior hearing or deposition was meaningful. [Fed. R. Evid. 804(b)(1)] Here, Plaintiff is offering the deposition testimony of Witt to prove the truth of the matter asserted therein; *i.e.,* that Defendant ran a red light at the time of the accident. Thus, the testimony is hearsay. Witt, the declarant, is unavailable because she is dead. Also, because the deposition was taken in connection with the same case that is currently the subject of the trial, there is an exact identity of parties and issues between the deposition and the trial. Thus, Defendant had an opportunity and a motive to develop the testimony of Witt at the time of the deposition by cross-examination. As a result, the elements of the former testimony exception are satisfied, and the deposition testimony of Witt is admissible in the trial. (B) is incorrect because the testimony of Witt does not constitute a dying declaration. In a civil action or a homicide prosecution, a statement made by a now unavailable declarant while believing her death was imminent, that concerns the cause or circumstances of what she believed to be her impending death, is admissible. [Fed. R. Evid. 804 (b)(2)] There is no indication that Witt's statements contained in the deposition were made at a time when Witt believed her death was imminent, or that such statements concerned the cause or circumstances of what Witt believed to be her impending death. Therefore, the requirements of a dying declaration are not met. (C) is incorrect because a statement need not be made in court to qualify under the former testimony exception to the hearsay rule. Deposition testimony is within the exception if the deposition is taken in compliance with law and the party against whom it is offered (or his predecessor in interest) had an opportunity and similar motive to develop the testimony. (D) is incorrect because it is not necessary for Defendant to have the opportunity to cross-examine Witt at the trial. It is only necessary that Defendant have had the opportunity to develop Witt's testimony at the prior proceeding; *i.e.,* at the deposition. Having been afforded this opportunity, Defendant cannot now obtain the exclusion of the proffered testimony on the ground that Witt cannot be cross-examined at trial.

Answer to Question 2

(D)   If offered to prove that Abigail stole the jewelry, the testimony by Winston would be hearsay and, thus, inadmissible. Hearsay is a statement, other than one made by the declarant while testifying at the trial or hearing, offered in evidence to prove the truth of the matter asserted. [Fed. R. Evid. 801(c)] A hearsay statement, to which no exception to the hearsay rule is applicable, must be excluded upon appropriate objection. [Fed. R. Evid. 802] The proffered testimony of Winston relates a statement made by Charles other than while testifying at the instant trial. Therefore, if Charles's out-of-court statement is offered to prove that Abigail stole the pieces of jewelry, the statement is hearsay. Since no exceptions to the hearsay rule apply, the statement is inadmissible. (A) is incorrect because the statement is not against the interest of the declarant (Charles). Under the statement against interest exception to the hearsay rule, statements of a person, now unavailable as a witness, against that person's pecuniary, proprietary, or penal interest when made are admissible. [Fed. R. Evid. 804(b)(3)] Here, Charles may be deemed to be unavailable because he has testified to a lack of memory of the subject matter to which his original statement to Winston relates. However, the statement contained in the proposed testimony of Winston is not against any interest of Charles, who is the declarant, but is rather against the interest, both penal and civil, of Abigail. Therefore, the statement does not qualify for admissibility as a statement against interest by Charles. (B) is incorrect because Charles has simply testified that he does not remember either seeing Abigail take the jewelry or telling Winston that she did so. Impeachment refers to the casting of an adverse reflection on the truthfulness of a witness. One form of impeachment is to show that a witness has, on another occasion, made statements that are inconsistent with some material part of his present testimony. If Charles in his testimony had denied seeing Abigail take anything or telling Winston that she had done so, then the testimony of Winston as to Charles's previous statements would be admissible as a prior inconsistent statement, thus serving to disprove the credibility of Charles. However, because Charles has merely testified to a lack of memory concerning these matters, Winston's testimony probably would not be considered a prior *inconsistent* statement. Although (B) could be correct in some jurisdictions, most would not consider introduction of a prior inconsistent statement an appropriate response to a claim of lack of memory unless the court believed the witness was being deliberately evasive. Since (D) is a completely accurate statement, it is the better answer. (C) is incorrect because Winston's testimony is relevant. Evidence is logically relevant if it tends to make the existence of any fact of consequence to the determination of an action more probable than it would be without the evidence. [Fed. R. Evid. 401] Winston's testimony that he was told that Abigail stole jewelry from his store would certainly tend to make it more probable that Abigail took the jewelry than would otherwise be the case. This fact is of great consequence to the determination of Winston's action against Abigail for the value of the missing jewelry. Thus, the proffered testimony is relevant. Although relevant, however, the testimony runs afoul of the hearsay rule, and is thus inadmissible.

Answer to Question 3

(C)   The Fifth Amendment of the United States Constitution provides that a witness cannot be compelled to testify against herself. Pursuant to this privilege, a witness may refuse to answer any question the answer to which might tend to incriminate her. Testimony is incriminating if it ties a witness to the commission of a crime or would furnish a lead to evidence tying the witness to a crime. The privilege against compelled self-incrimination can be claimed at any proceeding, whether civil or criminal, at which the witness's appearance and testimony are compelled. Here, Abigail's answer to a question as to whether she stole jewelry from the store might tend to incriminate her by tying her to the commission of a crime (*e.g.,* theft or larceny). Thus, Abigail is privileged to refuse to answer the question posed by Winston. (B) is incorrect because, as noted above, a witness may claim the privilege against self-incrimination in a civil proceeding. If the testimony might expose the witness to criminal liability, then the privilege applies even in a civil proceeding. (A) is incorrect because, where testimony might be incriminating, the witness may refuse to answer a question, regardless of whether the witness has a reasonable fear of prosecution. There is no basis for the judge predicating her ruling on a determination that Abigail has a reasonable fear of prosecution. Also, the privilege against self-incrimination allows Abigail to refuse to answer any questions at all relating to whether she stole jewelry. As a result, Abigail cannot be compelled to disclose such matters, even in an in camera proceeding. Similarly, (D) is incorrect because the applicability of the privilege against self-incrimination does not depend on the likelihood of actual criminal prosecution of the witness. Testimony that might tend to incriminate the witness triggers the privilege, without regard for whether the witness is a likely target of criminal prosecution.

Answer to Question 4

(C)   The record of Abigail's conviction should be excluded because Abigail has given no testimony to be impeached. Impeachment involves the casting of an adverse reflection on the truthfulness of a witness. Although Abigail has been called as a witness, she has not given any testimony at this point. Consequently, Winston is unable to introduce evidence that would otherwise constitute proper impeachment evidence. (B) is incorrect because, as has been noted, evidence cannot be used for impeachment purposes before there is anything to be impeached. (A) is incorrect because evidence of character to prove the conduct of a person in the litigated event is generally not admissible in a civil case. Circumstantial use of prior behavior patterns for the purpose of infer-ring that, at the time and place in question, a person probably acted in accord with such patterns raises the danger of unfair prejudice and distraction from the main issues. Consequently, even if the grand larceny of which Abigail was convicted involved dishonest acts toward an employer, the record of such a conviction is not admissible to show that she acted similarly with regard to Winston. (D) is incorrect for two reasons. First, it is unnecessary to address the issue of whether the conviction constitutes proper impeachment evidence, because impeachment is not even called for on these facts. Second, if properly offered to impeach testimony by Abigail, the con-viction would not be considered too remote. Under the Federal Rules, for example, a conviction is not too remote if fewer than 10 years have elapsed since the conviction or release from prison.

Answer to Question 5

(B)   The court should admit the letter and instruct the jury that it is up to the jury to decide whether the letter is authentic. Before a writing may be received in evidence, it must be authenticated by proof showing that the writing is what the proponent claims it is. All that is necessary is proof sufficient to support a jury finding of genuineness. The authenticity of a document is a prelimi-nary fact to be decided by the jury. Here, Winston's testimony that he is familiar with Abigail's handwriting and that he recognizes her signature on the letter is sufficient to support a jury finding of genuineness. Thus, the letter should be admitted and authenticity should be left to the jury to decide. (A) is wrong because a lay witness who has personal knowledge of the handwrit-ing of the supposed writer may state his opinion as to whether the document is in that person's handwriting. (C) is wrong because, as noted above, where there is a dispute as to the authenticity of a document, the issue of authenticity is a fact determination for the jury, not the judge, to decide. (D) is wrong because authentication of documentary evidence requires only enough evidence to support a jury finding that the matter is what its proponent claims it is. It is not required that the proponent establish its genuineness by a preponderance of the evidence.

Answer to Question 6

(A)   Wanda may properly authenticate Donald's voice if she is now familiar with Donald's voice. *Any* person familiar with an alleged speaker's voice may authenticate a recording of the voice by giving an opinion as to its identity. Thus, if Wanda is now familiar with Donald's voice, she may give her opinion as to whether it is Donald's voice on the tape. (B) is incorrect because lay opinion testimony is sufficient to identify a voice (assuming the lay witness is familiar with that voice). Expert testimony is appropriate only when the subject matter is one where scientific, technical, or other specialized knowledge would assist the trier of fact in understanding the evidence or determining a fact in issue. [Fed. R. Evid. 702] Here, identification of Donald's voice does not require such specialized knowledge; rather, all that is required is familiarity with Donald's voice. (C) is incorrect because Wanda's testimony would not be hearsay at all. Hearsay is a statement, other than one made by the declarant while testifying at the trial or hearing, offered in evidence to prove the truth of the matter asserted. [Fed. R. Evid. 801(c)] Wanda is not going to be testifying to an out-of-court statement. Rather, Wanda will testify that, being familiar with the voice of Donald by virtue of having heard that voice before, she can now identify the voice on the tape as being that of Donald. Because Wanda will not be testifying as to any particular statement made by Donald, there is no hearsay problem. (D) is incorrect because, as long as Wanda is familiar with the voice of Donald, it makes no difference that Wanda acquired such familiarity only after Donald was arrested. Thus, Wanda may properly authenticate the voice.

Answer to Question 7

(C)   Of the persons listed, the police officer is the only one who would not have: (i) personal familiarity with Darrin's handwriting; (ii) a basis for forming an opinion as to the handwriting derived from specialized knowledge; or (iii) a particular fact-finding function, such as that assigned to the jury. (A) and (B) are incorrect because an expert witness or a trier of fact can determine the genuineness of a writing by comparing the questioned writing with another writing proved to be genuine. Since a police officer is neither an expert witness nor a trier of fact, (C) does not come within this rule. (D) is incorrect because lay opinion testimony is admissible to identify handwriting if the witness is familiar with the handwriting. A secretary employed by Darrin for five years would have the requisite familiarity with Darrin's handwriting to permit the secretary to offer an opinion as to the genuineness of the writing at issue. Since the police officer was not previously familiar with Darrin's writing, he cannot testify as a lay witness either.

Answer to Question 8

(C)   The Dead Man Act will have no effect on the admissibility of Beatrix's conversation with Henrik because Simonson is not a protected party. A typical Dead Man Act provides that a party or person interested in the event, or her predecessor in interest, is incompetent to testify to a personal transaction or communication with a deceased, when such testimony is offered against the representative or successor in interest of the deceased. Such statutes are designed to protect those who claim directly under the decedent from perjured claims. Here, Simonson is not a representative or successor in interest of Henrik, such as an executor, administrator, heir, legatee, or devisee. Therefore, Simonson is not a protected party for purposes of a Dead Man Act. Because the testimony of Beatrix is not being offered against a representative or successor in interest of the decedent (Henrik), the Dead Man Act is inapplicable. Regarding (A), it is true that the bar to competency created by a Dead Man Act applies only to civil cases. However, the mere fact that a civil action is involved will not trigger applicability of a Dead Man Act. As explained above, the absence of someone who is deemed to be a protected party will prevent a Dead Man Act from having any effect. Thus, (A) is incorrect. Regarding (B), it is true that Beatrix is an interested party (*i.e.,* she stands to gain or lose by the direct and immediate operation of a judgment in this case). Nevertheless, (B) is incorrect because a Dead Man Act requires not only an interested person but a protected party. As has been noted, Simonson is not a protected party. (D) is incorrect because it is based on the assumption that a Dead Man Act does not apply to civil cases. In fact, such statutes apply only to civil cases, and not to criminal cases.

Answer to Question 9

(B)   Emma's statement was an admission, which is nonhearsay under the Federal Rules. An admission is a statement made or an act done that amounts to a prior acknowledgment by one of the parties to an action of one of the relevant facts. Although the statements would otherwise be hearsay, courts allow admissions by a party-opponent on the theory that if the party said or did something that now turns out to be inconsistent with his contentions at trial, he should be estopped from preventing the earlier statement's admission into evidence. Here, the statement that the plaintiff wants to testify to would ordinarily be barred as hearsay because it was made by an out-of-court declarant (Emma) and is being offered to prove the truth of what was stated; but because Emma is one of the defendants in this action, the statement will be admissible as an admission by a party-opponent. (A) is incorrect because a witness cannot be impeached before she testifies. The woman is the first witness of plaintiffs, who present their case first, so Emma, a defendant, has not yet testified. If the woman were to testify after Emma, however, she could introduce the statement for impeachment purposes even if it were otherwise hearsay and inadmissible as substantive evidence. (C) is incorrect because lack of personal knowledge does not necessarily exclude a party's admissions. Emma can attempt to discredit her statement in her case-in-chief by explaining that she had no foundational knowledge when she made the statement, but she cannot bar its admission. (D) is incorrect because the admissibility of admissions by a party-opponent is not dependent on whether the party knew she was speaking to a potential trial opponent; it is irrelevant to whom the admission is made.

Answer to Question 10

(D) Kathy's statement is admissible as an admission of a party-opponent. The Federal Rules treat admissions by a party-opponent as nonhearsay (whereas most states consider admissions to be an exception to the hearsay rule). An admission is a statement made or act done that amounts to a prior acknowledgment by one of the parties to an action of a relevant fact. Such a statement need not have been against interest at the time it was made. Some statements are considered admissions even if not made by the party against whom they are offered. One such vicarious admission is a statement by an agent concerning a matter within the scope of her agency, made during the existence of the agency relationship. [Fed. R. Evid. 801(d)(2)(D)] Here, Bystander's testimony as to Kathy's statement is offered to prove the truth of the matter asserted therein; *i.e.,* that Kathy had not properly fixed the brakes. Thus, Kathy's statement would normally be considered hearsay. However, Kathy made the statement while she was an agent of Arrow, and the statement concerned a matter within the scope of her agency (*i.e.,* whether Kathy had properly performed the job for which she was employed by Arrow). Consequently, Kathy's statement may be introduced against Arrow, as an admission by a party-opponent of negligence in the repair of the brakes. (A) is wrong because Kathy's statement is admissible against Arrow as a vicarious admission. (B) is wrong because it is irrelevant to the issue of whether Bystander's testimony is admissible. The fact that Elmer failed to stop at the stop sign, and thus was negligent, will not prevent introduction of testimony that Kathy admitted that she was negligent. (C) is wrong because the statement against interest exception to the hearsay rule is applicable only where the declarant is unavailable as a witness. Here, Kathy is available as a witness. In addition, as noted above, a statement is admissible as an admission by a party-opponent even if not against interest when made. Thus, Kathy's statement would be admissible against Arrow even if it were not against Arrow's interest when made.

Answer to Question 11

(D) Evidence that Kathy had readjusted the brakes after the accident is inadmissible because, for public policy reasons, evidence of repairs or other precautionary measures made after an injury is inadmissible to prove negligence or culpable conduct. [Fed. R. Evid. 407] The purpose of this rule is to encourage people to make such repairs. Here, Elmer is offering the evidence to prove Kathy's negligence in the original repair of the brakes, by showing the need to readjust them. Thus, this evidence is inadmissible, and Arrow's objection to it should be sustained. (A) is wrong because, as discussed above, the evidence may not be used to show Kathy's negligence. Thus, the tendency of the evidence to prove Kathy's negligence would constitute a reason for sustaining

Arrow's objection, rather than overruling it. (B) is wrong because Kathy's state of mind is not at issue. In addition, the proffered evidence does not really tend to prove anything relative to Kathy's state of mind. (C) is wrong for two reasons: (i) Even if the act of readjusting the brakes constituted assertive conduct, it would not be hearsay. If Kathy's conduct was a statement, it would be an admission by the agent of a party-opponent, and thus it would be nonhearsay. (ii) The act of readjusting the brakes is not assertive conduct constituting a statement under the hearsay rule. Assertive conduct is conduct intended by the actor to be a substitute for words. Kathy was not trying to communicate anything by fixing the brakes.

Answer to Question 12

(A)   The driving record is inadmissible because it is being offered as character evidence. In a civil case, evidence of character to prove the conduct of a person in the litigated event is generally not admissible. The slight probative value of character is outweighed by the dangers of prejudice and distracting the jury from the main issues. Therefore, circumstantial use of prior behavior patterns for the purpose of drawing the inference that a person has a particular character trait and that, at the time and place in question, she probably acted in conformity with it is not permitted. Evidence of Kathy's good driving record is being offered to show that she is a careful driver and to raise the inference that, when the accident occurred, she was acting in conformity with that trait. This constitutes impermissible use of character evidence and is inadmissible. (B) is incorrect because evidence is not excludable because it is self-serving. Virtually all evidence is self-serving to the party offering it. (C) is incorrect because it is based on the mistaken assumption that character evidence is admissible. As stated above, character evidence is generally inadmissible in a civil case. It is admissible in a civil case only when a person's character is directly in issue (*e.g.,* in a defamation case). Kathy's character is not in issue, so the driving record is inadmissible. (D) is incorrect because this is not habit evidence. Habit describes one's regular response to a specific set of circumstances. Character describes one's disposition in respect to general traits. Kathy's good driving record describes a general behavior pattern of careful driving, rather than a regular response to a specific set of circumstances. Thus, this is character evidence, rather than habit evidence.

Answer to Question 13

(C)   Allen's testimony is admissible as evidence of habit. Habit describes a person's regular response to a repeated specific situation. Evidence of a person's habit is relevant to prove that the conduct of the person on a particular occasion was in conformity with that habit. [Fed. R. Evid. 406] According to Allen's testimony, Elmer regularly fails to obey the stop sign at the intersection at which the collision occurred, and in fact, Elmer regularly disregards any stop sign. This regular response to a specific circumstance constitutes a habit. Consequently, Allen's testimony, which is evidence of this habit, is admissible, and so Elmer's objection should be overruled. (A) is incorrect because the best evidence rule is inapplicable to this question. Under the best evidence rule, where the terms of a writing are material, the original writing must be produced in proving the terms of the writing. Here, there is no writing material to the case; thus, the best evidence rule does not come into play. (B) is incorrect because the offered testimony is not character evidence. Character describes one's disposition in respect to traits or general patterns of behavior. If Allen's testimony were that Elmer is generally a careless driver, it would be inadmissible character evidence. Allen's testimony, however, describes a repeated response by Elmer to repeated specific circumstances, which is admissible habit evidence. (D) is incorrect because the fact that an objection is self-serving does not form a basis for overruling (or sustaining) the objection. In a sense, all objections are self-serving to the party making them, just as the evidence to which an objection is made is self-serving to the party offering it.

Answer to Question 14

(D) Pamela's testimony as to Violet's statements is admissible because the statements were made when Violet feared impending death and so they qualify under the dying declaration exception to the hearsay rule. Hearsay is a statement, other than one made by the declarant while testifying at the trial or hearing, offered in evidence to prove the truth of the matter asserted. [Fed. R. Evid. 801(c)] Upon appropriate objection, a hearsay statement to which no exception is applicable must be excluded. Under the dying declaration exception to the hearsay rule, a statement made by a now unavailable declarant while believing her death was imminent that concerns the cause or circumstances of what she believed to be her impending death is admissible. [Fed. R. Evid. 804(b)(2)] The declarant need not actually die as a result of the circumstances giving rise to her belief of imminent death. Here, testimony as to Violet's statements would be hearsay, because they are out-of-court declarations offered for the truth of the matter asserted; *i.e.,* that the driver of the car that hit Violet ran a red light. However, these statements related to the circumstances of what Violet believed to be her impending death and Violet (who is now unavailable due to her death) made these statements under a fear of imminent death, as indicated by her condition and her statement "I know I'm going to die." Consequently, all of the elements of the dying declaration exception are present, and Pamela's testimony as to Violet's statements is admissible. (A) is incorrect because the declarant need not actually die as a result of the incident that gives rise to the statements. Indeed, the declarant need not die at all. All that is required is that the declarant be unavailable at the time the statements are offered. (B) is incorrect because it reflects the traditional view, which limited the admissibility of dying declarations to homicide cases, rather than the position of the Federal Rules, which allow such declarations in both civil cases and homicide prosecutions. (C) is incorrect because Violet's statements do not qualify under the present sense impression exception to the hearsay rule. A present sense impression is a comment made by a person while perceiving an event that is not particularly shocking or exciting that concerns the event she is observing. Violet's statements were made at least one half-hour after the accident. This time lapse between the accident and the statements means that such statements were not made either at the time Violet received a sense impression or immediately thereafter; thus, the present sense impression exception is inapplicable to these facts.

Answer to Question 15

(C) Wrench's testimony regarding the speed of the cars should be admitted only if he qualifies as an expert in accident reconstruction. If the subject matter is such that scientific, technical, or other specialized knowledge is required to render an opinion, expert testimony is admissible and appropriate. In fact, in such an area, opinions by laypersons would not be permitted. To testify as an expert, a person must have special knowledge, skill, experience, training, or education sufficient to qualify him as an expert on the subject to which his testimony relates. The expert must possess reasonable certainty or probability regarding his opinion. Wrench is being asked to testify as to the speed of the cars, not based on actually viewing the cars while in motion (in which lay opinion is often accepted), but on his observation of the spinning wheels after the accident. Determination of the speed of vehicles based upon observation of the spinning wheels of such vehicles after a collision would certainly call for the application of technical or specialized knowledge, thus making the subject matter appropriate for expert testimony. To testify as an expert, Wrench must be qualified by virtue of having special knowledge or experience regarding accident reconstruction, which encompasses rendering opinions on the speed of vehicles based on the spinning of their wheels. Wrench's experience as an auto mechanic would not suffice to establish him as an expert in accident reconstruction. If Wrench is not qualified as an expert, his opinion testimony as to the speed of the cars based upon his observation of the spinning wheels will not be admitted. (A) is incorrect because, as has been explained, Wrench's personal opinion is not admissible without proper qualification of Wrench as an expert. (B) is incorrect because, if Wrench is not qualified as an expert, the fact that his opinion is supported by a proper factual basis (*i.e.,* personal observation) will not render that opinion admissible. (D) is incorrect because the presence of a witness at the scene of events to which his testimony relates need not be corroborated by another witness.

Answer to Question 16

(A) The court should strike the statement as unresponsive to any question asked. An unresponsive answer by a witness is subject to a motion to strike by examining counsel, but not by opposing counsel. Thus, examining counsel can adopt an unresponsive answer if it is not objectionable on some other ground. Here, Davidson's attorney asked Laura a question that was very specific and called for a specific answer (*i.e.,* whether there was broken glass on the pavement at the time and place of the accident). Thus, Laura should only have stated whether there was any glass. Laura's volunteered information regarding the speed of the cars bore no connection to the question posed and was totally unresponsive to that question (or to any other question asked). Therefore, Davidson's attorney, as examining counsel, is entitled to move to strike the statement, and this motion should be granted. (B) is incorrect for two reasons: (i) Laura's comment should be stricken as unresponsive regardless of whether she could have known how fast the cars were traveling. Even if Laura was highly experienced in estimating vehicle speeds, her comment was still not in response to any question. (ii) It is not true that Laura could not offer an opinion on the speed of the cars (if she were asked a question on this). A lay witness is permitted to estimate in miles per hour the speed of a moving vehicle, if it is shown that she has some experience in observing the rate of speed of moving objects. Thus, if Laura can establish such experience, her statement would be admitted into evidence (providing it was made in response to a question posed by examining counsel). (C) is incorrect because it misstates the concept of "opening the door." One who introduces evidence on a particular subject thereby asserts its relevance and cannot complain, except on grounds other than relevance, if her adversary thereafter offers evidence on the same subject. This is what is meant by "opening the door." Davidson's attorney is not complaining of evidence being offered by opposing counsel. Rather, the motion to strike is directed at a totally unsolicited comment from a witness. (D) is incorrect because the prejudicial nature (or lack thereof) of an unresponsive answer does not form the basis for a motion to strike. It is true that, in most cases, an attorney would move to strike only if the witness has made a statement harmful to his case. However, as noted above, the option of moving to strike rests entirely with the examining attorney, and he may move to strike based solely on the unresponsive character of the statement, without showing any prejudice.

Answer to Question 17

(D) The state court is least likely to take judicial notice of the Australian law. Most state courts will not take judicial notice of the law of a foreign country. Note that foreign law is a legislative fact and thus would not be covered by Federal Rule 201, which covers only adjudicative facts, even if the case were in federal court. (A) and (B) are incorrect because they are notorious facts (*i.e.,* facts of common knowledge in the community), and (C) is incorrect because it is a manifest fact (*i.e.,* fact capable of certain verification by resort to easily accessible sources of unquestionable accuracy). Both manifest and notorious facts are appropriate for judicial notice, and under the Federal Rules, notice *must* be taken of these facts if so requested by a party.

Answer to Question 18

(C) Sarge's testimony is inadmissible because it is not probative of a material issue (*i.e.,* whether Richman is a thief). Relevant evidence tends to prove or disprove a material fact in issue. Sarge's testimony tends to prove that Richman is brave and selfless, but it is not relevant as to the fact in issue, which is whether Richman is honest. (A) is incorrect because character evidence is admissible in a civil suit only when, as here, a person's character is directly in issue, but even when character is in issue, the evidence must be relevant to the particular character trait in issue; here, it is not relevant to the issue of Richman's being a thief. (B) is incorrect for the same reason; to be admissible, the evidence must be relevant. (D) is incorrect because proof of specific instances of a person's conduct is admissible when character is directly in issue. [Fed. R. Evid. 405(b)]

Answer to Question 19

(D) Porter's objection should be overruled because the testimony sought is relevant and otherwise admissible. Evidence is relevant if it tends to make the existence of a material fact more probable or less probable than it would be without the evidence. Don's answer to Debra's question will tend to make it either more or less probable that Goering was the dog that bit Pat, and that Don had notice of the dog's propensity to bite, both of which are material facts. Thus, this evidence is relevant. Relevant evidence may be admitted unless there is some specific rule against its admission (*e.g.,* hearsay). Here, there is nothing to prohibit the admission of this evidence. (A) is wrong because character evidence relates to human traits. The rules concerning character are completely inapplicable to animals. (B) is incorrect because the direct examination concerned the identity of the dog that bit Pat, and this question bears on that issue. Cross-examination is proper on matters brought out on direct examination and the inferences naturally drawn from those matters. Here, the inference from the direct examination is that it was Don's dog that bit Pat. On cross-examination, Don's attorney is trying to show that it was not Don's dog because Don's dog has a gentle disposition. (C) is wrong because the mere fact that the dog was brought up on direct examination does not mean that Don may be cross-examined on any subject relating to the dog; the question must be relevant and concern a matter brought out on direct.

Answer to Question 20

(C) The court should overrule the objection because Pontius is suing for personal injuries. A person cannot invoke the physician-patient privilege, which prohibits the doctor from divulging information acquired while attending a patient, where that person has put his physical condition in issue (*e.g.,* by suing for personal injuries). Pontius is suing Driver for personal injuries allegedly incurred as a result of being struck by the car driven by Driver. Therefore, Pontius himself has put his physical condition in issue and cannot avail himself of the physician-patient privilege. While it is true that the physician-patient privilege belongs to the patient (*i.e.,* the patient decides to claim or waive the privilege), (A) is wrong because, as discussed above, the privilege does not apply in this situation. (B) is incorrect because the testimony of Dr. Diaz is relevant to the present condition of Pontius. Evidence is relevant if it tends to make the existence of any fact that is of consequence to the determination of an action more probable than it would be without the evidence. [Fed. R. Evid. 401] The testimony of Dr. Diaz will indicate whether the physical condition of Pontius immediately after the accident would suggest that Pontius had suffered lower back injuries. For example, if the doctor's testimony would indicate the absence of a condition of injury at the time of the observation, then this would make it more probable than not that any current pain experienced by Pontius was not caused by the accident. (D) is incorrect because the privilege does not require that the physician be the patient's personal physician prior to an accident or other cause of injury. It is sufficient if the physician attended the patient in a professional capacity, even if he has never seen the patient before. Thus, the fact that Dr. Diaz was not Pontius's personal physician prior to the accident will not constitute a ground for overruling the objection.

Answer to Question 21

(A) The jacket is admissible as relevant evidence linking Doohan to the crime. Generally, all relevant evidence is admissible if offered in an unobjectionable form or manner (*i.e.,* if it is not subject to an exclusionary rule). Clearly, the bloodstained jacket makes it more probably true that Doohan committed the murder than it would have been without the jacket; therefore, the jacket is relevant evidence. Since it is not subject to an exclusionary rule, the jacket is admissible. (B) is incorrect because neither spousal immunity nor the privilege for confidential marital communications applies in this situation. Spousal immunity prohibits the prosecution from compelling one spouse to testify against the other in a criminal proceeding; that clearly is not at issue here. The privilege for confidential marital communications protects communications (*i.e.,* expressions intended to convey a message) between spouses made in reliance on the intimacy of the marital relationship. Nothing in the facts suggests a confidential communication with respect to the jacket. No privilege applies to observations of a spouse's condition, actions, or conduct. Furthermore, this is a ***testimonial*** privilege and probably would not prevent Winniehaha from handing over real evidence. (C) is incorrect because a jacket is not a "statement," and the hearsay rule excludes out-of-court statements that are offered for their truth. (D) is incorrect because the jacket does not incriminate Winniehaha, and she is the person who gave it to the police. More importantly, the privilege against self-incrimination applies only to testimony, not real evidence.

Answer to Question 22

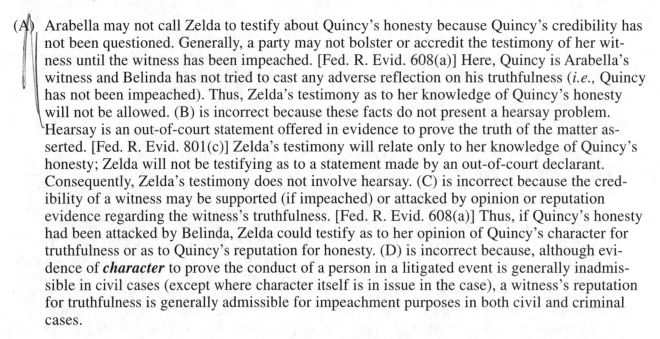

(A) Arabella may not call Zelda to testify about Quincy's honesty because Quincy's credibility has not been questioned. Generally, a party may not bolster or accredit the testimony of her witness until the witness has been impeached. [Fed. R. Evid. 608(a)] Here, Quincy is Arabella's witness and Belinda has not tried to cast any adverse reflection on his truthfulness (*i.e.,* Quincy has not been impeached). Thus, Zelda's testimony as to her knowledge of Quincy's honesty will not be allowed. (B) is incorrect because these facts do not present a hearsay problem. Hearsay is an out-of-court statement offered in evidence to prove the truth of the matter asserted. [Fed. R. Evid. 801(c)] Zelda's testimony will relate only to her knowledge of Quincy's honesty; Zelda will not be testifying as to a statement made by an out-of-court declarant. Consequently, Zelda's testimony does not involve hearsay. (C) is incorrect because the credibility of a witness may be supported (if impeached) or attacked by opinion or reputation evidence regarding the witness's truthfulness. [Fed. R. Evid. 608(a)] Thus, if Quincy's honesty had been attacked by Belinda, Zelda could testify as to her opinion of Quincy's character for truthfulness or as to Quincy's reputation for honesty. (D) is incorrect because, although evidence of ***character*** to prove the conduct of a person in a litigated event is generally inadmissible in civil cases (except where character itself is in issue in the case), a witness's reputation for truthfulness is generally admissible for impeachment purposes in both civil and criminal cases.

Answer to Question 23

(A) The judge should admit the FAA report because it clearly qualifies for admissibility under the public records exception to the hearsay rule. Hearsay is an out-of-court statement offered in evidence to prove the truth of the matter asserted. [Fed. R. Evid. 801(c)] If a statement is hearsay, and no exception to the hearsay rule applies, the evidence must be excluded upon appropriate objection to its admission. [Fed. R. Evid. 802] Under the public records exception to the hearsay rule, records, reports, statements, or data compilations in any form of public offices or agencies are admissible if they set forth: (i) the activities of the office or agency; (ii) matters observed pursuant to a duty imposed by law (excluding police observations in criminal cases); or (iii) factual findings resulting from an investigation made pursuant to authority granted by law, in civil actions and against the government in criminal cases. [Fed. R. Evid. 803(8)] The source of information and other circumstances must not be such as to indicate its lack of trustworthiness. In this case, the factual finding of the report (*i.e.,* that the crash was caused by the pilot's negligence) is an out-of-court statement offered to prove the truth of the matter asserted, and thus would be hearsay. However, because these findings result from an investigation made pursuant to authority granted by law, and are contained in a report compiled by a public agency, the elements of the public records exception have been satisfied, and the report is admissible. (B) is incorrect because the FAA report is admissible as substantive, as well as impeachment, evidence. There is nothing in the Federal Rules limiting the use of this type of agency report to impeachment evidence. (C) is incorrect because the report is admissible as a hearsay exception (*i.e.,* a public record). Also, the pilot's unavailability to testify has no bearing on the admissibility of the report. (D) is incorrect because the best evidence rule is inapplicable to these facts. In proving the terms of a writing, where the terms are material, the best evidence rule requires that the original writing be produced. The rule applies where the writing is a legally operative or dispositive instrument such as a contract, deed, or will, or where the knowledge of a witness concerning a fact results from having read it in the document. The rule does not apply where the fact to be proved has an existence independent of any writing. Here, negligence of the pilot (which Eve seeks to prove) does not depend on the FAA report. The report may be very strong evidence of such negligence, but the pilot either was or was not negligent independent of the report. Thus, the report is not the type of legally operative instrument to which the best evidence rule applies. Also, the rule prohibits secondary evidence in the form of copies (unless the original is shown to be unavailable for some reason other than the serious misconduct of the proponent). Eve is not seeking to introduce a copy of the FAA report, but rather the report itself. Thus, even if the best evidence rule were applicable, there is no attempt here to offer prohibited secondary evidence of the contents of the document.

Answer to Question 24

(C)   The photograph is not admissible unless a proper foundation is laid. To be admissible a photograph must be identified by a witness as a portrayal of certain facts relevant to the issue, and verified by the witness as a correct representation of those facts. It is sufficient if the identifying witness is familiar with the scene or object that is depicted. Here, the photograph taken by Paulette must be verified by a witness who is familiar with the accident scene as an accurate representation of that scene. Absent such verification and identification (*i.e.,* a proper foundation), the photograph is not admissible. (A) is incorrect because a photograph's admissibility does not require that the photographer be a police officer or that the photograph be taken for an official report. The identity of the photographer and the purpose for which the photograph was taken are irrelevant to the issue of admissibility of the photograph. (B) is incorrect because the photographer need not be called to authenticate a photograph; any person familiar with the scene may authenticate the photograph. (D) is incorrect because the best evidence rule (also known as the original documents rule) is inapplicable to these facts. The best evidence rule states that in proving the terms of a writing (including a photograph), where the terms are material, the original writing must be produced. Secondary evidence of the writing, such as oral testimony regarding the writing's contents, is permitted only after it has been shown that the original is unavailable for some reason other than the serious misconduct of the proponent. [Fed. R. Evid. 1002] Here, the admissibility of the original photograph taken by Paulette is in issue. A copy of the photograph is not being offered. Thus, no problem arises under the best evidence rule.

Answer to Question 25

(A) The letter is admissible as evidence of Dennoyer's intent to go to Vermont on January 12. Hearsay is an out-of-court statement offered to prove the truth of the matter asserted. Upon objection, hearsay must be excluded unless it falls within a recognized exception to the rule. The letter is an out-of-court statement, and it is being offered to prove its truth, *i.e.,* that Dennoyer intended to be in Vermont on January 12. The letter, therefore, is hearsay. However, there is an exception for declarations of state of mind, including declarations of intent offered to show subsequent acts of the declarant; *i.e.,* a statement of intent to do something in the future is admitted as circumstantial evidence that the intent was carried out. Dennoyer's letter was a statement of intent to go to Vermont on January 12 and is admissible as circumstantial evidence that he did so. (B) is wrong because it states the wrong hearsay exception. A present sense impression is a comment made concurrently with the perception of an event that is not particularly exciting concerning the event perceived. Clearly this exception does not apply to these facts because Dennoyer was not perceiving an event and describing it in his letter; rather he was expressing his state of mind at the time he was writing. (C) is wrong because the letter is relevant. Evidence is relevant if it tends to make the existence of a material fact more probable than it would be without the evidence. Dennoyer's whereabouts on the day of the crime are certainly a fact of consequence to the determination of this action. The letter makes the fact that he was in Vermont on January 12 more probable than it would be without the letter; thus, the letter is relevant. (D) is wrong because the letter falls within the state of mind exception to the hearsay rule (*see* above).

Answer to Question 26

(B) The court should allow the prosecutor's question because it is appropriate to show bias or interest on the part of the witness. Evidence that a witness is biased or has an interest in the outcome of the case tends to show that the witness has a motive to lie. Bias or adverse interest can be proved by cross-examination or extrinsic evidence, and in some cases, both. Here, the fact that Wiener is being prosecuted for the same crime tends to show that he has a motive to lie in saying that the fire started accidentally. Thus, it is proper impeachment for the prosecutor to cross-examine Wiener about Wiener's own prosecution. (A) is wrong because all witnesses are subject to impeachment, and evidence (including character evidence) that bears on truthfulness is always admissible (although the means of proof may be restricted). This choice confuses the basis for the prosecution's introduction of substantive character evidence against a defendant in a criminal trial with valid impeachment of a witness for bias or interest. (C) is wrong because conviction of a crime is not a requisite for introduction of evidence showing bias or interest. A felony conviction or a conviction for a crime involving dishonesty is an entirely separate method of impeachment. (D) is wrong for two reasons: (i) the answer to the question could in no way incriminate Wiener; and (ii) even if the answer could tie Wiener to the commission of the crime, he could invoke the privilege to refuse to answer—the question itself would not be objectionable.

Answer to Question 27

(A) Hugo's testimony should be admitted because it is proper opinion testimony by a lay witness. Where an event is likely to be perceived as a whole impression, rather than as more specific components, opinions by lay witnesses are generally admitted. Lay opinion testimony is admissible when: (i) it is rationally based on the perception of the witness; (ii) it is helpful to a clear understanding of his testimony or to the determination of a fact in issue; and (iii) it is not based on scientific, technical, or other specialized knowledge. [Fed. R. Evid. 701] One matter about which a lay witness may testify is the general appearance or condition of a person. In contrast, expert opinion testimony is called for when the subject matter is such that technical or other specialized knowledge will assist the jury in understanding the evidence or determining a fact in issue. Here, Hugo is not being asked to describe specific injuries that may have been incurred by Plaintiff; that would more appropriately be left to the specialized knowledge of an expert. Rather, Hugo is being asked to testify as to Plaintiff's general condition (*i.e.,* Plaintiff was conscious or unconscious). Having been on duty in the emergency room when Plaintiff was brought in, Hugo had the opportunity to observe Plaintiff. Thus, Hugo is in a position to offer an opinion as to Plaintiff's unconscious condition based on Hugo's own perception. It is easier for Hugo to express his testimony this way than to go into detail about specific manifestations of Plaintiff's condition. Also, this opinion aids in the determination of a disputed factual issue (*i.e.,* whether Plaintiff ever lost consciousness). Therefore, Hugo's testimony is admissible as proper lay opinion testimony. (B) is wrong because, as noted above, this testimony does not relate to a matter the understanding of which requires resort to specialized knowledge. Status as an expert is not necessary to be able to state whether a person was conscious. Therefore, Hugo's status as a nonexpert constitutes no basis for the exclusion of his testimony. (C) is wrong because, if anything, Hugo's testimony will assist the jury, rather than intrude upon its province. Generally, the jury is to make fact determinations. Hugo's opinion testimony is helpful to the determination of a disputed fact. The jury relies on such testimony to enable it to reach a conclusion as to whether Plaintiff was unconscious. (D) is wrong because the best evidence rule does not apply to these facts. In proving the terms of a writing, where its terms are material, the best evidence rule requires that the original writing be produced. This question does not involve a writing of any type. Hugo would simply be testifying to what he personally observed. Thus, the best evidence rule does not come into play.

Answer to Question 28

(A) Testimony regarding Dillon's attempt to bribe Weiss is admissible as substantive evidence against Dillon. An admission is a statement made or act done that amounts to a prior acknowledgment by one of the parties of one of the relevant facts. Under the Federal Rules, admissions by parties are not hearsay. Various kinds of conduct, including attempts to bribe witnesses, may be held to manifest an awareness of liability or guilt. Since Dillon's liability is the issue (*i.e.,* a relevant fact) in the case, his attempt to bribe Weiss is admissible as an admission of a party-opponent. (B) is wrong because, as discussed above, the offer is also admissible as an admission, and thus is not limited to impeachment. Moreover, Weiss's testimony would not be admissible as evidence of a specific instance of misconduct to impeach Dillon. A specific act of misconduct can be elicited only on cross-examination; extrinsic evidence is not permitted. The facts do not even indicate that Dillon has testified. (C) is wrong because the offer to bribe Weiss is relevant. Evidence is relevant if it tends to make the existence of a fact of consequence to the action more probable than it would be without the evidence. Evidence that Dillon tried to bribe a witness to testify falsely makes it more probable that the accident was his fault; thus, it is relevant. (D) is wrong because the fact that relevant evidence is misleading or prejudicial is not a sufficient reason, by itself, to exclude the evidence. Under Federal Rule 403, the judge has discretion to exclude otherwise admissible, relevant evidence if its probative value is substantially outweighed by the danger of unfair prejudice, confusion of the issues, misleading the jury, or by considerations of undue delay, waste of time, or needless presentation of cumulative evidence. Here, the choice states only that the evidence is misleading and prejudicial; it does not state that the probative value of the evidence is substantially outweighed by these facts. Furthermore, bribing a witness is highly probative of guilt, so it is unlikely to be misleading. Although the evidence is prejudicial, it is not at all clear that the prejudice would be unfair since there are few reasons other than guilt for bribing a witness.

Answer to Question 29

(C) The evidence of Daffy's conviction is inadmissible to prove Daffy was intoxicated because the crime was punishable by imprisonment of at most 90 days. Despite the fact that copies of judgments are hearsay (because they are out-of-court statements used to prove the truth of the matter asserted), the Federal Rules of Evidence provide that judgments of felony convictions are admissible in both criminal and civil actions to prove any fact essential to the judgment. The Rules define felony convictions as crimes punishable by death or imprisonment in excess of one year. [Fed. R. Evid. 803(22)] Here, the crime for which Daffy was convicted carries a maximum term of imprisonment of 90 days. Thus, Daffy's conviction is not a felony conviction for purposes of the Federal Rule, and the conviction is inadmissible hearsay as proof of the fact asserted (*i.e.,* that Daffy was driving his car while intoxicated when he struck Porky's car). (A) is incorrect because the copy of the judgment of conviction is not a record, report, statement, or data compilation of a public office or agency, setting forth: (i) the activities of the office or agency; (ii) matters observed pursuant to a duty imposed by law; or (iii) factual findings resulting from an investigation made pursuant to authority granted by law. Therefore, the copy of the judgment is not deemed to be a public record for purposes of the hearsay exception for public records and reports. (B) is incorrect because a final judgment offered to prove a fact essential to a point in controversy is admissible under the Federal Rules only if the judgment is a felony conviction. As noted above, Daffy's conviction is not a felony conviction. (D) is incorrect because a properly authenticated copy of a court judgment would be the best evidence of Daffy's conviction. The best evidence rule states that, in proving the terms of a writing, where the terms are material, the original writing must be produced. [Fed. R. Evid. 1002] One class of situations to which the rule applies is that in which the writing is a legally operative or dispositive instrument such as a contract, deed, will, or judgment. Such writings are viewed as essential repositories of the facts recorded therein, and as such are within the rule. Furthermore, duplicates (*e.g.,* photocopies) are admissible the same as originals, unless: (i) the authenticity of the original is challenged; or (ii) circumstances exist that would render it unfair to admit the duplicate in place of the original. [Fed. R. Evid. 1003] Here, a properly authenticated photocopy of the judgment of conviction would be as admissible as the original judgment for purposes of proving that such a judgment has been entered. Therefore, there is no violation of the best evidence rule.

Answer to Question 30

(C) The objection should be overruled because Wanda's testimony is proper opinion testimony. Although opinions by lay witnesses are generally inadmissible, they may be admitted when an event is likely to be perceived as a whole impression rather than as more specific components. Under the Federal Rules, lay opinion testimony is admissible when: (i) it is rationally based on the perception of the witness; and (ii) it is helpful to a clear understanding of her testimony or to the determination of a fact in issue. [Fed. R. Evid. 701] The witness must have had the opportunity to observe the event that forms the basis of her opinion. A witness who has seen a person and is able to describe that person's actions, words, or conduct may express an opinion as to whether that person was or was not intoxicated. Here, Wanda had an opportunity to personally observe Daffy and his words and conduct at the time of the accident. Her opinion that Daffy appeared intoxicated is helpful to an understanding of her testimony because it is easier and clearer to simply state that Daffy appeared intoxicated than to describe his gait, speech, eyes, and diction. Also, Wanda's opinion is helpful to the determination of a fact in issue—*i.e.,* Daffy's intoxication at the time of the accident. Thus, Wanda's opinion as to Daffy's intoxication is proper lay opinion testimony, and the objection of Daffy's attorney should be overruled. (A) is incorrect because, as has been explained, lay opinion testimony as to whether or not a person who has been observed by the witness was intoxicated is admissible. (B) is incorrect because expert testimony is appropriate and necessary only when the subject matter of testimony is such that scientific, technical, or other specialized knowledge would assist the finder of fact in understanding the evidence or determining a fact in issue. [Fed. R. Evid. 702] A determination as to whether a person was intoxicated can easily be based on observation of that person by a layperson and does not require any technical or specialized knowledge. Therefore, Wanda's status as an expert or nonexpert has no bearing on the admissibility of her testimony. (D) is incorrect because it states an exception to the hearsay rule, and there is no hearsay problem here. Hearsay is an out-of-court statement offered to prove the truth of the matter asserted. Wanda is not testifying to an out-of-court statement made by herself or anyone else, but rather is testifying as to what she observed concerning Daffy's intoxicated state.

Answer to Question 31

(C) Trinette's testimony should be admitted because it is probative evidence relating to an issue of consequence to the case. Phil's physical whereabouts at the time of the rape are of obvious consequence to the determination of this rape prosecution, particularly since his defense is that he was hundreds of miles away at the time of the rape. Trinette's testimony tends to make Phil's presence in the area more probable than it would be without her testimony. Thus, Trinette's testimony is relevant as to the identity of the rapist and should be admitted. (A) is incorrect even though it is true that Phil has not put his character in issue. In a criminal case, the prosecution cannot initiate evidence of the defendant's bad character merely to show that he is more likely to have committed the crime of which he is accused; the prosecution may only offer such evidence in rebuttal after the defendant has offered evidence of his good character to show his innocence. However, (A) is incorrect because Trinette's testimony is offered, not as evidence of Phil's bad character, but as evidence that he was near the city at the time of the rape rather than hundreds of miles away. Consequently, Trinette's testimony is admissible despite the fact that Phil has not put his character in issue. (B) is incorrect for two reasons. First, although they are inadmissible to establish criminal disposition or to infer bad character, prior crimes or misconduct may be admissible for other purposes; *e.g.,* to show motive, intent, opportunity, preparation, plan, knowledge, identity, or absence of mistake whenever these issues are relevant (and identity is relevant here because Phil has denied being the rapist). Thus, the fact that evidence pertains to a prior uncharged offense does not necessarily call for the exclusion of such evidence. Second, Trinette's testimony is not being offered to show character, but is rather offered to show that Phil was seen by Trinette near the rape scene shortly before the rape. The fact that Trinette's testimony also pertains to an uncharged offense (soliciting a prostitute) will not result in the exclusion of that testimony. (D) is incorrect because evidence is inadmissible if offered solely to establish a criminal defendant's disposition or propensity to commit the crime charged. If Trinette's testimony were only offered to show that, because Phil was seeking sexual gratification near the time of Andrea's rape, it was more likely that Phil committed that rape, the evidence would be inadmissible.

Answer to Question 32

(B) The prosecutor's question is aimed at discovering bias, which tends to show that June has a motive to lie. Impeachment involves the casting of an adverse reflection on the veracity of a witness, and it may take several forms. Evidence that a witness is biased tends to show that she has a motive to lie, and is thus a well-recognized method of impeachment. Inferences of bias may be shown by evidence of family or other relationship. Here, the prosecutor is attempting to show that, due to a family relationship or friendship with Robert's wife, June may be biased and would thus have a motive to lie on behalf of Robert. Therefore, the prosecutor is engaging in an accepted method of impeachment. (A) correctly states that the prosecutor's question attacks June's truth and veracity. However, not all methods of attacking a witness's truth and veracity are admissible. (B) is a better answer than (A) because it identifies the specific method of impeachment that the cross-examiner is using. (C) is incorrect because evidence that tends to prove or disprove the credibility of a witness is relevant. The information sought to be elicited by the prosecutor's question will reflect on a possible motive that June may have to lie. Therefore, such information is relevant. (D) incorrectly states that the answer to the prosecutor's question would create prejudice that would outweigh its probative value. Under Federal Rule 403, evidence may be excluded if its probative value is substantially outweighed by the danger of unfair prejudice, confusion of the issues, or misleading the jury. While any material evidence introduced by a party will probably be prejudicial to the adverse party's case, it is only *unfair* prejudice (*i.e.,* suggesting a decision on an improper basis) that may be excluded under this rule. Here, the answer to the prosecutor's question would clarify the matter of whether June had a motive to lie. This would not be unfairly prejudicial because it would tend to make June's testimony as to Robert's whereabouts at the time of the alleged crime more or less believable, which is the proper basis on which the trier of fact should accept or reject her testimony.

Answer to Question 33

(C) Shari should be allowed to testify as to what she perceived. To be admissible under the Federal Rules, evidence must be probative of a material issue in the case and must be competent (*i.e.,* not otherwise excludable). Evidence is material if it relates to an issue in the case, and it is probative if it tends to prove the fact for which it is offered. Evidence is competent if it does not violate a specific exclusionary rule. At issue here is whether Louise started the restaurant fire. If gasoline was used to start the fire, the fact that Louise was seen near the fire and smelled like gasoline makes it more likely that she started the fire; so the proffered evidence is material and relevant. It is also competent: under the Federal Rules, opinion testimony by lay witnesses is admissible when (i) it is rationally based on the perception of the witness, and (ii) it is helpful to a clear understanding of her testimony or to the determination of a fact in issue. Matters involving sense recognition, such as what something smelled like, are common subjects of opinion testimony. Here, Shari's testimony satisfies both elements of the test and should be admitted. Thus, (C) is correct and (A) is incorrect. (D) is incorrect because to testify as an expert one must have special knowledge, skill, experience, or education on the subject of her testimony, and if everyone who drives a car knows the smell of gasoline, there is nothing special about that knowledge. (B) is incorrect because the best evidence rule requires that the original document be produced only when the terms of the document are material and sought to be proved. The fact to be proved—that gasoline was used—exists independently of any written record of the chemical tests; therefore, the best evidence rule does not apply.

Answer to Question 34

(B) The fact that Main Street runs in a north-south direction is the most appropriate item for the judge to apply the doctrine of judicial notice to because it is a matter of common knowledge in the community. The Federal Rules conform to the existing state rules governing judicial notice. Federal Rule 201(b) defines a fact that may be noticed as "one not subject to reasonable dispute in that it is either (i) generally known within the territorial jurisdiction of the trial court, or (ii) capable of accurate and ready determination by resort to sources whose accuracy cannot reasonably be questioned." To be considered generally known within the community, the fact must be something that well-informed people generally know and accept. Although usually facts of common knowledge are known everywhere, it is sufficient for judicial notice if they are known in the community where the court is sitting. Because the fact that Main Street runs in a north-south direction is generally known by the community in which the courts sits, judicial notice may be taken of it. (A) is incorrect because judicial notice may not be taken of a fact solely because it is personally known by the judge. A judge may have to ignore facts that he knows as a private person if those facts are neither commonly known in the community nor capable of certain verification by resort to easily accessible sources of indisputable accuracy. Therefore, the judge may not take judicial notice of the wet pavement based solely on his recollection. (C) is incorrect because the fact that the brakes were faulty is subject to reasonable dispute. As discussed above, judicial notice may only be taken of matters of common knowledge in the community where the court sits or facts capable of certain verification. Here, the fact that Dawn's brakes were faulty was not a matter of common knowledge in Humberton. They were only faulty in the opinion of two witnesses. Also, the condition of the brakes is not easily verified by resorting to well-established sources. Even though their testimony was uncontroverted, the auto mechanic and engineer would not be considered such sources because their conclusions could be reasonably questioned. Therefore, the condition of the brakes would be considered to be subject to reasonable dispute and not appropriate for judicial notice. (D) is also incorrect because Dawn's speed at the time of the accident was subject to reasonable dispute. As discussed above, judicial notice may only be taken of facts not subject to reasonable dispute—*i.e.,* matters of common knowledge in the community or facts capable of certain verification. Whether Dawn exceeded the speed limit is not a matter of common knowledge in the community. In fact, there was conflicting testimony concerning Dawn's speed. The speed also was not a fact capable of certain verification from well-established sources. The skid marks would not be considered certain enough to be such a source.

Answer to Question 35

(B) The officer's testimony should be admitted because it is an admission by a party-opponent. Generally, evidence is admissible if it is relevant, *i.e.,* if it has a tendency to prove any fact of consequence to the action. The testimony here is relevant because it makes it more likely that the defendant committed the acts complained of. It is also competent because its admission does not violate any exclusionary rule of evidence. Evidence law generally prohibits admission of hearsay—out-of-court statements offered to prove the truth of the matter asserted—but the rule does not apply to admissions by party-opponents—they are treated as nonhearsay under the Federal Rules. Thus, the testimony is admissible and (B) is correct. (A) may be a true statement—past instances of misconduct may be used to impeach a witness, at least if they are probative as to whether he is worthy of belief—but it is an incorrect answer because it focuses on impeachment, and Amy's father is not being impeached here. (C) is incorrect because the best evidence rule is not applicable here. The rule requires that when the contents of a writing are sought to be proved, the writing itself should be admitted if it is available. Here, however, the witness is not trying to prove that the defendant has been convicted, but rather that he made the admission. (D) is incorrect for reasons similar to why (C) is incorrect. It is true under the Federal Rules that convictions generally are not admissible for impeachment of a witness if more than 10 years old, but the officer is not trying to admit the defendant's conviction here (and is not trying to impeach the defendant, who may not even have testified). Rather, Amy is seeking to admit the defendant's confession. The confession is an admission by a party-opponent and is admissible as substantive evidence.

Answer to Question 36

(B) Edgar's testimony is only relevant if the conditions of the experiment were substantially similar to the conditions at the time and place of the accident. Evidence of pretrial experiments that does not require expert testimony is treated no differently under the Federal Rules from other evidence. It will be admissible if it is relevant (*i.e.,* if it has any tendency to prove or disprove a fact that is of consequence to the action) and if it is not barred by a specific exclusionary rule or the general balancing test of Rule 403. To the extent that the conditions of Edgar's experiment replicated the conditions of the accident, the experiment is relevant because whether Edgar's linoleum was wet after 45 minutes tends to establish whether Store's floor was wet when Jack walked on it, and this fact is of major consequence to Jack's personal injury action. To the extent that the conditions of Edgar's experiment are not similar, the minimal probative value of his testimony probably would be outweighed under Rule 403 by considerations of unfair prejudice or waste of time. (A) is incorrect because the Federal Rules do not require a representative of the adverse party to be present at the experiment; Jack's attorney can subject the conditions of the experiment to scrutiny through cross-examination of Edgar. (C) is incorrect for the same reason: Jack's attorney can effectively cross-examine Edgar even without having conducted his own experiments. (D) is incorrect because the person conducting the experiment need not be an independent observer. If Edgar is an employee, his potential bias can be elicited on cross-examination.

Answer to Question 37

(A) Willis's testimony is admissible as relevant opinion testimony by an expert witness. The Federal Rules permit witnesses qualified as experts to testify in the form of an opinion if the subject matter is one where scientific, technical, or other specialized knowledge will assist the jury in understanding the evidence or determining a fact in issue. [Fed. R. Evid. 702] Under Federal Rule 703, the expert may base his opinion on facts not known personally but supplied to him outside the courtroom (*e.g.,* reports of other experts). Such facts need not be admissible in evidence as long as the facts are of a kind reasonably relied on by experts in the particular field. Here, Willis, as a state licensed engineer, probably qualifies as an expert on the subject of his testimony and therefore can state his opinion as to the cause of the collapse of the excavation wall. As choice (A) states, he may base his opinion on the building plans, the geologist's report, and the engineer's report if civil engineers in his field rely on this type of data in reaching conclusions such as his. Thus, choice (D) is incorrect. Choice (B) is incorrect because whether this analysis is negligent is irrelevant to its admissibility; this fact can be brought out by cross-examination. A prudent analysis will still be inadmissible if it was based on materials that experts in his field did not reasonably rely on. Choice (C) is incorrect; Federal Rule 704(a) provides that otherwise admissible opinion testimony is not objectionable because it embraces the ultimate issue to be decided by the trier of fact.

Answer to Question 38

(B) The court should rule Statement 1 admissible and Statement 2 inadmissible. Statement 1 is admissible as an admission by a party-opponent, while Statement 2 is inadmissible as an offer to pay medical expenses. An admission is a statement made or act done that amounts to a prior acknowledgment by one of the parties to an action of one of the relevant facts. The Federal Rules treat such statements as nonhearsay. [Fed. R. Evid. 801(d)(2)] In Statement 1, Deft acknowledges that he ran the red light, and that the incident resulting in Plain's injuries was his fault. This statement clearly amounts to an acknowledgment of relevant facts (*i.e.,* that Deft was at fault) and qualifies as an admission by a party-opponent. Evidence that a party paid (or offered to pay) an injured party's medical bill is not admissible to prove liability for the injuries. [Fed. R. Evid. 409] Such payment (or offer to pay) might be prompted solely by humanitarian motives. Statement 2 is clearly an offer by Deft to pay the medical bills of Plain, an injured party. Thus, the statement is not admissible to prove liability for Plain's injuries (and proving liability appears to be the only reason Plain has for attempting to introduce the statement into evidence). Note that had this been a single statement, the outcome would have been the same since an admission of fact accompanying offers to pay medical expenses is admissible. (A) is wrong because, as explained above, Statement 2 is inadmissible. (C) is wrong as to both statements because Statement 1 is admissible and Statement 2 is inadmissible. (D) is wrong because Statement 1 is admissible.

Answer to Question 39

(A) Since this was not a confidential communication between husband and wife, the testimonial privilege would be applicable. In federal court, the testimonial privilege is viewed as belonging to the witness-spouse. (B), (C), and (D) are therefore incorrect.

Answer to Question 40

(B) Since Warren did not testify, and he is charged with a crime of violence, his character for honesty and veracity is not at issue, and the proffered evidence is irrelevant. Thus, (C) is incorrect. A criminal defendant may offer evidence of character relevant to the charges, and so (A) is wrong. (D) is a misstatement of law.

Answer to Question 41

(D) Under the Federal Rules, this prior inconsistent statement may be used to impeach and as substantive evidence. A prior inconsistent statement made while under oath and subject to penalty of perjury in a deposition or prior hearing is not hearsay under Federal Rule 801. (A) is therefore incorrect. (B) is incorrect because the Federal Rules permit a party to impeach its own witness, even if not "surprised." (C) is incorrect because it is too narrow.

Answer to Question 42

(C) Federal Rule 407 makes evidence of subsequent remedial measures inadmissible to show negligence. Rule 407 is based on the public policy of safety. The law wants to encourage people to make repairs or take other remedial measures after an accident. Thus, (A) and (B) are incorrect. (D) is wrong because Carla is not trying to impeach Art or anyone else.

Answer to Question 43

(A) Federal Rule 609 permits the prosecution to inquire into prior convictions of crimes involving dishonesty if they are less than 10 years old. Since the conviction in (A) is more than 10 years old, it would be subject to objection as being too remote. (B) relates to the witness's ability to perceive and would be a legitimate question on cross-examination. (C) shows a possible bias on the part of the witness, which is an acceptable method of impeachment. (D) relates to a prior bad act that shows dishonesty. Such acts may be asked about on cross-examination of the witness.

Answer to Question 44

(C) Videotape evidence is treated the same as photographic and tape-recorded evidence. If it is properly authenticated, it is admissible, but it may not be properly admitted without the proper foundation first being established. (A) is wrong because the tape constitutes an admission and, therefore, is not hearsay. (B) is wrong because the privilege against self-incrimination applies only to testimonial evidence. (D) is nonsensical.

Answer to Question 45

(A) The accused may introduce evidence of his good character for the trait involved in the case to show his innocence of the alleged crime. Since this evidence is not restricted to impeachment purposes, (B) and (D) are incorrect. Under Federal Rule 405, the witness for the defendant may testify to the defendant's reputation for the trait in question, and he may also give his personal opinion. (C) is therefore incorrect.

Answer to Question 46

(B) This is a variation of the famous *Hillmon* case, where it was held that state of mind was admissible to show that the declarant acted in conformity with his expressed declaration. (A) is wrong because even though it is hearsay it is subject to a specific exception. (C) is wrong because state of mind is an exception to the hearsay rule. (D) is wrong because an alibi is relevant.

Answer to Question 47

(C) Jurors are incompetent as witnesses, but only as to the case in which they are currently sitting or at a later time to impeach their verdict. This is not the case here. The evidence could be excluded, however, if the judge determines that the probative value of the evidence would be substantially outweighed by its tendency to mislead. (A) is wrong because a leading question is permitted on cross-examination. (B) is wrong because the question goes to bias, so it cannot be excluded on the issue of scope of direct examination. (D) is wrong because it makes no sense.

Answer to Question 48

(D) All witnesses are competent unless physically or mentally impaired in some fashion not applicable here, or unless they are too young to understand the oath and the need to testify truthfully. Therefore, (A) and (B) are incorrect. (C) is wrong because there is no precise age at which an infant is deemed competent to testify; it depends on the capacity and intelligence of the particular child.

Answer to Question 49

(C) McKenzie's attempt to bribe Bob would be considered an admission by conduct. Under the Federal Rules, an admission is not considered hearsay. Alternatively, McKenzie's conduct could be classified as conduct not intended as an assertion. Such conduct is not considered hearsay under the rules. Thus, (A) is clearly wrong. (B) is wrong. The evidence helps establish that the defendant believed that he acted negligently. (D) is wrong. Since admissions are not hearsay, the evidence would not come in under an exception to the hearsay rule. Also, declarations against interest can only be used when the declarant is unavailable.

Answer to Question 50

(A) The contents of a document are sought to be proven and the document is not collateral; thus, the judge must find that the document itself is not available for testimony on the issue to be admissible. (B) is wrong because, as stated, the document itself must be produced unless it is not available. (C) and (D) are wrong because the judge, not the jury, makes these types of determinations.

Answer to Question 51

(B) Winston's statement was made while he was still under the stress of excitement of the startling event, and it concerns the immediate facts of the occurrence. (The tipoff that Winston's statement was made under the stress of excitement of the event is the exclamation mark at the end.) Therefore, it is an excited utterance and an exception to the hearsay rule. Thus, (C) is incorrect. (A) is incorrect because a prior consistent statement is admissible only to rebut a charge that the witness is lying or exaggerating because of some motive. The facts do not indicate such a charge against Winston. (D) is incorrect because the opinion of a lay witness is admissible if it is based on the perception of the witness, helpful in determining a fact in issue, and not based on scientific, technical, or other specialized knowledge.

Answer to Question 52

(C) The evidence tends to show that the bus company was not acting prudently when it hired the bus driver who injured Lucy; thus (A) is wrong. (B) is not a good answer because only *subsequent* remedial measures (*i.e.*, those taken after the injury to the plaintiff occurred) may not be proven as evidence of negligence. (D) is not accurate—the evidence does not show that the bus driver was incompetent, but rather that the company did not investigate his competence when he was hired, an issue related to Lucy's negligent hiring claim.

Answer to Question 53

(D) Each of the other picks presents a situation wherein leading questions are generally allowable, at the discretion of the court: (A) is a preliminary matter as to which there is no dispute; (B) is cross-examination; (C) is examination of a very young child. Leading questions are generally not permitted on direct examination of a disinterested witness, and thus (D) is correct.

Answer to Question 54

(C) Federal Rule 409 excludes offers to pay medical expenses, but not statements made in connection with such offers. The president of ChemCo, obviously authorized to speak for that entity, has made an admission of negligence, and that admission is admissible. Thus, (B) is wrong. (A) is wrong because the statement is an admission, which is nonhearsay under the Federal Rules. (D) is wrong because there was no offer to compromise—ChemCo merely said that it would pay medical expenses, without bargaining for anything in return. In addition, if it were an offer to compromise, a statement made in connection therewith would not be admissible.

Answer to Question 55

(B) Evidence is relevant if it helps decide an issue in dispute. Since the issue is whether it was Gary's car that hit Rob, the fact that Gary had speed equipment on his car would probably be considered irrelevant. While that point might be debated, (B) is still the correct answer because (A), (C), and (D) are clearly wrong. (A) is wrong. If the question was asked on cross-examination, it is not objectionable as leading; if the question was asked on direct exam, it would be unobjectionable as leading because the opposing party would be considered a hostile witness. (C) is wrong because evidence of a character trait of irresponsibility would be inadmissible. (D) is wrong. The issue is whether the evidence is relevant, not whether the best evidence rule applies.

Answer to Question 56

(B) Gary's answer could only reflect his opinion of what Rob did or thought, and is thus impermissible opinion evidence. A lay person's opinion is admissible if it is rationally based on the perception of the witness, helpful to a clear understanding of the witness's testimony on the determination of a fact in issue, and not based on scientific, technical, or other specialized knowledge. Gary's opinion does not meet those requirements. (A) is wrong because the question does not call for an out-of-court declaration. (C) is wrong because, although relevant, the answer would still be improper. (D) is wrong because the form of the question is improper.

Answer to Question 57

(C) If Gary "always" takes a specific route home, the evidence is offered as habit and is admissible. (D) is wrong, because the evidence is admissible to establish habit even if it is not offered for impeachment. (B) is wrong because the evidence may tend to show Gary could not have been the one who hit Rob. (A) is wrong because "self-serving" is not a valid objection.

Answer to Question 58

(D) Most likely the evidence violates the best evidence rule. Since Leslie testified that there was a written agreement, to prove its terms she would be required to produce the written agreement or explain its absence. (A) is not correct; the out-of-court agreement would be a "legally operative fact," not considered hearsay. (B) is wrong because she is not claiming the agreement is a will. (C) is wrong because she is testifying concerning the existence of a written agreement.

Answer to Question 59

(C) Any lay witness who is familiar with the signature of a person may testify as to his opinion as to its genuineness. Therefore, (A) is wrong. (B) is wrong because it goes to the weight of the testimony, not the admissibility. (D) is wrong because the lay witness may testify in support or against the genuineness.

Answer to Question 60

(B) A criminal defendant who takes the stand puts her credibility in issue the same as any other witness; thus, she may be impeached by proof of a prior felony conviction. (A) is wrong both because the question asked how the judge should rule on the "question," not whether Tammy would have to answer, and also, because the question is not even directed to any matter on which she can be incriminated. (C) is wrong because many proper questions seek "prejudicial" information. (D) is wrong because a party is not prohibited on cross-examination from inquiring into a witness's credibility.

Answer to Question 61

(B) This is a criminal matter, and the accused is permitted to introduce evidence of her good character for the trait involved in the case in support of the probability that she did not commit the crime alleged. Thus, (C) and (D) are wrong as misstatements of the law. (A) is wrong because just the fact that evidence is not hearsay is no reason to admit it.

Answer to Question 62

(B) The testimony is hearsay, but admissible within the state-of-mind exception. (A) is incorrect because a "dying declaration" must be made while in fear of "impending" death. (C) is incorrect because Barbara is not a psychiatrist, and there is no evidence that Tammy's husband assumed her to be one. (D) is wrong because the state of mind need not be as of the time of the incident to be relevant.

Answer to Question 63

(B) Persons interested in a lawsuit are no longer disqualified as witnesses. (A) is wrong because Linda need not be the personal representative of Bob's estate to testify. (C) is incorrect because she is testifying as to what she saw, not as to her opinion. In any event, a lay witness may testify as to an opinion if she is a percipient witness. (D) is wrong because the common law spousal incapacity has been abolished.

Answer to Question 64

(B) The evidence is not hearsay since it is an admission made by and offered against a party; therefore (A) is incorrect. (C) is wrong because Linda is available to testify. (D) may be relevant, but the facts show that it was merely an offer to compromise a disputed claim, and therefore public policy encouraging settlements precludes the introduction of such evidence.

Answer to Question 65

(A) An admission by a party-opponent is the party's own statement offered against him by the opposing side, and under the Federal Rules, it is not hearsay. Thus, (D) is incorrect. (B) does not state a proper basis for admissibility; besides, the only way the statement could be admitted by way of the report is as an admission. (C) is wrong. If the statement qualifies as an admission—made by a party, offered by the opponent and relevant—it will be admissible even if the admitting party had no rational basis for the statement.

Answer to Question 66

(D) Under Federal Rule 801(d)(2), an out-of-court statement of an agent or an employee can be introduced as an admission against the principal or employer if it concerns a matter within the scope of the agency or employment, made during the existence of the relationship. Relief's statement constitutes an admission by a party-opponent and is not hearsay. (A) and (C) state requirements for admissibility that have no basis in law. Admissibility of an admission is not conditioned on the availability of the declarant; (B) is therefore incorrect.

Answer to Question 67

(C) The accused in a criminal prosecution may always introduce evidence of his good character for the trait involved in the case to show that he might not have committed the crime of which he is charged. This is true whether or not he takes the witness stand on his own behalf, and so (B) is incorrect. (A) is wrong. The defendant's evidence of relevant good character must be established by reputation or opinion evidence, not by evidence of specific acts. The defendant presented appropriate reputation evidence. (D) is wrong. There is no such rule and the testimony is not questionable.

Answer to Question 68

(A) The testimony would be hearsay, but it would be admissible under the exception of a declaration of an intent to do a future act, sometimes referred to as a declaration of present mental state. [Fed. R. Evid. 803(3)] (D) is therefore incorrect. The trip provides an alibi defense and is therefore relevant; so (C) is thus incorrect. (B) is wrong because this is not a verbal act; verbal acts are out-of-court statements that when spoken have legal significance, *e.g.*, words of contract or defamation.

Answer to Question 69

(A) Impeachment is always proper on cross-examination, and evidence of bias can always be used to impeach a witness. (B) is wrong because relatives are competent to testify. Under the Federal Rules, a witness is competent if he has personal knowledge and declares he will testify truthfully. (C) is wrong because impeachment is not limited to the scope of direct examination. (D) is wrong because evidence of bias developed on cross-examination would never be considered collateral.

Answer to Question 70

(A) The clothing is circumstantial evidence because the trier of fact is being asked to draw an inference that the clothes are Digby's based on the proven fact that the clothes were found in a dumpster at Digby's building. Direct evidence is evidence that, if believed, will by itself establish one of the propositions in the case; no inference will be necessary. Thus, (B) is incorrect. (C) is incorrect because finding the clothing matching the description of the robber's clothes near Digby's apartment tends to make it more probable that Digby committed the robbery than it would be without the clothing. (D) is incorrect because it states the standard for proving guilt, not for the admissibility of evidence.

Answer to Question 71

(D) Aunt Minnie's comment is an out-of-court statement offered for its truth, and it does not fall within a recognized exception to the hearsay rule. (A) is incorrect because a present sense impression must be communicated while perceiving the event or object, or immediately thereafter. Minnie was telling Katrina about something she had seen earlier in the day. (B) is incorrect because, even if the statement is relevant, it is still hearsay, and Aunt Minnie's unavailability does not bring it within an exception to the hearsay rule. (C) does not state a reason for excluding the evidence; circumstantial evidence is admissible.

Answer to Question 72

(B) It is proper to impeach a witness by showing that the witness has a possible bias. Evidence that the witness is being paid to testify would be proper impeachment through bias. (A) states the requirement for introduction of a prior inconsistent statement; this is obviously inapplicable here. The credibility of a witness is not collateral, and so (C) is incorrect. Leading questions are proper on cross-examination; thus (D) is incorrect.

Answer to Question 73

(A) (A) is the only acceptable answer. (B) is incorrect because the opinion was based on the percep-tion of the witness and would be helpful to the determination of a fact in issue—the negligence of Parker. (C) is wrong because Tod is not a party. (D) is wrong because Tod did not testify and therefore the statement cannot qualify as a prior inconsistent statement. The statement is clearly hearsay. It could be argued that it qualifies as an "excited utterance," but admissible as an excited utterance is not one of the four picks. Therefore (A) is the winner because (B), (C), and (D) are clearly wrong.

Answer to Question 74

(C) Statements made under the stress of some exciting event and relating to that event are admissible as exceptions to the hearsay rule. Hence, (A) is incorrect. (D) is incorrect because even in those jurisdictions that permit dying declarations to be admitted in civil trials, the declaration must have been made by the decedent in the awareness that he was dying and it must have concerned the circumstances of his death. (B) is wrong because this statute only limits the admissibility of testimony *against* a decedent. The testimony in this case would not subject Vance's estate to any liability.

Answer to Question 75

(C) Gustave is going to have to offer more evidence to connect the medicine he took to the injuries that he and Dr. Hamilton's other patients suffered, but there is no reason to exclude Dr. Hamilton's testimony at this point. This question is best handled by determining the incorrect answers. (A) is obviously wrong because the hearsay objection is not applicable to percipient observations of a witness. (B) is wrong because the best evidence rule applies when a party is attempting to prove the contents of a writing, recording, or photograph. (D) is wrong because Dr. Hamilton is testifying about matters of which she has personal knowledge, and she is not giving opinion testimony; thus, she does not have to be qualified as an expert.

Answer to Question 76

(A) Where Sam has introduced part of a writing, Bill would be entitled to cross-examine or introduce rebuttal evidence as to any other part of the same writing necessary to make it understood. (B) is an incorrect statement of the law. (C) is incorrect because the evidence tends to make it more probable that Bill complied with the contract than it would have been without the evidence. (D) is incorrect because the contract is not hearsay; it is a legally operative fact.

Answer to Question 77

(B) Under the Federal Rules, Bill may compel the proponent of the evidence to introduce any part thereof that ought, in fairness, to be considered contemporaneous with it. (A) is incorrect because no foundation need be laid. (C) is incorrect because Federal Rule 106 does not require proof of relevance. The standard is fairness. (D) is incorrect because, although it is hearsay, it is within the business records exception to the hearsay rule.

REAL PROPERTY QUESTIONS

Question 1

George and Harry owned large adjoining properties in the mountains. The boundary line between the properties was never clearly marked.

Twenty-five years ago, George dug a water well on a section of the property that he thought was his, but in fact was Harry's. George has continued to use the water and to maintain the well on a regular basis ever since.

Harry was adjudicated mentally incompetent 15 years ago. He died recently, and his executor has filed suit to eject George and quiet title. The jurisdiction's statute of limitations for adverse possession is 20 years.

With respect to the land on which the water well was dug:

(A) George has acquired title by adverse possession.

(B) George cannot claim title as an adverse possessor because he did not enter with hostile intent.

(C) George is in adverse possession but has not acquired title because the statute of limitations was tolled by Harry's incompetency.

(D) None of the above.

Questions 2-3 are based on the following fact situation:

For many years, Oscar owned one large parcel of land in a rural area. He built his home on the northern half of the property, and developed a large orchard of fruit trees on the southern portion.

Oscar became ill and was forced to spend his declining years in a convalescent hospital. Shortly before his death, he decided to make gifts of his property. He divided the property into two parcels: Parcel 1 comprised of the northern property containing the house, and

Parcel 2 comprised of the orchard property. First, he conveyed Parcel 1 by grant deed to his friend, Frank, as follows: "To Frank, for life, and then to his widow for her life, remainder to Frank's children then alive." Later, he conveyed Parcel 2 to his friend, Sara.

Oscar died intestate and his sole heir at law was his brother, Bob.

The house on Parcel 1 was old and in need of repair. After months of trying, Frank was unable to rent the house in its current condition. Frank did not wish to make the necessary repairs or pay the higher residential taxes. For this reason, Frank proposed to tear down the house and plant fruit trees on Parcel 1 and thus produce an income for himself and his family. The property would be worth substantially more as a fruit orchard than in its present condition. However, Bob feels that Oscar's old house has sentimental value and wants Frank to leave the land as it is. The common law Rule Against Perpetuities is unmodified by statute in the jurisdiction.

2. Does Bob have standing to sue to enjoin Frank from tearing the house down?

   (A) Yes, because he holds a reversion by operation of law that will take effect on the death of Frank's widow.

   (B) Yes, because he holds an executory interest that will become possessory if Frank dies without surviving children.

   (C) No, because Bob has no interest in Parcel 1.

   (D) No, provided Frank was married at the time of Oscar's conveyance, and has some children now living.

3. Assuming that Bob had standing to sue, which of the following actions could the court properly take, assuming Bob requested the appropriate relief?

I.   Enjoin Frank from tearing down the house.

II. Order Frank to pay the taxes on the property.

III. Order Frank to make the necessary repairs.

IV. Allow Frank to tear down the house, but order him to pay damages to Bob.

(A) IV. only.

(B) II. and III. only.

(C) I., II., and III. only.

(D) I. only.

Question 4

Heathcliff and Sonia were good friends who lived together in an apartment for three years. They decided to purchase a home and bought Loveacre, taking the property as joint tenants. Two years after taking up residency on Loveacre, Sonia became pregnant. Heathcliff and Sonia married, and soon after the wedding a son was born whom the couple named Clyde. Heathcliff and Sonia had strong disagreements as to how Clyde should be raised. These disagreements led to heated arguments, which led to a divorce.

After the divorce, Sonia had custody of Clyde. Loveacre, though occupied by Sonia, remained in the names of both Heathcliff and Sonia. Heathcliff moved out of the state and conveyed all his title and interest in Loveacre by deed to Clyde. Shortly thereafter, Heathcliff was killed in an automobile collison. Heathcliff died intestate.

Who has title to Loveacre?

(A) Sonia.

(B) Sonia owns one-half and Heathcliff's heirs own one-half.

(C) Sonia and Clyde as joint tenants.

(D) Sonia and Clyde as tenants in common.

Question 5

Owen owned a small manufacturing business in Metroville. When Owen decided to retire, he put the business up for sale. Stephen was interested in purchasing an existing factory for his expanding widget business. After inspecting Owen's property, Stephen made an offer of $150,000, which Owen accepted. They entered into a written contract for the sale of the plant that set the closing date for 30 days from the date of the contract. During the 30-day period, Stephen found a site that was better suited to his widget business. Looking for a way to get out of his contract with Owen, Stephen did some research. He discovered that Owen's building did not comply with the Metroville building code, that the zoning ordinance that covered the area where the plant was located would forbid the heavy trucks that Stephen used in shipping his widgets, and that the plant violated by one foot the setback from the street required by the zoning ordinance. Stephen notified Owen that he would not be going through with the closing. Owen sued Stephen for specific performance.

If Stephen prevails, which of the following would be the proper basis for the court's ruling?

I.   The violation of the building code renders the title unmarketable.

II. The zoning ordinance forbids the use of the type of truck Stephen uses in the area where the plant is located.

III. The building violates the setback requirement by one foot.

(A) I. only.

(B) III. only.

(C) I., II., or III.

(D) I. or III. only.

Question 6

Bob entered into a written contract to purchase Arthur's house for $50,000. The contract called for Arthur to deposit a deed in escrow forthwith, and for payment of the purchase price and delivery of the deed through escrow within 30 days thereafter. Arthur immediately deposited the deed with the escrow holder. On the 29th day, Arthur was injured in a car accident and rendered comatose; he remains in this state to date. On the 30th day, the sale closed pursuant to the contract; Arthur's deed was delivered to Bob, and the $50,000 was paid over to Arthur's account.

Arthur's incapacity:

(A) Has no effect on Bob's title.

(B) Constitutes a lien on Bob's title.

(C) Allows his court-appointed guardian to set aside Bob's deed.

(D) Prevented passage of title to Bob.

Question 7

Phoebe owned a large parcel of land located quite a distance from the town of Pine Valley. Langley, a retired man of advanced years and modest means, desired a quiet retreat in which to spend his retirement years. He decided to purchase a small plot of land from Phoebe. The land was located near the center of Phoebe's large parcel of land and was completely surrounded by it. However, Langley liked the rustic cabin that was located on the land he wanted to buy. The deed to the land, which Phoebe delivered to Langley for fair consideration, did not specifically grant an easement over Phoebe's property to reach the public highway bordering her land. There were two means of access to the cabin from the public roads: a driveway from the county road on the south, and a private road from Highway 10 on the east. Phoebe told Langley that he could use the private road from Highway 10. Twice during his first two years at the cabin, Langley felt too tired to drive to the private road and took the driveway from the county road instead.

At the end of his second year at the cabin, Langley became strapped for cash and began reading tarot cards to supplement his retirement income. He was very popular, and had a steady stream of clients coming to his home at all hours of the day and night. Most of the clients came in on the driveway from the county road, which ran close to Phoebe's home. Phoebe objected, and told Langley that neither he nor his clients had any right to use that driveway. She instructed him that in the future he should advise his clients that they must use the private road from Highway 10. Langley refused, and he and his clients continued to use the driveway from the county road. This went on for three years. Finally, Phoebe could not stand the noise from the traffic passing by her window any longer. Phoebe began blocking off the driveway from the county road with her limousine. Langley brought suit to enjoin this practice. The prescriptive period in this jurisdiction is five years.

Who will most likely prevail?

(A) Phoebe, because the tarot business has changed the nature of the use of the easement by necessity.

(B) Phoebe, because she may select the location of the easement.

(C) Langley, because he has a valid easement by necessity in the driveway from the county road.

(D) Langley, because he has acquired an easement by prescription in the driveway from the county road.

Questions 8-10 are based on the following fact situation:

Ogden is the owner of an apartment house. He executes a deed of the property "to my son, Sam, for his life, and, upon Sam's death, to the children of Sam, except that if Sam becomes bankrupt, to my daughter, Diane, then to the children of Diane, upon Diane's death." Sam is alive and well and not bankrupt at the time of the grant.

8. At the time of the grant, Sam's interest is best described as:

   (A) An estate for indefinite period.

   (B) A determinable life estate pur autre vie.

   (C) A life estate subject to an executory interest.

   (D) A defeasible nonfreehold estate.

9. Assume for purposes of this question only that Sam has two children, Woody and Norm. At the time of the grant, the interest of Woody and Norm is best described as:

   (A) A contingent remainder.

   (B) A vested remainder subject to open and to total divestment.

   (C) A vested remainder subject to open.

   (D) An executory interest.

10. Assume for purposes of this question only that Sam becomes bankrupt and that Diane takes possession of the property. The interest of Diane's children, Carla and Cliffy, is best described as:

    (A) A contingent remainder.

    (B) A vested remainder subject to total divestment.

    (C) An executory interest.

    (D) A vested remainder subject to open.

Questions 11-12 are based on the following fact situation:

Owner holds a fee simple interest in 2,000 acres of land. He wants to develop 1,500 acres as a residential subdivision. He wants to hold the remaining 500 acres for a long period, hoping they will appreciate in value. In the meantime, he plans to use the tract as an inducement in the marketing of the lots in the 1,500-acre subdivision. Owner's market analysis leads him to conclude that the greatest inducement he can offer is to hold the 500 acres as an area in which purchasers in the subdivision can ride horseback, hike, camp, and fish. Business judgment indicates that he can make these 500 acres available for these purposes for 20 years if he can be assured that after such period he will be free to do with the land as he chooses.

11. The best device to implement the purpose of Owner with respect to the 500 acres (assuming that any device chosen will receive judicial recognition and enforcement) is:

    (A) Covenant.

    (B) Easement.

    (C) Leasehold.

    (D) Personal contractual obligation of Owner.

12. Assume that at the end of 20 years Owner sells the 500-acre tract to Waste, Inc., which plans to use the tract to dispose of low-level radioactive waste. The statute of limitations for adverse possession and prescriptive rights is 10 years. If the subdivision homeowners seek to enjoin this use, they will:

    (A) Prevail, because they have acquired an easement by prescription for recreational use.

    (B) Prevail, because they have acquired the tract by adverse possession.

    (C) Not prevail, because they have no interest in the property.

(D) Not prevail, because damages, not an injunction, is the appropriate remedy.

Question 13

Theodora owned Grayacre. She sold Grayacre to Buzz, who paid her a fair price for the property. Buzz failed to record the deed and left for an extended trip to the Indian Ocean. Two days after Buzz departed, Theodora was struck by a car. She died in the hospital two hours later, having never regained consciousness. Her will was duly probated, and one provision of the will read, "I leave Grayacre to my daughter, Daphne." Daphne knew nothing about the sale of Grayacre to Buzz, and she properly recorded her title to Grayacre in the county recorder of deeds office. Daphne wanted to start her own business, and asked the chief loan officer at Greenback Bank & Trust Company to advance her $50,000 to start up. The loan officer felt that Daphne's proposal was somewhat risky, but offered to make the loan if Daphne put up sufficient collateral. Daphne offered a mortgage on Grayacre as collateral. The bank checked the recorder's records showing Daphne to have sole title to Grayacre, and the loan and mortgage were executed.

Daphne opened "Daphne's Duncecaps," a company to manufacture and distribute duncecaps to public schools. Unfortunately for Daphne's business, her idea was not popular with school purchasing agents and Daphne's Duncecaps failed. Daphne was unable to repay her loan to Greenback, and the bank went to court to demand that Grayacre be foreclosed, and any proceeds from the sale be turned over to Greenback in satisfaction of Daphne's debt. Just as Grayacre was about to be sold, Buzz returned from the Indian Ocean, deed in hand. The state in which Grayacre is located has the following statute:

No conveyance or mortgage of an interest in land is valid against any subsequent purchaser for value without notice thereof, unless it is recorded.

May Greenback successfully take Grayacre?

(A) Yes, because Greenback succeeds to Daphne's rights in Grayacre.

(B) Yes, because the bank is a mortgagee for value.

(C) No, because Daphne never owned the land.

(D) No, because the bank knew or should have known that Daphne's business was very risky, and an intelligent loan officer would not have loaned the money in the first place.

Questions 14-16 are based on the following fact situation:

Harold and Wilma, a married couple, own Blackacre as a tenancy by the entirety. Harold transfers to Albert, by quitclaim deed, his interest in Blackacre. Wilma is away at the time of the transfer. When she returns, she mortgages her interest to Charlie.

14. What interest, if any, does Albert have?

(A) No interest.

(B) An undivided one-half interest with right of survivorship.

(C) An undivided one-half interest held in tenancy in common.

(D) The entire fee.

15. What interest, if any, does Charlie have?

(A) A lien against the entire property.

(B) A secured interest against Wilma's one-half interest as tenant in the entirety with Albert.

(C) A secured interest against Wilma's one-half interest as tenant in the entirety with Harold.

(D) No interest.

16. If Wilma predeceases Harold, leaving a will devising her interest to Charlie, who takes her interest?

   (A) Albert.

   (B) Charlie.

   (C) Harold.

   (D) Wilma's heirs.

Question 17

For many years, Allison owned Lot A, a parcel of land bordered on the west by a public road, and Barbara owned Lot B, which is located immediately to the east of Lot A. Barbara also had an easement to cross Lot A to enter the public road adjoining Lot A. Lot B is surrounded by swampland on the north, south, and east. Thus, the only route of ingress to and egress from Lot B over dry land passed through Lot A.

Twelve years ago, Barbara decided to move out of state. Thus, Allison purchased Lot B from Barbara and proceeded to use both lots as a common tract. Ten years later, Allison sold Lot B to Carla.

Does Carla have an easement over Lot A?

(A) Yes, she has an easement in gross.

(B) Yes, because her only access to Lot B is across Lot A.

(C) No, because the easement was extinguished when Allison purchased Lot B.

(D) No, because she has not used the property long enough to gain an easement by prescription.

Question 18

Jet inherited Shaleacre, a parcel of land, from Luz. Bick owned Rockacre, a much larger piece of property, which was adjacent to Shaleacre.

Bick began to drill for oil on Rockacre, but all of Bick's exploratory wells were nonproductive "dry holes." Bick was certain that there was oil in the area and he importuned Jet to grant him a lease to drill on Shaleacre. Jet turned down Bick's offer. After Jet's refusal, Bick drilled an exploratory well on Rockacre. However, Bick drilled the well on a slanted angle, so that he was actually drilling under Shaleacre, even though his rig was located on Rockacre. Bick struck oil, but shortly thereafter Jet discovered that the oil was coming from underneath Shaleacre.

Does Jet have an action for damages against Bick?

(A) Yes, because Bick has invaded Jet's subterranean rights.

(B) Yes, but only if Bick's drilling interferes with Jet's use and enjoyment of Shaleacre.

(C) No, because oil is a free-flowing liquid and may be captured wherever it flows.

(D) No, because Bick's action does not interfere with Jet's right to drill for oil on Shaleacre.

Question 19

Barbara purchased a house from Stewart. It turned out that the concrete used to pour the foundation had been improperly mixed and the foundation was crumbling. Barbara discovered that the cost of repairing the defective foundation would be over $10,000. She filed suit against Stewart for the cost of repairs.

Which of the following additional facts, if true, will give Barbara the best chance of winning her suit?

(A) The crumbling foundation makes the house unsafe or uninhabitable.

(B) Stewart was the builder of the house.

(C) Barbara took title to the house by warranty deed.

(D) Barbara had no knowledge of the defect when she purchased the house, and the defect was not reasonably apparent.

Question 20

Mike conveyed two 30-acre parcels of land, known together as Mixtacre, to Suzanne. The deed contained an accurate legal description of the property as well. Suzanne paid Mike $60,000 for the land. Unbeknownst to either Mike or Suzanne, Mike had taken his title deed to the Mixtacre parcels through a forged deed. The two parcels of Mixtacre were separated by a private gravel road. The south 30-acre parcel consisted of arable land, which Mike, and later Suzanne, used for farming. The north 30-acre parcel of Mixtacre was undeveloped woodland. Suzanne never used the "North 30" for timbering or for anything else. On very rare occasions, Suzanne would take a walk in the woods, but outside of those occasions Suzanne never set foot on the "North 30" of Mixtacre. Fifteen years after Mike conveyed Mixtacre to Suzanne, Orrin appeared on the scene. Orrin's name had been signed by a forger on the deed conveying Mixtacre to Mike, and Orrin was, in fact, the true owner of the property at that time. The state in which Mixtacre was located has a 10-year statutory adverse possession period, and Orrin admits that Suzanne now has title to the "South 30" of Mixtacre by adverse possession. However, Orrin claims ownership of the "North 30."

In an action to quiet title, the court will determine that the "North 30" of Mixtacre belongs to:

(A) Orrin, because Suzanne did not actually occupy the "North 30."

(B) Orrin, because one may not obtain color of title through a forged deed.

(C) Suzanne, because her farming of the "South 30" was constructive occupation of the entire Mixtacre tract, including the "North 30."

(D) Suzanne, because Mike did not know his deed to Mixtacre was forged, and he acted in good faith when he conveyed to Suzanne.

Question 21

Duke and Earl each hold an undivided one-half interest in Baronacre. By terms of their agreement, each has the right to possess all portions of the property and neither has the right to exclusive possession of any part. Duke wrongfully ousts Earl from the property.

In an action against Duke, Earl can recover:

(A) The fair rental value of the property for the time excluded.

(B) One-half of the fair rental value of the property for the time excluded.

(C) One-quarter of the fair rental value of the property for the time excluded.

(D) Nothing, because each co-tenant has the right to possess all portions of the property and neither has the right to exclusive possession of any part.

Question 22

Oscar borrowed $30,000 from Big Bank to help set up a small business. The economy in the community was a bit shaky and, although Oscar's business was starting to make it, he had cash-flow problems because he was carrying a large number of accounts receivable. There was an acceleration clause in Oscar's loan agreement with Big Bank, which the bank could exercise any time after six months, unless Oscar provided security for the loan. Big Bank, which had a lot of bad loans outstanding, invoked the acceleration clause. Oscar did not have the cash on hand to repay the loan, so he offered Big Bank a mortgage on Homeacre, property owned by Oscar which included the house in which Oscar lived. The loan officer at Big Bank found this acceptable and the $30,000 mortgage was duly recorded. There were no other mortgages on Homeacre, which Oscar had inherited from his parents.

The economy improved and Oscar's business picked up. In addition, real estate values climbed. Meyer offered Oscar $200,000 for Homeacre, and Oscar promptly accepted. Oscar and Meyer entered into a written land sale contract, setting the closing date as May 24. Meyer contracted to tender the $200,000 on that date and Oscar contracted to convey "marketable title, free of encumbrances." On May 15, Meyer's attorney conducted a title search in the county recorder's office. He wrote Meyer a letter, which Meyer received on May 18, informing Meyer that there was a mortgage on Homeacre. Meyer immediately called Oscar and asked him about it. Oscar told Meyer, "Don't worry. I'm planning to use the money you give me on the closing date to pay off the mortgage." Meyer found this unacceptable and failed to appear at the appointed time and place of closing, although Oscar was there on time with a deed of conveyance in hand.

If Oscar files an appropriate suit against Meyer demanding specific performance and wins, it will most likely be because:

(A) A mortgage used to secure a debt does not constitute a legal "encumbrance."

(B) The vendor of real property need not have marketable title until the time of the closing.

(C) The mortgage was unenforceable ab initio, because a preexisting debt is not adequate consideration.

(D) A mortgage of the type described does not follow the land and Meyer would have taken the land free of the mortgage even if Oscar did not pay it off.

Question 23

Sam, a wealthy bond trader resident in the state of New Lancaster, owned a number of properties. His residence was his townhome in New Lancaster City, but modem technology allowed Sam to engage in his business far from the city's trading pits via computer link up. Sam frequented his other residential properties, including land and a cottage near the resort town of Glenfield, in a region of New Lancaster famous for its mountains, lakes, and autumn colors. Sam enjoyed fishing, and his Glenfield property was located near well-stocked lakes. A fine trout stream ran through the land. Although thousands of tourists visited Glenfield every autumn, Sam limited his visits to the area to the warm summer months. During the 15 years Sam owned the Glenfield property, he had never seen the place during the "fall colors" season.

The year after Sam purchased his land and cottage at Glenfield, Dale purchased an adjacent piece of land, which contained a cottage and a large number of maple trees. Each autumn, when the dry leaves fell, Dale would rake the leaves into a large pile and burn them. Dale would always invite the whole town to view his annual "autumn bonfire" and to roast wieners and marshmallows. Unbeknownst to Dale, the site he always chose for his leaf pile and bonfire was partially across Sam's property line.

After years of their importuning, Sam finally agreed to take his family to Glenfield in the autumn. During Sam's visit, Dale began raking leaves onto the same spot he had used for 14 years. Sam demanded that Dale cease and desist. Dale refused. Sam hired an attorney to file suit in county court to enjoin Dale from raking leaves onto Sam's property and staging his annual bonfire. Assume that no applicable laws, ordinances, or regulations make the burning of leaves illegal and that the adverse possession period in New Lancaster is 10 years.

Will Sam prevail?

(A) No, because Dale has acquired a portion of Sam's land by adverse possession.

(B) No, because Dale has obtained an easement by prescription.

(C) Yes, because Dale's use of Sam's property was not continuous.

(D) Yes, because Sam had no prior notice of Dale's use of the land, so Sam cannot be said to have acquiesced in Dale's activities.

Question 24

Building 1 and Building 2 were connected to each other, but the stairway used to reach the second floor of each building was located entirely within Building 1. Building 2 was commercially-oriented, with a number of shops renting space on both the first and second floors. There is no access to the second floor other than the common stairway. Oscar owned both buildings, until he conveyed Building 2 to Amy. Amy continued to rent space on both floors of Building 2 to commercial tenants, and the tenants and their customers continued to use the common stairway. A number of years later, Oscar conveyed Building 1 to Bob. There was no mention of the stairway in Bob's deed from Oscar. Both Amy's deed and Bob's deed were properly recorded. A few years after Bob bought Building 1, the stairway had become dilapidated. Many of the steps were loose, and the bannister was about to become detached. Amy was concerned about the stairway's condition of disrepair, because she felt it reduced the value of Building 2, and also feared that customers of her tenants could be injured using the stairs. Amy approached Bob about repairing the stairs, and even offered to pay for half the cost. Bob summarily told her to mind her own business, that the stairs were his property, and that he would repair them when he felt like it, which was not going to be any time soon. Amy went to a reputable construction firm and was told it would cost $2,500 to fix the stairs. Amy then told Bob she was willing to pay the entire cost of fixing the stairs. Bob again told her to mind her own business and that he was not going to allow any repair workers on his property.

If Amy files suit against Bob, can she compel him to allow her to repair the stairs?

(A) Yes, because Amy has an easement, which implies the power to repair.

(B) Yes, because Amy may protect herself from the possibility of tort suits from her tenants' business customers.

(C) No, because Amy's interest in the stairs is only for the reasonable lifetime of the structure.

(D) No, because Amy has no right to enter Bob's property.

Question 25

Oldd owned Groundacre, a large urban property that had previously served as a parking lot next to a now-defunct amusement park. Oldd subdivided Groundacre into 10 lots and numbered them 1 through 10. Each lot was equal in size. Oldd conveyed Lot 1 to Anthony. The deed contained a restriction banning commercial use of the property. Oldd subsequently conveyed Lots 2 through 7 to six separate purchasers. Each of the deeds to these purchasers also contained the restriction on commercial use.

Anthony left Lot 1 undeveloped, but the purchasers of Lots 2 through 7 all used their lots for commercial purposes. Oldd subsequently conveyed Lot 8 to Tanja. Tanja's deed contained the restriction banning commercial use of the lot, but Tanja decided that she wished to use Lot 8 commercially. Oldd retains ownership of Lots 9 and 10. Tanja wants to bring suit to establish her rights to use Lot 8 for commercial purposes.

Which of the following best describes the parties Tanja should join in her lawsuit?

(A) Oldd only.

(B) Oldd and Anthony only.

(C) The other commercial users only.

(D) All landowners in the subdivision.

Question 26

Oberroth owned and operated Grainacre, a productive working farm, for many years. His children showed no great interest in farming, but he hoped that they might change their minds as they matured. He placed his greatest hopes on his eldest daughter, Rhonda, but thought it might take a few years. He took these things into consideration when, after being diagnosed with a terminal illness, he drafted his will. Oberroth died a few months after executing the will. The will devised Grainacre "to my best friend and good neighbor, Rye, for life, and then to my daughter, Rhonda, in fee simple absolute." The rest of Oberroth's property was divided equally among his children, his wife having died three years earlier.

For two years Rye occupied and operated Grainacre at a modest profit. However, he then discovered that there was a rich gravel deposit deep below the surface of Grainacre. Rye sank a deep shaft on the property and began to remove the gravel and sell it. Rhonda discovered this and asked Rye to cease and desist his gravel operations. Rye refused, telling her, "Grainacre is mine as long as I live. After that you can do what you darn well please with it, but I'm still alive and kicking." Rhonda filed an appropriate suit against Rye.

The court will:

(A) Partition the property.

(B) Enjoin Rye from mining the gravel and award damages to Rhonda.

(C) Order a sale of the property and a division of the proceeds between Rye and Rhonda.

(D) Allow Rye to mine the gravel and keep his profits from the mining operation.

Questions 27-28 are based on the following fact situation:

Davis owned Lot One, which adjoined a public road. Edsel owned Lot Two, an undeveloped piece of property immediately adjacent to Lot One but from a different original tract. The easiest practical access to Lot Two was from the public road adjoining Lot One. This required, however, that Edsel cross Lot One to reach the road. Davis granted an easement to Edsel, allowing Edsel to "pass through" Lot One on his journeys between Lot Two and the road. Edsel also wanted to develop Lot Two, but he faced a problem because no power lines had been installed to provide utility service for Lot Two. Edsel consulted Davis, but Davis refused to alter the wording of the easement. Although Power Company had a statutory power of eminent domain, it refused to run power lines to Edsel's property without Davis's permission.

27. Can Edsel require Davis to allow the power lines to be installed on Davis's property?

   (A) Yes, by exercising Power Company's right of eminent domain.

   (B) Yes, because the need for utility service is a sufficient basis for an easement by necessity.

   (C) No, because Edsel's easement is for a different purpose.

   (D) No, because the property is undeveloped and there is no established necessity for power service.

28. Does Power Company need Davis's permission to install power lines on Lot One?

   (A) Yes, because no easement exists allowing them to do so without such permission.

   (B) Yes, unless they are willing to post a bond against any possible damage to the property.

   (C) No, but only because they have the power of eminent domain.

   (D) No, if there is no other suitable power line access route.

Question 29

Blueacre, a property in State Blue, was owned by Oberstahr. Oberstahr's title to Blueacre was duly recorded in the office of the county recorder of deeds, as prescribed by State Blue laws.

Oberstahr then conveyed Blueacre to Warren by warranty deed. Warren did not record the deed.

One year later, Oberstahr mentioned Blueacre to his old friend, Quisling, who had performed many favors for Oberstahr over the years. Oberstahr entered into a written contract with Quisling to convey Blueacre to Quisling for "one dollar." On the closing date provided in the contract, Quisling handed Oberstahr a certified check for one dollar. Oberstahr handed Quisling a quitclaim deed conveying Blueacre to Quisling. Quisling promptly recorded the deed.

A statute in State Blue provides: "Any conveyance of an interest in land, other than a lease for less than one year, is not valid against any subsequent purchaser for value without notice thereof whose conveyance is first recorded."

In an action to establish ownership of Blueacre, Quisling's greatest obstacle to prevailing will be:

(A) A quitclaim deed is not a valid transfer of title.

(B) Proving that the transaction was a transfer for value.

(C) Warranty deeds are superior in right to quitclaim deeds.

(D) A quitclaim deed is not a recordable instrument.

Question 30

Oscar's will provided: "I leave my beloved lakefront estate, Moneyacre, to my butler Fred for life, remainder to my niece Nora, so that she may live out her days in the house she loves so much." Moneyacre is a 40-acre estate that includes a mansion, a 20-acre orchard, a beach, and gardens. At the time of Oscar's death, Fred was 40 years old and of modest means. Nora was 18 years old and quite wealthy. Moneyacre was encumbered by a mortgage that was not entitled to exoneration. The income from the orchards could barely pay the taxes. After the first year, Fred could no longer make the mortgage payments. Nora cheerfully agreed to pay the mortgage payments, telling Fred that she

was looking forward to retiring to Moneyacre and enjoying the beach and the glorious grounds.

Ten years after Oscar's death, the town in which Moneyacre was located became a hot resort area. A major resort chain approached Fred with a fabulous, multimillion-dollar offer for the easternmost 20 acres of Moneyacre, which included the residence and beach. The resort chain planned to raze the mansion to erect a high-rise hotel. The resort chain was aware that Fred was only a life tenant, but believed that it would make enough profit to cover any possible loss when Nora's interest became possessory. Fred approached Nora about the offer and proposed to give her most of the money, keeping only a few million dollars for himself. He pointed out to her that there was still plenty of land to erect a new house if Nora still wanted to retire there. In fact, Fred offered to build any house Nora desired on the remaining land. Nora refused to go along with the plan. Fred, needing the money to send his children to college, decided to proceed with the sale. Nora brought a suit to enjoin Fred's proposed actions.

Which of the following is Nora's best argument?

(A) The eventual use of the property by the remainderman will be as a residence.

(B) Destruction of the mansion constitutes waste.

(C) Because Nora paid the mortgage payments, Fred is subrogated to her rights.

(D) Fred has no right to transfer his life estate.

Question 31

In 1992, Herschel obtained a change in zoning for the 240-acre parcel of land he owned on the edge of Middletown, from agricultural to commercial and residential. He prepared and recorded, after obtaining approval from all appropriate agencies, a subdivision plan that included a commercial center, a number of lots for single-family residences, two multistory condominium buildings, an expensive apartment complex, and a 20-acre area in the center of the parcel that was designated "public sports arena." The theme of the entire development was "Early Southwest," and the list of covenants, conditions, and restrictions recorded with the plan included provisions that required every building constructed in the subdivision to be a "simulated adobe style" architecture approved in advance by the Downtown Merchants Association.

In 1993, Herschel sold many of the lots in the commercial center, including several to Development Associates, a real estate firm specializing in commercial properties. Each deed prepared by Herschel contained a reference to the design restriction in the recorded plan. Herschel also sold almost all of the residential lots, whose deeds contained the same reference to the restriction.

Development Associates held the lots it purchased until 1994, when one was sold to Weldon, who owned a SpeedyBurger franchise. The deed conveying the lot from Development Associates to Weldon contained no reference to the design restriction. SpeedyBurger was famous nationwide for its logo, mounted on the roof of every blue and white SpeedyBurger outlet, which was a giant burger with four wheels speeding into an equally giant open mouth. SpeedyBurger restaurants were constructed by SpeedyBurger Construction, Inc., a wholly owned subsidiary of SpeedyBurger, Inc. Weldon had already entered into a contract with the construction company, and the prefabricated restaurant, complete with logo, was constructed over the weekend, shortly after escrow closed on the lot transaction between Weldon and Development Associates.

Bruce, who purchased a lot in the commercial center from Herschel in 1992 and thereafter built an approved store in which he sold leather goods, owned the lot next to Weldon's SpeedyBurger. He did not learn of construction of the SpeedyBurger restaurant until he came in to work at the leather shop on a Monday, and saw the giant SpeedyBurger. Bruce brings an action

seeking a mandatory injunction compelling Weldon to demolish the SpeedyBurger restaurant. At trial, Bruce proves that Weldon did not seek or obtain approval of the Merchants Association for his building.

Should the court issue the injunction?

(A) No, because destruction of the restaurant would be a tremendous waste of resources.

(B) No, because Weldon's deed contained no restriction on the type of building that could be constructed on the lot.

(C) Yes, because the restrictive covenant runs with the land.

(D) Yes, unless Weldon can establish to the court's satisfaction that the SpeedyBurger design has at least as much aesthetic merit as any "Early Southwest" design.

Question 32

Wilhelm owned two adjacent lots in downtown Quaintville, one fronting directly on Main Street and the other behind the first. Wilhelm ran a small dry cleaning business on the lot next to Main Street, and had built a restaurant on the rear lot. Since the rear lot had no access to any public street, Wilhelm used the parking lot of the dry cleaning business, which extended from Main Street all the way back to the restaurant lot, for access to the restaurant. Since the restaurant could only attract enough customers to be profitable in the summer tourist season, it was closed from October through April.

After several years, Wilhelm sold his restaurant and the lot it was on to Becky. Becky insisted as part of the transaction that Wilhelm include an easement over the westernmost 30 feet of driveway of the retained lot running from Main Street to the purchased lot, to be used as an accessway to the restaurant for Becky and her customers. The deed from Wilhelm to Becky contained the grant of easement, and Becky promptly recorded it.

Two years later, in February, Wilhelm sold the dry cleaning property to Allan. The deed from Wilhelm to Allan did not mention the easement previously granted to Becky. Allan immediately demolished the small dry cleaning building and constructed a SpeedyBurger franchise restaurant. An outdoor patio area for use by the Speedy-Burger customers extended to the western boundary of Allan's lot, and completely blocked access to the lot of Becky to the rear. Because Becky's restaurant was closed for the winter, nothing came of the SpeedyBurger construction until April, when Becky returned to Quaintville to open her restaurant for the summer season.

Becky brings an action to compel Allan to demolish the outdoor patio so that she can use her easement. The SpeedyBurger restaurant occupies the entire lot upon which it is built, and the shortest alternate route over other parcels from Becky's lot to a public street would have to pass through several buildings and lots. How should the court rule?

(A) For Allan, because his deed contained no mention of the access easement.

(B) For Allan, because construction of the outdoor patio extinguished Becky's rights to the access easement.

(C) For Becky, because ownership of the easement gives her the right to use it for access to her lot.

(D) For Becky, because she has no other access to her lot.

Question 33

Anderson sold the mortgage to Greenacre and its accompanying note to Baker Mortgage Brokerage ("BMB"). Shortly thereafter, BMB sold both the mortgage and the note to Caldwell County Bank ("CCB"). CCB duly recorded the assignment in the offices of the Caldwell County Recorder of Deeds, as prescribed by state statute. However, CCB decided to use BMB as its collection agent for the payments as they came due. Therefore, CCB left the mortgage and note documents in the hands of BMB. BMB had

made a number of improvident real estate transactions, and as a result, BMB developed cash-flow and liquidity problems. To try to save BMB from bankruptcy, BMB's president sold the mortgage to Greenacre and the accompanying note to McElligot. This transaction was not enough to save BMB from insolvency. During the winding up of BMB's affairs CCB discovered BMB's sale of the mortgage and note to McElligot. CCB also learned that BMB never told McElligot about CCB's interests in the mortgage and note. CCB files suit against McElligot for the return of the mortgage and note.

The court will decide that:

(A) CCB owns both the mortgage and the note.

(B) McElligot owns both the mortgage and the note.

(C) CCB owns the mortgage, but McElligot owns the note.

(D) McElligot owns the mortgage, but CCB owns the note.

Question 34

Owen owned Blackacre in fee simple. Shortly after his wife died, Owen conveyed Blackacre as follows: "I hereby convey Blackacre to my only child, Ethyl, for life, remainder to the children of Mary in fee simple." Mary was Ethyl's only child at the time of the conveyance. Both Ethyl and Mary were married. Mary had no children.

What interest, if any, is created in favor of Mary's unborn children at the time of the conveyance?

(A) None.

(B) A springing use.

(C) A contingent remainder.

(D) A vested remainder subject to divestment.

Question 35

Samuel owned Redwood, a two-acre tract of land, on which he has built a single-family residence. Samuel entered into a contract to sell Redwood to Benson for $80,000. The contract provided that Samuel was to deliver marketable title to Benson, subject only to conditions, covenants, and restrictions of record, and all applicable zoning laws and ordinances. Redwood was subject to a 15-foot sideline setback originally set forth in the developer's duly recorded subdivision plan. The applicable zoning ordinance zones the property for single-family residences, and requires a six-foot sideline setback. One week before closing, Benson had a survey of the property made. It revealed that a portion of Samuel's house was 5.98 feet from the sideline. Benson refused to go ahead with the purchase of Redwood on the ground that Samuel's title was not marketable, and that if the sale was completed it could subject Benson to a lawsuit.

If Samuel brings suit against Benson for specific performance, will he prevail?

(A) Yes, because any suit against Benson concerning the setback would be frivolous.

(B) Yes, because the setback violation falls within the doctrine *de minimis non curat lex.*

(C) No, because any variation, however small, amounts to a breach of contract.

(D) No, because the fact that Benson may be exposed to litigation is sufficient to make the title unmarketable.

Question 36

A field, owned by the city, was used as a municipal parking lot for many years. When a new parking facility was constructed, the field was no longer used for that purpose. A parcel of land constituting a small portion of the field at the easterly end was never officially vacated by the municipality. Lee, the adjoining owner on both sides of the field, went into possession of the parcel, fenced it, and cultivated the parcel for a period of time in excess of the period required for adverse possession.

In an appropriate action brought by Lee to establish his title to the parcel, which of the following must he establish if he is to prevail?

I. Real property interests can be lost by a municipality by adverse possession.

II. His use of the parcel was proof of his assertion of dominion over the parcel.

III. Fee interests in real property can be abandoned by a municipality without an official vote.

IV. Lack of use of the parcel by the municipality created an irrevocable license in him.

(A) I. and II. only.

(B) I. and IV. only.

(C) II. and III. only.

(D) III. and IV. only.

Questions 37-38 are based on the following fact situation:

Art was the owner in fee simple of Redacre, a vacant tract of land. He told his favorite nephew, Phil, "I've always liked you, so I'm going to leave you Redacre when I die."

Phil was being pressured by Sandy to pay off an old debt. To satisfy Sandy, he executed and delivered to her a general warranty deed to Redacre. Sandy immediately recorded the deed. Sandy built a house on Redacre and has resided there ever since.

Art died shortly thereafter. His will left Redacre to Phil. Phil, needing money badly, sold Redacre to Mary by general warranty deed, which Mary promptly recorded. Mary paid Phil a reasonable value for Redacre. Mary purchased Redacre solely as an investment and never visited Redacre. She therefore never knew that Sandy was living there.

37. Which of the following best describes the effect of Phil's deed to Sandy at the time it was recorded?

   (A) It was ineffective as a conveyance of either legal or equitable interest in Redacre.

   (B) It effectively conveyed legal title to Redacre since it was recorded.

   (C) It effectively conveyed equitable title to Redacre.

   (D) It was effective as a quitclaim, conveying to Sandy Phil's expectancy of title.

38. Which of the following best describes the status of titles at the time of Art's death?

   (A) Sandy has title to Redacre.

   (B) Sandy has title if Art was aware of Phil's transfer to her.

   (C) Phil has title, but Sandy can sue to recover title on an estoppel theory.

   (D) Phil has title, and Sandy has no enforceable claim to Redacre.

Questions 39-40 are based on the following fact situation:

   Proctor and Gamble owned large adjoining tracts of land. The boundary line between the two properties was never properly determined or clearly known.

   In 1967, Proctor installed a gas-powered generator on land he thought he owned, but which was in fact owned by Gamble. Proctor ran electrical wires from the generator across land he knew belonged to Gamble. Gamble orally consented to the wiring crossing his land.

   In 1980, Gamble was found to be mentally incompetent. He died in 1991, and his executor filed suit to eject Proctor and quiet title. The statute of limitations for ejectment is 20 years.

39. With respect to the land on which the generator was installed:

   (A) Proctor cannot claim title by adverse possession because the statute of limitations was tolled by Gamble's incompetency.

   (B) Proctor cannot claim title by adverse possession because his occupation was not open and notorious.

   (C) Proctor has acquired title by adverse possession.

   (D) None of the above.

40. With respect to the land over which the electrical wires were laid:

   (A) Proctor has acquired title by adverse possession.

   (B) Proctor has acquired a prescriptive easement.

   (C) Proctor has acquired both title by adverse possession and a prescriptive easement.

   (D) Proctor has acquired neither title by adverse possession nor a prescriptive easement.

Question 41

   Jasper owned a 40-acre tract of land in a now booming area of Metroville. Jasper had inherited 30 acres and had acquired the other 10 acres by adverse possession from Myra. Jasper entered into a land sale contract promising to convey the 40 acres to Chandler. The contract provided that

Jasper would convey marketable title. Chandler paid Jasper the purchase price and accepted a deed from Jasper. Chandler promptly recorded the deed. Myra, having learned of the sale, brought a successful action against Chandler to quiet title. Chandler realizes for the first time that there were no covenants for title in his deed. Chandler brings an action against Jasper.

What is the most likely outcome of the suit?

(A) Chandler will win, because Jasper breached the terms of the contract.

(B) Chandler will win, because Jasper misrepresented the size of the tract.

(C) Jasper will win, because the terms of the deed control his liability.

(D) Jasper will win, because Chandler was negligent in not checking the covenants of title at the time of closing.

Question 42

When Walter purchased his new home, he decided to keep his old residence for a few months to see if the real estate market would improve, since he had not received any acceptable offers during the time he was looking for a new residence. When Todd noticed Walter moving out of his old home, he asked if Walter would be willing to rent it. Walter told Todd that he was intending to sell the house in a few months and that Todd would have to move if the new owners so desired. Todd agreed and moved in, paying Walter the agreed rent of $100 per week by dropping off cash at Walter's new house every Friday.

During the next few months, Walter's investment business suffered several serious reverses, and Walter decided that it would be prudent to retrench economically and attempt to ride out the financial storm. He put his new home, which had been extensively mortgaged, on the market for the amount owing and soon obtained a buyer. When he informed Todd that Todd would have to vacate the old home, Todd refused. The

next Friday, when Todd brought by the $100 rental payment, Walter refused to accept it.

The following Monday, Walter's lawyer commenced an action to evict Todd from Walter's old home. The jurisdiction requires that a statutory written notice be served upon any tenant whose term is for less than month-to-month or is not for a fixed term at least three days prior to commencement of eviction proceedings. No written notice of any kind was given to Todd.

Walter is most likely to gain immediate possession of his home by arguing that Todd is:

(A) A tenant from month-to-month.

(B) A tenant at sufferance.

(C) A licensee.

(D) A trespasser ab initio.

Questions 43-44 are based on the following fact situation:

In 1952, Alvin inherited a 200-acre undivided tract of land from his grandfather. The land remained vacant until 1988 when Alvin decided to subdivide the property into 80 two-acre lots. He prepared and duly recorded a subdivision plan that showed the 80 two-acre lots, and the remaining 40 acres in the center of the tract was designated "future public golf course." Alvin named the subdivision Fareway Greens and began to market the 80 two-acre lots. He prepared and distributed a brochure promoting Fareway Greens. The brochure provided that one of the benefits of living in Fareway Greens would be the proximity of the public golf course. Property bordering the 40-acre tract sold for a higher price because it was overlooking the golf course. Alvin sold 60 of the lots to individual purchasers. Each deed referred to the recorded plan and also contained the following clause: "No swimming pools shall be installed on any lots within Fareway Greens." In 1992, wishing to rid himself of the remaining Fareway Greens acreage, Alvin sold the remaining 20 acres and the 40-acre tract to Kerry by a deed that referred to the plan and contained the restriction relating to swimming pools. Kerry sold the 20 two-acre lots to individual purchasers and the 40-acre tract to Donna. None of the deeds from Kerry referred to the plan or contained any reference to the swimming pool restriction.

43. Assume for this question only that Donna has announced her intention of erecting a shopping mall on the 40-acre tract. Benny, an owner of a two-acre lot purchased from Alvin, brings suit to enjoin Donna. If Benny wins, it will be because:

(A) Donna will be deemed to have taken with actual notice because of the location of the tract.

(B) Benny can sue in equity to enforce the plan against Donna.

(C) Benny is a creditor beneficiary of Alvin's promise with respect to the tract.

(D) Benny was economically benefited by the existence of a golf course within the Fareway Greens development.

44. Assume for this question only that Sally, who purchased her lot from Kerry, decided to install a swimming pool on the rear quarter of her lot. Benny, who owns the adjoining lot, discovers that the pool has been installed and files suit against Sally to force her to remove it. Who will prevail?

(A) Benny, because the restrictive covenant in his deed runs with the land.

(B) Benny, because his land is not benefited by the existence of a swimming pool on the adjoining tract.

(C) Sally, because her deed did not contain the restrictive covenant.

(D) Sally, because she had no notice of the restriction on the installation of swimming pools.

Question 45

Peter and James inherited Orangeacre as joint tenants from their parents. Only half of the acreage was planted with oranges, and Peter decided that to increase productivity, the balance of the land should be planted with a different variety of oranges.

James refused to participate in the project, and Peter brought an action for declaratory relief alleging that he was entitled to be reimbursed for half of the cost of the improvement.

Which of the following correctly describes the result in the action?

(A) Peter will be denied the requested judgment.

(B) Peter will be granted the requested judgment.

(C) The result depends upon whether James will receive an economic benefit.

(D) The result depends upon whether the improvements will produce sufficient income to amortize their cost.

Question 46

Even though Ed Jones and Edith Smith had never been formally married, they lived together for 10 years as husband and wife. During this time Edith identified herself as "Mrs. Jones," with the knowledge and consent of Ed. For the entire period, Ed and Edith maintained joint checking accounts and filed joint income tax returns as Mr. and Mrs. Ed Jones. During this period of cohabitation, Ed Jones decided to buy a home. The deed identified the grantees as "Ed Jones and Edith Jones, his wife, and their heirs and assigns forever as tenants by the entirety." Ed made a down payment of $20,000 and executed a mortgage for the unpaid balance. Both he and Edith signed the note for the unpaid balance as husband and wife. Ed continued to make the monthly payments as they became due until he and Edith had an argument and decided to separate. Ed abandoned Edith and the house.

Edith then made the payments for six months. At the end of this period, Edith brought an action against Ed for partition of the land in question. Assume that the jurisdiction does not recognize the common law marriage. Assume further that the jurisdiction has no applicable statute on the subject.

Edith's request for partition should be:

(A) Granted, because the estate created by the deed was not a tenancy by the entirety.

(B) Granted, because the tenancy by the entirety that was created by the deed was severed when Ed abandoned Edith.

(C) Denied, because a tenant by the entirety has no right to partition.

(D) Denied, because Ed has absolute title to the property.

Question 47

Billings conveyed Green Acre "To Samuels, his heirs and assigns, so long as the premises are used for agricultural purposes, then to Richards, his heirs and assigns."

As a consequence of the conveyance, Billings's interest in Green Acre is:

(A) A right of entry.

(B) A possibility of reverter.

(C) A fee simple absolute because the conveyance violates the Rule Against Perpetuities.

(D) Nothing.

Question 48

Tom leased an apartment from Lon for a period of one year. At the end of the year, Tom continued occupying the apartment, paying Lon the $250 rent in advance each month. Tom had continually complained to Lon about the facilities provided for trash disposal behind the apartment house. Finally, after receiving no

response from Lon, Tom complained to the Health Department, who in turn mandated that Lon substantially improve the trash facilities for the apartment building. Shortly thereafter, Lon notified Tom that his rent was being increased to $400 per month. Tom protested and pointed out that all of the other tenants in the apartment building paid rent of $250 per month. Lon then gave Tom the required statutory notice that the tenancy was being terminated at the earliest possible time. By an appropriate action, Tom contested Lon's right to terminate.

If Tom succeeds, it will be because:

(A) The doctrine prohibiting retaliatory eviction is part of the law of the jurisdiction.

(B) A periodic tenancy was created by implication.

(C) A landlord must generally charge the same rent for all units located in one complex.

(D) Lon failed to establish a valid reason why Tom's rent needed to be raised.

Question 49

Employer owned Blackwood in fee simple. Employer was very happy with the service Employee had given him over the years. As a bonus, Employer decided to give Blackwood to Employee. Employer presented a deed conveying Blackwood to Employee. The deed was never recorded. Six months later, Employer found that he was in dire financial straits and needed Blackwood back to complete a sale of the tract of land. He asked Employee to please destroy the deed, which Employee dutifully and voluntarily did. Shortly thereafter, Employer and Employee were killed in an explosion of the factory where they both worked. Each of the successors in interest claimed title to Blackwood.

The probable outcome will be that:

(A) Employer was the owner of Blackwood, because Employee had voluntarily destroyed the deed.

(B) Employer was the owner of Blackwood, because the destruction of the deed by Employee relates back and redates the present transfer of the deed to Employee.

(C) Employee was the owner of Blackwood, because the deed was merely evidence of his title and its destruction was insufficient to cause title to pass back to Employer.

(D) Employee was the owner of Blackwood, because his destruction of the deed to Blackwood was under the undue influence of Employer.

Question 50

Luke and Linda were not married, but lived together for two years. As they felt that their relationship was very stable, they decided to leave their leased apartment and purchase a home. Luke and Linda each put up 50% of the down payment on Whiteacre. They took title as tenants in common, and each orally promised the other that the survivor should take title to Whiteacre. Luke and Linda lived at Whiteacre for three years, equitably dividing mortgage payments and maintenance expenses. They were then involved in a serious car accident. Linda was killed almost instantly and Luke died in the hospital one week later. Neither Luke nor Linda left a will. Linda was survived only by her mother, Meghan. Luke was survived only by his brother, Bobby.

Who owns Whiteacre?

(A) Meghan owns the whole.

(B) Bobby owns the whole.

(C) Meghan and Bobby each have a one-half interest as tenants in common.

(D) Meghan and Bobby each have a one-half interest as joint tenants.

Questions 51-52 are based on the following fact situation:

Ophelia wished to install an in-ground swimming pool in her backyard. She hired the Acme Pool Company to do the installation. Ophelia chose to locate the pool on the west end of her rather large backyard, close to the property line dividing her yard from her neighbor Norbert's property. She told Norbert that she intended to install the pool, and she told him that, when it was completed, she would invite him and his family to use it.

On the day that Acme began excavation for the pool, Norbert was at home. He stood outside in his backyard to watch the workers to be sure that they did not drive their equipment over his property. The workers wisely kept to Ophelia's property. Unfortunately, when the excavation was nearly completed, subsidence on Norbert's property, caused by the excavation, caused part of Norbert's backyard lawn to collapse. Norbert was understandably upset.

51. If Norbert sues Ophelia for the damage to his lawn, how will a court most likely rule?

(A) For Norbert, because Ophelia is absolutely liable for the damage to Norbert's land.

(B) For Norbert, but only if Ophelia's excavation was negligent.

(C) For Ophelia, because only the lawn was damaged, not any of the buildings located on the property.

(D) For Ophelia, because she had no duty to provide support for Norbert's land.

52. Assume for purposes of this question only that Ophelia's excavation caused Norbert's garage to collapse. What is Ophelia's best defense to an action by Norbert for damage to the garage?

(A) Ophelia gave notice to Norbert of her intention to excavate and he made no objection.

(B) Ophelia had hired Acme based on good recommendations.

(C) Ophelia's excavation was done in a proper manner, and there would have been no subsidence except for the fact that the garage was there.

(D) Norbert's garage was made of solid concrete and thus was unusually heavy.

Question 53

The Pacifica Railroad Company operated freight and passenger service over the line running from Bay City to Metropolis for over 70 years, but the increasing use of autos and planes for passenger travel and trucks for freight forced the railroad to cease all rail service in 1977. A portion of the rail line ran over the westernmost portion of 40 acres of farmland owned by Johnson pursuant to an easement granted by Johnson's predecessors in interest, and subject to which Johnson purchased the land in 1974.

In 1990, Johnson constructed several large structures for use in housing chickens and began operating a chicken farm, producing eggs and fryers for markets in Bay City. Johnson learned in 1993 that Pacifica intends to institute passenger rail service between Bay City and Metropolis, and he is afraid that the noise and vibration of the passing trains will adversely affect his egg production. He brings an action in state court to quiet title to the area of the rail easement and to enjoin Pacifica from entering upon his property. The statutory prescriptive period is 10 years.

How should the court rule?

(A) For Johnson, because Pacifica has abandoned the easement.

(B) For Johnson, because Pacifica's use of the easement will interfere unreasonably with his egg production.

(C) For Pacifica, because it has not abandoned the easement.

(D) For Pacifica, because Johnson's failure to use the land under the easement precludes him from asserting that the easement has been abandoned.

Questions 54-56 are based on the following fact situation:

In the mid-1980s, Sidney entered into a partnership with Jay to develop some land that had been in Sidney's family for many years.

In 1989, in compliance with all applicable laws, and after receiving all necessary permits, the partnership, BayShore Development, began construction on two projects. The first, BayShore Heights, consisted of 500 single-family residences built on 250 acres. The second, BayShore Mall, was a shopping center built on 100 acres next to the north end of BayShore Heights.

54. With consideration of likely court enforcement of the following, which method should BayShore Development use to ensure that BayShore Heights retains its residential character?

(A) All deeds should contain negative easements.

(B) All deeds should be subject to conditions subsequent.

(C) All deeds should include covenants.

(D) Ensure the residential character by developing the area in accordance with zoning laws.

55. Immediately to the west of BayShore Heights, Sidney owned additional acreage on which, in 1993, he desired to build another group of 250 single-family homes. To ensure their marketability, Sidney desired to sell them like BayShore Heights homes, and to that extent, intended that the deeds to the new homes contain the same restrictions as those in BayShore Heights and be enforceable in the same manner by owners in both developments. Will Sidney be successful in this plan?

(A) No, zoning restrictions will control.

(B) No, because in order to have such restrictions, the entire project must have been built at the same time.

(C) Yes, the restrictions will be equally enforceable for this new project as they were for BayShore Heights.

(D) Yes, provided that a court considers this new project to be part of a common development scheme with Bay-Shore Heights.

56. Clay, a developer who wanted to build high-rise condominiums on the remaining acreage owned by Sidney, seeks to purchase the property. Assuming that the condominiums will block the view of the bay of many of the homes in BayShore Heights, what is the effect the original BayShore Heights project may have on Clay's title to this property?

(A) Clay, who received title from Sidney, is restricted from using the property for anything but single-family dwellings.

(B) Clay will be subject to an implied easement for light and air, and the BayShore Heights owners can enjoin the building of high-rise condominiums.

(C) The creation of the original BayShore Heights project gives the owners of those homes a right, enforceable at law, of first refusal to buy the acreage offered to Clay.

(D) Clay takes title free of any claim by the owners of BayShore Heights because the owners have no enforceable claim against Sidney.

Questions 57-58 are based on the following fact situation:

Lou owned Blackacre, a large parcel of land. In 1960, Lou decided to subdivide Blackacre into 20 separate lots. Lou sold Lots 1-19, retaining Lot 20 for himself to live on. The deeds for each of the 19 lots sold by Lou contained the following restriction: "All lots within the Blackacre subdivision shall be used for residential

purposes only." The purchasers of Lots 1-19 each built residences on their property. Lou lived on Lot 20 in the Blackacre subdivision until his death, when it was sold without any restrictions to Al. In 1980, Al sold Lot 20 to Neil, without any restrictions. In 1990, Neil decided to build a grocery store on Lot 20. Sherry, an adjoining owner in the Blackacre subdivision, informed Neil of the restriction and told him that he would be unable to build the grocery store.

57. If the restriction to use the land for residential purposes only is held to apply to Lot 20, it will be because the restriction is:

(A) An equitable servitude.

(B) A covenant running with the land.

(C) A reciprocal negative servitude.

(D) Part of a general plan.

58. Assume that when Neil purchased Lot 20 from Al in 1980, he was furnished with an abstract of title by Al and was assured by Al that the land was unrestricted. The abstract of title showed that Lot 20 was not restricted. Neil contends that he cannot be bound to the residence restriction, because he had no notice of the restriction when he purchased Lot 20. If Sherry brings suit seeking an injunction against Neil's building of the grocery store, will Neil's contention of lack of notice create a valid defense?

(A) Yes, because Neil had neither actual nor constructive notice of the restriction.

(B) Yes, because he relied on the abstract of title and Al's representation in good faith.

(C) No, because the property owners in the Blackacre subdivision have a right to keep the subdivision in the condition that they want it.

(D) No, because Neil would be charged with notice as a result of the residential character of the Blackacre subdivision.

Questions 59-60 are based on the following fact situation:

Emma was the owner in fee simple of Greenacre, a tract of land. In 1965, Emma conveyed Greenacre to Martha, "for life and then to the first child of Martha's sister, Vera, who shall reach the age of 21." Vera was unmarried and childless in 1965. In 1971, Vera married, and in 1973, Vera gave birth to a son, Oscar. In 1994, Oscar reached the age of 21, and Martha was still alive and living on Greenacre.

59. Oscar now seeks to obtain possession of Greenacre and brings an action in ejectment against Martha. Martha's best defense against Oscar's attempt to eject her is that:

   (A) Martha's life estate was not subject to termination during her lifetime.

   (B) Oscar has no claim to Greenacre, because he was not living at the time of Emma's original conveyance.

   (C) A conveyance of Greenacre to Oscar violates the Rule Against Perpetuities.

   (D) Oscar's interest, if any, would be that of a contingent remainder, and the contingency is Martha's death.

60. Assume that Martha died before Oscar became 21. Assume also that the jurisdiction has abolished the common law rule of destructibility of contingent remainders. Who would be the owner of Greenacre?

   (A) Oscar.

   (B) Oscar's court-appointed guardian ad litem.

   (C) Emma and her heirs in fee simple.

   (D) Emma and her heirs would take the estate until Oscar became 21 years of age.

Question 61

The recording statute in the state of New Ayrshire reads, in relevant part, as follows:

   Any conveyance of an interest in land shall not be valid against any subsequent purchaser for value without notice thereof who first records.

Orris, the owner of Greenacre, was badly in need of money to make his April 15 income tax payment. Without telling Lorna, the chief loan officer at Salem National Bank, about his tax problems, he took out a loan of $30,000, secured by a mortgage on Greenacre. The mortgage papers were signed by Orris and by Lorna as agent for the bank on March 18. Lorna filled out the appropriate recordation form and gave it to Clarence, a bank clerk, on March 19. Lorna instructed Clarence to file the papers at the County Recorder's Office. Clarence was familiar with recording procedures, but inadvertently misplaced the papers. He discovered the papers on April 10 and filed them with the County Recorder. At the Recorder's Office, Clarence discovered a conveyance of Greenacre from Orris to Root dated April 5. It bore an official stamp of the County Recorder indicating that the conveyance had been filed in the Recorder's Office on April 8. Subsequent inquiry reveals that Root paid Orris $150,000 for Greenacre after a diligent title search and that Root had no knowledge of the mortgage on the property until Lorna contacted Root on April 11. In an appropriate action filed in state court, Salem National Bank seeks a declaration from the court that Root owns Greenacre subject to a $30,000 mortgage with Salem National Bank.

Is Salem National Bank's position likely to be upheld by the court?

(A) Yes, because the bank's interest was acquired for value prior to the date when Root recorded.

(B) Yes, because the mortgage was merely security for a loan.

(C) No, because Root recorded first.

(D) No, unless New Ayrshire is a title theory state.

Question 62

Hermann and Willa were a married couple who wanted to buy an expensive home. Unfortunately, the mortgage bank demanded a higher down payment than they could afford since many of Hermann's investments were tied up in non-liquid assets and also because the stock market had taken a plunge. Therefore, they went to Willa's mother, Maisie, and asked her if she would help them with the down payment by advancing them one-third of the money that the bank required. Hermann added, "I don't want my favorite mother-in-law to have to worry about this at all, so we'll put your name on the title and keep it there until you get paid back. That'll protect you if Willa and I get killed in a plane crash or an auto accident." Maisie advanced the money, and title was issued in the name of: "Hermann, Willa, and Maisie, as joint tenants with rights of survivorship." Maisie was very impressed by her son-in-law's willingness to make sure that she would not lose her money— so impressed that over the next three years Maisie paid one-third of all the upkeep expenses of the house, including state and local real estate taxes. Willa died suddenly of a stroke. Her will, which she had not revised in five years, stated: "All my interests in real property, wherever situated, pass to my son, Samuel." Samuel is Willa's son from a previous marriage. The probate court has been asked to rule on the distribution of the house. Hermann tells the court that he can prove orally that Maisie's name was put on the title only to give her a security interest.

How should the court rule regarding title to the property?

(A) The property belongs to Hermann, as sole tenant.

(B) The property belongs to Hermann and Maisie, as joint tenants.

(C) The property belongs to Hermann and Maisie, as tenants in common.

(D) The property belongs to Hermann, Maisie, and Samuel, as tenants in common.

Question 63

Thirty years ago, the Monopole Power & Light Company constructed a power dam on the Goon River. At the time the dam was constructed, Monopole solicited easements from all the landowners in the Goon River Valley, an agricultural area of approximately 200,000 acres. The power company paid fair value for the easements, which would allow the company to release water from the dam at certain times of the year, resulting in flooding of the land in the Goon River Valley. Most of the landholdings in the valley are large, averaging 10,000 acres each, but Faust, a small farmer, owned a mere 200 acres. At the time he signed the instrument granting Monopole the easement, Faust grumbled, "I feel like I'm selling my soul, but I've got to go along or be the pariah of Goon Valley."

In the 30 years since the dam was constructed, Faust's property has never been flooded. The only land Monopole has flooded is the 40,000 acres closest to the dam. Now, however, Monopole wants to substantially increase power production from the Goon Valley Dam. All landowners in the valley were notified by Monopole that henceforth all 200,000 acres (including Faust's 200 acres) would be flooded in accordance with Monopole's rights under the easement.

Faust consulted Nick Mephisto, a clever attorney, asking Nick if there was any way that Monopole's flooding plan could be stopped. Faust had not done anything special to improve his land, and he was using it in the same way as he did 30 years ago. Mephisto, however, made a visit to the Goon County Recorder of Deeds Office to check on the legality of the easements. He discovered that all of the easements were in order, except one. The large landowners' easements were all duly recorded and worded in the proper manner. The easement for Faust's property, however, lacked the requisite grantor's acknowledgment and thus was improperly recorded. Upon learning of this, Faust telephoned Monopole and told an officer of the company, "You folks better change your plans about generating more power from the Goon River Dam, because that easement you think you have to flood on my land is no good!"

May Monopole properly flood Faust's land under the terms of the easement?

(A) Yes, because Monopole has a valid easement, and such flooding is within the terms of the easement.

(B) No, because Monopole has failed to exercise its rights under the easement for 30 years, and the easement has lapsed.

(C) No, because the easement was not properly acknowledged and recorded.

(D) No, unless the state's adverse possession statute requires hostile occupation for a longer period than 30 years.

Questions 64-66 are based on the following fact situation:

Stevens owned Goldacre, a large tract of land, in fee simple. In 1985, Stevens deeded Goldacre as follows: "To Kent for life; if Roberts and Morris are discharged from the Army before Kent's death, to Roberts and Morris and their heirs. If they are not discharged from the Army before Kent's death, then the remainder is to go to my heirs." In 1994, Stevens and Kent died. Stevens's will left his entire estate to the American Cancer Society. Stevens's nearest relative is his brother, Philips.

64. In a jurisdiction that has codified common law principles, the interests of Morris and Roberts at the time the deed was executed are best described as:

(A) Mere expectancies.

(B) Contingent remainders.

(C) Absolutely vested remainders.

(D) Vested remainders subject to a condition subsequent.

65. Assume that Roberts and Morris were discharged from the Army prior to Kent's death. At the time of their discharge, their interest in Goldacre would be classified as:

(A) Tenants in common to a vested remainder.

(B) Joint tenants to a vested remainder.

(C) Tenants in common to a fee simple absolute.

(D) Tenants by the entirety to a fee simple absolute.

66. Assume the same facts as in the previous question. Assume also that Kent is now deceased. Assume further that Roberts predeceased Morris. Morris had a daughter named Cathy, who was the only heir. After Morris's death, Cathy's interest in Goldacre would be:

(A) Ownership of all Goldacre in fee simple.

(B) Ownership of one-half of Goldacre in fee simple.

(C) Ownership of an undivided one-half interest in Goldacre along with the heirs of Roberts who own the same interest.

(D) Ownership of one-half of Goldacre as a tenant in common with the heirs of Roberts.

Questions 67-69 are based on the following fact situation:

Anson and Barker were adjoining landowners. Anson's property was situated to the west of Barker's property. On the east of Barker's property was Clear Lake. In 1972, Anson purchased a boat to use for fishing on Clear Lake. Anson asked Barker if it would be all right if Anson moved his boat across an eight-foot patch of land leading from Anson's property to Clear Lake. Anson told Barker that the only other way to get to the lake was to take the highway, which involved a six-mile trip. Barker agreed, and Anson used the strip of land regularly to move the boat from his property to the lake and back again. Over the next few years, Anson's continued use of the eight-foot strip created a dirt roadway leading from his property to Clear Lake. In 1991, Barker sold his property to Samuels. Samuels noticed the dirt road on the eight-foot strip of his property and noticed Anson moving the boat across the dirt road. Even though Samuels knew that this was his property, he said nothing to Anson and let Anson continue for eight months. During the ninth month, Anson and Samuels had a violent argument, and Samuels told Anson that he was never to use the roadway on the eight-foot strip again. Anson continued to use the road until 1994, when Samuels sought an injunction to prevent Anson from using the roadway. The statutory period for adverse possession in this jurisdiction is 20 years.

67. When Barker gave Anson permission to use the eight-foot strip of land leading from Anson's property to Clear Lake, Anson's interest in Barker's property was:

   (A) An easement in gross.

   (B) An easement appurtenant to Barker's property.

   (C) An easement by necessity.

   (D) Not an easement.

68. Which of the following arguments would best support Samuels's action against Anson to enjoin the use of the road?

   (A) The selling of the property to Samuels terminated any claim Anson might have under adverse possession.

   (B) Anson was told to stop using the road prior to the time that the 20-year statute of limitations period had run.

   (C) Anson could not acquire any interest in Samuels's land because his original agreement was oral.

   (D) Anson's use of Samuels's land was permissive during the ownership of Barker.

69. Assume that Anson was held to have a valid easement over the eight-foot strip leading from his property to Clear Lake. The easement would be:

   (A) An easement in gross.

   (B) An easement appurtenant.

   (C) An easement by necessity.

   (D) An easement by implied reservation.

Question 70

Mark owned a 100-acre tract of land. Eighty acres were devised to him by his father 22 years ago. Mark had acquired title to an adjacent 20 acres from Prospector by adverse possession. On January 3, Mark entered into a land sale contract in which he promised to convey the 100 acres to Developer. The contract stated that closing was to occur on March 30. The contract otherwise listed the description of the property and was otherwise definite and certain as to the transaction. The contract did not state the nature of the title that Mark was to convey to Developer. At the time of closing on March 30, Developer paid the purchase price and accepted the deed conveyed by Mark. Six months later, Prospector returned to the area and brought a successful action in ejectment against Developer for the 20 acres. Developer now sues Mark for damages.

Which of the following statements would most accurately describe Developer's rights?

(A) Developer's rights are based on the implied covenant contained in a marketable title.

(B) Developer could bring an action for reformation of the deed with an abatement of the price of the land.

(C) The terms of Developer's deed control Mark's liability.

(D) Developer could bring an action against Mark for fraud.

Question 71

On April 15, Van entered into a valid written agreement with Bernie that provided that Bernie would buy Van's home for $75,000. The provisions of the agreement provided that closing would be at Bernie's attorney's office on May 15, and that Van would deliver to Bernie marketable title, free and clear of all encumbrances. On the date of closing, Van offered to Bernie the deed to the house, but Bernie refused to go ahead with the purchase because his attorney told him that Clifford, a contractor who had done work on the house, had recorded a lis pendens on May 1 against the property regarding a $10,000 contract dispute he had with Van. Van indicated that he was unaware of the lien, but that he was willing to go ahead with the sale and set aside funds from the purchase price to cover Clifford's claim until the dispute was resolved. Bernie still refused to proceed, stating that Van had breached the contract.

If Van brings an action against Bernie for specific performance, the probable result will be:

(A) Bernie prevails, because the title to the property was not marketable as of the date of closing.

(B) Bernie prevails, because an encumbrance was on the title as of the date of closing that was subject to litigation.

(C) Van prevails, because under the doctrine of equitable conversion, Bernie was the owner of the property when the lis pendens was recorded, and therefore, it was invalid.

(D) Van prevails, because an implied term of their contract was that he could use the proceeds to clear any encumbrance on the title.

Question 72

Margaret and Sarah lived together in Sarah's home for 20 years. Subsequently, Sarah became disabled because of a heart ailment and Margaret had to take care of her. Sarah told Margaret that she wanted to be sure that Margaret got her house after she died, so she gave Margaret a quitclaim deed. Margaret did not record the deed, but put it in her safe-deposit box.

Four months later, Irma, Sarah's daughter, found out about this and told her mother that if she would sell the house to her, she could live there for the rest of her life. Sarah, who wanted the money, agreed, and told Margaret that she had changed her mind and decided to leave the home to her children. Margaret promised to destroy the deed, and the next day, she did. Several days later, however, as Margaret and Sarah were driving to the store, their car was hit by a train and they both died. Sarah's and Margaret's heirs claim title to the house.

In an appropriate action to resolve this dispute, the most likely finding by the court will be:

(A) Margaret was owner of the house, because Sarah did not tell her the truth about why she was revoking her agreement.

(B) Margaret was still owner, because she did not retransfer title to Sarah.

(C) Sarah was the owner, because Margaret agreed to return the title, and did in fact destroy the deed.

(D) Sarah was the owner, because Margaret, as a donee, would not be able to prevail against Irma, who was a bona fide purchaser.

Question 73

Tyrone had rented Leona's home from her for seven years. When the time came to sign a new lease, Leona decided that since Tyrone had always been a quiet tenant, she would continue to charge him only $350 per month rent instead of the $500 to $550 she could probably get otherwise. The new lease was for a period of five years, and by its terms, Tyrone was specifically prohibited from assigning the lease without Leona's specific written consent. About a year later, Tyrone got married and moved into his new wife's home. Instead of giving up his lease with Leona, Tyrone sublet the property to Jack for $500 a month. Tyrone did not get Leona's permission to sublease the property.

If Leona brings an action to either eject Jack from the premises or to recover damages from Tyrone for subletting the premises without her consent, Leona most likely would:

(A) Be able to recover damages and to eject the new tenant.

(B) Be able to eject the new tenant only, because she has suffered no money damages.

(C) Not be able to eject the new tenant because, although Tyrone did not have the right to sublet, he had the power, but she will be entitled to recover the full rent paid by the new tenants because it would be unfair to let Tyrone profit from his wrongful act.

(D) Have no cause of action for either ejectment or damages.

Question 74

Sara was in a nursing home and asked Al, her attorney, to draft a deed that would give her farm to her son, Michael. Al drew the deed, had Sara properly execute it, and thereafter properly recorded the deed. Al then told Michael what he had done. Michael immediately went to the nursing home and told his mother, "I'm no farmer and I want nothing to do with the farm. Please take the deed back." A week later Sara returned home. Shortly thereafter, Michael died without a will, leaving his wife, Wanda, as his only heir. Sara has brought an action against Wanda to quiet her title to the farm.

If Sara is successful in this action, it will be because:

(A) Michael's statement to Sara was a constructive reconveyance of the farm.

(B) The presumption of delivery arising from Al's recording of the deed had no effect because Michael was unaware of what was happening.

(C) Wanda is subject to a constructive trust to carry out Michael's intent.

(D) Michael never effectively accepted delivery of the deed.

Questions 75-76 are based on the following fact situation:

Jake, who owned two houses on five acres of land, entered into a written agreement with Bob which stated:

> I agree to sell my house and sufficient land for a pool and garage to Bob for $75,000. Received from Bob $200.
>
> > Signed June 10.
> > Jake
> > Bob

On June 15, Bob entered into a written agreement with Marsha to sell her the house for $125,000.

75. Assume for purposes of this question only that Jake learns of Bob's contract with Marsha and decides to sell her the house for $125,000. Bob sues for specific performance. What will the result most likely be?

(A) Jake will prevail because $200 is only nominal consideration and cannot support the contract.

(B) Jake will prevail because the contract is ambiguous.

(C) Bob will prevail because Jake agreed to the purchase price in writing.

(D) Bob will prevail because Jake's contract with Marsha is sufficient evidence to show which house he agreed to sell to Bob.

76. Assume that Bob actually purchased the house from Jake and then decided that he could sell the house for more than $125,000; he therefore refused to sell it to Marsha according to their agreement. If Marsha sues for specific performance, how will a court hold?

(A) Judgment for Marsha, because she did not know Bob was purchasing the house from Jake for less than its market value.

(B) Judgment for Marsha, because Bob had marketable title at the time she sought to enforce the contract.

(C) Judgment for Bob, because he had no title to the house as of the date he entered into the agreement with Marsha.

(D) Judgment for Bob, because his agreement with Marsha was fraudulent to Jake at the time it was entered into, and therefore unenforceable.

Question 77

Mary owned 400 acres of land which she inherited from her late husband. About half of the property was densely wooded, and the rest was almost entirely occupied by a large gravel pit. Until his death, Mary's husband Clyde had operated Clyde's Sand and Gravel. Clyde had often thought of cutting the trees and selling the timber but by the time of his death had not done so.

Two years after Clyde's death, Mary transferred the 400 acres to her son Clyde Jr. for life, with the remainder to go to the State Land Trust for Historic Preservation.

Now Clyde Jr. wants to resume gravel production and to cut and sell the trees. Land Trust, the holder of the remainder, sues to block Clyde Jr. on a theory of waste.

How will the court most likely rule?

(A) Land Trust can stop both the gravel mining and the tree cutting.

(B) Land Trust can stop neither the gravel mining nor the tree cutting.

(C) Land Trust can stop the tree cutting but not the gravel mining.

(D) Land Trust can stop the gravel mining but not the tree cutting.

REAL PROPERTY ANSWERS

Answer to Question 1

(A)   George has acquired title to the land by adverse possession. George has been in possession of the land on which the well was dug openly, exclusively, continuously, and hostilely for a period in excess of the statutory limitations period for adverse possession. Such title results from the running of the statute of limitations for trespass to real property. If an owner of real property fails to take legal action within the statutory period to eject a possessor who claims adversely to the owner, title to the property vests in the possessor, and the owner is barred from suing for eject-ment. Adverse possession must be open and notorious (*i.e.,* such as the usual owner would make of the land and sufficiently apparent to put the true owner on notice that a trespass is occurring). Also, the possession must be actual and exclusive (*i.e.,* the possessor is not sharing with the true owner or the public at large). The possession must also be continuous throughout the statutory period. Finally, the possessor must occupy the property and enter without the owner's permis-sion. The possessor need not believe that he has a right to possession. Here, George has pos-sessed the subject property openly and notoriously by digging a well. This is something that the usual owner would do on the land, and it is sufficiently apparent to put Harry on notice that a trespass is occurring. George's possession has also been exclusive, because he has not shared it with Harry or the public. This possession has been continuous for 25 years, which is longer than the limitations period of 20 years. Finally, possession has been hostile because George has entered the land without Harry's permission and has acted as would an owner. Thus, George has satisfied all the elements required to obtain title by adverse possession. (B) is incorrect because hostile intent does not require that the possessor realize that the land is not his own. For purposes of adverse possession, George's possession was hostile by virtue of the fact that it was without permission and in derogation of Harry's rights. (C) is incorrect because the statute of limitations for adverse possession is tolled by the owner's disability only if he was under the disability at the time his cause of action accrued (when the claimant begins the adverse possession). Harry was not adjudicated to be mentally incompetent until 10 years after George began his possession of the well property. Thus, Harry's disability will not toll the statute. (D) is incorrect because, as has been explained above, (A) accurately states that George has acquired title to the land by adverse possession.

Answer to Question 2

(A)   Bob has standing to sue because he holds the reversion by operation of law that will take effect upon the death of Frank's widow. The remainder to Frank's children is void under the Rule Against Perpetuities. Thus, Bob inherits Oscar's reversionary interest, giving him standing to enjoin Frank. A person owning an estate in real property can create and transfer a lesser estate. The residue left in the grantor, which arises by operation of law, is a reversion. A reversion is transferable, devisable by will, and descendible by inheritance. The holder of a reversion may sue a possessory owner for waste. Pursuant to the Rule Against Perpetuities, no interest in property is valid unless it must vest, if at all, not later than 21 years after one or more lives in being at the creation of the interest. The validity of an interest under the Rule is determined at the time the interest is created, taking into account the facts then existing. In circumstances involving a deed, the perpetuities period begins to run on the date the deed is delivered with the intent to pass title. If a situation can be imagined in which the interest might not vest within the perpetuities period, the interest is void. One such problem is presented by the situation of the unborn widow. The term "widow" is a technical term referring to the person to whom someone is married at the time of death. A widow cannot be identified until the husband's death. Here, Frank has a life estate. Frank's widow has a contingent remainder in a life estate because, until her identity and existence are ascertained, there is no one to take possession should Frank's life estate come to an end. Also, there is a contingent remainder in fee simple in Frank's children, because their interest is contingent on their surviving Frank and his widow. This remainder violates the Rule Against Perpetuities, because Frank (even if he is presently married) might (after divorce or death of his current spouse) marry someone who was not alive at the time the interest was created. Frank might have a child by this person, after which everyone now connected with the vesting of this interest might die. Then, Frank's widow might live for more than 21 years after the death of all lives in being, leaving at her death the afterborn child as "Frank's children then alive." Thus, the interest of the child (or children) would, under these circumstances, vest outside the perpetuities period, rendering the interest void. When Oscar conveyed Parcel 1, he had a reversion by operation of law. This reversion was inherited by Bob, Oscar's only heir. Because the interest of Frank's children is void, the property will revert to Oscar (or his successors) on the death of either Frank or Frank's widow if he has one. As the holder of the reversion, Bob will have standing to attempt to enjoin the life tenant from committing waste on the property. (C) incorrectly states that Bob has no interest in Parcel 1, when in fact he holds a reversion. (D) is incorrect because, as detailed above, even if Frank was married at the time of the conveyance, and has some children now living, there is a scenario under which Frank might eventually die leaving a widow who was not yet born at the time of creation of this interest. In turn, this widow might die at such a time as to result in the vesting of the children's interest outside the perpetuities period. (B) is incorrect because Bob holds a reversion rather than an executory interest. An executory interest is a future interest created in a transferee that is **not** capable of taking on the natural termination of a preceding life estate. An executory interest divests the preceding interest or follows a gap in possession. Neither situation applies here. Furthermore, Bob is not a transferee of Parcel 1. Rather, Bob derives his interest by virtue of inheriting it from Oscar under the laws of intestacy.

Answer to Question 3

(D) The court could properly enjoin Frank from tearing the house down if Bob requests the appropriate relief. A life tenant has a duty not to change the premises in a way that the holders of subsequent estates have a reasonable ground to object to. Any changes or alterations could constitute a reasonable ground for objection unless changed neighborhood conditions deprive the land in its current form of reasonable productivity or usefulness. Here, there is no mention of changed neighborhood conditions. There is merely a change in the improvement on the property itself. Generally, this is not sufficient to prevent a life tenant who razes the structure from being charged with waste. Since a court could find that Bob, the reversioner, had a reasonable ground to object to the demolition of the house, the court could properly enjoin the destruction. (A) is wrong because Bob will not suffer any monetary damages from the destruction; the facts state that Frank's plan will actually increase the value of the property. Thus, despite the fact that the court could properly refuse to enjoin the demolition, it could not award damages, and (A) is therefore wrong. (B) and (C) are wrong because Frank cannot be ordered to pay the taxes or make the repairs. Although it is true that a life tenant is obliged to preserve the land and structures in a reasonable state of repair and to pay ordinary taxes, he is obligated only to the extent of rents and profits (or fair rental value if the life tenant occupies the property). Here, Frank is not occupying the property, and there are no rents or profits. Thus, Frank cannot be compelled to pay for the repairs or taxes. Furthermore, a life tenant is not required to make repairs that were necessary at the time the property passed to him.

Answer to Question 4

(D) Sonia and Clyde have title to Loveacre as tenants in common. Heathcliff and Sonia took Loveacre as joint tenants. An inter vivos conveyance by one joint tenant of his undivided interest severs the joint tenancy, so that the transferee takes the interest as a tenant in common and not as a joint tenant. Here, there was an inter vivos conveyance by Heathcliff to Clyde of all of Heathcliff's interest in the property held in joint tenancy with Sonia. This conveyance destroyed the joint tenancy, so that Clyde takes his interest in the property as a tenant in common with Sonia, rather than as a joint tenant. (A) is incorrect because the severance of the joint tenancy destroyed the right of survivorship. A joint tenancy carries with it a right of survivorship, whereby the death of one joint tenant frees the property from his concurrent interest, so that the surviving joint tenant retains an undivided right in the property that is no longer subject to the interest of the decedent. Had Heathcliff died without having conveyed his interest in Loveacre, Sonia would have held an undivided interest in the property, free of Heathcliff's interest. However, because the joint tenancy had been terminated prior to Heathcliff's death, there is no right of survivorship. Note also that the estate held by Heathcliff and Sonia was not a tenancy by the entirety, which is a marital estate similar to a joint tenancy between husband and wife. This estate arises presumptively (in some states) in any conveyance made to husband and wife, and carries a right of survivorship. Here, Heathcliff and Sonia took title to Loveacre prior to their marriage, and their subsequent marriage does not affect the nature of their title. This is important, because in a tenancy by the entirety, one spouse cannot convey any interest. (B) is incorrect because Heathcliff conveyed to Clyde his interest in the land. Thus, there is no interest or right in Loveacre to which the heirs of Heathcliff can succeed under the intestacy laws. In addition, even if there had been no conveyance, Heathcliff's heirs would not have succeeded to his interest in Loveacre. Rather, Sonia would have taken an undivided interest in the property by means of the right of survivorship. (C) is wrong because one joint tenant cannot convey his right of survivorship. When a joint tenant conveys his interest, it automatically becomes a tenancy in common interest. This is because the unity of time (one of the four unities required for creation of a joint tenancy) is lacking. To be joint tenants, the interests of the co-tenants must vest at the same time. Here, Sonia and Heathcliff's interest vested at the same time, but Clyde's vested much later. Thus, Clyde and Sonia cannot be joint tenants.

Answer to Question 5

(B) The fact that the building violates the setback allowance in the zoning ordinance renders the title unmarketable, breaching the implied warranty of marketability found in every contract for the sale of land. Generally, zoning restrictions do not affect the marketability of title, but an existing violation of a zoning ordinance does render title unmarketable. I. is incorrect because it is generally held that the violation of subdivision, housing, or building codes does not constitute an encumbrance on title. Zoning is treated differently. Thus, (A), (C), and (D) are wrong because they include I. II. is wrong because only an existing violation of the zoning ordinance, not a potential one, will render title unmarketable. Moreover, the truck restriction will not make Stephen's intended use impossible (he can use different trucks); thus, that contract argument also fails. The fact that II. is inaccurate is an additional reason that (C) is incorrect.

Answer to Question 6

(A) Arthur's incapacity has no effect on Bob's title. Generally, in an escrow transaction, title does not pass to the grantee until performance of the specified conditions (*e.g.*, the payment of money). There is a valid conditional delivery of the deed placed in escrow, and title will transfer automatically upon the occurrence of the condition. However, where justice requires, the title of the grantee is deemed to relate back to the time of the deposit of the deed in escrow. One situation in which the relation-back doctrine applies is when the grantor becomes incompetent (to avoid the rule that an incompetent cannot convey title). Here, title would ordinarily not have passed to Bob until the purchase price was paid, at which time the deed would be delivered through escrow. However, at the time the money was paid and the deed was delivered to Bob, Arthur was comatose and incompetent to actually convey title. This situation would lead to the unjust result that Bob would be prevented from taking title simply due to the unfortunate circumstances of Arthur's sudden incapacitation. Such a result triggers application of the relation-back doctrine, so that title is deemed to have passed to Bob at the time Arthur deposited the deed in escrow. Therefore, Arthur's incapacity has no effect on Bob's title to the house. (D) is incorrect because the prevention of passage of title is precisely the result designed to be avoided by application of the relation-back doctrine. (B) and (C) both incorrectly assume that Arthur's incapacity somehow interferes with or prevents the passage of title to Bob. As explained above, pursuant to "relation back," Bob has had clear title going back to the time at which the deed was deposited with the escrow holder, prior to Arthur's incapacity. Thus, there is no basis for concluding (as does (B)) that Arthur's incapacity constitutes a lien encumbering Bob's title, or that (as (C) states) Arthur's guardian is entitled to set aside the deed.

Answer to Question 7

(B) Phoebe will prevail in a suit because she, as the holder of the servient estate, has the right to choose the location of an easement by necessity. Phoebe has chosen the private road from Highway 10; thus, Langley has no right to use the driveway from the county road. Both (A) and (C) are incorrect because Langley has no easement by necessity in the driveway. As stated above, the owner of the servient parcel has the right to locate the easement, provided the location is reasonably convenient. Phoebe has located the easement in the private road; thus, no easement in the driveway exists. (D) is incorrect because Langley's use has not been continuous for the five-year period. To acquire an easement by prescription, the use must be: (i) open and notorious; (ii) adverse; and (iii) continuous and uninterrupted for the statutory period. Continuous adverse use does not mean constant use. Periodic acts that put the owner on notice of the claimed easement fulfill the requirement. In this case, however, two uses in the first two years would not be sufficient to put Phoebe on notice that Langley intended to claim an easement in the driveway. Therefore, Langley has not acquired a prescriptive easement in the driveway from the county road.

Answer to Question 8

(C) Sam has a life estate subject to an executory interest. The life estate is clear, and the language "except that if" indicates a condition subsequent. Upon the happening of that condition, Sam's estate is divested in favor of Diane or her children. Although it is true that Sam's interest is of indefinite duration, (A) is not the best description of his interest. Several kinds of interests are estates for indefinite periods. Thus, this choice is too broad. (B) is wrong for two reasons: (i) This is not a determinable life estate. Durational language such as "for so long as" and "until" creates a determinable estate. Such language is not used here. (ii) A life estate pur autre vie is a life estate measured by the life of another. The life estate here is for Sam's own life. (D) is wrong because a life estate is a freehold estate; possession is under title or right to hold.

Answer to Question 9

(B) Woody and Norm have a vested remainder subject to open and subject to complete divestment. They have a remainder because it is capable of taking in possession upon the natural termination of the preceding estate. It is not subject to a condition precedent and the beneficiaries are ascertainable; so the remainder is vested, not contingent. The remainder is subject to open because it is subject to diminution by Sam having more children. The remainder is subject to total divestment because the children's right to possession is subject to being defeated by the happening of a condition subsequent; *i.e.,* Sam's bankruptcy. (A) is wrong because the remainder is vested, not contingent; *i.e.,* it is not subject to a condition precedent, and the beneficiaries are ascertainable. (C) is not the best answer because it is incomplete. The vested remainder here is also subject to total divestment (*see* above). (D) is wrong because the children's interest does not divest Sam's estate, which would indicate an executory interest. Rather, their interest is capable of taking in possession on the natural termination of Sam's estate, and thus, it is a remainder.

Answer to Question 10

(D) If Sam has become bankrupt and Diane has possession, Diane's children have a vested remainder subject to open. Diane now has a possessory interest in the property for her life; at her death, the property will pass to her children. Since the children's interest will become possessory upon the natural termination of Diane's estate, it is a remainder. It is a vested remainder because it is not subject to a condition precedent and the takers (Carla and Cliffy) are ascertainable. However, Diane could have more children, and these children would also be entitled to the property. Therefore, the remainder is subject to open, to include any additional children. (A) is wrong because, as explained, it is not a contingent remainder since it is not subject to a condition subsequent and the takers are ascertainable. (B) is wrong because the remainder is not subject to total divestment. Total divestment would mean that Carla and Cliffy would lose their interests and that is not the case here; they may have their interests reduced but they will not lose them. (C) is wrong because the interest is not an executory interest; it does not divest the previous estate, but rather naturally follows Diane's life estate. (If Diane were not in possession—if Sam were not yet bankrupt—then this interest would be an executory interest since it would not naturally follow Sam's life estate, but would divest it if Sam became bankrupt.)

Answer to Question 11

(B) A 20-year easement for recreational purposes, granted to the homeowners of the subdivision, will best achieve Owner's goals. The holder of an easement has the right to use the tract of land for a special purpose, but has no right to possess or enjoy the land. If Owner grants the homeowners a 20-year easement, he may limit the permitted uses to whatever he wishes, and at the end of the 20 years, the homeowners' right to use the land ends. Owner may then dispose of the land as he wishes, free of the easement. (A) is incorrect because a real covenant is a promise to do, or refrain from doing, something on one's property that one would otherwise be privileged to do. A covenant does not grant a right to use or possess someone else's property. Therefore, a covenant would not be the appropriate legal device to allow the homeowners the use of the 500-acre tract. (C) is incorrect because a lease is not as effective as an easement in accomplishing Owner's goal. A leasehold is a possessory interest in land; so Owner would be giving up his right to possess the land. Thus, a lease to the homeowners would result in Owner's unnecessarily relinquishing much of his control over the tract, whereas the easement option allows him to do as he pleases with the property while granting the homeowners the right to use the tract. (D) is incorrect because the personal contract obligation of Owner does not adequately protect the homeowners' interests. It will not be much of an inducement if a prospective purchaser realizes that the right to use the land will terminate if Owner dies or sells the land. In the case of a land sale, the homeowners could be entitled to damages, but in contrast to the easement situation, would not be able to enforce the right to use the tract.

Answer to Question 12

(C) The homeowners will not prevail because they have no enforceable property interest. This answer is reached by the process of elimination. Although the homeowners may be able to get an injunction against the proposed use, it would not be because they have a property interest in the 500-acre tract, and the other options assume this fact. (A) is wrong because the homeowners have not acquired an easement by prescription. To acquire an easement by prescription, the use must be open and notorious, adverse, and continuous and uninterrupted for the statutory period (here 10 years). The use by the homeowners was **with** Owner's permission and, thus, was not adverse. (B) is wrong for similar reasons. Adverse possession requires the same basic elements as a prescriptive easement plus actual and exclusive possession. As explained above, the homeowners' use was not adverse. Also, they did not have actual possession (only the right to use the property), nor did they have exclusive possession since Owner could also use the property. Therefore, the homeowners did not acquire the property by adverse possession. (D) is wrong because the homeowners have no claim at law, which would make damages, rather than an injunction, the appropriate remedy.

Answer to Question 13

(B) The bank may successfully take Grayacre. A purchaser for value without notice of the prior conveyance at the time of the transaction is protected by the recording statute, which is a "notice" type of statute. Under a notice statute, a subsequent bona fide purchaser (*i.e.,* one who gives valuable consideration and has no notice of the prior instrument) prevails over a prior grantee who failed to record. Mortgagees are considered "purchasers"; thus Greenback Bank is a bona fide purchaser and is entitled to the protection of the recording act. Since Buzz was a prior grantee who failed to record his deed, and since Greenback Bank did not have any notice of Buzz's interest in the land, Greenback Bank will prevail over Buzz under the notice statute. (A) is wrong because Daphne's rights would be insufficient to protect the bank because Daphne was not a bona fide purchaser and would not be protected by the notice statute. She was not a BFP because she did not pay value for Grayacre. She inherited Grayacre under her mother's will. (C) is wrong because even though Buzz could have successfully challenged Daphne's right to ownership of the land because she was not a BFP for value, a subsequent mortgagee for value and without notice is protected by the recording statutes. (D) is wrong because it is irrelevant to a determination of one's interest under any of the recording acts. Even if the bank was imprudent in loaning money to Daphne in the first place, if it lent the money it satisfied the requirements of the notice statute to acquire a priority interest in Grayacre.

Answer to Question 14

(A) Albert has no interest in Blackacre. Harold and Wilma hold their property in a tenancy by the entirety. This type of tenancy is a special joint tenancy held by a married couple. It carries the right of survivorship, and can be terminated only by death of a spouse, divorce of the spouses, mutual agreement, or execution by a joint creditor of both spouses. Neither spouse alone can convey his interest to another. The spouses basically hold the property as one person, and thus severance by one is impossible. Therefore, Harold alone had no interest to convey to Albert. (B) is wrong because, as explained above, Harold had no power to convey his interest. Note, however, that even if this were a joint tenancy (rather than a tenancy by the entirety), the right of survivorship would not survive the conveyance to Albert. (C) is wrong because Harold's actions alone cannot cause a severance of a tenancy by the entirety and thus cannot turn this into a tenancy in common. (D) is wrong for all of the above reasons, plus the fact that Harold did not own the entire fee and thus had no power to convey it.

Answer to Question 15

(D) Charlie has no interest in Blackacre. Both spouses must join in the mortgage, because one spouse acting alone cannot convey or encumber the property. Thus, Wilma lacked the power to grant Charlie any interest in Blackacre. Even if Wilma could grant a mortgage interest, she could not encumber an interest greater than her own; so (A) is wrong. (B) is wrong because Wilma could not mortgage the property to Charlie, and Harold could not convey the property to Albert. Furthermore, a tenancy by the entirety is created by a conveyance to *spouses;* so Charlie could not hold the property as a tenant by the entirety with Albert. (C) is wrong because Wilma could not convey her interest without Harold's consent, and Charlie cannot be a tenant by the entirety with Harold.

Answer to Question 16

(C) Harold will succeed to Wilma's interest. Neither spouse in a tenancy by the entirety can defeat the right of survivorship in the other spouse. Therefore, Harold's right of survivorship is not affected by a contrary provision in Wilma's will. Thus, Charlie will not take her interest, and (B) is wrong. (A) is wrong because Albert has no interest. Even if Harold could have conveyed his interest, it would not carry the right of survivorship with it. (D) is wrong because Harold succeeds to Wilma's interest and, thus, Blackacre is not part of Wilma's intestate estate.

Answer to Question 17

(B) Carla has an easement by necessity over Lot A, because only by crossing over Lot A can she gain access to Lot B. When the owner of a tract of land sells a part of the tract and by this division deprives one lot of access to a public road, a right-of-way by absolute necessity is created by implied grant over the lot with access to the public road. The facts state that Lot B is surrounded by swampland on the north, south, and east. Thus, when Allison sold Lot B to Carla, there was an implied grant of an access easement across Lot A since Lot A was clearly her only access to a public road. (A) is wrong because an easement in gross does not have a dominant tenement. The holder of an easement in gross has a right to use the servient tenement independent of her ownership or possession of another tract of land. Here, the easement over Lot A arises solely as a consequence of Carla's ownership of adjacent Lot B. Thus, the easement is appurtenant, not in gross. (C) is wrong. Even though Barbara's easement was extinguished, Carla has acquired a new easement by necessity. When the ownership of the easement and the servient tenement is in one person, the easement is extinguished. Thus, when Allison bought Lot B, Barbara's easement was extinguished. After the easement was extinguished, however, a new easement was created by operation of law when the land was again subdivided into two lots and as a result of this subdivision one of the lot owners was deprived of access to a public road. (D) is wrong because Carla has an easement by necessity, which can arise any time the appropriate circumstances exist. Carla need not wait out the prescriptive period to gain the legal right to pass over Lot A.

Answer to Question 18

(A) Bick's action constitutes a trespass. A possessor of real property has the exclusive right to the use and possession of the surface, the air above the surface, and the land below the surface (including minerals). A trespass is a tangible physical intrusion that interferes with the possessor's right to exclusive possession of the land, and the possessor will be entitled to relief upon a showing of intentional, unprivileged physical intrusion. Here, Bick, without Jet's permission, physically invaded by drilling into property in which Jet had a right of exclusive possession. Thus, Jet would be entitled to damages resulting from Bick's trespass. Note that even if Bick had not struck oil, Jet could maintain a trespass action because trespass does not require actual damages to be established. (B) is incorrect because it states the nuisance grounds as the *only* theory of recovery. As noted above, Jet may also recover damages under a trespass theory. A nuisance is an activity that substantially and unreasonably interferes with a possessor's use or enjoyment of the property. Since Bick's conduct was unreasonable, and Jet's potential use of his mineral rights is being substantially interfered with (*e.g.,* by reducing the value of a lease he could make with another driller), Jet probably could recover damages under a private nuisance theory. However, as explained above, Jet may recover damages under a trespass theory, which would allow a recovery even though Jet's use and enjoyment were not interfered with; the physical invasion alone is sufficient for a recovery. (C) is a true statement of law and would be the correct answer if the well were entirely under Rockacre and oil from under Shaleacre were flowing into it. Bick's slanted well, however, is a trespass onto Shaleacre, and the "rule of capture" does not apply to cases of trespass. (D) is incorrect because it is irrelevant whether Jet's right to drill for oil is interfered with. Jet may recover damages for trespass simply because Bick has violated Jet's right to exclusive possession of the land.

Answer to Question 19

(B) Barbara will have the best chance of recovery against Stewart if Stewart was the builder of the house. Generally, a conveyance of real property contains no warranties of quality or fitness for the purpose intended, but there is now a recognized exception for the sale of a new house by the builder. There is an implied warranty that the new house is designed and constructed in a reasonably "workmanlike" manner and suitable for human habitation. Thus, in this case, Barbara would appear to have no claim against Stewart unless he was the builder, in which case she could claim that the house was not constructed in a reasonably "workmanlike" manner. (A) is wrong because the fact that the house was unsafe and uninhabitable would not by itself result in Stewart's liability unless he was the builder. (C) is wrong because the covenants contained in a warranty deed are covenants for title (*i.e.,* they protect the purchaser against competing claims for the title to the property); they offer no protection against defects on the property. (D) is wrong because Barbara's knowledge of the defect is not relevant to Stewart's liability under these facts. While a seller may be liable if he purposely conceals defects on the property or, in many states, if he does not disclose serious defects that he is aware of, he is not generally liable for defects in the absence of these circumstances. Since the facts do not indicate that Stewart acted to conceal the crumbling foundation, or was even aware of the problem, he will not be liable for the conditions unless he was the builder.

Answer to Question 20

(A) Orrin will prevail in an action to quiet title to the "North 30" because Suzanne did not actually occupy the "North 30." An adverse possessor will gain title only to the land she actually occupies. Actual possession is the kind of use the true owner would make of the parcel and is designed to give the owner notice of the trespass and the extent of the adverse possessor's claim. Mixtacre consists of two distinct parcels and Suzanne's use of the "North 30" parcel was not sufficient to put Orrin on notice of her trespass. (B) is wrong for two reasons: (i) Suzanne has color of title. Color of title merely means possession of a document purporting to convey title. (ii) Color of title is not necessary to gain title by adverse possession. In most jurisdictions, the possessor need not believe she has a right to possession; she can be a trespasser. (C) is wrong because Suzanne's possession and use of the "South 30" was not sufficient to constitute constructive possession of the "North 30." Possession of a portion of a unitary tract is sufficient adverse possession of the whole if there is a reasonable proportion between the part actually possessed and the whole and if the possessor has color of title. Suzanne has color of title, but she only occupied one-half of Mixtacre. Moreover, Mixtacre consists of two parcels separated by a road, so it is unlikely that it constitutes a unitary tract. In any case, Suzanne's possession of the "South 30" was not sufficient to put Orrin on notice of possession of the "North 30." (D) is wrong because, regardless of whether Mike acted in good faith, he did not have any title to convey to Suzanne. As noted above, color of title is not necessary for adverse possession, which is the only theory under which Suzanne could have title to the "North 30."

Answer to Question 21

(B) If one co-tenant wrongfully ousts another co-tenant from possession of the whole or any part of the premises, the ousted co-tenant is entitled to receive his share of the fair rental value of the property for the time he was wrongfully deprived of possession. Earl was wrongfully ousted and therefore, as one of two co-tenants, with right to possess all portions of the property, Earl would be entitled to one-half of the fair rental value of the property during the ousted period. (A) is incorrect because Earl is entitled only to his share (*i.e.,* one-half) of the fair rental value. (C) is incorrect as it also misstates the share of rental value to which Earl is entitled. Earl is entitled to one-half, not one-quarter, of the fair rental value of Baronacre. While (D) makes a correct statement, it addresses only the right of possession of the property. It is the share of ownership of the property, however, that determines the share of rents and profits. As Earl owned one-half of Baronacre, Earl is entitled to one-half the fair rental value for the time excluded.

Answer to Question 22

(B) If Oscar is granted specific performance it will be because he was prepared to deliver marketable title to Meyer at closing. The seller of real property need not have marketable title until the closing; *i.e.,* the buyer cannot rescind prior to that date on grounds that the seller's title is not marketable. In fact, the seller has the right to satisfy and eliminate title defects, such as a mortgage, at the closing with the proceeds from the sale. As long as the purchase price is sufficient and the mortgage is paid simultaneously with the transfer of title (*e.g.,* by use of an escrow), the buyer cannot claim that the title is unmarketable. The closing will result in marketable title. In this case Oscar intended to pay off a $30,000 mortgage at closing with a portion of the $200,000 purchase price. Thus, Meyer cannot claim that Oscar's title is unmarketable; he must proceed to closing. (A) is wrong because *any* mortgage or lien constitutes an encumbrance on the property. An encumbrance is any interest in land that diminishes its value. (C) is wrong because the fact that the mortgage was given for a preexisting debt does not mean it is unenforceable. The only possible negative effects of granting the mortgage for an antecedent debt is that the mortgagee is not considered a purchaser for value and, thus, is not protected by the recording statute. In this case, however, the recording statute does not even come into play. Even if it did, Meyer had notice of Big Bank's interest and could not cut off Big Bank's interest. Big Bank's loss of protection would only be a problem as against *prior* (of which there are none), rather than subsequent, grantees. Furthermore, it is not clear from the facts that the mortgage was granted merely in exchange for an antecedent debt. Big Bank agreed to forgo the immediate payment of the debt in exchange for the mortgage on Homeacre. (D) is wrong because all mortgages follow the transfer of land. Had the mortgage not been paid off and the sale proceeded, Meyer would not have been personally liable on the mortgage, but Homeacre would remain subject to foreclosure for default.

Answer to Question 23

(B) Sam will not prevail because Dale has acquired an easement by prescription. An easement is the right to use another's land for a special purpose, with no right to possess and enjoy the tract. One of the ways an easement can be created is by prescription, which is analogous to acquiring ownership through adverse possession. To acquire a prescriptive easement, the use must be: open and notorious; adverse and under claim of right; and continuous and uninterrupted for the statutory period. In this case, Dale's use was clearly open and notorious. He did not attempt to conceal his use; in fact, he invited the whole town to witness it. Dale did not have the owner's permission; hence, the use was adverse. Dale's use was under claim of right since it would appear to the community that he owned the property; *i.e.,* the use is such as the true owner would make of the land. Dale's use was continuous. Continuous adverse use does not mean constant use. A continuous claim of right with periodic acts that put the owner on notice of the claimed easement fulfills the requirement. Here, Dale made the same use of the property every year; the use was what a true owner would make of the property; and he invited the whole town to take note of it. This should be sufficient to put Sam on notice of Dale's claimed right. Finally, the use continued for the statutory period. The statutory period is 10 years, and Dale's use continued for 15 years. (A) is wrong because Dale did not exclusively possess Sam's property, and his use was not sufficient to satisfy the continuous possession requirement for adverse possession. In addition to the requirements for a prescriptive easement, to acquire title to property through adverse possession, the claimant must generally occupy the land to which he is claiming title. Here, Dale did not possess the property; he merely used it once a year. Similarly, the continuousness requirement for adverse possession differs somewhat from that required for a prescriptive easement. For adverse possession, intermittent periods of occupancy are generally not sufficient. (C) is incorrect because Dale's use was sufficiently continuous to acquire a prescriptive easement. As noted above, periodic acts that put the true owner on notice are sufficient for this purpose. (D) is incorrect because Dale's use of the land was sufficiently open and notorious to put the true owner on notice. It is of no consequence that Sam chose not to visit the property in autumn until this year. Sam cannot use the fact that he did not keep apprised of the use of his own property to thwart Dale's claim. Also, Sam's lack of acquiescence is irrelevant. Dale acquires his easement by prescription which occurs without the owner's acquiescence.

Answer to Question 24

(A) Amy has a right to repair the stairs because she has an easement. An easement by implication is created by operation of law rather than by written instrument. It is an exception to the Statute of Frauds. An easement is implied if, prior to the time the property is divided, a use exists on the "servient part" that is reasonably necessary for the enjoyment of the "dominant part," and the parties intended the use to continue after division of the property. The use must be continuous and apparent at the time the property is divided. Reasonable necessity is determined by many factors, including the cost and difficulty of alternatives, and whether the price paid reflects the expected continued use. The use of the stairs was continuous, apparent, and reasonably necessary to the use of Building 2 when Oscar conveyed Building 2 to Amy. Although the facts do not give enough information to determine whether Bob's purchase price reflected the continued use of the stairs, it seems clear that the alternatives would be very costly. Since there was no change in the use after Amy bought Building 2 and Oscar was still in possession of Building 1, it appears that they intended the use to continue. Thus, the implied easement from existing use arose when Oscar conveyed Building 2 to Amy. The burden of that easement passes with the transfer of the servient tenement, Building 1. The holder of an easement has a right, even a duty, to make repairs. Therefore, Amy has a right to repair the stairs in Building 1. (B) is wrong because no such right exists apart from the rights of an easement holder. Absent an easement, Amy would not have any right to enter Bob's property regardless of whether she would be subject to liability for injuries. (C) is wrong because easements are of perpetual duration, unless limited by the terms of a writing. Here there is no writing, so Amy's easement is perpetual. (D) is wrong because, as explained above, Amy has an easement implied from existing use. An easement gives Amy the right to enter Bob's property.

Answer to Question 25

(D) Tanja should join all of the landowners in the subdivision in a suit to terminate the servitude on the grounds of abandonment. If a covenant in a subdivision deed is silent as to who holds its benefit, any neighbor in the subdivision will be entitled to enforce the covenant if a general scheme or plan is found to have existed at the time he purchased his lot. In addition, a prior purchaser can enforce a restriction in a subsequent deed from a common grantor under either a third-party beneficiary theory or an implied reciprocal servitude theory. Under the implied reciprocal servitude theory, an implied reciprocal servitude attaches to the grantor's retained land at the moment he deeds a lot with the restriction. Thus, all of the other landowners in the subdivision could potentially enforce the covenant as an equitable servitude against Tanja. All parties would probably fail in an attempt to enforce the servitude, but Tanja should join them now to avoid multiple litigation. (Note that had the other landowners tried to enforce the equitable servitude against Tanja, they would all have been subject to the equitable defense of acquiescence, which provides that if a benefited party acquiesces in a violation of the servitude by one burdened party, he may be deemed to have abandoned the servitude as to other burdened parties. In addition, the other commercial users are subject to the defense of unclean hands. It is important to remember that these are defenses and do not terminate the servitude; therefore, it would be best for Tanja to join all possible complainants in a suit to have the servitude declared extinguished.) (A) is wrong because, as explained, the other landowners also could try to enforce the covenant. (B) is wrong for the same reason. Although Anthony has not violated the covenant and thus is not subject to the defenses possible against the other landowners, he and Oldd are not the only possible plaintiffs (remember the question in effect asks who can bring suit, not who can win it). (C) is wrong because Oldd and Anthony can also bring suit. (Note that the above discussion applies only to sparing Tanja from the enforcement of the restriction as an equitable servitude. Oldd may try to enforce the restriction as a real covenant. He will, however, be limited to recovering damages, which might be very difficult to prove under the circumstances.)

Answer to Question 26

(B) Rye will be enjoined from mining and liable for damages. Generally, a life tenant may not consume or exploit natural resources on the property. (There are several exceptions, none of which apply here.) If, as here, the life tenant does exploit the natural resources, it is considered voluntary waste, and the remainderman may sue for damages and an injunction (since damages are inadequate with respect to real property). Therefore Rhonda can get both damages and an injunction. (A) is incorrect because partition is generally a remedy for co-tenants, not holders of successive estates. A life tenant may ask for judicial *sale* in a partition proceeding if the land is practically worthless in the condition in which the life tenant receives it, but here Grainacre was not worthless as a farm. (C) is incorrect because a partition sale is not appropriate (*see* above). (D) is incorrect because depleting natural resources is considered waste; it diminishes the value of the land and thus injures the interest of the remainderman. Therefore, except under certain circumstances (not present here), a life tenant is not entitled to consume or exploit natural resources.

Answer to Question 27

(C) Edsel cannot require Davis to permit power lines to be installed on Davis's property. A basic change in the nature of use of an easement is not allowed. Thus, a power line cannot be added to Edsel's private easement of way across Lot One. (A) is incorrect because Edsel cannot exercise Power Company's right of eminent domain. (B) is incorrect because easements by necessity arise only when the owner of a single tract sells a portion of the tract that has no access to a public road. The facts in this question do not indicate that Davis ever owned both Lots One and Two; therefore, no easement by necessity can arise. (D) is incorrect because prior necessity is irrelevant. Necessity is determined at the time the parcel is divided. As noted above, the facts here indicate that the land was not part of a unitary tract; thus, a necessity analysis is impossible.

Answer to Question 28

(C) Power Company can install power lines on Davis's property without his permission only by exercising its power of eminent domain. Except for this power, neither Power Company nor Edsel has an easement or any other right to use Davis's land for this purpose. (A) is incorrect because it overlooks Power Company's statutory power of eminent domain. Absent this statutory power, however, (A) would be the correct answer. (B) is incorrect because, absent the power of eminent domain, Power Company has no right to use Davis's property regardless of whether it posts bond. (D) is incorrect because easements by necessity arise only upon the division of a unitary tract.

Answer to Question 29

(B) To be a bona fide purchaser for value, and thus entitled to the protection of the recording statute, the purchaser must prove that real—not merely nominal—consideration was paid. In other words, Quisling must prove that he is a purchaser rather than a donee. The consideration need not be adequate or the market value, but it must be of substantial pecuniary value. Quisling will have a difficult time proving that one dollar meets this test. (A) is wrong because title can be conveyed by quitclaim deed. (C) is wrong because a warranty deed is not superior in right to a quitclaim deed. The only difference between the two is that a warranty deed normally contains covenants for title, the breach of which gives rise to a cause of action against the grantor, and a quitclaim deed contains no assurances by the grantor. (D) is wrong because all instruments affecting title to real property are recordable and should be recorded.

Answer to Question 30

(B) Nora's best argument is that destruction of the residence constitutes waste. The other choices do not present arguments giving her a chance of success. A life tenant is entitled to all ordinary uses and profits of the land, but he cannot lawfully do any act that would injure the interests of the remainderman. A grantor intends that the life tenant have the general use of the land in a reasonable manner, but that the land pass to the owner of the remainder, as nearly as practicable, unimpaired in its nature, character, and improvements. Even ameliorative waste, which actually increases the value of the land, is actionable if there is no reasonable justification for the change. A life tenant can substantially alter or even demolish existing buildings if (i) the market value of the future interests is not diminished and *either* (ii) the remainderman does not object, or (iii) a substantial and permanent change in the neighborhood conditions has deprived the property in its current form of reasonable productivity or usefulness. Here, the market value of the property would not be diminished. The remainderman (Nora), however, is objecting, making option one unavailable. Furthermore, although the neighboring properties have been sold for hotels and resorts, it does not necessarily follow that the conditions have changed to such a degree that Moneyacre should be similarly converted. The property is large enough to be somewhat isolated from the changes in the surrounding areas; thus, despite the surrounding hotels, an owner could still enjoy the land as a private residence, orchard, and beach. Therefore, the property is still useful and the second option is also unavailable. In this case, the life tenant's desire to raze the mansion is not because the changes in the neighborhood have made the mansion uneconomical or impractical. The life tenant can make more money by tearing the mansion down, but its usefulness and value are apparently unaffected by the changes in the neighborhood. Thus, Nora will be able to enjoin Fred from allowing the resort chain to raze the mansion and build a hotel. (A) is wrong because the fact that Nora intended to use the property as a residence is irrelevant. Even if Nora intended to change the use of the property, she is still entitled to receive the land in the condition in which it passed to Fred. (C) is wrong because the fact that Nora made mortgage payments does not affect Fred's rights. Nora had to make the payments to protect her remainder interest. (D) is wrong because life estates generally are alienable. The transferee merely takes the same interest as the life tenant. In this case, Fred may convey his interest in the property. Of course, anyone taking Fred's interest would have only an estate for Fred's life, *i.e.,* a life estate pur autre vie.

Answer to Question 31

(C) The court should issue the injunction because the covenant runs with the land. A covenant will be enforceable as an equitable servitude—allowing a covenantee, covenantor, or successor to enforce the covenant in equity by way of injunction—when there is (i) a covenant in a writing satisfying the Statute of Frauds, that (ii) touches and concerns the land (*i.e.,* the effect of the covenant makes the land more useful or valuable to the benefited party) and that (iii) indicates an intention that the servitude exists, and (iv) notice is given to future owners of the burdened land. Here, the covenant was in writing in the subdivision plan and presumably it satisfied the Statute of Frauds. It touches and concerns the land—benefiting all of the lots and burdening all of the lots. The intention to create the servitude is established by the writing and can also be implied from the common scheme for development. There was sufficient record notice of the covenant since the plan was recorded and was noted in all of the original deeds prepared by Herschel, including the one in Weldon's chain of title. Thus, the covenant is enforceable and (C) is the best answer. (A) is incorrect because although an injunction is equitable in nature—so equitable principles govern—it is not a defense in equity merely to claim that granting an injunction will result in a waste of assets. (B) is incorrect. The court will enforce the restriction because Weldon had record notice of it—the deed from Herschel to Development Associates, which contained a reference to the restriction in the recorded plan, was in Weldon's direct chain of title and could have been discovered by him. (D) is incorrect because a court will not modify the covenant—it will enforce it or not enforce it, but will not substitute its judgment of what is aesthetically pleasing for the requirements of the covenant.

Answer to Question 32

(C) The court should rule for Becky because her easement gives her the right to use Allan's property for access to her lot. An easement is an interest in land which gives the holder a right to use the land for certain purposes. Here, Wilhelm granted Becky an easement to use a portion of his property for access to her lot. The presumption when an easement is granted is that it is perpetual unless otherwise stated. Thus, Becky's easement was perpetual and was not destroyed by the transfer of the servient tenement (Wilhelm's property) to Allan. Moreover, the easement is valid against Allan since it was recorded. Easements, like other interests in land, are good against subsequent holders of the burdened (servient) tenement as long as the interest is recorded. The facts here state that Becky properly recorded her easement, so it is good against Allan; thus, (C) is correct. (A) is incorrect because Becky's recorded deed is deemed to be constructive notice of the easement; mention of the easement need not be included in Allan's deed. A thorough search of the title index would have revealed that Wilhelm, Allan's predecessor in title, gave the easement to Becky. (B) is wrong because the obstruction of Becky's easement did not continue for the statutory period required to terminate easements by prescription. To terminate an easement by prescription, the owner of the servient tenement must openly and nonpermissively interfere with the use of the easement for the same statutory period as is necessary to acquire an easement by prescription. Although statutes vary, it would never be less than one year, and most statutes set the period at 10 or 20 years. (D) is incorrect. An easement by absolute necessity may be implied when the purchaser of part of a tract has no outlet to a public road or utility line except over the remaining land of the seller, but here, Becky does not need to rely on an implied easement since she has an express easement from Wilhelm.

Answer to Question 33

(A) CCB owns both the mortgage and the note. A mortgage is a security interest in property and a note is evidence of the underlying debt. Physical possession of the mortgage and note is not required for ownership. Thus, since CCB bought the mortgage and note and recorded its interest, CCB is the owner of both, even though it left possession of the documents with BMB. McElligot has no interest in the mortgage and note because he had record notice of CCB's interest (since CCB recorded the mortgage). Having notice of CCB's interest, McElligot cannot claim the protection of the recording act. (Note that CCB would prevail even under a pure race recording statute, where notice is not important, since it recorded first.) Also, McElligot cannot claim holder in due course status, since that status requires no notice of any other claims to the property. Therefore, McElligot has no interest in the mortgage and note. (B) is wrong because absent the protection of the recording act or holder in due course status, the first in time rule governs. CCB was the first to purchase the mortgage and note, and so it prevails. (C) and (D) are wrong because, as stated above, CCB holds both the mortgage and note, which were never separated.

Answer to Question 34

(C) Mary's unborn children have a contingent remainder. A remainder is a future interest created in a transferee that is capable of taking upon the natural termination of the preceding estates. A remainder must be expressly created in the instrument creating the prior possessory estate. The interest in Mary's children follows naturally upon the termination of Ethyl's estate; thus, it is a remainder. It is a contingent remainder because we do not know whether there will be any takers. A remainder created in favor of an unborn person has to be a contingent remainder. (A) is incorrect because the children do have an interest, a remainder. (B) is incorrect because a springing use cuts short an estate held by the grantor, which is not the case here. A remainder does not cut short a preceding estate. (D) is incorrect because a vested remainder can only be created in an existing person. A vested remainder may be subject to partial or total divestment, but it cannot be vested unless there is at least one remainderman in existence and ascertained.

Answer to Question 35

(D) Samuel will not prevail because his title was unmarketable. There is an implied warranty in every land sale contract that at closing the seller will provide the buyer with title that is marketable. It need not be perfect title, but it must be free from questions that might present an unreasonable risk of litigation. Since the placement of Samuel's house violated the 15-foot setback requirement in the original subdivision plan, Benson could be subject to suit. Most courts hold that violations of private restrictions imposed by covenant, servitude, or condition can render title unmarketable. The violation of the zoning ordinance is also a basis for finding the title unmarketable. (A) and (B) are therefore incorrect. (C) is an incorrect statement of law.

Answer to Question 36

(A) Lee's claim to the parcel would be based on adverse possession. First, it must be established that an adverse possession action against a municipality is possible in this jurisdiction, because government land generally cannot be obtained through adverse possession. His use should then be established to show the assertion of dominion required for adverse possession. Thus, (A) is correct. (C) and (D) are wrong because abandonment by the record owner (III.) is not an element of adverse possession. (B) and (D) are wrong because a license (IV.) need not be established, and could not be established by mere nonuse. A license, in fact, cuts against acquiring title by adverse possession since it is basically the owner's permission to use the land.

Answer to Question 37

(A) Since Phil did not acquire either legal or equitable title until after Art died, he had nothing to pass on to Sandy. Therefore, (B) and (C) are wrong. (D) is not the strongest answer based on the facts.

Answer to Question 38

(A) The majority of states would hold that, under the estoppel by deed theory, title would pass automatically to Sandy by operation of law. (B) is wrong because estoppel by deed applies regardless of the testator's knowledge of a prior deed. (C) is wrong because it states the minority position under estoppel by deed. Under the majority view, title passes to Sandy automatically; she need not bring suit to recover title. (D) is wrong because title passes to Sandy under the doctrine of estoppel by deed.

Answer to Question 39

(C) Since Proctor treated the land as his own for the statutory period, he acquired title to the land by adverse possession. (D) is therefore wrong. (A) is wrong because an intervening disability does not toll the statute of limitations. (B) is wrong because Proctor's occupation was indeed open and notorious under the facts.

Answer to Question 40

(D) Proctor used the land with Gamble's consent, and there were no facts to indicate that Proctor in any way manifested an intention to claim the land as his own. Therefore the "hostile" requirement is not met. (A), (B), and (C) are therefore wrong.

Answer to Question 41

(C) Jasper will win because the terms of the deed, not of the contract, control his liability. Under the doctrine of merger, the contract merges into the deed, and the terms of the contract are meaningless. Even though the contract specified a "good and marketable title," it is the deed that controls, and the deed contained no covenants of title. A deed does not incorporate the title terms of a contract. Thus, (A) is wrong. (B) is wrong; it is not supported by the facts. (D) is wrong because Chandler's negligence is irrelevant.

Answer to Question 42

(C) A license is a privilege to enter upon another's property. It may be revoked at any time merely by a manifestation of the licensor's intent to end it. A tenant at sufferance would be entitled to the statutory notice, and a month-to-month tenant would benefit from the common law right to a period of notice equal to the tenancy, i.e., one month. Thus, (A) and (B) are wrong. (D) is wrong because Todd is clearly not a trespasser ab initio since he entered onto the premises with permission.

Answer to Question 43

(B) Benny can enjoin Donna's actions only if he has an equitable servitude. (A) is wrong because the location of the tract will not be sufficient to establish notice. However, Benny will be able to enforce the restriction as an equitable servitude because Donna had *record* notice of it: a deed in her chain of title referred to the recorded plan that designated the tract as a golf course. (C) is wrong because Benny is not a third-party beneficiary of Alvin's promise. Instead, he is a direct promisee, since he dealt directly with Alvin. (D) is not sufficient to grant Benny an injunction against Donna.

Answer to Question 44

(A) The restrictive covenant runs with Benny's land, which is benefited, and with Sally's land, which is burdened. The essential ingredients are that the covenant touch and concern the land and that it be intended to run. Both are present here. (B) is therefore wrong. (C) is wrong because the restriction was contained in a previous deed relating to the property. (D) is wrong because Sally at least had constructive notice of the restriction.

Answer to Question 45

(A) A co-tenant has no duty to improve the property and cannot force the other co-tenants to contribute to the cost of improvements made by him. Thus, (B) is wrong. (C) and (D) are wrong because the results of an improvement are irrelevant; the co-tenant cannot force his other co-tenants to contribute to the improvement.

Answer to Question 46

(A) The estate could not have been a tenancy by the entirety since that estate can exist only between a legally married husband and wife. The estate created would probably be considered either a joint tenancy with right of survivorship or a tenancy in common, either of which may be partitioned. (B) is wrong because, even if the estate had been by the entirety, abandonment by one spouse does not cause a severance. (C) is wrong because although a tenant by the entirety cannot obtain a partition, that is not the type of tenancy involved here. (D) is wrong because Ed could not have absolute title under these facts.

Answer to Question 47

(B) Under the Rule Against Perpetuities, the attempt to give Richards an executory interest is void because Richards's interest could vest more than 21 years after a life in being. The courts will strike the gift over to Richards and will then read the rest of the conveyance as it stands. Thus, (C) is incorrect. The "so long as" language creates a fee simple determinable in Samuels, meaning that the grantor retains a possibility of reverter. Thus, (A) and (D) are incorrect.

Answer to Question 48

(A) In the present case, Lon is attempting to evict Tom for retaliatory purposes, and many jurisdictions prohibit such evictions. (B) is wrong because the fact that this is very likely a periodic tenancy will not save Tom from eviction, since the proper statutory notice has been given to terminate it. (C) is wrong because the amount of rent charged each tenant is a function of "freedom of contract," and a landlord is free to charge differing amounts of rents for the units. (D) is wrong because a landlord generally does not need to establish a valid reason to raise rent.

Answer to Question 49

(C) The deed, once it has been delivered, is merely evidence of title, and its destruction does not cause any change in the title. To transfer title, Employee would have had to deliver a new deed transferring title back to Employer. (A) and (B) are therefore wrong. (D) is not supported by the facts.

Answer to Question 50

(C) When Linda died, her one-half interest descended to her intestate heir, Meghan; and likewise, when Luke died, his one-half interest passed to his intestate heir, Bobby. There is no right of survivorship in a tenancy in common, and the oral agreement between Luke and Linda does not satisfy the Statute of Frauds or the Statute of Wills. The facts involving the closeness of Luke's death to Linda's is mere distraction, because no real simultaneous death issues arise here. It follows that (A) and (B) are incorrect. (D) is incorrect because a tenancy in common does not become a joint tenancy upon the death of the co-tenants.

Answer to Question 51

(A) A property owner has a right to the support of his land without any buildings on it. An adjoining neighbor is absolutely liable for any withdrawal of support. Thus, if Ophelia's excavation withdrew support for Norbert's land, she is absolutely liable for the damage. (B) is wrong because Ophelia's negligence is irrelevant; she is absolutely liable. (C) is wrong because damage to the land itself is recoverable if support has been withdrawn. (D) is wrong, because as indicated, adjoining landowners have a right of subjacent and lateral support.

Answer to Question 52

(C) If the land would not have subsided but for the structure, Ophelia is not absolutely liable. She would be liable only if she were negligent in excavating. (C) covers the lack of negligence and the fact that the structure contributed to the collapse; it is therefore her best defense. (A) is wrong because notice of the excavation, and lack of objection, does not preclude recovery by Norbert on the negligence. (B) is wrong because it concerns only the negligence issue. (D) is not as good an answer as (C) because even if the garage was unusually heavy, Ophelia could still be liable if she were negligent in excavating.

Answer to Question 53

(C) Easements are presumed to be of perpetual duration, and mere nonuse is not enough to constitute termination by abandonment. To abandon, the easement holder must demonstrate by physical action (e.g., removing the railroad tracks) an intention to permanently abandon the easement; this has not been done here, and so (A) is incorrect. (B) is wrong because it reaches the wrong result and relies upon a factor having nothing to do with abandonment. (D) is an incorrect statement of law—once abandoned, an easement cannot be revived simply because the owner of the underlying fee did not take some affirmative action.

Answer to Question 54

(C) Negative easements are of too limited a use to ensure that the project retains its residential character, so (A) is wrong. (D) is wrong because a governmental authority may change zoning laws. (B) is possible, but it is unlikely a court will enforce a forfeiture of an owner's estate, particularly since the same result could be accomplished by the use of covenants in the deeds. In addition, buyers may be reluctant to purchase lots subject to a condition subsequent that could cause the loss of their interest. Thus, (C) is the best method.

Answer to Question 55

(D) Prior purchasers may enforce restrictions in subsequent deeds from a common grantor if there is a general scheme evidencing the developer's intent to benefit the entire subdivision. Hence, (B) is wrong. (C) is wrong because it is too absolute; if a court finds there is no common development, the restrictions are not enforceable by the owners of BayShore Heights. (A) is wrong because zoning regulations do not limit the enforceability of private covenants.

Answer to Question 56

(D) The development of the original projects indicates no scheme or plan for development of the remaining acreage. Hence, (A) and (C) are not supported by the facts. (B) is a misstatement of law.

Answer to Question 57

(C) When a developer subdivides land into several parcels and some of the deeds contain negative covenants, but some do not, negative covenants or equitable servitudes, binding all the parcels in the subdivision, may be implied under the doctrine of reciprocal negative servitudes. Thus, (A) is not as complete an answer. (B) is incorrect because covenants require privity of estate and the remedy is damages, not an injunction. (D) is incomplete.

Answer to Question 58

(D) Since the facts state that the other purchasers of Lots 1-19 each built residences on their property, Neil would at least be charged with inquiry notice. Thus, (A) is incorrect. (B) is incorrect because Neil's reliance on the abstract of title and Al's representation would not negate the inquiry notice. (C)'s reasoning would not be sufficient to bind Neil to the covenant.

Answer to Question 59

(A) The conveyance clearly created an estate in Martha, lasting for Martha's life. (B) is incorrect because Oscar did not have to be alive at the time of the original conveyance in order to now claim an interest in Greenacre. (C) is incorrect because Oscar's interest would vest within 21 years of a life in being (Vera). (D) is incorrect because Oscar's interest would be a vested remainder.

Answer to Question 60

(D) Since Emma retained a reversionary interest in Greenacre, she would take possession of the land until Oscar became 21 years of age. Thus, (C) is wrong. (A) is wrong because Oscar is not entitled to possession until he reaches age 21. (B) is wrong. Oscar has no right to possession; thus, a guardian cannot possess for him.

Answer to Question 61

(C) Salem National Bank's position will not be upheld because Root, a bona fide purchaser, recorded first. The applicable recording statute is a race-notice statute, under which a subsequent purchaser for value without notice of any prior conveyance is protected if he records before the prior grantee. Here, the bank, as mortgagee, is a grantee of an interest in Greenacre prior to Root. However, Root purchased Greenacre for valuable consideration and without notice (either actual, record, or inquiry) of the prior conveyance to the bank. Root recorded his conveyance on April 8, prior to the time Clarence filed on behalf of the bank. Consequently, Root satisfies the statutory requirements, and he is protected against the bank's claim. (A) is incorrect because, to prevail, the bank must have *actually* recorded prior to Root. It is of no significance that the bank acquired its interest in the property—even for value—prior to the date of Root's recordation. The bank is not protected by the recording statute since it recorded its interest after recordation by another bona fide purchaser. (B) is incorrect because, although a mortgage is a security interest for a loan, it is still an instrument creating an interest in land. As such, a mortgage comes within the scope of the recording acts, so that a grantee thereof must record in order to give notice of the conveyance to subsequent purchasers. Having failed to record in time, the bank will lose against a subsequent bona fide purchaser who records first. (D) is incorrect because whether New Ayrshire is a lien theory or a title theory state is irrelevant to this question. Under either theory, the bank's mortgage is an instrument creating an interest in land, and is thus subject to the recording statute.

Answer to Question 62

(B) Hermann and Maisie hold the property as joint tenants. A joint tenancy carries the right of survivorship. When one joint tenant dies, the property is freed from her concurrent interest. The survivors retain an undivided right in the property, which is no longer subject to the interest of the deceased co-tenant. Since Hermann, Willa, and Maisie held the property as joint tenants with right of survivorship, Willa's death freed the property of her interest and Hermann and Maisie each hold an undivided one-half interest in the property. Their rights of survivorship continue. (A) is incorrect because, as stated above, Maisie also has an interest in the property. (A) might be a correct choice if Hermann were successful in proving his contention that Maisie's interest was only intended to be a security interest. The facts do not support this argument, however. The fact that Hermann intended that Maisie have a right of survivorship is evidence that she was intended as a joint tenant, not merely a secured lender. Maisie's payment of upkeep and taxes is further evidence that her interest was greater than that of a creditor. (C) is incorrect because the joint tenancy was not severed or partitioned. A conveyance by one joint tenant may sever a joint tenancy, resulting in a tenancy in common. However, a testamentary disposition by one joint tenant has no effect (*see* below) and thus does not work a severance. (D) is incorrect because Samuel does not have an interest in the property. A will is effective only at death and is inoperative as to joint tenancy property because, at the instant of death, the decedent's rights in the property evaporate. Thus, Willa had no interest in the property to convey to Samuel at her death.

Answer to Question 63

(A) Monopole has a valid easement entitling it to flood Faust's property. To create an easement by express grant, there must be a writing signed by the grantor. If validly created, an easement is presumed to be of perpetual duration. All of these requirements were complied with in the case of the easement to flood Faust's property. Faust signed the writing granting the easement, which is presumed to be of perpetual duration. (B) is incorrect because mere nonuse will not terminate an easement. To terminate an easement, the nonuse must rise to the level of abandonment, which requires physical action by the easement holder that manifests an intention to permanently abandon (*e.g.,* construction of a structure on the easement holder's property that would make it impossible to use the easement). Monopole has taken no physical action that could be characterized as an abandonment of the easement. (C) is incorrect because improper recordation does not affect the rights of the original parties to the transaction. Although an unacknowledged instrument does not impart constructive notice to subsequent purchasers, it has absolutely no effect on the validity of the easement as between the original parties. (D) is incorrect because the requirements for extinguishing an easement by adverse use for the prescriptive period have not been fulfilled. To extinguish an easement by prescription, the owner of the servient tenement must so interfere with the easement as to create a cause of action in favor of the easement holder. The interference must be open, notorious, continuous, and nonpermissive for the prescriptive period. Faust has done nothing (such as using his land in a different manner) that would indicate an interference with Monopole's easement so as to give rise to a cause of action in favor of Monopole.

Answer to Question 64

(B) "If Roberts and Morris are discharged from the Army before Kent's death" is a condition precedent to Roberts's and Morris's taking in possession. Thus, their interests are contingent rather than vested remainders, and (C) and (D) are incorrect. Stevens's deed constitutes a valid conveyance of a future interest to Roberts and Morris; therefore, they have more than mere expectancies, and (A) is incorrect.

Answer to Question 65

(A) Because the condition precedent to their remainder has been satisfied, *i.e.,* Roberts and Morris were discharged from the Army before Kent's death, their contingent remainder has "vested." Also, at common law, it was held that any conveyance to two or more persons was presumed to create a joint tenancy unless a contrary intention was clearly expressed. But today all courts hold that such a conveyance creates a tenancy in common. To create a joint tenancy, words such as "as joint tenants" or "in joint tenancy" must normally be used to show the necessary intent. Thus, Roberts and Morris are tenants in common to a vested remainder. (B) is therefore wrong. (C) is wrong because their estate is in a remainder interest, not a fee simple absolute, because the life tenant is still alive. (D) is wrong for the same reason and, additionally, because a tenancy by the entirety can be held only by a husband and wife—which may not be the case here.

Answer to Question 66

(C) When Roberts died, his one-half interest passed to his heirs. When Morris died, Cathy inherited Morris's interest in Goldacre. Therefore Cathy owns an undivided one-half interest in fee simple and the heirs of Roberts own an undivided one-half interest in fee simple. (A) is wrong because she does not own all of Goldacre in fee simple. (B) is wrong because she owns an ***undivided*** one-half interest, which is a one-half interest as to all of the tract, as opposed to one-half of Goldacre, which would be ***all*** interest in a one-half part of the tract. (D) is wrong for the same reason that (B) is wrong; she owns an ***undivided*** one-half interest therein.

Answer to Question 67

(D) In effect, Anson only had a "license" to use the land. Because the agreement between Anson and Barker was not in writing, the Statute of Frauds requirements for the creation of an express easement were not met. Also, since Anson's use of the land was permissive during Barker's ownership, he would not meet the adverse and hostile requirements of adverse use during that period; and therefore, Anson would not have satisfied the requirements of an easement by prescription. Thus, (A), (B), and (C) are wrong.

Answer to Question 68

(D) Since Anson's use of the land was permissive during Barker's ownership, he would not meet the adverse and hostile requirements of adverse possession during that period; and therefore, Anson would not have satisfied the requirements of an easement by prescription. (A) is wrong because changes in ownership of the land do not terminate adverse possession. (B) is wrong because, even though he was told to stop using the road, he continued to do so. (C) is wrong because it is too broad. While it is true that no express easement was created, the fact that the original agreement was oral would have no bearing on determining the creation of an easement by prescription.

Answer to Question 69

(B) Anson's easement is appurtenant because the right of special use benefits him in the use and enjoyment of another tract of land (his own property). An easement in gross is acquired independent of the ownership and enjoyment of another tract of land; there is no dominant tenement. Thus, (A) is incorrect. Even if the lake were considered a public way, Anson would not have an easement by necessity because he has other means of access. Therefore, (C) is incorrect. (D) is incorrect because the facts do not indicate that Anson once owned the entire parcel and conveyed part of it to Barker, impliedly reserving an easement in the conveyance.

Answer to Question 70

(C) The terms of the deed control Mark's liability. While the contract did not specify the quality of title, the law implies that a marketable title is to be conveyed, and since a title based on adverse possession is not marketable, although it may be good, Developer could have refused to perform. Once Developer accepted a deed, however, the doctrine of merger comes into play and the contract is merged into the deed. Any contract provisions for quality of title, express or implied, are no longer effective. Thus, (A) is incorrect. Developer must look to the terms of the deed for his rights. (B) is incorrect because the court will not rewrite the deed. The facts do not indicate that Mark made any misrepresentations, and so (D) is incorrect.

Answer to Question 71

(D) In a contract for sale of real property, the seller of the land is entitled to use the proceeds of the sale to clear title if he can ensure that the purchaser will be protected. Van's offer to escrow the funds in this case should act as such guarantee. Thus, (A) is incorrect. (B) is incorrect, because although there will be litigation over the contract dispute, the litigation will not affect the title to the land since Clifford is claiming only money damages and not an interest in the property. (C) is incorrect because the doctrine of equitable conversion is only applicable as against the seller and the buyer, and does not affect the right of some third party with regard to attaching property held in the name of a debtor.

Answer to Question 72

(B) The deed, once delivered, merely evidences title to the property, and its destruction has no effect on the title. Thus, Margaret was still the owner, and (C) is wrong. (A) is incorrect because Sarah cannot affect the ownership of the property after she delivered the deed to Margaret, regardless of the truth or falsity of her subsequent reasons for the attempted revocation. (D) is incorrect because

Irma was not a bona fide purchaser: She was aware of Margaret's deed. Also, it is only the **subsequent** bona fide purchaser, a purchaser for **value** and without **notice**, who gets the protection of the recording act. Margaret was the **first** grantee and, thus, her status as a donee would be irrelevant to the applicability of the recording act.

Answer to Question 73

(D) Restraints on alienation are traditionally strictly construed, and this prohibition against assignment would not be read to include a prohibition against subleasing. Hence, Leona would have no cause of action against Tyrone, and (A), (B), and (C) are incorrect.

Answer to Question 74

(D) If Sara prevails, it will be because Michael never effectively accepted delivery. (C) is wrong because neither Michael nor Wanda is guilty of any wrongdoing and there is no ground to impose a constructive trust. (A) is wrong because there is no such thing as a "constructive reconveyance" of land. (B) may look good at first, but it is a minority rule. In most states, acceptance is presumed if the conveyance is beneficial to the grantee, regardless of whether the grantee has knowledge of the conveyance. (D) is the best answer because even in those states that presume acceptance, the presumption is rebutted when the grantee expressly refuses to accept the conveyance.

Answer to Question 75

(B) Besides the fact that the contract does not specifically state which house is being sold, the phrase "sufficient land for a pool and garage" is too ambiguous to enforce by specific performance. (A) is wrong because $200 is not necessarily nominal consideration and, even if it were, the mutual promises to buy and sell would be sufficient consideration. (C) is wrong because the contract needs to include more than the purchase price to be enforceable; it must also describe the property. (D) is wrong because it is irrelevant which house Jake wants to sell to Marsha; that does not clear up the problem with enforcing the Jake-Bob contract.

Answer to Question 76

(B) There was no implied condition in the contract that Bob have marketable title at the time he entered into the agreement, just that he be able to deliver marketable title at the time of settlement. (C) is wrong for this reason. (A) is irrelevant. (D) is wrong because it is not fraudulent to buy property for resale.

Answer to Question 77

(C) A life tenant generally may not exploit natural resources on the property. The "open mine" exception exists for those uses existing prior to the granting of the life estate. Since the gravel quarry existed at the time of the grant, it is most likely that the grantor intended that the life tenant have the right to mine the gravel. The trees, on the other hand, cannot be cut by the life tenant because on these facts, there is no apparent intent on the part of the grantor that Clyde Jr. could do this. Thus, (C) is the correct choice, and (A), (B), and (D) are necessarily incorrect.

TORTS QUESTIONS

Questions 1-2 are based on the following fact situation:

The Ajax Missile Company was engaged in research and development of an interplanetary space shuttle, under contract with the United States Government. Over a period of years, it developed the prototype of a huge, solid-fuel rocket engine for use in this program. To evaluate the performance of this engine, it conducted a static test of the engine at a remote desert test site. The rocket engine was mounted on a concrete test stand, with the thrust of the engine directed downward into the ground. When the engine was fired up, huge clouds of flame and smoke filled the air, and particles of debris from the rocket fell onto an adjoining farm owned by Homesteader. The thrust of the rocket engine also caused heavy vibrations in the ground under the test site, which caused the slumping of subsurface earth structures surrounding the site, leading to the collapse of a water well on Homesteader's farm.

1. If Homesteader files an action against Ajax for trespass, which of the following facts, if proved, would be most helpful to Ajax in avoiding liability?

   (A) Homesteader bought and operated his farm knowing that Ajax used the adjoining property for testing its rocket engines.

   (B) Neither Ajax nor anyone in its employ set foot upon Homesteader's land.

   (C) Ajax had no reason to anticipate that the tests would cause any of the results that occurred.

   (D) The rocket testing program is essential to the national security, so that Ajax's conduct was completely privileged as a public necessity.

2. If Homesteader maintains his action against Ajax on the theory that Ajax was negligent,

which of the following would be the *most* helpful to Ajax in avoiding liability?

   (A) The subsurface earth structures that collapsed as a result of the tests were unstable before the tests took place.

   (B) Homesteader's farm is located at such a far distance from the test site that no risk to Homesteader was foreseeable.

   (C) Ajax exercised due care in selecting the personnel who chose the test site and conducted the tests.

   (D) Ajax built its test site and conducted the tests in conformity with safety procedures and standards used by all other companies engaged in similar tests.

Question 3

Poteet lent her automobile to her girlfriend DeeDee for the specific purpose of picking up a pizza that Poteet and DeeDee had ordered for dinner. DeeDee drove to the shopping mall where the pizzeria was located and parked Poteet's car there. Instead of going directly to the pizzeria, DeeDee went into a bookstore, browsed, and eventually purchased a book. DeeDee then went to the pizzeria and picked up the pizza, which had been ready for 15 minutes. Just as DeeDee left the pizzeria to return to the car, another car, driven by Tammy, struck Poteet's parked car, causing extensive damage to the car. Poteet did not carry collision insurance, and the car required $800 worth of body work.

If Poteet sues DeeDee on a negligence theory for damage to the car, who will prevail?

(A) Poteet, because DeeDee exceeded her authority when she went to the bookstore.

(B) Poteet, because but for DeeDee's delay in getting the pizza, Poteet's car would not have been damaged.

(C) DeeDee, because she did not create a foreseeable risk of damage to Poteet's car.

(D) DeeDee, because the family car doctrine imputes any of DeeDee's negligence to Poteet.

Questions 4-5 are based on the following fact situation:

Antoinette and Babette were high school classmates. After school, they went together to "Le Soda Shoppe," a short-order restaurant popular with students. Antoinette and Babette were seated in a booth near the front of the restaurant and were heavily engaged in conversation when Doug, another classmate, sat down at the booth immediately adjacent to theirs. Doug had a "crush" on Babette and wanted to scare her slightly to draw attention to himself. Therefore, he shot a spitball from his straw toward Babette, who was seated with her back toward him. Doug's shot went astray and struck Antoinette in the eye, causing her to suffer corneal damage.

When the missile struck Antoinette, she cried out loudly in pain. Upon hearing the cry, Marie, a waitress, rushed to Antoinette's assistance. Before Marie could reach the girl, she slipped on some pudding the busboy had failed to remove from the floor. Marie fell on top of Pantagruel, another restaurant patron, injuring him.

4. If Antoinette sues Doug, she can recover for:

(A) Assault.

(B) Battery.

(C) Intentional infliction of emotional distress.

(D) Nothing, because Doug did not intend to harm her.

5. If Pantagruel sues Marie, can he recover?

(A) Yes, because Marie had no duty to rescue.

(B) Yes, because Marie assumed the risk.

(C) No, because the touching was unintentional.

(D) No, but he may recover against the restaurant.

Questions 6-8 are based on the following fact situation:

Bill was walking along an unpaved road on his way to work. Suddenly, a school bus coming in the opposite direction began to careen toward him. This was due to the fact that the bus driver, Wally, had momentarily lost control of the bus while attempting to light a cigarette.

To avoid being hit by the bus, Bill jumped off the road into Carol's yard. Unfortunately, he landed in a bed of prize-winning zinnias and damaged them extensively.

6. In a suit by Carol against Bill for the damage to her zinnias:

(A) Bill is liable for any damage because he had no privilege to enter upon Carol's land.

(B) Whether Bill is liable depends on whether he was exercising due care.

(C) Bill may be held liable for damage to the zinnias.

(D) Bill is not liable for any damage to the zinnias because his entry was privileged.

7. Assume for purposes of this question only that in the process of dodging the bus, Bill's wallet fell out of his pocket, although he did not realize it at the time. Bill discovered the loss of his wallet that evening, and therefore returned the following day to look for it. Bill obtained Carol's permission to enter her land to look for his wallet.

While searching for his wallet on Carol's land, Bill brushed against an exposed electric wire that was partially hidden by some bushes and received a severe electric shock and burns. In a suit by Bill against Carol for these injuries:

(A) Carol is liable, because Bill entered with her permission.

(B) Carol is liable, because she failed to repair a dangerous condition on her property.

(C) Carol is liable if she failed to reasonably inspect the property and as a result was unaware of the dangerous condition of the wire.

(D) Carol is not liable unless she knew of the condition of the wire and failed to warn Bill of the danger.

8. In a suit by Carol against Wally, the bus driver, for the damages to her zinnias:

(A) Wally is liable for trespass because his driving caused Bill to enter onto Carol's land and damage her zinnias.

(B) Wally is liable on the theory of negligence.

(C) Wally is not liable because Carol's zinnias were not within the scope of any duty he owed in operating a bus on a public road.

(D) If Wally is held liable on any theory, he is entitled to indemnity from Bill, who did the damage.

Question 9

Rebecca was once a famous movie star, but in recent years her name and identity have faded from public attention. Jim, a freelance writer and photographer, decided to do a story on Rebecca's life in hopes of selling it to a movie magazine. After painstaking research, he found out that for many years there was a very close relationship between Rebecca and the great movie producer, Cecil, who is now deceased. Jim unreasonably surmised that Rebecca had been Cecil's mistress, although this was not true, and both were at all times happily married to other persons. Rebecca's husband died years ago and she is now unmarried.

Jim called upon Rebecca and asked for an interview, telling her that he wished to verify some facts about her background, including her relationship with Cecil. Rebecca slammed the door in Jim's face, telling him that she did not wish to discuss the past, and wanted complete privacy for the rest of her life. Jim interviewed other people about Rebecca and Cecil. What they told him made him think that his theory about Rebecca and Cecil's relationship was untrue, but he knew a good "romance" story sold better than one about a friendship, so he wrote that Rebecca was the former mistress of Cecil. Jim offered the story to a movie magazine for publication.

If the editor of the movie magazine rejects the story and returns it to Jim unpublished:

(A) No action for invasion of privacy or defamation will lie in favor of Rebecca.

(B) An action for invasion of privacy will lie in favor of Rebecca.

(C) An action for defamation will lie in favor of Rebecca.

(D) None of the above statements is correct.

Question 10

Porter worked in a petrochemical plant owned and operated by Cheminc. Porter did routine repair work around the Cheminc plant. As Porter was bending over to work on a fouled machine, a pipe carrying hot oil that was located behind Porter exploded. Porter was sprayed with the oil and suffered severe burns. Porter hired an attorney who made inquiries of the Cheminc plant manager and discovered that the exploding pipe had been manufactured by Pipeco. However, the plant manager refused to tell the attorney when the pipe had been installed in the plant.

If Porter brings a negligence action against Pipeco for his injuries, who will prevail?

(A) Porter, because the pipe manufactured by Pipeco exploded.

(B) Porter, if a reasonable inspection by Pipeco would have revealed a defect in the pipe that caused it to explode.

(C) Pipeco, if the pipe had burst because the oil had corroded it.

(D) Pipeco, because the pipe was in Cheminc's possession when it exploded.

Questions 11-12 are based on the following fact situation:

Hurts U-Drive rented one of its shiny new cars to Driver, for a leisurely cross-country vacation trip which Driver had planned for his family. While driving through a remote stretch of farmland, Driver decided to see how much power the rented car really had, and was driving in excess of 90 m.p.h. when he came to a curve. He applied the brakes and attempted to slow down, but the car went across the double line and struck head-on a station wagon coming in the opposite direction. Sam, the driver, was killed in the accident, and the station wagon was destroyed.

A "permissive use" statute is in effect making the bailor of an automobile liable for personal injury, death, or property damage caused by any person operating the automobile with his consent, up to a maximum of $25,000. The jurisdiction follows traditional contributory negligence and contribution rules.

11. If Sam's estate files suit against Hurts pursuant to the "permissive use" statute, and recovers the full $25,000, what rights if any would Hurts have against Driver?

(A) None, unless the rental agreement obligated Driver to assume any such liability imposed on the renter.

(B) Hurts may obtain contribution from Driver to the extent of $12,500, but not indemnity.

(C) Hurts may obtain indemnity against Driver for the full $25,000.

(D) Hurts may obtain contribution from Driver to the extent of Driver's relative fault, but not indemnity.

12. Assume for purposes of this question only that Sam's estate files suit against both Hurts and Driver, alleging that Driver was negligent in the operation of the rented automobile, and that Hurts was negligent in renting it to him, having reason to know that Driver was an incompetent and irresponsible driver. If the jury returns a verdict of joint and several liability against both defendants, and assesses damages in the sum of $100,000, how should the judgment be entered?

(A) $50,000 as against each defendant.

(B) $25,000 against Hurts and $75,000 against Driver.

(C) $100,000 against Hurts only.

(D) $100,000 against both defendants.

Questions 13-14 are based on the following fact situation:

As a result of interests traceable to his early career as a blacksmith, John's father acquired a large collection of anvils, which ultimately came into John's possession. John loaned the collection to the local museum and hired professional movers to transport the anvils to the second floor of the museum, where they would be displayed. The movers used an old rope and pulley apparatus to lift the anvils on the outside of the building to a second-story window. While one of the largest anvils was being lifted, it slipped and fell, crashing through the roof of Jane's parked car. Jane had just walked out of the drugstore across the street and saw the entire incident. Although the anvil was not even dented, Jane's car was extensively damaged.

13. If John brings a negligence action against the movers for allowing the antique anvil to fall, he can recover:

    (A) Nominal damages.

    (B) Punitive damages.

    (C) Both nominal damages and punitive damages.

    (D) Neither nominal damages nor punitive damages.

14. If Jane brings a claim for negligent infliction of emotional distress, she would:

    (A) Recover, if there were accompanying physical consequences.

    (B) Recover, because she was a foreseeable plaintiff.

    (C) Not recover, because she was not within the zone of danger.

    (D) Not recover, because there was no impact.

Questions 15-16 are based on the following fact situation:

Gilda Gammaray, a precocious student at Northcentral High School, was an "A" student in her chemistry class and was interested in developing a Science Fair project in the area of chemistry. She was inspired by an experiment conducted in class in which the teacher had the students mix three chemicals together to create a gas that caused the faces of the students to become grossly distorted. Gilda obtained an ample supply of the three chemicals and went to an abandoned building located on a street that had heavy pedestrian traffic. She mixed together the chemicals, and the fumes passed across the sidewalk, causing the pedestrians' faces to become grossly distorted, as if they suffered from physical defects. The effect of the gas was temporary and none of the pedestrians suffered any permanent damage. One of the pedestrians exposed to the gas was Parker.

15. If Parker wants to sue Gilda, which of the following best describes the tort she has committed against him?

    (A) Assault.

    (B) Battery.

    (C) Intentional infliction of emotional distress.

    (D) Invasion of privacy.

16. Assume for purposes of this question only that Parker was a rather vain man of middle years, and that in order to further her experiment, Gilda took pictures of the pedestrians affected by the gas and sent the pictures to the local newspaper. The newspaper ran a story describing Gilda's experiment and also ran a picture of Parker in which his face appeared highly contorted. If Parker sues the newspaper for false light publicity, he will:

    (A) Prevail, because the picture made him appear to be a grumpy old man.

    (B) Prevail, because the newspaper disclosed a private fact.

    (C) Not prevail, because he was on a public sidewalk when the picture was taken.

    (D) Not prevail, because he suffered no permanent harm.

Questions 17-18 are based on the following fact situation:

Matt looked out his front window one day and saw Rex standing on a narrow ledge on the second story of the house across the street. He also saw a ladder lying on the ground beneath where Rex was stranded. Matt turned away and pulled the drapes, muttering to himself, "Well, I'm not going to watch him fall off there." Later, Howard was walking down the street and saw Rex's situation and determined to help. Howard picked up the ladder and placed it against the side of the house. However, he set it atop a patch of ice. As Rex started down the ladder, a rotten rung broke and Rex fell to the ground and was injured.

17.   If Rex sues Matt for damages for his injuries, will he recover?

   (A)   Yes, because Matt had a duty to aid Rex when he saw that Rex was in peril.

   (B)   Yes, because a reasonably prudent person would have aided Rex under the circumstances.

   (C)   No, because Matt took no action to aid Rex.

   (D)   No, because Rex put himself in a position of peril.

18.   If Rex sues Howard, will he recover?

   (A)   Yes, because Howard's action caused the injury to Rex.

   (B)   Yes, because Howard assumed the duty of aiding Rex.

   (C)   Yes, because it was foreseeable that Rex would be injured as a result of Howard's negligent conduct.

   (D)   No, because Howard's negligence did not cause the injury to Rex.

Question 19

The Runtz Mansion was a large property that had once belonged to one of the founding families of Dodgeville, a city of 75,000 people. The mansion was purchased as a residence by Pangol, a vice president at Dodge State Bank, one of the three major banks in Dodgeville.

Pangol was extremely annoyed when he saw a headline in a local newspaper, *The Dodge Herald,* reading: "Local Banker Buys Old Runtz Mansion for 300 Grand." Hoppe, a reporter for the *Herald,* had noticed that the "for sale" sign had been removed from the spacious front lawn of the Runtz Mansion. He had gone to the County Recorder of Deeds' office and discovered the name of the buyer and the amount paid for the property from the deed, which was on file. Hoppe had then called the real estate agent and asked her about Pangol. The agent had told Hoppe that Pangol was a vice president at Dodge State Bank. In addition to the article in the *Herald,* which described the mansion and indicated Pangol's name and occupation and the amount paid for the property, the *Herald* published a picture of the front of the mansion, which one of its staff photographers had taken from the sidewalk in front of the mansion.

If Pangol sues the *Herald* for invasion of privacy, will he recover?

   (A)   Yes, because Pangol did not consent to publication of information about himself and his private residence.

   (B)   Yes, if a reasonable person of ordinary sensibilities would have been upset by publication of the story.

   (C)   No, because the *Herald* printed public facts.

   (D)   No, because the story in the *Herald* was true.

Questions 20-21 are based on the following fact situation:

Merchant contracted with Joe and Bill, professional painters who had their own partnership, to paint her furniture store. Midway through the job they ran out of paint, so Bill borrowed Joe's car to pick up more. On his way to pick up the paint, Bill decided to go to the library to get a book. After leaving the library, Bill, while driving negligently, ran into Di's parked car, causing extensive damage.

20. In a negligence action against Merchant, Di will most likely:

    (A) Recover under the theory of respondeat superior.

    (B) Recover, because Bill was on a detour, not a frolic.

    (C) Recover, because a principal is vicariously liable for the negligence of her agent.

    (D) Not recover.

21. If Di brings a negligence action against Joe, will she prevail?

    (A) No, because lending the car to Bill was not negligent.

    (B) No, because Bill was an independent contractor.

    (C) No, because a bailor is not vicariously liable for the torts of his bailee.

    (D) Yes, if Bill's stop at the library did not constitute a frolic.

Question 22

Sandra had 30,000 miles on her car when she purchased four new "Huggums" tires from Mac's Tire and Muffler Shop. It was widely known in the tire industry that purchasers of tires would, on occasion, exceed posted speed limits, and therefore tires were designed to perform at speeds higher than the maximum speed allowed in the United States. Although Sandra was a safe and careful driver, she sometimes exceeded the speed limit by as much as 10 m.p.h. if the traffic was light and weather conditions were favorable.

When Sandra's car had 32,000 miles on it, she sold the car to Pedro. Pedro immediately took the car on a 500-mile trip to visit his sister. During the course of the journey, Pedro often drove his car 10 m.p.h. over the posted limit. As Pedro approached his destination, he was driving 53 m.p.h. At that time his left front tire suddenly blew out. The car went out of control, crashed into another vehicle, and Pedro was severely injured.

If Pedro sues Sandra on a strict liability theory, Pedro should:

    (A) Recover, if the tire was defective when Sandra sold the vehicle to Pedro.

    (B) Recover, if the tire was defective when Mac's sold the tire to Sandra and Sandra could have discovered the defect with a reasonable inspection.

    (C) Not recover, because Pedro misused the tire by exceeding the posted speed limit on his trip.

    (D) Not recover, because Sandra is not a commercial supplier.

Questions 23-24 are based on the following fact situation:

Vic operated the corner hot dog stand, where he served Austria hot dogs. One day Hawker, a sales representative for Ballgame hot dogs, came to the stand and convinced Vic that he should buy Ballgame franks. He told Vic that Ballgame hot dogs were better than Austria's because they contained more beef and were more nutritious. Hawker also gave Vic a poster to put in his window showing actress Myrna Star with words to the effect that she always ate Ballgame hot dogs. Vic believed Hawker's statements about the superiority of Ballgame, so he bought the hot dogs and put the poster in the window. Two days later, the food and drug inspectors stopped by the stand and fined Vic $1,000 because the hot dogs were substandard; they contained no beef at all, a fact that Hawker knew. Vic filed suit against Hawker for misrepresentation.

23. Who will prevail in the suit?

    (A) Hawker, because Vic had a duty to determine the truth of the representations.

(B) Hawker, because Vic was not justified in relying on Hawker's statements.

(C) Vic, because violation of federal regulations makes this a misrepresentation per se.

(D) Vic, if he justifiably relied on Hawker's statements.

24. Myrna Star filed suit against Vic for invasion of privacy because, in fact, she was a spokesperson for a rival hot dog company. Will Myrna prevail?

(A) No, because Myrna is a public figure.

(B) No, because Vic gained no profit from using the poster.

(C) Yes, because Myrna had not given her permission to use the poster.

(D) Yes, because Vic was not reasonably justified in believing the poster was authorized.

Question 25

ConstructCo was involved in a landfill operation next to a busy public highway. At various times large heaps of dirt were piled up on the site. The construction superintendent noted that some children who lived in a nearby residential development had taken to sledding down the mounds of dirt. Since the dirt sloped down toward the highway, the superintendent realized that it might be dangerous for the children. He considered having the mounds of dirt removed, but decided instead to post signs around the landfill site. The signs were situated every 10 yards, and stated in bold letters, "NO TRESPASSING—NO SLEDDING." Despite the signs, which he saw and read, Peter, a 10-year-old neighborhood child, brought his sled to the development. He slid down one of the mounds of dirt and was propelled onto the highway, where he was struck by a car and seriously injured.

Is ConstructCo liable for Peter's injuries?

(A) Yes, if ConstructCo could have removed the piles of dirt at minimal cost.

(B) Yes, because ConstructCo created a public nuisance.

(C) No, because Peter was a trespasser.

(D) No, because Peter read and understood the warning signs and appreciated the danger.

Questions 26-27 are based on the following fact situation:

Dev was driving his car down the street when he ran down Paul, a 10-year-old boy who had darted into the road to retrieve a bouncing ball. After the accident, Paul's mother refused to take Paul to a physician because of moral scruples against the medical profession. As a result, Paul's injuries were more severe than they would otherwise have been.

26. Paul's best chance to recover for all of his injuries is to argue that:

(A) The doctrine of avoidable consequences at most bars recovery for the aggravation of but not for the original injury itself.

(B) Any negligence on the mother's part is not to be imputed to her child.

(C) Victims have no duty to take steps for their own safety after the accident.

(D) Defendants must take their victims as they find them, including their mothers' attitudes toward physicians.

27. Assume for purposes of this question only that the ball went into the road because Paul's friend had thrown it at a passing adult, who became angry and tossed it into the road. Which of the following best states the adult's liability?

(A) Paul may have a personal injury action against the adult for negligence.

(B) Paul may have a personal injury action against the adult for an intentional tort.

(C) Paul has no action against the adult, but Dev may obtain contribution from the adult.

(D) Paul has no action against the adult, but Dev may obtain indemnity from the adult.

Questions 28-29 are based on the following fact situation:

Prudence bought two new rear tires from The Tyre Centre, a retailer. The tires, manufactured by Rubko of Akron, were installed and balanced by employees of The Tyre Centre. Two weeks later, Prudence noticed that her right rear tire was very low on air and very close to going flat. Prudence was annoyed that this problem had developed on a new tire, and she planned to drive to The Tyre Centre to register a complaint. First, however, she decided to inflate the tire, because she was concerned that the tire would go flat if she drove all the way to The Tyre Centre.

Therefore, Prudence drove to the closest service station, located a block from her home. She backed her car up to the air pump and began to inflate the tire. Almost immediately, Prudence noticed that one spot on the tire was beginning to bulge. She checked the air pressure with a gauge and determined that the tire still needed seven pounds more pressure, so she continued to inflate the tire. After five more pounds of air were put into the tire, the bulge, which had continued to grow, ruptured. A piece of rubber flew off the tire and struck Prudence in the face, causing eye injuries and lacerations that required plastic surgery to correct. Prudence filed a lawsuit based on strict liability, naming both The Tyre Centre and Rubko of Akron as defendants. Assume the jurisdiction follows traditional contributory negligence rules.

28. Will Prudence prevail in her suit against The Tyre Centre?

(A) Yes, but only if the tire was improperly installed by The Tyre Centre's employees.

(B) No, if a reasonable person would not have driven the car with the tire close to being flat.

(C) Yes, but only if the defect in the tire could have been discovered by a reasonable inspection by the retailer.

(D) No, if Prudence knew the bulge was dangerous.

29. Will Prudence prevail against Rubko of Akron?

(A) No, if The Tyre Centre should have inspected the tire but failed to do so.

(B) No, if the tire was improperly installed.

(C) No, unless Rubko was aware of the defect in the tire and failed to notify The Tyre Centre thereof.

(D) Yes, if the tire was defective when it left the Rubko of Akron manufacturing plant.

Question 30

Albert and Barbara were both computer specialists, and each one owned a small computer consulting firm in a large Midwestern city. Albert and Barbara both attended Compuconference, the biggest trade meeting of computer industry people, which was held annually at different sites. This year the conference was in Santa Filomena, a West Coast resort town. At a cocktail party before the final banquet, Albert approached Barbara and said, "I've been meaning to get in touch with you; I've heard a lot of good things about your company. Maybe we could do some work together that would give small operations like ours a chance to bid on some big projects." Barbara replied to Albert, "I don't think so." Albert asked, "Why not?"

Barbara responded, "Because you're incompetent." Camille was standing near Albert and Barbara at the cocktail party and overheard Barbara's comment. Camille was a secretary at a computer supply firm in Atlanta who had been brought to the conference by her boss to keep track of any sales leads that he developed.

If Albert sues Barbara for defamation, will he prevail?

(A) Yes, if it was reasonably foreseeable that her remark would be overheard.

(B) Yes, but only if Barbara knew her remark would be overheard.

(C) No, because there was no publication.

(D) No, because Camille was not a party to the conversation.

Question 31

Trucko was driving a dumptruck containing gravel at a safe speed. From the other direction Crasher drove his big semitrailer truck. Crasher came around a curve and was confronted with a very slow-moving steamroller just in front of him. To avoid colliding with the steamroller, Crasher pulled his wheel to the left and crossed the center lane, where he bore down on Trucko, who was coming from the other direction. Crasher showed no propensity to yield, and there were other vehicles to Trucko's left. Trucko's only option was to turn his truck to the right, onto the land of Paget. The truck caused damage to Paget's lawn.

Which of the following best describes Trucko's liability to Paget?

(A) Trucko is liable for the damage to the lawn.

(B) Trucko is liable for public nuisance, because he has interfered with Paget's use and enjoyment of the land.

(C) Trucko is liable for both trespass and public nuisance.

(D) Trucko is liable for nothing, because the incident was not his fault, and he acted in a reasonable and responsible manner.

Questions 32-33 are based on the following fact situation:

Ekter owned a large engineering firm that specializes in the design of large buildings. Hotelier International Corporation asked Ekter to design a hotel for them. Ekter took into account weather conditions in New Bogota, where the hotel was to be built, and came up with two designs that would cost approximately the same amount to construct to specifications. One of them had the four large supporting pylons set so that it could withstand winds 20% higher than New Bogota had experienced in the 85 years that the weather bureaus kept records for the area. The other design set the pylons farther apart, but they would withstand winds 50% higher than New Bogota had experienced. Ekter decided to go with the first (20% margin) design, because he felt it was more aesthetically pleasing, and also because a 20% safety margin was usually considered adequate. Officers of Hotelier reviewed and approved Ekter's plans. The hotel was duly constructed and highly successful financially for Hotelier International.

Two years after the "Hotelier New Bogota" opened, a freak storm struck, bringing with it winds of hurricane force. The hotel suffered significant damage, which would have been avoided had the supporting pylons been placed farther apart. Additionally, Plimsoll, a guest in the hotel at the time of the storm, was injured while sitting in the hotel lobby when a decorative piece of masonry fell from the ceiling and struck him. Assume that the jurisdiction follows traditional contributory negligence and assumption of risk rules.

32. If Plimsoll sues Ekter for damages arising out of Plimsoll's injuries, who will prevail?

(A) Ekter, if the storm was not foreseeable.

(B) Ekter, because the storm was an act of God.

(C) Plimsoll, regardless of foreseeability, because of the special duty owed to hotel guests.

(D) Plimsoll, because Ekter is strictly liable for his design of the hotel.

33. If Hotelier International sues Ekter for the damage to the hotel, who will prevail?

(A) Ekter, because Hotelier assumed the risk by approving the plans.

(B) Ekter, because innkeepers, rather than engineers, are subject to strict liability.

(C) Ekter, if he acted in the manner of a reputable member of his profession.

(D) Hotelier, because the placement of the pylons resulted in extensive damage to the hotel.

Question 34

Porphyry and her friend Martha entered "Maison Mamselle," a women's clothing store. As the store was rather warm, both women removed their coats and carried them over their arms as they shopped. Porphyry's coat was a brown suede coat, which she had purchased on a recent trip to Italy. Suzie Sales, a clerk in the store, saw Porphyry and Martha looking at the rack where Maison Mamselle keeps its suede coats. Ten minutes later she saw Martha help Porphyry put on a brown suede coat, which happened to be the coat Porphyry bought in Italy, although Suzie did not know that. When Suzie saw Porphyry leaving the store wearing the brown suede coat, she immediately notified Dagobert, the store detective, telling him, "That woman stole that brown suede coat!" Dagobert accosted Porphyry and asked her to accompany him to a private room. As soon as Porphyry was in the room, Dagobert closed the door and stood in front of it. Dagobert did not examine Porphyry's coat, but started bombarding her with questions, such as: "How much other stuff have you stolen from us?" "Did you know that *this* store always prosecutes shoplifters?" "Are you married?" "How old are you?" Porphyry

was frightened and answered all of Dagobert's questions. She kept trying to tell him to look at her coat, but every time she finished answering one question, Dagobert quickly asked another. Finally, after half an hour, Dagobert looked at the coat and found the Italian label. He knew that all the suede coats sold by Maison Mamselle were made in Taiwan or Mexico, so he told Porphyry, "Sorry for the mix-up, but you'd be amazed how brazen some shoplifters are." Dagobert opened the door and Porphyry left the store.

If Porphyry sues Maison Mamselle for false imprisonment, will she prevail?

(A) Yes, because the detention was longer than necessary to establish that Porphyry had not stolen the coat.

(B) No, because Suzie had reasonable cause to believe that Porphyry had stolen the coat.

(C) No, because stores are allowed to detain people suspected of shoplifting and to question detainees about it.

(D) No, because Maison Mamselle should not be held liable for an intentional tort committed by Dagobert.

Question 35

The state of New Guernsey adopted a comparative negligence statute. Subsequent to passage of the law, Pons was injured in an automobile accident and suffered $100,000 worth of injuries, including $20,000 in hospital and physician's bills. Pons's medical insurance company paid Pons $20,000 to cover hospital and medical expenses. Later, Pons filed suit against Daley, who was driving the car that struck Pons's vehicle. When the case came to trial, the jury agreed with Pons's contention that her injuries were worth $100,000. The jury also determined that Pons was 30% negligent and that Daley was 70% negligent.

How much should Pons recover from Daley?

(A) $100,000.

(B) $70,000.

(C) $56,000.

(D) $50,000.

Question 36

Flowers usually received a ride home from work from a co-worker who lived nearby. On this particular day, however, Flowers became involved in a project that required a couple hours of overtime. After he had finished, he walked across the street to a tavern to get a drink. While there, he met Sluggo. During the course of their conversation, Flowers discovered that Sluggo lived only a short distance from Flowers. Sluggo offered to give Flowers a ride home. Flowers was hesitant because he knew Sluggo was probably too drunk to drive, but finally agreed. On the way home, Sluggo, driving in a dangerous manner, was involved in a collision with another car. Flowers was injured. The jurisdiction retains the traditional rules of contributory negligence.

If Flowers asserts a claim against Sluggo, Flowers will:

(A) Prevail, because Sluggo drove in a dangerous manner.

(B) Prevail if Sluggo's negligence was a proximate cause of Flowers's injury.

(C) Not prevail if the other driver involved in the collision was negligent.

(D) Not prevail, because Flowers knew that Sluggo was drunk.

Question 37

Mexzona is a state without a dramshop statute. Beerman was a bartender in "La Cantina," a tavern located in a medium-sized Mexzona city. At about 11:30 p.m., Donner entered La Cantina. Beerman served him drinks for two hours, at which point Donner left the tavern in a state of intoxication. Donner drove off. Several miles down the road, he fell asleep at the wheel. His car crossed the center line and struck a car driven by Perkins, who was severely injured. Donner drove away, only to be apprehended later by the police.

Is Beerman vicariously liable for Perkins's injuries?

(A) No, if Donner's actions were reckless.

(B) No, because there is no dramshop act in Mexzona to impose liability.

(C) Yes, because there is no dramshop act in Mexzona to limit liability.

(D) Yes, because Donner caused personal injuries.

Question 38

Paola and Dixon, who are otherwise unacquainted, happened to be riding the same crowded city bus during the evening rush hour. Neither Paola nor Dixon was able to find a seat, and they, along with about 15 other persons, were riding the bus as standees. When the bus braked suddenly, the standing passengers were thrown together, and Paola, who was wearing very high heeled shoes, began to stumble. Dixon tried to keep Paola from falling, and in doing so he placed his arm around Paola's waist.

If Paola sues Dixon for battery, will she recover?

(A) Yes, if Dixon intended to put his arm around Paola's waist.

(B) Yes, because Dixon touched Paola without her permission.

(C) No, but only if Dixon put his arm around Paola's waist by accident.

(D) No, because Dixon's conduct was socially acceptable.

Question 39

Marisa works for an agency that contracts with wealthy homeowners to clean their homes.

The agency is given a key to the house by the owner and sends its employees out on a schedule to clean and straighten up while the owners are away.

One day after Marisa had completed her work at the home of Nancy, she remembered that she had left some cleaning materials inside that she would need for her next assignment. Because she was already late for the next job, Marisa neglected to lock the door when she left Nancy's home. When Nancy returned home that evening, she discovered that her house had been ransacked and several items of jewelry stolen. The front door was open, and there were no signs of forced entry.

If Nancy brings an action against the agency that employed Marisa on a respondeat superior theory, will she likely prevail?

(A) No, because she is limited to claims for breach of contract based upon her agreement with the agency.

(B) No, because the act of the burglar was an independent supervening cause of Nancy's loss.

(C) Yes, because Marisa's failure to lock the door created the risk that someone might enter and take Nancy's valuables.

(D) Yes, because when Marisa returned after having completed her work, she was technically a trespasser and liable for any damage she caused to the premises.

Question 40

Pauline sought psychiatric treatment from Donald, a psychiatrist. During his treatment, which consisted of hour-long analysis sessions twice a week, Donald, unknown to Pauline, videotaped her. No sound recording was made of the sessions, but Donald was conducting a study on "body language" and planned to use the videotapes in those experiments. Pauline learned that Donald had been videotaping their analysis sessions and brought an action against him for battery.

If Pauline does not prevail as to this theory, it will probably be because:

(A) She did not suffer any injury as the result of Donald's actions.

(B) Donald had an implied consent to take the actions he did as part of the patient-physician privilege.

(C) She did not suffer an offensive touching.

(D) Donald intended that his actions would foster medical research.

Question 41

Roger owned two cars, one of which he regularly drove to work and one which he left at home for the use of his wife and teenage children. The car he usually left at home was a small foreign model, while he drove a station wagon. One month, the headlights on the foreign car went out, but since Roger was a little short of money and because the foreign car was only driven during the day, he did not worry about fixing it right away. One day during that month, Roger's wife had to take the children and some friends to a baseball game, so Roger took the foreign car to work. On the way there he was rear-ended by another driver who had been driving 20 m.p.h. over the speed limit posted on that stretch of road. The jurisdiction follows traditional contributory negligence rules and makes it a misdemeanor to drive a vehicle that does not have operating headlights.

If Roger brings an action against the other driver, will he prevail?

(A) Yes, unless the misdemeanor statute is intended to protect against cars being driven without headlights.

(B) Yes, because the other driver's violation of the speeding statute constituted negligence per se.

(C) No, because Roger violated the misdemeanor statute.

(D) No, unless Roger establishes that driving 20 m.p.h. over the speed limit created an unreasonable risk of injury to others.

Question 42

Bugslayers, Inc., is a specialized manufacturer of insecticides. Its only manufacturing plant is located in the state of New Burma. The main product of New Burma is rice, and the economy of the entire state is almost wholly dependent upon rice production. The Bugslayers plant is the only plant in the United States that manufactures "Bugbeater," which is the only insecticide effective in controlling the local population of the Egyptian Ricegobbler insect. When Bugslayers built its plant in 1936, the surrounding area was completely agricultural, with one large farm on either side of the 400-acre parcel on which the plant was and is located. As New Burma became more urbanized, the area in which the plant is located was zoned "commercial and manufacturing," although the area was still agricultural, except for the Bugslayers plant.

Two years ago, Clapboard and Chintzy ("C&C"), a real estate development company, purchased one of the farms adjacent to the Bugslayers property. C&C subdivided the land into tract housing designed for persons of relatively modest means. C&C failed, however, to tell prospective home buyers that the Bugslayers plant periodically emitted fumes that, although completely harmless, were particularly foul smelling. The residents of the houses near Bugslayers soon began to complain to Bugslayers about the horrible smells emanating from the plant. The management of Bugslayers hired engineers to determine if something could be done to eliminate the odors. The engineers concluded that it would be possible to install machinery to filter and scrub the plant emissions, but the nature of the fumes was such that several different types of equipment would be needed, and the cost of purchasing, installing, and operating the equipment would bankrupt the company and the plant would have to close, leaving New Burma without a supply of "Bugbeater" to prevent destruction of its rice crops by the Egyptian Ricegobbler. Bugslayers declined to install the equipment, and the residents of the housing tract bring an action for nuisance against Bugslayers.

Can the residents get injunctive relief?

(A) No, because the plant was there first, and the residents came to the nuisance.

(B) No, because the area is zoned for commercial and manufacturing activities.

(C) No, because the court would balance hardships, and the entire community would suffer drastically if the supply of "Bugbeater" was curtailed.

(D) Yes, because a method is available to eliminate the smelly fumes.

Question 43

Poleaxe was a member of the National Guard in the state of Montoming. He attended drills one weekend per month and spent two weeks every summer at an Army base where his National Guard unit received additional training and conducted field exercises. Poleaxe was paid regularly for his National Guard service, and he also received a uniform allowance, which was designed to be used to purchase the clothing he was required to wear while serving.

Shortly before the annual summer camp, the Army introduced a new plastic helmet, designed to replace the traditional heavy steel helmets. These new helmets were distributed by the Army to the quartermaster of the Montoming National Guard. Poleaxe used his uniform allowance to purchase one of the new helmets from the quartermaster. His helmet came in a cardboard box that had a picture of a National Guardsman in combat uniform on the cover. The Guardsman was depicted wearing the plastic helmet and riding a motorcycle. The box also had printed on it: "Manufactured by The Gung-Ho Corporation of Westbury, Connecticut— We're the tip of America's spear, since 1915." Poleaxe wore the helmet on his summer camp service and was very pleased to be free of the heavy steel helmet he used to be required to wear.

When he returned to Montoming, he decided to wear the Gung-Ho helmet while riding his motorcycle. In fact, the Gung-Ho helmet was designed for military combat use, rather than for motorcycle use. The patented "E-Z release" strap was ideal for certain combat conditions, such as allowing a medical corpsman to remove the helmet quickly to treat a head wound. However, straps designed for use on motorcyclists must be tighter and less easy to remove.

While riding, the front wheel of Poleaxe's cycle struck a rock. The motorcycle flew up in the air, and Poleaxe was thrown from the cycle. The helmet flew off Poleaxe's head when the strap released under stress, and Poleaxe suffered severe head injuries that his old motorcycle helmet would have prevented.

If Poleaxe brings a strict liability action against the Gung-Ho Corporation to recover for his injuries, who will prevail?

(A) Gung-Ho, because Poleaxe used the helmet for an improper purpose.

(B) Poleaxe, because Gung-Ho should have foreseen that someone might wear the helmet while riding a motorcycle when it put a motorcyclist's picture on the box.

(C) Gung-Ho, because the helmet was supplied through the National Guard, and suit would be barred by the doctrine of sovereign immunity.

(D) Poleaxe, unless Gung-Ho took reasonable precautions in designing and manufacturing the helmet.

Question 44

During the Miss Metropolis competition, the judges announced that Wilma was first runner-up and that Kerry was the winner. As the auditorium quieted for Kerry's acceptance remarks, Wilma said loudly, "You only won because you slept with all of the judges, you slut!" Kerry immediately slapped Wilma forcefully in the face.

Wilma brings an action for battery against Kerry. Who will prevail?

(A) Kerry, because she was provoked by Wilma's comment.

(B) Kerry, because a reasonable person would have slapped Wilma under the circumstances.

(C) Wilma, unless Kerry's slap was totally spontaneous.

(D) Wilma, because Kerry intentionally caused an offensive touching.

Question 45

Reedley owned a large commercial building in the downtown area of the city and a vacant lot next to his building. The leader of a Boy Scout troop for disadvantaged youths explained to Reedley that the Scouts can only afford to make the long trip to the mountains for camping once a year, but that it would be very beneficial if they could practice their outdoor skills and activities even in an urban environment. Reedley therefore agreed to let the Scout troop use the vacant lot to practice outdoor-type activities.

One weekend while Reedley was out of the city on business, the Scout leader asked Reedley's building manager if he would permit the Scouts to practice their archery. The building manager agreed, but insisted that the targets be set up against the building so that an errant shot would merely strike concrete and not injure someone on the streets bordering the lot. The building manager supervised the set-up of the targets and ensured that responsible adults were present to assist the Scouts, then left the area. One of the Scouts jokingly shot an arrow up into the sky, and it came down on the street next to the vacant lot, striking and injuring Dave, who was driving past on his motorcycle.

If Dave brings an action against Reedley for personal injuries, what is the likely outcome?

(A) For Reedley, because he had no personal knowledge of the archery practice by the Scouts.

(B) For Reedley, if he can show that the precautions taken by his building manager were those a reasonable person would have taken.

(C) For Dave, because a property owner is strictly liable for injuries to passersby caused by the activities of persons on the property.

(D) For Dave, because the Scouts used the vacant lot with Reedley's permission.

Question 46

In connection with an effort by the chamber of commerce and the city council to revitalize the downtown area, Harris entered into an agreement with Oates, a building contractor, to have a facade attached to the front of Harris's bookstore to simulate the architecture of the late nineteenth century. Oates constructed the facade and attached it to the storefront, using plans prepared by himself and his own employees. After completing the work, Oates was paid the contract price by Harris.

A week later, Diets was walking past the front of Harris's bookstore when the facade and a portion of the original building collapsed, striking Diets and injuring him.

Diets sued both Oates and Harris for damages arising from his injuries. The parties stipulated that the attachment of the facade to the storefront caused the building to collapse.

If Diets recovers against Harris, does the latter have any right of action against Oates?

(A) Yes, because Harris's conduct was not a cause in fact of the injuries to Diets.

(B) Yes, if Diets recovered from Harris on the basis of vicarious liability.

(C) No, because Harris selected Oates to perform the work.

(D) No, because payment for the work without reservation was acceptance by Harris.

Question 47

Hagler owned Greenacre, a 30-acre tract of land divided into three 10-acre segments. Hagler built a home on one of the segments and used the middle segment to raise crops. The third 10-acre segment remained undeveloped. The undeveloped 10-acre segment was covered by a number of small trees. Hagler decided to subdivide the undeveloped 10-acre segment into seven lots suitable for single-family residences. The first step in the development was the removal of the trees. Neighbor, who lived next to Hagler, knew that Hagler intended to remove the trees from his property. Because he needed firewood, Neighbor decided to cut down several of the trees on Hagler's property. The day before development was to start on Hagler's property, Neighbor went onto Hagler's land, cut down a number of trees, cut the wood into fireplace-sized pieces, and moved them onto his property. Hagler brought an appropriate action against Neighbor for damages.

Hagler most likely will:

(A) Recover only nominal damages, because the value of the land was not diminished.

(B) Recover nominal damages and the value of the trees removed.

(C) Not recover, because removal of the trees saved Hagler money in the development of the land.

(D) Not recover, because the value of the land was not diminished by the removal of the trees.

Question 48

Donamae lived alone except for her large Persian cat, "Fluffkins," in a single-family home in a fine subdivision in prosperous Lime County. Although Donamae had never had any problems with crime in the area, she bought a handgun to protect herself.

One night at about 11 p.m., Donamae heard a strange noise. She put on a robe, took the gun from her nightstand, and proceeded down her stairs, as her bedroom was located on the second floor of her house.

At about the same time, Donamae's next-door neighbor, Nathaniel, also heard a strange noise. He walked out of his house and onto Donamae's lawn, because he thought the sound came from the direction of Donamae's abode. He stood silently on Donamae's lawn, listening.

As Donamae reached the last step, Fluffkins playfully charged down the stairs. The 15-pound cat struck the back of Donamae's legs, causing her to lose her balance. Although Donamae did not fall, her loss of balance caused her to drop the gun. The gun hit the floor and discharged. The bullet went through Donamae's front window and struck Nathaniel in the shoulder.

If Nathaniel sues Donamae on a battery theory, he will:

(A) Prevail, because handguns are highly dangerous instrumentalities.

(B) Prevail, because the cat's actions are imputed to Donamae.

(C) Lose, because the firing of the gun was a nonvolitional act.

(D) Lose, because Nathaniel was a trespasser.

Questions 49-50 are based on the following fact situation:

Gardner purchased a new riding lawn mower, manufactured by Lawn Co., from Garden Center. Gardner decided to use the lawn mower that afternoon to mow her lawn. Although the instructions recommended against it, Gardner ran the mower at full throttle around her yard because she was in a hurry to finish. As she was nearing the edge of her property, she attempted to turn the mower. However, the steering wheel locked and she was unable to turn. Unable to stop in time, she hit her neighbor, Bystrom, who was watching from his property. The collision caused the mower to overturn. Both Bystrom and Gardner were injured. Assume that the

jurisdiction follows traditional contributory negligence rules.

49. If Gardner asserts a claim against Garden Center based on strict liability in tort, will Gardner prevail?

(A) Yes, because the steering locked while Gardner was riding the mower.

(B) Yes, if the steering locked because of a defect present when the mower left the factory at Lawn Co.

(C) No, if Gardner contributed to her own injury by running the mower at full throttle.

(D) No, if Garden Center carefully inspected the mower before selling it.

50. If Bystrom asserts a claim based on negligence against Lawn Co., and if it is established that the locking of the steering wheel resulted from a manufacturing defect in the mower, will Bystrom prevail?

(A) Yes, because Lawn Co. placed a defective product into the stream of commerce.

(B) Yes, if the defect could have been discovered through the exercise of reasonable care by Lawn Co.

(C) No, because Bystrom was not a purchaser of the mower.

(D) No, if Gardner was negligent in running the mower at full throttle.

Questions 51-52 are based on the following fact situation:

At home one January night, Scott heard something bang against the bay window in the room where he was reading the newspaper. When he heard another louder bang, he put down the paper and looked out the window. He saw eleven-year-old Roman, the neighborhood bully, out back packing a large snowball. Fearful that Roman would break the window, Scott went out the front door and walked around to the back. When Roman saw him, Scott said, "I want to talk to you, Roman." Roman ran in the other direction and jumped over the fence belonging to Scott's neighbor Tim. Tim had recently purchased a dangerous Rottweiler as a guard dog. Because it was dark, Roman landed on a birdbath, knocked it over, and woke up the dog. The Rottweiler attacked Roman, who received severe lacerations and suffered permanent scarring as a result.

51. Tim brings an action against Scott for trespass. If Scott prevails, it will most likely be because:

(A) Scott confronted Roman in order to defend his property.

(B) Scott did not enter onto Tim's land.

(C) Roman was the one who made the decision to jump over the fence.

(D) Scott did not intend to frighten Roman onto Tim's property.

52. If Roman asserts a claim against Tim to recover damages for his injuries, Roman will:

(A) Prevail, because Tim may not use a vicious dog to protect only his property.

(B) Prevail, because Tim is strictly liable for injuries caused by the vicious dog.

(C) Not prevail, because Roman was trespassing on Tim's property.

(D) Not prevail, if Tim had signs up warning about the dog.

Questions 53-55 are based on the following fact situation:

Aerodrome, Inc., operates a private airfield for general aviation aircraft. In connection with an expansion of its facilities, extensive excavation work was being done next to the landing field, resulting in large mounds of earth next to the excavations. The chain link fence surrounding the airfield had been removed in one location to permit entry of very large earth-moving equipment, and a makeshift barrier was erected of wooden traffic barricades. Several children from a nearby residential area, ranging in age from seven to nine, discovered the easily bypassable wooden barricades and began playing "king of the mountain" and other games on the huge mounds of earth after the airfield was closed in the evening. Aerodrome was aware of this activity.

One evening, Luke was flying his small, single-engine airplane on a cross-country flight and passed near the Aerodrome airfield. Due to a defect in the electrical system of the aircraft, which was not discovered by professional aircraft mechanics at Luke's home field when they inspected the plane and certified it operable, Luke was forced to seek an emergency landing area, and, as had occasionally been done by pilots in similar circumstances, glided toward the Aerodrome field. The electrical system defect rendered the aircraft very difficult to control, and as Luke made his landing he was unable to avoid striking and injuring Sally, who had been pushed onto the landing field during a game of "king of the mountain" on the mounds. If the electrical system defect had been discovered and remedied, in addition to probably not having to make an emergency landing, Luke would have been able to avoid Sally.

53. If Sally brings an action for personal injuries against Luke, what is Luke's best defense?

(A) He did not act willfully and wantonly.

(B) He could not reasonably foresee that he would have to make an emergency landing.

(C) He used reasonable care in the maintenance of his aircraft.

(D) His conduct was not the cause in fact of the injury to Sally.

54. If Sally brings an action against Aerodrome, Inc., what will be the probable outcome?

   (A) Judgment for Aerodrome, because Sally was a trespasser.

   (B) Judgment for Aerodrome, because Luke had the last clear chance to avoid the injury to Sally.

   (C) Judgment for Sally, because Aerodrome is strictly liable for an artificial condition on its property.

   (D) Judgment for Sally, because Aerodrome could have effectively prevented entry of the children on its property at minimal cost.

55. If Sally brings an action against the aircraft mechanics who certified Luke's plane as operable, what will be the probable outcome?

   (A) Judgment for the mechanics, because Sally was legally a bystander.

   (B) Judgment for the mechanics, because Aerodrome's negligence was an independent, superseding cause.

   (C) Judgment for Sally if the mechanics were negligent in inspecting the airplane.

   (D) Judgment for Sally, because the mechanics were strictly liable in tort.

Question 56

Gregory Richards, a well-known author, speaker, and civil rights activist, was addressing a community group on the disparate treatment afforded non-whites by the police as compared to their treatment of whites. In the course of his remarks, he said, "I'll bet that two kids, one white and one black, could do exactly the same thing at some suburban shopping center, and the cops would bust the black kid and not even bother the white one."

A group of teenagers of various races who were attending the address and who were friends decided to test Richards's theory at a nearby shopping mall. In pairs of varying racial composition, they approached shoppers and asked if they could carry their packages for a nominal fee. Many shoppers simply declined, some agreed, some thought the teenagers were soliciting for charity, and others thought they were panhandlers.

One elderly woman who had recently been the victim of a purse snatching in which she had received rather severe but noncrippling injuries was so frightened by the approach of two teenagers that she dropped her packages and screamed for assistance. Although immediately reassured by the teenagers and security personnel that nothing was amiss, she was so distraught that she had to be taken home by ambulance.

If the shopper seeks recovery from Gregory Richards, is she likely to prevail?

   (A) No, because the teenagers were not employees of Richards.

   (B) No, because Richards did not authorize the teenagers' acts.

   (C) Yes, if the teenagers would not have acted as they did but for hearing Richards's comments.

   (D) Yes, if her claim against the teenagers prevails on a theory of negligence.

Question 57

Adam drove into the parking lot of Bank and was about to pull into an empty spot when Ben cut in front of him with his automobile and took his parking place. Adam and Ben each got out of their car and Adam started to yell at Ben. After a heated argument, a fight broke out between them. Calib came out of the bank at that moment and saw that Adam was getting the better of Ben in the fight. Calib ran to his car, took a gun from the glove compartment, pointed it at Adam and said, "Stop this minute or I'll shoot."

If Adam asserts a claim against Calib based on assault, who will prevail?

(A) Adam, because Calib threatened him with deadly force.

(B) Adam, because Calib was unaware of who was the aggressor.

(C) Calib, because Adam was the original aggressor by starting the fight with Ben.

(D) Calib, if it was apparent that Adam was about to inflict serious bodily harm to Ben.

Questions 58-60 are based on the following fact situation:

Ham operates a shortwave radio in his home. Ham maintains a large radio antenna on the rear part of his lot. One day Ham noticed that the guide wires holding the antenna in place were frayed. Ham hired Fixer to replace the guide wires with new, stronger wire. Fixer replaced all of the guide wires as per his agreement with Ham. Four days after Fixer finished his work and Ham had paid him, the antenna fell over onto Neighbor's house, causing severe damage.

58. If Neighbor brings suit against Ham for damages to his home, Neighbor is most likely to prevail against Ham because:

    (A) Of respondeat superior.

    (B) He assumed responsibility when he paid Fixer for the repair.

    (C) He was in possession of the property from which the antenna fell.

    (D) Fixer was engaged in an inherently dangerous activity.

59. If Neighbor brings suit against Fixer for damage to his home, the best defense for Fixer is that:

(A) He was relieved of liability when Ham paid for the repair.

(B) He could not reasonably foresee that the antenna would fall.

(C) He did all the work under the direction of Ham.

(D) The antenna was on the property of Ham.

60. If Neighbor recovers a judgment against Ham, does Ham have any recourse against Fixer?

    (A) Yes, because Ham's conduct did not add to Neighbor's injury.

    (B) Yes, if the judgment against Ham was based on vicarious liability.

    (C) No, if payment by Ham was an acceptance of Fixer's work.

    (D) No, because of the doctrine of collateral estoppel.

Questions 61-62 are based on the following fact situation:

Bradley went to the local lumberyard late one Saturday afternoon to purchase some sheets of plywood. Hopson, a salesman for the lumberyard, escorted Bradley to the back end of the lot where the plywood was stored. While Bradley and Hopson were looking over the sheets of plywood, the custodian closed and locked the only gate out of the lumberyard, since it was closing time and he believed that all employees had gone home. The storage area of the lumberyard is surrounded by a 12-foot-high chain link fence. Bradley and Hopson soon discovered that they had been locked in the lumberyard. Since the storage area was located at the back of the property owned by the lumberyard, there was very little chance that they would be seen on the premises. Hopson informed Bradley that since the lumberyard was closed on Sunday, no one would be back to let them out until Monday morning. Hopson went into a small shed in the lumberyard to wait until help would come. However, Bradley, panicking at the thought of being trapped on the lumberyard property until Monday morning, tried to climb over the fence and in doing so, fell and was injured. Bradley asserted a claim against the lumberyard for damages for his injuries.

61. If Bradley's claim is based on negligence, is the defense of assumption of risk applicable?

   (A) Yes, because Hopson felt the most logical course of conduct would be to wait until help arrived.

   (B) Yes, if a reasonable person would have recognized that there was some risk of falling while climbing the fence.

   (C) No, because Bradley had an important engagement that evening.

   (D) No, if it appeared that there was no other practical way of escaping the lumberyard before Monday.

62. If Bradley's claim is based on false imprisonment, will Bradley prevail?

   (A) Yes, because he was harmed as a result of his confinement.

   (B) Yes, because he was confined against his will.

   (C) No, unless the custodian knew that someone was in the lot at the time he locked the gate.

   (D) No, unless the custodian was negligent in locking the gate.

Question 63

While practicing their target shooting at the firing range, Aaron and Dale got into an argument that almost erupted into physical combat, except that they were restrained and separated by bystanders. Later, in the parking lot of the range, Aaron shot Dale in the shoulder. At trial of Dale's civil action for battery against Aaron, the latter testified that Dale approached him, said, "We'll settle this once and for all, right now," and raised an object toward Aaron. Fearing that Dale was about to shoot him with a pistol, Aaron fired in self-defense. Bystanders who rushed to the scene immediately after hearing Aaron's shot found Dale on the pavement with a black metal flashlight in his hand. Dale's pistol was in his locker at the firing range.

If Aaron's testimony is believed by the trier of fact, judgment on Dale's claim for damages should be:

   (A) For Aaron, if he honestly believed that Dale was about to shoot.

   (B) For Aaron, if a reasonable person in the same circumstances would have believed that Dale was about to shoot.

   (C) For Dale, because he was not armed.

   (D) For Dale, because he was not the aggressor.

Questions 64-66 are based on the following fact situation:

When Nancy was jogging along a road by the beach, she came to a bike path that passed under a pier. A city code provided that only bicycles were to be used on this path and that pedestrians were prohibited. However, if Nancy were to continue her run along the road, she would have to detour around the pier; so her usual procedure when she jogged in the morning was to cut under the pier on the bike path and get back on the road on the other side. After she reached the road on the other side, she had gone about 15 feet when Al pulled out of the alley and hit her with his car, injuring her. There was a stop sign at the end of the alley, but Al had failed to see it and stop.

64. Nancy sued Al. On the basis of which standard of care will Al be judged?

   (A) Strict liability, because an automobile is an inherently dangerous instrument.

(B) That of a reasonable and prudent person under the facts of this situation.

(C) The standard set by the traffic ordinance, unless Al is excused from following its requirements.

(D) The doctrine of res ipsa loquitur, because it can be presumed that nobody would fail to stop at a stop sign in the absence of negligence.

65. Had Nancy not disobeyed the statute by using the bicycle path, she would not have been near the alley when Al drove out; thus, her violation of this ordinance can be said to be:

(A) The actual cause of her injury.

(B) A concurring actual cause of her injury.

(C) An intervening cause of her injury.

(D) An existing condition having no factual relationship to her injury.

66. Nancy's violation of the statute would not defeat her claim against Al because:

(A) Al's negligence occurred after Nancy's.

(B) Al should have known that joggers frequently used the bicycle path in spite of the ordinance.

(C) Accidents that occurred after the pedestrian left the bicycle path were not within the risk that the statute was designed to prevent.

(D) There is a greater chance of causing injury when a car driver violates a statute than when a pedestrian does.

Question 67

James was a geologist studying the land formations in and around a mountain that had undergone a volcanic eruption several years earlier.

When he came to town one day, he opened up a copy of the *National Newspaper* to find that he was in an ad for Mountain Cigarettes. The ad headline "quoted" James as saying, "They make you feel like you're in the mountains."

James is certain that it is his picture, but he never posed for the ad for Mountain Cigarettes. After further investigation of the photo, it appeared to James that they had used the image of his head on the body of someone else to give the impression that it was James.

James brings an action to recover damages against Mountain Cigarettes. Most likely his best cause of action is:

(A) Defamation.

(B) Invasion of privacy.

(C) Intentional infliction of emotional distress.

(D) Negligent infliction of emotional distress.

Question 68

Astrid is an artist of international reputation. Many years ago, she purchased a warehouse overlooking the East River, which she converted into a studio. Although for years most of the surrounding area was used for small manufacturing businesses, light industry, and warehouses, of late this particular area has become a kind of artist retreat, chiefly because of Astrid's presence. About four months ago, Earhaus Recording purchased a warehouse next door to Astrid's studio and converted it into a recording studio and rehearsal rooms. The studio opens at 10 a.m., but frequently stays open long past midnight, particularly on the weekends. Although the five recording studios are thoroughly soundproofed, the various rehearsal rooms are not. When bands are using them, the sound can easily be heard by Astrid when she is working in her studio.

Astrid had always done her work at night, but since the studio next door opened, she has found it very difficult to concentrate on her work. She is distracted by all the noise and activity from Earhaus Recording Studio. Astrid instructed her attorney to bring suit against the studio for private nuisance.

In this suit, the fact that Astrid owns her studio and has used it for 15 years is:

(A) Controlling on the issue of whether Earhaus Recording's use of its property is reasonable.

(B) Not controlling, but relevant to the issue of whether Earhaus Recording's use of its property is reasonable.

(C) Not controlling, and irrelevant since the surrounding area was used exclusively for industry and manufacturing when Astrid bought her property.

(D) Not controlling, and irrelevant since a landowner cannot establish the reasonableness of the use of property simply by being the first in the neighborhood.

Question 69

Torres Construction was employed by the city to repair a broken pipe under Central Street. As part of its work, Torres Construction dug a trench down the center of Central Street measuring 17 feet long by 5 feet wide by 7 feet deep. Warning signs and flashing lights were positioned at both ends of the trench to warn cars of the danger, but, except for two unlit warning signs along the sides, no barriers of any kind were put up on either side.

Clint, who had been away at college, was walking home along Central Avenue at about 11 p.m. after arriving at the downtown bus depot. A heavy rain started, and in an effort to avoid getting any more wet, Clint jaywalked instead of going to the corner to cross the street. In the dark and heavy rain, Clint did not realize that the road was dug up where he was crossing

and fell into the trench. Clint was knocked out when he hit the bottom of the trench and drowned when the water from the rain gathered at the bottom.

Clint's mother brought a wrongful death action against Torres Construction for the death of her son. Assume that this jurisdiction has a statute that makes it a misdemeanor for anyone to cross a main street such as Central Street at any place except in the marked crosswalks.

Torres Construction is likely to:

(A) Prevail, because Clint was negligent per se, and thus at fault for his own death.

(B) Prevail, because it had marked off its trench with warning signs.

(C) Not prevail, because a construction company is strictly liable for inherently dangerous conditions.

(D) Not prevail, because it left an open trench unprotected.

Questions 70-71 are based on the following fact situation:

Danny is a 10-year-old, and although his parents make sure he is home by 10 p.m. during the school week, they do not really enforce any sort of curfew on their son during the weekend. One Saturday night, when Danny's parents went to bed at midnight, Danny was still out. About 2 a.m., Danny and two other children were arrested by the police for breaking the windows and causing other damage to Bernadette's antique Cord automobile.

70. In a suit by Bernadette against Danny for the damages he caused to her automobile, Bernadette should:

(A) Prevail, because Danny, at the age of 10, should have been aware of the consequences of his action.

(B) Prevail, because Danny deliberately damaged her car.

(C) Not prevail, because Danny is presumed to be under the care of his parents and, therefore, is not legally responsible for his tortious conduct.

(D) Not prevail, unless she can show that Danny was mature enough to be aware of the consequences of his action.

71. Assume that the jurisdiction has no statute regarding parental liability. In a suit by Bernadette against Danny's parents for the damages caused to her automobile, Bernadette should:

(A) Prevail, because a minor's parents are vicariously liable anytime the minor commits a tortious act.

(B) Prevail, because Danny's parents did not ensure that Danny was home at a reasonable hour.

(C) Not prevail, unless she can show that Danny's parents were aware that Danny has done this sort of act before.

(D) Not prevail, because there is no reason to assume that Danny's parents could know that Danny might damage Bernadette's automobile.

Questions 72-73 are based on the following fact situation:

Clara has been having a running battle with her neighbor, Duncan, for several months over the fact that when he operates his ham radio at night, it interferes with her television reception. One night at about 2 a.m., Clara was watching one of her favorite old movies on television when Duncan started transmitting on his radio. Furious that he was again causing her to miss something she wanted to watch on television, Clara decided to fix him by cutting down his radio antenna. She got the ladder from her garage and climbed on top of Duncan's two-story house. However, just as she got to the antenna, her foot slipped and if she had not been able to grab hold of one of the support cables, she would have fallen to the street below. Duncan was unable to hear her cries for help because he was using earphones. Fortunately for Clara, the driver of a passing car, Eldon, saw her hanging from Duncan's roof. Eldon immediately came to her rescue and pulled her back onto the roof. However, as he straightened up after getting Clara back on the roof, he accidentally touched Duncan's antenna and suffered an electric shock. He fell from the roof and suffered severe burns on his back and a broken hip.

72. Eldon sued Clara for the injuries he suffered. Eldon should:

(A) Not prevail, because he voluntarily assumed the risk of injury.

(B) Not prevail, because the rescue of Clara was already over before he was injured.

(C) Prevail, because Clara was at fault in slipping from Duncan's roof.

(D) Prevail, because Clara may have been killed if she had fallen to the street.

73. Can Eldon assert a valid claim against Duncan for the injuries he suffered while trying to rescue Clara?

(A) Yes, because Duncan's refusal to take steps to insure that his radio would not interfere with Clara's television created this problem.

(B) Yes, if the facts show that Duncan could have taken steps to prevent his antenna from shocking someone.

(C) No, because Eldon voluntarily assumed the risks.

(D) No, because Duncan was not at fault.

Question 74

Worker entered into a written contract with Owner to install aluminum siding onto Owner's house. The contract called for all work to be completed by the following Tuesday. On that date, Worker finished installing the siding rather late in the afternoon. Wishing to get home as soon as possible, Worker decided that he would come back the next day and pick up his ladder and tools. Worker could not tell Owner of this plan, however, because Owner was out of town overnight on business. During the night, a thief used Worker's ladder and tools to gain entrance to Owner's home and steal Owner's television set and stereo. Owner has asserted a claim against Worker for damages for the loss of the television and the stereo.

In his claim against Worker, Owner will:

(A) Prevail, because by leaving the ladder and tools out, Worker created the risk that a person might unlawfully enter the house.

(B) Prevail, because Worker failed to get Owner's permission to leave his ladder and tools on Owner's property overnight.

(C) Not prevail, because the act of the thief was an independent superseding cause.

(D) Not prevail, because Owner's only recovery would be by way of an action for breach of contract.

Question 75

A city ordinance required that all dogs be leashed when taken outside of an enclosed area. Bee often allowed her dog, Bop, to run loose in front of Bee's house. One day, when Bop was running loose, Dina was driving her car up the street in front of Bee's house. The day was clear and sunny and Dina was driving carefully at a speed somewhat below the posted limit. Bop dashed out into the street from between two parked cars. Dina alertly applied her brakes, but could not avoid striking Bop. Pris, driving another vehicle behind Dina, promptly applied her brakes as soon as she saw the red lights glow on the rear of Dina's vehicle. However, Pris's

vehicle struck the rear of Dina's vehicle. Both of the vehicles suffered damage and both drivers suffered minor injuries which required x-rays and other medical attention.

If Pris sues Dina for her vehicle damage and personal injuries, Pris will:

(A) Prevail, because the ordinance was designed to prevent dogs from being hit by cars.

(B) Prevail, because Dina was a proximate cause of the accident.

(C) Not prevail, because Dina obeyed the traffic laws.

(D) Not prevail, unless Dina herself was negligent.

Question 76

Parker was enjoying a steak in a local restaurant when he started to choke. A waiter saw that Dr. Macmillan was sitting at a nearby table and the waiter ran over to her to ask her to help him save Parker. Dr. Macmillan stood up and told the waiter that she did not want to become involved, and she left the restaurant. Soon afterwards, the paramedics arrived and they were able to save Parker's life. Unfortunately, he suffered brain damage due to lack of oxygen.

Parker brings a suit against Dr. Macmillan seeking damages for his injuries. Parker's medical expert testified that had Parker received prompt medical attention there would have been no injuries at all. Can Parker recover damages from Dr. Macmillan?

(A) Yes, if the jurisdiction in which this accident occurred had a statute relieving doctors from malpractice claims when they give emergency first aid.

(B) Yes, if a reasonable doctor in Dr. Macmillan's position would have rendered first aid.

(C) No, because Dr. Macmillan was not responsible for Parker's condition.

(D) No, unless it can be shown that Dr. Macmillan knew that Parker was substantially certain to suffer injury unless he received medical assistance from a doctor.

Question 77

Paine and Duncan were playing tennis. Duncan became highly irritated because every time Duncan prepared to serve, Paine started talking loudly. Paine's loud talk distracted Duncan from his game, and Duncan usually faulted on his serves. Duncan told Paine to "cut it out," but Paine persisted in the behavior.

Standing several feet away, Duncan swung his tennis racket toward Paine's head. However, Duncan slipped as he swung the racket and it flew out of his hand as he lost his balance. The racket flew through the air and struck Paine in the head.

Has Paine grounds for a battery action against Duncan?

(A) Yes, if Duncan intended to create a reasonable apprehension in Paine.

(B) Yes, because the racket struck Paine.

(C) No, because Duncan did not intend the racket to strike Paine.

(D) No, but only if Duncan can prove that the owner of the tennis court had not maintained the court properly and this caused Duncan to slip.

TORTS ANSWERS

Answer to Question 1

(C)   If Ajax had no reason to anticipate that the tests would cause any of the results that occurred, then it cannot be said that Ajax intended to commit the act constituting trespass. Absent such intent, there is no cause of action for trespass. A prima facie case for trespass to land consists of: (i) an act of physical invasion of the plaintiff's real property by the defendant; (ii) intent on the defendant's part to bring about a physical invasion of the plaintiff's real property; and (iii) causation. The intent required is not intent to trespass; thus, mistake as to the lawfulness of an entry onto another's land is no defense as long as the defendant intended the entry upon that particular piece of land. Here, Ajax, in firing the rocket engine, caused debris to fall onto Homesteader's property. This would be a sufficient physical invasion for purposes of a trespass action. However, maintenance of this action requires a showing that Ajax intended to send this debris onto the land of Homesteader. If (as stated in (C)) Ajax had no reason to anticipate that its rocket engine tests would cause the debris to fall onto Homesteader's property, then Ajax did not intend to make any entry onto Homesteader's property (*i.e.,* Ajax neither acted with the goal of sending debris onto Homesteader's land nor did it know with substantial certainty that such a consequence would result from its tests of the engine). Consequently, under the circumstances set forth in (C), the element of intent would be missing, thereby precluding Homesteader from establishing a prima facie case for trespass. (A) is incorrect because the fact that Homesteader bought and operated the farm with knowledge that Ajax used the adjoining land for engine tests will not allow Ajax to commit an act that would otherwise be characterized as a trespass. Homesteader's knowledge of the use to which Ajax put the adjoining property cannot be taken as implied consent to the scattering of debris on Homesteader's land. (B) is incorrect because a physical invasion does not require that the defendant personally come onto the land. There is a trespass if, *e.g.,* the defendant floods the plaintiff's land or, as here, causes debris to settle on the plaintiff's land. (D) is incorrect because the defense of public necessity arises where the public good is threatened with injury, and the defendant's actions are reasonably and apparently necessary to avoid such injury. Also, the threatened injury must be substantially more serious than the defendant's interference with the plaintiff's property that seeks to avoid such injury. This defense presupposes a situation in which immediate action is required by the defendant to ward off an imminent threat to the public good. Testing rocket engines for eventual military use does not rise to the level of conduct necessary to avoid an impending injury to the public good. Thus, Ajax cannot successfully claim that its conduct is privileged as a public necessity.

Answer to Question 2

(B)   The distance from the test site to Homesteader's farm is most helpful to Ajax. Where an action is based on negligence, the plaintiff is alleging that the defendant has breached its duty of acting as an ordinary, prudent, reasonable person, and that such breach has actually and proximately caused injury to the plaintiff. No duty is imposed upon a person to take precautions against events that cannot reasonably be foreseen. Thus, if at the time of the defendant's conduct, no foreseeable risk of injury to a person in the position of the plaintiff is created by the defendant's act, the general duty of care does not extend from the defendant to the plaintiff. If (as (B) states) Homesteader's farm is located so far from the test site that no risk to Homesteader was foreseeable, then there would be no duty imposed upon Ajax to take precautions against the damage to Homesteader's property, which could not reasonably have been foreseen. Thus, the general duty of reasonable care would not extend from Ajax to Homesteader with respect to Ajax's testing operations. Absent such a duty, there can be no liability for negligence. (A) is incorrect because the prior instability of the subsurface earth structures will almost certainly not help Ajax. Such instability addresses the matter of causation of injury. Even assuming the instability of the structures, the facts indicate that the structures would not have slumped but for the firing of the rocket engine by Ajax. Thus, Ajax's conduct was the cause in fact (actual cause) of the damage to the water well on Homesteader's farm. The firing of the rocket by Ajax was also the proximate cause of Homesteader's injury because the damage was the direct result of Ajax's conduct. Hence, it will be of no help to Ajax to show that the subsurface structures were already unstable. (C) is incorrect because, even if Ajax exercised reasonable care in selecting the personnel involved in the testing, such personnel may still have acted negligently in the manner in which they conducted the tests or chose the test site. Under such circumstances, Ajax would be vicariously liable for the negligence committed by its employees within the scope of the employment relationship. (D) is incorrect because industry standards of conduct do not establish a conclusive test for determining whether specific actions constitute a breach of duty owed to someone. Industry standards are admissible as evidence of an appropriate standard of care, but they are not conclusive on this point (in fact, such standards may actually represent conduct that is negligent).

Answer to Question 3

(C) DeeDee is not liable for the damage to the car because a reasonable person would not have foreseen damage arising from the delay in getting the pizza. A prima facie case for negligence consists of: (i) a duty on the part of the defendant to conform to a specific standard of conduct for the protection of the plaintiff against an unreasonable risk of injury; (ii) breach of such duty by the defendant; (iii) that such breach is the actual and proximate cause of the plaintiff's injury; and (iv) damage to the plaintiff's person or property. No duty is imposed upon a person to take precautions against events that cannot reasonably be foreseen. Here, it is true that, had DeeDee gotten the pizza immediately, Poteet's car would not have been at the location it was at the time it was struck by Tammy. However, a mere delay in picking up a pizza while leaving a car properly parked does not create a foreseeable risk of damage to the car. Thus, there is no basis for holding DeeDee liable in negligence. (B) is incorrect because, as noted above, the fact that Poteet's car would not have been damaged if DeeDee had not delayed in getting the pizza is not enough to establish liability for negligence. The fact that the damage to Poteet's car was unforeseeable will preclude a finding that DeeDee acted negligently by delaying in getting the pizza. Likewise, (A) is incorrect because the mere fact that DeeDee stopped at the bookstore, when Poteet loaned her the car specifically to pick up the pizza, will not mean that DeeDee acted in a manner that created an unreasonable risk of damage to the car. The concept of "exceeding one's authority" might be relevant in the context of an employer trying to avoid vicarious liability for the tortious conduct of an employee by arguing that the employee acted outside the scope of her employment. However, in the context of this question, DeeDee's having stopped at the bookstore will not subject her to liability. (D) misstates the family car doctrine, which holds an automobile owner liable for tortious conduct of immediate family or household members who are driving with the owner's permission. This doctrine would not be used to relieve DeeDee of liability for any negligence on her part by imputing such negligence to Poteet. Note also that DeeDee and Poteet are not members of the same family or household.

Answer to Question 4

(B) Doug is liable for battery under the doctrine of transferred intent. Pursuant to this doctrine, where a defendant intends to commit a tort against one person but instead: (i) commits a different tort against that person; (ii) commits the same tort as intended but against a different person; or (iii) commits a different tort against a different person, the intent to commit a tort against one person is transferred to the other tort or to the injured person for purposes of establishing a prima facie case. Transferred intent may be invoked where the tort intended and the tort that results are both among the following: (i) assault; (ii) battery; (iii) false imprisonment; (iv) trespass to land; and (v) trespass to chattels. Assault requires: (i) an act by the defendant creating a reasonable apprehension in the plaintiff of immediate harmful or offensive contact to the plaintiff's person; (ii) intent on the part of the defendant to bring about in the plaintiff such apprehension; and (iii) causation. Battery requires: (i) an act by the defendant that brings about harmful or offensive contact to the plaintiff's person; (ii) intent on the part of the defendant to bring about such contact; and (iii) causation. Here, Doug intended either to commit battery against Babette (if he intended to hit her with the spitball) or to commit assault (if he merely intended to put Babette in apprehension of immediate harmful or offensive contact with the spitball). When Doug actually hit Antoinette, his intent as to Babette was transferred to Antoinette. Thus, Doug is liable to Antoinette for battery. (A) is incorrect because, with harmful contact having occurred, the tort for which Doug is liable is battery. Also, there is no indication that Antoinette was placed in apprehension of any harmful or offensive contact, as she apparently was unaware of what Doug was doing until she was struck by the spitball. (C) is incorrect because Doug's conduct is not extreme and outrageous (*i.e.,* transcending all bounds of decency), so as to qualify for the tort of intentional infliction of emotional distress. Also, Doug did not intend to cause severe emotional distress to anyone. Doug intended to simply frighten Babette slightly, not to cause her (or Antoinette) to suffer severe emotional distress. The doctrine of transferred intent does not apply where an assault or battery is intended toward one person, and emotional distress occurs in another person. (D) is incorrect because it fails to account for transferred intent. As detailed above, the fact that Doug did not intend to harm Antoinette will not relieve Doug of liability for battery, because his intent to commit a tort against Babette is transferred to the tort actually committed against Antoinette.

Answer to Question 5

(D) Marie is not liable because there is no indication of any fault on her part in injuring Pantagruel. However, the restaurant is vicariously liable for the negligence of the busboy in failing to remove the pudding. Marie fell on top of Pantagruel because she slipped on the pudding. Slipping and falling were not volitional acts by Marie, so it cannot be said that Marie acted with the intent to bring about any harm to Pantagruel, or that she knew with substantial certainty that such harm would occur. In addition, the facts do not indicate that the slip and fall occurred because Marie was not exercising ordinary, reasonable care. In her rush to assist a restaurant patron in distress, Marie inadvertently stepped on a slippery substance, the presence of which she had no reason to know. Thus, Marie did not act negligently. Because Marie's conduct was neither intentional nor negligent, she is without fault in the infliction of injury to Pantagruel. Consequently, Marie will not be held liable for the injury. However, the busboy who failed to remove the pudding from the floor did act negligently. The busboy owed a duty to restaurant patrons to act as an ordinary, reasonable person for the protection of the patrons against an unreasonable risk of injury. By leaving the pudding on the floor, the busboy created an unreasonable risk that a patron would be injured either by directly falling or by being near someone else who fell. Thus, the busboy breached his duty of due care. This breach, which caused Marie to fall on Pantagruel, actually and proximately caused physical injury to Pantagruel, who was a foreseeable plaintiff. This negligence on the part of the busboy was committed within the scope of his employment relationship with the restaurant. Under the doctrine of respondeat superior, the restaurant is vicariously liable for this tortious act of its employee. Thus, (D) correctly states that Marie is not liable, but the restaurant is liable. (A) is incorrect for two reasons. First, restaurateurs and others who gather the public for profit have a duty to use reasonable care to aid or assist their guests. Therefore, as a restaurant employee, Marie was under a duty to use reasonable care to assist Antoinette, a patron who was apparently in great distress and in need of assistance. Second, even if Marie was not under a duty to help Antoinette, her attempt to provide help will not render her liable for Pantagruel's injury. As noted above, Marie was not at fault in inflicting the injury on Pantagruel. Providing help despite not having a duty to do so is not a basis for imposing liability on Marie for the injury that befell Pantagruel. (B) is incorrect because it misapplies the principle of assumption of risk. A plaintiff may be denied recovery if she assumed the risk of any damage caused by the defendant's acts. Thus, assumption of the risk provides a defense to a plaintiff's claim, rather than a basis on which to hold a person liable. It is therefore meaningless to speak of Marie, the defendant, as having "assumed the risk." (C) is incorrect because, despite the fact that Marie's touching of Pantagruel was unintentional, she could still be held liable for his injuries if she had been negligent in causing them. Thus, the unintentional nature of Marie's conduct will not by itself relieve her of liability.

Answer to Question 6

(C) Bill is liable for damage to the zinnias even though he had a privilege to enter Carol's yard. Pursuant to the privilege of necessity, a person may interfere with property of another where it is reasonably and apparently necessary to avoid threatened injury from a natural or other force and where the threatened injury is substantially more serious than the invasion that seeks to avert it. In cases of private necessity (where the act is solely to benefit a limited number of persons rather than the public as a whole) the defense is qualified, so that the actor must pay for any injury he causes. Bill was faced with death or serious injury from being struck by the oncoming bus. Apparently the only way to avoid this injury was to jump into Carol's yard. The threatened injury to Bill was substantially more serious than Bill's entry into Carol's yard. Thus, Bill was privileged to enter the yard. However, because this is a private necessity situation, he will be required to pay for the damage he caused to the zinnias. (A) correctly states that Bill is liable for the damage, but incorrectly states that he was not privileged to enter upon Carol's land. On the other hand, (D) is incorrect because it concludes that Bill's privilege absolves him of liability for the damage he caused, which is not true in private necessity cases. (B) is incorrect because Bill's exercise of due care is irrelevant. Carol will be proceeding against Bill on a theory of intentional tort (either trespass or conversion). Due care is a concept that is applicable to a negligence action, but is not relevant to an action sounding in intentional tort. Therefore, Bill's liability is unaffected by whether or not he was exercising due care.

Answer to Question 7

(D) If Bill was on Carol's land with her permission, he is a licensee. A licensee is a person who enters land with the owner's permission, for his own purpose or business rather than for the owner's benefit. The owner or occupier of land has a duty to warn a licensee of a dangerous condition known to the owner or occupier that creates an unreasonable risk of harm to the licensee and that the licensee is unlikely to discover. However, the owner or occupier has no duty to a licensee to inspect for defects nor to repair known defects. Bill was a licensee because he entered Carol's land with her permission for his own purpose (retrieving his wallet) rather than for any benefit of Carol's. The exposed electric wire created an unreasonable risk of death or serious injury to Bill as he searched the yard. If Carol knew of the presence and condition of the wire, she should also have known that it posed an unreasonable risk of harm to Bill, and that, being obscured by bushes, it was unlikely to be discovered by Bill. Thus, the duty to warn Bill of the wire would be triggered. (D) accurately describes the duty owed by Carol to Bill as a licensee. (A) is incorrect because the mere fact that Carol gave Bill permission to enter her land will not subject her to liability for his injuries incurred thereon. Carol is not strictly liable for injuries to a licensee, but only for any injuries caused by a breach of her duty to warn of dangerous conditions known to her and that the licensee is unlikely to discover. (A) would impose liability even where Carol had no knowledge of the wire. (B) is incorrect because, as noted above, an owner of land does not owe a duty to a licensee to repair defects or dangerous conditions. Likewise, (C) is incorrect because the owner of land is not under a duty to a licensee to make an inspection to discover defects or dangerous conditions.

Answer to Question 8

(B) Wally is liable to Carol in a negligence action. The driver of a vehicle on a public road owes to foreseeable plaintiffs a duty of ordinary, reasonable care to refrain from creating an unreasonable risk of injury in the operation of the vehicle. In trying to light a cigarette while driving the bus, Wally created an unreasonable risk that he would lose control of the bus, thus endangering the physical safety and the property of other drivers on the road, pedestrians, and owners of property adjoining the road. There was a foreseeable risk of injury to Carol or her property arising from the manner in which Wally drove the bus; thus, the duty of care extended from Wally to Carol. This duty was breached when Wally drove the bus so as to create an unreasonable risk of injury to Carol or her property. It was reasonably foreseeable that a pedestrian endangered by the manner in which Wally drove the bus would be compelled to enter Carol's property and would damage the zinnias. By forcing Bill to jump off the road to save his life, Wally actually and proximately caused the damage to the zinnias; where a defendant's actions cause another to react, liability will attach for any harm inflicted by the reacting person on another. Thus, Wally can be held liable in negligence for the damage to Carol's zinnias. (C) is incorrect because the manner in which Wally operated the bus created a foreseeable risk of injury to the person or property of someone who owns property adjoining the road. Therefore, the general duty of due care owed by Wally in his operation of the bus extended to Carol and her zinnias. (A) is incorrect because Wally lacked the intent to bring about a physical invasion of Carol's property. Absent such intent, there can be no liability for trespass. Wally was negligent in his operation of the bus, and this caused Bill to enter Carol's land. However, Wally neither acted with the goal of forcing Bill onto Carol's land nor did he act knowing with substantial certainty that this consequence would result. Therefore, Wally did not have the intent needed to support an action for trespass. (D) is incorrect because none of the circumstances in which indemnity is available is present. Indemnity involves shifting the entire loss between or among tortfeasors. One held vicariously liable may obtain indemnification from the person whose conduct actually caused the damage. Wally will be held liable for his own negligence in driving the bus, not vicariously for any conduct of Bill's. Thus, this basis for indemnity does not apply. It is also possible for one tortfeasor to recover against a co-joint tortfeasor where there is a considerable difference in degree of fault. Here, Wally is primarily at fault. Wally was negligent in driving the bus, while Bill merely reacted to save himself from death or serious injury, and was apparently not negligent at all. Thus, it is Wally who is the "more wrongful" tortfeasor, thereby precluding recovery of indemnity from Bill on this basis as well.

Answer to Question 9

(C) Rebecca has an action against Jim for defamation. In a defamation context, a statement has been published when there is a communication to a third person who understands it. Here, Jim's sending the story to the magazine editor constitutes a sufficient publication for defamation purposes. Although Rebecca is not as much in the public eye as she once was, she is probably still a public figure. Thus, the elements of falsity and fault come into play. From the facts, we know that the story is false. The fault element is also satisfied because the story will have been published with malice (*i.e.,* with knowledge that it was false or with reckless disregard as to its truth or falsity). Reckless disregard is shown by the fact that Jim entertained serious doubts as to the truthfulness of the story. Publications made with malice are not entitled to constitutional protection, so the plaintiff is entitled to recover damages as permitted by state law. In most jurisdictions, general damages are presumed for libel, and need not be proved by the plaintiff. Here, the defamation is recorded in written form, so it is libel. Thus, general damages are presumed. (Note that if Rebecca is deemed not to be a public figure, the prima facie case is easier to establish because proof of malice would not be required.) Because all the other elements of defamation are present (*i.e.,* defamatory language concerning Rebecca and damage to her reputation), the sending of the story to the magazine would give rise to a defamation action in favor of Rebecca. With regard to a potential cause of action for invasion of privacy, the only branches of this tort that might be applicable are publication of facts placing the plaintiff in a false light and public disclosure of private facts about the plaintiff. Both of these torts require publicity concerning either "false light" facts or private facts. This requires more than publication in the defamation sense. Sending the story to the magazine and having it go unpublished does not constitute a public disclosure or any type of publicity regarding the matters contained therein. Thus, although there was a publication sufficient to support a defamation action, there was not a sufficient publication for purposes of invasion of privacy. Consequently, (B) is incorrect. (A) and (D) are incorrect because, as stated in choice (C), Rebecca does have a cause of action for defamation.

Answer to Question 10

(B) If a reasonable inspection by Pipeco would have revealed a defect in the pipe that caused the explosion, Pipeco was negligent either in failing to inspect the pipe or in failing to discover the defect pursuant to an inspection. Porter's action against Pipeco is a products liability action based on a negligence theory. In such a case, the prima facie case consists of: (i) a legal duty owed by the defendant to this plaintiff; (ii) breach of the duty; (iii) actual and proximate cause; and (iv) damages. Here, Pipeco owed a duty to those who could foreseeably be injured by a defect in the pipe that it manufactured. This duty was to exercise that degree of care to be expected of the ordinary reasonable pipe manufacturer, so as to take precautions against creating an unreasonable risk of injury. It was reasonably foreseeable that a defective pipe could explode and cause injury to someone who was working in a plant containing a pipe manufactured by Pipeco. Thus, Porter is a foreseeable plaintiff and the duty owed by Pipeco extends to him. If a reasonable inspection of the pipe by Pipeco would have revealed a defect that eventually caused the pipe to explode, it can be concluded that Pipeco either did not inspect the pipe at all or that any inspection that was conducted was not done with reasonable care. In either case, the conduct of Pipeco would not meet the standard of care required of the ordinary, reasonable pipe manufacturer, which resulted in Pipeco's supplying of a pipe that was so defective as to be unreasonably dangerous. But for this breach of duty, the pipe would not have exploded and injured Porter. The facts present no problem of proximate causation, as there appears to be no external intervening force. Thus, Pipeco's breach of duty actually and proximately caused the injuries incurred by Porter. Consequently, Porter will prevail in a negligence action under the circumstances set forth in (B). (A) is incorrect because it implies liability without fault. As a plaintiff in a negligence action, Porter must show that Pipeco breached a duty owed to him, and that such breach caused his injuries. The mere fact that a pipe manufactured by Pipeco exploded does not satisfy this burden. It is possible that the pipe could have exploded without any fault on the part of Pipeco. (C) is incorrect because it is possible that the hot oil corroded the pipe only because the pipe was not reasonably safe for its intended use. Presumably, the pipe should have been manufactured so as to resist corrosion from hot oil. We are not told that the oil was excessively hot or that there is any other reason that the pipe might have corroded. Thus, the bursting of the pipe from corrosion caused by hot oil might well be indicative of negligent manufacture on the part of Pipeco. (D) is incorrect because, despite the fact that the pipe was in Cheminc's possession at the time of the explosion, the explosion itself may have been caused by negligence on the part of Pipeco. If Pipeco is at fault in causing the explosion, then it will be liable, regardless of whose possession the pipe was in when the explosion occurred.

Answer to Question 11

(C) Hurts may obtain indemnity from Driver. One who is held liable for damages caused by another simply because of his relationship to that person may seek indemnification from the person whose conduct actually caused the damage. Hurts has been held liable for the damages caused by Driver solely because it rented a car to Driver. Such vicarious liability (imposed pursuant to the permissive use statute) being imposed on Hurts will entitle Hurts to be indemnified from Driver, whose conduct actually caused the damage. Thus, the entire loss will be shifted from Hurts to Driver. (A) is incorrect because a contractual promise to indemnify is not the only means by which a right of indemnification can come into existence. For example, a right of indemnity exists as a matter of law in the circumstances here, as detailed above. Thus, the absence of any obligation of Driver contained in the rental agreement will not mean that Hurts has no rights against Driver. (B) is incorrect because contribution is a device whereby responsibility is apportioned among those who are at fault. Contribution allows any defendant required to pay more than his share of damages to have a claim against any other jointly liable parties for the excess. Hurts is not really at fault in bringing about the injuries to Sam. Rather, Hurts can only be held liable by virtue of the permissive use statute. There is no responsibility to be apportioned here; instead, the entire loss should be shifted from Hurts to the person who actually caused the damage. Thus, indemnity is available, and contribution is not appropriate. (D) is incorrect for the same reasons that (B) is incorrect. In addition, (D) incorrectly provides for comparative contribution. Traditional contribution rules require all defendants to pay equal shares regardless of their respective degrees of fault.

Answer to Question 12

(D) The judgment should be entered in the full amount against both defendants. Where two or more tortious acts combine to proximately cause an indivisible injury to the plaintiff, each tortfeasor will be jointly and severally liable for that injury. Joint and several liability of such parties means that each is liable to the plaintiff for the entire damage incurred, so that the plaintiff may recover the entire judgment amount from any defendant (with the plaintiff of course being limited to one total recovery). Hurts and Driver have been found jointly and severally liable for the harm caused to Sam by their tortious acts. Thus, the entire damage amount of $100,000 is recoverable from either of these defendants. As a result, judgment in the amount of $100,000 should be entered against both Hurts and Driver. (A) and (B) incorrectly provide for each defendant to be liable for less than the entire damage incurred. It is only where the actions of each defendant are independent, the plaintiff's injury is divisible, and it is possible to identify the portion of injuries caused by each defendant that each will only be liable for an identifiable portion. Here, there is an indivisible injury, and the defendants have been found to be jointly and severally liable. Thus, there is no basis for entering judgment against either defendant for less than the entire amount of damages. (C) is incorrect because both defendants have been found liable, so there is no basis for entering judgment against Hurts only.

Answer to Question 13

(D) John cannot recover damages because his property was not harmed and because there are no grounds for punitive damages. The prima facie case for negligence requires damage to the plaintiff's person or property. Damages are not presumed in negligence cases; there must be **actual** harm or injury. In cases involving property damage, the measure of damages is the reasonable cost of repair, or, if the property has been almost or completely destroyed, its fair market value at the time of the injury. Punitive damages are recoverable only if the defendant's conduct was reckless, malicious, or willful and wanton. Here there is no indication that the movers intended injury to John's anvils; this is merely a case of negligence. Thus, John must show damage. The anvil has not been damaged in any way, so there are no actual damages available, and since nominal damages are not allowed for negligence, John cannot recover **any** compensatory damages from the movers. Also, there is no indication of willful and wanton, reckless, or malicious behavior on the part of the movers. Therefore, John cannot recover punitive damages either. (A) and (C) are wrong because, as stated, John cannot receive nominal damages. (B) and (C) are wrong because John cannot recover punitive damages.

Answer to Question 14

(C) Because Jane was across the street at the time of impact, she was not within the zone of danger, thus precluding her recovery for negligent infliction of emotional distress. A defendant breaches a duty to avoid negligent infliction of emotional distress when he creates a foreseeable risk of physical injury to the plaintiff through causing a threat of physical impact that leads to emotional distress. Damages are recoverable only if the defendant's conduct causes some physical injury, rather than purely emotional distress (although a severe shock to the nervous system that causes physical symptoms is considered a physical injury). If plaintiff's distress is caused by threat of physical impact, the threat must be directed at plaintiff or someone in her immediate presence. A bystander outside the zone of danger of physical injury who sees defendant negligently injuring another cannot recover for distress. Here, Jane witnessed the anvil striking her car from across the street. This vantage point placed Jane outside the zone of danger from the falling anvil, and the injury was to property rather than a person. Thus, Jane cannot recover for negligent infliction of emotional distress. It is true that, as implied by (A), there can be no recovery for this tort absent some accompanying physical consequences. However, even if Jane did suffer physical injury, she could not recover because she was not within the zone of danger. Therefore, (C) is a better answer than (A). (B) is incorrect because Jane's distance from the accident makes her an unforeseeable plaintiff. The "zone of danger" requirement precludes recovery by mere bystanders as to whom no foreseeable risk of physical injury arises from the defendant's conduct. It is unforeseeable that someone on the other side of the street would suffer physical impact or the threat thereof. Furthermore, even jurisdictions following the modern "foreseeability" approach permit bystander recovery only when witnessing injury to **another person** related to the bystander. (D) is incorrect because physical impact is not required for this tort; the threat of impact is enough. Therefore, even in the absence of impact, Jane could recover if she had been within the zone of danger from the movers' negligence.

Answer to Question 15

(B) Gilda has committed a battery because she intentionally caused an offensive contact to Parker. In order to establish a prima facie case for battery, the following elements must be proved: (i) an act by the defendant that brings about harmful or offensive contact to the plaintiff's person; (ii) intent on the part of the defendant to bring about harmful or offensive contact to the plaintiff's person; and (iii) causation. Certainly a reasonable person of ordinary sensibilities would consider contact with the gas to be offensive. The defendant is liable not only for "direct" contact, but also "indirect" contact; *i.e.,* it will be sufficient if she sets in motion a force that brings about harmful or offensive contact to the plaintiff's person. Thus, even though Gilda did not have direct contact with Parker, she allowed the chemical fumes to pass across the sidewalk and thereby caused the offensive contact to Parker. The fact that she wanted to replicate the class experiment and therefore went to an area with heavy pedestrian traffic evidences her intent to bring about the offensive contact. (A) is incorrect. In order to establish a prima facie case for assault, the following elements must be proved: (i) an act by the defendant creating a reasonable apprehension in plaintiff of immediate harmful or offensive contact to plaintiff's person; (ii) intent on the part of the defendant to bring about in the plaintiff apprehension of immediate harmful or offensive contact with the plaintiff's person; and (iii) causation. Here, Gilda's actions created actual contact but did not create an apprehension of contact on Parker's part; he was evidently not aware of the gas until he came into contact with it. Hence, the applicable tort is battery, not assault. (C) is incorrect. To establish a prima facie case for intentional infliction of emotional distress, the following elements must be proved: (i) an act by defendant amounting to extreme and outrageous conduct; (ii) intent on the part of defendant to cause plaintiff to suffer severe emotional distress, or recklessness as to the effect of defendant's conduct; (iii) causation; and (iv) damages. Actual damages are required. But it is not necessary to prove physical injuries to recover. It is, however, necessary to establish severe emotional distress (*i.e.,* more than a reasonable person could be expected to endure). According to the facts, the effect of the gas was temporary and none of the pedestrians suffered any permanent damage. Furthermore, the facts do not indicate that Parker suffered severe emotional distress. (D) is obviously incorrect, as Gilda has in no way tortiously interfered with the privacy of Parker, who was on a public sidewalk at the time. The tort of privacy includes the following four kinds of wrongs: (i) appropriation by defendant of plaintiff's picture or name for defendant's commercial advantage; (ii) intrusion by defendant upon plaintiff's affairs or seclusion; (iii) publication by defendant of facts placing plaintiff in a false light; and (iv) public disclosures of private facts about the plaintiff by the defendant. The facts do not suggest that Gilda committed any of these four kinds of wrongs.

Answer to Question 16

(A) Parker will prevail because unauthorized use of his picture wherein his face appears highly contorted would be objectionable to a reasonable person. To establish a prima facie case for invasion of privacy based on publication by defendant of facts placing plaintiff in a false light, the following elements must be proved: (i) publication of facts about plaintiff by defendant placing plaintiff in a false light in the public eye; and (ii) the "false light" must be something that would be objectionable to a reasonable person under the circumstances. Publication of the picture, conveying a distorted impression of Parker's physical appearance, would be objectionable to a reasonable person under the circumstances. It makes no difference that Parker is a vain man. This picture would still be objectionable to reasonable persons. Furthermore, Parker's facial contortion created the false impression that he was a grumpy old man. (B) cannot be correct because it is couched in terms of disclosure of private facts about the plaintiff. To establish a prima facie case for invasion of privacy based on public disclosure of private facts about plaintiff, the following elements must be proved: (i) publication or public disclosure by defendant of private information about the plaintiff; and (ii) the matter made public is such that a reasonable person of ordinary sensibilities would object to having it made public. Not only were private facts not disclosed here, but also the question refers to an action for false light publicity. (C) is incorrect. Because Parker was placed in a false light, it makes no difference that the picture was taken on a public sidewalk. An invasion of privacy based on false light can occur on public property as well as private property. (D) is incorrect. The absence of a permanent harm to Parker has no bearing on a privacy action. In an action for invasion of right to privacy, the plaintiff need not plead and prove special damages, providing the elements of a prima facie case are present. In other words, emotional distress and mental anguish are sufficient damages.

Answer to Question 17

(C) Rex will not recover from Matt because Matt, who was under no duty to aid Rex, did not cause Rex's injuries. Rex's action will sound in negligence. The prima facie case for negligence consists of: (i) a duty on the part of the defendant to conform to a specific standard of conduct for the protection of the plaintiff against an unreasonable risk of injury; (ii) a breach of that duty by the defendant; (iii) the breach must be the actual and proximate cause of the plaintiff's injuries; and (iv) damage to the plaintiff's person or property. Generally, there is no legal duty to affirmatively act for the benefit of others. This rule is subject to exception (*e.g.,* when defendant's negligence places another in a position of peril, defendant has a duty to use reasonable care to aid that person). Here, nothing in the facts shows that Matt was under a legal duty to act affirmatively to help Rex. Therefore, by not acting, Matt did not breach any duty to Rex. (Had Matt assisted Rex in a negligent fashion, with such negligence being a cause of Rex's injuries, then liability would ensue; but here, Matt did nothing at all.) Also, Matt's failure to act when he was under no duty to do so did not actually or proximately cause Rex's injuries. Thus, Matt is not liable for Rex's injuries. (A) is incorrect because it would impose upon Matt a duty to act affirmatively to assist Rex merely because Rex was in trouble. As explained above, no such duty exists. (B) is incorrect because, as stated, the law generally does not require someone to help another. Thus, the reasonably prudent person may do exactly what Matt did (*i.e.,* nothing), even if it seems rather hard-hearted. (D) is incorrect for two reasons: (i) it is uncertain that Rex put himself in a position of peril (it is possible that a passerby knocked down the ladder, thus creating the danger to Rex); and (ii) Matt is under no duty to assist Rex regardless of who created the danger (unless, of course, Matt created it). If a third party put Rex in his position of peril, Matt would still not be under a duty to help Rex. Note also that, even assuming that Rex put himself in this position, this would not automatically excuse Matt from liability for Rex's injuries. For example, if Matt had undertaken assistance to Rex, he would be liable for any resulting injuries if they were caused by his ***negligence*** in assisting Rex.

Answer to Question 18

(D) Rex will not recover from Howard because even if Howard was negligent in setting the ladder atop a patch of ice, this negligence did not cause the injury to Rex. As explained in the answer above, a person generally is under no duty to assist another. Therefore, Howard was under no duty to assist Rex. However, having gratuitously undertaken to do so, Howard came under a duty to act as an ordinary, reasonable person while rendering such assistance. Howard breached this duty by setting the ladder atop the patch of ice, thus creating an unreasonable risk that the ladder would slip while Rex was climbing down, causing him injury. However, Howard is not liable for Rex's injuries unless Howard's breach of duty caused those injuries. Before a defendant's conduct can be considered a proximate cause of the plaintiff's injury, it must first be a cause in fact (actual cause) of the injury. An act is the cause in fact of an injury when the injury would not have occurred but for the act. Here, Rex's fall and injuries would not have occurred but for the rotten rung. There is no indication that Howard's negligence in placing the ladder on the ice contributed in any manner to the injuries. If Howard had carefully placed the ladder on a solid, ice-free surface, Rex would have incurred the same injury by stepping on the rotten rung. Therefore, Howard's negligence was not a cause in fact of Rex's injuries. Because the element of causation is missing, Howard will not be liable for the injuries to Rex. (A) is wrong because Howard's negligent placement of the ladder was not the cause of Rex's injury. Rather, Rex fell as a result of stepping on the rotten rung. Thus, it cannot be said that Howard's negligent conduct caused the injury to Rex. (B) is wrong because Howard's assumption of the duty to aid Rex does not render Howard absolutely liable for all injuries incurred. As explained, Howard did assume the duty to act reasonably in aiding Rex, and Howard did breach his duty by placing the ladder on ice. Nevertheless, this breach of duty did not cause the injuries to Rex. Thus, if Howard's negligence did not cause the injury to Rex, Howard cannot be held liable, even if he was negligent. Regarding (C), while it is true that it was foreseeable that Rex would be injured as a result of Howard's negligent conduct (*i.e.,* that the ladder would slip on the ice causing Rex to fall and be injured), it is also true that Rex was not injured as a result of Howard's negligence. Howard cannot be held liable for something that was not in any way caused by his negligent conduct. Therefore, (C) is incorrect.

Answer to Question 19

(C) The disclosure of public facts about the plaintiff cannot be the basis of an invasion of privacy lawsuit. There are four categories of invasion of privacy: (i) appropriation of plaintiff's picture or name for defendant's commercial advantage; (ii) intrusion upon plaintiff's affairs or seclusion; (iii) publication of facts that place the plaintiff in a false light; and (iv) public disclosure of private facts about plaintiff by defendant. The first category would not be applicable here because the use of a person's name or photo in a newspaper article is not considered a commercial appropriation, in contrast to the use of his name in an advertisement of a product. The second category is inapplicable because the *Herald* gathered its information from public sources and took the picture of the house from a public sidewalk; it did not intrude on the plaintiff's private affairs or seclusion. The third category does not apply because the publication of these facts did not place Pangol in a false light. The fourth category is the most likely basis for Pangol's invasion of privacy action, but it would not succeed because none of the facts published about Pangol could be considered private. The sale price of a piece of property and the identity of the purchaser are matters of public record. A person's occupation would not be considered a private fact, nor would any description of the mansion in the article. Hence, Pangol will not recover against the *Herald* for invasion of privacy. (A) is incorrect. While the fact that Pangol did not consent to publication of the story would prevent the *Herald* from using the defense of consent, Pangol has not established a prima facie case here. The fact that the mansion is now Pangol's "private residence" does not make information about it "private facts." (B) is incorrect because the fact that a reasonable person would be upset by publication of the story is just one element of the prima facie case for the public disclosure action. The disclosure must also have been of private facts about the plaintiff; this element is not satisfied here. (D) is wrong because the fact that the story is true is not a defense to invasion of privacy actions. Public disclosure of private facts may subject the defendant to liability even if the facts are true.

Answer to Question 20

(D) Merchant is not liable for the tortious actions of Bill because Bill is an independent contractor. When there is a master-servant relationship between a principal and her agent, the master is vicariously liable for torts committed by the servant within the scope of the employment relationship. This is the doctrine of respondeat superior. On the other hand, the general rule is that a principal is not liable for tortious acts of an agent who is an independent contractor. An agent is likely to be an independent contractor if he: (i) is engaged in a distinct business of his own; (ii) controls the manner and method by which he performs his tasks; (iii) is hired to do a particular job; (iv) supplies his own tools and materials; (v) is paid a given amount for the job; and (vi) is hired to do a short-term, specific job. Despite the general rule, a principal can be held liable for the tortious acts of an independent contractor if: (i) the independent contractor is engaged in inherently dangerous activities; or (ii) the principal has a duty that is nondelegable on public policy grounds (*e.g.,* a land occupier's duty to keep her land safe for business invitees). Also, a principal can be held liable for her own negligence in selecting an incompetent independent contractor. Here, Merchant hired Bill, who is engaged in his own painting business (along with Joe), to perform one particular job (painting Merchant's furniture store). From the facts, it appears that Bill and Joe provide their own materials and control the manner and method in which they do their job. Therefore, Bill is, with respect to Merchant, an independent contractor rather than a servant. Bill was not engaged in an inherently dangerous activity, nor is there any nondelegable duty of Merchant involved. In addition, it does not appear that Merchant was negligent in hiring Bill. Thus, the general rule applies, and Merchant is not liable for the tortious conduct of Bill. (A) is wrong because recovery against Merchant on the theory of respondeat superior would require that either: (i) Bill was a servant of Merchant; or (ii) one of the exceptions to the rule of no vicarious liability for torts committed by independent contractors would be applicable. As has been explained above, neither of these factors is present here. (B) is wrong because the frolic-detour distinction is inapplicable to these facts. For a master to be vicariously liable the tort must have occurred within the scope of the servant's employment. To determine whether the tortious acts occurred within the scope of employment, a distinction is made based on whether the tortious conduct was committed while the servant was on a frolic or on a detour. (Small deviations from a master's directions (a detour) fall within the scope of employment, while major deviations (a frolic) fall outside the scope.) Because Bill was not a servant of Merchant, there is no "scope of employment" issue to be analyzed. Thus, it is meaningless to speak of Bill as having been on a frolic or detour. (C) is wrong because, as explained regarding (A) above, the principal is vicariously liable only if the agent is a servant or the exceptions for independent contractors apply. Neither of these is the case here. (C) is virtually a rephrasing of (A).

Answer to Question 21

(D) Di can recover if Bill was acting within the scope of the partnership business when he drove negligently. Vicarious liability for the conduct of another can arise in partnership and joint venture situations. Each member of the partnership is vicariously liable for the tortious conduct of another partner committed in the scope of the partnership's affairs. As with respondeat superior situations, if the tortfeasor has gone off on a frolic of his own, he is no longer acting within the scope of the partnership and the other partners will not be liable. On the other hand, a minor deviation from the partnership activity will not take it outside of the scope of the partnership's affairs. Here, Joe and Bill are partners in their painting business. If, as choice (D) indicates, Bill's detour to the library did not take his activity outside the scope of the partnership's affairs, Joe is vicariously liable simply because of his status as a partner. (A) is incorrect even though it is a true statement. Generally, an automobile owner is not vicariously liable for the tortious conduct of another driving his automobile (although statutes in some states alter this rule). An automobile owner can be held liable for his ***own negligence*** in entrusting the car to a driver. Here, there is apparently no statute that would render Joe (the car owner) vicariously liable for Bill's tortious conduct while driving Joe's car. Therefore, the general rule of no vicarious liability will apply. The other possible ground of recovery against Joe based on Bill's use of his car would be his own negligence in entrusting the car to Bill. There is no indication that Bill was a careless driver, or that Joe had any other reason to suspect that entrusting the car to Bill posed an unreasonable risk of danger to others. Consequently, Joe was not negligent in lending his car to Bill. Nevertheless, this is not a good choice because it overlooks the fact that Joe could be vicariously liable to Di because of his status as Bill's partner, as under the circumstances indicated in (D). (B) is incorrect because Bill's status as an independent contractor is irrelevant to this question. As detailed in the answer to the preceding question, Bill is, with respect to Merchant, an independent contractor. However, Bill is a partner rather than an independent contractor as to Joe. Since this question concerns Di and Joe, and has nothing to do with Merchant, Bill's status as to Merchant is irrelevant and would not save Joe from liability. (C) is a true statement (a bailor is not vicariously liable for the torts of his bailee). However, (C) is incorrect because it does not take into account the status of Bill and Joe as partners. It is because of their partnership status rather than their bailor-bailee status that Di might be able to recover.

Answer to Question 22

(D) Sandra is not strictly liable to Pedro because Sandra is not a commercial supplier of tires. Pedro's lawsuit against Sandra is alleging that Sandra is strictly liable for selling him a car with a defective tire. To establish a prima facie case for a defective product based on strict liability, the plaintiff must show: (i) a strict duty owed by a commercial supplier; (ii) breach of that duty by the sale of a product in a defective condition unreasonably dangerous to users; (iii) actual and proximate cause; and (iv) damages. While Pedro might be able to establish the other elements, he cannot establish that Sandra is a commercial supplier of either tires or automobiles. A casual seller who is not in the business of manufacturing, distributing, or selling the product does not owe a strict duty to subsequent purchasers; thus, Pedro will not recover against Sandra. (A) is incorrect because the fact that the tire was defective would establish breach of duty only if Sandra were a commercial supplier. Since she is only a casual seller, she has not breached a strict duty to Pedro. (B) is incorrect because Sandra's failure to discover the defect, even if negligent, has no relevance to whether she has a duty in strict liability. (C) is incorrect because misuse that is reasonably foreseeable, such as exceeding the posted speed limits, is not a defense to a strict products liability action. If Sandra were in breach of a strict duty owed to Pedro, Pedro's conduct would not preclude his recovery.

Answer to Question 23

(D) Hawker misrepresented a material fact regarding the hot dogs and if Vic justifiably relied on the misrepresentation, Vic will recover. A prima facie case of misrepresentation consists of: (i) a misrepresentation by the defendant; (ii) scienter; (iii) an intent to induce the plaintiff to rely on the misrepresentation; (iv) causation (*i.e.*, actual reliance on the misrepresentation); (v) justifiable reliance by the plaintiff on the misrepresentation; and (vi) damages. The misrepresentation must be of a material past or present fact. Although there is no general duty to disclose a material fact, if a defendant speaks and his utterance deceives the plaintiff, he will be under a duty to inform the plaintiff of the true facts. Scienter is present where the defendant made the representation knowing it to be false or with reckless disregard as to its truth or falsity. Actual reliance is shown where the plaintiff proves that the misrepresentation played a substantial part in inducing him to act as he did. The reliance must be "justifiable" but, as a practical matter, the plaintiff's reliance on representations of fact is almost always justified. (It is only where the facts are obviously false that reliance will be deemed not justified.) A plaintiff is not required to investigate the truth of the defendant's representation of fact. Finally, the plaintiff must have suffered actual pecuniary loss as a result of his reliance on the false statement. Here, Hawker made a misrepresentation to Vic when he told him that the hot dogs contained more beef than Austria hot dogs, when in fact Ballgame hot dogs contained no beef at all. Because Hawker knew that his statement was false, the statement was made with scienter. Hawker made the statement intending to induce Vic to buy the hot dogs in reliance on Hawker's representations as to the quality of the hot dogs. Vic actually relied on the statement because it played a substantial part in inducing him to purchase the hot dogs. Vic's reliance on Hawker's representation of fact was justified since it seemed reasonable to believe the sales representative's representations of fact and there is no general duty to investigate. Damages were incurred, in that Vic was fined $1,000 and he paid for hot dogs that were worth less than what was represented to him. Thus, Vic can establish the elements of a prima facie case for misrepresentation, and he will prevail against Hawker. (A) is wrong because (as stated above) a plaintiff is not under a duty to investigate the truth of a defendant's representation of fact. Thus, Vic's reliance on Hawker's statement was justified. (B) is wrong because reliance on a representation of fact is almost always justified. In this case, Hawker made a statement of fact concerning the beef content of the hot dogs. Although this statement was false, it was not obviously false, and Vic's reliance was justified. (C) is quite simply a fabrication of a legal principle. There is no such thing as "misrepresentation per se." A finding of misrepresentation requires proof of the necessary elements, rather than a mere showing of violation of federal regulations.

Answer to Question 24

(C) Myrna can recover for the unauthorized use of her picture for Vic's commercial advantage. There are four branches of the tort of invasion of privacy: (i) appropriation of the plaintiff's picture or name for the defendant's commercial advantage; (ii) intrusion upon plaintiff's affairs or seclusion; (iii) publication of facts that place plaintiff in a false light; and (iv) public disclosure of private facts about plaintiff. Of these four branches the only one applicable to these facts is the first. To establish a prima facie case for this type of invasion of privacy, a plaintiff need only prove the unauthorized use by the defendant of the plaintiff's picture or name for the defendant's commercial advantage. Generally, liability is limited to the use of the plaintiff's picture or name in connection with the promotion or advertisement of a product or service. Vic has used Myrna's picture to promote the sale of hot dogs. Myrna did not in any way consent to this use by Vic of her picture. Therefore, the elements that Myrna needs to prove are present, and she will prevail. (D) is wrong because it implies that if Vic had reasonably, but mistakenly, believed that use of the poster was authorized, Myrna would not prevail. However, mistake (even if reasonable) as to whether consent was given is not a valid defense. Thus, Myrna will prevail regardless of whether Vic was reasonably justified in believing the poster was authorized. (A) is wrong because Myrna's status as a public figure is irrelevant to this type of privacy tort. Public figure status could affect other types of invasion of privacy (*e.g.,* publication of facts placing the plaintiff in a false light and public disclosure of private facts about the plaintiff) if the published matter was of legitimate public interest. If so, the plaintiff would have to establish that the defendant acted with malice (*i.e.,* with knowledge of falsity or reckless disregard for the truth). If Myrna's action were based on one of these other types of privacy tort, her status as a public figure might be relevant. However, public figure status does not alter the elements needed to establish a case for unauthorized use of Myrna's picture, nor does it impose upon her the necessity of proving malice. (B) is wrong because there is no requirement that the defendant have actually gained a profit from using the picture. Vic is liable for this tort simply because he used Myrna's picture without her permission to promote and advertise the hot dogs.

Answer to Question 25

(A) ConstructCo will have breached its duty of ordinary care to Peter if it could have removed the piles of dirt at minimal cost. Most courts impose upon a landowner the duty to exercise ordinary care to avoid reasonably foreseeable risk of harm to children caused by artificial conditions on his property. Under the general rule, to assess this special duty upon the owner or occupier of land in regard to children on his property, the plaintiff must show the following: (i) there is a dangerous condition present on the land of which the owner is or should be aware; (ii) the owner knows or should know that young persons frequent the vicinity of this dangerous condition; (iii) the condition is likely to cause injury (*i.e.,* is dangerous) because of the child's inability to appreciate the risk; and (iv) the expense of remedying the situation is slight compared with the magnitude of the risk. If all of these elements are present, Peter has a cause of action under the "attractive nuisance" doctrine. Under these facts, the mounds of dirt sloping down toward the highway constituted a dangerous condition and the construction superintendent was aware that children were sledding down the mounds of dirt. The facts also state that he realized that this condition may be dangerous to the children. Thus, if ConstructCo could have removed the dirt at minimal cost, the expense of remedying the situation would have been slight compared to the magnitude of the risk, making ConstructCo liable under the attractive nuisance doctrine. (B) is incorrect because the mounds of dirt did not constitute a public nuisance, which is unrelated to the attractive nuisance doctrine. A public nuisance is an act that unreasonably interferes with the health, safety, or property rights of the community. The dirt did not unreasonably interfere with the safety rights of the community. The dirt was piled on a site next to a highway and did not create an obstruction for pedestrians or drivers. (C) is incorrect because even though Peter was a trespasser, infant trespassers come within an exception to the standard duty of care owed by an owner or occupier of land to a trespasser for artificial conditions. Thus, Peter's status as a trespasser does not prevent his recovery. (D) is incorrect because even though Peter read the sign, the sign did not alert Peter to the danger that the piles of dirt created, and there is no other evidence that he was aware of and appreciated the danger of sliding onto the highway. For assumption of the risk to be a defense, the plaintiff must be *aware of the risk* and then voluntarily assume that risk.

Answer to Question 26

(B) Paul's best argument is that his mother's refusal to take him to a physician, if deemed to be negligent, is not imputed to him. A plaintiff has a duty to take reasonable steps to mitigate damages. Thus, in personal injury cases, there is a duty to seek appropriate treatment to effect healing and to prevent aggravation. Failure to do so will preclude recovery for any particular item of injury that occurs or is aggravated *due to the failure to mitigate* (this is the avoidable consequences rule). Thus, Paul's not consulting a doctor could limit his recovery to the damages for the original injury only. However, Paul is a child and his mother decided not to seek medical help for Paul. If this was negligence on her part, is it imputed to Paul? In actions against a third party, a parent's negligence is not imputed to the child. Thus, the negligence of Paul's mother will not be imputed to Paul, and so Paul should receive a full recovery for *all* of his injuries. On the other hand, if Paul uses the argument in (A), then he will probably not recover for the aggravated injuries. (A) presents an accurate statement of law, relative to the effect of the avoidable consequences rule. If Paul avails himself of the avoidable consequences rule, then he will succeed in salvaging merely his right to recover for the original injury. Thus, (A) does not give Paul a chance to recover for *all* of his injuries, as does (B). (C) is incorrect because it directly contradicts the rule that a plaintiff must take all reasonable measures to mitigate damages after the original injury is inflicted. (D) is incorrect because it misstates the concept of "taking your victim as you find him." This concept refers to the *physical or mental condition of the victim* at the time of the injury (*e.g.,* the "eggshell skull plaintiff"); it does not cover the victim's relationship to others and their attitudes or actions. Thus, the attitude of a victim's mother toward physicians is not included in "taking your victim as you find him."

Answer to Question 27

(A) Paul may have a personal injury action against the adult for negligence because throwing the ball into the road would expose the children to an unreasonable risk of harm. A prima facie case for negligence consists of: (i) a duty on the part of the defendant to conform to a specific standard of conduct for the protection of the plaintiff against an unreasonable risk of injury; (ii) a breach of that duty by the defendant; (iii) the breach of duty was the actual and proximate cause of the plaintiff's injury; and (iv) damage to the plaintiff's person or property. A person is under a legal duty to act as an ordinary, prudent, reasonable person. It is presumed that an ordinary, prudent, reasonable person will take precautions against creating unreasonable risks of injury to other persons. Thus, if the defendant's conduct creates an unreasonable risk of injury to persons in the position of the plaintiff, then the general duty of care extends from the defendant to the plaintiff. Here, throwing the ball into the road created an unreasonable risk of injury to Paul and his friend. The adult knew, or in the exercise of reasonable care should have known, that one or both of the children would run after the ball, thus exposing them to the danger of being hit by a car. Thus, the general duty of ordinary, reasonable care extended from the adult to Paul, and the adult breached this duty by throwing the ball into the road. This breach actually caused Paul's injury because Paul would not have been in the road but for the adult throwing the ball there. The breach also proximately caused Paul's injury, despite the fact that the driver was possibly negligent in not watching the road. The driver's conduct was an independent intervening force; however, it was a foreseeable intervening force that brought about a foreseeable result, because the adult's act of throwing the ball into the road created a foreseeable risk that Paul would be hit by a car when chasing after the ball. Thus, the driver's conduct will not cut off the liability of the adult. The final element of a prima facie case for negligence is made out by the damage to Paul's person. (B) is wrong because the adult did not intend to bring about the harmful contact suffered by Paul. The intent required for intentional tort liability is present when either: (i) the actor's goal in acting is to bring about the consequences of his conduct; or (ii) the actor knows with substantial certainty that such consequences will result. Here, it does not appear that the adult's goal in throwing the ball into the street was to cause Paul to be hit by a car, nor did the adult know with substantial certainty that such harm would befall Paul. Therefore, the adult did not possess the intent required for intentional tort liability. (C) and (D) are both incorrect for the reason that one from whom contribution is sought or against whom indemnity is sought must be originally liable to the plaintiff. Contribution allows a defendant who is required to pay more than his share of damages to have a claim against other jointly liable parties for the excess. Indemnity involves shifting the entire loss between or among tortfeasors. If, as (C) and (D) state, Paul has no action against the adult, then the adult cannot be considered a joint tortfeasor with Dev. Consequently, Dev would have no right of contribution against the adult, nor would he be entitled to indemnification from the adult.

Answer to Question 28

(D) If Prudence knew that the bulge was dangerous, The Tyre Centre will be able to assert as a defense to strict liability that Prudence voluntarily assumed the risk. Assumption of risk is a valid defense to a products liability action based on strict liability. To have assumed the risk, either expressly or impliedly, the plaintiff must have known of the risk and voluntarily assumed it. If Prudence knew that the bulge was dangerous, her conduct was unreasonable when she continued to inflate the tire. By voluntarily proceeding with inflating the tire in the face of a known risk, she voluntarily assumed the risk. (A) is incorrect because it implies a necessity to show fault in terms of improper installation. To establish a prima facie case in products liability based on strict liability in tort, the following elements must be proved: (i) strict duty owed by a commercial supplier; (ii) breach of that duty; (iii) actual and proximate cause; and (iv) damages. To establish breach of duty for a strict liability action, the plaintiff need not prove that the defendant was at fault in selling or producing a defective product—only that the product in fact is so defective as to be "unreasonably dangerous." Thus, the element of negligence need not be proved in a strict liability case. (B) is incorrect. Even if it is a true statement, it is not a defense. If Prudence acted contrary to the reasonable person standard, at most she can be deemed contributorily negligent. Ordinary contributory negligence, however, is not a defense to strict liability in a jurisdiction following traditional contributory negligence rules. (C) is incorrect for the same reason as (A). (C) implies a necessity to show fault in terms of failure to discover the defect. A retailer, however, may be liable in strict liability even if it has no opportunity to inspect the manufacturer's product before selling it. Again, negligence concepts are irrelevant.

Answer to Question 29

(D) If the tire was defective at the time it left the Rubko of Akron manufacturing plant, Prudence will prevail against Rubko in a strict liability action because its defective condition made it unreasonably dangerous to users. To establish a prima facie case in products liability based on strict liability in tort, the following elements must be proved: (i) strict duty owed by a commercial supplier; (ii) breach of that duty; (iii) actual and proximate cause; and (iv) damages. To hold the commercial supplier strictly liable for a product defect, the product must be expected to, and must in fact, reach the user or consumer without substantial change in the condition in which it is supplied. Privity is not required; strict liability extends to suppliers in the distributive chain as well as to the ultimate buyer. To establish breach of duty for a strict liability action, the plaintiff need prove only that the product in fact is so defective as to be "unreasonably dangerous." To prove actual cause, the plaintiff must trace the harm suffered to a defect in the product that existed when the product left the defendant's control. As a manufacturer of tires, Rubko was a commercial supplier. The tire reached Prudence without substantial change in the condition in which it was supplied. The facts suggest that the tire was defectively manufactured since Prudence did not experience a problem with her other rear tire and there is no suggestion that other tires made by Rubko exhibited similar dangerous propensities. When a product emerges from a manufacturing process not only different from the other products, but also more dangerous than if it had been made the way it should have been, the product may be so "unreasonably dangerous" as to be defective because of the manufacturing process. To satisfy the causation element, Prudence must show that the tire was defective when it left the Rubko plant. (A) is incorrect. The negligent failure of an intermediary such as The Tyre Centre to discover the defect does not void the manufacturer's strict liability. Thus, if The Tyre Centre negligently failed to inspect the tire, such conduct would not constitute a superseding cause that would prevent a showing of proximate causation between the injury and the manufacturer's actions. Only if the intermediary's conduct becomes something more than ordinary foreseeable negligence would its behavior become a superseding cause. (B) is incorrect for the same reason as (A). While improper installation of the tire would constitute negligence on the part of The Tyre Centre, it would not be a superseding cause that would break the causal connection between Prudence's injury and the manufacturer's actions. (C) is incorrect. Rubko's failure to notify The Tyre Centre is irrelevant to its strict liability. Such failure to notify is relevant to the negligence concept of breach of duty, but in a strict liability case, negligence need not be proved.

Answer to Question 30

(A) If it was reasonably foreseeable that Barbara's remark would be overheard, the publication requirement for a defamation action will be satisfied. To establish a prima facie case for defamation, the following elements must be proved: (i) defamatory language on the part of the defendant; (ii) the defamatory language must be "of or concerning" the plaintiff (*i.e.,* it must identify the plaintiff to a reasonable reader, listener, or viewer); (iii) publication of the defamatory language by the defendant to a third person; and (iv) damage to the reputation of the plaintiff. Barbara's statement constitutes defamatory language because it adversely affects Albert's reputation by attacking his competency. Furthermore, a reasonable listener would understand that the defamatory language referred to Albert. The publication requirement is satisfied when there is a communication to a third person who understands it. If it was reasonably foreseeable that Barbara's defamatory statement would be overheard by Camille, and Camille has overheard and understood the statement, then the publication element is satisfied. Finally, damage to reputation is presumed because the statement is slander per se: it disparages Albert's abilities in his business or profession. (B) is incorrect. Albert will prevail even if Barbara did not know that her remark would be overheard as long as it was reasonably foreseeable that it could be overheard. The communication to the third person may be made either intentionally or negligently and (B) effectively states that Albert can prevail only if Barbara's communication was intentional. (C) is incorrect because there in fact was a publication, *i.e.,* there was a communication, albeit not intentionally made, to Camille, who would reasonably have understood it to be defamatory. (D) is incorrect because there is no requirement that the third party be a party to the conversation—the third party need only be a reader, listener, or viewer.

Answer to Question 31

(A) Even if Trucko can assert the defense of private necessity, he would still be liable for the damage to Paget's lawn. Trucko's entrance onto Paget's land constituted a prima facie case of trespass to land. The following elements must be proved for trespass to land: (i) an act of physical invasion of plaintiff's real property by defendant; (ii) intent on defendant's part to bring about a physical invasion of the plaintiff's real property; and (iii) causation. Intent to trespass is not required—intent to enter on the land is sufficient. Thus, even though Trucko did not intend to trespass onto Paget's land, he did intend to drive onto it to avoid hitting Crasher. Under the defense of private necessity, however, a person may interfere with the property of another where it is reasonably and apparently necessary to avoid threatened injury and where the threatened injury is substantially more serious than the invasion that is undertaken to avert it. Where the act is solely to benefit any person or protect any property from destruction or serious injury (rather than to benefit the public as a whole), the defense is qualified; *i.e.,* the actor must pay for any injury he causes. Here, Trucko was acting to avoid serious injury. However, he must pay for the damage to the lawn. (D) is therefore incorrect because negligence concepts are irrelevant to an action based on trespass to land. (B) is incorrect because a private nuisance is a substantial and unreasonable interference with another private individual's use and enjoyment of his land. Even if Trucko interfered with Paget's use of his lawn, the interference was neither substantial nor unreasonable. (C) is incorrect because there is no public nuisance in this case. A public nuisance unreasonably interferes with the health, safety, or property rights of the community. Trucko's actions affected one individual rather than the community.

Answer to Question 32

(A) If winds of hurricane force were not foreseeable, Ekter will prevail since he did not breach a duty of care to Plimsoll when he chose the design with a 20% safety margin. To establish a prima facie case for negligence, the following elements must be proved: (i) the existence of a duty on the part of the defendant to conform to a specific standard of conduct for the protection of the plaintiff against an unreasonable risk of injury; (ii) breach of that duty by the defendant; (iii) the breach of the duty by the defendant was the actual and proximate cause of the plaintiff's injury; and (iv) damage to the plaintiff's person or property. As a guest of the hotel, Plimsoll is a foreseeable plaintiff and therefore Ekter owed a duty of care to him. The issue under these facts is whether Ekter breached his duty of care to Plimsoll. To establish a breach of duty, Plimsoll must show that Ekter acted unreasonably. As a general rule a person is not required to take precautions against events that cannot reasonably be foreseen. Thus, if the storm was not foreseeable, Ekter's choice of design cannot be viewed as unreasonable and therefore he cannot be charged with a breach of duty. (B) is incorrect because an act of God may be a superseding intervening force that breaks the chain of proximate causation only if it is unforeseeable. (B) implies that the storm would absolve Ekter of liability regardless of whether it was foreseeable. However, even though the storm may be an act of God, if it was foreseeable, Ekter would have breached his duty of care to Plimsoll and would be an actual and proximate cause of Plimsoll's injury. (C) is incorrect. The higher duty of care owed to hotel guests runs from the hotel to the guest and not from the engineering firm to the guest. Because Plimsoll is suing Ekter rather than the hotel, any such special duty is inapplicable. (D) is incorrect. To establish strict tort liability, the plaintiff must prove that the defendant is a commercial supplier of a product. Ekter, however, provided a service of designing a hotel; since he is not a commercial supplier of a product, he cannot be held strictly liable.

Answer to Question 33

(C) If Ekter acted in the manner of a reputable member of his profession, he will not have breached the duty of care owing to Hotelier International. As the first two elements of its prima facie negligence action, Hotelier must establish the existence of a duty on the part of Ekter to conform to a specific standard of conduct for the protection of Hotelier against an unreasonable risk of injury, and a breach of that duty. A professional, such as an engineer, is required to possess and exercise the knowledge and skill of a member of the profession in good standing in similar localities. If Ekter exercised such knowledge and skill, he will have satisfied the applicable standard of care. (A) is incorrect. To have assumed the risk, either expressly or impliedly, the plaintiff must have known of the risk and voluntarily assumed it. Hotelier did not assume the risk of this damage because it could not have known of the risk. It merely reviewed and accepted the plans, relying on Ekter's professional opinion. (B) is incorrect because there is no general standard subjecting innkeepers to strict liability and, in any event, this has no bearing on Ekter's liability. Hotelier will prevail if it can establish a prima facie case for negligence. (D) is incorrect. While it may be true that the placement of the pylons resulted in damage to the hotel, there is no indication that Ekter breached a duty of care to Hotelier by choosing this particular design of placement.

Answer to Question 34

(A) A shoplifting detention that exceeds a reasonable period of time is not privileged and will constitute a false imprisonment. For a shopkeeper to detain a suspected shoplifter without liability for false imprisonment, all of the following conditions must be satisfied: (i) there must be a reasonable belief as to the fact of theft; (ii) the detention must be conducted in a reasonable manner and only nondeadly force can be utilized; and (iii) the detention must only be for a reasonable time period and only for the purpose of making an investigation. Suzie did have reasonable cause to believe that Porphyry had stolen the coat, and the initial detention appears to have been conducted in a reasonable manner. Under these facts, however, the privilege was lost by the length of detention. Dagobert could have discovered very quickly that the coat was not stolen if he had examined the label immediately, or if he had allowed Porphyry to explain. Also, his questions as to Porphyry's age and marital status were not asked for purposes of investigation. As a result, the detention was not for a reasonable time. (B) and (C) are true statements; however, all three conditions must be satisfied for the privilege to apply and the reasonable time period requirement was not satisfied here. (D) is incorrect. A master will be vicariously liable for tortious acts committed by its servant if the tortious acts occur within the scope of the employment relationship. While generally the intentional tortious conduct of servants is not within the scope of employment, a master will be liable for these torts in certain situations, such as where the servant intentionally chooses a wrongful means to promote the master's business. Such is the case here. Dagobert, as the store detective, was furthering the store's business and acting within the scope of his employment when he stopped Porphyry. His intentional tortious conduct in falsely imprisoning Porphyry will make the store liable.

Answer to Question 35

(B) Pons should recover $70,000 from Daley. Under a comparative negligence system, a contributorily negligent plaintiff is allowed to recover a percentage of her damages. The plaintiff's damages are reduced according to her proportionate share of the fault. Although the various jurisdictions differ as to the levels of a plaintiff's negligence that are allowable before her right to recover is cut off, all comparative negligence states would allow recovery when a plaintiff's negligence is only 30% and the defendant's negligence is 70%. Thus, Pons can recover 70% of her total of $100,000 in damages, leaving her with a recovery of $70,000. As a general rule, damages are not reduced or mitigated by reason of benefits received by the plaintiff from other sources, such as health insurance. Therefore, the $20,000 paid by Pons's insurance company will not reduce the $70,000 in damages to which she is entitled. (A) is incorrect because it fails to reflect the reduction in damages required under comparative negligence. Because Pons was 30% negligent, she cannot recover the entire $100,000. (C) is incorrect because it is derived from an initial reduction of damages by the amount of the insurance payments ($100,000 minus $20,000, leaving $80,000). This $80,000 figure is then reduced by the 30% negligence of Pons, leaving an amount of $56,000. However, as noted above, the insurance payments are not allowed to reduce damages. Thus, the 30% reduction is made from the figure of $100,000, not from $80,000. Similarly, (D) is incorrect because it is derived from a reduction of the $70,000 proportionate recovery by the $20,000 insurance payment.

Answer to Question 36

(D) Flowers will not prevail because he knew that Sluggo was drunk. Flowers assumed the risk of injury when he allowed Sluggo to drive him home. Implied assumption of risk requires that Flowers knew of the risk and voluntarily chose to encounter it, which is indicated here. Assumption of the risk is a complete defense to a claim based on negligence in a jurisdiction following traditional contributory negligence rules. (A) and (B) are therefore incorrect because Sluggo can claim assumption of risk as a defense. (C) is incorrect because negligence of other drivers is foreseeable and therefore is not a superseding cause that would cut off Sluggo's liability for his negligence. The negligence of the other driver cannot be used as an excuse for Sluggo's negligence; both drivers were actual and proximate causes of Flowers's injury.

Answer to Question 37

(B) Because Mexzona does not have a dramshop statute, Beerman will not be liable for the injuries caused to Perkins by Donner, the intoxicated vendee. At common law, no liability was imposed on vendors of intoxicating beverages for injuries resulting from the vendee's intoxication, whether the injuries were sustained by the vendee or by a third person as a result of the vendee's conduct.

Many states, in order to avoid this common law rule, have enacted "dramshop acts." Such acts create a cause of action in favor of any third person injured by the intoxicated vendee. Without a dramshop act, Beerman will not be vicariously liable. (A) is incorrect because it implies that Beerman would be vicariously liable if Donner was not reckless. Without a dramshop act, however, there can be no vicarious liability imposed on Beerman regardless of whether Donner's actions are characterized as reckless or simply negligent. (C) is incorrect because a dramshop act exists to *impose* liability rather than *limit* liability of a tavernkeeper. (D) is incorrect. While several courts have imposed liability on tavernkeepers even in the absence of a dramshop act, this liability is based on ordinary negligence principles (the foreseeable risk of serving a minor or obviously intoxicated adult) rather than vicarious liability. The question here is attempting to establish liability based on vicarious liability principles rather than negligence principles. Thus, without a dramshop act, Beerman cannot be vicariously liable for any personal injuries caused by Donner.

Answer to Question 38

(D) Paola will not recover in a suit for battery because Dixon's contact did not constitute a harmful or offensive contact. In order to establish a prima facie case for battery, the following elements must be proved: (i) an act by the defendant that brings about harmful or offensive contact to the plaintiff's person; (ii) intent on the part of the defendant to bring about harmful or offensive contact to the plaintiff's person; and (iii) causation. Judged by this standard, Dixon's conduct in trying to keep Paola from falling in a crowded bus would not be harmful or offensive. Contact is deemed "offensive" if the plaintiff has not expressly or impliedly consented to it. Consent may be implied from custom, conduct, or words, or by law. Under these facts the consent would be inferred as a matter of usage or custom. A person is presumed to consent to the ordinary contacts of daily life, which would include contact resulting from assistance to a fellow passenger in a crowded bus. (A) and (B) are incorrect. Even if Dixon intended to put his arm around Paola's waist or touched Paola without her permission, the touching was not harmful or offensive and therefore Dixon cannot be deemed to have committed a battery. (C) is incorrect. Even if Dixon's putting his arm around Paola's waist was not by accident, Dixon would not be liable for battery because under the circumstances the touching was not harmful or offensive.

Answer to Question 39

(C) Nancy will prevail because Marisa's negligence increased the risk of criminal conduct by a third party. Criminal acts and intentional torts of third persons are foreseeable independent intervening forces if the defendant's negligence created a foreseeable risk that they would occur. Here, Marisa's failure to lock the door created a risk of burglary; hence, the burglary does not cut off the agency's liability for Marisa's negligence. (A) is wrong because there is nothing in the facts to indicate that Nancy waived her right to bring tort claims against the agency. (B) is wrong because the burglary was not a superseding cause of the loss; it was within the increased risk caused by Marisa's negligence. (D) is incorrect because she reentered for purposes related to her employment and therefore was not a trespasser.

Answer to Question 40

(C) Pauline cannot make out a case for battery because she did not experience an offensive touching. To make out a prima facie case for battery, the plaintiff must show an intentional act by the defendant that caused harmful or offensive contact to the plaintiff's person. Here, nothing indicates that Pauline was touched in any way; thus, (C) is correct. (A) is incorrect because injury is not an element of battery; battery can be established even absent a showing of injury or damages. (B) is incorrect because if the elements of battery were present, the physician-patient privilege would not protect Donald here because Pauline did not impliedly consent to the taping. When a patient consents to a doctor's treatment, she impliedly consents to all necessary touching that goes along with the treatment. However, when the doctor goes beyond the scope of the acts consented to and does something substantially different, the defense of consent is no longer available. Here, Pauline consented to talk with Donald, but that is substantially different from agreeing to be the subject of an experiment. Thus, if taping Pauline were a battery, Donald could not rely on implied consent to relieve him of liability. (D) is incorrect because a benevolent motive is not a defense to a battery. If the other elements of battery were present, the fact that the battery occurred to foster medical research would not be a defense—that would allow psychiatrists to physically strike their patients merely to study their reactions!

Answer to Question 41

(B) Roger will recover because the other driver's violation of the statute constituted negligence per se. For a duty created by a criminal statute to replace the more general duty of care, the proponent of the statutory standard must show that (i) he is in a class intended to be protected by the statute, (ii) the statute was designed to prevent the type of harm that was suffered, and (iii) the statutory standards are clearly defined. Here, Roger can establish that the statutory standard regarding speeding should be applied against the other driver because Roger, as a fellow motorist, is in the class intended to be protected by the statute, it was designed to prevent accidents such as that which occurred, and the speed limit was posted. No excuse for violating the statute is present in the facts; thus, violation of the statute establishes negligence per se (*i.e.*, duty and breach of duty). Roger can establish causation and damages (at least property damage), completing the prima facie case. (A) is incorrect because while an applicable statute may establish plaintiff's contributory negligence, the headlight statute does not apply here. Even if the statute were intended to protect all drivers against cars being driven without headlights, it would be very difficult to show that it was designed to prevent rear-end collisions during the day, or that violation of the statute was a cause of Roger's injury. (C) is similarly incorrect; Roger's violation of the headlight statute does not establish contributory negligence. (D) is incorrect because Roger does not need to establish a breach of the general duty of care by the other driver. Here, the speed limit statute's specific duty replaces the more general common law duty of due care, and the other driver's violation of that statute constituted negligence per se.

Answer to Question 42

(C) The residents will not be successful in obtaining injunctive relief against the manufacturer of the insecticide because of the utility of the manufacturer's conduct. In deciding whether to issue an injunction against a nuisance, a court will consider the relative hardships resulting from granting or denying the injunction. Here, it is clear that the virtual destruction of the economy of an entire state must be avoided at the expense of creating foul-smelling fumes for some homeowners. In balancing these respective interests, courts take into account that every person is entitled to use his own land in a reasonable way, considering the neighborhood, the values of the respective properties, the cost to the defendant to eliminate the condition complained of, and the social benefits from allowing the condition to continue. Thus, in balancing the relative hardships, Bugslayers will prevail. The fumes are harmless, the cost to eliminate the fumes would be prohibitive, and Bugslayers has the only plant that produces an insecticide that can kill a pest that otherwise would devastate the rice crop and hence the economy of New Burma. (A) is incorrect. The mere fact that an activity creating a nuisance existed before the plaintiff came within its scope is ordinarily not a defense. The prevailing rule is that, in the absence of a prescriptive right, the defendant may not condemn surrounding premises to endure the nuisance; *i.e.,* the purchaser is entitled to reasonable use or enjoyment of his land to the same extent as any other owner as long as he buys in good faith and not for the sole purpose of a harassing lawsuit. (B) is incorrect. Conduct consistent with a zoning ordinance or other legislative license permits is highly persuasive, but not necessarily conclusive proof that the use was not a nuisance. Thus, even though the area is zoned for commercial and manufacturing activities, courts will still balance the hardships to determine if injunctive relief should issue. (D) is incorrect because even though a method is available to eliminate the smelly fumes, it would be prohibitively expensive and this is only one factor among several that the courts must weigh in determining whether a defendant's conduct is unreasonable.

Answer to Question 43

(B) Gung-Ho would be strictly liable in tort because it should have foreseen that a customer might use the helmet while riding a motorcycle and it failed to provide a warning to customers such as Poleaxe as to such impermissible use of the helmet. To establish a prima facie case in products liability based on strict liability in tort, the following elements must be proved: (i) strict duty owed by a commercial supplier; (ii) breach of that duty; (iii) actual and proximate cause; and (iv) damages. Gung-Ho was a commercial supplier and the helmet reached Poleaxe without substantial change in the condition in which it was supplied. To establish breach of duty for a strict liability action, the plaintiff need not prove that the defendant was at fault in selling or producing a defective product—only that the product in fact is so defective as to be "unreasonably dangerous." Although some products may be safe if used as intended, they may involve an unreasonable danger if used in other ways. Suppliers must anticipate reasonably foreseeable uses even if they are "misuses" of the product. In this case, Gung-Ho should have realized that, by depicting a National Guardsman riding a motorcycle while wearing the helmet, it was implying that the helmet was safe for such use. Although the helmet was clearly intended for combat use, it was reasonably foreseeable that it also might be used while riding a motorcycle (perhaps even while riding around the National Guard base). Thus, Gung-Ho should have included a warning with the box containing the helmet or changed the picture on the box. Either action would have been economically feasible and would have eliminated the reasonable customer expectation that the helmet would be safe for motorcycling. (A) is incorrect because without the requisite warning, Poleaxe would have no reason to believe he was using the helmet for an improper purpose. (C) is incorrect. Sovereign immunity does not apply because a private corporation is being sued, not the government or any agency thereof. Although government contractors may assert the federal government's immunity where the defect arose from government specifications in the design or manufacture of the product, the defect here is unrelated to the helmet's intended use. The defect here is the misleading picture on the box in conjunction with a failure to warn, neither of which had any relation to the government specifications for the product. (D) is incorrect because Gung-Ho's exercise of reasonable care is no defense in a strict liability action if the product is defective.

Answer to Question 44

(D) Wilma will prevail because Kerry intentionally caused an offensive touching. To make out a prima facie case for battery, Wilma need only show an act by Kerry that brings about harmful or offensive contact, intent by Kerry to bring about the contact, and causation. These elements are present here, and no defense is available (provocation is not a defense—insulting words do not give one the privilege to strike another). Therefore, (D) is correct. (A) and (B) are incorrect because, as indicated above, neither actual provocation nor reasonable provocation is a defense to battery. (C) is incorrect because even spontaneous acts are volitional movements, and that is all that is required to meet the "act" requirement. As long as the act is triggered by the conscious mind, it will be considered a volitional movement.

Answer to Question 45

(B) Reedley owed a duty of reasonable care to travelers on highways adjacent to his land, such as Dave. However, if Reedley's employee was not negligent, Reedley would not be liable. If the manager was negligent, Reedley's lack of knowledge would not prevent application of respondeat superior. Thus, (A) is incorrect. There is no strict liability for the use of property unless the activity is abnormally dangerous or ultrahazardous, and archery practice would probably not be classed as such. Thus, (C) is not as good a choice as (B). Merely giving the Scouts permission to use the lot would not establish negligence on the part of Reedley, so (D) is wrong.

Answer to Question 46

(B) Where one is vicariously liable for the torts of another, the former has a right of indemnity against the latter. Here, answers (C) and (D) reach a wrong result, and (A) does not provide any information about the theory upon which Diets recovered against Harris.

Answer to Question 47

(B) Neighbor trespassed onto Hagler's land and took the trees, which belonged to Hagler. However, Hagler is entitled to receive only nominal damages for the act of trespass, since the trespass caused no damage. Hagler is also entitled to receive the value of the trees removed by Neighbor since this amounted to a taking of Hagler's property. (A) and (D) are therefore incorrect. (C) is incorrect because the fact that Neighbor's actions benefited Hagler would not diminish Hagler's right of recovery.

Answer to Question 48

(C) To prevail in an action for battery, Nathaniel must show that Donamae engaged in volitional conduct with knowledge or desire to cause a battery. Here, the gun discharged without any volitional act, and so Nathaniel will lose. (A) is incorrect because even if a gun is considered to be a dangerous instrumentality, that fact is not relevant to a battery action, which is based on intent rather than strict liability. A cat's actions are not imputed to its owner; thus, (B) is incorrect. (D) is incorrect because Nathaniel's status as a trespasser would not necessarily prevent him from prevailing in an action for battery; Donamae did not have a right to use deadly force to protect her property here.

Answer to Question 49

(B) A retailer is strictly liable for injuries caused by a defect in a product sold by that retailer. This is true even if the retailer carefully inspects the product before selling it. (D) is therefore incorrect. (A) is incorrect because the fact that the steering locked is not enough to create liability without evidence that it was the result of a defect in the mower. (C) is incorrect because contributory negligence is not a good defense to strict liability in tort in jurisdictions retaining traditional contributory negligence rules.

Answer to Question 50

(B) The key is realizing that Bystrom is basing his claim on negligence. To recover, he must show that Lawn Co. failed to act reasonably with respect to the mower. (A) is incorrect because it speaks to strict liability in tort, not negligence. (C) is incorrect because there is no privity requirement in a negligence action. (D) is incorrect because Gardner's contributory negligence, assuming it was a cause in fact of the accident, was foreseeable and therefore not a superseding cause. Thus, it would have no bearing on Bystrom's potential recovery. (B) is the only alternative that speaks to the negligence of Lawn Co.

Answer to Question 51

(D) Scott will most likely prevail because he did not intend to frighten Roman onto Tim's property. For Tim to succeed in his trespass suit, he must show that Scott intended to bring about a physical invasion of Tim's property. Scott did not chase Roman onto Tim's yard, nor did Scott intend or know with substantial certainty that Roman would enter onto Tim's yard as a result of Scott's actions. (A) is incorrect because a landowner is not automatically privileged to chase or otherwise cause third persons to enter onto another's land to prevent the commission of a tort against his property. While the landowner may have a qualified defense if the trespass was reasonable and apparently necessary to protect his property from destruction or serious injury, the interference with Tim's property here did not result from necessity. (B) is incorrect because it is not necessary to establish a prima facie case for trespass to land that the defendant personally came onto the land; *e.g.,* trespass exists where the defendant floods the plaintiff's land, throws rocks onto it, or chases third persons upon it. (C) is incorrect because even though Roman made the decision to go over the fence, Scott could still be liable for trespass if Scott acted with the intention of causing Roman to enter upon Tim's land.

Answer to Question 52

(A) Roman will prevail because Tim may not intentionally use a vicious dog to protect only his property. One may use only reasonable force to defend property. A landowner may not use force that will cause death or serious bodily harm. Furthermore, one may not use indirect deadly force such as a trap, spring gun, or vicious dog when such force could not lawfully be directly used, *e.g.,* against a mere trespasser. (B) is incorrect because strict liability in such cases generally is not imposed in favor of undiscovered trespassers against landowners. Trespassers cannot recover for injuries inflicted by the landowner's abnormally dangerous domestic animals in the absence of negligence. (C) is incorrect because a landowner who protects his property from intruders by keeping a vicious watchdog he knows is likely to cause serious bodily harm may be liable even to trespassers for injuries caused by the animal. The liability is based on intentional tort principles: Because the landowner is not entitled to use deadly force in person to protect only property, he also may not use such force indirectly. (D) is incorrect because even if Tim put up warning signs, he could still be liable under intentional tort principles if he intentionally used the dog to protect his property, knowing that the dog is likely to cause serious bodily harm.

Answer to Question 53

(C) Luke's best defense is that he was not negligent. A forced landing is foreseeable, and Luke need not have foreseen the presence of anyone in particular on the ground. Thus, (B) is wrong. (A) is wrong because Luke need not have acted willfully or wantonly to be liable. (D) is wrong because Luke's conduct was the cause in fact of Sally's injury; *i.e.,* Sally would not have been injured but for Luke's landing of the plane. Causation alone is not enough to impose liability; there must also be a breach of duty, and Luke did not breach his duty of reasonable care.

Answer to Question 54

(D) Under the special rules for child trespassers (the attractive nuisance doctrine), a landowner who has reason to anticipate that children are likely to trespass and be injured by an artificial condition is under a duty of reasonable care to eliminate the danger. Sally might qualify under the attractive nuisance doctrine, so her status as a trespasser is not determinative. Thus, (A) is incorrect. There is no strict liability for conditions as described, so (C) is wrong. The doctrine of last clear chance applies to contributory negligence situations, not to insulate one tortfeasor from liability because of the acts of another tortfeasor; thus, (B) is wrong.

Answer to Question 55

(C) Sally will prevail if the mechanics were negligent. There is no strict liability in service transactions, so (D) is wrong. Privity of contract is not required to find liability for negligence, and Sally's presence on the landing field makes her a foreseeable plaintiff, so (A) is wrong. (B) is incorrect because this is not a superseding cause situation; the mechanics' potential negligence would not be cut off by Aerodrome's negligence.

Answer to Question 56

(B) Cause in fact is not a sufficient basis for Richards's liability on these facts, nor would he be liable vicariously for the teenagers' negligence. Thus, (C) and (D) are wrong. (A) is not as good a choice as (B) because the mere fact that they were not his employees does not alone insulate Richards from liability.

Answer to Question 57

(D) Calib will prevail if it reasonably appeared that Adam was about to inflict serious bodily harm to Ben. Deadly force in defense of others is acceptable if the other is being threatened with serious bodily harm; choice (D) presents that situation. (A) is therefore incorrect. (C) is wrong because the fact that Adam started the fight does not give Calib the right to use deadly force. (B) is wrong because it is irrelevant whom Calib thought was the aggressor; if it was apparent that Adam was about to inflict serious bodily harm on Ben, Calib would have the right to intervene.

Answer to Question 58

(C) Ham's duty as possessor of land makes him liable to Neighbor for the damage from the antenna. The fact that an independent contractor may have negligently created the danger does not relieve the duty Ham owes to adjoining landowners. [*See* Restatement (Second) §422] (A) is not correct because respondeat superior refers to an employer-employee relationship; Fixer was an independent contractor. (B) is wrong because no shifting of responsibility was created by the payment under these facts. (D) is wrong because there are not enough facts to establish that Fixer's work was an inherently dangerous activity.

Answer to Question 59

(B) If Fixer could not reasonably foresee that the antenna would fall, then he was not negligent. (A) is wrong because payment does not relieve an independent contractor from liability. (C) is wrong because even if Fixer did do the work under the direction of Ham, he would then be liable along with Ham. (D) is wrong because the location of the antenna would not affect Fixer's liability.

Answer to Question 60

(B)   If the judgment against Ham was based on vicarious liability, Ham will have an indemnity claim against Fixer. One who is vicariously liable for the tort of another has a right of indemnity against the person for whose tortious conduct he is strictly liable. (C) and (D) are, therefore, wrong. (A) is wrong because the absence of conduct by Ham contributing to Neighbor's harm does not by itself establish a basis for Ham's claim against Fixer (it is Ham's status as a nonnegligent *employer* that gives rise to his indemnification claim against his negligent employee), nor does the presence of such conduct necessarily preclude a claim against Fixer (even a negligent defendant can recover contribution against another negligent defendant).

Answer to Question 61

(D)   Bradley did not voluntarily consent to encounter the risk. The defense of assumption of risk generally is not available to a defendant whose negligence would require the plaintiff to forfeit a valuable right (here, the right not to be involuntarily confined) in order to avoid the risk. (A) is wrong, because what Hopson thought has no bearing on the applicability of assumption of a risk. (B) is wrong because mere appreciation of the risk is not sufficient; there must also be voluntary exposure. (C) is wrong because Bradley's plans are irrelevant.

Answer to Question 62

(C)   False imprisonment is an intentional tort requiring that the defendant have the intent to confine. (A) and (B) are therefore wrong, because the intent element is missing. (D) is wrong because negligence is not enough.

Answer to Question 63

(B)   One may act in self-defense not only where there is real danger but also where there is a reasonable appearance of danger. An honest but mistaken belief that Dale was about to shoot would justify the use of deadly force by Aaron if a reasonable person would have acted similarly under those circumstances. Thus, (C) is wrong. The test is an objective one—an honest belief alone is not sufficient. Thus, (A) is incorrect. (D) is wrong because it may incorrectly state the facts, and because it does not resolve whether Aaron had the right to use deadly force.

Answer to Question 64

(C)   When an applicable statute establishes the due care, the defendant's conduct is governed by the special statutory standard rather than the usual "reasonable person" standard. The statute is applicable because Nancy appears to be within the class of persons to be protected and the type of harm that occurred is what the statute was intended to prevent. Thus, (B) is wrong. (A) is wrong because an automobile is not an inherently dangerous instrument. (D) is a misstatement of law.

Answer to Question 65

(B)   Although probably not the proximate cause of her injury, the statutory violation was one of several contributing actual causes of her injury. Hence, (A) and (D) are wrong. (C) is wrong because Nancy's conduct in jogging on the bike path preceded Al's negligence in running the stop sign.

Answer to Question 66

(C) This is the best answer because it precludes applicability of the statute altogether. (A) and (B) assume that the statute imposes a special duty on Nancy but state reasons why breach of the statute did not cause Nancy's injuries. (D) does not state a legally recognized basis for this result.

Answer to Question 67

(B) James certainly is not defamed, nor do the facts indicate that he suffered any type of severe emotional harm. Thus, (A), (C), and (D) are wrong. The only cause of action would be for an invasion of privacy, specifically for commercial appropriation.

Answer to Question 68

(B) The fact that one type of land use was entered into before another is relevant but not conclusive evidence of the reasonableness of the use in a private nuisance action. Hence, (A) is incorrect. (C) is not correct because it is irrelevant what use the neighborhood was put to many years before if the facts show that, subsequently, the neighborhood has changed to another use that would be inconsistent with Earhaus Recording's use of its property. (D) is incorrect because the fact that Astrid was there first is still relevant to the issue of the reasonableness of Earhaus Recording's use of its property.

Answer to Question 69

(D) An excavator near a public road has a duty of due care to protect users of the road from straying and falling in. This duty is satisfied when the excavator has done everything reasonable to protect the open excavation by putting up barriers that are likely to prevent such accidents. Torres Construction may have reasonably protected cars driving on Central Street from falling in the trench, but no real step was taken to prevent pedestrians from falling into the trench at nighttime. Hence, (B) is incorrect. (A) is wrong, because although Clint may have violated the jaywalking statute, this is not the type of injury that these types of statutes are trying to prevent. (C) is not the best answer because all that is required with regard to artificial conditions is that the excavator exercise due care to warn persons of the danger.

Answer to Question 70

(B) A minor child will be held liable for the consequences of his intentional tortious conduct whether or not he is "aware" of the consequences of that conduct. Hence, (A) and (D) are wrong. (C) is a misstatement of the law.

Answer to Question 71

(C) The only basis on which to hold the parents liable here is if they had notice of their child's dangerous tendencies. (C) is a better answer than (D) because it holds out the possibility, not negated by the facts, that Danny's parents were on notice of Danny's tendency to misbehave. (A) misstates the law; in the absence of a statute, parents are not vicariously liable for the torts of their minor children. (B) is wrong because the mere failure to keep Danny in would not by itself amount to negligence with respect to Bernadette.

Answer to Question 72

(C) If a person, because of her wrongful conduct, gets herself into a position from which she must be rescued, that person is liable to the rescuer who suffers injuries while reasonably trying to aid her. (A) is wrong because a rescuer does not "voluntarily" assume the risk where the alternative is to allow the threatened harm to occur. (B) is wrong because although Clara had been pulled back on the roof, the rescue was not "over" until both she and Eldon were safely on the ground again. (D) is not a reason for imposing liability on Clara.

Answer to Question 73

(D) There is nothing in the facts which shows that Duncan did any negligent act that caused Clara to be put into a position of danger. Duncan's radio transmission was a cause of Clara's being up on his roof, but Duncan would not be required to have foreseen that she would go up there or otherwise be held legally at fault for her conduct in this case, so (A) is incorrect. (B) is incorrect because Duncan did not owe a duty to Eldon to take such steps, since he was not legally responsible for Clara's peril. (C) is wrong because an act of rescue is not deemed a voluntary assumption of the risk.

Answer to Question 74

(A) The intentional tortious or criminal conduct of a third person is not a superseding cause of the plaintiff's harm if it is foreseeable. Worker's actions have increased the risk that this criminal conduct will occur, making the theft a *foreseeable* intervening force; hence, Worker is subject to liability. (C) and (D) are, therefore, wrong. (B) is wrong because it does not go far enough toward establishing liability.

Answer to Question 75

(D) Even though Dina may have been a cause of the accident, she is liable only if she was negligent. Thus, (B) is incorrect, and (D) is correct. (A) is incorrect because Dina did not violate the applicable statute. (C) is incorrect because obeying a law does not preclude negligent conduct; *i.e.,* even though she obeyed the traffic laws, she would be liable if she had been negligent in some way (*e.g.,* driving within the speed limit but going too fast on a day when the streets were icy).

Answer to Question 76

(C) Because Dr. Macmillan did nothing to place Parker in a dangerous position, Dr. Macmillan had *no legal responsibility* to render first aid to Parker. Thus, she cannot be held liable for failing to help him. Therefore, (C) is correct, and (B) is wrong. Similarly, if Dr. Macmillan had no duty to render aid, it is immaterial that she would suffer no liability if she did render assistance. Likewise, the fact that she would be immune from liability does not mean that a *duty* to render emergency aid has arisen. Thus, (A) is not the best answer. (D) is a misstatement of the law, because even if Dr. Macmillan is shown to have been aware that Parker would suffer brain damage unless he received prompt medical care, she still would have no legal duty to render assistance.

Answer to Question 77

(A) If Duncan had the requisite intent for assault (creation of reasonable apprehension), that intent is sufficient for battery if contact occurs as the result of Duncan's actions. This is one ramification of the doctrine of transferred intent. (B) is incorrect because mere offensive contact will not suffice for battery if the requisite intent is absent. (C) is incorrect because of the doctrine of transferred intent and the fact that Duncan set in motion the process that resulted in Paine's being struck. (D) is incorrect because Duncan had the requisite intent to commit an intentional tort, making the negligence of a third party irrelevant.

BAR REVIEW

CONSTITUTIONAL LAW QUESTIONS

Question 1

A law of the state of Tenntucky provides that all persons who have been residents of Tenntucky for more than three years shall be entitled to free tuition at state-supported institutions of higher education. It further provides that persons who have resided in Tenntucky for three years or less shall pay the nonresident tuition rate, which is $4,000 per year. Sebastian was a student at Tenntucky State University, and a resident of Tenntucky for a little more than two years. Sebastian was annoyed that he was required to pay tuition and filed a class action suit on behalf of himself and other University students with less than three years' residency in federal district court for a declaratory judgment as to the constitutionality of the Tenntucky statute. In eight months, when the case actually came to trial, Sebastian had been a resident of Tenntucky for more than three years and was not required to pay tuition at the state university. However, Sebastian's case generated a great deal of interest, and a number of amicus curiae briefs were filed with the court, some of them supporting and some opposing Sebastian's position.

Should the state's motion to dismiss the case be granted?

(A) Yes, because Sebastian is now a three-year resident.

(B) Yes, because Sebastian lacks standing.

(C) No, because amicus curiae briefs have been filed.

(D) No, because there is a live controversy.

Question 2

Congress passed a law imposing a 50% excise tax on each pack of cigarettes manufactured for sale in the United States. An amendment was successfully added to the original bill requiring that all proceeds from the tax be used for anti-smoking educational programs in the audio, video, and print media and elsewhere. The amendment also provided for the establishment of federal stop-smoking clinics funded through the excise tax. The various tobacco companies were required to pay the tax directly to the federal government. Puffum Tobacco Company filed suit in the appropriate federal court, praying that the tax be struck down as unconstitutional.

The court is likely to rule:

(A) The tax is constitutional, because the tax is severable from its purpose.

(B) The tax is constitutional, because the broad provisions of the General Welfare Clause would condone it.

(C) The tax is unconstitutional, because it does not provide equal time for the tobacco companies to present their side of the smoking controversy.

(D) The tax is unconstitutional, because it abridges the First Amendment rights of tobacco manufacturers by forcing them to pay for messages they may not agree with.

Questions 3-5 are based on the following fact situation:

The state of Blue enacted a statute requiring the parents of every child to have the child vaccinated for smallpox before the child's third birthday. Failure to comply is a misdemeanor punishable by a fine of $500 or six months in the county jail. Mr. and Mrs. Jones object to the application of the statute to their infant children on the ground that any injections or vaccinations violate the tenets and beliefs of their religion.

3. Mr. and Mrs. Jones have commenced an action in federal court to declare the statute unconstitutional on the ground that it violates their right to the free exercise of their religion under the First Amendment to the United States Constitution. The best argument to defeat their action is that:

(A) A proceeding for declaratory judgment is not the proper vehicle for asserting this claim.

(B) The state of Blue legislature has repeatedly defeated bills to repeal the statute.

(C) There is no substantial threat that the statute will be enforced.

(D) The federal courts should abstain until the state courts have had an opportunity to construe the statute.

4. If the state commences a criminal prosecution against Mr. and Mrs. Jones for violation of the statute, the state court may constitutionally inquire as to whether:

(A) The tenets of the Jones family's religion are true.

(B) The Jones family's religion is a traditional, established one.

(C) Mr. and Mrs. Jones believe the tenets of their religion are derived from a supreme being or are merely internally derived.

(D) Mr. and Mrs. Jones sincerely believe the tenets of their religion.

5. The state's best argument to convict Mr. and Mrs. Jones is:

(A) The statute is a neutral law that incidentally burdens the rights of Mr. and Mrs. Jones under the First Amendment.

(B) The Free Exercise Clause applies only to belief and not to conduct.

(C) The state has a substantial and important interest in the health of its citizens and there is no other feasible way to achieve the legislative purpose.

(D) Making an exception for Mr. and Mrs. Jones on religious grounds would violate the Establishment Clause of the First Amendment.

Question 6

Because of a worldwide glut of corn, farmers in Illianda, a corn belt state, were unable to sell their corn at a profit. To prevent bankruptcies, the Illianda legislature decided that it would buy a large quantity of corn from local farmers. After arranging for the purchase, a legislative committee began searching for uses for the corn. It discovered that a small Illianda chemical company had recently devised a process for converting corn into biodegradable plastics. The process was untested, and so the state was able to purchase a license to use the process at a very low price. After Illianda successfully began converting its corn supply, a large demand for corn plastics developed. The chemical company charges new licensees a much higher license fee than Illianda had to pay; thus, Illianda can produce its plastic at a much lower cost than other licensees. To further stimulate the Illianda economy, the Illianda legislature decided that it would sell its plastics to Illianda purchasers at cost and that any surplus could be sold to nonresident purchasers at cost plus 25%.

Deeco is an out-of-state corporation that manufactures widgets. Its main competitor is Pakco, an Illianda corporation. Packaging is the most expensive cost of widget production, and both companies buy their plastic packaging from Illianda. Although Deeco cannot purchase packaging from any source at a price below the price it pays Illianda, the Deeco president feels that Pakco has an unfair advantage because it is able to buy packaging at cost and sell its widgets at a price lower than Deeco. Deeco brings an action in federal court challenging the Illianda policies.

Assuming that the court has jurisdiction, the court will most likely find the Illianda pricing scheme:

(A) Constitutional, because as a market participant Illianda is free to charge nonresidents more than residents.

(B) Constitutional, because Illianda is selling plastics at competitive prices outside Illianda.

(C) Unconstitutional, because the scheme discriminates against nonresidents in violation of the Commerce Clause.

(D) Unconstitutional, because charging non-residents more for plastics than residents pay violates the Privileges and Immunities Clause guaranteeing benefits of state citizenship.

Question 7

St. Minny, a town with a 30,000 population, was located on the west bank of a small river. Immediately across the river, on the east bank, was Paulopolis, a city of 60,000. Over the years, many civic improvement groups urged that the two municipalities be merged into "Minny-paulos," a single city of 90,000 souls. The arguments in favor of merger stressed savings to taxpayers accruing from the elimination of duplicate services. Proposals to merge the two places had appeared as referenda on the ballot on two separate occasions. Although the voters of Paulopolis approved each proposal by heavy margins, the voters of St. Minny, fearing that control of the government would be in the hands of more populous Paulopolis, rejected the referendum proposals by more than two-to-one.

To avoid the failure of yet another such referendum, a new proposal was made for the governance of the proposed combined city. For a period of 20 years, beginning at the date of the merger, the city council of the merged city would consist of six persons. The former Paulopolis would be divided into three council districts, as would the former city of St. Minny. Thus, each St. Minny council representative would be elected from a district with a population of 10,000, while the Paulopolis districts would contain 20,000 persons each. A mayor would be elected at large. Before this proposal was placed on the ballot, the state attorney general was asked her opinion of the proposal's legality. She issued an advisory opinion stating that the proposal was not in violation of any state statutory or constitutional provision. The proposal was placed on the ballot and was carried by large majorities in both St. Minny and

Paulopolis. Representatives from Paulopolis and St. Minny carved each former city into three council electoral districts. Three Paulopolis taxpayers filed suit to enjoin the holding of an election with council districts of such disparate proportions. The suit reached the state supreme court, which ruled that the governmental formula was constitutional under both the state and United States Constitutions. The plaintiffs wish to take the case to the United States Supreme Court.

The Supreme Court should:

(A) Rely on the attorney general's opinion and not hear the case on its merits.

(B) Not hear the case, because it was decided below on an independent state ground.

(C) Not hear the case, but remand it to federal district court.

(D) Hear the federal issues involved, but decline to rule on state issues.

Question 8

The state of Arkiana set up an intrastate message routing system to carry messages to and from the various state agency offices located throughout Arkiana. This proved to be cheaper and more efficient than reliance on the United States mail service. The state messengers wear distinctive turquoise colored uniforms and their trucks are painted turquoise and bear the "ASE" logo, which stands for Arkiana State Express.

The messenger service has been so successful that the governor got the state legislature to approve use of the "ASE" service as a fringe benefit for state employees. Thus, any Arkiana state employee could have a letter or package delivered to any address in the state, not just to another state agency address. The legislation allows state employees to use ASE for personal correspondence as well as for official business.

Is this legislation constitutional?

(A) Yes, because ASE's operation is entirely within the state borders of Arkiana.

(B) No, because the Commerce Clause prohibits states from unfairly competing with privately owned companies that could provide the same services.

(C) No, because the Equal Protection Clause prohibits this singling out of state employees for special benefits.

(D) No, because it violates the federal postal monopoly.

Question 9

Congress enacted a statute appropriating money to the states on condition that the states use the money to support "public performances of classical ballet open to the public." The statute provided that the money was not to be used to support any other type of dance, and that tickets to any performance paid for with these funds were to be distributed to the public on a first come, first served basis.

The state of Atlantic accepted a grant of $500,000 in these federal funds, $250,000 of the money being given to the Atlantic State Ballet Company, and the remaining sums divided among six local ballet companies. The Atlantic State Ballet had been started by the state in the 1960s and was part of a state effort to bring culture to poor areas in the inner city. Because the state had never before provided funds for ballet companies in these areas, state law required that no less than 35% of the tickets to each performance of the Atlantic State Ballet be distributed to the inner-city school systems to be given to minority school children.

The state method of distributing tickets to the Atlantic State Ballet is:

(A) Constitutional, because the Atlantic State Ballet is a state-operated ballet company, and the doctrine of federalism prohibits the federal government from interfering with a department of state government.

(B) Constitutional, because the Atlantic State Ballet ticket distribution system substantially conforms with the underlying purpose of the federal ticket distribution scheme.

(C) Unconstitutional, because the Supremacy Clause prohibits a state from this type of conduct.

(D) Unconstitutional, because the state distribution system violates equal protection.

Question 10

The President of the United States and the King of Buenaventura entered into a treaty that provided that Buenaventuran citizens who reside in the United States would not be taxed by the United States and that United States citizens who reside in Buenaventura would not be taxed by Buenaventura. The treaty was swiftly ratified by the United States Senate and the Royal Council of Buenaventura.

Two years after the treaty went into effect, Harold Weerdsma, an eccentric American billionaire, took up residence in Buenaventura. Seeing an excellent opportunity to enrich the royal coffers, the King of Buenaventura sent forth his tax collectors to levy Buenaventuran taxes on Weerdsma. Weerdsma, who had contributed a great deal of money to the campaign funds of supporters of the President, wired the President demanding relief. The President acted immediately. He declared the Buenaventuran tax treaty to be void and ordered the Internal Revenue Service to seek out all Buenaventuran residents in the United States and to impose taxes upon them. He also sent telegrams to the governors of all the states and territories and urged them to do likewise.

Is the President's action constitutional?

(A) Yes, under the Supremacy Clause.

(B) Yes, under the foreign policy powers of the President.

(C) Yes, because the President has emergency powers to protect United States citizens.

(D) No, unless the President receives the advice and consent of the United States Senate.

Question 11

New City is located on the eastern seaboard and the residents of New City are proud of their rich and diverse heritage. To promote such feelings, the city council approved the building of a city-run Ethnic Sculpture Garden. City residents and groups were encouraged to erect statues and other displays in the garden depicting ethnic, cultural, and religious heritage. Many of the displays include religious symbols. New City maintains the property and administers the affairs of the garden. While the garden is paid for primarily by a small admission fee, New City contributes about $1,000 a year for the garden's upkeep from general city funds.

Zealot, a local atheist, visits the garden one day and is appalled to see New City supporting religious displays. If Zealot brings an action against the city challenging its funding of the garden, the court should find the city's acts:

(A) Constitutional, because the amount of city funds spent on the garden is de minimis.

(B) Constitutional, because the New City garden also includes secular displays depicting the city's ethnic and cultural heritage.

(C) Unconstitutional, because New City is helping to maintain religious symbols in violation of the First Amendment.

(D) Unconstitutional, because New City does not have a compelling interest in running the garden.

Question 12

Congress enacted a statute that purported to ban all discrimination against African Americans 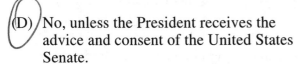 in any commercial transaction taking place within the United States.

The statute would most likely be held:

(A) Constitutional, under Thirteenth Amendment provisions barring badges or incidents of slavery.

(B) Constitutional, because the federal government has an important interest in furthering the equal protection provisions of the Fourteenth Amendment.

(C) Unconstitutional, because Congress's powers under the Commerce Clause do not extend so far as the statute would require.

(D) Unconstitutional, because commercial transactions are not among the privileges and immunities of national citizenship.

Question 13

Lola was one month pregnant and desired an abortion, but she was poor and her home state of Moralcopia did not provide financial assistance for abortions. However, the nearby state of Infamy provided public funds for performance of first trimester abortions on anyone who met certain financial criteria and had resided in Infamy for at least three months. Lola considered moving to Infamy, but before making the move she decided to see Doc, a doctor at an Infamy facility licensed to perform abortions. Doc advised Lola that while she met the state's financial criteria, she was not eligible for a state-paid abortion since she did not meet the state's residency requirement. Lola was upset and Doc told her that he believed that the residency requirement was unconstitutional and would like to see it challenged. Lola explained that she was afraid of going through the expense of moving to Infamy without knowing whether she would be successful in obtaining a state-paid abortion. Doc recommended that Lola bring an action challenging the residency requirement.

Lola brought the action in forma pauperis in federal court and named Doc as the only defendant. Doc responded that he thought the requirement was unconstitutional, and would like to be able to perform the abortion for Lola.

The court should:

(A) Dismiss the action because Lola lacks standing.

(B) Dismiss the action because there is no case or controversy.

(C) Abstain from hearing the action because deciding whether to fund abortions is a highly political issue.

(D) Issue a declaratory injunction upholding the residency requirement because the state has a compelling interest in preventing nonresidents from draining local welfare funds.

Question 14

The state of Xenia passed a statute requiring all commercial trucks passing through Xenia to use Type A tires, even though all other states permit the use of either Type A or Type B tires on commercial vehicles. The United States Supreme Court struck down the Xenia statute and stated in its opinion that Type A and Type B tires are equally safe. Subsequent to the Supreme Court decision, the legislature of the state of Zephyr enacted a statute requiring the use of Type B tires by commercial vehicles, and banning the use of Type A tires by commercial vehicles using the highways of Zephyr. The statute states that the reason for the prohibition is that Type A tires are dangerous.

The best argument for striking down the Zephyr statute as unconstitutional would be based upon:

(A) The fact that Type A and Type B tires are equally safe.

(B) Supremacy Clause.

(C) Commerce Clause.

(D) Res judicata.

Question 15

For many years, the United States government was involved in a dispute with a small Pacific island nation over the ownership of a small archipelago in the Pacific. Recently, a geological survey showed that this chain is a rich source of oil. The President decided that the United States and this island nation should jointly exploit the oil in this chain of islands, and share equally in its profits. Accordingly, he appointed ambassadors to negotiate a treaty to that effect.

A majority of the Senate, however, believed that the facts clearly showed that the United States was the sole owner of this island chain, having received it as part of a treaty entered into with the former government of this area of the Pacific. The Senate did not believe that the United States should be willing to give so much away; consequently, a majority of Senators announced their intent to vote against the ratification of any treaty not meeting the Senate's approval on this point. After a meeting of the Senate Foreign Relations Committee, a resolution was passed by the Senate requiring that the President include in this diplomatic mission a Senator to insure that the view of the Senate be introduced into any negotiation involving exploitation of the natural resources of this island chain.

What is the strongest constitutional ground for the President's refusal to do so?

(A) As commander-in-chief, the President has the exclusive power to determine how to protect our national interest abroad.

(B) This resolution is unreasonable because it includes a Senator and not any Representatives.

(C) The President has the exclusive power to select diplomatic representatives of the United States.

(D) The Senate, if it does not like the President's actions, can refuse to appropriate the necessary monies for the President to implement his policies.

Question 16

In which of the following cases is Sanjay, a citizen of India who received a bachelor's degree from The Ohio State University and is still residing in Ohio, most likely to prevail?

(A) Sanjay applies for a job at an Ohio public high school teaching political science, but is denied employment pursuant to a state law requiring that public school teachers be United States citizens. Sanjay sues to have the law declared unconstitutional.

(B) Sanjay applies for a job as a police officer for a city in Ohio, but is denied employment pursuant to a city ordinance requiring police officers to be United States citizens. Sanjay sues to have the ordinance declared unconstitutional.

(C) Sanjay applies for a job as a probation officer for a city in Ohio, but is denied employment pursuant to a city ordinance requiring probation officers to be United States citizens. Sanjay sues to have the ordinance declared unconstitutional.

(D) Sanjay applies for a job teaching political science at The Ohio State University, but is denied employment pursuant to a state law that requires university teachers to be United States citizens. Sanjay sues to have the law declared unconstitutional.

Question 17

A statute of the state of Xavier makes it a felony for anyone in the corridors or on the grounds of any building in which a court may be in session to make a speech or carry a sign intended to influence judicial proceedings. When Smith was on trial for murder, Brown was arrested for carrying a sign on the steps of the courthouse bearing the message: "Free Smith or the judge will die."

In the criminal proceeding against Brown, she:

(A) Cannot be convicted, because the statute could apply to others whose speech is constitutionally protected.

(B) Cannot be convicted, unless she personally intended to harm the judge.

(C) Can be convicted, if there was a clear and present danger that the judge would be influenced by the sign.

(D) Can be convicted, because the statute does not violate the freedom of expression guaranteed by the First Amendment.

Question 18

The state legislature of Calizona, concerned about the growing number of snakebite victims, passed a statute making the possession of rattlesnakes illegal. The legislative debates made clear that the purpose of the statute was to reduce the number of venomous snakebites in Calizona.

The Church of the Viper, located in the town of Flashflood, Calizona, promulgated the doctrine of rattlesnake worship, and members of the congregation handled rattlesnakes as an integral part of the Church's services. Serpentina Asp, head of the Church of the Viper, brought suit to have the statute declared unconstitutional for violating her right to practice her religion.

The court will most likely:

(A) Uphold the statute, because of the compelling state interest involved.

(B) Uphold the statute, because it is a neutral law of general application.

(C) Invalidate the statute, because it is not the least restrictive means of accomplishing the state's purpose.

(D) Invalidate the statute, because as applied to the Church, it interferes with an integral part of the Church's services.

Question 19

A corporation whose headquarters and plants are located within the state of Washaho manufactures a computerized telephone solicitation device that the corporation markets throughout Washaho. Those who purchase a subscription may use the device to boost sales through telephone solicitation. A database includes all the telephone numbers in the state of Washaho. The computerized solicitation device randomly dials such numbers and plays a recorded message soliciting purchases of the subscriber's product. If the person dialed is interested in the product, he may dial a number given on the recording and a live operator will take the order.

After sales of the device in Washaho, the Washaho legislature was besieged by letters from constituents complaining about an increase in annoying telephone sales pitches. In response to this barrage of mail, the Washaho legislature enacted a law banning the use of the computerized telephone solicitation device, and requiring that all telephone solicitation calls be dialed by human beings. Federal legislation and administrative regulations control only the rates to be charged for telephone calls.

The legislation is:

(A) Valid, because it involves wholly intrastate commerce that is not subject to federal regulation.

(B) Valid, because the statute does not conflict with federal legislation or the negative implications of the Commerce Clause.

(C) Invalid, because it is preempted by federal legislation under the Supremacy Clause.

(D) Invalid, because it is an unconstitutional attempt by a state to regulate interstate commerce.

Question 20

The large industrial city of Porkopolis, using its eminent domain power, condemned a decaying warehouse district on the banks of the Sludge River, which flows just north of the main business district of Porkopolis. The city council decided that it would be possible to rehabilitate the warehouse district by fixing up the old buildings and turning them into loft developments and trendy shops. To facilitate this, the city set up a separate entity, "The Warehouse District Development Authority." The Authority is completely controlled by the city. Anyone desiring to open a shop or a housing development must present his plan to the city council planning committee and if it is approved, the developer will be required to give his specifications to the Authority. The Authority will either use its own employees or hire subcontractors to prepare the space in the Warehouse District to the proposed specifications. The developer in turn will be charged a fee for this service by the Authority, with any profits made to be turned over to the general revenue fund of Porkopolis. In fact, the Authority has shown a substantial profit, and $3 million of Authority profits have been given to the Porkopolis general revenue fund during the first year of the Authority's existence.

Tackhammer, a private developer, has a plan to redevelop a block of the Warehouse District. He submitted his plan to the planning committee, and the plan was given preliminary approval. At that point, Tackhammer discovered the price that the Authority planned to charge to convert the block to Tackhammer's specifications. Tackhammer complained to the planning committee that he is an experienced contractor/developer, and that he is sure that he can rehabilitate the block to specifications for $150,000 less than the price proposed by the Authority. Tackhammer indicated that he is even willing to post a surety bond to insure that the work will meet the standards of the city building code. However, both the Authority and the planning committee turned Tackhammer down, telling him that the rehabilitation work will be done through the Authority or not at all. At no time was Tackhammer's ability to get the work done for less questioned, and it was made abundantly clear that he is being refused because Porkopolis wants the profits generated by the Authority.

If Tackhammer sues Porkopolis, what is his best argument for being allowed to do the rehabilitation work himself?

(A) Equal protection.

(B) Due process.

(C) Privileges and immunities protected by Article IV.

(D) None of the above, because the city has a right to protect its profits.

Question 21

To obtain key votes for passage of a military base closing bill, congressional leaders agreed to a provision relocating a special forces training center currently located in the state of Atlantica. A supplemental appropriations bill mandating that funds be spent for this purpose was also passed. The President signed the bills into law despite the protests of both Atlantica senators, whose votes the President would need on a tightly contested budget bill coming up. However, when the Secretary of Defense authorized expenditures and issued a timetable for base closings under the bill, relocation of the Atlantica training center was not listed and no funds were allocated for that purpose.

Which of the following statements is most accurate regarding the power of the President on this issue?

(A) The President has no power to decline to spend the funds because he is doing so for political reasons.

(B) The President has no power to decline to spend the funds because they were specifically appropriated for the relocation of the training center.

(C) The President, as part of his authority as commander in chief of the armed forces, has the power to leave the special forces training center open.

(D) The President, as part of his authority to balance the budget, has the power to decline to spend appropriated funds.

Question 22

Concerned over the growing number of murders, robberies, and other violent crimes being committed with guns, Congress enacted the Federal Firearm Control Act, which, inter alia, levied a tax of 5% of the sales price on every long weapon (rifle or shotgun) sold in the United States. The proceeds of the tax were earmarked for use by the Law Enforcement Assistance Administration. The Act provided for exceptions from its terms for police departments and the military. Ron, a shotgun collector and member of Americans for Freedom, a national gun owners' association, brings suit in federal district court seeking a declaration that the 5% tax on long weapons is unconstitutional.

How will the court likely rule?

(A) The tax is unconstitutional, because it infringes on the constitutional right of every citizen to bear arms.

(B) The tax is unconstitutional, because its effect is not limited to long weapons sold in interstate commerce, and thus will be applied to weapons sold entirely intrastate.

(C) The tax is constitutional as an exercise of the federal power to raise revenue.

(D) The tax is constitutional, pursuant to the Supremacy Clause of the federal Constitution.

Question 23

In connection with its agricultural products price support program, the United States Department of Agriculture regularly sent marketing and price information via telephone and teletype to its numerous field offices in the various states. Recently, problems arose because sophisticated criminals were using electronic devices to intercept the transmitted information, which they then used to gain an unfair advantage over other traders in the nation's commodities markets. To alleviate this situation, Congress enacted legislation making it a criminally punishable offense to "intercept marketing and/or price information in any fashion or to transmit such intercepted information to any other person in any fashion."

Delbert, who opposed the federal agricultural price support program, learned the identity of the individuals who were intercepting the Department of Agriculture transmissions, and, in exchange for not revealing their identities, obtained copies of every transmission they intercepted. He published these in his weekly newsletter, the "Market Ripoff Report."

If Delbert is prosecuted for violation of the federal statute prohibiting transmission of intercepted marketing or price information, and challenges that statute as unconstitutional as being not authorized by the enumerated powers of the federal government, which of the following is the government's strongest basis for supporting the statute?

(A) The General Welfare Clause.

(B) The Police Power.

(C) The power to tax and spend.

(D) The Commerce Clause.

Question 24

Among its other claims to fame, Dullsville contained a thriving panoply of adult-oriented businesses, such as bookstores and video arcades. The businesses were located in various areas of town, and the city council heard frequent complaints from citizens who asserted that the "secondary effects" of these businesses were lowering property values, increasing crime, and bringing unsavory people into their areas. In response to the individual letters and petitions circulated by community groups, whose assertions were supported by studies from other communities, the city council passed an ordinance banning the operation of adult-oriented businesses in any area of Dullsville zoned "residential" or "commercial." The ordinance specifically provided that such businesses would be allowed to operate in

areas zoned "industrial," provided that they complied with other laws, such as those against prostitution. The industrial zones in Dullsville where it would be possible for adult-oriented businesses to operate were in areas remote from the central business district and from other areas where there was good potential "walk-in" business. Kent, the owner of a highly profitable adult bookstore and video-rental operation located in a commercially zoned area on the seedier fringes of the downtown business district, did not want to close or move his business, and so he filed suit in federal court to prevent enforcement of the statute against him and others in adult-oriented businesses, claiming violation of his free speech rights.

The court's ruling is likely to favor:

(A) Dullsville, because speech-related activities may be regulated to prevent effects that are offensive to neighboring businesses and residents.

(B) Dullsville, because the ordinance is designed to serve a substantial governmental interest and does not unreasonably limit alternative avenues of communication.

(C) Kent, because the city is improperly regulating speech based on its content.

(D) Kent, because the city has not established that Kent is selling obscene materials.

Question 25

The city of Long Lake passed an ordinance prohibiting all of its police officers and firefighters from "moonlighting" (working a second job). The ordinance was passed because the city council determined that it wanted to have all police officers and firefighters readily available in case an emergency should arise and for overtime work when the situation warranted it, such as during the annual county fair, which brought many additional people into Long Lake. Other city employees, including members of the city council and the city manager, had no such restrictions placed on secondary employment.

Mikey, a police officer, sought to challenge the ordinance because he had a well-paying second job as a dancer at "Farthingmales," a nightclub featuring a "male strip review," where muscular male dancers performed with a limited amount of clothing for a predominantly female audience. The nightclub is within the city limits of Long Lake and follows all entertainment and liquor licensing policies. There has never been any suggestion that criminal or other illegal activity takes place at the club.

Applying constitutional principles, what is the likely result of Mikey's suit?

(A) Mikey prevails, because the ordinance restricts his First Amendment rights to freedom of expression.

(B) Mikey prevails, because the singling out of police officers and firefighters violates equal protection.

(C) Mikey loses, because the city has a significant interest that it seeks to regulate.

(D) Mikey loses, because there is a rational basis for the ordinance.

Question 26

Fox Reddogger worked as a reporter for a cable network news station during a recent Mideast war and gained instant notoriety for his battlefield reports. During the war, Fox became increasingly more frustrated by the way his reports were being censored by the military. After the war ended, Fox went home and began writing a factual novel describing places and events that he had not been permitted to televise.

Bob Snoops was a reporter for the *Washington Herald*. During the war, he wrote several articles criticizing the military leaders for over-censoring news from the war zone. Upon discovering that Fox had returned home to write a novel on the war, Snoops phoned Fox to arrange an interview. Fox invited Snoops to conduct the interview at his home and Snoops immediately went to Fox's home. Fox spoke freely of his battlefield experiences but refused to disclose any specific instances of censorship that he intended to include in his book. After Snoops had been interviewing Fox for about 45 minutes, Fox received a phone call and excused himself, leaving Snoops alone for a few minutes. Snoops immediately began searching and found a prepublication copy of Fox's book. He opened the book and quickly took photographs of several pages. Soon after taking the pictures, Fox returned and the two completed the interview.

Snoops returned to his office and had his film developed. He discovered that he had taken pictures of several pages describing several different instances of censorship. Snoops then wrote an article for the *Herald*'s Sunday magazine that included the photographed sections of Fox's book verbatim.

Fox read Snoops's article that Sunday and brought an appropriate action against Snoops for copyright infringement. Assuming that the court properly concludes that any fair use exception in the copyright laws is not applicable, it should:

(A) Not award Fox damages because his book included matters of public concern and so the *Herald* had a right under the First Amendment to publish it.

(B) Not award Fox damages because newspapers have an absolute right under the First Amendment to print whatever information they receive.

(C) Award Fox damages because he has a Fifth Amendment property right in his book.

(D) Award Fox damages because the newspaper did not get his permission to print the pages from his book.

Question 27

Under the "Gender Equality in Education Act" recently enacted by Congress, state-supported institutions of higher education that provide federal student loan funds to their students must achieve "gender equity" in the funding of intercollegiate athletic programs. Under a complex formula taking into account the average percentage of athletic department funds allocated to men's and women's programs over a five-year period, the percentage that each school must now allocate to women's athletics is determined. Depending on the school's past record of funding, this allocation may be greater than the percentage of women enrolled in the school. A state with any of its schools out of compliance will be penalized under the Act by being deprived of a portion of its federal education funding.

The Fortress is a state-supported military school in the state of Palmetto that only began admitting women five years ago. Presently, 10% of The Fortress's student body is female. However, to be in compliance under the federal athletic funding formula, The Fortress must now allocate 25% of its athletic budget to women's sports because it allocated less than the required percentage in several past years. Joe, a male student whose sports program is being discontinued because of the budget allocation, filed suit in federal court challenging the federal statute on various constitutional grounds.

In this case Joe is likely to:

(A) Prevail, because the government will be unable to prove that the discriminatory funding requirements required by the statute are necessary to achieve a compelling government interest.

(B) Prevail, because the federal government does not have the power to dictate the budget allocations of state-supported educational institutions.

(C) Not prevail, because remedying past discrimination is a legitimate government interest, and Joe will be unable to prove

that the statute's funding requirements are not rationally related to that interest.

(D) Not prevail, because the government will be able to prove that the statute's funding requirements are substantially related to an important government interest.

Questions 28-31 are based on the following fact situation:

Lobster fishing is a major industry in the state of Augusta. For many years, the world's largest and finest lobsters have been taken from the lobster beds which lie in Augusta's coastal waters. Recently, however, the number of lobsters caught annually has dropped dramatically. This is due in part to overfishing in the past, caused by increased demand for Augusta lobsters, and also to changing conditions in the coastal waters which deprived the lobsters of certain nutrients required for fast growth, so that it now takes several years longer for the lobsters to reach full size.

The situation prompted both state and federal action. The state of Augusta enacted a statute as follows: (1) No lobster shall be taken from lobster beds lying within three miles of the Augusta shoreline unless it is at least one pound in weight (the purpose of which is to enable young lobsters to reproduce before being caught), and (2) there shall be a tax of $1 per pound paid to the state on all lobsters taken from these waters, which shall be used for conservation and protection of the lobster beds.

At the same time, Congress enacted the Federal Lobster Conservation Act, which provides $5 million for research funds to develop and improve breeding grounds for lobsters. The Act also imposes a special excise tax of $1,000 on each lobster caught in violation of state law if later shipped in interstate commerce.

28. Consumers Alliance, a nonpartisan group dedicated to restoring fiscal integrity in the federal government, has filed suit in federal court against appropriate federal officials to enjoin their expenditure of the $5 million provided in the Federal Lobster Conservation

Act. The suit challenges the Act as an improper exercise of congressional power.

The suit is defended on the following grounds:

I. The federal court lacks jurisdiction to enjoin expenditure of funds voted by Congress, under the doctrine of separation of powers.

II. Consumers Alliance lacks standing to maintain the action (even though all of its members are admittedly federal taxpayers).

III. The Federal Lobster Conservation Act is a valid exercise of the federal taxing and spending powers.

Which of these grounds, if any, is valid?

(A) I. and III. only.

(B) II. and III. only.

(C) II. only.

(D) None of these grounds.

29. Georgia Greedy has shipped from Augusta to California 500 lobsters that weighed less than one pound each. The United States Attorney has filed suit against Greedy charging that the lobsters were taken in violation of Augusta law, and therefore Greedy owes $500,000 in taxes to the federal government under the Federal Lobster Conservation Act. Greedy challenges the constitutionality of the excise tax provision of the Act. Which of the following results is most likely?

(A) The Act will be upheld as a valid exercise of the federal taxing power.

(B) The Act will be upheld as a valid exercise of the federal commerce power.

(C) The Act will be held invalid because Congress does not have the power to tax for the purpose of regulation.

(D) The Act will be held invalid if the dominant purpose of the $1,000 per lobster tax is found to be regulatory rather than revenue raising.

30. Harriet Harris is a resident of the state of New Bedford, which borders on Augusta. She is engaged in the lobster fishing business and ships lobsters throughout the country. New Bedford law imposes no restrictions on the size of lobsters which may be taken from lobster beds lying in New Bedford waters. While fishing in coastal waters, Harris's boat crosses into waters lying within three miles of the Augusta coastline. She is arrested by Augusta law enforcement officers for taking from these waters lobsters that weigh less than one pound. Harris defends the charge by challenging the constitutionality of the provision in the Augusta statute which limits the size of lobsters that may be taken from coastal waters. Which of the following results is most likely?

(A) The statute will be upheld.

(B) The statute will be held invalid because it unduly burdens interstate commerce in lobsters.

(C) The statute will be held invalid because it violates the Interstate Privileges and Immunities Clause of Article IV, Section 2.

(D) The statute will be held invalid because it is preempted by the Federal Lobster Conservation Act.

31. John Jones, another New Bedford lobster fisherman, files suit to enjoin as unconstitutional the $1 per pound lobster tax imposed by the Augusta statute. Which of the following results is most likely?

(A) Jones will win because the state tax is invalid under the Commerce Clause.

(B) Jones will win because the tax is invalid under the Import-Export Clause.

(C) Jones will lose because the tax is valid under the Commerce Clause.

(D) Jones will lose because the tax is valid under the Import-Export Clause.

Questions 32-34 are based on the following fact situation:

A statute of the state of Plains provided that "any merchant desiring to sell within this state any product or goods manufactured in an Asian country must (i) obtain a special license from the state for $50, and (ii) clearly mark such goods as to specify the country of origin." The statute also makes it a misdemeanor for any merchant to "willfully sell goods" without complying with these statutory requirements.

Chipan is an Asian nation. A treaty exists between the United States and Chipan under which each country agrees to permit the "importation and sale of goods and products" from the other country.

Dang, a citizen of Chipan, was residing legally in the United States and had applied for naturalization. Dang owned and operated a boutique in Plains, in which he featured handcrafts and other goods imported from Chipan, but he never complied with the Plains statute noted above.

32. Plains commences a criminal prosecution against Dang for violating the statute. Dang defends on the ground that the Plains statute conflicts with the federal treaty with Chipan. Which of the following statements is most correct?

(A) The Plains statute is unconstitutional, and Dang should be acquitted.

(B) Dang will be acquitted only if the

treaty with Chipan preceded the Plains statute in point of time.

(C) The treaty with Chipan is no defense to a criminal prosecution in state courts for violating state laws.

(D) The treaty is no defense to the criminal prosecution in the absence of effectuating legislation by Congress.

33. Assume for purposes of this question only that Congress recently enacted a statute that specifically ends the permission for the free flow of goods from Chipan. Which of the following statements is most correct?

(A) The federal legislation is invalid because the agreement with Chipan was a treaty rather than an executive agreement.

(B) The federal legislation is invalid as interfering with the executive power over foreign affairs.

(C) The federal legislation works to repeal the substance of the treaty with Chipan.

(D) The federal legislation works to repeal the treaty with Chipan only if signed by the President (rather than being passed over his veto) and ratified by two-thirds of the Senate.

34. Assume for purposes of this question only that there is no treaty between the United States and Chipan. Dang now defends the criminal prosecution in Plains on the ground that the Plains statute discriminates against foreign commerce. Which of the following statements is most correct?

(A) The portion of the statute requiring the license fee can be sustained on the ground that reasonable inspection fees are proper; but the balance of the statute is invalid.

(B) The portion of the statute requiring that the goods be labeled as to country of origin can be sustained because it only requires disclosure; but the balance of the statute is invalid.

(C) The statute is constitutionally valid as long as the burden on foreign commerce is minimal and is justified by legitimate state interests.

(D) The statute is unconstitutional in its entirety.

Questions 35-36 are based on the following fact situation:

The First Church of Center City, East Dakota, planned a sex education program. The program was to be open to children of church members, ages 12 to 16. It would include lectures and slides. Some of the slides would depict explicit sexual activity between nude males and females. The parents would be required to give their consent before any child could participate. The program would be conducted by the Church Board, which consisted of the minister, a doctor, and a psychologist. The Church Board described the program as "an integral part of involving the church in the real world of a teenager."

An East Dakota statute provides in its entirety, "It is unlawful to sell, give, or display to any person under the age of 17 any lewd or obscene article, picture, or depiction."

35. If the district attorney threatens to prosecute the Church Board members under this statute if they carry out the planned program, and they seek relief in federal court:

(A) The federal court has power to grant a declaratory judgment that the statute is unconstitutional, either on its face or as applied to the church program.

(B) The federal court has power to enjoin the district attorney from prosecuting the Church Board members only if there is diversity of citizenship between the members and the district attorney.

(C) The federal court is more likely to grant an injunction or declaratory relief after the state criminal prosecution has commenced than beforehand.

(D) Under no circumstances will the federal court enjoin a state criminal prosecution.

36. If the Church Board members are convicted of violating the above statute and they appeal:

(A) Their convictions will be reversed because the freedom to engage in conduct connected with one's religion is absolutely protected under the First and Fourteenth Amendments.

(B) Their convictions will be upheld because the state's interest in regulating activities involving children necessarily outweighs any rights of the Church Board members under the Free Exercise Clause of the First Amendment.

(C) Their convictions will be reversed if it can be shown that the statute is being applied only to interfere with religion.

(D) Their convictions will be upheld because the members of the Church Board lack standing to challenge the statute on "free exercise of religion" grounds.

Question 37

Gloria was an unmarried 14-year-old who was two months' pregnant and living in the state of West Dakota. West Dakota required a female under the age of 18 who desired an abortion to obtain parental or judicial consent. Gloria did not want her parents to discover that she was pregnant and the local judge was an old family friend, so she decided to hitchhike to East Dakota, which has the following laws with respect to abortion:

Any person seeking to terminate a pregnancy must:

I. Have resided within the state for at least 30 consecutive days;

II. If it is a nontherapeutic abortion and is to be performed at a public hospital, obtain the services of a qualified physician;

III. Notify her parents or a court of the planned abortion; and

IV. Reimburse the state for the costs of a nontherapeutic abortion performed at a public hospital.

Which provision of the East Dakota statute is *least* likely to be constitutional?

(A) I.

(B) II.

(C) III.

(D) IV.

Questions 38-41 are based on the following fact situation:

As a result of rapid growth in population in the town of Pleasantville, there has been a disproportionately large increase in the number of families with school-age children, and this has put tremendous pressure on the Pleasantville school system. The newer families in town have been demanding increased classrooms and teaching staff. The "oldtimers" have been resisting any change in the school budget that would increase the tax rates on local property.

Under local statutes, the Pleasantville schools are administered by a school board consisting of five members, elected annually. To run for office, candidates are required to sign a loyalty oath, pay a $500 filing fee, and fill out a financial statement which is open for public inspection. Moreover, although the school board members are elected by the voters at large, one member is required to reside within each of the designated school districts within the town.

To be eligible to vote in school board elections, the statutes require that electors have resided in Pleasantville for at least one year prior to the date of the election, and that they own property subject to taxation by Pleasantville for school purposes.

38. Alan Ames is one of the "newcomers" to Pleasantville. He wishes to run for election to the school board, but the Town Clerk has refused to place Ames's name on the election ballot because Ames has not paid the $500 filing fee or provided the personal financial information required by the statute. Ames files suit to have his name placed on the ballot. Which of the following statements is most correct?

(A) The filing fee requirement is invalid if Ames is indigent, but the financial statement requirement is valid.

(B) The filing fee requirement is valid, but the financial statement requirement is unconstitutional because it impairs Ames's right of personal privacy.

(C) Both requirements are plainly unconstitutional and Ames is entitled to have his name placed on the election ballot.

(D) Ames will win unless the requirements are shown to serve some legitimate state purpose.

39. Barbara Bates has also applied to run for election to the Pleasantville school board. Her application for a place on the ballot was refused by the Town Clerk when she failed to execute the required loyalty oath. Bates now sues to have her name placed on the ballot. Which of the following statements is most correct?

(A) The loyalty oath requirement is valid if the candidate must merely affirm that she does not advocate the violent overthrow of the state or federal governments.

(B) The loyalty oath requirement is valid if the candidate must merely affirm that she will oppose the violent overthrow of the state or federal governments.

(C) The loyalty requirement is valid if the candidate must merely affirm that she has never been a member of any organization dedicated to the violent overthrow of the state or federal governments.

(D) No oath is constitutionally permissible as a condition for ballot qualification.

40. Charles Carter, another newcomer, attempted to register to vote in the forthcoming school board election. However, the Town Clerk refused to register Carter because he will not have resided in Pleasantville for a full year prior to the election. Carter files a class action on behalf of all of the new residents of Pleasantville challenging the validity of the one-year residency requirement. Which of the following statements is correct?

(A) If Carter's suit is not heard before the election, it will be dismissed as moot, because Carter will have met the residency requirement by the time of the next annual election.

(B) Carter's suit will prevail even if the matter is not decided until after the forthcoming election.

(C) As long as there is some legitimate purpose for the one-year residency requirement, such as the need to prepare voting lists, the residency requirement will be upheld.

(D) Carter will lose because one-year residency requirements have been held permissible restrictions on the right to vote in local elections.

41. Ed Early, a registered voter, files suit challenging the constitutionality of the statutory provision which requires that school board members each reside in one

of five separate school districts within the town. Early presents uncontested proof that most of the Pleasantville population now resides in two of the five districts, whereas the other three districts are primarily rural and sparsely populated. The court will most likely rule that:

(A) The residency requirement is unconstitutional because it impairs the voters' equal protection rights in that it gives the voters in the less populous districts more effective representation on the school board.

(B) The residency requirement is unconstitutional because it violates the candidates' equal protection rights.

(C) The residency requirement is constitutionally permissible because school board members do not exercise legislative power and hence their election is not subject to the "one person, one vote" requirement.

(D) The residency requirement is constitutionally permissible because the board members are elected at large.

Question 42

Which of the following suits is *least* likely to be properly instituted pursuant to the United States Supreme Court's original jurisdiction under Article III, Section 2?

(A) *State of Nevada v. The President of the United States,* seeking to assert the interest of Nevada citizens in retaining diplomatic relations with Taiwan.

(B) *Oregon v. California,* seeking to protect Oregon's timber from allegedly illegal cutting by California residents.

(C) *State of Illinois v. The President of the United States,* seeking to enjoin enforcement of an allegedly unconstitutional executive order that will greatly limit the state's authority to make policy decisions regarding admission to state universities.

(D) *United States v. Pennsylvania,* seeking to enjoin state construction of a bridge over a navigable waterway.

Question 43

The state of Arkota passed a law stating that "only persons living with their parents or guardians who are bona fide residents of Arkota shall be entitled to free public education in Arkota; all others who wish to attend Arkota public schools may do so, but they must pay tuition of $3,000 per semester." It happened that Arkota had very good schools, and the surrounding states had poor schools. Penelope's parents lived in neighboring Montoming, but Penelope had moved in with her friend Frieda, who was an Arkota resident, so that Penelope could attend high school in Arkota. The Arkota legislature passed the tuition statute just as Penelope completed her junior year. Penelope wants to complete her senior year in the Arkota high school, but cannot afford to pay tuition.

If Penelope sues in federal court to strike down the tuition statute, the court is likely to rule that the statute is:

(A) Constitutional, provided that Arkota can show that the statute is necessary to promote a compelling state interest.

(B) Constitutional, unless Penelope can show that the statute is not rationally related to a proper state interest.

(C) Unconstitutional, because it infringes on Penelope's fundamental right to an education.

(D) Unconstitutional, because it interferes with Penelope's fundamental right to interstate travel.

Question 44

Baxter, an employee of the United States Department of Labor, was instructed by his superior to solicit subscriptions to the Department's bulletin on a door-to-door basis in the city of Centerville. While doing so, Baxter was arrested for violation of a city ordinance that prohibited commercial solicitation of private residences.

Baxter's best defense is:

(A) Intergovernmental immunity.

(B) The First Amendment freedom of expression as it applies to the states through the Fourteenth Amendment.

(C) The Equal Protection Clause as it applies to the states through the Fourteenth Amendment.

(D) The city ordinance effectively restricts interstate commerce.

Question 45

A federal statute taxing residential real property will most likely be upheld if it:

(A) Is applied to residences located in the various Indian lands in the United States.

(B) Is enacted under the Commerce Clause.

(C) Applies to residences located in the District of Columbia.

(D) Is applied uniformly throughout the United States.

Questions 46-48 are based on the following fact situation:

The legislature of Mississippi recently enacted statutes regulating the auto repair business. Numerous problems had arisen with unprincipled auto repair operations that were opened in the state by nonresidents who would leave the state to avoid civil liability for their fraud. The new legislation provided, among other things, that all auto mechanics or auto repair business owners must be licensed by the state department of consumer affairs, and it also established licensing standards. Licensees must be residents of Mississippi, defined as any

United States citizen whose domicile has been that state for one year prior to the application for a license. Any applicant for an auto repair business license must demonstrate financial responsibility by purchasing business failure insurance from an insurance company whose principal place of business is in Mississippi. To become a licensed auto mechanic, the applicant must demonstrate one year of related experience within the state of Mississippi or five years of auto mechanic experience elsewhere.

Wilcox, who just moved to Mississippi from the state of New York, where he has been an auto mechanic for two years, wants to open an auto repair business in which he will be the sole mechanic. He applies to the state department of consumer affairs for a license and is denied one. He decides to open his garage anyway and does excellent business, with no dissatisfied customers. The state department of justice brings an action in state court to enjoin Wilcox's business and for civil penalties.

46. If Wilcox attacks the state legislation's provision that licensees be residents of the state for a year prior to the application, his challenge should be based upon:

(A) The Privileges and Immunities Clause of Article IV.

(B) The Commerce Clause.

(C) The Equal Protection Clause of the Fourteenth Amendment.

(D) All of the above.

47. Assume for the purposes of this question only that Wilcox had lived in Mississippi for the last five years. If Wilcox challenges the power of the state to require him to obtain a license to practice his livelihood, he will probably:

(A) Lose, because the state has plenary power regarding commerce.

(B) Lose, because licensing is within the police power of the state and infringes no specific constitutional prohibition.

(C) Win, because the license requirement substantially burdens interstate commerce.

(D) Win, because the license requirement violates the Equal Protection Clause of the Fifth Amendment.

48. Assume for the purposes of this question only that Wilcox meets all the requirements for a mechanic's license, but when he seeks to purchase the necessary insurance, he discovers that Mississippi insurance firms charge about three times as much for business insurance as firms that operate out of New York. He purchases insurance by mail from a reputable New York firm and is denied a business license. His challenge to this aspect of the state legislation will:

(A) Succeed, because the requirement that the insurer be a Mississippi firm violates the Due Process Clause of the Fourteenth Amendment.

(B) Succeed, because the requirement constitutes discrimination against interstate commerce.

(C) Fail, because the state can enforce its laws governing the sale of insurance only if the firm is located in Mississippi.

(D) Fail, because the requirement is reasonably related to the legislation's purpose to protect auto repair consumers.

Question 49

Lois, a reporter, received an anonymous tip that Jimmy Olson, a former photographer and currently the mayor of Metropolis, was taking kickbacks on city contracts with the Krypton Construction Co. Lois was thrilled to get this information because she had vowed to get even with Olson for causing the breakup of a romance between Lois and another reporter. Lois called her usual sources, but none of them could confirm the rumor. Finally, she called Krypton Construction and spoke with Mr. Krypton's secretary, Clara. Clara told Lois that Mr. Krypton had admitted to her that he was paying the mayor, but Clara did not want her name in the paper. Lois agreed to keep Clara's name out of print.

Lois wrote the story and it was published. The story was in fact false. As it turns out, Clara had been fired that day and was cleaning out her desk when Lois called. She thought that confirming the rumor would be a good way to get back at Mr. Krypton for firing her.

Jimmy Olson sues Lois for libel and establishes the above facts at trial. His suit should:

(A) Succeed, because Lois's vow of revenge indicates that she acted with malice.

(B) Succeed, because the story was false and Olson was damaged by it.

(C) Fail, because Olson is a public official.

(D) Fail, because newspaper reporters are protected from libel suits by the First Amendment.

Questions 50-51 are based on the following fact situation:

Following a number of poisoning incidents of consumers of over-the-counter headache remedies, Congress enacted legislation prescribing in great detail the specifications for various types of containers that all manufacturers, wholesalers, and retailers of nonprescription drugs were required to use in marketing their products. The containers mandated by the new legislation were considerably more expensive than those formerly in wide use in the industry and would result in considerably smaller sales volumes. The same legislation established a Commission on Nonprescription Drug Use whose purpose was to gather information about the number, type, and costs to the consumer of nonprescription drugs used in the United States and report its findings on an annual basis to Congress. The members of the

commission were all Representatives or Senators who served on the committees in their respective chambers concerned with legislation relating to food and drugs.

50. General Ingestion, a manufacturer of pharmaceuticals, objects to the notion of having to supply the government with any information about the manufacture and sale of nonprescription drugs and so resists a subpoena for its chief executive officer to testify before the commission. Insofar as Congress's power to investigate is concerned, the general rule is:

(A) The power of Congress is limited only by the concept of separation of powers.

(B) Congress's power to investigate is coextensive with its power to legislate.

(C) Congress's power to investigate is limited to the appointment of its own members to make such investigations.

(D) There are no limitations upon Congressional powers of investigation as to the domestic economy.

51. Congress's power to prescribe standards for the manufacture of nonprescription drug packaging is derived from:

(A) The Necessary and Proper Clause.

(B) The Commerce Clause.

(C) The General Welfare Clause.

(D) The Tenth Amendment.

Question 52

The legislature of the state of Blue enacts a statute that provides for loaning certain textbooks on secular subjects to students in all public and private schools. In accordance with the statute, the state board of education distributes textbooks to Redbrick School, a private school that offers religious instruction and admits only Caucasian students.

Which of the following is the strongest argument against the constitutionality of free distribution of textbooks to the students at Redbrick School?

(A) A state may not constitutionally aid private schools through distribution of textbooks.

(B) Segregation is furthered by the distribution of textbooks to these students.

(C) The distribution of textbooks advances religion because it is impossible to separate their secular and religious uses.

(D) The distribution of textbooks fosters excessive government entanglement with religion.

Questions 53-54 are based on the following fact situation:

In response to a growing number of injuries and fires occurring as the result of the improper manufacture and use of fireworks, Congress adopted the Federal Firework Control Act, which established certain safety and performance standards for all fireworks manufactured in the United States. The Act also created a seven-member safety commission to investigate firework safety, to make recommendations to Congress for new laws, to make further rules for establishing safety and performance standards, and to prosecute violations of the Act. The chairman of the committee was appointed by the President. Three members were selected by the Speaker of the House of Representatives and three members were selected by the President pro tempore of the Senate. Big Blast, Inc., a manufacturer of fireworks offered for sale in the northeastern portion of the country, seeks to enjoin enforcement of the Commission's rules.

53. The best argument that Big Blast can make is that:

(A) The commerce power does not extend to the manufacture of fireworks sold solely within a state.

(B) Legislative power may not be delegated by Congress to an agency in the absence of clear guidelines.

(C) Big Blast is denied due process of law because it is not represented on the commission.

(D) The commission lacks authority to enforce its standards, because some of its members were appointed by Congress.

54. The appropriate decision for the court is to:

(A) Forbid the commission to take any action under the Act.

(B) Order that all members of the commission be appointed by the President by and with the advice and consent of the Senate.

(C) Allow the commission to prosecute violations of the act but not allow it to issue rules.

(D) Allow the commission to continue investigating firework safety and making recommendations to Congress.

Questions 55-56 are based on the following fact situation:

Oral is a member of the legislature of State. He is prosecuted in federal court for violating the civil rights of a member of the janitorial staff of the state legislature's building in connection with a sexual assault that occurred in Oral's office late at night during the Christmas recess. Oral raises as a defense the claim that the allegedly wrongful acts were committed in the course of legislative business and are immune from scrutiny by the federal government.

55. Which of the following is the strongest constitutional argument in favor of Oral's defense?

(A) The application of federal civil rights statutes to state legislators would violate the Due Process Clause.

(B) A federal court must follow state law respecting the scope of legislative immunity.

(C) State legislators enjoy the protection of the Speech and Debate Clause of the United States Constitution.

(D) Because of doctrines of federalism, federal law generally cannot be applied to state legislators acting in the course of their official duties.

56. Which of the following is the strongest argument against Oral's constitutional defense?

(A) Congress may impose liability on state legislators by virtue of the Necessary and Proper Clause.

(B) Congress does not significantly interfere with state government by applying the civil rights statutes to state legislators.

(C) Congress may impose liability on the state legislators as a means of guaranteeing a Republican form of government.

(D) Congress has plenary power under the General Welfare Clause.

Questions 57-58 are based on the following fact situation:

Congress enacted legislation providing, among other things, that "federal courts shall not order any public educational institution to establish athletic activities or to modify existing athletic activities on the grounds that such activities are not provided on an equal basis to both men and women."

57. Which of the following is the strongest argument for the constitutionality of the federal legislation?

(A) Congress provides financial support for public educational institutions and is therefore empowered to place conditions upon the expenditure of federal funds.

(B) Athletics involves tremendous amounts of money and the occasional use of interstate means of transportation, thus falling within the commerce power.

(C) Under Article III, Congress may restrict the jurisdiction of the federal courts.

(D) The Fourteenth Amendment authorizes Congress to define governmental conduct that violates the Equal Protection Clause.

58. Which of the following is the strongest argument that the federal legislation is unconstitutional?

(A) The courts, not Congress, have the primary responsibility for defining the minimum requirements of the Equal Protection Clause of the Fourteenth Amendment.

(B) The Privileges and Immunities Clause of the Fourteenth Amendment prohibits Congress from limiting the forms of relief afforded by federal courts.

(C) Congress cannot limit the authority of federal courts to hear and decide cases properly presented for decision.

(D) The legislation unduly burdens interstate commerce.

Questions 59-60 are based on the following fact situation:

Hoping to help control a growing gang problem and to give teenagers a place to go, the city of Centreville established a youth center. Originally, the center was open to all young people between the ages of 13 and 19, but trouble often occurred when male gang members showed up at the youth center. There were frequent fights and incidents of alcohol and drug abuse. The City Council threatened to close the center, but social workers who work at the center suggested a compromise, pointing out that the trouble invariably involved single men who came to the center without dates. Therefore, the Council passed an ordinance forbidding any male between the ages of 13 and 19 to enter the center unless accompanied by a female.

Rick, an 18-year-old who was new to Centreville, went to the youth center to try to meet new friends. He was refused admission because he was not escorted by a female.

59. Angered, Rick filed suit in federal district court seeking admission to the center and asking the court to strike down the ordinance as unconstitutional. The court should find the ordinance:

(A) Constitutional, because in these situations, the government is performing a parens patriae function.

(B) Constitutional, if the city can show a rational relationship between the ordinance and maintaining order at the center.

(C) Unconstitutional, if Rick can show that the ordinance was not necessary to promote a compelling government interest.

(D) Unconstitutional, unless the city can show that the ordinance is substantially related to important government objectives.

60. Assume for purposes of this question only that by the time the trial date arrived, Rick was 20 years old and married. Furthermore, after receiving numerous complaints about the ineffectiveness of the ordinance (the gangs simply moved their activity outside the doors of the center), the City Council has slated a vote to repeal the ordinance within a month of Rick's trial date.

When Rick's suit comes before the federal district court, the court should:

(A) Dismiss, because Rick is 20 years old.

(B) Dismiss, if Rick has been permitted to enter the center with his wife.

(C) Hear the case on the merits, because regardless of any change in Rick's circumstances, he has already suffered a deprivation of his constitutional rights.

(D) Dismiss, if it appears that the City Council will repeal the ordinance.

Questions 61-63 are based on the following fact situation:

The state of Pacific enacted legislation that permits parents to pay for the education of their children at the school of their choice by means of a voucher system. The system provides that when a residential real property owner pays his state real property tax, the taxpayer is given a voucher that can be used to pay the tuition at the school in which his children are enrolled. The school, if accredited by the state, can turn in the vouchers to the state and receive funds represented by these vouchers. If the taxpayer has no children in school, the taxpayer can assign the voucher to a relative by blood or marriage who has children in school, but the voucher cannot otherwise be sold or assigned except to the state. Residential taxpayers who have neither children nor close relatives with children can return the vouchers to the state and receive a 50% credit on their real property taxes.

In addition, Pacific raised its state sales tax from 3% to 5%, the additional 2% to be used exclusively to pay the costs of the public school system in addition to any voucher payments made for those children attending private school.

Roberts, a state legislator who fought against the enactment of the bill, brought suit in federal court to have the voucher system declared unconstitutional. In his suit, Roberts contends that parents are using the vouchers to send their children to parochial school and to send their children to segregated private schools. Roberts also alleged that 60% of the residential real property taxpayers are white, and 53% of the blacks in Pacific are inner-city dwellers who live in rental property.

61. For Roberts to bring suit against Pacific, at the very least Roberts must show that:

   (A) He rents his home.

   (B) He rents his home and has children who are of school age.

   (C) He owns residential real property on which he pays taxes.

   (D) He owns residential real property, on which he pays taxes, and has children who are of school age.

62. To prevail in his contention that the voucher system is unconstitutional with regard to the segregated private schools, Roberts is *least likely* to rely on which of the following arguments?

   (A) The purpose of the legislation was to promote segregation.

   (B) Voucher funds are being used by the majority of parents to send their children to segregated schools.

   (C) The voucher system has no valid purpose other than to promote segregation.

   (D) Segregation is furthered by the use of the voucher system.

63. Of the following, which is Pacific's best argument in support of its use of tax money to pay tuition at religious schools?

   (A) The Equal Protection Clause requires that both private and public schools be treated in the same manner.

   (B) Private religious schools, like public schools, fulfill a function important to the general welfare of the citizens of the state.

   (C) The purpose and effect of the taxes is secular in nature and is not intended to involve the state in religious institutions.

   (D) Only the taxes of the parents of the children who attend private religious schools are used to pay tuition at those schools; general tax revenues are not.

Questions 64–65 are based on the following fact situation:

A statute in the state of San Carlos prohibited speechmaking, noisy picketing, or other public gathering within 250 feet of the state's Legislative House when the legislature was in session to vote or debate on any legislation. The statute did permit silent picketing or silent vigils at any time, as long as the pickets did not interfere with pedestrians or traffic. The nearest place to the Legislative House where speeches could be made during a session was a large public park directly opposite the House.

During a controversial debate on a proposed bill to reinstate the death penalty in San Carlos, supporters of the bill gathered for a rally and speeches. George, one of the leaders of the group of about 250, was giving a speech when he was informed that the legislature had decided to send the bill back to committee and that there would be no vote on the bill until the next legislative session. George became very angry and upset at what he considered to be a ploy by the legislature to avoid "responding to the will of the people." He delivered a loud harangue to the crowd during which he said, "We are the ones who must live in fear because murderers and rapists walk the streets. We are the ones who must suffer. Well, maybe it's about time our legislators learn what it is to live in fear; to be afraid for their own lives!" At that, he told the crowd that they should all go across the street and let the legislators hear the voices of the people. When the chanting crowd reached the front of the House, the state police dispersed them and arrested George, charging him with violating the statute.

64. This statute would probably be held to be:

(A) Constitutional on its face and as applied to George.

(B) Constitutional on its face, but not as applied to George.

(C) Unconstitutional on its face, because a state's citizens have a right to take their complaints to their state legislature.

(D) Unconstitutional on its face, because it permits silent picketing while prohibiting other picketing.

65. George is also charged under a state statute that makes criminal "a threat against any state official in the performance of his duty." In a trial on this charge, George would most likely be found:

(A) Not guilty, because the statute is unconstitutional on its face.

(B) Not guilty, because George could not constitutionally be punished under this statute for his speech.

(C) Guilty, because George threatened the legislators.

(D) Guilty, because the crowd was moved to action in response to George's speech.

Questions 66-68 are based on the following fact situation:

A statute in the state of Utopia makes it unlawful to sell soft drink beverages in any type of container except refundable glass containers. A violation of the statute is a misdemeanor, subjecting the violator to a fine of up to $1,000.

66. Assume that CanCo, an out-of-state corporation that manufactures aluminum soft drink

cans, brings suit in a state court contesting the constitutionality of the statute. The highest court in Utopia ruled against CanCo's claim that the statute was unconstitutional. If CanCo sought to appeal the matter to the Supreme Court, the Court may:

(A) Deny a hearing, because the Eleventh Amendment forbids the exercise of judicial power by the federal government in a suit prosecuted against any state by a citizen of another state.

(B) Deny the hearing, because the highest court of any state is the final arbiter of the constitutionality of its own laws.

(C) Grant a hearing, because a federal question is involved.

(D) Grant a hearing, because jurisdiction exists on the basis of diversity.

67. Assume that CanCo is a manufacturer doing business in Utopia, and it brings suit for declaratory judgment in the federal court, contending that the bottle statute violates a constitutional prohibition. The federal court should:

(A) Entertain the suit, because a federal question is involved.

(B) Entertain the suit, because an action for declaratory relief is a proper method of deciding constitutional questions.

(C) Abstain from the assertion of jurisdiction until a state court has the opportunity to construe the statute.

(D) Dismiss the suit, because CanCo is not being prosecuted for the violation of the statute.

68. Assume that in addition to fines, the statute provides for the suspension or revocation of a retail business license where there have been "repeated violations" of the statute by any one individual or business.

Allman, a store owner, had already been fined three times under the statute when an inspector purchased from him a soft drink in a can. Several days later, Allman received a notice from the regulatory agency that was created by the statute stating that his business license was suspended for 21 days for violation of the statute. In a suit filed by Allman in the court to set aside the suspension, the most likely finding a court would make is that Allman:

(A) Prevails, because the statute fails to set forth the exact number of violations that a business would have to make before its business license was revoked.

(B) Prevails, because he was not given a hearing before the agency.

(C) Does not prevail, because the agency could by its rules construe the term "repeated violations" in such a manner as to comport with due process requirements.

(D) Does not prevail, because the agency is merely a regulatory agency, and therefore Allman has no right to a hearing.

Questions 69-70 are based on the following fact situation:

Lawrence, a chief commissioner on a federal trade board, is cited for contempt of the Senate for refusing to answer certain questions concerning discussions during a closed meeting of the board. The contempt citation is prepared and given to a federal grand jury for indictment. The grand jury returns the indictment, but the United States Attorney General refuses to prosecute Lawrence.

69. Can the Senate force the Attorney General to prosecute Lawrence in accordance with the grand jury indictment?

(A) Yes, provided that two-thirds of the Senate concur in the resolution.

(B) Yes, because the indictment charges Lawrence with a crime against the Senate.

(C) No, because the Attorney General is a member of the executive branch, and he has the exclusive right to determine whether to prosecute.

(D) No, because Lawrence, as a federal trade commissioner, is a member of the executive branch, and it violates the separation of powers doctrine for the Senate to seek testimony from him.

70. If Lawrence were prosecuted for this contempt charge, he would *least likely* be convicted if he is able to show that:

(A) The questions he refused to answer related to his duties as a member of the executive branch.

(B) If he answered the questions, he could be subject to dismissal from his position as chief of the board.

(C) The questions do not relate to any matter concerning which the Senate intended to legislate.

(D) Disclosure of the substance of the discussions that occurred during the closed meeting of the board would have a chilling effect on the free exchange of views.

Question 71

Fritz was appointed as an administrative judge to review claims against the federal government made by Indians under the congressional statute, the Indian Claims Arbitration Act of 1957. For 20 years Fritz heard, reviewed, and arbitrated disputed claims made against the government by various Indian tribes and their citizens. When Fritz found a claim to be valid, he would make a recommendation to the Bureau of Indian Claims that the claim be paid. If Fritz found the claims to be without merit, or if the Bureau decided against his recommendation, the claimant would have the right to bring suit in a federal court. Last year, a presidential commission recommended the abolition of the Bureau of Indian Claims as a cost-cutting measure. The commission reasoned that whatever increase there may be in litigation in the federal court would be balanced by the decrease in claims because individual Indians would not have the money to retain a lawyer to pursue the claims. Congress acted on this recommendation and repealed the Act. Fritz was offered a position as an attorney in the Department of Transportation, but he turned it down and brought suit against the government.

What is the likely result of this suit?

(A) Fritz prevails, because it violates the doctrine of separation of powers for the executive branch to interfere with a congressional act by recommending its repeal.

(B) Fritz prevails, because it violates the Constitution to terminate the tenure of a federal judge during good behavior.

(C) The government prevails, because it established Fritz's position and it can terminate it at will.

(D) The government prevails, because Fritz had no judicial discretion or powers in his position with the Bureau.

Question 72

The ravages of inflation and its effects on interest rates have caused some states to pass (and enforce) usury laws. These laws have retarded industrial growth in some states with low interest rates to benefit consumers because capital is attracted to states where it would get the most return. As a result of this, Congress has enacted legislation establishing a uniform usury rate. The legislation, in essence, establishes that the usury rate will be determined by the Federal Reserve Board on the date of the loan. The law is intended to be of great assistance to the private home market as well as commercial building.

The state of Oma has a usury law that permits the charging of interest in excess of that which Congress has provided. The state of Oma brings an action in federal court seeking to avoid the law with respect to the state. Oma is able to produce evidence that loans made in the state during the last two years for the purpose of housing all were at rates exceeding those permissible under the provision of the federal law. The state alleges that to enforce the federal law would be to bring the housing industry to a stop.

The federal judge should:

(A) Rule that he has no jurisdiction to hear the case.

(B) Rule that the state law is invalid as a result of the Supremacy Clause.

(C) Rule that granting temporary relief by enjoining the federal act pending a decision on the merits would be proper.

(D) Impanel a three-judge court because of the seriousness of the issue.

Question 73

Which of the following clauses of the Constitution would most likely permit Congress to impose upon the states a uniform child custody law?

(A) The Commerce Clause.

(B) The Police Power Clause.

(C) The Privileges and Immunities Clause.

(D) The Taxing and Spending Power Clause.

Questions 74-76 are based on the following fact situation:

To practice acupuncture in the state of Missouri, one must have a license issued by the Missouri Board of Health. Missouri statutes specify that an applicant for an acupuncture license must establish that (i) he was trained, in

Missouri, by a person licensed to practice acupuncture; (ii) he has been a resident of Missouri for the three years preceding the date of application for the license; and (iii) he is a citizen of the United States.

Victor Chan, a citizen of the United Kingdom permanently admitted as a resident alien to the United States, has recently moved from San Francisco, California, to South Rabbit's Foot, Missouri, at the request of that town's only physician. When Victor Chan applied to the Missouri Board of Health for a license to practice acupuncture, his application was denied because he was not trained in Missouri (having been trained in Hong Kong), has not resided in Missouri for the preceding three years, and is not a United States citizen. The citizens of South Rabbit's Foot and Victor Chan bring an action in federal district court against the Missouri Board of Health and the state of Missouri seeking to compel them to issue a license to practice acupuncture to Mr. Chan.

74. If the plaintiffs challenge the constitutionality of the Missouri statute that predicates issuance of a license on United States citizenship, their best argument would be:

   (A) That it is a bill of attainder.

   (B) That it violates the Equal Protection Clause of the Fifth Amendment.

   (C) That it violates the Equal Protection Clause of the Fourteenth Amendment.

   (D) That it invades the foreign policy power reserved to the federal government.

75. Chan's strongest argument against the requirement that an applicant be trained in Missouri is:

   (A) The requirement violates the Privileges and Immunities Clause of the Fourteenth Amendment.

   (B) The requirement violates the Privileges and Immunities Clause of Article IV.

   (C) The requirement burdens his fundamental right to practice a particular profession.

   (D) The requirement bears no relationship to the interests the state seeks to protect.

76. The plaintiffs' challenge to the residency requirement of the Missouri statutes will probably:

   (A) Succeed, because the requirement violates the Privileges and Immunities Clause of the Fourteenth Amendment.

   (B) Succeed, because the requirement violates the Equal Protection Clause of the Fourteenth Amendment.

   (C) Succeed, because the requirement violates the Due Process Clause of the Fourteenth Amendment.

   (D) Fail, because the state has a compelling interest in furthering the welfare of its residents.

Question 77

For the past two years, Professor has been employed as a teacher in the Biology Department of State University. By law, a professor does not acquire tenure until after he or she has completed three consecutive years of teaching. Shortly after Professor completed her second year, she was informed that she was not being rehired for the following year. Applicable state law did not require either a statement of reasons or a hearing, and the State University administration refused to give either to Professor.

Which of the following, if established, sets forth the strongest constitutional argument Professor could make to compel the college to furnish her a statement of reasons for the failure to rehire her and an opportunity for the hearing?

   (A) She purchased a home in anticipation of renewal of her contract, since most professors who had taught two years were rehired.

(B)   She had been voted the most popular
      professor on campus in each of her first
      two years of teaching.

(C)   She was the only teacher at State Univer-
      sity whose contract was not renewed that
      year.

(D)   There is evidence to indicate that the
      decision not to rehire Professor was not
      based on her ability to teach.

CONSTITUTIONAL LAW ANSWERS

Answer to Question 1

(D)   There is a live controversy and the case is not moot. A federal court will not hear a case unless there is a real, live controversy at all stages of the proceeding, not merely when the case is filed. Since Sebastian is no longer required to pay nonresident tuition, there is arguably no controversy and the case may seem moot. However, a class action is not moot, and the class representative may continue to pursue it—even if the representative's own controversy has become moot— because the claims of others in the class are still viable. Here, Sebastian filed his suit as a class action for University students with less than three years' residency; undoubtedly some of those students will still have a real controversy at this time. Thus, the case is not moot. (A) is wrong although it states a true fact. (A) implies that the case should be dismissed because Sebastian's claim is moot. As explained above, this is a class action and other members of the class have a viable case. Thus, even though Sebastian's case by itself would be moot, he may continue the case as a representative of the class action. (B) is wrong because standing (the requirement that a plaintiff have a concrete stake in the outcome of the case) is determined at the beginning of a lawsuit. At the beginning of Sebastian's case, Sebastian had standing because he had suffered an injury (*i.e.,* had to pay nonresident tuition), caused by the government, that was remediable by the court. Thus, he had a concrete stake in the outcome of the case and had standing. (C) is wrong because it is irrelevant; the fact that amicus curiae briefs have been filed has no effect on mootness. A moot case will not be heard simply because amicus briefs have been filed.

Answer to Question 2

(B)   The tax is constitutional because it represents a proper exercise of the power of Congress to tax and spend for the general welfare. Pursuant to the Constitution, Congress may tax and spend to provide for the general welfare. A congressional tax measure will be upheld if it bears some reasonable relationship to revenue production or if Congress has the power to regulate the taxed activity. Congress may spend for any public purpose, not merely the accomplishment of other enumerated powers. The tax at issue here bears a reasonable relationship to revenue production. Also, the purchase and sale of cigarettes in the United States is subject to congressional regulation, as an activity having a substantial economic effect upon interstate commerce. Thus, the tax itself is valid. The amendment to the original tax bill is also valid, as a reflection of a congressional determination to use the proceeds of the tax for the promotion and implementation of an antismoking program, presumably in furtherance of public health. This is a public purpose for which Congress can spend pursuant to the General Welfare Clause. (A) is incorrect because it implies that the purpose of the tax is not constitutional. The purpose of the tax is to raise revenue to fund a federal antismoking program. As explained above, this is a proper exercise of the congressional taxing and spending power. Therefore, the constitutionality of the tax does not hinge on the severability of its purpose. (C) is incorrect because there is no "fairness doctrine" under the Constitution; *i.e.,* when Congress determines a course of action pursuant to its power to tax and spend for the general welfare, it need not provide equal time for opponents of the action to express their views. (D) is incorrect because the tax in no way abridges the First Amendment rights of the manufacturers. While the freedom of speech is very broad and includes the freedom to not speak and to refrain from endorsing views with which one does not agree, it does not invalidate the tax here because the tax does not force the tobacco companies to endorse the stop-smoking clinics or the government's antismoking stance. Neither does the tax forbid or control the tobacco manufacturers from endorsing a pro-smoking message. The manufacturers' First Amendment rights are simply not burdened here.

Answer to Question 3

(C) If there is no substantial threat that the statute will be enforced, then there are no constitutional issues ripe for review. A federal court will resolve only constitutional issues that are necessarily presented, ripe for review, and unavoidable for decision of the case. Someone seeking a declaration that a statute is unconstitutional must demonstrate that she has engaged (or will engage) in specific conduct, and that the challenged statute poses a real and immediate danger to her interests. The court will not determine the constitutionality of a statute when the statute has not been enforced and there is no immediate threat that it will be enforced. Thus, if the state of Blue statute is not likely to be enforced, it is not a substantial threat to the Joneses and so they will be unable to demonstrate any real and immediate harm (or threat thereof) to their interest. Therefore, this case is not ripe, and this choice gives the state a chance to defeat the Joneses' argument. The other choices do not present the state with viable arguments. (A) is incorrect because, if ripeness were present, an action for declaratory judgment *would* be proper. A federal court may not issue advisory opinions, but where there is a real controversy, it may issue a final judgment declaring the rights and liabilities of the parties even though no affirmative relief is sought. Maintenance of such an action requires an actual dispute between parties with adverse legal interests. If the Joneses were being prosecuted for violating the statute (or threatened with prosecution), the requisites for a declaratory judgment would be met and it would be an appropriate means of determining the constitutionality of the state of Blue statute. (B) is incorrect because the refusal of the state legislature to repeal the statute indicates a legislative intent that the statute remain in effect, thus implying a greater likelihood that the statute *would be enforced*. This would make the Joneses' case ripe and so would help them rather than defeat their action. (D) is incorrect because the grounds for abstention are absent. When a federal constitutional claim is premised on an unsettled question of state law, the federal court should abstain, to give the state courts a chance to settle the underlying state law question. Here, there is no unsettled question of state law. Therefore, abstention by the federal court would be inappropriate.

Answer to Question 4

(D) The sincerity of the Joneses' religious beliefs is a factor that can be inquired into as a way of determining whether the Joneses can avail themselves of the protection of the Free Exercise Clause. The Free Exercise Clause of the First Amendment, applicable to the states through the Fourteenth Amendment, prohibits punishing people for their religious beliefs. When a person claims that he is being punished for his religious beliefs, the court may consider whether the person challenging the law sincerely holds those beliefs. Thus, the court may consider whether the Joneses' beliefs are sincerely held. (A) is incorrect because the First Amendment forbids a court from determining whether a person's religious beliefs are true. A court must respect a sincerely held religious belief, even if it appears to be illogical or incapable of proof. (B) is incorrect because the Free Exercise Clause protects all sincerely held religious beliefs, regardless of whether a specific religion is deemed to be "established" or "traditional." (C) is incorrect because religious beliefs need not be theistic to qualify for constitutional protection. An asserted religious belief must occupy a place in the believer's life parallel to that occupied by orthodox religious beliefs. Even an internally derived belief is entitled to protection.

Answer to Question 5

(A) The Free Exercise Clause does not afford a right to a religious exemption from a neutral law that happens to impose a substantial burden on religious practice, if the law is otherwise constitutionally applied to persons who engage (or fail to engage) in the particular conduct for nonreligious reasons. Here, the Joneses claim that the state of Blue vaccination statute interferes with their religious beliefs. However, the statute requires **all parents** to obtain vaccinations for their children. Thus, if the state argues that the law was enacted to ensure the health of its children and not merely to interfere with the religious beliefs of people such as the Joneses, the state will succeed. (B) is incorrect because conduct is protected (although the protection is limited). For example, the government cannot punish conduct merely because it is religious (although if the law affects both religious and nonreligious conduct, it is generally valid). [*See, e.g.,* Employment Division v. Smith (1990)] (C) is incorrect because it states the former rule in these cases. In the past, the Court used a balancing test to determine whether a religious exemption had to be granted from a law with a secular purpose that happened to burden religious practices or beliefs. The Court would consider the severity of the burden, the strength of the state's interest, and the existence of alternative means. Now, however, the Court no longer uses a balancing test; the state need not establish a strong interest or a lack of alternative means if the challenged statute is neutral. (D) could be successfully argued, but its chances for success are not as certain as for the argument in (A). The Establishment Clause prohibits laws respecting the establishment of religion. If a law includes a preference for one religious sect over another, the law will be held invalid unless it is narrowly tailored to promote a compelling interest. If there is no sect preference, the law is valid if: (i) it has a secular purpose; (ii) its primary effect neither advances nor inhibits religion; and (iii) it does not produce excessive government entanglement. Here, no sect preference appears, since nothing indicates that the state of Blue would exempt only members of the Joneses' religion. It could be argued, however, that the only purpose for the exemption here is to favor religious believers over nonbelievers. If that is the purpose, the exemption would not have a secular purpose and would fail the secular purpose test above. On the other hand, the state could argue that free exercise of religion is also protected, and the exemption protects sincerely held religious beliefs. [*See, e.g.,* Wisconsin v. Yoder (1979)] Thus, the outcome of the argument in (D) is uncertain, and (A) is the state's best argument.

Answer to Question 6

(A)   The court will likely reject Deeco's challenge to the Illianda pricing scheme. Although the Commerce Clause generally prohibits states from discriminating against out-of-state businesses to benefit local economic interests, the market participant exception applies here. The Commerce Clause does not prevent a state from preferring its own citizens when the state is acting as a market participant (*e.g.,* buying or selling products, hiring labor, giving subsidies, etc.). Since the pricing scheme here involves the sale of goods, Illianda can constitutionally charge whatever prices it desires to whomever it desires. Therefore, (A) is correct and (C) is incorrect. (B) reaches the right result but for the wrong reason. But for the market participant exception, the Illianda pricing scheme would violate the Commerce Clause for discriminating against nonresidents. It would not matter that Illianda's prices outside of Illianda are lower than anyone else's price, since Illianda is charging its own residents an even lower price. (D) is incorrect. Although the Privileges and Immunities Clause of Article IV entitles citizens of each state to the privileges and immunities of citizens of the several states, and thus prohibits discrimination by a state against nonresidents, the Clause does not apply to corporations, such as Deeco. Therefore, the Clause cannot be the basis for the court's ruling here.

Answer to Question 7

(D)   The Supreme Court may grant certiorari to review a case from the highest court in a state that can render an opinion on the matter if a state statute's validity is called into question under the federal Constitution. [28 U.S.C. §1257] The Court may decide the federal issues, but cannot rule on the state law issues. (A) is incorrect for several reasons: (i) the attorney general evaluated only the proposal's validity under the state constitution; and (ii) even if her opinion had addressed the proposal's federal constitutional validity, the Supreme Court is not bound by advisory opinions of state attorneys general. (B) is incorrect even though the state supreme court may have had an independent state ground for finding the law constitutional under its state constitution. The Supreme Court will refuse to hear the case only if the state ground is *adequate* by itself to support the decision as well as independent, so that the Court's review of the federal ground for the decision would have no effect on the outcome of the case (such as if the state court had found the law invalid under both the state and federal Constitutions). Here, the Supreme Court's review of the state court opinion on the law's federal constitutional status may have an outcome on the case regardless of the state court's decision on the state constitutional issue; the Court therefore will hear the federal issues involved. (C) is incorrect because 28 U.S.C. section 1257 provides that appellate review of a matter from a state's highest court is to the Supreme Court by petition for a writ of certiorari, rather than to a federal district court.

Answer to Question 8

(D) The legislation is unconstitutional because it violates the federal postal monopoly. Article I, Section 8, Clause 7 of the Constitution grants Congress the power to establish post offices and post roads. This power grants Congress a monopoly over the delivery of mail. No other system for delivering mail—public or private—can be established absent Congress's consent. Congress has delegated to the Postal Service the power to decide whether others may compete with it, and the Postal Service has carved out an exception to its monopoly for extremely urgent letters. However, this exception would not apply to the state messenger service here since the Arkiana service extends to every letter or package of an employee deliverable within the state. (A) is irrelevant because the postal monopoly applies even to wholly intrastate competing systems. The rationale is that the Postal Service must be protected from companies that would deliver only on profitable routes at a low cost, leaving the Postal Service only expensive, money-losing routes. (B) is a misstatement of the law. The Commerce Clause does not prohibit states from competing; rather, it merely prohibits states from interfering with interstate commerce by either protecting local economic interests or unduly burdening interstate transactions. (C) is incorrect because the Equal Protection Clause would not prohibit the special treatment here. Since no suspect class or fundamental right is involved, the program would be judged under the rational basis standard. Under this standard, a law is upheld if it is rationally related to *any* legitimate government interest. Here, the law would be upheld since there is a conceivable rational basis for the program (*e.g.,* to make government employment more attractive), and the law is rationally related to that interest.

Answer to Question 9

(C) The state ticket distribution system is unconstitutional because of the Supremacy Clause. A valid act of Congress supersedes any state or local action that conflicts with it. The act here is valid since Congress has the power to spend for the general welfare, and in so doing may place conditions on grants as it sees fit. The state law directly conflicts with the federal law since the federal law requires that tickets be distributed on a first come, first served basis and the state law requires that 35% of the tickets be given to minority school children. Since the state law conflicts with the federal law, it is invalid. (A) is based on the Tenth Amendment, and is incorrect because even if Congress lacks the power to directly regulate the distribution of the tickets in question, the regulation here would still be valid as a spending power condition. The Supreme Court has held that Congress may condition grants under the spending power even where it cannot directly regulate. [*See* South Dakota v. Dole (1987)—conditioning federal highway grants on prohibiting minors from drinking] (B) is incorrect because the Supremacy Clause invalidates **all** conflicting state laws where there is a clash, no matter how complementary the state law may be viewed. (D) is incorrect because the state program probably is valid under the Equal Protection Clause. State programs that ***favor*** racial and ethnic minorities are subject to the same strict scrutiny standards as programs that discriminate against minorities: they must be narrowly tailored to promote a compelling government interest. There is a compelling government interest in remedying past discrimination, and the facts indicate that the ballet company was established to remedy the prior lack of cultural opportunity that existed in the inner city. The program also appears to be narrowly tailored, and so would likely survive an equal protection challenge.

Answer to Question 10

(B) The President's action is constitutional pursuant to his power over treaties and foreign relations. The power to enter into treaties is vested in the President, and his power to act for the United States in day-to-day foreign affairs is paramount. Even as to foreign relations that require congressional consent, the President's powers are much broader than in the realm of internal affairs. No significant judicial control has been exercised over such declarations. Thus, this action is allowable under these broad powers. (A) is incorrect because the Supremacy Clause, by itself, grants no power to the federal government. It merely provides that the Constitution, laws, and treaties of the United States are the supreme law of the land, and conflicting state or local laws must yield. Thus, the President must find his authority to act elsewhere in the Constitution. (C) is incorrect because the President's emergency power to protect United States citizens is unclear. While he has power to act concerning foreign nations, it is unclear whether he could "legislate" concerning the internal affairs involved here (*e.g.,* tax collection) merely because he thought that United States citizens needed protection. In any case, the power to act here more properly arises from the President's power over foreign affairs and not from a power to protect United States citizens. (D) is incorrect because the Constitution only requires the President to obtain the advice and consent of the Senate to enter into treaties; it does not require him to obtain Senate consent to void a treaty.

Answer to Question 11

(B) New City may continue to operate the garden because the display is not primarily religious in nature. In a case such as this, where state action does not involve a preference of one religious sect over another, the action is valid under the Establishment Clause if (i) it has a secular purpose, (ii) its primary effect neither advances nor inhibits religion, and (iii) it does not involve excessive government entanglement with religion. These tests are met here: The secular purpose is to promote pride in heritage and perhaps to encourage people to learn about the heritage of others. The primary effect does not promote or inhibit religion, but merely acknowledges the religious backgrounds of New City residents. Finally, the maintenance and administration of the garden by the city does not constitute excessive entanglement between government and religion. Therefore, (B) is correct and (C) is incorrect. [*See* Lynch v. Donnelly (1984)—permitting government-maintained Christmas display that includes religious as well as nonreligious symbols] (A) is incorrect because if the garden did fail one of the above tests, the fact that only a relatively small amount of municipal funds were used would not remedy the constitutional violation; de minimis is not a defense. (D) is incorrect because it states the wrong test. Establishment Clause cases not involving a sect preference are resolved under the above three-part test and not under the compelling interest test.

Answer to Question 12

(A) The statute is constitutional as a legitimate exercise of congressional enforcement powers under the Enabling Clause of the Thirteenth Amendment. The Thirteenth Amendment prohibits slavery. The Enabling Clause of the amendment has been held to confer upon Congress the authority to proscribe almost any private racially discriminatory action that can be characterized as a badge or incident of slavery. Because the statute at issue bans *all* discrimination against African Americans in commercial transactions, it necessarily reaches private conduct. Such congressional action is constitutionally permissible pursuant to the Thirteenth Amendment. (B) is incorrect. Application of the Fourteenth Amendment has been limited to cases involving state action. [*See* United States v. Morrison (2000)] The statute here reaches private action, and so the Thirteenth Amendment is the correct source for the law, since that amendment addresses private action. (C) is incorrect because even if Congress's power over interstate commerce would not reach every commercial transaction, the statute would be enforceable under the Thirteenth Amendment, as discussed above. (D) is incorrect because it is irrelevant. While it is true that the commercial transactions here are not among the privileges and immunities of citizenship (which include rights such as the right to petition Congress for redress and the right to interstate travel), the law can be based on the Commerce Clause or the Thirteenth Amendment, and thus is constitutional.

Answer to Question 13

(B) The federal court should dismiss the action since there is no case or controversy. The federal courts will not issue advisory opinions and so will not hear collusive actions. The fear is that if interested parties are not on both sides of an issue, the court will not have an opportunity to fairly address all of the sides to each issue. Here, there is no interested party opposing Lola, and so the federal court should dismiss. (A) is incorrect since Lola has standing. To have standing, a person must have a concrete stake in the outcome of the controversy. A plaintiff will have to show an injury in fact caused by the government that can be remedied by a decision in her favor. Lola would be able to get an abortion in Infamy if the statute is stricken, and so she has standing. (C) is incorrect because a political question is not involved. A political question is an issue committed by the Constitution to another branch of the government or an issue inherently incapable of resolution and enforcement by the political process. Whether a residency requirement is constitutional is not a political question. (D) is incorrect. When a state uses a durational residency requirement (a waiting period) for dispensing benefits, the government usually must show that the requirement is tailored to promote a compelling interest because it interferes with an individual's fundamental right to migrate from state to state. However, even assuming that the community interest in preventing nonresidents from draining local welfare funds is compelling, the court should decline jurisdiction since there is no case or controversy here.

Answer to Question 14

(C) The best argument for striking down the statute as unconstitutional is the Commerce Clause. Under the Commerce Clause, states may regulate local aspects of interstate commerce as long as the regulation does not discriminate against interstate commerce or unduly burden interstate commerce. The statute here does not discriminate against interstate commerce since it treats all trucks alike. To determine whether the statute unduly burdens interstate commerce the court will balance the incidental burden on interstate commerce from the statute against the benefits produced by the legislation. Here, the burden on commerce is great, because the statute will force everyone who wants to travel through Zephyr to have Type B tires. The Supreme Court, in its opinion on the benefit produced by the statute from the previous case, found Type A tires and Type B tires equally safe. Thus, the statute provides little, if any, benefit. Since the burden on interstate commerce outweighs the benefits of the statute, the statute will be struck down. (A) is incorrect because the fact that tires are equally safe does not itself render a ban against one type of tire unconstitutional. Such an argument might arise under the Due Process Clause (*i.e.,* the law is arbitrary), but the issue is not fully discussed in choice (A). In any case, the mere fact that the tires are equally safe is not itself a constitutional rationale for striking down a law. (B) is incorrect because the Supremacy Clause is used to strike down state laws that conflict with federal laws or regulations or that involve a field that Congress has preempted. Under the facts here, there is no conflicting federal law and nothing indicates that Congress has preempted the field. Rather, the actual basis for invalidating this law is the "dormant" or "negative" Commerce Clause. (D) is incorrect because res judicata (the fact that the issue has been litigated before) is not a constitutional doctrine, and the Court need not follow its previous decision.

Answer to Question 15

(C) The President's strongest argument is that the power to select ambassadors is vested by the Constitution in the President, and the Senate's only power in this respect is to advise and give (or withhold) its consent. The Senate is not given the power to force ambassadors on the President. (A) is not a strong argument because the President's power as commander-in-chief is not involved here. That power involves the President's role as the supreme military leader, and military issues are not involved under the facts. (B) is not a strong argument because as far as foreign relations are concerned, the Senate does have more powers than the House. As stated above, ambassadors may be selected only with the advice and consent of the Senate, and the President's treaty power is also similarly limited. Thus, but for the fact that the resolution is not within the Senate's power to enforce, it would be appropriate to exclude the House from participating, since foreign affairs are involved. (D) may be a true statement, since Congress controls appropriations, but it is not a strong argument because it merely states that the Senate has another remedy (*i.e.,* besides forcing an ambassador on the President), and the fact that the Senate has another method for achieving its goals has no bearing on whether its action here is permissible.

Answer to Question 16

(D) Sanjay is most likely to prevail in his attempt to obtain a teaching position at the university. State or local laws based on alienage are subject to strict scrutiny. A state generally may not discriminate against aliens absent a compelling state interest, and no compelling interest is served by prohibiting aliens from teaching at a state university. However, where the discrimination relates to participation of aliens in the functioning of state government, the rational basis test applies. The Supreme Court has upheld statutes similar to those in (A), prohibiting aliens from teaching primary or secondary school on the rationale that teachers at the elementary and high school level have a great deal of influence over the attitudes of students toward government, the political process, and citizenship. While the court has not decided a challenge to a state law restricting aliens from teaching at the university level, it is likely to find that the rationale for the ban at the lower-level schools is not as applicable to university students. Thus, although it is not certain whether he would prevail, Sanjay has a better chance in challenging the ban at the university level than at the high school level. (B) and (C) are incorrect for the same reason as (A)—the Court has upheld statutes prohibiting aliens from serving as police or probation officers, because those officers have a direct effect on the functioning of government.

Answer to Question 17

(D) Brown can be convicted because the statute does not violate the First Amendment. Certain public property (*e.g.,* public streets or parks) is so historically associated with the exercise of First

Amendment rights that speech thereon can be regulated only by content neutral proscriptions. Other places controlled by the government, however, are not so historically linked to speech activities, and in such locations free speech might interfere with the intended use of such locations. Thus, the government can regulate access to these nonpublic forums based on the subject matter of the speech, as long as the regulation is reasonably related to the purpose served by the property and is not designed merely to suppress a particular point of view. A courthouse and its grounds are not a public forum. (The surrounding sidewalks are, but that is not in issue here.) The statute, although based on the subject matter of speech, is viewpoint neutral and reasonably related to the courthouse purpose of promoting a stable, orderly atmosphere in which judicial proceedings can take place, free of improper outside influence or coercion. Thus, the statute is valid and Brown can be convicted for her actions. (A) is wrong because it is based on an overbreadth argument and the statute here is not overbroad. A regulation of speech that restricts substantially more speech than necessary is unenforceable, even if the speech in question could have been properly restricted by a narrower statute. This doctrine is inapplicable here because the statute is not overbroad: it reaches only speech *in the courthouse or on its grounds* and only that speech *that might improperly influence the judicial proceedings*; it does not limit all speech at that location. (B) is wrong because Brown's personal intent to harm the judge is irrelevant. The statute makes it a crime to make a speech or carry a sign intended to influence the judicial proceeding. The statute does not require that the violator intend to harm anyone. Since the state is entitled to regulate speech or conduct in the courthouse or on its grounds that might interfere with the judicial proceedings, it is entitled to convict Brown for her actions here regardless of her intent to harm the judge. (C) is wrong because it improperly applies the "clear and present danger" test to these facts. Under the current version of the "clear and present danger" test, a state cannot forbid advocating the *use of force or violation of law* unless such advocacy is (i) directed to producing or inciting imminent lawless action, and (ii) likely to produce such action. The state statute here does not purport to punish advocacy of force or lawlessness, but rather seeks to further the purpose of maintaining the stability and integrity of the judicial proceedings by regulating access to certain nonpublic areas. Therefore, the restrictions are constitutionally valid and the "clear and present danger" test is inapplicable.

Answer to Question 18

(B) The court will most likely uphold the statute because it is a religiously neutral law of general application. The First Amendment provides that the free exercise of religion shall not be abridged; however, the prohibition is far from absolute. The Supreme Court has stated that the amendment prohibits the government from outlawing religious beliefs and probably from outlawing conduct merely because it is religious (*i.e.,* the state could not forbid the handling of snakes only in religious ceremonies), but states may validly proscribe general conduct; *i.e.,* a law of general application will not be held invalid under the First Amendment merely because it happens to proscribe conduct that is required by one's religious beliefs. Neither will the state be required to provide religious exemptions from the statute. [Employment Division v. Smith (1990)] Thus, the statute here is probably valid. (A) is incorrect because the state need not show a compelling interest to have the statute upheld; it will be held valid as long as it is a religiously neutral law of general application. (Note that before *Smith,* the Court often purported to apply a balancing test to cases such as the one here, and the state had to show a compelling interest for a statute that interfered with religious conduct.) (C) is incorrect because the state need not show that a statute is the least restrictive means for achieving its legislative goal merely because the statute happens to burden religious conduct. (This was sometimes required under the balancing test formerly used.) (D) is incorrect because it is irrelevant whether the religious practice interfered with is an integral function of a religion or merely a minor belief—the Court will not assess the centrality of religious belief, but will only inquire into whether a person's belief is sincere.

Answer to Question 19

(B) The legislation is valid because the statute does not conflict with federal legislation or violate the Commerce Clause. The states may regulate local aspects of interstate commerce as long as Congress has not adopted regulations concerning the subject matter or preempting the entire area of regulation. Even absent federal legislation, under the negative implications of the Commerce Clause the state regulation must not discriminate against interstate commerce or unduly burden it. Here, there is no federal legislation directly conflicting with the state law, since the facts state that the federal government only regulates the rates that may be charged by phone companies. Neither has Congress preempted the field. Preemption occurs when Congress shows an intent to occupy an entire field, thus precluding any state regulation. If the law does not state whether state law is to be preempted, the Court will look to the comprehensiveness of the scheme and whether Congress has created an agency to administer over the area. Here, the legislative scheme does not seem comprehensive, and although the facts indirectly mention the existence of an agency (since there are relevant administrative rules), it may be presumed that Congress did not intend to preempt the field here (the agency's only power presumably is over rate regulation). Finally, the state law does not discriminate against out-of-state competition, since the manufacturer of the device is located in the state, and the law does not unduly burden interstate commerce, because the incidental burden on interstate commerce does not appear to outweigh the legitimate local benefits produced by the regulation. Thus, (B) is correct. (A) is incorrect because the federal commerce power allows regulation of any activity, local or interstate, that either in itself or in combination with other activities has a substantial economic effect on interstate commerce. Here, it would be within Congress's power to regulate such a device even though it is being used only within the state. (C) is incorrect for the reasons stated above regarding preemption. (D) is incorrect because, as indicated above, states may regulate local aspects of interstate commerce under certain circumstances.

Answer to Question 20

(D) Tackhammer has no good argument for doing the rehabilitation work himself. (A) is incorrect because Tackhammer has no equal protection claim. The Equal Protection Clause guarantees that similarly situated persons will not be treated differently, absent sufficient justification. Here, the city treats all would-be developers in the same manner, requiring them all to use the city's Development Authority to implement their plans; thus, (A) is not a good argument. (B) is incorrect because the Due Process Clause has not been violated here. The substantive portion of the Due Process Clause requires that laws or other government action not be arbitrary. If a fundamental right is involved, the strict scrutiny standard is applied, and the action will be invalid unless it is necessary to a compelling interest. If no fundamental right is involved, the action will be upheld as long as it is rationally related to a legitimate governmental interest. Here, no fundamental right is involved, and the requirement that developers use the Development Authority is rationally related to the city's legitimate interest in raising revenue. Therefore, substantive due process is not violated. The procedural portion of the Due Process Clause forbids denying a person of life, liberty, or property without fair process. It would require that Tackhammer be heard before some neutral decisionmaker on the question of whether he should be allowed to develop the block himself. However, the Clause is not applicable here because Tackhammer has no legitimate property interest in developing the block. "Property" in this context includes more than personal belongings, but there must be some legitimate claim or entitlement to a government benefit for a property interest to arise in it. Tackhammer has no such claim here; rather, he has only an expectation of deriving the benefit. Thus, (B) is not a good argument. (C) is incorrect because the Privileges and Immunities Clause is not applicable here. The Article IV Privileges and Immunities

Clause prohibits states from discriminating against nonresidents regarding "fundamental" rights, and here there is no such discrimination. Therefore, this is not a good argument.

Answer to Question 21

(B) The President has no power to decline to spend funds specifically appropriated by Congress when Congress has expressly mandated that they be spent, regardless of Congress's reason for making the appropriation. The President has no "legislative" power in internal affairs, and has a duty under Article II to "see that the laws are faithfully executed." In contrast, Congress clearly has the power to spend to "provide for the common defense and general welfare." [U.S. Const. art. I, §8] Hence, the Supreme Court has ruled that there is no constitutional basis for the President to "impound" (*i.e.,* refuse to spend) funds whose expenditure Congress has expressly mandated. [Kendall v. United States (1838)] Here, since Congress passed a separate appropriations bill mandating that funds be spent on the relocation of the training center, the President must carry out the congressional directive. (A) is wrong because there is no requirement that the President exercise in a nonpolitical manner any power that he has over expenditures; the fact that he may have refused to authorize expenditures to obtain votes on an unrelated matter would not by itself invalidate his action. (C) is wrong because the President's authority is very limited when he is taking action in the domestic arena against the express will of Congress. [*See* Youngstown Sheet & Tube v. Sawyer (1952)] Here, Congress has specifically directed that the training center be relocated, and there is no indication in the facts that there is a military necessity in keeping the center at that location. (D) is incorrect because the scope of the President's authority on budget matters does not extend to refusing to spend funds specifically appropriated by Congress.

Answer to Question 22

(C) The tax is a constitutional exercise of the federal power to raise revenue. The Constitution gives Congress the power to raise revenue and collect taxes, and a tax measure will be upheld as long as it bears some reasonable relationship to revenue production. Moreover, even if the tax does not relate to revenue production, it will be upheld if Congress has the power to otherwise regulate the subject taxed. Here, the tax appears to be related to revenue production, since its revenues are earmarked to help law enforcement. And even if the law were not related to revenue production it would still be upheld because it involves goods in interstate commerce, and Congress has plenary power to regulate interstate commerce. Thus, (C) is correct. (A) is incorrect because the constitutional right to bear arms probably refers only to the rights of the states to maintain militias. However, even if it gives each citizen the right individually to bear arms, that right, like any other right under the Constitution, is not absolute, and the tax suggested would not greatly infringe on the right, so it would be valid. (B) is incorrect because federal taxes are not limited to interstate activities. Moreover, even if the tax relies upon the Commerce Clause for its validity, it is still valid. Although the tax will regulate intrastate activities, the Commerce Clause has been held to give Congress the power to regulate any activity that has a substantial cumulative effect on interstate commerce, and almost all intrastate sales of goods, taken together, may be found to have such an effect on interstate commerce. (D) is incorrect because it is irrelevant. The Supremacy Clause makes federal law supreme over conflicting state law, but there is no conflicting state law here.

Answer to Question 23

(D) Congress's broad powers under the Commerce Clause provide the strongest basis for supporting the statute. The Commerce Clause gives Congress plenary power to regulate interstate commerce.

The transmission of information across state lines via telephone or teletype lines has been held a sufficient basis for invoking the commerce power of the federal government. Hence, it would permit regulation of the activity being conducted over those lines, such as the interception of market information prohibited by the statute. (A) is incorrect because the General Welfare Clause is a limitation on Congress's enumerated power to tax and spend rather than an independent source of congressional power (*i.e.,* Congress's power to tax and spend must be carried out for "the general welfare"). (B) is incorrect because Congress has no enumerated police power. Other than for the District of Columbia, all general police powers to provide for citizens' health, welfare, etc., are vested in the state rather than in Congress. (C) is incorrect because the power to tax and spend permits taxing and spending measures but not statutes that directly regulate and prohibit an activity, as the statute in question does.

Answer to Question 24

(B) Dullsville is likely to prevail because the zoning ordinance is a constitutional restriction on the operation of adult-oriented businesses. The Supreme Court has held that businesses selling material that is sexually explicit, although not necessarily obscene, may be regulated through land use ordinances designed to reduce the secondary effects of such businesses. Thus, a zoning ordinance prohibiting the location of adult bookstores and theaters in areas close to residential zones and restricting such theaters to a limited area of the city is permissible if it is designed to promote substantial government interests (*e.g.,* property interests) and does not prohibit all such entertainment in the community. [City of Renton v. Playtime Theaters, Inc. (1986)] Because Dullsville's ordinance is a legitimate part of its zoning scheme and does not prevent the businesses from operating in other areas of the town, it will probably be upheld. (A) is incorrect because it is too broad. The type of regulation in this question cannot be based simply on what residents find "offensive"; only regulations that are based on substantial government interests and do not entirely prohibit the activity have been permitted by the Supreme Court. (C) is incorrect because the regulation here, even if it is arguably content-based, is permissible because it is based on the legitimate local interest of preserving property values from the secondary effects of such businesses. (D) is incorrect because a city may restrict the location of speech-related businesses under the circumstances here without having to establish that the content of the speech is obscene.

Answer to Question 25

(D) Because the ordinance is not related to the exercise of a fundamental right or based on a suspect trait, it need only rationally relate to some legitimate governmental interest. Under the Equal Protection Clause, which is implicated because the ordinance treats some city employees differently from others, a governmental classification must be necessary to promote a compelling state interest when it relates to who may exercise a fundamental right or when it is based on a suspect trait (*e.g.,* race or national origin). If a quasi-suspect classification (*e.g.,* gender or legitimacy) is involved, the classification will be upheld if it is substantially related to an important government interest. In all other cases, the classification is valid if there is any conceivable basis upon which it might relate to any legitimate governmental interest. This "rational basis" test is used for all classifications that only relate to matters of economics or social welfare. The right of police officers and firefighters to hold second jobs is not a fundamental right that will trigger strict scrutiny. In addition, the ordinance is not based on a suspect or quasi-suspect classification. Therefore, the validity of the ordinance is judged according to the "rational basis" test. A party attacking a classification under this test bears the difficult burden of demonstrating to the court that the classification does not have a rational relationship to a legitimate interest of government. The ordinance is intended to and does in fact promote the legitimate governmental interests of public safety and social welfare—it increases the likelihood that there will be sufficient numbers of police and firefighters to deal with emergencies and to maintain order during times of increased population. Thus, the ordinance is valid. (C) is incorrect because, as detailed above, the test applicable here is the "rational basis" test, which requires only that the city have a "legitimate" interest rather than a "significant" interest. (B) is incorrect. Although the ordinance treats police officers and firefighters differently from other city employees, this treatment, as discussed above, is rationally related to legitimate governmental interests. Regarding (A), it is doubtful from the facts that Mikey's job as a male dancer was a means of exercising his freedom of expression. However, even if Mikey was "expressing" himself by means of this job, the ordinance's content-neutral restriction on this freedom is only incidental, is in furtherance of the governmental interests of public safety and social welfare, and is narrowly tailored to the furtherance of those interests. Note also that the city is not prohibiting Mikey from expressing himself by means of the dance art form as such, but is only prohibiting him from holding a job in addition to that of police officer. Presumably, Mikey is free to join a dance troupe or otherwise engage in dance, as long as such activities do not involve his being employed outside the police force. For these reasons, (A) is incorrect.

Answer to Question 26

(D) Fox can obtain damages from Snoops because he had a property right in his manuscript that can be protected by the copyright laws regardless of the public importance of the content. The best way to answer this question is to eliminate the wrong choices. (A) is wrong because there is no First Amendment exception to copyright laws. It does not matter that Fox may have been a public figure or that his book discussed a matter of public concern; magazines have no right to publish copyrighted material without permission beyond the statutory fair use exception, not the case here. [Harper & Row Publishers v. Nation Enterprises (1985)] (B) is wrong because it is too broad; the press generally has no greater freedom to speak than does the public. (C) is wrong because the Fifth Amendment is not applicable here. The Fifth Amendment prohibits *government* from taking private property without due process or just compensation, and here a private party has acted. Therefore, (D) is correct; Fox will prevail in an appropriate action for copyright infringement against Snoops because Snoops published portions of Fox's work without permission.

Answer to Question 27

(D) Joe is not likely to prevail because the statute's attempt to compensate for past discrimination against women is substantially related to an important government objective. When examining federal government action involving classifications of persons, the Supreme Court, using the Due Process Clause of the Fifth Amendment, applies the same standards that it applies to state actions under the Fourteenth Amendment Equal Protection Clause. When analyzing government action based on gender classifications, the Court will apply an intermediate standard and strike the action unless the government proves, by an exceedingly persuasive justification, that the action is substantially related to an important government interest. Applying this standard, the Court has generally upheld classifications benefiting women that are designed to remedy past discrimination against women, because remedying past gender discrimination is an important government interest. Here, the federal statute establishes a formula designed not only to insure current "gender equity" in funding of intercollegiate athletic programs but also to correct specific past inequities, and The Fortress's required funding allocation in favor of women is designed to correct inequitable allocations by the school in prior years. Hence, even though the statute's allocation requirement may discriminate against Joe and other males at the school, the government can satisfy its burden of showing a substantial relationship to an important government interest. (A) is incorrect because classifications based on gender are subject to an intermediate standard rather than a strict scrutiny standard; in other words, the government need not show that the classification is necessary to achieve a compelling interest, only that it is substantially related to an important interest. Furthermore, if the classification were one subject to strict scrutiny, remedying past discrimination based on the classification would probably be considered a compelling government interest. (B) is incorrect because Congress may "regulate" states through the spending power by imposing conditions on the grant of money to state governments. Even if Congress lacked the power to directly regulate the activity that is the subject of the spending program, attaching conditions on the spending does not violate the states' Tenth Amendment rights. (C) is wrong because it imposes the burden of proof on the wrong party and relies on the wrong standard. Because the Act results in gender discrimination, the government has the burden of proof, and that burden is to prove that the Act is substantially related to an important government interest.

Answer to Question 28

(B) II. is a valid defense—Consumers Alliance lacks standing to maintain the action because its interest is too remote. As an organization representing the interests of its members, Consumers Alliance would have standing to challenge government actions that injure the organization or its members. A party must have standing to mount a constitutional challenge; *i.e.,* the party must demonstrate a concrete stake in the outcome of a controversy. To show the existence of such a stake, the plaintiff must be able to assert that it is injured by a government action or that the government has made a clear threat to cause injury to it if it fails to comply with a law, regulation, or order. Also, the plaintiff must show that the injury in fact will be remedied by a decision in its favor. As a general rule, people do not have standing as taxpayers to challenge the manner in which the federal government spends tax dollars, because their interest is too remote. Under an exception to this general rule, federal taxpayers have standing to challenge federal appropriation and spending measures if they can establish that the challenged measure: (i) was enacted under the taxing and spending power of Congress; and (ii) exceeds some specific limitation on the power. The only such limit found by the Court to date on the taxing power is the Establishment Clause. Here, Consumers Alliance, as a group of taxpayers trying to challenge the way in which the federal government is spending tax money, falls within the general rule that such people cannot demonstrate a sufficient stake in the outcome of the controversy as to confer upon them standing. In addition, Consumers Alliance cannot claim standing under the exception to this rule, because the challenge raised by the group does not allege that the Establishment Clause, or any other specific limitation on the taxing and spending power, has been exceeded. Thus, II. represents a valid defense to the suit. III. also is a valid defense. Pursuant to the taxing and spending powers, Congress may lay and collect taxes, as well as spend to provide for the common defense and general welfare. Such a spending may be for any public purpose, not merely for the accomplishment of other enumerated powers. The enactment of the Federal Lobster Conservation Act represents spending for the public purpose of promoting the vitality of the major industry of lobster fishing. Consequently, the Act is a valid exercise of the federal taxing and spending powers, and III. is a valid defense. I. does not provide a valid ground of defense because although there is no explicit constitutional statement of the power of federal courts to determine the constitutionality of acts of other branches of government, such judicial review of other branches of the federal government was established in *Marbury v. Madison.* The Constitution is law, and the judiciary has the authority and duty to declare what the law is. For instance, if a plaintiff can show that a particular spending measure exceeds the limitations of the Establishment Clause, a federal court has the power to prevent such an unconstitutional expenditure of funds. Thus, (B), II. and III. only, is the correct choice.

Answer to Question 29

(B)   The Act will be upheld under the Commerce Clause. Congress clearly has the power to regulate interstate commerce and also has the power to tax and spend for the general welfare. The Act here is primarily regulatory in nature and, as part of that regulatory scheme, allocates funds for research. Since the provisions under which Greedy is being assessed are characterized as an "excise tax," there is an initial temptation to label the measure as "penal" or "prohibitive" and, accordingly, outside the parameters of the taxing power. Nevertheless, because the excise tax provision has a regulatory purpose rather than a primarily revenue-raising purpose, the Act will be upheld under the commerce power, rather than the taxing power. Congress has the power to lay and collect taxes, imposts, and excises. A tax measure will be upheld if it bears some reasonable relationship to revenue production *or* if Congress has the power to regulate the taxed activity. Thus, if Congress has the power to regulate the subject or activity taxed, the tax can be upheld as a necessary and proper exercise of one of Congress's regulatory powers (even though enacted for a regulatory rather than a revenue-raising purpose). One of Congress's enumerated powers is the commerce power, pursuant to which Congress may regulate commerce with foreign nations and among the several states. "Commerce" includes almost every form of economic or commercial activity involving or affecting two or more states. It has been held that Congress has the power to regulate any activity, local or interstate, that either in itself or in combination with other activities has a substantial economic effect upon interstate commerce. The excise tax at issue here, when viewed in the context of the Federal Lobster Conservation Act as a whole, appears to be aimed at regulating the catching of lobsters rather than producing revenue. The activity regulated (*i.e.,* the catching of lobsters and subsequent shipping of the lobsters in interstate commerce) will be deemed to have a substantial economic effect upon interstate commerce because the cumulative effect of many such instances could be felt on the supply and demand of the interstate commodity market. Consequently, this activity falls within the regulatory authority of Congress under its commerce power. The tax is therefore a necessary and proper means of carrying out the commerce power. (A) is incorrect because, as a regulatory measure (rather than one geared to raising revenue), the Act's validity is directly based on the authority of Congress to regulate activities impacting commerce. The tax is only valid as a means of implementing this regulatory power. Therefore, it is incorrect to base the validity of the Act directly on the taxing power. (C) and (D) are both incorrect because they advance the notion that a tax cannot be imposed for regulatory purposes. As has been explained above, a tax may be imposed by Congress as a means of effectuating its regulatory powers held pursuant to the Commerce Clause. Thus, a tax is not invalid simply because its purpose is regulatory, whether such a purpose is dominant or otherwise.

Answer to Question 30

(A)   The statute will be upheld because it does not discriminate against out-of-state economic interests and it is not unduly burdensome. A state or local government may regulate local aspects of interstate commerce if such regulation: (i) does not discriminate against out-of-state competition to benefit local economic interests; and (ii) is not unduly burdensome (*i.e.,* the incidental burden on interstate commerce does not outweigh the legitimate local benefits produced by the regulation). The Augusta statute does not discriminate against out-of-state elements of the lobster fishing industry. The statute is designed to maintain the lobster population by allowing lobsters to reproduce. By maintaining the lobster population, Augusta is attempting to further the legitimate interest of reviving its faltering lobster fishing industry, rather than trying to protect a local business against interstate competition. In addition, the statute is applied evenhandedly (*i.e.,* it does not merely regulate the activities of out-of-state lobster fishers while exempting Augusta fishers from those same regulations). Therefore, the statute does not discriminate against interstate commerce. The statute may impose some incidental burden on interstate commerce by requiring out-of-state lobster fishers to refrain from taking lobsters weighing less than one pound from lobster beds within three miles of the Augusta shoreline. However, this burden should not result in any great difficulty for out-of-state lobster fishers who wish to catch lobsters in Augusta waters. There is nothing especially burdensome or restrictive about the statute's provisions, and certainly the incidental burden that does exist does not outweigh Augusta's legitimate interest in maintaining its lobster population and the vitality of its lobster fishing industry. Consequently, the statute is not unduly burdensome. Because the statute is not unduly burdensome and is nondiscriminatory against out-of-state competition, it does not violate the Commerce Clause. (B) is incorrect because, as explained above, the statute does not unduly burden interstate commerce. (D) is incorrect because the statute is not preempted by the federal act. Under the Supremacy Clause, a state law that directly conflicts with a federal law will be held invalid. Even if a state law does not directly conflict with a federal law, it may still be held invalid if it appears that Congress intended to preempt the entire field of regulation. Preemption may be explicit in the federal law or the Court might find preemption from a pervasive federal scheme. In any case, the state statute here seems to be in harmony with the federal act, since both seek to preserve lobster fishing. Moreover, no preemption will be found since the Act recognizes and reinforces state laws on the subject by providing a penalty for shipping lobsters taken in violation of state law. Thus, (D) is incorrect. (C) is incorrect because the Interstate Privileges and Immunities Clause prohibits discrimination by a state against nonresidents when such discrimination concerns fundamental rights, such as those involving important commercial activities or civil liberties. The Augusta statute does not discriminate in favor of its own citizens, because *no one* is permitted to take a lobster from a lobster bed lying within three miles of the Augusta shoreline unless the lobster weighs at least one pound, regardless of whether that person is a resident of Augusta. Therefore, the statute confers no advantage on Augusta residents. As a result, there is no violation of the Privileges and Immunities Clause of Article IV, Section 2.

Answer to Question 31

(C) Jones will lose because the tax is valid under the Commerce Clause. A tax is valid under the Commerce Clause if: (i) the tax does not discriminate against interstate commerce; (ii) there is a substantial nexus between the activity taxed and the taxing state; (iii) the tax is fairly apportioned; and (iv) the tax fairly relates to services or benefits provided by the state. The Augusta tax is applicable equally to residents of Augusta and nonresidents. Thus, there is no discrimination against interstate commerce. Because the lobsters are taken from coastal waters of Augusta, there is a substantial nexus between the activity taxed and the taxing state. There is fair apportionment if a tax is based on the extent of the taxable activity or property in the state. Here, the catching of any lobsters within three miles of the Augusta shoreline must obviously occur entirely within Augusta coastal waters. Thus, the Augusta tax is fairly apportioned. Also, there is a fair relationship between the tax and any benefits provided by the taxing state, because Augusta is permitting those engaged in lobster fishing to take from the dwindling supply of lobsters in its coastal waters, in return for a rather modest amount of $1 per pound. That revenue, in turn, is used to preserve and protect the lobster beds, which directly benefits Jones and other lobster fishermen. Thus, the Augusta tax meets all the requirements for validity under the Commerce Clause. (A) incorrectly states that the tax is invalid under the Commerce Clause. (B) and (D) are both incorrect because the Import-Export Clause applies to the authority of a state to tax foreign commerce. This question here does not deal with imported or exported goods. Thus, the Import-Export Clause is inapplicable to these facts.

Answer to Question 32

(A) The statute is unconstitutional and Dang should be acquitted. Like other federal law, a treaty is the supreme law of the land. Consequently, any state action or law that conflicts with a United States treaty is invalid. Some treaties are expressly or impliedly self-executing (*i.e.*, they are effective without any implementation by Congress). Others are not effective unless and until Congress passes legislation to effectuate their ends. The federal treaty with Chipan, pursuant to which the United States and Chipan agree to permit the importation and sale of goods and products from each other, does not appear to be in need of congressional action to implement its terms. The treaty on its face allows goods from Chipan to be imported and sold in this country. With the permission for such importation and sale having thus been granted, there should be no need for any further action to bring about the terms of the treaty. Thus, the treaty is impliedly self-executing, and it has supremacy status over any conflicting state law. Because the Plains statute places obstacles in the way of the sale of products from countries such as Chipan, the statute is in conflict with the treaty, and is therefore invalid. (D) is incorrect because, as explained above, there is no indication that effectuating legislation is necessary with relation to this treaty. (C) is incorrect because, if the statute under which Dang is prosecuted is invalid by reason of a conflict with the federal treaty, then obviously the prosecution can proceed no further. Thus, the treaty does provide a defense to the state criminal prosecution. (B) is incorrect because a federal treaty has supremacy over conflicting state law regardless of the time sequence in which the treaty and the state statute came into being. Consequently, Dang will be acquitted even if the treaty was made after the enactment of the Plains statute. The result would be different if the statute were a federal statute, as in the next question.

Answer to Question 33

(C) The federal statute would work to repeal the treaty. Although a treaty has supremacy over conflicting state law, a treaty is only on a supremacy parity with an act of Congress. Any conflict between an act of Congress and a treaty is resolved by order of adoption; *i.e.*, the last in time prevails. Here, the congressional legislation conflicts with the treaty by specifically terminating the permission to freely import and sell goods from Chipan that was conferred by the treaty. Because this statute was enacted after the treaty, the terms of the statute prevail, thus repealing the substance of the treaty with Chipan. (A) is incorrect because the legislation has the same effect in this case regardless of whether the agreement was a treaty or an executive agreement; as discussed above, the legislation will prevail over the treaty. (B) is incorrect because there is no unconstitutional interference with the executive's powers here. Both the President and Congress have some authority over foreign relations (*e.g.,* the Commerce Clause allows Congress to regulate foreign commerce), and Congress has a right to exercise its power here. As stated above, the last expression of the sovereign (here, the statute) controls. (D) states the requirements for adoption of a treaty (*i.e.,* the treaty power is granted to the President by and with the advice and consent of the Senate, providing two-thirds of the Senators present concur). Legislation that has the effect of repealing a treaty need not be signed by the President (*i.e.,* it may be passed over the President's veto), nor must such legislation be ratified by two-thirds of the Senate (unless an attempt is being made to override a presidential veto, in which case a two-thirds vote of each house is required). Therefore, (D) is incorrect.

Answer to Question 34

(D) The statute is an unconstitutional violation of the Commerce Clause. Regulation of foreign commerce is exclusively a federal power because of the need for the federal government to speak with one voice when regulating commercial relations with foreign governments. The existence of legitimate state interests underlying state legislation will not justify state regulation of foreign commerce. The Plains statute, in imposing requirements for a license costing $50 and for a clear marking of goods as being from an Asian country, clearly is an attempt by the state of Plains to restrict or even eliminate the flow of such goods in foreign commerce. Thus, the statute is unconstitutional. (A) is incorrect because even if the $50 fee represents a reasonable inspection fee, the fee would still constitute an interference with foreign commerce. In addition, the facts do not indicate that the license fee has anything to do with inspection, or that the amount of the fee bears any relation to legitimate inspection purposes. (B) is incorrect because the labeling requirement imposes a burden on goods that flow in the stream of foreign commerce. Although this burden may be relatively small, it is still impermissible in light of the exclusive power held in this area by the federal government. (C) is incorrect because it states factors that would be relevant in a matter involving regulation of interstate commerce, rather than foreign commerce. Congress's power over interstate commerce is shared with the states, so that a state law may regulate local aspects of interstate commerce if it does not discriminate against out-of-state competition to benefit local economic interests and its incidental burden on interstate commerce does not outweigh the legitimate local benefits arising therefrom. However, Congress's power over foreign commerce is exclusive, so that factors such as a minimal burden on foreign commerce and the presence of legitimate state interests will not save a state law from a challenge based on the power to regulate foreign commerce.

Answer to Question 35

(A) The federal court may grant a declaratory judgment that the statute is unconstitutional. A federal court has the authority to issue a final judgment declaring the rights and liabilities of parties (*i.e.*, a declaratory judgment) only if there is an actual controversy. A complainant must show that he has engaged (or wishes to engage) in specific conduct and that the challenged governmental action poses a real and immediate danger to his interests. Here, the Church Board members are planning to present a program of sex education and they are presented with an immediate danger of criminal prosecution from the district attorney. This threat of prosecution presents an immediate threat of interference with the Board members' First Amendment rights; *i.e.*, as is commonly stated in the First Amendment context, their rights have been "chilled." Thus, there is an actual dispute such as to authorize a court to issue a declaratory judgment that the East Dakota criminal statute (under which a prosecution is genuinely threatened) is unconstitutional, either on its face or as applied. (C) is incorrect because the commencement of a state criminal prosecution actually makes it less likely that a court will grant an injunction or declaratory relief. Generally, a federal court will not enjoin *pending* state criminal proceedings, because of principles of equity, comity, and federalism. Thus, commencement of a state criminal prosecution would have the opposite effect of that described in (C). (D) is incorrect because it is too broad. Although a federal court will generally refrain from enjoining a *pending* state criminal prosecution, it could enjoin a prosecution before it is brought. Moreover, even if a prosecution is pending, a federal court could enjoin the proceeding in cases of proven harassment or prosecutions undertaken in bad faith (*i.e.*, without hope of a valid conviction). (B) is incorrect because a federal court has jurisdiction over a civil action arising under the Constitution or laws of the United States (federal question jurisdiction). Here, if the Board members are alleging a right that is founded on federal constitutional law, the court will have jurisdiction over the matter regardless of the existence of diversity of citizenship.

Answer to Question 36

(C) The convictions will be reversed if it can be shown that the statute is being applied only to interfere with religion. The Free Exercise Clause prohibits government from punishing religious belief. The Clause prevents government from punishing conduct merely because it is religious and from regulating conduct for the purpose of interfering with religion. However, the Clause does not prohibit government from regulating general conduct, even if the regulation happens to interfere with a person's ability to conform conduct to sincerely held religious beliefs. Thus, if it can be shown here that the statute is not really a regulation of general conduct but rather is being applied only to interfere with religion, the convictions will be reversed. (A) is incorrect because, as stated above, a person's conduct can be regulated by a generally applicable conduct regulation; religiously motivated conduct has very narrow protection. (B) is incorrect because it implies that the court will balance the interests involved in determining the validity of the application of the statute here. Under the former constitutional test, the Court would make such a determination, but since *Employment Division v. Smith* (1990), the Court has abandoned the balancing approach in favor of the approach discussed above. (D) is incorrect because the Church Board would have standing. All that is required is a concrete stake in the outcome of the litigation; having been prosecuted for violating the statute, the Board's stake is about as concrete as it can get.

Answer to Question 37

(A) The 30-day residence requirement to obtain an abortion is least likely to be constitutional because it violates the rights to privacy and to travel. Certain constitutional rights are deemed to be fundamental and can be interfered with only to promote compelling government interests. Among these are the right to privacy and the right to travel interstate. The right to privacy, among other things, protects a woman's constitutional right to have an abortion. Thus, a government cannot restrict a woman's decision to have an abortion except to promote a compelling interest (*e.g.,* protecting the life and health of the pregnant woman or protecting a viable fetus). Where, as here, the fetus is not yet viable, the state may not adopt regulations that impose an "undue burden" on the woman's right to have an abortion. The duration requirement here does not appear to serve any purpose other than to deter obtaining an abortion, and so it violates the right of privacy. The requirement also appears to violate the right to travel as well. The right to travel interstate protects a person's right to migrate from state to state. Generally, government action interfering with the right to migrate from state to state (*e.g.,* durational residency requirements) must be narrowly tailored to a compelling interest. A short durational requirement (*e.g.,* 24 hours) to obtain an abortion might be justified, but the 30-day waiting period here burdens a woman's ability to migrate for no apparent legitimate reason; rather, as stated above, the purpose appears to be to deter abortions. Thus, the right to travel is violated. (B) is constitutional because, as explained above, the government has a compelling interest in protecting a pregnant woman's health, and a requirement of obtaining a qualified physician seems to be narrowly tailored to promote that interest. (C) has been held to be constitutional as long as the court bypass procedure is available. (D) is constitutional because while government is restricted in its ability to interfere with a woman's right to have an abortion, it is not required to fund abortions. Thus, a state may require reimbursement for nontherapeutic abortions performed in public hospitals.

Answer to Question 38

(A) The filing fee is invalid if Ames is indigent, but the financial statement requirement is valid. A state may not impose on candidates a fee that renders it impossible for indigents to run for office. Even as applied to nonindigent candidates, an unreasonably high filing fee that is not tailored to promote a substantial or overriding state interest might be held invalid. However, even a reasonable and otherwise valid fee would have to be waived for an indigent candidate unable to pay the fee. If Ames is indigent, then a $500 filing fee would certainly preclude his running for office. Other types of restrictions on the ability of persons to be candidates must be examined to see if the restrictions violate either the First Amendment right of political association or the Fourteenth

Amendment Equal Protection Clause. A ballot access regulation must be a reasonable, nondiscriminatory means of promoting important state interests (such as running an honest, efficient election system). The financial statement requirement here is a reasonable means of promoting the important state interest of disclosing possible conflicts of interest that might compromise the integrity of elected officials. (It also might be a legitimate method for determining whether a candidate is truly indigent, thus justifying waiver of the filing fee.) This requirement is nondiscriminatory because it is applied to all candidates, rather than only some candidates. Any impairment of a candidate's right of privacy resulting from this requirement is slight in comparison to the important governmental interest served thereby. Thus, the financial statement requirement is valid. (B) is incorrect in stating the invalidity of the financial statement requirement. Also, (B) is incorrect because it cannot be said with any certainty that the filing fee requirement is valid. The fee requirement will certainly be invalid as applied to indigent candidates, and it might be so high and lacking in promotion of a substantial state interest that it will be invalid as applied to all candidates. (C) is incorrect because it states that the financial statement requirement is unconstitutional in addition to the filing fee requirement. As noted above, the requirement of a financial statement is valid. (D) is incorrect because the validity of restrictions on the ability of persons to be candidates is determined by a balancing test: a severe restriction such as a filing fee making it impossible for indigents to run for office would require a **compelling** state purpose to be valid.

Answer to Question 39

(B) The loyalty oath is valid if it merely requires the candidate to affirm that she will oppose the violent overthrow of the government. The government may require employees and other public officers to take a loyalty oath. Such an oath must not be overbroad, so as to prohibit constitutionally protected activities, nor can it be vague. An oath has been upheld that requires state employees to oppose the overthrow of the government by force, violence, or by an illegal or unconstitutional method. [Cole v. Richardson (1972)] This type of oath (which is virtually the same as that set forth in (B)) was deemed to be similar to an oath requiring the taker simply to commit herself to live by the constitutional processes of our system. (D) is incorrect because, as noted above, a requirement for a loyalty oath as a condition of holding public office or employment is valid, as long as the oath is within constitutionally acceptable limits. (A) is incorrect because it has been held that a loyalty oath that disavows **advocating** the violent overthrow of the government as an abstract doctrine is invalid. The First Amendment prohibits statutes regulating advocacy that are not limited to advocacy of action. [Communist Party v. Whitcomb (1974)] The oath in (A) appears to be overbroad in that it regulates mere advocacy of violent overthrow of the government, rather than regulating only advocacy of action. Therefore, the oath is invalid. (C) is incorrect because only knowing membership in an organization with specific intent to further unlawful aims is unprotected by the First Amendment. [Keyishian v. Board of Regents (1967)] The oath in (C) would in effect punish mere membership in an organization, without showing knowledge of or a specific intent to further any unlawful aims of the organization.

Answer to Question 40

(B) Carter's suit will prevail even if the matter is not decided until after the election, because the suit is not moot and the residency requirement is unconstitutional. Carter's suit is not moot even if the matter will not be decided until after the election because other members of the class might have a live controversy. Under the case and controversy requirement of the Constitution, there must be a real, live controversy at all stages of the suit. If through the passage of time, the controversy between the parties is resolved, the case is said to be moot. However, there are exceptions to the mootness doctrine. In a class action, it is not necessary that the suit by the named plaintiff be viable at all stages, as long as the claim is viable by some member of the class. Thus, the suit here would not be moot. Moreover, the residency requirement here violates Carter's fundamental rights to vote and to interstate travel. A restriction on the right to vote is subject to strict scrutiny and is valid only if it is necessary to achieve a compelling state interest (otherwise the restriction violates the Equal Protection Clause by treating new residents differently from old residents). Relatively short residency requirements (*e.g.,* 30 days) have been upheld as being necessary to promote the compelling interest of assuring that only bona fide residents vote. However, the Supreme Court has struck down longer durational requirements for lack of a compelling justification. Thus, the one-year requirement here probably unconstitutionally impinges on the right to vote. The residency requirement also impinges on the fundamental right to travel in the same manner (*i.e.,* it discourages people from migrating by denying them the right to vote without a compelling reason). Thus, the requirement is invalid. (A) is incorrect because, as indicated above, the case will not be moot since other members of the class might have a live controversy. (C) is incorrect because it applies the wrong standard. Because fundamental rights are affected by the residency requirement here, the government must show a ***compelling*** justification; a mere rational or legitimate basis is not enough. (D) is incorrect because, as stated above, the Supreme Court has found that there was no compelling interest for a one-year residency requirement in order to vote.

Answer to Question 41

(D) The residency requirement is permissible because the board is elected at large. The Equal Protection Clause prohibits state dilution of the right to vote, so that when a governmental body establishes voting districts for the election of representatives, the number of persons in each district may not vary significantly. This is known as the principle of "one person, one vote." This principle applies to almost every election where a person is being elected to perform normal governmental functions (*e.g.,* an election for trustees for a junior college district). However, the principle of one person, one vote generally is inapplicable where there is an at-large system of election (except where the system is adopted for discriminatory purposes). Here, the school board members are elected by all of the qualified voters in the Town of Pleasantville in an at-large system (rather than having the voters of each individual district select one board member apiece), and no discriminatory intent is evident. Thus, the statutory provision requiring board members to reside in each of the five districts does not result in an imbalance or a dilution of the voting rights of the citizens of Pleasantville. Consequently, (A) is incorrect, and (D) presents an accurate statement of the constitutionality of the residency requirement. (Note that the answer might be different under federal ***statute*** because the town would have to prove a valid, nondiscriminatory purpose.) (C) is incorrect because school board elections are generally subject to the requirements of one person, one vote. As noted above, these requirements apply to most elections for persons to perform normal governmental functions. Thus, these requirements apply not only to legislators, but also to elected administrative and executive officials (*e.g.,* members of a school board). (B) is incorrect because, even assuming that the residency requirement violates the candidates' equal protection rights, Early would not have standing to raise the issue. Generally, a claimant must assert his own constitutional rights and cannot assert the rights of third parties.

Answer to Question 42

(A) The suit to assert state citizens' rights is not within the Supreme Court's original jurisdiction. Under Article III, Section 2, the United States Supreme Court has original jurisdiction in all cases affecting ambassadors, other public ministers, and consuls, and in which a state is a party. In (A), Nevada is not really seeking to advance or protect any interest of its own. Rather, the state is attempting to act in parens patriae (*i.e.,* to act as a representative of its citizens, thereby asserting their interests). Thus, Nevada is not an actual party in this case in the sense that the Supreme Court has traditionally required to justify exercise of original jurisdiction. (B) would be a proper case for institution under the Supreme Court's original jurisdiction because it involves an attempt by a state (Oregon) to protect its own economic interest rather than to assert the interests of its citizens in a representative capacity. Similarly, (C) sets forth a situation in which Illinois is attempting to defend its asserted right to render decisions affecting admissions policies relative to its own state universities. Thus, in (C) Illinois is an actual party to the case. Finally, (D) describes an attempt by the federal government to prevent state construction of a bridge (presumably pursuant to the admiralty power). Clearly, this case involves an alleged grievance that will be directly committed by a state. Therefore, Pennsylvania is an actual party. From the foregoing, it is clear that (A) presents the only case in which it can be said that a state is not actually involved as a party.

Answer to Question 43

(B)   A bona fide residence requirement, such as this statute, that is not based on a suspect classification and does not limit the exercise of a fundamental right, is judged by the rational basis test. Thus, (A) is incorrect. The statute provides free education for all children who are bona fide residents of Arkota. Thus, it uniformly furthers the state interest in assuring that services provided for its residents are enjoyed only by residents. (C) is incorrect because education is not a fundamental right. (D) is incorrect because this statute does not impair the right of interstate travel. Any person is free to move to the state and establish residence there. This statute does not deter people from moving into the state.

Answer to Question 44

(A)   State and local governments cannot tax or regulate the activities of the federal government. This principle is often termed "intergovernmental immunity." The arrest and prosecution of a federal employee who was on the job violates this principle, which is based on the supremacy of the federal government and federal law. (B) is not a bad answer because door-to-door solicitation is protected by the First Amendment. However, at best, (B) would subject the city's actions to strict scrutiny and allow the city to prevail if it could prove that its action was necessary to achieve a compelling government purpose. In contrast, (A) would automatically invalidate the city's enforcement of the law against Baxter, and so (A) is a better answer. (C) is irrelevant because the Fourteenth Amendment's restriction on the states has to do with persons, not the federal government, and here there is no claim that the city was discriminating against Baxter. The city's ordinance, as briefly described, does not seem to provide the basis for an equal protection claim. (D) is wrong because nothing in the facts shows any burden on interstate commerce. Moreover, at most such a claim would trigger heightened scrutiny; it would not automatically invalidate the enforcement of the law as would (A).

Answer to Question 45

(C)   This is the safest answer since, under Article I, the right of Congress to legislate over the District of Columbia is the same as the state legislatures' right to regulate their internal matters. This has been held to include the right to tax real property. (A) is incorrect since the Indian lands are considered independent sovereignties and as such could not be taxed by a "foreign" government. (B) could conceivably be correct given Congress's plenary powers over interstate commerce. (D) is also arguably correct for the same reason, that is, assuming Congress acted pursuant to its plenary power a "uniform" tax would be valid. But the question asks for the "most likely" result, and (C) is the best answer given the choices.

Answer to Question 46

(C) Classifications distinguishing between residents and nonresidents of a state are not suspect, provided the focus is, as here, on individuals who are "citizens" and the challenge is not posed by an alien. Since the state could probably show a rational relationship between most provisions in the law and the state's interest in protecting its citizens from unscrupulous mechanics, the measure would pass constitutional muster. However, the durational residency requirement arguably burdens the fundamental right to interstate travel, thus triggering strict scrutiny analysis. (A) is wrong because Wilcox is now a resident of Mississippi, which takes him outside the operation of the Article IV Privileges and Immunities Clause and, in any case, most of the regulations are closely related to the substantial state purpose of protecting its citizens from fraudulent business persons. Thus, (D) is also wrong, since it postulates that "all" of the challenges are appropriate. (B) is wrong because there is no indication that Congress has preempted the field, and the residency provision probably does not constitute an invasion of the federal commerce power, since it is largely a valid exercise of the police power whose benefits outweigh any incidental burdens that might be imposed on commerce.

Answer to Question 47

(B) Licensing of persons who deal with the general public is a valid exercise of the state's police power. Since there could be circumstances within which the various requirements, including five years' experience, could be rationally related to the state's objectives, the licensing scheme as a general matter is valid. (A) is a misstatement of law; Congress, not the states, has plenary power over interstate commerce. (C) is not supported by the facts. While an argument could be made that Wilcox's activities have some impact on commerce, there is nothing here to indicate that these regulatory requirements fail applicable tests. (D) is wrong because the equal protection guarantee of the Fifth Amendment applies only to federal government action.

Answer to Question 48

(B) Since the state seeks simply to protect its citizens, which will presumably occur if insurance is provided by a reputable company, there are reasonable alternatives to the discriminatory regulation challenged here. Thus, the insurance regulation violates the Commerce Clause. (A) is incorrect. Since this case involves a classification, it does not implicate due process, which is concerned with how individuals are treated as an absolute matter. (C) is wrong because Mississippi can enforce its regulations within the state even if the insurer is from out of state, provided it does not discriminate when it does so. (D) is incorrect, because even if there is a rational relationship between the state interest and the particular requirement that Wilcox is challenging, there are reasonable nondiscriminatory alternatives available to regulate the out-of-state insurers.

Answer to Question 49

(C) Olson's suit will fail because, as a public official, he has to establish a higher level of fault on Lois's part than what he has shown. The Supreme Court, in *New York Times v. Sullivan* (1964), held that the First Amendment bars a civil libel judgment for criticism of a public official unless the plaintiff shows actual malice by clear and convincing evidence. "Actual malice" requires a showing that the publication was known to be false or that it was published with reckless disregard as to its truth or falsity. Here, Lois believed her report was true, and since she confirmed the rumor by talking to an apparently reliable source, she was not reckless as to the truth or falsity of her report. Traditional malice or ill will is not an element of "actual malice," which has a distinct meaning in defamation cases; thus, (A) is incorrect. (B) is wrong because falsity and damages alone are insufficient; Olson must also prove actual malice. (D) is wrong because the First Amendment will not protect reporters who act with knowledge of falsity or reckless disregard as to truth or falsity.

Answer to Question 50

(B)   (B) states the general rule: the power of Congress to investigate is coextensive with the power to legislate created by Article I, Section 8 of the Constitution. (A) and (D) are accordingly incorrect statements of the limitations on this power. (A) is wrong since it postulates that "only" separation of powers doctrines bear. (D) is wrong because it is too sweeping. Congressional investigation is limited to matters over which the Congress has jurisdiction. (C) is simply wrong. Congress may use appropriate means to investigate, provided the means selected do not themselves violate separation of powers principles.

Answer to Question 51

(B)   The Supreme Court has construed the scope of the commerce power very broadly, so that it covers the regulation of drug packaging, which has a substantial economic effect on interstate commerce. (A) is wrong because this type of regulation definitely falls under the Commerce Clause, and there is no need to imply a power (under the Necessary and Proper Clause) when an enumerated power controls. (C) is wrong because the General Welfare Clause presents a limitation on Congress's spending and taxing powers which is not relevant here. (D) is wrong because the Tenth Amendment generally does not bar Congress from exercising its powers under the Commerce Clause, even when the legislation might arguably invade areas that might have traditionally been left to the state via its police powers.

Answer to Question 52

(B)   State provision of textbooks to the segregated private school violates the Equal Protection Clause by giving state support to a racially segregated educational process. (A) is wrong because a state may, under certain situations, aid a private school. (C) and (D) are parts of the test for violation of the Establishment Clause. The Supreme Court has held that a state lending textbooks on secular subjects to all students, including those at religious schools, does not violate the Establishment Clause. Thus, (C) and (D) are incorrect.

Answer to Question 53

(D)   The Appointments Clause of the Constitution permits Congress to vest appointments of inferior officers only in the President, the courts, or the heads of departments. Enforcement is an executive act; therefore, Congress cannot appoint members of a commission that exercises enforcement powers. Legislative power can be delegated under very vague guidelines without creating an unconstitutional delegation. Thus, (B) is incorrect. (A) is incorrect because the commerce power would probably extend to the manufacture of fireworks, whether or not the fireworks were actually sold in interstate commerce, because, taken as a whole, the activity has a substantial economic effect on interstate commerce. There is no constitutional provision requiring that a party or group to be regulated be represented on the commission that regulates it. (C) is therefore incorrect.

Answer to Question 54

(D) Congress may appoint its own members to a legislative or investigative commission; therefore, for the limited purposes indicated, the Appointments Clause is not violated. Thus, (B) is incorrect. (C) is incorrect because prosecution of violations is an executive act and the Appointments Clause governs. (A) is incorrect because forbidding the commission to take any action is too strong a remedy and is not constitutionally required.

Answer to Question 55

(D) The general principles of intergovernmental immunity prevent federal interference with state governmental functions. There is no indication of any violation of due process, and federal courts need follow state law only in cases where jurisdiction is based upon diversity of citizenship or when a federal statute specifically incorporates state law. Thus, (A) and (B) are incorrect. (C) is incorrect because the protection of the Speech and Debate Clause extends only to federal legislators.

Answer to Question 56

(B) Even though the claim of "legislative business" is raised, the facts indicate that Oral's activities cannot have had much to do with the operation of state government. Oral may, accordingly, be subject to sanction under a variety of federal statutes that either proscribe such conduct or characterize it as a violation of the victim's civil rights. The courts have consistently refused to decide what a "republican form of government" specifically entails. (C) is therefore incorrect. (A) is incorrect because the Necessary and Proper Clause alone does not furnish authorization for federal action. Congress must be acting in the exercise of one of its express powers, and the answer as phrased does not indicate that this is the case. (D) is incorrect because the general welfare power is a taxing and spending authorization, and would not justify criminal sanctions.

Answer to Question 57

(C) Congress is explicitly authorized to restrict the jurisdiction of the federal courts under Article III. (D) is incorrect because Congress cannot define conduct that will violate the Fourteenth Amendment's Equal Protection Clause; it may only enact laws to prevent or remedy violations of rights already recognized by the courts. [City of Boerne v. Flores (1997)] (B) is incorrect because the statute does not regulate interstate commerce, but rather limits the power of the courts to order certain remedies. Neither does the statute affect the expenditure of any federal educational funds, since it is directed at the courts. Therefore, (A) is incorrect.

Answer to Question 58

(A) If the Equal Protection Clause requires that athletics in education be administered fairly according to sex, then Congress could not constitutionally interfere with the fashioning of a judicial remedy to achieve constitutionally required conduct. (D) is wrong because Congress may burden interstate commerce, since it has plenary power on that subject. (C) is wrong because Congress may limit the jurisdiction of federal courts. (B) is wrong because the Privileges and Immunities Clause has always protected individual rights against infringement by state government, not limited the powers of Congress vis-a-vis the federal courts.

Answer to Question 59

(D) Classifications based on gender are quasi-suspect and violate equal protection unless the government shows by exceedingly persuasive justification that they are substantially related to an important government objective. (A) is incorrect; even if the government were performing a parens partriae function, it would not be permitted to violate equal protection. (B) states the wrong equal protection test. (C) states the wrong test and places the burden of proof on the wrong party.

Answer to Question 60

(A) A real, live controversy must exist at all stages of review, not merely when the complaint is filed. If a true controversy no longer exists, the court will dismiss the complaint as moot. A case becomes moot, for example, when, as here, a party can no longer be affected by the challenged statute. The fact that parties unconnected to the litigation may still be affected by the ordinance does not affect this lawsuit's mootness. (C) is therefore incorrect. (B) is incorrect because the fact that Rick was permitted to enter the center with his wife is not the reason that there is no longer a controversy. Had he attempted to enter alone, he would have been allowed in because he is now 20 years old. (D) is incorrect because what the City Council might do in the future should not affect the court's decision.

Answer to Question 61

(C) One of Roberts's challenges in the suit against Pacific is that the funds collected from the property taxes are used to send children to parochial schools. In general, a taxpayer has no standing to challenge the expenditure of the taxes. The major exception to this rule is where the taxpayer alleges that the taxes were enacted under Congress's taxing and spending power, and exceed some specific limitation on that power, in particular the Establishment Clause. Roberts would not have to have children to make this challenge; hence (D) is wrong. (A) and (B) are wrong, because Roberts is only challenging the voucher system and not the sales tax increase. Therefore, he must show that he is paying the taxes he contends are being spent for unconstitutional purposes.

Answer to Question 62

(B) State taxes used to pay tuition to segregated private schools would sanction discrimination and arguably violate the Equal Protection Clause. It makes no difference how many parents send their children to such schools: the question is whether the program was intended to have, and did in fact have, the discriminatory effect. (B) is therefore the weakest argument, since (A) and (C) illustrate the intent requirement and (D) indicates that the effect is present.

Answer to Question 63

(C) The only argument that the state can use to support this scheme is that there is neither a religious purpose nor an effect on religion; thus, the government does not violate the Establishment Clause. (A) is wrong because the Fourteenth Amendment does not change the prohibition of the First Amendment. (B) is wrong because the fact that private religious schools fulfill an important function does not justify a violation of the Establishment Clause. (D) is wrong because when the parents pay the tax to the state, it becomes state funds. The prohibition goes to the state's involvement in its most basic sense. The fact that the state is arguably acting in accordance with the wishes of the taxpayers involved makes no difference.

Answer to Question 64

(A) The statute looks more like a time, place, and manner restraint on speech-related activities in a public forum than it does a burden on a fundamental right. This is so, despite its breadth of coverage, since it applies only to times when the legislature is in session and likely to be disturbed by noisy picketing. The application of the statute to George does not make it unconstitutional as applied; there is no reason why he could not have spoken as noisily as he wanted to in the park. Thus, (B) is incorrect. (C) is wrong because there are many methods to direct complaints to a legislator without yelling through his window. (D) is incorrect because silent picketing can be considered to be reasonable at the same time that noisy picketing is prohibited.

Answer to Question 65

(B) A state may prohibit speech that specifically advocates conduct that is dangerous to society or to the government and is likely to produce such conduct. [Brandenburg v. Ohio (1969)] George does not appear to have been actually encouraging the crowd to injure the legislators. His statement that maybe the legislators should know what it feels like to be in fear of their own lives appears to be no more than hyperbole, since the reason why he urged the crowd to go across the street was not to injure anyone, but merely to let the legislature "hear" their disapproval of its actions. (A) is incorrect because the statute itself is constitutional; it merely cannot be applied against George on these facts. (C) and (D) are incorrect because the facts do not support either conclusion, for the reasons discussed above.

Answer to Question 66

(C) (A) is wrong because the purpose of the Eleventh Amendment is to protect the sovereignty of a state by preventing lawsuits against that state being brought in a federal court; the appeal in this case deals only with the constitutionality of a state statute. (B) is wrong because the highest court in a state is only the final arbiter on a state law decided in accordance with the state's constitution, not the federal Constitution. (D) makes no sense, since diversity refers only to the jurisdictional basis of the federal district court.

Answer to Question 67

(D) This question tests your ability to spot procedural problems. Under the rationale of *Poe v. Ullman* (1961), the suit should be dismissed because of the ripeness problem. The statute in question forbids only the sale of soft drink beverages in aluminum cans within the state, not the manufacture. There is no showing in the facts that CanCo even sells its cans to bottling companies that sell soft drinks within Utopia, so there is no reason to assume that CanCo is being affected by the statute. (A) and (B) are wrong because they discuss only the most general reason why the court can assert jurisdiction, not why it should. (C) is wrong because there is no reason, under these circumstances, for the federal court to defer to a state court. The statute in question is not ambiguous or complex, and thus the constitutional question is fairly obvious.

Answer to Question 68

(B) The most obvious problem in this situation is that Allman was not afforded the right to a hearing either before or after his license was suspended. A business license is a valid property right, and procedural due process requires a hearing if it is suspended. Thus, (C) is wrong. The agency obviously had enforcement powers; thus (D) is wrong. (A) is an arguable complaint by Allman, but since there appears to be a regulatory agency that can make rules regarding the enforcement of the statute, the agency can construe "repeated violations" so as to comport with due process requirements.

Answer to Question 69

(C) The exercise of prosecutorial discretion is an exercise of executive power, and the doctrine of separation of powers forbids legislative interference with its exercise. (A) is wrong because the number of senators voting for the resolution is irrelevant; the question is one of constitutional power, not degree of support. (B) is wrong for much the same reason; it does not matter that the alleged criminal act was committed against the Senate. (D) is a misstatement of law; Congress can seek testimony from members of the executive branch without violating the separation of powers doctrine.

Answer to Question 70

(C) Congress's power to investigate is limited to matters on which it can legislate. These facts do not state that the Senate could not legislate concerning the subject matter of these questions, but only that it did not *intend* to legislate. However, the question asks under which facts would Lawrence be *least* likely to be convicted of a contempt charge, and out of these answers this will be his best choice. (A) is wrong because Congress can question a member of the executive branch concerning his duties. (B) is wrong because he would only have a privilege not to answer if he is subject to criminal liability. Merely because he may get fired is not sufficient grounds for him to refuse to answer a lawful question posed by a member of the Senate in an appropriate hearing. (D) seems to have some validity, because it speaks to a question of freedom of speech. However, there is nothing in the facts that shows that the board has a right to have closed meetings and confidential discussions. Generally, the workings of a federal board are a matter of public record, so unless there is some fact that shows that the board had the right to have an unrecorded meeting, this is not the best answer.

Answer to Question 71

(D) Under Article III of the Constitution, a federal judge is protected from termination of tenure during good behavior. This necessarily requires that a person who seeks protection under this provision be able to show that he is a federal "judge." From the facts, Fritz was clearly no more than an administrative hearing officer, without discretion or power. Thus, he would not be a judge within the meaning of this article, and its provisions would not apply to him. Therefore (B) is wrong. (A) is wrong because anybody can recommend that Congress enact or repeal a statute. Just because an executive branch's commission does so, it does not mean that there is a violation of the separation of powers doctrine. (C) is factually incorrect and does not explain the proper reason for the result.

Answer to Question 72

(B) The court should rule that the Act of Congress is valid under Congress's commerce powers, and under the Supremacy Clause of the Constitution, the state law is invalid. It is possible that the court would enjoin the application of the federal law pending a trial on its merits, but highly unlikely. Thus, (C) is wrong. (A) is wrong; the court has jurisdiction. (D) is ridiculous.

Answer to Question 73

(D) The most likely method the United States could use to impose a uniform child custody law upon all the states is through the taxing and spending power, making an allocation of funds available to each state that adopts the uniform law. No other selection would pass constitutional muster. The Commerce Clause has not been applied to child custody matters, and it is unlikely that Congress would use its commerce powers to regulate in this area. Indeed, were it to do so, such a measure might well lead the Court to find a violation of this power. Thus (A) is not the most likely basis for such a statute. (B) is wrong; there is no general federal police power. (C) is wrong because neither of the Privileges and Immunities Clauses would apply to this matter: Article IV does not apply, since this is an action of the federal government, and the Fourteenth Amendment does not apply since child custody matters are not among the list of privileges or immunities the Court has recognized under that provision.

Answer to Question 74

(C) Alienage is a suspect classification when used by the states in matters not involving the self-government process, and must be justified by a compelling state interest or be considered a violation of the Equal Protection Clause of the Fourteenth Amendment. (B) is wrong because the Fifth Amendment applies only to the federal government. While the federal government is responsible for foreign policy, and as a consequence, is given great latitude in that area by the courts, this alone would not be a reason to invalidate the citizenship requirement. Thus, (D) is wrong. (A) is wrong because a bill of attainder is a legislative determination of guilt.

Answer to Question 75

(D) Chan's best argument is that the requirement bears no rational relationship to the state's interest in making certain that individuals in the health professions are qualified to practice. The classification here, between those trained in the state and those trained elsewhere, does not on its face implicate either a suspect class or a fundamental right. Chan will, accordingly, need to argue that it is either irrational in and of itself, or is unconstitutional as applied to him, a resident alien. (C) is wrong because there is no fundamental right to practice a profession. (A) and (B) are wrong because both Privileges and Immunities Clauses protect citizens, and Chan is not a citizen.

Answer to Question 76

(B) Residency requirements have been successfully challenged as violative of the Equal Protection Clause. These durational residency requirements can be construed as burdening the fundamental right of interstate travel, thus triggering a strict scrutiny analysis. The desire to benefit state residents is not alone a compelling state interest. Thus, (D) is wrong. This requirement might even be struck down under the traditional mere rationality test. (A) is wrong because the Privileges and Immunities Clause does not apply to aliens. (C) is wrong because the classification makes an equal protection analysis more appropriate.

Answer to Question 77

(D) Professor is an at-will employee, and under most circumstances may be discharged "for any reason or no reason at all." Thus, normally, evidence regarding the motives for dismissal is irrelevant. The question here, however, is what is the ***strongest*** argument that Professor could make, and (D) creates at least an inference that an impermissible motive might be present (gender, free speech, etc.). (A) is a weaker answer because Professor has no property interest in continued employment; a mere expectation in continued employment is not enough, even when coupled with reliance (her buying a house). There must be a legitimate claim or entitlement—created by a contract or clear policy—that employment can be terminated only for cause. The bases alleged in (B) are arguably irrelevant; her popularity may or may not have anything to do with her ability, and even if it does, she remains an at-will employee. (C) might under some circumstances offer an argument, but there could be any number of valid explanations for keeping others and letting her go, including budget constraints, subject needs, etc. (D) is, accordingly, the strongest of the possibilities.

CONTRACTS QUESTIONS

Questions 1-4 are based on the following fact situation:

Builder and Owner entered into a valid written contract under which Builder agreed to erect a house according to certain plans and specifications, for which Owner agreed to pay the sum of $200,000, upon completion.

1. Assume for purposes of this question only that during the course of construction, building costs increased significantly. Builder informs Owner of the increased costs, and the parties agree in writing that Builder may omit installing the air conditioning unit called for by the specifications (thus saving Builder approximately $10,000) and nevertheless receive the full construction contract price. Under the general rule, this subsequent written agreement is:

   (A) Unenforceable for lack of consideration, even though in writing.

   (B) Enforceable as a novation, which superseded the original construction contract.

   (C) Enforceable, because an agreement modifying a contract for the sale of goods (the air conditioning unit) needs no consideration to be binding.

   (D) Enforceable, on the theory that Builder gave up his right to breach the contract (walking off the job and refusing to complete the building) in reliance on Owner's agreement to the modification.

2. Assume for purposes of this question only that in light of substantial increased building costs, Owner and Builder orally agree that Builder may omit installation of the air conditioning unit (saving Builder $10,000), and that the contract price will be reduced to $195,000. Builder completes the building in reliance thereon. Most courts would hold that this subsequent oral agreement is:

   (A) Unenforceable, because a contract in writing cannot be modified orally.

   (B) Unenforceable under the Statute of Frauds.

   (C) An enforceable contract.

   (D) Unenforceable under the parol evidence rule.

3. Assume for purposes of this question only that Builder has completed the building, except that a good faith dispute has arisen between Owner and Builder as to the workmanship on several items. Owner sends Builder a check for $190,000 marked "payment in full." If Builder indorses and cashes the check, and then sues Owner to recover the $10,000 balance, most courts would hold:

   (A) Builder's cashing the check constituted an accord and satisfaction, discharging Owner's duty to pay the balance.

   (B) Builder can recover the $10,000 balance from Owner.

   (C) Builder is estopped to sue for the balance because he cashed the check knowing it was being tendered in full settlement.

   (D) Builder's indorsing a check so marked constituted a written release, thereby discharging the contract.

4. Assume for purposes of this question only that the building has been completed except for the final interior painting and finishing the roof. At this point, the entire structure is destroyed by a fire set by vandals. Under traditional contract law principles, Builder can recover from Owner:

   (A) The full contract price, less the value of the work remaining to be done when the building was destroyed.

(B) The actual value of labor and materials expended, plus a proportionate amount of the profits he would have earned on completion, his further performance having been excused by impossibility.

(C) Nothing, unless he builds another building.

(D) The reasonable value of his labor and materials on the building, but without any allowance for profits.

Questions 5-6 are based on the following fact situation:

Wrangler was a famous breeder of racehorses who owned Sir Marathon and Lady Luck, both retired sweepstakes champions. Bettum owned a racing stable and was anxious to obtain the offspring of Wrangler's horses for his stable.

After considerable negotiations, Wrangler and Bettum signed the following document:

It is hereby agreed that Bettum shall have the first right to purchase all colts foaled out of Lady Luck by Sir Marathon during the next three years. Price to be determined on the basis of sex, weight, height, and bone structure at time of delivery.

Six months later, the first colt was born to Lady Luck, and it had all the markings of a champion. Bettum immediately tendered $25,000 to Wrangler for the colt, which was a good faith approximation of its value. However, Wrangler refused to deliver the colt unless Bettum paid $100,000. Bettum sued Wrangler.

5. If Wrangler defends on the ground that there is no enforceable contract obligating him to sell, the court would most likely hold:

(A) There is no enforceable contract because Bettum was not obligated in any way under the signed writing.

(B) There is an enforceable contract because, by signing the document, Bettum impliedly promised to purchase.

(C) Regardless of whether the writing was an enforceable contract, Bettum's good faith tender of $25,000 created an enforceable contract.

(D) The agreement is enforceable as a firm offer between merchants under the U.C.C.

6. Assume that there is otherwise an enforceable contract. If Wrangler defends on the ground that no price was fixed in the agreement and the parties have been unable to agree on a price, the court should hold:

(A) Bettum is entitled to purchase the colt at whatever price the court determines to be reasonable.

(B) The provision requiring the price to be negotiated can be enforced by appointment of an arbitrator to set the price.

(C) Bettum is entitled to purchase the colt for $25,000.

(D) Bettum is entitled to purchase the colt for $100,000.

Question 7

Induscorp was a manufacturer of machine tools. Barney, a factory owner, telephoned Induscorp's order department and placed an order for two of Induscorp's standard "Type-A" machines. Barney and Induscorp came to an oral agreement whereby the total price for both machines was agreed to be $10,000. The first machine was to be delivered on May 1, with payment of $5,000 due 30 days after delivery, and the second machine was to be delivered on June 1 on the same terms (payment of $5,000 due 30 days after delivery). Although Induscorp did not carry the machine in stock, no retooling was required because the Type-A machine was a standard model.

The first machine was duly delivered on May 1. The second machine arrived on June 1, but Barney refused to accept delivery and also refused to pay for the first machine. Assume that it cost Induscorp $3,000 to manufacture each Type-A machine, and that Induscorp could resell the machine for only $3,000.

If Induscorp sues Barney on June 2, what damages should be awarded aside from any incidental damages?

(A) $3,000.

(B) $5,000.

(C) $7,000.

(D) $10,000.

Question 8

Odivia owned Homeacre, on which both a house and a garage were located. Odivia did not own an automobile, and she decided that she would turn the garage into an exercise area, including a modern sauna and spa. Odivia entered into a written agreement with contractor Eero, who agreed to do the job personally for $12,500, which included all requisite plumbing, electrical, and carpentry work. Eero was to begin work by May 14. On May 15 Eero had not yet appeared to start the job. Odivia telephoned Eero, who told her, "I've got a big job with Developers Incorporated that's going to pay me a lot more money than that marginal project of yours, so I'm not going to work on your garage." Over a period of several months, Odivia made many calls to local contractors, but none of them would agree to do the job for the price agreed upon by Eero. On June 3 of the following year Odivia filed suit for specific performance against Eero.

Which of the following represents Eero's best argument in his defense against Odivia's suit?

(A) Specific performance is an equitable remedy, and because Odivia waited for over a year to sue, the equitable defense of laches will apply.

(B) Specific performance is inappropriate, because a contract for personal services is involved.

(C) Specific performance is not an appropriate remedy if nominal legal damages are available to Odivia.

(D) Specific performance is inappropriate, because Odivia's failure to obtain another contractor for the job is an indication that $12,500 was an unfair price.

Question 9

Sam and Bam entered into negotiations over the telephone. They reached a general understanding that Bam would buy widgets from Sam. Following their conversation, Sam sent Bam a contract, already signed by Sam, agreeing to sell 1,000 widgets to Bam for a total contract price of $10,000. Upon receipt of the contract in the mail, Bam signed the contract and deposited an envelope containing the contract in the mailbox located in front of Bam's office building.

Before Sam received the contract, Bam had a change of heart. He telephoned Sam and said, "Look, Sam, I just can't make a profit on those widgets. I'm not interested in that contract we talked about." Sam replied, "That's all right, I understand. Maybe we can do business some other time." The next day, the signed contract was delivered to Sam's office. Sam, also having had a change of mind, decided that he wanted to enforce the contract.

Is the contract enforceable against Bam?

(A) Yes, because the acceptance occurred prior to rejection.

(B) Yes, because of the parol evidence rule.

(C) No, because the offer to rescind was accepted and that discharged the original contract.

(D) No, because the rejection by telephone voided the acceptance by mail.

Questions 10-13 are based on the following fact situation:

Gibbons operated a health food store in the City of Euphoria. Vita-Crest was a manufacturer and distributor of health foods. On March 1, they entered into a written agreement whereby Vita-Crest agreed to supply Gibbons with whatever quantity of natural foods he might order, at Vita-Crest's published wholesale prices, for a period of 12 months and he agreed to purchase from no other source during that period of time. The agreement contained the following provision:

> Both parties desire to further the cause of improving the American diet. Hence, it is agreed that payment for any purchases made under this agreement during the month of April only shall be made to the American Diet Institute, a nonprofit corporation, to carry on the good works of the Institute.

On April 1, Gibbons ordered and Vita-Crest shipped 20 cases of health food products, at a wholesale price of $4,000, which remains unpaid.

On April 15, Gibbons sold his store, inventory, and accounts receivable to Standard Food Stores, Inc., a chain operation. As part of the sale, he assigned to Standard the contract with Vita-Crest. Standard promptly notified Vita-Crest of the sale and assignment.

10. If, on May 1, American Diet Institute commences suit to collect the $4,000 owing for the April 1 transaction:

   (A) The action will lie only against Gibbons.

   (B) The action can be maintained against Gibbons or Standard for the full $4,000.

   (C) The action can be maintained only against Standard.

   (D) It cannot maintain the action against either Gibbons or Standard.

11. Assuming that the American Diet Institute sues Vita-Crest in an attempt to collect the $4,000, which of the following, if any, is the best defense to such action?

   (A) There was no consideration for Gibbons's promise to make the payments to American Diet Institute.

   (B) The American Diet Institute owes Gibbons more than $4,000.

   (C) The goods shipped by Vita-Crest to Gibbons were not of merchantable quality.

   (D) Vita-Crest was simply attempting to confer a gift upon the American Diet Institute.

12. Assume for purposes of this question only that Vita-Crest and Gibbons had both become disillusioned with the American Diet Institute prior to April 1, and had made a subsequent written agreement to eliminate the provision for payments to the Institute. What effect would this have on the Institute's right to maintain an action for $4,000 (assuming that it otherwise had standing to collect the same)?

   (A) No effect, because the Institute's rights vested when the contract was made.

   (B) The Institute can still sue if it can prove that it had detrimentally relied on the parties' agreement before the Institute found out that they had changed the agreement.

   (C) The subsequent agreement would, upon its execution, cut off the Institute's right to maintain any action under the original agreement.

   (D) The Institute can still sue if it could prove that it had learned of the original agreement between Vita-Crest and Gibbons before they changed it.

13. Assume for purposes of this question only that on May 1, Standard sends Vita-Crest an order for 5,000 cases of food products "on the terms and conditions of your agreement with Gibbons, which has been assigned to us." Vita-Crest refuses to deliver. If Standard brings suit, the court should hold that:

    (A) Standard is entitled to enforce the agreement, as it gave Vita-Crest prompt notice of the assignment from Gibbons.

    (B) There was no mutuality of obligation in the original agreement between Vita-Crest and Gibbons and hence there was nothing to "assign" to Standard.

    (C) Standard cannot compel Vita-Crest to fill the order for 5,000 cases.

    (D) Standard is entitled to enforce the agreement if it is willing to pay cash, as one person's credit is not necessarily as good as another's.

Questions 14-15 are based on the following fact situation:

Warden, a wholesaler, sold quality shoes to retailers in a six-state region. Warden ordered 1,000 pairs of shoes from Michael, a shoe manufacturer. The shoes cost $50 per pair, so the total contract price was $50,000. It happened that Michael owed $50,000 to Tyree, a supplier of leather. Michael assigned, in writing, "all proceeds from the contract with Warden" to Tyree. Michael notified Warden that he had assigned the proceeds of the contract to Tyree and then shipped the 1,000 pairs of shoes to Warden. Upon receipt of the shoes, Warden discovered that 10% of the shoes were defective. He sent a check for 90% of the contract price ($45,000) to Michael. Michael deposited the check. Realizing that the business was in deep trouble, Michael withdrew all funds from his bank account and took off for a country with which the United States has no extradition treaty. Tyree demands payment from Warden.

14. If Tyree sues Warden for the $45,000 that Warden paid on the contract, will Tyree prevail?

    (A) Yes, because Warden had notice from Michael that the contract had been assigned to Tyree.

    (B) Yes, unless there was a nonassignment clause in the contract.

    (C) No, because Warden fulfilled his obligations under the contract by paying Michael.

    (D) No, because Tyree could not have performed the other side of the contract by furnishing shoes.

15. Assume for purposes of this question only that there was no agreement with Tyree, and that Michael neither deposits the check nor departs for a foreign country. Has Warden made a proper rejection?

    (A) Yes, because the shoes were defective.

    (B) Yes, because he made only partial payment.

    (C) No, because Warden accepted the shoes, and failed to seasonably notify Michael of any rejection due to the defects.

    (D) No, unless the defects were substantial.

Question 16

Pontecorvo, a wealthy art collector, was noted for his acumen in selecting the works of "up-and-coming" contemporary painters and sculptors. Often, but not invariably, the mere news that Pontecorvo had purchased a young artist's piece caused the market value of that artist's work to increase substantially. One day, Pontecorvo visited the gallery and studio of Dal Vidor-Holly, a painter whose work had already attracted considerable attention in the fashionable art markets on both coasts. Pontecorvo admired one of Vidor-Holly's paintings, which was titled "Mother's Whistler." Vidor-Holly told Pontecorvo on August 31 that Pontecorvo could have the painting for $30,000. Although Pontecorvo liked the painting and thought Vidor-Holly had promise, Pontecorvo was not sure he wanted to buy it. Therefore, Pontecorvo entered into a written agreement with Vidor-Holly whereby Vidor-Holly agreed to keep his offer to sell the painting to Pontecorvo at $30,000 open for 30 days. Pontecorvo paid Vidor-Holly $500 for this, and the terms of the agreement provided that the offer would expire at 11:59 p.m. on September 30 if Pontecorvo failed to accept by that time.

On September 20, Pontecorvo telephoned Vidor-Holly and told him, "The more I think about it the less I think that 'Mother's Whistler' is what I want." Vidor-Holly responded, "That's your decision to make, Mr. Pontecorvo."

On September 26, art collector Trista visited Vidor-Holly's gallery and offered Vidor-Holly $35,000 for "Mother's Whistler."

On September 27, Vidor-Holly mailed a $50 check to Pontecorvo, with a letter stating, "I am hereby terminating my offer to you regarding the painting 'Mother's Whistler' and I am refunding 10% of the money you paid me to keep the offer open." The artist mailed his letter at 11:59 p.m. on the 27th. Pontecorvo received the letter at 11:30 a.m. on September 29.

On September 28, at 9:30 a.m., Pontecorvo mailed a letter to Vidor-Holly, stating, "I've decided to purchase 'Mother's Whistler' from you. Find enclosed my certified check in the amount of $30,000." Two hours later, Vidor-Holly sold the painting to Trista. Vidor-Holly received the letter on October 1 and immediately mailed the check back to Pontecorvo.

Can Pontecorvo maintain a successful legal action against Vidor-Holly?

(A) Yes, because Vidor-Holly sold the painting after Pontecorvo's effective acceptance, and before Vidor-Holly's revocation became effective.

(B) Yes, because in his revocation Vidor-Holly did not refund the full $500 to Pontecorvo.

(C) No, because Vidor-Holly effectively revoked his offer before Pontecorvo accepted.

(D) No, because Pontecorvo's power to accept lapsed before Pontecorvo effectively accepted.

Question 17

Baxter advertised in the newspaper that he wished to sell 40 acres of land at $1,000 per acre. Campbell and Wilson were interested, so they came out to inspect the property. They inspected the land with Baxter and his father, Bill. After the inspection, Campbell agreed to purchase the land for $40,000. A contract for the sale of the 40 acres was prepared and signed by Baxter and Campbell. The contract failed to state the purchase price. Later, Campbell had a change of heart and refused to complete the purchase. Baxter now brings a lawsuit for breach of contract.

The court should hold for:

(A) Baxter, because the parol evidence rule will not bar testimony that Campbell agreed to pay $40,000.

(B) Baxter, because the Statute of Frauds can be satisfied by combining the original advertisement and the written contract.

(C) Campbell, because the parol evidence rule will bar all evidence that he agreed to pay $40,000 for the land.

(D) Campbell, because the Statute of Frauds would require the contract to contain the price in order to be enforced.

Questions 18-20 are based on the following fact situation:

On November 3, Bunker sent a fax message to Sachs, a dealer in precious metals: "Please quote your best price on 800 troy ounces platinum bars for immediate delivery at my bank."

At 10 a.m. the next morning (November 4) Sachs replied by fax, "My best price is $475 per ounce." Bunker received Sachs's message at 3 p.m. on November 4, and he immediately responded via fax, "Deal is okay, confirming letter follows." This message did not reach Sachs until 10 p.m. on November 5. In the meantime, during the afternoon of November 4, Sachs had offered 800 ounces of platinum bars to Hunter at $478 per ounce, and Hunter had accepted. When Sachs received Bunker's second fax message, Sachs faxed back to Bunker: "My offer canceled. Have agreed to sell platinum to Hunter. No more platinum in stock." Bunker immediately replied via fax: "Reject your cancellation. We have agreement for 800 ounces platinum at $475 per ounce." All of the faxes included the parties' respective letterheads.

18. The first two communications between Bunker and Sachs are best characterized as:

    (A) An offer and an acceptance.

    (B) A request for an offer and an offer.

    (C) An offer and a price quotation.

    (D) A request for an offer and a price quotation.

19. Assume for purposes of this question only that Sachs's November 4 fax message to Bunker was: "Will sell platinum at $475 per ounce. Price F.O.B. my vault." Bunker's reply was as above. On November 5, Bunker has a contract for 800 ounces of platinum at $475 per ounce. Who must pay the freight charge from Sachs's vault to Bunker's bank?

    (A) Sachs.

    (B) Bunker, unless he reasonably objects to the new term covering freight.

    (C) Bunker, unless the new term regarding freight constitutes a material alteration of the agreement.

    (D) Bunker.

20. Assume for purposes of this question only that Sachs's November 4 fax to Bunker provided: "Best price $475 per ounce. Firm for 48 hours." Assume also that Bunker was aware of Sachs's agreement with Hunter at the time Bunker sent his fax to Sachs on November 4. On November 5, Sachs has which of the following obligations?

    (A) A contract with Bunker only, because platinum constitutes "goods" under the Uniform Commercial Code.

    (B) A contract with Hunter only, because platinum is not within the Uniform Commercial Code definition of "goods."

    (C) A contract with Bunker and a contract with Hunter, because Sachs's fax to Bunker was a firm offer.

    (D) A contract with neither Bunker nor Hunter.

Questions 21-22 are based on the following fact situation:

Mary purchased a small house in West Key. The house had been unoccupied for a period of time and the plumbing in the house's only bathroom did not function, and there were similar problems with plumbing in the kitchen. Mary entered into a written agreement with Pipes whereby Pipes agreed to repair the plumbing in Mary's house. The contract also contained a clause requiring that all plumbing work be completed by noon on October 1. Mary had this clause inserted because she had to vacate her apartment by noon on October 1, and her house was not habitable without functioning plumbing. The contract further provided that Mary would pay Pipes $1,200 for his work.

21. Assume for purposes of this question only that Pipes had planned to start work on Mary's plumbing on September 27, because that would give him adequate time to do the work with some leeway for any

unexpected problems. However, the 27th was a beautiful day, and Pipes decided to go on a picnic with his girlfriend. After the picnic, Pipes and his girlfriend went dancing at a bar featuring country and western music. Pipes drank a great deal and woke up on the 28th with a terrible hangover. He spent the day in bed and did not start the plumbing work until the 29th. That evening Pipes called Mary and told her, "I'm not going to be able to get your plumbing finished by noon on October 1 unless I get my friend Joe to help me and that will cost about $150." Mary told Pipes, "I have to have a place to live, so do whatever you need to do to get the house ready." Pipes hired Joe to help him, and the job was finished at 11 a.m. on October 1. As soon as the job was done, Pipes paid Joe $150. Pipes sent Mary a bill for $1,350. She sent him a check for $1,200 and refused Pipes's repeated demands for an additional $150. If Pipes sues Mary for $150, who will prevail?

(A) Pipes, because Mary agreed to pay the $150.

(B) Pipes, because he completed performance by noon on October 1.

(C) Mary, because her statement to Pipes was ambiguous.

(D) Mary, because Pipes gave her no new consideration.

22. Assume for purposes of this question only that Pipes began working diligently on Mary's plumbing on September 27. When he quit working for the day on the afternoon of September 28, half of the job was completed. Shortly thereafter, it started to rain. The rain continued and became so heavy that a nearby reservoir overflowed and burst the dam restraining the water. A flash flood ensued. Mary's house was in the path of the flood, which struck Mary's house at 2 a.m. on September 29. The house was completely washed away. Which of the following best describes the obligations of the parties to the contract after the flood?

(A) Neither Pipes nor Mary is discharged from their obligations under the contract.

(B) Mary is obliged to pay Pipes $1,200.

(C) Pipes is discharged from his obligation, but is entitled to recover from Mary the fair value of the work he performed prior to the flood.

(D) Both Pipes and Mary are discharged from all contract obligations.

Question 23

Patrick was exasperated with the smog in Big City and sent Andrew the following letter on January 1:

> Andrew, my family and I are moving out of here and going to live on a tropical island. Do you want to buy the stuff in our house? The price is $25,000.

Andrew received the letter on January 2, and on January 3 sent Patrick a letter accepting the offer. The next day Andrew changed his mind. He called Patrick and told him to forget the deal. Later that day, Patrick received the letter that Andrew had sent on January 3.

Is there a contract between Patrick and Andrew?

(A) Yes, because the contract is for the sale of goods for more than $500 and Patrick's attempted rejection is oral.

(B) Yes, because Andrew's letter of acceptance was effective when he mailed it.

(C) No, because Andrew's rejection was communicated to Patrick before his letter of acceptance was received.

(D) No, because the description of the subject matter as "the stuff in our house" is not sufficiently definite and certain.

Question 24

Sabrina owned Maroonacre and put it up for sale. Bertram entered into negotiations to purchase Maroonacre and they agreed upon a sale price of $100,000. Sabrina told Bertram, "I'll drop a contract in the mail this afternoon and have Artemesia, my attorney, draw up a deed." Sabrina signed a land sale contract, which only described the property as "Maroonacre," without a metes and bounds legal description. She mailed the contract to Bertram that afternoon, although it was mailed too late for the last mail pickup of the day. Artemesia promptly drew up a deed and dropped it in the mail to Sabrina, who did not sign it. Bertram received the contract the next day.

After Sabrina mailed the contract, she received an offer from Bella to purchase Maroonacre for $150,000. Sabrina called Artemesia and told her to come to Sabrina's office with a deed for Maroonacre, conveying to Bella for $150,000. Artemesia brought the deed to Sabrina's office and both Sabrina and Bella signed the deed and Bella promised to pay the full amount in two days. Artemesia sent a letter to Bertram, stating, "Sabrina has found another purchaser for Maroonacre; all matters regarding your offer for Maroonacre are hereby rescinded." Sabrina later received the signed contract from Bertram.

Bertram wishes to compel Sabrina to convey Maroonacre to him for $100,000. Is Bertram entitled to specific performance?

(A) Yes, because Sabrina signed the land sale contract.

(B) No, because the land sale contract does not contain the complete legal description of Maroonacre.

(C) No, because the deed was not signed by the party to be charged.

(D) No, because contracts involving land are governed by the Statute of Frauds.

Question 25

Tom leased a piece of business property from Leonora. Tom told Leonora, "If you ever decide to sell this property, I'd be very interested in purchasing it, if the price is within reason." Leonora told Tom, "There's a good chance that I will be putting it up for sale within the next six months." Tom gave Leonora $5,000 and told her, "Here's $5,000 to give me an option to buy the property for $35,000 if it is put on the market within the next year. If you decide not to sell during that period, give me back the $5,000, but keep any interest you've earned on it." Leonora agreed to this arrangement.

Three months later, a business deal in another state came through for Leonora, and Leonora told Tom, "I've just put the property you wanted up for sale, but we have to move quickly because I have to leave the state in two weeks." Tom agreed to buy for $35,000, with the $5,000 he had already given Leonora to serve as earnest money to be used toward the total purchase price. Leonora drew up a contract to sell the land to Tom; it included a "time is of the essence clause," requiring Tom to appear with the $30,000 balance on or before noon on June 15.

On the night of June 14, Tom learned that his daughter, Donna, was hospitalized for a serious illness in Collegetown, a city 200 miles away. Tom got a late-night flight to Collegetown. The physicians attending Donna assured Tom that she would recover, but encouraged him to stay on to see her the next day during visiting hours. Tom agreed to do so. At 9:15 a.m. on June 15, Tom visited the Collegetown branch of the State Bank and Trust Co., a large bank with branches throughout the state. Tom banks with State Bank in his city of residence, and the Collegetown branch issued Tom a certified check on his account, payable to Leonora. At 10 a.m., Tom telephoned Leonora's office. Although Leonora had not yet arrived, Tom told Leonora's private secretary, "I'm in Collegetown, because my daughter is ill, but tell Leonora not to worry, because as soon as I leave this phone booth I'm dropping a certified check for $30,000 in the mailbox across the street. She should get the money in tomorrow morning's mail." Leonora arrived in her office at 10:30 a.m., and received Tom's message.

At 11 a.m., Leonora received a phone call from Pamela, who offered to pay $40,000 for the property. Leonora asked, "How long will it take you to raise the money?" Pamela replied, "Fifteen minutes!" Leonora told Pamela to come in with the $40,000 at 1:30 p.m. Pamela arrived at 1:30 p.m. with $40,000 in cash. Leonora ripped up the contract with Tom, and drew up a new one in favor of Pamela.

On the morning of June 16, Tom's check arrived in Leonora's office. Leonora mailed the $30,000 check back to Tom, along with her own check, payable to Tom, in the amount of $5,000. Pamela took possession of the property.

If Tom sues Leonora for specific performance, will he prevail?

(A) Yes, because he tendered the money in a timely manner by mailing the check before noon on June 15.

(B) Yes, because he had notified Leonora that it was impossible for him to be at the closing.

(C) No, because he did not tender the money at the set closing date.

(D) No, because he could not accept an offer under an option contract using the mailbox rule.

Questions 26-27 are based on the following fact situation:

Winston, well known in the community to be wealthy, went to Rudder, a boatbuilder, and told Rudder that he wanted a yacht built to his specifications. They agreed orally that the price would be $400,000, and that Winston was to make payment in full within 30 days after Winston had accepted delivery of the yacht. They further agreed that Rudder would not subcontract any of the work. Rudder, however, contacted Genoa, a master sailmaker, and subcontracted the sails for the yacht to Genoa. They agreed orally that Rudder would pay Genoa $25,000 for the sails within 10 days after Winston had accepted and paid for the yacht. Rudder did not tell Genoa of his agreement

with Winston regarding subcontracting. Genoa made the sails and delivered them to Rudder. Rudder completed the yacht and delivered the boat to Winston, who accepted it as being to his specifications. Now, the 30-day payment period has expired, but since Winston's huge speculation in precious metals futures went sour and he became insolvent, he has not paid Rudder.

Genoa went to Rudder and demanded $25,000 for the sails. Rudder told Genoa, "Under our agreement, you don't get paid until I get paid."

26. Is there an enforceable contract between Rudder and Genoa?

(A) Yes, because they are merchants under the Uniform Commercial Code.

(B) Yes, because Genoa fully performed.

(C) No, because Rudder had agreed not to subcontract.

(D) No, because of the Statute of Frauds.

27. If Genoa alleges that a contract exists between him and Rudder and sues Rudder, how much can Genoa recover?

(A) The fair market value of the sails, based upon a quasi-contract.

(B) The cost of materials and labor.

(C) $25,000.

(D) Nothing.

Questions 28-30 are based on the following fact situation:

Builder contracted with Owner to construct a house on property owned by the latter for a contract price of $100,000.

28. Assume for purposes of this question only that Owner committed a total breach of the contract at a time when Builder had already

incurred costs of part performance of $30,000, and Builder would have to spend an additional $60,000 to finish the job. Builder is entitled to recovery in the amount of:

(A) $10,000.

(B) $30,000.

(C) $40,000.

(D) $60,000.

29. Assume for purposes of this question only that the contract between Owner and Builder provided that Owner would pay one-third of the contract price (*i.e.,* $33,333) on completion of the foundations, another third ($33,333) on completion of the walls and roof, and the balance ($33,334) when the entire job was completed. If Builder had properly completed the foundations, and then stopped working because he became insolvent, Builder could recover:

(A) $33,333, the contract price.

(B) $33,333 offset by whatever damages Owner suffered in getting the job completed by someone else.

(C) Nothing because he has committed a material breach of the contract.

(D) Nothing on the contract because this construction contract is not divisible in nature; but he might be entitled to quasi-contractual relief.

30. Assume for purposes of this question only that shortly after beginning performance, Builder had assigned to Supplier his right to all monies due under the contract (*i.e.,* $100,000) and that Supplier had promptly notified Owner of this assignment and Owner had acknowledged the same. Assume further that Builder has now completed the entire house, except for small items which would cost $2,500 to

repair. If Supplier were to sue Owner, Supplier would be entitled to recover:

(A) $100,000, the amount assigned; Owner may look to Builder for a recovery for minor breach.

(B) The reasonable value of the labor and materials expended by Builder on the job.

(C) $97,500, on a theory of substantial performance.

(D) Nothing, because Owner's duty to pay is subject to a constructive condition precedent, and the assignee takes subject to the defense that the condition has not been satisfied.

Questions 31-33 are based on the following fact situation:

Steelmaker Corp. purchased a tube rolling machine from Toolcorp, a manufacturer of heavy machinery. The machine was sold unassembled for a price of $150,000, with $25,000 payable upon delivery and the balance ($125,000) to be paid in 10 monthly installments of $12,500 each. After the machine parts were delivered, Steelmaker contacted Assembly, Inc., a company that specialized in assembly and installation of large and complex manufacturing machinery, and told Assembly that "it must have the machinery up and running within 45 days," or Steelmaker would be in breach of one of its major contracts. Assembly agreed, in a written contract with Steelmaker, to assemble and install the tube rolling machine within 45 days at a price of $15,000. Three weeks into the assembly and installation job, Assembly estimated in all honesty that it would lose from $2,000 to $3,000 on the Steelmaker job, because the union representing Assembly's employees forced a new wage agreement on Assembly by threatening a long and costly strike. Assembly approached Steelmaker and told it that the job could not be finished for less than $17,000. After some discussion, Steelmaker and Assembly executed a writing under which Steelmaker agreed to pay Assembly an additional $2,000 upon completion of the job. In the meantime, Toolcorp had heard about Assembly's labor problems, and was advised that Assembly was about to stop work. Toolcorp orally offered Assembly a $3,500 "bonus," if Assembly would agree to finish the job for Steelmaker. Assembly accepted Toolcorp's promise and scheduled the assembly and installation of the tube rolling machine as planned, within the 45-day time limit set in the agreement between Assembly and Steelmaker.

31. If Toolcorp refused to pay Assembly the $3,500 bonus, and Assembly therefore sued Toolcorp, which of the following would be Assembly's strongest argument?

   (A) Assembly owed Toolcorp no preexisting duty to complete the job for Steelmaker, and such completion was sufficient bargained-for consideration for Toolcorp's promise to pay the additional $3,500.

   (B) Since the $3,500 payment was characterized as a "bonus," no further consideration was required and Toolcorp is bound to its promise.

   (C) Assembly would not have completed the job for Steelmaker except in reliance on Toolcorp's promise to pay the additional $3,500.

   (D) By completing the job for Steelmaker, Assembly conferred a benefit on Toolcorp worth at least $3,500, because such performance assured Steelmaker's ability to pay Toolcorp the balance on the installment purchase agreement for the tube rolling machine.

32. If Steelmaker refused to pay Assembly the additional $2,000, in a suit by Assembly against Steelmaker, which of the following would be Steelmaker's strongest position?

   (A) Steelmaker came under no duty to pay Assembly more than $15,000, because this was a contract for services and not for goods.

   (B) Since Assembly knew that Steelmaker needed its machinery up and running in 45 days, the modification is voidable because Assembly took advantage of Steelmaker's duress.

   (C) Toolcorp's offer to pay the bonus assured that Assembly's performance would be profitable.

   (D) During initial contract negotiations, Assembly assured Steelmaker that the tube rolling machine would be assembled and installed for no more than $15,000.

33. Assume for purposes of this question only that Steelmaker refused to let Assembly continue with the work when Assembly asked for a higher installation price and that Steelmaker sued Assembly for breach of contract. Which of the following evaluations is correct?

   (A) Steelmaker would not have a cause of action, because Assembly did not unequivocally repudiate the contract.

   (B) Steelmaker would not have a cause of action, because Assembly was legally excused by the union's threatened strike and a new wage agreement.

   (C) Steelmaker would have a good cause of action if it alleged and proved that Assembly would not have lost money under the original agreement.

   (D) Steelmaker would have a good cause of action regardless of whether Assembly's estimate that it would cost more money than under the original agreement was accurate.

Questions 34-35 are based on the following fact situation:

Michelle, a woman of advancing years, owned Greenacre, a property worth approximately $150,000. Michelle told her daughter, Dolly, who lived with her and took care of her, that she wanted as little "tied up in the courts" as possible when she died. "That's why," she said, "I've put your name alongside mine on the title to Greenacre, but I want you to understand that I want you to share the property equally with your brother, Billy." Dolly told Michelle that she would.

Michelle had an elder sister, Anne, who owned Rougeacre, a property worth approximately $200,000. Dolly regularly corresponded with her Aunt Anne, who had been very lonely since her only child was killed while on duty as an officer of the French Foreign Legion. Anne appreciated the correspondence, and she sent Dolly a letter that included this statement: "Because you have been so good to me and you take such good care of your mother, I plan to leave everything I own, including Rougeacre, to you and your brother; you can count on it." Dolly continued with her kindnesses to Anne. In addition to letters, Dolly sent Anne little gifts from time to time. Although the gifts were inexpensive, Anne considered them an indication of Dolly's thoughtfulness. Dolly also spent a lot of her time attending to Michelle's daily needs.

Eventually, Anne died, and her will left all of her property (most of which is represented by the value of Rougeacre) to Billy. Billy wrote Dolly a letter stating, "I know that you were always very kind to Aunt Anne, and I feel really bad about being the only person named in her will. I don't want you to worry about that, because I'm going to share her estate with you. We can discuss the details at Anne's funeral."

Dolly spent $800 on a round-trip ticket and flew off to Anne's funeral. After the funeral, Dolly talked to Billy. Billy told her, "I've been thinking about things, and I rescind what I told you in the letter, because I was emotionally upset at the time I wrote it. I would be willing to share Anne's estate with you, if you'll agree to share Mom's estate with me." Without hesitating, Dolly told Billy, "Mom has already signed over all her property to me, and it's only fair, because I'm the one who's been taking care of her." Billy replied, "In that case, I think it's best we follow Aunt Anne's last wishes as expressed in her will—I'm keeping Rougeacre and the rest of Anne's property myself." Dolly did not tell Billy about her oral agreement with Michelle to share Greenacre (which represents almost the entire value of Michelle's property). However, Billy later discovered the oral agreement regarding Greenacre in a telephone conversation with Michelle. Dolly sued Billy for a 50% share of Anne's estate before Billy learned of the oral agreement.

34. What amount should Dolly realize from her suit?

    (A) Nothing, because Anne's will left everything to Billy, and Billy's letter is an insufficient basis to compel him to share.

    (B) $800, because this represents Dolly's actual expenses incurred in reliance on Billy's letter.

    (C) $100,000 (half of Anne's estate), because Billy promised her that in the letter.

    (D) $100,000, but only if she shares Michelle's estate with Billy.

35. Assume for purposes of this question only that Dolly sued Anne's estate. What is the result most likely to be?

    (A) Dolly will recover one-half the value of Rougeacre because her acceptance of Anne's offer to leave Dolly Rougeacre in exchange for Dolly's continued care to Michelle created a contract.

    (B) Dolly will recover the value of her services if the only reason she continued to care for Michelle was because of Anne's promise to Rougeacre.

(C) Dolly will recover nothing because she had "unclean hands" since she was preventing Billy from taking his rightful share of Greenacre.

(D) Dolly will recover nothing because, under the parol evidence rule, the will cannot be contradicted by a prior writing.

Questions 36-37 are based on the following fact situation:

Miller, a grain dealer and processor, contracted with Baker, a commercial baked-goods manufacturer. The written agreement provided that Miller would supply "One carload milled baking flour, F.O.B. Miller's place of business." The contract included terms describing the quality of the flour and the contract price. Another clause in the contract made it contingent upon Baker's obtaining a "letter of credit from Big Bank at an interest rate of no more than 2.5%."

36. Which of the following facts would discharge Miller's duty to perform and place Baker in breach?

(A) Big Bank is insolvent.

(B) Big Bank refused to supply a letter of credit on the terms specified in the contract.

(C) Baker did not apply for the letter of credit.

(D) Baker obtained a 2.5% letter of credit from Large Bank, a bank of comparable size and solvency to Big Bank.

37. Assume for purposes of this question only that Baker received a letter of credit from Big Bank at 3% interest. Upon hearing of this, Miller refused to ship the flour to Baker. If Baker sues Miller for breach, who will prevail?

(A) Miller wins, because the 2.5% is a material term of the contract which Baker breached.

(B) Baker wins, because the interest-rate term was included in the contract for Baker's benefit.

(C) Miller loses, because the .5% differential between the interest rate stated in the contract and the rate obtained on the Big Bank letter of credit is not material.

(D) Baker loses, unless a 2.5% interest rate was unavailable at a comparable bank.

Question 38

Alan wanted to have his driveway resurfaced. He called a number of commercial establishments which do such work and received bids ranging from $4,200 to $5,000. Bert submitted a bid to do work for $4,000, and Alan entered into a contract with him to have the driveway resurfaced.

Shortly before Bert was scheduled to begin work, he called Alan and said, "I just found out my secretary made a mistake in adding figures. I know we signed a contract, but I couldn't possibly do the work for less than $4,400 or it would not be worth it."

If Alan sues Bert for breach of contract, who will prevail?

(A) Alan, but only if it is too late for Alan to accept the bid of the next lowest bidder.

(B) Alan, but only if Alan did not have reason to know of the error in Bert's bid.

(C) Bert, because he had not yet commenced performance under the contract.

(D) Bert, because he can successfully assert the defense of mistake.

Question 39

Pearly had neglected her teeth for a long period of time, but she finally decided to attend to her dental health. She went to Boris, a highly reputable dentist, to have her teeth cleaned and to determine the course of dental work she needed. Boris honestly told her that she needed a lot of dental work, some of it involving complex procedures. When she asked Boris what the cost would be, Boris told her "about $3,500." Pearly agreed to use Boris as her dentist and he began her treatment. During the course of that treatment, Boris determined that he would use "precious" metal material instead of the "semi-precious" metal that he had planned to use for Pearly's inlays. Boris had sound medical reasons for his decision. When Pearly's treatment was finished, Boris sent her a bill for $4,100. An angry Pearly demanded to know why the bill was more than $3,500. Boris explained to Pearly that the higher bill was because more expensive inlays were used, and he carefully documented the cost of his materials. Pearly honestly believed that it was unfair for Boris to charge her $4,100. Therefore, she sent Boris's invoice back to him, along with a check for $3,500. On the check Pearly had clearly written "Payment In Full." Boris read the notation on the check. He then went to his own bank and deposited the check. Boris made no notation of his own on the check other than his signature on the back as an indorsement. Two weeks later Boris called his bank to make sure that Pearly's check had cleared. He then immediately filed suit against Pearly for $600.

Will the court award Boris $600?

(A) Yes, because Boris merely estimated the cost of the dental work to be $3,500.

(B) No, because there is an account stated.

(C) No, because there has been an accord and satisfaction of the original debt.

(D) Yes, if Boris can prove to the court that the precious metal inlays were medically necessary and that he charged a fair price for them.

Questions 40-41 are based on the following fact situation:

Integrated Circuit Technology, Inc. ("ICT") was having difficulty finding qualified engineers to work in its expanding production facilities because the hardware needed to train top-flight engineering students was so expensive that most colleges could not afford to purchase more than a minimal amount of such equipment, which limited program sizes and held down the number of applicable engineering degree candidates. ICT's chief executive officer, Cruz, wrote the following letter to the heads of several universities: "If you will commit your institution to accepting in your engineering degree program every junior-year undergraduate who wishes to pursue that major, ICT will provide your institution with all the necessary electronic hardware to instruct such students. Our engineers have informed me that one set of equipment (*i.e.*, one each of every machine used by ICT in its production process) is sufficient for use by five students; therefore, for every five engineering degree majors you accept in excess of your current engineering degree population, ICT will provide one such set of equipment."

40. Marchand, chancellor of Middle States University ("MSU"), received a letter from Cruz and immediately mailed a reply letter accepting ICT's generous offer. A few weeks later, Marchand received another letter from Cruz explaining that the response to his original letter had been so overwhelming that schools such as MSU who had no history of supplying graduates to ICT as employees would have to be omitted from ICT's equipment program. If MSU brings an action for breach of contract against ICT, what result?

(A) Judgment for ICT, because it could not be determined with sufficient specificity what MSU's needs for equipment would be, there having been no time to ascertain how many new engineering degree students would apply to the expanding degree program.

(B) Judgment for ICT, because MSU's obligation under any contract is illusory—no additional students will necessarily apply to an expanded engineering degree program.

(C) Judgment for MSU, because ICT is classified as a merchant under the U.C.C. and its offer was therefore irrevocable.

(D) Judgment for MSU, because Marchand's letter was an effective acceptance of ICT's offer and an enforceable contract was thereby formed.

41. Jackson, chancellor of Seaport College of Engineering ("SCE"), also received a letter from Cruz. The ICT letter arrived during SCE's annual budget review process, and Jackson was called upon to decide how much of the college's limited funds to apply to engineering equipment purchases. The day that she received Cruz's letter, Jackson informed the budget committee that no funds would be needed from that year's budget for engineering equipment purchases. A few days later, as Jackson was dictating the acceptance letter to ICT, she received a second letter from Cruz indicating that the ICT equipment program was being canceled due to an influx of qualified foreign engineers to the United States. Because the budget had been approved and all available funds had been committed to nonengineering equipment purchases, Jackson mailed the acceptance letter anyway and it was delivered to Cruz at ICT. If SCE brings a breach of contract action against ICT, what result?

(A) Judgment for SCE, if Jackson's removal of funds from the engineering department's budget was a reasonable and foreseeable response to ICT's offer.

(B) Judgment for SCE, because Jackson's removal of funds from the engineering department's budget converted ICT's offer into an express option.

(C) Judgment for ICT, because its promise to supply equipment to SCE was not supported by consideration.

(D) Judgment for ICT, because its revocation was received by Jackson before she dispatched the acceptance letter.

Questions 42-43 are based on the following fact situation:

Upon graduation from high school, Nephew could not decide whether he wanted to go on to college or start working for a living. Uncle told Nephew that if Nephew would attend college, Uncle would pay his tuition and expenses for the full year, and that Uncle would pay him a $1,000 bonus for each "A" Nephew earned as a final grade in a class. Nephew told Uncle that he would attend college. The next day, Grandfather called Nephew and told him that he had learned of the offer that Uncle had made him and that if Uncle failed to pay Nephew as promised he (Grandfather) would. Nephew attended college and earned "A"s as final grades in three classes. Shortly thereafter, Uncle died, and the executor of Uncle's estate refused to pay Nephew the bonus for each of the three "A"s.

42. Nephew will be unsuccessful in trying to enforce Grandfather's promise because:

(A) The contract was illusory.

(B) The contract was oral.

(C) There was no consideration flowing to Grandfather.

(D) The fact that Nephew received a year's worth of free education and tuition was sufficient compensation for Nephew's efforts in earning the three "A"s.

43. If Nephew brings suit against Uncle's estate for failure to pay $1,000 for each "A" as a bonus, will Nephew succeed?

(A) Yes, because there was a bargained-for exchange between Nephew and Uncle.

(B) Yes, because Uncle, had he been alive, clearly would have paid the bonus to Nephew.

(C) No, because Uncle's promise was personal, and the obligation was extinguished at Uncle's death.

(D) No, because the agreement between Uncle and Nephew was oral, and it would be impossible for Nephew to prove up its terms after Uncle's death.

Questions 44-46 are based on the following fact situation:

On July 1, Sam offered to sell Durham, his prize bull, to Bill for $15,000. In return for $100 which Bill paid Sam, Sam handed to Bill a signed written statement that recited the offer and stated that Sam promised not to revoke for a period of 30 days. Both Bill and Sam are cattle ranchers.

On July 10, Bill wrote Sam as follows: "I cannot pay more than $12,500 for Durham. If you cannot accept this amount, I will not be able to go through with the deal."

Bill did not know that Sam had already sold Durham to another party on July 9.

On July 27, Bill wrote Sam: "I accept your offer to sell Durham. Enclosed is my check for $15,000."

Sam received Bill's letter of July 27 on July 29.

44. In a suit by Bill against Sam for damages, a court would most likely find that:

(A) No contract was formed because Bill's letter of July 10 terminated Sam's offer.

(B) No contract was formed because Sam had already sold Durham, and this operated as a revocation of his offer since Sam was no longer able to perform.

(C) A contract was formed because the acceptance was effective prior to the expiration of 30 days.

(D) A contract was formed because Sam had no power to sell Durham to another party.

45. Assume Sam had not sold Durham on July 9 but instead sold Durham on July 20 after receiving Bill's letter of July 10. Also assume that Bill learned of the sale on July 21. Bill's power to accept the offer:

(A) Terminated when Sam received Bill's letter of July 10.

(B) Terminated when Sam sold the bull.

(C) Terminated on July 21 when Bill learned of the sale.

(D) Continued until July 30 because Bill paid $100 for a 30-day option.

46. Assume Bill's letter of July 10 had read:

I have decided to take Durham. A check for $15,000 is enclosed. I am leaving for Canada for six months and will pick up Durham on January 1. I will pay you for his board and care.

Bill's letter is:

(A) A counteroffer, because it changes the terms of the offer.

(B) A counteroffer, because it was not a definite expression of acceptance.

(C) An acceptance, and Sam must board the bull but is entitled to the reasonable value of that service.

(D) An acceptance, and Sam may refuse to board the bull.

Questions 47-50 are based on the following fact situation:

Wholesale Electronics Supply ("WES"), located in Los Angeles, California, sells integrated circuits to manufacturers of electronic components throughout the United States. Last year, these sales brought in gross revenues of $100 million. WES also operates a chain of retail outlets in the Southern California area which sell stereo equipment and electric guitars manufactured by others with components purchased in part from WES. WES purchases integrated circuits from five or six different Japanese and American firms, one of which is Silicon Industries ("Silicon"), a corporation with its main offices in San Jose, California. On January 19, WES mailed an order for $200,000 worth of 64-byte microprocessors to Silicon, specifying that the account was payable in full on or before March 1 and that delivery was to be not later than February 25, F.O.B. Southern Pacific Railroad Depot, San Jose, California. Silicon delivered the microprocessors to the railroad depot on February 15 and notified WES by fax that their order was scheduled to arrive at the Southern Pacific Railroad Depot in Los Angeles on February 20. On February 17 Silicon learned that WES had defaulted on a $700 million loan from the United States Government and that the Attorney General is considering filing an involuntary petition for bankruptcy against WES.

47. Assume that Silicon wires WES that it demands immediate payment in cash for the microprocessors. Is this permissible?

   (A) No, but Silicon may refuse to tender delivery of the goods by stopping them in transit.

   (B) No, because the contract terms specifying delivery F.O.B. at the Southern Pacific Railroad Depot passed title of the goods to WES.

   (C) No, because the payment terms were expressly stated in the purchase order of January 19.

   (D) Yes, if WES is in fact insolvent.

48. Assume that the microprocessors were picked up by WES at the Los Angeles Southern Pacific Depot. Two days later, Silicon learned of the default by WES on

the government loan and learned that, according to Dunn & Bradstreet, WES is unable to pay its debts as they become due. Silicon now seeks to reclaim the goods. Is this permissible?

   (A) No, because the date specified for payment of the account, March 1, has not yet passed.

   (B) Yes, unless WES assures Silicon that it will make payment on or before March 1.

   (C) Yes, because Silicon relied on WES's representations of solvency.

   (D) Yes, if WES is in fact insolvent.

49. Assume for the purposes of this question that Silicon successfully reclaimed the goods from WES after learning that WES was unable to pay its debts as they became due. Silicon then attempted to resell the microprocessors to computer manufacturers in New York. Shortly after Silicon reclaimed the microprocessors, electronics manufacturers announced the availability of a 128-byte microprocessor that renders 64-byte chips obsolete for those purposes. Silicon quickly sold the reclaimed goods for $25,000 and now seeks to recover $175,000 from WES in an action at law. Will Silicon prevail?

   (A) No, because a seller who reclaims waives all other remedies.

   (B) No, because the measure of damages is the market value of the goods at the time and place of delivery.

   (C) No, because the measure of damages is the market value of the goods on the date that payment was originally to be made.

   (D) Yes, because WES's insolvency was a breach of the purchase contract.

50. Assume that on February 21, WES wired Silicon that it was rejecting the microprocessors because they did not meet quality

control standards specified in the purchase order. Also assume that this rejection is proper. Silicon discovered that the defects in the goods shipped to WES were caused by an impure batch of silicon and that by using untainted microprocessors made from other batches it can make a perfect tender of conforming goods by February 25. Silicon timely notified WES of its intention to cure. Silicon delivers conforming microprocessors to the Southern Pacific Railroad Depot on February 25, as required by the purchase order. WES refuses to accept these microprocessors. Is this permissible?

(A) No, because if Silicon notified WES of its intent to tender conforming goods, such tender on or before the date specified in the contract for tender cures the previous imperfect tender.

(B) Yes, because the right to cure an imperfect tender is waived if delivery is to be to a common carrier instead of directly to the buyer.

(C) No, unless WES had purchased conforming goods from another manufacturer before the date Silicon tendered the conforming goods.

(D) Yes, because tender of the original nonconforming goods permitted WES to rescind the purchase contract.

Questions 51-54 are based on the following fact situation:

Frank, doing business as Cleveland Business Machines, agreed with Herbert, an accountant, to lease to Herbert a small business computer system, provide software and support, and maintain the system. Their oral agreement included that the lease would be for a term of three years, and that Herbert would pay a monthly charge of $500 for all services. Frank and Herbert further agreed that $100 of the monthly charge would be paid by Herbert

directly to Noel, in satisfaction of a debt Frank owed him.

Frank prepared a written copy of the agreement on his own word processor, but accidentally printed the monthly rental and service charge as $400 rather than $500. He did not include the agreement that called for the direct payment to Noel in the written copy. Frank sent the copy of the written agreement, signed by him, to Herbert, who also signed it without discovering the error in the amount of the monthly rental and service charge.

51. If Herbert refused to make any payments to Noel, and the latter brings an action against Herbert for damages as a consequence, which of the following, if true, would be most harmful to Noel?

(A) The obligation of Frank to Noel was subject to a statute of limitations which had run prior to the date the agreement between Frank and Herbert was first discussed.

(B) Noel never notified Frank or Herbert that he accepted their agreement to have Herbert make payments to him.

(C) No consideration supported the obligation owed by Frank to Noel.

(D) Before Noel learned of the agreement between Frank and Herbert, they agreed that Herbert would pay the entire $500 directly to Frank.

52. In Noel's action against Herbert, which of the following, if any, are correct?

I. Enforcement of the agreement for Herbert to pay $100 per month is precluded by the Statute of Frauds because the agreement was to answer for the debt of another.

II. Herbert could successfully raise the Statute of Frauds because his agreement with Frank could not by its terms be performed within one year.

(A) I. only.

(B) II. only.

(C) Both I. and II.

(D) Neither I. nor II.

53. If Noel brings an action against Herbert, which of the following will have the greatest effect on the outcome?

(A) Whether Noel was a party to the agreement between Frank and Herbert.

(B) Whether the agreement between Frank and Herbert was completely integrated.

(C) Whether Frank was negligent in not discovering that the agreement omitted mention of the payment of money directly to Noel.

(D) Whether Herbert was negligent in not discovering that the agreement omitted mention of the payment of money directly to Noel.

54. Herbert refused to pay more than $400 per month for rental of the computer system and ancillary services. If Frank brings an action for the difference between the payment as orally agreed and as memorialized in the contract, which of the following, if proven, would most benefit Frank?

(A) The parties made a mistake in integration.

(B) The writing was only a partial integration.

(C) The writing was intended as a sham.

(D) Frank or Herbert misunderstood the amount the rental and service payment was to be.

Questions 55-56 are based on the following fact situation:

Lex, the owner of a semi-pro baseball team (the Supermen) needed a new team manager. He entered into contract negotiations with Luther. Luther was concerned about his salary, and Lex was concerned about losing his new manager in mid-season. After explaining to Luther that it would cause unknown harm if Luther were to leave during the season and would cost him several hundred dollars more to replace a manager after the season had begun, the parties agreed that Luther would be paid $300 per week, plus 5% of all gate receipts from home games to be paid as a bonus at the end of the season. Also, Luther agreed to pay a "penalty" of $200 per week for each week that he did not manage the team. The parties' written contract included both of these agreements.

Luther managed the team for 18 weeks with mixed success. Although the Supermen had a winning record, they were in third place and attendance at home games was poor. Nevertheless, with 10 weeks left in the season, Luther was offered and accepted a job as manager of a professional ball team, whose former coach, Jimmy Olson, had just been fired. Fortunately for Lex, Olson agreed to manage the Supermen for the rest of the season. Jimmy had great success with the Supermen: they climbed to first place and attendance skyrocketed.

55. If Lex brings suit against Luther to recover $2,000, the amount due under the "penalty" provision, what result?

(A) Luther will prevail, because "penalty" clauses in contracts are not enforceable.

(B) Luther will prevail, because Lex was not harmed by Luther's breach.

(C) Lex will prevail, because Luther can be penalized for his willful breach.

(D) Lex will prevail, because the "penalty" provision is enforceable.

56. At the end of the season, Luther brings suit against Lex to recover 5% of gate receipts for the games he managed. Who will prevail?

   (A) Luther, because his breach was not substantial.

   (B) Luther, because Lex's only remedy was the "penalty" clause.

   (C) Lex, because finishing the season with the team was an implied condition of the contract.

   (D) Lex, because finishing the season with the team was an express condition of the contract.

Questions 57-58 are based on the following fact situation:

On January 2, Smith borrowed $1,000 from his friend Jones, agreeing in writing to repay the loan within a year. In September, it became clear to Smith that he would have difficulty meeting the year deadline, and so Smith approached Brown with the following proposition: Smith would perform 200 hours of work for Brown during the next six months at the special rate of $5 per hour, if Brown would agree to pay $1,000 for the entire 200 hours to Jones on the following January 1. Brown agreed.

By January 1, Smith had only worked five hours for Brown, and Brown stated to Smith that he would not pay Jones because Smith had not worked enough. Smith responded, "That's okay, just hold onto the money until I get 200 hours in, then pay Jones." Brown agreed.

57. Subsequently, Jones learns of the arrangements between Smith and Brown and he sues Brown for $1,000. The probable result of this action will be:

   (A) Judgment for Jones, because he was a third-party beneficiary to the original contract between Smith and Brown and there was no consideration for the modification of the contract.

   (B) Judgment for Jones, because he was a third-party beneficiary to the original agreement between Smith and Brown and he did not agree to the modification.

   (C) Judgment for Brown, because his contract was with Smith and therefore he cannot be liable to Jones.

   (D) Judgment for Brown, because the original agreement had been modified before Jones knew of the original agreement.

58. Assume for purposes of this question that after the agreement between Smith and Brown was entered into in September, Smith informed Jones of the arrangement. Jones's response was, "I don't care who pays me but if I don't get my money by January 2, I'll sue." The January 1 modification between Smith and Brown occurs, and after learning of the modification, Jones sues Brown for $1,000. What is the probable result of this action?

   (A) Judgment for Jones, because he was informed of the original agreement and did not participate in the modification.

   (B) Judgment for Jones, because he assented to the original agreement.

   (C) Judgment for Brown, because the original agreement was modified before Jones's rights became vested.

   (D) Judgment for Brown, because his contract was with Smith, not Jones.

Questions 59-60 are based on the following fact situation:

Producer hired Fiddler to play in an orchestra that was to leave on a 10-week tour of the United States. Fiddler, a musician, turned down another job opportunity in order to accept Producer's job offer. One week after the start of the tour, Fiddler was hospitalized with a bad back and was unable to perform. Producer hired Player to take Fiddler's part in the orchestra.

Four days later, Fiddler recovered but Producer refused to allow Fiddler to rejoin the orchestra or to complete the tour. Fiddler then sued Producer for breach of contract.

59. Which of the following is Fiddler's best legal theory?

    (A) His reliance on the job offered by Producer by declining another job opportunity created an estoppel against Producer.

    (B) His failure to perform with the orchestra for four days was not a material failure so as to discharge Producer's duty to perform.

    (C) His performance with the orchestra for the four-day period was physically impossible.

    (D) Fiddler was never told that an injury might jeopardize his continued employment with the orchestra.

60. Which of the following, if true, would adversely affect Fiddler's rights in his action against Producer?

    (A) Most of the orchestra members felt that Player was a better addition to the orchestra than Fiddler.

    (B) Producer had offered Fiddler a job in the ticket office at a higher salary but Fiddler had declined.

    (C) Producer could not find any substitute except Player, who demanded a contract for a minimum of 10 weeks if he was to perform at all.

    (D) Fiddler was not pleased about his continued employment by Producer because he did not like to travel.

Question 61

Jim owned a hardware store. In one section of his store, he had bins full of loose nuts, bolts, screws, and washers. On August 1, Jim noticed that he was running low on half-inch carriage bolts and their corresponding nuts. He called Acme Screw Co. and ordered 1,000 half-inch carriage bolts and nuts to be delivered by August 15. On August 15, the 1,000 bolts were delivered, but the nuts were missing. Jim called Acme and was told that they had been temporarily out of nuts when they had filled Jim's order, and had reduced the amount he owed to reflect this, as they had done in the past with Jim in similar circumstances. Jim protested and Acme offered to send the nuts by overnight carrier so that Jim would get them the next day.

May Jim cancel the contract?

    (A) Yes, because he was entitled to a perfect tender.

    (B) Yes, because the time for performance has passed.

    (C) No, because the one-day delay is not material.

    (D) No, because Acme has a reasonable amount of time within which to cure.

Questions 62-65 are based on the following fact situation:

Shortly after a series of rapes took place within Big City, the city council of Big City approved the offering of a $25,000 reward for the arrest and conviction of anyone guilty of the rapes. Information concerning the reward was broadcast by Big City's sole radio station once daily for one week. Shortly thereafter, Karen, a victim of one of the rape attacks, hired Stevens, a private detective, to find the person responsible for perpetrating the rapes. Karen had agreed to pay Stevens $100 per each day spent investigating the rapes. The next year, the city council of Big City passed a resolution repealing its reward offer. The city council caused this resolution to be telecast once daily for a week over Big City's local television station, the local radio station, meanwhile, having ceased operations. One month later, Philip voluntarily confessed to Stevens to having committed all of the earlier rapes. Philip was arrested and ultimately convicted of all the rapes. Karen thereupon paid Stevens at the agreed-on rate and suggested also that Stevens claim the city's $25,000 reward, of which Stevens had been previously unaware. Stevens immediately made the claim. The city refused to pay Stevens anything, although he swears that he never heard of the city's repeal of the reward offer before claiming the reward. Assume that Big City has no immunity to suit.

62. In which of the following ways could Big City's reward offer be effectively accepted?

   (A) Only by an offeree's making the arrest and assisting in the successful conviction of a rapist within the scope of the offer.

   (B) Only by an offeree's return promise to make a reasonable effort to bring about the arrest and conviction of a rapist within the scope of the offer.

   (C) By an offeree's communication of assent through the same medium (radio) used by the city in making its offer.

   (D) By an offeree's supplying information leading to arrest and conviction of a rapist within the scope of the offer.

63. If Big City's reward offer was revocable, revocation could be effectively accomplished only:

   (A) In the same manner as made or by a comparable medium and frequency of publicity.

   (B) In the same manner as made only.

   (C) By simply passing the resolution, since the events that transpired at the city council meeting are considered to be of public notice.

   (D) By notice mailed to all residents of the city and all other reasonably identifiable potential offerees.

64. If Stevens sues Big City to recover the $25,000 reward, which of the following would be most helpful to Stevens?

   (A) Big City was benefited by Stevens's services.

   (B) The attempted revocation of the reward was against public policy.

   (C) Big City's offer was in the nature of a bounty so that the elements of contract are not essential to the city's liability.

   (D) Big City is estopped from denying the reward to Stevens because he acted in the public interest.

65. If Stevens sues Big City to recover the $25,000 reward, which of the following would be least helpful to Big City?

   (A) The consideration furnished by Stevens, if any, for the city's reward promise, was legally insufficient under the preexisting duty rule.

   (B) Stevens was already compensated by Karen for his investigative services.

   (C) Big City's offer had effectively been revoked prior to Stevens's attempted acceptance.

   (D) Stevens failed to communicate his acceptance of the offer to Big City.

Questions 66-69 are based on the following fact situation:

Ace Business Supplies sold office equipment and supplies to various companies in the area. Ace entered into a written agreement with Typitrite, Inc. to purchase from Typitrite all of Ace's monthly requirements of printers for a period of five years at a specified unit price. The agreement also provided that:

1. The parties covenant not to assign this contract.

2. Payments coming due hereunder for the first six months shall be made directly by Ace Business Supply to Commercial Bank, a creditor of Typitrite, Inc.

Shortly thereafter, Typitrite, Inc. made an "assignment of the contract" to Equitable Loan Co., as security for a $50,000 loan. Ace Business Supplies subsequently ordered the delivery of and paid Typitrite the agreed price of $10,000 for Ace's requirement of printers for the first month of the agreement.

66. Which of the following accurately states the legal effect of the covenant not to assign the contract?

(A) The covenant as properly interpreted was not breached, and the assignment was effective.

(B) The covenant made the assignment to Equitable Loan Co. ineffective.

(C) Typitrite's assignment was a breach of its contract with Ace Business Supplies, but was nevertheless effective to transfer to Equitable Loan Co. Typitrite's rights against Ace Business Supplies.

(D) The covenant is effective if the parties can establish a rational reason for including the covenant into their agreement.

67. Assume for this question only that the assignment from Typitrite to Equitable Loan was effective and that Ace Business Supplies was unaware of the assignment when it paid Typitrite the $10,000. Which of the following is correct?

(A) Ace Business Supplies and Typitrite are each liable to Equitable Loan for $5,000.

(B) Typitrite is liable to Equitable Loan for $10,000.

(C) Ace Business Supplies is liable to Equitable Loan for $10,000.

(D) Neither Ace Business Supplies nor Typitrite is liable to Equitable Loan for any amount.

68. Assume for this question only that the assignment from Typitrite to Equitable Loan was effective and that Commercial Bank did not become aware of the original agreement between Ace Business Supplies and Typitrite until after Typitrite accepted the $10,000 payment from Ace Business Supplies. Which of the following, if any, is (are) correct?

I. Commercial Bank has a prior right to Ace Business Supplies's $10,000 payment as against either Typitrite or Equitable Loan.

II. Commercial Bank was an incidental beneficiary of the Ace Business Supplies-Typitrite agreement.

(A) I. only.

(B) II. only.

(C) Both I. and II.

(D) Neither I. nor II.

69. Assume for this question only that two weeks after making the $10,000 payment to Typitrite, Ace Business Supplies, by written notice to Typitrite, terminated the agreement for purchase of printers, because the demand upon Ace Business Supplies for office supplies was so great that Ace decided to no longer carry office equipment. If Equitable Loan brings suit against Ace Business Supplies for total breach, which of the following would be useful for Ace Business Supplies's defense?

(A) Ace Business Supplies ceased in good faith to have any further requirement for printers.

(B) Typitrite's "assignment of the contract" to Equitable Loan to secure a loan would normally be interpreted as a delegation of Typitrite duties under the contract as well as an assignment of its rights, and its duties owed to Ace Business Supplies were personal and therefore nondelegable.

(C) Typitrite's rights under its agreement with Ace Business Supplies were personal and therefore nonassignable.

(D) The original contract between Ace Business Supplies and Typitrite was unenforceable by either party for want of a legally sufficient consideration for Typitrite's promise to supply Ace Business Supplies's requirements of printers.

Questions 70-73 are based on the following fact situation:

Martha needed a new pair of shoes. She went to her local Skysheim shop and told the salesperson that she worked in the city's downtown area and had to walk eight blocks to get from her house to her commuter train and then six blocks from her train to her office. During the workday, she had to climb up and down stairs several times. She wanted shoes that were suitable for walking on concrete, had gripping power for stairs, and were comfortable. The salesperson went into his stockroom and brought out four different styles of Skysheim's "Clouds," reputably the most comfortable shoe on the market, designed for the type of use that Martha had in mind. Martha tried on each of the four pairs but did not like the way any of them looked. While walking around the store, however, Martha saw a shoe she did like—"Hobblers," Skysheim's high-fashion shoe. She told the salesperson to bring her a pair to try. He did so and explained to Martha that Hobblers were completely made of the finest leather and would probably last for years. Martha tried on the shoes and told the salesperson that she would take them.

70. Assume for this question only that the salesperson took the shoes back to the register with him and collected Martha's

money. As he was putting the shoes into a bag, a person brandishing a gun entered the store, forced the salesperson to put all of the money in the register into the bag with Martha's shoes, and fled with the bag, the money, and the shoes. After the police had come, Martha asked the salesperson to get her another pair of shoes. He told Martha that she would have to pay for them again. Martha refused. If Martha sues Skysheim for another pair of shoes, who will prevail?

(A) Martha, because she did not yet have possession of the shoes.

(B) Martha, because the purpose of the contract had been made impossible by an unforeseen event.

(C) Skysheim, because title to the shoes had already passed to Martha.

(D) Skysheim, because the contract goods had already been identified.

71. Assume for this question only that Martha bought the shoes and wore them twice. She decided that they were too uncomfortable for her daily commute. She took the shoes back to the Skysheim shop and demanded her money back. Skysheim refused. If Martha sues to get her money back, under which theory would she most likely prevail?

I. Breach of the implied warranty of fitness for particular purpose.

II. Breach of the implied warranty of merchantability.

III. Breach of express warranty.

(A) I. and II., but not III.

(B) I. and III., but not II.

(C) II. and III., but not I.

(D) None of the above.

72. Assume for this question only that Martha bought the shoes. She wore them to work regularly, but after a week she wore a hole through one shoe's sole. She took it to a shoe repair shop and was told that the sole was vinyl. If Martha sues Skysheim for a refund, under which theory would she most likely prevail?

    I.   Breach of an express warranty that the shoes were leather.

    II. Breach of an express warranty that the shoes would last for years.

    III. Breach of the implied warranty of merchantability.

    (A) I. and II., but not III.

    (B) I. and III., but not II.

    (C) II. and III., but not I.

    (D) I., II., and III.

73. Assume for this question only that Martha paid for the shoes and walked out of the store. A few moments later, she sat down to look at her new shoes in the sunlight. On close inspection, she noticed a small nick in the leather of one of the shoes. She immediately went back to Skysheim and demanded a refund. The salesperson refused. If Martha sues for a refund, who will prevail?

    (A) Martha, because there was a breach of contract.

    (B) Martha, because she had a reasonable time after purchase in which to inspect.

    (C) Skysheim, because Martha accepted the goods.

    (D) Skysheim, because Martha did not give written notice of the breach.

Questions 74-77 are based on the following fact situation:

Indegas wanted to ensure that it had sufficient stocks of gasoline and oil for its independent dealerships; it therefore entered into contracts with various refineries to purchase the gasoline they produced. In 1991, it entered into an agreement with Cal-Tex by which terms Indegas was given the right to purchase all gasoline refined by Cal-Tex for the next five years at a price set at 95% of the domestic market price at the time of delivery. Indegas agreed to purchase no less than 5,000 gallons a week and to use its own tankers to transport the gasoline from Cal-Tex's refinery to its storage facilities. At the time this contract was signed, Indegas gave written notice to Cal-Tex that it intended to buy all gasoline produced by Cal-Tex until further notice.

For the first year, Indegas continued to purchase all gasoline produced by Cal-Tex. However, at the end of that year Cal-Tex purchased an out-of-state refinery that refined all its gasoline from domestic shale oil. As a result of this merger and of more efficient plant methods, Cal-Tex doubled its production of gasoline by 1992. At a meeting between Cal-Tex and Indegas, Cal-Tex's president noted that Indegas was getting as much gasoline as it needed, and that Cal-Tex intended to sell the extra gasoline it was producing on foreign markets at a higher price than Indegas was paying. Indegas agreed with this proposal and signed an addendum to the original agreement reflecting this change.

Thereafter, Indegas continued to purchase one-half Cal-Tex's total capacity until 1993 when, as a result of a foreign oil boycott, Cal-Tex was unable to purchase sufficient foreign oil to operate profitably its local refinery. Cal-Tex, by letter, notified Indegas that it could no longer deliver gasoline to it in accordance with their agreement. Nevertheless, Cal-Tex's other refinery was able to increase its production by 25% and continue to sell to foreign markets.

74. The 1991 agreement between Cal-Tex and Indegas was:

(A) Unenforceable because of the failure to set a specific price for the gasoline.

(B) Unenforceable because it was for an unreasonable period of time.

(C) Enforceable as to price, but not as to the amount of gasoline Cal-Tex agreed to sell.

(D) Enforceable in all respects.

75. Assuming Indegas had an enforceable agreement in 1991, the modification of this contract made by the addendum was:

(A) Enforceable to the extent that Indegas purchased the gasoline.

(B) Enforceable in all respects.

(C) Unenforceable, because there was no consideration for Indegas's agreement to take only one-half of the gasoline produced.

(D) Unenforceable, because the contract did not state the amount of gasoline produced by each refinery.

76. Assume that a contract existed between Indegas and Cal-Tex. Cal-Tex's refusal to deliver gasoline to Indegas is:

(A) Justifiable, because it was refining no gasoline at the local refinery.

(B) Justifiable, because its performance was excused because of the foreign boycott of oil.

(C) Justifiable, because Indegas was aware of the possibility of an oil boycott when it entered into the agreement.

(D) Not justifiable and a breach of contract.

77. Assume that the oil boycott ended, but that Cal-Tex sold both its refineries to a large oil company. What is the effect of this sale on Cal-Tex's obligation to Indegas?

(A) The sale discharges its obligation to Indegas because there has been a full performance.

(B) Cal-Tex is liable for damages if the other oil company fails to deliver gasoline to Indegas.

(C) Cal-Tex is excused from further performance because it has no more refineries to produce gasoline.

(D) Cal-Tex breached its contract with Indegas.

CONTRACTS ANSWERS

Answer to Question 1

(A) The agreement is unenforceable because modification of the contract must be supported by consideration, and Builder has given no consideration. While consideration is generally necessary to modify a contract, even when the modification is in writing, consideration is usually found to exist where the obligations of both parties are varied. However, a modification solely for the benefit of one of the parties is unenforceable. The modification here is solely for the benefit of Builder because he receives the same amount of money from Owner even though the air conditioning unit will not be installed. Builder is not giving any new or different consideration because he was already obligated to finish the house, and the performance of an existing legal duty is not sufficient consideration. While courts will sometimes find consideration where severe and unforeseen hardships make full performance impracticable, increased construction costs are not within that category. Therefore, the subsequent written agreement is unenforceable. (B) is incorrect because there is no novation here. A novation occurs where a new contract substitutes a new party under the terms of an old contract. Clearly, the agreement here does not involve such a substitution. (C) is incorrect because consideration is required for modification of a construction contract. Modification of a contract for the *sale of goods* under the U.C.C. may be effective without consideration [U.C.C. §2-209(1)], but the contract here only incidentally involves the sale of goods (all things movable at the time they are identified to the contract). Primarily, the contract is a construction contract and is not subject to the U.C.C. rule. Therefore, consideration is required for its modification. (D) is incorrect because Builder does not have a legal right to breach the contract. The majority of courts adhere to the view that detriment to the promisee is the exclusive test of consideration. Legal detriment will result if the promisee refrains from doing something that he has a legal right to do. Because Builder does not have a legal right to breach the contract, his refraining from walking off the job is not sufficient consideration to support the modification. While a number of cases have held that unforeseen hardships may justify enforcing an agreement for more than the originally bargained-for consideration, most courts require the hardship to be so severe that the contract could be discharged on impracticability grounds (so that a new promise to perform for more money is supported by refraining from exercising the right to discharge the contract). The test for impracticability requires that the party encounter *extreme and unreasonable* difficulty and/or expense and that this difficulty was not anticipated. The substantially increased building costs would probably not be considered an extreme and unreasonable expense. Furthermore, Builder arguably should have anticipated possible increases in costs.

Answer to Question 2

(C) The agreement is enforceable because both Builder and Owner gave new consideration to support the modification. If parties agree to modify their contract, consideration is usually found to exist where the obligations of both parties are varied. It is usually immaterial how slight the change is, because courts are anxious to avoid the preexisting duty rule. Here, the obligations of both Builder and Owner are varied—Builder will not install the air conditioning unit and Owner will pay a construction price reduced by $5,000. Consideration is therefore found in the promise of both parties to forgo their rights under the original contract—Builder's right to full contract price and Owner's right to the air conditioner. (A) is incorrect because a contract in writing may be modified orally unless the modification brings the contract within the Statute of Frauds or, in U.C.C. cases, the contract provides that modifications must be in writing. The contract here is not within any provision of the Statute of Frauds (is not for the sale of goods of $500 or more, can be completed within a year, etc.), and does not fall under the U.C.C. Even if the contract had prohibited oral modifications, parties in non-U.C.C. cases may alter their agreement orally in spite of such a provision as long as the modification is otherwise enforceable. (B) is incorrect because this modified construction contract does not have to be in writing since it can be completed within a year. A promise that by its terms cannot be performed within a year is subject to the Statute of Frauds and must be evidenced by a writing signed by the parties sought to be bound. If the contract can be completed within one year, it need not be in writing. Here, it can be assumed that Builder could complete the house within a year. Therefore, the modification does not have to be in writing. (D) is incorrect because the parol evidence rule does not apply to *subsequent* oral agreements. The parol evidence rule states that where the parties to a contract express their agreement in a writing with the intent that it embody the full and final expression of their bargain, any other expressions—written or oral—made prior to the writing, as well as any oral expressions contemporaneous with the writing, are inadmissible to vary the terms of the writing. Parol evidence can be offered to show *subsequent* modifications of a written contract, such as the oral agreement between Builder and Owner, because the rule applies only to prior or contemporaneous negotiations.

Answer to Question 3

(A) Most courts would hold that there was a good faith dispute and the check thus proposed an accord; Builder's act of cashing it is a satisfaction. A contract may be discharged by an accord and satisfaction. An accord is an agreement in which one party to an existing contract agrees to accept, in lieu of the performance that she is supposed to receive from the other party, some other, different performance. Satisfaction is the performance of the accord agreement. An accord and satisfaction generally may be accomplished by tender and acceptance of a check marked "payment in full" where there is a bona fide dispute as to the amount owed. Here, there is a good faith dispute between Owner and Builder as to the workmanship on several items. Therefore, Owner's tender of the check marked "payment in full" and Builder's cashing of the check constituted an accord and satisfaction, discharging Owner's duty to pay the balance. (B) is incorrect because the debt is unliquidated. Generally, payment of a smaller sum than due will not be sufficient consideration for a promise by the creditor to discharge the debt. However, the majority view is that payment of the smaller amount will suffice for an *accord and satisfaction* where there is a "bona fide dispute" as to the claim. As discussed above, because Owner and Builder had a good faith dispute about the workmanship on several items, Owner's tender of the check and Builder's cashing of the check constituted an accord and satisfaction, which discharged Owner's duty to pay the balance. (C) is incorrect because a promissory estoppel situation does not exist in that there was no change of position by Owner based on any act or statement by Builder. Whenever a party to a contract indicates that he is "waiving" a condition before it is to happen or some performance before it is to be rendered, and the person addressed *detrimentally relies* upon the waiver, the courts will hold this to be a binding (estoppel) waiver. Here, there is no indication that Owner detrimentally changed position as a result of Builder cashing the check. Therefore, Builder's act of cashing the check could not be considered an estoppel waiver. (D) is incorrect because Builder's indorsement is not sufficient to meet the writing requirement for a release. A release that will serve to discharge contractual duties is usually required to be in writing and supported by new consideration or promissory estoppel elements. While the good faith dispute between Builder and Owner would meet the consideration requirement for a release, the indorsement does not show the kind of circumspection and deliberateness that the writing requirement was intended to insure. Therefore, the better answer is that the acceptance of the check by Builder was a satisfaction, as discussed above, rather than a release.

Answer to Question 4

(C) Builder will recover nothing because Builder's duty to construct the building for Owner is not discharged by the fire. Contractual duties will be discharged where it has become impossible to perform them. While contractual duties will generally be discharged if the contract's subject matter is destroyed, a contractor's duty to construct a building is not discharged by destruction of the work in progress unless the buyer has assumed that risk. The rationale behind this rule is that the construction is not rendered impossible; the contractor can still rebuild. The risk of loss during construction, absent contrary provisions, lies with the builder, who is generally in a better position to acquire insurance during the construction process. Therefore, because Builder inserted no provision in the contract relieving him of liability in the case of fire, his duty to build the house is not discharged by the fire. (A) is incorrect because there has not been a breach by Owner during the construction, nor had Owner assumed the risk of the fire. If the owner breaches a construction contract during the construction, the builder is entitled to the contract price minus the cost of completion. However, the facts here involve risk of loss from fire, not a breach by Owner. Also, while Builder might have recovered the contract price less the value of the work remaining to be done if Owner had assumed the risk of a fire, Owner had not done so and Builder's duty to complete the house is not discharged. (B) is incorrect because Builder's duty of performance has not been rendered objectively "impossible" by the fire, as discussed above. Moreover, even if the construction contract were discharged, Builder would not be entitled to a proportionate amount of the profits he would have earned. At best, he would be reimbursed only for the value of his labor and the materials used on the building (*see* below). (D) is incorrect because, while Builder might be entitled to this recovery if the construction contract were discharged by impossibility, his duty was *not* discharged by the fire. When the duties of parties to a contract are excused on account of impossibility, restitution or quasi-contractual remedies are available to the parties to put them back into the original status quo in order to prevent unjust enrichment. However, as discussed above, Builder's duty of performance has not been rendered objectively "impossible" by the fire. (It is also unlikely that Builder could show that Owner has been unjustly enriched since the construction was destroyed.) Therefore, Builder can recover nothing from Owner until he builds another house.

Answer to Question 5

(C) An enforceable contract was created because even though the document standing alone does not appear to be supported by any consideration, it still may be construed as an *offer* to sell, which was accepted before it was revoked. In general, a contract must be supported by valuable consideration on both sides to be fully enforceable from the moment of formation. The majority of courts adhere to the view that detriment to the promisee in performing an act or making a promise is the exclusive test of consideration. Here, the writing was not supported by consideration on both sides because Bettum was not clearly obligated to purchase the colts. However, the writing still may be construed as an offer to sell. The fact that the price of the colts was left open to be determined later does not prevent the writing from being considered an offer because a reasonable price at the time of delivery will be supplied by the court. [U.C.C. §2-305] Because the offer had not been revoked, Bettum's good faith and prompt tender would constitute the acceptance, creating an enforceable contract (although the contract may or may not be enforceable at the price tendered). (A) is incorrect because, as discussed above, Wrangler became obligated to sell the colt when Bettum accepted the offer to purchase the colt by tendering the $25,000. (B) is incorrect because Bettum did not impliedly promise to purchase a colt by signing the agreement. The terms of the document clearly show that Wrangler and Bettum did not intend that Bettum would be obligated to purchase; Bettum merely was given a right of first refusal. The courts will not imply from the signing of a document a promise that is contrary to the parties' intent. Because Bettum was not obligated to purchase a colt, the written document was unenforceable as a contract for lack of consideration. (D) is incorrect because the U.C.C. limits the duration of irrevocability of merchants' firm offers to three months. Even without consideration, an offer by a merchant to buy or sell goods in a signed writing that, by its terms, gives assurances that it will be held open is not revocable during the time stated or for a reasonable time if no period is stated (but in no event may such period exceed three months). [U.C.C. §2-205] Wrangler, as a famous breeder of horses, would be considered a merchant under the U.C.C. because he holds himself out as having special knowledge of horses. [U.C.C. §2-104(1)] However, because such an offer can only be considered irrevocable without consideration for three months, the six-month-old written agreement is not enforceable as a firm offer.

Answer to Question 6

(A) Bettum may purchase the colt, and the court will supply the missing price. In a contract for the sale of goods, the failure to state the price does not prevent the formation of a contract if the parties intended to form a contract without the price being settled. In such a case, if the price is left to be agreed to by the parties and they fail to agree, a reasonable price at the time of delivery will be supplied by the court. [U.C.C. §2-305] Here, Bettum and Wrangler had a contract for the sale of goods (colts), with the price of the colts to be determined later. Because they have failed to agree on a price, Bettum is entitled under the U.C.C. to purchase the colt at whatever price the court determines to be reasonable. (B) is incorrect because there is no provision for arbitration in the agreement. As stated above, if the price is left open in a contract for sale of goods, and the parties are unable to agree later on a price, the court will imply a reasonable price. [U.C.C. §2-305] (C) is incorrect because even though $25,000 was a good faith tender, it may or may not be the "reasonable" price determined by the court. As discussed above, if the price in a contract for sale of goods is left to be agreed by the parties and they fail to agree, the court will determine and supply a reasonable price. [U.C.C. §2-305] (D) is incorrect because $100,000 does not appear to be a reasonable price and it has not been supplied as a reasonable price by the court. As discussed above, the U.C.C. provides that if the price is left to be agreed upon by the parties and they fail to agree, the court will supply a reasonable price. [U.C.C. §2-305] Bettum would have to pay $100,000 only if the court determined that $100,000 was a reasonable price.

Answer to Question 7

(B) Induscorp should recover $5,000 because the oral contract between Induscorp and Barney is enforceable to the extent Barney received and accepted the goods. A promise for the sale of goods of $500 or more is not enforceable unless evidenced by a writing signed by the party to be charged. [U.C.C. §2-201(1)] However, an oral contract for such goods is enforceable to the extent of goods received and accepted by the buyer. [U.C.C. §2-201(3)(c)] Oral contracts for specially manufactured goods not suitable for sale in the ordinary course of the seller's business also are enforceable when the seller has begun substantially to perform. Here, the parties' agreement was oral. Barney accepted one machine, but neither machine was specially manufactured. Barney is bound to pay the $5,000 contract price for the accepted machine, but he is not bound to pay for the rejected machine. (A) is incorrect because Induscorp is entitled to the contract price for the machine Barney accepted, not just restitution. If a contract is unenforceable because of noncompliance with the Statute of Frauds, a party can generally sue for the restitution of any benefit that has been conferred. However, as discussed above, an oral contract for the sale of goods of $500 or more is enforceable to the extent of goods received and accepted by the buyer. Therefore, because Barney accepted one machine, Induscorp is entitled to the $5,000 contract price of that machine, not just $3,000 in restitutionary damages. (C) is incorrect because Induscorp is not entitled to any damages as to the rejected machine. As indicated above, Induscorp is entitled to $5,000 for the first machine. There is no enforceable contract regarding the second machine, and Induscorp is not entitled to damages for that machine. If there were an enforceable contract for the second machine, (C) would state a proper measure of damages—if a buyer breaches by refusing to accept goods, the seller is entitled to recover the difference between the contract price ($5,000) and the market or resale price ($3,000), here, $2,000. Thus, Induscorp would be entitled to $5,000 for the accepted machine and $2,000 for the rejected machine, or $7,000. (D) is incorrect for the same reason that (C) is incorrect—Induscorp is only entitled to the contract price of the machine accepted by Barney. If the contract for the second machine were enforceable, (D) would still not be a proper measure of damages. Under the U.C.C., the seller has a right to force goods on a buyer who has not accepted them only if the seller is unable to resell the goods or if the goods have been lost or damaged after the risk of loss passed to the buyer. [U.C.C. §2-709] Because Induscorp can resell the second machine, which has not been lost or damaged, it could not recover the full price of the second machine from Barney even if the contract was fully enforceable.

Answer to Question 8

(B) Eero's best argument is that a personal services contract is not specifically enforceable. Thus, Odivia cannot obtain specific performance of Eero's agreement to perform personal plumbing, electrical, and carpentry work for her. One of the prerequisites to obtaining specific performance is that a plaintiff must show that the legal remedy is inadequate. Where the plaintiff has contracted for something rare or unique, money damages are inadequate compensation for loss of the bargain. Generally, services to be performed under a personal services contract are not unique and money damages can remedy a breach. Thus, specific performance is not available in such cases. In addition, even in the case of unique services, a court will not order a defendant to work for the plaintiff, in part because of the difficulty of enforcement and because such an order is tantamount to unconstitutional involuntary servitude. Another requirement for specific performance is that enforcement must be feasible. Enforcing a personal services contract generally would create complicated and time-consuming supervision problems that courts are reluctant to undertake. In this case, Eero agreed to personally perform for Odivia plumbing, electrical, and carpentry work. Thus, this was a personal services contract. However, the services to be performed by Eero were not unique or capable of being performed solely by Eero. Odivia could obtain adequate compensation by receiving the amount, above her contract price with Eero, that it will cost to have someone else perform the required work (plus reasonable compensation for the delay in performance). Thus, specific performance is inappropriate here. (A) is incorrect because circumstances that would permit the defense of laches do not appear to be present. Laches is available as an equitable defense if the plaintiff has unreasonably delayed in bringing the action and the delay is prejudicial to the defendant. There is no automatic invocation of laches by a delay of one year before suit is filed. Here, there is no showing that Odivia's delay in filing suit was unreasonable, given that she spent several months trying to find another contractor, nor that Eero has been prejudiced by the delay. Therefore, laches will not provide Eero with a strong defense. (C) is incorrect because, if only nominal damages are available, Odivia will not have an adequate legal remedy. Nominal damages are appropriate where there is a breach, but no actual loss. Here, nominal damages would fail to compensate Odivia for the amount she will have to pay above the price agreed to by Eero. Thus, the availability of nominal damages would not, by itself, render specific performance an inappropriate remedy. Regarding (D), a court of equity may inquire into the relative values of agreed-upon consideration and deny an equitable remedy if it finds a contract to be unconscionable. Nevertheless, the mere fact that Odivia could not find another contractor to do the job for the price agreed upon by Eero does not establish that her contract with Eero was unconscionable. Thus, Eero will not be successful in his contention that specific performance should be denied on the basis that the price for which he agreed to do the work was too low.

Answer to Question 9

(A) The contract is enforceable because the "mailbox rule" applies here. Acceptance by mail creates a contract at the ***moment of posting***, properly addressed and stamped, unless the offer stipulates that acceptance is not effective until received, or an option contract is involved. If the offeree sends an acceptance and then rejects the offer, the mailbox rule applies; *i.e.,* a contract is created upon dispatch of the acceptance. Because no option contract is involved here, and Sam's offer did not state that Bam's acceptance would only be effective when received, Bam's acceptance was effective the moment he placed the envelope containing the contract in the mailbox. Bam's attempt to reject occurred after acceptance took place. Thus, a valid contract was formed and Sam may enforce it. (B) is incorrect because nothing in the parol evidence rule would serve to validate the contract. Ostensibly, this choice implies that there is a contract because the parol evidence rule will prevent Bam from introducing the oral rescission. However, as discussed below, the rescission is ineffective because there was no meeting of the minds. The parol evidence rule would not prevent introduction of the rescission if it were otherwise valid. The parol evidence rule of the U.C.C. merely prohibits a party to a goods contract from contradicting an integrated writing with evidence of any prior agreement or contemporaneous oral agreement. Subsequent agreements such as the attempted rescission here can be introduced. Therefore, the parol evidence rule does not serve to validate the contract here. (C) is incorrect because there is no "meeting of the minds" concerning the rescission. A contract may be discharged by an express agreement between the parties to rescind; the agreement to rescind is itself a binding contract. Because Sam did not know that Bam had accepted the contract, Sam's statement that "that's all right" cannot be construed as acceptance of Bam's offer to rescind. Therefore, a contract to rescind was not formed. (D) is incorrect because the telephone rejection did not void the acceptance by mail. As discussed above, if the offeree sends an acceptance first, followed by a rejection, the mailbox rule applies; *i.e.,* a contract is created upon dispatch of the acceptance. Because Bam's telephone rejection took place after his acceptance by mail, his acceptance was effective and a contract was created when the letter was mailed. While an ***offeree*** will be estopped from enforcing the contract if the offeror receives the rejection first and changes his position in reliance on it, Sam is the one wanting to enforce the contract here.

Answer to Question 10

(B) Gibbons remains liable based on his contract with Vita-Crest, and Standard is liable based on its assumption of the contract with Vita-Crest. American Diet Institute (ADI) is expressly designated in the contract between Gibbons and Vita-Crest as a party to whom payment for any April purchases is to be directly made. Thus, the portion of the contract providing for payment is primarily for the benefit of ADI. Consequently, ADI is an intended third-party beneficiary of Gibbons's promise to make the April payment. As the third-party beneficiary, ADI has a right of action against the promisor (Gibbons) for enforcement of the promise to pay. When Gibbons assigned to Standard his contract with Vita-Crest, Standard was deemed to have assumed Gibbons's duties under that contract as well as being assigned the rights thereunder. Thus, Standard can be held to the duty to pay for the health food products that were ordered in April. Although Standard is deemed to have assumed the duties of Gibbons under the contract, Gibbons (the delegator) remains liable on the contract. Consequently, ADI has a right of action for the April payment against Gibbons and Standard (although ADI will be limited to only one recovery). (A) and (C) are incorrect because they conclude that, as between Gibbons and Standard, only one of them has the duty to tender the required payment. As explained above, **both** Gibbons and Standard are under this duty. (D) is incorrect because, as the intended third-party beneficiary of the promise to pay, ADI can maintain an action to collect the April payment. A third-party beneficiary has a right of action in his own right.

Answer to Question 11

(D) If Vita-Crest was attempting to confer a gift upon ADI, then ADI is a donee beneficiary. A third-party donee beneficiary may not sue the promisee, whose act is gratuitous (except under very limited circumstances where: (i) the promisee tells the beneficiary of the contract and should foresee reliance, **and** (ii) the beneficiary reasonably relies to its detriment). Consequently, under the circumstances set forth in (D), ADI has no sustainable cause of action against Vita-Crest, the promisee, for the $4,000 that was intended to be a gift. By establishing ADI as a donee beneficiary, (D) provides a complete defense for Vita-Crest. If ADI is a creditor beneficiary, then it may sue Vita-Crest on the existing obligation between them. In such case, ADI's right to recover from Vita-Crest would be unaffected by any defenses that could be raised on behalf of Gibbons. Thus, it will be of no help to Vita-Crest if ADI owes Gibbons more than $4,000, or if the goods shipped were not merchantable. Consequently, (B) and (C) are incorrect. Similarly, (A) is incorrect because if ADI is a creditor beneficiary, the enforceability (or lack thereof) of Gibbons's promise to make the payments to ADI would not affect Vita-Crest's obligation to ADI. Also, the promise of Gibbons to pay ADI is not required to be supported by consideration separate from the consideration given in support of the original agreement between Gibbons and Vita-Crest. Thus, the lack of separate consideration would not under any circumstances provide a defense to an action brought by the third-party beneficiary.

Answer to Question 12

(B) The institute can still sue if it detrimentally relied on the agreement. An intended third-party beneficiary can enforce a contract only after her rights have vested. Vesting occurs when the beneficiary: (i) manifests assent to the promise in a manner invited or requested by the parties; (ii) brings suit to enforce the promise; or (iii) materially changes position in justifiable reliance on the promise. Thus, if ADI detrimentally relied on the agreement between Gibbons and Vita-Crest, ADI's rights will have vested and the parties' right to modify their agreement will have been eliminated, at least with respect to payment to ADI. Thus, (B) presents an accurate statement of applicable legal principles. (A) is incorrect because, as noted above, the third-party beneficiary's rights do not vest until occurrence of one of the specified conditions. Vesting does not automatically occur upon execution of the contract. (C) is incorrect because it fails to account for the possibility that ADI may have taken action causing his rights to vest prior to the later agreement between Gibbons and Vita-Crest. Had this been the case, the later agreement would not have cut off ADI's right to maintain an action on the original agreement. (D) is incorrect because simply learning of an agreement, without taking any of the required actions for vesting, will not result in the vesting of the rights of a third-party beneficiary.

Answer to Question 13

(C) Standard cannot compel Vita-Crest to fill the order. An assignment of rights is barred if it will substantially change the obligor's duty. At common law, the right to receive goods under a requirements contract generally was not assignable because the assignment could change the obligation of the parties. Under the U.C.C., such a right might be assignable if the quantity requirement is not unreasonably disproportionate to the quantity originally contemplated by the parties. [U.C.C. §2-306] Here, there is no good indication of the quantity the parties intended; however, Gibbons owned only one store and his requirements for the month of April were only 20 cases. Standard, on the other hand, is a chain and its requirements are 5,000 cases, a disproportionately large increase. Therefore, the assignment here would be unenforceable even under the Code. (A) is incorrect because prompt notice of the assignment does not obviate the problem of the unreasonably disproportionate requirements. (B) is incorrect because there is mutuality of obligation (consideration on both sides) here. The parties entered into a requirements contract whereby Vita-Crest agreed to sell Gibbons all of Gibbons's natural foods requirements and Gibbons promised to buy natural foods only from Vita-Crest. (Gibbons's promise to buy only what he "desires" is not illusory because Gibbons agreed to not purchase natural foods from any other source.) A requirements contract is not illusory because the U.C.C. imposes a duty to purchase requirements in good faith. (D) is incorrect because it implies that the assignment here is not assignable because the assignee poses a different credit risk from the assignor (and the risk can be eliminated through cash payment). However, as discussed above, the contract here is not assignable because of the unreasonably disproportionate requirements of Standard, not because of Standard's creditworthiness.

Answer to Question 14

(A) Tyree will be able to recover the $45,000 from Warden because Warden had notice of the assignment. Most contract rights may be assigned, and the right assigned here (to receive money) falls within the general rule. Once the assignment is effective, the assignee (Tyree) becomes the real party in interest, and he alone is entitled to performance under the contract. (The assignor has been replaced by the assignee.) Once the obligor (Warden) has knowledge of the assignment, he is bound to render performance to the assignee. Here, the assignment was effective as soon as Michael (the assignor) manifested his intent that the right should be assigned (*i.e.,* in his written assignment to Tyree). Warden was given notice of the assignment. Thus, Warden was bound to pay Tyree. Warden breached his duty by paying Michael instead of Tyree; thus, Tyree may recover from Warden for his failure to perform. (B) is wrong because provisions prohibiting "assignment of the contract" will be construed as barring only the delegation of the assignor's duties, and here only an assignment of the right to the proceeds was made. Furthermore, the U.C.C., which governs the contract here since goods are involved, specifically provides that an assignor's right arising out of his performance under the contract can be assigned despite an agreement to the contrary (although this may breach the assignor's contract with the obligor). (C) is wrong because, as stated above, once Warden had notice of the assignment, he owed the duty to pay to Tyree (the assignee), and payment to any third party, even Michael (the assignor), does not discharge this duty. (D) is wrong because it is irrelevant whether the assignee could perform under the contract; the relevant question is whether the assignor could and did properly perform.

Answer to Question 15

(C) Warden did not properly reject, because he accepted the shoes and failed to give proper notice of rejection. A buyer who receives nonconforming goods generally has the right to accept all, reject all, or accept any commercial units and reject the rest. Here, 10% of the shoes shipped were defective, so Warden had a right to reject. To properly reject, the rejecting party must, within a reasonable time after delivery and before acceptance, seasonably notify the seller of the rejection. If the notice fails to state a defect, the buyer cannot rely on that defect if the seller could have cured by supplying conforming goods. Here, Warden failed to notify Michael of the defects; he merely sent a check for less than the contract price. Since the contract did not have a particular delivery date, Michael probably had time to cure and, presumably, would have. Thus, Warden cannot rely on the defect in claiming a breach; therefore, his rejection was improper. (B) is wrong because, as explained above, partial payment did not give notice of the specific defect, and so Warden could not rely on that defect in rejecting. Thus, the rejection was not proper. (D) is wrong because the right of rejection exists for *any* defect, whether substantial or minor. The U.C.C., which governs sales contracts such as this one, gives buyers the right to a ***perfect tender***.

Answer to Question 16

(D) Pontecorvo's power to accept lapsed because it had to be exercised prior to 11:59 p.m. on September 30. The so-called mailbox rule does ***not*** apply to the exercise of options. In such cases acceptance is effective when ***received*** by the offeror. Thus, (D) is correct. (A) is wrong because, for the reasons discussed above, Pontecorvo did not effectively accept before his option expired. (C) is wrong for two reasons: (i) a revocation is not effective until received; and (ii) because the contract is an option, the offeror's power to terminate the offer through revocation is limited. Even if the revocation had arrived earlier, Vidor-Holly lacked the power to revoke. (B) is irrelevant. Returning the consideration, in and of itself, would not give the offeror the power to revoke in an option situation.

Answer to Question 17

(D) Under the Statute of Frauds, contracts for the sale of land must be in writing. The writing must contain all essential terms, and the price is considered an essential term. (A) is wrong because although the parol evidence rule might not bar the testimony, the Statute of Frauds will prevent recovery. (B) is wrong; the advertisement was not signed by Campbell, the party charged with breaking the contract. Thus, it is not a memorandum. Furthermore, the ad could not be considered part of the contract because there is nothing in the question indicating that it was attached to or referred to in the contract, or that it was assented to by the parties as part of the contract. In fact, an ad is a mere offer to deal; the actual price term may be very different by the time parties to a contract reach an agreement. (C) is wrong; the parol evidence rule would not bar the testimony, and in any event, that is not the reason Campbell will win.

Answer to Question 18

(B) Bunker's first communication was a request for an offer and Sachs's response was an offer. For a communication to be an offer, it must create a reasonable expectation in the offeree that the offeror is willing to enter into a contract on the basis of the offered terms. The first communication by Bunker does not pass the test since it is clear on its face that Bunker did not want to be bound by whatever price Sachs came up with, but rather wanted to find out what Sachs would offer. Sachs's communication, on the other hand, passes the test. While it said nothing more than the price, it was sent in response to a request containing specific delivery terms and a specific quantity. Under the circumstances, Sachs's response would have created a reasonable expectation in Bunker that Sachs was willing to enter into a contract under the terms of the two communications. (A) is wrong because, as indicated above, Bunker's communication was not an offer since it did not indicate the requisite intent to be bound. Thus, Sachs's communication could not be an acceptance, since an acceptance must be in response to an offer. (C) and (D) are wrong because, as explained above, Sachs's communication was not merely a price quotation; given that it was sent in response to a very specific inquiry, it was sufficient to be an offer.

Answer to Question 19

(D) Bunker must pay the freight because that is what the offer stated, and Bunker accepted the offer. The term "F.O.B." is a delivery term under the U.C.C., which governs the contract here because it is a contract for the sale of goods. That term means "free on board," and it obligates the seller to get the goods to the location indicated after the term. Here, the term indicates that the goods are "F.O.B. my [Sachs's] vault," so Sachs is only obligated to get the platinum to his vault, and Bunker must pay the freight from there. (A) is incorrect because Bunker must pay the freight, for the reasons given above. (B) and (C) are incorrect because they condition the answer on factors that are not relevant here. The conditions relate to whether the offer terms or the acceptance terms will govern a contract between merchants where the acceptance terms differ from the offer terms. Here, the acceptance did not vary the terms of the offer. Sachs offered to sell for $475 per ounce, price F.O.B. his vault, and Bunker accepted those terms ("Deal is okay . . . "). Thus, it is unnecessary to consider the conditions under (B) and (C).

Answer to Question 20

(C) If Sachs's fax provided a firm price for 48 hours, Sachs would have a contract with both Bunker and Hunter because the offer to Bunker would have been an irrevocable firm merchant's offer during the 48 hours. Under the U.C.C., which governs here because goods are involved, a written offer signed by a merchant giving assurances that it will stay open will be irrevocable for the time stated. Sachs qualifies as a merchant of platinum (one who deals in goods of that kind sold) and his offer was written and signed (the letterhead satisfies the signature requirement under the U.C.C.), and contained words of firmness ("firm for 48 hours"), so it was irrevocable for 48 hours. Thus, Bunker accepted the offer before it was terminated, and Hunter's acceptance was valid because the offer to him was never revoked. Therefore, Sachs is obligated to both Bunker and Hunter. (A) is incorrect because while platinum qualifies as "goods," the result under the U.C.C. is as described above. Also, (A) would probably be incorrect even if platinum were not goods, since Bunker's acceptance was effective under common law rules. Under the common law, Sachs's offer was revocable despite the words of firmness (since no consideration was given to keep the offer open), but it was not revoked until *after* Bunker accepted—Bunker's knowledge of the offer to Hunter was not sufficient to revoke Sachs's offer (unless Bunker also knew of Sachs's limited supply, not the case here). Thus, even under the common law, Sachs would have a contract with both Bunker and Hunter. (B) is incorrect because platinum qualifies as goods, and even if it did not, Sachs would be obligated to both Bunker and Hunter, as explained above. (D) is incorrect because, as explained above, Sachs has a contract with both Bunker and Hunter.

Answer to Question 21

(D) The modification of the contract between Mary and Pipes was not supported by consideration, because Pipes gave nothing other than what he was already legally obligated to give. A contract may be subsequently modified by the parties, thus serving to discharge those terms of the original contract that are the subject of the modification. A modifying agreement must be mutually assented to. In addition, consideration is necessary to modify a contract. Although courts often find consideration present in that each party has limited her right to enforce the original contract as is, if a modification would operate to benefit only one of the parties, it may be unenforceable without some consideration being given to the other party. Generally, the promise to perform or the performance of an existing legal duty will not be sufficient consideration. One exception to this rule is that if a promisee has given something in addition to what he already owes in return for the promise he now seeks to enforce, or has in some way agreed to vary his preexisting duty (as by accelerating performance), there is consideration. Pipes is seeking to enforce a modified version of the contract, the modification being that Mary now owes an additional $150. This modification does not benefit Mary at all, as she is simply getting what she originally bargained for at a higher price. The modification does benefit Pipes because without it he would be unable to complete his work as per the contract. Thus, the modification is unenforceable without consideration on the part of Pipes. No consideration is present, as Pipes merely performed his preexisting contractual duty. Pipes gave nothing in addition to what he already owed, nor did he vary his duty in any manner. Therefore, the promise of Mary to pay is unenforceable as modified. (A) is therefore incorrect. (B) is incorrect because the fact that Pipes completed performance by October 1 does not entitle him to the extra money. Only if Mary's modified promise is found to be enforceable will Pipes be entitled to the $150. (C) is incorrect because, although Mary did not specifically tell Pipes that she would pay the $150, her statement strongly implies that she would do so. In any event, it is clear that the requisite consideration was absent, so it is unnecessary to consider the potential ambiguity of Mary's assent to the proposed modification.

Answer to Question 22

(C) The destruction of Mary's house discharges Pipes's duties due to impossibility, but Pipes has a right to recover for the reasonable value of the work he performed. Contractual duties are discharged where it has become impossible to perform them. The occurrence of an unanticipated or extraordinary event may make contractual duties impossible to perform. If the nonoccurrence of the event was a basic assumption of the parties in making the contract, and neither party has assumed the risk of the event's occurrence, duties under the contract may be discharged. Impossibility must arise after entering into the contract. If there is impossibility, each party is excused from duties that are yet to be performed. If either party has partially performed prior to the existence of facts resulting in impossibility, that party has a right to recover in quasi-contract at the contract rate or for the reasonable value of his performance if that mode of valuation is more convenient. Here, the house on which Pipes was to perform plumbing repairs was totally destroyed in a flood. The facts indicate that this flood was of such an unexpected nature that its nonoccurrence was a basic assumption of the parties, and neither party was likely to have assumed the risk of its occurrence. Thus, it has become literally impossible for Pipes (or anyone else) to complete the job. This impossibility will discharge both Mary and Pipes from performing any contractual duties still to be fulfilled. Therefore, Pipes need not finish the repair work, and Mary is not obligated to pay the entire amount of $1,200. (A) and (B) are therefore incorrect. However, because Pipes rendered part performance prior to the flood, he may recover for the work that was performed. (D) is incorrect because it fails to account for the fact that Mary will have to pay Pipes for the value of the work already performed.

Answer to Question 23

(B) Andrew accepted Patrick's offer when he mailed his letter on January 3, and thus, a contract was formed. Under the "mailbox" rule, acceptance of an offer by mail creates a contract at the moment the acceptance is posted properly stamped and addressed. If the offeree sends both an acceptance and a rejection, whether the mailbox rule will apply depends on which the offeree sent first, the acceptance or the rejection. If the offeree *first sends an acceptance* and later sends his rejection, the mailbox rule does apply. Thus, even if the rejection arrives first, the acceptance is effective upon mailing (and so a contract is formed) unless the offeror changes his position in reliance on the rejection. Here, Andrew first sent an acceptance, then called with his rejection. The mailbox rule applies, and since there is nothing in the facts to show that Patrick relied on the rejection, a contract was formed. (A) is wrong because it implies that a rejection must be in writing. There is no such requirement. Also, the rejection (absent detrimental reliance) has no effect on the contract since the offer had already been accepted and the contract formed. (C) is wrong because, as stated above, under the mailbox rule the fact that the rejection was received before the acceptance is irrelevant (unless there has been detrimental reliance on the rejection, which was not the case here). The contract was formed when Andrew sent his acceptance. (D) is wrong because the description, although somewhat ambiguous, can be made reasonably certain by evidence of the subjective understanding of the parties and extrinsic evidence of what was in the house, which a court will consider to clarify an ambiguous term.

Answer to Question 24

(A) Bertram is entitled to specific performance since Sabrina signed the land sale contract. A contract was formed here when the parties orally agreed to the sale of Maroonacre. However, the contract was unenforceable at that time because, under the Statute of Frauds, a contract for the sale of land is unenforceable unless a memorandum containing the contract's essential terms is signed by the party to be charged. Here, the party to be charged is Sabrina, and she signed the land sale contract, a writing sufficient to satisfy the Statute of Frauds (a memorandum for the sale of land is sufficient if it contains the price, a description of the property—which need not be a "legal" description—and a designation of the parties). Thus, the contract was enforceable. Specific performance is allowed when the legal remedy (damages) would be inadequate (usually with contracts to purchase land). Therefore, Bertram is entitled to specific performance. (B) is incorrect because to satisfy the Statute of Frauds, a description need not be a complete legal description, but need merely be sufficient to reasonably identify the subject of the contract. It is sufficient that the property was identified by its name. (C) is incorrect because it does not matter whether the deed was signed by Sabrina, since the land sale contract was sufficient under the Statute, and Sabrina signed it. (D) is incorrect because while it is true that contracts involving the sale of land are governed by the Statute of Frauds, the Statute was satisfied here by the written sale contract.

Answer to Question 25

(C) Tom will not prevail because his failure to tender the money was a breach of contract, which released Leonora from her duty to convey the property. A party's obligation to perform her duties under a contract will be excused by a material breach of the contract by the other party. Here, Tom breached the contract by failing to tender $30,000 on or before noon on June 15, as the contract required. Although generally a one-day delay in a land sale contract is a minor breach, this breach was material since the parties *specifically agreed* to make time of the essence. Tom's performance was a condition concurrent to Leonora's duty to perform; so Leonora was free to sell the property after the time for Tom's performance had passed. (A) is incorrect because the money was not tendered in a timely manner. The contract specifically required the money to be paid by noon on June 15, and here it would not arrive until June 16, a day late. The mailbox rule (*i.e.,* an ***acceptance*** is effective upon dispatch) does not save the tender here because the tender is not an acceptance of the contract; the contract was accepted when the parties bilaterally promised to exchange $35,000 for the property. Rather, the tender was a condition concurrent to Leonora's duty to transfer the property, and there is no mailbox rule for fulfillment of conditions. (B) is incorrect because impossibility will not excuse his late performance. To excuse a condition because of impossibility, the impossibility must be objective (the condition cannot be fulfilled by ***anyone***). There is no indication here that it was impossible for Tom to get the money to Leonora by the time set. He could possibly have made arrangements for someone else to deliver the check, or since his daughter was out of danger, he could have come himself. It was not impossible for him to perform. Tom might argue that the notice was a modification of the contract, but he gave no consideration to obtain the modification, nor did Leonora agree to the modification since Tom spoke only with Leonora's secretary. Tom might also argue that his notice constituted a waiver of the "time is of the essence clause," but again Leonora did not agree to such a waiver. (D) is incorrect because, while it is true that the mailbox rule does not apply to option contracts (*i.e.,* an offer under an option contract is not accepted merely by dispatching the acceptance), tendering the $30,000 here was not an acceptance of an offer but rather a condition concurrent to a bilateral contract. The option was accepted when the parties entered into a bilateral contract for the sale of the land. Thus, the mailbox rule is irrelevant. (D) would have been correct if the offer were stated differently (*e.g.,* Tom has the option of purchasing the property by tendering $30,000 before noon on June 15), since the tender then would have been an acceptance of the option.

Answer to Question 26

(B) There is an enforceable contract between Genoa and Rudder since Genoa fully performed. The contract here was for the sale of goods (sails) for the price of $500 or more; thus, the contract is within the Statute of Frauds. A contract within the Statute of Frauds is generally unenforceable absent a memorandum signed by the party to be charged containing the contract's essential terms. However, there is an exception to the general rule for goods received and accepted. Here, although the contract was oral, Rudder accepted the sails, and so he is bound despite the Statute. Note that Rudder might also be bound under another exception to the Statute—for specially manufactured goods if the sails were made specially for the yacht and were not suitable for sale to others. (A) is incorrect because the U.C.C. does not exempt merchants from the Statute of Frauds. It does, however, provide a special confirmatory memo rule by which a merchant may be bound even if his signature does not appear on the writing evidencing the contract, although the special rule is not applicable here because here there is no writing at all. (C) is incorrect because it is irrelevant. The fact that Rudder agreed not to subcontract is relevant to whether he breached his contract with Winston, but it does not affect his contract with Genoa. (D) is incorrect because, as stated above, the contract here falls within an exception to the Statute of Frauds since Rudder accepted the sails.

Answer to Question 27

(C) Genoa will be able to recover the full $25,000 contract price. Under the U.C.C., the contract is enforceable, despite the absence of a writing, to the extent of the goods accepted, which here is the entire amount contracted for. The proper remedy is the agreed-upon price of $25,000, which Genoa will be able to prove by parol evidence. [*See* U.C.C. §2-201, comment 2] (A) is incorrect because the recovery will be under the contract, since the promises are enforceable under an exception to the Statute of Frauds; thus, the quasi-contract remedy will not be applied. Note that if the contract had been unenforceable, this could be a proper basis for a recovery. (B) is incorrect because it also is a possible quasi-contract measure of damages, and as stated above, Genoa will be able to recover under the contract here. (D) is incorrect because the court will construe Rudder's agreement as a promise rather than a condition. If it were a condition, Rudder would not have a duty to pay because he was not paid. However, where an agreement provides that a duty is to be performed once an event occurs, if the event is not within the control of the promisee, it is less likely that he will have assumed the risk of its nonoccurrence and therefore less likely to be a condition of the promisor's duty to perform. In doubtful situations, courts will more likely hold that the provision is a promise rather than a condition because this supports the contract and preserves the reasonable expectations of the parties.

Answer to Question 28

(C) Builder is entitled to his profit plus costs. Where an owner breaches a construction contract after construction has been started but before construction is completed, the builder is entitled to recover any profit he would have derived from the contract plus any costs he has incurred to the date of the breach. Here, Builder's profit would have been $10,000 and his costs up to the time of the breach are $30,000. Thus, he can recover $40,000. Another way of saying this is contract price minus the cost of completion. Here, the contract price was $100,000 and the cost of completion was $60,000. Thus, Builder is entitled to $40,000. (A) is incorrect because that amount ($10,000) reflects only Builder's profit and he is also entitled to his costs. (B) is incorrect because that amount ($30,000) reflects only Builder's expenses, and he is also entitled to profits. (D) is incorrect because Builder is not entitled to recover the cost of completion since he has not done the work.

Answer to Question 29

(D) Builder cannot recover on the contract but he may recover some compensation for the work he did on a quasi-contractual basis. The issue here is whether this contract is divisible. A contract is divisible if: (i) the performance of each party is divided into two or more parts under the contract, (ii) the number of parts due from each party is the same, and (iii) the performance of each part by one party is the agreed-upon equivalent of the corresponding part from the other party. The third requirement is the problem here. There is no indication that the parts Builder is to perform are the equivalent of the payments Owner is to make. Rather, these payments appear to be unrelated to the actual work and merely progress payments. Thus, this contract is not divisible in nature. Since Builder breached the contract by ceasing performance when he became insolvent, he is not entitled to his contract price. However, Builder may be entitled to quasi-contractual relief. In cases of a failed contractual relationship between the parties, quasi-contractual relief is possible where a party has conferred a benefit on the other that will result in unjust enrichment of the other if no compensation is required. Here, Builder properly completed the foundations, and this conferred a benefit on Owner. Therefore, quasi-contractual relief may be available to Builder. (A) is wrong because, as mentioned, Builder is not entitled to the contract price since this is not a divisible contract. Even if it were divisible, (A) would be wrong because Owner would be able to offset his damages for Builder's breach and thus would not be obliged to pay him the full amount. (B) would be the correct answer if the contract were divisible. As explained above, this contract is not divisible merely because it calls for three payments. The payments must be the equivalent of the work performed; otherwise the payments are mere progress payments and the times set for payment are simply convenient times to pay. (C) is wrong because although the breach was material, Builder could recover something on a quasi-contractual basis (*see* above).

Answer to Question 30

(C) Supplier will be able to recover the contract price less damages for Builder's minor breach. Generally, an assignee has whatever rights his assignor would have against the obligor. Similarly, the assignee is subject to any contract-related defenses that the obligor has against the assignor. Thus, Supplier will have whatever rights Builder would have against Owner. Here, Builder completed the house but certain small items needed repair. If the repairs are minor, Builder will be seen as substantially performing his contract, and substantial performance will discharge his duty to perform and obligate payment by Owner. Since the facts state that the cost of repair was small (less than 3% of the cost of the contract), it will probably be seen as a minor breach. Thus,

Owner cannot avoid payment of the contract price. However, despite the substantial performance, the other party to the contract may recover damages for the less than complete performance. Thus, Owner will be able to offset her damages from the breach. Supplier then will be able to recover $97,500 (the contract price less the damages). (A) is incorrect because, as stated above, the obligor may offset damages directly against the assignee; he does not have to pay the full contract price and then seek damages from the assignor. (B) is incorrect because this suggests a quasi-contract remedy, but as stated above, Supplier, the assignee of Builder, would be able to recover the contract price less damages since Builder substantially performed. (D) is incorrect because the constructive condition precedent to Owner's duty to pay (Builder's performance) has been satisfied here by substantial performance.

Answer to Question 31

(A) Assembly's best argument is that they owed Toolcorp no preexisting duty to complete the job, and such completion was sufficient bargained-for consideration. Generally, a promise is unenforceable unless it is supported by consideration; thus, for Toolcorp's promise to be enforceable, there must be consideration supporting it. Consideration is defined as a bargained-for exchange of something of legal value. Most courts hold that the thing exchanged will have legal value if it causes the promisee to incur a detriment. A minority of courts hold that a benefit to the promisor is also sufficient. Thus, Assembly's best argument would be one that includes the idea that they incurred a bargained-for detriment, and this is reflected by (A). The problem with (A) is the preexisting legal duty rule. Traditionally, courts have held that performance of an existing legal duty is not sufficient consideration. However, the rule is riddled with exceptions, and one exception recognized in many jurisdictions applies when, as here, the preexisting duty is owed *to someone other than the promisor*. Thus, (A) is the best argument because it provides for a full contract recovery. (D) is wrong because it merely reflects the fact that Toolcorp received a benefit. As indicated above, it is the presence of consideration—defined as a bargained-for exchange of something of legal value—that permits the contract to be fully enforced. (A) is a better answer than (D) because it more clearly reflects the basis for finding consideration here. (B) is wrong because merely identifying a promise to pay as a "bonus" does not obviate the need for consideration. For a promise to be enforceable, there must be consideration. (C) is wrong because mere reliance on a promise is not enough to make a contract enforceable. For reliance to provide a substitute for consideration, under the doctrine of promissory estoppel, the promisor must reasonably expect that its promise will induce reliance, and such reliance must reasonably be induced. However, the promise will be enforceable *only to the extent necessary to prevent injustice*. Here, since Assembly had a duty to complete the work even without Toolcorp's promise, there is no indication that justice would require payment of the $3,500; there is nothing in the facts to show Assembly incurred more costs, etc. Thus, the recovery to Assembly under a promissory estoppel theory would undoubtedly be less than the contract recovery possible under (A).

Answer to Question 32

(A) Steelmaker's strongest position is that Steelmaker came under no duty to pay because this was a contract for services rather than goods. The general rule is that a modification of a contract must be supported by consideration. Since a preexisting legal duty is not consideration, for a modification to be enforceable there must be a new promise made by each side. Here, Steelmaker has agreed to pay an additional $2,000, but Assembly has promised nothing in return. Thus, the modification is unenforceable. Note that the U.C.C. enforces a good faith modification even without consideration, but the U.C.C. applies only in the sale of goods, and the contract here was for services (assembly of the machine). (B) is an arguable position, but the majority of jurisdictions would not find duress under the facts here, where one party is merely taking economic advantage of the other party's pressing need to enter into the contract. (C) is not the best position because whether Assembly's performance is profitable is irrelevant. Toolcorp's offer does not affect the rights and duties of Steelmaker and Assembly. Because of the preexisting legal duty rule, Assembly would not have had a right to the additional $2,000 from Steelmaker even if Toolcorp had never offered to pay the bonus. Toolcorp's offer is therefore irrelevant. Note that if the contract had been within the U.C.C. (which permits good faith modification without consideration), Steelmaker could claim that because the bonus would make Assembly's performance profitable, Assembly had not acted in good faith in obtaining the modification from Steelmaker, but, as mentioned above, the U.C.C. does not apply here since this is a contract for services, not goods. (D) is not the best position because what was discussed at the negotiations is irrelevant; the parol evidence rule would prohibit introduction of such statements (when there is an integrated writing, prior and contemporaneous oral statements are inadmissible to vary its terms).

Answer to Question 33

(A) Steelmaker would not have a cause of action because Assembly did not unequivocally repudiate the contract. Steelmaker refused to allow Assembly to perform under the contract, which itself is a breach of contract that would excuse Assembly from performing its contractual duties. Thus, an action for breach by Steelmaker will be successful only if Assembly did something to breach the contract before Steelmaker breached. Steelmaker would argue that Assembly breached by anticipatory repudiation, since it asked for more money to complete the work. However, the facts do not support this argument because excuse from a contract for anticipatory repudiation is available only where the repudiating party *unequivocally indicates* that it will not perform under the contract, and the contract must be executory on both sides. Here, Assembly did not unequivocally state that it would not perform, but rather merely asked for more money for its performance. Moreover, Assembly had already begun to perform, and so the contract was no longer executory on both sides. (B) is incorrect because the mere threat of a strike is not a sufficient excuse to release Assembly from its contract. Impossibility sometimes excuses a party from a contract, and a strike might render a contract impossible to perform. However, here there was no strike—merely a threatened one—and so Assembly would not have been excused. (C) is incorrect because it seeks to negate the repudiation, but as established above, there was no repudiation here. (C) might also be taken to mean that Steelmaker is not liable for breach because it really saved Assembly money. However, saving the other party's money is not a valid excuse that would release Steelmaker from its contractual duties. (D) is incorrect because it states no reason for excusing Steelmaker from its duties under the contract. Without a repudiation, there was no breach, and thus Steelmaker had no right to refuse to let Assembly continue the work.

Answer to Question 34

(A) Dolly should not recover in her suit because there is no enforceable promise (*i.e.*, no contract) here. Generally, a contract will not be enforced unless consideration has passed between the parties. Consideration is defined as a bargained-for exchange of a benefit to the promisor or a detriment to the promisee. Here, Billy offered Dolly half of Anne's estate, which is certainly a detriment to him, but Dolly offered nothing in return. While Billy told Dolly that they would discuss the details at the funeral, Dolly's purchasing a ticket to attend the funeral is not a bargained-for detriment to her (*i.e.*, it is not the price of the exchange) because it does not appear that Billy's motive for the promise was to induce Dolly to come to the funeral. Rather, Billy's offer was simply to make a gift. Thus, Billy's offer was not an enforceable promise. (B) is incorrect because Dolly would be able to recover her reliance damages only under a promissory estoppel theory, and there are no grounds for promissory estoppel here. Under promissory estoppel, a promise is enforceable, at least to the extent necessary to prevent injustice, even though there was no consideration for it, if the promisor should reasonably expect to induce action by his promise and that action is in fact induced. Here, Billy did not promise to give Dolly half of Anne's estate *if* she came to the funeral; rather, he only promised to share the estate and said they would talk about it at Anne's funeral. It is not reasonably foreseeable that, based on the promise, Dolly would make a special trip to attend the funeral. Indeed, it is not clear that Dolly was induced to go to the funeral by the promise; she may have been planning to attend in any case. (C) is incorrect because, as explained above, Billy's letter was an offer to make a gift; without consideration for that offer, it is unenforceable. (D) is incorrect because it relies on the existence of a contract between Billy and Dolly (Billy will share Anne's estate with Dolly in exchange for Dolly's sharing Michelle's estate with Billy), and there is no such contract here. Billy certainly made an offer to make such a contract, but Dolly probably rejected the offer by saying that Michelle's property was already hers. Even if Dolly's statement was not sufficient to amount to a rejection, Billy's next statement was certainly a revocation (". . . it's best [if] we follow Aunt Anne's . . . will"). Thus, a contract was not formed by the exchange, so Dolly's performance (sharing Michelle's estate) has no effect on whether she can recover from Billy on his promise.

Answer to Question 35

(B) Dolly can recover the value of her services if she detrimentally relied on Anne's letter. Although there was no enforceable contract between Anne and Dolly because there was no consideration on Dolly's part (*see* below), Dolly can recover under a theory of promissory estoppel. If a person making a promise should reasonably expect to induce action of a definite and substantial character, and such action is in fact induced, the promise is enforceable to the extent necessary to prevent injustice. Here, Anne's letter could reasonably be construed as a promise to make a will, and it was reasonable to expect that Dolly would rely on it (the letter said "you can count on it"). Thus, promissory estoppel will allow the promise to be enforced *if Dolly relied on it*. However, the recovery under this theory is not necessarily the contract remedy; rather, it is the amount necessary to prevent injustice. A court *could* find that the amount necessary to prevent injustice is half the value of Rougeacre but that is not clear from the facts. Dolly will recover at least the value of her services. (A) is wrong because it states that there is a contract between Anne and Dolly. However, there is no consideration on Dolly's part. For a contract to be enforceable, there must be consideration, but here Dolly has not given anything in exchange for Anne's promise to leave her Rougeacre. Dolly did not promise to continue to care for her mother, and Dolly incurred no other detriment (there is nothing in the facts to show that she continued to care for her mother because of the letter). The care Dolly had been giving her mother would not be sufficient consideration for a contract because it would be past consideration. (C) is wrong because Dolly's treatment of Billy regarding Greenacre is irrelevant to a suit against Anne's estate. (D) is wrong because the parol evidence rule is not applicable here. The parol evidence rule forbids the use of a prior writing to contradict the terms of a contract. Here, a will is involved. It is true that under wills law, the letter could not be used to alter the terms of the will, but it could be used to show a contract between the parties giving rise to a breach of contract action.

Answer to Question 36

(C) Miller's duty to perform would be discharged and Baker would be in breach if Baker did not apply for the letter of credit. The terms of the contract made the contract contingent upon Baker obtaining a letter of credit from Big Bank. Thus, obtaining a letter of credit was a condition precedent of the contract. Where a party whose duty to perform is subject to a condition precedent prevents that condition from occurring, he no longer has the benefit of the condition. Thus, if Baker did not even try to obtain a letter of credit, he will be in breach for failure to fulfill the condition, and Miller will be discharged because of Baker's actual breach. (A) and (B) are both incorrect for the same reason—Baker did not guarantee that he would be able to obtain a letter of credit from Big Bank; rather he was obligated merely to attempt to get a letter. Having tried but failed to get the letter (because of bankruptcy of the bank in (A) and the bank's refusal in (B)), the condition precedent to the contract failed and *both* parties will be discharged. (D) is incorrect because the court will probably construe the provision regarding the bank from which the letter of credit was to be obtained as a promise rather than a condition, and breach of the promise here would not be sufficient to discharge Baker. Failure of a condition prevents the parties' duties to perform from arising under a contract. Breach of promise discharges the nonbreaching party from a contract only if the breach is material. Here, the parties were probably more interested in the type of bank that Baker was to obtain a letter from than his actually obtaining a letter from Big Bank. Thus, a court will most likely find that obtaining the letter of credit from Big Bank (as opposed to any other bank) was merely a promise and not a condition. Since Baker obtained a letter of credit from a bank similar to Big Bank, there was a breach of the promise. However, the breach was not material, and so it would not be sufficient to discharge Miller from its duties under the contract.

Answer to Question 37

(B) Baker will prevail because the limitation on the interest rate was placed in the contract for his protection and he was free to waive it. As established in the preceding answer, a condition precedent to the contract here was that Baker was to obtain a letter of credit from Big Bank at no more than 2.5% interest. The limit on interest was clearly for Baker's benefit—he would not have to enter into the contract unless he could find a satisfactory loan. One having the benefit of a condition may by words or conduct indicate that he will not insist upon the condition, and the courts will enforce such a waiver. (A) is incorrect because the 2.5% term was material, but was material to the condition precedent to the contract, and not to the contract itself. (C) is incorrect because while the extra .5% is immaterial, it would be sufficient to prevent the contract; the court would give the condition a literal meaning, and the fact that the variance was immaterial would not alter the fact that the condition precedent was not met. (D) is incorrect because it is immaterial whether a lower interest rate was available, since Baker is free to waive the condition and obtain a letter of credit at a higher rate.

Answer to Question 38

(B) If Alan knew or had reason to know of the computation error, the mistake will prevent formation of a contract. A mutual mistake going to the heart of the bargain may prevent formation of a contract. However, where only one of the parties is mistaken about facts relating to the agreement, such a unilateral mistake will not prevent formation of a contract. Nevertheless, if the nonmistaken party knows or had reason to know of the mistake made by the other party, he is not permitted to take advantage of the offer. Here, there was such a unilateral mistake, as Bert (due to his secretary's error) was mistaken as to the price for which he could resurface Alan's driveway at a profit. Thus, there is a contract for the price of $4,000. However, if Alan had reason to know of the error in the bid, Bert will be able to successfully defend on the ground that the mistake prevents formation of the contract. (B) is the only answer that reflects this. (D) is incorrect because, as explained above, Bert *cannot* successfully assert mistake as a defense unless Alan knew or had reason to know of the error. (A) is incorrect because, even if it is not too late for Alan to accept the next lowest bid, Alan is still entitled to be put where he would have been had Bert's promise been performed. Had the promise been performed, Alan would have had his driveway resurfaced for $4,000. If Alan can still accept the next lowest bid ($4,200), he is entitled to receive as damages the amount, above the price of his contract with Bert, that it will cost to resurface the driveway ($200). (C) is incorrect because Bert is bound to fulfill the terms of his contractual obligation, regardless of whether he has commenced performance under the contract. Had Bert discovered the error prior to Alan's acceptance of the offer, Bert could have revoked the offer. However, once the contract was formed, Bert must live up to his contractual duties or be liable for breach.

Answer to Question 39

(C) A contractual duty may be discharged by an accord and satisfaction. An accord is an agreement in which one party to an existing contract agrees to accept, in lieu of the performance that she is supposed to receive from the other party, some other, different performance. Satisfaction is the performance of the accord agreement. The effect of this performance is to discharge both the accord agreement and the original contract. An accord and satisfaction may be accomplished by a good faith tender and acceptance of a check conspicuously marked "payment in full" where there is a bona fide dispute as to the amount owed. Boris and Pearly agreed that Boris would perform the dental work needed by Pearly in return for Pearly's promise to pay "about $3,500." The facts indicate that, following the actual dental work, there ensued a good faith dispute as to whether Pearly owed only $3,500 or the additional $600 as well. Pearly in good faith tendered to Boris a check marked "payment in full," which notation Boris saw before he deposited the check into his account. Boris's acceptance of Pearly's check gives rise to an accord and satisfaction with regard to the disputed original debt. Thus, Boris is deemed to have accepted the amount tendered by Pearly as full payment for the dental services performed, and Pearly's duty to pay for the services is discharged. (A) is incorrect because, even if Boris could have successfully asserted that $4,100 was within the range of the amount "about $3,500," his actions with respect to the check constitute an acceptance of the amount tendered therein. (B) is incorrect because an account stated is a contract whereby parties agree to an amount as a final balance due. For an agreement to be an account stated, there must be more than one prior transaction between the parties. The dispute between Pearly and Boris involves only one transaction. Thus, there is no account stated. (D) is incorrect because, with the existence of an accord and satisfaction, Pearly's duty to pay is deemed to be discharged. Thus, it is irrelevant at this point that the inlays may have been medically necessary or that Boris charged a fair price for them.

Answer to Question 40

(D) Marchand's letter of acceptance created an enforceable contract. (A) is wrong because requirements contracts are now recognized as sufficiently definite to be enforced. (B) is incorrect because MSU's promise was not illusory; it agreed to expand its degree program and to accept anyone who applied. (C) is not the best answer because ICT's offer was accepted before the purported revocation, and so the revocability of the offer is immaterial.

Answer to Question 41

(A) Under the modern, majority view, where the offeror could reasonably expect that the offer would induce the offeree to detrimentally change position in reliance on the offer, the courts will hold the offer to be an irrevocable option due to the detrimental reliance. (D) would be the correct answer under the older, minority view, which did not recognize the application of promissory estoppel in this situation, and would thus apply the rule that the revocation, effective on receipt, predated dispatch of the acceptance. (B) is wrong because the offer is converted into an equitable option, not an express option. (C) is incorrect because SCE's agreement to expand its degree program and accept applying students is adequate consideration to support ICT's promise.

Answer to Question 42

(B) Grandfather's promise was a promise to answer for the debt of another, which is required to be in writing under the Statute of Frauds. (A) is wrong because the contract clearly is not illusory; Uncle promised to pay if Nephew received "A"s. Uncle would be paying money and Nephew would be giving Uncle the satisfaction of Nephew's receiving "A"s. (C) is wrong because the consideration for Grandfather's promise is Nephew's act of getting "A"s. (D) is incorrect because this was not the bargained-for exchange Nephew expected.

Answer to Question 43

(A) Nephew and Uncle had entered into a valid contract, and Uncle's estate would be liable to pay the consideration promised by Uncle. (B) is irrelevant and is not supported by the facts. (C) is an incorrect statement of the law. (D) is wrong because Nephew could still prove the existence of the oral agreement, even after Uncle's death.

Answer to Question 44

(C) Bill has an option for 30 days. His July 10 counteroffer does not terminate that option. (A) is therefore wrong. His July 27 acceptance forms a contract between Sam and himself. Sam cannot perform the deal because he has already sold the bull to an innocent third party. He had the power but not the right to sell. Thus, (D) is wrong. Therefore, Sam has breached his contract with Bill. Thus, (B) is wrong because sale of the bull constitutes breach of the option contract; the offer was irrevocable for 30 days.

Answer to Question 45

(B) The rejection of the offer in an option contract does not terminate the power to accept the offer. Nevertheless, if the optionor (Sam) detrimentally relies upon the rejection, the power to accept the offer terminates at the time of reliance; *i.e.*, when Sam sells the bull. Thus, (B) is correct and (C) is wrong. (A) is wrong because, as stated, the rejection of the offer does not terminate the power of acceptance. (D) is wrong because Sam detrimentally relied on the rejection and thus the power of acceptance terminated earlier than 30 days.

Answer to Question 46

(D) Under U.C.C. section 2-207, proposed new terms in a deal between merchants do not terminate the offer (*i.e.*, do not constitute a counteroffer) and they become part of the deal unless (i) the offer is limited to its own terms, (ii) the new terms materially alter the deal, or (iii) the offeror objects within a reasonable time. (D) is correct and (C) is incorrect because Bill's proposal would materially alter the terms of the contract. (A) and (B) are wrong because the letter is not a counteroffer.

Answer to Question 47

(D) If a buyer is actually insolvent, U.C.C. section 2-702 permits the seller to refuse to deliver except for cash, including payment for all goods previously delivered under the contract. Thus, it does not matter that title passed on delivery to the Southern Pacific Depot. (A) is wrong because while Silicon could stop the goods in transit under U.C.C. section 2-705, even after title passes (thus rendering (B) wrong), it could also demand cash payment. (C) is wrong because the U.C.C. provisions allow the above modifications to payment terms upon finding the buyer insolvent.

Answer to Question 48

(D) U.C.C. section 2-702(2) permits the seller to reclaim goods upon demand within 10 days after the buyer receives them if the seller discovers that the buyer received the goods on credit while insolvent. (A) is incorrect because it does not matter whether the time for payment has passed. (B) is incorrect because, when the buyer is actually insolvent, the U.C.C. allows the seller to do more than merely demand assurances. (C) is incorrect because reliance upon a representation of solvency is not important unless more than 10 days have elapsed since delivery.

Answer to Question 49

(A) U.C.C. section 2-702(3) provides that the successful reclamation of goods from an insolvent buyer excludes all other remedies with respect to them. Thus, (A) is correct and (D) is incorrect. (B) and (C) are incorrect because they do not accurately state remedies for the seller. If the seller did have a right to recover damages, it would be measured by the *difference* between the contract price and the market value of the goods.

Answer to Question 50

(A) U.C.C. section 2-508 provides that where a tender of goods by the seller is rejected because of nonconformance of the goods and the time for performance has not passed, the seller may sea-sonably notify the buyer of his intention to cure and may then make a conforming delivery within the time specified in the contract. Thus, (A) is correct and (D) is incorrect. (B) is an untrue statement. (C) is incorrect because Silicon timely notified WES of its intention to cure.

Answer to Question 51

(D) The parties to a contract that benefits a third party may validly modify the contract before the beneficiary learns of the contract and relies upon it to his detriment. (A) and (C) are incorrect because, if Frank intended to confer a benefit on Noel by entering into the contract with Herbert, Noel could enforce the agreement as a donee third-party beneficiary whether or not an enforce-able obligation existed between Frank and Noel. (B) is incorrect because a third-party beneficiary is not obligated to notify the parties that he accepts the benefit of their agreement, especially when the agreement merely calls for the payment of money to him.

Answer to Question 52

(B) The portion of the Statute of Frauds requiring that a contract to answer for the debt of another be in writing applies only to sureties or guarantors—Herbert is not guaranteeing any debt of Frank; he is promising to pay a portion of what he will owe Frank to Noel. As to the requirement that contracts not performable by their terms within one year be in writing, the agreement to pay money to Noel could be seen as collateral to the main agreement, but since it calls for payments over the same three-year period, it is not performable within one year either.

Answer to Question 53

(B) The effect of a completely integrated agreement, meaning that the writing embodies the entire agreement of the parties, is that evidence could not be introduced to show a prior or collateral oral agreement. (A) is incorrect since Noel need not be a party to the contract since he has rights as a third-party beneficiary. (C) and (D) are incorrect since the negligence of either of the parties has no bearing on whether the collateral oral agreement can be proved or enforced.

Answer to Question 54

(A) Where the parties make a mistake in integrating their agreement into a writing, the courts will permit the error to be corrected. (B) is wrong because, while it is conceivable that the additional term ($100 to Noel) was left out, the correction of the mistake in price ($500 instead of $400) would *most* benefit Frank. If the writing was a sham, no rights would arise from it; hence, (C) is wrong. (D) is wrong because if one of the parties made a mistake as to the payment amount, he would not necessarily be entitled to relief.

Answer to Question 55

(D) Although the $200/week damages was denominated a "penalty" by the parties, in fact it operates as a reasonable liquidated damages clause. The parties to a contract may stipulate what damages are to be paid in the event of a breach if: (i) damages are difficult to ascertain at the time the contract is formed and (ii) the amount agreed upon is a reasonable forecast of compensatory damages in the case of a breach. These conditions have been met here. (A) is wrong because while it is true that penalties will not be enforced, a court would not construe the provision here as a penalty since it meets the requirements above. (B) is irrelevant. (C) is a misstatement of the law.

Answer to Question 56

(C) In construing the contract, the court will attempt to give effect to the reasonable expectations of the parties. Even though they did not expressly so provide, the parties probably intended the bonus to be incentive for Luther to stay and that it be paid only if Luther completed the season. Thus, such a condition will be implied. Therefore, (D) is wrong. (A) is contrary to the facts since there were 10 weeks left in the 28-week contract. (B) is wrong because Lex's remedy does not affect Luther's right to payment.

Answer to Question 57

(D) An agreement affecting a third-party beneficiary may be modified without the third party's consent if his rights have not yet vested. If Jones did not know of the original agreement, his rights could not yet have vested. (A) is wrong. It is true that Jones was a third-party beneficiary, but Smith and Brown are free to modify the agreement without consideration. (B) is wrong because, as stated, although Jones must agree to the modification if his rights have vested at the time of the modification, Jones's rights had not vested when the agreement was modified. (C) is wrong because it is too broad a statement; under some circumstances there can be liability to the third party.

Answer to Question 58

(B) A modification of the contract can take place without the consent of the third-party beneficiary prior to the time the third-party beneficiary's rights become vested. The rights become vested when the third party assents in a manner requested by the parties, detrimentally relies on the contract, or brings a lawsuit to enforce it. Here, the parties asked Jones to assent and, although his answer may have been grumbling, he assented. Since Jones's rights were then vested, the contract could not subsequently have been modified without his consent. Thus, (C) and (D) are wrong. (A) does not go far enough; mere knowledge of the original arrangement is not enough to vest rights.

Answer to Question 59

(B) The contract extended for a 10-week period. Missing only four days of a performance to run for 10 weeks would not be considered a total material breach of the contract. (A) is wrong because this would tend to go more to a formation problem. Here the contract has already been validly formed. (C) is wrong because a claim of impossibility could conceivably discharge the entire contract, and, therefore, Fiddler would have no claim. (D) is wrong because Fiddler need not be warned of the consequences of a breach.

Answer to Question 60

(C) Producer is entitled to find a substitute to perform in Fiddler's absence. If this was the only way Producer could acquire a substitute, then Producer's actions would be proper. (A) is wrong because this would not relieve Producer from liability to Fiddler. (B) is wrong because Fiddler does not have to accept any job under the contract, only the job that was the subject of the contract or a similar job to mitigate damages. (D) is wrong because this factor would not excuse Fiddler from his liability under the contract.

Answer to Question 61

(D) The general rule in contracts for the sale of goods is that the buyer is entitled to a perfect tender. A few exceptions to this rule exist, including where the seller has reason to think that nonconforming goods will be acceptable to the buyer, which reason can arise from the parties' past dealings. In such a case, upon notification of its intention to cure, the seller must be given a reasonable time within which to cure, which may extend beyond the original time for performance. Thus, (A) and (B) are wrong. (C) is wrong because, but for the above exception, the perfect tender rule would apply and the day's delay would be fatal.

Answer to Question 62

(D) The language of the reward offer should not be read with total literalness, but rather in the context of what Big City was seeking to obtain and the normal duties required to accept an offer of this kind. Therefore, (A), which would require that the offeree actually participate in the arrest, can be eliminated. Offers of this type normally require only that the offerees supply information leading to the arrest and conviction of the culprit. (B) and (C) can be ruled out without difficulty because they would envision a bilateral contract under which the offeree would be promising or assenting to Big City's proposal. In this kind of word context the offer is obviously the unilateral proposal that can be accepted only by performance.

Answer to Question 63

(A) This kind of reward offer can be revoked by comparable publicity as to the revocation by the offeror. (B) is wrong because the facts make it impossible to use the same manner to revoke the offer. (C) does not go far enough in communicating the revocation effectively to anyone who heard the offer originally. (D) would be too onerous a task.

Answer to Question 64

(C) Stevens cannot successfully recover on a contract theory because he was unaware of the offer. An offeree must be aware of the offer before he can, by his actions, accept it. Big City, therefore, would not be liable on a contract theory. The bounty idea has sometimes been used in reward cases when the offeree is a governmental agency. Therefore, (C) is the best answer. (A) does not go far enough because a party will not be liable for benefits gratuitously lavished upon it. (B) is wrong because public policy cannot limit a party's right to revoke an offer. (D) is incorrect because estoppel requires detrimental reliance on the other party's conduct, and here Stevens could not rely on the offer since he was unaware of it.

Answer to Question 65

(D) (D) is least helpful because the contract with Big City was unilateral and did not require a notice of acceptance; rather, performance was sufficient. (A) is helpful because the fact that Stevens was already under contract might have impact with respect to the preexisting duty rule. (B) is helpful because the fact that Stevens had been compensated already would not have a bearing on a contract theory but might on a quasi-contractual theory. (C) is helpful because the broadcast of the revocation on the television station would most likely have effectively revoked Big City's offer.

Answer to Question 66

(A) Under U.C.C. section 2-210(3), which governs this sale-of-goods case, "unless the circumstances indicate the contrary, a prohibition of assignment of 'the contract' is to be construed as barring only the delegation to the assignee of the assignor's performance." In other words, the covenant "not to assign this contract" would be interpreted as barring *only* the delegation of Ace's *duty to pay* to some other party, not the assignment of the right to receive Ace's payment. Therefore, when Typitrite "assigns the contract" to Equitable, since Typitrite has assigned only the right to payments, it has not breached its contract with Ace. (B) and (C) are therefore wrong. (D) is wrong because the covenant would not stand or fall on its rationale.

Answer to Question 67

(B) When an assignment has been made, but the obligor on the contract has not been informed of the assignment, he is still obligated to pay the party with whom he originally dealt—the assignor. Therefore, Ace Business Supplies would not be liable to Equitable Loan, and (C) is therefore wrong. However, it appears that Typitrite is responsible to Equitable Loan for the $10,000 payment that it has received, at least in the event of default in their financing arrangement if the agreement so provides.

Answer to Question 68

(D) Neither of these factors is correct. I. is wrong, because Commercial Bank would be claiming as a third-party beneficiary, and Typitrite's subsequent acceptance of the payment indicates that it is modifying its original intent that Commercial Bank be paid. A contract with respect to which there is a third-party beneficiary can be modified to affect the third-party beneficiary's rights provided that the third-party beneficiary has not justifiably relied upon its status. Here the key is that Commercial Bank did not know of the original agreement until the modification occurred. II. is wrong, because Commercial Bank could not be described as an incidental beneficiary. It was a directly named intended beneficiary of the contract. Therefore (D) is the correct answer.

Answer to Question 69

(A) The obligation of a buyer under a requirements contract is to act in good faith. This is the U.C.C.

rule. (B) and (C) are wrong, because the rights involved here are clearly assignable since the payment of money does not involve personal responsibilities. (D) is wrong because the U.C.C. regards requirements contracts as being supported by sufficient consideration.

Answer to Question 70

(A) Where the seller is a merchant, the risk of loss does not pass to the buyer until the buyer takes physical possession of the goods. (B) is wrong because performance was not impossible; Martha had already performed and Skysheim could perform by tendering another pair of shoes. (C) is wrong because passage of title does not shift the risk of loss in this case. (D) is wrong because while a buyer gains some rights once the goods are identified, identification does not shift the risk of loss.

Answer to Question 71

(D) An implied warranty of fitness for particular purpose arises where a seller knows that the buyer is relying on the seller to pick suitable goods for the buyer and the buyer relies on the seller's expertise. Here, Martha asked the seller to pick suitable goods, but declined the seller's advice and picked out her own shoes. Therefore, this warranty did not arise. The implied warranty of merchantability arose but was not broken. This warranty arises in every sale of goods by a merchant and ensures, generally, that goods shall be fit for ordinary purposes. Nothing in the facts indicates that the shoes here are not fit for ordinary purposes. The only express warranties here arose from the statement that the shoes were leather and, perhaps, from the sample shoe on the sales floor. However, nothing in the facts indicates that there has been a breach of either of these express warranties. Therefore, (D) is the correct answer.

Answer to Question 72

(B) An express warranty will arise from any statement of fact or promise. Here, the salesperson said that the shoes were completely made of leather and would last for years. The former is a statement of fact that will give rise to a warranty; thus, I. is a good theory. The latter is not a statement of fact, but a prediction of the future. Moreover, it is not specific—how long is "years"? This statement amounts to mere puffery and will not give rise to a warranty. Therefore, II. is not a good theory. An implied warranty of merchantability will arise in every sale by a merchant unless disclaimed. To be merchantable, goods must be fit for ordinary purposes, and arguably shoes that wear out in a week are not fit for ordinary purposes. Therefore, III. is a good theory.

Answer to Question 73

(C) Once a buyer has accepted goods, her right to reject for nonconformance generally lapses and her only remedy is a suit for damages. Acceptance usually occurs when the buyer takes possession of the goods. In some cases, the buyer can revoke acceptance, but the breach must be substantial and the buyer must have a good reason for accepting the goods (*i.e.*, something more than not taking the time to carefully inspect). Here, Martha accepted the goods and the breach appears minor. (A) entitles Martha only to damages, not a full refund. (B) is a misstatement of the law. (D) is wrong because written notice is not required; oral notice is acceptable.

Answer to Question 74

(D) This is an output contract. (A) is wrong because there is a price term, although it is dependent on future events. (B) is wrong because there are no facts that show the five years to be "unreasonable" and even if there were, parties are free to enter into unreasonable contracts. (C) is wrong because Indegas agreed to buy at least 5,000 gallons a week by the original agreement, and all the gasoline by its notice. Such output contracts are enforceable.

Answer to Question 75

(B) Although there was no consideration for Indegas to take only one-half of the bargained-for production, none is required because this is a contract for the sale of goods, and subject to U.C.C. section 2-609 (which provides that good-faith modification is enforceable regardless of lack of consideration). (C) is therefore wrong. (A) and (D) make no sense.

Answer to Question 76

(D) The lack of foreign oil did not constitute an objective impossibility of performance, since Cal-Tex's other refinery was producing gasoline. (B) is therefore wrong. The contract did not contemplate a particular refinery producing the gasoline, and therefore (A) is wrong. (C) is wrong because Indegas's knowledge was not a condition of the contract, but the purpose for entering into it.

Answer to Question 77

(B) Since delivery of gas is not personal in nature, that duty can be assigned. The quantity will be measured by Cal-Tex's original output. However, when a duty is delegated to a delegate, the delegator remains liable should the delegate fail to perform. (A) is incorrect because the contract was for five years, and five years have not yet elapsed. (C) would be correct only if Cal-Tex went out of business without delegating its duties to another by selling the other the business, not the case here. (D) is wrong because, as indicated above, such a delegation is proper.

CRIMINAL LAW QUESTIONS

Question 1

Snoops was tried for the forcible rape of Betty Lou. His defense was that she had consented to have intercourse with him. Over his objection the trial judge charged the jury that while the prosecution must prove the overall case beyond a reasonable doubt, Snoops had the burden of proving his defense by a preponderance of the evidence.

The judge's instructions were:

(A) Correct, if state law places the burden of proving lack of consent on the defendant.

(B) Correct, as long as the judge emphasized that the state must prove the entire case beyond a reasonable doubt.

(C) Incorrect, because the instruction placed a burden on the defendant that denied the defendant due process of law.

(D) Incorrect, because in a criminal trial the defendant cannot be required to prove any critical issue by a preponderance of the evidence.

Questions 2-4 are based on the following fact situation:

Delbert owned and operated a large construction business. He frequently carried large sums of cash on him so that he could pay his workers, located at various sites throughout the city. Because of this, he kept a loaded pistol in the glove compartment of his car. However, Delbert had no permit to carry the gun, and by statute it is a felony to possess a loaded handgun without a permit.

Delbert was a hot-tempered individual, and very jealous of his wife, Victoria, and of any contact she had with other men. Harry, Delbert's business partner, knew of Delbert's jealous attitude and suspicions concerning Victoria. Harry also knew that before her marriage to Delbert, Victoria was engaged to marry Vincent.

Harry found out that his own wife, Harriette, was having an affair with Vincent. Harry was determined to avenge himself upon Vincent. To achieve this end, he arranged to have Vincent receive a bogus telegram that purported to be from Victoria (Delbert's wife). The telegram stated that her life was in danger and pleaded with Vincent to come to her house that night at 11 p.m. Harry then met Delbert at a previously arranged business meeting, and around 10:55 p.m., he told Delbert that he had information that Vincent and Victoria were having an affair, and indeed that they were probably sleeping together that very night, because they knew Delbert would be tied up with Harry at the business meeting. As Harry expected, Delbert flew into a rage, dashed out of the meeting, and drove to his home nearby.

At 11 p.m., Vincent arrived at Delbert's house. He rang the bell, and Victoria, who had been asleep and was in her nightgown, invited him into the living room. Vincent was in the middle of explaining the telegram to her when she heard Delbert drive up. Fearing that he would misconstrue the situation, she urged Vincent to hide in her bedroom closet. Delbert burst in on them in the bedroom before Vincent could reach the closet, and seeing Victoria in her nightgown, shouted, "I'll murder the both of you." He ran to his car, grabbed the pistol from the glove compartment, returned to the house, and shot and killed Vincent. Just as he was about to fire the gun at Victoria, a neighbor, Terrance, rushed in and tried to persuade Delbert to drop the gun. Delbert shot and killed Terrance.

The jurisdiction defines murder in the first degree to include premeditated and deliberate killings and all killings that take place during the commission of a dangerous felony. Premeditation and deliberation is defined as requiring some meaningful reflection prior to the killing. All other common law murder is classified as murder in the second degree.

2. If the jury finds that Delbert was unreasonable in his erroneous belief that Vincent

and Victoria were together for the purpose of adultery, Delbert's killing Vincent was:

(A) Voluntary manslaughter.

(B) Involuntary manslaughter.

(C) First degree murder.

(D) Second degree murder.

3. Delbert's killing of Terrance was:

(A) First degree felony murder based on his commission of the felony of carrying a loaded handgun without a permit.

(B) First degree murder if Delbert was unreasonable in his belief that Victoria and Vincent were together for adulterous purposes.

(C) Second degree murder whether Delbert was reasonable or unreasonable in his belief that Victoria and Vincent were together for adulterous purposes.

(D) Voluntary manslaughter if Delbert was reasonable in his belief that Victoria and Vincent were together for adulterous purposes, because he had been adequately provoked.

4. With respect to the killing of Vincent, Harry is guilty of:

(A) First degree murder.

(B) Conspiracy and first degree murder.

(C) Only whatever crime Delbert is found to have committed in killing Vincent.

(D) Solicitation and first degree murder.

Questions 5-6 are based on the following fact situation:

Ned, a college student, was the sole lifetime beneficiary under a large trust administered by Banker, whose office was across the country. Ned received a large monthly distribution from the trust, and whenever he ran short, he simply called Banker for extra funds, because the trust provided that Ned was to receive whatever he needed from income or principal.

Ned's roommate Dan found out about Ned's trust arrangement and decided to see if he could make it pay off for him. Dan sent a telegram to Banker, which appeared to be from Ned, and which read as follows:

> Have to go into hospital tomorrow for emergency surgery; am short of funds and need at least $5,000 to cover medical bills; am sending my friend Dan to pick up money; please give him $5,000. Ned.

The next day, Dan showed up at Banker's office and obtained $5,000 on the promise that he would take the money to Ned. Dan absconded with the funds.

5. When Dan sent the telegram to Banker, he committed:

(A) No common law crime.

(B) No completed crime, but a criminal attempt.

(C) Solicitation.

(D) Forgery and uttering.

6. When Dan obtained the $5,000 from Banker, he committed:

(A) False pretenses.

(B) Embezzlement.

(C) Larceny by trick.

(D) Larceny.

Question 7

State W's supreme court recently ruled unanimously in *People v. Ambrose* that one who drives off in a car to go for a joy ride, intending to return the car, is not guilty of attempted larceny even though he believes he is committing larceny.

In a later situation occurring in State W, Dan, intending to kill a police officer in circumstances amounting to malice, fired a bullet at the officer's heart. Unbeknownst to Dan, the officer was wearing a bullet-proof vest, and the bullet did not penetrate. Dan was charged with attempted murder of the police officer. At trial, Dan's attorney produced an expert who testified that the vest worn by the officer could not have been pierced by the bullet fired by Dan. The prosecution did not dispute this testimony.

The trial judge, considering himself bound to apply the precedent discussed above to any case in which it was applicable, should:

(A) Rule that the *Ambrose* case had no bearing on the case before him because the precedent involves a crime against property, whereas Dan is charged with a crime of violence.

(B) Rule, on the basis of the *Ambrose* case, that Dan is not guilty of attempted murder.

(C) Rule that, notwithstanding the *Ambrose* case, Dan is guilty of attempted murder.

(D) Distinguish the *Ambrose* case on the basis that here Dan has not performed a true act of perpetration, whereas in the precedent case, the defendant there clearly did so.

Questions 8-9 are based on the following fact situation:

Because all of the other members of his fraternity were smoking marijuana, Ernie decided that he also would do so. He was aware that a statute was in effect that makes it a crime to possess or smoke marijuana, but decided to risk breaking this law. After making several inquiries, Ernie learned that he could make a purchase from Charlie at the pool hall, and he approached Charlie for that purpose. However, Charlie was suspicious and told Ernie that a single marijuana cigarette would cost $50. Ernie did not have this much money, but he knew he had a counterfeit $50 bill, and he gave this to Charlie, whereupon Charlie gave Ernie a "marijuana cigarette," which was in fact only an ordinary tobacco cigarette.

As Ernie left the pool hall, he lit the cigarette, whereupon he was immediately apprehended by a detective who was keeping all of Charlie's visitors under surveillance. After being fully advised of his constitutional rights, Ernie admitted that he purchased the "marijuana cigarette" from Charlie. Later, the police determined that there was no marijuana in the cigarette.

8. Assume that the state supreme court has held in the case of *State v. Bierce* that one who receives property believing it to be stolen is guilty of an attempt to receive stolen property, even though it turns out the property was in fact not stolen.

    If Ernie is charged with attempt to smoke a marijuana cigarette, the court should rule that:

    (A) The *Bierce* decision is not binding precedent in this case because a completely different crime is involved.

    (B) The *Bierce* decision is distinguishable because the present case involves "legal impossibility" rather than "factual impossibility."

    (C) Based on the *Bierce* decision as precedent, Ernie can be convicted of an attempt to violate the statute.

    (D) The *Bierce* decision is not applicable because the crime was malum in se, whereas smoking marijuana is only malum prohibitum.

9. Based on his dealings with Ernie, Charlie could be convicted of:

    (A) Larceny by trick.

    (B) False pretenses.

(C) Embezzlement.

(D) No theft offense.

Questions 10-11 are based on the following fact situation:

The police had probable cause to believe that Rhino was running a gambling operation out of his home at 1313 Broccoli Street. Thus, the police presented their evidence to a magistrate, who issued them a warrant to search that address for gambling slips and other gambling paraphernalia. The police went to Rhino's house, which contained two stories and a basement. They entered the premises and discovered "numbers" slips, racetrack betting records, and football pool cards on the first floor. Two of the officers then went upstairs, while the third went down to the basement. While there were no police on the first floor, Rhino's friend Hippo entered the house, carrying a briefcase. He set the briefcase on the floor and had opened up the top of the case, when he heard a police officer yell to her partner, "Hey, there's more gambling stuff in the bedroom." Hippo became frightened and left the briefcase sitting in the middle of the floor, while he hid himself in the hall closet. The police officers returned to the first floor and immediately spotted the briefcase, which they knew had not been there when they first entered the premises. Since the top of the briefcase was open, the officers saw the betting slips in the briefcase and seized them. Because they knew that someone had entered the house since they arrived, they re-searched the first floor. They found Hippo hiding in the closet. They informed him that he was under arrest, clapped handcuffs on him, and read him his *Miranda* warnings. One of the officers patted down Hippo, checking for weapons. The officer noticed a bulge in Hippo's pocket. Although the officer knew that the bulge was unlikely to be a weapon, he reached into the pocket anyway, and discovered a package that appeared to be (and later proved to be) heroin. Hippo chose to remain silent and demanded to see a public defender. His request was granted promptly. Hippo was charged with possession of narcotics.

10. At the preliminary hearing, Hippo's public defender contends that Hippo's arrest was illegal. Is her contention correct?

(A) Yes, because the police officer who searched Hippo knew that Hippo did not have a weapon in his pocket.

(B) Yes, because Hippo's mere presence in the house did not give the police probable cause to believe Hippo had committed a crime, and they had no basis for searching Hippo at all, because he did not act toward them in a threatening manner.

(C) No, because the contents of the briefcase gave them probable cause to arrest Hippo.

(D) No, because they had a right to search Hippo for gambling slips, and the discovery of the heroin was merely incidental to a lawful search.

11. Assume for the purposes of this question only that the public defender's motion at the preliminary hearing was denied and that Hippo is brought to trial. The public defender moves to suppress the admission of the heroin. How should the court rule?

(A) For Hippo, because the warrant only entitled the police to search the premises.

(B) For Hippo, because the heroin was seized during an unlawful arrest.

(C) For the state, because the evidence was taken during a lawful arrest.

(D) For the state, because Hippo did not ask for assistance of counsel until after the patdown.

Question 12

Barney and his neighbor Fred were both fond of woodworking and often worked together making lamps, tables, and other household items. Because Fred's garage was much larger than Barney's garage, all of their woodworking equipment was in Fred's garage, although some of the machinery and tools had been purchased by Barney, some by Fred, and some jointly by Barney and Fred. The home shop included a lathe, a drill press, a band saw, and all the other items required for a well-equipped home shop. Fred had given Barney a key to the garage, so that Barney would have equal access to the shop equipment and be able to work on his carpentry projects any time he wished.

One day Barney took the afternoon off from his regular job and arrived home to find Pebbles, the precocious babysitter, there by herself. Pebbles told Barney that his son was at a neighborhood "play group" and would not return until 3 p.m. Pebbles, who was one week short of her 17th birthday, often acted provocatively toward Barney, and this time was no exception. She made it abundantly clear that she was interested in having sex with Barney. Barney wanted to avoid being caught if his wife happened to come home from work early, so he took Pebbles to Fred's garage. Barney used his key to unlock the garage door and brought Pebbles inside. Barney opened the unlocked doors of one of Fred's cars and proceeded to engage in a sexual act with Pebbles on the front seat. After they were through, but unbeknownst to Barney, Pebbles impulsively took a pair of fuzzy dice hanging from the car's rear-view mirror, put them in her purse, and kept them as a "trophy" of her sexual encounter with Barney. Assume that the jurisdiction in which these events took place maintains the common law definitions of property crimes, and that the state statutes define the "age of consent" as 17 years of age.

Which of the following best describes the criminal liability, if any, of Barney and Pebbles?

(A) Barney is guilty of burglary, and Pebbles is guilty of larceny.

(B) Both Barney and Pebbles are guilty of burglary, and Pebbles is guilty of larceny.

(C) Barney is not guilty of burglary, but Pebbles is guilty of larceny.

(D) Neither Barney nor Pebbles is guilty of larceny or burglary.

Question 13

Landry, a locksmith, knew that his friend Morton had been having marital troubles. Morton, who was a stock clerk at the hardware store where Landry worked, had told Landry that he suspected his wife was having an affair with Vorner, another clerk at the store, and Morton had even borrowed some of Landry's tools to break into a locked chest of his wife's to try to find evidence of the affair. One afternoon at the store, Morton, visibly upset, ran up to Landry and asked to borrow some of his tools, telling him that Vorner took the afternoon off and was probably going to meet up with his wife. Landry gave him the tools, telling him, "Don't do anything you'll regret later." Morton patted something under his jacket as he was leaving, saying, "I think some other people are going to have the regrets." Landry, who knew that Morton had been working on a display case for hunting knives that morning, began to have second thoughts about giving Morton the tools, but he did not do anything immediately because he did not want to get himself and Morton into trouble. Meanwhile, Morton went to Vorner's apartment and picked the door lock with Landry's tools. He found his wife and Vorner in bed together and stabbed Vorner, seriously wounding him. A few minutes later Landry called Vorner's apartment to try to warn Vorner that Morton might come over.

After Morton was arrested, he agreed to plead guilty to aggravated battery and attempted voluntary manslaughter in exchange for testifying against Landry, who was charged as an accomplice to attempted murder.

Can Landry be convicted of that charge?

(A) Yes, because he recklessly disregarded a substantial risk to human life and was not provoked.

(B) Yes, because his failed attempt to neutralize his assistance did not prevent the crime from occurring and therefore did not constitute an adequate withdrawal.

(C) No, because he did not have the requisite intent to be liable as an accomplice.

(D) No, because an accomplice cannot be found guilty of a more serious offense than that for which the principal has been convicted.

Questions 14-16 are based on the following fact situation:

Alice, Betty, and Carol agreed to hold up a newsstand attendant. Alice waited in their car around the corner while Betty and Carol approached the stand, with knives drawn. The attendant gave them all the money in his possession, a sum of $20. As Betty and Carol turned away, the attendant grabbed a gun and fired several times. He intended only to wound Betty and Carol but instead killed Carol. Meanwhile, Alice had long since become frightened and had fled the scene with the car.

14. If the attendant cannot be prosecuted for manslaughter, it will be because:

(A) He only intended to wound Carol.

(B) The robbery constituted a provocation.

(C) The attendant was trying to get his $20 back.

(D) He was apprehending a fleeing wrongdoer.

15. If Betty is accused of felony (robbery) murder, her most promising defense would be:

(A) She had not the slightest desire to see her partner harmed.

(B) The fatal attack itself was performed by the attendant.

(C) The killing occurred after the robbery was over.

(D) The robbery did not constitute a felony since only $20 was involved.

16. Alice is charged with robbery and conspiracy to commit robbery in a state that retains the common law definitions of these crimes. Her most promising partial defense is:

(A) She cannot be tried for both offenses; the prosecutor must choose between them.

(B) She cannot be convicted of conspiracy if Betty was insane and Carol was an undercover police officer.

(C) She cannot be convicted of conspiring with Carol, since Carol, now dead, cannot be convicted with her.

(D) She abandoned the conspiracy prior to the commission of the robbery.

Question 17

As Wife was straightening out the contents of a drawer where Husband kept his business papers, she came across a sealed envelope marked "Private" in Husband's handwriting. Since she was curious as to its contents, she slit the envelope open and found enclosed a torrid love letter to Husband from Secretary (who worked for Husband), plus some nude photographs of Secretary. Wife was incensed. She went to another drawer where she knew Husband kept his handgun and, assuming it was loaded because Husband always told her, "You're safe around here because I've always got a loaded gun ready," she headed off to Husband's office (which was just down the street) with the intent to do away with Secretary. When Wife arrived, she burst into the office, pulled the gun out of her purse, and pointed it at Secretary, saying, "Here's your direct ticket to Hell, you homewrecker!" Wife pulled the trigger, but nothing happened. This was because the handgun contained no ammunition. Wife ran from the office, after first shouting, "I wish I'd killed you." Secretary called the police and Wife was arrested.

The jurisdiction's criminal code defines assault as "(1) an attempt to commit a battery; or (2) the intentional creation of a reasonable apprehension in the mind of the victim of imminent bodily harm." The code uses the common law definitions of homicide crimes.

Of which of the following crimes could Wife be convicted?

I. Assault.

II. Attempted murder.

III. Attempted manslaughter.

(A) I. and III., but not II.

(B) III. only.

(C) I. and either II. or III.

(D) II. or III., but not I.

Question 18

Partnerdum and Partnerdee operated "Electroland," a retail business that sold stereos, computers, and other electronic devices. They had been the dominant electronic business in Middleville, a town of 40,000 people, until "Fong's Electrictown" opened six months ago. Fong, the owner of Fong's Electrictown, sold the same or better quality merchandise as Electroland, but at lower prices and with better service contracts. Partnerdum and Partnerdee were very upset at the subsequent decline in business at Electroland. They were unwilling to cut their prices, so Partnerdum suggested to Partnerdee, "Why don't we do something to scare off Fong so he'll leave town?" Partnerdee readily agreed, and they came up with a plan to hire someone to intimidate Fong. They hired Karl Kriminal, who had just finished serving a term for armed robbery in the state penitentiary. They instructed Kriminal to "scare the socks off Fong" by robbing him, but also told him, "no rough stuff, because we only want to scare him out of town." Kriminal loitered near Fong's Electrictown, waiting for it to close at 9 p.m. The lights in the store window went out, and Lee, an employee of Fong's Electrictown, left the store. Kriminal mistook Lee for Fong, approached Lee, drew a gun, and demanded money. Lee, who had martial arts training,

kicked the gun from Kriminal's hand and struggled with Kriminal. He threw Kriminal to the ground, but Kriminal's gun also struck the ground and accidentally discharged. The bullet struck Lee, who died after giving the police a description of Kriminal. Kriminal told the police that Partnerdum and Partnerdee hired him, and the partners were arrested.

Partnerdum and Partnerdee are guilty of:

(A) Conspiracy to commit robbery only.

(B) Conspiracy to commit robbery and robbery.

(C) Conspiracy to commit robbery and felony murder.

(D) Conspiracy to commit robbery, robbery, and felony murder.

Question 19

It was a dark and rainy night. Out of the gloomy darkness Deirdre Defendant approached Vladimir Victim from behind. She stuck a gun in Vladimir's back and shouted, "Your money or your life!" Vladimir was scared out of his wits and collapsed in a faint on the spot. Deirdre lifted Vladimir's wallet and stuck it in the back pocket of her coveralls. Deirdre took off at a trot, but after she had traveled about 10 feet from Vladimir, the wallet slipped out of Deirdre's pocket and fell to the ground. Deirdre did not realize this until she arrived home and found the wallet missing. In the meantime, Vladimir revived; he found the wallet with all its contents intact. Vladimir called the police to report the crime and later identified Deirdre in a lineup at the police station.

Deirdre should be convicted of:

(A) Larceny only.

(B) Robbery only.

(C) Larceny and robbery.

(D) Nothing.

Questions 20-21 are based on the following fact situation:

John planned to hold up his neighborhood market. One day he sat at the bus stop, near the market, watching to see when would be the best time. When he saw the market was empty, he got up, walked over to the market, opened the door, and went inside. He walked up to the counter with his hand in his jacket pocket to simulate a gun. Before the clerk could turn around to see what John wanted, Sara entered the market, startling John, who turned and ran out the door.

John jumped into Sara's car, which was standing unlocked with the motor running outside the market, and sped off to the bus station. He was later captured in another state.

20. On a charge of attempted robbery, John should be found:

(A) Not guilty, because he used no actual force on the clerk nor threatened any.

(B) Not guilty, because he withdrew successfully from the robbery attempt.

(C) Not guilty, because he never entered the zone of perpetration.

(D) Guilty, whether or not he totally abandoned his plan when Sara entered the market.

21. If John is charged with the theft of Sara's car, he should be found:

(A) Not guilty of larceny, because Sara was grossly negligent in leaving it unlocked and running.

(B) Guilty of larceny, because using the car for his escape subjected it to a substantial risk of loss.

(C) Not guilty of larceny, because he only intended to use it for his escape.

(D) Guilty of larceny, because it was taken to aid in the commission of an inherently dangerous felony.

Question 22

A law passed by the legislature of State Green required that all businesses in the state report any deposits of toxic waste discovered on property owned by the reporting firm. Another provision of the law required that the toxic waste reports be made on state form SG-TW-430 and that duplicate copies of the form should be filed with both the state department of labor and the state environmental protection agency. The statute provided that after each report was filed, the relevant state agencies would ensure that any dangerous area was cordoned off and work out a plan with the reporting firm for the clean-up of the waste deposit. The effective date of the statute was June 15.

Inez was a safety inspector employed by the Effluvium Chemical Works ("ECW"). ECW operated a number of chemical plants in State Green. Inez was making her first visit to the plant in Verdi, on June 17, when she noticed a strange gooey substance covering a six-foot area just inside the chain-link fence that surrounded the plant. Inez filed no report to the state agencies regarding the gooey area. On June 20, Jason, an employee of ECW, was walking along the chain-link fence when he slipped and fell face first into the gooey area. The gooey substance was highly toxic Prolene Hexagizmo. Jason's skin contact with the substance was sufficient to kill him in a matter of minutes. Inez was charged with murder.

Which of the following facts, if true, would provide the strongest argument in Inez's defense?

(A) Inez did not know that the gooey substance was toxic.

(B) Inez was unaware of the state reporting law.

(C) The state printing office did not produce any copies of form SG-TW-430 until July 6.

(D) It would have been impossible to clean up the toxic waste deposit before the time when Jason encountered it.

Question 23

Abbott approached Fred on a street, pulled out a gun, and said: "See that store over there. If you don't go over and set fire to it right now, I'm going to shoot you." Fred walked over to the store, with Abbott still pointing the gun at him, went inside to the store's office, poured gasoline on all the office furniture, and set fire to the office. Shortly thereafter Smith, the owner of the store, rushed in trying to save her important papers. In doing so, she was overcome by smoke and died in the fire. Fred is charged with the criminal homicide of Smith.

The most likely result is that Fred will be found to be:

(A) Guilty of murder.

(B) Guilty of manslaughter.

(C) Not guilty of murder, because duress is a defense to arson.

(D) Not guilty of murder, because Fred never intended to kill anyone.

Questions 24-25 are based on the following fact situation:

Aragon and Benitez were traveling in Mexico toward the United States border in an automobile owned by Aragon. Before they reached the border, Aragon told Benitez, "You owe me a favor. Keep this package for me." Aragon gave Benitez a small foil package. Benitez put the package in his coat pocket, saying, "O.K., but don't tell me what's in it." Aragon and Benitez crossed the border and passed over into the United States without any problem. However, about 25 miles north of the border, at a fixed checkpoint, U.S. Border Patrol officers were stopping cars, looking for undocumented persons. The officers stopped Aragon's car, and before they even began to question the occupants, Aragon became frightened and blurted out, "I'm clean, man, but *he* has a stash," pointing at Benitez. The officers searched Benitez and found the foil package, which contained heroin. Benitez was arrested, but Aragon was not.

24. Was the stopping of Aragon's car by the Border Patrol legal?

(A) Yes, because the car was stopped at a fixed checkpoint.

(B) No, because it was a random stop.

(C) No, because there was no probable cause to stop the vehicle.

(D) No, because the stopping occurred too far from the border.

25. Is the evidence found on Benitez admissible?

(A) Yes, under the automobile exception.

(B) Yes, because due process imputes knowledge where there is willful ignorance.

(C) No, because due process forbids granting of immunity to the more culpable defendant.

(D) No, if Benitez did not know the package contained heroin.

Questions 26-27 are based on the following fact situation:

Droole's wife, Marcie, telephoned Droole and told him she would be out of town on an overnight business trip. Marcie had had an unprecedented number of supposed business trips recently, and Droole was growing suspicious. He parked his car near Marcie's place of employment and saw Marcie get into a car with Bob, her boss. Droole followed the car and determined that instead of going to the airport, Bob was taking Marcie to the Golden Hours Motel, a local establishment that had become notorious as a place for lovers' trysts. An angry Droole decided to get even with Bob. He drove to a gas station, where he purchased several metal gallon cans, which he proceeded to fill with gasoline. Shortly after sundown, Droole used a crowbar to break into the back door of Bob's home. He went into Bob's basement and poured the gasoline on the concrete floor. Droole, a nonsmoker, then realized that he had nothing with him to ignite the gasoline. He drove back to the filling station and purchased a disposable lighter for 50¢. Just then, a sudden thunderstorm broke. A bolt of lightning struck near Bob's house. Bob's house and another house on the block burned to the ground. When Droole drove from the filling station to Bob's house, he found Bob's house already ablaze. He got out of his car, watched the fire, and started laughing hysterically. Police in the area saw him and discovered that he smelled like gasoline. Droole was arrested and charged with burglary and arson. At Droole's trial, Frieda, the town fire marshal, gives uncontroverted testimony regarding the findings of the fire department's routine investigation into the destruction of Bob's house.

26. Assume for purposes of this question only that Frieda testifies: "The officials conducting the investigation concluded that the combustible substance in the basement of the dwelling had only a minimal effect. The lightning bolt set off a conflagration that would in all likelihood have destroyed Bob's home anyway." The jury should convict Droole of:

    (A) Burglary only.

    (B) Burglary and arson.

    (C) Burglary and attempted arson.

    (D) Attempted burglary and attempted arson.

27. Assume for purposes of this question only that Frieda testifies: "The officials conducting the investigation concluded that under normal circumstances the fire department could have prevented significant fire damage to Bob's dwelling and the other house on the block. However, the presence of a flammable substance in Bob's basement created a sudden explosion that caused the fire to rage out of

control." The jury should convict Droole of:

    (A) Burglary only.

    (B) Burglary and arson.

    (C) Burglary and attempted arson.

    (D) Attempted burglary and attempted arson.

Question 28

Massahampshire takes the "bifurcated trial" approach to insanity defense cases. The first part of the trial determines the defendant's guilt or innocence, and the second part determines whether the defendant was legally sane at the time the crime was committed. It also takes a "modern" approach to criminal law, and much of its Criminal Code follows the Model Penal Code.

Dupre was on trial for murder. The prosecution produced three witnesses who testified that they had seen Dupre shoot Vellum on a city street. The defense put Dupre on the stand, and Dupre's attorney asked Dupre, "Did you shoot this man, Vellum?" Dupre answered, "I shot no man; there was a tiger; the tiger was coming down the street at me; the tiger would have clawed me and eaten me, so I shot it . . . and shot it . . . and shot it." The prosecution immediately objected, and moved that Dupre's testimony be stricken.

How should the court rule on that motion?

(A) Granted, because Dupre's purported delusions are only relevant to the second part of the trial.

(B) Granted, if the judge is convinced that Dupre is lying.

(C) Not granted, because the testimony is relevant to Dupre's mens rea.

(D) Not granted, because the testimony is relevant to Dupre's conduct.

Question 29

Dolph, who was indigent and employed part-time at a minimum-wage job, was charged with a crime for which the maximum punishment is six months in prison and a fine of $500. When asked how he wished to plead, Dolph said, "Innocent." The judge asked Dolph who was representing him, and Dolph indicated that he wished to represent himself. The judge told Dolph that the court would appoint an attorney to represent him if he needed counsel. He further explained that the state has a policy of appointing private attorneys to defend indigents, and that if such defendants are acquitted or imprisoned, there is no charge for the court-appointed lawyer. If, however, the defendant is sentenced to probation, the defendant must pay "reasonable attorney's fees," which it is presumed the defendant will be able to pay out of job earnings while on probation. Dolph told the judge that paying for an attorney would be difficult, and that he still wished to defend himself. The judge told Dolph, "Haven't you ever heard the old maxim—'a lawyer who defends himself has a fool for a client'?—believe me that I'm acting in your best interests. I am going to appoint an attorney for you, because that power is in my discretion." The judge duly appointed List, an attorney with criminal defense experience, to defend Dolph. Dolph fully cooperated with List. List did a highly competent job, but the evidence heavily favored the state. Dolph was convicted, but List's plea for leniency was effective, and Dolph received a suspended sentence and probation. Two weeks later, Dolph received a bill for $500 for legal services, a figure that represented about half the sum a lawyer not appointed by the court would have charged for similar work.

Although Dolph would be able to pay the fees over a long period of time via installments, he is angry that he has been billed at all, and feels he could have gotten probation if he had been allowed to argue his own case. He consults Artemis, another attorney, and asks her to appeal both his conviction and the imposition of the legal fees.

Artemis should advise Dolph that the appellate court would most likely:

(A) Affirm both his conviction and the imposition of fees, because there is no reversible error, since List competently represented him, and the state has a right to recoup costs from those able to pay.

(B) Affirm the conviction because there was no reversible error, but reverse the imposition of fees, because Dolph could have gotten probation for himself as easily as List did.

(C) Reverse the conviction, because Dolph was denied the right to defend himself, but affirm the imposition of fees because List was competent and the state has a right to recoup costs from those able to pay.

(D) Reverse both the conviction and the imposition of fees, because Dolph was denied the right to defend himself.

Question 30

After a busy business lunch at "The Sign of the Raider," a restaurant popular with local stockbrokers and corporate attorneys, Hugh went to the restaurant's cloakroom. He removed a coat he believed to be his own from the coat rack. The coat was of similar color and of the same brand ("Nantucket Fog") as Hugh's own coat, but it actually belonged to another patron of the restaurant. Hugh walked the three blocks back to his office. He removed the coat, and, just as he was hanging it on the rack in his office, he noticed that another person's name was written on the inside of the collar. Hugh immediately left the office and sprinted back in the direction of the restaurant, intending to return the coat and pick up his own. As he crossed the street, Hugh was struck by a car. Although his injuries were minor, the coat was destroyed.

If Hugh is acquitted of larceny, what is the best reason for his acquittal?

(A) The coat was destroyed through no fault of his own.

(B) The coat looked so much like Hugh's coat that his mistake was reasonable.

(C) Hugh thought the coat was his when he took it.

(D) When he realized the coat was not his, Hugh tried to return it.

Questions 31-32 are based on the following fact situation:

Asher planned to rob a bank, but he was constrained from doing it because his car was immobilized, and thus he lacked a getaway vehicle. He, therefore, approached his friend Frederick and told Frederick of his plan. He asked Frederick to join him in the robbery and proposed that Frederick supply his car and driving skills to assist in getting to the bank and making a successful escape. Frederick thought Asher's idea was a harebrained scheme. Although Frederick had no desire to participate in the robbery, he pretended to agree to aid Asher and planned to report Asher's plan to the police before Asher could commit the crime.

On the day that Asher had appointed for the crime, Frederick drove to Asher's house and picked up Asher. Asher told Frederick to drive him to the Third National Bank. Frederick took a direct route, but approximately two miles from the bank he told Asher that he needed a pack of cigarettes and drove into the parking lot of a convenience store. Inside the store, Frederick used a pay telephone to call the local police. He told them that a robbery was about to take place at the Third National Bank and that units should be assigned there to prevent the crime. The desk sergeant, Stella, thought that Frederick was making a "crank call." She laughed at him and hung up the phone. Frederick made another attempt to call the police, but Stella answered again, laughed at him, and hung up. Frederick was now out of quarters and he went back to the parking lot, intending to talk Asher out of going to the bank. When he reached the lot, he found the car missing. Frederick had left his keys in the ignition and also had left the engine running. When Frederick did not emerge from the store

in five minutes, Asher had grown nervous and had driven off in the car. Asher drove to the bank, entered it, and drew a gun. He demanded money from one of the tellers and a shooting match ensued, during the course of which both Asher and one of the bank guards were killed. The police traced the car to Frederick, who freely told the police the truth.

31. If Frederick is charged with conspiracy, the trial court is most likely to find him:

(A) Guilty, because his withdrawal was ineffective since it was not communicated to Asher in time for him to change his plans.

(B) Guilty, because he provided Asher with an instrumentality of the crime.

(C) Not guilty, because Frederick withdrew from any conspiracy.

(D) Not guilty, because Frederick lacked criminal intent.

32. If Frederick is tried for the death of the security guard, should he be convicted?

(A) Yes, because he provided Asher with the car used in the crime.

(B) Yes, because it was foreseeable that Asher would drive the car to the crime scene after Frederick left the keys in the ignition.

(C) No, because Frederick lacked the requisite intent.

(D) No, because Frederick effectively withdrew from participation in the crime.

Question 33

Harfo, Groufo, and Chifo met in a room in the Hotsheetz Hotel on a Saturday night and agreed that they would rob a nearby branch of the Last Bank and Trust Company on the following Tuesday. Harfo was assigned the task of stealing a car to be used for the getaway, Chifo agreed to procure weapons, and Groufo would "case" the bank to determine the location of cameras, guards, and other security devices. On Sunday night, Harfo stole a car and parked it in a lot behind his girlfriend's apartment building. While visiting his girlfriend on Monday night, Harfo complained of severe chest pain and shortly thereafter suffered a series of convulsive seizures. Harfo's girlfriend called an ambulance and Harfo was rushed to the hospital. Harfo was placed in the intensive care unit and heavily sedated. Groufo and Chifo, unaware of Harfo's illness, met at the appointed place of rendezvous and decided to rob the bank on their own, despite the absence of Harfo and a getaway car. They robbed the bank, but were quickly apprehended as they tried to escape on foot. Groufo and Chifo implicated Harfo under police questioning.

Harfo can be charged with:

(A) Theft of the car only.

(B) Conspiracy to commit robbery and theft of the car only.

(C) Robbery and theft of the car only.

(D) Theft of the car, conspiracy to commit robbery, and robbery.

Question 34

Archie Delphinium and his wife, Edith, were taking an extended motor tour of the United States. Through his local automobile club in eastern Pennsylvania, Archie received a set of maps with routes marked out. Archie prudently arranged to make motel reservations in advance at their proposed stopover points, because Archie and Edith were traveling in the summer season when an abundance of tourists sometimes meant there would be "no room at the inn" in more popular vacation areas, such as the Grand Canyon region.

When the Delphiniums were driving through the sparsely populated high plains of the Western state of Arapahoe, Edith complained to Archie of severe pains in her abdominal area. She asked if he would please stop in Crow City, the next town of any consequence, to have a doctor examine her. Signs on the interstate highway indicated that Crow City had an emergency hospital facility. Signs on the highway also stated: "Next food, gas, and lodging at Dry Gulch, 118 miles." It was getting to be late in the afternoon, and Archie had a reservation at the Highway Inn in Dry Gulch that would be automatically canceled if the Delphiniums did not arrive before 6 p.m. He, therefore, refused to stop at Crow City and drove on toward Dry Gulch. In fact, Edith was suffering from an attack of acute appendicitis. Her appendix burst about 30 miles from Dry Gulch, and she was on the point of expiring when Archie arrived at the Dry Gulch Clinic. A nurse attended to Edith and called Dr. Holiday, the only physician in the county. He arrived 30 minutes later. A weakening Edith told Dr. Holiday that Archie had refused to stop at Crow City. Holiday concluded that it was too late to save Edith's life and she died two hours later. After a coroner's inquest into the death of Edith, Archie was charged with murder.

Which of the following, if true, would be the fact most beneficial to Archie's defense?

(A) Although Edith held herself out as "Mrs. Delphinium," and the couple had lived together for many years, Archie and Edith were never legally married.

(B) The Dry Gulch Clinic had adequate operating facilities and an adequate supply of pharmaceuticals to save Edith's life, but Dr. Holiday acted incompetently when he failed to make a more serious attempt to save Edith's life.

(C) An autopsy following Edith's death disclosed that she had cancer, from which she would have died within a few months.

(D) Archie did not believe that Edith's complaints of abdominal pain signaled a serious medical problem.

Question 35

State Blue makes "exploitation of a minor for sexual purposes" a felony. A minor is defined as anyone under the age of 18.

Norma Kay was a physically and emotionally mature 15-year-old sophomore at Arjay High School, which was located in State Blue. She was befriended by Byron Thomas, a 25-year-old amateur filmmaker, who had dreams of some-day "making it big" in Hollywood. After a few dates, Byron and Norma Kay became sexually intimate. Byron then suggested that Norma Kay might be interested in performing in some of his films. She already had viewed a number of Byron's films in private with him and was well aware that Byron specialized in making films and videos of couples involved in sexual acts. Norma Kay had dreams of stardom and felt that pornographic films were as good a place as any to start. Byron made several films where Norma Kay engaged in sexual intercourse with Byron and another older actor. Byron sold videotape prints of his productions and gave Norma Kay a small percentage of his profit from each of the movies in which she was featured, calling it a "royalty." Norma Kay also helped Byron make copies of the tapes and fill orders. Byron and Norma Kay continued to be sexually intimate off the screen as well. At a bachelor party for Arjay High's assistant football coach, a video-tape was shown featuring Norma Kay. She was quickly recognized by several Arjay High faculty members attending the party, one of whom brought the film to the police. Byron was charged with exploitation. Although the prosecutor's officer offered Norma Kay immunity if she agreed to testify against Byron, she consistently refused to do so. The prosecutor decided to charge Norma Kay as well.

Norma Kay can be tried with Byron as:

(A) A principal.

(B) An accessory after the fact.

(C) An accomplice.

(D) None of the above.

Question 36

Under which of the following circumstances would the named defendant most likely be found ***not guilty*** of larceny?

(A) Upon leaving his police science class, Jack sees the bicycle of another student leaning against the building, and, without the owner's knowledge or permission, rides away on the bike, intending to sell it at a local swap meet.

(B) Jill, who is moving permanently to Afghanistan, asks an acquaintance if she can borrow the latter's backpack and frame. Jill immediately leaves for Afghanistan after obtaining the backpack and frame.

(C) Reginald, who learned that an accountant had embezzled $100,000 from his employer, went to the accountant's apartment and took the cash, intending to spend it on a wild weekend in Mallorca.

(D) Sherri, needing a ride to work, hot wires her neighbor's Cadillac and drives it into town. Sherri intends to drive the car back at the end of the workday and return it to the neighbor, who is away on vacation.

Question 37

Willie lived in a very exclusive section of Suburb and had grown into a willful, undisciplined teenager.

One of Willie's neighbors purchased one of the few goldplated DeLorean sports cars ever built and parked it in his attached multicar garage. Willie, whose aptitude for electronics was as thoroughly developed as unlimited time and money made possible, had manufactured a radio device that could be programmed to open any automatic garage door opener, and Willie used the device to open the neighbor's garage one night. Using other specialized tools, Willie cut a key to the DeLorean and drove it away, intending to cruise by a few of his friends' favorite nighttime haunts in the opulently exotic car and then return it to its owner with no one the wiser.

After driving the car to a local bar and having several drinks, Willie decided to take his friends for a ride to the nearby seacoast. When the party arrived at the bluffs above the beach, Willie impulsively decided to push the DeLorean over the cliff, making a spectacular golden wreck of the sports car.

The jurisdiction's penal statutes simply codified the common law without alteration of any kind.

Willie is guilty of:

(A) No crime.

(B) Burglary.

(C) Larceny.

(D) Both burglary and larceny.

Question 38

In which of the following situations is Defendant *least* likely to be found guilty of murder?

(A) Not intending to kill, Defendant hits Victim over the head with a lead pipe, and Victim dies from the wound. 2nd

(B) Not intending to kill, Defendant while at a party pushes Victim, a 10-year-old child, into the swimming pool, and Victim drowns.

(C) Not intending to kill, Defendant drops bricks from the top of a tall building into the crowd below; one of the bricks strikes and kills Victim.

(D) Not intending to kill, Defendant committing a robbery, pushes Victim, a store clerk; Victim falls, strikes her head on the counter, and dies.

Question 39

Diane was driving her car on a city street when she was stopped by Officer, who clocked her going 42 m.p.h. in a 30-m.p.h. zone. As Officer reached Diane's car, he saw her put something into her purse. Officer told Diane, "Ma'am, you were speeding; that's why I

stopped you. I'd like your driver's license, and, by the way, what did you just put into your purse?" Diane responded, "It's just a marijuana cigarette, but don't worry, Officer, I've only had two and my driving judgment hasn't been impaired." Officer took Diane's purse, removed the "joint," and charged Diane with possession of marijuana as well as speeding.

At Diane's trial for marijuana possession, the prosecution seeks to introduce the marijuana cigarette into evidence. Diane's attorney moves to suppress the evidence. The defense motion should be:

(A) Granted, because the cigarette is fruit of the poisonous tree.

(B) Granted, because Officer did not have a valid search warrant.

(C) Denied, because Officer's asking about the contents of Diane's purse did not constitute custodial interrogation.

(D) Denied, provided Officer had a reasonable suspicion of criminal activity.

Question 40

After much discussion Axle, Bowers, and Crandall decided to burglarize the home of King, a prominent businessman. The three agreed that the crime would be committed the following Saturday night. On Thursday, Crandall stole a gun for "insurance" in case they encountered trouble during the burglary. On Friday, Crandall was arrested and jailed for a previous, unrelated crime. He was kept in confinement over the weekend. Axle and Bowers decided to go ahead with the burglary. On Saturday night, as they were about to break open the front door to King's home, they were arrested by a passing police officer.

Crandall is guilty of:

(A) Larceny of the gun only.

(B) Larceny of the gun and conspiracy only.

(C) Larceny of the gun and attempted burglary only.

(D) Larceny of the gun, conspiracy, and attempted burglary.

Question 41

Deal has had a history of epileptic seizures over the last five years. Each seizure comes upon him without warning. One day, Deal decided to attend an afternoon movie in town. As he was driving to the theater he had a seizure. He lost control of the car and struck a pedestrian who was lawfully crossing the street. The pedestrian died on the way to the hospital as a result of his injuries. Deal is charged with involuntary manslaughter.

He will most likely be found:

(A) Guilty, because the law presumes that a person intends the natural and probable consequences of his acts.

(B) Guilty, because he knowingly and recklessly chose to drive his car.

(C) Not guilty, because his failure to control the car was not a voluntary act.

(D) Not guilty, because he had no intent to harm anyone.

Question 42

Print kept a small printing press in one room of his home. He used the printing press to help him in his business. Trout was a classmate of Print's son, Donny. She had been in Print's home on many occasions to visit with Donny and had seen the printing press. Trout decided to print a one-page newsletter critical of the local school board's policies and distribute it around town. On an evening when she knew Print and his family were not at home, Trout broke into Print's home intending to use the printing press to print her newsletter. She believed that the unauthorized use of the printing press constituted a crime, but she was mistaken in this belief. Print and his family returned home while Trout was still in the house. She was arrested and charged with burglary. The jurisdiction defines burglary as the breaking and entering of the dwelling house of another at nighttime with the intent to commit a crime.

Trout should be found:

(A) Guilty, because her mistake was one of law, not of fact.

(B) Guilty, because she broke and entered Print's home believing she was going to commit a crime.

(C) Not guilty, because even if she had been successful, no crime would have occurred.

(D) Not guilty, because there was no dangerous proximity to success.

Question 43

Murphy was convicted after a jury trial of violation of federal statutes prohibiting the sale of automatic weapons to foreign nationals, in connection with his activities as a procurement officer for the Provisional Wing of the Irish Republican Army. It was established at trial that Murphy had purchased a number of stolen U.S. Army heavy machine guns and attempted to ship them to Ireland in crates marked "machine parts." The trial court expressly based its imposition of the maximum possible sentence for the conviction on Murphy's refusal to reveal the names of the persons from whom he purchased the stolen weapons.

You are a court of appeals justice authoring the opinion in Murphy's appeal of the sentence imposed. His counsel argues that the trial court's consideration of Murphy's failure to name the sellers of the stolen weapons is reversible error. You should:

(A) Reverse the trial court, because the consideration of Murphy's silence violates his Fifth Amendment privilege against self-incrimination.

(B) Reverse the trial court, because the consideration of collateral circumstances in sentencing violates his due process rights.

(C) Affirm the trial court, because the right to silence of the Fifth Amendment does not include the right to protect others from incrimination.

(D) Affirm the trial court, because citizens must report violations of the criminal statutes.

Question 44

At Dale's trial for battery, it is established that Viola was struck in the face by Dale's fist. Which of the following, if true, would *least* support a finding that Dale had committed battery?

(A) Dale had just been awakened by Viola, and, still groggy, he thought she was a burglar and struck her before he realized the truth.

(B) Dale was at a party where an amateur hypnotist placed him in a highly suggestible state and instructed him that Viola was Adolf Hitler, whereupon Dale struck her.

(C) Dale was showing a friend how Muhammad Ali knocked Sonny Liston down, and being somewhat tipsy, became too exuberant and struck Viola, who was standing nearby.

(D) In setting up equipment for a polygraph examination of Dale, Viola accidentally touched a live electrical wire to Dale's armpit, causing him to involuntarily twitch his arm forward, striking her in the face.

Question 45

Mark was deer hunting with some friends when he thought he saw a deer in a copse of trees a few hundred yards away. To approach the trees, Mark had to climb over a fence posted with "no hunting" and "no trespassing" signs. Mark carefully stalked the fleet-footed forest creature, fired, and discovered to his chagrin that he had just shot a large bull. Homer, owner of the property, heard the shot and grabbed his shotgun, fearing that hunters had shot another one of his cattle. When he arrived at the copse of trees and discovered that Mark had killed his prize bull, he became enraged and ordered Mark to get off his property in extremely abusive language. Instead of leaving immediately, Mark said, "It's just a damn cow!" Homer raised his shotgun and fired at Mark, narrowly missing him. When Homer operated the pump-action of the shotgun and raised it again, Mark shot and killed him.

In Mark's prosecution for murder, he should be found:

(A) Guilty, because he was a trespasser on Homer's land.

(B) Not guilty, because Homer attacked him with deadly force.

(C) Guilty, because Homer's attack was provoked by Mark.

(D) Not guilty, because Homer had no right to defend his property with deadly force.

Question 46

While hiking through an area that had been recently devastated by a fire, Hiker discovered a sign that stated: "Now entering State Wilderness Area." Thinking that the sign would make a nice decoration, Hiker took the sign home with him. He was arrested and charged with violating the state statute that provides, "Any person who appropriates to his own use property owned by the state shall be guilty of a crime and shall be punished by a fine of not more than $5,000 or by imprisonment for not more than two years or by both such fine and imprisonment." At trial, Hiker admitted taking the sign, but claims that he believed the sign had been abandoned since the area had recently been devastated by a fire. In fact the sign had not been abandoned.

Hiker will most likely be found:

(A) Guilty, because this is a strict liability offense.

(B) Guilty, because intent is not placed in issue by this statute.

(C) Not guilty, unless the jury finds that the state had taken adequate steps to inform the public that the sign had not been abandoned.

(D) Not guilty, if the jury finds Hiker honestly believed the sign had been abandoned.

Question 47

Jim and Sandy had recently separated, although they had not yet filed for a divorce. Jim lived in a hotel in the downtown area while Sandy resided in the house that was jointly owned by Jim and Sandy. Shortly after the period of separation began, Sandy started to date Nick, whom she had recently met. Upon bringing Sandy home from a date, Nick would quite often stay for a drink before leaving for home. One night while Sandy and Nick were in the house having a drink, Jim burst in and told Nick, "Get out." When Nick refused, Jim said, "Then let's go outside and settle this right now." Nick again refused. Jim then pulled a knife from his pocket and moved toward Nick. Nick immediately grabbed a chair and hit Jim on the head, killing him instantly. Nick was arrested and charged with murder.

Nick will most likely be found:

(A) Guilty, if Nick could have retreated safely once Jim pulled out a knife.

(B) Guilty, because Nick's failure to obey Jim's order to leave the house made Nick a trespasser.

(C) Not guilty, because Jim attacked Nick with a deadly weapon.

(D) Not guilty, because Sandy had invited Nick into the house.

Question 48

In which of the following cases is a conviction of the named defendant for robbery *least likely* to be upheld?

(A) Having induced a woman to return home with him, Philips tells her that she will not be allowed to leave unless she gives him all of her money. Fearing for her safety, the woman gives Philips all of the cash she has in her possession.

(B) While in a bar, Ericson noticed the wallet of the man sitting next to him laying on the counter. Ericson waited until the man was looking away and then picked up the wallet and put it into his pocket. Shortly thereafter, the man realized his wallet was gone and accused Ericson of taking it. Ericson pretended to be insulted, slapped the victim, and went off with the wallet.

(C) Sanders broke into a home he believed was unoccupied. Upon finding a man inside, he tied him up and forced him to tell Sanders where he kept his money. Sanders went to the spot, took the money, and fled.

(D) Billings hired a friend to bump into people at an airport hard enough to cause them to drop their luggage. Billings would then pick up the luggage and run off with it.

Question 49

Drury parked his car on a city street and entered a local tavern. While Drury was inside, vandals broke the ignition motor on his car and smashed the taillights. Later that night Drury left the tavern and attempted to start his car, but was unable to because of the vandals' actions. Police in a patrolling squad car noticed Drury entering the car and attempting to start it. When Drury got out of the car, the police approached him and asked him to identify himself. When he refused, he was arrested and charged with attempting to drive an automobile at night without functioning taillights.

Drury's best defense is:

(A) Entrapment.

(B) Legal impossibility.

(C) Factual impossibility.

(D) Lack of requisite intent.

Question 50

Prex, the president of a private college, received a report that there was a great deal of cocaine use occurring on the second floor of the old dormitory. Prex persuaded the school security officers to place several concealed microphones in the second-floor student lounge. Conversations occurring in the lounge were monitored by the security officers. Security officers recorded a conversation in which Jackson, a student at the college, offered to sell cocaine to another student. A security officer took a tape of the conversation to the local police, who played it for a local judge. The judge issued a warrant to search Jackson's room. While searching the room the police discovered a large amount of cocaine. Jackson was arrested and charged with unlawful possession of narcotics. Jackson's attorney moved to prevent the introduction of the cocaine into evidence.

The motion will most likely be:

(A) Granted, because Jackson's privacy was unreasonably invaded.

(B) Granted, because the electronic surveillance was "fundamentally unfair."

(C) Denied, because the police properly obtained a search warrant.

(D) Denied, because Prex was acting on behalf of the college population in general.

Questions 51-52 are based on the following fact situation:

Mary was walking her dog one evening when the leash slipped out of her hand and the dog began to run away. Mary reached out, trying to grab the leash, and in so doing narrowly missed striking Anne, who was walking along the street in the opposite direction. Anne, believing that she was being attacked by Mary, pushed Mary away. Statutes in the jurisdiction defined criminal assault as "an attempt to commit a criminal battery" and criminal battery as "causing an offensive touching."

51. If charged with criminal assault, Mary should be found:

(A) Guilty, because she should have realized she might strike someone by reaching out to recapture the leash.

(B) Guilty, because she caused Anne to be apprehensive of an offensive touching.

(C) Not guilty, because she did not hit Anne.

(D) Not guilty, because she did not intend to hit Anne.

52. If charged with criminal battery, Anne should be found:

(A) Guilty, because she intentionally pushed Mary.

(B) Guilty, because Mary did not intend to assault her.

(C) Not guilty, because she was justified in pushing Mary.

(D) Not guilty, because a push is not an offensive touching.

Question 53

In which of the following situations is Defendant most likely to be guilty of larceny?

(A) Unreasonably mistaking another man's hat for his own, Defendant takes the hat off the hat rack and walks off with it.

(B) Wishing to collect on a long-time debt, Defendant went into Fred's house and took $50 in cash, the amount Fred owed him.

(C) Defendant took Phil's car with the intention of returning it the next day. However, he was involved in an automobile accident and totaled the car before he could return it.

(D) Mistakenly believing that larceny only involves the taking of items over $100 in value, Defendant takes his neighbor's lawn mower worth $75 and sells it to a third person.

Questions 54

Acting on a hunch, Officer Blue went to Mildred's apartment, broke in, and searched it. Officer Blue found exactly what she was looking for under Mildred's bed: a red velvet sack filled with jewels. The attached note read, "Millie, here are the goods from the Winthrop heist. Johnny." It was well known in the community that Mildred's boyfriend was a jewel thief named Johnny Lightfingers. Officer Blue also knew that the Winthrop estate had been burglarized three days ago.

Just as Officer Blue finished reading the note, Mildred returned. Officer Blue immediately placed Mildred under arrest as an accessory to the Winthrop burglary. Based on the evidence obtained from Mildred's apartment, a search warrant was issued for Johnny's apartment. The search yielded burglar tools and more jewels from the Winthrop estate. Johnny was immediately arrested and charged with the Winthrop burglary.

At Johnny's trial for the Winthrop burglary, Johnny's attorney files a motion to suppress the evidence consisting of the bag of jewels and note, the tools, and the jewels from Johnny's apartment. The court should:

(A) Grant the motion as to the bag of jewels and note, but deny it as to the evidence found in Johnny's apartment.

(B) Grant the motion, because all of this evidence is fruit of the poisonous tree.

(C) Deny the motion, because the police would have caught Johnny with the goods eventually.

(D) Deny the motion, because the police had a warrant to search Johnny's apartment.

Question 55

Darwin, on trial for robbing Victoria of some jewelry, relied on the defense that he was only trying to recover property that Victoria had previously stolen from him. The trial court instructed the jury that the prosecution must prove guilt beyond a reasonable doubt, and that if the jury should find that the defendant had established by a preponderance of the evidence that he was only trying to recover his property, they should find him not guilty. After he was convicted of robbery, Darwin asserts that the instruction to the jury was error.

His conviction should probably be:

(A) Reversed, because Darwin need only convince the jury of any defense to a reasonable certainty, not by a preponderance of the evidence.

(B) Reversed, because the instruction put a burden on Darwin that denied him due process of law.

(C) Affirmed, because Darwin's burden to show that he was trying to recover his property was not one of ultimate persuasion, but only to produce evidence to rebut the legitimate presumption that the robbery was conducted with the intent to permanently deprive Victoria of the jewelry.

(D) Affirmed, because the instruction was an accurate statement of the law.

Question 56

Nan ran a boarding house for local factory workers. One evening she smelled what she believed to be a suspicious odor coming from the room of a young boarder, Hal. She telephoned her daughter Yolanda, who was a police officer, and told her of the smell. Her daughter, suspecting that it was marijuana, told her mother that she wanted her to inspect the room the next day when Hal was at work, and if she found anything, to bring it to her.

The next morning, after Hal had gone, Nan took the master key and went into his room. In a drawer next to his bed, she found a box of tablets and some white powder. She took these to her daughter, who checked with the narcotics division and confirmed that they were drugs. Yolanda had her mother return the items, swear out an affidavit, and she had a search warrant issued.

When Hal returned that night, the police arrested him and searched his room. A quantity of drugs was found, and Hal was charged with possession of narcotics for sale.

At trial Hal moved to prevent the evidence of the drugs from being introduced. The trial judge should:

(A) Grant Hal's motion, because once the drugs had been taken to the police department, they had to be kept there and could not be returned to Hal's room for the purpose of finding them there.

(B) Grant Hal's motion, because his reasonable expectation of privacy had been unreasonably invaded.

(C) Deny Hal's motion, because Nan, as owner of the boarding house, had a legal right to inspect the rooms.

(D) Deny Hal's motion, because even without the drugs found by Nan, the police had reasonable cause to seek a search warrant.

Question 57

In which of the following situations is Defendant most likely to be guilty of common law burglary?

(A) Defendant, attempting to defraud his insurance company, breaks a window in his own house one night and takes some silverware.

(B) Defendant is a mail carrier making afternoon deliveries. She sees a valuable watch near a window, opens the window and with a stick, lifts the watch up and steals it.

(C) Defendant, angry at his girlfriend, steals her key, and while she is away one night, goes into her house and takes back the television he gave her.

(D) Defendant is a safepicker. Using a skeleton key, he opens the door to George's office and breaks into the safe.

Questions 58-61 are based on the following fact situation:

Gene, learning that his old friend Bart was out of prison, left the following note in his mailbox: "I'm glad to see that you are finally out. Have just found out that Larry is getting a shipment of stolen fur coats at Walker & Son's Warehouse next Saturday. I have a way of stealing them late Saturday night when no one is around. Interested? Contact me at 555-1234. Gene."

Bart, however, had gone to see some friends in another city and had left the apartment to Ray, who also just got out of prison. Ray, after reading the note, called Ginger and told her to meet him in her car and bring a gun, because he had just overheard at a bar about this shipment of fur coats that was being delivered on Saturday.

Saturday morning, as Larry was opening the warehouse, Ginger and Ray jumped him. However, the police, who had heard of the shipment, were staking out the warehouse, and when they saw Larry get jumped, they moved in and arrested all of them before the shipment arrived.

On Friday, Gene investigated why Bart had not called. When he learned that Bart had gone out of town, he decided it would be impossible to steal the furs himself. But when the police found his note on Ray, they picked up Gene and arrested him.

58. Gene is charged with conspiracy in a jurisdiction that follows the common law

rules. At Gene's preliminary hearing, the best argument his attorney can make to quash the charge is that:

(A) The note did not contain sufficient details of a "plan" to commit an unlawful act.

(B) Gene did not know Ray.

(C) Gene had made no agreement with Ray or Bart.

(D) Ray and Ginger had been arrested before the shipment arrived, so no crime had been committed.

59. Gene's attorney argued that even if it is assumed that Ray and Gene had agreed to steal the furs, Gene was innocent of the conspiracy because he decided not to go ahead with the plan. A jury could find Gene:

(A) Not guilty of conspiracy, because he did not commit an overt act.

(B) Not guilty of conspiracy, because he decided not to go ahead with the plan before Saturday.

(C) Guilty, because Ginger and Ray had attempted to steal the fur coats.

(D) Guilty, because Ray agreed to attempt to steal the coats.

60. Gene is charged with being an accessory to the assault and battery of Larry. Gene's attorney argued that even if it is assumed that Ray and Gene had agreed to steal the furs, Gene was not guilty because:

(A) He had withdrawn from the plan.

(B) He knew nothing about the assault and battery of Larry.

(C) Gene's plan did not involve assaulting or battering Larry.

(D) Ginger and Ray were arrested before the shipment ever arrived.

61. Ginger and Ray may be charged with:

(A) Attempted robbery and conspiracy to rob.

(B) Conspiracy to rob only, because they were arrested before the shipment of furs arrived.

(C) Attempted robbery only, because the facts indicate that their co-conspirator, Gene, may not have been planning a robbery.

(D) Battery only.

Question 62

Barney had been seeing Hank's wife for several weeks. One night they were drinking together in a bar, when suddenly Hank walked in. Seeing them together, he yelled, "I'm going to kill you!" and put his hand into his coat. Seeing his actions, Barney grabbed a heavy ashtray from the table and hit him in the head. As a result of the blow, Hank, who had a plate in his head, died. No weapon was found on his person.

Barney is charged with manslaughter. Of the following, which is the best defense Barney can assert?

(A) He did not intend to seriously injure Hank.

(B) He thought Hank had a weapon.

(C) He did not know that Hank had a plate in his head.

(D) He had no time for deliberation or premeditation.

Questions 63-64 require you to assume that you are in either a TYPE A or a TYPE B jurisdiction.

CRIMINAL LAW 451.

TYPE A. The homicide statute in this jurisdiction reads in part as follows:

Murder is the unlawful killing of a human being with malice aforethought. Such malice may be express or implied. It is express when there is manifested a deliberate intention to unlawfully take away the life of a fellow creature. It is implied when no considerable provocation appears or when the circumstances attending the killing show an abandoned and malignant heart.

TYPE B. The homicide statute in this jurisdiction reads in part as follows:

Murder is the unlawful killing of a human being with malice aforethought. Such malice may be express or implied. It is express when there is manifested a deliberate intention to unlawfully take away the life of a fellow creature. It is implied when no considerable provocation appears or when the circumstances attending the killing show an abandoned and malignant heart. All murder that is perpetrated by willful, deliberate, or premeditated killing or committed in the perpetration of or attempt to perpetrate arson, rape, robbery, or burglary is murder of the first degree. All other kinds of murders are of the second degree.

Both TYPE A and TYPE B jurisdictions have a statute reading as follows:

Manslaughter is the unlawful killing of a human being without malice. It is of two kinds:

1.   Voluntary—upon a sudden quarrel or heat of passion.

2.   Involuntary—in the commission of an unlawful act, not amounting to a felony; or in the commission of a lawful act that might produce death in an unlawful manner or without due caution and circumspection.

Manslaughter is punishable by imprisonment in the state prison for a period not exceeding 15 years.

Louis and Rob were both teenagers, old enough to be held legally responsible for a crime in the particular jurisdictions. Even before either of them had gotten a driver's license, they had been car-racing enthusiasts. They both owned their own cars, equipped with racing-type equipment.

Although it was against the law, Louis and Rob, along with other teenagers, would frequently race their cars on a little-used highway just outside of town. One night, after the group had been drinking beer and racing their cars against each other, Louis challenged Rob to a game of "chicken." He and Rob would drive their cars at each other at a speed of 50 m.p.h., and the first to turn away would have to pay the other $25. Although other kids they knew had played this game, neither Rob nor Louis had.

Rob did not really want to participate, but because he did not want any of the girls he knew to think he was afraid to do so, he agreed. He and Louis got into their cars, drove off in opposite directions a designated distance, and then turned around. When the starters flashed their lights, Rob and Louis raced toward each other. When the cars were about 40 feet apart, Louis suddenly turned his car to the right. But Rob, going too fast to stop, crashed into the side of the car, killing Louis instantly.

63.   Rob is charged with first degree murder in a TYPE B jurisdiction. Of the following, which defense would be Rob's best theory?

(A)   An automobile is not a dangerous weapon, and therefore there can be no deliberate killing.

(B)   Rob, because of his youth, could not have formed the necessary malice aforethought to support a conviction for murder.

(C)   Rob is guilty of murder, but not first degree murder.

    (D) Rob cannot be guilty of any degree of murder because he did not intend to kill Louis.

64. If Rob is charged with criminal homicide in a TYPE A jurisdiction, the trial judge could properly give a charge to the jury on the following theories.

    (A) Involuntary manslaughter only.

    (B) Murder and involuntary manslaughter.

    (C) Murder and voluntary manslaughter.

    (D) First degree murder, second degree murder, and involuntary manslaughter.

Question 65

In response to a telephone call, a report went out over the police radio requesting an ambulance because of a shooting. Several officers who heard the broadcast arrived at the subject residence and knocked on the front door, identifying themselves as police officers. Believing that someone inside the house had been shot, one of the officers entered the building through an unlocked window and opened the front door for the other officers to enter. While searching for victims, the officers saw, in plain view, several containers of cocaine. Defendant, the occupant of the house, was arrested and charged with possession of narcotics. At his trial, Defendant moved to suppress the evidence of the narcotics on the ground that the police officers' warrantless entry into his residence was improper.

Did the police officers have a right to enter the building without a warrant?

(A) Yes, because exigent circumstances existed as a result of the shooting.

(B) Yes, because the police officers were acting in their official function.

(C) No, because there were no factors to indicate that there was not enough time to obtain a warrant.

(D) No, because there was no probable cause to enter without a warrant.

Question 66

After receiving a telephone call that a gunshot was heard there, the police went to a warehouse. There they found Davis standing over Vic's body. They immediately arrested Davis, gave him his *Miranda* warnings, and when he requested his attorney, took him to jail. At trial, Davis testified in his own defense. He claimed that he was in the warehouse alone when he was attacked by Vic, and that he shot Vic in self-defense. The prosecution, on cross-examination, asked Davis why he did not tell the police when they arrived there that he had shot Vic in self-defense. Davis's attorney objected to this question, but he was overruled. Davis was unable to give a very satisfactory answer, and the prosecution suggested that he was lying.

Davis was convicted. He appealed, contending that the prosecutor's cross-examination was improper. His conviction would most likely be:

(A) Reversed, because once Davis had asked for an attorney, he had no obligation to talk with the police while he was in custody.

(B) Reversed, because post-arrest silence constitutes Davis's exercise of his *Miranda* rights and use of that silence against him at trial would violate due process.

(C) Affirmed, because Davis's silence when the police arrived is tantamount to a prior inconsistent statement, giving rise to an inference that the story was fabricated.

(D) Affirmed, because by taking the stand, Davis waived any right he may have had not to testify against himself.

Question 67

A statute in this jurisdiction makes it a felony for any "married person to enter into a new marriage with another when such married person knows, or should know, that his former marriage has not been terminated by a divorce decree or by the death of a former spouse."

Annie is charged with bigamy when it is discovered that she married Gerald while still being married to Rodney. Annie's best defense to this charge is that:

(A) She filed for a divorce but just never got around to requesting the court to enter a divorce decree.

(B) Rodney left home one night after a bad argument, and she has not seen or heard from him in three years.

(C) She retained an attorney to get her a divorce from Rodney, and she believed she had received a divorce.

(D) When she and Rodney were first married, she was underage and so she believed her first marriage to have been invalid.

Question 68

Mervin, a professional jewel thief, sold some stolen goods, including a sterling silver cigar box, to Giles, an antique dealer who frequently purchased stolen goods from Mervin. Several weeks later, acting on an anonymous tip, the police raided Giles's store and arrested him. In this raid, the police seized the goods Mervin sold to Giles and some records in which Giles had recorded this transaction. However, at Giles's subsequent trial for receiving stolen goods, the charges against him were dismissed when the court ruled that the search warrant had been improperly issued.

The police were able to trace the stolen goods to Mervin because of fingerprint identification and the information contained in Giles's record book. At his trial, Mervin made a motion to suppress the stolen goods and record book.

The judge should:

(A) Grant the motion, because the evidence is the fruit of the poisonous tree in that the search of Giles's store was improper.

(B) Grant the motion, because the trial court in Giles's case has already ruled that the evidence was improper.

(C) Deny the motion, because Mervin's fingerprints on the stolen goods were what led to his identification.

(D) Deny the motion, because Mervin has no standing to object to the search.

Question 69

Gregg was invited over to his friend Jud's house for drinks. After they both had consumed several beers each, Jud told Gregg that he wanted to show him something that he just got. Jud went into his bedroom and brought out a pre-WWII German Luger. Jud told Gregg that he had stolen the gun from a local museum several days before. Gregg asked him if he was interested in selling it, but Jud said no.

They continued to drink for a couple of hours and then decided that they would go out to a bar. As they got to Gregg's car, Gregg realized that he had left his coat in the house and told Jud that he was going back to get it. Gregg went back into the room, and as he picked up his coat, he saw the stolen pistol on the table. He quickly picked it up and put it in his pocket.

Gregg is charged with larceny and burglary. In this jurisdiction, burglary is defined as the breaking and entering of the dwelling place of another with the intent to commit any theft or felony.

Assuming that the evidence at trial shows that in fact the pistol was stolen, Gregg should be convicted of:

(A) Both larceny and burglary.

(B) Burglary only.

(C) Larceny only.

(D) Neither larceny nor burglary.

Question 70

Delbert overheard from some friends that Vanessa was suffering from a rare blood disease. Delbert told Vanessa that he could cure her by giving her a special elixir he had invented. Delbert charged Vanessa $500 for the elixir. The elixir had no effect on the blood disease. Delbert is charged with obtaining money by false pretenses.

Each of the following, if true, will absolve Delbert of guilt for obtaining money by false pretenses except:

(A) Delbert was playing a practical joke on Vanessa and intended to return the money.

(B) Delbert honestly believed that the elixir would cure the blood disease, but his belief was unreasonable.

(C) Vanessa honestly believed that the elixir would cure the blood disease, but her belief was unreasonable.

(D) Vanessa was an undercover police officer and did not believe that the elixir would cure the blood disease.

Question 71

Dorian is on trial for a federal offense. The government has subpoenaed crucial documents from Dorian's bookkeeper. The documents will clearly incriminate Dorian, and so Dorian wishes to invoke her Fifth Amendment privilege against self-incrimination to prevent the documents from being admitted.

Will Dorian succeed in preventing admission of the documents?

(A) Yes, because the documents will incriminate Dorian.

(B) Yes, because the documents belong to Dorian; the bookkeeper merely has custody of them.

(C) No, unless the documents include records required to be kept by legislation.

(D) No, because the Fifth Amendment privilege applies only to compelled testimony.

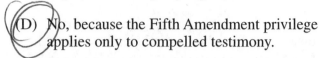

Questions 72-74 are based on the following fact situation:

The statutes of State Z define the following crimes (with the most serious listed first):

> First degree murder—Premeditated or intentional killing.

> Felony murder—Killing while in the act of committing a common law felony.

> Second degree murder—Killing with reckless disregard for the safety of others.

> Manslaughter—Killing with adequate provocation or through criminal negligence.

State Z has another statute that states: "It shall be a felony to dispense prescription drugs without a prescription."

Alyce, a student activist vehemently opposed to nuclear power, suggested to her boyfriend, Bob, that they put nitroglycerine in the sugar bowls at their college cafeteria so that some of their fellow students would become sick to their stomachs and the anti-nuclear group could claim that toxic emissions from a nearby nuclear power plant were the cause. Bob told Alyce that people could become very ill, or even die, if they consumed too large a quantity of nitroglycerine. Alyce said that they would only put a little nitroglycerine in each bowl and asked Bob to get the drug from his friend Phil, a pharmacist. Bob at first refused, but when Alyce threatened to break up with Bob if he did not get the drug, Bob agreed to obtain nitroglycerine. Bob told Phil that his doctor had prescribed nitroglycerine pills for him, that Bob had lost the prescription, and that the doctor was on an extended visit to Tierra del Fuego and could not be reached. Phil did not know about the statute making it a felony to dispense drugs without prescription and gave Bob a bottle of nitroglycerine pills. Bob gave the bottle to Alyce. Before Bob awoke the next day, Alyce broke open the pills, went to the cafeteria, and put small quantities of nitroglycerine in several sugar bowls. She unintentionally put a much larger amount in the sugar bowl at one table. A number of people became slightly ill from ingesting the drug. However, four persons who sat at the table where Alyce had put a large amount in the bowl became extremely ill, and one of the four eventually died.

72. The most serious crime for which Alyce may be convicted is:

(A) First degree murder.

(B) Felony murder.

(C) Second degree murder.

(D) Manslaughter.

73. In the death of the student, Bob may be liable as:

(A) An accessory before the fact.

(B) A principal in the first degree.

(C) A principal in the second degree.

(D) An accessory after the fact.

74. The most serious crime for which Phil may be convicted is:

(A) Felony murder.

(B) Second degree murder.

(C) Dispensing drugs without a prescription.

(D) No crime, because Phil did not know what Bob was going to do with the drugs and was unaware of the drug dispensing statute.

Question 75

John Johnson was a security guard at a local department store. Under applicable state law, private security guards are allowed to carry a gun on the job and while proceeding between their place of residence and work.

While driving home from work one evening, Johnson was involved in a car accident with Victor. The accident was clearly Johnson's fault, and an enraged Victor started swinging wildly at Johnson, twice hitting him in the face. Johnson pulled his gun and fired at Victor, intending to shoot him in the arm. The bullet struck Victor in the heart, killing him instantly.

Johnson will most likely be found guilty of:

(A) Felony murder, because the shooting of Victor was a felony.

(B) Voluntary manslaughter, if the jury found that Johnson was enraged when he shot Victor.

(C) Involuntary manslaughter, because Johnson did not intend to kill Victor.

(D) No crime, because Johnson was justified in using deadly force to prevent a physical attack.

Question 76

Deft left his horse with Fillmont's Stable while he went on vacation. When he returned, he went to the stable to pick up his horse and was informed by Fillmont that the bill was $500. Deft told Fillmont that he would have to go home and get more money. Deft believed that he was being overcharged by Fillmont; instead of paying Fillmont, he arranged to have Neighbor pick up the horse from the stable. Neighbor thought that the stable bill had been paid and Deft had a right to the horse; thus, Neighbor took the horse without Fillmont's knowledge. Halfway to Deft's house, Neighbor decided to keep the horse and rode away on it to his own home.

456. INTERMEDIATE QUESTIONS

Is Neighbor guilty of larceny in taking the horse from Fillmont?

(A) Yes, because Deft had not paid the stable bill.

(B) Yes, because Fillmont had possession of the horse.

(C) No, because Deft was the rightful owner of the horse.

(D) No, because he did not know that Fillmont had not been paid for the stable bill.

Question 77

The police received information linking Dullard to drug trafficking. A team of two officers went to Dullard's residence, where Dullard lived with his mother, Mae. The police found Mae at home, and she told them that Dullard was not expected back until 5:30 p.m. The police informed Mae that they suspected Dullard of selling drugs and asked if they could search his room. At that point Mae stated, "I'm finished with that no-good bum; not only is he into drugs but he has been stealing my money to pay for them, and all the time I'm making his bed and fixing his food. You can search his room. He likes to keep his private stuff under his pillow. I hope he goes to jail." The police searched Dullard's room and discovered eight ounces of marijuana under the pillow of his bed.

Dullard's motion to suppress the marijuana should be:

(A) Granted, because Dullard had a reasonable expectation of privacy in the area searched, and the police did not have a warrant.

(B) Granted, because Mae's consent was given at a time when police knew her interests were in conflict with Dullard's.

(C) Denied, because Mae had the authority to consent to the search of Dullard's room.

(D) Denied, because with Mae's statement the police had probable cause to search the room.

CRIMINAL LAW ANSWERS

Answer to Question 1

(C) The judge's instructions resulted in a violation of defendant's due process rights. The Due Process Clause requires that in all criminal cases the state prove guilt beyond a reasonable doubt. This requirement means that each element of a crime must be proved beyond a reasonable doubt. Snoops is charged with rape, which is the unlawful carnal knowledge of a woman by a man not her husband, without her effective consent. Thus, lack of consent is an element of the offense, and the state must prove lack of consent beyond a reasonable doubt. To require Snoops to prove consent would violate the due process requirement that the state prove all elements of an offense beyond a reasonable doubt. (B) is incorrect because lack of consent is part of the entire case that the state must prove where the charge is rape. To say that the state must prove "the entire case" is really to say that the state must prove each element of the offense. It is impermissible for a judge to segregate one element of the offense from other elements, and to impose upon the defendant the burden of proving that element. (A) is incorrect because if state law were to place the burden of proving lack of consent on the defendant, such a law would violate the Due Process Clause and would therefore be invalid. (D) is incorrect because a state may impose upon a criminal defendant the burden of proof regarding certain issues; *e.g.,* an affirmative defense such as insanity or self-defense.

Answer to Question 2

(D) Delbert intended to kill Vincent, but he did not act in a deliberate and premeditated manner, nor was he acting under a provocation that would have aroused a sudden and intense passion in the mind of an ordinary person (given the jury finding). Thus, of the crimes listed, Delbert can be guilty only of second degree murder. Murder is the unlawful killing of a human being with malice aforethought. Malice aforethought exists if the defendant has: (i) intent to kill; (ii) intent to inflict great bodily injury; (iii) awareness of an unjustifiably high risk to human life; or (iv) intent to commit a felony. Statutes such as the one in this question often divide murder into degrees. Thus, first degree murder here consists of a deliberate and premeditated taking of life, with all other murders relegated to second degree status. An intentional killing is reduced from murder to voluntary manslaughter if: (i) the defendant acts under a provocation that would arouse sudden and intense passion in the mind of an ordinary person such as to cause him to lose self-control; (ii) there is insufficient time between the provocation and the killing for the passions of a reasonable person to cool; and (iii) the defendant in fact did not cool off between the provocation and the killing. Here, the facts are clear that Delbert shot Vincent with the intent to kill him. This eliminates (B) as a correct answer. Involuntary manslaughter occurs when death is caused by criminal negligence, rather than an intentional act. Delbert's shooting of Vincent goes far beyond mere criminal negligence. (A) is incorrect because of the unreasonableness of Delbert's belief that Vincent and Victoria were together for the purpose of committing adultery. For purposes of voluntary manslaughter, the discovery of one's spouse in the act of adultery constitutes adequate provocation. However, as noted above, the provocation must have been such as to arouse the passions of an ordinary person. If, as this question states, Delbert's belief regarding Vincent and Victoria was unreasonable, the passions of an ordinary person would not have been aroused upon seeing Vincent and Victoria together. Therefore, Delbert's killing will not be reduced to voluntary manslaughter. (C) is incorrect because the quickness and anger with which Delbert acted would preclude the notions that he meaningfully reflected on the idea of killing Vincent, as required by the definition of premeditation and deliberation in the statute. This absence of deliberation and premeditation takes the killing outside the ambit of first degree murder. Consequently, Delbert's intentional killing of Vincent must be considered second degree murder, as choice (D) states.

Answer to Question 3

(C) Delbert's killing of Terrance was second degree murder. Terrance engaged in no provocation against Delbert. Thus, any provocation potentially produced by Delbert's finding Victoria and Vincent together would not reduce Delbert's killing of Terrance to voluntary manslaughter. Delbert's firing of a gun at Terrance indicates either intent to kill or to inflict great bodily injury. Thus, Delbert acted with the malice aforethought required for murder. (D) is incorrect because the issue of whether Delbert was reasonable or unreasonable in his belief that Vincent and Victoria were together for adulterous purposes is relevant only to the shootings committed against those two people. A reasonable belief that adultery was about to take place, or had already taken place, would be adequate provocation to arouse intense passion in an ordinary person so as to reduce an intentional killing from murder to voluntary manslaughter. However, although Delbert may have been provoked by the sight of Vincent and Victoria together, such provocation will not affect the killing of Terrance. No provocation emanated from Terrance, who was not at all involved in the "adulterous" scene. Because Terrance did not provoke Delbert, there are no grounds for reducing Delbert's killing of Terrance from murder to voluntary manslaughter. (A) is incorrect because, although a felony in the jurisdiction at issue, carrying a loaded handgun without a permit is not the type of inherently dangerous felony that will form the basis for a first degree felony murder conviction. Typically, such felonies include arson, robbery, burglary, rape, mayhem, and kidnapping. (B) is incorrect for two reasons. First, (B) links Delbert's guilt of the killing of Terrance to the issue of whether there was a reasonable belief as to whether Victoria and Vincent were together for adulterous purposes. As noted above, any provocation produced by an apparent adulterous relationship between Victoria and Vincent is irrelevant to the killing of Terrance. Second, Delbert is not guilty of first degree murder because the killing of Terrance was not committed in a deliberate and premeditated manner as defined by the statute (*i.e.,* it was not done after meaningful reflection). (C) is the only answer reflective of the fact that this is second degree murder, and that the possibly adulterous situation involving Vincent and Victoria is of no significance to the killing of Terrance.

Answer to Question 4

(A) Harry is guilty of first degree murder. Harry intended to kill Vincent, and the arrangements Harry made to achieve this goal (*i.e.,* setting up the meeting between Vincent and Victoria, and misinforming Delbert as to an affair taking place between Vincent and Victoria) indicate that Harry reflected on the idea of killing Vincent, and decided to do so in a cool and dispassionate manner. Acting with a deliberate and premeditated state of mind as defined by the statute, Harry used an unknowing agent, Delbert, to bring about the death of Vincent. Thus, Harry is guilty of first degree murder. (D) is incorrect because solicitation merges into the completed crime. At common law, solicitation consisted of inciting, counseling, advising, inducing, urging, or commanding another to commit a felony with the specific intent that the person solicited commit the crime. One who solicits another to commit a crime cannot be convicted of both the solicitation and the completed crime. Here, the crime was completed with the killing of Vincent. Thus, Harry cannot be guilty of solicitation. (B) is incorrect because there was no conspiracy. A conspiracy is an agreement between two or more persons to accomplish some unlawful purpose, or to accomplish a lawful purpose by unlawful means. The parties must agree to accomplish the same objective by mutual action. Here, Harry and Delbert did not agree to act together to accomplish the killing of Vincent. Rather, Harry used Delbert as his unwitting agent for this purpose. Thus, there is no guilt of conspiracy. (C) is incorrect because Harry's guilt is based on the fact that he caused the death of Vincent (using Delbert as his agent) after premeditation and deliberation. Thus, Harry has committed murder in the first degree regardless of what crime Delbert is found to have committed in killing Vincent.

Answer to Question 5

(D) Dan committed forgery and uttering when he sent the telegram. Forgery consists of the making of a false writing or the altering of an existing writing with intent to defraud. Uttering consists of offering as genuine an instrument that may be the subject of forgery and is false, with intent to defraud. Any writing that has apparent legal significance is a potential subject of forgery. The writing must represent itself to be something that it is not. The telegram sent by Dan had apparent legal significance, because it appeared to be a request by Ned for a disbursement of funds from the trust, which Banker was required to comply with according to the trust terms. Also, the telegram appeared to set forth an agency relationship between Ned and Dan, at least for purposes of picking up the money. In addition, the telegram was false, because it represented itself to be a request for disbursement of trust funds by one with authority to make such request. Dan made out this telegram with intent to defraud the trust and the sole lifetime beneficiary of $5,000. Consequently, Dan is guilty of forgery. When Dan sent the telegram to Banker, Dan offered the false instrument as genuine, again with the intent to defraud. This constituted uttering. (A) is incorrect because Dan has committed forgery and uttering, which are common law crimes. (B) is incorrect because the crimes of forgery and uttering were completed upon sending the telegram. Therefore, Dan's acts went beyond a mere attempt. (C) is incorrect because solicitation consists of inciting, counseling, advising, inducing, urging, or commanding another to commit a felony with the specific intent that the person solicited commit the crime. Here, Dan sent the telegram, not as a means of inducing Banker to commit an offense, but rather as part of Dan's plan to trick Banker into giving him the money. Banker was totally unaware of the scheme concocted by Dan. Thus, Dan did not commit solicitation.

Answer to Question 6

(C) Dan committed larceny by trick because Banker's consent to Dan's taking the money was induced by the misrepresentation that Dan would take the money to Ned. Larceny consists of a taking and carrying away of tangible personal property of another by trespass, with intent to permanently (or for an unreasonable time) deprive the person of his interest in the property. If the person in possession of property has not consented to the taking of it by the defendant, the taking is trespassory. However, if the victim consents to the defendant's taking possession of the property, but such consent has been induced by a misrepresentation, the consent is not valid. Under such circumstances, the larceny is called larceny by trick. Here, Dan obtained the money from Banker on the promise that he would take it to Ned. This misrepresentation induced Banker to give possession of the money to Dan. Dan then proceeded to take the money and carry it away, intending all the while to permanently deprive one who had a possessory interest superior to Dan's of his interest in the money. Thus, all the elements of larceny are present. Because the original wrongful taking resulted from consent induced by misrepresentation, the specific larceny committed by Dan is more precisely characterized as larceny by trick. Consequently, although Dan has in fact committed larceny, (C) is a better answer than (D). Regarding (A), false pretenses consists of obtaining title to the property of another by an intentional (or knowing) false statement of past or existing fact, with intent to defraud the other. If a victim intends to convey only possession of the property to the defendant, the offense is larceny by trick. However, if the victim intends to convey title, the offense is false pretenses. Here, Banker intended to convey possession of the money to Dan so that Dan could give the money to Ned. Banker did not intend to convey title to Dan. Because Dan did not obtain title by means of his misrepresentation but simply obtained possession, the offense of false pretenses was not committed. (B) is incorrect because embezzlement is the fraudulent conversion of property of another by a person in lawful possession of that property. In embezzlement, the misappropriation of the property occurs while the defendant has lawful possession of it. In larceny, the misappropriation occurs generally at the time the defendant obtains wrongful possession of the property. Dan did not have lawful possession of the money because his possession of the money resulted from his misrepresentation to Banker. Thus, Dan's taking of the money was wrongful from the outset. Because Dan had wrongful, rather than lawful, possession of the money, there was no embezzlement.

Answer to Question 7

(C) The *Ambrose* case is irrelevant to Dan's case, because *Ambrose* deals with a different type of impossibility than the factual impossibility present in the case involving Dan. In determining whether impossibility is a defense to attempt, a distinction is made between factual and legal impossibility. It is no defense to a charge of attempt that it would have been impossible for the defendant to do all of those things that he intended to do. Such impossibility is characterized as factual impossibility. Legal impossibility, which is a defense, occurs where a defendant sets out to do something he mistakenly believes constitutes a crime. In Dan's case, it was impossible for Dan to complete the intended killing of the police officer simply because of the fact that the officer was wearing a bulletproof vest. This is a classic case of factual impossibility, which will not provide Dan with a defense to the charge of attempted murder. *Ambrose*, on the other hand, is a legal impossibility decision. There is no crime in the books to cover either the defendant's behavior or his intended behavior. Since he intended to return the car, he cannot be guilty of larceny or attempted larceny. The fact that he thought he was committing a crime does not change that result. (B) is incorrect because, as explained above, *Ambrose* is based on a different form of impossibility from that which is present in Dan's case. *Ambrose* does not hold that factual impossibility is a good defense to attempt. Consequently, *Ambrose* provides no basis for finding that Dan is not guilty. (A) is incorrect because it sets forth an insignificant reason for distinguishing *Ambrose* from the instant case. Although *Ambrose* involves a property offense, it would have precedential value as to the crime of violence with which Dan is charged if it addressed the issue of factual impossibility, which is a salient issue in Dan's case. Similarly, (D) incorrectly focuses on a meaningless distinction between the two cases. It is irrelevant that the defendant in *Ambrose* actually drove off in the car he intended to steal, while Dan did not actually kill the officer. What is important is the reason that Dan did not perpetrate the intended crime; *i.e.*, it was impossible for him to do so because of the bulletproof vest. As stated previously, the distinction between the two cases is that *Ambrose* does not address such factual impossibility.

Answer to Question 8

(C) Ernie can be convicted of an attempt to violate the statute. The *Bierce* decision stands for the proposition that an accused is guilty of criminal attempt where he has performed all the acts he intended to accomplish with the requisite intent, and but for facts beyond his knowledge he would have committed a crime. This is precisely what happened with Ernie's attempt to smoke what he thought was a marijuana cigarette. Whether impossibility of success constitutes a defense to a charge of criminal attempt depends on the type of impossibility at issue. It is no defense to a charge of criminal attempt that it would have been impossible for the defendant to do all of those things that he intended to do. This is known as factual impossibility, and includes situations in which a defendant engages in conduct while mistaken about certain attendant circumstances, such that, had such circumstances been as he believed they were, what he set out to do would be a crime. It is this type of impossibility that is present in the *Bierce* case and also in Ernie's case. In *Bierce*, the defendant believed the property he received was stolen, and had it been so, he would have been guilty of receiving stolen property. Although the property actually was not stolen, the court held that the defendant was still guilty of attempt to receive stolen property. Similarly, Ernie smoked a cigarette, believing that it contained marijuana. Had the cigarette actually contained marijuana, Ernie would have violated the law by smoking it. Although Ernie did not commit the completed crime of smoking marijuana, he will still be guilty of attempt to smoke marijuana, following the precedent of *Bierce*. (B) is incorrect because legal impossibility, which is a defense to attempt, covers only those situations in which what the defendant sets out to do would not actually be a crime, but defendant mistakenly believes that it is a crime. Both Ernie's case and the *Bierce* decision involve circumstances that a majority of courts deem to be factual impossibility, rather than legal impossibility. (A) is incorrect because the precedential value of a case is not determined by the fact that it relates to a different crime than is involved in a currently pending case. The principle for which *Bierce* stands (*i.e.,* impossibility due to a mistake about attendant circumstances is no defense to a charge of attempt) is applicable to all cases involving similar circumstances, regardless of the crime involved. Similarly, (D) is incorrect because the applicability of the *Bierce* principle to the instant case is not affected by the fact that the crime in *Bierce* was malum in se (*i.e.,* inherently evil, because it requires criminal intent to deprive someone of his interest in property), whereas smoking marijuana is malum prohibitum (*i.e.,* wrong only because it is prohibited by legislation).

Answer to Question 9

(B) Charlie has committed false pretenses because his misrepresentation concerning the contents of the cigarette induced Ernie to convey title to the counterfeit $50 bill. The offense of false pretenses consists of obtaining title to the property of another by an intentional (or knowing) false statement of past or existing fact, with intent to defraud the other. Charlie falsely represented to Ernie that the cigarette he gave him contained marijuana, intending that Ernie would rely upon such misrepresentation by paying money for the cigarette. Ernie, acting in reliance upon this misrepresentation, conveyed to Charlie title to the counterfeit $50 bill. Although the bill was counterfeit, it still constitutes property for purposes of a prosecution for false pretenses, because it is personal property capable of being possessed and having some value. Despite its counterfeit nature, the bill has value because its apparent genuineness allows its owner to pass it off as real money. Thus, all of the elements of false pretenses are present in Charlie's dealings with Ernie. Because Charlie has committed false pretenses, which is a theft offense, (D) is incorrect. (A) is incorrect because Charlie obtained title to the counterfeit bill rather than mere possession. If a victim consents to someone's taking possession of property, but such consent is induced by a misrepresentation, the consent is not valid. The resulting offense is larceny by trick. False pretenses differs from larceny by trick in what is obtained. If the victim intends to convey only possession of the property, the offense is larceny by trick. However, if the victim intends to convey title, the offense is false pretenses. Here, Ernie intended to convey title to the counterfeit bill, acting in reliance upon Charlie's false representation that the cigarette contained marijuana. Because Charlie obtained title, the offense of which he can be convicted is false pretenses rather than larceny by trick. (C) is incorrect because embezzlement consists of the fraudulent conversion of property of another by a person in lawful possession of that property. In embezzlement, misappropriation of the property occurs while the defendant has lawful possession of it. Here, Charlie did not convert the counterfeit bill while he was in lawful possession of it; rather, he obtained title to the bill by means of a misrepresentation. Because Charlie did not have lawful possession of the bill, he has not committed embezzlement.

Answer to Question 10

(C) The contents of the briefcase supplied probable cause to believe that Hippo was involved in the gambling operation, and thus, Hippo's arrest was lawful. A police officer may arrest a person without a warrant if she has reasonable grounds to believe that a felony has been committed and that the person before her committed it. The police had searched Rhino's house for gambling paraphernalia, pursuant to a search warrant. Having already found such paraphernalia in the house, and seeing still more in the briefcase, which was not previously present, the police had reasonable grounds to believe that the person who left the briefcase was involved in the gambling operation. When the officers found Hippo, who had not been present during the initial search of the first floor, they had reasonable grounds to believe that he had left the briefcase and was therefore involved in the commission of gambling offenses. Thus, the arrest of Hippo was lawful. (A) focuses on the propriety of the search that uncovered the heroin, rather than on the lawfulness of the arrest itself. Do not be sidetracked. The call of the question concerns the legality of the arrest. As has been explained above, Hippo's arrest is lawful and is based on grounds entirely independent of the legality of the subsequent search and seizure. Thus, (A) is incorrect. Although it is true that, as (B) states, Hippo's mere presence in the house did not give probable cause to believe he had committed a crime, his arrest was not based on his mere presence. As has been explained, reasonable grounds to believe that Hippo was part of the gambling operation arose from the presence of betting slips in the briefcase and the great likelihood that Hippo was the person who brought the briefcase into the house. Thus, (B) incorrectly states the basis for Hippo's arrest. Also, (B) incorrectly states that there was no basis to search Hippo, because he had not behaved threateningly. In fact, the police may conduct a search incident to a lawful arrest without actually fearing for their safety. Note also that this second part of (B), similarly to (A), incorrectly focuses on the search of Hippo, rather than on the arrest itself. (D) incorrectly asserts a right to search Hippo independent of any probable cause to arrest him. A search warrant does not authorize the police to search persons found on the premises who are not named in the warrant. However, if the police have probable cause to arrest a person discovered on the premises, they may search him incident to the arrest. Consequently, any right that the police had to search Hippo arose from their arrest of him, which was based on probable cause. (D) ignores the necessity of probable cause to arrest. Of course, (D) also attempts the same distraction as (A) and (B); *i.e.,* it focuses on the search of Hippo as a means of either justifying or attacking the arrest, rather than on the grounds for the arrest itself.

Answer to Question 11

(C) The heroin was discovered during a search incident to a lawful arrest and is admissible. A search warrant does not authorize the police to search persons found on the premises who are not named in the warrant. However, if the police have probable cause to arrest a person discovered on the premises, they may search him *incident to the arrest.* This search may be of the person and areas into which he might reach to obtain weapons or destroy evidence (his "wingspan"). Also, the police may make a protective sweep of the area beyond the defendant's wingspan if they believe accomplices may be present. The arrest of Hippo was lawful because the presence of the betting slips in the briefcase he brought into Rhino's house gave the police probable cause to believe that Hippo was involved in the illegal gambling being investigated. Because the arrest of Hippo was lawful, the police were entitled to conduct a search incident to that arrest. Such a search was permissible even though the police did not actually fear for their safety. Consequently, the heroin discovered as a result of this search is admissible, and the motion to suppress will be denied. (A) is incorrect because, although the warrant only authorized a search of the premises, this does not preclude the police from also searching persons found on the premises as to whom there exists probable cause to arrest. Once Hippo was lawfully arrested, the police were fully entitled to search him incident to the arrest. (B) is incorrect because, as has been explained earlier, the arrest of Hippo was lawful. Thus, the heroin cannot be suppressed as the product of an unlawful arrest. (D) is incorrect because the police may conduct a search incident to a lawful arrest regardless of a defendant's request for counsel. Even if Hippo had requested counsel before the patdown, the police could search him for weapons or evidence before getting him a public defender.

Answer to Question 12

(C) Pebbles is guilty of larceny for having taken the dice. However, the elements of burglary are not present. At common law, burglary consists of a breaking and entry of the dwelling of another at nighttime, with the intent of committing a felony therein. While perhaps Barney had the intent to commit the felony of statutory rape when he entered the garage, he did not commit a "breaking" because he had access to the garage at any time. Also, Pebbles and Barney entered Fred's garage and car during the daytime, rather than at night, and the garage and car are not "dwellings"; *i.e.,* structures regularly used for sleeping. From the foregoing, it follows that there was no burglary committed on these facts. Larceny is the taking and carrying away of tangible personal property of another by trespass with intent to permanently (or for an unreasonable time) deprive the person of his interest in the property. Pebbles took the dice belonging to Fred and put them in her purse. In doing so, Pebbles obtained control of the property and moved it without the consent of the person in possession of the property. Because Pebbles wanted to keep the dice as a "trophy," she had the intent to permanently deprive Fred of his property at the time of the taking. Thus, the requisite elements of larceny are present, and Pebbles is guilty of this crime. (A) is incorrect because, although Pebbles is guilty of larceny, Barney (as detailed above) is not guilty of burglary. (B) is similarly incorrect. (D) is incorrect because, although Barney is not guilty of either crime listed, Pebbles is guilty of larceny.

Answer to Question 13

(C) Landry cannot be convicted as an accomplice because he did not have the requisite intent for attempted murder. To be convicted as an accomplice under the prevailing rule, a person must have given aid, counsel, or encouragement with the ***intent*** to aid or encourage the principal in the commission of the crime charged. Mere knowledge that a crime would result from the aid provided is generally insufficient for accomplice liability. Here, Landry did not provide the tools to Morton with the intent that he kill Vorner. His knowledge that Morton might be intending harm to Vorner is not sufficient to establish the intent to kill required for attempted murder. (A) is wrong because even if Landry's conduct constituted reckless disregard of high risk to human life, that state of mind is not sufficient for attempted murder. Unlike murder, ***attempted*** murder is a specific intent crime and requires an intent to kill. (B) is incorrect. While Landry's attempt to neutralize his assistance would not have been enough to raise the defense of withdrawal if he had incurred liability as an accomplice, here he did not have the requisite intent for accomplice liability. (D) is an incorrect statement of law; the degree of liability of a principal is irrelevant to the potential liability of an accomplice. If Landry had had an intent to aid Morton in killing Vorner, the fact that Morton could show adequate provocation to reduce his offense to attempted voluntary manslaughter would have no effect on Landry's liability for attempted murder.

Answer to Question 14

(D) If the attendant cannot be prosecuted for manslaughter, it will be because he was privileged to use deadly force to apprehend a fleeing felon. A private person may use deadly force to apprehend a fleeing felon if the felon threatens death or serious bodily harm and deadly force is necessary to prevent her escape. Also, for a private person to use force to effect an arrest, the person harmed must actually be guilty of the felony for which the arrest was made; *i.e.,* it is not sufficient that it reasonably appeared that the person was guilty. Here, Betty and Carol actually committed the felony of robbery. Because they were armed with knives, Betty and Carol threatened death or serious bodily harm, and deadly force was necessary to prevent their escape. Thus, the newsstand attendant's best argument is that he had the right to use deadly force to apprehend them, and this serves as a defense to a charge of manslaughter. (A) is incorrect because acting with the intent to inflict serious bodily injury is a sufficient mens rea for voluntary manslaughter. Thus, the fact that the attendant intended only to inflict great bodily injury is no defense to manslaughter. (B) is incorrect because the existence of provocation is not a defense to manslaughter. Rather, provocation must be found to reduce a killing from murder to manslaughter. Thus, the fact that the attendant may have been provoked by the robbery would, if anything, provide a basis for a manslaughter prosecution, rather than a defense thereto. (C) is incorrect because deadly force may not lawfully be used merely to regain possession of property. Deadly force could only be justified by another basis of privilege such as to effectuate an arrest.

Answer to Question 15

(B) Liability for felony murder cannot be based upon the death of a co-felon from resistance by the victim or police pursuit. Under the felony murder doctrine, a killing committed during the course of a felony is murder, malice being implied from the intent to commit the underlying felony. However, under the majority view, liability for murder cannot be based on the death of a co-felon from resistance by the victim or police pursuit. Thus, because Carol's death resulted from an act by the attendant (the victim of the robbery), Betty will not be found guilty of the felony murder of Carol, a co-felon. (A) is incorrect because any desire (or lack of desire) by Betty to see her co-felon harmed is irrelevant to liability for felony murder. The only mens rea required is the intent to commit the underlying felony. Here, Betty had the intent to commit robbery, the underlying felony. From this intent, the malice required for murder is implied. (C) is incorrect because the fact that the felony was technically completed before Carol's death does not prevent the killing from being felony murder. A death caused while fleeing from the crime is considered to have been caused during the commission of the felony. (D) is incorrect because robbery is a felony regardless of the value of the property that is taken.

Answer to Question 16

(B) If Betty was insane and Carol was an undercover police officer, then Alice cannot be said to have conspired with them to commit the robbery. A conspiracy consists of: (i) an agreement between two or more persons; (ii) an intent to enter into an agreement; and (iii) an intent to achieve the objective of the agreement. The parties must agree to accomplish the same objective by mutual action. This agreement requires a meeting of at least two "guilty minds"; *i.e.,* two persons who are actually committing themselves to the scheme. If Betty was insane, then she lacked the capacity to intentionally enter into an agreement to rob the newsstand attendant and to intend to achieve the robbery. If Carol was an undercover police officer, then she did not intend to achieve the robbery, but was, rather, trying to prevent it. Under these circumstances, Alice was the only one who was actually committed to the holdup of the newsstand attendant and who intended to bring it about. Because there was no meeting of Alice's "guilty mind" with at least one other, Alice cannot be convicted of conspiracy under the common law rule. (A) is incorrect because a defendant can be tried and convicted of both conspiracy and the crime she commits pursuant to the conspiracy (here, robbery). (C) is incorrect because a conviction of conspiracy does not require that all parties be tried and convicted. While an *acquittal* of all persons with whom a person is alleged to have conspired precludes conviction of the remaining defendant, that is not the case here. Carol was not acquitted, and the facts do not indicate whether Betty will be acquitted. Also, note that a state's decision to discontinue prosecution would not be deemed to be an acquittal, and thus most likely a state's *inability* to prosecute because of a co-conspirator's death would not be an acquittal. (D) is incorrect for two reasons: (i) withdrawal from a conspiracy is not a defense to a charge of conspiracy, and (ii) withdrawal is a defense to *subsequent crimes* committed by other members of the conspiracy only if the withdrawing party performs an affirmative act notifying all members of the conspiracy in time for them to have the opportunity to abandon their plans. Here, Alice simply drove away, without notifying Betty or Carol that she was abandoning the plan. Therefore, Alice's actions in abandoning the conspiracy afford her no defense to either the conspiracy or the robbery committed pursuant thereto.

Answer to Question 17

(C) Wife could be convicted of assault and either attempted murder or attempted manslaughter. To be liable for either attempted murder or attempted manslaughter, defendant must have acted with the intent to kill and have committed an act beyond mere preparation for the offense. The fact that it is not possible to complete the intended offense (factual impossibility) is not a defense to liability for attempt. Here, Wife clearly intended to kill Secretary and did everything in her power to carry out the killing. The fact that the gun was not loaded is no defense. Choices (B) and (D) are wrong because Wife could also be convicted of assault. Assault is either: (i) an attempt to commit a battery; or (ii) the intentional creation (other than by mere words) of a reasonable apprehension in the mind of the victim of imminent bodily harm. Here, Wife has committed both types of assault: she attempted to commit a battery against Secretary and intentionally placed her in fear of imminent bodily harm. While she could not be convicted of the first type of assault if she were also convicted of attempted murder or attempted manslaughter (because that type of assault is a lesser-included offense that merges into the greater offense), she could be convicted of the second type of assault (it does not merge because it contains elements not encompassed by attempted murder or attempted manslaughter). Choice (A) is wrong because Wife could be convicted of attempted murder instead of attempted manslaughter if she cannot establish adequate provocation. An intentional killing can be reduced from murder to voluntary manslaughter if (i) there exists a provocation that would arouse sudden and intense passion in the mind of an ordinary person so as to cause her to lose self-control; (ii) the defendant in fact was provoked; (iii) there was insufficient time for the passions of a reasonable person to cool; and (iv) the defendant in fact did not cool off between the provocation and the killing. Many common law courts recognized the existence of provocation in only two instances: exposure to a threat of deadly force and discovery of one's spouse in bed with another person. Furthermore, some provocations, such as "mere words," were defined as inadequate provocation as a matter of law. Modern courts tend to be more reluctant to take such cases from juries and are more likely to submit to the jury the question of whether "mere words" or similar matters constitute adequate provocation. These principles apply in this case even though Wife's liability is only for attempted murder or manslaughter rather than the completed offense. Here, Wife's discovery of the love letter and nude photographs might be sufficient to make it a jury question as to whether adequate provocation existed. However, the jury might still conclude that the provocation was not sufficient and find Wife liable for attempted murder rather than attempted manslaughter.

Answer to Question 18

(C) Partnerdum and Partnerdee are guilty of conspiracy (along with Kriminal) to commit robbery and of felony murder. A conspiracy consists of: (i) an agreement between two or more persons; (ii) an intent to enter into an agreement; and (iii) an intent to achieve the objective of the agreement. Most states also require an act in furtherance of the conspiracy, although an act of mere preparation will suffice. Each conspirator is liable for the crimes of all other conspirators if: (i) the crimes were committed in furtherance of the objectives of the conspiracy; and (ii) the crimes were a natural and probable consequence of the conspiracy (*i.e.,* were foreseeable). Partnerdum,

Partnerdee, and Kriminal entered into an agreement to rob Fong. All three of these persons intended to enter into this agreement, and they intended to achieve the objective of the agreement (*i.e.,* to rob Fong). Kriminal's act of waiting by the store for Fong and attacking Lee would be sufficient overt acts. Thus, all the elements of conspiracy are satisfied, and Partnerdum and Partnerdee are guilty of conspiracy to commit robbery. A killing (even if accidental) committed during the course of a felony is murder. If, in the course of a conspiracy to commit a felony, a death is caused, all members of the conspiracy are liable for murder if the death was caused in furtherance of the conspiracy and was a foreseeable consequence of the conspiracy. Here, although there was to be no physical harm, and Kriminal mistook Lee for Fong, it was foreseeable that death would result from the commission of a dangerous felony such as robbery. Lee's death occurred in furtherance of the conspiracy to rob Fong. Because this death occurred in furtherance of the conspiracy and was a foreseeable consequence thereof, the other conspirators (Partnerdum and Partnerdee) are also liable for felony murder. Robbery was not committed here because there was no taking of personal property from Lee. Robbery consists of a taking of the personal property of another from the other's person or presence by force or intimidation with the intent to permanently deprive him of the property. Although Kriminal demanded Lee's money, the ensuing struggle prevented him from actually taking it. This would be attempted robbery, because Kriminal committed an act with the intention of committing robbery, but he fell short of completing the crime. However, this is not robbery. Therefore, (A) is incorrect because it fails to account for the fact that Partnerdum and Partnerdee are guilty of felony murder as well as conspiracy to commit robbery. (B) and (D) are incorrect because they would find Partnerdum and Partnerdee guilty of robbery, despite the fact that there was no taking of personal property. Also, (B) ignores the fact that Partnerdum and Partnerdee are guilty of felony murder.

Answer to Question 19

(B) Deirdre should be convicted of robbery but cannot also be convicted of larceny because larceny is a lesser included offense of robbery. Robbery consists of a taking of the personal property of another from the other's person or presence, by force or intimidation, with the intent to permanently deprive him of it. Deirdre took Vladimir's personal property (his wallet) from his person at gunpoint, intending to permanently deprive him of his property. Although Vladimir fainted, this taking was accomplished by force, because Deirdre's threat of shooting Vladimir precipitated his fainting. Thus, Deirdre can be convicted of robbery. Larceny consists of a taking and carrying away of the tangible personal property of another by trespass, with intent to permanently deprive the person of his interest in the property. Although Deirdre carried Vladimir's wallet only 10 feet before it slipped out of her pocket, this is a sufficient carrying away for purposes of larceny. Thus, Deirdre could be convicted of larceny. However, one may not be convicted of both a greater offense and a lesser included offense. A lesser included offense is one that consists entirely of some, but not all, elements of the greater crime. Larceny is a lesser included offense of robbery because larceny consists of all the elements of robbery except for force or intimidation. Indeed, robbery can be considered an aggravated form of larceny, in which the taking is accomplished by force or threat of force. Thus, Deirdre cannot be convicted of **both** larceny and robbery. Therefore, (C), which would allow conviction of both crimes, is wrong. (A) is wrong because it would preclude a conviction for robbery and, as has been explained, Deirdre can be convicted of robbery. (D) is wrong because Deirdre can be convicted of robbery.

Answer to Question 20

(D) John should be found guilty of attempted robbery because, with the specific intent to commit a robbery, John went beyond mere preparation for the offense, and having done so, abandonment is not a defense. A criminal attempt is an act that, although done with the intention of committing a crime, falls short of completing the crime. The defendant must have the intent to perform an act and obtain a result that, if achieved, would constitute a crime. Also, the defendant must have committed an act beyond mere preparation for the offense. If a defendant has, with the required intent, gone beyond preparation, the general rule is that abandonment is not a defense. Even in those jurisdictions in which abandonment is a defense, such abandonment must be: (i) fully voluntary and not made because of the difficulty of completing the crime or because of an increased risk of apprehension; and (ii) a complete abandonment of the plan made under circumstances manifesting a renunciation of criminal purpose, not just a decision to postpone committing it or to find another victim. Here, John intended to take money from the clerk at the market by means of the threat of having a gun (*i.e.,* by simulating a gun). Thus, John intended to commit a robbery. In walking up to the market counter while simulating a gun with his hand, John committed an act that was a substantial step toward commission of the intended crime, and that strongly corroborated his intent and purpose to commit the crime. All that was missing to complete the crime was for the clerk to turn around and, upon seeing John apparently armed, be forced to give up the money. Thus, John went far beyond mere preparation for the crime of robbery. Having gone beyond mere preparation, with the intent to commit robbery, John is guilty of attempted robbery. And, as explained above, even if John abandoned his plan when Sara entered the market, such abandonment will not afford him a defense. Even in those jurisdictions in which abandonment is a defense, John will not have a defense because his abandonment apparently occurred when Sara's sudden presence increased the risk of apprehension. Thus, the abandonment did not really manifest a renunciation of criminal purpose. (A) is incorrect because, to be guilty of attempted robbery, events need not have progressed to the point where the defendant has used or threatened to use force. Since John had the requisite intent for attempt and went beyond mere preparation by standing at the counter and simulating a gun, he should be found guilty of attempted robbery. (B) is incorrect because, as detailed above, abandonment of an attempt does not afford a defense, and in any event, John's abandonment here did not really come about by way of renouncing his criminal purpose. (C) is incorrect because a conviction of attempt does not require entry into a "zone of perpetration." Rather, a defendant (with the requisite intent) need only have committed an act beyond mere preparation. The Model Penal Code and most state criminal codes require that the act constitute a substantial step towards commission of the crime and strongly corroborate the actor's criminal purpose.

Answer to Question 21

(C) Because John only intended to use Sara's car briefly (to get to the bus station), he lacked the intent to permanently deprive Sara of the car. Larceny consists of a taking and carrying away of the tangible personal property of another by trespass, with intent to permanently (or for an unreasonable time) deprive the person of her interest in the property. If the defendant intends to deal with the property in a manner that involves a substantial risk of loss, this intent is sufficient for larceny. Although John wrongfully took and carried away Sara's car, he did not have the requisite intent for larceny. John intended only to use Sara's car as a means of getting to the bus station, where he would leave the car. Thus, John intended to use the car for a short time and to leave it in a public place, where it was likely to be easily and quickly recovered and restored to Sara. Therefore, John lacked the requisite intent for larceny. (B) is wrong because there is no indication that the circumstances of the escape were such that there existed a substantial risk of loss of the car. John was not going to drive the car a great distance, nor was he going to abandon it in some dangerous or obscure location. Admittedly, there may have been *some* risk of loss involved in John's use of the car. However, the risk was not so substantial as to indicate that John possessed the intent to deprive that is required for larceny. (A) is incorrect because the negligence of the owner of property does not constitute a defense to a charge of larceny. Although it may have been unwise for Sara to leave her car unlocked with the motor running, a taking of the car without her consent would still be wrongful. (D) is incorrect because the taking of property to aid in the commission of an inherently dangerous felony does not in and of itself constitute larceny. (D) implies the existence of a "felony larceny" rule, similar to felony murder. There is no such rule. Therefore, it must be shown that John possessed the requisite intent before he will be found guilty of larceny.

Answer to Question 22

(A) If Inez did not know that the substance was toxic, she did not have the state of mind necessary for murder. Ignorance or mistake as to a matter of fact will serve as a defense to a crime if it shows that the defendant did not have the state of mind required for the crime. Where the mistake is offered as a defense to a malice crime, the mistake must be reasonable; *i.e.,* it must be the type of mistake that a reasonable person might make under the circumstances. While the statute itself may create a strict liability offense, for which Inez's mistake as to the identity of the substance would not be a defense, Inez here is being charged with murder, which is a malice crime. For Inez to be convicted of murder, it must be shown that she had: (i) intent to kill; (ii) intent to inflict great bodily injury; (iii) reckless indifference to an unjustifiably high risk to human life; or (iv) intent to commit a felony. If she knew that the substance was toxic, the prosecution would have an argument that she acted with reckless indifference to an unjustifiably high risk to human life by not taking any action. However, if she did not know that the substance was toxic, her failure to act is far less likely to establish reckless indifference. In other words, Inez was operating under such ignorance as to a matter of fact that she did not have the requisite state of mind for murder. This would provide Inez with a defense. (B) is incorrect because it is not a defense to crime that a defendant was unaware that her acts were prohibited by the criminal law, or that the law compelled her to do something. Thus, even if Inez was unaware of the reporting law, such ignorance of the law is no defense. Furthermore, regardless of her awareness of the reporting law, Inez, as a safety inspector for ECW, may have owed a duty to Jason and other ECW employees to act to clean up toxic waste. For this reason as well, Inez's ignorance of the reporting law would not provide her with a strong argument. (C) does not provide a strong defense argument because the requirement of filing the reports on a specified form is a mere administrative detail. The fact that the forms were not yet available would not relieve Inez of her duty to report any known deposits of toxic waste or to otherwise act to safeguard ECW employees from such waste. (D) is incorrect because, even if it would have been impossible to clean up the waste deposit by the time Jason encountered it, an immediate report by Inez on the existence of the deposit would at least have resulted in warning ECW employees to stay away from the area, perhaps leading also to the cordoning off of the area.

Answer to Question 23

(C) Fred is not guilty of arson (since he acted under duress) and therefore he is not guilty of Smith's homicide. A person is not guilty of an offense, other than homicide, if he performs the otherwise criminal act under the threat of imminent infliction of death or great bodily harm and his perception of the threat is reasonable. Here, Fred set fire to the store because Abbott ordered him to do so or he would shoot Fred. Since Abbott had a gun, Fred's perception of Abbott's threat of imminent death or great bodily harm was reasonable. Therefore, Fred acted under duress and is not guilty of arson. If Fred is not guilty of arson, then he cannot be guilty of murder. Murder requires a mental state of malice aforethought (*i.e.,* an intent to kill or inflict great bodily harm, an awareness of an unjustifiably high risk to human life, or the intent to commit a felony). Here, the state's only basis for showing malice aforethought would be to use the felony murder doctrine. Under that doctrine, a killing, even an accidental one, that occurs during the course of a felony is murder. The only felony here is arson (which includes the burning of buildings other than dwellings in most jurisdictions), and since Fred is excused from criminal liability for that crime due to duress, he cannot be convicted of murder under the felony murder doctrine because he did not commit the underlying felony. Thus, (C) is correct and (A) is incorrect. (B) is incorrect because Fred did not commit either voluntary or involuntary manslaughter. Voluntary manslaughter is an intentional killing distinguishable from murder by the existence of adequate provocation. As explained above, Fred did not have the requisite intent for murder (malice aforethought) and thus he cannot be guilty of voluntary manslaughter. Nor is Fred guilty of involuntary manslaughter. Involuntary manslaughter consists of either criminal negligence or "unlawful act" manslaughter. Since Fred acted under duress, he was not criminally negligent nor was the burning a "malum in se" (inherently wrongful) act necessary for "unlawful act" manslaughter. Therefore, there is no basis to find Fred guilty of manslaughter. (D) is incorrect because one can be convicted of murder without intending to kill (*e.g.,* in the case of a felony murder). Thus, if Fred were guilty of arson, he could be found guilty of murder despite the fact that he did not intend to kill anyone.

Answer to Question 24

(A) Because the stop was at a fixed checkpoint, it was a legal stop. Border officials may stop an automobile at a fixed checkpoint inside the border to question the occupants even without a reasonable suspicion that the automobile contains persons who are illegally present in the United States. This is in contrast with roving patrols inside the United States border, which may stop an automobile to question the occupants only if the officer reasonably suspects that the automobile may contain persons who are illegally present in the United States. Because Aragon's car was stopped at a fixed checkpoint, the Border Patrol officers were entitled to stop the car to question Aragon and Benitez, even if the officers did not reasonably suspect that the car contained persons illegally present in the United States. (B) is incorrect because a random stop at a fixed checkpoint is legal. As explained above, reasonable suspicion of the presence of persons who are illegally in the United States is not required at a fixed checkpoint, and so the Border Patrol officers were entitled to make a random stop of the car. (C) is incorrect because, as explained, probable cause to stop a vehicle at a fixed checkpoint is not required. (D) is incorrect because a stop at a fixed checkpoint is permissible even if the checkpoint is not located particularly close to the border. In addition, 25 miles is, relatively speaking, not that far from the border.

Answer to Question 25

(A) The evidence is admissible because the search was valid. As explained in the answer to the preceding question, border officials may *stop* an automobile at a fixed checkpoint inside the border even without reasonable suspicion that the car contains persons whose presence in the United States is illegal. However, to conduct a *search* at a fixed checkpoint, border officials must meet the requirements of one of the exceptions to the warrant requirement, such as the automobile exception (which requires probable cause) or consent. The automobile exception comes into play when the police have probable cause to believe that the vehicle contains evidence of a crime. The statement of Aragon to the Border Patrol officers gave them probable cause to believe that the car contained evidence of a crime (*i.e.,* that Benitez had drugs on his person). Thus, the requirement for application of the automobile exception was present, providing validity for the warrantless search conducted by the Border Patrol. Because the search was valid, the evidence found on Benitez is admissible. Besides being an incorrect statement of law, (B) is incorrect because it focuses on Benitez's knowledge of the contents of the package. Whether Benitez knew that heroin (or some other illegal substance) was in the package is irrelevant to the admissibility of the heroin. Even assuming that Benitez knew of the contents, the search would not be valid unless there was probable cause for the search. (D) similarly links Benitez's knowledge of the package's contents to the admissibility of the evidence. As noted above, the admissibility of the evidence is dependent on the validity of the search that produced the evidence, rather than on the knowledge of the defendant as to the existence of the evidence. (C) is incorrect for three reasons: (i) due process does not prohibit granting of immunity to a more culpable defendant; (ii) there is no indication that immunity was even granted here (immunity from prosecution may be granted to compel a witness to answer questions. The facts merely state that Aragon was not arrested; this does not necessarily mean that he was granted immunity); and (iii) the call of the question relates to the admissibility of the evidence, and a grant of immunity does not relate to the question of the admissibility of the evidence found *on Benitez*; such admissibility is determined by the validity of the search of Benitez by the Border Patrol officers.

Answer to Question 26

(C) Droole should be convicted of burglary, which is a breaking and entry of the dwelling of another at nighttime, with the intent of committing a felony therein. After sundown, Droole broke into and entered Bob's house, intending at the time of entry to commit the felony of arson. Whether the arson was ever carried out by Droole is immaterial to the crime of burglary. What is important is Droole's intent at the time of entering the house. Thus, all of the elements of burglary are present. Arson is the malicious burning of the dwelling of another. Droole set out intending to burn Bob's house, but Frieda's testimony indicates that the burning that occurred was not caused by the gasoline that Droole poured on the floor of the basement. When a crime is defined to require not merely conduct but also a specified result of that conduct, the defendant's conduct must be the cause-in-fact of that result; *i.e.,* the result would not have occurred *but for* defendant's conduct. Here, the result (the burning) would have occurred regardless of defendant's conduct. Thus, it cannot be said that Droole committed arson. Nevertheless, Droole is guilty of attempted arson. An attempt is an act that, although done with the intention of committing a crime, falls short of completing the crime. Attempt requires a specific intent to commit the completed crime, as well as an act beyond mere preparation for the offense. Droole certainly had the specific intent to burn Bob's house, and his pouring the gasoline onto the floor of the basement was an act that went well beyond mere preparation for the crime of arson. It was only due to the fact that he had no means to ignite the gasoline that Droole did not actually set fire to the house. Consequently, the elements for a conviction of attempted arson are present. (A) is incorrect because Droole should be convicted of attempted arson *as well as* burglary. (B) is incorrect because Droole fell short of completing the crime of arson. (D) is incorrect because the crime of burglary was completed at the time of entry. Thus, there was not merely an *attempted* burglary.

Answer to Question 27

(B) Regarding burglary, the analysis set forth in the preceding question applies here as well. Thus, Droole should be convicted of burglary because he broke into and entered Bob's house after dark with the intent to commit the felony of arson. Regarding arson, the testimony of Frieda on which this question is based requires a causation analysis. Problems of proximate causation arise only when the harmful result that is an element of the crime occurs because of the defendant's acts, but in a manner not intended or anticipated by the defendant. The general rule is that a defendant is responsible for all events that occur as a natural and probable consequence of his conduct, even if he did not anticipate the precise manner in which they would occur. Droole did not actually ignite the fire that burned Bob's house. However, according to Frieda's testimony, there would have been no significant fire damage but for the fact that Droole poured gasoline on the basement floor. Thus, Droole's conduct was the cause-in-fact of the burning of Bob's house. In acting as he did, Droole intended to bring about the burning of Bob's house, and such burning was within the scope of risk created by his conduct. Although the burning actually occurred in a manner that was unanticipated by Droole, such burning was a natural and probable consequence of Droole's pouring the gasoline, and the harm that resulted is the type that was likely to occur from Droole's actions. Therefore, the burning of Bob's house was proximately caused by Droole. Having caused the burning of Bob's house, with the intent that the house burn, Droole is guilty of arson. (A) is incorrect because as detailed above, Droole is guilty of burglary *and* arson, rather than just burglary. (C) is incorrect because Droole should be convicted of the completed crime of arson, rather than simply attempted arson. (D) is incorrect for the same reason, as well as for the reason that Droole has committed the completed crime of burglary, not just attempted burglary.

Answer to Question 28

(C)   Dupre's testimony makes it more likely than not that he did not intend to kill or inflict great bodily injury to a human being, thus negating the malice aforethought required for murder. The events here take place during the first stage of the bifurcated trial process. During this stage, there is a determination of the defendant's guilt; *i.e.,* did the defendant perform a criminal act with the requisite mental state? Dupre is on trial for murder. Murder is the unlawful killing of a human being with malice aforethought. Malice aforethought exists if the defendant has any of the following states of mind: (i) intent to kill; (ii) intent to inflict great bodily injury; (iii) awareness of an unjustifiably high risk to human life; or (iv) intent to commit a felony. Thus, at this first stage of the bifurcated process, it must be determined whether Dupre shot Vellum with malice aforethought, thus causing the death. Although the bifurcated trial process is designed to separate, as much as possible, the issues of a defendant's guilt and his sanity, Dupre's testimony is being offered not as evidence of his insanity, but rather as evidence that, because he believed he was shooting at a tiger, he did not have the intent to kill or inflict great bodily injury to a human being. The distinction may be somewhat fine, but the modern trend in criminal law, which we are told is followed by Massahampshire, views such evidence as admissible on the issue of intent. Because Dupre's testimony tends to show that, at the time of shooting Vellum, he did not have the requisite mens rea for murder, such testimony is admissible in the "guilt" phase of the bifurcated trial process, and the prosecution's motion to strike the testimony is denied. (A) is incorrect because, as has been explained, Dupre's purported delusions are relevant to the first phase of the trial, as well as the second, because they relate to his malice aforethought, or lack thereof. (B) is incorrect because the judge's opinion as to whether a witness is lying does not determine the admissibility of the witness's testimony (but will affect the weight to be given that testimony if the judge is the trier of fact). Dupre's testimony is relevant to his mens rea and is thus admissible even if the judge believes that Dupre is lying. (D) is incorrect because the testimony is not relevant to his conduct, in that it does not make more or less probable anything concerning the conduct itself. It is apparently undisputed that Dupre shot Vellum. At issue is the existence of intent on the part of Dupre at the time of the shooting. It is to this matter that Dupre's testimony is relevant.

Answer to Question 29

(D)   Although a waiver of the right to counsel will be carefully scrutinized to ensure that the defendant has a rational and factual understanding of the proceeding against him, a defendant has an absolute right to waive counsel and represent himself. The waiver must be knowing and intelligent, and the defendant need not be found capable of representing himself effectively—the defendant's ability to represent himself has no bearing on his competence to choose self-representation. Where the state provides counsel in cases of indigence, it may then seek reimbursement from a convicted defendant who subsequently becomes able to pay. Although the facts give no indication as to Dolph's competence to represent himself, it does appear that his desire to represent himself was based on full information as to the various ramifications of proceeding either pro se or with counsel. Therefore, Dolph's waiver of counsel was knowing and intelligent, and the judge was bound to honor the waiver. Violation of Dolph's right to represent himself will result in a reversal of Dolph's conviction. Although, as stated above, the state may recoup costs of appointed counsel from indigents who become able to pay, the state cannot recover from Dolph the costs of an attorney who was appointed against Dolph's will and in violation of his right to represent himself. Had effect been given to Dolph's right to represent himself, there would have been no attorney's fees to be assessed against him. (A) is incorrect because the denial of Dolph's right to represent himself does constitute reversible error, regardless of the competence with which List represented him. Also, as explained above, the state's right to recoup costs from indigents who become able to pay does not extend to those defendants who have had appointed counsel imposed on them against their will. (B) is incorrect because it states that the conviction involved no reversible error, when denial of Dolph's right to represent himself is reversible error. (B) also incorrectly states that the imposition of fees should be reversed because Dolph could have gotten probation for himself as easily as List did. There is no way to know that Dolph could have gotten probation for himself as easily as List did, and it is not really at issue whether Dolph could have done so. What is at issue is that the costs were imposed as part of an unconstitutional forced representation by appointed counsel. Thus, even if List obtained probation for Dolph when Dolph would have been unable to do so, the costs should be reversed, because Dolph should have been free to proceed pro se, even if this meant risking imprisonment. Similarly, (C) is incorrect because it states that List's competence is a reason for affirming the imposition of fees. As stated above, Dolph had the right to proceed pro se if his decision was knowing and intelligent, regardless of the fact that appointed counsel may have been highly competent. The state cannot force Dolph to forgo a constitutionally protected right by accepting appointed counsel, and then further force him to pay for such counsel.

Answer to Question 30

(C) Because Hugh believed the coat to be his own, he lacked the intent to commit larceny. Larceny consists of a taking and carrying away of the tangible property of another by trespass, with the intent to permanently deprive the person of his interest in the property. The intent to deprive the owner of his property generally must exist at the time of the taking (except for the continuing trespass situation; *see* below). Here, Hugh took and carried away a coat belonging to another. But when he took it, Hugh believed that the coat was actually his own coat. Thus, Hugh did not take the coat with the intent to permanently deprive the owner of his property. Absent this intent, Hugh cannot be guilty of larceny. (A) is incorrect because although Hugh did not actually destroy the coat himself, he could still be guilty of larceny. As mentioned, larceny requires the intent to permanently deprive the owner of the property. This intent includes intentionally dealing with property in such a way as to create a substantial risk of loss. Thus, even if Hugh did not destroy the property himself, if he dealt with it in a way as to risk its destruction, he could still be guilty of larceny, and so this is not the best reason for his acquittal. (B) is incorrect because the reasonableness of the mistake is not relevant. The test for whether a defendant has the intent for larceny is a subjective one—what this defendant intended. Thus, even if the mistake was reasonable, if Hugh knew the coat was not his, he could still be guilty of larceny. (D) is incorrect because it attempts to negate the continuing trespass situation, which is not applicable here. Under the continuing trespass theory, if a defendant *wrongfully* (*i.e.,* with a "bad" mental state) takes the personal property of another *without* the intent to permanently deprive the owner, but later, while still in possession of the property, he decides to keep it, he is guilty of larceny. This theory does not apply here because Hugh's taking of the coat was not wrongful. Thus, it is irrelevant that he was trying to return the coat; even if he had decided to keep it, he would not be guilty of larceny, although he would be guilty of some other crime. Therefore, (D) is not the best reason for Hugh's acquittal because it raises irrelevant issues.

Answer to Question 31

(D) Frederick never had the required mental state for conspiracy. Conspiracy requires three elements: (i) an agreement between two or more persons; (ii) an intent to enter into an agreement (which is often inferred from the act of agreement); and (iii) an intent to achieve the objective of the agreement. The two intent elements indicate that conspiracy is a specific intent crime. A defendant must have had both intents to be found guilty. Here, since Frederick planned to contact the police before Asher could commit the crime, he never intended to achieve the criminal objective of robbing the bank. Thus, he cannot be found guilty of conspiracy. (A) is incorrect because Frederick never entered into the conspiracy to begin with (because he lacked the requisite intent); thus, he did not need to withdraw. (B) is incorrect because merely providing the instrumentality to commit the crime is insufficient by itself to establish liability for conspiracy; there must also be some intent to facilitate the crime. The facts show that Frederick *never intended* to commit the crime, and thus he cannot be guilty of conspiracy. (C) is incorrect because, as stated above, Frederick never entered into the conspiracy. If he had, (C) would still be incorrect because at common law and in most states withdrawal is not a defense to the conspiracy charge itself, merely a limitation on liability for the subsequent acts of the co-conspirators.

Answer to Question 32

(C) Frederick lacked the requisite intent to be liable as either an accomplice to the robbery or as a conspirator with Asher; thus, he cannot be convicted of the death of the security guard. A defendant may, by virtue of his aid, counsel, or encouragement of the principal who commits the crime, be liable as an accomplice for the crime that he assisted the principal to commit, as well as other crimes that were probable or foreseeable. In addition, each conspirator is liable for the crimes of all other conspirators if the crimes were committed in furtherance of objectives of the conspiracy and were a natural and probable consequence of the conspiracy (*i.e.,* foreseeable). Here, Asher would have been liable for the death of the security guard since it occurred during the course of an armed robbery. Thus, Frederick would be liable if he were an accomplice or co-conspirator. However, Frederick is not a co-conspirator because he lacked the requisite intent for conspiracy (as discussed in the previous question). He also lacked the intent required for accomplice liability, which requires providing aid with the intent to see the crime committed. Although Frederick provided the car to allow Asher to commit the robbery, he planned to have the police at the bank to prevent the crime from being committed. Hence, he provided the car without the necessary intent. (A) is incorrect because merely providing the assistance is not enough. Frederick must also have had the requisite intent. Here, he lacked the intent to be liable as an accomplice. (B) is incorrect because foreseeability suggests a mental state of negligence for accessory liability. While it may have been negligent for Frederick to leave the keys in the ignition, he was still acting with an intent to prevent the crime from being committed rather than to facilitate its commission. Thus, he did not have the mental state for conspiracy or accomplice liability, and cannot be convicted for the guard's death. (D) is incorrect. It is true that Frederick's attempt to notify the police probably would have been an effective withdrawal for accomplice liability (even though it did not neutralize the assistance he provided) and for a co-conspirator's liability for the subsequent crimes of the other members. But since Frederick never had the intent required for any type of culpable participation in the crime, the court would not be required to consider Frederick's defense of withdrawal.

Answer to Question 33

(D) Harfo can be charged with theft, conspiracy, and robbery. The facts clearly show that Harfo is guilty of the theft of the car that was to be used for the getaway. Conspiracy requires: (i) an agreement between two or more persons; (ii) an intent to enter into the agreement; and (iii) an intent to achieve the objective of the agreement. Most states also require an overt act in furtherance of the conspiracy. Harfo conspired to commit robbery, because he entered into an agreement with Groufo and Chifo to rob the bank, intending both to enter into such an agreement and to achieve the objective thereof. Harfo's theft of the car constituted an overt act in furtherance of the conspiracy. Thus, Harfo can be charged with conspiracy. Each member of a conspiracy is liable for the crimes of all other conspirators if: (i) such crimes were committed in furtherance of the objectives of the conspiracy; and (ii) such crimes were a natural and probable consequence of the conspiracy. A conspirator may **_limit his liability for subsequent acts_** of the other members of the conspiracy **_if he withdraws_** from the conspiracy by performing an affirmative act that notifies all members of the conspiracy in time for them to have the opportunity to abandon their plans. However, withdrawal is not a defense to a charge of conspiracy. Harfo's absence from the robbery scene with the getaway car was due to his sudden illness, rather than any voluntary decision on his part to withdraw from the conspiracy. Having failed to make a legally effective withdrawal from the conspiracy, Harfo continued to be liable for any crimes committed by Groufo and/or Chifo that were in furtherance of the conspiracy and were foreseeable consequences of the conspiracy. The facts state that Groufo and Chifo robbed the bank. Certainly, the robbery of the bank, which was the sole object of the conspiracy, was a crime committed in furtherance of the conspiracy's objectives and was a natural and probable consequence of the conspiracy. Therefore, Harfo is liable for this robbery committed by his co-conspirators. Because Harfo can properly be charged with all three crimes, (A), (B), and (C) are incorrect.

Answer to Question 34

(D) If Archie did not believe that Edith's complaints indicated a serious medical problem, he did not have the mental state required for murder. Murder is the unlawful killing of a human being with malice aforethought. Malice aforethought is present if the defendant acts with: (i) intent to kill; (ii) intent to inflict great bodily injury; (iii) reckless indifference to an unjustifiably high risk to human life; or (iv) intent to commit a felony. Assuming that, as stated in (D), Archie did not believe that Edith's complaints of abdominal pain were indicative of a serious medical problem, it cannot be said that in bypassing the Crow City emergency facility Archie acted with the intent to kill or seriously injure Edith, or that he even acted with reckless indifference to a high risk to Edith's life. If Archie did not believe there was a serious medical problem, he could not have thought he was placing Edith in great danger of death by driving on to Dry Gulch. Under such circumstances, Archie lacked the mens rea required to sustain a murder conviction. (A) refers to the matter of whether Archie had a duty to assist Edith in her distress. A defendant's failure to act will not result in criminal liability unless the defendant has a legal duty to act under the circumstances. Such a duty may exist where there is a sufficiently close relationship between the defendant and the victim; *e.g.,* a spouse has a duty to prevent harm to his or her spouse. Even if Archie and Edith were not legally married, the fact that they had lived together for many years as if they were married indicates that they were in a relationship of such a close nature as to give rise to a duty to act to prevent harm to each other. Thus, the facts set forth in (A) will not be helpful to Archie. Regarding (B), a defendant is responsible for all results that occur as a natural and probable consequence of his conduct, even if he did not anticipate the precise manner in which they would occur. All such results are proximately caused by the defendant's act, and the chain of causation is broken only by a superseding factor. An intervening act will shield the defendant from liability if the act is a mere coincidence or is outside the foreseeable sphere of risk created by the defendant's conduct. Negligent medical care is a foreseeable risk. Being injured or even dying due to incompetent medical care was a risk to which Archie exposed Edith when he refused to stop at Crow City, thereby exacerbating an already serious situation. Although Archie may not have anticipated that Edith would die because of Dr. Holiday's incompetence, Edith's death was a natural and probable consequence of Archie's refusal to stop at Crow City. Thus, the additional fact of Dr. Holiday's incompetent treatment of Edith does not establish any defense for Archie. (C) is incorrect because an act that hastens an inevitable result is still considered a legal cause of that result. Although it may be true that Edith would have died of cancer within a relatively short time, Archie's failure to get her proper care as quickly as possible actually caused her death.

Answer to Question 35

(D) Norma Kay cannot be tried with Byron for the exploitation offense. If a statute is intended to protect members of a limited class from exploitation or overbearing, members of that class are presumed to have been intended to be immune from liability, even if they participate in the crime in a manner that would otherwise make them liable. While the facts do not specify what conduct constitutes exploitation of a minor for sexual purposes, Byron's conduct undoubtedly qualifies. He can be charged as a principal, because he actually engaged in the act that caused the criminal result by making and selling films of Norma Kay engaging in sexually explicit acts with him and another person. Norma Kay cannot be deemed a principal, as she did not actually exploit a minor. (A) is therefore incorrect. The prosecution probably would seek to try her as an accomplice. An accomplice is one who aids, counsels, or encourages the principal before or during the commission of the crime, with the intent that the crime be committed. It is true that Norma Kay aided and encouraged Byron both before and during his commission of the crime of exploitation by willingly cooperating with him in the making of the films and helping with their distribution. However, the statute regarding exploitation of a minor is intended to protect minors from the type of actions engaged in by Byron. As a member of the class to be protected by the statute, Norma Kay is presumed to be immune from liability under the statute, despite the fact that she participated in the crime in a manner that would otherwise render her liable as an accomplice. Thus, (C) is incorrect because Norma Kay is not subject to conviction as an accomplice. Regarding (B), an accessory after the fact is one who receives, relieves, comforts, or assists another knowing that he has committed a felony, in order to help the felon escape arrest, trial, or conviction. Norma Kay has not assisted Byron in an effort to escape, nor has she harbored him. The simple refusal to testify against Byron does not render Norma Kay an accessory after the fact. Consequently, (B) is incorrect.

Answer to Question 36

(D) Sherri is most likely to be found not guilty of larceny because she did not have the intent to permanently (or for an unreasonable time) deprive her neighbor of his interest in the Cadillac. Larceny consists of a taking and carrying away of tangible personal property of another by trespass, with intent to permanently (or for an unreasonable time) deprive the person of his interest in the property. The intent to permanently deprive must exist at the moment of the taking. If the defendant intended to return the property within a reasonable time, and at the time of the taking had a substantial ability to do so, the unauthorized borrowing is not larceny. If, however, the defendant intended to deal with the property in a manner that involved a substantial risk of loss, this is sufficient for larceny. In (D), Sherri did not intend to permanently deprive her neighbor of his interest in the Cadillac. Rather, she intended to return it at the end of the workday, and had no intention of dealing with it in a manner that involved a substantial risk of loss. This intent to borrow and to return the car within a reasonable time is insufficient to support a charge of larceny. Thus, Sherri will be found not guilty. (A) is incorrect because Jack, at the time of taking and riding away on a bicycle belonging to another, intended to sell it. Thus, Jack committed the requisite acts, with the intent to permanently deprive, so as to be guilty of larceny. (B) is incorrect, because it is an example of larceny by trick. Larceny requires that the taking be trespassory. In (B), the owner of the backpack and frame consented to Jill's taking them. However, if the victim consents to the defendant's taking possession of the property, but this consent has been induced by a misrepresentation, the consent is not valid. The resulting larceny is called larceny by trick. Jill misrepresented to her acquaintance that she merely wanted to borrow the items, but actually intended to keep them when she left for Afghanistan. Because the victim's consent was induced by this misrepresentation, such consent is not valid. Therefore, Jill's taking was wrongful, and she is guilty of larceny. (C) is incorrect because larceny can be committed even against someone who has previously stolen the property from the true owner. Larceny is a crime against possession, so it is only necessary that the person from whom the property is taken have a possessory interest in the property superior to that of the defendant. Although the accountant from whose apartment Reginald took the money had embezzled the cash, the accountant had possession of the money and thus had a possessory interest in it that was superior to that of Reginald. Consequently, Reginald's taking of the cash, accompanied by the requisite intent to deprive, constitutes larceny.

Answer to Question 37

(C) Willie is guilty of larceny only. Larceny is the taking and carrying away of the tangible personal property of another by trespass, with the intent to permanently deprive the person of his interest in the property. Under the continuing trespass doctrine, if a defendant takes property with a wrongful state of mind but without the intent to steal, and later, while still in possession of it, forms the intent to steal it, the trespass involved in the initial wrongful taking is regarded as "continuing" and the defendant is guilty of larceny. Here, Willie's initial wrongful taking continued to the time Willie intentionally destroyed the car, thereby permanently depriving the owner of possession. Therefore, Willie committed larceny and (A) is incorrect. Burglary requires the breaking and entering of the dwelling of another at nighttime with the intent to commit a felony therein. Willie is not guilty of burglary because, when he entered the attached garage, he did not intend to commit a felony therein; he merely intended to borrow the car. Thus, (B) and (D) are incorrect.

Answer to Question 38

(B) If a person recklessly causes the death of another, the crime is manslaughter. If a person causes the death of another under circumstances that show a "wicked or depraved heart," reckless indifference to a very high risk of death or serious injury, the crime is murder. While it would be a judgment for the jury as to how to characterize the behavior in (B), manslaughter is the probable crime. (B) is therefore correct because (A), (C), and (D) would clearly be murder. (A) is incorrect because hitting someone over the head with a lead pipe demonstrates an intent to inflict great bodily injury, and that is enough to satisfy the malice aforethought requirement for murder. Dropping a brick from a tall building into a crowd demonstrates that Defendant acted in the face of an unusually high risk that his conduct would cause death or serious bodily injury. Thus, malice aforethought is implied, and (C) is incorrect. (D) is incorrect because malice aforethought can also be implied from an intent to commit a felony.

Answer to Question 39

(C) Persons temporarily detained for routine traffic stops are not in custody for *Miranda* purposes. Therefore, Diane was not entitled to *Miranda* warnings, and her statement about the marijuana was not tainted. Her statement thus properly provided the probable cause for the search of her purse. (A) is therefore wrong. (B) is wrong because this case falls within the automobile exception to the warrant requirement. (D) states the test for a stop, not a search. An automobile search requires probable cause.

Answer to Question 40

(D) Crandall stole the gun; thus, he is guilty of larceny of the gun. Since he agreed with Axle and Bowers to burglarize King's home, he is guilty of conspiracy. And since Crandall never communicated a withdrawal from the conspiracy to either Axle or Bowers, he would be vicariously liable for the attempted burglary of King's home. (A), (B), and (C) are therefore incorrect.

Answer to Question 41

(B) Since Deal was aware of the fact that he might experience a seizure while driving, his actions constituted criminal negligence (also called recklessness), which is a sufficient state of mind for the crime of involuntary manslaughter. (A) is an incorrect statement of the law. (C) is incorrect because he voluntarily drove knowing that he might experience a seizure, which is sufficient for involuntary manslaughter. (D) is incorrect because the state of mind for involuntary manslaughter can be established by criminal negligence.

Answer to Question 42

(C) Under the statute, Trout could not be convicted of burglary unless she actually intended to commit a crime when she entered Print's home. Since what she intended to do was not a crime, there can be no burglary, even though she thought she was committing a criminal act. (A) and (B) are therefore incorrect. (D) is incorrect because she had "broken" and "entered," which, except for the mental element, is all that is required to complete the crime.

Answer to Question 43

(C) The United States Supreme Court held, in *Roberts v. United States* (1980), that a defendant's refusal to cooperate with an investigation of the criminal conspiracy of which he was a member may properly be considered in imposing sentence because the Fifth Amendment right to silence does not afford a privilege to refuse to incriminate others.

Answer to Question 44

(D) Battery is a general intent crime which may be committed recklessly or with criminal negligence. In (D), Dale's act was involuntary, thus negating criminal liability. (A) might result in a battery conviction. If Dale was reasonable in his belief that he was under attack, he would have the defense of self-defense. If he was unreasonable in that belief, he would be guilty of battery. It would be a jury question as to whether his belief was reasonable or unreasonable. (B) might result in a battery conviction. It is not clear whether Dale was actually placed under hypnosis, and even if he was, some courts do not accept that as a defense. (C) might result in a battery conviction. A jury could find that Dale recklessly struck Viola.

Answer to Question 45

(B) Mark acted in self-defense in response to Homer's deadly attack. This is not affected by the fact that Mark was a trespasser or that Homer was enraged by Mark's negligence. (D) is a correct statement of the law but is irrelevant to Mark's guilt.

Answer to Question 46

(D) Although the statute does not clearly indicate what state of mind is required, the statute appears to be a larceny-type offense. Larceny requires a specific intent to steal. Therefore, if Hiker honestly believed that the sign was abandoned property, he did not have the intent to steal and so will be found not guilty. (A) and (B) are wrong because a statute that closely resembles a traditional common law offense requiring mens rea is seldom held to be a strict liability offense; rather, it is interpreted to require the mens rea of the common law crime. (C) is incorrect because, even if the state had taken those steps, Hiker would not be guilty if he honestly believed that the sign had been abandoned. A mistake of fact need not be reasonable when offered as a defense to a specific intent crime.

Answer to Question 47

(C) Nick will most likely be found not guilty. A person is justified in using deadly force in self-defense when he reasonably believes that it is necessary to prevent the use of unlawful deadly force against him. It seems clear from the facts that Nick has killed in self-defense. Even if striking Jim with the chair were seen as the use of deadly force, it could be justified as a necessary response to Jim's use of deadly force. (A) is wrong because the majority rule is that there is no duty to retreat before using deadly force in self-defense against an initial aggressor threatening deadly force. (B) and (D) are incorrect. Regardless of whether Nick had a right to be on the premises, he was entitled to defend himself against the use of unlawful deadly force. One cannot use deadly force against a trespasser in one's dwelling unless the trespasser poses a threat to a person.

Answer to Question 48

(B) Robbery is the taking and carrying away of the personal property of another from the other's person or presence by force or intimidation. In (A), (C), and (D), a jury could find the defendant guilty of robbery because there are facts to prove each element of the crime. In (B), however, a conviction for robbery is unlikely. The taking of the property was not by force or intimidation; the crime was already completed when Ericson slapped the victim.

Answer to Question 49

(D) The crime of attempt is a specific intent crime, requiring the specific intent to carry out the crime in question. Since Drury did not know that vandals had smashed his taillights, he never intended to drive an automobile at night without functioning taillights. (A) is incorrect because Drury did not attempt to drive the automobile at the instigation of the police. (B) is incorrect because legal impossibility is not applicable to these facts. (C) is incorrect because factual impossibility is not a good defense to a charge of attempt.

Answer to Question 50

(C) A search warrant must be based on probable cause. Here, there was sufficient information for a judge to conclude that there was probable cause to believe that evidence of a crime would be found in Jackson's room. Thus, the warrant was properly obtained. (A) is wrong because Jackson had no reasonable expectation of privacy in a dormitory's lounge. Also, even if his privacy had been invaded, any invasion here was done by private persons, not the state, and thus would not prevent introduction of the evidence. (B) is wrong because it is untrue as a matter of law. (D) is wrong because it is not a sufficient basis to deny Jackson's motion. It is irrelevant that Prex acted on behalf of the college population.

Answer to Question 51

(D) The statutes define assault as "an attempt to commit a battery." Attempt requires the specific intent to commit the crime. There is no indication that Mary had such intent; therefore, (D) is the best answer.

Answer to Question 52

(C) Anne clearly committed a battery; therefore, (D) is wrong. The question is whether it was justified. Since she is permitted to use nondeadly force when she reasonably believes it is necessary to avoid the danger of harm from an aggressor, and the facts indicate this was her position, the best answer is (C). (A) is wrong because the pushing was justified. (B) is wrong because even if Mary did not intend to assault Anne, Anne could use reasonable nondeadly force if she reasonably believed she was under attack.

Answer to Question 53

(D) Larceny is the taking and carrying away of the personal property of another with the intent to permanently deprive the other of his interest in the property. Defendant's mistake is as to the coverage of the criminal law, and this would not be an excuse to the crime of larceny. (A) is wrong because Defendant clearly did not intend to steal another's property. (B) is wrong because Defendant's intent to obtain repayment of a debt does not satisfy the intent required for larceny. (C) is wrong because the intent to "permanently deprive" did not exist.

Answer to Question 54

(D) Johnny's expectation of privacy extended only to his own home, which was searched under a warrant. Johnny does not have standing to assert a Fourth Amendment claim regarding the search of Mildred's apartment because Mildred's apartment was not Johnny's home, and Johnny did not own it or have a right to possession of it. Thus, (A) is incorrect. Since Johnny cannot object to the search that provided the probable cause for the search of his apartment, (B) is also incorrect. (C) is not a valid justification because there is nothing to indicate that the seizure would fall under the "inevitable discovery" exception to the exclusionary rule.

Answer to Question 55

(B) Robbery requires an intent to permanently deprive the victim of her property. An intent to recover property that the defendant believes is his would not be a sufficient intent. The prosecution must prove every element of the crime beyond a reasonable doubt, and putting the burden of persuasion to show an innocent intent on the defendant would deprive him of due process of law, since it would relieve the prosecution of its burden to show the required intent for robbery. (A) and (C) are wrong. The defendant does not carry any burden of proof with respect to an element of the crime. The burden is on the prosecution to prove each element beyond a reasonable doubt.

Answer to Question 56

(B) Hal had an expectation of privacy with respect to the room he rented from Nan, and the police had no reason to believe that Nan was authorized to invade his privacy. (C) is wrong because although Nan, as the owner of the building, may have had limited rights to inspect a boarder's room, it cannot be said that she is authorized, at the instructions of the police, to go through the private property of her boarders. (D) is wrong because Nan's testimony concerning a "suspicious odor" would not be sufficient to uphold a search warrant. (A) is wrong; there is no such rule of law.

Answer to Question 57

(C) Common law burglary was the breaking and entering of the dwelling house of another in the nighttime with the intent to commit a larceny or other felony inside. In (C) the defendant would be guilty of burglary. Opening a closed door was enough for a "breaking," and since the defendant used a key, clearly a closed door was opened. (A) is incorrect because the dwelling place must be the dwelling place of someone other than the party breaking into it. (B) is wrong because at common law, the breaking had to be done at nighttime, and the mail carrier is working during the day. (D) is wrong because the place broken into had to be a dwelling at common law.

Answer to Question 58

(C) The note only outlined a proposal. Gene made no agreement with Ray, nor, technically, did the note make an "offer" to Bart since it did not state that he wanted Bart to participate in any plan. (A) is wrong; it is no defense to a conspiracy charge that the agreement did not specify the details of the projected criminal activity. (B) is wrong; if Ray had contacted Gene and agreed to participate in the plan, a conspiracy would have been committed in spite of the fact that they had not known each other before. (D) is wrong; the crime of conspiracy requires only the commission of an unlawful act, not that the parties accomplish the intended purpose of the conspiracy. Besides, although they were unsuccessful in their plan to steal the fur coats, they did assault, and maybe batter, Larry.

Answer to Question 59

(D) The facts of this question assume that Gene and Ray agreed to steal the furs. At that moment, Gene is guilty of a conspiracy, and his later conduct has no effect on his guilt of conspiracy. (A) is wrong; even in jurisdictions where an overt act is required, any of the co-conspirators may commit it. (B) is wrong; his decision was made after he entered into the conspiracy. (C) is wrong; if there was a conspiracy, Gene is guilty at the time the parties agree to the unlawful act. The fact that the unlawful act was attempted is evidence only of the intent of the conspiracy, not of the fact.

Answer to Question 60

(C) If Gene agreed to steal the furs, the plan he agreed to did not involve assaulting Larry. He planned to steal the furs at night, "when no one was around." Therefore, he cannot be held liable for this subsequent offense merely by virtue of his membership in a conspiracy; the offense must be a reasonably foreseeable result of the conspiracy, and here assault and battery were not foreseeable. (A) is wrong because his withdrawal would have had to have been communicated to Ginger or Ray to be effective. (B) is wrong because a co-conspirator is liable for reasonably foreseeable crimes committed by co-conspirators in furtherance of the conspiracy. It is not necessary that Gene actually be present or know about the crime; if the crime is foreseeable, he is liable. (D) is irrelevant.

Answer to Question 61

(A) Even though Gene may not have contemplated robbery, Ginger and Ray did. They could be guilty of attempted robbery because they had the intent to commit that crime and a jury would find they came close to completing it. Conspiracy does not merge with an attempt charge; thus, the defendants can be found guilty of both crimes. (B) is wrong; this is a misstatement of law.

(C) is wrong; even if it is arguable that Gene did not intend to rob Larry, Ginger and Ray did. The fact that Gene may not be guilty of conspiracy to rob does not mean that his co-conspirators cannot be. (D) is wrong; although they may be also charged with battery, this is not the only crime of which they may be charged.

Answer to Question 62

(B) Of the defenses, the best defense Barney would have is self-defense. If he were reasonable in his belief that Hank had a weapon and intended to "kill" him, he could use deadly force to protect himself. (A) is not a good defense because it is unreasonable to assume that hitting a person in the head with a heavy ashtray could not seriously injure him. In addition, manslaughter can be established with a reckless mental state, so Barney could be guilty even if he did not intend to seriously injure. (C) is incorrect because even if he did not know that Hank had a plate in his head, he could be guilty of manslaughter if the jury found that he recklessly caused Hank's death. (D) is wrong because Barney is not charged with murder in the first degree.

Answer to Question 63

(C) The only theory of first degree murder applicable is that the murder was "willful, deliberate, or [and] premeditated." This type of murder requires an actual intent to kill, which Rob did not have. (A) is wrong because an automobile can be a dangerous weapon when used as one, and the intentional driving of an automobile at another can support and permit, though not require, an inference that Rob intended to kill. At common law, 14 is the cutoff age for youthfulness to be a factor. Since Rob had been driving for several years, it must be presumed he is over age 14. Thus, (B) is wrong. (D) is clearly wrong. While Rob might be able to avoid liability for first degree murder because of his lack of intent to kill, he could be liable for second degree murder.

Answer to Question 64

(B) A jury could find Rob guilty of murder under the theory that the circumstances show an "abandoned and malignant heart," or of involuntary manslaughter under the theory of an unlawful act, or a lawful act done "without due caution and circumspection." (A) is wrong; it would be proper to charge the jury on murder as well as manslaughter. (C) is wrong because there is no way that Rob would be guilty of voluntary manslaughter, which would involve an unjustified, unexcused, but mitigated intentional homicide. Rob did not intend to kill or seriously injure; moreover, if he did so intend, there is no factor of mitigation present. (D) is wrong because this question is based on a Type A jurisdiction, which has adhered to the common law by not dividing murder into degrees.

Answer to Question 65

(A) A shooting is deemed to create a necessity situation to the extent that a motive to enter and search premises to preserve the life of a person thought to be on the premises and in immediate danger is a recognized exception to the warrant requirement. Therefore, the officers had a right to enter the building without a warrant. Since the officers were legitimately on the premises, they had a right to seize all illegal items in plain view. Thus, (C) and (D) are wrong. (B) is wrong because the fact that the officers were acting in their official function is not enough to allow them to enter a building without a warrant.

Answer to Question 66

(B) After arrest a defendant has a right to remain silent, and his silence cannot be used against him. The Supreme Court has held that the prosecution cannot comment to the jury on the fact that an arrested defendant exercised the privilege against self-incrimination. (A) is not entirely accurate. Even if Davis had not asked for an attorney, he could have invoked the privilege against self-incrimination and refused to talk while in custody. Thus, (A) is not as good an answer as (B), which speaks directly to the reason the conviction will be reversed. (C) is wrong. Even though the silence might give rise to the inference that the story was fabricated, the arrested defendant has a "right" to remain silent and the silence cannot be used against him. (D) is wrong. By testifying he waived his right to be silent at the trial; he did not waive his right to silence before the trial.

Answer to Question 67

(C) Of all the possible defenses, (C) is the one most clearly showing that Annie was justified in her belief that her former marriage was already terminated when she married Gerald. (A) is not the best answer, because Annie should know that if she does not get the divorce decree entered she is not legally divorced. (B) is not the best answer, because although many jurisdictions will accept a reasonable mistake of fact based on the prolonged absence of a spouse, three years would probably not be considered a "prolonged" absence. (D) is not the best answer, because although it is arguable that her marriage to Rodney may have been void, most jurisdictions would find the marriage only voidable while Annie was still a minor. Thus, in these jurisdictions, if neither party sought to annul the marriage until the minor spouse reached majority, they would no longer be able to annul their marriage. Although it can be argued that Annie is operating under a mistake of fact that her first marriage was invalid, most jurisdictions would not find the first marriage void as a matter of law.

Answer to Question 68

(D) Mervin had no ownership interest in Giles's store; he had no legitimate expectation of privacy with respect to it, *i.e.*, he was not present when the search was made; and he had no ownership interest in the stolen goods. Thus, he lacks the standing to object to their illegal seizure. Giles does have such standing and was successful in having the evidence suppressed at his trial, but what occurred at Giles's trial is not relevant to Mervin's motion. Therefore, (A) and (B) are incorrect. (C) is incorrect because the only evidence containing Mervin's fingerprints were the stolen goods. If it is found that these items were illegally seized, it would follow that the evidence arising out of this illegal seizure, including Mervin's fingerprints, was also illegally seized.

Answer to Question 69

(C) Larceny is the taking and carrying away of the personal property of another with the intent to permanently deprive the other of the property. However, larceny is a trespass against *possession*, not ownership, and therefore, in most jurisdictions, a defendant can be convicted of larceny even when he takes property from someone who only has possession of that property because of some wrongful act. However, Gregg would not be guilty of burglary because there is no evidence that he entered the house with the intent to steal the gun. Therefore, (A), (B), and (D) are incorrect.

Answer to Question 70

(C) It is not a defense to obtaining money by false pretenses that the victim unreasonably relied on the defendant's misrepresentation. The test for reliance is a subjective one. (A) is incorrect because the obtaining of mere possession that the defendant expects to be temporary does not constitute false pretenses. (B) is incorrect because false pretenses requires that the misrepresentation be knowingly false, and this is not the case when the defendant sincerely, but unreasonably, believes that the misrepresentation is true. (D) is incorrect because false pretenses requires reliance by the victim to be actionable.

Answer to Question 71

(D) The privilege against self-incrimination bars the government from procuring **compelled testimony**. Since the documents here were voluntarily prepared, they cannot be considered to be compelled. Furthermore, documents are considered to be real or physical evidence, not testimonial evidence, and thus are outside the scope of the privilege. Thus, (A) is incorrect. (B) is irrelevant since the documents are beyond the scope of the privilege. (C) is wrong because records required by statute that have a lawful administrative purpose are not protected by the Fifth Amendment.

Answer to Question 72

(C) Alyce consciously disregarded a substantial and unjustifiable risk that the drug she was placing in food could be seriously harmful or even fatal. (A) is wrong because Alyce lacked the necessary intent to kill. (B) is wrong because Alyce did not commit a common law felony; battery was not a felony at common law. (D) is not as good an answer as (C). While a jury could find that her actions were criminally negligent, resulting in manslaughter, a jury could also find that she acted with reckless disregard, resulting in second degree murder. Thus, under the call of the question, (C) is correct.

Answer to Question 73

(A) Bob is an accessory before the fact, and thus subject to the same penalty as Alyce. An accessory before the fact provides assistance before the crime but is not actually or constructively present during the crime. (B) is incorrect because a principal in the first degree actually perpetrates the crime. (C) is incorrect because a principal in the second degree must be actually or constructively present during the commission of the crime, and here, Bob was sleeping. (D) is wrong because Bob's aid was before, not after, the fact.

Answer to Question 74

(C) Phil did not commit felony murder because (i) he did not commit a common law felony and (ii) he did not have the necessary mens rea to be liable as an accomplice. Thus, (A) is incorrect. Not knowing the use to which the nitroglycerine was to be put, he did not act with the reckless disregard for the safety of others required for second degree murder, and, again, he lacked the mens rea required for accomplice liability. Thus, (B) is incorrect. (D) is incorrect because it is generally not a defense to crime that the defendant was unaware that his acts were prohibited by the criminal law (assuming that the statute proscribing his conduct was made reasonably available prior to the conduct). Thus, (C) is correct. Phil dispensed the drugs to Bob without a prescription and so he violated that law.

Answer to Question 75

(B) Voluntary manslaughter occurs when the actor kills another person but acts in the "heat of passion" after "sufficient provocation." At common law, provocation could be established by showing that the victim had committed a serious battery on the defendant. If as a result of the battery (provocation) the defendant killed the victim while in a rage (heat of passion), the criminal liability was voluntary manslaughter. Therefore, (B) is the correct answer; a serious battery was committed on Johnson, and *if* the jury found that Johnson was enraged when he shot Victor, sufficient provocation would be established for voluntary manslaughter. (A) is wrong. For criminal liability to attach under the felony murder rule, it must be established that the actor was engaged in a felony "independent" of the homicide when the death occurred. There was no independent felony here. (C) is wrong because it is too broad a statement. Even though the defendant did not intend to kill the victim, he might be guilty of murder under a theory of "intent to cause serious bodily harm" or "depraved heart." (D) is also too broad a statement and cannot be correct in light of the facts set out in the question. A person is justified in using deadly force only if he reasonably believes such force is necessary to prevent death or serious physical injury.

Answer to Question 76

(D) Neighbor would not be guilty of larceny when he took the horse from Fillmont because Neighbor did not have the mens rea necessary for the crime. Common law larceny required the trespassory taking and carrying away of personal property in the possession of another, with the intent to permanently deprive the other of lawful possession. The intent to permanently deprive was often referred to by the courts as the "intent to steal." If the actor believed that he had a right to the property or was taking the property on behalf of someone who had that right, the actor could not be found guilty of larceny, since there would be no intent to permanently deprive another of lawful possession. As Neighbor thought the bill had been paid and the horse rightfully belonged to Deft, Neighbor did not have the "intent to steal" necessary for larceny at the time he took the horse from Fillmont. (A) is wrong. Even though the bill had not been paid, Neighbor is not guilty if he believed Deft had a lawful right to the horse. (B) is wrong. Even though the horse was in the possession of Fillmont, Neighbor is not guilty if he believed Deft had a lawful right to the horse. (C) is wrong because a person can be guilty of larceny of his own property if another person (usually a bailee) has a superior right to possession of the property at the time of the taking.

Answer to Question 77

(C) Dullard's motion to suppress should be denied because his mother had the authority to consent to the search of Dullard's room. A search of a residence can be based on the voluntary consent of the occupant. Where a parent has general access to a room occupied by a son or daughter, the parent can give a valid consent to a search of the room even if the son or daughter is an adult. The facts in the question indicate Mae had general access to Dullard's room ("and all the time I'm making his bed"). Therefore, her consent is valid and eliminates the need for probable cause and a warrant. (A) is wrong. Dullard had a reasonable expectation of privacy in the area searched, but the consent of Mae eliminated the need for a warrant. (B) is wrong. At one time, some courts required an "amicable relationship" between the parties before the police could rely on a third party's consent. The "amicable relationship requirement" is no longer recognized by the courts. (D) is not a good answer. It is true that with Mae's statement the police had probable cause to search Dullard's room. However, probable cause alone would not validate the search. The police would need probable cause *plus* a warrant or a valid consent. In this question the search would have to be based on consent.

EVIDENCE QUESTIONS

Questions 1-3 are based on the following fact situation:

Plain and Deef were involved in a two-car collision. Deef was indicted for drunken driving, a crime that carries a maximum sentence of two years' imprisonment. Walter, an eyewitness, testified before the grand jury. Deef pled guilty to the charge of drunken driving and was fined $500. After the criminal charge was disposed of, Plain sued Deef for negligence and sought personal injury damages.

1. In the negligence action against Deef, Walter testified for Plain that Deef was on the wrong side of the highway at the time of the collision. On cross-examination, Deef seeks to question Walter about Walter's sworn grand jury statement that Deef was driving normally at the time of the accident.

    Upon proper objection the court should rule Walter's statement before the grand jury:

    (A) Admissible for impeachment only.

    (B) Admissible as substantive evidence only.

    (C) Admissible for impeachment and as substantive evidence.

    (D) Inadmissible, because it is hearsay not within any exception.

2. Assume that Walter did not testify at the trial of the negligence action because he could not be located. Witt, another eyewitness, was produced and gave trial testimony similar to that given by Walter before the grand jury. Deef offers in evidence as part of his defense case, without prior notice to Plain, a properly authenticated transcript of the testimony given earlier by Walter before the grand jury. The transcript of Walter's grand jury testimony is:

    (A) Admissible under the former testimony exception to the rule against hearsay.

    (B) Admissible nonhearsay.

    (C) Admissible to rehabilitate the testimony of Witt if Witt has been impeached by a charge of recent fabrication or improper motive.

    (D) Inadmissible hearsay.

3. Thereafter, Plain offered the properly authenticated record of Deef's conviction for drunken driving. The record should be:

    (A) Admitted as proof of Deef's character in order to infer negligence.

    (B) Admitted as proof of Deef's intoxication.

    (C) Excluded, because the conviction was not the result of a trial.

    (D) Excluded, because it is hearsay not within any exception.

Question 4

In a criminal trial the prosecution called Wayne, an expert witness, to the stand. The prosecutor conducted a direct examination of Wayne that lasted one-half hour. The defense attorney cross-examined Wayne for three days and told the court that he planned to spend at least another day in cross-examination. The prosecutor moved that the cross-examination be terminated by the court.

May the court approve the prosecutor's motion?

(A) Yes, unless the court determines the testimony to be relevant.

(B) Yes, if the court finds that the defendant had an adequate opportunity for meaningful cross-examination.

(C) No, if the questioning relates to the subject matter of direct.

(D) No, because in a criminal trial the consideration of judicial economy is outweighed by due process.

Questions 5-7 are based on the following fact situation:

Ped sued Derrick and Derrick's employer for personal injuries. Ped claimed that she was struck on the head by a wrench dropped by Derrick from a high scaffold, on which Derrick was working in the course of a construction project.

5. To prove that it was Derrick who dropped the wrench, Ped offers the wrench itself as evidence: The wrench bears the brand name "Craftsman" on the handle, and other evidence shows that the wrenches used by Derrick on the job are "Craftsman" brand wrenches. Which of the following best describes this evidence?

(A) But for the word "Craftsman," the wrench would be irrelevant. The word "Craftsman" is hearsay, and it is not admissible under any exception to the hearsay rule. The wrench should therefore be excluded.

(B) The wrench is direct evidence that it was Derrick who dropped the wrench. It is not hearsay and should be admitted.

(C) The wrench is irrelevant because it fails to show that it is more likely than not that Derrick was the person who dropped it.

(D) The wrench is relevant circumstantial evidence and is not hearsay when offered to prove that it was Derrick who dropped the wrench.

6. As evidence that Ped assumed the risk of injury, Derrick's employer offers the testimony of the construction foreman. He will testify: "Just before the accident, I stopped Ped and said: 'If you walk under that scaffold without a hard hat on, it may be the last walk you take.'" Which of the following best characterizes this testimony?

(A) The evidence is not hearsay because the declarant is testifying as a witness at the hearing.

(B) The evidence is hearsay, but it should be admitted as part of the res gestae.

(C) The evidence is hearsay, but it should be admitted under the present state of mind exception to the hearsay rule.

(D) The evidence is not hearsay because the statement is not offered for its truth.

7. A safety officer from the State Commission on Industrial Safety interviewed all of the people connected with the accident. The safety officer's written report quotes several damaging admissions made by Derrick's employer during the interview. Which of the following is **not** among the foundational facts Ped will have to establish if she wants to have the report admitted under the past recollection recorded exception to the hearsay rule?

(A) That the report was written while the interview was fresh in the memory of the safety officer.

(B) That the report accurately records what was said by Derrick's employer.

(C) That the report was written by the safety officer or adopted by him.

(D) That the safety officer is not available and cannot be called as a witness at trial.

Questions 8-9 are based on the following fact situation:

Pat sued Delivery Co. for damages suffered when a load of bricks fell off one of Delivery's trucks directly in front of Pat while Pat was driving on a highway. Pat charged that Delivery Co. was negligent in supplying its truck with a defective load chain clamp, which helped tie the load to the bed of the truck, and also under a respondeat superior theory that Delivery's truck driver, Yogi, was negligent in failing to secure the load properly on the truck.

8. Pat calls as a witness Xenon, who testifies that he was formerly employed as a truck driver at Delivery Co. and is an acquaintance of Yogi. Xenon further testifies that immediately prior to the accident he had coffee with Yogi at a cafe, and mentioned to Yogi that the tie chains holding Yogi's load of bricks "looked kind of loose." Assuming proper objection by Delivery's attorney, such testimony is:

   (A) Admissible under an exception to the hearsay rule.

   (B) Admissible nonhearsay.

   (C) Inadmissible hearsay.

   (D) Inadmissible opinion evidence.

9. Delivery Co. has a rule that any driver involved in an accident must file a report to the company within 12 hours. Pat has demanded that Delivery produce Yogi's original handwritten report, which Delivery does. Pat then calls Yogi to the stand as an adverse witness, and Yogi identifies the report as his, testifies to the existence of the rule requiring such reports and that Yogi routinely filled it out only a few minutes after the accident. Because it states that the faulty load chain clamp caused the accident, Pat offers it in evidence. Delivery objects on appropriate grounds. The report is:

   (A) Admissible, but only if Yogi testifies that he cannot remember the details in the report.

   (B) Inadmissible, because the record was not prepared in the course of Delivery's primary business.

   (C) Inadmissible, because only statements of fact in business records are admissible, and the conclusion that the clamp was "faulty" and that it "caused" the accident are not statements of fact.

   (D) Admissible as nonhearsay.

Question 10

Vickie was raped and beaten by Dean. She called the police and provided an accurate description of Dean, who was arrested shortly thereafter and charged with the attack on Vickie. After the attack, Vickie was examined by Dr. Dornfeld. When Dean came to trial, Vickie refused to cooperate with the prosecution and steadfastly refused to testify against Dean. To establish that Vickie was raped and beaten, the prosecution put Dr. Dornfeld on the stand, planning to have him testify as to Vickie's physical condition after the attack and as to how she said she received her injuries. Vickie wishes to prevent Dr. Dornfeld from so testifying by invoking the physician-patient privilege.

Under which of the following circumstances is the court *least* likely to allow Vickie to use the physician-patient privilege to keep Dr. Dornfeld from testifying?

(A) Vickie visited Dr. Dornfeld for the purpose of diagnosis and treatment, and her statements to him were made for that purpose.

(B) Vickie is married to Dean.

(C) Vickie's statements to Dr. Dornfeld were made public by Dr. Dornfeld in a previous statement to the police.

(D) At the time Vickie visited Dr. Dornfeld, she knew that his license to practice medicine was revoked two years prior to her visit.

Questions 11-13 are based on the following fact situation:

Pike sues Dever to rescind a contract for fraud and damages. Pike alleged in his complaint that, pursuant to a written contract, he had bought a business known as Bilkum Autos from Dever, and that he had purchased it in reliance on Dever's fraudulent representations as to the value of Bilkum Autos's inventory and cash on hand.

At trial, without objection, Pike introduced the written contract, which included, as Paragraph 2, recitals of facts containing the statement: "Bilkum Autos, hereafter referred to as the Company, is a solvent company with inventory and cash assets valued at $200,000 . . ." and, as Paragraph 43, a boilerplate integration clause (*i.e.,* "no other representations have been made," etc.). It is conceded that Dever is a lawyer but Pike is not.

11. Pike proposes to testify that during negotiations Dever said the real value of Bilkum Autos in cash and inventory was about $500,000, but that tax laws made it inexpedient to recite the real value. Dever objects. The offered evidence is:

(A) Inadmissible, as violative of the parol evidence rule.

(B) Inadmissible because it is hearsay.

(C) Admissible hearsay, unaffected by the parol evidence rule.

(D) Neither hearsay nor violative of the parol evidence rule.

12. Pike next seeks to call Dever's ex-wife to testify that Dever told her of the fraud on Pike. Dever objects on the ground of privilege. Dever's ex-wife:

(A) Can be called and can testify against Dever over the objection.

(B) Can be called and must testify because the privilege applies only in criminal cases.

(C) Cannot be directed to testify against Dever over Dever's objection if the facts were told to her in confidence during the marriage.

(D) Cannot be called as a witness at all over Dever's objection.

13. In his defense, Dever calls Dr. Wizard as a financial expert. To qualify Wizard as an expert, Dever asks Wizard about his education, training, and experience in finance. Dr. Wizard testifies that he has received "a B.A. and Ph.D. in economics and business finance from Shoestring State." On cross-examination concerning qualifications, Pike asks, "Isn't it a fact, Dr. Wizard, that you flunked out of Shoestring State at the end of your freshman year?" to which Wizard replies, "No." Pike then offers the registrar of Shoestring State to introduce a transcript of the college's records to show that Wizard studied only one year and was awarded no degrees. Dever objects.

Which of the following best states the reasoning to be followed in determining whether to admit the transcript?

(A) Denying the witness's claim to degrees is impeachment on a collateral matter, which cannot be proved by extrinsic evidence.

(B) The judge should admit the transcript and decide himself whether Wizard is an expert and allow him to testify further only if the judge believes Wizard to be an expert.

(C) A dispute about the qualifications of an expert witness is a question of fact for the jury; therefore, the judge should admit the transcript and instruct the jury that they are to disregard Wizard's testimony if they conclude that he is not an expert.

(D) Whether Wizard was awarded a B.A. and Ph.D. is a fact irrelevant to the main issues, and the transcript therefore should be excluded.

Question 14

Ephor, the owner of a small business, was injured in a traffic accident. A month after the accident, Ephor asked Archon, an employee, to take a photograph of the intersection where the accident occurred. Archon took the photograph and gave it to Ephor, who in turn gave it to his lawyer, Leonidas. Leonidas wishes to introduce the photograph into evidence at trial of Ephor's lawsuit against Diogenes, the defendant. Leonidas plans to have Archon testify that he took the photograph. Leonidas also plans to call Nestor as a witness. Nestor lives in the neighborhood of the accident scene and arrived at the intersection shortly after the accident occurred. Nestor is willing to testify that the scene in the photograph is in fact the intersection where the accident happened.

Whose testimony is necessary to introduce the photograph into evidence?

(A) Archon's testimony is necessary and Nestor's is unnecessary.

(B) Nestor's testimony is necessary and Archon's is unnecessary.

(C) The testimonies of both Archon and Nestor are necessary.

(D) The picture is inadmissible.

Question 15

While working on a construction project, Potter was injured when a heavy object struck his knee. Potter was fully compensated for his medical expenses, time off from work, and related damages, but he now seeks disability payments from the construction company, because he has developed arthritis in the same knee. The construction company claims that the arthritis has nothing to do with Potter's on-the-job injury and refuses to pay him disability money. Potter sues. Dr. Orthopod takes the stand to testify for Potter. He is qualified as an expert witness, and during direct examination, Dr. Orthopod states, "It is my opinion that the blow to Potter's knee caused his arthritis." On cross-examination, Dutch, the construction company's attorney, produces a treatise on arthritis written by Dr. Rheum. Dutch asks Dr. Orthopod if Dr. Rheum's treatise is considered to be authoritative.

Dr. Orthopod responds, "I recognize Dr. Rheum's treatise as a standard authority in the field, but I did not rely on it in forming my professional opinions regarding Mr. Potter's condition." Dutch then seeks to introduce into evidence a statement in Dr. Rheum's treatise that "the idea that arthritis can be caused by a single traumatic event is purely folklore, although it is widely believed by the ignorant who have no scientific basis for their beliefs." Potter's attorney objects.

The court should find the statement from the treatise:

(A) Admissible, but only for the purpose of impeaching Dr. Orthopod's testimony.

(B) Admissible, but only as substantive evidence.

(C) Admissible, both as substantive evidence and for purposes of impeaching Dr. Orthopod.

(D) Inadmissible.

Questions 16-18 are based on the following fact situation:

In the prosecution of Dwight for bank robbery, it is established that as the robber came out of the bank, he was seen entering a car by a group of people including Wesley, Xavier, and Yancy.

16. Wesley is prepared to testify that as the car drove off, someone yelled, "Get that number," whereupon Xavier screamed, "I've got it. The number is 07771!" Wesley's testimony is:

(A) Admissible only if Xavier fails or refuses to testify to such facts, because Xavier's testimony would be the best evidence thereof.

(B) Admissible hearsay.

(C) Inadmissible hearsay.

(D) Inadmissible because there is no proper foundation or identification of the hearsay declarant.

17. Assume for purposes of this question and the next that Wesley's testimony is admitted, and that Yancy now wishes to testify for the defense that he was there and does not remember hearing Xavier say anything. Yancy's testimony is:

(A) Inadmissible as irrelevant to any issue in the case.

(B) Proper impeachment of Wesley.

(C) Improper impeachment of Wesley because it relates to a collateral matter.

(D) Improper impeachment because it does not positively controvert Wesley's testimony, as Yancy merely says he does not remember.

18. Because Xavier cannot be located at the time of trial, the prosecution seeks to introduce a transcript of testimony given by Xavier before the grand jury that indicted Dwight. (Xavier's testimony was that, at the time of the robbery, he had screamed, "I've got it. The number is 07771!") The transcript of Xavier's testimony before the grand jury is:

(A) Admissible to rehabilitate Wesley if Wesley has been impeached by Yancy's testimony.

(B) Admissible nonhearsay.

(C) Hearsay, but admissible under the former testimony exception to the hearsay rule.

(D) Inadmissible hearsay.

Question 19

Child was injured in an automobile accident. Child's parent, Father, brought Child, age 12, to see Attorney to bring suit against Defendant.

During the visit to Attorney's office, the seriousness of Child's injuries was discussed with candor. After the discussion, Attorney told Father and Child that they would be better off with a lawyer who specialized in personal injury work. Eventually, another attorney was hired to bring Child's lawsuit against Defendant.

Defendant's counsel has reason to believe that Child's injuries are not serious at all. He therefore subpoenas Attorney for an oral deposition. During the course of the deposition he asks Attorney about his discussion with Child regarding Child's injuries.

May Attorney invoke the attorney-client privilege?

(A) No, because Child never hired Attorney as her counsel.

(B) No, because the privilege is held by the client rather than the attorney.

(C) Yes, unless Child did not pay Attorney for consultation.

(D) Yes, because the presence of a third party did not negate the privilege.

Question 20

Except under extraordinary circumstances, the judge conducting a trial in federal district court:

(A) May not question a sworn witness who is one of the actual parties to the "case or controversy."

(B) May not question a sworn witness regarding ultimate issues of the case.

(C) May not question a sworn lay (nonexpert) witness.

(D) May question a sworn witness in any of the above circumstances.

Question 21

During the course of his trial for assault, Danny placed professional sociologist Sato on the stand. Sato testified that he had scientifically polled the community in which Danny lived and that Danny had a high reputation for being a peaceable man in a rather rough community. On cross-examination, the prosecutor asked Sato, "Isn't it true, Mr. Sato, that last year you filed a false income tax return?" The defense immediately objected.

Should the court require Sato to answer the question posed to him?

(A) Yes, but only if Sato has been convicted of filing a false tax return.

(B) Yes, because the question is relevant to the truthfulness and credibility of the witness.

(C) No, because specific instances of conduct are inadmissible.

(D) No, because the question does not go to a relevant character trait.

Question 22

Penny was riding up an escalator in Dirk's Department Store, when suddenly the escalator sped up and then came to a very quick stop, throwing people against each other and then down the escalator. Penny tried to hold on to the railing but was unsuccessful. She was thrown violently to the left, felt a horrible pain in her back, and then tumbled down the escalator to the bottom. Officials of Dirk's promptly called their industrial health nurse, who examined Penny and summoned an ambulance. When the ambulance arrived, paramedics placed Penny on a stretcher, and just as they picked up the stretcher to take her to the hospital, Penny heard Clara, a customer of the store, say, "Yesterday I heard Cora, another customer, tell Dirk that the escalator was acting funny. You know, speeding up and stopping." Penny was treated at the hospital and must undergo rehabilitation treatment for her badly injured back. Penny now sues Dirk's

Department Store for her injuries, and at trial calls Clara to testify to Cora's remark. The lawyer for Dirk's objects.

How should the court rule?

(A) Admissible, as a statement against interest.

(B) Admissible, as relevant evidence that Dirk's was aware of the defect and did nothing to correct it.

(C) Inadmissible, unless Cora cannot be located as a witness.

(D) Inadmissible, as hearsay not within any exception.

Question 23

Pluto was injured as a result of Duck's negligence. Pluto went to Amy, an attorney, who agreed to file suit on his behalf on a contingent fee basis. Amy sent Pluto to see Dr. Sawbones, a physician, for the purpose of examining Pluto prior to trial and assessing the extent of his injuries. During the course of the examination, Pluto made some statements to Sawbones indicating that he was not completely free from negligence when the accident occurred. Duck seeks to call Sawbones to testify to the statements Pluto made to Sawbones. Amy objects.

The objection should be:

(A) Overruled, because Pluto made an admission.

(B) Overruled, because a physician qualifies as an expert witness.

(C) Sustained, because the attorney-client privilege applies.

(D) Sustained, because the physician-patient privilege applies.

Question 24

Dorcas was involved in an accident in which Dorcas's car struck the rear end of the car driven by Pippin. The police issued tickets to Dorcas, charging her with reckless driving and speeding. When Dorcas's case came before the traffic court, Dorcas's attorney entered into a plea bargain with the prosecutor. Under the plea bargain, Dorcas agreed to plead guilty to speeding and to pay a fine of $100, and the prosecution agreed to drop the reckless driving charge. Accordingly, Dorcas pleaded guilty and the court fined her $100.

In the later civil suit, where Pippin sues Dorcas for personal injuries, is Dorcas's guilty plea before the traffic court admissible?

(A) Yes, because it is an admission.

(B) Yes, because it is a statement against interest.

(C) No, because there is a public policy in favor of plea bargaining to promote court efficiency.

(D) No, because no felony was involved.

Questions 25-28 are based on the following fact situation:

Diamond is being prosecuted for the rape of Pearl. The issues at the trial are the identity of Pearl's attacker and whether Pearl consented.

25. Upon the issue of whether Diamond was Pearl's attacker, Pearl is called to the witness stand and testifies that Diamond resembles her assailant, but she cannot be positive because the attack occurred so long ago. The prosecutor then shows Pearl a written statement that she gave the police shortly after the crime containing a detailed description of her attacker. The prosecutor then asks her whether, having read the statement, she can be more certain about the identification of Diamond. Diamond's attorney objects. The court should:

(A) Sustain the objection, because the writing itself should be read into evidence.

(B) Sustain the objection, on the ground that the question regarding identification has already been asked and answered.

(C) Overrule the objection, as long as Pearl can now testify without reading from the statement.

(D) Overrule the objection only if it appears that the prosecutor was legitimately surprised by Pearl's adverse testimony regarding identification.

26. On the issue of Pearl's consent, which of the following statements most accurately states the prevailing view as to the burden of proving consent or lack thereof?

(A) Diamond must establish Pearl's consent by a preponderance of the evidence.

(B) The prosecution must establish that Pearl did not consent by a preponderance of the evidence, although otherwise Diamond's guilt must be proved beyond a reasonable doubt.

(C) The prosecution must prove beyond a reasonable doubt that Pearl did not consent even if Diamond remains silent on the issue.

(D) The prosecution must prove beyond a reasonable doubt that Pearl did not consent only if Diamond produces some evidence that Pearl did consent.

27. On the issue of Pearl's consent, Diamond's attorney calls Warburton as a witness and asks him, "Do you know Pearl's reputation in the community for chastity?" Warburton laughs and then declares, "It's a joke! She's been to bed with everyone—including me!" The prosecution moves to strike Warburton's testimony. The judge should:

(A) Deny the motion as not timely.

(B) Deny the motion, because Warburton's testimony is relevant to the issue of consent.

(C) Grant the motion, because the issue is not Pearl's reputation, but rather whether she consented.

(D) Grant the motion, because this kind of character evidence is prohibited in rape cases.

28. Assume for purposes of this question only that Warburton was permitted to testify as to Pearl's poor reputation for chastity. On cross-examination of Warburton by the prosecution, which of the following questions would *not* be proper (assume appropriate objections by Diamond's counsel)?

(A) "Isn't it true that you're maligning Pearl because your wife and Pearl have been enemies since childhood?"

(B) "Isn't it true that you were charged last year with assault for striking your wife?"

(C) "Have you heard that Pearl teaches Sunday School classes on morality and has received an award from her church based on her outstanding moral character?"

(D) "Do you know that Pearl teaches Sunday School classes on morality and has received an award from her church based on her outstanding moral character?"

Questions 29-30 are based on the following fact situation:

Paul applied for a $250,000 life insurance policy and was required to submit to a physical examination to qualify for the policy. During the course of the examination, he told Dr. Dan, a physician approved by the life insurance company who had never seen Paul before, "I used to have some back trouble, but that's all cleared up now." A few weeks after Dr. Dan's examination, David's automobile struck the rear end of a car in which Paul was riding as a passenger. Paul now claims that he suffers persistent lower back pain and sues David for damages.

29. David calls Dr. Dan as a witness and seeks to have him testify as to Paul's statement to him. Paul's attorney objects on the ground of physician-patient privilege. The testimony as to Paul's statement is:

(A) Admissible, but only if a proper foundation is laid establishing that Paul is attempting to perpetrate a fraud.

(B) Admissible, because Paul was not seeking diagnosis or treatment.

(C) Inadmissible, because the statement was made to a physician who was attending Paul in a professional capacity.

(D) Inadmissible, as irrelevant, because the statement was made prior to the accident.

30. Assume for purposes of this question only that before the accident, Paul told his friend, Freddy, "My general health is pretty good, but I have a lot of back trouble; in fact I'm in considerable pain right now." If David seeks to have this statement introduced into evidence, it will be:

(A) Admissible, as an excited utterance.

(B) Admissible, as a statement of present bodily condition.

(C) Inadmissible, unless Paul has waived the physician-patient privilege by talking about his back pain.

(D) Inadmissible, because Paul was not seeking diagnosis or treatment.

Question 31

Dutch was on trial for burglary, and he took the stand in his own defense. On direct examination Dutch vigorously denied having committed the burglary. Also on direct examination, Dutch's attorney asked Dutch questions about his employment history in an attempt to portray Dutch to the jury as a "solid citizen" who would not commit a burglary. Dutch stated that his last regular employer was XYZ Corporation, where Dutch worked as a bookkeeper. On cross-examination, Cora, the county prosecutor, asked Dutch if he had embezzled funds from XYZ Corporation. Dutch denied that he had embezzled from XYZ or from anyone else. Cora then wanted to call Lamb, a police officer, to the stand. Lamb would testify that when Lamb arrested Dutch for embezzlement, Dutch admitted to Lamb that he had embezzled money from XYZ Corporation.

Assuming that Dutch has not yet been tried on the embezzlement charges, may Cora call Lamb to the stand?

(A) Yes, but only for purposes of impeachment.

(B) Yes, both for impeachment of Dutch and as substantive evidence.

(C) No, because Dutch has not yet been convicted of embezzlement.

(D) No, because the evidence would be extrinsic.

Question 32

Humphrey and Wilhelmina were good friends. One evening, while Wilhelmina was visiting Humphrey's apartment, a visitor named Victor came to see Humphrey. Humphrey and Victor engaged in a conversation relating to the distribution of illegal narcotics in Wilhelmina's presence. Two months later, Humphrey and Wilhelmina married. Subsequent to the marriage, Humphrey was arrested and charged under federal law with the sale and distribution of drugs. Peter Prosecutor wants Wilhelmina to testify about the conversation between Humphrey and Victor.

May she so testify?

(A) Yes, because the conversation occurred prior to the marriage of Humphrey and Wilhelmina.

(B) Yes, but only if she chooses to do so.

(C) No, unless Humphrey permits her to do so.

(D) No, unless both Humphrey and Wilhelmina agree that she may testify.

Question 33

Diana, a sole proprietor of a small business, was the subject of an investigation by the Internal Revenue Service and was subsequently charged with tax fraud. Diana gave all of her canceled business checks to Astrid, her attorney. Palsgraf, the federal prosecutor, wants the court to issue a subpoena duces tecum to bring Diana's canceled checks into evidence.

The subpoena will be:

(A) Denied, because of the attorney-client privilege.

(B) Denied, because of the privilege against self-incrimination.

(C) Granted, because of the business records exception to the hearsay rule.

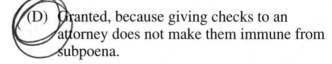
(D) Granted, because giving checks to an attorney does not make them immune from subpoena.

Question 34

At trial questions have been raised whether the proposed testimony of Wilma Witness is relevant and whether it falls within the present sense impression exception to the hearsay rule.

As to a preliminary determination of the admissibility of Wilma's testimony:

(A) A judge should determine whether the proposed testimony falls within the exception before it is heard by the jury, and in making that determination she is limited by the rules of evidence.

(B) A judge should decide whether the testimony falls within the present sense impression exception, but in making that determination she is not limited by the rules of evidence other than privilege.

(C) The jury, after being instructed on the rules of evidence by a judge, should determine whether the testimony falls within the scope of the present sense impression exception.

(D) The jury should determine whether the testimony falls within the scope of the exception and the judge should then instruct the jury on the appropriate uses for that evidence.

Question 35

Priscella and Wanda were best friends. Two years ago, Wanda informed Priscella that she had named Priscella beneficiary of a $100,000 insurance policy issued on Wanda's life. Wanda told her sister Sally what she had done. Sally said that Wanda owed it to her family to name a family member as beneficiary and demanded that Wanda do so. Wanda refused, which greatly angered Sally. Six months ago, Wanda was found strangled in the front seat of her car. Priscella was charged with Wanda's murder. At trial, Sally testified that she had seen Priscella riding in the front seat of Wanda's car with Wanda driving one hour before Wanda was found dead. Priscella was acquitted of Wanda's murder. Priscella asked Insurance Co. to pay her the proceeds from the insurance policy on Wanda's life. When Insurance Co. refused, Priscella sued to force payment. Insurance Co. defended on the grounds that Priscella had killed Wanda. Because Sally had died by the time of the trial on the insurance policy, Insurance Co. offers into evidence a duly authenticated transcript of Sally's testimony from the murder trial.

That transcript should be found to be:

(A) Admissible, because it is a record of Sally's former testimony.

(B) Admissible, because it is a past recollection recorded.

(C) Inadmissible, because on the same evidence, Priscella was acquitted of murdering Wanda.

(D) Inadmissible, because the motive to cross-examine in the former trial was not the same as in this trial.

Question 36

Diablo was arrested and charged with the murder of Flores, a member of the Centerville Athletic Club. Flores was found dead near the locker room inside the club. Diablo allegedly entered the club, killed Flores, and left before anyone discovered the body. At trial, the prosecution called the doorman of the club who testified that, although he could not identify Diablo by sight, he remembered admitting a member the day of the murder who showed a membership card bearing the name of Arnold Kramer. The prosecution then sought to admit the testimony of a police officer that a membership card to the Centerville Athletic Club bearing the name of Arnold Kramer was found on Diablo's person at the time of his arrest.

Diablo's best argument in seeking to exclude the police officer's testimony is that it:

(A) Violates the best evidence rule.

(B) Violates the hearsay evidence rule.

(C) Is about a purely collateral matter.

(D) Violates Diablo's privilege against self-incrimination.

Question 37

Pete is suing David for personal injuries sustained when Pete slipped and fell on the floor in David's office. Pete called Ike to testify that he was on duty in the hospital emergency room when Pete was admitted and that he saw Dr. Gwen treat Pete's skull. As he was getting ready to testify, Ike refreshed his recollection by studying Pete's copy of the hospital records. These records had not been admitted into evidence.

Ike's testimony concerning the treatment should be:

(A) Admitted, as evidence of the extent of Pete's injury.

(B) Admitted, as past recollection recorded.

(C) Excluded, because it is not the best evidence.

(D) Excluded, because it is based on hearsay not within any exception.

Question 38

Duncan was arrested for driving a car while intoxicated. The police took a videotape of Duncan as he attempted to walk a straight line and touch his nose at the time of the arrest. The prosecution seeks to introduce this tape at Duncan's trial.

The videotape is:

(A) Admissible, because it is more substantive than prejudicial.

(B) Inadmissible, because it is hearsay not within any exception.

(C) Inadmissible, because it violates Duncan's privilege against self-incrimination.

(D) Inadmissible, because a specific instance of misconduct cannot be proved by extrinsic evidence.

Questions 39-40 are based on the following fact situation:

Dave, while driving north on Grand Avenue, collided with Peter, who was driving east on Sixth Street. A police officer present at the scene cited Dave for running a red light, which is a misdemeanor offense.

At the preliminary hearing, Dave initially pleaded guilty, but he withdrew his plea when the judge told him what she had in mind for a sentence. The judge let Dave change his plea to innocent. Dave, however, had no success at his trial and was convicted.

Peter is now suing Dave in a civil action for the injuries he sustained in the accident.

39. If Peter tries to introduce evidence of Dave's original guilty plea, on proper motion, this evidence will be:

(A) Excluded, because it is hearsay not within any exception.

(B) Excluded, because the plea was withdrawn.

(C) Admitted, because an admission is not hearsay.

(D) Admitted, because it described Dave's state of mind.

40. If Peter tries to introduce a certified copy of the record of Dave's conviction to corroborate his testimony that Dave ran the red light, on proper motion, this evidence will be:

(A) Excluded, because it is not the best evidence of what happened at the time of the accident.

(B) Excluded, because it is hearsay not within any exception.

(C) Admitted, because a conviction is evidence of the facts necessary to sustain the judgment of the court.

(D) Admitted, because it is an official record.

Questions 41-43 are based on the following fact situation:

Prudhome purchased some engine additive manufactured by Motorglide. While driving his automobile to the mountains to go skiing, the car engine began to overheat. Prudhome stopped the car immediately and started to open the hood when the engine burst into flames. Prudhome suffered minor burns on his arms and hands. His car and everything in it were destroyed in the fire.

Prudhome brings suit against Motorglide, contending that Motorglide was negligent and in breach of warranty. He seeks damages for the loss of his personal property and for the burns on his hands and arms.

41. Compton, an automobile engineer, sat in court while Prudhome testified to the events concerning the engine fire. Prudhome's testimony was not challenged or rebutted. Prudhome calls Compton to the stand and asks him whether, based on Prudhome's prior testimony, it was possible for a car engine to burst into flames as it did. Compton's testimony would be:

(A) Inadmissible, because Compton's opinion was not elicited by means of a hypothetical question.

(B) Inadmissible, because Compton was in the court while Prudhome testified concerning the engine fire.

(C) Admissible, because Compton was in the court while Prudhome testified concerning the engine fire.

(D) Admissible, as long as Compton's opinion is based only on admissible evidence.

42. Prudhome also called Taylor, a chemical engineer, and asked her whether in her opinion, based upon laboratory reports made concerning the engine additive, it was possible for the additive to have caused the car engine to overheat and burst into flames. Motorglide's attorney objected to Taylor's testimony on this point. The court should rule that the testimony is:

(A) Admissible, if such reports are reasonably relied upon by chemical engineers in the course of their profession.

(B) Admissible, if Taylor has the reports with her and offers them into evidence.

(C) Inadmissible, because Taylor's testimony embraces the ultimate issue in the case.

(D) Inadmissible, because the contents of the laboratory reports are hearsay and not admissible under any exception.

43. Prudhome testified that although he had purchased the additive several days before his skiing trip, he did not add it to his oil until the morning he left for the mountains. During this testimony, Prudhome noted that he remembered that he purchased the additive on January 5 because that was the only day he had been to the auto store, and, furthermore, he had a credit card receipt at home that would show the date. Motorglide objected to Prudhome's testimony concerning the date on the credit card receipt. Of the following, how would a judge most likely rule on this objection?

(A) Sustained, because the actual receipts are the best evidence of the date the additive was purchased.

(B) Sustained, because the information in the credit card receipt is hearsay, not subject to any exception.

(C) Overruled, because the date the additive was purchased is not material to any issue at trial, and Prudhome had independent recollection of the date.

(D) Overruled, because the information in the credit card receipt is admissible under the past recollection recorded exception to the hearsay rule.

Question 44

An indictment was filed in federal district court charging Warren with violations of federal statutes prohibiting bank robbery. At trial, the government attempted to introduce into evidence the testimony of Warren's wife, Faye, who would testify that she had seen Warren arm himself on several occasions with weapons identical to those used in the bank robberies, had seen him return to their home carrying sacks filled with money with the markings of the robbed banks, and had overheard, while serving meals, Warren and his co-defendants discussing plans for robbing the various banks and concealing the loot. Warren's attorney objected, and the district court judge ruled that Faye's testimony was within the spousal privilege and could not be admitted over Warren's objection.

Was this ruling correct?

(A) No, because the spousal privilege may only be asserted by the testifying spouse—she may not be compelled to testify nor foreclosed from testifying.

(B) Yes, because the privilege not to testify may be asserted by either the testifying or nontestifying spouse.

(C) The question cannot be answered, because state law of spousal privilege controls, and the state law is not presented in the question.

(D) No, because there is no federal common law, and the spousal privilege is a creation of the common law.

Question 45

Engineer Thornton is called as a witness in a professional malpractice action. During direct examination by the attorney for the party who called her, she is asked leading questions. The opposing party objects.

Which of the following is *least* likely to persuade the trial court to permit the leading questions?

(A) The question is necessary to refresh recollection.

(B) The questions relate to preliminary information, such as name, address, etc.

(C) Thornton was called as an adverse witness.

(D) The questions relate directly to an issue of ultimate fact in the lawsuit.

Question 46

Paula sued her neighbor Doris over a 10-foot-high stockade fence that Doris was building adjacent to Paula's backyard. The local zoning ordinance permitted a fence of this height unless it was a "spite fence," defined as a fence erected solely for the purpose of interfering with neighboring landowners' use and enjoyment of their property. Paula alleged that Doris was building the fence to block sunlight to the bonsai garden that Paula had planted because Doris was anti-Japanese. Doris denied that she was building the fence for that purpose. Paula wishes to introduce evidence that Doris had sprayed herbicide towards the garden previously.

Should the judge permit Paula's testimony?

(A) Yes, because Doris's character is at issue in the case.

(B) Yes, because it pertains to Doris's motivation in building the fence.

(C) No, because Paula's testimony is evidence of specific conduct, which is not admissible in this case because Doris's character is not in issue.

(D) No, because character evidence generally is not admissible in a civil case.

Questions 47-49 are based on the following fact situation:

Peter was lawfully crossing the street when he was struck and seriously injured by a car driven by Tony. Tony had run a red light. At the time, Tony was on his way home from Donna's Tavern. Peter brings suit against Donna's Tavern for his injuries, claiming that Tony was permitted to drink too much liquor at Donna's Tavern before leaving.

47. Peter calls Wanda to the stand. Wanda testifies that she and a friend had visited Donna's Tavern on the night in question. Wanda seeks to testify that she remarked to her friend, "Look at that guy. He's so drunk he can't even stand up." Wanda's testimony concerning her remark to her friend is:

   (A) Admissible as a prior consistent statement.

   (B) Admissible as a statement by Wanda regarding the condition she observed made while she was observing it.

   (C) Admissible as relevant nonhearsay testimony.

   (D) Inadmissible as hearsay not within any exception.

48. Donna's Tavern calls Tony to the stand, expecting him to say that he was sober when he left Donna's Tavern on the night in question. However, on direct examination, Tony testifies that he "may have had a few too many" at Donna's Tavern that evening. Donna's Tavern then seeks to confront Tony with his statement made on deposition that he was sober when he left Donna's Tavern on the night in question. The statement contained in the deposition is:

   (A) Inadmissible, because Donna's Tavern cannot impeach its own witness.

   (B) Inadmissible, because it is hearsay not within any exception.

   (C) Admissible for impeachment and as substantive evidence that Tony was sober.

   (D) Admissible, but only for the purpose of impeachment.

49. Peter then offers evidence that after the accident in question, the owner of Donna's Tavern called him at home and offered to pay all of Peter's medical expenses, saying, "I guess I owe you that much after letting Tony leave here drunk last night." The statement that Tony was drunk when he left the bar on the night in question is:

   (A) Admissible as a statement against interest.

   (B) Admissible as an admission by the owner of Donna's Tavern that Tony was drunk when he left the bar.

   (C) Inadmissible as hearsay not within any exception.

   (D) Inadmissible on public policy grounds.

Question 50

Beekeeper purchased from Fabrico a specially designed helmet and faceguard that was designed to protect the wearer from bee stings. Shortly thereafter, as Beekeeper was wearing the helmet and faceguard, he was stung on the left cheek by a bee that had entered through a small tear in the faceguard. One hour later, Beekeeper suffered a heart attack. Beekeeper brought suit against Fabrico to recover for the bee sting and the heart attack.

Doctor Able, a physician, having listened to Beekeeper testify to the foregoing facts, is called by Beekeeper and asked whether, assuming the truth of such testimony, Beekeeper's subsequent heart attack could have resulted from the bee sting. His opinion is:

(A) Admissible, only if Doctor Able was Beekeeper's treating physician.

(B) Admissible, as a response to a hypothetical question.

(C) Inadmissible, because a proper foundation has not been laid.

(D) Inadmissible, because an expert's opinion may not be based solely on information provided by lay persons.

Question 51

Allen brings suit against Berry for a libelous letter received by Employer. Berry allegedly sent the letter. The authenticity and contents of the letter are disputed at the jury trial. In response to a question from Allen's attorney, Employer states that: "I received a letter from Berry, which I seem to have lost, but I remember exactly what it said."

Employer will be allowed to testify as to the contents of the letter if:

(A) Allen's attorney lays a proper foundation by proving Employer's good character for truth.

(B) The judge finds that the original letter is lost.

(C) The jury is satisfied that the original letter is unavailable.

(D) Employer can recall the contents of the letter from his own memory without looking to any other document.

Question 52

In an action for breach of contract, which of the following questions, if asked of a witness for plaintiff on cross-examination by counsel for defendant, would most probably be ruled improper by the trial court?

(A) "Weren't you fired last year after your employer learned you had been using its computerized accounting system to divert company funds to your personal bank account?"

(B) "As a creditor of the plaintiff, isn't it true that you stand to gain several thousand dollars if plaintiff prevails in this lawsuit?"

(C) "Isn't it true that you are currently a resident of the City Detoxification Hospital recovering from addiction to Valium?"

(D) "Weren't you convicted six years ago in the court of Neighboring County of forgery?"

Question 53

In a contract action between Ted and Violet, brought in federal court on the basis of diversity jurisdiction, the major issue is the value of Greenacre. Ted's attorney calls Realtor to the stand and qualifies her as an expert on property valuation. Since Realtor had not personally inspected the property, Ted's attorney was prepared to ask Realtor a hypothetical question based on evidence adduced at the trial. However, the trial had already dragged on longer than expected, and to save time, Ted's attorney merely asks Realtor, "In your expert opinion, how much is Greenacre worth?" Violet's attorney objects.

The objection should be:

(A) Sustained, because an expert may not render an opinion on an ultimate issue.

(B) Sustained, because an expert must disclose the basis for her opinion.

(C) Overruled, because qualification as an expert creates a presumption of a proper basis for the opinion.

(D) Overruled, because Violet is entitled to immediate cross-examination of Realtor.

Questions 54-58 are based on the following fact situation:

Jim and Mike were helping Jon as he unloaded pallets of brick from a truck onto a forklift at a construction site. The site was downtown in a large city, and as Jon moved from the back of the truck with his load, the forklift and Robin's car collided, causing the bricks to fall and injure Robin. Sherry, who was driving in her taxi on the same street, called her dispatcher to send the police. A police officer came and took down the statements of all witnesses.

Robin sued Jon for negligence, alleging that she was driving in a proper lane when Jon's forklift turned into her car. Jon alleges that Robin swerved into a closed lane and hit the front of the forklift. All witnesses are available to testify.

54. Robin's counsel called the police officer to testify that Jim had said, in Jon's presence, that "Jon accidentally went too far into traffic" and Jon did not say anything. The trial judge should rule that this evidence is:

   (A) Admissible, because Jim was working for Jon, and as his agent, could make a statement against Jon's interest.

   (B) Admissible, because silence may be deemed an admission.

   (C) Inadmissible, because Jim's statement was hearsay, and Jon's silence is also hearsay.

   (D) Inadmissible, because Jim has not yet testified to his statement.

55. In support of her claim for damages for injuries, Robin's attorney sought to introduce evidence of Robin's testimony made to her boyfriend several days after the accident that "I must have sprained my neck because it hurts so much." The judge ruled the testimony:

   (A) Inadmissible, because it is hearsay.

   (B) Inadmissible, because Robin is not qualified to give testimony as to her medical condition.

   (C) Admissible, but only if Robin also puts on medical evidence that her neck was sprained.

   (D) Admissible, to show that Robin had suffered physical pain.

56. Jon's attorney sought to have the police officer testify that she took the statement of Sherry, who stated that Robin had attempted to pass her cab and went into the closed lane where she hit the front of the forklift. The judge should rule the testimony:

   (A) Inadmissible, because the police report is the best evidence.

   (B) Inadmissible, because it is hearsay.

   (C) Inadmissible as oral testimony, but the report may be introduced into evidence.

   (D) Admissible, because the officer was testifying as to past recollection recorded.

57. Robin's attorney sought to have the police officer testify that Mike had made a statement to her that, "All of us probably had too many beers at lunch and were in a hurry to finish the unloading." The trial judge should rule this evidence:

   (A) Inadmissible, as it is not relevant to the issues presented in the trial.

   (B) Inadmissible, because it is a hearsay declaration.

   (C) Admissible, because it is an admission.

   (D) Admissible, because it is a statement against interest.

58. Since Sherry had a passenger in her cab, she did not stay at the scene of the accident but made her statement the next day. She did, however, jot down her recollection of the accident when she dropped off her

passenger. At trial, when she was having difficulty remembering some of the facts, Jon's attorney sought to let her review the notes she had made. The court should rule this:

(A) Permissible, because it is a present recollection refreshed.

(B) Permissible, because it is a past recollection recorded.

(C) Impermissible, because Sherry is required to report all accidents to her employer, and the record is thus privileged.

(D) Impermissible, because there is no showing that Sherry had used her notes when she gave her statement to the police officer.

Question 59

Elbert sued Max for battery. Max claimed that he was attacked for no reason by Elbert and that he hit Elbert with a pipe in self-defense.

Frances was called to testify that on the night in question she was watching Max and Ralph across her back fence. She heard Ralph tell Max that Elbert had been flirting with Max's girlfriend, Maxine, and Max seemed very angry.

Max's attorney objected to this testimony. The court should find the evidence:

(A) Admissible, to show provocation for the battery.

(B) Admissible, as a legally operative fact.

(C) Inadmissible, because it is hearsay.

(D) Inadmissible, because it is an opinion.

Questions 60-61 are based on the following fact situation:

Trixie was on her way home from work when, while stopped at an intersection, she saw a yellow sports car run a red light, strike a woman in the crosswalk, and proceed through the intersection. Trixie gave a very detailed description of the driver to the police officer at the scene. Based on this description, the police apprehended Irwin and charged him with several criminal counts for the accident that seriously injured Prudence, the pedestrian. Trixie testified at the trial, but Irwin was acquitted. Prudence then filed a civil suit against Irwin to recover for her injuries.

Before the trial of Prudence's suit, Trixie was run down in the crosswalk of the very same intersection by a car driven by Neal. In the ambulance on the way to the hospital, Trixie said, "Irwin can't get away with it . . . . He hit Prudence that day . . . . I'll never forget his face." Trixie was dead on arrival at the hospital.

60. In her suit against Irwin, Prudence offers into evidence the police report containing Trixie's description of the driver. Irwin objects. The court should find the report:

(A) Admissible, because the report is relevant, and it is not hearsay.

(B) Admissible, because the report falls within the business records exception to the hearsay rule.

(C) Inadmissible, because the report is hearsay not within any exception.

(D) Inadmissible, because the report is not the best evidence.

61. Prudence then calls the ambulance attendant who accompanied Trixie on her final ride, and asks him to recount Trixie's statements made en route to the hospital. Irwin objects. The attendant's testimony is:

(A) Admissible, because Trixie's statement constitutes a dying declaration.

(B) Admissible, because Trixie's statement is an excited utterance.

(C) Inadmissible, because of the physi-cian-patient privilege.

(D) Inadmissible, because it is hearsay not within any exception.

Question 62

Phillipe was shopping at the Big Department Store. While riding down an escalator, the escalator malfunctioned, causing Phillipe to fall forward to the floor. After hitting the floor, Phillipe was in too much pain to move. Bert, another customer in the store, called an ambu-lance. Bert had no medical training, and so he simply tried to make Phillipe comfortable until the ambulance arrived. While waiting for the ambulance, Phillipe told Bert, "My left arm is numb and I have chest pains. I'm afraid I'm having a heart attack." Upon being taken to the hospital, it was determined that Phillipe had not suffered a heart attack, but had sustained severe damage to his chest and to the nerves affecting feeling in his left arm. Phillipe sued Big Depart-ment Store for his injuries. Big Department Store denies that Phillipe was injured as serious-ly as alleged in the complaint. At trial, Phillipe called Bert to testify to the statement made by Phillipe.

Bert's testimony as to Phillipe's statement is:

(A) Admissible to prove the extent of Phillipe's injuries at the time.

(B) Inadmissible, because Phillipe did not suffer a heart attack.

(C) Inadmissible, because Bert is not a doctor.

(D) Inadmissible, because it is hearsay not within any exception.

Question 63

In 1950, Abe purchased a life insurance policy on his life, naming his brother Ben as beneficiary. In 1980, Abe went on a game-viewing safari to Africa. Abe was supposed to return within six months, but failed to do so. By 1995, Abe had still not been heard from. Ben

contacted the insurance company about recover-ing the benefits under the policy, but the insur-ance company refused to pay the claim on the basis that there was no evidence that Abe was dead. Ben filed suit against the insurance com-pany to collect the proceeds under the policy. The jurisdiction in which the action has com-menced has a statute that states that a person is presumed dead if missing from the jurisdiction for seven years, and if no one in the jurisdiction has heard from the person in those seven years.

Assume that no other evidence is admitted at the trial on the issue of Abe's death. Which of the following is the most accurate statement?

(A) The jury will be permitted to find that Abe is alive.

(B) The jury will be permitted to find that Abe is dead.

(C) The judge must rule as a conclusive pre-sumption that Abe is dead.

(D) The jury must find that Abe is dead.

Question 64

Felix has filed a petition in the probate court to contest the validity of his brother Millard's will. Felix contends that when Millard executed the will eight years before, he was an alcoholic and was incapable of forming a valid testamen-tary intent. In support of this contention, Felix seeks to offer an affidavit prepared by Millard's former attorney, April, which states that she was asked to prepare a will for Millard just four months before this will was made. She had refused to do so because it was her opinion that Millard suffered from severe mental deficiency as an apparent result of his chronic alcoholism.

The judge should rule this affidavit to be:

(A) Admissible.

(B) Inadmissible, as being violative of the attorney-client privilege.

(C) Inadmissible, because it is hearsay not within any exception.

(D) Inadmissible, because it is improper opinion evidence.

Question 65

Pamela was injured in an automobile accident when her car was hit by the pickup truck driven by Dennis. At trial of her personal injury action, Pamela alleges that Dennis was driving on the wrong side of the road and that he was driving in excess of the posted speed limit. Dennis denies these allegations and denies liability for the accident. At trial, Pamela seeks to introduce evidence that Dennis has a reputation in the community for being a daredevil and for being somewhat irresponsible. In fact, Pamela's witness would testify that Dennis is known by all his friends as "Dennis the Menace."

The proffered testimony is:

(A) Admissible, because reputation evidence is a proper method of proving character.

(B) Inadmissible, to show that Dennis was negligent on this occasion.

(C) Inadmissible, because it is irrelevant.

(D) Admissible, if Dennis introduces evidence of his reputation for carefulness.

Question 66

Preston sued Dayton Elevator Company for injuries he suffered when his foot caught in one of its moving walkways. Dayton Elevator Company's chief engineer prepared a report of the accident at the request of its insurance company, and the report was given to the attorney who was hired to represent the elevator company in this trial. As part of its case-in-chief, Dayton's attorney seeks to introduce the report into evidence. The report states that the walkway was in good mechanical condition at the time of Preston's injury. Preston's attorney objects.

The report is:

(A) Admissible, as a business record.

(B) Admissible, if relied upon by a testifying expert witness.

(C) Inadmissible, because the insurance company is an interested party.

(D) Inadmissible, because it is hearsay not within any exception.

Questions 67-69 are based on the following fact situation:

Vance is charged with the murder of his employer, Mary. At the trial, the prosecution offered the testimony of another employee, Art, that he had accidentally picked up the phone when Vance was talking to an unidentified man who said, "I hear Mary's going to confess about the money you and she embezzled from the company. What are you going to do about it?"

67. Vance's attorney objects to Art's testimony on the ground that it is irrelevant. The judge should:

(A) Sustain the objection.

(B) Sustain the objection, on the grounds that whatever probative value the testimony has is substantially outweighed by the danger of unfair prejudice, confusion of the issues, or misleading the jury.

(C) Overrule the objection.

(D) Overrule the objection; but if Vance's attorney so requests, instruct the jury not to consider Art's testimony as evidence of Vance's involvement with any embezzlement of funds.

68. Vance's attorney also objects to Art's testimony on the ground that it is hearsay. The judge should:

(A) Sustain the objection.

(B) Overrule the objection, because the testimony, although hearsay, is being introduced to show Vance's state of mind, a hearsay exception.

(C) Overrule the objection because the testimony, although hearsay, qualifies as a business record since the call was made during business hours on a business phone.

(D) Overrule the objection if the evidence is offered to help prove Vance's motive.

69. Assume the judge holds that Art's testimony is admissible. Vance then attempts to testify that the "embezzlement incident" Art referred to in his testimony was in fact a proper reimbursement that Vance was entitled to. The prosecution objects to the testimony, claiming it is irrelevant. The judge should rule that Vance's testimony is:

(A) Admissible, because it is relevant in determining whether Vance had a motive to kill Mary.

(B) Admissible, because it is relevant in establishing Art's credibility.

(C) Inadmissible as irrelevant, because it would tend to impeach Art's testimony on a collateral matter.

(D) Inadmissible as irrelevant, because the probative value of Vance's testimony is substantially outweighed by the danger of unfair prejudice, confusion of the issues, waste of time, or needless presentation of cumulative evidence.

Questions 70-73 are based on the following fact situation:

Travis is on trial in federal court for the armed robbery of a casino. Travis claims that he was out of town at the time of the robbery.

70. Travis calls Erica to the stand as an alibi witness to testify that she was with him on the trip. When asked where she was and who she was with on the date in question, Erica stated that she could not recall. She said she recalls spending a weekend at the Lovebird Motel this spring, but she does not recall the date or her traveling companion. Travis's attorney then showed her a letter written by her on Lovebird Motel stationery, and asks her to look at it and try to answer the question again. The prosecution objects. The objection should be:

(A) Overruled, because this is a past recollection recorded.

(B) Overruled, but Erica cannot depend on the terms of the letter when answering.

(C) Sustained, because the letter is hearsay.

(D) Sustained, because the letter has not been properly authenticated.

71. Erica responded to the above question by stating, "I do recall that it was the weekend of the robbery that I was at the Lovebird, because I now remember that it was the same weekend as my mother's birthday; but I would not go around the block with a cad like Travis, let alone a romantic trip." Travis's attorney then asks, "Didn't you in fact state at Travis's preliminary hearing that you were with him for the entire weekend, and it was one of the most memorable weekends of your life?" The prosecution objects. The question is:

(A) Proper, if the judge finds that Erica is hostile.

(B) Proper, because it constitutes refreshing the witness's recollection.

(C) Improper, because this is a leading question on direct examination.

(D) Improper, because Travis cannot impeach his own witness.

72. Travis's attorney then seeks to introduce the transcript of Erica's statement from the preliminary hearing. The prosecution objects. The transcript is:

(A) Admissible, for impeachment purposes only.

(B) Admissible, for impeachment purposes and as substantive evidence.

(C) Inadmissible, because it is hearsay.

(D) Inadmissible, because Erica is not unavailable.

73. The prosecution calls Barbara, Travis's wife, to testify that just before the robbery, Travis purchased a gun. She will also testify that she found a casino floorplan in Travis's dresser drawer. Travis's attorney objects. The objection should be:

(A) Sustained, because spousal privilege belongs to the party-spouse.

(B) Sustained, because Travis acted in reliance upon the intimacy of the marital relationship.

(C) Overruled, because the Federal Rules do not recognize testimonial privileges.

(D) Overruled, because Barbara may choose to testify.

Questions 74-77 are based on the following fact situation:

Buyer entered into a written contract with Farmer to purchase Farmer's dairy farm. The contract contained a provision that "Farmer's land and inventory are valued at $175,000." The contract also contained a provision that stated, "This contract represents the entire agreement between the parties. No other promises or representations have been made."

Buyer alleges that he purchased the farm only because Farmer had assured him that the land and inventory were worth $350,000, when they were in fact worth only $175,000.

74. Buyer seeks to testify that during negotiations Farmer had said repeatedly that the value of the land and the inventory was $350,000, but at the advice of Farmer's attorney, he was going to list the value at $175,000 in the contract for tax purposes. Farmer's attorney objects. The evidence is:

(A) Inadmissible hearsay.

(B) Inadmissible under the parol evidence rule.

(C) Neither hearsay nor violative of the parol evidence rule.

(D) Admissible hearsay, unaffected by the parol evidence rule.

75. Buyer's attorney next calls Farmer's ex-wife to testify that during their marriage Farmer told her about the fraud he had pulled on Buyer. Farmer's attorney objects on the grounds of privilege. The court should rule that Farmer's ex-wife:

(A) Can be called as a witness and can testify against Farmer because she and Farmer are no longer married.

(B) Can be called as a witness but cannot be directed to testify against Farmer if the facts were told to her in confidence.

(C) Cannot be called as a witness at all.

(D) Must testify, because the privilege applies to criminal cases only.

76. Farmer's attorney, by way of defense, attempts to call to the stand Cattleman, as an expert on farm management and finance. To qualify Cattleman as an expert, Farmer's attorney asks Cattleman about his

training, education, and experience in the field. Cattleman responds that he was "certified by the State Board of Agriculture in 1962 as an expert on Farm Management." On cross-examination concerning qualifications as an expert, Buyer's attorney asks, "Isn't it true, Cattleman, that you failed the certification exam given by the State Board of Agriculture on Farm Management in 1962?" Cattleman replies, "No!" Buyer's attorney then attempts to submit into evidence the official pass-fail list published by the State Board for the 1962 farm management certification exam. Farmer's attorney objects. The court should:

(A) Admit the list in order for the trial judge to evaluate whether Cattleman is qualified as an expert, and permit Cattleman to testify only if the judge concludes that Cattleman is sufficiently qualified.

(B) Admit the list as relevant to Cattleman's qualifications, and instruct the jury that the list may also be considered in determining Cattleman's truthfulness as a witness.

(C) Exclude the transcript as irrelevant, since it tends to impeach Cattleman on a collateral issue.

(D) Exclude the transcript because Buyer's attorney failed to lay a proper foundation for the evidence.

77. Farmer's attorney then offers a report prepared shortly after Buyer and Farmer signed the contract and purportedly signed by Stillwell, a well-known local CPA. While reports of this kind were not normally prepared by Stillwell, he prepared this one as a favor to Farmer. The report contains an extensive analysis of the financial condition of Farmer's farm and concludes that "it is entirely possible, in my opinion, that, using the right accounting methods, the value of the land and inventory of Farmer could be placed at $350,000 instead of $175,000." Buyer's attorney objects to the introduction of the report as evidence of the value of the farm. The court should rule that the report is:

(A) Admissible nonhearsay, since the report constituted the opinion of Stillwell.

(B) Hearsay, but admissible as a past recollection recorded.

(C) Hearsay, but admissible as a business record.

(D) Inadmissible hearsay.

EVIDENCE ANSWERS

Answer to Question 1

(C) The grand jury statement is admissible both as impeachment evidence and as substantive evidence. A prior inconsistent statement made under oath at a prior proceeding or deposition is admissible nonhearsay, and thus may be used as substantive evidence as well as for impeachment. The credibility of a witness may be impeached by showing that the witness has, on another occasion, made statements that are inconsistent with some material part of his present testimony. Because it is made by the declarant other than while testifying at the trial or hearing, a prior inconsistent statement will usually constitute hearsay if offered to prove the truth of the matter asserted therein. Under such circumstances, the statement would be admissible only to impeach the witness. However, where the statement was made under oath at a prior proceeding, including a grand jury proceeding, it is admissible nonhearsay (*i.e.,* it may be considered as substantive proof of the facts stated). [Fed. R. Evid. 801(d)(1)(A)] Walter's sworn statement before the grand jury that Deef was driving normally at the time of the accident is inconsistent with his later in-court testimony that Deef was on the wrong side of the highway at the time of the collision. Thus, this statement can be inquired into by Deef to cast doubt on Walter's credibility. Because the statement was made at a prior proceeding, and was made under oath, it is nonhearsay, and is also admissible as substantive proof that Deef was in fact driving normally at the time of the accident. (C) is the only answer that reflects the fact that the grand jury statement may be used both for impeachment and for substantive purposes. (A) reflects the view of prior law, which was that prior inconsistent statements were limited to impeachment regardless of the circumstances under which they were made. As noted above, Federal Rule 801(d)(1)(A) deems such statements made under oath at a prior trial or other proceeding to be nonhearsay, and as such, to be admissible as substantive evidence. (B) is incorrect because it precludes use of Walter's grand jury testimony for impeachment purposes. A prior inconsistent statement may always be used to impeach the credibility of a witness. (D) is incorrect for two reasons. First, even if deemed to be hearsay, a prior inconsistent statement would be admissible to impeach the witness. Second, because the prior inconsistent statement of Walter was made under oath at a grand jury proceeding, it is admissible nonhearsay.

Answer to Question 2

(D) The transcript of Walter's grand jury testimony is inadmissible hearsay. Hearsay is a statement, other than one made by the declarant while testifying at the trial or hearing, offered in evidence to prove the truth of the matter asserted. [Fed. R. Evid. 801(c)] A hearsay statement, to which no exception to the hearsay rule is applicable, must be excluded upon appropriate objection to its admission. [Fed. R. Evid. 802] The transcript of Walter's grand jury testimony is being offered to prove the truth of the matter asserted therein (*i.e.,* that Deef was driving normally at the time of the accident). The grand jury testimony of a person who is not now testifying is deemed neither nonhearsay nor within any recognized exception to the hearsay rule. (A) is wrong because grand jury testimony does not fall within the former testimony exception. Under that exception, the testimony of a now unavailable witness given at another hearing or in a deposition taken in accordance with law is admissible in a subsequent trial if there is a sufficient similarity of parties and issues so that the opportunity to develop testimony or cross-examine at the prior hearing was meaningful. [Fed. R. Evid. 804(b)(1)] Grand jury proceedings do not afford an opportunity for cross-examination. Consequently, Plain (the party against whom the grand jury transcript is offered) did not have the opportunity to develop Walter's testimony. Absent a meaningful opportunity to cross-examine Walter at the time of his grand jury testimony, the transcript of such testimony will not be admissible under the former testimony exception. (B) is incorrect because Walter's statement is an out-of-court statement being offered for its truth and does not fall within any special category of nonhearsay under the Federal Rules. Therefore, the grand jury testimony is hearsay. Note that Walter's testimony cannot be nonhearsay under Rule 801(d) because Walter is not currently testifying at Deef's trial; thus, the grand jury transcript cannot be the prior statement of a *witness*. (C) is incorrect because the rehabilitation of Witt (if he has been impeached by a charge that he was lying or exaggerating because of some motive) would have to be accomplished through the introduction of a prior consistent statement made by Witt, rather than Walter. A party may rehabilitate a witness by showing a prior consistent statement if opposing counsel has impeached the credibility of a witness by making a charge that the witness is lying or exaggerating because of some motive. Under Federal Rule 801(d)(1)(B), the prior consistent statement may be used not only to bolster the witness's testimony, but also as substantive evidence of the truth of its contents (*i.e.,* it is nonhearsay). If Witt has been charged with lying or exaggerating, then Deef's counsel may rebut such a charge by introducing a prior consistent statement made by Witt before the time of any such alleged lying or exaggerating. However, a statement by Walter cannot be used to rehabilitate Witt.

Answer to Question 3

(B) The record of Deef's conviction should be admitted to prove Deef's intoxication. The record of conviction is hearsay; *i.e.,* it is a statement, other than one made by the declarant while testifying at the trial or hearing, offered to prove the truth of the matter asserted. Under the Federal Rules, however, such judgments fall within the hearsay exception for records of felony convictions. Under the Federal Rules, judgments of felony convictions are admissible in both criminal and civil actions to prove any fact essential to the judgment, whether the judgment arose after trial or upon a plea of guilty. [Fed. R. Evid. 803(22)] For purposes of this Rule, a felony is any crime punishable by death or imprisonment in excess of one year. The drunken driving charge to which Deef pleaded guilty was punishable by a maximum of two years' imprisonment and is, thus, a felony. Consequently, a properly authenticated copy of Deef's conviction of this crime is admissible to prove the fact of Deef's intoxication, which was a fact essential to the judgment of conviction. Note that the actual plea of guilty is also admissible as an admission of a party-opponent. This type of judicial admission is not conclusive, and the defendant may explain the circumstances of the plea. The plea, being an admission, is nonhearsay under the Federal Rules. (A) is incorrect because, in a civil case, evidence of character to prove the conduct of a person in the litigated event is generally not admissible. Circumstantial use of prior behavior patterns for the purpose of inferring that, at the time and place in question, a person probably acted in accord with such patterns creates a danger of prejudice and distraction from the main issues. Therefore, the record of Deef's conviction cannot be used to infer negligence by showing Deef's character. (C) is incorrect because, as noted above, a judgment of a felony conviction is admissible under Federal Rule 803(22) regardless of whether the conviction resulted from a trial or a guilty plea. (D) is incorrect because, as discussed above, the judgment is within the exception to the hearsay rule for records of felony convictions.

Answer to Question 4

(B) Although a party is entitled as of right to some cross-examination, the extent or scope of cross-examination is a matter of judicial discretion. The judge may exercise reasonable control over the examination of witnesses to aid the effective ascertainment of truth, to avoid wasting time, and to protect witnesses from harassment or undue embarrassment. Specifically, the trial court has the authority to cut off cross-examination when it determines there has been an adequate opportunity for meaningful cross-examination. Here, the defense attorney has the right to cross-examine Wayne, who is an adverse witness. However, carrying on such cross-examination for three days, with the prospect of at least one more day, would probably be considered excessive in light of the limited direct examination of the witness. Cross-examination is limited to: (i) matters brought out on direct examination and inferences naturally drawn therefrom; and (ii) matters affecting the credibility of the witness. [Fed. R. Evid. 611(b)] (A) is incorrect because, even if the testimony is relevant, the court may terminate or otherwise control the cross-examination to avoid wasting time or harassing a witness. (C) is incorrect for a similar reason. Although matters relating to the subject matter of direct examination may properly be brought out on cross-examination, the court has the discretion to terminate such questioning to avoid wasting of time or harassment or embarrassment of a witness. Therefore, it is incorrect to state that, if the questioning of Wayne relates to the subject matter of direct examination, the court lacks the authority to terminate the cross-examination. (D) is incorrect because, although due process considerations are of undisputed significance, the facts here do not appear to present any real conflict between due process and judicial economy. If the defense attorney has had an adequate opportunity for cross-examination of Wayne, then there is no deprivation of due process if principles of judicial economy now dictate that the questioning be cut short.

Answer to Question 5

(D) The word "Craftsman" is not hearsay, and the wrench is relevant circumstantial evidence on the issue of whether Derrick dropped the wrench that struck Ped. Evidence is relevant if it tends to make the existence of any fact of consequence to the action more probable than it would be without the evidence. [Fed. R. Evid. 401] If Derrick uses "Craftsman" wrenches on the job, and the wrench that struck Ped bears the brand name "Craftsman," it is more probable than would otherwise be the case that the wrench that struck Ped was dropped by Derrick. Thus, the wrench is relevant to prove that Derrick dropped the wrench. The wrench is circumstantial, rather than direct, evidence because a fact about it is being proved as a basis for an inference that another fact is true; *i.e.,* the fact that the wrench bears the name "Craftsman" is proved to form a basis for inferring that Derrick dropped the wrench. Direct evidence is offered to prove a fact about the object as an end in itself. Here, the wrench bearing the name "Craftsman" is not being offered as a means of proving, for example, that the wrench is in fact a "Craftsman" brand. Consequently, the wrench constitutes circumstantial evidence. In addition, when offered for the stated purpose, the wrench is not hearsay. Hearsay is a statement, other than one made by the declarant while testifying at the trial or hearing, offered in evidence to prove the truth of the matter asserted. [Fed. R. Evid. 801(c)] The wrench is not being offered to prove the truth of the matter asserted (*i.e.,* that the wrench is actually a "Craftsman"). It is of no significance whether the wrench being offered is a genuine "Craftsman." What is important is that it bears the same name as those wrenches used by Derrick on the job. Thus, introduction of the wrench into evidence will not violate the rule against hearsay. (A) is incorrect because it states that the word "Craftsman" on the wrench creates a hearsay problem. As noted, the wrench is not being offered to prove its genuineness as a "Craftsman," but rather to form the basis for an inference that it was dropped by Derrick. Thus, there is no hearsay problem. (B) is incorrect because the wrench is circumstantial, rather than direct, evidence that Derrick dropped the wrench that struck Ped. (C) reaches the incorrect conclusion that the wrench is not relevant. As has been explained above, the fact that the wrench that struck Ped bears the name "Craftsman" tends to make more probable the material fact that Derrick is the person who dropped the wrench. Therefore, the wrench is relevant. Also, (C) states an incorrect test for relevance. To be relevant, the wrench need not show that it is more likely than not that Derrick dropped it; rather, the wrench must have some tendency to make it more probable than it would be without this evidence that Derrick dropped it.

Answer to Question 6

(D) The evidence is not hearsay because the statement is not offered for its truth; the statement of the foreman is offered to show its effect on Ped. Hearsay is a statement, other than one made by the declarant while testifying at the trial or hearing, offered in evidence to prove the truth of the matter asserted. [Fed. R. Evid. 801(c)] If a statement is hearsay, and no exception to the hearsay rule is applicable, the evidence must be excluded upon appropriate objection to its admission. [Fed. R. Evid. 802] A statement that would be inadmissible hearsay to prove the truth of the statement may be admitted to show the statement's effect on the hearer or reader. Thus, in a negligence case, where knowledge of a danger is at issue, a statement of warning is admissible for the limited purpose of showing knowledge or notice on the part of a listener. Here, the defense of assumption of the risk has been raised. Whether Ped knew of the danger involved in walking under the scaffold is an issue. Consequently, the statement of the construction foreman is admissible to show that Ped had knowledge of the possible danger. The statement is not hearsay because it is not offered to prove that it was in fact dangerous for Ped to walk under the scaffold. (A) incorrectly states that the reason the statement is not hearsay is that the declarant is testifying as a witness. The fact that the declarant is now testifying does not alter the hearsay nature of a statement. Any out-of-court statement offered for its truth is hearsay in most jurisdictions (the Federal Rules have a few specific statements characterized as nonhearsay) regardless of whether the declarant is testifying. The reason hearsay is excluded is that there is no opportunity for cross-examination *at the time* the statement was made. The key in this case is not that the declarant is testifying, but that the statement is not being offered for its truth. (B) characterizes the testimony as hearsay, which is incorrect because it is not being offered for its truth. Even if this testimony were hearsay, it is incorrect to state that it is "part of the res gestae." Formerly, a wide class of declarations was loosely categorized under the label of res gestae exceptions to the hearsay rule. This group included the following exceptions: (i) present state of mind; (ii) excited utterances; (iii) present sense impression; and (iv) declarations of physical condition. The testimony of the foreman would not come within any of these exceptions. (C) incorrectly characterizes the testimony as hearsay. In addition, this statement, even if hearsay, would not come within the present state of mind exception. A statement of a declarant's then-existing state of mind is admissible when the declarant's state of mind is directly in issue and material to the controversy, or as a basis for a circumstantial inference that a particular declaration of intent was carried out. The declarant here is the foreman. There is no indication that the foreman's state of mind is at all relevant to this litigation, nor is the statement offered indicative of any particular intent on the part of the foreman. Thus, the present state of mind exception is inapplicable.

Answer to Question 7

(D) The past recollection recorded exception to the hearsay rule is one of a class of hearsay exceptions that do not require unavailability of the declarant. If a witness has insufficient memory of an event to enable him to testify fully and accurately, even after consulting a writing given to him on the stand, the writing itself may be introduced into evidence if a proper foundation is laid for its admissibility. The foundation for receiving such a writing into evidence must include proof that: (i) the witness at one time had personal knowledge of the facts recited in the writing; (ii) the writing was made by or under the direction of the witness or has been adopted by him; (iii) the writing was timely made when the matter was fresh in the mind of the witness; (iv) the writing is accurate; and (v) the witness has insufficient recollection to testify fully and accurately. [Fed. R. Evid. 803(5)] Ped need not establish the unavailability of the safety officer. (A), (B), and (C) each correspond to one of the foundational requirements. (A) corresponds to requirement (iii), (B) corresponds to requirement (iv), and (C) corresponds to requirement (ii). Because (A), (B), and (C) reflect foundational facts that Ped will have to establish to have the report admitted under the past recollection recorded exception, they are incorrect.

Answer to Question 8

(B) Xenon's testimony is admissible nonhearsay. The statement by Xenon is not being offered to prove the truth of the matter asserted therein and thus is not hearsay. Hearsay is a statement made out of court by the declarant, offered in evidence to prove the truth of the matter asserted. [Fed. R. Evid. 801(c)] Although hearsay is inadmissible (unless an exception to the hearsay rule is applicable), a statement that would be inadmissible hearsay to prove the truth thereof may be admitted to show the statement's effect on the hearer or reader. Thus, in a negligence case, where knowledge of a danger is at issue, a person's warning statement is admissible for the limited purpose of showing knowledge or notice on the part of a listener. Here, one of the theories of recovery underlying Pat's lawsuit is that Yogi negligently failed to secure the load. Therefore, Pat must show that Yogi either knew or should have known that the load was not properly secured. Consequently, Xenon's statement that the chains looked loose is admissible to show that Yogi had notice of the possible danger. If this same out-of-court statement were offered to show that its contents were true (*i.e.,* that the chains were in fact loose), then it would constitute hearsay, but because the statement is offered to show notice to Yogi of a possible danger, it is nonhearsay and (C) is incorrect. (A) is incorrect because the admissibility of the statement arises from its status as nonhearsay. If a statement is nonhearsay, then there is no need to refer to hearsay exceptions in determining the statement's admissibility. (D) is incorrect for two reasons. First, the statement by Xenon is not being offered to show Xenon's opinion that the chains were loose. Rather, the statement is offered to show that Yogi had notice of a possible danger involving the chains. Because the testimony of Xenon simply relates this statement made to Yogi, such testimony cannot be characterized as opinion testimony. Second, (D) incorrectly implies that opinion evidence is inadmissible. Even opinions of lay witnesses are admissible when they are: (i) rationally based on the perception of the witness; (ii) helpful to a clear understanding of the witness's testimony or to the determination of a fact in issue; and (iii) not based on scientific, technical, or other specialized knowledge. [Fed. R. Evid. 701] Certainly, Xenon would be permitted to testify that the chains looked loose at the time he observed them, as such an opinion would be based on personal observation, would be helpful to the determination of a fact in issue (*i.e.,* whether the load was properly secured), and would not be based on technical knowledge.

Answer to Question 9

(D) The report is admissible nonhearsay. The report is an admission by a party-opponent because it is a statement by an agent concerning a matter within the scope of his agency, made during the existence of the employment relationship. Yogi's statement constitutes a prior acknowledgment of a relevant fact, and is admissible against Yogi's principal, Delivery Co. Such an admission is considered nonhearsay under the Federal Rules. (A) is wrong because, as discussed above, the report is admissible as an admission and no foundation is necessary. If the report were not made by a party, Pat could seek to have it admitted as past recollection recorded, but several foundational requirements would have to be met. A writing may be introduced under this exception to the hearsay rule if: (i) the witness at one time had personal knowledge of the facts recited in the writing; (ii) the writing was made by the witness or under his direction, or was adopted by the witness; (iii) the writing was timely made when the matter was fresh in the mind of the witness; (iv) the writing is accurate; and (v) the witness is presently unable to remember the facts sufficiently to testify fully. Here, Yogi has not testified that the writing is accurate or that he has insufficient recollection of the accident to testify fully. Without this foundational testimony, the report could not be admitted as a past recollection recorded. (B) is wrong because it implies that the report could be admitted only as a business record, and that one of the elements for that exception is lacking. As discussed above, the writing is admissible as an admission; so there is no need to rely on the business record exception. Furthermore, even if the report were not an admission and Pat were seeking to admit it as a business record, a court might find that it was made in the regular course of business. In *Palmer v. Hoffman,* the United States Supreme Court held that a similar routine accident report was prepared in anticipation of litigation, and litigation was not the railroad's primary business. Most courts, however, have applied this rule only when the report is offered by the preparer's side. If it is offered against the party that prepared it, most courts find it within the regular course of business. The Federal Rules give the trial court discretion to exclude a business record of this nature where its source indicates a lack of trustworthiness. Thus, since the report is being offered against Delivery Co., most courts would find it sufficiently trustworthy and admit it. (C) is wrong because, as discussed above, the report is admissible as an admission and thus no foundational requirements for the business record exception need be met. Moreover, even under the business record exception, opinions are allowed as long as they are in the regular course of business.

Answer to Question 10

(D) The court would never permit invocation of the physician-patient privilege if the patient knew that the person she was consulting was not a licensed physician. The physician-patient privilege requires that a licensed physician be present for purposes of treatment, that the information be obtained while attending the patient, and that the information be necessary for treatment (*i.e.,* that it deal with medical matters). While some jurisdictions do not apply the privilege to criminal proceedings, the question appears to assume that such a privilege would be applicable in criminal cases in this jurisdiction. In all jurisdictions, though, the existence of a licensed physician, or the patient's reasonable belief that the consultant is a licensed physician, is a prerequisite for the privilege to apply. (A) is incorrect because it states one of the requirements for the privilege to apply. Thus, under this circumstance the court would be *most* (rather than least) likely to allow Vickie to use the privilege. (B) is incorrect simply because it is irrelevant. Whether Vickie is married to Dean does not affect the applicability of the physician-patient privilege to Dr. Dornfeld's testimony. Thus, that circumstance does not make it either more likely or less likely that the court will allow the privilege. (C) is wrong because the privilege belongs to the patient and she may decide whether to claim it or to waive it. Hence, Dr. Dornfeld's prior disclosure would not make the court less likely to allow Vickie to assert the privilege.

Answer to Question 11

(D) Pike's testimony does not violate the hearsay rule or the parol evidence rule. Hearsay is a statement other than one made by the declarant while testifying at the trial or hearing, offered in evidence to prove the truth of the matter asserted. A hearsay statement must be excluded upon objection, if no exception to the hearsay rule is applicable. However, an out-of-court statement introduced for any purpose other than to prove the truth of the matter asserted is not hearsay. Thus, a statement that would be inadmissible hearsay if offered to prove its truth may be admitted to show the statement's effect on the person hearing it. Here, Pike is offering to testify to Dever's out-of-court statement, not to prove the truth of that statement (*i.e.,* that the real value of the business was $500,000), but rather to show the effect of the statement on Pike (*i.e.,* that Pike relied on the statement in entering into the transaction). Thus, the offered evidence is not hearsay. Under the parol evidence rule, if an agreement is reduced to a writing, all prior or contemporaneous negotiations or agreements are merged into the written agreement. Extrinsic evidence is not admissible to add to, detract from, or alter the agreement as written. However, the parol evidence rule does not bar admission of parol evidence to show that an apparent contractual obligation is not an obligation at all—*e.g.,* to show that a contract was void or voidable. Consequently, parol evidence is admissible to establish or disprove a contract attacked on grounds of fraud, duress, or undue influence inducing consent. The testimony in this case does not violate the parol evidence rule because it is offered to show the existence of fraud that induced Pike to enter into the contract. (A) is wrong because it states that the evidence violates the parol evidence rule, which is not true (*see* above). (B) is wrong because it characterizes the evidence as hearsay and it is not since it is not offered for its truth. (C) is also wrong because it characterizes the evidence as admissible hearsay, and the evidence is not hearsay at all.

Answer to Question 12

(C) If the facts were told to Dever's ex-wife in confidence during her marriage to Dever, Dever has a privilege to prevent her from disclosing such facts. Either spouse has a privilege to refuse to disclose, and to prevent another from disclosing, a confidential communication made between the spouses while they were husband and wife. Both spouses hold this privilege. The communication must be made in reliance upon the intimacy of the marital relationship, and must be made during a valid marriage. Divorce will not terminate the privilege retroactively. If Dever told his ex-wife of the fraud on Pike during their marriage, and he did so in reliance upon the intimacy of their relationship, then Dever may prevent his ex-wife from disclosing this confidential communication. The divorce of Dever and his ex-wife subsequent to disclosure of the fraud does not terminate the privilege. (A) is incorrect because it ignores Dever's privilege to prevent the testimony if the testimony reveals a confidential marital communication. (B) is incorrect because the applicability of the privilege for confidential marital communications extends to civil cases. Thus, Dever's ex-wife can refuse to disclose the contents of such a communication, or Dever can prevent her from making such a disclosure. (Note that in criminal cases, there is a separate concept of spousal immunity under which a married person may not be compelled to testify against her spouse, and if a spouse is a criminal defendant, the other spouse may not even be called as a witness. In federal court, this privilege belongs to the witness-spouse; *i.e.,* she may not be compelled to testify, but neither may she be foreclosed from testifying (except as to confidential communications). Spousal immunity, unlike that for confidential marital communications, terminates upon divorce or annulment. (Care should be taken to avoid confusing these two privileges.)) (D) is incorrect because it is too broad. Dever can only prevent his ex-wife's testimony as to matters revealed as a confidential marital communication. Dever cannot prevent her from being called as a witness.

Answer to Question 13

(B) The qualification of a witness as an expert is a preliminary fact to be determined by the judge. The existence of preliminary facts (*e.g.,* competency of testimony or evidence privilege) other than those of conditional relevance must be determined by the court. These questions are withheld from the jury out of a fear that, once the jury hears the disputed evidence, the damage has been done, rendering ineffective an instruction to disregard the evidence if the preliminary fact is not found. One of these foundational facts that must first be determined by the judge is the qualification of a witness as an expert. Thus, in this question it is the province of the judge to determine whether Dr. Wizard is an expert in the field of finance, so as to allow him to testify further. Also, the judge is free to consider any relevant evidence in making the determination; so he should consider the transcript. (A) is incorrect because Dr. Wizard's claim to degrees is not a collateral matter. Where a witness makes a statement not directly relevant to the issues in the case, the rule against impeachment on a collateral matter bars the opponent from proving the statement untrue either by extrinsic evidence or by a prior inconsistent statement. However, a witness's competence to testify and credibility are always relevant. A test for deciding whether a matter is collateral is to ask whether the evidence would be admissible absent the contrary assertion by the witness. If it would be, it cannot be excluded as impeachment on a collateral matter. In this case, Pike could present evidence that Dr. Wizard is not qualified as an expert regardless of whether Dr. Wizard asserted that he had obtained certain degrees. Thus, the transcripts are admissible. (C) is incorrect because it assigns to the jury the function of deciding the qualifications of an expert witness, which is a question for the court. The jury decides those preliminary facts where the answer to the preliminary question determines whether the proffered evidence is relevant at all. In such instances, the court may instruct the jury to determine whether the preliminary fact exists, and to disregard the proffered evidence unless the jury finds that the preliminary fact does exist. If the jury were allowed to hear Dr. Wizard's testimony, it would be virtually useless to instruct the jury to disregard the testimony if it concluded that Dr. Wizard is not an expert. (D) is incorrect because the credibility of Dr. Wizard and his qualifications as an expert witness may be attacked by showing that he did not receive the claimed degrees from Shoestring State. Any matter that affects the credibility or competency of the witness is relevant.

Answer to Question 14

(B) Only Nestor's testimony is necessary to introduce the photograph. To be admissible, a photograph must be identified by a witness as a portrayal of certain facts relevant to the issue, and verified by the witness as a correct representation of those facts. It is sufficient if the witness who identifies the photograph is familiar with the scene or object depicted. It is not necessary to call the photographer to authenticate the photograph. Here, the actual physical appearance of the intersection is most likely relevant to the manner in which the accident occurred. As a resident of the neighborhood in which the accident took place, and as someone who was at the scene of the accident shortly after its occurrence, Nestor is sufficiently familiar with the scene to testify that the photograph is an accurate representation of the accident scene. Such identification by Nestor is needed for the photograph to be admissible. (A) incorrectly categorizes Archon's testimony as necessary. Generally, a photographer's testimony is not necessary to authenticate a photo. In this case, it is particularly unhelpful because Archon is not familiar with the scene as it was when the accident occurred. Also, the testimony of Nestor is necessary as a verification by one who is familiar with the scene. (C) is incorrect because, as stated above, the testimony of Archon, the photographer, is not necessary. (D) is incorrect because the photograph is admissible if properly identified by Nestor.

Answer to Question 15

(C) The statement from Dr. Rheum's treatise is admissible to impeach and as substantive evidence. Under the Federal Rules, learned treatises can be used either for impeachment or as substantive evidence. One way the credibility of an expert witness may be attacked is by cross-examining him as to his general knowledge of the field in which he is claiming to be an expert. This can be done by cross-examining the expert on statements contained in any scientific publication that is established as reliable authority. Reliability of a publication may be established by: (i) the direct testimony or cross-examination admission of the expert; (ii) the testimony of another expert; or (iii) judicial notice. The Federal Rules recognize an exception to the hearsay rule for learned treatises and admit them as substantive evidence if: (i) the expert is on the stand and it is called to his attention, and (ii) it is established as reliable authority (*see* above). Dr. Orthopod has admitted on cross-examination that Dr. Rheum's treatise is authoritative in the field. Thus, Dutch may use the statement in the treatise to attack Dr. Orthopod's general knowledge of the field of arthritis by showing that Dr. Orthopod's opinion that the blow to Potter's knee caused his arthritis is considered by the author of the treatise to be ignorant and unfounded. As noted above, such an attack on Dr. Orthopod's general knowledge of the field is a proper means of impeaching his credibility. In addition, pursuant to the Federal Rules, the statement may be read into the record as substantive evidence (*i.e.,* as a means of proving that Potter's arthritis could not have been caused by a single traumatic event, such as the blow to his knee). The statement may be used as substantive evidence because it has been brought to the attention of Dr. Orthopod during cross-examination and he established it as a reliable authority, and it will be read into evidence while he is on the stand. (A), which reflects the traditional view, is incorrect because the Federal Rules permit the use of the statement in the treatise as substantive evidence. (B) is incorrect because it precludes use of the statement for impeachment purposes. (D) is incorrect because it would not allow introduction of the statement for either impeachment or substantive evidentiary purposes, and thus it is an incorrect statement of the law.

Answer to Question 16

(B) Xavier's statement is admissible under the excited utterance exception to the hearsay rule. Although hearsay is generally inadmissible, certain kinds of hearsay are deemed to be reliable enough to be admitted. Among these exceptions is one for excited utterances. Under this exception, a declaration made during or soon after a startling event is admissible. The declaration must be made under the stress of excitement produced by the startling event (*i.e.,* before the declarant has time to consciously reflect on the occurrence. Also, the declaration must concern the immediate facts of the startling occurrence). [Fed. R. Evid. 803(2)] Here, Xavier's statement (to be testified to by Wesley) is an out-of-court declaration, offered to prove the truth of the matter asserted (*i.e.,* that the license plate number of the getaway car was 07771). Thus, Xavier's statement is hearsay. However, this statement was made during the course of a bank robbery, an event startling enough to produce nervous excitement in Xavier. The statement was made under the stress of the excitement produced by the robbery, and concerned the immediate facts of the robbery (*i.e.,* it referred to the car in which the robber was making his escape). Therefore, the statement qualifies as an excited utterance, rendering Wesley's testimony admissible. (A) is wrong because it represents an incorrect application of the best evidence rule. The best evidence rule applies only when a party is trying to prove the terms of a writing. Here, there is no writing involved; thus, the best evidence rule is inapplicable. (C) is wrong in characterizing Xavier's statement as inadmissible. Although the statement is hearsay, as explained above, it is admissible as an excited utterance. (D) is wrong because no foundation is required for Wesley to testify to the excited statement he heard. Also, note that the hearsay declarant (Xavier) is, contrary to the language of (D), identified as the person who made the statement.

Answer to Question 17

(B) Yancy's testimony should be admitted as proper impeachment of Wesley. Impeachment is the casting of an adverse reflection on the veracity of a witness. A witness may be impeached by either cross-examination or extrinsic evidence, such as by putting other witnesses on the stand who contradict the witness's testimony. Here, the defense is using Yancy's testimony to impeach Wesley's testimony as to what Xavier said. This is proper. (A) is wrong because a witness's credibility is always relevant. Furthermore, Yancy's testimony relates to a crucial issue in the case, the identification of the vehicle used in the crime. Thus, the testimony is relevant. (C) is wrong because this is not a collateral matter. Impeachment on a collateral matter is prohibited, but a collateral matter is one that arises when a witness makes a statement not directly relevant to the issues in the case. Wesley's statement about the license plate number of the getaway car is directly relevant to the issues in the case and, thus, is a proper subject of impeachment. (D) is wrong because impeachment evidence need not positively controvert the prior testimony; it need only tend to discredit the credibility of the prior witness.

Answer to Question 18

(D) The transcript of Xavier's testimony before the grand jury is inadmissible hearsay. Hearsay is a statement, other than one made by the declarant while testifying at the trial or hearing, offered in evidence to prove the truth of the matter asserted. If a statement is hearsay and no exception to the rule is applicable, the evidence must be excluded upon appropriate objection. The reason hearsay is excluded is because the adverse party was denied the opportunity to cross-examine the declarant. Xavier's statement was not made while testifying at Dwight's trial and is being offered for its truth. Since it does not fall within any exception, it is inadmissible hearsay. (A) is wrong because inadmissible hearsay is not admissible even for the purpose of rehabilitation. To the extent that Wesley was impeached by Yancy's testimony, it was through evidence contradicting Wesley's assertion. To be effective as a rehabilitation of Wesley's testimony, the transcript would be offered to prove the truth of the matter asserted, and thus it would constitute hearsay. (B) is wrong because, as discussed above, the transcript is hearsay. Note that the Federal Rules consider a prior consistent statement made by the witness to be nonhearsay if introduced to rebut a charge of recent fabrication or improper motive. This is not applicable to this case because the prior statement is Xavier's, not that of the witness testifying at trial (Wesley). Moreover, the facts do not indicate that the defense is attacking Wesley's testimony as a recent fabrication or that he has improper motive. (C) is wrong because grand jury testimony does not fall within the former testimony exception to the hearsay rule. For a statement to qualify under this exception, the party against whom the former testimony is offered must have had the opportunity to develop the testimony at the prior proceeding by direct, cross, or redirect examination. Grand jury proceedings do not afford such an opportunity, so the grand jury testimony of an unavailable declarant is not admissible.

Answer to Question 19

(D) Attorney may invoke the attorney-client privilege because the presence of a minor client's parent does not waive the privilege. A client has a privilege to refuse to disclose, and to prevent others from disclosing, confidential communications between herself and her lawyer. The attorney-client privilege requires that, at the time of the communication, the client be seeking the professional services of the attorney. Disclosures made before the lawyer has decided to accept or decline the case are covered if the other requirements of the privilege are met. A communication is confidential if it is not intended to be disclosed to third persons; thus, communications made in the known presence and hearing of a stranger are not privileged. However, statements made in front of third persons whose presence is reasonably necessary to the consultation (e.g., this client's parent) are still considered confidential. Here, Child was consulting with Attorney for the purpose of seeking Attorney's professional services. During this consultation, Child made disclosures concerning her injuries that were not intended to be disclosed to third persons. Thus, Child's communication would be deemed confidential. This confidentiality would not be lost by virtue of the fact that the communication was made in the presence of Father, whose presence was reasonably necessary given Child's age. Because the elements of the attorney-client privilege are thus satisfied, Attorney may invoke the privilege on behalf of Child to refuse to disclose his discussion with Child concerning Child's injuries. (A) is incorrect because the attorney-client privilege does not depend on an actual hiring of the attorney. The requisite relationship exists simply by virtue of the fact that, at the time of the communication, Child was seeking Attorney's professional services. (B) is incorrect because the person who was the attorney at the time of the communication can claim the privilege on behalf of the client. The attorney's authority to do this is presumed in the absence of any evidence to the contrary. (C) is wrong because application of the privilege does not hinge on payment for services. The confidential communications of a client receiving a professional consultation free of charge are protected to the same extent as those made to a lawyer charging for her time.

Answer to Question 20

(D) The judge may call witnesses upon her own initiative and may interrogate any witnesses who testify. [*See* Fed. R. Evid. 614] The judge has total discretion in this area as long as no partisanship for a particular side is shown. (A), (B), and (C) are incorrect because none of these circumstances would preclude a judge from questioning the witness. As stated above, a judge may question or cross-examine any witness at any time as long as she does not demonstrate partisanship for one side of the controversy.

Answer to Question 21

(B) The court should require Sato to answer the question because it is relevant to the truthfulness and credibility of the witness. Any matter that tends to prove or disprove the credibility of a witness is relevant and should be admitted. Specific "bad acts" that show the witness unworthy of belief (*i.e.,* acts of deceit or lying) are probative of truthfulness. Filing a false income tax return reflects on the witness's veracity and, thus, his credibility. Therefore, Sato should be required to respond. (A) is incorrect because inquiry into bad acts *to impeach a witness's credibility* is permitted even if the witness was never convicted of a crime. (C) is incorrect because Federal Rule 608 permits inquiry about specific acts of misconduct, within the discretion of the court, if they are probative of truthfulness. However, extrinsic evidence is not admissible to prove the act. (D) is incorrect because the question relates to truthfulness, and a witness's credibility is always relevant.

Answer to Question 22

(B) The court should find the testimony admissible as relevant evidence that Dirk's was aware of the defect. Hearsay is a statement, other than one made by the declarant while testifying at the trial or hearing, offered in evidence to prove the truth of the matter asserted. [Fed. R. Evid. 801(c)] A hearsay statement to which no exception to the hearsay rule is applicable must be excluded upon appropriate objection to its admission. [Fed. R. Evid. 802] A statement that would be inadmissible hearsay may be admissible to show the effect of the statement on the hearer or reader. For example, in a negligence case where knowledge of a danger is in issue, a third person's statement of warning is admissible to show notice or knowledge on the part of a listener. Here, Cora's remark to Dirk is an out-of-court statement. However, the statement can be offered to show that Dirk's had notice of a possible danger posed by the escalator. (Note that Cora's remark would be inadmissible hearsay if offered to prove the escalator was speeding up and stopping.) (A) is incorrect because it states an exception to the hearsay rule, and the testimony offered is not hearsay (*see* above). Even if the testimony were offered to prove the escalator was malfunctioning, this exception would not apply because the declarant (Cora) made no statement against *her* interest. Also, she is possibly available to testify, which takes her statement out of the exception. (C) is incorrect because Clara's testimony is admissible nonhearsay. In addition, the unavailability of a declarant is only significant with regard to certain hearsay exceptions that require unavailability (*e.g.,* the statement against interest). If Clara's testimony is offered to show notice to

Dirk's of a potential problem with the escalator, there is no hearsay problem. The absence of a hearsay problem precludes resort to a hearsay exception and the availability of Cora is of no significance. (D) is incorrect because Cora's statement is not hearsay since it is not offered to prove the truth of the matter asserted (*i.e.,* that the escalator was malfunctioning) but to show notice of the defect.

Answer to Question 23

(C) The objection should be sustained because the attorney-client privilege applies. A client has a privilege to refuse to disclose, and to prevent others from disclosing, confidential communications between himself (or his representative) and his lawyer (or her representative). A "representative of a lawyer" is one who is employed to assist in the rendition of legal services. If a physician examines a client at the request of the attorney (*e.g.,* to assess the extent of injury), the attorney-client privilege applies to communications made to the physician because the physician is deemed to be a representative of the attorney. (A) is incorrect because the statements are privileged under the attorney-client privilege. Absent this privilege, the statements would be admissible as admissions of a party-opponent. An admission is a statement made or act done that amounts to a prior acknowledgment by one of the parties of a relevant fact. Pluto's negligence is a relevant fact and his statements to Sawbones constitute an acknowledgment thereof. (B) is incorrect because whether Sawbones qualifies as an expert is irrelevant. This situation does not call for expert testimony. Expert opinion testimony is appropriate when the subject matter is such that scientific, technical, or other specialized knowledge would assist the finder of fact in understanding the evidence or determining a fact in issue. Sawbones is not being called to give his opinion on some matter that calls for specialized knowledge, such as matters pertaining to medicine. Rather, Sawbones is being called to testify that Pluto acknowledged his negligence. Thus, the principles of expert opinion testimony are inapplicable to these facts. (D) is incorrect for two reasons: (i) The physician-patient privilege protects only information that is necessary to enable the physician to act in his professional capacity. Thus, if information given by the patient deals with a nonmedical matter, the information is not privileged. Pluto's statements concerning his negligence were not necessary to enable Sawbones to treat or diagnose his condition. Therefore, this information obtained by Sawbones is not covered by the privilege. (ii) The privilege is not applicable where the patient has put his physical condition in issue by, for example, suing for personal injuries. Pluto is suing Duck for personal injuries. Consequently, even if Pluto's statements to Sawbones constituted information that would be deemed privileged, the privilege is not applicable in this case.

Answer to Question 24

(A) Dorcas's guilty plea is an admission by a party-opponent and thus is admissible. Under the Federal Rules, an admission by a party-opponent is not hearsay. [Fed. R. Evid. 801(d)(2)] An admission is a statement made or act done that amounts to a prior acknowledgment by one of the parties to an action of a relevant fact. A plea of guilty to a traffic infraction is a formal judicial admission. The admission is conclusive in a prosecution for that infraction, but if the plea is used in another proceeding, it is merely an evidentiary admission (*i.e.,* it is not conclusive and can be explained). Here, Dorcas has acknowledged by her guilty plea that she was speeding at the time of the accident. This fact is relevant to Pippin's suit for personal injuries because it increases the likelihood that Dorcas was at fault in the accident that caused those injuries. Therefore, Dorcas's guilty plea is admissible in the current civil action as an evidentiary admission. (B) is wrong because there is no indication that Dorcas is unavailable. Statements of a person, now unavailable as a witness, against that person's pecuniary, proprietary, or penal interest when made are admissible under the statement against interest exception to the hearsay rule. [Fed. R. Evid. 804(b)(3)] A declarant is unavailable if: (i) she is exempt from testifying due to a privilege; (ii) she refuses to testify; (iii) she testifies to lack of memory of the subject matter; (iv) she is dead or ill; or (v) she is absent and the statement's proponent has been unable to procure her attendance or testimony by process or other reasonable means. [Fed. R. Evid. 804(a)(1)-(5)] Since Dorcas apparently is available as a witness in the suit, the statement against interest exception is inapplicable. Although it may be true that public policy favors plea bargaining, (C) is incorrect because there is no attempt here to offer a statement made during the plea bargaining process. Under the Federal Rules, **withdrawn** guilty pleas, pleas of nolo contendere, offers to plead guilty, and evidence of statements made in negotiating such pleas are not admissible in any proceeding. [Fed. R. Evid. 410] However, there is no prohibition against admitting the guilty plea itself. This question asks whether the guilty plea is admissible, not whether statements made in negotiation thereof are admissible. Thus, the policy favoring plea bargains is irrelevant. (D) is wrong because the question asks about the admissibility of the plea rather than a copy of the conviction. Convictions may be introduced to prove any fact essential to the case only if they are felony convictions. [Fed. R. Evid. 803(22)] Because the conviction is not being offered, the fact that a felony is not involved is of no consequence. Dorcas's **plea** is admissible as an admission even though a felony was not involved.

Answer to Question 25

(C) The court should overrule the objection because counsel is permitted to attempt to refresh a witness's recollection. A witness may use any writing or thing for the purpose of refreshing her present recollection. However, she generally may not read from the writing while she actually testifies, because the writing is not authenticated, is not in evidence, and may be used solely to refresh her recollection. Here, Pearl has testified that she cannot positively identify Diamond as her attacker, thus indicating that she has an incomplete recollection of the attacker. The prosecutor is entitled to show Pearl her written statement in an attempt to refresh her memory about the rapist. With Pearl having read the statement, the prosecutor may now ask her whether her memory of the rapist has been sufficiently refreshed so as to allow her to be more certain regarding the identity of Diamond as the rapist. She may testify as long as the writing refreshed her present recollection. (A) is incorrect because it confuses present recollection refreshed with past recollection recorded. The writing itself is read into evidence only as past recollection recorded, when a witness is unable to refresh her recollection after consulting the writing. Here, Pearl should be permitted to testify as long as her recollection was refreshed by the writing. (B) is incorrect because, as explained above, a witness who testifies to a lack of recollection regarding a particular matter may be asked if her recollection has been refreshed after having been shown a writing. The fact that Pearl has previously indicated an uncertainty as to the matter of identification allows the prosecutor to attempt to refresh Pearl's memory of this point. Thus, the objection is not sustainable on the ground that the question has been asked and answered. (D) confuses the concepts of refreshing a witness's recollection and impeaching one's own witness. Under the Federal Rules, the credibility of a witness may be attacked by any party, including the party calling her. [Fed. R. Evid. 607] Under the traditional rule, a party could impeach his own witness only if the witness: (i) was an adverse party; (ii) was hostile; (iii) was one required to be called by law; or (iv) gave damaging surprise testimony. Here, the prosecutor is trying to refresh Pearl's recollection, rather than to cast an adverse reflection on her credibility. There is no requirement that the examiner be surprised by adverse testimony in order to attempt to refresh the memory of a witness. Therefore, the objection by Diamond's attorney should be overruled even in the absence of prosecutorial surprise as to Pearl's testimony.

Answer to Question 26

(C) The prosecution must prove beyond a reasonable doubt that Pearl did not consent even if Diamond remains silent on the issue. In a criminal prosecution, the state is required to establish the guilt of the defendant beyond a reasonable doubt. This requirement means that the state must establish every element of the offense beyond a reasonable doubt. The defendant is not required to establish the nonexistence of any element of the crime. This is a rape case. Under the common law definition, rape consists of: (i) the unlawful carnal knowledge; (ii) of a woman by a man not her husband; and (iii) without her effective consent. Thus, lack of consent by the victim of a rape is an element of the offense, and as such, must be proven beyond a reasonable doubt by the prosecution. Diamond need not raise the issue to trigger the prosecution's burden of establishing lack of consent. (A) is incorrect because, as explained above, the burden is not on Diamond to establish consent; rather, the burden is on the prosecution to establish lack of consent. (B) is incorrect because Pearl's lack of consent is an element of the crime charged, and the prosecution must establish it beyond a reasonable doubt. (D) is incorrect because it would require Diamond to disprove (or at least challenge) the element of lack of consent prior to the prosecution's being required to prove lack of consent.

Answer to Question 27

(A) A motion to strike is effective only where there was no basis or opportunity for an earlier objection. An objection ordinarily must be made after the question is asked, but before the witness answers. If the question is not objectionable, but the answer is, a motion to strike is appropriate. Here the question was clearly objectionable and the prosecution had time to object. In most states reputation or opinion evidence of the past sexual behavior of an alleged rape victim or evidence of the rape victim's sexual relations with persons other than the defendant is not admissible. The Federal Rules also exclude such evidence. Thus, the testimony of Warburton regarding Pearl's reputation for chastity would have been inadmissible. At the time Diamond's attorney asked this question, it was clear that Warburton's answer would necessarily involve inadmissible matter. Therefore, the prosecutor was required to make an objection before Warburton answered the question, rather than waiting to see if the answer was damaging to his case. Because the prosecutor failed to make a timely objection despite the opportunity to do so, the testimony of Warburton is admissible, and there is no basis for a motion to strike such testimony. (D), although it states the correct rule of law, is incorrect because the prosecutor's failure to object to this evidence in a timely manner resulted in its admission, and the motion to strike Warburton's testimony is ineffective. (B) is wrong. While consent is a material issue because the state must prove the absence thereof to establish guilt of rape, whatever probative value Warburton's testimony may have is deemed to be outweighed by the dangers of unfair prejudice arising from such evidence of unchastity. Therefore, the relevance of Warburton's testimony to the issue of consent would not constitute a basis for denying the motion to strike. As has been explained, the motion is denied because of a lack of timely objection by the prosecutor. Thus, (B) reaches the correct result, but for an incorrect reason. (C) is incorrect because as discussed above, the motion should not be granted because objection to Warburton's testimony was not timely.

Answer to Question 28

(B) Asking Warburton about the assault charge is an improper method of impeachment. A witness may be interrogated upon cross-examination with respect to an act of misconduct only if it is *probative of truthfulness*. An assault is not probative of truthfulness, so it would not be proper impeachment evidence. Had he been convicted of the assault, the conviction would have been admissible, provided it was a felony. (A) is incorrect because it is an example of proper impeachment by showing bias. Evidence that a witness is biased tends to show that he has a motive to lie. Warburton's close relationship to his wife gives rise to an inference that he would be hostile toward Pearl if she and his wife had a longstanding personal enmity. Consequently, the question posed in (A) represents a proper method of impeaching Warburton's credibility by probing into a possible bias against Pearl. (C) and (D) are incorrect because these questions represent proper means of rebutting the evidence of Pearl's character for unchastity, as well as trying to impeach Warburton's credibility based on lack of knowledge. Evidence of a character trait of the alleged crime victim may be offered by the prosecution to rebut a defendant's evidence of bad character of the victim. [Fed. R. Evid. 404] The prosecution may prove such a trait by reputation evidence as well as by opinion evidence. On cross-examination, the prosecution may inquire into relevant specific instances of conduct. [Fed. R. Evid. 405(a)] Traditionally, asking a witness if he has heard of a particular instance of conduct represents a means of testing the accuracy of the hearing and reporting of a ***reputation*** witness, who relates what he has heard. Asking a witness if he knows of a particular instance of conduct is a means of testing the basis of an ***opinion*** expressed by the witness. Here, Warburton's testimony indicates both that he has heard that Pearl has a bad reputation for chastity and that his own opinion is that Pearl is a person of unchaste character. Thus, in attempting to rebut this testimony, the prosecution may test the accuracy of what Warburton has heard concerning Pearl's character by asking him if he has heard of specific instances of her teaching Sunday School and receiving a church award. Also, the prosecution may test the basis for Warburton's opinion as to Pearl's unchastity by asking if he knows of these specific instances that are indicative of Pearl's good character.

Answer to Question 29

(B) Dr. Dan's testimony regarding Paul's statement is admissible because an examination for insurance purposes is not considered to be for diagnosis and treatment. To be privileged, the information must be acquired by the physician in the course of treatment. Some states have expanded this to include a consultation for diagnosis, but an insurance examination would not qualify as diagnostic either. Thus, Paul's statement to Dr. Dan is not privileged. Since it is not privileged and qualifies as an admission by a party-opponent for hearsay purposes, the statement is admissible. (A) is wrong because an attempt by Paul to perpetrate a fraud is not the only way that Dr. Dan could testify to Paul's statement. It is true that the physician-patient privilege does not apply if the physician's services were sought or obtained in aid of planning a crime or tort, but that is not the only time it is inapplicable. Moreover, it is nearly impossible to believe that Paul could have been attempting to lay the groundwork for a fraudulent claim, given the facts that the insurance examination occurred before the accident and the statement was against his interest. As noted above, the privilege never attached since Paul was not seeking diagnosis or treatment. Even if it had, the mere fact that Paul has put his physical condition in issue by suing for injuries is sufficient to abrogate the privilege. There would be no need to resort to proof of an attempted fraud. (C) is wrong because Paul's statement, despite having been made while Dr. Dan was attending to Paul in a professional capacity, is not privileged for two reasons: (i) Paul was not seeking diagnosis or treatment, and (ii) Paul put his physical condition in issue. (D) is wrong because the preexisting back injury is relevant on issues of causation and damages.

Answer to Question 30

(B) Paul's statement will be admissible as a statement of present bodily condition. Paul's statement is an out-of-court statement offered to prove the truth of the matter asserted (*i.e.,* that Paul had bad back pain before the accident); thus, it is hearsay. The statement may be admitted, however, under an exception to the hearsay rule, as a statement of present bodily condition. Statements of symptoms being experienced, including the existence of pain, are admissible even if not made to a doctor or other medical personnel. Paul's statement concerns the back pain he was experiencing when he made the statement and thus falls within this exception. The statement is therefore admissible. (Note that the statement is also admissible as an admission by a party-opponent, which is nonhearsay, but that is not given as a choice in this question.) (A) is wrong because this statement is not an excited utterance. To qualify as an excited utterance, the declaration must be made during or soon after a startling event and must concern the immediate facts of the startling event. It must be made under the stress produced by the startling event. [Fed. R. Evid. 803(2)] There is no indication that Paul's statement to Freddy, which was made before the accident, was made during or soon after a startling event. Thus, the statement is not an excited utterance. (C) is wrong because the physician-patient privilege does not apply here because this is a personal injury case and Paul has placed his physical condition in issue. (D) is wrong because Paul's statement need not be made in seeking diagnosis or treatment to be admissible; as long as it concerns a present bodily condition—even if not made to a doctor—it is admissible.

Answer to Question 31

(D) Lamb may not testify about the embezzlement because it constitutes impeachment by extrinsic evidence of a specific instance of misconduct. A specific act of misconduct offered to attack the witness's character for truthfulness can be elicited only on cross-examination. If the witness denies the act, the cross-examiner cannot refute the answer by calling other witnesses or producing other evidence. Since the alleged embezzlement is admissible, if at all, only as impeachment evidence, when Dutch denied it, Cora could not call Lamb to testify. (A) is wrong because extrinsic evidence, such as Lamb's testimony, of an instance of misconduct is not admissible. (B) is wrong because when a person is charged with one crime, extrinsic evidence of other crimes or misconduct is inadmissible to establish criminal disposition. Since nothing in the facts indicates that such evidence is being offered to prove something other than disposition (*e.g.*, motive, identity, common plan or scheme), Lamb's testimony is not admissible as substantive evidence. As discussed above, for impeachment, Cora is limited to inquiry on cross-examination regarding the embezzlement. (C) is wrong because, even if Dutch had been convicted of the embezzlement, Lamb's testimony would not be the proper way to introduce it. The fact that a witness has been convicted of a crime is proved by eliciting an admission on cross-examination or by the record of conviction.

Answer to Question 32

(B) Wilhelmina may testify if she chooses to do so. In federal court, the privilege of spousal immunity belongs to the witness-spouse. There are two privileges based on the marital relationship. Under spousal immunity, a person whose spouse is the defendant in a criminal case may not be called as a witness by the prosecution, and a married person may not be compelled to testify against her spouse in any criminal proceeding. In federal court, one spouse may choose to testify against the other in a criminal case, with or without the consent of the party-spouse. Spousal immunity lasts only during the marriage and terminates upon divorce. However, as long as a marriage exists, the privilege can be asserted even as to matters that occurred prior to the marriage. Since Humphrey is a criminal defendant, Wilhelmina cannot be compelled to testify about Humphrey's conversation with Victor. She may, however, choose to testify, and Humphrey cannot stop her. The other choices reflect elements of the privilege for confidential marital communications. Under this privilege, either spouse (whether or not a party) may refuse to disclose, and may prevent another from disclosing, a confidential communication made between the spouses while they were husband and wife. The communication must be made during a marriage, and must be in reliance upon the intimacy of the marital relationship, which is presumed in the absence of contrary evidence. This privilege is not afforded to a communication that is made in the known presence of a stranger. Both spouses jointly hold this privilege. The conversation between Humphrey and Victor cannot qualify as a confidential marital communication for several reasons. Most importantly, it was not a communication between Humphrey and Wilhelmina. Moreover, the incident did not occur during the marriage. Thus, the privilege for confidential marital communications does not apply, and Humphrey cannot prevent Wilhelmina's testimony should she choose to testify. (A) is wrong because it states a reason why the privilege for confidential marital communications does not apply. Spousal immunity still applies; thus (B) is a better choice because it reflects the fact that Wilhelmina's testimony cannot be compelled. (C) is wrong because, in federal court, spousal immunity does not permit the defendant-spouse to foreclose testimony by the witness-spouse. As discussed above, the privilege for confidential marital communications, under which both spouses may prevent disclosure, does not apply here. (D) is wrong for the same reason.

Answer to Question 33

(D) The subpoena will be granted because giving the checks to an attorney does not confer privileged status upon them; thus, they are not immune from subpoena. The attorney-client privilege, which confers upon the client the right to refuse to disclose and to prevent others from disclosing confidential communications between herself and her lawyer, does not apply to preexisting documents. The checks in this question were in existence at the start of the professional relationship and, therefore, are not covered by the attorney-client privilege. (A) is wrong because, as just noted, the attorney-client privilege does not apply to preexisting documents. (B) is wrong because the privilege against self-incrimination is a privilege not to testify at a proceeding at which the witness's appearance is compelled. It does not apply to evidence other than testimony. Since the prosecutor is subpoenaing documents, not testimony, the privilege against self-incrimination does not apply. (C) is wrong because it states an exception to the hearsay rule, which is irrelevant for purposes of obtaining a subpoena. The hearsay rule would be important if the prosecution seeks to introduce the checks into evidence at trial, but at this point, their status as business records is not important.

Answer to Question 34

(B) The judge determines whether the testimony falls within an exception to the hearsay rule, and is generally not limited by the rules of evidence in making that determination. The Federal Rules of Evidence distinguish between preliminary facts to be decided by the jury, which involve whether the proffered evidence is relevant, and preliminary facts decided by the judge, which involve whether the evidence is competent, *i.e.,* not barred by an exclusionary rule. All preliminary fact questions that determine the applicability of an exception to the hearsay rule must be determined by the judge, because the competency of the evidence will depend on that preliminary fact determination. In making this preliminary fact determination, the trial court may consider any nonprivileged relevant evidence, even though it would not otherwise be admissible under the rules of evidence. [Fed. R. Evid. 104(a)] In this case, then, the judge should decide whether the testimony falls within the present sense impression exception, and she is not limited in making this determination by the rules of evidence other than privilege. (A) is incorrect because the judge's preliminary fact determination does not need to be based on the rules of evidence (other than privilege rules). (C) and (D) are incorrect because, as discussed above, determining whether the testimony falls within the scope of the hearsay exception is a determination of whether the evidence is competent, and this determination is made by the judge rather than the jury.

Answer to Question 35

(A) Prior testimony is admissible as an exception to the hearsay rule if the testimony was given under oath and the party against whom the evidence is now offered either offered the testimony or had the testimony offered against her at the former trial, and had an opportunity and similar motive to develop the testimony either on direct or cross-examination. [Fed. R. Evid. 804(b)(1)] (B) is wrong because a past recollection recorded requires testimony from the witness whose statement was recorded. (C) is wrong because the disposition at the previous trial has no bearing on the admissibility of prior testimony. (D) is wrong because the motive to cross-examine was identical at each trial—to discredit Sally's testimony.

Answer to Question 36

(A) The membership card would be a writing within the meaning of the best evidence rule. As such, secondary evidence as to its existence could only be introduced if the original is shown to have been lost or destroyed, unobtainable, or within the control of the opponent. (B) is incorrect because the police officer's testimony about the name on the card would not violate the hearsay rule. The evidence is not being offered to prove the truth of the matter asserted in the card. It is being offered to show that the defendant possessed the card, and is circumstantial evidence that the defendant committed the crime. (C) is incorrect because the existence of the membership card on Diablo's person is not collateral to the issues involved. (D) is incorrect because the privilege against self-incrimination prevents a witness from being compelled to testify against himself, which is not the case here.

Answer to Question 37

(A) Ike's testimony should be admitted as evidence of the extent of Pete's injury, because it relates to his firsthand observations and is otherwise admissible. (B) is wrong because he is not reading from the records as he testifies, and the record is not being introduced. In addition, a proper foundation has not been laid for the introduction of the records as a past recollection recorded. (C) is wrong because his testimony is about what he saw, not about the contents of the records. (D) is wrong because anything (even hearsay statements) can be used by a witness to refresh his recollection.

Answer to Question 38

(A) The videotape is admissible as relevant and material evidence not excluded by any rule. Furthermore, (A) is the correct pick by process of elimination. (B) is incorrect. The tape is not hearsay because it is not a statement offered to prove the truth of the matter. It is nonassertive conduct offered to show Duncan's mental and physical condition. (C) is incorrect because the privilege against self-incrimination applies only to testimonial evidence. (D) is silly, since almost all crimes (*i.e.*, instances of misconduct) are proven by extrinsic evidence. For the record, since this videotape would be considered documentary evidence, a proper foundation will have to be laid before it can be admitted.

Answer to Question 39

(B) A plea of guilty which is later withdrawn may not be used against the defendant who made the plea, except in special cases not applicable to this fact pattern. [Fed. R. Evid. 410] (A) is wrong; since Dave's statement would be considered an admission, it cannot be excluded by the hearsay rule. It will be excluded under Rule 410, which prohibits the use of the withdrawn guilty plea, even if it does qualify as an admission. (C) is wrong because, although an admission is not hearsay, this evidence is excluded by Rule 410. (D) is wrong. While Dave's state of mind might be relevant in the civil suit, the evidence will still be excluded under Rule 410.

Answer to Question 40

(B) The certified copy of the record of Dave's conviction will be excluded because it is inadmissible hearsay. A misdemeanor conviction is hearsay not admissible under any exception. A felony conviction, on the other hand, is admissible under an exception to the hearsay rule. [Fed. R. Evid. 803(22)] Thus, (C) and (D) are incorrect. (A) is incorrect because under the Federal Rules a certified copy of the record of conviction satisfies the best evidence rule.

Answer to Question 41

(C) Compton's testimony is admissible because it is based on knowledge gained by him at trial. Facts or data upon which expert opinions are based may be derived from presentation at trial. One acceptable method of doing this is to have the expert attend the trial and hear testimony establishing the facts. Thus, (B) is incorrect. (A) is incorrect. Under the Federal Rules, a hypothetical question is not required to elicit an expert's opinion. (D) is incorrect because an expert may also base his opinion on facts supplied to him outside the courtroom, including types of facts not admissible in evidence, as long as they are reasonably relied on by experts in the field.

Answer to Question 42

(A) The basis of an expert's opinion need not be admissible into evidence for the expert's testimony to be admissible, provided that the information is of a type reasonably relied upon by experts in the particular field. [Fed. R. Evid. 703(B)] (B) is incorrect because Taylor need not offer the reports into evidence in order to base her opinion on them. In fact, the proponent of the expert opinion is not permitted to disclose the reports if they are inadmissible, unless the court determines that their probative value in assisting the jury to evaluate the expert's opinion substantially outweighs their prejudicial effect. (C) is wrong because the Federal Rules reject the traditional prohibition on opinions embracing the ultimate issue in the case, as long as the opinion is helpful to the trier of fact. (D) is wrong because Taylor is only relying on the reports as the basis of making her opinion; she is not offering the reports themselves into evidence. Hence, they would not be governed by the hearsay rule.

Answer to Question 43

(C) A judge would most likely permit this testimony because (i) Prudhome had independent recollection of the date, and (ii) the date on which the additive was purchased is really "collateral" to the issues at trial. At most, the two important facts would be that the additive was used in Prudhome's car, and perhaps, the date when he added it to his oil. Thus, it seems that the date when he purchased it is completely irrelevant, and since Motorglide objected to the testimony only on this point, the trial judge would probably overrule its objection. (A) is incorrect because the best evidence rule is not applicable when the facts "testified" to regard only collateral matters. (B) is weak because Prudhome is not really testifying as to the facts contained in the credit card receipts, but that he remembered the date independently, and could prove it if it was necessary. Thus, the hearsay rule would probably not apply to what Prudhome testified to in this instance. (D) is incorrect. Even if the credit card receipt were considered hearsay, it would not qualify under the past recollection recorded exception.

Answer to Question 44

(A) Federal Rule 501 provides that federal courts shall apply rules of privilege developed at common law except in diversity cases, wherein state law controls, but this is not a diversity case. The United States Supreme Court has held that the privilege not to testify may be asserted only by the testifying spouse, and if she is willing to so testify against her husband, the marital relationship is so disharmonious that there is nothing left for the privilege to preserve.

Answer to Question 45

(D) The substantive relation of the questions to the issues of the lawsuit has no bearing on whether leading questions are permitted. Use of leading questions on direct examination to refresh the recollection of a witness or to establish preliminary matters is permitted in the discretion of the trial court. Thus, (A) and (B) are incorrect. Where a witness is hostile to the party calling him, the examination is treated as cross-examination, and leading questions may be used. Thus, (C) is incorrect.

Answer to Question 46

(B) The judge should permit Paula's testimony because evidence of specific acts of misconduct is admissible to show motive. Under Federal Rule 404(b), evidence of other acts may be admissible in a criminal or civil case if they are relevant to some issue other than character, such as motive. Here, whether Doris was motivated by an improper purpose in building the fence is the key issue in the lawsuit by Paula. Doris's prior misconduct in spraying herbicide toward Paula's garden is circumstantial evidence that her hostility toward the garden motivated her to build the fence. (A) is not correct because even though Doris's motivation and intent are at issue in the case, her character is not. In the absence of character being directly in issue in the case, evidence of character to prove the conduct of a person in the litigated event is not admissible. (C) and (D) are wrong even though they correctly state general rules: evidence of specific acts of misconduct is generally inadmissible, and character evidence is generally inadmissible in a civil case. However, when the specific acts are being offered for a purpose other than to show bad character or conduct in conformity to character, they are admissible in both criminal and civil cases.

Answer to Question 47

(B) Wanda's remark is admissible under the present sense impression exception to the hearsay rule. [Fed. R. Evid. 803(1)] (A) is wrong. A prior consistent statement can be used to rebut evidence that the trial testimony is a lie or an exaggeration because of some motive to falsify that has arisen since the event. The facts do not indicate such a claim was made. The statement is hearsay because the witness is relating an out-of-court statement that she made; therefore, (C) is wrong. (D) is wrong because the statement comes within the present sense impression exception to the hearsay rule.

Answer to Question 48

(C) Under the Federal Rules, depositions can be used more broadly than under the rules in many states. Here the prior inconsistent statement can be used for impeachment purposes and as substantive evidence. (A) is wrong because the Federal Rules permit impeachment of your own witness. (B) is wrong because under the Federal Rules, prior inconsistent statements, made under oath and subject to the penalty of perjury in a deposition or prior hearing, are admissible as nonhearsay. (D) is wrong because the statement can be used for more than impeachment.

Answer to Question 49

(B) The offer to pay medical expenses in itself is not admissible as an admission. Here, however, there is a statement that follows such an offer. This statement is admissible as an admission by the owner of Donna's Tavern that Tony was drunk when he left the bar. Since this is an admission, under the Federal Rules it is not hearsay. (A) is an exception to the hearsay rule and is thus unnecessary. Furthermore, it is an exception requiring the unavailability of the declarant, and there is no indication in the facts that the owner is now unavailable. (C) is wrong because, as mentioned, the statement is not hearsay under the Federal Rules. (D) is a misstatement of the law; only the offer to pay medical expenses is inadmissible on public policy grounds.

Answer to Question 50

(B) Under the Federal Rules, an expert witness may learn the basis for the opinion at or before the hearing. (A) is wrong because the basis for an expert's opinion need not be personal observation. (C) is wrong because under the Federal Rules, an expert witness may testify in the form of an opinion without prior disclosure of the underlying facts or data. In addition, here the basis of the expert's testimony was based on evidence already introduced at trial. (D) is wrong because expert opinion may indeed be based on information provided by lay people.

Answer to Question 51

(B) This is a best evidence rule question; it is an attempt to prove the contents of a document that is the basis of the suit. The best evidence rule applies and therefore the party must produce the original document or offer a satisfactory excuse for not producing it. Under Rule 1004, if the original is lost that is considered a reasonable excuse for not producing the original. Whether the letter is in fact "lost" would be a preliminary question of fact to be determined by the court under Rule 104(a), rather than the jury. Thus, (B) is correct and (C) is wrong. (A) is wrong; there is no such requirement under the rules. (D) is wrong; there is no such rule of law.

Answer to Question 52

(C) Federal Rule of Evidence 608(b) permits cross-examination relating to prior bad acts if, in the discretion of the trial court, they are probative of truthfulness. Thus, (A) is wrong. (D) is wrong because Federal Rule 609 permits inquiry into prior crimes involving dishonesty which are less than 10 years old. Since the bias involved in a pecuniary interest is always relevant and admissible, (B) is wrong. Only the question relating to drug abuse—a marginally relevant topic, relating possibly to the witness's ability to perceive or remember—appears improper.

Answer to Question 53

(D) Federal Rule 705 provides that a hypothetical question need not be asked. Examining counsel may ask the expert for an opinion and then immediately allow the opposing side to cross-examine, without any disclosure of the data underlying the opinion (unless the trial court requires advance disclosure). It follows that (B) is incorrect. (A) is incorrect because the Federal Rules repudiate the ultimate issue limitation. (C) is simply an incorrect statement of the law.

Answer to Question 54

(B) Although it is arguable that a person who may be liable for negligence would reasonably remain silent when in the presence of a police officer, this is the best answer because silence may be deemed an admission in a situation in which a reasonable person would have responded to an accusation. (D) is wrong because there need be no foundation evidence. (C) is wrong; the silence is deemed the adoption of the statement, thus Jim's statement would be an admission. (A) is incorrect because the facts do not indicate that Jim was Jon's agent, and the statement against interest exception to the hearsay rule requires the unavailability of the declarant.

Answer to Question 55

(D) Robin's testimony was to show she was suffering pain, and is an exception to the hearsay rule as a declaration of present physical sensation. Thus, (A) is incorrect. (B) is wrong because Robin is not testifying that she suffered a "sprained" neck, which would require an expert witness. (C) is wrong because Robin's statement is admissible to show current physical condition even if she does not introduce medical evidence.

Answer to Question 56

(B) Sherry's statement is hearsay, and just because it has become part of a police report, it does not stop being hearsay. (A) and (C) are wrong because although the police report itself may qualify under some exception, Sherry's statement contained in the report is still hearsay. (D) is wrong because the facts do not indicate that the police officer is testifying from her report, and it does not change the hearsay character of the testimony.

Answer to Question 57

(B) The statement is inadmissible hearsay. (A) is wrong, because the statement may tend to show a reason for the accident. (C) is wrong because Mike is not a party, and the statement is not attributable to Jon. (D) is wrong because the statement against interest exception requires that the declarant be unavailable to testify; nothing in the facts suggests that Mike is unavailable.

Answer to Question 58

(A) Under the rule of present recollection refreshed, a witness may be shown any writing that may refresh her memory of an event. (B) is wrong because the doctrine of past recollection recorded refers to the admissibility of the contents of a writing, and a proper foundation must be laid. (C) is a misstatement of the law and makes no sense in this situation. (D) is wrong because Sherry is not testifying to the contents of her statement, but to her recollection of the accident.

Answer to Question 59

(A) Frances's testimony about Ralph's and Max's conversation is not being offered for its truth (*i.e.*, to prove that Elbert had been flirting with Maxine), but rather to show its effect on Max. Thus, it is not hearsay, and (C) is incorrect. When the words themselves are in issue (*e.g.*, words of contract, gift, defamation, etc.), they are legally operative facts. This concept does not apply to these facts, and so (B) is wrong. (D) is incorrect because opinion testimony by lay witnesses is admissible if it is based on the perception of the witness, helpful in determining a fact in issue, and not based on scientific, technical, or other specialized knowledge. Here, Frances saw Max, and he appeared angry. Whether Max was angry could help determine whether he acted in self-defense or struck the first blow.

Answer to Question 60

(C) The report contains an out-of-court statement being offered for its truth; *i.e.*, that the person who hit Prudence fits the description given by Trixie. Thus, (A) is incorrect. The report does not fall within any exception to the hearsay rule. It is not a business record because Trixie was not under a business duty to convey the information to the police. (B) is therefore incorrect. (D) is incorrect because the report is the original document, and the best evidence rule expresses a preference for originals.

Answer to Question 61

(D) Trixie's statement is an out-of-court declaration offered for its truth, and it does not fall within any hearsay exception. It is not a dying declaration because the declaration does not concern the immediate circumstances causing Trixie's grievous injuries. Likewise, an excited utterance must concern the immediate facts of the startling event. (A) and (B) are therefore incorrect. (C) is incorrect because, even if the privilege attached to an ambulance attendant, the information that is privileged is limited to that necessary for treatment. Trixie's statements are clearly beyond the scope of the privilege.

Answer to Question 62

(A) Declarations of present bodily condition are admissible as an exception to the hearsay rule, even if not made to a physician. Such statements relate to symptoms, such as pain. Here, Phillipe's statement was one of present bodily condition and is admissible to prove the extent of his injuries, which is an issue in the case. It follows that (D) is incorrect. (C) is incorrect because, as noted above, a declaration of present bodily condition is admissible even if not made to a physician. (B) is incorrect, because Phillipe's statement is admissible as a declaration of present pain, not as proof he had a heart attack.

Answer to Question 63

(D) The jury must find that Abe is dead. Since the basic facts that support the presumption were proven at trial, and no other evidence was introduced, the jury must find in accordance with the presumption, because the other party did not meet its burden of going forward with rebuttal evidence. (A) and (B) are therefore wrong. (C) is wrong because the presumption regarding Abe's death is a rebuttable presumption. A conclusive presumption is really a rule of substantive law.

Answer to Question 64

(C) This affidavit is clearly hearsay, and there is nothing in the facts that shows that it is admissible under any of the exceptions to this rule. Hence, (A) is wrong. (B) is wrong because, for this purpose, the attorney-client privilege terminates upon the death of the client, and also, because the observations of the attorney would not be deemed a "communication received from the client." (D) is incorrect because a lay person could probably testify to her opinion in this situation since it is rationally based on her own perception, it is helpful to a determination of a fact in issue, and it is not based on scientific, technical, or other specialized knowledge.

Answer to Question 65

(B) Character evidence as proof of conduct in the litigated event is not admissible in a civil case unless character is directly in issue (*e.g.*, in a defamation action). Character is not directly in issue here, and so (A) and (D) are incorrect. The defendant in a criminal, but not a civil, case can introduce evidence of good character, which can then be rebutted. (C) is wrong, because such evidence is clearly relevant.

Answer to Question 66

(D) The report is an out-of-court statement being offered for its truth, and it does not fall within any exception to the hearsay rule. It does not qualify as a business record because the report was not made in the course of a regularly conducted business activity, so (A) is incorrect. (B) is incorrect because an expert may rely on inadmissible evidence, but relying on it does not make it admissible. (C) is incorrect because interest goes to the weight, not the admissibility, of the evidence.

Answer to Question 67

(C) Evidence is relevant if it tends to establish a material proposition in the case. This evidence, which would help establish a motive, which in turn would help establish the guilt of the defendant, would clearly be relevant. Therefore, an objection based solely on the relevance of the evidence should be overruled. Therefore (A) and (B) are wrong. (D) is wrong. On the facts of this case, the involvement of Vance in embezzlement would be relevant, and since the objection was based on grounds of relevance, the limiting instruction would not be required. The statement might be hearsay when used for that purpose, but it would probably qualify as an admission by silence on the part of the defendant. In any event, the objection was not on hearsay grounds.

Answer to Question 68

(D) Out-of-court statements offered for the purpose of proving knowledge on the part of the listener are not objectionable as hearsay. In addition, the evidence may be admissible as an admission by silence. Therefore, (A) is incorrect. (B) is wrong; the state of mind exception to the hearsay rule applies when the out-of-court statement helps establish the declarant's state of mind. (C) is wrong; phone calls during business hours on business phones do not qualify as a business record.

Answer to Question 69

(A) Evidence that there was no embezzlement would help establish that there was no motive for Vance to kill Mary. Therefore, it would be relevant. The testimony would have no effect on Art's credibility, so (B) and (C) are incorrect. (D) is not a very good answer. First, the objection is on relevancy, not on Rule 403. In addition, rejecting the evidence on Rule 403 grounds would be extremely unlikely on the facts presented.

Answer to Question 70

(B) If a witness's memory is incomplete, the examiner may seek to refresh her memory by allowing her to refer to a writing or anything else—provided she then testifies from present recollection and does not rely on the writing. (A) is incorrect because past recollection recorded is a hearsay exception that applies when a party is seeking to introduce a particular kind of writing. Here, Travis is not seeking to introduce the writing; he merely wants Erica to look at it. Thus, (A) is incorrect. (C) and (D) are incorrect because the letter is not being offered into evidence.

Answer to Question 71

(A) Under the Federal Rules, either party may impeach a witness, and leading questions are permitted when a witness is hostile. Thus, (C) and (D) are incorrect. (B) is incorrect because the examiner is not trying to refresh Erica's recollection of the trip; rather, he is talking about a preliminary hearing and is trying to impeach her with an inconsistent statement.

Answer to Question 72

(B) Under Federal Rule 801(d)(1), if the prior inconsistent statement was made at a trial or hearing while the declarant was under oath and subject to the penalty of perjury, it is not hearsay. The statement is admissible to impeach Erica *and* as substantive proof that Erica spent the weekend in question with Travis on an out-of-town trip. Thus, (A) and (C) are incorrect. (D) is incorrect because it imposes the unavailability requirement of the former testimony exception to the hearsay rule. Since this evidence is not hearsay, the exception and its requirements do not apply.

Answer to Question 73

(D) In federal court, one spouse may testify against the other in a criminal case, without the consent of the party-spouse. Thus, (A) is incorrect. (B) states an element of the privilege for confidential marital communications, which belongs to both spouses. Unfortunately for Travis, Barbara is not testifying about communications between them; she is testifying about facts that she observed. (C) is incorrect because, although the Federal Rules do not set out specific privileges, they specifically state that the witness's privilege is governed by the common law as interpreted by the courts of the United States.

Answer to Question 74

(C) The statement by Farmer is not hearsay, because it is not offered to prove that the statement was true; rather, it is evidence of words which are a fraudulent representation, and hence themselves actionable. It is not within the parol evidence rule, because the plaintiff is not trying to prove the meaning of the contract, but rather is alleging fraud. (A), (B), and (D) are therefore wrong.

Answer to Question 75

(B) Under the privilege for confidential marital communications, a person can refuse to disclose, or object to another person disclosing, confidential communications made during the marriage. Under the husband-wife privilege, a spouse cannot be forced to testify against a spouse in a criminal case. (A) is incorrect; the privilege for confidential communications applies even though the parties are divorced, as long as the communication took place during the marriage. (C) is wrong; the spouse can be called as a witness, but cannot be compelled to testify to confidential communications. (D) is wrong; the privilege for confidential communications applies to both civil and criminal cases.

Answer to Question 76

(A) The judge must himself determine whether a witness is sufficiently expert to testify. For this purpose, he should allow the transcript into evidence. (C) and (D) are therefore wrong. (B) is wrong because the court cannot permit the witness to testify at all, until he is qualified.

Answer to Question 77

(D) The testimony is hearsay on the issue of the value of the land and inventory. (A) is wrong because the value in the report is being offered as a fact due to Stillwell's expertise. In addition, even if the report only contained an opinion, it would still be hearsay. (B) is wrong, because a past recollection recorded is a record about a matter about which the witness once had knowledge but now has insufficient recollection. Here, Stillwell has not been called as a witness. (C) is wrong because such a report is not made in the normal course of business, since Stillwell does not normally make such reports.

REAL PROPERTY QUESTIONS

Questions 1-2 are based on the following fact situation:

For many years, Oscar owned one large parcel of land in a rural area. He built his home on the northern half of the property, and developed a large orchard of fruit trees on the southern portion. The county road ran in front of the northern portion. To service his orchard, Oscar built a driveway directly from the county road across the northern portion of the property to the orchard.

When he built his house, Oscar ran an overhead power line across the orchard property to hook up to the only available electric power pole located on the far southern side of the property.

Oscar became ill and was forced to spend his declining years in a convalescent hospital. Shortly before his death, he decided to make gifts of his property. He divided the property into two parcels: Parcel 1, comprised of the northern property containing the house, and Parcel 2, comprised of the orchard property. First, he conveyed Parcel 1 by grant deed to his friend, Frank, as follows: "To Frank, for life, and then to his widow for her life, remainder to Frank's children then alive." Later, he conveyed Parcel 2 to his friend, Sara.

1. Finding no recorded document granting an easement for the power line, Sara has decided to remove it. Which of the following facts, if proved, would be the most helpful to Frank in preventing Sara from doing so?

    (A) Sara knew that the power line ran across the land when she accepted the deed from Oscar.

    (B) Frank's alternative access to power is much less convenient and would cost 100 times as much.

    (C) Sara told Oscar that she did not mind having the power line on the property.

    (D) Sara is acting in retaliation against Frank for blocking the driveway, and not in any good faith belief that she has the right to remove the power line.

2. Assume for purposes of this question only that Sara has an easement in the driveway and that it is plainly visible. Which if any of the following would extinguish her easement?

    (A) Nonuse of the driveway for the statutory period applicable to prescriptive easements.

    (B) Sale of Parcel 1 to a purchaser for value who is unaware of her easement.

    (C) Excessive use of the driveway easement, which unreasonably increases the burden on Parcel 1.

    (D) None of the above.

Questions 3-5 are based on the following fact situation:

Developer Don created an exclusive residential subdivision, Woodlake. In his deed to each lot, the following language appeared: "Grantee agrees for himself and assigns to use this property solely as a single family residence, to pay monthly fees as levied by Woodlake Homeowners' Association for upkeep and security guard services, and that the backyard of this property shall remain unfenced so that bicycle paths and walkways may run through each backyard, as per the Woodlake master plan [adequately described], for use by all residents of Woodlake."

Don sold lots to Able, Baker, and Caspar. All deeds were recorded. Able in turn sold to Arnold by deed that omitted any mention of the foregoing covenants, and Arnold had no actual knowledge thereof. Shortly thereafter, Arnold started operating a commercial swimming pool sales operation out of his home.

Baker in turn sold to Bates, who knew of but refused to pay the monthly fees levied by the homeowners' association.

Caspar leased her property for 10 years to Calvin, who erected a fence around the backyard, unaware of the covenant against such fencing.

Answer the following questions according to common law principles:

3. If Don, still owning unsold lots, sues for all appropriate relief from Arnold's operation of the swimming pool sales business, which of the following statements regarding the covenant restricting the lots to single family use is correct?

   I. The covenant is enforceable against Arnold as a covenant running with the land, even though there is no contractual agreement between Don and Arnold.

   II. The covenant may be enforceable against Arnold as an equitable servitude because he had at least constructive knowledge when he purchased from Able.

   III. The covenant is enforceable even if it is contained in a deed signed only by the grantor (Don), and not signed by the grantee (Able).

   (A) II. only.

   (B) I. and III. only.

   (C) I. only.

   (D) I., II., and III.

4. If the homeowners' association files suit against Bates to collect the monthly fees for upkeep and security guard services:

   (A) Bates would win because there is no privity between Baker and the association.

   (B) Bates would win because the covenant regarding fees does not touch and concern the land.

   (C) The homeowners' association would win because the covenant regarding fees created an equitable servitude binding on Bates.

   (D) The homeowners' association would win because the covenant regarding fees created a burden that runs with the land at law.

5. If Bates sues Calvin to remove his backyard fence:

   (A) Calvin would win because there is no privity between Baker and Calvin.

   (B) Calvin would win because he erected the fence in good faith and without knowledge of the restrictions.

   (C) Bates would win because Bates is in vertical privity with Baker.

   (D) Bates would win because the deed language about fencing created an equitable servitude, which is enforceable against Calvin.

Question 6

Tim, a small business owner, found his business was foundering. However, Tim hoped that an upturn in the economy would improve his business position. Tim's sales started to pick up, but Tim had a serious cash flow problem and needed cash to buy the inventory he needed to fill the orders. Tim went to Julie, a wealthy acquaintance, and asked her for a loan. Julie was willing to make the loan if Tim could put up adequate collateral to assure her that she would not lose her money. She refused an offer of shares in Tim's business, but was willing to accept Agateacre, a property worth $100,000, that Tim had inherited from his mother, to guarantee the loan. Tim gave Julie a deed to Agateacre, which was duly recorded in the office of the county recorder of deeds. Julie gave Tim $50,000, and Tim signed a promissory note agreeing to repay the $50,000 within eight months. Tim continued to occupy Agateacre, where his home was situated, and Julie agreed to reconvey Agateacre to Tim as soon as he repaid the $50,000.

Although the economy continued to prosper, Tim's business did not. Tim continued to lose money and was unable to pay Julie when the note came due. Tim asked Julie for an extension, but she refused because it was clear to her that Tim's business was finished, and that Tim had no other prospects for raising the necessary funds.

If Julie seeks to take possession of Agateacre, may she do so?

(A) Yes, because she has clear record title.

(B) Yes, but only if she institutes foreclosure proceedings and is the successful purchaser at the foreclosure sale.

(C) No, because $50,000 does not reflect the fair market value of Agateacre.

(D) No, Julie is limited to a contract claim against Tim because the law does not recognize this type of security agreement.

Questions 7-8 are based on the following fact situation:

Otto and Gretchen lived together for many years, but never married. The state in which they lived did not recognize common law marriages.

Gretchen was entirely dependent on Otto for support. Due to Otto's advancing age, she became increasingly concerned about her own economic security in the event anything should happen to Otto. He repeatedly promised to take care of her in his will, but Gretchen insisted that Otto must "do something now" to provide her with some security.

One day, Otto asked Gretchen to meet him at his bank. There, he showed her a deed to the

Imperial Hotel, which he owned. The deed was properly executed and named Gretchen as grantee.

7. Assume for purposes of this question only that in front of Gretchen, Otto handed the deed to his banker, Brad, stating, "You are aware of my relationship with Gretchen. I want Gretchen to know that you will be holding this deed, and that when I die you are to give the deed to her." Brad accepted the deed, and assured Gretchen that he understood the situation and would handle everything. A few months later, Otto and Gretchen had a violent quarrel. Otto prevailed upon Brad to return the deed. In a suit by Gretchen against Otto to establish her claim to an interest in the hotel:

(A) Gretchen will win because the deed gave her a present right to possess the hotel.

(B) Gretchen will win because the facts show that Otto intended her to have an interest in the property when he gave the deed to Brad.

(C) Otto will win because there was no lawful consideration given for the deed and hence it was revocable.

(D) Otto will win because the agreement with Brad did not satisfy the Statute of Frauds.

8. Assume for purposes of this question only that instead of handing the deed to Brad, Otto simply handed it to Gretchen. Included in the language of the deed was the following: "Title to the property herein conveyed shall not pass to the named grantee until the death of the grantor named herein." Shortly thereafter, Otto died, leaving no will. In a suit by Otto's administrator against Gretchen to quiet title to the Imperial Hotel:

(A) Otto's administrator will win because the deed was never properly delivered.

(B) Otto's administrator will win because, regardless of delivery, the transaction between Otto and Gretchen violates the Statute of Wills.

(C) Gretchen will win only if she can produce further evidence that Otto intended her to have some actual interest in the property during his lifetime.

(D) Gretchen will win because the deed conveyed to her a future interest in the hotel, which now becomes possessory.

Questions 9-10 are based on the following fact situation:

Fred needed money. His neighbor Tom agreed to loan Fred the money he needed if Fred would give adequate security for the loan. Fred made out a note payable to Tom and secured it with a first trust deed on his house, which Fred owned free and clear of monetary encumbrances. Tom recorded the trust deed.

Fred decided to move to California, and so he sold his house to Bob. Fred wanted Bob to assume the existing trust deed, but in return for a $1,000 increase in the purchase price, Fred agreed that Bob could take the house subject to the mortgage.

The next year, Bob needed money to build a swimming pool and borrowed it from Samuel, securing the loan with a second trust deed on the house. This trust deed was recorded.

Several years later, Bob got into financial trouble and was unable to make payments to either Tom or Samuel on the notes they held. Both Tom and Samuel commenced foreclosure proceedings.

To protect his credit, Fred paid Tom, and Tom assigned him the note and first trust deed. Fred recorded the assignment of the trust deed.

In the foreclosure proceedings, Bob and Samuel argued that Fred has either paid off his own note, which extinguished the first trust deed, or that the first trust deed is junior to Samuel's because the assignment from Tom was recorded after Samuel recorded his trust deed.

9. Which of the following arguments offers the *least* support for Fred's position that his interest has the first priority?

(A) Fred is subrogated to the rights of Tom to the extent of Fred's payment to Tom.

(B) Fred, as assignee, may enforce the note and trust deed that were owned by Tom.

(C) If Fred were denied a first priority, Bob or Samuel would be unjustly enriched.

(D) Even though Fred was the maker of the note, Fred's payment to Tom did not discharge the note.

10. Assume for purposes of this question that only Samuel is foreclosing on the property. The balance on the loan from Samuel is $10,000. The day before the judicial sale, Bob inherited $25,000 from his Aunt Miranda. He quickly contacted Samuel and offered to pay off the loan in full. Samuel refused because he is hoping to buy the now valuable property at the judicial sale. If Bob seeks to force Samuel to accept his offer, he will:

(A) Win, if the jurisdiction has a statutory right of redemption.

(B) Win, because equity requires a creditor to accept such an offer.

(C) Lose, if his agreement with Samuel waived his right to redeem.

(D) Lose, because he lost all of his rights in the property when he defaulted on the loan.

Question 11

Anne and Burton entered into a written land sale contract, under which Burton agreed to purchase a home from Anne for $200,000. When the closing date arrived, Burton duly tendered $200,000 to Anne, and Anne conveyed the property to Burton. Burton took up residence in the home on May 15. Shortly after Burton took up residence in the home, an electrical fire broke out. Fortunately, the fire department arrived promptly and the damage was minimal, but the fire inspector told Burton that the fire had started because the wiring system was defective and that Burton was fortunate that death or more serious property damage had not occurred. Constance, a competent local contractor, confirmed the fire inspector's judgment. She agreed to rewire the house for $8,000. Burton had Constance rewire the house. He then sued Anne for the cost of repairs. Anne's defense is that she had no knowledge that the wiring was defective.

Which of the following facts, if true, would be most significant in establishing a case for Burton against Anne?

(A) The fire occurred prior to June 15.

(B) The wiring problem was a dangerous latent defect that would have deterred Burton from purchasing the home for that price had the defect been disclosed to him.

(C) Anne was the builder of the recently completed house.

(D) Anne conveyed the property to Burton via warranty deed.

Question 12

Stockton owned a hotel in Jodhpurboot, a resort town. Stockton was approached by Eddie Oh, founder and promoter of "Eddie Oh Assertiveness Training for Success Seminars." Eddie wanted to run a two-week seminar in Jodhpurboot and wanted to lease space in which to conduct the seminar. Stockton leased Eddie the hotel's "grand ballroom," the period of the lease being August 1 through August 14. To provide the proper atmosphere for the seminars, Eddie attached curtain rods to the walls of the ballroom, using lightweight screws to attach the rods. Eddie then strung light blue ring curtains through the rods. After the seminar, on August 16, Eddie arrived to remove the curtains and rods. Stockton brought an action to enjoin Eddie from removing the curtains and the rods from the grand ballroom.

The court should rule:

(A) In favor of Eddie, because he had a short-term lease and the curtains and rods were easily removable.

(B) In favor of Eddie, because curtains and rods are trade fixtures.

(C) In favor of Stockton, because the curtain rods were attached by screws, and as such were fixtures, which became part of the realty.

(D) In favor of Stockton, because Eddie did not remove the curtains and rods before the lease expired.

Question 13

Alton owned Sandacre, and his brother, Bruce, owned Sodacre, an adjoining property. Alton drew up an instrument that stated, "Upon my death, I wish Sandacre to pass to my wife, Carla, but should she or her heirs ever attempt to sell Sandacre, the right of first refusal is hereby granted to my brother, Bruce, his heirs and assigns." Bruce drew up a similar instrument granting Alton the same rights over Sodacre. Both instruments were executed with all proper formalities.

Alton died, and Carla enjoyed possession of Sandacre. She decided, however, that she would rather live in the city with her daughter, Domitia. Therefore, she placed an ad in the newspaper offering Sandacre for sale. Lattimore responded to the ad and offered to buy Sandacre for $200,000. Bruce learned of this and demanded that he be allowed to exercise his option to purchase Sandacre. Carla had never liked Bruce, and she told him, "I'll sell my property to whomever I wish, and I want to sell to Mr. Lattimore. He at least cleans his fingernails." Bruce stomped off in a rage and filed suit to compel Carla to sell him Sandacre.

Assuming that the state in which the property is located strictly follows the common law Rule Against Perpetuities and the common law rule against restraints on alienation, will Bruce prevail?

(A) Yes, because his arrangement with Alton was reciprocal.

(B) Yes, because he has the equivalent of a possibility of reverter in Sandacre.

(C) No, because the right of first refusal violates the Rule against Perpetuities.

(D) No, because a right of first refusal is an improper restraint on alienation.

Questions 14-15 are based on the following fact situation:

On December 1, Amy rented an apartment to Bette for one year, commencing January 1. Bette paid first and last month's rent. Both Amy and Bette realized that, at the time of the making of the lease, the apartment in question was occupied by Colin, who had a lease on the premises until December 31. Colin refused to leave the apartment on December 31, and Amy served the appropriate legal notices to vacate the premises. Colin still did not vacate the apartment, and Amy was therefore forced to institute an unlawful detainer action against Colin. Amy was successful in the action and succeeded in getting the marshal to enforce the judgment and take possession of the apartment. Bette received possession of the apartment on February 1. The lease between Amy and Bette contained the following statement: "Bette, on payment of the monthly rent and compliance with all of the covenants and conditions stated herein, shall have the quiet enjoyment of the premises."

14. Bette now sues Amy for damages resulting from the delay in Bette's possession of the premises. Which of the following would provide Bette with the best argument?

(A) Amy expressly promised Bette that possession of the premises would be available on January 1.

(B) Amy breached the covenant of quiet enjoyment stated in the lease by not delivering up possession of the premises to Bette at the beginning of the term of the lease on January 1.

(C) The jurisdiction follows the majority view, and Amy was required to deliver actual possession.

(D) Bette took no part in the holdover tenancy or the attempts to terminate the holdover tenancy of Colin.

15. Amy's best defense to an action by Bette for damages resulting from Bette's delay in receiving possession of the apartment is that:

(A) Amy is not liable, because she did not breach any specific promise to deliver the premises on January 1.

(B) Amy is not liable for damages, because the jurisdiction follows the majority rule and she acted properly and quickly, doing everything within her power to eject Colin in a timely manner.

(C) Amy's obligation to Bette ends with the signing of the lease.

(D) Amy incurred no obligation, because the jurisdiction follows the minority view regarding the landlord's duty to deliver possession and, under the terms of the new lease, Bette had the right to possession, not Amy, and a continued occupancy by Colin was a wrong to the interests of Bette.

Questions 16-18 are based on the following fact situation:

In 1990, Harvey, the owner of Blueacre, a vacant parcel of land located in Wyorado, executed a warranty deed granting "all of my property in Wyorado to my favorite nephew, Mitch." Harvey placed the deed in his bedroom closet and told his friend, Curt, to get the deed and give it to Mitch if Mitch survived Harvey.

In 1994, Harvey became angry at Mitch, since Mitch seemed so interested in horses and cars that he no longer paid any attention to his Uncle Harvey. Therefore, Harvey conveyed Blueacre by quitclaim deed to Ursula for $20,000. Harvey told Ursula about the earlier deed to Mitch, and he told Ursula that he planned to tear it up, but Harvey never did so.

Harvey died in 1995, leaving Mitch as his sole surviving heir. Curt thereupon delivered Harvey's deed to Mitch, which was the first time Mitch knew of the deed. Mitch moved onto Blueacre, living in a concrete building shaped like a Native American tepee, which Mitch built on the property. The concrete tepee cost Mitch $15,000 to build, but due to its unusual design did not really enhance the value of Blueacre at all.

At no time did Harvey own any land in Wyorado other than Blueacre.

16. The deed from Harvey to Mitch was:

   (A) Effective as a conveyance of title when executed in 1990, because Curt accepted the deed on behalf of Mitch.

   (B) Effective as a conveyance of title on Harvey's death in 1995.

   (C) Ineffective as a conveyance, because Harvey failed to deliver it to Mitch.

   (D) Ineffective as a conveyance, because the description of the land was inadequate.

17. The deed from Harvey to Ursula was:

   (A) Effective as a conveyance of title when delivered.

   (B) Effective upon recordation, to cut off Mitch's interest in the property.

   (C) Ineffective as against Mitch, because Ursula knew of the deed from Harvey to Mitch when she became a grantee.

   (D) Ineffective as against Mitch, because Ursula took by quitclaim deed and thus stands in the shoes of Harvey.

18. Assume for purposes of this question only that Ursula prevails over Mitch as to ownership of Blueacre. As between the parties:

   (A) Ursula is entitled to retain the tepee installed by Mitch and can also re-cover the reasonable rental value for Mitch's use and possession.

   (B) Ursula is entitled to retain the tepee, but must reimburse Mitch for the $15,000 it cost him to build the tepee.

   (C) Mitch is entitled to remove the tepee he built.

   (D) Mitch is entitled to a lien on Blueacre for $15,000, less the fair rental value of his use and possession of the property.

Questions 19-20 are based on the following fact situation:

Helen and Wilbur were a couple who lived together for many years but never got around to getting married. Although Minnekota, the state in which they reside, does not recognize com-mon law marriage, it has statutes that prohibit discrimination on the basis of marital status. Both Helen and Wilbur had good jobs, and Wilbur was also fortunate enough to win a large prize in the Minnekota State Lottery. The pro-ceeds of the prize were used for many purposes, among them the purchase of Niceacre, a large property containing a fine old mansion. Title to Niceacre was duly recorded and Helen and Wilbur held title as joint tenants.

Unfortunately, Wilbur's success in the lottery encouraged Helen to believe that it was easy to make money by gambling. Although Helen was sometimes successful, she ran into a streak of bad luck and had to raise a quick $20,000 to pay off her bookmaker. Helen was too embarrassed to tell Wilbur, but she was able to convince the loan officer at Trustme Federal Savings to hold a mortgage on Niceacre in exchange for the money. The officer was also willing to accept Helen's signature alone, and Wilbur never learned about the mortgage.

Two years later, Helen died without having paid off the mortgage.

Helen left no will, and her only heir at law is her sister, Sonia. Minnekota is a "lien theory" mortgage state.

19. Who has title to Niceacre?

  (A) Wilbur.

  (B) Wilbur and Trustme Federal Savings.

  (C) Wilbur and Sonia.

  (D) Wilbur, Sonia, and Trustme Federal Savings.

20. What would be the state of title to Niceacre if Minnekota subscribed to the "title theory" of mortgages?

  (A) Wilbur and Trustme Federal Savings would have title, because the joint tenancy would have been severed.

  (B) Wilbur would have title, because the joint tenancy would not have been severed.

  (C) Sonia would have a legal interest in Niceacre.

  (D) The same as under the lien theory, because the mortgage theory of the jurisdiction has no effect on whether joint tenancies are severed.

Question 21

On February 10, Ohner took out a $10,000 mortgage on Whiteacre with First Bank. On February 15, Ohner conveyed Whiteacre to Byyer for $50,000. On February 17, First Bank recorded its mortgage interest in Whiteacre. On February 21, Byyer recorded his deed to Whiteacre.

Does Byyer hold Whiteacre subject to First Bank's mortgage?

  (A) Yes, in a race-notice jurisdiction.

  (B) No, in a race-notice jurisdiction.

  (C) Yes, regardless of the type of recording statute.

  (D) No, because Byyer was a bona fide purchaser for value who bought Whiteacre before First Bank recorded the mortgage.

Question 22

Frogsmith was a wealthy and philanthropic resident of Hightown. Frogsmith's pride was the Frogsmith mansion, which Frogsmith had built to his exact specifications on Froggy Hill 40 years ago. A special feature of the mansion was a pipe organ that was built into the wall of the music room. The organ was impressive, with beautiful handcarved wood scrollwork. The same European artisans who carved the organ carved its accompanying bench, designed to seat the person playing the organ. The bench was made from the same wood as the organ and was carved to match the patterns on the organ. The bench was fully movable and could be slid into a niche beside the organ when not in use, although Frogsmith usually left the bench in front of the organ for its matching effect, even when the organ was not being played.

Frogsmith died, and his will left all of his personal property to his only child, Chuckles, and all of his real property to the Hightown

Community Trust, a local community fund charity. After the will was admitted to probate, Chuckles had a large moving truck driven to the Frogsmith mansion. Chuckles proceeded to remove all the furniture, silver, linen, and other movables from the mansion. Among the items taken by Chuckles was the organ bench. Snootnose, the president of the Hightown Community Trust, noticed that the organ bench was gone. Snootnose asked Chuckles to return the bench to the mansion. Chuckles refused.

If the Hightown Community Trust brings suit against Chuckles to replevy the bench, the court will rule in favor of:

(A) Chuckles, because the bench is personalty because it was not bolted to the floor.

(B) Chuckles, because removing the bench does not damage the real property.

(C) The Trust, because the bench is an accession to a fixture and cannot be removed.

(D) The Trust, because removal of the bench reduces the value of the devise to the Trust.

Question 23

Verdugo placed Blancoacre, a suburban lot and home, for sale for $155,000. Verdugo spent about $3,000 to "spruce the place up" prior to placing the property on the market. Verdugo knew that the roof of the home on the property was in very bad shape. During the last rainy period, there had been several major leaks in the roof, which had left ugly water marks on the ceiling and walls in the home. At about the time Verdugo thought he would have to repair the roof, a drought began. He put off repairs. A roofing contractor told Verdugo that it would cost an additional $4,500 for a new roof. Instead, Verdugo painted the shingles that could be seen from the street to make them appear new, and covered the watermarks on the interior. Verdugo reasoned that, with any luck, the drought would last beyond the closing date, and the buyer would not discover the problem until it was too late. After a realtor showed Pringle a number of properties, Pringle decided on Blancoacre. He offered Verdugo $150,000 for

the property, and they entered into a written contract for the sale of Blancoacre for $150,000. The contract included a clause making Pringle's obligation to tender the purchase price at the closing date "subject to approval by an inspector of Pringle's choosing."

Prior to closing, Pringle inspected the property with his friend Izzy, a local tradesman with a good reputation. Neither Pringle nor Izzy climbed onto the roof, but Izzy mentioned that the roof looked fairly new. Izzy also looked for signs of water damage to the ceilings and walls on the interior, but found none. Izzy found a few minor defects inside the home, which Verdugo agreed to correct. Verdugo did so at a cost to himself of $350. When the closing date arrived, Pringle tendered the purchase price to Verdugo, and Verdugo conveyed Blancoacre to Pringle by warranty deed.

Three months after Pringle moved into Blancoacre, a major rainstorm occurred. The roof leaked like a sieve and much of Pringle's personal property was damaged. Pringle replaced the roof at a cost of $8,000. Pringle's homeowner's insurance covered the cost of the water damage to Pringle's floors and personal property, but would not reimburse his expenses incurred in installing the new roof, which the insurance carrier deemed "normal maintenance and repair."

If Pringle sues Verdugo for the $8,000 cost of installing a new roof, the court is likely to rule in favor of:

(A) Pringle, because Verdugo breached an implied warranty that the house was fit for the purpose intended.

(B) Pringle, because Verdugo concealed the defects in the roof from Pringle.

(C) Verdugo, because Pringle had an ample opportunity to inspect the property before tendering the purchase price, and Verdugo had no duty to disclose defects to him.

(D) Verdugo, because the property conveyed to Pringle was not a new house constructed by Verdugo.

Question 24

Arnold, a developer, purchased Bigacre from Otto. He had plans to make the large, but undeveloped, property profitable. Thus, Arnold built 10 homes on the rural property and rented them out to tenants. Because Bigacre was too far from the city to be hooked up to the city's water supply network, Arnold drilled a well on Bigacre to supply the domestic needs of all 10 Bigacre homes. The well provided an adequate water supply and none of the tenants ever had reason to complain of water shortages.

Subsequently, Beth, the owner of Smallacre, built a home on her property, which was located immediately adjacent to Bigacre. Beth took up residency in the home on Smallacre and drilled a well to supply her water needs. Although all of Beth's water usage was domestic, she drew a large quantity of water from her well. Six months after Beth took up residency on Smallacre, the well on Bigacre ceased producing enough water to adequately supply Arnold's tenants on Bigacre. Both wells draw percolating water.

If Arnold sues Beth, asking that the court enjoin her from interfering with Arnold's supply, what is the court likely to order Beth to do?

(A) Cut back her water use sufficiently so that Arnold's tenants can be adequately supplied.

(B) Pay money damages to Arnold.

(C) Transfer water from Beth's well to Arnold's property.

(D) Nothing.

Question 25

Oliver conveys Greenacre "to Manuel and his heirs, but should Manuel or his successor attempt to convey this property, then to Quigley and his heirs." During his lifetime, Quigley's interest in the property is best described as:

(A) An executory interest.

(B) A contingent remainder.

(C) A vested remainder.

(D) None of the above.

Questions 26-27 are based on the following fact situation:

Gina owned Greenacre. She conveyed Greenacre as follows: "To my friend Flicka for life, then to the heirs of my son, Sebastian." At the time of the conveyance, Sebastian had not yet married and had no children. At the time of Flicka's death, Gina was still living, and Sebastian was still unmarried and childless.

26. At the time of the conveyance, what interest do Sebastian's heirs have?

(A) Shifting executory interest.

(B) Springing executory interest.

(C) Contingent remainder.

(D) Nothing.

27. At Flicka's death, who is entitled to possession of Greenacre?

(A) Sebastian.

(B) Gina.

(C) Flicka's heirs.

(D) Sebastian's heirs.

Question 28

Tomasz lived in Michiana, and all the property he owned was located within the boundaries of Michiana. The Michiana recording statute reads, in relevant part: "No conveyance is good against a subsequent purchaser for value, without notice, who first records." Tomasz drew up a deed conveying Duneacre to his son, Stashu. Tomasz never recorded the deed and left it in the top drawer of his desk in his study. Two years later, Tomasz died. He left a will, which declared that all of his property be divided equally between Stashu and Tomasz's daughter, Danuta.

While going through his father's personal effects, Stashu discovered the deed to Duneacre. He showed the deed to his sister and the two of them agreed not to record the deed. Stashu put the deed in a desk drawer in his home. A year later, Stashu died. Stashu's lawyer, Laine, was named executor in Stashu's will. As Laine perused Stashu's personal papers, he came across the deed and promptly recorded it. He then entered into a contract to sell Duneacre to Andy. Danuta discovered this and promptly filed suit, claiming an interest in Duneacre.

The court will rule:

(A) In favor of Danuta, because there was no proper delivery of the deed to Duneacre.

(B) In favor of Danuta, because Laine violated his fiduciary duty as a lawyer and executor when he recorded.

(C) Against Danuta, because Laine and Andy are protected by the recording act.

(D) Against Danuta, because Danuta is not a bona fide purchaser.

Question 29

Gretna Green divided her 25-acre property, Greenacre, into 100 quarter-acre residential lots. Green was a staunch advocate of all forms of environmentalism. Therefore, she included in the deed of all 100 grantees the following provision:

> Grantee covenants for herself and her heirs and assigns that all aluminum cans, glass bottles, and grass clippings of Grantee and her heirs and assigns shall be recycled. This covenant runs with the land and shall remain in effect as long as there is a recycling center within five statute miles of the Greenacre Development.

At the time Gretna sold her lots, there was a recycling center about one mile from the western boundary of Greenacre. Gretna advertised Greenacre as "An Environmentally Sound Place to Live and Raise Kids," and proudly pointed out the recycling covenant to all prospective purchasers. Therefore, the Greenacre Development tended to attract persons who considered themselves "environmentally aware." Betsy Brookfield was active in many environmental causes. She sold her house in the city and purchased a lot in the Greenacre Development. Her deed contained the recycling clause. She had a home built at 15 Spotted Owl Street and happily recycled her bottles, cans, and clippings. Two years later, Betsy won the state lottery and decided to move to Brazil, where she could directly involve herself in rain forest preservation activities. She gave the Spotted Owl Street property to her niece, Nancy Niles, as a gift. Nancy's deed to the property contained the recycling covenant. Shortly after Nancy took possession of the house, the recycling center moved its location to a new site about four and a half miles from Greenacre. Nancy continued to recycle, but she was less enthusiastic about such matters than her aunt. She had fallen in love with Stan Stickney, the owner of a tallow-rendering plant. When Stan asked Nancy to marry him, she moved in with Stan and put the house up for sale. On the advice of her real estate agent, Nancy said nothing to prospective buyers about recycling. The house was purchased by Vito Veteran, who had lost the use of his legs from wounds received in Vietnam. Vito was impressed that the house was wheelchair-accessible with only a few minor alterations required. Vito's deed did not contain the recycling clause, and Vito hired a local disposal service to carry away his garbage and trash. He hired a landscaper-gardener to maintain the yard. The landscaper bagged the grass clippings and they were removed by the disposal service, which put all Vito's trash and clippings in a landfill. Watching the disposal service trucks drive up to Vito's property infuriated many of the neighbors. They formed a committee and informed Vito of his duty to recycle. Vito told them he knew nothing of the covenant and that it would be difficult for a person in his physical condition to haul cans, bottles, and clippings to the recycling center. Unfazed, the neighbors filed suit to require Vito to comply with the covenant or pay damages.

Vito's best defense is which of the following?

(A) Vito's deed did not contain the covenant.

(B) The covenant does not touch and concern the land.

(C) An intelligent inspection of the neighborhood would raise no inference that the covenant existed.

(D) Vito's physical condition requires a balancing of hardships by the court.

Question 30

A statute in State Red provided: "No conveyance is valid against any subsequent purchaser for value without notice unless the conveyance is recorded. No lease for three years or more is valid against a subsequent purchaser for value without notice unless the lease has been recorded."

Father was a successful businessman in Magenta, a city of 150,000 residents, located in State Red. Father's oldest child, Son, was in his second year of law school when Father leased him an office building in Magenta. The lease had a 10-year term, and Father advised Son to record the lease. Son told Father, "Hey Dad, I'm the lawyer in the family. I don't have to record because it's going to be obvious to any prospective purchaser that I'm in possession of the property. Any buyer is going to inspect the property. When he does, I'll tell him about the lease and that will put him on notice. That recording statute doesn't mean a thing when the buyer's got notice. I learned all this in my property course last year."

Shortly thereafter, Father entered into a contract to sell the leased property to Able. Before purchasing the property Able merely drove by it. Able eschewed a closer inspection because of Father's reputation in Magenta as an honest and highly ethical businessman and his reputation for maintaining any properties he owned in top condition. Because Able's inspection was merely a drive-by, he did not notice Son's occupancy, and the standard title search did not reveal the lease because it was unrecorded. Able tendered the purchase money to Father, and Father conveyed to Able the property by warranty deed. Able subsequently found Son in possession of the premises and ordered Son to vacate. Son refused and asked Able where he should send the rent checks.

In an action by Able to evict Son, the court should rule that:

(A) Son wins, because Able's drive-by inspection will be deemed to confer actual notice on him.

(B) Son wins, because Able had a duty to properly inspect the property.

(C) Able wins, because Able is a subsequent purchaser for value and Son failed to record.

(D) Able wins, because Son knew of the statute and willfully failed to record.

Question 31

Selma owned a large piece of property known around town as the "Old Carter Compound," despite the fact that no member of the Carter family had owned the property since World War I. At that time, the compound, which consisted of the several buildings comprising the family's estate, was sold to Kincaid. Kincaid turned the family home into an inn and built a profitable bakery at the back of the property that supplied fresh baked goods to the inn and several stores in the area. The property passed by inheritance to Kincaid's daughter, Katherine, and from Katherine to her daughter, Selma. Selma decided to retire to a warmer climate and entered into a contract to sell the property to Bolton for $1 million. The contract was recorded. Bolton gave Selma $200,000 as earnest money. The closing date was set for September 10, two months after the signing of the contract.

On August 10, in a fit of resentment, Phipps Carter, a poor descendant of the original owners of the property, set fire to the inn, which was closed for the day. The inn burned to the ground. On September 10, Selma appeared at the closing and tendered the deed to the property. Bolton refused to tender the remaining $800,000 of the purchase price and demanded the return of his earnest money. Selma, who was counting on the proceeds of the sale to pay for her retirement home, sued Bolton for specific performance of the sale contract. Bolton countersued for the return of his earnest money. Both parties stipulate that the value of the property without the inn is $600,000.

At trial, Selma will most likely:

(A) Not prevail on the issue of specific performance, but will be allowed to keep the earnest money.

(B) Not prevail on the issue of specific performance and will be ordered to return the earnest money.

(C) Prevail on the issue of specific performance, but the price will be abated to $600,000.

(D) Prevail on the issue of specific performance for the full contract price.

Question 32

Tammy devised her two-acre parcel in downtown Smallville to her daughter Bertha, her heirs and assigns, "so long as the property is used for residential purposes, then to Wilma, her heirs and assigns." Wilma was Tammy's niece. The remainder of Tammy's property passed through the residuary clause of her will to her grandson, Exeter. Bertha lived on the two acres for 25 years, then upon her death, ownership passed to her daughter, Beulah. In the meantime, Wilma had also died, leaving her entire estate to her son, Wesley. Beulah has moved to Metropolis and has leased the two acres in Smallville to a developer who has obtained the necessary permits to build a shopping center on it. Exeter and Wesley both file quiet title and ejectment actions against Beulah, and the cases are consolidated.

How should the court, applying common law, rule as to ownership of the two acres?

(A) For Beulah.

(B) For Wesley.

(C) For Exeter, because he received a right of reversion from his grandmother.

(D) For Exeter, because he received a possibility of reverter from his grandmother.

Question 33

Farmer owned a 70-acre tract of land on the outskirts of Boomtown, a rapidly growing municipality. Boomtown was famous, or in the minds of some, "infamous," for its lack of land-use regulations and a zoning code that allowed almost anything to be built anywhere. When Farmer was ready to retire to Florida, she sold the entire 70-acre parcel to Greedy. The conveyance to Greedy contained no restrictions. Upon taking possession of Farmer's property, Greedy divided the property into two parcels, 40-acre Grandacre and 30-acre Petitacre. Greedy then subdivided Grandacre into 80 one-half-acre lots and put them on the market. Under Boomtown's liberal land-use provisions there was no zoning code limitation on the use of either parcel, nor was Greedy required to file a plat map with local officials. However, each purchaser of a Grandacre lot received a deed containing a clause labeled "Restrictive Covenant," which stated that use of the lot was limited to "no more than one single-family dwelling and one garage." In addition, Greedy's staff gave every prospective purchaser a brochure depicting the 80-lot subdivision upon its completion, with a drawing of a house on each lot. The lots sold briskly and soon a number of homes were constructed on the Grandacre lots. Two years later, Otto, who owned one of the first lots sold on Grandacre, was transferred by his company to an out-of-state location. He sold both the lot, and the house he had built thereon, to Scott. Scott's deed did not contain the restrictive covenant.

Soon after, when the last Grandacre lot was sold, Greedy sold the adjacent Petitacre to Barker. The deed from Greedy contained no restrictions as to the use of Petitacre. Barker planned to construct an "auto mall" on the site and lease the property to a number of new and used car dealers. Two weeks after Scott moved into his home on Grandacre, Barker began building the auto mall. Scott was angry that the busy mall was to be right next door to his home. He filed suit against Barker to enjoin his construction of the auto mall.

Which of the following is the best argument in Barker's defense?

(A) Greedy did not expressly promise in writing that he would restrict the remaining lots when he conveyed the lot to Otto.

(B) Scott and Barker are not in each other's chain of title.

(C) Scott's deed contained no restrictive covenant.

(D) Petitacre was not part of a common scheme of development.

Question 34

Stanley, after a lengthy negotiation, agreed in writing to sell Goldacre to Byron. The contract called for Stanley to deliver a good and marketable title to Byron within 90 days from the date of this contract, and at that time Byron was to deliver to Stanley $50,000 in cash. One month later, Byron discovered that the owner of record was not Stanley, but Trask. At the time set for closing, Stanley tendered a deed in the form agreed to in the contract. Byron refused to pay the purchase price or to take possession because Stanley was not the record owner of Goldacre. Stanley correctly explained that he had been in adverse possession of Goldacre for 25 years, five years longer than the jurisdictional requirement. Byron still refused to complete the sale.

If Stanley brings suit against Byron for specific performance, Stanley will:

(A) Prevail, because Stanley's action for specific performance is an action in rem, even though Trask is not a party.

(B) Prevail, because Stanley has obtained "good and marketable title" by adverse possession.

(C) Not prevail, because Stanley's failure to disclose his lack of record title constitutes fraud.

(D) Not prevail, because Byron cannot be required to buy a lawsuit, even if the probability is great that Byron would prevail against Trask.

Question 35

LaRue owned property in City on which was located a vacant building with street access. Tong sought to open a bakery in City. Tong asked LaRue about the building's availability and, after a period of negotiations, LaRue leased the building to Tong for 10 years, commencing January 1, 1988, at a monthly rental of $1,700. The lease stated in part, "Tong may not sublet or assign this lease without first receiving written permission from LaRue to do so. Any attempt to sublet or assign the lease without first receiving written permission shall constitute a breach entitling LaRue to terminate this lease." In June of 1993, Tong's bakery began experiencing severe financial difficulties. Stringer believed that Tong's financial difficulties were the result of mismanagement by Tong. Believing he could do much better, Stringer approached Tong and offered to purchase the bakery if Tong would agree to sublet the premises to him. Tong agreed and executed a sublease on July 1, 1993. Stringer took possession the same day. On July 3, Tong approached LaRue and asked for written permission to sublet the premises to Stringer. LaRue said he had no real objection to the sublease and would execute the document requested by Tong, but only if Stringer would sign a five-year extension of the existing lease. Stringer refused to extend the lease, but remained in possession of the building. At no time did LaRue accept rent from Stringer. After notice was given to all parties and the applicable grace period in the lease had elapsed, LaRue brought an appropriate action against Tong and Stringer to evict Tong and Stringer from the premises and to declare the lease terminated because it had been breached.

The result of this action should be:

(A) Against LaRue, because LaRue's withholding consent is an invalid restraint on alienation.

(B) Against LaRue, because LaRue's conditional consent operated as a waiver of the term of the lease requiring LaRue to give written permission for subletting.

(C) For LaRue, because Tong has breached the lease.

(D) For LaRue, because his oral consent to sublet is not enforceable because of the Statute of Frauds.

Question 36

Michael owned a large parcel of land that he divided into two equal parcels called Acreone and Acretwo. In 1967, Michael deeded Acretwo to Nancy by warranty deed, including an easement over the south 25 feet of Acreone for access to the navigable river that ran along the westerly boundary of Acreone. Michael acknowledged the deed and easement, and Nancy recorded the document. The recording officer maintains an alphabetical grantor-grantee index, but no tract index.

Nancy made no use of the easement until March 1990, which was after Laura had purchased Acreone from Michael in April 1989. Laura had paid at least market value for Acreone and was not aware of Nancy's easement.

Laura objected to Nancy's use of the easement shortly after Nancy began using it, but Nancy paid no attention, and in June 1994, Laura sued Nancy to quiet her title and to restrain Nancy from using Acreone. Nancy has

reasonable access to a public highway on the easterly boundary of Acretwo.

If Nancy is successful, it will be because:

(A) The absence of a tract index requires that Laura make inquiry regarding the riparian rights of owners abutting her property.

(B) Laura and Nancy trace their title to a common grantor, Michael, whose covenants of title run with the land and estop Laura from denying Nancy's title.

(C) An easement is a legal and incorporeal interest that is not just attached to an estate in the land, but runs with the land itself and therefore binds successive owners of the servient estate regardless of notice.

(D) The easement is a legal interest in Laura's chain of title even though there is no tract index.

Questions 37-38 are based on the following fact situation:

Katherine and Amanda were sisters who held record title to Lakeacre as joint tenants with right of survivorship. Katherine moved out of Lakeacre shortly after conveying her interest in Lakeacre to her brother Jeff by quitclaim deed. Jeff did not record his deed.

Several years later, Amanda died, leaving her adopted son Chris as her sole heir.

Shortly after Amanda died, Katherine asked Jeff to return his deed and give up his interest in Lakeacre. Jeff agreed and returned the deed, which Katherine destroyed.

37. Who has title to Lakeacre?

(A) Jeff and Chris as co-tenants.

(B) Katherine and Chris as co-tenants.

(C) Katherine as sole owner.

(D) Jeff as sole owner.

38. Assume for this question only that after Jeff returned his deed to Katherine, Katherine executed and delivered a deed conveying Lakeacre to Paul. The jurisdiction has the following recording act:

> A conveyance of an interest in land shall not be valid against any subsequent purchaser for value, without notice thereof, unless the conveyance is recorded.

Paul promptly and properly recorded his deed. In a suit between Paul and Jeff, Paul will prevail, if at all, because:

(A) Paul recorded his deed.

(B) Jeff's interest terminated when he returned his deed to Katherine.

(C) There has been no severance because Amanda adopted Chris.

(D) Paul is a bona fide purchaser.

Question 39

Olsen and Larsen were negotiating over the proposed purchase by Olsen of a new home constructed by Larsen in a subdivision owned by Larsen. The subdivision contained four types of floor plans. Houses constructed according to the same floor plan were identical, but the different plans varied in square footage and cost.

Olsen could not decide whether he wanted a house with a swimming pool or one located on an extra-large cul-de-sac lot. Both houses were of the same floor plan and both were offered for sale at $100,000. Larsen, who had many other sales transactions to negotiate, prepared a validly executed deed that was ready for recording but did not identify the property conveyed. He told Olsen to decide which house he wanted, identify it in the deed, and then record the deed. Olsen agonized for a few days, then decided that he liked a house with a more expensive floor plan better than either of his original choices. He entered its description in the deed and recorded

the deed. The house described had a fair market value of and had been offered for sale by Larsen at $125,000.

Two weeks later, Olsen offered the house for sale to Snyder for $110,000. A real estate agent working for Snyder reported that Olsen had title of record and that it was marketable and free of encumbrances. Olsen told Snyder that the same type of house was selling for $125,000 in the subdivision, but did not describe how he had come to own it or how much he had paid for it. Snyder agreed to purchase the home, and Olsen conveyed by a validly recorded warranty deed.

If Larsen brings an action against Snyder to quiet title to the house originally sold to Olsen, which of the following is the most probable reason for a judgment for Snyder?

(A) Larsen is guilty of unclean hands.

(B) Recording of the deed by which Olsen conveyed to Snyder precludes any attack on its validity.

(C) Evidence of Larsen's oral instructions to Olsen is barred by the Statute of Frauds.

(D) Larsen is estopped from relying upon his agreement with Olsen because Snyder is a bona fide purchaser for value.

Questions 40-42 are based on the following fact situation:

Lamont owned a 40-acre farm bordering the city limits of Gridley when the local authorities annexed his land to the city and rezoned it from agricultural to residential use. Nathan, the moving force behind the annexation and rezoning, purchased the 40 acres from Lamont and obtained approval of, filed, and recorded a subdivision map dividing the former farm into 120 quarter-acre lots with two five-acre "city parks." He then announced the opening of "Parkland" and proceeded to sell the quarter-acre lots with houses built by his construction subsidiary.

Parkland included a set of covenants, conditions, and restrictions that had been approved by the local land use planning agencies and filed as part of the subdivision map. Among these was a covenant that all purchasers of the lots promised not to engage in any commercial activity (the zoning applicable to Parkland permitted certain types of businesses).

Nathan's real estate operation sold 100 of the quarter-acre lots over the next two years to individual purchasers; each deed referred to the covenants, conditions, and restrictions filed with the subdivision map. When the last 20 lots—located adjacent to one of the areas originally designated as a city park—did not move, Nathan sold the lots and the park in a single 10-acre package to a large national real estate corporation. The deed from Nathan to the corporation omitted any reference to the covenants, conditions, and restrictions. The corporation sold the quarter-acre lots to individual purchasers via deeds also not mentioning the covenants, etc., and then sold the five-acre "park" to a fundamentalist church.

40. After the sale of the five-acre park, but before the church began construction of its Born Again Worship Center and Christian Education Complex, the city of Gridley passes a resolution designating the two "park" areas in Parkland as the Richard Gridley and Gertrude Gridley Memorial Parks, respectively, and soliciting bids from local landscaping firms to prepare the parks for use by the public. When the church learns of the city's plans, it brings an action to quiet title to the five-acre parcel it purchased from the national corporation. How should the trial court rule?

(A) For the city, since the church had constructive notice that the parcel was to be used for park purposes.

(B) For the church, since the deed by which it purchased the parcel did not contain any reference to the subdivision map that designated the area a "park."

(C) For the city, since Nathan dedicated it and the city accepted the two parcels designated as a "park."

(D) For the church, since the city has committed laches in waiting so long to develop the park.

41. Assume for the purposes of this question only that the city has taken no action with respect to the parks, but Winslow, who purchased an individual lot from Nathan, brings an action seeking to enjoin construction of the Born Again Christian Education Complex, alleging that it violates the covenant against conducting commercial activities. The trial court makes a preliminary determination that the Education Complex is a commercial activity. Should the injunction issue?

(A) Yes, because the church cannot be considered a bona fide purchaser.

(B) Yes, because Winslow is a creditor third-party beneficiary of the promise made by Nathan with respect to all the lots in Parkland.

(C) Yes, because Winslow has an equitable servitude concerning use of the land within Parkland.

(D) No, because the covenant not to conduct commercial activity applies only to purchasers of individual quarter-acre lots.

42. One of the purchasers of a quarter-acre lot from the large real estate corporation was Madame Zorka, a self-proclaimed psychic. She places a tasteful neon sign in the front window of her residence and begins giving psychic readings for a fee, an activity in conformity with the applicable zoning regulations. If Winslow seeks to enjoin this activity, will he succeed?

(A) No, because the deed from the corporation to Zorka did not refer to the covenants, conditions, and restrictions.

(B) No, if Zorka relied on the zoning regulations before purchasing her property.

(C) Yes, because the restrictive covenant relating to commercial activity runs with the land.

(D) Yes, if Winslow can show reciprocal negative servitudes implied from a common scheme.

Question 43

Abner conveyed Purpleacre, a large tract of land, to Bosco and Canfield by a deed that created a co-tenancy in equal shares with right of survivorship. Bosco, by deed, then conveyed "My undivided, one-half interest in Purpleacre" to Dansford. Bosco has since died. The jurisdiction has no statute directly applicable to this situation.

In an action between Canfield and Dansford, in which both claim sole title to Purpleacre, Canfield will prevail only if:

(A) The co-tenancy created in Bosco and Canfield was a tenancy by the entirety.

(B) He was once the sole owner of Purpleacre.

(C) Bosco and Canfield owned Purpleacre as tenants in common.

(D) He had knowledge of the conveyance prior to Bosco's death.

Questions 44-45 are based on the following fact situation:

Blackwood and Redwood were two adjoining undeveloped tracts of land. Art owned Blackwood, and Baker owned Redwood. Art decided to develop a recreational facility that would be open to the public on Blackwood. He prepared a development plan outlining the areas on Blackwood designated for recreational use. The plan provided for main access to the facility to be by way of a road to be constructed around the perimeter of Blackwood and to be known as

Circle Drive. The plan was fully approved by all necessary governmental agencies and duly recorded. However, construction of the facility and of Circle Drive has not yet begun, and according to a local ordinance, Circle Drive cannot be opened as a public way until construction is finished on the recreational facility. Baker for many years had attempted to sell Redwood. However, since Redwood had no access to any public roadway except a narrow gravel road that was in very poor condition, its market value was minimal. Baker knew that he could sell Redwood for a higher price if he improved the access road, but to do so would cost a great deal of money. Shortly after Art's plans for development of Blackwood were announced, Baker sold Redwood to Carl. The description used in the deed from Baker to Carl was the same as that used in prior deeds except that the portion of the description that formerly said, "thence by land of Art South Easternly at a distance of 250 feet more or less" was changed to "thence by Circle Drive as laid out on the plan of Blackwood, South 10 degrees East 254 feet," with full reference to the plan and recording data. Carl now seeks a building permit that would allow him to construct access from Redwood to Circle Drive. Art objects to the granting of the building permit on the grounds that he never granted any rights to Baker or Carl to use Circle Drive. There are no applicable statutes dealing with this situation. Carl brings an appropriate action to determine his rights to build an access connecting Redwood and Circle Drive.

44. The best argument for Art in this action is that:

(A) The Statute of Frauds prevents the introduction of evidence that might prove the necessity for Carl to use Circle Drive.

(B) Carl would be unjustly enriched if he were permitted to use Circle Drive.

(C) Carl's right must await the action of appropriate public authorities to open Circle Drive as a public street since no private easement arose by implication.

(D) Carl's right to use Circle Drive is restricted to the assertion of a way by necessity, and the facts preclude the success of such a claim.

45. The best argument for Carl in this action is that:

(A) The deed from Baker to Carl referred to the recorded plan and therefore created rights to use this street delineated on the plan.

(B) The recording of the plan is a dedication of the street shown on the plan to public use.

(C) There is a way by necessity over Blackwood to gain access to a public road.

(D) The fact that Carl could only gain access to Redwood by expending a large amount of money to repair and improve the one-lane gravel road creates a sufficient need for an easement across Blackwood to gain access to a public road.

Question 46

Carol leased 130 square feet of space in a commercial building owned by Barbara pursuant to a written contract specifying a term of three years, renewable at Carol's option for an additional three years. Carol installed sinks, tile, mirrors, special chairs, and other equipment related to her hairstyling business. During the second year of the lease term, Barbara borrowed $60,000 from Commercial Credit Company, and executed a mortgage in that company's favor on the building. Carol was not informed of the existence of the mortgage.

In the last month of her three-year term, Carol decided not to renew and began removing the equipment and other items that she had installed at the beginning of the lease. Barbara had defaulted on the payments due Commercial Credit, and that company had commenced

foreclosure proceedings two months earlier. Commercial Credit now brings an action to enjoin removal of the equipment, naming as defendants both Carol and Barbara.

If the trial court refuses to issue the injunction, it will probably be because:

(A) The Statute of Frauds precludes Commercial Credit from asserting any interest in the equipment.

(B) In the absence of an agreement to the contrary, a commercial tenant is entitled to remove any property she voluntarily brings upon the premises.

(C) Chattels installed for the purposes of trade generally may be removed by the tenant if she pays for any damages occasioned thereby.

(D) Carol was given no notice of the mortgage.

Question 47

Otto conveyed Brownacre to Jack for life, then to Susan and Richard as joint tenants with the right of survivorship. Jack, Susan, and Richard were riding together in an automobile that was struck by a truck. They were rushed to the emergency room of Local Hospital on the night of July 28. Although all three were alive when they arrived at the hospital, the hospital records establish that Richard died at 10:28 p.m., Susan died at 10:29 p.m., and Jack died at 10:30 p.m. that same evening. The jurisdiction has not adopted the Uniform Simultaneous Death Act or any local modification of that Act.

Who takes Brownacre?

(A) Jack's heirs.

(B) Susan's heirs.

(C) Richard's heirs.

(D) Otto or his heirs.

Question 48

Bill's will left his ranch, the Bar None, to Winchester, his heirs and assigns, so long as the property was used exclusively for ranch purposes, then to Bill's grandson Charlie. The remainder of Bill's property passed through the residuary clause of the will to Charlie. Seven years after Bill's death, Winchester began strip mining operations on the Bar None. Charlie brought an action to quiet title to the ranch against Winchester, and Winchester counterclaimed on the same theory.

Who should prevail?

(A) Winchester, because the condition imposed on his interest under the will is void as against the Rule Against Perpetuities.

(B) Charlie, because the condition imposed is valid and he takes according to the subsequent provision.

(C) Charlie, pursuant to the residuary clause.

(D) Winchester, because the condition imposed is a restraint against alienation.

Question 49

Tuttle rented an older two-story residence that had been converted into office space for his law practice and subleased most of the building to three other lawyers. He paid $2,000 per month to the owner, Otto, and charged his subtenants $600 per month each.

After having been in the building for three years, Tuttle and Otto orally agreed that Tuttle would purchase it for a price of $120,000, to be paid in monthly installments of $2,000 over a five-year period. It was further agreed that title would remain in Otto's name until $48,000 had been paid on the total price, whereupon Otto would deliver a deed to Tuttle.

Shortly thereafter, Tuttle redecorated his suite, installing new carpeting, wall paneling, a bar, and other improvements costing about $4,000. During the course of the next two years,

he hired an associate and placed him in one of the offices formerly occupied by one of the lawyer-tenants, and raised the monthly rental he charged the other two lawyers to $700.

Two years after the agreement with Otto, Tuttle demanded that Otto convey the building by delivery of a deed. Otto refused, denying that any oral agreement for sale had ever existed.

Tuttle brings an action for specific performance against Otto, who pleads the Statute of Frauds as a defense. If Otto wins, it will be because:

(A) Tuttle did not obtain Otto's approval before making the improvements to his offices.

(B) The original violation of the Statute of Frauds was incurable.

(C) Tuttle's actions in paying $2,000 per month and making improvements were as consistent with being a tenant as with the oral contract.

(D) Otto received no unconscionable benefit entitling Tuttle to equitable relief.

Questions 50-53 are based on the following fact situation:

Joann entered into a written lease-option to purchase Norm's house. Under the terms of the agreement, Joann was to pay a fixed monthly rent plus all taxes and reasonable maintenance charges for the upkeep of the house. The option to purchase the home could be exercised at any time during the five-year term of the lease by giving Norm a written 30-day notice of the intent to exercise the option.

About three years after Norm entered into the lease, he died, leaving his entire estate to his late wife's sister, Sara. Several days before Norm's death, Joann had assigned her lease-option to Al by written agreement. Although Joann properly set forth the terms concerning the option, she failed to properly state that Al was liable to pay the real property taxes on the residence during the period of the lease.

50. Sara was informed that there was a tax lien on the residence. She paid the lien and brought suit against Al for the amount. Judgment for:

(A) Al, because under the terms of his assignment with Joann he is not liable for the taxes.

(B) Al, because the agreement to pay taxes was collateral, and thus is not a covenant running with the land.

(C) Al, because in order for the agreement to be a covenant running with the land it must be expressly stated in the original agreement.

(D) Sara, because payment of property taxes touches and concerns the land.

51. Al became very upset because Sara brought suit against him for the taxes, and he abandoned the residence. Can Sara bring a suit against Joann for this breach of the lease?

(A) No, because Joann is no longer a tenant.

(B) No, because Joann was not a tenant at the time Sara gained her interest in the property.

(C) Yes, because Joann's assignment to Al did not terminate her obligations.

(D) Yes, because Joann had caused the problem by failing to include the tax payment provisions in her assignment.

52. If Al had fully performed under the lease, including paying the taxes, could Al exercise the option to purchase that was given to Joann?

(A) Yes, because both the burden and benefit of the covenant to convey run with the land.

(B) No, because the covenant to convey does not touch or concern the land.

(C) No, because the option to purchase was personal to Joann.

(D) No, because the burden of the covenant to convey given in a lease does not run with the land.

53. Assume that instead of abandoning the premises, Al assigned the lease to Howard. If Howard fails to pay the rent, including payment of taxes, can Sara bring suit against Al to recover this money?

(A) Yes, because Al remains in privity of estate with Sara.

(B) Yes, because Al remains in privity of contract with Sara.

(C) No, because Al is no longer in privity of estate with Sara.

(D) No, because the fact that Joann was allowed to assign the lease means that Al is allowed to assign it also.

Questions 54-58 are based on the following fact situation:

Randy, having suffered a recent heart attack, asked his old friend Hilda to come by to visit him. When she got there, Randy told her that he was in very poor health and that, because he knew that she had wanted for a long time to start a riding school, he wanted to give her some property on which she could build the school. He then gave Hilda an envelope containing two grant deeds purchased in a stationery store and filled in and signed by Randy in ink. The first deed purported to give to Hilda "My property known as Twelve Oaks, with its five acres of land and the stable and dressage course located thereon." The second gave to Hilda "four acres of wooded land on the northwest section of my property located at Forest Knoll, adjacent to Twelve Oaks for use by Hilda in connection with her proposed riding school." Both deeds contained standard warranties, including a covenant against encumbrances, the right to convey, and the right of quiet enjoyment. Randy told Hilda that he was giving the property to her, but since he did not have a better description, he wanted to keep the deeds until his attorney could review them. Hilda agreed and gave them back to him.

Unfortunately, Randy suffered another heart attack the next day and died without seeing his attorney. However, when Hilda spoke with the administrator of Randy's estate, she learned that Randy had, as part of another deed 12 years before, sold that part of Twelve Oaks on which was located the stable and dressage course. The purchaser, Ruth, was also given an easement to cross over Randy's property to get to the property she purchased, although there is no evidence that Ruth had ever used this "right of way" since she preferred to reach her property by riding cross-country on her horse. Thus, there was no trail or road ever made across Randy's property.

54. Randy's heirs bring an action for declaratory relief against Hilda asserting that the deed to Twelve Oaks is void because it contained an inaccurate and ambiguous description. A trial court would enter judgment:

(A) Against Hilda, because the deed failed to give an accurate description of the property owned by Randy at the time of his death.

(B) Against Hilda, because Randy informed Hilda that he did not know the description of his property and he wanted his attorney to prepare the deeds.

(C) Against Hilda, because the deed purports to transfer more property than Randy owned and thus is void as a matter of law.

(D) For Hilda, because the error in description was not sufficient to put in doubt what Randy intended to convey to her.

55. If, in the suit for declaratory relief, Randy's heirs attempt to void the deed to the Forest Knoll land, Hilda will:

(A) Prevail, because Randy intended for Hilda to choose the appropriate acreage, and she can therefore select the four acres that satisfy her needs.

(B) Prevail, because the deed clearly states what property Randy intended to grant to Hilda.

(C) Not prevail, because the phrase "wooded land" is too uncertain.

(D) Not prevail, because the description is too vague.

56. Assuming that a court finds the descriptions in both deeds to be sufficient, with regard to Hilda's interest in the property, which of the following findings is a court likely to make?

(A) An interest was transferred to Hilda, because even though there was no actual delivery, the deeds can be treated as wills.

(B) An interest was transferred to Hilda because there were valid deeds and a valid delivery.

(C) No interest was transferred to Hilda because Randy kept both the deeds; thus, there was no delivery.

(D) No interest was transferred to Hilda, because Randy did not have the chance to have his attorney review the deeds.

57. If Ruth has the right of way over the property Randy gave to Hilda, it is possible that Randy's estate would be liable for breach of the covenant:

(A) Against encumbrances.

(B) Of quiet enjoyment, if such a right of way exists whether or not Ruth is using it.

(C) Of right to convey, because Randy, by not mentioning the right of way in Hilda's deed, implied that there were no easements.

(D) Of right to convey, because the existence of the right of way by Ruth is inconsistent with Randy's alleged title.

58. Randy's son Phil introduces evidence that Randy had promised him in writing that, if he was ever going to get rid of Twelve Oaks, Phil would have the right to purchase it first. The trial court will:

(A) Void the deed to Hilda.

(B) Require Hilda to convey to Phil if he tenders market price for the property.

(C) Not affect Hilda's deed, but Phil may have a cause of action against Randy's estate.

(D) Not affect Hilda's deed because Phil has no claim against either her or Randy's estate.

Question 59

Shortly before their wedding, Harvey and Winona bought Pinkacre, taking title in both names. They had intended to build a summer cottage there, but many years after their marriage Pinkacre was still a vacant lot. Harvey decided that their introverted son, Sampson, would have more confidence if he were a landowner; thus, Harvey drew up a deed conveying a one-quarter interest in Pinkacre to Sampson. Not wanting to show favoritism, two weeks later, Harvey drew up a deed conveying a one-quarter interest in Pinkacre to their daughter, Delilah.

Who owns Pinkacre?

(A) Harvey and Winona share ownership of Pinkacre with rights of survivorship, and Sampson and Delilah have no interests.

(B) Sampson has a one-quarter interest, Delilah has a one-quarter interest, and Winona has a one-half interest.

(C) Sampson has a one-quarter interest, Delilah has a one-quarter interest, and Winona has a one-half interest, with rights of survivorship.

(D) Winona owns Pinkacre.

Questions 60-62 are based on the following fact situation:

Madge was a wealthy widow who had worked for many political and charitable causes. When she died in 1991, her will, dated 1969, left all of her property, including real property, to her dear friend, Leonard.

However, when Leonard met with the executor of the estate, he learned that the two pieces of real property Madge had owned had been deeded to other parties. Her large home and country estate had been deeded in 1974 to Dr. Thaddeus "for so long as the property is used as an animal shelter, but if the property is used for any other purpose, it is to go to the Asthmatic Children's Association." A small office building she owned was deeded just before her death in 1991 to the Women's Rights Organization ("WRO") for use by them as operating quarters for "as long as they worked to promote the passage of the Child Support Amendment until the year 1999," but the deed also stated that in 1999, or if the Amendment was passed before 1999, the property was to go to Helping Hand, Inc., a private organization that made loans and gave advice to women who were starting their own businesses.

Madge's only heir is her daughter, Lucy, who had been left nothing in the will because she was wealthy in her own right. Neither Dr. Thaddeus nor WRO is a charitable organization. Although this jurisdiction is a common law jurisdiction with respect to all real property considerations, the state's probate laws provide that future interests or estates in real property may be passed by will or descent in the same manner as present or possessory interests.

60. In 1993, Dr. Thaddeus approached Lucy and asked her to join with him to sell the home in a fee simple absolute to Marvin, who wanted to build a shopping center on the land. Dr. Thaddeus and Lucy entered into a contract of sale with Marvin. However, after consultation with an attorney, Dr. Thaddeus decided against the sale. Marvin sued Lucy and Dr. Thaddeus for specific performance. The requested relief will be:

(A) Denied, because the Asthmatic Children's Association did not join in the contract of sale.

(B) Denied, because Leonard did not join in the contract of sale.

(C) Granted, because Dr. Thaddeus had the power to sell his interest.

(D) Granted, because together, Lucy's and Dr. Thaddeus's interests would merge and they would have a fee simple estate.

61. Leonard's interest in the home as of the date of Madge's death could best be described as:

(A) An executory interest.

(B) A power of termination or right of entry.

(C) A possibility of reverter.

(D) A contingent interest.

62. In 1994, WRO and Helping Hand, Inc. joined together to sell the office building in fee simple absolute to Reynold. Leonard filed suit to prevent the sale of the property to Reynold. In this action, judgment will be for:

(A) WRO and Helping Hand, Inc., because together they own a fee simple absolute in the building.

(B) WRO and Helping Hand, Inc., because the attempted restrictions on the use of the property violate the Rule Against Perpetuities.

(C) WRO and Helping Hand, Inc., because the deed restriction was an unlawful restraint on alienation.

(D) Leonard, because he did not sign the contract of sale.

Questions 63-65 are based on the following fact situation:

In 1975, Leland purchased Whiteacre, a vacant tract of land, from Mabel, by warranty deed. Unknown to Leland, Mabel did not own Whiteacre. Whiteacre was owned in fee simple by Norris. Shortly after the purchase, Leland built a house on the northwest corner of Whiteacre. Other than that portion, Whiteacre remained vacant. In 1980, Leland decided to build a barn. He placed the barn on five acres of land that he believed to be a part of Whiteacre. The five acres actually belonged to Otis, an adjoining landowner. Otis did not live within the state, and so he was unaware that Leland had built the barn on his property. In 1990, Otis died, still without knowledge that Leland had built a barn on his land. His will left all of his property to his 5-year-old son, Pierre. In 2000, Norris died and left all her property to Quigley. The relevant statutory period for adverse possession is 20 years.

63. Leland brings suit to quiet title to Whiteacre. The court should decide that:

(A) Leland is the owner of Whiteacre.

(B) Quigley is the owner of Whiteacre, because as to him, adverse possession began in 2000.

(C) Quigley is the owner of Whiteacre, because Leland only occupied a part of Whiteacre.

(D) Quigley is the owner of Whiteacre, if Leland did not pay the property taxes on Whiteacre.

64. Assume that in 2002 Leland discovered that the five acres on which he built his barn were not part of Whiteacre. Leland brings a quiet title action against Pierre. Who will prevail?

(A) Pierre, because Leland did not pay the property taxes on the five acres.

(B) Pierre, because his status as a minor would toll the adverse possession statute until he reached his majority.

(C) Leland, because he honestly believed that the five acres were part of Whiteacre.

(D) Leland, because he was in continuous possession of the five acres for the statutory period.

65. Assume for purposes of this question only that in 1977 Norris learned of Mabel's transaction with Leland and prevented Leland from entering Whiteacre thereafter. This led to a costly court battle. When Leland notified Mabel and told her that he thought it was her duty to straighten this out, she told him to "get lost." Leland would succeed in a suit for damages against Mabel for breach of which of the following covenants of title?

(A) The covenant of quiet enjoyment only.

(B) The covenants of seisin, right to convey, quiet enjoyment, warranty, further assurances, and the covenant against encumbrances.

(C) The covenants of seisin, right to convey, quiet enjoyment, warranty, and further assurances.

(D) The covenants of seisin and right to convey only.

Question 66

In an effort to preserve the family farm, Grey willed his farm to his daughter Gwendolyn. The will stated that the property would go to Gwendolyn for her life with a remainder to each of her children living at the time of Grey's death. The will further provided that "No child of Gwendolyn shall have the right to mortgage or sell any part of his or her interest prior to attaining the age of 35. The interest of any child who attempts to mortgage or sell his or her interest shall immediately terminate and shall pass to and become the property of the remaining children of Gwendolyn who are alive at the time of my death, in equal shares."

Several weeks later Grey died. Geoffrey, one of Gwendolyn's three children, wants to sell his interest in the farm. Gwendolyn and the two other children object to the sale. Presume that Geoffrey is under the age of 35.

In an action for declaratory relief by Geoffrey that the stated restriction on the sale is void, what would be the probable result?

(A) The suit would be dismissed, because Geoffrey is under 35 years of age, and therefore, has no interest in the property.

(B) The gift to Gwendolyn's children is void in its entirety, because it violates the Rule Against Perpetuities.

(C) The restriction would be stricken, because it unlawfully restricts the alienation of real property.

(D) The restriction is proper, because all Geoffrey has is a defeasible estate.

Questions 67-68 are based on the following fact situation:

Oona owned Big Acre, a large tract of undeveloped land. Big Acre had a stream, which was not navigable, running across it in an east to west direction that eventually flowed into the Blue River. Beatrix was interested in buying the northern one-half of Big Acre to use as a cattle ranch. Oona and Beatrix eventually agreed upon the price, and in a cash transaction, Oona conveyed by deed to Beatrix according to the following description: "The upper portion of Big Acre from the northern boundary to the stream."

67. In determining the exact boundaries of the portion of Big Acre purchased by Beatrix, which of the following would be the most accurate?

   (A) Oona retained all of the stream as part of her portion of Big Acre.

   (B) Oona and Beatrix each own one-half of the stream bed.

   (C) Beatrix owns all of the stream because of the rule interpreting the words of a deed most stringently against the grantor.

   (D) Because the description is invalid, the ownership interest of Oona and Beatrix in the stream cannot be determined.

68. Assume for the purpose of this question only that the deed from Oona to Beatrix stated that the acreage of the land was 557.7 acres. It was subsequently determined by survey that the land conveyed to Beatrix was in fact 563.2 acres. In a dispute between Oona and Beatrix as to the mistake, which of the following is most accurate?

   (A) The deed is invalid because of the mutual mistake of the parties.

   (B) The deed is invalid unless the court admits parol evidence as to the amount of acreage conveyed.

   (C) The deed is valid, and Beatrix is the owner of 557.7 acres.

   (D) The deed is valid, and Beatrix is the owner of 563.2 acres.

Questions 69-71 are based on the following fact situation:

Nicholas owned a tract of land in Red Valley that he leased to Realty Corp. for 99 years. Realty Corp. built a 60-story office complex on the property. Realty Corp. then sold the building to Rasputin, Inc., assigning the lease with Nicholas's approval. Ten years into the lease, Nicholas conveyed the property in joint tenancy to his twin sons, Alexander and Vladimir, as a birthday present. Unfortunately, a few years after the conveyance, Nicholas and his sons had a serious falling out over how to run the family business. Nicholas no longer wished the sons to control valuable commercial property, and so he demanded that they return the deed with which he conveyed the Red Valley property to them. The sons returned the deed, and Nicholas destroyed it. A few months later, Vladimir learned that he was seriously ill and not likely to live much longer. He executed a quitclaim deed conveying "any interest I have in the Red Valley property" to his daughter, Anastasia. Vladimir subsequently died.

69. Who owns the reversion in the Red Valley property?

   (A) Alexander.

   (B) Nicholas.

   (C) Alexander and Anastasia as tenants in common.

   (D) Alexander and Anastasia as joint tenants.

70. Assume for the purposes of this question only that Rasputin, Inc. has failed to make a rent payment for several months and has also failed to build the road that Realty Corp. agreed to build in the original lease. The landlord of the Red Valley property has a cause of action against:

   (A) Rasputin for the rent only, because the rent covenant runs with the land.

(B) Rasputin for the rent and the road, but only if Rasputin expressly assumed performance of all covenants.

(C) Rasputin and Realty Corp. for both the rent and the road.

(D) Rasputin for the rent only, and Realty Corp. for the road only.

71. Assume for purposes of this question only that, after Vladimir died, Nicholas sold and conveyed the Red Valley property to Olga. Assume also that the deed from Nicholas to Alexander and Vladimir was never recorded and that the jurisdiction's recording act states the following: "No conveyance or mortgage of an interest in land is valid against any subsequent purchaser for value without notice thereof whose conveyance is first recorded." If Olga brings a quiet title action and is successful, which of the following best explains this result?

(A) As owner of the property, Nicholas was entitled to convey it to Olga.

(B) Alexander and Vladimir failed to record the deed they took from Nicholas.

(C) Alexander and Vladimir failed to record their deed, and Olga was unaware of their interest when she paid Nicholas market value for the property.

(D) Alexander and Vladimir failed to record their deed, Olga was unaware of their interest when she purchased the property, and Olga recorded her deed.

Question 72

Garth owned some property along the waterfront in Giles Bay, a small city on the coast that catered mostly to tourists. He rented his property to Flora, a pottery maker, who intended to use the back part of the building for living quarters, and the front part as a pottery studio to make the pottery she sold to the tourists in town. Flora installed a kiln, some lights, and some storage units in the front part of the building for her use. Sometime later, Garth mortgaged the property to First City Bank to secure a loan. The mortgage was recorded, but Garth did not personally tell Flora that he had done so. In fact, she only learned of it when Garth defaulted on the loan and the bank foreclosed on the mortgage and told her that she would have to quit the premises. Flora began removing the equipment and fixtures that she had installed in the house. The bank objected and sought an injunction to prevent her from doing so.

Under these circumstances the court should deny Bank the injunction because:

(A) There was no contrary provision in the agreement between Garth and Flora, and therefore, she is entitled to remove any personal property which belongs to her.

(B) Bank had no perfected security interest in the personal property belonging to Flora.

(C) The equipment was installed for Flora's exclusive benefit and she did not intend for it to stay.

(D) Garth had never given Flora notice of the mortgage.

Question 73

Leila owned 150 acres of farmland that she leased to the Thurman Produce Company for 15 years. Thurman used the land for crops along with several other contiguous acres that it owned or leased. About four years after the parties entered into this lease, the state condemned a portion of Leila's property because it intended to build a highway. As a result, too little of Leila's property remained for Thurman to profitably farm, although there still existed the farmhouse on the property, which was being used by one of its foremen. Thurman gave Leila 30 days' written notice that it considered the lease to have been terminated because of the condemnation.

In a suit for breach of contract, Leila would probably:

(A) Lose, because the condemnation made it economically undesirable for Thurman to continue to lease the property.

(B) Lose, because when there is a condemnation, the tenant's obligation to pay rent is extinguished.

(C) Win, because Thurman can still use the farmhouse, and the rental value would be adjusted accordingly.

(D) Win, because the condemnation did not affect Thurman's obligation to pay the full rental price, although it is entitled to share in the condemnation award.

Question 74

Stefan, who is married to Madge, entered into a written contract with Phil to sell Phil a vacation house, which was purchased by Stefan during his marriage to Madge, but held in his name alone.

The contract expressly required Stefan to provide "good, clear, and marketable title" to the vacation home. Phil paid the purchase price and was given a deed to the property from Stefan. According to the marital property laws of this jurisdiction, both husband and wife own an interest in any real property purchased during their marriage. However, another statute provides that when real property is held in the name of one spouse alone, that spouse may convey that real property to another, and any interest in the property owned by the spouse whose name does not appear on the recorded title is terminated, unless that spouse brings an action within one year to set aside the conveyance.

Six months later, Madge successfully set aside the conveyance on the ground that Stefan had conveyed her marital interest in the vacation home without her consent.

What would be the result of an action for damages by Phil against Stefan for breach of this agreement?

(A) Stefan would prevail, unless the deed expressly covenanted title.

(B) Stefan would prevail, if the facts show that Phil had knowledge that Stefan was married.

(C) Phil would prevail, because Madge was able to set aside the conveyance.

(D) Phil would prevail, because the terms of the contract are incorporated in the deed when the contract requires marketable title.

Question 75

Orbit owned Blackacre. Gasco asked Orbit if it would be possible for Gasco to run pipes over Blackacre to supply natural gas to a new housing development. It would be complex and expensive, but possible, for Gasco to use another route. Gasco offered Orbit what Orbit considered a generous price to run the pipes over a 15-foot strip of Blackacre. Therefore, Orbit granted Gasco and its "heirs and assigns" an easement over the 15-foot strip of Blackacre "for pipeline purposes." The easement was duly recorded in the office of the County Recorder of Deeds. The housing development was delayed for several years due to financing difficulties and Gasco did not use the easement during that period. By the time the housing development needed utility services, Orbit had sold Blackacre to Astro. Astro received a warranty deed from Orbit, and the deed specifically mentioned the easement to Gasco.

Without objection from Astro, Gasco laid the pipe across the 15-foot strip of Blackacre. For the next 10 years, Gasco supplied natural gas to the housing development through Blackacre pipes. However, continuing residential development in the area made it economically feasible for Gasco to place a major main line on the other side of the housing development adjacent to Blackacre. This meant that Gasco no longer needed the lines that ran across Blackacre. Gasco sold its rights in the easement to Petroco, an oil company that wished to run a crude oil pipeline across Blackacre. Shortly after Gasco had finished laying its pipe, Astro had planted a number of trees and a beautiful flower garden on the 15-foot strip. Now, although Petroco confined its activities to the strip, it drove trucks onto the land, uprooted the trees, and tore up the flower garden in order to excavate for the laying of a larger pipe than Gasco had installed. An exasperated Astro filed suit to enjoin Petroco from further activities on the 15-foot strip and for damages for the destruction wrought on Blackacre.

Is Astro likely to succeed in this suit?

(A) Yes, because Gasco's sale of the easement to Petroco was without Astro's permission.

(B) No, because Gasco had the right to assign its interest.

(C) No, as to the injunction, because Petroco is using the land for pipeline purposes, but Astro is entitled to damages.

(D) No, as to the injunction and damages, because the use is for pipeline purposes and this obviously implies the right to excavate in order to lay pipe.

Question 76

Fischer owned a piece of land on which he developed and built a large apartment house. After the apartment house was completed, Fischer conveyed the building and the land to Thompson for life, remainder to Herrera; subject, however, to Bank's mortgage. Bank held a mortgage on the building for $17,000, payable in annual installments of $2,000 plus interest.

Thompson moved into the manager's apartment and began to manage the day-to-day maintenance of the building as well as to collect rents. Despite Thompson's best efforts, the vacancy factor reached an unanticipated high when two large automobile plants in the area closed. The rental income was not sufficient to cover the annual mortgage payment.

Who is responsible for the mortgage payments and in what amount?

(A) Thompson pays all.

(B) Herrera pays all.

(C) Thompson pays the interest and Herrera pays the principal.

(D) Herrera pays the interest and Thompson pays the principal.

Question 77

Rosalie purchased a lovely new tract home in the Pleasantville development. When Rosalie purchased the home, she put up 20% of the purchase price as a down payment and financed the rest of her purchase through a mortgage with Thrifty Federal Savings. Rosalie lived in her home for three years and always made her mortgage payments promptly. However, her employers offered her a major promotion if she would move to another city. Rosalie accepted the offer and put her house on the market. While the house was being marketed, Rosalie continued to make all mortgage payments promptly. Rosalie sold the house to Vitus, who purchased the property subject to the mortgage. After Vitus took possession, Thrifty Federal Savings received no further mortgage payments from either Rosalie or Vitus.

In most states, which of the following best describes the remedy or remedies available to Thrifty Federal Savings?

(A) Thrifty Federal Savings may foreclose on the land, but may not sue either Rosalie or Vitus on the underlying debt.

(B) Thrifty Federal Savings may foreclose on the land or it may sue Rosalie on the underlying debt.

(C) Thrifty Federal Savings may foreclose on the land or it may sue Vitus on the underlying debt.

(D) Thrifty Federal Savings may foreclose on the land or it may elect to sue either Rosalie or Vitus on the underlying debt.

REAL PROPERTY ANSWERS

Answer to Question 1

(B)   If proved, the fact that would be the most helpful to Frank in preventing Sara from removing the power lines is that Frank's alternative access to power is much less convenient and would cost 100 times as much as the current arrangement. This helps to prove that there was an easement implied by operation of law ("quasi-easement"). An easement may be implied if, prior to the time the tract is divided, a use exists on the "servient part" that is reasonably necessary for the enjoyment of the "dominant part," and a court determines that the parties intended the use to continue after division of the property. To give rise to an easement, a use must be apparent and continuous at the time the tract is divided. In this case, Oscar used the servient part of his property (Parcel 2) to run a power line to the dominant part of his property (Parcel 1). This use was reasonably necessary to the enjoyment of the dominant parcel because electricity is important to the enjoyment of the property, and the cost and difficulty of the alternatives are excessive. Whether a use is reasonably necessary depends on many factors, including the cost and difficulty of the alternatives. Since the alternative would be much less convenient and cost 100 times as much, the use of Parcel 2 is reasonably necessary. Thus, this fact, if proved, would bolster Frank's case. (A) is wrong because Sara's actual knowledge is irrelevant. Sara need not be aware of the use; it need only be shown that the use was apparent. Overhead wires are clearly visible and would be readily discoverable on reasonable inspection. The lines are, therefore, apparent. (C) is similarly wrong. Oral statements made to the grantor after Parcel 1 had been conveyed have little effect. They show Sara's knowledge, but as discussed above, that has little relevance with respect to an implied easement. (D) is wrong because Sara's motive for removing the power line is also irrelevant. If no easement is established, Sara may remove the lines for whatever reason she likes. If, however, the requirements for an implied easement are satisfied, Sara may not remove the lines regardless of how good her reasons are.

Answer to Question 2

(D)   There are several recognized circumstances under which an easement will be terminated, and none of the alternatives listed fits within any of these circumstances. (A) is incorrect because mere nonuse of an easement will not result in its extinguishment, even if such nonuse continues for the statutory period applicable to prescriptive easements. An easement can be extinguished where the holder demonstrates by a physical action that she intends to permanently abandon the easement. However, nonuse of the easement, without more, will not constitute a manifestation of an intent never to make use of the easement again. Furthermore, the statutory period of limitations is relevant only to prescriptive termination of an easement by actions undertaken by the holder of the servient tenement, not action or nonaction of the holder of the dominant tenement. (B) is incorrect because, just as the benefit of an easement appurtenant passes with a transfer of the benefited land (regardless of whether the easement is mentioned in the conveyance), so also does the burden of an easement appurtenant pass with the servient land when transferred. Note that a subsequent purchaser without actual or constructive notice of an easement may take free of the easement by virtue of a recording act. In this case, however, the recording act will not aid a purchaser. The mere existence of the driveway across Parcel 1 to Parcel 2 puts any purchaser on inquiry notice of an easement. Thus, even if Parcel 1 is sold to a purchaser for value who is unaware of the easement, the burden of the driveway easement passes with the transfer of Parcel 1. (C) is incorrect because, if a court were to find that there is now an unreasonably excessive use of the easement, the proper remedy would be to enter an order conforming use of the easement to a proper scope. Excessive use would not, however, result in the extinguishing of the easement.

Answer to Question 3

(D) All of the statements are correct. The covenant regarding use as a single family residence runs with the land, thus binding Arnold as effectively as if he had himself expressly agreed to be bound. The original covenanting parties (Don and Able) intended that successors in interest to the covenantor would be bound by the terms of the covenant. Such intent is inferred from the language of the covenant ("grantee agrees for himself and assigns"). Although Arnold did not have actual knowledge of the covenant, he had constructive notice by virtue of the fact that the original deed (from Don to each grantee) was recorded and in his chain of title. There was horizontal privity between the original covenanting parties because, at the time Able entered into the covenant with Don, they shared an interest in the land independent of the covenant (*i.e.,* they were in a grantor-grantee relationship). Arnold holds the entire interest held by Able at the time Able made the covenant; thus, there is vertical privity. Finally, the covenant touches and concerns the land because it restricts the holder of the servient estate in his use of that parcel of land (*i.e.,* the owner of the lot cannot use the land for other than single family residential purposes). Thus, all the requirements have been met for the burden of the covenant to run, and Arnold, as the successor in interest to the burdened estate, is bound by the arrangement entered into by Able in the same way as if Arnold had expressly agreed to be bound. Consequently, I. is a correct statement and (A) is incorrect. II. is correct because the elements for an equitable servitude are met, and Arnold had constructive (*i.e.,* record) notice. An equitable servitude is a covenant that equity will enforce against assignees of the burdened land who have notice of the covenant. Equitable servitudes are created by covenants contained in a writing that is sought to be enforced in equity. For the burden of an equitable servitude to run with the land, the covenanting parties must have intended that the servitude be enforceable by and against assignees. As noted previously, the language of the covenant indicates the existence of such intent. Also, the servitude must touch and concern the land. This covenant does touch and concern the land because it restricts the landholder in his use of the land. Finally, running of the burden requires the assignee have notice (actual, record, or inquiry) of the servitude. Here, although the covenant was not mentioned in the deed, Arnold had record notice of the servitude at the time he purchased the property because the original deed to each lot was recorded. Thus, (B) and (C) are incorrect. III. is correct because, with respect to both real covenants and equitable servitudes, acceptance of a deed signed only by the grantor is sufficient to bind the grantee as promisor.

Answer to Question 4

(D) The homeowners' association will win because the covenant created a burden that runs with the land at law. A covenant to pay a homeowners' association an annual fee for, *e.g.,* upkeep or security, is deemed to impose a burden that runs with the land. The requirements for running of a burden are present here. The language of the covenant indicates that the parties intended successors in interest to the covenantor to be bound by the terms. Bates had actual and constructive notice of the covenant at the time he purchased the land. Horizontal privity is present in that at the time the promisor entered into the covenant with the promisee, the two shared an interest in the land independent of the covenant (*i.e.,* Don and Baker were in a grantor-grantee relationship). There is vertical privity because Bates holds the entire interest held by Baker at the time Baker made the covenant. Finally, the burden of the covenant to pay fees to the homeowners' association touches and concerns the land, because the fees are a charge on the land, increasing the landowner's obligations in connection with the use and enjoyment of the land. Moreover, these fees touch and concern the land because the upkeep and security of the subdivision enhances the value of each lot. (B) incorrectly concludes that the covenant does not touch and concern the land. (A) is incorrect because, if the deed is silent as to who may enforce the covenant, any neighbor in the subdivision is entitled to enforce the covenant if a general scheme or plan existed at the time he purchased his lot. Here, the covenants in all the deeds relating to payment of fees to the homeowners' association are evidence of a general plan of restrictions at the outset of the sales of these lots. Furthermore, Don created the subdivision before he sold the lots, so there is probably a good deal of evidence on his plan when he sold the lots. Thus, any of the residents of Woodlake could bring an action for the enforcement of this covenant. Particularly because it is referred to in the deeds, the homeowners' association can be deemed to be bringing this action on behalf of the subdivision residents, who are the real parties in interest. Thus, the fact that there is no privity between Baker and the homeowners' association will not preclude the association from suing to enforce the covenant. (C) is incorrect because the remedy sought is the payment of money. Breach of a real covenant is remedied by an award of money damages, whereas breach of an equitable servitude is remedied by equitable relief, such as an injunction or specific performance. Because the homeowners' association seeks to obtain from Bates the payment of money, it is inaccurate to refer to this as a situation involving an equitable servitude.

Answer to Question 5

(D) Bates would win because the deed language about fencing created an equitable servitude, which is enforceable against Calvin. The deed language about fencing was intended by the original parties to be enforceable by and against assignees. Such intent is shown by the specific language of the covenant ("Grantee agrees for himself and assigns"), as well as by the purpose of the covenant and the surrounding circumstances. This covenant was meant to assure that, pursuant to the subdivision's master plan, there would be bicycle paths and walkways running through each backyard, for the use of all subdivision residents. Bates, as a resident of Woodlake, is therefore entitled to enforce the covenant so as to obtain access to bicycle paths and walkways. The burden of the covenant touches and concerns the land occupied by Calvin, because it restricts the landholder in his use of the parcel (*i.e.*, his rights in connection with the enjoyment of the land are diminished by being unable to fence in the backyard). Also, the benefit of the covenant touches and concerns Bates's property because it increases his enjoyment thereof by providing him with a bicycle path and a walkway. Calvin had constructive notice of the restriction. Since all of the original deeds were recorded, the restriction is in Calvin's chain of title, giving him record notice. In addition, Calvin could be deemed to have notice of the restriction if the subdivision is sufficiently developed, had fences, and the bicycle paths and walkways running through each backyard were in place in accordance with a general plan for the subdivision. This would put Calvin on inquiry notice of a deed restriction. Any neighbor in a subdivision can enforce a covenant contained in a subdivision deed if a general plan existed at the time he purchased his lot. As has been noted, the maintenance of access to all backyards for use as bike paths and walkways was part of such a general plan. All of the requirements are in place for the existence of an equitable servitude, which can be enforced by Bates against Calvin. (B) is incorrect because, although Calvin did not have actual knowledge of the restriction at issue, he had record notice, and possibly inquiry notice, of the fence restriction. (A) and (C) both incorrectly assume that privity is a significant factor. However, unlike situations in which a covenant at law is involved, privity is not required to enforce an equitable servitude. Bates is seeking an order compelling Calvin to remove the fence. This is an equitable remedy; thus, the law of equitable servitudes applies. Privity of estate is not needed to enforce an equitable servitude, because the servitude is enforced not as an in personam right against the owner of the servient tenement, but as an equitable property interest in the land itself. Consequently, it is irrelevant to the determination of this action whether there is privity between either Baker and Calvin (as referred to in (A)), or between Bates and Baker (as referred to in (C)).

Answer to Question 6

(B) Julie may take possession of Agateacre only if she institutes foreclosure proceedings and is the successful purchaser at the foreclosure sale. Julie must institute foreclosure proceedings because the deed is, in reality, an equitable mortgage. A landowner needing to raise money may "sell" the land to a person who pays cash and may give the lender an absolute deed rather than a mortgage. However, if a court concludes that the deed was really given for security purposes, it will treat it as an equitable mortgage and require that the creditor foreclose it by judicial action, like any other mortgage. The following factors indicate an equitable mortgage: (i) the existence of a debt or promise of payment by the deed's grantor; (ii) the grantee's promise to return the land if the debt is paid; (iii) the fact that the amount advanced to the grantor/debtor was much lower than the value of the property; (iv) the degree of the grantor's financial distress; and (v) the parties' prior negotiations. Here, Tim has agreed by his promissory note to repay Julie the amount she purportedly paid to purchase the property, and Julie has promised to return Agateacre upon repayment. The sum of money given by Julie to Tim is only one-half of the value of the property. In addition, Tim was in fairly serious financial condition at the time of his dealings with Julie. Finally, the discussions between Tim and Julie prior to the exchange of money and the deed indicate quite clearly that the parties intended that Agateacre serve as security for Julie's loan to Tim. These facts give rise to the conclusion that the deed, absolute on its face, is really an equitable mortgage, thus requiring Julie to foreclose it by judicial action. At a foreclosure sale, the highest bidder takes the property. Therefore, to take possession of Agateacre, Julie must not only institute foreclosure proceedings but also be the successful bidder at the sale. (A) is incorrect because, pursuant to the foregoing analysis, the deed given to Julie will not be dealt with by the court as an absolute deed conveying title, but rather as an equitable mortgage giving Julie a security interest in the property. Consequently, Julie does not have clear record title. (C) is incorrect because, while the fact that Julie gave Tim a sum of money lower than the market value of Agateacre will be considered as one of several factors indicating that this is an equitable mortgage situation, it will not, by itself, preclude Julie's taking possession of the property. If this were a situation involving a true absolute conveyance of the property, the conveyance would not be set aside simply because the purchase price is less than the market value. No consideration is necessary for a valid deed. (D) is incorrect because, as discussed above, the court will treat this as an equitable mortgage.

Answer to Question 7

(B) Gretchen will win because the facts show that Otto intended her to have an interest in the property when he gave the deed to Brad. To effectively transfer an interest in realty, a deed must be delivered. There is a delivery when there are words or conduct evidencing the grantor's intention that the deed have some present operative effect; *i.e.,* that title pass immediately and irrevocably, even though the right of possession may be postponed until the future. A conditional delivery becomes effective only upon the occurrence of a condition, but the transfer then relates back to the date of the conditional delivery. When the grantor gives the deed to a third party (rather than directly to the grantee), conditional delivery is permissible. If the grantor executes a deed to the grantee and gives it to a third party with instructions to give it to the grantee upon the grantor's death, most courts hold that the grantor cannot get the deed back because his intent was to presently convey a future interest to the grantee (either a remainder with a life estate reserved in the grantor, or an executory limitation). Here, the facts indicate, in response to Gretchen's insistence on doing "something now" to provide for her security, Otto intended that the deed have the effect of immediately conveying to Gretchen a future interest in the hotel (although Gretchen's taking of possession of the hotel and of the deed itself were to be postponed until Otto's death). Consequently, the delivery is irrevocable and Otto is precluded from taking back the deed. (C) is incorrect because the revocability of this deed is not affected by the fact that no consideration was given. Consideration is not required to render a deed valid, nor is consideration required to render the delivery of a deed irrevocable. (D) is incorrect because instructions to a person acting as custodian for the donee (in this case, Brad) can be oral. Even though a deed is unconditional, the general rule is that parol evidence is admissible to show the conditions and terms upon which a deed was deposited with a third party. (A) is incorrect because the facts actually indicate that Otto had no intention of transferring to Gretchen a present possessory right in the hotel. The entire purpose of Otto's words and conduct was to convey some immediate right in the hotel, but to postpone the actual right of possession until the future (*i.e.,* upon Otto's death). Thus, Gretchen will prevail in establishing an interest in the hotel, not because she is entitled to presently possess the hotel, but because she was given a future interest in the property.

Answer to Question 8

(D) Gretchen will win because the deed conveyed to her a future interest in the hotel, which now becomes possessory. Where a deed, otherwise properly executed and delivered, contains an express provision that title will not pass until the death of the grantor, the effect is to create a present possessory life estate in the grantor and a future estate in the grantee. The deed here was properly executed and manually delivered by the grantor to the grantee. The language of the deed stating that title shall not pass until Otto's death actually created a life estate in Otto and a future interest in Gretchen that will become possessory upon Otto's death. Thus, the language of the deed shows an intent to make the instrument legally effective at the moment of delivery. As a result, the requirements for a valid delivery are met, and Gretchen is now entitled to take possession of and title to the hotel, thereby defeating the claim of Otto's administrator. Because the foregoing analysis shows that there was a proper delivery, (A) is incorrect. (B) is incorrect because the deed in this question was intended by the grantor to be immediately effective in conveying a future interest in the hotel during the lifetime of the grantor. If the deed language was interpreted to mean that Otto intended that no interest would be transferred until his death, the deed would be testamentary in nature and its validity would require that it have been executed with all testamentary formalities (*e.g.,* that it be signed by an appropriate number of witnesses). However, because the deed is deemed to have immediately conveyed an interest in the hotel to Gretchen, it is effective as a deed and need not comply with the formalities required of a will. Consequently, the deed is a valid will substitute and does not violate the Statute of Wills. (C) is incorrect because, if the effect of this deed is to create in Gretchen an immediate future interest in the hotel, then Gretchen need not come forth with any other evidence concerning Otto's intent that she receive an interest during his lifetime.

Answer to Question 9

(D) Payment of the note by the maker discharges the note and, thus, this argument offers the least support for Fred's position that he has a first priority. The best way to get the correct answer is to use a process of elimination. (A) is wrong because it supports Fred's position: the purchaser of a note and trust deed is subrogated to (*i.e.,* takes over) the interest of the seller, thus giving Fred Tom's priority. (B) is wrong because it is saying essentially the same thing as (A). (C) is wrong because it is the policy reason behind the rules stated in (A) and (B). Thus, (A), (B), and (C) are wrong because they do offer support for Fred's priority position.

Answer to Question 10

(B) Bob will win because he is exercising his equity of redemption rights. Under the doctrine of the equity of redemption, at any time prior to the foreclosure sale, the borrower has the right to free the land of the deed of trust by paying off the amount due. Here, Bob's offer is adequate even if the deed of trust contains an acceleration clause. (A) is wrong because a statutory right of redemption, recognized in about half the states, gives the borrower a right to redeem for the foreclosure price *after* the foreclosure sale. (C) is wrong because this right to redeem cannot be waived in the agreement establishing the security interest. (D) is wrong because a defaulting debtor under a deed of trust does not lose the equity of redemption.

Answer to Question 11

(C) The fact that Anne was the builder of the house would be the most significant fact in establishing Burton's case. Generally, absent concealment, misrepresentation, or nondisclosure of a known serious defect, a seller is not liable for defects on the property sold. An exception is made for sales of new homes by the builder. If the builder of the new home sells it, most courts imply a warranty of fitness or quality; *i.e.,* the builder is deemed to warrant that the house is designed and constructed in a reasonably workmanlike manner and is suitable for human habitation. Here, the dangerously defective condition of the wiring would constitute a breach of that warranty, and so if Anne were the builder she could be held liable to Burton. (A) is wrong for two reasons: (i) if the defect were covered by a warranty, it would not be limited to 30 days; and (ii) without the fact that Anne is the builder of a new house, Anne would not be liable no matter when the defect was discovered—even if it was discovered one hour after the closing. (B) is wrong because Anne did not know of the defect. A majority of states require the seller to disclose serious defects where the defects are not easily discoverable by the buyer, but the seller has to know or have reason to know of the defect, and that is not indicated by these facts. (D) is wrong because under a warranty deed, a grantor gives the grantee assurances regarding title; these warranties having nothing to do with the physical condition of the property.

Answer to Question 12

(D) The court should rule in Stockton's favor. A tenant must remove annexed chattels before the termination of the tenancy or they become the property of the landlord. Although Eddie was probably entitled to remove the curtains and rods at the end of the lease, he forfeited them by waiting for two days after the lease expired to remove them. (A) is wrong because it goes to whether the curtains and rods were intended to be fixtures. Because of the delay in their removal, whether the curtains or rods were fixtures is irrelevant. This choice would be correct, however, had Eddie attempted to remove the curtains on August 14. The short-term lease and the fact that the rods are easily removable constitute evidence that Eddie lacked the requisite intent to permanently improve the property and thus he could have removed them if he had acted promptly. (B) is wrong for the same reason. The delay in the removal of the items results in their becoming the property of the landlord regardless of whether they are trade fixtures. Trade fixtures (*i.e.,* fixtures installed for the purpose of carrying on a trade or business) are removable prior to the end of the lease term. Thus, since Eddie installed the curtains to carry on his business, this would have been a correct choice had Eddie attempted to remove the curtains prior to the end of his lease term. (C) is wrong because the mere fact that the curtain rods were attached by screws does not make them fixtures that must remain with the realty. "Fixtures" are chattels affixed to the land that become part of the land. The intent of the person affixing the chattel is relevant. The curtains and rods would probably not be considered fixtures because Eddie did not have the requisite intent to permanently improve the property, as evidenced by the short-term lease and the easily removable nature of the attached chattels. In the absence of an express agreement to the contrary, if removal of the chattel does not cause substantial damage to the premises or destruction of the chattel, the tenant has not manifested an intention to permanently improve the property. Here, removing the screws, rods, and curtains would not result in substantial damage to the premises or destruction of the chattels. Also, even if the curtains and rods were found to be fixtures, they would be trade fixtures, which are removable by the tenant.

Answer to Question 13

(C) Bruce will not prevail because the right of first refusal created in the instrument executed by Alton violates the Rule Against Perpetuities. Under the common law Rule Against Perpetuities, no interest in property is valid unless it must vest, if at all, within 21 years after a life in being at the time the interest is created. Because a right of first refusal is specifically enforceable, it is considered an equitable interest in property. As such, rights of first refusal are subject to the Rule Against Perpetuities. Thus, if the right may be exercised beyond the perpetuities period, it is void. In this case, the right of first refusal extends to Bruce's heirs and assigns. These heirs and assigns could exercise the right well after the perpetuities period of a life in being plus 21 years. Therefore, Bruce's right is void. (A) is wrong because it suggests that the reciprocity of the arrangement resulted in an enforceable contract. Even if the instrument was a contract, it is not enforceable because it creates an interest in land that violates the Rule Against Perpetuities. (B) is wrong because Bruce's interest is nothing like a possibility of reverter aside from the fact that Bruce's interest and a possibility of reverter are both future interests. A possibility of reverter is the reversionary interest left in the grantor after he conveys a fee simple determinable. Bruce is not a grantor, and his interest is not one retained upon the granting of a lesser estate. The most important difference between a possibility of reverter and a right of first refusal, however, is that a possibility of reverter is vested and not subject to the Rule Against Perpetuities, while a right of first refusal is subject to the Rule. (D) is wrong because rights of first refusal are generally excepted from the application of the common law rule against restraints on alienation, which prohibits any restriction on the transferability of property.

Answer to Question 14

(C) Under the majority view, the landlord has a duty to deliver actual possession to the tenant. One of the tenant's remedies for a breach of this duty is to continue the lease and recover damages that accrue until the landlord delivers possession. (A) is incorrect because it misstates the facts. (B) is incorrect because the right of quiet enjoyment is interfered with when a tenant is actually evicted by the landlord or someone with paramount title or is constructively evicted by acts of the landlord or those claiming under her. Here, Bette's possession is being interfered with by Colin, who is not the landlord or one claiming under her (since his tenancy has terminated) and who does not have paramount title. Thus, the covenant was not breached by Amy. (D) is incorrect because under either the majority view or the minority view, in which the landlord does not have the obligation to put the tenant in actual possession, Bette's inactivity in the unlawful detainer action is irrelevant to the issue of liability.

Answer to Question 15

(D) Under the minority approach, the landlord has no duty to deliver actual possession at the commencement of the term, and hence is not in default under the lease when the previous tenant continues wrongfully to occupy the premises. (A) is incorrect because the fact that Amy did not breach an express promise would not relieve her of liability. (B) is incorrect because, under the majority view, Amy would be liable for damages that accrued between January 1 and February 1. (C) is incorrect because a landlord's obligations to a tenant continue throughout the lease term.

Answer to Question 16

(C) The deed from Harvey to Mitch was ineffective as a conveyance because there was no valid delivery. If a grantor executes a deed but fails to deliver it during his lifetime, no conveyance of title has occurred. "Delivery" refers to the grantor's intent; it is satisfied by words or conduct showing that the grantor intended that the deed have a present operative effect—*i.e.,* that title pass immediately and irrevocably, even though the right of possessing the land may be postponed until some future time. To make an effective delivery, the grantor must relinquish control. Here, Harvey clearly did not intend to relinquish Blueacre since he executed the deed but retained it, and merely told his friend to deliver it, at his death, to his nephew, provided that the nephew was still alive. Thus, since Harvey did not intend to relinquish control of Blueacre until his death, there was no valid delivery of the deed. (Note that the deed did not convey a future interest to Mitch.) To convey a future interest (*i.e.,* a present interest in the property, but where possession is postponed until some future time), there must also be a ***present intent*** to convey an interest. Here, Harvey has shown no intent to presently convey an interest since he retained the deed. Generally, in cases where the grantor has retained the deed, the condition that title will not pass until the grantor's death must be contained in the language of the deed itself for a future interest to be conveyed. (A) is wrong because the conveyance was not effective when the deed was executed. As explained above, Harvey did not intend to pass title to Blueacre, and thus there was no valid delivery. Although a delivery to an agent of the grantee may pass title, this did not occur here. There is nothing to show that Curt was Mitch's agent; rather if he was anyone's agent it would most likely be Harvey's (his duties were to give the deed to Mitch at Harvey's death). Also, even if Curt were Mitch's agent, there was still no delivery. Curt did not receive the deed; he only learned where Harvey intended to retain the deed. Furthermore, delivery would require the intent to relinquish title, and as explained above, Harvey had no such intent. (B) is wrong because even assuming that now there was a delivery of the deed to Mitch, there was no interest for the deed to convey. Since Harvey had not effectively delivered the earlier deed to Mitch, Harvey was the sole owner of the property in 1994, when he conveyed it to Ursula. Thus, at Harvey's death in 1995, Ursula, not Harvey, owned the property and so the deed was ineffective to pass any interest to Mitch. (D) is wrong because the description here is probably adequate to convey the land. A description is sufficient if it provides a good lead as to the identity of the property sought to be conveyed. The deed provided a sufficient means by which the property could be located, since Blueacre was the only property Harvey owned in Wyorado.

Answer to Question 17

(A) Ursula's deed was effective to convey title from Harvey to Ursula immediately on delivery. A quitclaim deed transfers whatever right, title, or interest in the property the grantor has. Thus, when Ursula took by quitclaim deed, she acquired Harvey's interest in Blueacre. Since, as explained in the previous answer, there was no delivery of Harvey's first deed (to Mitch), Harvey was the sole owner of the property; therefore, Ursula took full title to Blueacre. (B) is wrong because recordation of Ursula's deed is irrelevant. Mitch never had an interest that could be cut off (*see* preceding answer). Thus, Ursula prevails because she acquired valid title from Harvey in 1994, rather than because of any priority in recording. Had Ursula not recorded her deed, she would still have prevailed. (C) is wrong because it is irrelevant that Ursula knew of the earlier deed to Mitch. The earlier deed to Mitch was not a valid conveyance of the property because there was no delivery. Since no interest passed to Mitch, her notice of the deed is meaningless. This choice would be relevant only if Mitch had an interest in the property; if the conveyance to Mitch had been effective, then Ursula's notice of it would have prevented her from prevailing against Mitch under a notice-type recording statute. (D) is wrong because the fact that the conveyance was by quitclaim deed is not important; she is the full owner of Blueacre. This choice implies that Ursula's quitclaim deed is somehow ineffective against Mitch's warranty deed, but the fact that Ursula took by quitclaim does not in any way lessen her interest in Blueacre. A quitclaim deed effectively conveys all interest in the property the grantor has. In this case, Harvey had a fee simple absolute, and so that is what passed to Ursula under the deed. Mitch's warranty deed was never delivered and thus it was worthless.

Answer to Question 18

(A) Ursula is entitled to retain the tepee installed by Mitch and can also recover the reasonable rental value for Mitch's use and possession. Even though Mitch was acting in good faith when he built the tepee, he was still a trespasser. Whether installed in good faith or not, in the absence of a statute, trespassers' annexations on the property of another are lost to them. This follows from the intention test; *i.e.,* the good faith trespasser, believing the land to be his own, normally intends annexation of an item to be permanent. Therefore, the annexed item becomes part of the property. Here, there is no mention of a statute changing this rule, so Mitch loses his tepee despite the fact that he believed in good faith that he owned the land. A trespasser can also be held liable for the reasonable rental value of the property. (B) is wrong. Although some courts allow a good faith improver to recover in a case like this, those courts limit such recovery to the *value added* to the land by the improvement, rather than building costs. As noted in the facts, Mitch's tepee added no value to the land. Thus, he cannot recover his $15,000. (C) is wrong because, as explained above, a trespasser may not recover his annexed item. (D) is wrong. Since Ursula is entitled to retain the tepee and Mitch cannot recover any monetary amount since he added no value to the land, he therefore would not be entitled to a lien on the property.

Answer to Question 19

(A) Wilbur takes sole title to Niceacre under his right of survivorship. A joint tenancy carries the right of survivorship. Thus, when one joint tenant dies, the property is freed of her interest and the surviving joint tenant holds the entire property. Therefore, Wilbur owns Niceacre. (B) is wrong because Trustme has no interest. Most states regard a mortgage as a lien on title. In these states, when one joint tenant mortgages the property that does not, by itself, sever a joint tenancy until default and foreclosure proceedings have been completed. Trustme Federal Savings' rights were lost when Helen died prior to foreclosure. When Helen died, her interest in the property evaporated, and with it the bank's security interest. (C) is wrong because Sonia has no interest in Niceacre. Surviving joint tenants, rather than heirs at law, succeed to a deceased joint tenant's interest. Even if Helen had left a will naming Sonia as devisee of the property, the joint tenancy between Helen and Wilbur would not have been terminated. A will is a testamentary conveyance (effective only at death) and hence is inoperative as to joint tenancy property, because at the instant of death the decedent's rights in the property evaporate. (D) is wrong because, as discussed above, only Wilbur had title to Niceacre.

Answer to Question 20

(A) Mortgaging property in a "title theory" state severs a joint tenancy. In a title theory state, a mortgage is considered to be an actual transfer of title to the property, rather than just a lien on the property. Thus, a mortgage by a joint tenant transfers the legal title of the joint tenant to the mortgagee (the money lender). This action destroys the unity of title and thus severs the joint tenancy. Here, Helen's mortgage to Trustme severed the joint tenancy, and so Wilbur and Trustme hold title to the property as tenants in common. (B) is wrong because, as explained, the joint tenancy was severed. (C) is wrong because if Sonia inherited any interest at all in Niceacre, it would be an equitable interest. When property is mortgaged in a title theory state, the borrower retains an equity of redemption. Thus, when a joint tenant mortgages property and severs the joint tenancy, she can regain title as a tenant in common upon paying off the mortgage. At most, Sonia inherited the right to pay off the mortgage and hold Niceacre as a tenant in common with Wilbur. This is an **equitable,** not legal, interest. (D) is wrong because the mortgage theory has a great effect on the issue of severance; a mere lien on the property (lien theory) does not cause a severance, but a transfer of title (title theory) does.

Answer to Question 21

(A) Byyer takes subject to First Bank's mortgage in a race-notice jurisdiction because it was recorded first. All recording acts apply to mortgages as well as deeds. Thus, a subsequent purchaser of the property will take subject to a prior mortgage unless the recording act changes the result. A race-notice recording act would change this result only where a subsequent purchaser did not have notice of the mortgage at the time of purchase **and** recorded his deed before the mortgage was recorded. Here, Byyer probably did not have notice of the mortgage but he recorded **after** First Bank; thus, he takes subject to First Bank's interest. (B) is wrong because Byyer did not win the race to record, which is one of the two requirements for a subsequent purchaser to prevail in a race-notice jurisdiction. (C) is wrong because Byyer would not take Whiteacre subject to First Bank's mortgage in a pure notice jurisdiction. Under a notice recording act, a subsequent bona fide purchaser with no actual or constructive notice prevails over a prior grantee or mortgagee who has not recorded at the time of the conveyance to the subsequent purchaser. (D) is not the best answer because it would only be true in a notice jurisdiction. Byyer would take subject to the mortgage in a pure race or race-notice jurisdiction because the mortgage was recorded before Byyer's deed (even though Byyer did not have notice of the mortgage when he bought Whiteacre).

Answer to Question 22

(C) Hightown Community Trust will win because the organ is a fixture and the bench is integrally connected to the organ. Under the concept of fixtures, a chattel that has been annexed to real property is converted from personalty to realty. As an accessory to the land, it passes with owner-ship of the land rather than with a transfer of the personal property of an estate. The manifest intent of the annexor determines whether the chattel becomes a fixture. The factors for evaluating the annexor's intent are: (i) the relationship between the annexor and the premises, (ii) the degree of annexation, and (iii) the nature and use of the chattel. Under this analysis the organ itself is clearly a fixture: (i) Frogsmith was the fee owner of the mansion and had the organ built to his specifications when the mansion was constructed; (ii) the organ was built into the wall of the mansion and could not be easily removed; and (iii) the appearance of the organ and how it comple-mented the rest of the mansion probably were more important to Frogsmith than its function. An accession is an addition to personal property that becomes an integral part of the property in the same sense that a fixture becomes an integral part of the realty. The doctrine is fully applicable in this case even though the accession goes with an item of property that is itself converted from personalty to realty, as the organ was here. The bench is an accession because it was created as an integral part of the organ and significantly contributes to an important aspect of the organ: its overall appearance. Removing the bench and replacing it with a bench made of different wood or carvings would damage the aesthetic value of the organ. Thus, Hightown Community Trust will succeed in obtaining the bench because it is not severable from the organ. (A) is incorrect because the fact that the bench was not bolted to the floor is not determinative. The bolting goes to whether the bench alone is a fixture. This is irrelevant since it is an accession to (and thus a part of) the organ, which is clearly a fixture. (B) is incorrect because the fact that removing the bench does not damage the building itself does not give Chuckles the right to remove it. Removing the bench will damage the organ because the bench is an accession to the organ. The organ, as a fixture, is part of the real property; thus, removal of the bench will damage the property. (D) is incorrect because harm to the parties is not an issue in determining whether an item is a fixture. The relevant question is whether removal damages the real property. If the bench were found to be personalty, the fact that its removal would reduce the value of the Trust's gift would have no impact on Chuckles's right to remove it.

Answer to Question 23

(B) The court is likely to rule in favor of Pringle because Verdugo concealed the defects in the roof from Pringle. Although the general rule is that a sale of real property carries no implied warranties of quality or fitness, a seller may be liable where he has actually concealed conditions on the property. Here, Verdugo knew the roof was in need of major repair, yet he made inexpensive, cosmetic repairs to the roof. These repairs hid from casual inspection the defects that caused the roof to leak. Thus, Verdugo concealed from Pringle a defective condition on the property. Had Pringle known of this condition, he would have either refused to purchase the property or would have insisted that appropriate repairs be made at Verdugo's expense. Therefore, Pringle will prevail in his lawsuit. (A) is incorrect because the implied warranty of fitness or quality applies only to the sale of a new house by the builder. (This is an exception to the general rule of no such warranties, above.) Blancoacre is not new, nor (as far as we know) is Verdugo its builder. Thus, the implied warranty does not cover the sale from Verdugo to Pringle. Although (C) states the general rule, it is incorrect as applied to these facts because of Verdugo's act of concealment. A seller is generally not required to disclose defects (at least those easily discoverable upon inspection), but he may not make misrepresentations or conceal known defects. Consequently, the rule stated in (C) does not apply here. Although (D) correctly sets forth grounds for the non-applicability to these facts of an implied warranty of fitness, Verdugo's concealment of the defects will make him liable for damages. Therefore, (D) is incorrect in concluding that the court will rule in favor of Verdugo.

Answer to Question 24

(D) Under the reasonable use theory, which is followed in most states, the landowner can use as much percolating water as she wants as long as it is used for beneficial purposes of the overlying land. She will be liable only if the purpose is malicious or the water is simply wasted. (Note that the result is the same under the absolute ownership theory, still followed in several eastern states, which permits the landowner to extract as much water as she wishes for any nonmalicious purpose, including export.) (A) is wrong because Beth may take as much water as she wishes for use on Smallacre. This answer might be correct under the prior appropriation doctrine, a minority approach employed by some western states, since Arnold's beneficial use was first in time. (B) is also wrong under the majority view, although it would probably be the best answer under the minority prior appropriation view. Since domestic use is a preferred beneficial use, Beth probably would be allowed to extract the water under that theory, but because water rights are considered property rights, she would have to compensate Arnold for diminishing his supply. (C) is incorrect under all theories of water law.

Answer to Question 25

(D) Quigley has no interest in Greenacre; thus, none of the other choices is correct. The language of the grant creates a fee simple subject to a condition subsequent in Manuel and an executory interest in Quigley. The condition subsequent, however, attempts to restrict the transferability of a legal interest in property. This restriction is an invalid restraint on alienation and therefore is void. When the condition is stricken, Manuel has a fee simple absolute, and Quigley is left with nothing. Thus, (A) is incorrect because, as explained, Quigley's interest is void. (B) and (C) are incorrect for the same reason, and also because a remainder cannot follow a fee simple interest; it can only follow a fee tail or a life estate. Here, Manuel was conveyed a fee simple estate.

Answer to Question 26

(C) Sebastian's heirs have a contingent remainder. A remainder is a future interest created in a transferee that is capable of taking in present possession and enjoyment (*i.e.*, capable of becoming a present interest) upon the natural termination of the preceding estates created in the same disposition. A remainder must be expressly created in the instrument creating the intermediate possessory estate. Remainders almost always follow life estates. A remainder is *contingent* if it is created in favor of unborn or unascertained persons, because until the remainderman is ascertained, there is no one ready to take possession should the preceding estate come to an end. Since the interest of Sebastian's heirs is capable of taking possession upon the natural termination of Flicka's life estate, which was created in the same instrument, it is a remainder. The same result is reached merely by noting that the interest of Sebastian's heirs follows a life estate and, thus, must be a remainder. The remainder is contingent because Sebastian is still alive and so has no ascertainable heirs. (A) is incorrect because a shifting executory interest *divests* the interest of another transferee; it cuts short rather than follows naturally the prior estate. Here, at the time of the conveyance, the heirs' interest follows naturally; it does not cut short Flicka's prior estate. (B) is incorrect because a springing executory interest follows a gap in possession or divests the estate of the transferor. At the time of the conveyance, the interest of Sebastian's heirs followed an estate in another transferee; it did not follow a gap or divest the transferor. Therefore, their interest, at that time, could not be a springing executory interest. (Note, however, that if Flicka dies during Sebastian's life, the interest in Sebastian's heirs will become a springing executory interest (*see* below).) Since Sebastian's heirs have a contingent remainder, (D) is obviously incorrect.

Answer to Question 27

(B) Gina is entitled to possession of Greenacre at Flicka's death. A reversion is a future interest left in the grantor after she conveys a lesser vested estate than she has. If the reversion was not expressly retained, it will arise by operation of law where no other disposition is made of the property after expiration of the lesser estate. Since Sebastian is still living at Flicka's death, meaning his heirs are unascertained and so unable to take possession when Flicka dies, Gina acquires possession of Greenacre under a reversionary interest by operation of law. Note that at common law, the heirs' contingent remainder would have been destroyed since no one was ready to take possession when the prior life estate ended. Today, however, most states have abolished the destructibility doctrine. Thus, if Sebastian later dies survived by heirs, the heirs will be entitled to the land. Gina's reversion would give way to a springing executory interest (*i.e.*, one that divests the estate of the transferor) in Sebastian's heirs when Sebastian dies. (A) is wrong because the conveyance from Gina did not create an interest in Sebastian; it provided only for his heirs. (C) is wrong because Flicka's interest, a life estate, terminated upon her death. She had no interest to pass to her heirs. (D) is wrong because, during Sebastian's life, his heirs do not exist.

Answer to Question 28

(A) Danuta will prevail because the deed executed by Tomasz to Stashu was never properly delivered. A deed is not effective unless it is delivered. Unless there is some clear expression of intent that the grantor envisioned the passage of title to the grantee (*i.e.,* that the grantor intended to relinquish control over the property), the continued possession of the deed raises a presumption of nondelivery. Tomasz did not do anything to indicate an intent to pass immediate title to Stashu. The presumption of nondelivery is not rebutted and Tomasz retained title. Therefore, Duneacre was part of Tomasz's estate and Danuta and Stashu inherited it as tenants in common. (Multiple grantees are presumed to take as tenants in common.) Danuta has an undivided one-half interest in Duneacre. (B) is wrong because whether Laine violated his fiduciary duty has no bearing on the ownership of Duneacre. That fact would be relevant only if Danuta were seeking damages from Laine. Laine's recording of the void deed did not damage Danuta because it did not affect her rights. (C) is wrong for two reasons: (i) Andy cannot be protected by the recording act because he has not yet recorded and this is a race-notice jurisdiction. To prevail in a race-notice jurisdiction a party must be a subsequent purchaser for value, without notice of an adverse claim, and must record first. Andy has not yet recorded. It is not clear from the facts whether he has received the deed. If he has not, he cannot qualify as a bona fide purchaser since he now has notice of Danuta's claim. (ii) Laine cannot claim the protection of the recording act because he is acting as Stashu's agent. Stashu was a donee with notice and as such was outside the protective provisions of the recording act. (D) is wrong because, as explained above, Danuta need not be a bona fide purchaser (*i.e.,* need not turn to the recording act) to prevail. She inherited an undivided one-half interest in Duneacre, which has not been cut off by the subsequent acquisition and recording by a bona fide purchaser.

Answer to Question 29

(B) The covenant does not clearly "touch and concern" the land. While recycling may benefit the community at large, "touch and concern" involves the relationship between landowners at law. Recycling by Vito does not directly benefit the other landowners in the use and enjoyment of their land. Thus, (B) is correct. (A) is wrong because even though Vito's deed does not contain the covenant, Vito has record notice because the restriction is in Vito's chain of title. (C) is wrong because servitudes implied from a common scheme apply only to negative covenants and the recycling requirement is an affirmative covenant. Thus, this defense does not go to the point. (D) is wrong because it goes only to issues in equity. The suit includes a claim for damages at law. In any case, balancing of hardships is not generally applied in such cases (although some courts might elect to do so).

Answer to Question 30

(B) Son will prevail because Able did not properly inspect the property. A title search is not complete without an examination of possession. If the possession is unexplained by the record, the purchaser is obligated to make inquiry. The purchaser is charged with knowledge of whatever an inspection of the property would have disclosed *and* anything that would have been disclosed by the possessor. Thus, Able is on constructive notice of Son's possession and anything that would have been disclosed by inquiring of Son. Since Able had this notice, he is not protected by this recording statute, and he will take subject to Son's lease. (A) is wrong because "actual notice" means that Able was aware of Son's possession. The facts make clear that Able did not know of Son's possession. Furthermore, the act of driving by has no legal consequence; thus, it would not be deemed to confer anything on Able. (C) is wrong because Able had constructive notice of Son's possession, and therefore, is not protected by the recording statute. (D) is wrong because Son's state of mind is irrelevant for purposes of applying the recording statute.

Answer to Question 31

(D) Selma will succeed in her suit for specific performance at the full contract price. Where property subject to a contract for sale is destroyed without fault of either party before the date set for closing, the majority rule is that the risk of loss is on the buyer. Thus, the buyer must pay the contract price despite a loss due to fire, unless the contract provides otherwise. Here, the inn was destroyed by fire after Selma and Bolton entered into their contract for the sale of the property, but before the closing date. The contract apparently was silent regarding risk of loss. Thus, under the majority rule, the risk of loss is on Bolton, the buyer. As a result, Selma is entitled to receive specific performance of the contract, meaning that Bolton must pay the full contract price. (A) and (B) are incorrect because they conclude that Selma is not entitled to specific performance. As explained above, Selma *is* entitled to specific performance because the risk of loss is on Bolton. (B) is also incorrect because it states that Selma must refund the earnest money. Selma is entitled to the full contract price; thus, there is no reason for her to return the earnest money. (C) is incorrect because it allows Bolton to tender less than the full contract price. With Bolton bearing the risk of loss, he must pay the $1 million contract price despite the decrease in the property's value due to the fire.

Answer to Question 32

(D) The attempted gift to Wilma and her successors fails under the Rule Against Perpetuities because Wilma's interest could vest in possession more than 21 years after a life in being. Thus, (B) is incorrect. Bertha and her successors have a fee simple determinable and Tammy retained a possibility of reverter, which passed to Exeter through the residuary clause in Tammy's will. When Beulah, Bertha's successor, ceased using the property for residential purposes, the possibility of reverter matured, leaving ownership in Exeter. (A) is therefore incorrect. (C) is incorrect because a possibility of reverter, not a right of reversion, is the interest left in the grantor when a fee simple determinable is created.

Answer to Question 33

(D) Scott cannot enforce the restriction against Barker because Petitacre was not part of the common scheme of development. Since neither Barker's deed to Petitacre, nor any deed in his chain of title contains the restrictive covenant, to succeed Scott must show the existence of an implied reciprocal negative servitude that can be enforced on Petitacre. When a developer subdivides land into several parcels and some of the deeds contain negative covenants but some do not, equitable servitudes (negative covenants enforceable by injunction) binding on all of the parcels may be implied if: (i) there is a **common scheme** of development and (ii) the grantee has **notice** of the restrictive covenant. In this case, both requirements are lacking. A common scheme of development is proven by evidence that the developer intended that all parcels in a subdivision be developed within the terms of the negative covenant. The key in this case is that Petitacre was not part of the subdivision intended to be so restricted. The same evidence that proves the common plan for the subdivision shows that Petitacre was not intended to be included; *i.e.,* the brochure shows only Grandacre—80 lots with single-family homes—and nothing at all about Petitacre. In addition, the mere fact that Greedy bothered to divide the property into two parcels before he subdivided the 80 lots on Grandacre shows that he intended to develop the parcels separately. Last, Petitacre's disproportionate size, 30 acres compared with one-half-acre lots, further shows that, at the time Otto bought his lot (and Scott's rights are derived from Otto), Greedy did not intend to include Petitacre in the subdivision. Therefore, the common scheme requirement is not met. Also, it is unlikely that Barker had the requisite notice to be bound by the covenant. He did not have record notice (since the restriction was not in his chain of title);

nothing in the facts shows that he had actual notice; and because his parcel does not appear to be part of the neighborhood (being 30 acres and on the periphery), he did not have inquiry notice. Thus, Barker is not bound by the single-family home restriction in the subdivision deeds. (A) is wrong for the above reasons, but would be wrong even if Petitacre were within the common scheme. A prior purchaser of a burdened lot generally cannot enforce the promise against a subsequent purchaser unless the developer promised the prior purchaser that he would restrict his remaining lots. This promise need not be in writing, however; it may be implied from many things, including: a map or plat shown to the purchaser, oral representations, or sales literature. In this case, the brochure, as well as the overall appearance of the development, would suffice to infer a promise on the part of Greedy to restrict his remaining lots of Grandacre. (B) is wrong because, had Petitacre been part of the common scheme, the fact that Scott and Barker are not in each other's chain of title would not matter. That is not a requirement for enforcing an equitable servitude; in fact, it is almost never the case that the party seeking enforcement is in the other party's chain of title. If that were true, only the developer could enforce the restraints. (C) is wrong because the fact that Scott's deed did not contain the restriction is irrelevant. The important thing is that Scott's property is bound by the restriction. The restriction is in his record chain of title; thus Scott took subject to the restriction and is bound by it.

Answer to Question 34

(D) Stanley will not prevail because his title is not marketable. There is an implied warranty in every land sale contract that at closing the seller will provide the buyer with a title that is marketable. Historically, title acquired by adverse possession was not considered marketable because the purchaser might be later forced to defend in court the facts that gave rise to the adverse possession against the record owner. While most recent cases are contra, for purposes of the bar exam the rule is that one who obtains title by adverse possession must bring an action to quiet title in order for that title to be marketable. Thus, (B) is incorrect. (C) is incorrect because Stanley's action does not amount to fraud; marketable title can be based on adverse possession (although a quiet title suit may be necessary). He never represented that he had record title. (A) makes no sense. A third party with an interest in Goldacre would not be barred from enforcing that interest subsequent to Stanley's specific performance action.

Answer to Question 35

(C) LaRue should prevail because Tong has breached the lease. Generally, if a tenant transfers (assigns or sublets) in violation of a prohibition in the lease against transfers, the transfer is not void. However, the landlord usually may terminate the lease under either the lease terms or a statute. Here, since Tong has breached the provision of the lease prohibiting assignment or sublease, and the lease contains a forfeiture clause, LaRue was within his rights to terminate the lease. (A) is incorrect because clauses restricting assignment or sublease are not considered to be restraints on alienation. (B) is incorrect because a conditional consent is not a waiver where the condition is not agreed to. (D) is incorrect because an oral consent, if made, is sufficient to waive the provision. Here, LaRue's consent was conditioned on Stringer signing an extension of the lease, which he did not do.

Answer to Question 36

(D) If Nancy prevails, it will be because the easement is a legal interest in Laura's chain of title. This is a recording act problem. (A), (B), and (C) all sound fascinating, but they are all misstatements of law. Even though Laura had no actual or inquiry notice, the recorded easement by her grantor Michael would give her constructive notice of Nancy's interest in Acreone, regardless of the absence of a tract index.

Answer to Question 37

(A) Jeff takes because Katherine conveyed her interest to him, and Chris takes by inheritance. Thus, (A) is correct, and (C) is wrong. (B) is wrong because Katherine has transferred her interest to Jeff. The destruction of his deed has no effect on his interest. For Katherine to have her interest back, Jeff would have to reconvey by deed to her. (D) is wrong because when Katherine conveyed her interest to Jeff, the joint tenancy was severed and the interest became a tenancy in common. Since a tenancy in common has no right of survivorship, when Amanda died, her interest passed to Chris, her heir.

Answer to Question 38

(D) Paul will prevail because he is a bona fide purchaser. (A) is speaking to the right theory, *i.e.*, the recording act, but *if* Paul is to prevail under the recording act, he must take without notice of Jeff's interest **and** pay value; in other words, he must be a bona fide purchaser. That is why (D) is the best answer. (A) is wrong because the recording act is a "notice" statute. Paul would prevail against Jeff even if Paul had not recorded (in contrast to the result under a "race-notice" statute). (B) is wrong because Jeff's return of his deed does not affect his interest. (C) is nonsense.

Answer to Question 39

(D) Snyder has relied to his detriment upon the agency given by Larsen to Olsen, so Larsen is estopped to deny that it was exercised validly. (B) is incorrect because recording of a deed does not insulate it from attack on its validity. (C) is incorrect because the Statute of Frauds, relating to the *enforceability* of conveyances, would not prevent evidence of Larsen's instructions to Olsen from being proved. (A) is incorrect because Larsen had done nothing inequitable that would raise an unclean hands issue.

Answer to Question 40

(C) Recording of the subdivision map containing the designated city parks was an offer of dedication, and the city's action in naming and preparing them was an acceptance of dedication sufficient to give the city good title. Laches would not be a factor over a two-year period, so (D) is incorrect. The church is bound because it had constructive notice of the dedication (not of the proposed use) through its chain of title. Thus, (A) and (B) are incorrect.

Answer to Question 41

(C) Winslow has an equitable servitude—the right to enforce the covenant in equity. He is not a third-party beneficiary of Nathan's promise, but rather he is a direct promisee. (B) is therefore incorrect. Whether the church is a bona fide purchaser is immaterial, since it would be bound by the covenant because of its presence in public records. Thus, (A) is incorrect. The covenant was never restricted to any particular lot or type of lot in the subdivision. (D) is therefore incorrect.

Answer to Question 42

(C) A covenant runs with the land if it touches and concerns the land and is intended to run. Use of land for commercial purposes touches and concerns, and it is evident that Nathan and Winslow intended it to run with the land. Zorka is bound even though her deed did not refer to the covenant and she did not purchase directly from Nathan. The covenant is in the public records and it runs with the land. Thus, (A) is incorrect. (B) is incorrect because compliance with zoning regulations does not excuse noncompliance with an enforceable covenant; both must be complied with. (D) is incorrect. Winslow need not show a servitude implied from a common scheme to prevail; the covenant was recorded and runs with the land, so Winslow can enforce the covenant as an equitable servitude.

Answer to Question 43

(A) The somewhat ambiguous description of the conveyance given in the problem could apply either to a joint tenancy with a right of survivorship or to a tenancy by the entirety. If the conveyance is a tenancy by the entirety, then further conveyance by Bosco to Dansford would not cause a severance and, upon Bosco's death, Canfield would be the sole owner of the land. On the other hand, if it were initially a joint tenancy, Bosco's conveyance would sever it, converting the estate of Canfield and Dansford into a tenancy in common. (B) is irrelevant because the form of concurrent ownership, *i.e.,* tenancy by the entirety or joint tenancy, not the status of prior ownership, is determinative of the rights of the parties. (D) is also irrelevant because the form of concurrent ownership is controlling regardless of knowledge or lack of knowledge of the subsequent conveyance to Dansford. Under (C), Canfield and Dansford would each have an undivided *one-half* interest.

Answer to Question 44

(C) Carl's rights clearly depend on the existence of a public street. (A) is wrong because no issue of Statute of Frauds is present. There has been no purported conveyance to Carl of rights in the street by anyone who owns such rights. (B) is wrong since there is no legal objection to the enrichment that results if persons other than the dedicator are permitted to use a public street. (D) is wrong since, if a public street exists, Carl need not assert a way by necessity.

Answer to Question 45

(B) Generally, a city accepts a dedication when it approves the plans. (A) is wrong because a simple referral to a recorded plan does not automatically create rights. (C) is wrong because Carl does not need a way of necessity since he has other access to his land. (D) is wrong because the alternative access exists, and the amount of money required to improve the access does not determine need for an easement by necessity.

Answer to Question 46

(C) Equipment installed for the purposes of trade by a tenant is usually removable if it is not an integral part of the premises and if the tenant pays any damages caused by the removal. Tenants who attach tools of the trade do not generally intend to improve the real property. The Statute of Frauds does not preclude the mortgagee from claiming an interest in property that has become an integral part of the premises, and so (A) is wrong. (D) is wrong because the mortgagee has the same rights as the former owner, regardless of the tenant's knowledge of the mortgage. (B) is wrong because the usual rule is that personal property that becomes affixed to the real property is a fixture, subject to the "trade fixtures" exception described in (C).

Answer to Question 47

(B) Susan and Richard held an indefeasibly vested remainder as joint tenants. There is no condition, stated or implied, that they survive Jack in order to take. Because Richard predeceased Susan, Susan took the property interest pursuant to the right of survivorship. Upon Susan's death, the remainder passed to her heirs. In turn, Susan's heirs took Brownacre upon the death of Jack, the life tenant. (A) is wrong because Jack had only a life estate; he had no interest to pass to his heirs at his death. (C) is wrong because Susan survived Richard and thus owned all of the remainder at her death; Richard owned nothing. (D) is wrong because Otto, having granted a life estate and an absolutely vested remainder, retained no interest in Brownacre.

Answer to Question 48

(C) Charlie prevails because the ranch passed through the residuary clause. Under the Rule Against Perpetuities, the attempt to give Charlie an executory interest is void, so (B) is incorrect. However, the courts would simply read the conveyance without the language of the executory gift, leaving a possibility of reverter in the grantor, Bill. Thus, (A) is incorrect. Since Charlie succeeded to Bill's interest as grantor via the residuary clause of the will, he will prevail. (D) is wrong because there is no restraint on alienation contained in the will.

Answer to Question 49

(C) The doctrine of part performance may be used to enforce an otherwise invalid oral contract of sale provided the acts of part performance unequivocally prove the existence of the contract. Here, Tuttle's actions are explicable even if he had remained a tenant, since he continued to pay the same amount per month as had been previously paid as rent, and the improvements he made are a kind frequently made by long-term tenants. (A) is incorrect because Otto's approval was not needed to make such improvements. (B) is incorrect because if Tuttle had taken actions that clearly indicated the presence of an oral contract, the doctrine of part performance would have applied. The benefit to Otto is irrelevant for purposes of the Statute of Frauds; the issue is part performance. Thus, (D) is not the best answer.

Answer to Question 50

(D) An assignee is in privity of estate with the lessor, and is liable for those covenants in the original lease that run with the land. Hence, (A) is wrong. (B) and (C) are wrong because an agreement to pay taxes touches and concerns the land, and thus runs with the land.

Answer to Question 51

(C) The tenant-assignor remains in privity of contract with the lessor and is liable for the rent reserved in the lease. (A) and (B) are incorrect because Joann's status as a tenant is immaterial. (D) is incorrect because Joann's failure to include the tax payment provision in her assignment to Al does not affect her liability as the assignor under privity of contract.

Answer to Question 52

(A) A covenant to convey touches and concerns both the leasehold and reversion, and therefore runs with those respective interests in the land. Thus, (B) is incorrect. (C) is incorrect because there is nothing about the option in the facts that shows it to be personal. (D) is incorrect because, as explained above, the burden of the covenant to convey does run with the land.

Answer to Question 53

(C) Absent an express assumption, an assignee is not liable on covenants in the original lease once he reassigns. Hence, (A) is wrong. (B) is wrong because an assignee is not in privity of contract with the lessor unless the assignee expressly assumes the lease obligations. (D) is incorrect because Al's ability to subsequently assign the lease is unrelated to the issue of liability. Al, as an assignee of Joann, is liable for covenants running with the land on the basis of privity of estate. Once Al assigns the lease to Howard, privity of estate ends and Al's liability is terminated.

Answer to Question 54

(D) A description in a deed is sufficient if it furnishes a good lead as to the identity of the property. Hence, (A) is wrong. (C) is incorrect because a deed purporting to convey more land than the grantor owns does not invalidate the deed. (B) fails to conform to the facts.

Answer to Question 55

(D) The description is too vague in its entirety; there may be difficulty determining **which** four acres in the northwest section. Thus, (B) is wrong. (C) is wrong because the "wooded land" language is not the only vague part; which four acres in the northwest section is a problem. (A) is wrong because whatever Randy's actual intent, he failed to accomplish it with this deed.

Answer to Question 56

(B) (A) is wrong because an undelivered deed cannot be sustained as a valid testamentary disposition under the Statute of Wills. (C) is wrong because the original giving of the deeds to Hilda constituted "delivery" and she accepted; the fact that she returned the deeds to Randy to hold does not change the fact that a delivery was made. (D) is irrelevant.

Answer to Question 57

(A) The existence of the easement breaches the covenant against encumbrances and Randy's estate is in breach of this covenant. (B), (C), and (D) are incorrect because the existence of an easement burdening the land does not breach the covenant of quiet enjoyment or right to convey, respectively. The covenant of quiet enjoyment is breached when the grantee is evicted by a third party with **paramount** title, *i.e.,* title or ownership of the estate conveyed that is superior to the grantor's title. The covenant of right to convey is breached if the grantor lacks title, *i.e.,* ownership of the estate conveyed, at the time of the grant.

Answer to Question 58

(C) If a "right of first purchase" is found to be valid, the agreement is merely a promissory restraint, the breach of which may give Phil a cause of action against Randy's estate, but will not affect Hilda's interest unless she had knowledge of the agreement at the time she acquired her deed from Randy. Thus, alternatives (A), (B), and (D) are incorrect.

Answer to Question 59

(B) There is a presumption that Harvey and Winona are tenants in common. For a joint tenancy to exist, there must be an express creation of such tenancy; thus, there is a presumption of tenancy in common unless the conveyance is to a husband and wife in a state that recognizes tenancy by the entirety. Here, Harvey and Winona were not married when they took title to Pinkacre. Each tenant in common has an undivided interest, which may be conveyed by inter vivos transfer. Harvey started with an undivided one-half interest, one-half of which he conveyed to Sampson and the other half of which he conveyed to Delilah. Harvey has thus conveyed all of his interest in Pinkacre, and so (A) is incorrect. There is no right of survivorship in a tenancy in common; therefore, (C) is incorrect. (D) is not supported by the facts.

Answer to Question 60

(B)   The executory interest in the Asthmatic Children's Association is void under the Rule Against Perpetuities because it might vest beyond lives in being plus 21 years; the charity-to-charity exception to the Rule Against Perpetuities does not apply because Dr. Thaddeus is not a charitable organization. Therefore Madge retained a possibility of reverter, which passed to Leonard. Hence, alternatives (A) and (D) are wrong. (C) is wrong because, although Dr. Thaddeus had the power to sell his interest, he did not own a fee simple absolute.

Answer to Question 61

(C)   Striking out the Asthmatic Children's Association's void interest left Madge with a possibility of reverter, which need not be expressly retained in the conveyance. Since all future interests are devisable under the state statute, Madge's interest passed to Leonard upon her death. (A) is wrong because Leonard's interest is not an executory interest; it is an interest in the grantor, and an executory interest is held by someone other than the grantor. (Leonard takes his interest by inheriting it from the grantor.) (B) is wrong because no right of entry was reserved in the grantor. Unlike a possibility of reverter, which automatically follows a fee simple determinable, a right of entry must be expressly retained. (D) is wrong because the possibility of reverter is always a vested interest, which is the reason why the Rule Against Perpetuities does not invalidate it.

Answer to Question 62

(D)   Leonard may enjoin the sale because he has an interest in the property. WRO's interest in the estate lasts as long as it is working to promote the passage of the Child Support Amendment. The grant does not provide for the contingency of WRO ceasing to promote passage of the amendment before 1999. This gap would be filled by a possibility of reverter retained by Madge. Since she passed that interest to Leonard in her will, there can be no contract to sell the property without his signature. Hence, (A) is wrong. (B) is wrong because the interest in the estate will pass to Helping Hand, Inc., if at all, within 21 years. (C) is wrong because WRO could pass a defeasible fee.

Answer to Question 63

(A)   Leland would be declared the owner of Whiteacre on the basis of the application of the rule of constructive adverse possession. The rule states that where the claimant goes into actual possession of some portion of the property under color of title, he will be deemed in adverse possession of the entire property described in the instrument on the basis that his adverse possession is constructive possession of the extended parts of the property not actually occupied. Thus, (C) is incorrect. (B) is incorrect because a transfer in ownership does not interrupt the statutory period for adverse possession. (D) is incorrect because only a minority of states require the adverse possessor to pay taxes on the property.

Answer to Question 64

(D)   Since Leland was in continuous possession for the statutory period and has met all of the other requirements of adverse possession, he would be declared the owner of the five acres. (A) is incorrect because only a minority of states require the adverse possessor to pay property taxes. (B) is incorrect because the disability of Otis's successor in the interest will not toll the running of the statute. For a disability to stop the clock, the disability must have been in existence on the day the adverse possession began in 1980. (C) is incorrect because Leland's state of mind is irrelevant under the majority view. Even if he had possessed the land knowing he was trespassing, he could still claim it by adverse possession.

Answer to Question 65

(C)   Since Mabel neither owned Whiteacre nor was acting as Norris's agent, she breached the covenants of seisin and right to convey at the time of the conveyance to Leland. Thus, (A) is incorrect. There is nothing in the facts to suggest the property is encumbered; thus, she did not breach the covenant against encumbrances. (B) is therefore incorrect. Under the covenants of quiet enjoyment, warranty, and further assurances, Mabel promised that (i) Leland would not be disturbed in his possession of Whiteacre; (ii) she would defend Leland's title against lawful claims; and (iii) she would perform whatever acts are necessary to perfect Leland's title. Mabel has obviously breached these covenants. Thus, (D) is incorrect.

Answer to Question 66

(C)   There are two gifts to Gwendolyn's children. The first is a vested remainder that follows Gwendolyn's life estate, and the second is the executory interest that is given to the other children if one purports to sell or mortgage his or her interest. This second restriction is an attempt to restrain the alienation (sale) of property, which is void. Thus, (D) is incorrect. (A) is incorrect because Geoffrey and the other children have interests that are vested at Grey's death. (B) is incorrect for the same reason. The children's interests vested and their class closed at the time of Grey's death and thus are not subject to the Rule Against Perpetuities.

Answer to Question 67

(B)   Each party owns one-half of the stream bed. The general rule is that where a stream is a boundary, abutting owners each own one-half of the bed. Thus, (C) and (A) are wrong. (D) is incorrect; the description is not invalid.

Answer to Question 68

(D)   The physical description takes precedence over the quantity description unless there are grounds for reformation of the underlying deal. Thus, (C) is incorrect. The facts indicate that Oona and Beatrix were bargaining for a specific physical location and not for a specific number of acres. Thus, there appear to be no grounds for reformation. A conflict in description does not invalidate a deed, so (A) and (B) are incorrect.

Answer to Question 69

(C)   A conveyance of a co-tenant's interest in joint tenancy property severs the joint tenancy, and that interest is subsequently held as a tenancy in common with the other co-tenants. Thus, (D) is incorrect. Since the joint tenancy with right of survivorship was severed before Vladimir's death, (A) is incorrect. Returning the deed to Nicholas did not return ownership of the property to him; that would require a reconveyance. Thus, (B) is incorrect.

Answer to Question 70

(C) An assignment does not release the tenant from his contractual obligations to the landlord; thus, Realty Corp. is still liable for all of the lease provisions. Thus, (D) is incorrect. An assignee is in privity of estate with the landlord and is liable on all covenants in the lease that run with the land. His assumption of these duties is implied; it need not be expressed in the assignment. Covenants to pay money run with the land, as do covenants to perform physical acts on the property. Therefore, Rasputin, Inc. is liable for both the rent and the road even if it did not expressly assume performance of the covenants. Thus, (A) and (B) are incorrect.

Answer to Question 71

(D) Nicholas had no interest in the property that he conveyed to Olga; thus, (A) is wrong. However, if Olga is a bona fide purchaser for value who records first, the deed to Alexander and Vladimir (now to Alexander and Anastasia) would not be good against Olga's. (B) and (C) are incorrect because they do not contain every element necessary for Olga to prevail.

Answer to Question 72

(C) Since Flora installed the equipment without any intention to benefit her landlord, she is entitled to remove it when the lease terminates, provided that she repairs any damage such removal may cause. (A) is incorrect because personal property attached to real property may become a fixture (and thus a part of the realty, not to be removed) if the one who attached it intended that it become part of the real property. It is presumed that chattels used in a trade or business are not intended to be fixtures and, thus, may be removed. (D) is immaterial since notice to the tenant is not necessary. The mortgagee stands in the same position as the landlord-mortgagor, so the issue involved in this case could arise without there being a mortgage at all. (B) is incorrect in that but for the fixtures being trade fixtures, they would have been considered part of the real property and subject to the bank's mortgage.

Answer to Question 73

(D) In partial condemnation cases, the landlord-tenant relationship continues, as does the tenant's obligation to pay the entire rent for the remaining period of the lease. The tenant is, however, entitled to share in the condemnation award to the extent that the condemnation affected the tenant's rights under the lease. Therefore, (B) and (C) are incorrect. (A) is not correct because the law of landlord and tenant traditionally refuses to recognize frustration of purpose as grounds for termination of a lease.

Answer to Question 74

(A) Under the doctrine of merger, all covenants not collateral to the land sale contract are "merged" in the deed. Thus, acceptance by the buyer of the deed discharges the seller of all liability under the contract. Therefore, unless the deed contains the covenants of seisin, right to convey, or right to quiet enjoyment, Stefan would prevail. Therefore, (C) and (D) are incorrect. (B) is also incorrect because Phil's knowledge that Stefan was married has no effect on the doctrine of merger or liability on the covenants of title.

Answer to Question 75

(C) An easement in gross that is commercial may always be transferred, and the permission of the holder of the servient estate is not needed. Thus, (A) is wrong. Since Petroco was within its rights under the terms of the easement, the laying of pipe is permissible and no injunction will lie. It is, however, the obligation of the holder of the easement to reasonably restore the surface following the excavation. Thus, (C) is correct, and (B) and (D) are wrong.

Answer to Question 76

(C) The doctrine of waste governs the obligations between a life tenant and the holder of the remainder regarding the payment of a mortgage on the property. The life tenant pays the interest and the holder of the remainder pays the principal. (C) correctly states that rule, and (A), (B), and (D) are necessarily wrong.

Answer to Question 77

(B) In most jurisdictions, when a sale is made "subject to" the mortgage, the mortgagee has the option of foreclosing on the land or suing the mortgagor (in this case, Rosalie) on the debt. (A) is incorrect because it fails to allow for the remedy of suing on the debt. (C) and (D) are incorrect because one who purchases subject to a mortgage (Vitus) is not personally liable on the underlying debt.

TORTS QUESTIONS

Questions 1-3 are based on the following fact situation:

Puro Water Co. markets water in lightweight plastic bottles, specially designed to be taken along on camping trips. Each bottle is marked "100% pure spring water—recommended by the American Campers Association." These bottles are sold by grocery stores, sporting goods stores, and other retail outlets.

Eager purchased several containers of Puro water from dealer Don's Sports Store, and took them with him on a camping trip to Yellowrock National Park. While Eager was away from his campsite, a neighboring camper, Beaver, took one of the unopened containers without Eager's knowledge or consent. Later, Beaver opened the container and drank some of the Puro water, and immediately became violently ill. Tests were run on the water and showed that it contained impurities.

1. If Beaver maintains a negligence action against Puro, which of the following arguments would be the most helpful to Puro in avoiding liability?

    (A) Dealer Don had ample opportunity to test and inspect the bottled water for purity and failed to do so.

    (B) Puro bottled its water in compliance with numerous statutes that regulate the process of bottling water for human consumption.

    (C) Beaver has failed to introduce any evidence at trial as to how the impurities got into the water he drank, and therefore has not met his burden of proof.

    (D) No reasonable person would have foreseen that the water would have been stolen and consumed by a thief.

2. If Beaver maintains an action against Puro on the basis of strict tort liability, which of the following would be the most helpful to Puro in avoiding liability?

    (A) The impurity in the water was an amoeba that was so rare that it could not be detected by tests commonly used for establishing whether water is safe for human consumption.

    (B) The water was sold in its natural state, and had not been manufactured or processed by Puro in any way.

    (C) In answer to an interrogatory, Beaver has admitted that he has no evidence that his illness was caused by the impurities in the water.

    (D) Although marketed under Puro's label, the water had been bottled by another company and any impurity in the water was the other company's fault.

3. If Beaver maintains an action against the American Campers Association, on which theory would he be most likely to recover, if at all?

    (A) Express warranty.

    (B) Implied warranty of merchantability.

    (C) Strict tort liability.

    (D) Negligence.

Questions 4-5 are based on the following fact situation:

Fatherlode Mining Co. operated a mine for many years that produced a mineral used in the manufacture of high-grade steel alloys. Because of distressed conditions in the steel industry, Fatherlode's orders dropped dramatically and it was no longer profitable to operate the mine. Fatherlode closed down operations and informed Public Light & Power Co. that electricity to the mine should be cut off. The mine was quite isolated and a special line of power poles brought electricity to the mine.

Despite its knowledge of the mine's abandonment, Public left the power running through its lines to the mine. This was standard company policy, because Public knew that whenever its lines were turned off, thieves were likely to steal valuable transformers and cables. Thus, it maintained power even on branch lines that no longer had customers. Public never told Fatherlode of its policy and Fatherlode was unaware that power was still flowing to the mine.

Poindexter, a hitchhiker, was dropped off at a crossroad about a half mile from the mine entrance. Poindexter walked along the road and spotted a sign saying "Fatherlode Mining Co.," with a smaller sign, reading "Closed," nailed beneath it. Poindexter entered onto Fatherlode's land and saw that the mine was, in fact, abandoned. He decided to steal some transformers and to try to sell them. He climbed up a power pole and suffered an electric shock when he tried to detach a transformer. Although Poindexter survived the shock, his fall from the pole after being shocked caused permanent injuries.

4.   If Poindexter sues Public Light & Power Co. for his injuries, will Poindexter prevail?

(A)   Yes, because Public used unreasonable force to protect its property.

(B)   Yes, because force applied by mechanical devices may not be used to protect property alone.

(C)   No, because Public owed no duty to a trespasser.

(D)   No, because Poindexter assumed the risk.

5.   If Poindexter sues Fatherlode Mining Co., which of the following is Fatherlode's strongest defense?

(A)   Poindexter was a trespasser.

(B)   Poindexter was a thief.

(C)   Fatherlode asked Public to turn off the power.

(D)   Fatherlode was unaware that Public had not turned off the power.

Questions 6-7 are based on the following fact situation:

Harold wanted to decorate his house with hanging plants. He bought some plants and baskets at Norman's Nursery and then visited Sam's Sports and Hardware Store, where he bought "20-pound test" fishing line which he planned to use to hang the plants. The line was manufactured by Ketchum Industries, a specialized manufacturer of fishing tackle.

In fishing terms, "20-pound test" means that fishing line will not break under an initial stress of up to 20 pounds when a hooked fish tugs against the line. It does not mean that it will support a constant 20-pound weight. Most sportfishers are aware of this technical meaning, but most laypersons are not. Ketchum put no warnings or explanations on the package in which the line was sold.

Harold went home and proceeded to hang plant baskets around his home. Harold hung a 15-pound basket from his front porch, directly above an old-fashioned porch swing. Harold's friend, Giselle, came to visit Harold, and she sat down on the swing. While she conversed with Harold, the line holding the basket broke, causing the plant to fall and strike Giselle on the head. Giselle suffered severe head injuries.

6.   Will Giselle prevail in a suit against Ketchum?

(A)   Yes, because Ketchum had a duty to include warnings for all potential uses of its product.

(B)   Yes, if Ketchum knew its product was used for purposes other than fishing.

(C) No, if it is customary in the fishing tackle industry not to place warnings on fishing line.

(D) No, because Harold was negligent in hanging the plant directly above a place where a person was likely to sit.

7. Will Giselle prevail in a suit against Harold?

(A) Yes, because she was a social guest.

(B) Yes, because Harold was negligent in hanging the plant.

(C) No, because Harold could not be expected to know the technical meaning of "20-pound test."

(D) No, because she was not a foreseeable plaintiff.

Question 8

Digby was employed by the collection department of Cardshark, Inc., a wholesale distributor of greeting cards. He was assigned to collect money owed on a consignment account by Mary, the elderly sole proprietor of a card shop named "Sensitive Greeting Cards." Digby strode into the shop while Mary was waiting on some customers and demanded to know why she had not paid her account. Mary, distressed by his intrusion, assured him that her account was fully paid and asked him to wait until her customers had left to continue the discussion. Digby, undeterred, continued in a loud voice, "We're not going to put up with freeloaders like you anymore. I'm going to come back with a truck and repossess your entire inventory if you don't pay up." Mary, in tears, begged Digby to leave but he only became angrier. Pounding his fist on the counter, he shouted, "And then we're going to prosecute you for fraud and put you in jail!" Digby then left, but by then Mary was severely distraught.

If Mary sues Digby for her emotional distress, who will prevail?

(A) Mary, if Digby's conduct was extreme and outrageous.

(B) Mary, if she felt subjected to a threat of physical injury.

(C) Digby, if he did not intend for Mary to suffer severe distress.

(D) Digby, if Mary owed the money that Digby demanded.

Question 9

Wanda's father died after a long illness. In accordance with his wishes, she arranged with Divine Rest Mortuary to bury him next to the body of his wife, who had died several years before. Wanda selected the most ornate casket available and spared no expense in the arrangements. Because her father's illness had caused his physical condition to deteriorate, Wanda insisted that the casket remain closed during the wake, and she could not bring herself to view the body before the funeral. At the cemetery, however, she decided to view the body before it was buried. She was horrified to discover that the body in the casket was dressed in a clown costume and a bright orange wig. In fact, it was not her father but Zobo the Clown, who had died the same day as her father and had requested to be buried in his costume. Although the mortuary was able to retrieve her father's body and bury it, Wanda was greatly distressed by the episode and suffered nightmares as a result. However, she did not seek medical or psychiatric care because of it. The mortuary apologized for the incident, but insisted that Wanda pay all of the agreed-to charges for the funeral.

Wanda brings an action against the mortuary to recover for her emotional distress. The mortuary is prepared to stipulate to its negligence. Can Wanda recover damages?

(A) No, because Wanda did not have to obtain medical or psychiatric care.

(B) No, because Wanda suffered no physical injury.

(C) Yes, because of the known sensitivity of people concerning the death of a family member.

(D) Yes, because the mortuary is requiring Wanda to pay the bill for the funeral expenses.

Question 10

Percy and Donald were both honor students at Upstate Law School. After passing the bar examination, both Percy and Donald were granted interviews by Big Law Firm, a prestigious firm located in the state's largest city, which was well-known for paying larger salaries to its beginning associates than any other firm in the state. During law school, both Percy and Donald were on the Law Review, where Percy became editor-in-chief and published a "case comment" that received favorable attention from members of the bar throughout the state. Donald's grades were slightly higher than Percy's, but this was largely because Donald did not have to devote as much time to the Law Review as did Percy in his role as editor-in-chief. Both Percy and Donald were interviewed by Anneliese, the hiring partner of Big Law Firm. During the course of her interview with Donald, Anneliese asked Donald his opinion of Percy's notable case comment. Donald told her, "There's a rumor around school that Percy got outside help on that comment." Based at least in part on this, Anneliese recommended Donald for an associate's position at Big Law Firm. Donald accepted the job offer that followed, and Percy received a polite letter of rejection from Anneliese. Six months later, Percy discovered that Donald had made the statement to Anneliese about the case comment. Percy filed a slander action against Donald.

Assuming that there was never a rumor around Upstate Law School that Percy had received outside help and that Percy did not receive outside help on the comment, will Percy prevail in his suit against Donald?

(A) Yes, because Donald's statement to Anneliese was false.

(B) Yes, because Donald showed reckless disregard for the truth or falsity of the statement.

(C) No, because Anneliese asked Donald for his opinion.

(D) No, unless Percy can prove special damages.

Question 11

Scientific Light and Illumination, Inc. ("SLI") manufactured a laser for home hobbyist use. The SLI lasers were distributed by retail outlets of scientific equipment and by direct mail sales. Lycurgus purchased an SLI laser from a retail outlet in Suburb, where he lived. An amateur inventor, Lycurgus was attempting to develop a means by which personal computers could be "networked" via satellite transmission of encoded laser beams. Since the SLI laser was the only such device available at anything other than astronomical prices, Lycurgus bought it despite its very low power output. He had already purchased a readily available voltage booster from his local Radio Hut store, and attached the booster to the SLI laser to obtain the level of emissions he desired. One night, Lycurgus attempted to bounce a laser signal off an old Telstar satellite passing high overhead. Because of a defective voltage regulation device, present in the SLI laser when it left the SLI production facilities, the voltage booster Lycurgus was using caused the laser to overheat and explode. A fragment of molten quartz fell on the roof of the neighboring residence, owned by Virgil, and set it aflame. Since it was late, Virgil was asleep and was barely able to escape from his burning home. He suffered severe lung damage from the combustion products he inhaled in his flight from the flames.

Virgil brought an action against SLI for the physical injuries he suffered as a result of the SLI laser explosion. Which party will probably win this lawsuit?

(A) Virgil, unless SLI can prove that the SLI laser was never intended to be used at the power levels necessary for satellite transmission.

(B) SLI, because Virgil was neither a purchaser nor a user of the laser.

(C) SLI, if it exercised due care in the manufacture of the laser.

(D) Virgil, because he was injured by the defective SLI laser.

Question 12

During a trip to Vail, Colorado, Polly's ankle was injured in a skiing mishap. Upon her return to Biggston, her hometown, she consulted Dr. Ace, an orthopedic specialist with staff privileges at Sawbones Hospital. Ace told her that the injury would require a relatively simple operation to assure that she would not walk with a pronounced limp in the future. Ace was known in the community as a highly skilled and respected orthopedic specialist, and Polly agreed to the operation. Upon her admission to Sawbones Hospital, Polly signed the standard consent forms and liability waivers releasing Dr. Ace, Dr. Baker (the anesthesiologist), Dr. Chase (the assistant surgeon), and the surgical nursing staff. Two hours before the operation was scheduled to be performed, one of Ace's patients was brought into the emergency room with numerous orthopedic injuries that required immediate attention. Dr. Ace quickly called Dr. Deuce and asked him to perform Polly's operation. Dr. Deuce was, like Dr. Ace, a highly skilled orthopedic specialist with wide respect in the community. When Dr. Deuce arrived at the hospital, Polly was already sedated. He performed the operation with his usual skill. The operation was a complete success and no complications occurred. However, when Polly discovered that she had been operated on by Deuce rather than Ace, she became upset and consulted an attorney.

The attorney should advise Polly that if she sues Deuce for battery, the likely result is:

(A) Polly will win, but she may be entitled only to nominal damages.

(B) Polly will win, unless a reasonable person similarly situated would have consented to the operation.

(C) Polly will lose, because Deuce performed the operation competently.

(D) Polly will lose, because she suffered no harm.

Questions 13-14 are based on the following fact situation:

Cyril conveyed Cityacre to Olga. Cityacre was a corner lot in a residential area, but there was a lot of traffic on both of the streets bordering Cityacre because it was quite close to the central business district. When Olga took possession, Cityacre contained a modest home, in which Olga took up residence. There was a small hedge at the apex of the lot. During the course of the 20 years Olga lived on Cityacre, the hedge grew so large that it obstructed the view around the corner for motorists at the intersection of the streets bordering Cityacre. However, the city had made the intersection a four-way stop, and all of the stop signs were clearly visible to motorists.

One afternoon two motorists, Donna and Edmund, were driving inattentively and each ran a stop sign at the intersection bordering Cityacre. Their cars collided in the intersection and both Donna and Edmund were injured. The jurisdiction in which Cityacre is located has adopted pure comparative negligence.

13. If Donna sues Olga for her injuries, who is likely to prevail?

(A) Donna, as long as her percentage of fault is not as great as Olga's percentage of fault.

(B) Donna, if it was foreseeable that motorists could be injured if the hedge was not cut back.

(C) Olga, because Donna ran the stop sign.

(D) Olga, if Olga's fault was slight compared with Donna's fault.

14. If Edmund sues Donna for his injuries, what is the likely result?

   (A) Edmund wins, if his percentage of fault is less than Donna's.

   (B) Edmund loses, unless Donna had the last clear chance to avoid the accident.

   (C) Donna wins, because Edmund ran the stop sign.

   (D) Donna loses, regardless of whether Edmund's fault was greater or less than Donna's.

Question 15

Viola, a nine-year-old girl, attended Academic Academy, a private school. Academic Academy was located in an area of the city where traffic was very heavy. Therefore, a number of parents complained to school authorities that it was dangerous for their children to walk to the school. The school, an exclusive school with many children of prominent citizens in attendance, put pressure on the city to install more traffic lights in the area of the school. In response to the pressure, a traffic light was installed across the street from the school. However, the city decided that the light should only be in operation from September through June, the normal school year. Although Academic Academy had a "Summer Enrichment Program," which approximately 10% of its students attended, it made no complaint to the city about the suspension of traffic light operation during the summer.

Viola attended the Summer Enrichment Program. One morning, as she walked to school, she entered the crosswalk where the nonoperative light controlled traffic during the regular school year. When she was three feet into the street, she was struck by a car driven by David and was seriously injured. When the police arrived on the scene, David admitted to them, "I was driving too fast; I didn't have time to stop when I saw the kid in the crosswalk."

Viola's mother, Litigatia, wants to file suit against the school on Viola's behalf. Can the school be held liable?

   (A) Yes, unless Viola's parents were negligent.

   (B) Yes, because Viola was an invitee.

   (C) No, unless the school knew of the risk and owed a duty to Viola.

   (D) No, because of David's negligence.

Question 16

Cisneros was sailing down the deep water channel to Lake Washington using the kicker on his sailboat when LeBeau roared by in his cabin cruiser at about 20 knots, nearly swamping Cisneros. Cisneros raised his middle finger in the timeworn salute of the impotently angry and shouted a few well-chosen references to LeBeau's anatomy and ancestry. LeBeau happened to glance back at Cisneros during the latter's tirade and, perceiving that Cisneros was being less than complimentary, swung about and pulled alongside the much smaller sailcraft. The two skippers exchanged further hostilities centering on each other's lack of seamanship, whereupon LeBeau powered away, made a tight circle, and steamed at high speed directly at Cisneros's bow. Cisneros was convinced that the boats would collide, so he steered close to the edge of the channel and abruptly ran aground on a shallow sand bar. LeBeau's mocking guffaws rose above the rumble of his engine as he sailed away from the stranded but uninjured Cisneros.

If, after freeing his craft, Cisneros brings an appropriate action against LeBeau for damages, the probable outcome will be:

   (A) Cisneros will win, unless he was himself responsible for provoking LeBeau during the relevant events.

   (B) Cisneros will win, because he believed that LeBeau's maneuvers threatened imminent danger of harm to him.

(C) LeBeau will win, because Cisneros suffered no physical injury or property damage.

(D) LeBeau will win, unless Cisneros suffered severe emotional distress from LeBeau's conduct.

Questions 17-18 are based on the following fact situation:

As soon as Wanda moved into her new house, she went to the local animal shelter and selected two dogs to keep her company. The dogs were housebroken but barked constantly at birds and squirrels in the yard. Their barking was particularly incessant during the day, while Wanda was at work. Morlock, who lived next door and worked nights, was aggravated by the constant barking, which disturbed his sleep, and decided to let Wanda know how he felt. One evening, upon learning that Wanda was entertaining her boss and several clients, Morlock came to her front door with a tape recorder and an electrically amplified bullhorn. He started playing a tape of the dogs barking, putting it at full volume and amplifying it with the bullhorn. When Wanda came to the door, he began yelling at her through the bullhorn and berating her in front of her guests for having no consideration for her neighbors. Wanda, very upset, slammed the door shut. The door struck the bullhorn and jammed it against Morlock's face, knocking out two of his teeth.

17. If Wanda asserts a claim based on intentional infliction of emotional distress against Morlock, what will be the probable result?

(A) Wanda will prevail, because Morlock's conduct was extreme and outrageous.

(B) Wanda will prevail if she suffered pecuniary harm from Morlock's conduct.

(C) Morlock will prevail, because Wanda suffered no physical harm.

(D) Morlock will prevail if the barking from Wanda's dogs constituted a nuisance.

18. If Morlock asserts a claim based on battery against Wanda, will Morlock prevail?

(A) Yes, unless Wanda did not foresee that the bullhorn would knock out Morlock's teeth.

(B) Yes, if Wanda knew that the door was substantially certain to strike the bullhorn.

(C) No, because Wanda was entitled to use force to protect herself.

(D) No, if Morlock's conduct provoked Wanda's response.

Question 19

Rollerball Wreckers was in the process of demolishing a large office building that had been built in the 1920s. Unlike in a normal demolition, large chunks of masonry were apt to fall unpredictably as the wrecking process took place because of the unusual construction methods used for that building. Therefore, Rollerball surrounded the wrecking site with large signs reading "Danger! No Pedestrians in the Wrecking Area! Please Use the Sidewalk on the Opposite Side of the Street!" In addition to the signs, Rollerball placed amplified bullhorns all around the wrecking site. Each constantly broadcast a message warning of the dangers and encouraging pedestrians to avoid the wrecking site. Poohbah was in a hurry to make an appointment to play racquetball at the Downtown Athletic Club. He noticed the signs and heard the broadcasts over the bullhorns, but he did not wish to expend the additional time required to cross to the other side of the street. Poohbah moved a barricade that Rollerball had placed across the sidewalk to block it and walked past the wrecking site. When he had walked about 20 feet, a large piece of masonry fell off the building and struck Poohbah, causing him to be seriously injured. Once Poohbah was released from the hospital several weeks later, he sued Rollerball for his injuries and lost time from work. Poohbah suffers permanent disabilities from the mishap. The jurisdiction in which the accident occurred retains traditional contributory negligence doctrines.

The prevailing party in Poohbah's suit against Rollerball is likely to be:

(A) Poohbah, if Rollerball was engaged in an ultrahazardous activity.

(B) Poohbah, because the doctrine of res ispa loquitur applies.

(C) Rollerball, because Poohbah assumed the risk of injury.

(D) Rollerball, because Poohbah was contributorily negligent.

Questions 20-21 are based on the following fact situation:

Orwell, the owner of a high-rise office building, leased one-half of the 16th floor to a law firm. As part of this lease, Orwell agreed to refurbish the leased space to meet the law firm's needs and specifications. Consequently, Orwell hired Conrad to do the reconstruction work necessary.

Conrad, an experienced contractor, took the designs and specifications given to him by Orwell and prepared the work orders necessary to get bids for the subcontract work. One of the requirements for this job was that the walls and ceiling in the office space be insulated. Conrad asked for various bids for the insulation work, and Simpson was awarded the subcontract.

Simpson used a liquid-foam type of insulation substance that solidified after application on the surface of the walls and ceilings. But because the insulation material contained a flammable substance when it was wet, Simpson decided to do the spraying on a Saturday when the office building was closed.

On the day that Simpson did the spraying, he posted signs on the 16th floor saying, "Caution: Insulation spraying in progress. No smoking or open flames." Barbara, an employee who worked in one of the offices on the other side of the 16th floor, came into work on that Saturday. Although she saw the signs put up by Simpson, she decided to get her work done anyway. When she got into her office, Barbara turned on the air conditioner. But, because some vapors from Simpson's spraying had gotten into the open ventilation system, the vapors were pulled into Barbara's office when she turned on the air conditioner, and Barbara's eyes were injured by those vapors.

The insulation material used by Simpson was manufactured by National Chemical. On the can containing the material there was a label that stated "Danger. This material is extremely hazardous and volatile. Do not use near open flame. Use only with adequate ventilation." This material also contained a chemical known to be harmful to people's eyes. But in the 10 years that the product had been on the market, there was no reported case of anyone suffering an eye injury.

20. Barbara brings suit against National Chemical for the injury to her eyes on a theory of strict liability. The most likely result is that Barbara will:

(A) Prevail, because the label did not warn the user that the vapors can cause bodily harm.

(B) Prevail, because the product was being used for its intended purpose and Barbara was injured.

(C) Not prevail, because Barbara's use of the air conditioner is a superseding negligent act.

(D) Not prevail, because the long history of no injuries demonstrates that the warning on the label was adequate.

21. If Barbara sues Orwell for the injuries that she suffered, she will:

   (A) Recover, because she is an invitee of a tenant in this building.

   (B) Recover, if she can recover against National Chemical.

   (C) Not recover, unless Orwell was negligent.

   (D) Not recover, because the insulation came in a closed container.

Question 22

Mildred Minor was a three-year-old child attending nursery school. Tom Tease, who attended the same nursery school, teased Mildred every day because she wore glasses. One day when Tom's teasing was particularly vicious, Mildred slugged Tom in the face, knocking out his two newly acquired front teeth.

If Tom's parents sue Mildred's parents for damage to Tom's teeth, the best defense would be:

(A) Tom was the initial aggressor.

(B) Mildred is too young to be responsible for her actions.

(C) A parent cannot be liable for damages due to the child's conduct.

(D) They were unaware of any potentially violent behavior by Mildred.

Question 23

Tom contracted AIDS through a blood transfusion. As the disease took hold, Tom steadily weakened and had to be admitted to the hospital. During Tom's stay in the hospital, his physician, Dr. Alucard, often appeared in the hospital room with a camera. Alucard took pictures of Tom each time, documenting his weight loss and otherwise deteriorating condition. Finally, Tom's wife, Tina, was told that

Tom had only a few hours to live and so she remained at Tom's bedside. Tom weakened gradually, but then he went into a series of spasms. The nurse told Tina that Tom would only last a few minutes more. Just as Tom was about to whisper his last goodbye to Tina, Alucard entered the room with a camera. Tina asked him, "Please, Doctor, leave us alone these last few minutes." Alucard ignored Tina's pleas. He brought a large sheet of blue cardboard and said, "I need a good photo background; I'm going to put this under the pillow." As Alucard approached Tom, Tom feebly raised his hand and clenched his fist. However, his action had no effect, as Alucard raised Tom's head to slide the cardboard underneath the pillow. Alucard snapped a photograph just as Tom expired. After Tom's interment, Tina, his sole heir, wished to file suit against Alucard. She discussed the following tort actions with her attorney, Shelley:

I.   Assault and battery.

II. False light publicity.

III. Intrusion on seclusion.

IV. Publication of private facts.

Shelley should advise Tina that she is likely to recover from Alucard on a suit based on:

(A) I. only.

(B) I. and III. only.

(C) II., III., and IV. only.

(D) I., II., III., and IV.

Question 24

Dorothy was riding her bicycle along a public road when a violent storm came up. She hurried toward her home but saw a funnel cloud approaching from that direction. She immediately turned off the road and took cover in a picnic shelter that she had seen through the trees. Although the tornado passed a few hundred yards away, the shelter remained intact and Dorothy was uninjured. Unfortunately, however, a new cement floor had recently been poured for the shelter. Dorothy's footprints and tire tracks left permanent impressions in the cement, requiring the owner of the property, Putnam Enterprises, Inc., to repour the entire floor of the shelter.

What will be the result if Putnam sues Dorothy for the damages to the floor?

(A) Putnam will not prevail because Dorothy had a privilege to enter the shelter.

(B) Putnam will prevail but will only recover nominal damages because of Dorothy's privilege.

(C) Putnam will not prevail because Dorothy's entry onto Putnam's property was caused by an act of God.

(D) Putnam will recover for the damage to the floor because Dorothy's entry onto Putnam's property was for her own benefit.

Question 25

Sterling was offering to sell his three-year-old house with a large detached garage because he had just been transferred to a job in another city. Barbara saw his listing and visited the house, and then returned the next day to talk to Sterling. She asked him numerous questions about the flammability of the materials used to construct the garage, explaining that her aunt, Penelope, was considering storing some valuable antiques in that building. Sterling, who was anxious to sell, assured Barbara that all of the lumber and wallboard had been treated with a flame retardant that made the garage almost impervious to an accidental fire. At the time he said this, Sterling had no knowledge of whether the materials used for the garage had been treated with anything; in fact, they had not. Barbara purchased the house and her aunt moved all of her antiques into the garage. Three months later, the garage caught fire and burned to the ground.

In an action by Penelope against Sterling to recover for the loss of her antiques, will she prevail?

(A) Yes, because Penelope suffered pecuniary loss from the fire.

(B) Yes, if Penelope relied on the statements made to Barbara by Sterling.

(C) No, because Sterling's statements were not made in a business or professional capacity.

(D) No, because Sterling owed no duty to Penelope regarding his statements.

Question 26

Since his recent divorce, Stanley had been feeling very despondent. He drove out into the country, parked his car in an isolated area, and channeled the exhaust inside the car. Stanley got back in the car, rolled up the windows, and left the engine running, hoping that carbon monoxide would put him out of his misery.

Meanwhile, Blanche, a jogger, happened to be taking a run in the country and came upon Stanley's car. She saw a hose going into the trunk from the exhaust pipe and concluded that perhaps someone was trying to commit suicide. She looked through the windshield and saw Stanley passed out on the front seat. She tried to open the car doors, but finding them locked, she broke a window to get into the car and cut her hand badly in the process. Stanley was hospitalized for the effects of the gas and Blanche's hand required surgery to repair damaged tendons.

Is Stanley liable to Blanche for her injuries?

(A) Yes, because it was foreseeable that someone would try to rescue him.

(B) Yes, because she saved his life.

(C) No, because she did not place him in peril.

(D) No, because she was a volunteer.

Question 27

Patrick was driving north on Jambalaya Road at a speed that was seven miles per hour in excess of the legal limit. Patrick knew he was speeding, but wasn't worried about it, because he was a longtime resident of the area and he knew that all the streets crossing Jambalaya Road for the next two miles had stop signs.

Duffy had recently been transferred to the city from the Midwest and was still not completely familiar with local street arrangements and traffic patterns. Duffy's car was proceeding east on Gumbo Street, approaching its intersection with Jambalaya Road. Duffy was traveling at only 25 miles per hour, but he failed to see the stop sign at Jambalaya Road and entered the intersection without stopping. Even though Patrick was speeding, he would have had adequate time to either stop his car or swerve to avoid Duffy's vehicle, had he been paying attention. However, Patrick's mind was preoccupied with thoughts of how to rearrange his stock portfolio. Thus, Duffy's car struck Patrick's. Duffy received a few minor cuts and abrasions and one headlight of his car was shattered. Patrick suffered back and neck injuries and a broken leg, while his car was a total loss. The jurisdiction follows traditional contributory negligence and assumption of the risk rules.

If Patrick sues Duffy, what is Duffy's best defense?

(A) Duffy's running the stop sign was unintentional.

(B) Patrick was negligent in purchasing a car that would suffer heavy damage when struck at low speed.

(C) Patrick was contributorily negligent.

(D) Patrick had the last clear chance to avoid the accident.

Question 28

Willy Himan was a well-liked, middle-aged salesman in a highly competitive field. One evening Willy received a telephone call from the Middletown police. The police officer on the telephone told Willy that his son, Bippy, had been arrested for possession of a small amount of marijuana. Willy drove down to the police station to post bond for Bippy. It so happened that the *Middletown-Megaphone*, a local tabloid newspaper, kept a reporter and a photographer stationed at the central police station in Middletown. As Willy was posting bond for Bippy, the photographer took a picture of Willy. The picture showed Willy flanked by two bulky police officers, and was quite similar to pictures that newspapers often print of criminals being taken into custody. The city editor of the *Middletown-Megaphone*, faced with a dearth of news for the morning edition, decided to print the picture of Willy on page one. The picture took up close to a quarter of the page. It was accompanied by a very small caption, which read, "Willy Himan's son arrested for possession of narcotics." Willy's boss was hypersensitive about the reputation of his company and fired Willy when he saw the picture in the morning *Middletown-Megaphone*.

If Willy sues the newspaper, will he recover?

(A) Yes, for intrusion upon seclusion.

(B) Yes, for false light publicity.

(C) No, because the caption was true.

(D) No, because printing the picture was in the public interest.

Question 29

Dieter and Freya were recently engaged to be married. They went to "Katzenjammer," a popular local nightclub, to celebrate their engagement. While at Katzenjammer, they met their friend, Ingrid, who joined them at their table. Although Freya and Ingrid had several drinks, Dieter drank very moderately, telling the waiter, "I have to drive." Freya asked Dieter to give Ingrid a ride home and he readily agreed. A statute in the jurisdiction makes it an offense to drive a vehicle on any public road in the state without a valid driver's license. Dieter's license recently expired, but he was too busy with wedding plans to go to the local branch of the State Department of Motor Vehicles to renew the license. The trio left Katzenjammer and they entered Dieter's car. Dieter and Freya sat in the front seat, while Ingrid sat in back. Dieter began driving on what he felt was the best route to Ingrid's house. Ingrid told Dieter that he was going the wrong way. Dieter disagreed. Ingrid became more insistent and began yelling at Dieter. Freya agreed with Ingrid and impulsively grabbed the steering wheel. The car swerved and struck Pike, a pedestrian, injuring Pike.

If Pike sues Dieter, who will prevail?

(A) Pike, because Dieter violated a statute by driving without a valid license.

(B) Pike, because Dieter failed to control his passenger, Freya.

(C) Dieter, because Dieter did not start the argument.

(D) Dieter, because Freya's action was the proximate cause of the injury.

Questions 30-31 are based on the following fact situation:

Driver Alpha was proceeding south on the highway in his automobile. He was driving close to the shoulder and his vehicle skidded and hit a support column beneath a bridge that crossed over the highway. The impact from Alpha's car caused structural damage to the support column, and this in turn caused the bridge to drop 18 inches. The sag of the bridge was clearly visible from the highway. Alpha lay unconscious in his heavily damaged car as a result of the accident. At the time Alpha's car struck the bridge support, Beta was proceeding south on the same highway as Alpha, but Beta was five miles from the bridge at the time. When driver Beta came upon the scene of Alpha's accident, he pulled his car off the road and stopped the engine. He got out of his car and walked to Alpha's vehicle, hoping that he might be able to assist whomever was in the battered auto.

Shortly thereafter, Truckdriver ("TD") approached the scene of the accident in his semi-trailer truck. TD saw that an accident had occurred near the bridge. Under ordinary circumstances, TD's truck could have passed easily under the bridge, but the 18-inch lowering now left insufficient clearance for large trucks. TD had adequate time to slow down or stop after he noticed that there was an accident, but he proceeded ahead without reducing speed. TD's vehicle struck the lowered bridge, causing TD's truck to tip over on its side. It fell on the roof of Alpha's auto, crushing the car and killing Alpha. The impact of the truck with the bridge also caused chunks of concrete to fall from the bridge. One of these chunks struck Beta in the head, injuring Beta seriously. TD was also injured. Personal injury actions survive in this jurisdiction, and the jurisdiction follows traditional contributory negligence rules.

30. If Alpha's estate sues TD, who will prevail?

(A) Alpha's estate, but only if TD saw the dangerous condition.

(B) Alpha's estate, if a reasonable truck driver should have seen the dangerous condition.

(C) TD, because Alpha's own negligence placed Alpha in peril.

(D) TD, because the bridge clearance was usually adequate.

31. Assume for purposes of this question only that Alpha was negligent in hitting the support column. If Beta sues Alpha's estate, who will prevail?

(A) Alpha's estate, because TD's actions caused Beta's injuries.

(B) Alpha's estate, because Beta was not a foreseeable plaintiff, as Beta was five miles away when the initial accident occurred.

(C) Beta, because he stopped to render assistance.

(D) Beta, because Alpha's negligence was the proximate cause of Beta's injuries.

Question 32

Farmer hired Prufrock, a 16-year-old, for a summer agricultural labor job. Although Prufrock lived in a nearby city and was unfamiliar with rural life, both he and his parents felt that working on a farm during the summer would be beneficial to Prufrock, both physically and spiritually.

Because the type of agricultural work for which Prufrock was hired was exempt from child labor and minimum wage laws, Farmer paid Prufrock two dollars per hour. Prufrock worked part-time and was able to take a bus home to the city, provided he reached a rural bus stop on the highway before 5:30 p.m.

One afternoon, Farmer was driving a tractor, while Prufrock rode on the hayrack being towed behind Farmer's tractor. They were going up a hill, and as the tractor neared its crest, storm clouds formed suddenly. It began to rain and there were loud claps of thunder. Farmer knew that the safest place to be during an electrical storm was the low ground. Prufrock, however, had never seen an electrical storm in open country (except as a passenger inside an automobile) and had never been told how to act safely during such a storm. When the storm began, Farmer stopped his tractor, jumped off without saying anything, and ran swiftly down the hill toward the low ground. Prufrock was struck by lightning and seriously injured as he stood at the crest of the hill watching Farmer run.

Is Farmer liable to Prufrock for the injuries caused by lightning?

(A) Yes, because Prufrock was an employee, acting within the scope of his employment.

(B) Yes, because Prufrock was a minor.

(C) No, because Prufrock was injured by an act of God.

(D) No, because lightning is never foreseeable.

Question 33

Rosalie was shopping in the Ladies' Boutique, a store specializing in expensive women's clothing. Bruno, a security guard at the store, saw Rosalie holding up a blue sweater in front of a mirror and comparing its color to that of a blue scarf that she was holding in the other hand. Bruno immediately recognized the scarf as an expensive "D'Alpini" designer scarf imported from Italy and which was stocked by the Ladies' Boutique and by a few other retailers in the area. Bruno saw Rosalie put the scarf in her purse, and he discreetly kept an eye on her. Rosalie took the sweater to the cashier and paid for it. She then walked toward the exit door, only to find her way blocked by Bruno, who weighed at least twice as much as the petite Rosalie. Upon being asked by Bruno about the scarf, Rosalie pulled the scarf from her purse as well as a sales receipt showing that she had purchased the scarf two days before at the Ladies' Boutique. Bruno said to her, "That's fine, sorry to trouble you," and Rosalie left the store.

Can Rosalie successfully recover in a suit against the Ladies' Boutique?

(A) Yes, because Bruno unlawfully detained Rosalie.

(B) Yes, if the detention caused Rosalie mental distress.

(C) No, because the detention was reasonably prompted and lasted no longer than necessary.

(D) No, because the detention was insufficient to constitute an imprisonment.

Questions 34-35 are based on the following fact situation:

Sam Starr, a detective, recently retired from the St. Paul, Minnesota, Police Department. Starr had been instrumental in solving many important crimes committed in the Twin Cities area and had received many commendations from his own police superiors, the Mayor of St. Paul, and national police associations. A year after Starr's retirement to Florida, he turned on his television set and Zeta Broadcasting System ("ZBS") was presenting a docu-drama entitled "To Nab a Crook." At the beginning of the show, Starr saw among the credits, "This story is based upon the life of Detective Sam Starr of the St. Paul, Minnesota, Police Department; however, this is a dramatization and in order to enhance the dramatic effect of the show as entertainment, not every event depicted in this show actually happened as portrayed by the professional actors in the show." Once the show was over, Starr was furious. Some parts of the show dealt fairly accurately with some of the crimes Starr had helped solve in Minnesota, but other parts, under the rubric of "enhancing the dramatic effect," portrayed "Detective Pat Smith" (the Starr-like character) as being involved in several James Bond-type sexual escapades.

34. If Starr sues ZBS for invasion of privacy, who will prevail?

   (A) Starr, because his name was appropriated by ZBS for a commercial purpose.

   (B) Starr, because the seclusion of his retirement has been upset.

   (C) Starr, because he has been portrayed in a false light.

   (D) ZBS, if the show as a whole was complimentary to Starr.

35. Assume for purposes of this question only that the court finds that ZBS has defamed Starr. To what damages would Starr be entitled?

   (A) Nominal damages only, unless Starr can show actual pecuniary loss.

   (B) General damages, even without actual proof of injury.

   (C) Only damages based on competent evidence of actual injury.

   (D) No damages, unless Starr can prove actual malice on the part of ZBS.

Question 36

   Martha, the wife of the president of a small but very prestigious private college located in Boston, Massachusetts, was an instructor at the college. While doing research for an article profiling Martha's husband, a reporter for a Boston newspaper discovered and revealed in a published news story that Martha had falsified her academic credentials when she applied for a position with the college, before she married the president. The story stated that she had attended the state university of a midwestern state, and not the London School of Economics, as her resume had claimed, and that her credentials were not properly verified because the president of the college, a former United States Secretary of State, had been courting Martha at the time she applied for her position as an instructor.

   As a result of the news story, Martha was widely ridiculed in the media and subjected to numerous jokes and innuendo among her colleagues. She asserted a cause of action against the newspaper for defamation. A deposition of the reporter who wrote the story revealed that he had obtained his information from a member of the State Department and that Martha's attendance at the midwestern university had been verified by telephone with its registrar.

   Will Martha prevail at trial?

   (A) Yes, if the story printed by the newspaper was false.

   (B) Yes, because the story revealed facts about her private affairs not generally known to the public.

   (C) No, because the newspaper did not publish the story with knowledge that it was false or with reckless disregard for its truth or falsity.

   (D) No, if the newspaper was not negligent.

Questions 37-39 are based on the following fact situation:

Greg was a seven-year-old boy who often came onto Mr. Smith's property to play with Mr. Smith's dog. Mr. Smith was aware that this occurred. When Mr. Smith decided to put in a swimming pool, a couple of large pieces of equipment were left in his backyard overnight by Jones Corp., the construction company. The equipment was not owned by Jones Corp. but was leased from Brown Co., which was responsible for its repair and maintenance. After the workers had left, Greg came onto the Smith property to play. Eventually, he climbed up on one of the pieces of equipment, which had no safety locking device on the ignition, and began pushing buttons and moving levers. The engine started and the equipment began to move. Greg became frightened and jumped off, falling into the hole that had been dug that day, and was injured. Greg's parents brought suit against Mr. Smith and Jones Corp. in a jurisdiction that retains joint and several liability.

37. In Greg's suit against Mr. Smith, who will prevail?

 (A) Greg, because Mr. Smith is strictly liable for ultrahazardous activity on his property.

 (B) Greg, because his presence on Mr. Smith's property was reasonably foreseeable.

 (C) Mr. Smith, because Greg was a trespasser.

 (D) Mr. Smith, because he had no duty to inspect the safety features of the equipment.

38. If Jones Corp. is held liable for Greg's injuries, Jones Corp. could:

 (A) Obtain indemnity from Brown Co. if the equipment was negligently maintained in an unsafe condition.

 (B) Obtain contribution from Brown Co. if the equipment was negligently maintained in an unsafe condition.

 (C) Obtain indemnity from both Brown Co. and Mr. Smith.

 (D) Not recover any damages it paid from any other party.

39. Assume for the purposes of this question only that Greg's parents filed suit against both Jones Corp. and Brown Co. but not against Mr. Smith, and that the jury found the defendants jointly and severally liable for Greg's injuries in the amount of $6,000. Which of the following is a correct statement of the defendants' liability?

 (A) Both defendants would be liable for the full amount.

 (B) The defendants would be liable for damages based upon their relative fault.

 (C) Each defendant would be liable for $3,000.

 (D) Greg could recover $6,000 from each defendant.

Questions 40-41 are based on the following fact situation:

While driving his car down the road, Ashton experienced a heart attack. Because of this, Ashton's car crossed the center line of the highway and headed directly at a car driven by Simpson. Simpson, seeing Ashton's car heading toward him, swerved to avoid the collision. In so doing, Simpson's son, Russell, was thrown through the sun roof of the car when a latch on the sun roof sprung open. Russell landed in a ditch beside the road, filled with water. He suffered severe injuries and almost drowned in the ditch. The automobile driven by Simpson was manufactured by the Modo Automobile Company.

40. If Russell brings suit against Ashton for the injuries sustained in the accident, Russell will:

    (A) Prevail if Ashton's act was a substantial factor in causing the car driven by Simpson to swerve.

    (B) Prevail if Ashton violated a statute by crossing the center line.

    (C) Not prevail if Ashton had no prior history of heart trouble.

    (D) Not prevail, because Ashton's actions did not create a foreseeable risk of harm from driving.

41. If Russell brings suit against the Modo Automobile Company for the injuries sustained in the accident, Russell will:

    (A) Prevail if it was economically feasible to install a more secure latch.

    (B) Prevail, because the latch sprang open when the car swerved.

    (C) Not prevail, because the car was not being used in the normal manner when the roof came open.

    (D) Not prevail if Simpson was negligent in swerving the car.

Questions 42-44 are based on the following fact situation:

One of the employees of Department Store informed the head of security that he suspected a customer of shoplifting. The employee pointed out Wilma as the suspected shoplifter. The head of security, unfortunately, thought the employee was pointing at Martha. He waited until Martha had left the store and then followed her outside. He went up to Martha, pulled a gun, and requested that Martha return with him to the Department Store offices. Martha did so, even though she insisted that she had not done anything wrong. Martha was kept waiting in the Department Store offices for an hour, until the employee informed the head of security that he had arrested the wrong woman. Martha was terribly embarrassed by the entire incident because a number of her friends had seen the guard take her into the offices.

42. If Martha sues Department Store on the theory of assault, she will:

    (A) Prevail if she saw the gun pointed at her.

    (B) Prevail if Department Store's belief that she was the right woman was unreasonable.

    (C) Not prevail, because Martha suffered no injury.

    (D) Not prevail if there was no intent to injure.

43. If Martha sues Department Store on the theory of false imprisonment, she will:

    (A) Prevail, unless Department Store was reasonable in believing that she was the right woman.

    (B) Prevail, because she was intentionally detained.

    (C) Not prevail, because the period for which Martha was detained was the minimal period necessary to establish her identity.

    (D) Not prevail, because Martha suffered no harm.

44. If Martha sues Department Store for damages for her humiliation, Martha will:

    (A) Prevail if she was falsely imprisoned.

    (B) Prevail if Department Store was negligent in identifying her.

    (C) Not prevail, because humiliation is not actionable.

    (D) Not prevail, unless Department Store's conduct was extremely outrageous.

Question 45

Mineralco owned a tract of land believed to be rich in mineral deposits. It contracted with Digger for the removal of soil from the property and delivery of the soil to Mineralco's laboratories. While one of Mineralco's trucks was on the way to the laboratory, the rear gate broke loose, dumping three tons of soil onto the highway. Turner, who was driving a short but safe distance behind the truck, was unable to stop in time and collided with the soil, causing serious injury to Turner. The rear gate had been negligently secured by one of Digger's employees.

If Turner sues Mineralco for his injuries, will he prevail?

(A) No, because the rear gate was secured by Digger's employee.

(B) No, if Digger had a license to transport soil on the highway.

(C) No, unless Mineralco was subject to a nondelegable duty in respect to the movement of its soil on the highway.

(D) No, if in the area where the accident occurred the transportation of soil on the highways was common practice.

Question 46

Able and Baker owned adjacent parcels of land in an area that was zoned for commercial use. Baker constructed four tennis courts on his property and equipped them with bright lights for night use. The tennis court operated 365 days a year and was kept open until 2 a.m. Five years later, a new shopping center was built one mile from Able's and Baker's properties, making their parcels highly desirable for residential purposes. Able decided to construct several residential units on his property, but his architect informed him that, because of the lights, the residences facing the tennis courts would have to be equipped with light-proof draperies that would have to be kept closed until after the tennis courts close each night.

If Able asserts a claim based on nuisance against Baker, who is likely to prevail?

(A) Able, because the residences will constitute higher use of the property than the tennis courts.

(B) Able, because the glitter from the lights interferes with the use and enjoyment of Able's property.

(C) Baker, because the area was zoned for commercial use when the tennis courts were built.

(D) Baker, because the tennis courts were built before Able planned his residential development.

Questions 47-48 are based on the following fact situation:

One Saturday, Joseph, age 10, was walking past an office building being constructed when he saw several of his playmates from school climbing on the large concrete pipes used by the construction company to install the sewer system for the building. Joseph decided to join his friends, and was soon enjoying the game of "superheroes" they all were playing. During one particularly fierce confrontation between Tammy, also age 10, and Joseph, Tammy struck Joseph in the face with her "sword" (a piece of sheet metal left as scrap by the builders) and seriously injured his eye.

47. Joseph's parents bring an action against Tammy and her parents for negligence and intentional tort. The insurance company representing Tammy's family raises the defense of contributory negligence as to the negligence cause of action, alleging that Joseph was engaged in a mock battle with Tammy with his own pretend "sword," another piece of metal. When the court instructs the jury as to the standard to be applied to Joseph's conduct, it should state that:

(A) Joseph's conduct is judged by what a person of ordinary prudence and caution would have done in the same circumstances.

(B) Joseph's conduct is judged by what a child of similar age, experience, and intelligence would have done in similar circumstances.

(C) Joseph's conduct is immaterial, because Tammy committed an intentional tort when she purposely struck Joseph in the eye.

(D) Joseph's conduct is immaterial, because it is presumed that a child under the age of 14 cannot be negligent.

48. Assume for the purposes of this question only that Joseph was negligent in engaging in the combat with Tammy. The action against Tammy's family is brought by Joseph's mother on his behalf as his guardian ad litem. Joseph's father also brings an action against Tammy's family for the cost of the medical treatment he paid for his son. If the jurisdiction follows traditional rules of contributory negligence, Joseph's father will:

(A) Not recover, because Joseph was contributorily negligent.

(B) Not recover, because Joseph suffered the injuries, not his father.

(C) Recover, because his action is independent of Joseph's, not derivative of it.

(D) Recover, because contributory negligence does not apply to a child under the age of 14.

Questions 49-50 are based on the following fact situation:

Rancher owned a large parcel of vacant land just outside City which motorcyclists frequently used for impromptu motorcross competitions. Rancher knew about this use of his land and while he was not particularly happy about it, he had no immediate plans for the parcel and took no action. The motorcyclists had been riding there every weekend for about two years. One weekend, Rancher drove out to the parcel to do some target shooting with a new .22 caliber rifle he had just bought. He set up some beer cans left by the motorcyclists and was plinking away when Rider arrived at the area with his dirt bike. Rider had been drinking and continued to drink beer as he drove his bike around Rancher's parcel. Just as Rider was trying a particularly dangerous stunt on his dirt bike, one of Rancher's shots struck a rock and ricocheted, passing through Rider's upper arm. Rider was able to ride his bike one-handed to nearby Hospital, where he was treated for a gunshot wound. The jurisdiction has adopted a "pure" comparative negligence statute and retained joint and several liability.

49. Rider brings an action for negligence against Rancher. Rider will probably:

(A) Recover all of his damages.

(B) Recover a portion of his damages, because he was negligent in driving his motorcycle while drunk and attempting the dangerous stunt.

(C) Not recover, because driving while drunk is gross negligence or worse.

(D) Not recover, because he was a trespasser on Rancher's land.

50. Assume for the purposes of this question only that when Rider was treated at Hospital, the emergency room physician was negligent, and as a result, Rider never recovered full use of his arm and could not ride his motorcycle in motorcross ever again. Rider's earnings as a carpenter were also permanently reduced. It is stipulated at trial that Rancher was negligent in target shooting in the same area as the motorcycle riders. The result will be:

(A) Rider will recover all of his damages, including the permanent disability, from Rancher.

(B) Rider will recover the portion of his damages attributable to a properly treated .22 caliber gunshot wound from Rancher.

(C) Rider will recover nothing from Rancher.

(D) Rider will recover all of his damages from Rancher only if he (Rider) joins the negligent doctor as a defendant and the doctor fails to satisfy that portion of the judgment attributable to his negligence.

Question 51

In response to a number of accidents involving pedestrians in the local business district, City enacted a statute making it illegal for a pedestrian to walk through City's central business district anywhere other than on the sidewalk. City also enacted a statute making it illegal for any business to obstruct the sidewalk in front of its establishment. As Turner was walking along the sidewalk in the central business district on his way to lunch, he discovered that Loader had stacked a pile of boxes in front of his establishment in such a way that it totally obstructed the sidewalk. Turner stepped into the street to walk around the obstruction of boxes. While in the street, Turner was struck by a taxicab, negligently driven by Cabbie. The jurisdiction follows traditional contributory negligence rules.

If Turner asserts a claim against Cabbie, Turner's act of leaving the sidewalk and walking into the street will have which of the following effects?

(A) It will bar Turner's recovery as a matter of law.

(B) It will bar Turner's recovery unless Cabbie saw Turner in time to avoid the impact.

(C) It may be considered by the trier of fact on the issue of Cabbie's liability.

(D) It is not relevant in determining the rights of Turner.

Questions 52-54 are based on the following fact situation:

Fixit owns and operates a small repair store. In addition to repairing virtually any broken item, Fixit occasionally purchases items in need of repair, rebuilds them, and resells them. Cutter, who runs a gardening service, stopped by Fixit's shop to purchase a lawn mower. He saw a lawn mower that had been originally manufactured by Lawnco for sale in Fixit's shop. The lawn mower had a sign on it which read, "Totally reconditioned." While inspecting the lawn mower, Cutter noticed that the lawn mower had a heavy duty blade on it designed for cutting thick weeds. Knowing that he needed the lawn mower for lawn cutting only, Cutter told Fixit that he would buy the lawn mower if Fixit could put a lighter weight blade on the lawn mower. Fixit agreed and installed a lightweight blade designed for lawn cutting onto the lawn mower. The blade was manufactured by Grass Master Company and was not designed to be used on a Lawnco mower. Two weeks later, Worker, an employee of Cutter's gardening service, was injured while using the lawn mower. Worker's leg was severely cut. As a result, Cutter had to give up half of his customers for a two-week period until a replacement for Worker could be found. Assume that the jurisdiction follows traditional contributory negligence rules.

52. If Worker was injured because the blade flew off the lawn mower when a restraining bolt holding the blade in place broke, and if Worker asserts a claim based on strict liability in tort against Lawnco, Worker will probably:

(A) Recover, because Lawnco put the lawn mower in the stream of commerce.

(B) Recover if the restraining bolt that broke was a part of the lawn mower when it was new.

(C) Not recover, because the lawn mower had been rebuilt by Fixit.

(D) Not recover, because Worker was not in privity of contract with Lawnco.

53. If Worker was injured because the blade flew off the lawn mower when the restraining bolt holding the blade in place broke, and if Cutter asserts a claim based on strict liability in tort against Fixit for loss of business because of the injury to Worker, Cutter will probably:

(A) Recover, because the reconditioned lawn mower was the actual and proximate cause of Cutter's loss of business.

(B) Recover, because Fixit knew the lawn mower was to be used in Cutter's gardening business.

(C) Not recover, because economic loss from injury to an employee is not within the scope of Fixit's duty.

(D) Not recover, because Fixit was not the manufacturer of the lawn mower.

54. Assume for purposes of this question only that while Worker was using the lawn mower to cut through a patch of heavy weeds, the blade broke and a piece of it flew off the lawn mower and severely cut Worker's leg. If Worker asserts a claim based on strict liability in tort against Grass Master Company, the defense most likely to prevail is:

(A) Worker was not in privity of contract with Grass Master Company.

(B) Worker was contributorily negligent in using the lightweight blade to cut heavy weeds.

(C) Grass Master used every available means to inspect and discover defects in the blade.

(D) Grass Master could not foresee that the grass blade might be used on heavy weeds.

Questions 55-58 are based on the following fact situation:

Linda sprained her ankle while skiing and went to the emergency clinic at Hospital. A nurse had Linda soak her ankle in ice water to bring down the swelling, and told her to wait in the room as the doctor would be in to check her ankle in a half hour after the swelling had gone down. Only several minutes later, however, Myron came into her room and told her he was her doctor. In fact, Myron was a harmless mental patient who was in an outpatient program at Hospital's mental health section.

Myron proceeded to examine Linda's hurt ankle, causing her some discomfort but no injury. However, when he decided to bandage the ankle, Myron made the bandage too tight and Linda was in pain. When Linda complained, Myron told her he would give her a shot that would stop the pain. But Linda was afraid of shots and told Myron she would prefer pain pills instead. Myron said that pain pills would take too long to be of any use, and started to give Linda the shot, but the nurse came back and caught him.

55. In a suit by Linda against Myron for battery, Myron asserted as a defense that he was a mental patient. This defense is:

(A) Not valid, because Myron was only an outpatient.

(B) Not valid, if Myron had the state of mind to commit battery.

(C) Valid, because mental patients cannot be held responsible for their actions.

(D) Valid, if Myron really believed he was a doctor.

56. Myron contends as a defense that Linda consented to his touching her. This defense is:

(A) Invalid, because Linda thought he was a doctor.

(B) Invalid, because Linda did not want a shot.

(C) Valid, because Linda was not injured by Myron's conduct.

(D) Valid, because in an emergency situation, consent is presumed.

57. If Linda sued Myron for false imprisonment, she is most likely to:

(A) Prevail, because her injuries prevented her from leaving the room without being harmed.

(B) Prevail, because she would not have stayed in the room if Myron had not pretended to be a doctor.

(C) Not prevail, because Myron would have let her leave if she wanted.

(D) Not prevail, because she had no reason to believe that she could not leave.

58. If Linda sued Hospital for negligence, which of the following defenses would most likely show that Hospital is not liable?

(A) Linda had been told the doctor would not see her until the swelling had gone down; therefore, she was not justified in believing Myron was a doctor.

(B) Myron's conduct was an independent intervening cause that cuts off Hospital's liability.

(C) Hospital had no reason to believe Myron would impersonate a doctor, and had otherwise taken every precaution.

(D) Linda was not really injured by anything Myron did.

Questions 59-62 are based on the following fact situation:

Ken and Steve worked together for many years as night countermen in Liquor Store. In the last few months, however, Steve became very upset over personal problems and began to drink on the job. Ken knew of Steve's personal problems, so he covered for Steve at the store and would send Steve home when he became too drunk to work. Then one day Ken realized that Steve had been taking money from the cash register. Ken did not want to get Steve fired, so he decided to quit and find another job. He did not tell his employer about Steve because there had not been very much money taken, and Ken believed that if Steve had the sole responsibility of running the store at night he would quit his drinking.

Not long after Ken left, Jose, a friend of his, who knew the reasons why Ken had quit, came into the store one night to buy some beer and cigarettes. Steve, who obviously had had something to drink, started to talk with him about the store. When Jose asked Steve if he found it difficult to be the only counterman at night now that Ken was gone, Steve said, "Yes, but when we found that Ken was stealing from the cash register we had no choice but to let him go."

59. If Ken sues Steve for defamation, Ken must show:

(A) He suffered special damages by reason of Steve's oral statement.

(B) He was fired from his new position as a liquor clerk.

(C) His former employer at Liquor Store did not think he was a thief.

(D) Only that Steve accused him of being a dishonest employee.

60. The fact that Jose knew the truth of why Ken really left:

(A) Acts as a complete defense to the claim of relief for defamation.

(B) Establishes that Ken has not suffered any injury.

(C) May diminish the damages Ken would be entitled to recover.

(D) Proves that Steve had no reasonable ground for believing that Ken was fired for dishonesty.

61. If Steve had accused Ken of the thievery without any other person being present, Ken may:

(A) Sue Steve for defamation, because Steve had no reason to believe that the accusation was true.

(B) Sue Steve for defamation, because the money was really missing, and Ken might have been arrested for embezzlement.

(C) Sue Steve for intentional infliction of emotional distress.

(D) Sue Steve for negligent infliction of emotional distress.

62. If Ken sued Steve for defamation, and Steve defended the action by alleging that it was true that Ken stole money from the cash register, Ken would:

(A) Be able to sue Steve in another defamation action because there is a new publication.

(B) Be able to sue Steve in another defamation action only if he can show that Steve did not believe the allegation to be true.

(C) Not be able to sue Steve in another defamation action because the accusation is absolutely privileged.

(D) Not be able to sue Steve in another defamation action because of the doctrine of collateral estoppel.

Questions 63-68 are based on the following fact situation:

One night when Dean and Alice had been drinking at a party, they decided they would take Dean's new four-wheel-drive vehicle for a test drive off the road. The nearest open area where they could drive the vehicle was in a large county park area near their home. A county ordinance, however, restricted the area for use by hikers, bike riders, and horse riders; vehicle traffic was totally prohibited on any of the riding or hiking trails.

In spite of the posted signs prohibiting vehicles on the bridle paths, Dean and Alice entered the county park by way of a narrow bridle path. A little while later, when trying to negotiate a sharp turn, the vehicle slipped and fell down a steep incline. As the vehicle fell, it turned over several times, landing on its tires when it reached the bottom of the incline. The vehicle was equipped with a roll bar, which was intended to protect the passengers in the event the vehicle turned over, but on the first or second turn-over the roll bar had collapsed. Dean was killed in the accident, and Alice suffered severe head and back injuries.

The vehicle was manufactured overseas by Musashi Motors and exported to the United States without the roll bar. When the vehicle arrived in the United States, a manufacturer of recreational safety equipment, Saf-T, installed the roll bars on Musashi's four-wheel-drive vehicles. Musashi had factory representatives at Saf-T to inspect samples of the manufactured roll bars and to conduct tests on a sample number of the vehicles after installation.

Alice sued both Musashi and Saf-T for her injuries. The jurisdiction follows traditional contributory negligence rules. Evidence at trial shows that Musashi had tested a sample of the roll bars in the same series as the one installed in Dean's vehicle, and had conducted its normal tests with regard to the installations. The particular roll bar installed on Dean's car, however, had a series of hairline cracks in the welded area of the brace that weakened the roll bar to the extent that it would collapse when the vehicle turned over.

63. In a negligence action by Alice against Musashi, Musashi cites as a defense the violation of the county ordinance by Dean. This violation of the ordinance will have the following effect:

(A) It bars recovery by Alice.

(B) It bars recovery by Alice only if it can be shown that she agreed with Dean to go driving in the county park.

(C) It will not bar recovery by Alice, because at the time she and Dean went into the park it was closed.

(D) It will not bar recovery by Alice.

64. Assume Musashi can show that Dean was negligent. Such proof would have the following effect on Alice's claim against Musashi:

(A) It would totally bar recovery by Alice.

(B) It would bar recovery by Alice if it is shown that Dean was the sole legal cause of Alice's injuries.

(C) It would bar recovery by Alice if it is shown that there is a direct connection between Dean's negligence and Alice's injuries.

(D) It would have no effect if Musashi had failed to test the roll bar.

65. In a suit for negligence, Alice must at least be able to show the following facts to establish a case against Musashi:

(A) Musashi failed to inspect the roll bar on Dean's vehicle.

(B) The roll bar on Dean's vehicle was defective.

(C) The roll bar on Dean's vehicle was defective, and Musashi inspected the

roll bar but failed to discover the defect.

(D) The roll bar on Dean's vehicle was defective, and Musashi could have discovered the defect if it had inspected the vehicle properly.

66. Of the following, the best defense Musashi could assert against Alice in her negligence action is that:

(A) Saf-T had guaranteed the reliability of its product, and, therefore, Musashi was under no obligation to inspect.

(B) The roll bar was not designed to withstand the type of stress it suffered in the accident.

(C) Musashi's inspection procedures were reasonable under the circumstances.

(D) Saf-T manufactured the roll bar, and, therefore, it must be held solely liable for any defects.

67. To establish a showing of strict liability against Saf-T, Alice must:

(A) Show that the roll bar was defective and failed to work in the proper manner, causing her injuries.

(B) Show that her head and back injuries occurred as a result of the accident.

(C) Show that she was wearing a seatbelt at the time of the accident.

(D) Rely on the doctrine of res ipsa loquitur.

68. In the negligence suit by Alice, Saf-T asserts that it is not liable for the accident because the defect could have been found if Musashi had properly inspected. As against Alice, this defense would:

(A) Protect Saf-T from liability, because it no longer had a "duty" to Alice.

(B) Protect Saf-T from liability, because under the reasonable person test, it was justified in relying on Musashi's testing.

(C) Not protect Saf-T from liability, because Musashi had no obligation to test every roll bar.

(D) Not protect Saf-T from liability, because Saf-T could be liable for negligence regardless of Musashi's inspection.

Questions 69-70 are based on the following fact situation:

Eb was driving his car negligently along a mountain road. He lost control of his car and careened over the side of a cliff. Tom, a passing motorist, saw Eb's car go off the road and stopped to see if he could help. Tom started to climb down the cliff to render aid to Eb. In doing so, Tom slipped and broke his leg.

69. If Tom sues Eb to recover damages for his broken leg:

(A) Tom's best chance of recovery would be on the basis of an intentional tort.

(B) Tom would have to show that Eb breached a duty to Tom not to place himself in a position of danger that might invite a rescue.

(C) Tom could recover under the Andrews view of duty.

(D) Tom could not recover under the Cardozo view of duty.

70. Regarding any defenses Eb might raise, which of the following statements is correct?

(A) A rescuer acts at his own peril.

(B) The excitement of the accident and the speedy response of the rescuer would be considered in a case such as this.

(C) Assumption of the risk cannot be invoked against rescuers.

(D) Eb would not have a valid defense.

Questions 71-72 are based on the following fact situation:

Fred was rushed from work to the Charity Hospital emergency room with excruciating pain in his lower left side. The emergency room doctor on duty quickly diagnosed the problem as a ruptured spleen. Fred was immediately taken to the operating room, and Doctor operated on Fred. Fred recovered from the operation and was released. Nine years later, Fred was promoted to a classified job that required a complete physical. One of the x-rays detected foreign metallic matter in his left side. Upon further examination and x-rays, it was determined that Fred had a small surgeon's clamp lodged in his left side. Recovery for negligence in the jurisdiction is limited to two years.

71. Fred brings an action joining Charity Hospital and Doctor as defendants, alleging negligence. In his complaint, he alleges that he does not know which of the defendants is responsible for the damages. Which of the following theories of law would be most helpful to Fred's suit?

(A) Respondeat superior.

(B) Res ipsa loquitur.

(C) Contribution.

(D) Indemnity.

72. Charity Hospital and Doctor file a general denial and a special affirmative defense alleging that the statute of limitations is a bar to the action. Fred's attorney makes a motion to strike the special affirmative defense. The motion should be:

(A) Granted, because the statute of limitations is tolled under the circumstances.

(B) Granted, because of the common law rule that one must know of a wrong in order to have a remedy.

(C) Denied, because the facts do not present an exception to the statute of limitations.

(D) Denied as to Doctor, but granted as to Charity Hospital.

Questions 73-74 are based on the following fact situation:

Michael asked Oscar if he could borrow the latter's pickup truck to use for hauling some firewood, and Oscar agreed. Michael drove his car to Oscar's house, parked it, and left in Oscar's truck. While Michael was driving back to his home to pick up his wife, Sally, Oscar remembered that the linkage in the truck's steering had been damaged in a recent off-road excursion, so he telephoned Sally and told her to warn Michael that the steering might fail in any violent maneuvering. Michael arrived home about 20 minutes later, and he and Sally prepared to drive to the mountains to cut wood. Sally, in the bustle of packing a picnic lunch and loading tools into the pickup, forgot to tell Michael about the steering. As Michael and his wife approached a gas station near their home, intending to refuel the pickup for the wood cutting trip, Inez, driving her car, made a left turn directly in front of Michael without looking to see if any cars were approaching. Michael jerked the pickup's wheel sharply to the left, and the steering gave way. The truck smashed into the rear of the car, and Michael suffered injuries. If the steering of the pickup had not been defective because of the damaged linkage, Michael could have swerved around the car, avoiding a collision.

73. If Michael asserts a claim for personal injuries against Oscar, who will prevail?

(A) Oscar, because the failure of Sally to tell Michael about the steering on the pickup was the cause in fact of Michael's injuries.

(B) Oscar, because as a gratuitous lender, his duty of care to Michael was very slight.

(C) Michael, because Oscar was strictly liable for any damages caused by the defective steering in his truck.

(D) Michael, because Oscar failed to tell him that the steering on the pickup was defective.

74. Assume for purposes of this question only that Inez had borrowed her friend Trudy's car to go on a job interview, and the accident occurred while Inez was rushing to the interview. If Michael asserts a claim against Trudy for personal injuries, he will probably:

(A) Not recover, because the immediate cause of the collision was the failure of the pickup's steering.

(B) Not recover, because Sally's negligence in not telling him about the steering defect will be imputed to him.

(C) Recover, because a car owner is vicariously liable for the tortious acts of the driver.

(D) Recover, if the jurisdiction has enacted a permissive use statute.

Questions 75-76 are based upon the following fact situation:

Homer was very proud of the spacious and superbly maintained landscaping around his home in a suburban neighborhood. But as he grew older, walking behind the mower during his frequent lawn cutting sessions gradually became an unbearable ordeal. When he saw a three-by-five card on the bulletin board at the senior citizens' center advertising a "practically new" riding mower at about half the price of a similar machine from a dealer, Homer immediately contacted the seller, who he discovered lived just two blocks away in the same neighborhood, and bought the mower for cash.

Unknown to Homer, although the mower was in good mechanical condition and suffered from no structural problems, it contained a design defect that caused it to topple over if the steering wheel were turned too sharply while the machine was in motion. One day, as Homer was using the riding mower to cut the grass in front of his residence, a group of college students, one of whom lived nearby, came roller blading down the sidewalk bordering Homer's front lawn. All of the students had been drinking, and Biff, something of a showoff, was quite intoxicated. Just as the group passed near Homer, mowing near the sidewalk, Biff shouted, "Look, I'm Dorothy Hamill!" and attempted to do a double axel. Flailing about in the air, Biff tumbled onto Homer's lawn directly in the path of the mower. Homer attempted to swerve violently to the left to avoid him, but the mower toppled forward, dumping Homer and itself over and giving Homer a concussion.

75. Homer brings an appropriate action against Biff for damages in state court. Will Homer recover for his injuries?

(A) No, if Biff can show that the manufacturer of the mower is strictly liable for Homer's injuries.

(B) No, if Biff can prove that Homer would not have been injured but for the existence of the design defect in the mower.

(C) Yes, because Homer was injured as a result of trying to avoid running over Biff.

(D) Yes, because Biff was negligent in trying to do the difficult skating maneuver while intoxicated.

76. Assume for the purposes of this question only that Homer had also named the private seller of the mower as a defendant in his action for personal injuries. Will Homer recover against the seller?

(A) No, unless the seller knew of the design defect when he sold the mower to Homer.

(B) No, because the mower worked properly in ordinary use.

(C) Yes, because the mower contained the design defect when the seller transferred ownership to Homer.

(D) Yes, if the seller had warranted to Homer that the mower had been well-maintained.

Question 77

While at a party, Becky came up behind Tanya, grabbed her by her arm, and accused Tanya of having an affair with Becky's husband. Becky knew that her accusation was not true.

Of the following facts, which would be most helpful to Tanya in a suit against Becky for intentional infliction of emotional distress?

(A) Becky knew that Tanya is very religious, and her religious beliefs strongly condemn adultery.

(B) When Becky grabbed her arm, it caused Tanya great pain and she has suffered an upset stomach from the trauma of it.

(C) Other people at the party overheard Becky's accusation.

(D) Tanya's employer heard of the accusation and did not give her a promotion.

TORTS ANSWERS

Answer to Question 1

(B)   Evidence that Puro complied with applicable statutes will be admissible to show that Puro acted with ordinary, reasonable care, and is the only one of the listed arguments that would be helpful to Puro. Puro is being sued on a negligence theory; thus, Beaver must prove that Puro failed to exercise ordinary, reasonable care in bottling and distributing the water. Violation of a statute will establish a conclusive presumption of duty and breach of duty. However, compliance with an applicable statute does not necessarily establish due care, because due care may require more than is called for by the statute. Nevertheless, compliance with a statute is admissible as evidence that a defendant may have acted with due care. Thus, Puro could use its compliance with the water bottling statutes as a means of establishing that it conformed with its duty to use ordinary, reasonable care. (A) is incorrect because a products liability action based on negligence uses the same causation analysis as a standard negligence case. Thus, a defendant's liability is not cut off by a foreseeable intervening force that comes into motion after the defendant's original negligent act. Consequently, an intermediary's negligent failure to discover a defect is not a superseding cause, and the defendant whose original negligence created the defect will be held liable along with the intermediary. Hence, Don's negligent failure to inspect the water for purity will not relieve Puro of liability for the consequences of its own negligence, if any. (C) will not be helpful to Puro because this question allows for use of res ipsa loquitur. Under this doctrine, if a plaintiff shows that his injury is of a type that would not normally occur in the absence of negligence, and that such negligence is attributable to the defendant (*e.g.*, by showing that the instrumentality causing the injury was in the exclusive control of the defendant), the trier of fact is permitted to infer the defendant's negligence. Here, impurities would not normally get into the bottled water in the absence of negligence, and the fact that the container from which Beaver drank was unopened allows the trier of fact to infer that the impurity entered the water due to negligence on the part of Puro. Therefore, Beaver is not required to introduce evidence as to how the impurity got into the water in order to prevail. (D) is incorrect because Puro's duty of due care in the context of products liability arises from having placed the water into the stream of commerce. Having done so, Puro owes a duty to any foreseeable plaintiff, whether such person be an actual purchaser of the water or merely a user thereof. With the placing of the water into the stream of commerce, Beaver is a foreseeable plaintiff as a drinker of the water, regardless of the fact that he obtained the water by means of theft.

Answer to Question 2

(C)   One of the elements of a prima facie case for products liability based on strict liability is causation of some harm to the plaintiff by a defective product. Beaver must show that Puro owed a strict duty as a commercial supplier of water, and that Puro breached such duty by marketing a product that was so defective as to be unreasonably dangerous. In addition, the defect must have actually and proximately caused some harm to the plaintiff, and there must be damages. If, as (C) states, Beaver can produce no evidence that the illness he suffered was caused by the water's impurities, then he cannot prove the element of causation. Absent causation, a cause of action for strict liability will not lie. (A) is not as helpful to Puro as (C) because it does not preclude Beaver from establishing a prima facie case for strict liability. The fact that the impurity in the water was a rare amoeba might allow Puro to claim that it was not feasible to make the water safer than it was (*i.e.,* a "state of the art" defense), but the success of this argument is much less certain than the argument of no causation raised by choice (C). (B) is incorrect because Puro owes a strict duty as a commercial supplier to refrain from selling a defective product. There is no requirement that the defendant in a strict liability action have manufactured or processed the product, only that the defendant be a commercial supplier of the product. Puro is a commercial supplier of the water by marketing it to retail outlets. Therefore, Puro can be strictly liable even if the water is sold in its natural state. (D) is incorrect because, even if the water was actually bottled by another company, Puro also owes a strict duty as the company that markets the water to retail outlets and is thus part of the distributive chain.

Answer to Question 3

(D) Liability under (A), (B), or (C) would require that the American Campers Association be either a commercial supplier or a seller of the water. Because the Association is neither, negligence provides the only possible basis for recovery of the alternatives listed. Here, the Association may occupy such a position of prominence in the field of camping equipment and accessories that it was reasonably foreseeable that a person might be influenced by the recommendation on the bottle into drinking the water. It might be deemed reasonably foreseeable that such a person would be injured if the Association failed to exercise ordinary, reasonable care in checking out the quality of the product being endorsed. If, in fact, the Association failed to so investigate, this could create an unreasonable risk of injury to a person in the position of Beaver, who would consume a product that was tainted, thinking it to be free of impurities. Such facts would give rise to a finding that Puro had breached a duty of reasonable care owed to Beaver, thereby causing his illness. (A) is incorrect because an express warranty arises where a seller or supplier makes any affirmation of fact or promise to the buyer relating to the goods that becomes part of the basis of the bargain. Although the Association may have made an affirmation of fact that the water was "100% pure spring water," the Association is not a seller or supplier of the water, but is simply endorsing the product. Thus, an express warranty did not come into existence. (B) is incorrect because a warranty of merchantability is implied in a sale by a merchant who deals in goods of the kind sold. This warranty is that the goods are generally fit for the ordinary purposes for which such goods are used. As noted above, however, the Association did not sell the water (nor, for that matter, is the Association a merchant dealing in goods of this kind). Consequently, the facts do not give rise to an implied warranty of merchantability on the part of the Association. Similarly, (C) is incorrect because strict liability requires that the defendant be a commercial supplier of the product in question (*e.g.,* manufacturer, retailer, assembler, or wholesaler). Because the Association is merely an endorser of the water rather than a commercial supplier, there can be no recovery against it in strict liability.

Answer to Question 4

(A) Poindexter will prevail because Public used unreasonable force to protect its property. One may use reasonable force to prevent the commission of a tort against her property, real or personal. However, force that will cause death or serious bodily harm may not be used. In addition, indirect deadly force may not be used when such force could not lawfully be directly used. Here, Public kept the power running to prevent the theft of its transformers and cables. In effect, this amounts to the use of indirect deadly force as a means of preventing a tort to personal property. As explained above, use of such force to protect property is not permitted. Thus, Poindexter will prevail in his suit against Public. (B) is incorrect because it is too broad. Force may be used to protect only property if such force is reasonable, regardless of whether it is directly applied or indirectly applied by mechanical devices. The problem here is that the force used by Public was unreasonable because it was deadly force. Regarding (C), it is true that an owner or occupier of land owes no duty to an undiscovered trespasser. However, Public is not an owner or occupier of the land on which the abandoned mine sits, but simply the owner of the electricity transmission facilities and possibly an easement across the land. Thus, Public is held to the general duty of due care regardless of Poindexter's status, rather than the more limited duty applicable to a landowner or occupier. (D) is incorrect because the facts do not indicate that Poindexter assumed any risk. To have assumed a risk, a plaintiff must have known of the risk and must have voluntarily gone ahead in the face of the risk. Here, the facts indicate that Poindexter did not know that electric power to the mine was still running. Indeed, because the mine was abandoned, Poindexter undoubtedly assumed that the power was not running. Thus, Poindexter did not know of the risk involved in detaching the transformer and could not have voluntarily assumed such a risk. (Note that, although the question does not indicate the theory on which Poindexter is basing his cause of action, it may be based on a theory of intentional tort (specifically battery). If the suit is based on intentional tort, the factors mentioned in (C) and (D) would not even be relevant to the case.)

Answer to Question 5

(A) Choice (A) is Fatherlode's strongest defense because Poindexter's status as an undiscovered trespasser means that Fatherlode owed no duty to Poindexter, thereby completely relieving Fatherlode of any liability for Poindexter's injuries. An owner or occupier of land owes no duty to an undiscovered trespasser. However, with regard to a discovered trespasser, the owner or occupier must warn of or make safe artificial conditions known to the landowner that involve a risk of death or serious bodily harm and that the trespasser is unlikely to discover. Poindexter, having come onto the land owned by Fatherlode without permission or privilege, is a trespasser. Because Fatherlode had no notice of Poindexter's presence on the property, Poindexter is deemed to be an undiscovered trespasser. Consequently, Fatherlode owes no duty to Poindexter with regard to the injuries incurred on its property. (C) and (D) each present factors that would be helpful to Fatherlode, but they are not as strong as (A). The fact that Fatherlode asked Public to turn off the power, as well as Fatherlode's being unaware that Public had not turned off the power, would be indicative of the exercise of due care on the part of Fatherlode (*i.e.,* it took every reasonable step to see that the power was not left running in the abandoned mine, and could not reasonably have known that in fact the power was still on). However, if it is shown that no duty of care extended from Fatherlode to Poindexter, then the first element of a prima facie case for negligence is absent, thus eliminating any need for Fatherlode to attempt to show that it acted with ordinary, reasonable care. As a result, (A) is a much stronger defense than (C) or (D). (B) is incorrect because the fact that Poindexter tried to commit theft of Public's transformers is not relevant to any duty that may have been owed to him by Fatherlode. It is relevant that Poindexter was a trespasser, because this means that Fatherlode owed him no duty. However, Poindexter's status as a thief is of no significance.

Answer to Question 6

(B) Knowledge on the part of Ketchum that its fishing line was being used to hang objects would give rise to a duty to place warnings on the packages containing the product. The fishing line was manufactured to withstand a certain amount of stress for purposes of catching fish. However, if the manufacturer knew that members of the public were using the line to support a constant amount of weight, it was on notice that marketing the product without including warnings as to such use created an unreasonable risk of injury that might occur when the line broke. Under these circumstances, Ketchum breached its duty of ordinary, reasonable care by failing to include appropriate warnings with the product. As a guest of a purchaser of the product, Giselle is a foreseeable plaintiff; thus, the duty was owed to her. This breach of duty actually and proximately caused Giselle to suffer severe head injuries. Therefore, Ketchum is liable to Giselle in a products liability action based on negligence. Giselle also would prevail if she pursued an action based on strict liability. As is the case in a negligence action, courts in a strict liability case require a supplier to anticipate reasonably foreseeable uses even if they are misuses of the product. Thus, the lack of warnings accompanying the fishing line would also subject Ketchum to strict liability. (A) is incorrect because the facts do not establish that Ketchum was under a duty to place the warnings on its fishing line. Such a duty would exist if (as (B) states) Ketchum knew of the nonfishing uses being made of the product. Ketchum had no duty to put warnings on the product unless it knew or should have known of the other uses to which the fishing line was being put. (C) is incorrect because industry custom does not conclusively establish the applicable standard of care in a given case (although such customs are admissible as evidence of the standard to be applied). Here, the custom of the fishing tackle industry may be violative of the appropriate standard of care (*i.e.*, manufacturers of fishing lines may be under a duty to add the warnings to the product). Thus, the statement set forth in (C) will not by itself mean that Giselle does not prevail. (D) is incorrect for two reasons. First, there is no indication that Harold was negligent. Harold neither knew nor had reason to know that the fishing line would not support the plant basket. Thus, even if Harold were negligent, such negligence would not be a superseding cause of the injury because it would be ordinary foreseeable negligence. Consequently, Ketchum would not be relieved of liability for the results of its own wrongful conduct, but would be held liable along with Harold.

Answer to Question 7

(C) Giselle will not prevail in a suit against Harold. As a social guest of Harold's, Giselle is deemed to be a licensee; *i.e.*, one who enters onto land with the owner's permission for her own purpose or business rather than for the owner's benefit. The owner has a duty to warn a licensee of a dangerous condition known to the owner that creates an unreasonable risk of harm to the licensee and that the licensee is unlikely to discover. The owner has no duty to a licensee to inspect for defects nor to repair known defects. Harold, as a person who was not involved with fishing, had no reason to suspect that a fishing line that was "20-pound test" could not support the constant weight of a 15-pound basket. Thus, Harold did not know of the dangerous condition present in the form of the basket overhanging his porch. Because Harold was unaware of the danger, he was under no duty to warn Giselle, a licensee, of the dangerous condition. Having violated no duty owed to Giselle, Harold will not be held liable for her injuries. (A) is accurate in stating that Giselle was a social guest. However, as detailed above, the duty owed to a guest is simply to warn of concealed dangerous conditions of which the owner is aware. Harold had no duty to warn of a danger that he neither knew of nor had reason to know of. (B) is incorrect because there is no indication either that Harold hung the basket in a negligent manner or that he was negligent in failing either to warn Giselle or to be aware of the danger. Harold appears to have acted as would a reasonable person with no knowledge of the meaning of technical terms of fishing. (D) is incorrect because a social guest would indeed be a foreseeable plaintiff. If Harold had been negligent in hanging the basket directly above the swing, it would have been reasonably foreseeable that an injury would befall any person who sat on the swing. Thus, (D) reaches the correct result that Giselle will not prevail, but for an incorrect reason.

Answer to Question 8

(A) Digby will be liable to Mary for intentional infliction of emotional distress if his conduct is judged to be extreme and outrageous. To establish a prima facie case for intentional infliction of emotional distress, plaintiff must prove (i) an act by defendant amounting to extreme and outrageous conduct, (ii) intent to cause severe emotional distress or recklessness as to the effect of defendant's act, (iii) causation, and (iv) damages, *i.e.*, severe emotional distress. If Digby's conduct is judged to be extreme and outrageous, he is liable because the other elements of the tort are present: Given Digby's conduct and Mary's response, Digby was at least reckless as to whether his conduct would cause severe distress, and the facts indicate that it did cause such distress. Thus, Mary will prevail under the circumstances in choice (A). (B) is incorrect because a threat of physical injury is not required to establish intentional infliction of distress. Nor would threat of physical injury be sufficient to create liability for negligent infliction of emotional distress—that tort requires also that some physical injury result, which is not the case here. (C) is wrong because Digby could be liable even if he did not intend for Mary to suffer emotional distress, as long as he was reckless as to the effect of his conduct. (D) is incorrect because the fact that Mary owed the money would not excuse Digby's conduct if it was extreme and outrageous.

Answer to Question 9

(C) Wanda can recover damages for her emotional distress, even though she suffered no physical injury and did not require medical care, because of the known sensitivity of people concerning the death of a family member. In the usual case, the duty to avoid negligent infliction of emotional distress is breached when defendant creates a foreseeable risk of physical injury to plaintiff, typically by causing a threat of physical impact that leads to emotional distress, and plaintiff can recover for physical injury caused solely by the distress. In special situations, however, courts have permitted plaintiff to recover in the absence of physical injury where defendant's negligence creates a great likelihood of severe emotional distress. One of these situations is the mishandling of a relative's corpse, because it is certainly foreseeable that a person will suffer severe emotional distress if the corpse of a family member is negligently mishandled. In this case, the mortuary was negligent in putting the wrong body in the casket, creating a foreseeable risk of severe emotional distress to Wanda under the circumstances. Despite the fact that she suffered no physical injury, she can recover damages from the mortuary. (C) is therefore correct and (B) is incorrect. (A) is incorrect because the fact that Wanda did not obtain medical or psychiatric care does not prevent her from recovering damages. She can establish proof of her emotional distress through her own testimony and the testimony of others. (D) is incorrect because the fact that the mortuary is charging Wanda for the funeral is irrelevant. Regardless of the mortuary's conduct regarding the bill, its negligence in handling the body of her father makes it liable for her emotional distress.

Answer to Question 10

(A) Donald's statement constitutes slander per se and therefore Donald will be liable. To establish a prima facie case for defamation, the following elements must be proved: (i) defamatory language on the part of the defendant; (ii) the defamatory language must be "of or concerning" the plaintiff (*i.e.,* it must identify the plaintiff to a reasonable reader, listener, or viewer); (iii) publication of the defamatory language by the defendant to a third person; and (iv) damages to the reputation of the plaintiff. Here, Donald's suggestion that Percy received outside help on an article Percy authored impeaches his integrity and legal skills. The defamatory language directly related to Percy. The publication requirement is satisfied when there is a communication to a third person who understood it. Thus, when Donald made the statement to Anneliese, who clearly understood it, there was a publication. In ascertaining whether the damages element of the plaintiff's prima facie case has been satisfied, the type of defamation involved must be identified. For slander, injury to reputation is not presumed. Thus, ordinary slander is not actionable in the absence of pleading and proof of special damages. If, however, the spoken defamation falls within one of four categories, characterized as slander per se, an injury to reputation is presumed without proof of special damages. Thus, a defamatory statement adversely reflecting on the plaintiff's abilities in his business, trade, or profession is actionable without pleading or proof of special damages. Donald's statement adversely reflected upon Percy's honesty and capability in his profession, and as such is slander per se. (B) is incorrect because it states a standard for public figure plaintiffs, not private persons. Public figure plaintiffs must show malice, defined by the Supreme Court in *New York Times v. Sullivan* as knowledge that the statement was false, or reckless disregard as to its truth or falsity. Private persons such as Percy need not prove malice as part of the prima facie case. (C) is incorrect because the mere fact that the interviewer asked Donald his opinion does not justify a defamatory response. Donald did not have a common law qualified privilege to make the statements because he was not a former employer of Percy and was not yet a member of Anneliese's firm (negating any common interest privilege). Furthermore, once publication is established, it is no defense that the defendant had no idea that the publication was defamatory. It is the intent to publish, not the intent to defame, that is the requisite intent. Thus, even if Donald thought his comments did not constitute defamation because they were in response to the interviewer's question, he could still be found liable for defamation assuming all other elements of the tort were satisfied. (D) is incorrect. As noted above, Donald's defamatory statement adversely reflecting on Percy's abilities in his profession is actionable without proof of special damages.

Answer to Question 11

(D) Virgil will prevail in an action against SLI because the manufacturer of an unreasonably dangerous defective product is strictly liable to foreseeable plaintiffs injured by the product. To establish a prima facie case in products liability based on strict liability in tort, the following elements must be proved: (i) strict duty owed by a commercial supplier; (ii) breach of that duty; (iii) actual and proximate cause; and (iv) damages. All of those elements are satisfied here. SLI was a commercial supplier of the lasers. To hold the commercial supplier strictly liable for a product defect, the product must be expected to, and must in fact, reach the user or consumer without substantial change in the condition in which it is supplied. The facts establish that the defective voltage regulation device was present in the SLI laser when it left SLI production facilities. A majority of courts extend the protection from defective products not only to buyers, but also to members of the buyer's family, guests, friends, and employees of the buyer, and foreseeable bystanders. Here, Virgil was a foreseeable bystander. A defective laser could foreseeably cause an explosion and fire to surrounding property, thereby injuring residents of such property. (A) is incorrect. Some products may be safe if used as intended, but may involve serious dangers if used in other ways. Courts have required suppliers to anticipate reasonably foreseeable uses even if they are "misuses" of the product. Thus, misuse of the product will not preclude a products liability claim by Virgil if the misuse was reasonably foreseeable, and answer (A) omits consideration of the foreseeability of Lycurgus's misuse. Since SLI's defective laser actually and proximately caused injury to Virgil, Virgil will prevail in a strict tort liability action against SLI. (B) is incorrect because one need not be a consumer or user of the defective product to recover in products liability. As noted above, foreseeable bystanders can sue under strict liability. (C) is incorrect. To establish breach of duty for a strict liability action, the plaintiff need not prove that the defendant was at fault in selling or producing a defective product—only that the product in fact is so defective as to be "unreasonably dangerous." The element of negligence need not be proved in a strict liability case. Thus, the manufacturer of a defective product is liable even if the manufacturer was entirely without negligence.

Answer to Question 12

(A) Polly can establish a prima facie case for battery. The fact that the operation was a success and that she may not be able to prove actual damages will not bar her recovery. The prima facie case for battery requires: (i) an act by defendant that brings about a harmful or offensive contact to plaintiff; (ii) intent on the part of defendant to do the act; and (iii) causation. Here, Dr. Deuce's performing the operation on Polly's ankle would be harmful or offensive contact because Polly had selected Dr. Ace to perform the operation and did not consent to Dr. Deuce's participating in any way. Even if evidence of her distress is not adequate to prove actual damages, she will still be entitled to a judgment in her favor and nominal damages, because damages is not an element of the prima facie case for battery. (B) is wrong because the fact that a reasonable person would have consented is irrelevant in a nonemergency situation. If Polly had been brought into the emergency room requiring immediate surgery, her consent to the operation would be implied by law if she was incapable of consenting and a reasonable person similarly situated would have consented. Here, however, the operation was not an emergency and Polly's express consent should have been obtained. (C) is wrong because the fact that Deuce performed the operation competently is irrelevant where Polly did not consent to his involvement at all. (D) is wrong because, as discussed above, the prima facie case for battery does not require harm (damages) to be shown. Even if she cannot prove actual harm, she will be entitled to a judgment for nominal damages.

Answer to Question 13

(B) Donna may recover some damages from Olga if Olga should have foreseen that motorists could be injured if the hedge was not cut back. Olga, as the owner and occupier of Cityacre, owes a duty to those off the premises for unreasonably dangerous artificial conditions. In contrast to overgrown weeds, which are a natural condition for which no duty is owed, a hedge is considered an artificial condition, analogous to a fence. Hence, by letting the hedge become so large that it created a foreseeable danger to motorists by obstructing their vision, Olga has breached her duty to Donna. The other elements of Donna's negligence action (besides a duty and a breach of the duty) are actual and proximate cause, and damages. Donna can establish actual cause by showing that, although she failed to notice the stop sign, she would have noticed another car traveling on a collision course with hers; *i.e.,* but for the overgrown hedge, Donna would have been able to avoid the accident. Proximate cause in an indirect case such as this can be established by showing that any intervening forces were foreseeable and not superseding. Edmund's negligent failure to stop may also have been caused in part by the overgrown hedge and is a foreseeable intervening force that does not break the chain of causation. Assuming that Donna can establish damages, the final element of her prima facie case, Donna can recover some of her damages from Olga regardless of how much at fault Donna was, because the jurisdiction has adopted pure comparative negligence. (A) is incorrect because a pure comparative negligence jurisdiction allows plaintiff to recover no matter how great her negligence is. Thus, if Donna and Edmund are each 45% at fault and Olga is only 10% at fault, Donna can recover 10% of her damages from Olga. (C) is incorrect because Donna's conduct, even if it were considered "reckless," does not preclude her recovery from Olga if Olga was at all at fault because this is a pure comparative negligence jurisdiction. (D) is wrong because Olga is still liable for some damages in a pure comparative negligence jurisdiction even if her fault was only slight.

Answer to Question 14

(D) Edmund can prevail in a lawsuit against Donna regardless of whether his fault was greater or less than hers. Edmund will be able to establish a prima facie case of negligence against Donna, because her inattentive driving breached her duty of care to other drivers and was a direct cause of Edmund's damages. Donna's defense that Edmund's contributory negligence also caused the accident does not bar his recovery; comparative negligence jurisdictions allow recovery despite contributory negligence by the plaintiff, and *pure* comparative negligence rules allow recovery no matter how great plaintiff's negligence is. While Donna could counterclaim against Edmund for the percentage of her damages that Edmund was responsible for, Edmund could still have a net recovery—regardless of his greater fault—if his damages are significantly greater than Donna's (*e.g.,* if Edmund is 60% at fault and has suffered $100,000 in damages, while Donna is 40% at fault and has suffered $10,000 in damages, Edmund would recover $34,000 in damages). (A) is wrong because the jurisdiction follows a *pure* comparative negligence approach, which allows recovery no matter how great plaintiff's negligence is. If *partial* comparative negligence had been adopted instead, Edmund's success would depend on a comparison of his fault and Donna's fault. (B) is wrong because last clear chance is a mitigation of the "all or nothing" effect of traditional contributory negligence; it permits plaintiff to recover despite his own contributory negligence. Because a comparative negligence jurisdiction rejects the "all or nothing" approach, most comparative negligence jurisdictions do not use the last clear chance doctrine. (C) is incorrect because Edmund's running of the stop sign, whether it is considered negligent or reckless, does not bar him from recovering in most pure comparative negligence jurisdictions; it merely reduces his recovery.

Answer to Question 15

(C) The school can be held liable if Litigatia can establish a prima facie case for negligence. Negligence requires: (i) a duty on the part of the defendant to conform to a specific standard of conduct to protect the plaintiff against an unreasonable risk of injury; (ii) a breach of that duty; (iii) actual and proximate causation; and (iv) damages. The element at issue here—the existence of a duty—is present only if defendant's conduct created an unreasonable risk of harm to persons in the position of the plaintiff. Specifically, Litigatia would have to show that the school's conduct in running the summer program without the traffic light in operation created an unreasonable risk of injury to schoolchildren, and therefore the school had a duty to take precautions against such risk. If this duty can be shown to exist, the school will be liable for negligence because the other elements of the prima facie case (breach of the duty, causation, and damages) can be readily established from these facts. Thus, the school's liability will depend on whether it had a duty to take proper safety precautions on behalf of students, such as Viola, who attend the summer program. (A) is wrong because even if Viola's parents were negligent in not ensuring that Viola was safely escorted to school during the summer when the light was not in operation, the school is not absolved from liability. The parents' negligence was a foreseeable intervening force that caused a foreseeable result; hence, it is not a superseding intervening force that would break the causal connection between the school's conduct and Viola's injury. Nor would the parents' negligence preclude them from suing on Viola's behalf; contributory negligence of a parent is not imputed to the child in actions against a third party. (B) is wrong because Viola's status is irrelevant. An invitee is a person who enters onto the premises in response to an express or implied invitation of the landowner. In this case, the traffic light appears to be located outside the school property, on a public street. The school is therefore not an owner or occupier of the land on which the injury occurred. Thus, Viola's status as an invitee, licensee, or trespasser is irrelevant in an action against the school. (D) is wrong for the same reasons as (A). David's negligence was an independent intervening force because it occurred after the time of the school's alleged negligence and was not a response or reaction to it. However, it was a foreseeable intervening force because it was within the scope of the increased risk created by the school's alleged negligence; in fact, it was precisely the type of conduct that the school would have to protect the children against if the school is deemed to have a duty under these facts.

Answer to Question 16

(B) Cisneros will win because LeBeau's actions constituted an assault. A prima facie case for assault consists of: (i) an act by the defendant creating a reasonable apprehension in the plaintiff of immediate harmful or offensive contact; (ii) intent on the part of the defendant to bring about that apprehension; and (iii) causation. Here, if Cisneros reasonably believed that LeBeau's boat was about to hit his boat (and thus cause a harmful or offensive contact with him), there is a basis for assault because the other elements (intent on the part of LeBeau and causation) were present. The only issue is whether the belief was reasonable. In determining whether the apprehension was reasonable, the courts usually apply a reasonable person test. Here, a reasonable person certainly could believe that LeBeau's actions constituted a threat of an immediate harmful contact (*e.g.,* a crash). Thus, there would be a basis for assault. (A) is wrong because unless Cisneros's initial actions were such as to justify LeBeau's acting in self-defense, it is immaterial that Cisneros made insults provoking LeBeau's tortious conduct. Self-defense is permitted when a person reasonably believes he is being or is about to be attacked. Here, it is clear that Cisneros's conduct would not justify LeBeau's actions in self-defense. Cisneros made no threat to LeBeau. Words alone (in the heated conversation between two parties) do not cause reasonable apprehension of harmful contact, and there is no showing that any acts indicated harm. Also, self-defense would not apply because LeBeau's conduct was clearly not defensive; he repeatedly came after Cisneros despite Cisneros's attempts to leave. (C) is wrong because damages are recoverable for assault without the plaintiff's suffering actual physical injury. Assault is the causing of *apprehension* of contact; it does not require actual contact. (D) is wrong because Cisneros does not need to rely on an intentional infliction of emotional distress to recover. He can prevail on an assault claim even if he did not suffer severe emotional distress.

Answer to Question 17

(A) Wanda will probably prevail on a claim for intentional infliction of emotional distress because Morlock's conduct was sufficiently extreme and outrageous and the other elements of the tort are present. Intentional infliction of emotional distress requires: (i) an act by defendant amounting to extreme and outrageous conduct; (ii) intent to cause severe emotional distress or recklessness as to the effect of defendant's conduct; (iii) causation; and (iv) damages. "Outrageous conduct" is extreme conduct that transcends all bounds of decency. Morlock's use of the bullhorn to amplify the recording and his insults against Wanda for the benefit of her guests would probably qualify as extreme and outrageous conduct, particularly since there is no evidence that he had previously tried to resolve the problem with Wanda in a more civilized manner. Morlock had the requisite intent (either he intended to cause emotional distress, as shown by use of the bullhorn, or he was reckless as to its effect), there was causation, and Wanda suffered damages (*i.e.,* she was severely distressed) as a result of Morlock's actions. (B) is wrong because pecuniary harm is not required for purposes of this tort—all that is required is severe emotional distress. (C) is wrong because, in contrast to negligent infliction of distress, intentional infliction of distress does not require proof of physical harm to recover. (D) is wrong because the fact that the barking constituted a nuisance would not be a defense to conduct amounting to intentional infliction of distress; abatement of a private nuisance by self-help must be preceded by notice to the other party and must be conducted in a reasonable manner.

Answer to Question 18

(B) If Wanda knew the door would strike the bullhorn, she could be liable to Morlock for battery. Battery requires: (i) an act by defendant that causes a harmful or offensive contact to plaintiff's person; (ii) intent to cause the harmful or offensive contact; and (iii) causation. Here, there was a harmful contact caused by Wanda. The only consideration is whether Wanda had the requisite intent. If a person knows with substantial certainty the consequences of her action, she has the intent necessary for this type of tort. Thus, if Wanda knew that the door was substantially certain to hit the bullhorn Morlock was holding, Wanda had the intent necessary for battery. (For purposes of battery, anything connected to or being held by the plaintiff is part of plaintiff's person.) (A) is wrong because if Wanda intended to cause a harmful contact (a battery), she is liable for all the consequences of her actions, whether she intended them or not. A defendant need not foresee the extent of the injuries caused by her intentional act to be held liable for them. (C) is wrong because this is not a case of self-defense. Self-defense is appropriate when a person reasonably believes that she is being or is about to be attacked. Nothing in the facts shows any basis for Wanda to believe that Morlock was going to harm her. Thus, self-defense is not appropriate here. (D) is wrong because it does not provide Wanda with a defense. Morlock's conduct angered Wanda and may have triggered her actions, but since Morlock's conduct was not sufficient to allow Wanda to act in self-defense, Wanda's use of force here is not excused.

Answer to Question 19

(C) Rollerball has a valid defense of assumption of risk because Poohbah voluntarily encountered a known risk when he walked past the construction site. The facts indicate that Rollerball probably is engaged in an ultrahazardous activity, because the demolition involves a risk of serious harm, cannot be performed with complete safety, and is not a commonly engaged-in activity (because of the unusual aspects of this building). Rollerball therefore is subject to strict liability for injuries caused by the demolition, regardless of the care it took to keep pedestrians away. However, assumption of risk is a valid defense to strict liability. The defense of assumption of the risk requires that plaintiff know of the risk and voluntarily assume it. Here, Poohbah assumed the risk; *i.e.,* he voluntarily encountered the abnormal risk regarding this building despite knowing of the danger. Thus, Rollerball will prevail. (A) is incorrect because the fact that Rollerball was engaged in an ultrahazardous activity just establishes that a strict liability standard will apply. Rollerball will still prevail in the suit if it can establish assumption of risk on Poohbah's part. (B) is wrong for several reasons. Res ipsa loquitur, which allows a plaintiff to establish a prima facie case for negligence without direct proof of a breach of duty, requires that the accident causing the injury be unlikely to occur in the absence of negligence, whereas the facts suggest that the unpredictable falling of chunks of masonry would occur regardless of the care Rollerball took in the demolition process. In addition, res ipsa loquitur requires plaintiff to prove freedom from fault on his own part, and here Poohbah clearly was at fault in voluntarily and unreasonably proceeding in the face of a known danger. (D) is incorrect because ordinary contributory negligence in failing to realize the danger or guard against its existence is not a defense to strict liability in jurisdictions retaining traditional contributory negligence. Contributory negligence is a defense if plaintiff knew of the danger and proceeded to act unreasonably by encountering it, but such conduct is better described as a type of assumption of risk than as contributory negligence, and thus (C) is a better answer than (D).

Answer to Question 20

(A) Barbara will prevail because the lack of a warning about eye injuries made the product unreasonably dangerous. A strict liability products liability action requires: (i) a strict duty by a commercial supplier; (ii) a breach of that duty by the sale of a product in a defective condition that makes the product unreasonably dangerous; (iii) causation; and (iv) damages. Here, National Chemical is a commercial supplier of a "defective" product. Although the insulation substance was not actually defective in that it apparently performed as it was meant to do, it is legally defective if it was unreasonably dangerous and could be made safer by adequate warnings. Here, National Chemical knew of the danger and could easily have placed a warning on the label. That could have alerted Simpson to the danger, enabling him to take precautions that would have prevented Barbara from being injured. Thus, National Chemical breached its duty. Since the other elements (causation and damages) are present, Barbara will prevail. (B) is wrong because even in a strict liability action, liability will be found only if the product is defective, not just because someone was injured when it was used for its intended purpose. (C) is wrong because there is no showing that Barbara was or should have been aware of the danger she faced when she turned on the air conditioner; hence, her conduct did not constitute contributory negligence. (D) is wrong because the manufacturer must warn of the danger, and its duty is not satisfied merely because there have been no injuries to date by following the instructions on the label.

Answer to Question 21

(C) Barbara cannot prevail unless Orwell was negligent. A defendant cannot be held liable in strict liability unless the defendant is a commercial supplier of the **product**. Orwell is not a supplier of the product, but is only the user. Thus, Orwell cannot be held in strict liability to Barbara. He can be liable only if he was somehow negligent, such as being negligent in hiring the contractors. (A) is wrong because Barbara's status alone is not a reason for recovery. A lessor who has covenanted to repair leased premises has a duty to everyone authorized to be on the premises to protect against unreasonably dangerous conditions. Here, Barbara, an employee of a tenant, has the right to be on the premises but nothing in the facts indicates that Orwell or the people he hired negligently created the dangerous condition. Therefore, Barbara's status alone does not give her a right to recover. Orwell must be negligent in some way. (B) is wrong because it implies that Orwell is liable if National Chemical is liable. However, even if National Chemical is liable on a strict liability theory, Orwell is not automatically liable. He is not involved in the products liability case and thus his liability, if any, can only be based on his own negligence. (D) is wrong because it suggests that Orwell cannot be liable because he did not have the opportunity to inspect the insulation. In a products liability case based on negligence, a dealer is not liable unless he knew or should have known of the defect. Here, Orwell is not a dealer and he did not have any idea of the defect. Therefore, the fact that the containers were closed is irrelevant.

Answer to Question 22

(D) Mildred's parents' best defense is that they were unaware of any potentially violent behavior by Mildred. At common law, parents are not vicariously liable for the torts of their child. (Statutes in most states allow for limited liability for intentional torts, but there is no indication of such a statute here.) Parents can be liable, however, for their own negligence, *i.e.,* in not exercising due care under the circumstances. Thus, if the parents know their child may be violent, they could be negligent if they do not take precautions to prevent that behavior or injury from that behavior. However, if the parents have no reason to know their child could be violent, they have no duty to protect against such behavior. Here, if Mildred had never done anything like this before, and her parents had no idea that she would be violent, they were not negligent in allowing her to attend nursery school. (A) is wrong because although Tom's teasing may have provoked Mildred, he did not initiate the violence. He did nothing to allow Mildred a right of self-defense, and so his actions would not provide Mildred's parents with a good defense. (B) is wrong because there is no general tort immunity for children. As long as the child is old enough to intend the act, she can be held liable. Here it seems that Mildred intended to cause a battery. She either intended or knew with substantial certainty that swinging her fist would strike Tom in the face; *i.e.,* would cause a harmful or offensive contact. Thus, this choice does not present the best defense for defendants. (C) is wrong because parents can be liable for damages due to their child's conduct. As explained above, although the parents are not vicariously liable at common law, they can be liable based on their own negligence (*e.g.,* for negligent supervision).

Answer to Question 23

(B) Tina is likely to recover from Alucard based on assault and battery (I) and intrusion on seclusion (III). Assault and battery are both intentional torts. Battery requires: (i) an act that brings about harmful or offensive contact; (ii) intent to bring about the harmful or offensive contact; and (iii) causation. Whether a given contact can be considered harmful or offensive is judged by how it would be viewed by a reasonable person of ordinary sensibilities. Most contact that a doctor has with his patient is for purposes of treatment and would not be considered offensive; in fact, the law implies consent to the contact in such cases. However, Alucard's lifting of Tom's head during his dying moments for a purpose unrelated to treatment went far beyond the scope of any implied consent. Most persons would judge his act to be an offensive contact. Intent for battery is satisfied by showing that Alucard knew with substantial certainty that the offensive contact would occur. He need not have intended injury or committed the act for a bad motive; the fact that both Tom and Tina indicated to Alucard that the contact was not consented to is enough to establish his intent. Assault requires: (i) an act by defendant creating a reasonable apprehension in plaintiff of immediate harmful or offensive contact to plaintiff's person; (ii) intent to create the apprehension or bring about the contact; and (iii) causation. Tom's feeble attempt to ward off Alucard indicates his apprehension of the imminent offensive contact, and Alucard's intent to commit the contact satisfies the intent element for assault. Causation is easily established for both torts, and actual damages are not required; also, actions for these torts do not expire on the victim's (Tom's) death. Thus, Tina can recover in an action for assault and battery to Tom. Tina's other action would be her own action for intrusion on plaintiff's seclusion. This tort requires an act of intruding on the seclusion of the plaintiff in her private matters, and that the intrusion be objectionable to a reasonable person. While a doctor usually is not intruding on seclusion by entering a patient's room, Alucard ignored Tina's reasonable request to be alone with her husband during his final minutes, just so he could take another photograph. This kind of intrusion would be highly objectionable to a reasonable person. Thus, since the facts establish this tort, (A) is wrong. (C) and (D) are wrong because Alucard is not liable for false light publicity (II) or publication of private facts (IV). Both of these privacy torts require some type of publicity or publication, and the facts do not indicate that Alucard did anything with the photographs. In contrast, intrusion on seclusion does not require any use or publication of the photograph; the intrusion itself makes Alucard subject to liability.

Answer to Question 24

(D) Putnam will recover damages from Dorothy even though she had a privilege to enter the shelter. The privilege of necessity arises when a person interferes with the property of another because it was reasonably and apparently necessary to avoid threatened injury from a force of nature or some other force. The threatened injury must be substantially more serious than the invasion that is undertaken to avert it. However, in private necessity cases, where the action taken is solely to benefit the actor or some other person from serious injury (rather than to benefit the general public), the defense is incomplete—the actor must pay for any injury she causes. Here, Dorothy had a privilege to enter Putnam's property and take refuge in the shelter to protect herself from the storm. However, her privilege is not absolute because her entry onto the property was for her own benefit. Hence, she will be liable to Putnam for the damages she caused. (A) is incorrect because Dorothy's privilege will not absolve her from liability for the damages. The only effect of the privilege of private necessity is to give the actor the right to enter the land of another without being classified as a trespasser; the landowner therefore has no right to eject the actor as he would a trespasser. (B) is incorrect because Putnam can recover all damages caused by Dorothy's entry. (C) is incorrect because the fact that an act of God was involved does not mean that Dorothy is not liable to Putnam. If not for the private necessity defense, Dorothy would have committed the tort of trespass, because she committed an act that caused a physical invasion of Putnam's property, and had the intent to commit the act.

Answer to Question 25

(B) Penelope will recover against Sterling if she relied on his statements to Barbara. The elements of a prima facie case for intentional misrepresentation consist of (i) a misrepresentation, (ii) scienter, (iii) an intent to induce plaintiff's reliance, (iv) causation (*i.e.,* actual reliance), (v) justifiable reliance, and (vi) damages. Here, Sterling made a false statement knowing that he did not know whether it was true; this satisfies the scienter requirement. Regarding intent to induce reliance, statements made to one person can be the basis of an intentional misrepresentation action by another person where the defendant could reasonably foresee that that person would rely on the statement. Based on what Barbara had said, Sterling had reason to foresee that Barbara's aunt might rely on his assertions of fire resistance in storing her antiques. Finally, given the assumption stated in choice (B), Penelope can establish causation (actual reliance) and justifiable reliance. Thus, she can recover for any pecuniary damages she suffered as a result of the fire. (A) is incorrect because the fact that Penelope suffered pecuniary loss is not enough to establish her right to recover for intentional misrepresentation. She also has to establish that she actually relied on Sterling's statements to Barbara, which is established by the assumption in choice (B). (C) is incorrect because the fact that Sterling did not make the statements in a business or professional capacity will only preclude recovery for *negligent* misrepresentation. The fact that Sterling knew that he did not know the truth or falsity of his statement establishes the scienter required for intentional misrepresentation. (D) is incorrect because, as stated above, Sterling owed a duty to Penelope because he could reasonably foresee that she would rely on his statements.

Answer to Question 26

(A) Because Blanche was a foreseeable plaintiff, Stanley owed her a duty of care against an unreasonable risk of injury and therefore Stanley is liable to Blanche for her injuries. To establish a prima facie case for negligence, the following elements must be proved: (i) the existence of a duty on the part of the defendant to conform to a specific standard of conduct for the protection of the plaintiff against an unreasonable risk of injury; (ii) breach of that duty by the defendant; (iii) the breach of the duty by defendant was the actual and proximate cause of plaintiff's injury; and (iv) damage to plaintiff's person or property. A duty of care is owed only to foreseeable plaintiffs. A rescuer is a foreseeable plaintiff as long as the rescue is not wanton. Hence, a defendant will be liable if he negligently puts himself or a third person in peril and plaintiff was injured in attempting a rescue. Stanley's actions created a risk that someone might be injured in an attempt to rescue him. Blanche was a rescuer and her actions in assisting Stanley were not wanton. Blanche looked through the windshield and saw Stanley passed out on the front seat. She then attempted to open the car doors, but finding them locked she had no choice but to break a window to get into the car. Stanley's actions were the actual and proximate cause of her injuries and therefore she can recover on a negligence theory. (B) is incorrect because Stanley's (or his estate's) liability would exist regardless of whether Blanche succeeded in saving his life. (C) is incorrect. The fact that Blanche did not place Stanley in peril would, if anything, increase the likelihood of his liability. (D) is incorrect. Blanche, as a volunteer, was under no duty to come to Stanley's aid. However, her status as a volunteer does not relieve Stanley of liability for her injuries. As a volunteer rescuer, Blanche was a foreseeable plaintiff to whom Stanley owed a duty of care. Further, persons who undertake to save the lives of others are generally not held to have voluntarily assumed the risk of injury.

Answer to Question 27

(C) Since Patrick was driving in excess of the legal speed limit, Patrick was contributorily negligent. Under traditional rules, plaintiff's contributory negligence is a complete defense to negligence (*i.e.,* it completely bars plaintiff's right to recover). Patrick is contributorily negligent here because he was both exceeding the speed limit and not paying attention to his driving. If he had been paying attention, he probably would have had adequate time to either stop his car or swerve to avoid Duffy's vehicle. (A) is incorrect because even if Duffy alleges that his running the stop sign was unintentional, that defense would only apply for intentional torts and not to torts based on negligent conduct. (B) is incorrect. Patrick was not under any duty to purchase a car that would be able to sustain minimal damage when struck at a low speed; therefore, the first element for establishing a prima facie case of negligence is absent—the existence of a duty on the part of the defendant to conform to a specific standard of conduct for the protection of the plaintiff against an unreasonable risk of injury. (D) is also incorrect. The doctrine of last clear chance permits the plaintiff to recover despite his own contributory negligence. Under this rule, the person with the last clear chance to avoid an accident who fails to do so is liable for negligence. (In effect, last clear chance is plaintiff's rebuttal against the defense of contributory negligence.) Thus, the doctrine of last clear chance would not be available to Duffy as a defense.

Answer to Question 28

(B) Willy will recover in a suit against the newspaper since the newspaper published facts about Willy that placed him in a false light. To establish a prima facie case for invasion of privacy based on publication by defendant of facts placing plaintiff in a false light, the following elements must be proved: (i) publication of facts about plaintiff by defendant placing plaintiff in a false light in the public eye; and (ii) the "false light" must be something that would be objectionable to a reasonable person under the circumstances. The large picture of Willy flanked by two bulky police officers implied that Willy committed a crime because it looked like pictures that newspapers often print of criminals being taken into custody. This "false light" would clearly be objectionable to a reasonable person under the circumstances. (A) is incorrect. The branch of invasion of right to privacy, intrusion upon plaintiff's affairs or seclusion, requires (i) an act of prying or intruding on the affairs or seclusion of plaintiff by defendant; (ii) the intrusion must be something that would be objectionable to a reasonable person; and (iii) the thing to which there is an intrusion or prying must be "private." Here, the photograph of Willy was taken at the police station, which is a public place. Hence, the intrusion was not into anything of Willy's private domain and is not actionable under this branch of invasion of privacy. (C) is incorrect. The impression that Willy committed a crime was not dispelled by inclusion of the small explanatory caption. As a result, the caption will not serve as a valid defense. (D) is incorrect because printing the picture would probably not qualify as being in the public interest. Willy was a salesman rather than a public official or public figure; his picture was printed because there was a dearth of news. His posting bond for the arrest of his son for possession of a small amount of marijuana is not the type of information that is of general public interest.

Answer to Question 29

(D) Dieter will prevail because Freya's grabbing of the wheel is the negligent conduct that caused Pike's injuries. To establish a prima facie case for negligence, the following elements must be proved: (i) the existence of a duty on the part of the defendant to conform to a specific standard of conduct for the protection of the plaintiff against an unreasonable risk of injury; (ii) breach of that duty by the defendant; (iii) the breach of the duty by defendant was the actual and proximate cause of plaintiff's injury; and (iv) damage to plaintiff's person or property. While it is unlikely that Dieter's driving with an expired license breached a duty to Pike (*see* discussion of choice (A) below), the issue raised by choice (D) is whether Dieter's conduct was the actual and proximate cause of Pike's injuries. Before the defendant's conduct can be considered a proximate cause of plaintiff's injury, it must first be a cause in fact of the injury. An act or omission to act is the cause in fact of an injury when the injury would not have occurred but for the act. The "but for" test applies where several acts combine to cause the injury, but none of the acts standing alone would have been sufficient. But for any of the acts, the injury would not have occurred. But for Dieter's driving and Freya's grabbing the steering wheel, the injury to Pike would not have happened. Thus, Dieter's actions would be considered a cause in fact of the injury. However, Freya's grabbing of the steering wheel would be a superseding intervening force. A superseding force is one that serves to break the causal connection between the initial wrongful act and the ultimate injury, and itself becomes a direct immediate cause of such injury. Thus, the first actor would be relieved of liability from the consequences of his antecedent conduct. Freya's conduct in grabbing the steering wheel was an unforeseeable intervening force creating an unforeseeable harmful result, and thus constituted a superseding force. Consequently, Dieter would be relieved of any negligence liability since Freya's actions were the proximate cause of the accident. (A) is incorrect. A specific duty imposed by a statute may replace the more general common law duty of due care when (i) the plaintiff is within the class to be protected by the statute, (ii) the statute was designed to prevent the type of harm suffered, and (iii) the statutory standard of conduct is clearly defined. The statute probably does not apply here because it is intended to keep unsafe drivers off the streets, and there is no indication that Dieter is an unsafe driver, or that any driver could have prevented the injury when Freya grabbed the steering wheel. Even if the statutory standard were applicable, a violation means only that plaintiff will have established a conclusive presumption of duty and breach of duty. It does not, however, establish causation or damages. Here, the fact that Dieter does not have a valid license is not the proximate cause of Pike's injury. (B) is incorrect because Dieter had no way of knowing that Freya would grab the steering wheel. Dieter's conduct will be measured against the reasonable, ordinary, prudent person who drives a vehicle. Dieter's moderate drinking at the nightclub evidences his prudent behavior. A reasonable, prudent person would not have foreseen that one of his passengers would impulsively grab the steering wheel and therefore there are no special safety precautions that Dieter should have taken as part of his duty of care toward pedestrians. (C) is incorrect, because even if Dieter had started the argument, this would not justify Freya's grabbing of the steering wheel. In either case, Freya's actions rather than Dieter's would be considered the proximate cause of Pike's injuries.

Answer to Question 30

(B) If a reasonable truck driver should have seen the dangerous condition, then TD's striking the bridge constitutes negligent conduct. To establish a prima facie case for negligence, the following elements must be proved: (i) the existence of a duty on the part of the defendant to conform to a specific standard of conduct for the protection of the plaintiff against an unreasonable risk of injury; (ii) breach of that duty by defendant; (iii) the breach of the duty by defendant was the actual and proximate cause of plaintiff's injury; and (iv) damage to plaintiff's person or property.

TD's conduct will be measured against that of the reasonable, ordinary, prudent truck driver. Under these facts, TD saw that an accident had occurred near the bridge. He also had adequate time to slow down or stop after he noticed that there was an accident. However, he proceeded ahead without reducing speed. It is unclear from the facts if, at the time TD spotted the accident, he should have seen the dangerous condition of the bridge. However, if a reasonable truck driver would have seen the dangerous condition, TD would have breached his duty to conform to the conduct of a reasonable truck driver so as to avoid subjecting foreseeable plaintiffs to an unreasonable risk of injury. (A) is incorrect because even if TD did not see the dangerous condition, it is possible that he should have seen it. To be free from negligence liability, TD's duty of care must conform to that of the reasonably prudent truck driver. (C) is incorrect because it appears that TD had the last clear chance to avoid the accident, and there is no clear indication that Alpha acted negligently in any case. Assuming that Alpha was negligent, the doctrine of last clear chance permits the plaintiff to recover despite his own contributory negligence. Under this rule, the person with the last clear chance to avoid an accident who fails to do so is liable for negligence. Alpha is in a position of "helpless peril" from which he cannot extricate himself. Under these circumstances, TD will be liable if he either had actual knowledge or should have known of Alpha's predicament. If Alpha were not negligent, (C) would be incorrect for the simple reason that TD could not avail himself of a contributory negligence defense. (D) is incorrect because even if the clearance is usually adequate, on this occasion it was not; the issue is whether TD should have seen the dangerous bridge condition after spotting the accident.

Answer to Question 31

(D) Beta will prevail against Alpha's estate because he can establish a prima facie case of negligence against Alpha. One of the elements of negligence is a showing that defendant's breach of duty was the actual (cause in fact) and proximate cause of plaintiff's injury. An act or omission to act is the cause in fact of an injury when the injury would not have occurred but for the act. Alpha's accident was the actual cause of Beta's injury because but for the accident, Beta would not have stopped to assist Alpha. Alpha's accident was also a proximate cause of Beta's injury. Not all injuries actually caused by defendant will be deemed to be proximately caused by his acts. The general rule of proximate cause is that defendant is liable for all harmful results that are the normal incidents of and within the increased risk caused by his acts. This is an indirect cause case because an independent intervening force (TD's truck) came into motion after defendant's negligent act and combined with it to cause plaintiff's injury. Independent intervening forces are foreseeable (and thus do not cut off defendant's liability) where defendant's negligence increased the risk that these forces would cause harm to the plaintiff. Once Alpha negligently put himself in peril on the highway, he created a foreseeable risk that a rescuer would be injured in some way by the act of another motorist while assisting Alpha. Thus, TD's negligence was a foreseeable intervening force that combined with Alpha's negligence to create a foreseeable harmful result to Beta. Alpha's estate, therefore, is not relieved of liability by TD's conduct. (A) is incorrect because even if TD's actions caused Beta's injuries, they were a foreseeable risk created by Alpha's conduct and thus do not constitute a superseding intervening force that would cut off Alpha's liability to Beta. (B) is incorrect. Alpha owed a duty of care to Beta under the general rule that a rescuer is a foreseeable plaintiff as long as the rescue is not wanton. Hence, a defendant will be liable if he negligently puts himself in peril and plaintiff is injured in attempting a rescue. The fact that, at the time Alpha's car struck the bridge support, Beta was five miles from the bridge does not make Beta an unforeseeable plaintiff. He could still be considered a foreseeable rescuer. (C) is incorrect because the fact that Beta stopped to render assistance merely establishes Beta as a foreseeable plaintiff. The critical issue is whether Beta can establish proximate cause.

Answer to Question 32

(A) As an employer, Farmer breached his duty of care owing to Prufrock and therefore is liable for Prufrock's injuries on a negligence theory. To establish a prima facie case for negligence, the following elements must be proved: (i) the existence of a duty on the part of defendant to conform to a specific standard of conduct for the protection of the plaintiff against an unreasonable risk of injury; (ii) breach of that duty by defendant; (iii) the breach of the duty by defendant was the actual and proximate cause of plaintiff's injury; and (iv) damage to the plaintiff's person or property. The first issue raised by these facts is whether Farmer owed a duty of care to his employee. As a general matter, no legal duty is imposed upon any person to affirmatively act for the benefit of others. However, the existence of a special relationship between the parties may create a duty. Modern cases extend the duty to employers when employees are injured in the course of employment. Thus, Farmer owed Prufrock a duty to protect him against an unreasonable risk of injury while acting within the scope of his employment. Farmer breached this duty by not warning and instructing Prufrock in how to act safely during an electrical storm. The breach of Farmer's duty was the cause in fact and proximate cause of Prufrock's injuries. Before the defendant's conduct can be considered a proximate cause of plaintiff's injury, it must first be a cause in fact of the injury. An act or omission to act is the cause in fact of an injury when the injury would not have occurred but for the act. The "but for" test applies where several acts combine to cause the injury, but none of the acts standing alone would have been sufficient. But for any of the acts, the injury would not have occurred. Thus, but for Farmer's failure to instruct Prufrock on how to act during an electrical storm, Prufrock would not have been injured. Farmer's failure to instruct is also the proximate cause of Prufrock's injuries. The general rule of proximate cause is that defendant is liable for all harmful results that are the normal incidents of and within the increased risk caused by his acts. This is an indirect cause case because an independent intervening force (the lightning) came into motion after Farmer's negligent conduct and combined with it to cause Prufrock's injury. Independent intervening forces are foreseeable (and thus do not cut off defendant's liability) where defendant's negligence increased the risk that these forces would cause harm to the plaintiff. Farmer's negligent failure to instruct Prufrock about the need to seek low ground during an electrical storm greatly increased the risk that Prufrock would be struck by lightning when the storm came up. Because the lightning was foreseeable and brought about a foreseeable harmful result to Prufrock, it was not a superseding force that would cut off Farmer's liability for Prufrock's injuries. (B) is incorrect because Prufrock's minority does not create a duty toward him by Farmer. The duty of care arises out of the employer/employee relationship. (C) is incorrect because, as noted above, the act of God (the lightning) would not be a superseding intervening force since it was foreseeable. Here, Farmer was negligent in not seeking to minimize the chances of Prufrock's being struck by lightning, when Farmer knew that such danger existed and owed Prufrock such duty as a result of his relationship (employer/employee) with Prufrock. (D) is incorrect because lightning can be foreseeable and was foreseeable here. The rain and loud claps of thunder were a clear signal that lightning might occur, and Farmer's failure to warn Prufrock created a foreseeable risk that the lightning would strike him.

Answer to Question 33

(C) Rosalie cannot successfully maintain a false imprisonment action against the store because the detention was privileged. The elements of a prima facie case for false imprisonment are: (i) an act by the defendant that confines or restrains the plaintiff to a bounded area; (ii) intent on the part of the defendant to confine or restrain the plaintiff; and (iii) causation. However, a privilege exists for shopkeepers to detain for investigation someone suspected of shoplifting. For the privilege to apply, the following conditions must be satisfied: (i) there must be a reasonable belief that a theft has been committed; (ii) the detention must be conducted in a reasonable manner; and (iii) the detention must be only for a reasonable period of time and for the purpose of making an investigation. Here, while the prima facie case for false imprisonment can be established by Rosalie, the detention was privileged because the store's security guard reasonably believed that a theft was being committed and detained Rosalie in a reasonable manner and only long enough to determine that she had not stolen the scarf. Hence, the store would not be liable to Rosalie in a false imprisonment action. (A) is incorrect because Bruno's detention was not unlawful but rather was privileged under the circumstances, as discussed above. (B) is incorrect because mental distress is not an element of a false imprisonment action. Had Bruno's conduct not been privileged, Rosalie could recover even if she had not suffered mental distress or other actual damages. Nor is mental distress sufficient to establish an intentional infliction of emotional distress action here, because Bruno's conduct under the circumstances was not "extreme and outrageous" as that tort requires. (D) is incorrect because Bruno's conduct in blocking Rosalie's exit from the store was a sufficient confinement for purposes of false imprisonment. In the absence of the shopkeeper's privilege, the store would be liable to Rosalie for the tort.

Answer to Question 34

(C) Starr will prevail in a suit for invasion of privacy since ZBS has published facts about Starr which place him in a false light in the public eye by attributing to him actions that he did not take. To establish a prima facie case for invasion of privacy based on a publication by defendant of facts placing plaintiff in a false light, the following elements must be proved: (i) publication of facts about plaintiff by defendant placing plaintiff in a false light in the public eye; (ii) the "false light" must be something that would be objectionable to a reasonable person under the circumstances; and (iii) malice on the part of defendant where the published matter is in the public interest. A fact will be deemed to present plaintiff in a false light if it attributes to him: (i) views that he does not hold, or (ii) actions that he did not take. The facts reveal that several parts of the ZBS docudrama portray the Starr-based character as being involved in several James Bond-type sexual escapades. Thus, they attribute to Starr actions he did not take. Furthermore, this false light would be objectionable to a reasonable person under the circumstances. Finally, Starr does not need to show malice because the episodes he is objecting to are not in the public interest. (A) is incorrect. To establish a prima facie case for invasion of privacy based on an appropriation of plaintiff's name, only one element need be proved: unauthorized use by defendant of plaintiff's picture or name for defendant's commercial advantage. Liability is generally limited to the use of plaintiff's name in connection with the promotion or advertisement of a product or service. The mere use of a personality's name in a TV show or magazine story, even though motivated by profit, does not suffice for liability. While Starr's name was listed in the credits, there is no evidence that his name was used in connection with the promotion or advertisement of the program and therefore this particular type of invasion of right to privacy is not as applicable as a false light action. (B) is incorrect. To establish a prima facie case for invasion of privacy based on an intrusion upon the plaintiff's affairs or seclusion, the following elements must be proved: (i) act of prying or intruding upon the affairs or seclusion of the plaintiff by the defendant; (ii) the intrusion must be something that would be objectionable to a reasonable person; and (iii) the thing to which there is an intrusion or prying must be "private." This tort does not provide special protection for the seclusion of a retirement. There is nothing in the facts to suggest that ZBS invaded plaintiff's private affairs in creating the scenes that he is objecting to. The accurate material in the show was drawn from Starr's crimefighting activities, which are not in his private domain. Thus, this branch of the privacy tort is inapplicable. (D) is incorrect because if Starr's privacy has been invaded, it is no defense that the program as a whole was not offensive. The invasion of privacy torts do not involve a balancing of complimentary and offensive statements to determine overall whether plaintiff's privacy was invaded.

Answer to Question 35

(B) Starr can recover presumed general damages because the defamation was libel and did not involve a matter of public concern. At common law, if all other elements of defamation in the form of libel have been established, plaintiff can recover damages for the general injury to his reputation without offering any proof; *i.e.,* general damages are presumed by law for all libel in most jurisdictions. Defamatory material in a television program, at least if it is not ad-libbed, is treated as libel. Thus, Starr can recover general damages even without proof of actual injury for the defamatory broadcast. (A) is incorrect because it states the rule for slander not within one of the slander per se categories: plaintiff must show actual pecuniary loss (*i.e.,* special damages) or else he can recover only nominal damages. (C) is incorrect. Under *Gertz v. Robert Welch, Inc.* (1974), a private figure suing on a matter of public concern not only must show that the defendant was negligent in ascertaining truth or falsity but also must prove "actual injury," *i.e.,* competent evidence of some personal or reputational damages. (Presumed damages are barred unless actual malice rather than negligence is established.) Here, however, the defamatory scenes that are the subject of Starr's suit are not on a matter of public concern—they are merely "enhancing the dramatic effect." Thus, the damages rules of *Gertz* do not apply and general damages are presumed according to common law. [Dun & Bradstreet, Inc. v. Greenmoss Builders, Inc. (1985)] (D) is incorrect because Starr is not a public figure and is no longer a public official; thus, he does not have to prove actual malice on the part of ZBS to recover damages.

Answer to Question 36

(D) Martha will not prevail if the newspaper was not negligent. Although at common law defamation liability could be strict, a number of Supreme Court decisions based on the First Amendment now impose a fault requirement in cases involving public figures or matters of public concern. A defendant may not be held liable for defamation on a matter of public concern not involving a public figure unless, in addition to publishing a false story, it was at least negligent in ascertaining the truth or falsity of its facts. Here, a story about an instructor at a prestigious college falsifying her academic credentials is a matter of public concern. Thus, (A) is incorrect. Knowledge or reckless disregard is the standard applicable to public figures, and Martha does not qualify as such merely because she is married to a public figure. Therefore, (C) is incorrect. (B) is incorrect because it describes a type of invasion of privacy—public disclosure of private facts. Invasion of privacy is not relevant to a defamation action.

Answer to Question 37

(B) Because Mr. Smith was aware that Greg often came onto his property, he should have taken steps to avoid the risk of harm posed by the equipment. Greg's suit sounds in negligence. A prima facie case for negligence consists of: (i) a duty on the part of the defendant to conform to a specific standard of conduct for the protection of the plaintiff against an unreasonable risk of injury; (ii) a breach of that duty by the defendant; (iii) the breach of duty was the actual and proximate cause of the plaintiff's injury; and (iv) damage to the plaintiff's person or property. A landowner has a special duty to exercise ordinary care to avoid reasonably foreseeable risk of harm to children caused by artificial conditions on his property. This duty is imposed upon the landowner if the plaintiff shows: (i) there is a dangerous condition on the land of which the owner is or should be aware; (ii) the owner knows or should know that young persons frequent the vicinity of this dangerous condition; (iii) the condition is likely to cause injury (*i.e.,* is dangerous) because of the child's inability to appreciate the risk; and (iv) the expense of remedying the situation is slight compared with the magnitude of the risk. Here, Mr. Smith knew or should have known that the equipment was on his land. Likewise, he should have known about its dangerous condition (*i.e.,* no safety locking device on the ignition); *i.e.,* he should have asked Jones Corp. whether it was safe to leave the equipment unattended, knowing that Greg often came onto the property. The equipment without the locking device is dangerous because a seven-year-old child would not appreciate the risk; he would probably believe that it is like a car, which will not start unless there is a key. The magnitude of the risk to Greg outweighed the expense of alleviating the danger, which could have been done in a number of ways (*e.g.,* by denying Greg access to the machinery, by specifically warning Greg of the danger, or by checking with the construction company to make sure that the machinery could not be started). Having failed to take any such precautions, Mr. Smith breached the duty he owed to Greg. This breach actually and proximately caused Greg's injuries. Thus, Greg will prevail against Mr. Smith. (A) is incorrect because building a swimming pool is not an ultrahazardous activity. An ultrahazardous activity is one that: (i) involves a risk of serious harm to persons or property; (ii) cannot be performed without risk of serious harm no matter how much care is taken; and (iii) is not a commonly engaged-in activity in the community. Building a swimming pool is probably a common activity in Mr. Smith's community, should not generally pose a risk of serious harm, and can be performed safely with the exercise of proper caution. Thus, there is no basis for holding Mr. Smith strictly liable for engaging in an ultrahazardous activity. (C) is incorrect because being a trespasser does not prohibit Greg's recovery. As explained above, as an infant trespasser, Greg was owed the duty of ordinary care to avoid a reasonably foreseeable risk of harm caused by the construction equipment. Having breached this duty, Mr. Smith will not prevail. (D) is incorrect because, regardless of whether Mr. Smith is deemed to have had a duty to inspect the safety features of the equipment, he breached his duty of ordinary care by failing to take any precautionary measures at all to guard against the foreseeable risk of harm to Greg.

Answer to Question 38

(B) If Brown Co. negligently maintained the equipment, Jones Corp. could obtain contribution from Brown Co. When two or more tortious acts combine to proximately cause an indivisible injury to a plaintiff, each tortious actor will be jointly and severally liable for that injury. Joint and several liability permits a plaintiff to recover the entire judgment amount from any defendant. Contribution allows a defendant required to pay more than his share of damages to recover from the other jointly liable parties for the excess. In other words, contribution apportions responsibility among those who are at fault. Here, if Jones Corp. is held liable for Greg's injuries, it will be because of its negligence in leaving unattended a piece of equipment without a safety locking device. However, if Brown Co., which was responsible for repair and maintenance of the equipment, negligently performed such maintenance, resulting in the absence of the safety locking device, then Brown Co.'s negligence would have combined with that of Jones Corp. to proximately cause Greg's injuries. This would render Jones Corp. and Brown Co. jointly and severally liable to Greg for the entire damage incurred. Thus, if Jones Corp. is held liable for the injuries, it has a claim against Brown Co., as a jointly liable party, for the amount it pays in excess of its share of damages. (A) is incorrect because indemnity is not available here. Indemnity involves shifting the entire loss between or among tortfeasors, and is available where: (i) there is a contractual promise to indemnify; (ii) there is a special relationship between the defendants that would allow for vicarious liability; or (iii) the defendant is a supplier in a strict products liability case who is liable to an injured customer, thus giving the supplier a right of indemnification against previous suppliers in the distribution chain. In addition, some states allow a joint tortfeasor to recover indemnification from a co-joint tortfeasor where there is a considerable difference in degree of fault. Here, there is no evidence of a contractual right to indemnity between Jones Corp. and Brown Co., there is no relationship between them that causes Jones Corp. to be held vicariously liable for Brown Co.'s negligence, and this is not a strict products liability case. Also, there is no indication of a considerable difference in degree of fault between Jones and Brown. Therefore, none of the circumstances in which indemnity is available is present. (C) is incorrect because it would allow for indemnity in this situation and, as explained above, the circumstances allowing for indemnity are simply not present here. (D) is incorrect because, as explained above, Jones Corp. can recover from Brown Co. based on contribution rules.

Answer to Question 39

(A) Where there is joint and several liability, both defendants are *liable* to the plaintiff for the entire amount of damages incurred, not just a portion of it. Of course, double recovery is not allowed. Thus, since Jones Corp. and Brown Co. have been found jointly and severally liable for Greg's injuries, each is liable for the full amount of $6,000. (D) is incorrect because it would result in a double recovery. Although each defendant is liable for the full $6,000, Greg's total recovery from the defendants cannot exceed $6,000. Thus, if Greg recovers $6,000 from one defendant, he cannot recover anything from the other defendant. (C) is incorrect because it would limit the liability of each defendant to only one-half of the total damage incurred. As stated above, joint and several liability means that each defendant is liable for the entire amount of damages. (B) is incorrect because it confuses joint and several liability with contribution among tortfeasors. Contribution allows a defendant who pays more than his share of damages to recover the excess from the other jointly liable parties; responsibility for the total damages is thus apportioned among those at fault. Traditional contribution rules require all defendants to pay equal shares regardless of their respective degrees of fault, while states with a comparative contribution system impose contribution in proportion to the relative fault of the various defendants. Nevertheless, this simply means that Jones and Brown have contribution rights *against each other* (*i.e.,* one can recover from the other for damages paid in excess of the amount proportionate to the defendant's relative fault). This does not, however, mean that these defendants' liability *to Greg* is based on their relative fault. In fact, if one defendant were judgment-proof, the other would be required to pay Greg the full $6,000 despite the fact that the judgment-proof defendant was mostly at fault.

Answer to Question 40

(C) For Russell to prevail in a claim against Ashton, Russell is going to have to show some fault on Ashton's part. Generally, a person would not be deemed at fault if he had a surprise heart attack while driving, which, of course, opens the issue of whether that person should have known of the possibility that he might have a heart attack. If Ashton had no prior history of heart problems, it is hardly likely that he would have any reason to believe that he might have a heart attack while driving, so (C) is the proper answer. None of the other answers deals with the threshold problem of whether Ashton is at fault in the first place since he had a heart attack; therefore, they are wrong.

Answer to Question 41

(A) In a suit for strict liability, a plaintiff will win if he shows that the latch was defective and it was that defect that made the product unreasonably dangerous. Plaintiff can show that the design of the latch was defective by showing that a less dangerous modification or alternative was economically feasible. (B) is wrong; the mere fact that the latch came open does not satisfy the test. (C) is wrong because reasonably foreseeable misuse is not a defense to strict liability. While the car may not have been used in the normal manner, it was certainly being used in a reasonably foreseeable manner and that is all that is required. (D) is wrong because Simpson's actions are irrelevant to Modo's strict liability in tort.

Answer to Question 42

(A) Department Store could be liable to Martha for assault if its employees caused Martha to be in apprehension of an immediate battery. (C) is incorrect because there need be no actual injury for Martha to recover for assault. She is entitled at least to nominal damages, and depending on the nature of the defendant's conduct, she might be entitled to punitive damages. (B) is completely wrong. Deadly force is never permitted in making a misdemeanor arrest, and so there would be no privilege to the assault in this case. (D) is wrong because intent to injure is not an element of the tort of assault.

Answer to Question 43

(B) The facts satisfy the requirements of false imprisonment. (A) is wrong because reasonable belief is not sufficient by itself to establish a shopkeeper's privilege to detain a suspected shoplifter; the means of restraint must be reasonable and deadly force may not be used. (C) is wrong because the period of confinement, no matter how short, is irrelevant to the tort of false imprisonment. (D) is wrong because "harm" is not required.

Answer to Question 44

(A) Since Martha was falsely imprisoned, she can recover damages for the humiliation she suffered. (C) is incorrect on that point. (D) is an incorrect statement because while Department Store's outrageous conduct might be important with regard to Martha's right to recover for intentional infliction of emotional distress, she can recover humiliation damages because of the false imprisonment even without that showing. (B) is not quite an accurate statement. The fact that Martha was falsely imprisoned may be attributable to the fact that Department Store was negligent in identifying her, but her cause of action arises out of the fact that she was falsely imprisoned regardless of how it came about that she was.

Answer to Question 45

(C) If Mineralco was subject to a nondelegable duty, it would be liable for the negligence of Digger in the transportation of the soil. (A) is therefore incorrect. (B) is incorrect because the possession of a license would not excuse Mineralco from liability. (D) is incorrect because the fact that the transportation of soil was common to the area would not excuse liability for negligence.

Answer to Question 46

(C) This is clearly the best of the possibilities. Conduct consistent with what a zoning ordinance permits is highly persuasive evidence that the use is not a nuisance. (A) is incorrect because higher use of property may be a factor considered when the courts balance the respective uses, but it is not in itself a conclusive argument. (B) is incorrect because the interference with another's use and enjoyment must be substantial and unreasonable to be actionable. (D) is incorrect because coming to the nuisance is not a good defense.

Answer to Question 47

(B) Most jurisdictions follow the rule that a child's conduct is judged by the standard of care applicable to a child of similar age, experience, and intelligence in similar circumstances. Thus, (A) is wrong. Formerly, many jurisdictions would conclusively presume that a very young child was incapable of negligence, and that an older child was rebuttably presumed not to have acted negligently. Most courts today, however, do not fix these presumptions at an arbitrary age. Thus, (D) is a misstatement of law. (C) is wrong because the question refers to the negligence cause of action.

Answer to Question 48

(A) In a contributory negligence jurisdiction, Joseph's negligence would be a complete defense to his recovery, and any derivative action based on his injuries would also be barred. A parent's action for his or her child's medical expenses is a derivative action; hence, (C) is wrong. (B) is irrelevant. (D) is a misstatement of the law (*see* discussion in previous question).

Answer to Question 49

(A) Rider's negligence was not a substantial factor in causing his injuries since it did not create a foreseeable risk of being shot by Rancher (*i.e.,* a sober, careful Rider arriving at the same place at the same time would still have been shot). Therefore, none of Rider's damages would be attributable to his negligence, and his recovery from Rancher would be total. Thus, (B) and (C) are wrong. (D) is wrong because Rancher owes Rider a duty of reasonable care in his activities, because Rider is a "discovered trespasser."

Answer to Question 50

(A) Because the damage resulting from medical malpractice was a foreseeable result of Rancher's negligence, he is liable for such damage even though the negligent doctor contributed to Rider's damages; *i.e.,* Rancher does not escape liability because of the malpractice. Therefore, (C) is wrong. Rider would not be permitted to recover in full from both Rancher and the doctor, but could maintain an action for all his damages directly against Rancher with no need to join the doctor. Thus, (B) and (D) are wrong.

Answer to Question 51

(C) Since Turner was not where Cabbie might have expected him to be, it would be relevant in judging the reasonableness of Cabbie's conduct. For this reason, (D) is wrong. (A) and (B) are wrong since Turner's violation would probably be excused under the circumstances. While (B) raises the issue of last clear chance, which would negate a contributory negligence defense, the facts do not establish that Turner was contributorily negligent.

Answer to Question 52

(C) A product manufacturer is not strictly liable for defects that were not present when the product left the manufacturer's control. (A) is therefore wrong. (B) is wrong because Fixit altered the use of the bolt by attaching a nonconforming blade. (D) is wrong because the majority of courts do not require privity of contract in a strict liability in tort action.

Answer to Question 53

(C) Most courts have refused to extend strict products liability to cases in which plaintiffs suffer only economic loss when not accompanied by physical harm to the plaintiff. (A) is therefore wrong.

(B) is wrong because it would have no bearing on a strict liability in tort action. (D) is wrong because strict liability extends to retailers.

Answer to Question 54

(D) A product manufacturer is not liable if the injury results from an unintended and unforeseeable misuse of the product. (A) is wrong since strict liability extends to foreseeable users. (B) is wrong because the facts do not indicate that Worker knew about the lightweight blade, and, in any case, states retaining traditional contributory negligence rules hold that ordinary contributory negligence is not a defense to strict products liability. (C) is wrong since the care exercised by the manufacturer is irrelevant in a strict liability action.

Answer to Question 55

(B) Mental incompetency does not preclude a showing that a defendant "intended" to inflict or to cause apprehension of a harmful touching. Hence, (C) is wrong. (D) is wrong because it makes no difference who Myron thought he was; it is only relevant that he intended to do what he did. (A) is irrelevant.

Answer to Question 56

(A) Consent to an intentional tort is ineffective if procured by fraud. Linda thought Myron was a doctor, and that is the only reason why she allowed him to treat her. (B) is arguable, but the facts really do not show Myron to have given her a shot and the facts only stated that Linda preferred to have pills instead of a shot. (C) is wrong because there is no need to show injury to prove battery. (D) is inconsistent with the facts; Linda was capable of giving consent.

Answer to Question 57

(D) Linda was in the room willingly and no facts show that she was there against her will. (A) is wrong because although a plaintiff need not risk harm by trying to escape, Linda was not trying to escape. (B) is incorrect, because whatever the reason for her conduct, there are no facts that tend to show Myron intended to falsely imprison her. (C) is not as good a choice as (D) because, while it is unlikely that Myron would have attempted to keep her locked in the room, the facts do not establish what his state of mind was.

Answer to Question 58

(C) Of all the defenses, the best defense is that Hospital acted reasonably under the circumstances and had no reason to know of Myron's conduct. (A) is incorrect; it goes only to the issue of Linda's conduct, not whether Hospital was negligent. (B) is wrong, because Myron's conduct is not "intervening" but is the circumstance upon which Hospital's breach of its duty to Linda may be shown. (D) is contrary to the facts—Linda suffered at least some discomfort.

Answer to Question 59

(D) Steve's statement imputing dishonesty in a person's profession or business is slander per se and hence requires no proof of special damages. Thus, (A) and (B) are incorrect. (C) is irrelevant in an action against Steve.

Answer to Question 60

(C) As long as it is understood in its defamatory sense, an accusation need not be believed to be actionable. Hence, (A) is wrong. (D) is wrong because the fact that Jose does not believe the statement does not prove lack of basis for Steve to have made it. (B) is wrong because damages are presumed to exist if it is slander per se.

Answer to Question 61

(C) Defamation requires a publication to third persons; hence (A) and (B) are incorrect. (D) is incorrect because negligent infliction of emotional distress requires a showing by the plaintiff that defendant created a foreseeable risk of physical injury to plaintiff, typically by causing a threat of physical impact that leads to emotional distress. No such risk was present here. In contrast, the scope of intentional infliction of emotional distress is broad enough to allow recovery for emotional distress caused by defendant's intentional insults and indignities. While it is by no means certain that Ken would prevail, it is the only theory that offers Ken a chance of recovering.

Answer to Question 62

(C) Since Steve's allegation is relevant to a lawsuit, it is absolutely privileged regardless of its truth or falsity. Thus, (A) and (B) are wrong. (D) makes no sense; a different statement would be involved in the second action.

Answer to Question 63

(D) Violation of the ordinance will not bar recovery by Alice. When an applicable statute establishes a duty of care, a tortfeasor's conduct will be governed by that statutory duty of care. However, in order for Musashi to be able to assert the statute as a defense (to establish contributory negligence of the plaintiff), it will have to show that plaintiff was one of the class of persons who were intended to be protected by the statute. In all likelihood, the statute was intended to protect the hikers, horseback riders, and bicyclists who use the trails, not the occupants of vehicles. Furthermore, it was Dean, not Alice, who violated the statute, and there is no basis for imputing Dean's negligence to Alice. Hence, the violation of the statute would not bar recovery by Alice. Thus, (A) is wrong. (B) is wrong. Even if it were shown that she had agreed with Dean, it would not bar recovery. (C) is wrong because there are no facts that show the prohibition against vehicular traffic was limited to the hours the park was open.

Answer to Question 64

(B) Dean's negligence is relevant in determining the cause of Alice's injuries. Hence, (D) is wrong. However, only if Dean's negligence is the sole proximate cause of Alice's injuries would it preclude Alice's suit against Musashi. Thus, (A) and (C) are incorrect.

Answer to Question 65

(D) The standard of care in a negligence action is reasonable care, and the plaintiff must show that the defendant has failed to exercise such care. (A) is wrong because it does not refer to the standard of care. (C) is wrong because it does not show that Musashi's standard of conduct was unreasonable. (B) is wrong because it does not refer to Musashi's conduct at all, which is critical to an action based on negligence.

Answer to Question 66

(C) Defendant's exercise of due care in the performance of a duty owing to plaintiff is a good defense in a negligence action. The fact that Saf-T guaranteed the product is irrelevant to Musashi's liability; thus (A) is wrong. (B) is not supported by the facts, which suggest that this roll bar collapsed because it was weakened by hairline cracks. (D) is a misstatement of the law in products liability cases.

Answer to Question 67

(A) Strict liability requires proof only that an unreasonably dangerous defective condition in defendant's product caused plaintiff's injury. (D) is wrong because res ipsa loquitur is applicable only in a negligence action. (B) is wrong because it only shows that Alice was injured, not that the bar was defective. (C) is wrong because whether Alice wore a seatbelt is not part of her prima facie case; at most, her failure to wear a seatbelt would be admissible in some states as evidence of contributory negligence.

Answer to Question 68

(D) The suit against Saf-T is for negligent manufacturing and installation of the roll bar. This negligence would not be superseded by any negligent conduct by Musashi, and there is no indication that Musashi discovered the defect but sold the vehicle anyway. (A) is wrong because the contract between Musashi and Saf-T cannot extinguish Saf-T's liability to third persons. (B) is wrong because the negligence of an intermediary does not relieve the manufacturer of liability for negligence. (C) is irrelevant.

Answer to Question 69

(B) This is a correct statement of the rescuer rule of duty. If Tom could show a breach of that duty, then he could recover from Eb on a negligence theory. (A) is therefore wrong. (C) and (D) are wrong because these theories apply to the unforeseeable plaintiff problem, which is not the case here because a rescuer is foreseeable.

Answer to Question 70

(B) All of the circumstances will be considered when evaluating the conduct of the rescuer. Thus, (A) and (D) are wrong. (C) is an incorrect statement of law; assumption of risk may be applicable, depending on the circumstances.

Answer to Question 71

(B) Res ipsa loquitur means the thing speaks for itself. It is appropriate in situations where an injury does not usually occur unless someone was negligent and plaintiff does not know which of the defendants caused the injury. While res ipsa loquitur is not always available where more than one person may have been in control of the instrumentality causing the injury, it is available in a case where a particular defendant had the power of control over the site of the injury. Even if Fred does not know who left the clamp in his body, Doctor, as the surgeon in charge, would be responsible and res ipsa loquitur could be used. (B) is thus the correct answer.

Answer to Question 72

(A) The general rule in malpractice actions is that the patient must know of the injury before the statute of limitations begins to run. Here, the subsequent examination for the promotion he received is the first indication of the negligence. The statute would begin to run from the time of that examination and would be tolled until that point in time.

Answer to Question 73

(D) Oscar's failure to ensure that Michael was made aware of the steering defect was negligent. In a gratuitous bailment, the bailor has a duty to inform the bailee of known dangerous defects. This duty is neither slight care nor strict liability. Thus, (C) and (B) are wrong. Sally's negligence in not telling Michael of the steering defect was a cause in fact, but would not supersede Oscar's negligence so as to relieve him of liability, because such negligence would not be so unforeseeable as to be a superseding cause. Thus, (A) is also incorrect.

Answer to Question 74

(D) The general rule is that an automobile owner is not liable for torts committed by another person driving the automobile. (C) is therefore incorrect. A permissive use statute, however, imposes liability for damage caused by anyone driving with the car owner's consent. (A) is wrong because Inez's negligence was also a causal factor. (B) is wrong because Sally's negligence will not be imputed to Michael.

Answer to Question 75

(D) Homer will recover because Biff's conduct created an unreasonable risk of harm to a foreseeable victim, and such harm proximately occurred. (A) is incorrect because the existence of a concurrent tortfeasor who is also liable for a plaintiff's injuries does not relieve another tortfeasor of liability. (B) is incorrect for a similar reason—Biff's actions were a concurrent cause of Homer's injuries, so he is liable even though the design defect was also a cause. (C) is wrong because it does not include the element of Biff's negligence—if Biff had been acting prudently or was operating under some privilege, the fact that Homer was injured while trying to avoid hitting him would not create liability. Thus, (D) is the best answer.

Answer to Question 76

(A) While a casual seller of personal property is not strictly liable for injuries caused by the defect, a seller who knows that the property has a dangerous defect has a duty to warn the buyer of the defect, and will be liable in a negligence action for failing to do so. (C) is wrong because it does not mention the necessary element that the seller knew of the design defect when he sold the mower to Homer. (D) is not correct because good maintenance had nothing to do with the accident that injured Homer. (B) is wrong because it was foreseeable that a user might have to turn sharply while riding the mower.

Answer to Question 77

(A) The tort of intentional infliction of emotional distress requires at least a reckless disregard that the conduct would cause emotional distress. The statement in (A) is most helpful to establish that requirement because it shows that the defendant knew of plaintiff's peculiar susceptibility to such an accusation. (B) is incorrect because, while one of the damages in an action for battery may be for emotional suffering caused by the battery, Tanya is suing for intentional infliction of emotional distress. (C) is not the best answer, because while evidence that it happened in front of other people may show the "outrageousness" of the conduct, an act is not outrageous just because it occurs in the presence of others. (D) is wrong because this tort does not require proof of economic damages.

BAR REVIEW

CONSTITUTIONAL LAW QUESTIONS

Question 1

State Green enacted the "Citizen Encouragement Act," which was designed to encourage long-time resident aliens to become American citizens. Under the Act, numerous state and municipal jobs were to be denied to persons who had been resident aliens for longer than 10 years. Those already in the state had to apply for American citizenship within a year after the law took effect. Persons who had acquired resident alien status prior to achieving the age of majority had until their thirtieth birthday to acquire such status or be automatically disqualified from obtaining such a job.

Pleczyk had fled a dictatorship in his native land and sought political asylum in the United States. Pleczyk was 40 years old and had been a resident alien for 15 years. He did not file for citizenship within the one-year grace period because he hoped to return to his native country when democracy was restored. Pleczyk, who was an expert on telecommunications, saw an ad in the newspaper describing a civilian position with a police department in Gruenwald, a medium-sized city in State Green. The position involved supervising and maintaining the department's emergency communications and response network. The chief of police was highly impressed when he received Pleczyk's application and even more impressed after interviewing Pleczyk. He told Pleczyk, "You've got the job, subject to the usual background check." The next day, an embarrassed chief called Pleczyk and told him, "I'm sorry, I can't hire you. Our legal department tells me I can't hire a long-term resident alien for any job with the Police Department." The law department was correct, because the new law banned long-term resident aliens from employment with "any state, county, or municipal agency involved with public safety." Pleczyk consults with an attorney.

The attorney should advise Pleczyk that, as applied to him, the State Green law is:

(A) Constitutional, because a police department is an integral governmental function and the state law does not discriminatorily classify resident aliens by race or ethnicity.

(B) Constitutional, because aliens are not entitled to the privileges and immunities of state citizenship.

(C) Unconstitutional, because the law does not apply equally to all aliens.

(D) Unconstitutional, because the reasons for application of the law to Pleczyk do not appear compelling.

Question 2

Congress was concerned about the quality of education at the lower grade school level. Believing that if local school boards had more flexibility in hiring and firing teachers, the caliber of teachers would be improved, Congress passed a law providing that school districts no longer needed to recognize the tenure of elementary school teachers; in other words, at a school board's discretion, all tenured teachers in a school district would lose their status and would be treated the same as nontenured teachers. The effects of the law would be to allow all teachers (tenured and nontenured) to be fired more easily if their performance was not adequate. The law would also allow the salaries of tenured teachers to be lowered, at least until a new contract with the teachers could be negotiated. This law will not take effect for two years, to give schools and teachers time to adjust to the law, but it specifically provides that once the law is in effect, school board actions under the law supersede any existing contract terms.

The Brookside Public Elementary School District is in the first year of a three-year contract with its teachers. Teachers in that district are represented by a teacher's union, to which all of the teachers belong. The union is not affiliated with any national unions or active in any other school districts. The union claims that when the law takes effect and the school board decides to implement it, numerous terms of the teacher's contract will be invalidated. (The contract provides for various rights and benefits for tenured teachers and has salary requirements set up on the basis of tenured/nontenured categories.) The school board has stated that it plans to abolish tenured positions as soon as the law takes effect. The union files an action in federal court on behalf of the teachers, asking for an injunction to prevent the school board from abolishing tenured positions and for a declaratory judgment stating that the law is invalid.

Should the federal court hear the case?

(A) No, because a ruling on the law at this point is premature.

(B) No, because the union does not have standing to sue on behalf of the teachers.

(C) Yes, because the federal law encourages improper interference with a contract in violation of the Contract Clause of the Constitution.

(D) Yes, because the teachers' rights and benefits are threatened by the law and school board's stated plans.

Question 3

Members of Congress were concerned about the rising use of chemical pesticides in populated areas and the danger to the environment from their runoff into waterways. After studying the matter, a congressional committee suggested, and the full Congress adopted, a law that prohibits the use of various pesticides in areas with a certain population density near navigable waters.

Iammi, a city located in the southeastern United States, was plagued by a sharp increase in disease-carrying mosquitoes. The city's board of health recommended that all residential areas be sprayed with chlorfin, a pesticide proven to be highly effective against mosquitoes. Despite the fact that the federal law would prohibit use

of chlorfin in these areas, the city council passed an ordinance adopting the board of health plan, relying on the opinions of several independent experts that the health benefits of reducing the mosquito population outweighed the risks of spraying. Yoga Yesiega, an Iammi citizen and committed environmentalist, is outraged by the ordinance, and brings an action in federal district court challenging the ordinance.

Assuming that Yesiega has standing, the court will most likely find the ordinance:

(A) Valid, because pursuant to the police power, cities have a compelling interest in laws designed to protect the health, safety, and welfare of their citizens.

(B) Valid, because controlling health hazards is an integral governmental function.

(C) Invalid, because it is superseded by the power of Congress to adopt laws to protect the health, safety, and welfare of citizens.

(D) Invalid, because it conflicts with a federal law that Congress had the power to make under the Commerce Clause.

Question 4

After the federal government closed a large military base near Blueville, unemployment figures for the city soared and tax revenues plummeted precipitously. Desperate to raise revenue, the City Council voted to erect billboards on the sides of all government buildings and to sell the space for commercial advertising. The city ordinance provided that any advertiser could rent the space, provided that the activity or product advertised was legal and had "nothing to do with religion or politics" because the Council sought to "avoid controversy."

Priscilla belonged to no organized religion, but considered herself a "spiritual" person. Priscilla operated and owned the Many Roads Bookstore and Meeting Center. Many Roads specialized in books on religious and generally "spiritual" subjects, but did not limit itself to any one religion or set of beliefs. In addition to selling books, Many Roads conducted reading and study groups on all of the major religions. Priscilla wished to place an ad on one of the new billboards. The ad was to read "Come to Many Roads Bookstore and You May Find Your Own Path to God. Study Groups Every Evening at 6 p.m." The ad was rejected by city officials.

If Priscilla files an appropriate suit against Blueville in federal district court asserting violation of her First Amendment rights, she is likely to:

(A) Win, because the City Council has made the sides of civic buildings public forums.

(B) Win, because restrictions on commercial speech must be narrowly tailored to serve a substantial government interest directly advanced by the restriction.

(C) Lose, because the restriction is viewpoint neutral and reasonably related to a legitimate government purpose.

(D) Lose, because the city must avoid excessive entanglement with religion.

Question 5

The state of Indiago required all automobile drivers to carry liability insurance; however, because of the high number of auto accidents in the state, the cost of insurance became prohibitive. The Indiago legislature sponsored a study on the problem. The results of the study showed that males under the age of 21 were four times more likely to get into automobile accidents than any other group, including females in the same age group. The study predicted that prohibiting males under the age of 21 from driving would result in a 15% reduction in all other persons' automobile insurance rates. The legislature held hearings on the pros and cons of prohibiting males under age 21 from driving and ultimately raised the minimum age for obtaining a driver's license to age 21 for males. Females were still allowed to obtain licenses at age 16.

Mario was an 18-year-old male living in Indiago when the driving age limit was raised. He worked as a delivery person for Tiddlywinks Pizza. He was a skilled driver and had never had an accident. Since Mario can no longer drive, he was fired from his job and replaced by a 17-year-old female.

If Mario sues to have the law set aside and prevails, it will most likely be because the state could not prove that the law was:

(A) The least restrictive means of achieving a compelling government purpose.

(B) Rationally related to a legitimate government purpose.

(C) Substantially related to an important government interest.

(D) Necessary to achieve a compelling government purpose.

Question 6

Lotco is the exclusive provider of lottery supplies (*e.g.,* tickets, sales terminals, etc.) for Wisconsota, a northern midwestern state. Wisconsota closely regulates the manufacture and distribution of lottery equipment by Lotco in order to prevent frauds. One lottery regulation requires Lotco to submit to the state resumes of persons being considered for employment. The state runs background checks on the prospective employees to ensure that they do not have a criminal record. If the state informs Lotco that a prospective employee has not passed the background check, the regulation forbids Lotco from hiring the person.

Pam has been working for Lotco for two years. Her performance has been marginally acceptable, but she often calls in sick. Last Friday, Pam called in sick. That evening, Pam's supervisor saw Pam dancing at a local bar. He immediately informed Pam that she should consider her employment terminated. Pam begged the supervisor to allow her to explain, but the supervisor refused to listen. Pam in fact had been sick on Friday morning but began feeling well by mid-afternoon.

A Wisconsota law provides that employees of the state cannot be fired from their positions except for cause.

Pam sues in the federal district court for Wisconsota, claiming that she was constitutionally entitled to a hearing to determine whether her supervisor had cause to fire her.

If the court rules correctly, it will probably find Pam's termination:

(A) Constitutional, because no hearing was required since the supervisor witnessed Pam's misconduct.

(B) Constitutional, because Lotco is free to fire employees at will.

(C) Unconstitutional, because it violates Pam's right to procedural due process.

(D) Unconstitutional, because of the state's regulation of the hiring process.

Question 7

A movie, *Last Rhumba in Havana*, was critically acclaimed and received the coveted Golden Bratwurst award at the Sheboygan International Film Festival. The film was heavily attended in the nation's large metropolitan areas and eventually worked its way to smaller towns. *Last Rhumba* has portrayals of nudity and scenes involving sexuality, but its advertising is very tasteful and concentrates on its critical acclaim and its receipt of seven Academy Award nominations. However, when *Last Rhumba* opened in Bleaton, Michinois, there was a public outcry against the film. Picketers appeared in front of the local theater carrying signs such as "Keep Filth Out of Bleaton!"

Bleaton was founded in the late nineteenth century by a fundamentalist religious group. Although the original religious group has faded from the scene, Bleaton remains a very conservative and highly religious community. Bleaton is the only community in Michinois where a consensus of the community would find *Last Rhumba* to be an obscene film. The Bleaton police, however, responding to community pressure, went to the local court seeking an injunction to halt the showing of the movie in Bleaton. Cecil B. Selwyn, owner of the theater, refused to voluntarily stop showing the film and appeared in court to defend against the proposed injunction.

What is Selwyn's best defense?

(A) The proper "community standards" should be those of the entire state rather than of the town.

(B) The film has some redeeming social value.

(C) The Establishment Clause of the First Amendment prevents the state from enforcing a particular set of religious beliefs.

(D) The film has proven artistic merit.

Question 8

Yessir Township is located in a farming community in a midwestern state. Most people who live in the township are Yessirrites, a religious group whose main religious tenet is that authority must be strictly obeyed. To maintain order in the classroom and help instill proper respect for authority in children, the Yessir Township School Board has voted that teachers within the township shall have the power to inflict corporal punishment on their students for certain offenses. Ricky is a fourth grader who attends a Yessir Township school. Neither he nor his parents are Yessirrites. Last week Ricky's teacher saw Ricky pull the hair of the girl sitting in front of him. The teacher called Ricky to the front of the class, made him bend over, and hit him on the rear with a ping pong paddle. Ricky received no permanent injury other than embarrassment. When Ricky got home, he told his parents of the ordeal. Ricky's father was very upset and hired an attorney. Rather than suing the teacher for battery as permitted under state law, the attorney brings an action against the teacher under a federal statute providing a cause of action for damages against any government employee who deprives a person of his constitutional rights. The attorney argues that the teacher deprived Ricky of:

I. His First Amendment rights under the Establishment Clause.

II. His right to procedural due process under the Fourteenth Amendment.

III. His right to be free from grossly disproportionate punishment under the Eighth and Fourteenth Amendments.

On which ground(s) is it likely that Ricky will prevail?

(A) I. and II.

(B) I. and III.

(C) II. and III.

(D) None of the above.

Question 9

Texlahoma is a large cattle-producing state. Farmers in Texlahoma recently have been having financial difficulty, chiefly because Argentinean beef can be imported to the United States for 20¢ per pound less than United States beef can be produced. To counteract the deleterious effects of Argentinean beef on the local economy, the Texlahoma legislature adopts a statute requiring any food service business operating in the state to serve beef raised in the United States.

Jeff is a licensed hot dog vendor at Airmen's Field, a municipally owned football stadium located in a major city in Texlahoma. Over the past several years Jeff has served "Viener's All Beef Dogs," which are made primarily from Argentinean beef. When Jeff discovers that switching to an all beef hot dog made from United States beef will reduce his profits by 10%, he comes to you, an attorney, for advice.

In researching Jeff's case, you discover that most of the footballs that are used at Airmen's Field are made of Argentinean leather.

Which of the following grounds is the best argument against the constitutionality of the Texlahoma statute?

(A) The statute burdens foreign commerce.

(B) The statute violates equal protection guarantees since it is not rational to prohibit the sale of Argentinean beef but not Argentinean leather.

(C) The statute substantially interferes with Jeff's right to earn a living under the Privileges and Immunities Clause of the Fourteenth Amendment.

(D) The statute constitutes a taking without due process of law.

Question 10

The state of Mediocre has modeled its constitution on the United States Constitution, adopting federal constitutional provisions verbatim wherever possible. Article VI of the state constitution's Bill of Rights follows the corresponding section of the United States Constitution and provides for speedy trials. Derrick was arrested in Mediocre for armed robbery. A combined preliminary hearing to determine probable cause and initial appearance was held within 20 hours of his arrest. Probable cause was found, and bail was properly denied under the state's Bail Reform Act. A state statute provided that when a defendant is in custody, his trial must begin within 50 days of his arrest. After 50 days had passed since Derrick's arrest and no trial had been held, he filed a motion for dismissal for violation of his right to a speedy trial under the state constitution. The trial judge held that he was bound to follow federal interpretations of the speedy trial provision and granted Derrick's motion on that basis. On appeal, the state supreme court agreed with the trial judge. The state prosecutor seeks to challenge the ruling in the United States Supreme Court.

If the Supreme Court thinks that the state court wrongly decided that Derrick was denied his right to a speedy trial under federal standards, it should:

(A) Reverse the decision because the state speedy trial provision cannot be interpreted in a manner different from federal interpretations.

(B) Reverse the decision and remand it to state court because the state speedy trial issue was so intertwined with the federal question that it would be difficult to determine on which ground the state court relied.

(C) Decline jurisdiction because the Eleventh Amendment prohibits a state from challenging a decision of its supreme court in federal court.

(D) Reverse the decision and remand the case to be decided on the independent state grounds only.

Questions 11-12 are based on the following fact situation:

Floracania is a large and populous western state that contains several national parks, including Morgue Valley, a hot and barren wasteland that stretches for nearly 100 miles on the western edge of the state. Unemployment is on the rise in Floracania, and the state offers a $25,000 prize to anyone who can devise a scheme to create at least 200 jobs within the state and demonstrate its viability. While hiking through Morgue Valley, Rick, an aircraft designer, notices some interesting rock along the valley's walls. On close inspection it appears that the rock contains rutile, a shiny mineral that contains titanium. Knowing that titanium is commonly used in military aircraft built within Floracania and that mining and refining titanium could provide the state with thousands of jobs, Rick chips out a sample of the ore and takes it back to the State Bureau of Employment. After reviewing Rick's ideas, the state announced that Rick was the first recipient of the $25,000 prize. The press quickly found Rick, interviewed him

about his find, and carried his story that evening. Upon seeing the story, Ronnie, the federal ranger in charge of Morgue Valley, was outraged since he knew of the rutile but never thought of its potential.

11. Ronnie has Rick arrested for violating a federal law making it illegal to remove any "plants, animals, or minerals from federal lands." Rick is convicted and fined $5,000. Rick appeals his conviction to the federal court of appeals, claiming that the fine was unconstitutional. How should the court rule?

(A) For Rick, since the state has a compelling interest in reducing unemployment and the federal statute unreasonably interferes with the state interest.

(B) For Rick, since removing the rutile was a purely intrastate act and had no effect on interstate commerce.

(C) For the government, since the federal statute providing for the fine is constitutional under the Property Clause of Article IV, Section 3 of the federal Constitution.

(D) For the government, since the federal statute providing for the fine is constitutional under the Commerce Clause.

12. To get some credit for the discovery, Ronnie informs his superiors of the titanium supply. To help support other national parks, the national park service builds a titanium smelting plant within Morgue Valley. The smelting plant is built to satisfy federal pollution regulations and will provide 300 jobs. A Floracania statute provides that all smelting plants within the state must be inspected by a Floracania inspector. Ronnie allows the inspection, assuming that if the plant is built to federal standards it surely will pass the state's tests. However, unbeknownst to Ronnie, the Floracania standards are much more strict than the federal standards (because Floracania residents are very concerned

about health and environmental issues and the state tourism industry depends on a clean environment). A Floracania inspector inspects the plant and refuses to approve it for operation. Ronnie begins to operate the plant anyway, and Floracania fines Ronnie $5,000. Which of the following will be Ronnie's best defense?

(A) The state does not have a compelling interest in regulating the plant, since it is within a federal park.

(B) The state regulation is invalid since Congress has preempted the field of pollution control.

(C) The state pollution regulation is invalid since it is inconsistent with the state's compelling interest in providing jobs.

(D) The state law violates the principles of intergovernmental immunity as applied to Ronnie.

Question 13

The city of Zenith, located in the state of West Dakota, was the national headquarters of the Curyist religion. Adherents of the religion played a leading role in the civic and business affairs of the city, in part because many of the teachings of the religion's founder, Cury, focused on one's conduct in business and commercial activities. Another tenet of the religion was that only males had the capacity to interpret these teachings in an authoritative manner; female members of the church were permitted to worship but not to participate in "Cury groups," small study groups where the topic of discussion was applying the founder's writings and teachings to current business activities. Zenith Community College, a branch of the state university system, permitted numerous student groups to use its facilities for extracurricular activities during times when classes were not in session. However, the school administration denied a request to a group of students in the business department to hold "Cury group" meetings in a classroom, claiming that it would be in violation of a state statute forbidding any group using public facilities to discriminate on the basis of race or gender.

The students bring an action in federal court challenging application of the statute to them by the school administration. If the court finds the actions of the school valid, it would most likely be because:

(A) Permitting the religious group to hold the meeting in a public school facility would violate the Establishment Clause, applicable to West Dakota under the Fourteenth Amendment.

(B) The statute is the least restrictive means of advancing West Dakota's compelling interest in ending discrimination by groups using public facilities.

(C) Allowing student groups to use classroom facilities when classes are not in session does not constitute state action for purposes of the Fourteenth Amendment.

(D) The right of freedom of association does not apply to groups involved in business and commercial activities.

Question 14

Which of the following named defendants could constitutionally be punished under a state statute that made criminal the "incitement of others to perform any criminal act"?

(A) Daniel, who tells a noontime rally of several hundred students at the university that "the corporate political structure of the United States reeks with its own corruption and will, when the time is right, be cleansed by the purifying fire of violent revolution. And I will lead that revolution, brothers and sisters; I will lead you in that glorious, purifying bloodbath!"

(B) Norman, who tells a clandestine meeting of 17 followers that "I believe that the non-white races are vermin created by Satan and should be eradicated on sight by right-thinking white Americans."

(C) Bruce, who tells the several thousand members of a protest march that "the racist war in Central America is illegal and immoral, and you should all go to the draft board offices right now and burn their records as a symbol of our contempt for their illegal war."

(D) Lucy, a member of the Khadafi People's Revolutionary Army ("KPRA"), whose Manifesto states that "each soldier of the Khadafi People's Revolutionary Army will take constant and immediate action to destroy the government of the fascist United States and to execute the officials of that government." Lucy joined the KPRA two years ago during her first semester of college away from her hometown of Dayton, Ohio, and has attended one weekly meeting and one KPRA bake sale since.

Question 15

Because of the rise in crime over recent years, the installation of burglar alarms has become a major business. Congress has recognized that the quality of alarm systems and installation personnel varies greatly. Since many people depend on burglar alarms to protect not only their possessions but their lives as well, Congress created the National Agency for Burglar Alarms ("NABA"). It gave NABA the power to regulate both burglar alarm hardware and installation personnel.

NABA adopted a regulation requiring that all burglar alarm installation companies be licensed. The regulation provided that anyone installing an alarm without a license could be fined, and that any company in the installation business on the day the regulation was adopted automatically would receive a license, but to obtain a license thereafter, an applicant would have to show that he has worked as an installer at a licensed company for at least three years.

Jim has been installing alarm systems for eight years. He had his own installation company, but because of difficulties in collecting his fees, he sold the business to Alarmco a few months before the NABA regulation was adopted and went to work for Alarmco servicing his old accounts. A few months after the NABA regulation was adopted, a representative from a national department store chain approached Jim and told him that the chain would like to hire Jim as an independent contractor to revamp the chain's alarm systems, explaining that he was very impressed with an alarm system that Jim had installed in one of their stores two years ago. Jim quit his job and applied for an NABA installer's license. His application was denied because he was not in business on the day the NABA regulation was adopted and had worked for a licensed installer for only a few months. Jim decided to install the alarm systems anyway.

Can Jim properly be fined for installing alarms?

(A) Yes, because the NABA was established under Congress's power to legislate for the general welfare, and Congress may take whatever steps are necessary and proper to enforce its laws.

(B) Yes, because the regulation falls within the scope of Congress's commerce power and Congress may delegate its authority to regulate as it has done here.

(C) No, because the regulation interferes with Jim's fundamental right to earn a living without a substantial justification and so violates the Privileges and Immunities Clause of Article IV, Section 2.

(D) No, because a government agency cannot itself levy fines for a violation of its regulations.

Question 16

The state of Florissippi prohibits publication of the identity of victims of sexual crimes, but allows trials of such cases to be televised, as long as the victim's face is blocked out. Recently, Billy K. Callahan, the nephew of a United States Senator, was accused of raping a woman at his family's estate in Florissippi.

Because of the notoriety of the Callahan family, the press was eager to enlighten the public as to all aspects of the Callahan case. Edward R. Burro, a reporter for a metropolitan newspaper published in Florissippi, discovered the name of Billy's victim from a police report that inadvertently included the victim's name and published the victim's identity in the next edition of the paper. Burro and the paper were fined $2,500 for violating the statute.

If Burro and the paper challenge the fine, the court should rule:

(A) For the state, because it has a compelling interest in protecting the privacy of its citizens.

(B) For the state, because inclusion of the victim's identity in the police report was inadvertent.

(C) For Burro and the paper, because the state does not have a compelling interest in prohibiting the dissemination of the lawfully obtained information here.

(D) For Burro and the paper, because the First Amendment allows the press to print any information that it legally obtains.

Question 17

Patton, an attorney, was employed by the United States Department of Health and Human Services in a regional office located in the leading tobacco-growing state. A labor contract between the agency and the clerical workers union contained a policy providing for termination of union employees only for certain specified grounds. Patton, however, was not a member of the union and not covered by such a policy. Patton was angered by the regional director's refusal to adopt a no-smoking policy for employees and visitors in the office. She posted a notice in the employee cafeteria ridiculing what she called the hypocrisy of an agency promoting health issues and nonsmoking programs while refusing to provide its employees with those same opportunities. The notice prompted a great deal of debate among the

employees and was brought to the attention of the regional director, who was very displeased.

Which of the following statements is most accurate regarding the director's right to dismiss Patton?

(A) Patton has a liberty interest in the exercise of her First Amendment rights that entitles her to a hearing to contest the grounds of her dismissal.

(B) Patton has a property interest as a public employee that precludes her from being fired without notice and an opportunity to respond.

(C) Patton has no right to a hearing because her statements were not an expression of views on public issues.

(D) Patton has both a liberty interest and a property interest that entitles her to a pre-termination evidentiary hearing.

Question 18

The state of Coronado provided for a public school system based primarily on property tax revenues from the various districts. School districts that had a property tax base below a certain threshold received supplemental funds from the state that were derived from state lottery revenues. The school districts receiving the supplemental funds served a predominately Hispanic population as compared to the school districts funded only from property tax revenues.

Because of a series of natural disasters in the state in recent years, as well as a substantial drop in lottery revenues, the state was facing a serious budget deficit. To help balance the budget, the Coronado state legislature passed a statute terminating the supplemental funds program and earmarking the lottery revenues for deficit reduction. A group of parents of Hispanic schoolchildren in one of the school districts formerly receiving supplemental funds filed suit in federal court, alleging that the state's action in terminating the funding violates the Equal

Protection Clause of the Fourteenth Amendment.

Which of the following best describes the appropriate standard by which the court should review the constitutionality of the state action?

(A) Because the state statute results in discrimination against a suspect class, the state will have to demonstrate that the statute is necessary to vindicate a compelling state interest.

(B) Because the right to education burdened by the statute is not a fundamental right, the parents will have to demonstrate that the statute is not substantially related to an important state interest.

(C) Because no suspect class or fundamental right is improperly burdened in this case, the parents will have to demonstrate that the statute is not rationally related to any legitimate state interest.

(D) Because the state statute is not discriminatory in intent, the state will have to demonstrate only that the statute is rationally related to a legitimate state interest.

Question 19

Since the oil crisis in the late 1970s and early 1980s, inventors have been attempting to develop products to improve fuel economy in automobiles. Recently, Vette, an automotive engineer, announced that he had developed a carburetor that will enable cars to achieve 100 miles per gallon of fuel, and that he will allow the carburetor to be inspected next May at the Indianapolis 500. Maro, another automotive engineer and former employer of Vette, brings an action to prohibit Vette from displaying the carburetor, claiming that Vette probably had stolen the carburetor's design from Maro. The court grants Maro a temporary restraining order prohibiting Vette from disclosing any mechanical details of his carburetor and orders a hearing to be held in one week to determine whether a preliminary injunction should be issued. Since

each party will have to reveal the mechanical details of his designs at the hearing, Maro requests that the hearing be closed to the public and that the record be sealed to avoid revelation of his designs. The court grants the request.

Stewart, a reporter for *Popular Cars Magazine,* hears about the case and wants to attend the hearing. When Stewart is told that the hearing will be closed, he files an action to have it opened.

What is Stewart's best argument for opening the hearing?

(A) Closure is not necessary to preserve an overriding interest here.

(B) The right of freedom of the press is extensive and allows the press to attend all hearings of interest to the public.

(C) Closure here amounts to a prior restraint.

(D) Under the fairness doctrine, the magazine will be required to give each litigant an opportunity to present his side of the case.

Question 20

As part of the Domestic Security Act, Congress established a permanent commission to evaluate the security of federal government buildings located in the District of Columbia. The commission would have the authority to evaluate current security conditions, establish new security guidelines, and coordinate security procedures among various governmental agencies. The legislation provided that three members of the commission were to be appointed by the President, two members by a committee of the House of Representatives, and two members by the United States Supreme Court. The President had the authority to veto any of the selections to the commission made by the congressional committee or the Supreme Court.

If a party with the requisite standing challenges the legislation and it is found unconstitutional, it will most likely be because:

(A) The President's power to veto a particular selection made by the congressional committee constitutes an improper exercise of the veto power.

(B) The commission will be exercising administrative powers.

(C) The judiciary does not have the power to make appointments to an advisory commission.

(D) The legislation does not provide for Senate confirmation of the presidential appointees.

Question 21

The zebra mussel is a small, prolific mussel first introduced into the Great Lakes by a foreign cargo ship. The mussels attach themselves to smooth, hard surfaces, and because of their small size they often make water intake pipes their home. After conducting a study, Congress determined that the mussels pose a great threat to the economic welfare of the Great Lakes region. To combat the mussels, Congress passed a statute requiring that all water intakes in the Great Lakes be coated with zebronium, a chemical compound that repels zebra mussels.

The Society for the Preservation of the Great Lakes ("SPGL") has also been studying the zebra mussel problem. Its studies show that while zebronium is effective, it is toxic to other aquatic life. The SPGL recommends that Great Lakes intake pipes be coated with a less toxic copper-based paint.

Because zebronium may harm aquatic life in the Great Lakes and copper-based paint is cheaper than zebronium, three Great Lakes states adopt laws permitting municipal water districts to coat their intake pipes with copper paint. Can municipalities using copper-based paint on their intake pipes successfully be prosecuted for violating the federal law?

(A) No, because the Tenth Amendment prevents Congress from interfering with integral government functions.

(B) No, because the municipalities are taking effective steps to combat zebra mussels in compliance with the spirit and purpose of the federal law.

(C) Yes, because Congress is in a better position to regulate the entire Great Lakes region than the individual states.

(D) Yes, because Congress may adopt laws regulating navigable waters.

Question 22

Harbor City is an old city located on the southern shores of Lake Michigan. Although the city was home to a thriving garment manufacturer, jobs were becoming scarce. To boost the local economy, the city council began developing its lakeshore. A beautiful marina was built, which attracted boaters from a nearby major metropolitan area, and shopping malls and eating establishments then began to spring up. To further increase tourism, the council began sponsoring laser light shows. Dancing laser lights were shown on a giant smokestack near the lakeshore. The shows proved to be very popular, and several charitable organizations approached the council requesting that they be allowed to sponsor a show and charge admission to raise money to help support their causes. One charity that was allowed to sponsor a show was Thousand Points of Light Against Blindness ("TPLAB"). To make its show outstanding, TPLAB hired Randy Warhal, a well-known laser light artist, to give the show.

When Randy arrived in Harbor City, he began setting up his lasers for the show. A city official soon stopped Randy, informing him that he could only use the city's lasers, explaining that the city feared that outsiders might use powerful lasers that could cause eye damage to viewers or disturb the nearby boaters. Randy called the TPLAB office and explained that the success of his art depends on the power of his lasers and that he could not produce desirable effects using the city's lasers. TPLAB appealed to the city council for help, but the council held fast to its rule requiring all laser light artists performing at its lakefront park to use the city's lasers.

If TPLAB files an action against Harbor City, the court will most likely:

(A) Find for TPLAB, since art is protected by the First Amendment and the city rule interferes with Randy's freedom of expression.

(B) Find for TPLAB, since the city rule is not the least restrictive method for achieving the city's goals.

(C) Find for Harbor City, since the laser light show is not speech and therefore is not protected by the First Amendment.

(D) Find for Harbor City, since the rule is a reasonable time, place, and manner restriction.

Question 23

Due to an ongoing economic slump, Congress was searching for new ways to raise revenue without offending the common taxpayer. A brilliant idea came to Stan Rostinsheepski, the chairman of the House Ways and Means Committee, while vacationing in Cozumel. He noticed that people were eager and willing to spend their hard-earned money on vacations. When he got back to Washington, he proposed that the federal government place a tax of $25 on each person flying into airports in the five most popular vacation destinations in the country, which his staff determined to be Orlando, Anaheim, Las Vegas, Maui, and San Francisco (the District of Columbia was also considered, but was eliminated so that the tax would not affect members of Congress). The tax was implemented, and officials in the five destinations were outraged, fearing that the number of vacationers to the taxed destinations would decrease due to the tax.

If the tax is challenged in federal court by an official with standing, the most likely result is that the tax will be held:

(A) Unconstitutional, because it makes it significantly more difficult for persons to travel between the states.

(B) Unconstitutional, because the tax unfairly discriminates against certain vacation destinations by taxing them and not taxing other, similar vacation destinations.

(C) Unconstitutional, because it is not rationally related to raising revenue since travel to those destinations probably will decrease.

(D) Constitutional, because Congress has plenary power to impose taxes to raise revenue.

Question 24

Many members of Congress have become increasingly displeased with the way the current Supreme Court has been whittling away protections that previous Supreme Court decisions created for individuals accused of crimes. To prevent further dilution of these protections, Congress passed a law eliminating from Supreme Court jurisdiction all cases in which a state supreme court has decided that a defendant's federal constitutional rights have been violated.

If the statute is held unconstitutional, it will most likely be because:

(A) The determination of the extent of constitutional rights is precisely the domain of the Supreme Court.

(B) Congress's power to limit jurisdiction applies only to cases originating in the federal courts.

(C) To be effective, the action taken by Congress here would require a constitutional amendment.

(D) Congress may not eliminate all avenues for Supreme Court review of issues vested within the judicial power of the federal courts.

Question 25

Charles Brown, the mayor of the town of Moralmous, has received several complaints from Moralmous residents regarding the growing number of adult theaters and nude dancing establishments in the nearby town of Decadents. To allay fears, he asked the town's attorney what can be done to prevent or at least limit such establishments from setting up business in Moralmous. Moralmous currently follows a zoning plan that provides for residential, commercial, and light industrial uses.

Which of the following most correctly describes the town's constitutional options?

(A) The town may revise its zoning ordinance to prohibit adult theaters and nude dancing establishments since erotica is unprotected speech.

(B) The town may revise its zoning ordinance to limit the location of adult theaters and nude dancing establishments only if this serves a compelling interest.

(C) The town may revise its zoning ordinance to limit the location of adult theaters and nude dancing establishments to control the secondary effects of such businesses.

(D) The town may not limit the location of either adult theaters or nude dancing establishments in any manner different from limitations on other commercial establishments.

Question 26

Venada is a western desert state. Most people in the state are employed by mining companies, the United States military, and gambling establishments. Many Venada residents grew tired of what they considered to be the immoral state of things in Venada and formed an organization called Citizens Against Gambling, Arming, and Mining ("CAGAM"). Members of CAGAM looked for an area in Venada where they would be free of all of the immoral activities in the state. A CAGAM officer soon discovered Peaceful, a sleepy Venada town. CAGAM members moved to Peaceful in large numbers, and soon controlled the village council. To ensure that the decadence of Venada did not invade Peaceful, the village council adopted an ordinance prohibiting "any gambling, mining, or military activities within village limits" and also prohibiting any devices related to such activities from entering the village. Unfortunately, Peaceful was located on a road that served as the most convenient exit from a nearby military base. In the past, the military would drive tanks and trucks with armed troops through Peaceful to go to training exercises in the Venada desert.

Can the military continue to drive through Peaceful?

(A) Yes, because the village ordinance interferes with the federal right to bear arms.

(B) Yes, because states and municipalities may not interfere with legitimate federal operations.

(C) No, if other routes are only slightly less convenient.

(D) No, because the village ordinance is a legitimate exercise of the municipality's police power to protect the health, morals and safety of its citizens.

Question 27

John and Mary were married five years ago. When they were first married, John had been working as a carpenter and Mary had been a receptionist. About two years after they were married, John and Mary had twins and Mary was forced to stay home to care for her children because of the prohibitive cost of day care. Money became tight for the family and John did not handle the added pressure well. Soon, John began drinking and lost his job. The family lost its apartment and was forced to move into public housing. John then started to become abusive. Mary filed for divorce with the state, but was told that she must pay a $150 court fee to obtain her divorce. Mary challenges the required fee.

Which of the following statements is most correct concerning Mary's challenge?

(A) Because Mary is poor, the state will have to show that its divorce fee is necessary to achieve a compelling interest.

(B) Because Mary is poor, she will have to show that requiring her to pay the divorce fee is irrational.

(C) Because Mary has a compelling interest in obtaining a divorce, the state will have to show that its divorce fee is narrowly tailored to serve an important state interest.

(D) Because Mary has a fundamental right to a divorce, the state will have to prove that requiring Mary to pay the fee is necessary to achieve a compelling state interest.

Question 28

Olympia is a large city within the state of Olympus. The Olympia Board of Aeronautics ("OBA") oversees the running of Olympia International Airport. Because of recent economically harsh times, OBA has received an unusually large number of requests for vendor licenses to operate shops and pushcarts in the airport. To give new applicants an opportunity, OBA has adopted a policy of reviewing current vendor licensees every three years. During the process, OBA reviews customer comments, assesses the utility of the vendor's services, and reviews the profitability of the vendor (licensees pay rent based on a percentage of their gross profit). The licensee is entitled to present evidence on all of the issues reviewed.

Pete owns a Currency Cart (a franchised currency exchange on wheels). He cashes checks, processes credit card advances, and exchanges foreign money for people passing through the airport. Pete had an OBA license to operate the cart within the airport until last week, when his license came up for review. After an appropriate hearing, OBA refused to renew Pete's license mainly because of an excessive number of customer complaints. Nevertheless, Pete continued operating his Currency Cart pursuant to a license granted to him under the Federal Borders Act that allowed him to operate his cart at all borders or their functional equivalent.

An Olympia police officer sees Pete and demands to see Pete's license. Pete shows his federal license, but the officer issues Pete a citation because he does not have an OBA license.

Which of the following is Pete's best constitutional defense?

(A) OBA deprived Pete of his license without due process of law.

(B) OBA's licensing scheme was arbitrary and capricious.

(C) OBA's licensing scheme substantially interferes with interstate and foreign commerce.

(D) OBA's license requirement here was superseded by Pete's federal license.

Question 29

A study by the Legislative Research Bureau of the state of New Foria indicated that an inordinately high percentage of homeless in the state were afflicted by alcoholism or addiction to illegal drugs. The legislature, therefore, decided to levy a special tax, with all proceeds marked for rehabilitative services for the homeless. However, the budget committee of the lower house concluded that further direct taxes on alcoholic beverages would be deeply resented by the citizenry. Also, lobbyists from the state's growing wine industry objected to anything that would retard the industry's development. There were no breweries or distilleries located in New Foria. The tax that was eventually passed required that newspapers and magazines of general circulation published in the state be taxed at a rate of 20% on all advertising space sold for beer or distilled spirits promotions.

For certain historical reasons, a high proportion of the advertising revenue of the *New Bremen Clarion* came from beer and wine ads. The *Clarion* was a weekly journal published in a small New Foria municipality far from the state capital. Several lawsuits were filed after imposition of the tax. The plaintiffs included the publisher of the *Clarion,* a major wholesale beer and liquor distributor located in New Foria's largest city, and several out-of-state brewers and distillers who sold and advertised their products in New Foria.

If the tax is declared unconstitutional, it will most likely be because:

(A) The tax burdens interstate commerce by exempting advertisements for the local wine industry from the tax, while the ads of out-of-state brewers and distillers are subject to the tax.

(B) The tax infringes on freedom of the press, which is guaranteed by the First and Fourteenth Amendments.

(C) The tax is unconstitutional because it is not properly apportioned.

(D) The tax violates the Equal Protection Clause of the Fourteenth Amendment, because it does not treat all alcoholic products equally.

Question 30

Pursuant to its power under the Commerce Clause, Congress adopted legislation requiring all employers to pay employees at least $8 per hour and prohibiting employers from requiring any employee to work more than a 12-hour day. The legislation also provided that any employee whose rights under the legislation are violated by his employer may bring a cause of action for damages against the employer in the federal district court in the district where the employee resides. The legislation defined "employer" to include "all commercial employers, all charities that compensate workers for their time, and all state and local governments."

Roy Desota worked as a paramedic for the Aridzona state police. Because of the nature of the job, Aridzona required its state police paramedics to work a 24-hour shift. They would then be off for 48 hours. Roy was unhappy with this arrangement and preferred to work a regular 10- or 12-hour day. A friend of Roy told him about the federal legislation discussed above, and Roy immediately brought an action against the state of Aridzona in federal district court.

The district court should hold:

(A) In favor of Roy, because under the Commerce Clause, Congress can create a federal court cause of action for damages against state governments.

(B) In favor of Roy, because Congress has the power to regulate the jurisdiction of the federal courts pursuant to Article III.

(C) Against Roy, because the federal legislation was not enacted pursuant to Congress's power to enforce the Fourteenth Amendment.

(D) Against Roy, because Congress has no power to remove the states' Eleventh Amendment immunity from suit in federal court.

Question 31

The state of Picayune sought to cut back spending wherever it could. One study revealed that an inordinate amount of resources were spent on elections. The study revealed that the fewer the candidates, the less was spent. It also revealed that a candidate who did not have at least 4% of the voters supporting him or her initially has never won an election. To avoid a useless waste of state funds in this area, the state legislature adopted a law requiring a candidate in a general election to collect on a petition supporting his or her candidacy the signatures of at least 4% of the voters eligible to vote for the office for which the candidate was running.

Debra lived in Picayune and was sick and tired of the way the state had slashed funding for school programs and environmental projects. She decided to run for the office of governor. Since Debra was not a member of either of the major parties in Picayune, she decided to run as an independent. Debra did not have as much money to run her campaign as the major party candidates, but her stand on the issues proved to be very popular. Several polls showed that 35% of the voters favored Debra. Nevertheless, while Debra's campaign was rapidly gaining support, her workers were inexperienced and few, and so they were able to obtain only 3.5% of the eligible voters' signatures by the filing deadline. Based on Debra's petition, the board of elections refused to put Debra's name on the ballot.

If Debra sues to have her name placed on the ballot, claiming that the Picayune petition requirements are unconstitutional, which of the following statements is most accurate?

(A)   Debra will have to show that the petition requirement is not rationally related to a legitimate state purpose.

(B)   Debra will have to show that the petition requirement is not necessary to achieve a compelling state interest.

(C)   Picayune will have to show that the petition requirement is narrowly tailored to achieve a compelling state interest.

(D)   Picayune will have to show that the petition requirement is rationally related to a legitimate state interest.

Question 32

Apathy is a large metropolitan city located on the ocean. In recent years the crime rate in Apathy has steadily increased, especially among teenage boys. Recently, groups of concerned citizens met to discuss their options for lowering the crime rate. Father Sarduchi, the administrator of a local parochial school, suggested that "idle hands are the devil's playground, and so the key to keeping teens from crime is to give them something to do." He suggested that they get the local teenage boys interested in scouting. To get the scouting program off the ground quickly, it was decided that all of the boys of scouting age in Apathy would be invited to an overnight jamboree, to be held in Lant Park, a large city park located on the oceanfront. Since it was Father Sarduchi's idea and he had some experience working with teenage boys, he was put in charge of the program.

Father Sarduchi met with Isaac, the Apathy parks commissioner, and requested a permit to camp at the park. Isaac told Father Sarduchi that while he could obtain a permit to use part of the park during daylight hours, a city ordinance prohibited large organized use of the park during the evening and all overnight camping. Isaac explained that the city wished to keep the park open for general use during the evening, when most people were off work, and the park was cleaned overnight. Father Sarduchi felt that the city's time restrictions would jeopardize the success of the jamboree and so brought an action in federal district court seeking to compel the city to allow overnight camping for this one special occasion.

If the court determines that the ordinance is valid, what will be the basis for its decision?

(A)   The ordinance is rationally related to a legitimate government interest and burdens the First Amendment rights involved no more than is reasonable under the circumstances.

(B)   The ordinance is narrowly tailored to serve a significant government interest and does not unreasonably limit alternative channels of communication.

(C)   The ordinance is substantially related to a legitimate government interest and burdens the First Amendment rights involved no more than is reasonable under the circumstances.

(D) The ordinance is rationally related to a legitimate government interest and does not unreasonably limit alternative channels of communication.

Question 33

Because of numerous complaints from minorities, Congress created a committee to investigate private discrimination. The committee found that minority race members were often discriminated against in private contracts of every sort, including contracts for housing, services, and goods. To help alleviate the problem, Congress passed a bill providing that "It shall be unlawful to discriminate against minority race members in the making and enforcement of any public or private contract, of every kind whatsoever. Any person whose rights under this statute are violated may bring a cause of action against the party that has so violated the person's rights in the federal district court for the district in which he resides, seeking treble damages or $1,000, whichever is greater." Several large banks that have been accused of discriminatory loan practices challenge the federal statute.

If the court finds that Congress had the power to enact the statute, the court most likely will find that the power arose from:

(A) The Contract Clause.

(B) The Thirteenth Amendment.

(C) The Fourteenth Amendment.

(D) The Commerce Clause.

Question 34

The state of Atlantic enacted a statute to provide financial aid for residents of the state who attend public or private colleges and universities in the state. Under this statute eligible students receive varying amounts of money, depending upon need. Sam, who is a resident of Atlantic, applied for a grant of funds under this statute to attend a private college in the state of Pacific. His application was denied because the college was outside Atlantic.

Sam files suit in federal court against the appropriate Atlantic official, challenging the constitutionality of the denial on equal protection grounds and to compel granting of his application. Which of the following statements is most correct?

(A) The suit is barred by the Eleventh Amendment.

(B) Sam has standing to maintain the action despite the fact that he has never paid taxes in Atlantic.

(C) The federal court will not grant the injunctive relief sought by Sam in the absence of "extraordinary circumstances."

(D) The doctrine of sovereign immunity bars Sam's action.

Question 35

LEGAL/EAGLE, a Delaware corporation with its business headquarters in Chicago, Illinois, conducts bar preparation courses for law school graduates. In addition to its national headquarters, LEGAL/EAGLE rents local administrative headquarters in at least one city in each state.

Its instructors are law school professors and other lawyers who are paid an hourly, or occasionally, bi-annual fee, but each instructor is considered an independent contractor and prepares his or her own lecture outlines and respective study outlines that are provided to students. Some instructors lecture only in one or more cities in the same state, while other instructors lecture in cities throughout the United States. Professor Morton Scholar is a resident of the state of Virginia, but he gives lectures on Constitutional Law in more than 20 states, including California.

Zenger Publishers prints all of LEGAL/ EAGLE's instructional materials in New York

State and ships the materials by commercial carriers to the respective state offices of LEGAL/ EAGLE. Zenger does not solicit business and does not have officers or agents outside of New York.

Which of the following taxes is *most* likely valid?

(A) A Virginia income tax on all of Professor Scholar's income.

(B) An Illinois income tax on all of Professor Scholar's income.

(C) A New York use tax on instructional materials shipped to and sold in California.

(D) A California ad valorem property tax on each item of instructional material received in that state.

Question 36

As part of a program to meet the needs of a growing homeless population, the city council of River City appropriated funds to construct a shelter and community center in the downtown area, and sought bids from organizations interested in operating the center. The group submitting the lowest bid was The First Church of the Good Samaritan, which ran a number of shelters and food kitchens in adherence to the religion's central tenet of aiding the needy. While church members never actively preached to people using the shelters, it did make available reading materials about its religion. The only other bidder, Reliance, Inc., was a local nonprofit foundation not affiliated with any church. Reliance concluded that it was underbid because it was subject to a state tax imposed on all facilities offering overnight lodging, whether run for profit or not-for-profit; the only exemption was for facilities run by an organized religion.

Reliance seeks to challenge the application of the state tax to its operation of the homeless shelter. Which of the following statements is most correct?

(A) Imposing the tax on the church's operation of homeless shelters, which is mandated by the religious beliefs of its members, would improperly inhibit their free exercise of religion.

(B) Maintaining the tax exemption for the church's operation of homeless shelters is a proper means of avoiding excessive government entanglement with religion.

(C) Permitting a tax exemption for the church-run shelter and not for a shelter run by other not-for-profit institutions has the unconstitutional effect of advancing religion.

(D) The tax exemption only for church-run shelters violates the Equal Protection Clause of the Fourteenth Amendment because the state does not have a compelling interest justifying application of the tax to some organizations that operate shelters and not others.

Question 37

After almost a year of legislative maneuvering, Congress finally passed a comprehensive health-care reform statute, which the President signed into law. Among other things, the statute created a Federal Health Policy Board, which was directed to monitor the fees charged for various medical procedures covered by insurance, and had the power to subpoena records to determine whether fee increases were a true reflection of cost increases. Nothing in the statute provided for caps on fee increases.

Because of the continuing escalation of health-care costs while the statute was being debated, several states had passed health-care legislation on their own. The state of Arkota had passed legislation prohibiting most fee increases of 10% or more per year for specified health-care services covered by insurance and creating a health-care review board to regulate these costs and impose monetary penalties on health-care providers or insurers that tried to circumvent the cap.

Which of the following would be the best basis for finding the Arkota provision unconstitutional?

(A) The federal legislation was passed after the state legislation and therefore supersedes it.

(B) The Federal Health Policy Board was constituted with many of the same powers as the Arkota board but was not given the power to impose sanctions.

(C) The state provision impairs existing contracts between health-care providers and insurers in violation of the Contract Clause.

(D) Health-care fee caps create an undue burden on interstate commerce even in the absence of federal regulation.

Question 38

Residents of the city of Parsimonia were beginning to feel the same economic pressures as residents of other cities. However, unlike other cities, Parsimonia officials had prepared for hard economic times and had a small budget surplus. To boost the morale of Parsimonia residents, city officials contracted with several builders to tear down some old buildings within the city and erect a park. Before the contracts were made, in order to garner the greatest political benefit from such projects, the Parsimonia council adopted an ordinance requiring that 35% of the workforce of contractors working on city-funded projects be Parsimonia residents.

Frank Wright, doing business as Wright Construction, was one of the contractors working on the park project. Wright employed several people from Parsimonia, but most of his employees came from Lake Grabowski, a town in a neighboring state that was a few miles west of Parsimonia and was the headquarters of Wright Construction. When the Parsimonia projects inspector discovered that Wright did not employ the required 35%, he gave Wright an ultimatum—hire enough Parsimonians to reach

the requirement within 20 days or forfeit the opportunity to work on the project. Wright immediately filed an action in federal district court seeking to have the Parsimonia employment requirement declared unconstitutional.

The court should rule in favor of:

(A) Parsimonia, because it is acting as a "market participant" here.

(B) Parsimonia, because there is a rational basis for favoring Parsimonia residents here.

(C) Wright, because the requirement interferes with his rights under the Privileges and Immunities Clause of Article IV.

(D) Wright, because the requirement interferes with his Contract Clause rights.

Question 39

A federal law requiring that all automobiles driven on United States military bases be equipped with air bags would most probably be justified by:

(A) The Property Clause of Article IV, Section 3.

(B) The General Welfare Clause of Article I, Section 8.

(C) The Supremacy Clause of Article VI, Section 2.

(D) The Commerce Clause of Article I, Section 8.

Question 40

Congress has recently enacted legislation that makes it a federal crime for any person to interfere with any right conferred by the Equal Protection Clause of the Fourteenth Amendment. Under which of the following circumstances would the named defendant be most likely to be validly convicted of violating the new statute?

(A) Roger bribes a federal official so that he fails to distribute free dairy products to otherwise eligible Asians because Roger hates Vietnamese immigrants.

(B) James, who believes women are inferior to men, persuades the dean of a private school licensed by the state to deny admission to otherwise qualified women because of their sex.

(C) Marcus, by threats of violence, coerces the coach of a public high school's basketball team to exclude white athletes from the team solely because of their race.

(D) Charles, a homophobe, persuades the members of his church council to deny shelter and food to homosexual men who seek aid at the church-run downtown relief center.

Question 41

As an aide to a member of the Congress of the United States, you are expected to provide an analysis of the constitutionality of proposed legislation that your employer is called to vote upon. A bill has been proposed that would create a mandatory price schedule for every motor vehicle sold in the United States.

Which of the following should you tell your employer is the strongest constitutional basis for the proposed legislation?

(A) All motor vehicle transactions in the United States, taken as a whole, have a significant impact upon interstate commerce.

(B) Since the purchase or sale of a motor vehicle, by definition, involves commerce, the federal government may regulate such transactions under the commerce power.

(C) Congress has the power to regulate transportation in the United States.

(D) Congress has the power to legislate for the general welfare of the people of the United States.

Question 42

Speedit, Inc. is a package delivery service that operates throughout the United States. Speedit specializes in transporting packages to airports, where air freight companies or commercial airlines transport the packages to their cities of destination. Speedit operates its service in the state of Great Lakes. Its entire fleet of trucks that operate in Great Lakes are registered in Great Lakes and never leave that state. Speedit purchased the trucks from Great Lakes dealers. Speedit drivers pick up packages from shippers within Great Lakes, and the packages are then delivered to an airport located in Great Lakes, where employees of the airlines load the packages onto their planes. Each shipper is charged a service fee by Speedit. Great Lakes wishes to impose a 5% transaction tax on each of the fees collected by Speedit for its services rendered in Great Lakes.

The federal courts would probably rule that such a tax is:

(A) Constitutional, because the tax is imposed before the packages enter the stream of commerce.

(B) Constitutional, because the tax is severable from any effect it might have on interstate commerce.

(C) Unconstitutional, because the packages are already in the stream of commerce.

(D) Unconstitutional, because the tax exposes Speedit to the possibility of multiple taxation.

Question 43

It was common practice in the state of Odaroloc for those loaning money with land as security for the loan (mortgagees) to require the party to whom money was lent to convey title to the secured land to the lender via a deed absolute. The lender would reconvey only upon complete payment of the loan by the debtor party. Another aspect of the deed absolute transaction was that it allowed the lender to dispose of the land immediately upon any default by the debtor, thus avoiding the cost and delay involved in foreclosure proceedings. Various populist and consumer groups had lobbied against the legality of the deed absolute for years, but had never been able to overcome the power of the state's lending institutions, until Demo Gogg was elected governor by a landslide on a platform that was highly populist in nature. Given the mandate that Gogg received from the electorate, the legislature quickly enacted a bill that immediately outlawed use of the deed absolute, declaring that all such deeds would be considered mere liens against the secured property. The law applied not only to loans made in the future, but also to the thousands of such loans in existence at the time the legislation was passed. The lending institutions, and many individuals who had loaned money secured through deeds absolute, banded together to challenge the constitutionality of the new law.

Assuming that there are no problems regarding jurisdiction and standing, which of the following represents the best argument attorneys for the lending institutions can make against the constitutionality of the law abolishing deeds absolute?

(A) As applied to loans outstanding at the time the bill was enacted, the law is an ex post facto law, and such laws are banned by the federal Constitution.

(B) Lenders using the deed absolute have been singled out by Governor Gogg and his followers in the legislature as political scapegoats, and such discrimination against the lenders violates the Equal Protection Clause.

(C) Lenders had property rights in the secured property and such rights were summarily abrogated by the new law, constituting an unconstitutional taking of property without due process of law.

(D) As applied to loans outstanding at the time the bill was enacted, the law impairs the contract rights of the lenders and such

rights are guaranteed by the Contracts Clause of the federal Constitution.

Question 44

After the release of various news stories about the President's possible violation of political campaign funding laws, a federal grand jury investigation and an investigation by a special Senate subcommittee have begun. The Senate subcommittee has subpoenaed documents and records from several top officers of the executive branch. Learning of the subpoenas, the President orders all executive officials to refuse to turn over materials, claiming "executive privilege."

Which of the following statements is most accurate?

(A) The subpoena violates the constitutional principle of separation of powers.

(B) The President's executive privilege is absolute, except in cases of impeachment.

(C) The presidential papers are presumptively privileged, but the privilege must yield to a demonstrated specific need for evidence in a pending legislative proceeding.

(D) The President's executive privilege applies to proceedings by Congress, but not to proceedings by the courts.

Question 45

The legislature of the state of New Caledonia passed a bill requiring that anyone holding himself out to be a private investigator in the state must be licensed by the state. Licensure requirements included a thorough background check into the person's criminal record and mental health. It also required passing a test on ethical obligations of a private investigator. Finally, the investigator was required to sign a two-part oath. Part one was a loyalty oath, which stated: "I solemnly swear (or affirm) that I will be loyal to the United States and the State of New Caledonia, and will uphold their Constitutions." Part two stated: "I solemnly swear (or affirm) that I am not now a member of any organization that advocates illegal acts, nor will I become a member of any such organization while I am a licensed private investigator in New Caledonia."

Panza, a highly qualified citizen of New Caledonia with a master's degree in criminal justice administration, applied for a private investigator's license. He easily passed both background checks, but he refused to take the oaths, claiming that they inhibited his freedoms of speech and association as guaranteed by the federal Constitution. The New Caledonia professional licensure board denied him a private investigator's license solely on the basis of his refusal to take the oaths.

If Panza sues in federal court to require New Caledonia to grant him a license and to strike down the oath requirements in the licensure statute, the court is likely to find that:

(A) Both the loyalty oath and the membership oath are constitutional.

(B) The loyalty oath is constitutional, but the membership oath is unconstitutional.

(C) The membership oath is constitutional, but the loyalty oath is unconstitutional.

(D) Neither the loyalty oath nor the membership oath is constitutional.

Question 46

Members of the legislature of Arkasouri have been receiving complaints from their constituents that the current method of funding school districts in the state is unfair, because the schools located in District 101—the district in Arkasouri's wealthiest county—receive twice as much funding per pupil as do schools located outside that district. This is due to the fact that District 101 residents pay more in taxes than residents of other districts, and is in no way due to racial or ethnic discrimination. In response to public pressure, the legislature adopted a statute requiring that Arkasouri school districts be funded equally on a per capita basis.

Frump, a resident of District 101 whose children attend public schools, brought an action in state court to have the statute declared invalid. The case reached the highest court in Arkasouri, which ruled that, based upon a provision in the Arkasouri Constitution similar to the Equal Protection Clause of the Fourteenth Amendment to the United States Constitution, all school districts in the state must be funded equally on a per capita basis. Subsequent to this decision, Torrington, a taxpayer in the state of Geordia, sued in federal court, demanding equal per capita funding of Geordia school districts. Torrington's case eventually reached the United States Supreme Court, which ruled that the Fourteenth Amendment does not compel equal funding, provided there is no probable racial discrimination in the funding.

After the United States Supreme Court decision, Frump filed a petition for a writ of certiorari to have the Arkasouri high court's decision overturned. Frump is most likely to:

(A) Prevail, because the Supremacy Clause renders the state decision invalid.

(B) Prevail, because the issue is res judicata.

(C) Not prevail, because the state decision turned on state law grounds.

(D) Not prevail, because Frump lacks standing.

Questions 47-49 are based on the following fact situation:

The state of Green has a statute providing that no alien may own land within the state and that it is unlawful for anyone to give, sell, or otherwise convey land to an alien. Arthur, a citizen of Canada, legally resides in Green. Arthur has entered into a contract to buy a parcel of land, located in Green, from Danielle.

47. If Arthur and Danielle join in a declaratory judgment action to test the state of Green statute in a federal court:

(A) The case may not be heard because Arthur does not have standing.

(B) The burden of proof is on Arthur and Danielle to show that the statute is rationally related to a legitimate state interest.

(C) The burden of proof is on the state to show that the statute is necessary to achieve a compelling state interest.

(D) The burden of proof is on the state to show that the statute is substantially related to an important state purpose.

48. If Danielle, but not Arthur, brings the suit to test the statute, her best argument is that the statute:

(A) Denies the equal protection of the laws to aliens.

(B) Unconstitutionally impairs her contract for the sale of her land to Arthur.

(C) Is a direct restraint on the alienation of her real property.

(D) Deprives her of a property right without due process of law.

49. If Arthur, but not Danielle, brings the suit to test the statute, he will probably:

(A) Win, because the statute impinges on Congress's power to legislate with respect to aliens and foreign affairs.

(B) Win, because the statute denies the privileges and immunities guaranteed by Article IV of the Constitution even though he is not a citizen.

(C) Win, because the statute denies him equal protection of the laws even though he is not a citizen.

(D) Lose, because he is an alien.

Question 50

During extensive hearings, the legislature of the state of Green investigated the effects on its highway system and on traffic safety of double tractor-trailer rigs, the huge freight-carrying trucks commonly known as "eighteen wheelers," which consist of a tractor (the motorized portion) towing two large, connected trailers. The testimony of highway engineers established that such vehicles, because of their greater weight, caused the roadway to deteriorate faster than other freight vehicles and autos. Traffic safety experts produced evidence showing that double tractor-trailer vehicles were involved in more accidents than other freight vehicles, primarily due to "jackknifing," where the rear trailer loses traction and swerves violently, causing the entire vehicle to be upended. After lengthy debate, the legislature passed a statute requiring the owners and users of double tractor-trailer vehicles to pay a user's fee in addition to normal vehicle licenses of $10 per mile traveled over the highways of Green, and an annual registration fee of $5,000.

Wesley owns a freight hauling business in the state of Red. His 30 trucks, all of which are double tractor-trailer rigs, carry manufactured goods between major cities in the states of Red, Yellow, and Blue. The trucks must pass through Green to reach Yellow and Blue on economical routes, and about 30% of the total mileage of all Wesley's vehicles is accumulated in Green. The mileage fees and registration fees for 30 trucks in a year would be about 60% of Wesley's gross annual income.

Wesley brought suit in federal district court in Red seeking a judicial declaration that the Green statute imposing user and registration fees in the amounts selected by the legislature of that state is unconstitutional. At trial, attorneys for Green produced evidence of highway destruction and safety hazards establishing the dangers of double tractor-trailer rigs as found by legislative committee hearings. Wesley proved the relevant facts about his operations and the cost the statute would impose.

If the court finds the tax unconstitutional, it will most likely be because:

(A) It seeks to regulate by taxation what it could not do directly, *i.e.,* regulate interstate commerce.

(B) The state's interests in preserving its highways and in promoting traffic safety are outweighed by the interference with interstate transportation of goods.

(C) It violates Wesley's right to the equal protection of the laws.

(D) A use tax on companies engaged in interstate commerce violates the Commerce Clause.

Question 51

Under contract with the federal government, Vendo operated a concession in Bronco River National Park. Vendo operated a small restaurant and a store that sold various curios and souvenirs. All of the land upon which Vendo conducted her business was federal land within the boundaries of the National Park. Bronco River National Park is located entirely within the boundaries of the state of Wyovada. Vendo paid no property taxes to Wyovada, because the land she leased under the terms of the concession was all owned by the federal government. However, the Wyovada state legislature recently enacted a statute imposing a "land utilization tax" ("LUT") on those operating businesses within the state who paid no property taxes. Wyovada attempted to enforce the tax against Vendo, and she in turn filed suit in federal district court to prevent the imposition of LUT on her business activities within Bronco River National Park.

Which of the following is Vendo's best argument?

(A) Vendo has been denied the privileges and immunities of national citizenship, protected by the Fourteenth Amendment, because the state tax impairs her fundamental right to conduct business on federal lands.

(B) The tax is unconstitutional as applied to Vendo, because it interferes with interstate

tourism in violation of the federal commerce power.

(C) Vendo is being denied equal protection of law, because those operating businesses on federal lands in other states are not subject to LUT or similar state taxes.

(D) The tax is unconstitutional as applied to Vendo, because under the property power the federal government has plenary power to regulate federal lands.

Question 52

The Federal Communications Commission issued a lengthy set of regulations regarding personal radar detectors. The regulations deal with the safety of such detectors and the frequencies on which they may operate, so as not to interfere with FCC licensed radio and television stations or with radar used by commercial airliners and private aircraft. Speedy, a resident of the state of South Cornpone, owned a radar detector that complied fully with all FCC regulations. One day, Speedy turned on his radar detector as he drove on an interstate highway from his home in South Cornpone into North Cornpone, where he planned to visit his aunt. A North Cornpone state trooper, using an old-fashioned stopwatch, clocked Speedy going 90 miles per hour in a 55-mile-per-hour zone. The trooper pulled Speedy over and issued him a speeding citation. He spotted the radar detector on Speedy's front seat and promptly issued Speedy another citation for violation of a state statute making it illegal to possess a personal radar detector in the passenger compartment of a vehicle within the state of North Cornpone. Speedy is willing to plead guilty to the speeding violation but seeks to go to federal court to have his conviction for possession of the radar detector overturned.

The court is likely to rule:

(A) Speedy wins, because the regulation of radio transmissions is within the purview of the FCC rather than the states and preempts any state laws that attempt to regulate such devices as radar detectors.

(B) Speedy wins, because the North Cornpone law burdens interstate commerce.

(C) Speedy loses, because the North Cornpone statute does not conflict with the FCC regulations.

(D) Speedy loses, because the state has a legitimate interest in regulating the use of radar detectors in order to promote safe driving.

Question 53

The constitution of the state of Haze authorizes a state reapportionment board to redraw state legislative districts every 12 years. During the most recent reapportionment process, consultants had provided the board with two alternative plans for reapportionment. One plan provided for districts with less than 3% difference in proportional representation between districts. The other plan was drawn up to conform state legislative districts as nearly as possible to county borders, resulting in differences in proportional representation between districts of up to 12%. The current apportionment of legislative districts results in differences of up to 15% between districts. The board ultimately selected the reapportionment plan based on county borders, and this plan was approved by the state legislature.

Thompson, a Caucasian resident of Haze City and a registered voter, brought a constitutional challenge to the reapportionment in federal court. His claim was based on the fact that, as a result of the plan that the board selected, the percentage of the African-American voting population in the district in which he lived increased from 45% to 55%. Had the other plan been selected, the percentage would have been unchanged in his district.

In the absence of a federal statute applicable to the state, is Thompson likely to prevail?

(A) Yes, because an alternative plan with more equal apportionment is available.

(B) Yes, because any legislative apportionment discriminating in favor of or against racial minority groups is subject to strict scrutiny, and there is no evidence of past discrimination or any other compelling state interest to justify adopting the plan.

(C) No, because preserving political subdivisions is a legitimate state interest that justifies the plan's variance in representation.

(D) No, because the reapportionment plan results in less of an overall variance between districts than the current legislative apportionment.

Question 54

A statute of the state of West Plains has detailed classifications of civil servants for both state and city positions. It provides that all civil servants who have been employed for over 18 months may be dismissed only for "misconduct" and also requires that state and city agencies comply with all procedures set forth in any personnel handbook issued by that agency. The personnel handbook of the state tollway authority sets forth detailed procedures for dismissal of civil servant employees. The handbook provides that written notice of the grounds for dismissal must be given to the employee prior to dismissal, and that the employee must, upon request, be granted a post-dismissal hearing within three months after the dismissal takes effect. An employee is entitled to present witnesses and evidence at the post-dismissal hearing, and is entitled to reinstatement and backpay if the hearing board decides that the city has not shown by a preponderance of the evidence that the dismissal was justified.

Gilbert has been an employee of the state tollway authority for three years. After an investigation by state auditors, Gilbert was notified by registered letter that he was being dismissed because of evidence that he took bribes from construction firms in exchange for steering contracts to them. He was informed of his right to a hearing and requested one as soon as possible. Three weeks after his dismissal, the state personnel board conducted a hearing at which Gilbert denied the charges and presented witnesses to attest to his honesty. At the conclusion of the hearing, the board upheld his dismissal, finding that it was supported by a preponderance of the evidence.

If Gilbert files suit in federal court challenging his dismissal on constitutional grounds, will he be likely to prevail?

(A) Yes, because Gilbert had a right to a pre-termination hearing at which he could present witnesses to support his side of the story.

(B) Yes, because Gilbert had a right to have an opportunity to respond to the charges prior to his dismissal.

(C) No, because the state may establish the required procedures for terminating an interest that it created by statute.

(D) No, because the procedures taken for termination of Gilbert's job satisfied due process requirements.

Questions 55-56 are based on the following fact situation:

To combat rising insurance rates, State forms a state-owned insurance company ("State Company") that operates exclusively within the state. The company provides insurance on the basis of premiums calculated according to a schedule of fees. The schedule shows a higher rate by 25% for the city of Rockridge.

55. A group of Rockridge residents, angered by the fact that premiums are higher for their community than for any other in the state, brings suit in state court requiring State Company to make the premiums equal for everyone. Which of the following would be the most likely result?

(A) The residents will prevail, unless State Company shows a compelling reason for the discrimination.

(B) State Company will prevail, unless the residents show that there is no rational basis for higher premiums.

(C) The suit will be dismissed, because State Company is organized as a private business and thus is acting as a market participant.

(D) The suit will be dismissed, because it is an instrument of the state, and thus immune under the Eleventh Amendment from suits by citizens of the state.

56. Rockridge has a Mexican-American population of approximately 40% of the entire population of the city, compared with 15% in the rest of the state. In a suit by these Mexican-American citizens alleging that State Company's rate structure violates the Equal Protection Clause, which of the following would be the most likely result?

(A) The citizens will prevail, because the higher rates have the effect of discriminating against the Mexican-American population.

(B) The citizens will prevail, unless State Company shows a compelling reason for the discrimination.

(C) State Company will prevail, unless the citizens show that they pay higher rates than similarly situated non-Mexican-American citizens of Rockridge.

(D) State Company will prevail, because discriminatory economic regulations are not a suspect classification.

Question 57

In an effort to standardize laws pertaining to the solicitation of business by mail, Congress adopted the Uniform Mail Solicitation Act ("U.M.S.A."), which established certain requirements that must be met before an organization can solicit business through the mails.

A national religious organization solicits charitable contributions by mail. The federal statute would substantially interfere with the successful accomplishment of the organization's religious objectives.

If the organization files suit seeking a declaratory judgment that the federal law may not be applied to its solicitation activities, which of the following, as a matter of constitutional law, best describes the burden that must be sustained?

(A) The federal government must demonstrate that a rational legislature could believe that this law helps to achieve a legitimate national interest when applied to both religious and secular solicitation activities.

(B) The federal government must demonstrate that the application of this statute to the solicitation activities of this organization is necessary to vindicate a compelling governmental interest.

(C) The organization must demonstrate a specific congressional purpose to inhibit the accomplishment of the organization's religious objectives.

(D) The organization must demonstrate that no reasonable legislator could think that the application of the U.M.S.A. to this organization would be helpful in accomplishing a legitimate governmental objective.

Questions 58-60 are based on the following fact situation:

Wilbur's adult son was murdered and the confessed murderer was convicted after a jury trial and sentenced to death. Several years later, the state supreme court overturned the conviction for reasons relating to the procedures used by the police to obtain the confession of the accused murderer. The district attorney declined to reprosecute, citing lack of available admissible evidence.

Wilbur announced to the press that he was forming an organization to change the state

constitution to permit greater admissibility of relevant evidence in criminal prosecutions, and that the organization—Parents Against Murder ("PAM")—would hold its first rally on the steps of the state supreme court building.

At 10 a.m. on a Monday, Wilbur addressed a crowd of about 500 people on the steps of the supreme court building, while the court was in session inside. Using a hand-held voice amplification device, he exhorted his listeners to join PAM and to support his suggested changes in the state constitution. As he described the circumstances of his son's murder and the subsequent judicial proceedings, he became very emotional and shouted, "Each one of the so-called justices in that building are murderers, just like the bastard who killed my son. They're worse murderers, because they make it possible for more sons and daughters, fathers and mothers to be murdered. I'd like to see every one of them strung up, like they should have done to the creep that was set free, and if someone will give me a rope I'll go in there and do it myself. If there's a God in Heaven, the seven of them will burn in Hell!" After his speech, Wilbur handed out leaflets describing his organization and its aims, and then went home. The crowd had dispersed by 11 a.m.

58. A state statute, enacted in 1898, prohibits "the public utterance of any blasphemy or sacrilege," and provides criminal penalties for its violation. Wilbur is prosecuted for violation of this statute, only the third recorded such prosecution in the state's history. Which of the following constitutional defenses would *least aid* Wilbur's defense?

(A) Application of the statute to Wilbur infringes his freedom of speech in violation of the Fourteenth Amendment.

(B) Application of the statute to Wilbur denies him equal protection of the law in violation of the Fourteenth Amendment.

(C) The statute violates the Fourteenth Amendment because it is an establishment of religion.

(D) The statute violates the Fourteenth Amendment because it is vague.

59. Another state statute proscribes, with criminal penalties, "the making of any threat to the life or safety of a public official for any act he performed as part of his official duties in office." Which of the following is correct regarding the statute?

(A) Wilbur could constitutionally be punished under the statute, but only if the state court justices heard the threats he made.

(B) Wilbur could constitutionally be punished under the statute.

(C) Wilbur could not be constitutionally punished under these circumstances, but the statute is constitutional on its face.

(D) The statute is unconstitutional on its face.

60. A third state statute makes criminal "all speechmaking, picketing, or public gathering of any sort on the steps of the supreme courthouse Monday through Friday, between the hours of 8:30 a.m. and 4:30 p.m., when court is in session." If Wilbur is prosecuted for violation of that statute, which of the following best describes the applicable burden of proof?

(A) The state will have to show that there was a compelling need for the statute and that no less restrictive alternatives existed to meet that need.

(B) The state will have to show that the statute was narrowly tailored to serve a significant government interest and leaves open alternative channels of communication.

(C) Wilbur will have to show that there was no compelling need for the statute and that less restrictive alternatives were available to accomplish the same goals.

(D) Wilbur will have to show that there was no reasonable basis for enacting the statute.

Question 61

Federal District Judge Jones was accused of misconduct in office and was impeached by the House of Representatives. At trial in the United States Senate, Judge Jones was convicted and removed from office. However, the President then directed the Attorney General to institute criminal proceedings against the judge. After presentation to a federal grand jury, an indictment was issued against Judge Jones and signed by the Attorney General. At the opening of his trial, Judge Jones moved to have the indictment dismissed.

Most likely the trial judge would:

(A) Dismiss, because the President had told the Attorney General to prosecute.

(B) Dismiss, because the criminal proceeding violates the Fifth Amendment's proscription against double jeopardy.

(C) Deny the dismissal, because the federal grand jury issued the indictment.

(D) Deny the dismissal, because Judge Jones has not been previously tried in a criminal proceeding.

Question 62

Fassil was a foreign student who had entered the United States on a student visa four years ago. When Fassil's visa expired, he was notified by the Immigration and Naturalization Service that he was subject to being deported. Federal law provided that an alien who is subject to being deported has the right to appear before an administrative officer appointed by the Attorney

General's office for a hearing on whether he should be deported. This officer, appointed by the executive branch of the government, has the right under law to make a final order concerning whether the alien should be deported. After a hearing, the administrative officer entered an order allowing Fassil to remain in the United States as a permanent resident.

However, a congressional act allowed the House of Representatives, by resolution, to deport "undesirable aliens." After the administrative judge entered his order, the House passed a resolution that Fassil should be deported. Fassil petitioned the federal court to declare the legislative resolution invalid.

The court should find the resolution:

(A) Valid, because Congress has plenary powers with regard to aliens and naturalization.

(B) Valid, because aliens are not "citizens" within the meaning of the Fourteenth Amendment.

(C) Invalid, because the INS law removed congressional power with regard to aliens in this circumstance, and the resolution of the House violates the separation of powers doctrine.

(D) Invalid, because Fassil was denied due process when he was not given a hearing before the House of Representatives.

Question 63

Ford defeated Hudson in a close election to determine the president of the State Carpenters' Union. Shortly after the election, Hudson discovered that Ford had been a member of the Communist Party 15 years ago. The United States has a statute that prohibits a member of the Communist Party from serving as an officer of a labor union. Hudson revealed this information to the executive board of the Carpenters' Union, which declared Ford's election as president invalid. Ford brings suit in federal court

challenging the constitutionality of the United States statute.

The court will most likely hold the statute to be:

(A) Constitutional, because the statute bears directly on the internal security of the United States.

(B) Constitutional, if the government can show a rational basis for the adoption of the statute.

(C) Unconstitutional, because the federal government may never discriminate among persons on the basis of political affiliation.

(D) Unconstitutional, as a bill of attainder.

Questions 64-66 are based on the following fact situation:

The state of Red has long been known for the quality of its silver-tip fox furs. Recently, however, the size of the silver-tip fox population has dwindled to dangerously low proportions. This is due in part to increased hunting caused by the increased demand for the furs and also to a reduction in the size of the foxes' habitat caused by increased population in Red.

Both the government of Red and the federal government have decided to take action to protect the foxes. The state government has enacted a statute that reads as follows:

1. No fox shall be hunted or captured within the state unless it is at least 24 inches in length (the purpose being to allow young foxes to breed before being taken).

2. A tax of $5 per fox shall be levied on all foxes taken within the state. All fees so collected shall be used for conservation and protection of the foxes' habitat.

3. All hunters must report in person any foxes taken within the state to the nearest State Department of Fish and Game office, which shall then levy the $5 fee.

The federal government enacts legislation that provides $2.5 million for research into ways to increase the state's fox population. The legislation also imposes a special excise tax of $100 per fox taken in violation of state law if later shipped via interstate commerce.

64. Act Now, a consumer action group, brings suit in federal court to stop the expenditure of the $2.5 million on a "frivolous and unnecessary project." The suit challenges the expenditure as an improper exercise of congressional power. Which of the following defenses raised by the federal government are valid?

   I.   The legislation is a valid exercise of the federal taxing and spending powers.

   II. The federal court lacks jurisdiction to enjoin such expenditures voted by Congress, under the doctrine of separation of powers.

   III. Act Now lacks standing to sue (even though all of its members are federal taxpayers).

   (A) I. and II. only.

   (B) I. and III. only.

   (C) I. only.

   (D) III. only.

65. Hunter, who is engaged in the business of hunting and trapping foxes and selling the furs, is a resident of the state of Blue, which borders Red. Blue has no laws restricting the taking of silver-tip foxes. While hunting foxes in Blue, Hunter accidentally crossed into Red. She was arrested by Red game wardens for taking foxes less than 24 inches in length. If Hunter challenges the constitutionality of the Red statute, which of the following is the most likely result?

   (A) The statute will be held invalid because it violates the interstate Privileges and Immunities Clause of Article IV, Section 2.

   (B) The statute will be held invalid because it is preempted by the federal legislation regarding the taking of foxes.

   (C) The statute will be upheld because Congress may allow the states to adopt legislation that would otherwise violate the Commerce Clause.

   (D) The statute will be upheld because it is not unduly burdensome on interstate commerce.

66. Gamer, a resident of the state of Green who hunts foxes in Red and sells the furs in other states, filed suit challenging the constitutionality of the $5 per fox tax imposed by the Red statute. Which of the following is the most likely result?

   (A) Gamer will win, because the tax is invalid under the Commerce Clause.

   (B) Gamer will win, because the tax is invalid under the Import-Export Clause.

   (C) Gamer will lose, because the tax is valid under the Commerce Clause.

   (D) Gamer will lose, because the tax is valid under the Import-Export Clause.

CONSTITUTIONAL LAW ANSWERS

Answer to Question 1

(D) The law probably is unconstitutional as applied to Pleczyk. An equal protection issue is involved. Under the Equal Protection Clause, state classifications based on alienage are subject to strict scrutiny and so must serve a compelling interest to be constitutional. No compelling purpose seems to be present here. Thus, (D) is correct. (A) is incorrect because, although there is an exception from the strict scrutiny standard where a state or local government discriminates against aliens when hiring persons for jobs involving "self-government" process, the job here (emergency communications for a police department) is a technical position and probably would not be found to be related to the self-government process and, in any event, the statute applies to all positions and not just to jobs involving only the self-government process. (B) is incorrect because, although it is true that aliens are not entitled to the privileges and immunities of state citizenship, the law here is still unconstitutional under the Equal Protection Clause, as discussed above, which applies to aliens. (C) is incorrect because the discrimination would be unconstitutional even if it did apply to all aliens equally, as discussed above.

Answer to Question 2

(A) The federal court should not hear the case because it is not yet ripe for review. A federal court will not hear a case unless there exists a "case and controversy." This has been interpreted to mean, among other things, that a plaintiff generally is not entitled to review of his claim unless he has been harmed or there is an immediate threat of harm. This is to prevent the federal courts from hearing unnecessary actions. There is no immediate threat of harm to the union here since the law does not take effect for another two years. Before that happens, Congress might change the law or repeal it altogether, or the school board may decide to keep the old contract system after all. Thus, (A) is correct and (D) is incorrect. (B) is incorrect because the union would have standing. An association has standing if (i) there is an injury in fact to its members that would give them standing, (ii) the injury is related to the organization's purpose, and (iii) neither the nature of the claim nor the relief requested requires participation of the individual members in the lawsuit. All three of the conditions are met here; thus, the union would have standing. (C) is incorrect because the Contract Clause does not limit federal power, only state power, and since the state would be acting pursuant to a federal law here, there would be no Contract Clause violation. Moreover, even if the Contract Clause limited the state's actions here, it still is not clear that there would be a constitutional violation. The Clause bans only substantial interference with existing contracts (*i.e.,* destruction of almost all of a party's rights under a contract), and it is not clear here that the impairments would be sufficiently substantial.

Answer to Question 3

(D) Congress's power to regulate commerce has been construed broadly, so that it may regulate any activity, local or interstate, that either in itself or in combination with other activities has a substantial economic effect on interstate commerce. If Congress has determined that the use of chemical pesticides and their runoff into waterways (which are channels of interstate commerce) will have an overall detrimental impact on the environment, this determination will be sufficient in this case to satisfy the standards established by the Supreme Court. Therefore, the law probably is a valid exercise of the commerce power. Any state or local action that conflicts with a valid act of Congress is invalid under the Supremacy Clause. (A) is incorrect because while the police power (the power to adopt regulations for the health, safety, and welfare of citizens) belongs to the states, a police power regulation that conflicts with a federal law is invalid under the Supremacy Clause. (B) is incorrect because state and local government activities may be regulated by a general law that applies to both the public and private sectors, even if the regulation affects integral governmental functions, as long as there is a constitutional basis for the law. (C) is incorrect because Congress does not have a general "police power" to adopt laws on health and safety. The laws that Congress has passed banning activities that it has deemed harmful to public health have been based on its power to regulate interstate commerce.

Answer to Question 4

(C) The restriction will probably be upheld because it is viewpoint neutral and reasonably related to a legitimate government purpose. The billboards are not traditional public forums; rather, they will be found to be "commercial ventures" by the city. In a similar setting, the Supreme Court held that cities could differentiate between broad categories of speech in accepting advertising on city-owned buses (*i.e.,* the Court allowed a city to refuse political advertising and accept only commercial advertising) [*see* Lehman v. Shaker Heights (1974)], as long as the restriction was viewpoint neutral and reasonably related to a legitimate government interest. The city rule here is constitutional because it is viewpoint neutral (it distinguishes between broad categories of speech but does not distinguish based on content within a category) and it is reasonably related to the legitimate government interest of avoiding controversy. (A) is incorrect because the Supreme Court has held that allowing advertising on government-owned property does not make that property a public forum; rather, the property is a commercial forum. [*See* Lehman v. Shaker Heights, *supra*] (B) is incorrect because although it states the general rule for regulation of commercial speech, the more specific Supreme Court precedents regarding advertising on *city-owned* property used for a proprietary venture (discussed above) would apply here. (D) is incorrect because nothing in the city policy would cause an excessive entanglement with religion; rather, the policy seeks to avoid excessive entanglement by prohibiting religious ads on government property.

Answer to Question 5

(C) Mario will prevail if the state cannot establish that the restriction is substantially related to an important government interest. Classifications based on gender usually are tested against an intermediate standard of review; *i.e.,* the Supreme Court will strike down the classification unless the government offers an exceedingly persuasive justification that the classification is substantially related to an important government interest. Classifications intentionally discriminating against men generally are invalid, and (C) states the proper standard for review. (A) and (D) are substantially the same and incorrect because they state the standard to be applied to classifications involving a suspect class or fundamental right. However, a gender-based distinction is characterized as a *quasi-suspect* classification. (B) is incorrect because it states the standard to be applied when no fundamental right or suspect or quasi-suspect class is involved.

Answer to Question 6

(B) Lotco was free under the Constitution to fire Pam without a hearing because she was an employee at will. Unless prohibited by a state statute, a private employer usually can fire an employee for any reason or no reason at all, absent a contract providing otherwise. (C) and (D) are related to each other and are both incorrect. Most constitutional guarantees prohibit state action and do not impose duties on private parties. That is not to say that state action can never be found in the acts of a private party—it will be found if the private party performs exclusive public functions or has significant state involvement in its activities. However, there is no state action here. Running a lottery is not an exclusive public function and merely being the exclusive lottery supplier for a state does not constitute significant state involvement, even where the state controls who may be hired. State action will not be found merely because the state has granted a monopoly to a business or heavily regulates it. (A) is incorrect because whether a hearing is required does not turn on whether the supervisor witnessed the misconduct—if state action were involved, a hearing would have been required because a public employee who is subject to removal only for "cause" has a property interest in her job that cannot be taken without fair process. Since there was no state action, no hearing was necessary.

Answer to Question 7

(D) Selwyn's best defense is that the film has proven artistic merit. The First Amendment generally protects the right of freedom of speech, and this freedom includes the right to show movies. Thus, to enjoin the showing of the movie here, the city will have to prove that the speech involved is unprotected speech. Obscenity is the category of unprotected speech most relevant here. The Court has defined obscenity as a depiction of sexual conduct that, taken as a whole, by the average person, using contemporary community standards: (i) appeals to the prurient interest in sex; (ii) portrays sex in a patently offensive way; and (iii) using a rational, reasonable person standard, does not have serious literary, artistic, political, or scientific value. If Selwyn shows that the film has proven artistic merit, it cannot be held to be obscene because the third element of the above definition will have failed. Thus, (D) is his best argument. (A) is not as good an argument as (D) because the Supreme Court has held that while a statewide community standard *may* be used, it is not mandatory—a local community standard is sufficient to evaluate whether the film is "patently offensive." Thus, the town of Bleaton's community standards would be sufficient. (B) is not as good an argument as (D) because it is not sufficient that there is *some* redeeming social value; it must have *serious* redeeming value, as indicated above. For example, it would not be sufficient that an otherwise obscene movie included short tips on the importance of brushing teeth. (C) is not a good argument. The Establishment Clause forbids the government from adopting a law or program that establishes religion. It is inapplicable here because the town is not trying to enforce a particular set of religious views; rather, it is trying to prohibit obscenity. The Supreme Court has held that the government has a legitimate interest in prohibiting obscenity, and the fact that this happens to coincide with the beliefs of a particular religious group does not render such bans void. If (C) were true, laws against murder could be found invalid on similar reasoning.

Answer to Question 8

(D) Ricky probably cannot prevail on any of the constitutional claims presented. There is no Establishment Clause violation here. Under the Establishment Clause, if there is no sect preference, government action generally will be upheld if the action serves a secular purpose, its primary effect neither advances nor inhibits religion, and it does not excessively entangle government with religion. There is no sect preference under the school board's corporal punishment rule here, the rule has the secular purpose of maintaining order in the classroom (the fact that this coincides with the tenets of Yessirism is irrelevant), its main purpose neither advances nor inhibits religion, and there is no excessive entanglement. Thus, I. is not helpful. Neither is II., because there has been no deprivation of procedural due process. The Supreme Court has held that although corporal punishment may involve a liberty interest, no hearing is required prior to inflicting such punishment; the possibility of a common law action in tort is sufficient procedural protection. [Ingraham v. Wright (1977)] Finally, there is no Eighth Amendment violation because paddling students as a disciplinary measure has not been found to be cruel and unusual punishment. Therefore, III. is also of no use to Ricky.

Answer to Question 9

(A) The best argument against the constitutionality of the Texlahoma statute is that it burdens foreign commerce. For all practical purposes, the power to regulate foreign commerce lies exclusively with Congress. Therefore, a state that adopts legislation requiring private vendors to favor United States products over foreign products, as Texlahoma did here, may be acting outside the scope of its powers. (B) is incorrect because the statute is a rational method of protecting local beef interests. The rational basis standard applies when an economic law such as the one here is challenged on equal protection grounds. Under the standard, the Supreme Court will usually defer to a legislature's decision that the law is rational notwithstanding the fact that the statute is underinclusive. In other words, the law need not address all of the problems that prompted its passage; it will be upheld even if it is only a "first step" toward a legitimate goal. Here, prohibiting the use of foreign beef appears to be a rational method of protecting Texlahoma beef raisers. Thus, it is irrelevant that the statute is underinclusive in that it allows the use of both United States beef and Argentinean leather. (C) is incorrect because the right to earn a living is not a privilege under the Fourteenth Amendment, which protects against infringement of rights of national citizenship, such as the right to petition Congress for redress. (Neither would the statute violate the Privileges and Immunities Clause of Article IV, since that clause only prohibits discrimination against citizens of other states and the statute here treats citizens of all states the same.) (D) is incorrect because Jeff had all of the process that was due him. Since the government action here was a general act and not an individualized adjudication, Jeff had no right to an individual hearing; the normal procedure for adopting a statute is all the process that is due.

Answer to Question 10

(D) The best way to approach this question is to eliminate the wrong answers first. (A) is incorrect because state constitutional provisions do not have to be interpreted exactly the same as federal provisions; the federal Constitution provides the minimum rights that states must provide, but states are free to grant broader rights. Thus, even though a 50-day delay may be constitutional under the federal Constitution, it can still be held unconstitutional under a state constitution. (B) is incorrect because the facts make it clear that the state court was relying on federal case interpretations. Moreover, if the Supreme Court could not decide whether the case was based on federal or state grounds, it would not reverse the case, since a federal court will not hear a case that can be based on adequate and independent state grounds; rather, it would dismiss the case or remand it to the state for clarification. (C) is incorrect because the Eleventh Amendment generally prohibits federal courts from hearing actions by a private party or foreign government against the state government; it does not bar a state from appealing a ruling from its own court system. Thus, (D) is correct. The Supreme Court had jurisdiction to hear the case, since it has jurisdiction to hear appeals from a state's highest court concerning the constitutionality of a state statute, and as indicated above, the state court's decision was not based on independent state grounds since the decision was based on federal case law interpreting an identical federal provision. Thus, jurisdiction was proper and the Court could reverse the state court decision and hold that a 50-day delay does not violate the federal Constitution. However, the case should be remanded so that the state may decide whether the delay was too long under state law, since a state is free to provide its citizens with more civil protection than is required by the federal Constitution.

Answer to Question 11

(C) The court should affirm Rick's conviction. The fine is constitutional under the Property Clause, which gives Congress the power to "make all needful rules and regulations respecting the territory or other property belonging to the United States." This power permits Congress to acquire and dispose of all kinds of property, and to protect its property with a law such as the one here. (D) is not as good an answer as (C) because the Commerce Clause is not as directly applicable to regulation of acts on federal lands as is the Property Clause. Nevertheless, (B) is wrong because the fine could probably be upheld under the Commerce Clause. Under the Clause, Congress may regulate any act that may itself or in combination with other activities have a substantial effect on interstate commerce, even intrastate activities. If everyone removed minerals from federal lands, the necessary substantial effect on interstate commerce would be present. (A) is incorrect because, notwithstanding the state's compelling interest, by virtue of the Supremacy Clause a valid act of Congress supersedes any state or local action that actually conflicts with the federal rule.

Answer to Question 12

(D) The states have no power to regulate the activities of the federal government unless Congress consents to the regulation. Thus, instrumentalities and agents of the federal government are immune from state regulations that interfere with their federal functions. Here, the regulation clearly interferes with Ronnie's federal duties to run Morgue Valley operations. While it might be argued that Ronnie agreed to comply with the state regulations, because he allowed the state inspection, nothing indicates that Congress consented, and so the state regulation cannot be applied to Ronnie. (A) is factually incorrect; a state may still have a compelling interest in activities on federal lands, and the interest here of preventing pollution that may spread beyond federal lands probably is compelling. Nevertheless, the argument is without merit because it is irrelevant whether the state has a compelling interest in regulating federal activities; a state simply is not allowed to interfere with federal activities. (B) is incorrect because not enough facts are given to make this determination. The Supremacy Clause prohibits states from adopting laws that interfere with federal laws, and this prohibition extends to any law—even one that seeks to support the federal scheme—when Congress has preempted the field. In determining whether a field has been preempted, courts will consider the comprehensiveness of the federal scheme. The question does not give enough facts to make the determination here. (C) is incorrect because it is irrelevant. The Constitution does not require the state to favor one compelling interest over another, and so states are free to adopt laws that interfere or are inconsistent with other state goals, unless the laws are arbitrary, in which case they would violate substantive due process. The laws here do not appear to be arbitrary, and so (C) does not offer a viable defense.

Answer to Question 13

(B) If the school's action is valid, it will be because the state statute is the least restrictive means of advancing the state's compelling interest in ending discrimination by groups using public facilities. While schools are generally not public forums, they may become a designated public forum by being held open to student groups for meetings. In that case, the First Amendment may be violated if a college restricts use of its classrooms based on the content of a student group's speech. To justify content-based regulation of otherwise protected speech, the government must show that the regulation is necessary to achieve a compelling state interest that cannot be satisfied by less restrictive means. Similarly, the right to associate for expressive purposes is not absolute. Infringements on the right may be justified by compelling state interests, unrelated to the suppression of ideas, that cannot be achieved through means significantly less restrictive of associational freedoms. Here, the state's interest in not allowing its facilities to be used by groups practicing discrimination of various types is compelling. [See

Roberts v. United States Jaycees (1984)] The denial of access to the student group based on their religious principles, while it may be viewed as content-based discrimination, is the most narrowly drawn means of advancing the state's interest. [*See* Bob Jones University v. United States (1983)] (A) is incorrect because a school does not violate the Establishment Clause by permitting a religious student group the same after-class access to its facilities that other student groups have. [Good News Club v. Milford Central School (2001)] (C) is wrong because the actions of administrators of a state college in allowing or denying access to its facilities is clearly state action that brings the Fourteenth Amendment into play. (D) is incorrect. While the right to join together for expressive or political activity, which is protected by the First Amendment, may be less strong for large organizations that engage in both commercial and expressive activity than for smaller and more selective groups, it is still a recognized right. [*See* Roberts v. United States Jaycees, *supra*] Furthermore, the student group's discussion of business activity in this case is tied to its religion. Hence, the association rights of the student group are based on freedom of religion as well as freedom of expression. The state would probably have to show a compelling interest to support a restriction on the group's association rights.

Answer to Question 14

(C) Of all the defendants listed, Bruce is the only one who is advocating imminent illegal action and whose advocacy is likely to produce such action. A state cannot prohibit advocating the use of force or of violation of the law unless such advocacy: (i) is directed to producing or inciting imminent lawless action; and (ii) is likely to produce or incite such action. In (C), Bruce is advocating the immediate commission of an illegal act (burning the records of the draft board offices). Bruce's words are directed to producing such action. Because Bruce is addressing several thousand people who are there for the purpose of protesting government policy in Central America, many such people are likely to be stirred into action by Bruce's words, as a means of further demonstrating their opposition to the war. Thus, it is likely that a number of people will converge on the draft board office and attempt to disrupt its operations and burn its records. Consequently, Bruce's words are of the type that can be constitutionally proscribed by the state. In (A), Daniel's words simply relate his belief as to the nature of the political system in the United States, and they speak of some time in the indefinite future when, supposedly, Daniel will lead a violent uprising against that system. These words are not *directed* to inciting imminent lawless action, but are rather a prediction and an expression of Daniel's hope as to what will happen in the future. Also, it is highly unlikely that the several hundred university students listening to these words will be incited to immediately engage in violent revolution. Thus, Daniel's speech cannot constitutionally be punished. Similarly, in (B), Norman is expressing his beliefs that nonwhite people should be "eradicated." Although such words do advocate the use of force, the facts do not indicate that they are directed toward the incitement of such action *imminently* (*e.g.*, Norman is not advocating that his listeners kill a particular nonwhite person who is nearby). In addition, there is no indication that Norman's listeners are likely to be provoked by his words into the imminent use of force against nonwhite persons. Consequently, the state cannot, under the Constitution, punish Norman for his words. (D) is incorrect because Lucy has not even gone so far as to advocate the use of force or illegal action. The KPRA manifesto does state that members of the KPRA will constantly and immediately take illegal and violent action. However, mere membership in such an organization, with apparently no active promotion of its goals or interests, and no active participation in its operations, will not subject a person to punishment based on the advocacy of the organization. In two years of KPRA membership, Lucy's involvement with the organization consisted of attending one meeting and one bake sale. This falls far short of demonstrating an active promotion of KPRA's illegal and violent goals, or participation in activities designed to further those goals. Because Lucy has not personally advocated lawless or violent action, or personally participated in or otherwise furthered such advocacy by others, she cannot constitutionally be punished under the state statute.

Answer to Question 15

(B) Jim can be fined. Congress has the power to regulate alarm installation companies under the Commerce Clause because the clause permits Congress to regulate any local or interstate activity that, either in itself or in combination with other activities, has an effect on interstate commerce. Burglar alarm companies use instrumentalities of interstate commerce such as phone lines and have a cumulative effect on interstate commerce even though some may only do business locally. Hence, their activities can be regulated by Congress. The delegation to the NABA is valid since Congress has broad discretion to delegate its legislative power; the Supreme Court will uphold almost any delegation of congressional power. Therefore, Jim can be fined. (A) is incorrect because it improperly mixes two concepts. Congress does not have the power to *legislate* for the general welfare—there is no federal police power—rather, Congress has the power to *spend* for the general welfare. (C) is incorrect because even assuming that the regulation here interferes with Jim's right to make a living, it would not violate the interstate Privileges and Immunities Clause of Article IV because the clause restricts states, not the federal government. (D) is incorrect. Congress can provide that violation of an agency's regulations is a criminal offense that can be enforced through the imposition of fines. Furthermore, an agency has the power to impose civil fines and penalties for a violation of its regulations.

Answer to Question 16

(C) Burro and the paper should prevail. The Constitution prohibits Congress or the states from abridging freedom of the press. While this freedom is no greater than the freedom of speech granted to all citizens, the information printed by the paper here is protected. The media may not be punished for publishing a true fact once it is lawfully obtained from the public records or is otherwise released to the public. It does not matter that the release was inadvertent. Therefore, (C) is correct and (B) is incorrect. [*See* The Florida Star v. B.J.F. (1989)] (A) is partially true—a state might have a compelling interest in protecting the privacy of its citizens—but the state generally cannot protect the interest by prohibiting publication of public information; the most that the state may do is keep such records sealed. (D) is incorrect because it is too broad; freedom of the press is not absolute. For example, the press would not be allowed to reprint copyrighted material regardless of whether it was legally obtained.

Answer to Question 17

(A) If Patton is fired, she has a right to a hearing to determine whether her First Amendment rights were violated by her dismissal. Under the Due Process Clause of the Fifth Amendment, a person has a liberty interest in the exercise of specific rights provided by the Constitution, including freedom of speech. If a government employer seeks to fire an employee for speech-related conduct when the speech involved a matter of public concern, the courts must carefully balance the employee's rights as a citizen to comment on a matter of public concern against the government's interest as an employer in the efficient performance of public service. Under the Court's expansive interpretation of what is a public issue in this context [*see* Rankin v. McPherson (1987)], Patton's statement would probably qualify. At the very least, she can make a sufficient showing that her termination violates her free speech rights to be entitled to a hearing on the issue under procedural due process principles. [*See* Givhan v. Western Line Consolidated School District

(1979)] (B) is wrong because Patton does not appear to have a property interest in her job. A public employee who is subject to removal only for "cause" has a property interest in her job and generally must be given notice of the charges against her that are to be the basis for her job termination, and a pre-termination opportunity to respond to those charges. Here, however, Patton did not have a property interest in her job; she could have been dismissed for no reason at all. She was not covered by the labor contract between the agency and its clerical workers, and there appears to be no other basis for her to claim an entitlement to continued employment. (C) is wrong because Patton is entitled to a hearing as long as she can raise a prima facie claim that her speech, which was regarding an important health issue and the perception of her agency, was on a public issue and therefore protected by the First Amendment. (D) is wrong for two reasons. As discussed above, Patton does not have a property interest in her job. Also, due process does not necessarily entitle her to a pre-termination evidentiary hearing; a post-termination evidentiary hearing is probably sufficient. [See Cleveland Board of Education v. Loudermill (1985)]

Answer to Question 18

(C) To prevail, the parents will have to show that the statute does not meet the rational basis test. Under that test, a law is presumed to be valid and will be upheld unless the challenger can make the difficult showing that it is not rationally related to a legitimate state interest. Here, the statute terminating the funds did not target a suspect class and did not burden a fundamental right, so the rational basis test applies. (A) is incorrect because it is not enough to show that legislation has a discriminatory effect on a suspect class; there must be an intent to discriminate. To establish a racial, national origin, or ethnicity classification, the party challenging the law must show that (i) the racial classification appears in the law itself (facial discrimination), (ii) the law was applied in a purposefully discriminatory manner, or (iii) the law was enacted or maintained for a discriminatory purpose. None of these situations appears to be the case under these facts. (B) is incorrect because it states the wrong standard. As that choice indicates, the Supreme Court has not held education to be a fundamental right under the Due Process Clause, nor has it found classifications based on wealth to require strict scrutiny. Hence, the test that is applied is the rational basis standard; the standard in choice (B) is an intermediate scrutiny test applied to gender and legitimacy classifications. (D) is wrong because it imposes the burden of proof on the wrong party. For a statute that does not discriminate against a suspect class, the plaintiff bears the burden of proving that the statute is not rationally related to a legitimate state interest.

Answer to Question 19

(A) Stewart's best argument is that the closure here is not necessary to preserve an overriding interest because trials and pretrial hearings generally must be open to the public. The Supreme Court has held, at least in the context of criminal cases, that trials and pretrial proceedings can be closed only if closure is necessary to preserve an overriding interest and the closure order is narrowly tailored to serve the overriding interest. While the Court has not yet established the standard for civil matters such as the case here, several Justices and commentators have suggested that the same standard will be applied in civil cases since they too have historically been open to the public. (B) is a false statement of the law—freedom of the press is not absolute and does not allow the press unlimited access to any hearing of interest to the public; the hearing may be closed where an overriding interest in protecting the privacy of the parties is established. (C) is not as good an argument as (A) because while closure here would amount to a prior restraint (any government action that prevents a communication from reaching the public), the prior restraint would be justified if the government proves that it was narrowly tailored to achieve a compelling interest. The argument in (A) negates this possibility and so is a better argument. (D) is incorrect because the fairness doctrine is irrelevant to the issue of whether a hearing should be open to the public. It was a rule of the Federal Communications Commission that required, among other things, that the media give political candidates an opportunity to oppose candidates or views endorsed by the media.

Answer to Question 20

(B) If the legislation is found to be unconstitutional, it will be because the commission will be exercising administrative powers. Under Article II, Section 2, Congress may not appoint members of a body with administrative or enforcement powers. Such persons are "officers of the United States" and must be appointed by the President with senatorial confirmation unless Congress has vested their appointment in the President alone, in federal courts, or in heads of departments. Here, selection of two members of the commission by a committee of the House of Representatives would violate the Appointments Clause because the commission has investigative and administrative powers. (A) is incorrect because the problem with the legislation is not that the President is infringing on the legislative branch's power by being able to veto congressional appointments, but rather that the congressional appointments are infringing on the executive branch appointment power. (C) is incorrect because Congress may by law vest appointment power of inferior officers in the federal courts. Hence, the judiciary has been properly granted the power by Congress to appoint members of the commission. (D) is incorrect because only Cabinet-level officers require Senate confirmation for their appointment. Inferior officers, which would include members of this commission, may be appointed by the President without Senate approval if provided for by Congress, as is the case here.

Answer to Question 21

(D) The cities can be prosecuted because state or local government action that conflicts with valid federal laws is invalid under the Supremacy Clause. The federal law here could be found valid as an exercise of the commerce power (Congress can regulate any activity that either in itself or in combination with other activities has a substantial economic effect on interstate commerce) or under the admiralty power (Congress can regulate all navigable waterways). The action of the municipalities directly conflicts with the directives of the federal law and can therefore be stopped. (B) is incorrect because the fact that the copper paint may be as effective as the zebronium does not change the result. The action by the municipalities can be prohibited under the Supremacy Clause. (A) is incorrect because for regulations that apply to both the public sector and the private sector, the Supreme Court has held that states' Tenth Amendment rights are best protected by the states' representation in Congress; hence, the Tenth Amendment is not a likely ground for striking this federal legislation because it is not directed only at state or local governments. (C) is incorrect because it is irrelevant; the federal law is superior to the states' laws because it is within Congress's power, not because Congress is in a better position than the states to adopt the legislation involved.

Answer to Question 22

(D) Harbor City will prevail because its rule is a reasonable time, place, and manner restriction. Speech protected by the First Amendment includes not only verbal communication, but also conduct that is undertaken to communicate an idea. The laser light show, like other art, probably is protected speech. While the content of speech generally cannot be limited, the conduct associated with speech in public forums can be regulated by reasonable time, place, and manner restrictions. To be valid, the regulation must be content neutral, narrowly tailored, and leave open alternative channels of communication. Harbor City's rule meets these requirements: the types of images displayed are not controlled, just the means of showing them; the rule is narrowly tailored since it does not regulate substantially more speech than is necessary to further a significant government interest (here, preventing eye damage and disturbing boaters); and alternative channels of communication are available since Randy can use the city's equipment, albeit with less spectacular results. (A) is incorrect because while Randy's art is protected by the First Amendment, it may still be regulated by reasonable time, place, and manner regulations, as indicated above. (B) is incorrect because it states the wrong standard. To be valid, a time, place, and manner regulation need not be the least restrictive means for achieving the desired result, but rather only narrowly tailored to the result. [*See* Ward v. Rock Against Racism (1989)] (C) is incorrect because art, including performance art such as the laser light show, is protected by the First Amendment. As discussed above, the First Amendment guarantee of freedom of speech protects more than merely spoken or written words; it includes conduct and other forms of expression undertaken to communicate an idea.

Answer to Question 23

(D) The destination tax will likely be held constitutional under Congress's taxing power. Congress has the power to lay taxes under Article II, Section 2, and a tax measure will usually be upheld if it bears some reasonable relationship to revenue production or if Congress has the power to regulate the taxed activity. Despite the protest from the officials of the affected locations, the tax here does appear to be related to revenue production and so will be upheld. (C) is incorrect because whether the tax actually does have a revenue-enhancing effect is irrelevant as long as it reasonably appears to be a revenue-producing measure. (A) is incorrect because the extent of the right to travel is not clearly defined. The Supreme Court has established that the right to travel from state to state is a fundamental right that may be violated by *state* laws designed to deter persons from moving into a state; however, the Court has not specifically applied this rule to the federal government or to the type of tax legislation present here. (B) also is incorrect. While the federal government is not subject to the Equal Protection Clause of the Fourteenth Amendment, it is prohibited from unfair discrimination by the Due Process Clause of the Fifth Amendment. Nevertheless, the discrimination here is not unfair. If a governmental act, such as the tax here, does not involve a fundamental right or a suspect or quasi-suspect class, it will be upheld as long as it is rationally related to a legitimate governmental interest. The government has a legitimate interest in taxing, and so the tax will be upheld.

Answer to Question 24

(D) The most likely ground for holding the statute unconstitutional is that Congress may not limit all avenues for Supreme Court review of federal constitutional issues. Article III, Section 2 provides that the Supreme Court shall have appellate jurisdiction under such regulations as the Congress shall make. Although *Ex parte McCardle* (1868) gives Congress broad power to regulate the Supreme Court's appellate jurisdiction, it has been suggested that Congress may not eliminate all avenues for Supreme Court review of issues vested within the federal judicial power. This argument is the most likely basis for finding the law here unconstitutional because none of the other choices is viable. (A) is not the best argument. As indicated above, Congress has the power to regulate the appellate jurisdiction of the Supreme Court, and since the Supreme Court's primary role as an appellate court is to determine constitutional issues, it follows that Congress can eliminate from the Supreme Court's review the determination of certain cases involving constitutional issues, as long as jurisdiction remains in some lower federal courts. (B) is incorrect because Congress's power is limited to regulating the Supreme Court's appellate jurisdiction; it has no power to restrict or enlarge the Court's original jurisdiction. (C) is incorrect because Congress has the authority to adopt laws modifying appellate jurisdiction; modification of the Court's original jurisdiction would require a constitutional amendment.

Answer to Question 25

(C) This is the best answer since it most accurately reflects current law. A municipality may use zoning to limit the location of adult theaters and nude dancing establishments as long as the ordinance (i) is designed to promote important government interests (*e.g.,* eliminate the secondary effects of such businesses—lowering of property values, increased traffic, etc.) and (ii) does not prohibit all such entertainment in the community. [*See* City of Renton v. Playtime Theatres, Inc. (1986)] (A) is incorrect because nude dancing (and by implication other erotica) is marginally protected speech. The Supreme Court has held erotica to be symbolic conduct (*i.e.,* conduct undertaken to convey a message), and like other symbolic conduct, it can be regulated to serve important government interests unrelated to the suppression of speech. [*See* Barnes v. Glen Theatre, Inc. (1991)—allowing state to prohibit public nudity, including nude dancing] (B) reaches a correct result—municipalities can limit the location of such establishments—but uses the wrong standard. As discussed above, erotica is only marginally protected speech and can be regulated to serve important, rather than compelling, interests. Protecting community morals and property values are important enough to justify regulation. (D) is incorrect because the Supreme Court has allowed municipalities to treat adult theaters differently from other theaters, despite the fact that this appears to be regulation based on the content of speech. For example, in *City of Renton* the Court allowed the municipality to prohibit adult theaters from being located within 1,000 feet of residential zones, schools, and parks.

Answer to Question 26

(B) Peaceful's ordinance is invalid to the extent that it restricts the passage of troops through the town. The states have no power to regulate the activities of the government unless Congress consents. Thus, instrumentalities of the federal government are immune from state regulations relating to performance of their federal functions. A state or local law that attempts to restrict United States military traffic in this manner is not enforceable. (A) is incorrect. The precise meaning of the Second Amendment right to bear arms has not been established, but in any case the rights it protects are those of citizens, not the United States military. (C) is incorrect because it is irrelevant whether there are equally convenient alternative means of performing the military activities; as long as the activities are within the legitimate scope of federal activities (and military exercises certainly fall within the scope of federal power), they cannot be regulated by the states. (D) is incorrect because even assuming that the ordinance is a police power regulation, it cannot interfere with the legitimate functions of the federal government.

Answer to Question 27

(D) Because marriage and divorce are part of the fundamental right of privacy, the state will have to show that requiring Mary to pay the fee is necessary to achieve a compelling state interest. The Supreme Court applies one of three standards to determine whether state action that classifies people is valid. A classification based on suspect criteria (*e.g.,* race, religion, or nationality) or affecting a fundamental right will be strictly scrutinized—the state must prove that it is necessary to achieve a compelling state interest. A classification based on quasi-suspect criteria (*e.g.,* gender and legitimacy) will be given intermediate scrutiny—it must be established that the action is substantially related to an important state interest. All other classifications will be upheld unless the complainant shows that the classification is not rational. The law here has the effect of classifying people into those who can obtain a divorce and those who cannot. While the classification is based on wealth (those who can afford to pay the fee and those who cannot), which is neither a suspect nor quasi-suspect class, it also affects a fundamental right—the right to marry and be divorced, which is controlled by the state through access to its courts, is part of the fundamental right of privacy. [Boddie v. Connecticut (1971)] Therefore, the classification will be subjected to strict scrutiny and the state will be required to waive its divorce fee here, since Mary cannot afford to pay, unless the state can show that the fee is necessary to serve a compelling state interest. (A) is incorrect because while it states the proper strict scrutiny standard, it gives the wrong reason for applying the standard. Strict scrutiny will be applied here not because Mary is poor, but because the right to divorce is fundamental. (B) is incorrect because it states the wrong standard—while a classification based solely on wealth would be tested under the rational basis standard, the standard to be applied here is based on Mary's fundamental right to a divorce. (C) is incorrect because it states both the wrong standard to be applied (the intermediate standard) and an improper rationale for applying the standard—it is irrelevant that Mary has a compelling interest in obtaining a divorce; what is relevant is that the right to obtain a divorce is encompassed within the fundamental right of privacy.

Answer to Question 28

(D) Pete's best defense is that OBA's license requirement was superseded by Pete's federal license. The Supremacy Clause makes federal law the supreme law of the land. This means that whenever a valid federal law conflicts with a state law, the state law is inapplicable and the federal law controls. The federal law granting Pete a license here would be valid pursuant to Congress's power to regulate interstate and foreign commerce. In addition to actually regulating such commerce, Congress can adopt any law necessary or proper to implement its power, and providing licenses to vendors to ensure that people can exchange money at the border and its functional equivalents would certainly be within the scope of the broad federal power. Because the OBA license requirement interferes with the federal licensing scheme, it cannot be enforced against Pete. (A) is incorrect because Pete appears to have had all the process that was due. It may be that Pete had a property interest in his license under the Fourteenth Amendment Due Process Clause in that he could expect to keep the license as long as he performed well. He could not be deprived of his property interest in his license without due process of law, including a hearing. Here, he was given a hearing prior to revocation of his license at which he was allowed to present relevant evidence, and nothing in the facts indicates that the OBA was biased against Pete. Thus, due process was satisfied. (B) is incorrect because nothing in the facts indicates that the licensing scheme was arbitrary. An arbitrary licensing scheme would violate substantive due process, which requires at a minimum that laws be rational. Note also that this choice is somewhat of a red herring—the "arbitrary and capricious" standard is the standard that courts use in reviewing determinations of fact by administrative agencies that are not "on the record." (C) is incorrect because nothing in the facts indicates that Olympia's licensing scheme interferes with foreign or interstate commerce—nothing in the scheme favors local economic interests over out-of-state or foreign interests, so there is no unlawful discrimination, and the scheme appears to place little if any burden on interstate or foreign commerce.

Answer to Question 29

(B) The tax unconstitutionally burdens the freedom of the press. Press and broadcasting companies can be subject to general business taxes, but a tax applicable only to the press or based on the content of a publication will not be upheld absent a compelling justification. Mere need for revenue probably is not a sufficiently compelling interest. (A) is incorrect because there is no unconstitutional burden on interstate commerce here. The law treats all businesses subject to the tax (namely breweries and distilleries) equally, and so is not protecting local business against out-of-state competition. The fact that the law treats breweries and distilleries differently from wineries and that New Foria has no breweries or distilleries but does have wineries probably does not change this, because a court will probably find these to be distinct businesses for purposes of advertising. (C) is incorrect. When a sales tax is imposed on a sale taking place entirely within one state, there is no apportionment problem because the sale cannot be taxed by any other state (because no other state has a sufficient nexus). (D) is incorrect because there is no equal protection violation here even though brewers and distillers are being treated differently from wine makers. Since no suspect class or fundamental right is involved, nor is a quasi-suspect class involved, the tax will pass constitutional muster as long as it is rationally related to a legitimate government purpose, and the tax here certainly seems to be related to revenue production.

Answer to Question 30

(C) The court should hold against Roy because the Supreme Court has permitted Congress to remove the states' Eleventh Amendment immunity from suit only when it acts to enforce the Fourteenth Amendment. The Eleventh Amendment generally prohibits a federal court from hearing private parties' claims against the government, including claims for damages such as Roy's claim here. While Congress's power to prevent discrimination under the Fourteenth Amendment has enabled it to abrogate state immunity, it has no such power under the Commerce Clause. [*See* Seminole Tribe of Florida v. Florida (1996)] Hence, the court should dismiss the action as barred by the Eleventh Amendment, and (A) is therefore incorrect. (B) is incorrect because while Congress does have the power to regulate the jurisdiction of the federal courts, it does not have the power to grant jurisdiction in violation of another constitutional provision, such as the Eleventh Amendment in this case. (D) is wrong because Congress does have power under certain circumstances to remove the states' Eleventh Amendment immunity. Under the power given to Congress in the enabling clause of the Fourteenth Amendment (and perhaps the Thirteenth and Fifteenth Amendments), it could pass anti-discrimination legislation that permits a state to be sued in federal court.

Answer to Question 31

(C) Most likely, Picayune will have to show that its petition requirement is narrowly tailored to achieve a compelling state interest. The Supreme Court uses a balancing test in determining whether a regulation of the electoral process is valid: if the restriction on First Amendment activities is severe, the regulation will be upheld only if it is narrowly tailored to achieve a compelling interest. Requiring a candidate to obtain 4% of voters' signatures probably qualifies as a severe First Amendment restriction. Thus, the state must show that the regulation is narrowly tailored to achieve a compelling interest (*e.g.,* running an honest and efficient election system). Note that the Court has approved a requirement that candidates obtain 1% of the voters' signatures before being placed on the ballot. [*See* Munro v. Socialist Workers Party (1986)] In any case, the Court probably would not apply the rational basis standard under these facts, so (A) and (D) are incorrect. (B) is incorrect because when the Court applies heightened scrutiny, it requires the government to bear the burden of persuasion, not the person challenging the government's action.

Answer to Question 32

(B) The court will base its decision on its determination that the ordinance is narrowly tailored to serve a significant government interest and does not unreasonably limit alternative channels of communication. While the First Amendment protects the freedoms of speech and assembly, the government may reasonably regulate speech related conduct in public forums through content neutral time, place, and manner regulation. To be valid, government regulations on speech and assembly in public forums must be content neutral and narrowly tailored to serve a significant government interest, and must leave open alternative channels of communication. Here, the ban on camping overnight in the park, a content-neutral regulation of a public forum, would be evaluated by the court using the standard in choice (B). (A) and (D) are incorrect because the rational relationship test is used for restrictions on free speech rights in nonpublic forums. Here, because the park is a public forum, the more restrictive test stated in (B) is used. (C) is incorrect because it misstates both parts of the standard.

Answer to Question 33

(B) The court most likely will find that Congress had the power to enact the legislation under the Thirteenth Amendment. The Thirteenth Amendment simply provides that neither slavery nor involuntary servitude shall exist within the United States and gives Congress the power to adopt appropriate legislation to enforce the proscription. Since the amendment is not limited to proscribing state action, Congress may adopt legislation regulating private parties. Under the amendment, the Supreme Court has allowed Congress to prohibit any private conduct that Congress deems to be a "badge" or "incident" of slavery, and has upheld statutes regulating private contracts. [*See, e.g.,* Runyon v. McCrary (1967)] (A) is not a good basis for the statute because the Contract Clause is a limitation on *states'* rights to modify contracts retroactively; it is unrelated to Congress's power to regulate private contracts. (C)—the Fourteenth Amendment—is incorrect. The Fourteenth Amendment prohibits *states* from discriminating on the basis of race; it does not extend to private conduct. [*See* United States v. Morrison (2000)] (D)—the Commerce Clause—might also be a basis for the legislation here, but it is not as good an answer as (B) because the commerce power is limited to transactions that either in themselves or in combination with other activities have a substantial economic effect on interstate commerce, and by its terms the legislation here can reach wholly intrastate transactions. The interstate commerce requirement is a limit on congressional legislation and no such limit is present under the Thirteenth Amendment. Therefore, the Thirteenth Amendment is a better basis for the legislation here.

Answer to Question 34

(B) Sam has standing. A person challenging the constitutionality of a government action must have standing to raise the issue. To have standing, a person must show that he is injured by a government action (injury in fact) and that a favorable decision will eliminate the harm. Generally, a taxpayer does not have standing to challenge the way tax money is spent because any alleged injury is too remote. However, here Sam is not bringing suit as a taxpayer; rather he is alleging that the Atlantic policy of providing financial aid only for residents who attend schools in the state injures him by depriving him of such aid solely on the basis of attending a college outside Atlantic, thus violating his right to equal protection. A ruling in Sam's favor will eliminate the harm to him. Therefore, Sam has a concrete stake in the outcome of this controversy, entirely independent of whether Sam has ever paid taxes in Atlantic. Regarding (A), the Eleventh Amendment prohibits a federal court suit against a state by a citizen of that state or by a citizen of another state. However, the Eleventh Amendment does not bar a suit against a state official acting pursuant to state law but allegedly in violation of the plaintiff's constitutional rights. Here, Sam is seeking an order that a particular Atlantic official be compelled to act in conformity with Sam's right to equal protection. The lawsuit is not brought against Atlantic, nor does it seek a retroactive recovery from state funds. The prospective payment of Atlantic funds that Sam seeks through the compelled granting of his application for aid is not prohibited by the Eleventh Amendment. Thus, (A) is incorrect. Regarding (D), the doctrine of sovereign immunity refers to the rule that a governmental entity may not be sued unless it consents to be sued (which consent is generally afforded by statute). Here, the facts do not state whether Atlantic has consented to be sued. However, as detailed above, Sam is not actually suing the state. In reality, Sam is suing an Atlantic official who is allegedly enforcing an unconstitutional enactment, and is therefore deemed to be stripped of his official character. Because the suit is not against the state, the doctrine of sovereign immunity is not applicable. (C) is incorrect because it is only with regard to state criminal statutes or prosecutions that a party seeking to enjoin such statutes or prosecutions must show irreparable injury or exceptional circumstances (*i.e.,* a showing of significant harm that could not be avoided by state adjudication and appellate review of the proceedings). Here, there is no criminal statute or prosecution at issue. Thus, there is no need to show "extraordinary circumstances."

Answer to Question 35

(D)   An ad valorem tax on each item received in California is most likely to be held valid. An ad valorem property tax is a tax based on a percentage of the assessed value of the property in question. Although such a tax is generally valid, potential Commerce Clause problems arise when the property taxed moves in interstate commerce. Goods in transit are totally exempt from taxation. Interstate shipment usually ends when the goods reach their destination; thereafter, the goods are subject to local tax. Here, once each item of instructional material is received in California, it has clearly reached its destination, and the interstate shipment has come to an end. At this point, the materials become subject to the local ad valorem property tax. Thus, (D) sets forth a tax that is valid. (C) is incorrect because it misstates the concept of the use tax. A use tax is a tax imposed on the users of goods purchased out of state. Use taxes are imposed by the state in which the buyer resides. Here, New York is the state of Zenger, the publisher and seller of the instructional materials. New York has no basis for imposing a use tax on materials that are being used in California. The income taxes described in (A) and (B) are invalid because they fail to satisfy the three-part test for determining the validity of a non-discriminatory state tax affecting interstate commerce. The factors required to be satisfied are: (i) substantial nexus between the activity or property taxed and the taxing state; (ii) fair apportionment based on the extent of the taxable property or activity in the state; and (iii) a fair relationship between the tax and the services or benefits provided by the state. In (A), Professor Scholar is a resident of Virginia, and he also lectures in that state. Thus, there is a substantial nexus between Scholar's income-producing activity and the taxing state. However, Scholar's income-producing activity is carried on in more than 20 states. Therefore, a Virginia income tax on *all* of Scholar's income would not be fairly apportioned according to the extent of the taxable activity carried on in Virginia, and would potentially subject Scholar to cumulative tax burdens. Consequently, the tax is invalid. The Illinois income tax in (B) also fails to fairly apportion the tax, because it taxes *all* of Scholar's income. In addition, the Illinois tax is invalid because there is no indication of a substantial nexus between Illinois and Scholar's income-producing activity. We are not told that Scholar lectures in Illinois; indeed, the only mention of Illinois is a reference to its being the national headquarters of LEGAL/EAGLE, which in no way establishes any nexus between Illinois and Scholar's activity.

Answer to Question 36

(C)   The tax exemption in this case probably violates the Establishment Clause. To be valid under this clause, a law favoring religion or authorizing governmental benefits to a religiously affiliated institution (i) must have a secular purpose, (ii) must have a primary effect that neither advances nor inhibits religion, and (iii) must not produce excessive government entanglement with religion. Although religious associations may be included in tax exemptions available to a variety of secular and religious organizations, a tax exemption that is available only for religious organizations or religious activities and not for other organizations engaged in the same activity violates the Establishment Clause. [Texas Monthly, Inc. v. Bullock (1989)] Here, providing the tax exemption only to shelters run by religious groups and not to those run by other not-for-profit groups would seem to have a primary effect of advancing religion, since it provides religious groups with an advantage over nonreligious groups in providing services to the homeless. (A) is incorrect. While a broad exemption from property taxation for property used exclusively for religious, educational, or charitable purposes has been held not to violate the Establishment Clause [Walz v. Tax Commission (1970)], a narrower exemption applying only to religious groups is invalid, as discussed above. If the exemption here had applied to any not-for-profit group that operates a homeless shelter, it probably would have been valid. (B) is incorrect. While an exemption may involve less government entanglement than imposing the tax on church-run shelters, the other elements of the Establishment Clause test are not satisfied when shelters run by other groups are excluded from the exemption. (D) is incorrect because the state does not need to show a compelling interest to validate a tax classification that does not discriminate against a suspect class or burden a fundamental right. The tax exemption here need only have a rational relationship to a legitimate government interest.

Answer to Question 37

(B) The fact that the federal board was similar to the state board but was not given the power to restrict fee increases and impose sanctions in an otherwise comprehensive bill suggests that such provisions in the state law violate the Supremacy Clause. A state law may fail under the Supremacy Clause even if it does not directly conflict with a federal statute or regulation if it interferes with the achievement of a federal objective or the federal regulations occupy the entire field. The more comprehensive a federal scheme is, the more likely a finding of implied preemption. The fact that the health-care legislation was comprehensive but the federal board was not given regulatory or enforcement power suggests that Congress did not want specific restrictions in these areas and may have wanted free-market principles to determine fee increases at the outset. The state board's power to impose these restrictions may violate the Supremacy Clause under these circumstances. (A) is incorrect because the fact that the federal legislation was passed later does not automatically mean that the state legislation has been superseded. In areas of concurrent legislative power, a state regulation will be upheld if it does not conflict with and is not preempted by federal legislation. (C) is incorrect because the Contract Clause prevents only *substantial* impairments of existing contracts by state legislation, and only if the legislation does not serve an important and legitimate public interest or is not a reasonable and narrowly tailored means of promoting that interest. Here, the law has a prospective effect only, and even if existing contracts between health-care providers and insurers are affected by the legislation, the other requirements for the Contract Clause to apply are not likely to be satisfied. (D) is incorrect because states may regulate local aspects of interstate commerce in the absence of federal regulation as long as the regulation is nondiscriminatory and does not unduly burden interstate commerce, which is a case-by-case balancing test. Here, the legislation appears to be nondiscriminatory and there are insufficient facts to establish that it would constitute an undue burden; hence, (B) presents a stronger argument than (D).

Answer to Question 38

(C) The court should rule in favor of Wright because the pursuit of a livelihood is a right protected by the Privileges and Immunities Clause, and the requirement here substantially interferes with that

Fifteenth Amendment, does not curtail the actions of the federal government
has not interfered with any right conferred by the Fourteenth Amendment
Clause. (B) is incorrect because James has induced discriminatory actio
dean of a private school. The Fourteenth Amendment does not protec
private persons or institutions. The actions of a private entity may
state is significantly involved in the private entity. However, the
sufficient state involvement with a private entity so as to con
the fact that the private school in (B) is licensed by the sta
natory treatment of women state action. (D) is incorrect
tory action by his church, which is a private entity wit
As explained above, the Fourteenth Amendment E
the actions of such an entity. Thus, Charles has
Protection Clause.

Answer to Question 41

(A) As part of its power to regulate inte
interstate, which either in itself o
effect upon, or effect on move
tions in the United States, in
(as (A) states), Congress
enacting a mandatory
and sold in one state
involve more than
vidual transacti
the federal g
is incorre
tutes in
such
T

on federal property.

Answer to Question 40

(C) The facts of (C) are the only ones in which the named defendant has compelled a state official t
deny equal protection of the law to some person. The Fourteenth Amendment prevents states
from depriving any person of life, liberty, or property without due process of law and equal
protection of the law. Because the Equal Protection Clause protects against state action only, th
federal statute at issue prohibits only behavior that causes or induces a state official, agency, o
instrumentality to deny the equal protection of the law to some person. In (C), Marcus has coerced a state agent (the coach of a public high school basketball team) to exclude people from
participation in an activity at a state institution solely on the basis of race. Because this is a sta
governmental act that classifies people based on a suspect trait (race) in the absence of a comp
ling state interest, it violates equal protection. For bringing about this violation, Marcus is gu
of violating the federal statute. (A) is incorrect because Roger is inducing a *federal* official to
discriminate in the distribution of free dairy products. The Fourteenth Amendment, unlike th

. Therefore, Roger
Equal Protection
against women by the
against the actions of
constitute state action if the
mere granting of a license is not
ert its action into state action. Thus,
does not make the school's discrimi-
because Charles has induced discrimina-
h no apparent significant state involvement.
qual Protection Clause does not protect against
ot interfered with a right conferred by the Equal

state commerce, Congress may regulate any activity, local or
in combination with other activities has a substantial economic
ent in, interstate commerce. Because all motor vehicle transac-
the aggregate, have a significant impact upon interstate commerce
s constitutionally empowered to regulate such transactions by, e.g.,
rice schedule. (B) is incorrect because the price of a vehicle manufactured
may have no effect upon **interstate** commerce; *i.e.,* it may not affect or
one state. While Congress does have the power to determine that these indi-
ons do in fact have an impact on interstate commerce, they do not come within
overnment's commerce clause power merely because they involve "commerce." (C)
because it is too broad. Congress is empowered to regulate transportation that consti-
erstate commerce. However, there is no congressional power to regulate transportation as
(D) is incorrect because Congress may **tax and spend** to provide for the general welfare.
e General Welfare Clause does not, however, authorize Congress to enact nonspending legislation or regulations for the general welfare.

Answer to Question 42

B) The transaction tax in this case, which is being applied to the local activities of an interstate
company, is valid because it is not discriminatory and does not unduly burden interstate commerce. A "transaction tax" is essentially a privilege or occupation tax—*i.e.,* a tax on the privilege
of doing business in the state. This type of tax is constitutional if: (i) it does not discriminate
against interstate commerce; (ii) the activity taxed has a substantial nexus to the taxing state; (iii)
the tax is fairly apportioned; and (iv) the tax fairly relates to services provided by the taxing
state. Here, there is nothing in the facts to indicate that the tax is being imposed only on shipments being made in interstate commerce or only on interstate shippers; thus, no discrimination
against interstate commerce exists. The transaction tax is on fees paid by Great Lakes shippers to
Speedit for transport of the packages within Great Lakes using its Great Lakes-registered trucks;
hence, a substantial nexus exists between the taxed activity and the state. The tax is fairly apportioned because it is a percentage of the service fee that Speedit sets for its purely local activity (in
other words, it is severable from any effect it might have on interstate commerce). Finally,
Speedit's use of the Great Lakes transportation network (*e.g.,* roads and airport) in operating its
business indicates that the transaction tax fairly relates to the services provided by the state.
Therefore, this tax is valid. (A) is wrong because whether the packages have entered the stream

of commerce is relevant only to an ad valorem property tax on the packages themselves. A tax on the packages, if they were already in the stream of commerce, would be invalid. Here the tax is on the service of transporting the packages, and so a different test (*see* above) applies. (C) is wrong for a similar reason. The status of the packages in interstate commerce is not the critical factor for evaluating a tax on the shipping transaction; rather, the factors above are important. (D) is wrong because the tax on Speedit is being imposed only on its local activity in Great Lakes. A similar tax imposed on Speedit by other states would apply only to Speedit's local activity in those states; hence, this type of tax does not expose Speedit to the possibility of multiple taxation.

Answer to Question 43

(D) The best argument against the statute is that it violates the Contracts Clause. The Contracts Clause prohibits states from retroactively and substantially impairing contract rights unless the governmental act serves an important and legitimate government interest and is a reasonable and narrowly tailored means of promoting that interest. Here, the legislation by its terms affects existing contracts. It is arguable that the effect is a substantial impairment, since deeds absolute have been turned into mortgages by the statute. While protecting debtors may be a legitimate government interest, it could be argued that the statute is not narrowly tailored to that interest. It is doubtful that the plaintiffs' attorneys would win on this argument, but it is their best approach. (A) is not a good argument because ex post facto laws are laws that retroactively alter criminal law, and here the law is not criminal, but rather civil. (B) is not a good argument because the law does not violate the Equal Protection Clause. The law does not involve a suspect or quasi-suspect class or a fundamental right, and so its validity would be tested under the rational basis standard. A law that has any legitimate rational basis will be upheld under this standard, and as established above, the law here serves the legitimate government purpose of protecting debtors. Thus, equal protection is not violated. (C) is not a good argument because the Due Process Clause does not prohibit laws that "summarily take" property from a class in general; no individual hearing or other process is required for laws of general applicability. Substantive due process is not violated either; since no fundamental right is involved, the law will be judged under the rational basis standard, and as stated above, will be upheld.

Answer to Question 44

(C) Executive privilege is an inherent privilege necessary to protect the confidentiality of presidential communications. Under this privilege, presidential documents and conversations are presumptively privileged, but this privilege must yield to a demonstrated need for such materials as evidence in a criminal case in which they are relevant and otherwise admissible. [United States v. Nixon (1974)] Although the Supreme Court has not expressly decided that the privilege must also yield to a demonstrated need for evidence in a pending legislative proceeding, such an extension of *Nixon* is likely, and none of the other alternatives is at all accurate. (A) is incorrect because it is too broad. In *Nixon, supra,* the Court decided that an evidentiary subpoena to the President in a criminal case does not violate the separation of powers principle, and by extension a subpoena issued by a Senate subcommittee, pursuant to the well-established implied power of Congress to investigate, would not be deemed to violate separation of powers. (B) is also incorrect because it is too broad. As stated above, although a presumptive privilege applies to presidential documents and conversations, that privilege must yield to a demonstrated need in criminal cases. Thus, executive privilege is not absolute. (D) is incorrect because executive privilege does apply to proceedings by the courts; in fact, the privilege is overridden only upon a specific showing of need for specific information.

Answer to Question 45

(B) The loyalty oath is constitutional, but the membership oath is unconstitutional. The First Amendment protects the rights of association and speech. State infringements on these rights must be justified by a compelling state interest, unrelated to the suppression of ideas. In the area of public employment, neither standards of conduct nor loyalty oaths may be vague or overbroad. Precision is required because of the potential chilling effect on First Amendment rights. Here, Panza is not applying for public employment, but the state is requiring him to take the oaths to obtain a state license, which involves the same First Amendment issues. The loyalty oath is virtually identical to oaths that have been held to be constitutional. The state has a compelling interest in seeing that both constitutions are upheld and there is nothing vague about the oath. Oaths similar to the membership oath, however, have been struck down as overbroad. The state has a compelling interest only in preventing *knowing membership* with the specific intent to *further unlawful aims*. Persons cannot be denied a license because of mere membership in a particular group, and the state statute here addresses mere membership. Thus, (B) is correct and (A), (C), and (D) are incorrect.

Answer to Question 46

(C) Frump will not prevail because the state decision was based on state law grounds. The Supreme Court will hear a case from a state court only if it turned on federal grounds. If it finds adequate and independent state grounds for the decision, it will refuse jurisdiction. Here, the facts state that the Arkasouri decision was based on a provision of the state constitution. The fact that the state provision is similar to the federal Equal Protection Clause is irrelevant to determining whether the decision here was based on state law, since the state court did not base its decision on interpretation of the federal provision, but rather interpreted the state provision. Therefore, the Supreme Court will refuse jurisdiction, and Frump will not prevail. (A) is incorrect because the Supremacy Clause renders state laws invalid only if they conflict with federal law or if Congress has preempted the field. Nothing in the facts indicates that Congress has preempted the issue of school funding, and the state decision is not in conflict with the Supreme Court decision here; the Supreme Court held that the federal Equal Protection Clause does not *require* equal funding, not that equal funding violates equal protection. Thus, the state court was free to grant its citizens more protection under the state equal protection provision than is granted under the federal provision. (B) is incorrect because res judicata is not a constitutional issue. Moreover, the Supreme Court did not decide whether equal funding was invalid; only that it was not required. (D) is incorrect because Frump has standing. To have standing, a party must have a concrete stake in the outcome of a controversy. This requires an injury in fact caused by the government action that can be remedied by a decision in the litigant's favor. Frump has an injury in fact since his children are being deprived of educational money under the new state statute. This injury could be remedied by a decision in his favor, because if the statute is held invalid, the state would go back to the unequal funding system.

Answer to Question 47

(C) Because the state statute is based on alienage, it is subject to strict scrutiny and thus the state has the burden of proof. State laws based on alienage are subject to the strict scrutiny test, except when the law concerns alien participation in the functioning of the state government (and possibly "illegal" alien adults), in which case the rational basis test is applied. Under the strict scrutiny test, the government bears the burden of showing that the law is necessary to a compelling state interest. The state law here does not concern alien participation in the functioning of state government (or illegal aliens), and thus the strict scrutiny test will be used. The state of Green thus has the burden of proof. (A) is wrong because Arthur has standing. A person has standing if he can demonstrate a concrete stake in the outcome of the controversy; *i.e.,* he has been or will be injured by the governmental action and that a decision in his favor will remedy the situation. Arthur has standing because he has been injured (the statute directly impairs his right to own land and thus violates his right to equal protection). A declaratory judgment in his favor will remedy this situation; Arthur will be able to buy land if the law is declared unconstitutional. Thus, Arthur has standing. (B) is wrong because, as explained above, the burden of proof is on the government and not on Arthur and Danielle. (B) is also wrong because it implies that the validity of the statute would be determined by the rational basis test. However, since the statute is based on alienage and does not pertain to participation in the functioning of state government, the strict scrutiny standard, rather than the rational basis test, will be applied. (D) is wrong because, as discussed, the strict scrutiny standard applies.

Answer to Question 48

(A) Although the Green statute directly impairs the equal protection rights of Arthur rather than Danielle, Danielle can assert Arthur's rights. A person who challenges the constitutionality of a governmental action must have standing; *i.e.,* she must demonstrate a concrete stake in the outcome of the controversy and that the governmental action at issue impairs her rights. Generally, a claimant must have suffered (or may presently suffer) a direct impairment of her own constitutional rights. However, a plaintiff may assert a third party's rights where the plaintiff has suffered injury and the injury adversely affects her relationship with third parties, resulting in an indirect violation of their rights. Here, the Green statute causes injury to Danielle by prohibiting her from contracting to sell land to Arthur. Such an injury would adversely affect Danielle's relationship with aliens by prohibiting her from selling land to them, and would thus indirectly violate their right to equal protection. Consequently, Danielle may assert the equal protection rights of aliens. (B) is incorrect because under the Contract Clause, which prohibits states from passing any law impairing the obligation of contracts, there is no impairment unless the law is retroactive. Here, it appears that Arthur and Danielle entered into their contract after the enactment of the statute. Thus, the statute did not unconstitutionally impair that contract. (C) is incorrect because, even if the statute does constitute a direct restraint on the alienation of Danielle's property, such a restraint does not rise to the level of a constitutional violation. Thus, an argument based on (C) would not be as strong as the assertion of aliens' equal protection rights, as found in (A). (D) is incorrect because nothing here indicates that Danielle's due process rights have been violated. The procedural due process proscription against the governmental taking of property without due process of law applies to individualized takings—*i.e.,* when the government takes property to which the individual has a legitimate claim. Here, Danielle is not complaining about an action against her individually, but about a law of general application. Thus, a procedural due process argument is inapplicable. Substantive due process will not be helpful to Danielle either. If a law limits a fundamental right (*i.e.,* voting, privacy, right to travel, or a First Amendment right), the strict scrutiny test is used. However, if a fundamental right is not involved, as here, the rational basis test is used. Under the rational basis test, it is unlikely that Danielle can succeed with her claim since she will have the burden of proving that the government has no rational basis for its law. Since under this test almost any basis will support governmental action, this statute is likely to be upheld, and so this is not Danielle's best argument.

Answer to Question 49

(C) Arthur will win because legal aliens fall within the protection of the Equal Protection Clause. The Fourteenth Amendment prevents the states from denying any person within their jurisdiction equal protection of the laws. Legal aliens are "persons" within the meaning of this clause. The Green statute subjects Arthur to disparate treatment solely on the basis of his status as an alien. Thus, the state has denied Arthur equal protection of the laws. (A) is incorrect because the statute does not intrude on any congressional power respecting aliens or foreign affairs. Although Congress has exclusive power over naturalization and denaturalization, as well as plenary power over admission, exclusion, and deportation of aliens, the state statute does not impinge on any of these areas. Neither does the statute concern the conduct of foreign affairs. Thus, the statute does not conflict with or otherwise intrude upon any power belonging to Congress. (B) is incorrect because the Article IV Privileges and Immunities Clause does not protect the rights of aliens. This Privileges and Immunities Clause protects "citizens" of states from discrimination by other states. Aliens and corporations are not "citizens" for purposes of this clause. (D) incorrectly implies that Arthur's status as an alien excludes him from any protection under the Constitution. As noted above, legal aliens are protected by the Equal Protection Clause.

Answer to Question 50

(B) If the court should find the statute unconstitutional, it will be because the state's safety concerns are outweighed by the burden on interstate commerce. Where a state enacts a law that does not discriminate against interstate commerce, it may still be invalid if the benefits from the law are outweighed by the burdens the law places on interstate commerce. The determination is made on a case-by-case basis, depending on the facts. Here, there is no discrimination against interstate commerce, and the state has shown that tandem trailer trucks are more dangerous than other vehicles and they cause more road damage. However, Wesley has shown that the state law makes it expensive to operate his interstate trucks in Green. The court could easily find that the added expense on interstate carriers is not outweighed by the benefits to Green. (Note that the Supreme Court has twice addressed this issue in similar cases [Raymond Motor Transportation, Inc. v. Rice (1978); Kassel v. Consolidated Freightways Corp. (1981)] with a similar result.) (A) is incorrect because it assumes that the states cannot regulate interstate commerce in general or trucks in particular. As indicated above, safety aspects of interstate commerce can be regulated by the states as long as the regulation does not discriminate against or unduly burden interstate commerce. If a state has the power to regulate an aspect of interstate commerce, it has the power to tax it as well, and a tax such as the one here could be valid (see (D), below). (C) is incorrect because the Equal Protection Clause is not violated here. Under the Clause, a law that regulates economic interests where no suspect class or fundamental right is involved will be upheld as long as the classification is rationally related to any legitimate governmental interest. Preventing accidents and saving money on road repair are legitimate government interests; so the law here is valid. (D) is incorrect because states can impose use taxes on interstate businesses as long as the activity taxed has a substantial nexus to the taxing state; the tax is fairly apportioned; the tax does not discriminate against interstate commerce; and the tax is fairly related to the services provided by the state. The tax here appears to meet these conditions.

Answer to Question 51

(D) The best argument is that the tax interferes with the plenary power of Congress to regulate federal lands. Article IV, Section 3 of the Constitution gives Congress the power to make all necessary rules and regulations concerning property belonging to the federal government. Vendo would argue that this power, when combined with the Supremacy Clause (which makes federal law the supreme law of the land, superseding conflicting state law) would prevent any attempt by a state to tax persons on federal land, absent congressional consent to the tax. In fact, this argument will probably fail because the Court has indicated that while the states may not *directly* tax or regulate the federal government, they may indirectly do so by adopting taxes or regulations on persons dealing with the federal government, as long as the tax or regulation does not unduly burden the federal government. The tax here seems to fall into the permissible category; nevertheless, this is Vendo's best argument. (A) is not a good argument because the Privileges and Immunities Clause of the Fourteenth Amendment does not protect the right to conduct business on federal lands. The Clause protects a narrow range of privileges of United States citizenship, such as the right to *enter onto* federal lands, the right to petition Congress for redress, and the right to vote for federal officers. The Clause does not protect the entire Bill of Rights against infringement, and Vendo's right here falls outside the scope of the Clause. (B) is incorrect because the commerce power would not preempt the tax here. Generally, a state may adopt taxes that will affect interstate commerce as long as the tax does not discriminate against interstate commerce (the tax here does not), and (i) there is a substantial nexus between the state and the taxpayer (here, Vendo does business on land within the state), (ii) the tax is fairly apportioned (the tax here is fair since it merely equalizes the tax burden on users of land within the state), and (iii) there is a fair relationship between the tax and the benefits provided by the state (this requisite is met since Vendo gets the protection of doing business in the state in exchange for the tax). (C) is incorrect because there is no equal protection violation here. The Equal Protection Clause merely prohibits the states from treating similar people in a dissimilar manner without a valid reason. When, as here, the law does not involve a suspect or quasi-suspect class or a fundamental right, the law will be upheld as long as there is a rational basis for the discrimination. Here, it is questionable whether the law discriminates, since it is applicable to *all* persons using land in the state. Assuming that the law does discriminate on the basis of the location of land, the discrimination is permissible because it is rationally related to a legitimate state purpose (a state may impose taxes to raise revenues but may not impose a tax on land or activities outside of the state).

Answer to Question 52

(D) States may regulate local aspects of interstate commerce as long as the local regulation does not conflict with, or is not preempted by, federal regulation and the regulation meets the following tests: (i) the regulation does not discriminate against out-of-state competition in order to benefit local economic interests, and (ii) the incidental burden on interstate commerce does not outweigh the local benefits of the regulation. In this case, the federal regulations do not conflict with the state ban and are not so comprehensive as to preempt even nonconflicting state regulation. With regard to the two-part test, the first standard is met because the regulation is not discriminatory against out-of-state products (because it bans *all* radar detectors regardless of origin). The second part is a balancing test, in which the court will consider whether the regulation promotes legitimate state interests and whether less restrictive alternatives are available. Here, the ban clearly promotes the state's legitimate interest in highway safety by making it harder for speeding motorists to evade detection. Anything less than a ban would not be effective in preventing the use of the detectors, and their use makes radar, the state's best means of preventing speeding, much less effective. On balance, the ban's local safety benefits outweigh its burden on interstate commerce and transportation. (A) is incorrect because a field will be held to be preempted only where the federal statute is so comprehensive that Congress impliedly occupied the whole field, and here the federal regulations concern only safety of the devices and use of frequencies. (B) is incorrect because it is too broad—not every law that burdens interstate commerce is unconstitutional. Rather, a balancing test will be applied. (C) is incorrect because it addresses only the preliminary issue. It is not enough that a statute regulating local aspects of interstate commerce does not conflict with federal regulations; even in the absence of any conflicting federal regulations, the statute must meet the tests described above.

Answer to Question 53

(C) Thompson will not prevail because the reapportionment plan does not violate the Equal Protection Clause of the Fourteenth Amendment. That provision has been interpreted to prohibit state dilution of the right to vote, so that whenever a governmental body establishes voting districts for the election of representatives, the number of persons in each district may not vary significantly. However, for the purpose of electing representatives to a state or local governmental body, the variance in the number of persons included in each district can be greater than that permitted for congressional districts. If the deviation from mathematical equality between districts is reasonable and tailored to promote a legitimate state interest, the law establishing the districts will likely be upheld. The Court has held that maintaining the integrity of local political subdivision lines when establishing legislative districts is a legitimate state interest, as long as the final apportionment is substantially based on population. [*See* Mahan v. Howell (1973)—16% variance upheld] Here, the reapportionment attempted to conform legislative districts as nearly as possible to county borders and had a maximum variance of 12%. Thus, it will probably withstand Thompson's challenge. (A) is incorrect because the fact that an alternative plan has a lesser variance between the districts does not make the selected plan invalid. Because it satisfies the less stringent requirements for state and local governmental bodies discussed above, the plan does not violate the Equal Protection Clause. (B) is incorrect because race can be considered in drawing up new voting districts, even though it cannot be the predominate factor. If a plaintiff can show that a redistricting plan was drawn up predominately on the basis of racial considerations (as opposed to the more traditional factors, such as compactness, contiguity, and community interest), the plan will violate the Equal Protection Clause unless the government can show that the plan is narrowly tailored to serve a compelling government interest (such as eliminating past discrimination). However, if a legislative redistricting map can be explained in terms other than race, the Court will not find that the law constitutes racial discrimination on its face. In such a case, the person attacking legislative districts as being based on racial classifications would have to show that district lines were drawn predominately for a racially discriminatory purpose. Here, as discussed above, the state's interest in preserving political subdivisions (counties) is a legitimate government interest, and Thompson will be unable to prove that this was not the predominate factor in the reapportionment. (D) is incorrect because the fact that the reapportionment plan reduces the existing population variance among districts does not make it constitutionally valid. The plan must satisfy the equal protection requirements established by the Court in apportionment cases.

Answer to Question 54

(B) Gilbert will likely prevail because the procedures taken to terminate his employment did not satisfy due process. Under the Due Process Clause of the Fourteenth Amendment, a public employee who is subject to removal only for "cause" under a statute, ordinance, or personnel document has a property interest in continued employment that cannot be taken away without due process of law. The Court has held that such an employee generally must be given notice of the charges and *a pre-termination opportunity to respond to those charges*. The employee must also be given a subsequent evidentiary hearing regarding the termination (with reinstatement if the employee prevails). [Cleveland Board of Education v. Loudermill (1985)] Here, Gilbert was notified of the charges but was not given any opportunity to respond to the charges until after his termination. Hence, his termination did not satisfy due process requirements. (A) is incorrect because the employee does not have to be given a full, formal hearing before his termination, as long as he is given oral or written notice of the charges, an explanation of the employer's evidence, and an opportunity to tell his side of the story. (C) is wrong because the fact that the state created Gilbert's property interest in his job does not permit the state to define what procedures may be used to terminate the interest. The procedures to which Gilbert was entitled are determined by independent constitutional standards. (D) is incorrect because, as discussed above, the procedures followed here did not satisfy due process standards. The Supreme Court has held that an employee can be suspended from his job without a prior hearing if the government has a significant reason for removing the employee from the job and providing him with only a post-termination hearing. [Gilbert v. Homar (1997)—campus police officer suspended after being arrested and charged with felony drug offense] Here, however, there is no substantial reason why the employee could not have been given the opportunity to respond to the charges prior to dismissal.

Answer to Question 55

(B) The legislation here is merely economic in nature and economic legislation will be upheld as long as there is a rational basis for the legislation. The residents would have the burden of proving that there is not a rational basis for the higher premiums here. (A) is incorrect because the compelling interest standard is not used to judge economic legislation, such as that involved here. (C) is incorrect because the market participant rule is an exception to the Commerce Clause ban on state action burdening interstate commerce. Here, the issue is not interstate commerce. Because this is a state-created and operated company, it will be held to the same equal protection standards as any other arm of the state. The Eleventh Amendment refers to suits in federal court. Thus, (D) is not applicable since the facts indicate that the citizens sued in state court. This does not mean that the state is necessarily subject to the suit, since it might have its own sovereign immunity doctrines. However, even if that were an answer choice, the facts do not indicate to what extent the state has waived its sovereign immunity doctrines.

Answer to Question 56

(C) State Company will prevail unless the citizens can show that State Company charges Mexican-American citizens higher rates than other citizens of Rockridge who are similarly situated. The mere fact that legislation or governmental action has a discriminatory effect is not sufficient to trigger strict scrutiny. There must be intent to discriminate on the part of the government, which can be shown by the discriminatory application of a law or regulation that appears neutral on its face. If State Company is charging Rockridge's Mexican-American citizens higher rates than other Rockridge citizens who are otherwise situated the same, the court will find that there is an intent to discriminate in the rate-setting process, triggering strict scrutiny because a suspect class is involved. (A) is incorrect because, as stated above, the citizens must show more than a discriminatory effect to prevail. The classification will be subject to strict scrutiny only if an intent to discriminate is established, which can be shown by (i) facial discrimination, (ii) discriminatory application, or (iii) discriminatory motive. (B) is incorrect. If the strict scrutiny standard applied, proof of a compelling interest would be required to uphold the discriminatory classification. However, as discussed, strict scrutiny will be triggered only if an intent to discriminate is shown; a discriminatory effect is not sufficient. (D) is incorrect because government actions or regulations that improperly discriminate against a suspect class may violate equal protection even if they are "economic" in nature.

Answer to Question 57

(C) The organization must prove that the legislation was motivated by a desire to inhibit the accomplishment of the organization's religious objectives. The Free Exercise Clause cannot be used to challenge a law of general applicability unless it can be shown that the law was motivated by a desire to interfere with religion. [Employment Division v. Smith (1990)] Thus, states may regulate conduct even if the regulation happens to interfere with a person's religious practices, as long as that was not the purpose of the legislation. (A) is incorrect because the burden of proof is on the organization, as the party challenging the law, to show that it was motivated by improper considerations. Even if the rational basis test were applied, the burden of proof would be on the organization rather than the government. (B) is incorrect because it states the test for upholding a law that was designed to suppress conduct solely because it was religiously motivated. Such a law would only be justified if the government could show that it was necessary to further a compelling interest. (D) is incorrect because the rational basis test is not applied to a Free Exercise Clause challenge to a law regulating general conduct. As discussed above, the challenger must show that the legislation was motivated by a desire to interfere with religion.

Answer to Question 58

(B)   A Fourteenth Amendment equal protection defense would be least helpful to Wilbur. When a law treats a person or class of persons differently than others, it is an equal protection question. Here, the statute on its face does not treat different classes of persons differently, and there is nothing in the facts to suggest that the law, although infrequently enforced, has been applied to Wilbur in a discriminatory manner. Hence, an equal protection argument would be weak. (A) is incorrect because it is presumptively unconstitutional for the government to place burdens on speech because of its content. To prevail, the government would have to show that the statute was necessary to serve a compelling state interest and narrowly drawn to achieve that end. Thus, free speech rights would provide an effective challenge to the statute. (C) is incorrect because Wilbur could argue that the statute violates the Establishment Clause. A statute will be valid under that provision only if it (i) has a secular purpose, (ii) has a primary effect that neither advances nor inhibits religion, and (iii) does not produce excessive government entanglement with religion. Wilbur can argue that a statute prohibiting the utterance of "blasphemy" and "sacrilege" violates that rule. (D) is incorrect because Wilbur has a strong argument that the statute violates the Due Process Clause. If a criminal law or regulation fails to give reasonable notice as to what is prohibited, it violates the Due Process Clause. This principle is applied strictly when First Amendment activity is involved to avoid the chilling effect that a vague law might have on freedom of speech. Here, Wilbur can defend by asserting that the statute does not define the prohibited speech except in the most general terms, and therefore the statute is unconstitutionally vague.

Answer to Question 59

(C)   While Wilbur could challenge on constitutional grounds any prosecution of him under the statute, the statute is not unconstitutional. Content-based restrictions on speech are permitted in cases where the speech creates a clear and present danger of imminent lawless action. A state can forbid advocating the use of force or of law violation if such advocacy (i) is directed to producing or inciting imminent lawless action, and (ii) is likely to produce or incite such action. Thus, a statute proscribing threats to the life or safety of a public official is valid when applied to specific, immediate threats of harm. (D) is therefore incorrect. Wilbur could not be punished under the facts of the question because it does not appear that he was actually threatening the justices with harm or inciting the crowd to storm into the court building; he appeared to be merely venting his outrage and went home after handing out his leaflets. There was no indication that Wilbur's words were inciting imminent lawless action or were likely to produce such action; thus, (B) is incorrect. (A) is wrong because whether the justices actually heard the threats would be irrelevant if they were otherwise actionable.

Answer to Question 60

(D) Wilbur will have to show that the statute was not reasonably related to a legitimate government purpose. Other than streets, sidewalks, parks, and designated public forums, most public property (including a court building and its grounds) is considered to be a nonpublic forum. The government can regulate speech in such a forum to reserve the forum for its intended use. Regulations will be upheld as long as they are (i) viewpoint neutral, and (ii) reasonably related to a legitimate government purpose. Here, the statute prohibited public gatherings on the steps of the courthouse at specified times while the court was in session, which appears to be a reasonable, viewpoint-neutral effort to preserve government property for its intended use. Wilbur would have the burden of proving that there was no reasonable basis for the statute. (A) and (C) are incorrect because the strict scrutiny standard enunciated in those choices only applies to content-based restrictions, and here the statute was not content-based. (B) is incorrect because it states the test for restrictions on speech in public forums. Unlike sidewalks and parks, a courthouse building and grounds are not a public forum even if they are open to the public during specified times.

Answer to Question 61

(D) The trial judge will most likely deny Judge Jones's motion to dismiss the indictment. The Fifth Amendment right to be free of double jeopardy for the same offense applies to subsequent criminal actions, but not to civil actions or impeachment proceedings, which are distinct from criminal proceedings. Article I, Section 3 of the Constitution specifically states that a conviction by impeachment does not prevent the party convicted from being subject to indictment, trial, judgment, and punishment according to the law. Hence, (B) is incorrect. (A) is wrong because there is nothing in the facts to show that the Attorney General was not acting within his prosecutorial discretion even if he was complying with the wishes of the President. (D) is incorrect because the fact that the grand jury issued the indictment is irrelevant. If double jeopardy did apply or if the Attorney General had abandoned his prosecutorial discretion in instituting criminal proceedings, the fact that the grand jury issued an indictment would not prevent the indictment from being dismissed.

Answer to Question 62

(C) The court should find the resolution invalid. While Congress has broad power to delegate, the separation of powers doctrine forbids Congress from trying to control the exercise of the power delegated in various ways, such as by overturning an executive agency action without bicameralism (*i.e.*, passage by both houses of Congress). By enacting the federal law allowing the administrative law judge to enter a final order with regard to aliens, Congress has given up any control it may have had previously in these situations. The resolution by the House here is an unconstitutional legislative veto that violates the separation of powers doctrine. (A) is wrong because, while Congress does have plenary power over aliens with regard to immigration and naturalization, here it has given up control over this area by enacting a law allowing an administrative officer appointed by the executive branch to make a final order concerning whether an alien should be deported. (B) is incorrect because the fact that aliens are not citizens has no bearing on whether the House resolution violated the Constitution. (D) is incorrect because, while resident aliens are entitled to notice and hearing before they can be deported, Fassil did receive a hearing before the administrative officer. There is no requirement that persons affected by legislative action have the right to be heard by the legislative body taking the action. Thus, the better argument as to why the resolution was invalid is based on separation of powers.

Answer to Question 63

(D) The court will likely find that the statute is a bill of attainder. A bill of attainder is a legislative act that inflicts punishment without a judicial trial on individuals who are designated either by name or in terms of past conduct. Past conduct acts to define who those particular persons are. The prohibition against bills of attainder mandates the use of judicial machinery for trial and punishment of crime as well as the drafting of the definition of criminal conduct in such general terms that it will not single out a particular individual or small group for punishment because of past behavior. In *United States v. Brown* (1965), the Court found that a provision making it a crime for an officer of a labor union to have been a member of the Communist Party was an unconstitutional bill of attainder. Hence, (A) is wrong. (B) is wrong because regardless of whether a rational basis exists for the adoption of the statute, if it constitutes a bill of attainder it cannot be upheld. (C) is incorrect because it is too broad. While the right to join together with other persons for political activity is protected by the First Amendment, infringements on that right may be justified by compelling government interests.

Answer to Question 64

(B) The legislation is a valid exercise of federal power and Act Now lacks standing to sue. Congress has the power to lay and collect taxes (as long as they are uniform) and the power to spend to "provide for the common defense and the general welfare." A tax measure will be upheld if it bears some reasonable relationship to revenue production or if Congress has the power to regulate the taxed activity. Spending may be for any public purpose—not merely the accomplishment of other enumerated powers. These independent powers enable Congress to address matters it otherwise could not regulate directly under the commerce power. Both the excise tax and the appropriation are valid exercises of congressional power, so I. is a valid defense. III. is a valid defense because the organization has standing to sue on behalf of its members only if the individual members would have a right to sue on their own behalf. As a general rule, federal taxpayers have no standing to challenge the way tax dollars are spent by the federal government, because their interest is too remote. The only exception recognized by the Court has been expenditures under Congress's taxing and spending power that violate the Establishment Clause. Here, the appropriation does not violate the Establishment Clause or any other specific constitutional limitation. II. is not a valid defense because it is a well-established principle of judicial review that federal courts have the power to review and, if necessary, enjoin expenditures voted by Congress.

Answer to Question 65

(D) The statute will be upheld because it is a valid state regulation of commerce. In the absence of congressional action preempting the area of regulation, a state may regulate local aspects of interstate commerce if the regulation (i) does not discriminate against out-of-state competition to benefit local economic interests, and (ii) is not unduly burdensome (*i.e.*, the incidental burden on interstate commerce does not outweigh the legitimate local benefits produced by the regulation). Here, the federal legislation does not conflict with the state law, nor does it preempt state regulation of foxes; in fact, the excise tax supports state laws regulating fox hunting. The state law here does not discriminate against interstate commerce or out-of-state competition because it applies to all hunting of foxes within the state. Nor is the state law unduly burdensome because the state's legitimate interest in trying to preserve one of its natural resources outweighs the incidental burden on interstate commerce that is created by the law. (A) is incorrect because the Privileges and Immunities Clause of Article IV prohibits discrimination by a state against nonresidents engaging in commercial activities. Here, the law does not discriminate against nonresidents—it applies equally to hunters residing in the state of Red. (B) is incorrect because, as discussed above, the federal legislation regarding the taking of foxes supports the state statute; it has not preempted state laws in that area. (C) is incorrect because, while Congress may allow the states to adopt discriminatory regulations that would otherwise violate the Commerce Clause, that is not the case here. The state of Red statute is nondiscriminatory and would not violate the Commerce Clause even in the absence of any congressional regulation on the topic, and the fact that the congressional excise tax reinforces state laws regulating foxes does not establish a congressional grant to the states of power over interstate commerce.

Answer to Question 66

(C) Gamer will lose because the tax is valid under the Commerce Clause. The same general considerations applicable to state regulation of commerce apply to taxation. A nondiscriminatory state tax affecting interstate commerce will be deemed to be an undue burden on the free flow of commerce unless three criteria are met: (i) there must be a substantial nexus between the activity taxed and the taxing state, (ii) the tax must be fairly apportioned according to a rational formula, and (iii) the tax must be fairly related to the benefits or services provided by the state. Here, the tax satisfies all three tests because the capture of foxes within the state has a nexus to the state, it is imposed on a per fox basis, and it is used for the conservation of the foxes' habitat, a legitimate purpose for which a state may exercise its power to tax. Thus, (A) is incorrect. (B) and (D) are incorrect because the Import-Export Clause prohibits states from imposing taxes on goods imported from or exported to foreign nations. The Clause is inapplicable here because nothing in the facts suggests that Gamer exports fox furs to other countries.

CONTRACTS QUESTIONS

Question 1

Biddlebaum was a deacon at Community Church. Among the tasks assigned Biddlebaum by the pastor was leadership of the church young adults group. In addition to Bible lessons and matters directly related to faith and belief, the group had various charitable and "fun" activities that were planned and directed by Biddlebaum. Biddlebaum firmly believed that the greatest curse on American society was drugs, among which he included alcohol and tobacco. One afternoon Biddlebaum saw Wing, a member of his church group, walking down the street with a white cylinder in her mouth. He assumed that Wing was smoking a cigarette. In fact, Wing was enjoying a piece of candy manufactured to look like a cigarette. Wing was vehemently anti-smoking. She had never smoked a cigarette in her life and frequently chided her friends who had taken up the habit. However, Biddlebaum wished to encourage abstinence from drugs and was concerned about Wing based upon what he had seen her doing on the street. On Friday afternoon, the bus was about to depart for a weekend "Campout" involving Biddlebaum's young adults group and similar groups from neighboring churches. At that time, Biddlebaum told Wing, "I'll give you $50 if you don't smoke a single cigarette during the whole Campout Weekend." Wing agreed to this. Wing, of course, did not smoke during the Campout Weekend. On Sunday evening Biddlebaum told Parishioner how he had helped turn the course of a young person in the right direction through his stratagem with Wing. Parishioner correctly informed Biddlebaum that Wing never smoked cigarettes. Biddlebaum now refuses to pay Wing $50.

Is Biddlebaum legally obligated to pay Wing $50?

(A) Yes, because Wing fulfilled Biddlebaum's terms and her motive for doing so is unimportant.

(B) Yes, because Biddlebaum's anti-drug activities morally obligate Biddlebaum to pay Wing.

(C) No, because not smoking during the Camp-out Weekend was good for Wing's health and in no way a detriment to Wing.

(D) No, because Wing would not have smoked during the Campout Weekend in any case and cannot be said to have been induced into abstinence by Biddlebaum's offer.

Question 2

Cogburn, a breeder of quarter horses, entered into an agreement with Ringo to sell and deliver two quarter horses, "True" and "Grit." Ringo had initially wanted to buy only one horse, since that was all he had room for in his stables, but was persuaded to buy both so that he could surprise his fiancee, Derby, with the gift of a horse. Although the fair market value of each horse was $3,000, Cogburn agreed to sell True and Grit together for a total price of $5,000. Under the agreement that Ringo wrote out and both parties signed, Cogburn agreed to deliver True to Ringo on August 1, at which time Ringo agreed to pay Cogburn $5,000. Cogburn further agreed to deliver Grit to Derby on August 12.

On August 1, Cogburn delivered True to Ringo and, at the same time, Ringo gave Cogburn a certified check for $5,000, drawn on Last Chance National Bank. On August 12, Cogburn brought Grit to Derby's residence and told Derby, "Here's your new horse; he's a gift from Ringo." Derby told Cogburn, "I loathe quarter horses. Ringo ought to know that I'm only interested in Arabians. Take that ugly beast out of my sight." Cogburn brought Grit back to his farm and sent a telegram to Ringo, informing him that Derby refused delivery and that Cogburn could not keep the horse. Two weeks later, after not hearing from Ringo, Cogburn sold Grit to Trailboss for $3,000.

If Ringo sues Cogburn, Ringo should recover:

(A) $3,000, the value of Grit.

(B) $2,000, the difference between the value of True and what Cogburn received from Ringo.

(C) Nothing, because Ringo was not financially harmed.

(D) Nothing, because Cogburn performed his part of the contract.

Question 3

Dos Santos received a "hot tip" on the stock market from his friend Huckleberry that Technogen, a small biotechnology firm, was a "can't miss" proposition because Technogen's genetic research and engineering scientists would soon announce a major breakthrough. At the time Huckleberry spoke to Dos Santos, Technogen was selling at $5 per share. Dos Santos wanted to buy 1,000 shares of the stock, but he lacked the funds to do so. Therefore, Dos Santos borrowed $5,000 from Capistrano on February 1, agreeing in writing to repay the loan on or before August 1. Dos Santos then purchased the stock.

On February 23 the Food and Drug Administration announced that Technogen's "breakthrough" was based on faulty research and refused to certify the product for clinical trials. The price of Technogen stock immediately plunged to $2.50 per share and has remained there. On July 15 Dos Santos notified Capistrano that he would be unable to pay back the $5,000 on August 1. Dos Santos told Capistrano that he would sell his Technogen stock, but that would realize him only $2,500. However, he offered Capistrano an antique diamond ring that had been recently appraised at $2,200. Dos Santos showed Capistrano an article in a highly respected magazine predicting that political instability in leading diamond producing regions was likely to send the value of diamonds soaring. Capistrano agreed to accept $2,500 in cash plus the ring as payment for the loan.

On August 1 a bonded courier delivered the diamond ring and Dos Santos's certified check for $2,500 to Capistrano. Capistrano took the check, but he told the courier to return the ring to Dos Santos. Dos Santos got the ring back the same afternoon. Meanwhile, Capistrano deposited the check in his bank, and the next day filed suit against Dos Santos for $2,500. Dos Santos consulted an attorney as to whether he has any rights against Capistrano.

Assuming there are no Statute of Frauds issues, the attorney should advise Dos Santos that:

(A) Dos Santos has no remedy against Capistrano, because the amount of the debt was undisputed.

(B) Dos Santos has no remedy against Capistrano, who properly exercised his right to enforce the original agreement by refusing tender of the ring.

(C) Dos Santos has no remedy at law, but he may successfully sue in equity for specific performance if the ring is considered unique.

(D) Dos Santos has the option of suing for specific performance, or waiting until Capistrano obtains a judgment against him and then suing Capistrano for breach.

Question 4

Artemesia owned and operated a gallery that specialized in the sale of works by contemporary artists. Six months ago Artemesia underwent a serious operation. During her period of convalescence, Artemesia's good friend Crafty was of great help to her. Crafty brought Artemesia meals and flowers and ran numerous errands for her while Artemesia was laid up. Crafty sometimes purchased art from Artemesia's gallery. Most of the items Crafty bought were in the $200 to $700 range, because Crafty did not make a lot of money in his job as an editorial assistant. However, Crafty loved and appreciated art, and his modest apartment's walls were filled with originals and prints. One Saturday evening Artemesia and Crafty were discussing the work of several up-and-coming young artists. Crafty told Artemesia that he particularly liked the work of Van Dough. Artemesia said, "How would you like the Van Dough I've got in my gallery?" Crafty knew that Artemesia was referring to "The Watermelon Eaters," a painting the artist had just consigned to Artemesia's gallery. Crafty said, "I'd love it, but I've only got $2,700." Artemesia responded, "You give me $2,700 and the Van Dough is yours." Crafty knew that the Van Dough was priced at $7,000. He immediately wrote out a check for $2,700 and gave the check to Artemesia, who told Crafty to visit the gallery on Monday and pick up the painting. Since her illness, Artemesia had ceased going to the gallery on weekends. On Sunday, Artemesia's gallery manager, Morton, sold "The Watermelon Eaters" to MacRamay, a gallery customer. Neither Morton nor MacRamay knew of the agreement between Artemesia and Crafty. MacRamay took the painting with him on Sunday. When Crafty arrived at the gallery on Monday, the painting was gone.

Can Crafty obtain specific performance from Artemesia?

(A) Yes, because there was a bargained-for exchange of promises between Crafty and Artemesia.

(B) Yes, because Crafty's assistance to Artemesia during her illness should be considered part of the quantum of adequate consideration.

(C) No, because the painting was sold to a bona fide purchaser for value and enforcement against Artemesia is no longer feasible.

(D) No, because Artemesia's promise was essentially a gift to Crafty that Artemesia was free to revoke.

Question 5

Plumboco was a large-scale manufacturer of plumb bobs, which were used as components in a variety of industrial products. Plumboco regularly sent out circulars to customers and prospects in the various industries employing plumb bobs. The circulars included prices and descriptions of the various models of plumb bobs. All of Plumboco's prices were quoted "C.I.F." in the circulars. Middlemaker was one of the companies receiving Plumboco circulars. In the latest circular Plumboco quoted "Model Z16" plumb bobs at $3,500 per 100 plumb bob lot "C.I.F." Middlemaker used Z16-type plumb bobs and considered $3,500 per 100 to be a particularly good price. Middlemaker faxed an order to Plumboco reading: "As per your circular, ordering two 100 plumb bob lots, model Z16, at $3,500 per lot. Delivery by August 6." Plumboco mailed back its standard confirmation form, confirming quantity, price, and delivery date. However, Middlemaker's purchasing agent noticed that a rubber stamp impression in red ink had been placed on the bottom of Plumboco's confirmation. It read: "Acceptance of this order conditioned on a crating charge of $150 per 100 plumb bob lot."

Assuming no additional facts, which of the following best represents the relationship between Plumboco and Middlemaker immediately after Middlemaker received Plumboco's confirmation?

(A) There is a valid, enforceable contract between Plumboco and Middlemaker that includes the crating fee.

(B) There is a valid contract between Plumboco and Middlemaker, but it does not include the crating fee.

(C) There is no contract between Plumboco and Middlemaker, because there has been an alteration of a material term.

(D) There is no contract between Plumboco and Middlemaker, because Plumboco's confirmation letter was a counteroffer, which Middlemaker may accept or reject.

Questions 6-7 are based on the following fact situation:

Pitt, a large wholesale dealer in produce, had never done business with Greengrocer before. Greengrocer operated a small chain of markets in the Middle West. They entered into a written agreement whereby Pitt agreed to supply

Greengrocer the "fuzzy" variety of peaches at $35 per "standard crate." Both Pitt and Greengrocer understood the meaning of the term "standard crate," which was the usual way fuzzy peaches were shipped in the produce trade. The agreement contained a provision stating "Greengrocer will buy as many standard crates of fuzzy peaches as Greengrocer chooses to order."

6. Assume for purposes of this question only that Greengrocer has not yet placed any orders for peaches with Pitt. Is the agreement between Pitt and Greengrocer enforceable?

   (A) Yes, because it is a valid requirements contract and, as such, is enforceable under the Uniform Commercial Code.

   (B) Yes, because the Uniform Commercial Code will imply reasonable terms.

   (C) No, because the total quantity of the contract is not specified.

   (D) No, because there is no consideration on Greengrocer's part.

7. Assume for purposes of this question only that on June 1 Greengrocer ordered from Pitt "150 standard crates, C.O.D. June 10." Along with his order for the 150 crates, Greengrocer enclosed a letter stating, in relevant part, "I will order another 150 standard crates of fuzzy peaches on June 15, if you will supply them at a price of $30 per unit." Because of a late season freeze in the Southeast that damaged the crop, a relatively frequent occurrence, fuzzy peaches were in short supply. After receiving Greengrocer's communications, Pitt wrote to Greengrocer, "I am not going to ship you any fuzzy peaches, because I am going to take care of the needs of my old customers." Litigation ensues.

   The court should find:

   (A) There is no contract between Pitt and Greengrocer, because the original promises were unenforceable.

   (B) Greengrocer has a contract to buy 150 crates of peaches at $35 per unit.

   (C) Greengrocer has a contract to buy 150 crates of peaches at $35 per unit, and there is an offer by Greengrocer to buy another 150 crates at $30 per unit.

   (D) Greengrocer has a contract to purchase 300 crates of peaches at $35 per unit.

Question 8

Farm Fresh Dairy operated a small processing plant that supplied premium ice cream to nearby specialty shops and ice cream parlors. It entered into a written agreement with Patti's Parfait Parlor to sell "all output of Fancy Grade ice cream" to Patti's, and Patti's agreed to sell "exclusively Farm Fresh Dairy frozen desserts." The agreement stated that Patti's would pay $25 for each five-gallon container of Fancy Grade ice cream that it ordered from Farm Fresh. Several months after the parties entered into this contract, demand for the high-fat ice creams dropped sharply among the health-conscious consumers who had formerly patronized Patti's. Patti's had to throw out some of its product because the reduced demand meant that opened containers were not used up before the taste of the ice cream became affected. Patti's wanted to stop selling the Fancy Grade ice cream and instead sell a frozen yogurt product produced by another dairy.

Can Farm Fresh enforce the agreement against Patti's?

(A) Yes, because changing demand is one of the standard risks of business that both parties assumed.

(B) Yes, because the court will imply a promise on the part of Patti's to use its best efforts to sell Farm Fresh ice cream.

(C) No, because there was no consideration on the part of Patti's to support an enforceable contract.

(D) No, because the total price and total quantity terms were never established.

Question 9

Tarbel, a contractor, entered into a contract with Denhart College to remodel a residence hall during the summer. As specified by the contract, the work had to be completed before the fall semester began at the beginning of September. Because Tarbel received a great deal of other maintenance business from the college, his price of $400,000 was significantly lower than other contractors and he was not going to demand payment until the work was completed.

By the end of the first week in August, Tarbel had completed 75% of the project and had expended $350,000 in labor and materials. At that time, however, a labor dispute between Tarbel and his employees prompted most of the workers to walk off the job. Because prospects for a quick settlement of the dispute were doubtful, Tarbel informed the college that he would not be able to meet the completion deadline. A week later, the college obtained another contractor who was able to finish the project by the end of August. The college paid him $150,000, which included a substantial amount of overtime for his workers. The increase in value of the residence hall due to the remodeling was $425,000.

Tarbel, who had not been paid, files suit against Denhart College, which files a counterclaim against Tarbel. What should the ultimate recovery be in this action?

(A) Tarbel should recover nothing from the college because Tarbel breached the contract.

(B) Tarbel should recover $200,000 in quasi-contract from the college, which is the difference between its expenditures and the amount the college paid the other contractor to complete the work.

(C) Tarbel should recover $250,000 in quasi-contract from the college, which is the

contract price minus the amount the college paid the other contractor to complete the work.

(D) Tarbel should recover $275,000 in quasi-contract from the college, which is the difference between the value of the completed remodeling and the amount the college paid the other contractor to complete the work.

Question 10

Brandon and Marlowe entered into a written contract whereby Brandon agreed to buy and Marlowe agreed to sell for $7,500 "any painting by Bleu in Marlowe's art gallery." Marlowe operated a gallery specializing in the work of promising young artists and Brandon was an avid art collector. The contract was to be executed on July 6 according to its written terms. Brandon went to Marlowe's gallery on July 6 with a certified check in the amount of $7,500. Brandon pointed out a painting by Ruyter hanging on the wall, and told Marlowe, "That's the painting I want, and I'll also take the old fashioned $250 gilt frame over there." Marlowe responded that the contract specified a painting by Bleu rather than a painting by Ruyter, and Marlowe added: "You can have the $250 frame if you're willing to pay me $250 extra for it." An angry Brandon filed suit against Marlowe. Brandon asserts in his pleading that he remains able and willing to tender $7,500 to Marlowe. Brandon also asserts that prior to signing the contract Brandon and Marlowe agreed orally that Brandon could have a painting by Ruyter if he wanted one and that Marlowe would throw in a frame worth $250. Marlowe denied that any such conversation took place. There are no other witnesses.

The court should allow Brandon to testify regarding:

(A) The oral agreement for the painting, but not the oral agreement for the frame.

(B) The oral agreement for the frame, but not the oral agreement for the painting.

(C) Both the oral agreement for the painting and the oral agreement for the frame.

(D) Neither the oral agreement for the painting nor the oral agreement for the frame.

Questions 11-12 are based on the following fact situation:

Ernest wrote the following letter to his brother-in-law, Charles, who lived in a city about a half hour's drive from Ernest's metropolitan apartment:

Dear Charles,

I no longer have the time to pursue photography as a hobby, and I know you have admired my equipment for a long time. I will sell you all my camera equipment for $1,500. Let me know whether you are interested within one week, because I have been offered $1,500 for the equipment by a local camera shop and must let them know by the first of the month.

Sincerely,
Ernest

Two days after receiving the letter, Charles mailed a letter back to Ernest agreeing to purchase the camera equipment for $1,500. The next day, while describing the equipment to a friend who was very knowledgeable about photographic equipment, Charles learned that Ernest's equipment was second-rate and not worth more than $1,200. He immediately telephoned Ernest, stating, "I have no interest in purchasing your equipment." Ernest received Charles's letter agreeing to purchase the camera equipment a day after receiving the phone call.

11. If Ernest brings an action against Charles for breach of contract, and Charles defends on the grounds that no contract was formed, how should the court rule?

(A) For Charles, because the description of the subject matter of the contract was too indefinite to be enforced.

(B) For Charles, because Ernest received the telephone call before he received the letter.

(C) For Ernest, because Charles's letter accepting the offer was effective when mailed.

(D) For Ernest, because the contract is for the sale of goods over $500 in value and Charles's attempted rejection of the offer was oral.

12. Assume for the purposes of this question only that a valid contract was formed between Ernest and Charles by the exchange of letters. Charles refuses to accept the camera equipment and Ernest brings an action for breach. Should the trial court invoke the parol evidence rule to bar Charles from offering evidence that he was unduly rushed into making a decision because Ernest really did not need an answer within a week?

(A) Yes, because the proffered evidence contradicts a material term of the contract.

(B) Yes, because Charles is estopped from denying the truth of a contract that he has accepted.

(C) No, because the proffered evidence does not contradict a material term of the contract.

(D) No, because the proffered evidence establishes a fraud.

Question 13

In which of the four following fact situations would a court be most likely to find that an implied-in-fact contract existed?

(A) Dr. Hacksaw, a licensed physician, sees an unconscious pedestrian lying bleeding on the shoulder of the highway. Hacksaw stops his car, gets out, and renders emergency medical care to the injured pedestrian.

(B) Olivia, an octogenarian, asks her favorite niece, Nelda, a CPA, to fill out and file Olivia's state tax return. Olivia's only income is from social security and interest on a bank account. It takes Nelda five minutes to complete the form. She puts her own postage stamp on the envelope containing the return and mails the return.

(C) Cisco, a contractor, has a contract to repave Bruce's driveway. Cisco mistakes the home of Bruce's neighbor, Nicholas, for Bruce's home. As Cisco repaves Nicholas's driveway, Nicholas stands by watching until the job is done.

(D) Hobart, a homeowner, has already paid his annual county property taxes. A clerk in the county assessor's office mistakenly sends Hobart a bill that should have gone to Hobart's neighbor, Nils. Being a good citizen and thinking that the assessor would not have sent him the bill if he did not owe the money, Hobart writes out a check to the county assessor and pays the tax bill.

Questions 14-15 are based on the following fact situation:

Girder entered into a written agreement with Crane, whereby Crane agreed to supply heavy equipment and operators for a new state toll road project on which Girder was the general contractor. Among the duties Crane undertook to perform was the installation of the toll collection booths and automatic toll collection machinery. Other terms of the contract between Crane and Girder included the following:

Clause I: "Time is of the essence. Crane must have all toll booths and toll collection equipment in place and operable by August 20."

Clause II: "Any modification of the contract without written approval by Girder shall be void."

Clause III: "Exoneration—Crane shall be held harmless for any property

damage occurring while Crane is placing the toll booths and automatic toll collection machinery."

Clause IV: "Liquidated Damages— Failure to complete the job on time shall result in liquidated damages of $1,000 per day chargeable against Crane."

Before Crane began work on Girder's project, Crane was offered an extremely lucrative opportunity to work on a construction project in a war-ravaged Middle Eastern oil sheikdom. The rebuilding work would continue for several years and promised to bring Crane far more income than the work for Girder. Crane wished to assign his part of the contract with Girder to Derrick, who was equally experienced and qualified in heavy equipment contracting.

14. Which clause in the contract between Girder and Crane would be most likely to bar Crane from assigning to Derrick?

(A) The "time is of the essence" clause.

(B) The nonmodification clause.

(C) The exoneration clause.

(D) The liquidated damages clause.

15. Assume for purposes of this question only that Crane assigned his part of the contract to Derrick with Girder's written approval. On July 28, Derrick used his heavy equipment to place the toll booths and automatic toll collection machinery on permanent mountings. Unfortunately, Derrick did not put the booths or toll collection equipment in the proper location, even though the specifications were clear and exact regarding the correct locations. It will be quite expensive to uproot the toll booths and collection machinery and to move and reset them in their proper locations. Is Crane liable to Girder for the cost of removing and resetting the toll booths and collection machinery?

(A) Yes, because the assignment, in and of itself, does not relieve Crane of liability on the underlying contract.

(B) Yes, if the job of placing the booths and machinery in their correct locations cannot be completed until after August 20.

(C) No, because Crane transferred his duties to Derrick.

(D) No, if Girder's approval is construed as an offer of novation.

Question 16

Mable, a homeowner, entered into a written agreement with contractor Cedric, whereby Cedric agreed to completely remodel Mable's bathroom "to Mable's specifications" at a cost of $10,000. Mable's specifications were highly detailed and required custom-made fixtures that would not be usable in other bathroom remodeling jobs. Cedric ordered the custom-made fixtures and paid $4,000 for them when they were delivered to his place of business. Figuring up the cost of the fixtures and labor, Cedric estimated that he would make a total profit of $2,000 on the job after payment for materials and workers. Before Cedric began work on the project, but after he had paid for the fixtures, Mable told Cedric, "I've had a change of heart. I think I'm going to sell the house next year, so I won't be needing that custom bathroom." Cedric made no attempt to sell the fixtures to another contractor and filed suit against Mable for damages.

Cedric is likely to recover:

(A) Nothing, because he failed to mitigate damages.

(B) His expectation damages of $2,000.

(C) $4,000 for the cost of materials as restitution.

(D) $2,000 as expectation damages, plus $4,000 in reliance damages.

Question 17

Retailer entered into a written contract with Wholesaler whereby Wholesaler agreed to sell and Retailer agreed to buy 100 boxes of "Red Star" sunglasses, manufactured by Redblok Corporation. The agreed-upon price was $75 per box. Two weeks before the specified delivery date, Wholesaler notified Retailer, "Because of unexpected high demand for sunglasses this season, we will be unable to fill your order." Although Retailer learned that the needed quantity of "Red Star" sunglasses could be shipped within two days for $83 per box from a supplier in another area, Retailer instead purchased 100 boxes of "Red Seal" sunglasses locally at a cost of $90 per box. The "Red Seal" glasses were also manufactured by Redblok Corporation but were of a slightly higher quality than the "Red Star" model. A few days before the original delivery date, Wholesaler notified Retailer that it would fill the order, and tendered 100 boxes of "Red Star" sunglasses on the date of delivery. However, Retailer refused to accept them. At that time, the wholesale market price of "Red Star" sunglasses had declined to $80 per box.

If Retailer sues Wholesaler for damages based on Wholesaler's alleged breach, Retailer is likely to recover:

(A) $1,500, representing the difference between the cost of cover and the contract price.

(B) $800, representing the difference between the contract price and the nonlocal supplier's price.

(C) $500, representing the difference between the contract price and the wholesale market price at the time of performance.

(D) Nothing, because Retailer obtained cover without waiting a commercially reasonable time for Wholesaler to retract the repudiation.

Questions 18-19 are based on the following fact situation:

Chip ran a popular and profitable antique business. His large store, "Antique Boutique," had the widest selection of antiques in the western part of the state. Dale loved antiques, and her home was tastefully decorated with a variety of European and American pieces. Antique Boutique was about a two-hour drive from Dale's home, but she visited the store several times a year. Chip had a beautiful Early American bedroom ensemble that Dale coveted. It included an elegant four-poster bed, a large gilt-framed mirror, and two well-crafted dressers. Over a period of several weeks, Chip and Dale negotiated about the price, but they failed to come to an agreement.

18. Assume for purposes of this question only that on Dale's last visit to Antique Boutique both Chip and Dale signed a statement dated April 3, the day of Dale's visit: "Chip offers to sell Dale an Early American bedroom ensemble, manufactured in Ohio during the 1870s, recorded as items 20465, 20466, 20467, and 20468 in the registry of Antique Boutique. An enforceable agreement regarding the ensemble exists between Chip and Dale if Chip and Dale agree upon the price of the ensemble on or before April 12." On April 6, Chip sent a letter to Dale, stating: "You can have the bedroom ensemble for $22,000." Also on April 6, Dale sent a letter to Chip, stating: "I'm willing to pay you $22,000 for the bedroom ensemble." The addressees both received their letters on April 7. Without assuming any additional facts, which of the following statements is most correct as of April 8?

(A) Chip and Dale have had a valid contract from the moment the letters of April 6 were mailed.

(B) There is a contract between Chip and Dale, because Chip, a merchant, sent Dale an offer in writing.

(C) There is a contract between Chip and Dale, because the crossing offers were identical and received before April 12.

(D) There is no contract between Chip and Dale, because there is a lack of mutual assent.

19. Assume for purposes of this question only that Chip and Dale entered into a valid agreement for the bedroom ensemble with the ensemble to be delivered on May 20. One of the terms of the contract provided that Chip was to tender the ensemble to Dale's favorite niece, Priscilla, as a birthday present from Dale. Chip sent a photocopy of the contract to Priscilla. Priscilla received the copy on May 4. Priscilla had just purchased a modern bedroom set for $6,000, but she was so anxious to see the beautiful antique set in her bedroom that she gave her new bedroom set to a charitable organization. The charity picked up Priscilla's furniture on May 10. On May 15, Dale told Chip that she wanted to cancel the contract for the bedroom ensemble. Chip assented and sold the ensemble to Tex for $26,000. Priscilla rented a truck and appeared at Antique Boutique on May 20. Can Priscilla compel Dale to honor the original contract or pay her damages?

(A) Yes, because Priscilla is an intended beneficiary of a valid contract.

(B) Yes, because Priscilla reasonably relied on the contract between Chip and Dale.

(C) No, because Priscilla was merely an incidental beneficiary.

(D) No, because Priscilla was a donee beneficiary and Dale properly revoked the gift.

Questions 20-21 are based on the following fact situation:

Yott was a wealthy sportsman and sailing enthusiast. He purchased a large old wooden sailing ship for $200,000. Although the boat was a classic, Yott wanted the vessel to be modernized and made more comfortable. Yott entered into a written contract with Salty, a marine architect and engineer. Under the terms of the contract, Yott agreed to pay Salty $7,500, and Salty agreed to draw up the modernization plans and to be the contractor for the modernization of the ship.

20. Assume for purposes of this question only that at the time Yott and Salty entered into the agreement, Yott told Salty orally, "Of course, your modernization plan is subject to the approval of my sister, Marina. Although I'm sure she'll like any design of yours, we've got no deal unless your plans meet with her approval." Salty agreed to this. Salty finished his drawings and submitted them to Yott, who was enthusiastic about Salty's designs. Marina, a famous yachtswoman, was engaged in a trans-Pacific yacht race at the time and was not expected home for a number of weeks. Cheered by Yott's enthusiasm, Salty went ahead and modernized the ship according to his designs. When Salty finished the work, he submitted a bill to Yott. Yott refused to pay, pointing out that Marina had never approved the designs. If Salty sues Yott, which of the following issues of contract law is most likely to be decisive in determining the outcome of the case?

    (A) Statute of Frauds.

    (B) Parol evidence rule.

    (C) Rules of construction.

    (D) Conditions precedent.

21. Assume for purposes of this question only that the written agreement between Yott and Salty contained a clause stating: "Salty shall not begin the actual marine engineering and modernization without prior approval of the plans by Yott's certified public accountant, Counter." Salty submitted his designs to both Yott and Counter. Yott liked the plans, but Counter did not. Counter withheld his approval. Salty asked Yott if Yott wanted him to submit new designs. Yott told Salty orally, "No! Your

designs are great! Counter is a landlubber who wouldn't know a battleship from a bathtub. You go right ahead and modernize the sailboat." Salty modernized the boat. Yott now refuses to pay Salty, citing the clause requiring approval by Counter. If Salty sues Yott, Salty will recover:

    (A) The full contract price, because Counter's approval was not a condition precedent for the contract to take effect.

    (B) The full contract price, because once Salty began modernizing the ship after speaking with Yott, Yott did nothing to stop Salty.

    (C) The reasonable value of Salty's services and materials, because otherwise Yott would be unjustly enriched.

    (D) Nothing, because Yott's oral statement will be excluded by the parol evidence rule.

Question 22

Two years ago, Marquis, an expert on antique jewelry, told Sparkler that an antique star sapphire ring belonging to Sparkler was "probably worth about $6,000," although Marquis never gave a formal appraisal of the ring. Sparkler had meanwhile run up several thousand dollars of gambling debts and was looking for a way to scrape up some funds to satisfy the debts. Sparkler knew that his friend Beryl loved antique jewelry and offered to sell the ring to her. Beryl looked at the ring through a jewelers' loupe and truthfully told Sparkler, "This gemstone looks very nice to me, but I'm no expert. Why don't you take the ring to a reputable jeweler for an appraisal, and if the price isn't too high I'll buy it from you." Sparkler did not tell Beryl about Marquis's opinion regarding the stone's value, because he hoped the value might have increased in the ensuing two years. Sparkler took the ring to Rouge, a highly respected jeweler, for an appraisal. Rouge told Sparkler in good faith, "If the stone in this ring were perfect, it would be worth $6,200, but there's a very tiny, almost invisible flaw, and that flaw reduces the value of the ring to $4,800." Rouge gave Sparkler a formal appraisal document valuing the ring at $4,800. Although Sparkler was disappointed, he needed money and told Beryl she could have the ring for $4,800. Unbeknownst to Beryl or Sparkler, Rouge was suffering from a minor eye infection that caused him to find a "flaw" where none, in fact, existed. After she purchased the ring from Sparkler for $4,800, Beryl sought her own appraisal for insurance purposes. A reputable jeweler issued Beryl an appraisal document accurately stating the ring's value at $6,200. Sparkler learned of this before he paid off his gambling creditors. He demanded return of the ring from Beryl in exchange for the money Beryl paid. Beryl refused.

If Sparkler sues Beryl to replevy the ring, the court should rule in favor of:

(A) Beryl, because parties to a contract generally assume the risk of determining value.

(B) Beryl, because Sparkler should have known the ring was worth more than $4,800 based on his conversation with Marquis.

(C) Sparkler, because both parties mistakenly relied on an inaccurate appraisal in determining the ring's value.

(D) Sparkler, because accuracy of the appraisal was an express condition precedent.

Questions 23-24 are based on the following fact situation:

Cordero owned a beautiful home entertainment center, which included a large-screen television. Cordero worked very hard at two jobs, so he had little opportunity to enjoy the entertainment system. Cordero's friend, Tina, wanted an entertainment system so that she could watch her favorite daytime soap operas. She importuned Cordero, and he finally agreed to sell her his home entertainment system for

$2,500. Tina made a downpayment of $700 and took possession of the entertainment system. She agreed to pay the balance due to Cordero in 18 equal $100 installments, beginning on June 5, with subsequent installments due on the fifth of each month until the balance was paid in full.

Gabrielle owed Tina $2,000. On May 20, Tina entered into an oral agreement with Gabrielle whereby Gabrielle agreed to make the 18 $100 installment payments to Cordero. In exchange for this, Tina promised to forgive Gabrielle's $2,000 debt to her. On June 7, Cordero called Tina and asked where his first $100 installment payment was. At that time Tina told Cordero of her agreement with Gabrielle. Gabrielle has made none of the installment payments.

23. If Cordero files suit demanding payment from Gabrielle, who will prevail?

(A) Cordero, because he was a third-party beneficiary of the agreement between Tina and Gabrielle.

(B) Cordero, because he is an assignee of Tina's rights against Gabrielle.

(C) Gabrielle, because there was no consideration for her promise to Tina.

(D) Gabrielle, because the surety provision of the Statute of Frauds prevents Cordero from enforcing Gabrielle's promise.

24. Does Cordero have a right to recover the debt from Tina?

(A) Yes, if Cordero has not yet filed suit against Gabrielle.

(B) No, unless Cordero is not able to recover the money from Gabrielle.

(C) Yes, unless Cordero has expressly agreed with Gabrielle and Tina that Gabrielle would assume Tina's duties under the contract.

(D) No, because Gabrielle expressly assumed Tina's duties under the contract.

Question 25

Flipper was a wholesale distributor of pinball machines and other mechanical and electronic games. Flipper's headquarters were in Azura, the largest city in the state of Blue, but Flipper's business served the entire state. There were no plants manufacturing the types of machines that Flipper sold within a thousand miles of Blue, and certain very popular machines were in scarce supply. Arcade owned and operated two video game arcades in Slate, the third-largest city in Blue. Arcade also sold and leased machines to taverns and convenience stores in the Slate area.

On August 3, Flipper sent a letter to Arcade, which Arcade received on August 5. The letter stated, in relevant part: "I now have in stock those 20 electronic poker games that you wanted for your business. I can guarantee delivery until September 2 at $2,000 per machine."

On August 16, Flipper sold the 20 electronic poker games to Tilt at a price of $2,300 per machine. On August 17, Flipper telegrammed Arcade: "Am revoking offer regarding poker machines; have already sold same at higher price." Arcade received the telegram the same day.

During the month of August, the Blue legislature was in special session, mainly to deal with a budget crisis in public schools throughout the state. However, certain other legislation was also debated during the special session. The special session passed a bill declaring the sale of electronic gambling machines to be illegal in the state of Blue. The definition of electronic gambling machines included the poker machines distributed by Flipper. The governor signed the bill into law on August 28, and it became effective immediately.

On August 30, Arcade wired Flipper: "Accept your offer to sell me 20 poker games at $2,000

per machine." Flipper received the telegram the same day.

If Flipper is not obliged to sell Arcade 20 electronic poker machines at $2,000 each, it will be because:

(A) Flipper had already sold the machines at a higher price.

(B) The state law banning the sale of such machines operated to revoke the offer.

(C) Flipper revoked his offer before Arcade accepted.

(D) The state law banning the sale of such machines renders the performance of Flipper's duties impossible.

Questions 26-27 are based on the following fact situation:

Tella Vishun purchased a large tract of land outside of Dullsville. She successfully applied to the Federal Communications Commission for a license to operate a television station. She then entered into a written contract with Diggum, a general contractor. Diggum agreed to build Vishun's studio and broadcast transmitter for $3 million by July 1. Among the tasks Diggum undertook were building of access roads large enough to accommodate Vishun's new fleet of minicam vans and to install the underground cables and fiberoptic lines necessary to broadcast.

26. Assume for purposes of this question only that when digging the deep trench necessary to lay the conduit containing the fiberoptic lines, Diggum encountered a stretch of extremely soggy soil. This was an indication that an offshoot of the Dullsville aquifer underlay Vishun's property. This was not indicated on any of the geological survey maps available in the office of the Dull County Recorder of Deeds. Diggum told Vishun that it would cost an additional $50,000 to lay the conduit through that stretch of soil. Vishun had already launched an advertising

campaign with the theme: "U.S.A. Channel 86—Born on the Fourth of July," indicating that the station would begin broadcasting on July 4, which was rapidly approaching. Therefore, when Diggum threatened to quit the job without the additional $50,000, Vishun reluctantly agreed orally to Diggum's demand as long as Diggum promised that all of the work would be completed by the middle of June. Diggum agreed and proceeded to lay the conduit and completed building the studio and transmitter by June 15. Vishun then paid Diggum $3 million. Diggum demanded $50,000 more, but Vishun refused to pay it. If Diggum sues Vishun for the $50,000, who will prevail?

(A) Vishun, because the oral modification was not effective to alter the prior written agreement.

(B) Vishun, because no valid consideration was provided for the agreement to pay the additional $50,000.

(C) Diggum, because the additional $50,000 payment was a reasonable modification of the contract, given all of the surrounding circumstances.

(D) Diggum, if $3,050,000 was a fair price for the completed job.

27. Assume for purposes of this question only that after Diggum finished the job, Vishun discovered that Diggum had laid a portion of the conduit through a patch of magnetized rock. This meant that under certain conditions, such as magnetic storms generated by sunspot activity, a higher than normal level of interference with broadcast signals would occur. The written contract between Vishun and Diggum had specified that the conduit should be laid in a path that avoided the area of magnetized rock. Despite the defect, the studio and broadcasting transmitter are now worth about $4 million. Without the defect, their value would be $100,000 more. Vishun contracted with Kables, another contractor, to reroute the conduit around the magnetized rock for a cost of $50,000. How much is Diggum entitled to collect from Vishun?

(A) $2,900,000, because the actual value of the property is $100,000 less than the value it would have been if Diggum had not breached.

(B) $3 million, because the value of the property even with the defect is greater than the contract price.

(C) $2,950,000, because Vishun will have to pay $50,000 to correct Diggum's defective performance.

(D) Only the expenses Diggum incurred, but not his expected profit, because he breached the contract with Vishun.

Questions 28-29 are based on the following fact situation:

Claw died, leaving his nephew Scratch as his sole heir. Among the items inherited by Scratch were some old oil paintings that had been stored in Claw's attic for a number of years. Scratch knew nothing about art and had no place to put them in his home. He placed an ad in the paper offering to sell the paintings "at a price to be mutually agreed upon." Fang, a buyer for an art gallery, responded to the ad and examined the paintings. From the signature and the style, Fang recognized that the artist was William Hamilton, a renowned 19th century American portrait artist. Scratch and Fang agreed upon a price and executed a contract.

28. Which of the following facts, if true, would give Scratch the best basis for rescinding the contract with Fang?

(A) Scratch told Fang that Claw had dabbled in painting when he was younger and had undoubtedly painted them himself.

(B) Scratch did not know that Fang was a buyer for an art gallery and was very familiar with 19th century American art.

(C) Scratch told Fang that he wanted to get rid of the paintings as soon as possible because he was angry at his uncle for giving away most of his possessions to a TV evangelist just before he died.

(D) Fang falsely told Scratch that the paintings were going to be used to furnish Fang's country estate.

29. Which of the following facts, if true, would give Fang the best basis for rescinding the contract with Scratch?

(A) Several of the paintings cracked when they were being transported by Fang because they were brittle with age.

(B) The day after the purchase, a respected art historian announced in a press release that many William Hamilton paintings were actually done by his students and other associates, causing the value of all William Hamilton paintings to decline.

(C) Because of some experimental pigments that the artist had used, the colors began to fade rapidly as soon as the paintings were exposed to light; within a few days, virtually all of the colors had faded away.

(D) The gallery for which Fang had procured the paintings was destroyed by a fire shortly after the contract was executed.

Questions 30-31 are based on the following fact situation:

Chip was the owner of a company that manufactured very large, high-speed computers, and Data was a mid-level distributor of computers and computer support systems. Chip and Data entered into a written agreement whereby Data would purchase a Mark VII "Maxicomputer" from Chip for $50,000, with the delivery date set for November 4. At the time of the making of the contract, Chip and Data agreed orally that the written agreement would not become binding unless Data notified Chip, in writing, by October 7, that Data had obtained a buyer for the computer. Because of the complexity of the computer system and its expense, Chip did not wish to risk being stuck with the Mark VII in his inventory if Data was unsure of his ability to resell the computer to its ultimate user. On September 25, Data found a buyer, Garbagian, who needed a Mark VII Maxicomputer for her business, and who agreed to buy the Mark VII from Data. Due to a bitter strike at Chip's leading competitor in the large computer business, which severely limited supply, the price of large computers rose rapidly during the month of October. By the end of the month, the Mark VII Maxicomputer had a market value of $70,000, at which price Chip was taking orders from mid-level distributors such as Data.

30. Assume for purposes of this question only that when the agreement between Chip and Data concerning sale of the Mark VII was reduced to writing by Chip's office staff, a glitch in the word processor caused the printout to show the delivery date of the Mark VII as 12/4 instead of 11/4. Chip and Data signed the paper with the wrong delivery date. Also assume that Data did not inform Chip in writing that he had obtained Garbagian as a buyer until October 30. Because of the increase in the value of the computer, Chip wishes to be discharged from the contract with Data so that he can sell the Mark VII to another buyer at a price $20,000 higher. Which of the following provides the best argument that Chip should be discharged from his duties under the contract with Data?

(A) The increase in value of the computer constitutes commercial frustration.

(B) There has been a failure of a condition precedent.

(C) A case of mutual mistake exists because of the word processing error regarding the delivery date.

(D) There has been a failure of a condition subsequent.

31. Assume for purposes of this question only that on October 8 Data telephoned Chip. Data told Chip that Data had obtained Garbagian as a buyer for the Mark VII. Data also told Chip, "I wasn't able to get you written confirmation of that by October 7 because of the postal workers' slowdown and because my fax machine just broke down." Chip assured Data that this was no problem. After the increase in value of the computer, Chip wishes to be discharged from the contract with Data. Data's best argument in response would be based on:

  (A) Statute of Frauds.

  (B) Parol evidence rule.

  (C) Waiver of condition.

  (D) Excuse of condition by hindrance.

Question 32

Eider, a manufacturer of down coats and jackets, entered into a written agreement with Furry, a distributor, whereby Furry agreed to distribute Eider's products in the state of New Svalbard for a one-year period to begin on June 1. Eider's coats and jackets were of very high quality and were packed with more down than other manufacturers' products. This made Eider's coats very warm, but it also made them very bulky. As provided in the contract, Furry began distributing Eider's products in New Svalbard on June 1.

On September 1, Furry began distributing coats and jackets manufactured by Nolyn, one of Eider's competitors. Nolyn's coats and jackets were manufactured using space-age technology. They were sewn with man-made fabrics that provided exceptionally warm outerwear without the usual bulkiness of winter coats and jackets. Eider complained to Furry, demanding that Furry cease distributing Nolyn's products in New Svalbard. Furry refused Eider's demand, and Eider brought suit against Furry.

Which of the following facts, if established, would provide a basis for Eider's best case against Furry?

  (A) Nolyn's advertising campaign in New Svalbard emphasizes the theme: "Your winter coat shouldn't look fat, and you shouldn't look fat wearing it!"

  (B) Seasonally adjusted sales figures showed that Eider's sales in New Svalbard dropped 6% after Nolyn's products were introduced.

  (C) Before Eider signed the distribution contract with Furry, Furry told him, "This is an exclusive deal."

  (D) In the outerwear industry it has been a custom for many years for distributors to distribute only one brand of outerwear.

Question 33

Minx and Vixen entered into a written agreement whereby Minx, the owner and operator of an exclusive clothing salon, agreed to sell Vixen a certain full-length fake fur coat for $12,000, with delivery by December 7. On December 6, Vixen went to Minx's salon at 5:30 p.m. Minx told Vixen: "Your coat is ready and you can have it today." Vixen inspected the coat and discovered that a button was missing. Vixen told Minx that she would not accept the coat without the missing button. Minx informed Vixen that the tailor had gone home for the day at 5 p.m. and would not be back at the salon until 8:30 a.m. on December 8, because Congress had enacted a law declaring December 7 to be Pearl Harbor Day, a new federal holiday, and the tailor had the day off. Minx assured Vixen that the coat could be ready with the button sewn on by 9:15 a.m. on December 8.

Which of the following best states Vixen's position?

  (A) Vixen may reject the coat, because Minx failed to provide perfect tender.

  (B) Vixen may reject the coat, but Vixen must give Minx an opportunity to cure.

(C) Vixen must accept the coat, because its value is not substantially impaired by the missing button.

(D) Vixen must accept the coat, because the defect can be easily cured.

Questions 34-36 are based on the following fact situation:

On March 5, Triton Machine Works mailed the following signed communication to Banfield Machine Tools: "We hereby offer to sell you 500 diamond core drill bits, priced at $300 each. This is a firm offer." This offer was received by Banfield Machine Tools on March 7. On March 8, Triton mailed a notice to Banfield stating: "Please be advised that our offer of March 5 is revoked." This notice of revocation was received by Banfield on March 10. On March 11, Banfield wired Triton: "Consider you bound by your offer. Please enter our order as per your offer for 10 diamond core drill bits. Box two per case, hardwood casing only. Our draft for $3,000 has been sent under separate cover."

34. If Banfield sues Triton and Triton defends on the ground that it had revoked its offer, the court probably would hold:

(A) No contract exists because Triton's notice of revocation had been received by the offeree before acceptance was attempted.

(B) Having stated that it was extending a "firm offer," Triton's offer was irrevocable for three months as a matter of law.

(C) Banfield has an enforceable contract with Triton, unless the court determines that the March 11 telegram was not sent within a commercially reasonable time.

(D) Having received no consideration for its declaration that it had made a firm offer, Triton retained an unfettered election to revoke its offer at any time.

35. If Triton defends on the ground that its offer was for the sale of 500 diamond core drill bits in one lot only, rather than in small quantities (here, only 10 bits ordered by Banfield), the court should hold:

(A) Since Triton's offer failed to state that it was a single lot only, it was subject to partial acceptance at the buyer's option.

(B) Triton should prevail because the offer specifically offered 500 drill bits and it would be commercially unreasonable to hold the seller to piecemeal sales at the stated price.

(C) The attempted formation of a contract is flawed by ambiguity so that the minds of the parties never met and no enforceable obligation to sell was created by Banfield's acceptance.

(D) Parol evidence is admissible on the question whether the offer contemplated sale of the bits as a single lot or piecemeal.

36. If the court were to conclude that a contract came into existence between Triton and Banfield on the strength of Triton's letter of March 5, and Banfield's reply of March 11, its terms would include:

(A) Only those terms set forth in Triton's letter of March 5, because the offeror has not assented to any enlargement of the terms regarding mode of shipment.

(B) All terms set forth in Triton's offer plus consistent additional terms proposed in Banfield's acceptance.

(C) All terms set forth in Triton's offer plus those in Banfield's attempted acceptance, provided that Banfield's proposals did not amount to a material alteration of Triton's offer.

(D) The terms of the offer plus all those in the purported acceptance which did not amount to a material alteration of the offer and to which the offeror did not object within a reasonable time.

Questions 37-38 are based on the following fact situation:

Flatville was in the 150th day of its drought, with no end in sight according to the meteorologists, when Hank, a local farmer, learned about a scientist in another state who claimed to have perfected a rainmaking machine. Leon, the scientist, came to Flatville in response to Hank's telegram. Hank entered into an agreement with Leon to pay Leon to make it rain, but did not specify an amount of payment or any deadline by which it must rain. After several days of trying without success, Leon said that the machine might work better at a higher elevation, such as the farm of Hank's neighbor, Will. Will readily agreed to let Leon use the land and further told Leon, "If you make it rain by tomorrow night, I'll pay you $20,000." Leon placed the machine on Will's land. By nightfall, clouds had begun to gather over Flatville, and the next morning it was pouring rain.

37. If Hank refuses to pay Leon anything, can Leon recover damages from Hank?

(A) No, because Leon cannot prove conclusively that he caused it to rain.

(B) No, because Leon's agreement with Hank did not specify the amount to be paid.

(C) Yes, he will recover a reasonable price for his services under the contract.

(D) Yes, he will recover his normal fee for rainmaking.

38. If Will refuses to pay the $20,000 to Leon, can the latter enforce the promise to pay?

(A) Yes, because Will's promise was supported by the consideration that Leon make it rain by the next night.

(B) Yes, but only in the amount of the reasonable value of his services.

(C) No, because Leon had a preexisting duty to make it rain as a result of the agreement with Hank.

(D) No, because Will's promise constituted no legal detriment to him.

Question 39

Bill noticed that Sam had a For Sale sign on an old car parked in front of Sam's house. Bill, a tinkerer by nature, thought it would be fun to have an old car to fix up and customize. Bill rang Sam's doorbell. Sam answered the door, and Bill asked him, "How much do you want for that jalopy with the For Sale sign on it?" Sam said, "I'll take $400 for it." Bill said, "You've got a deal, but it's Sunday, so my bank is closed. I'll come by with the money after work tomorrow, about 6 p.m." Sam replied, "That's just fine with me." Bill and Sam exchanged telephone numbers. At 9:15 the next morning, Sam called Bill at work. Sam told Bill, "When I talked to you yesterday, I forgot that I'd just put two new tires on that car. I'll need an extra $50." Bill responded, "Okay, I'll bring $450 in cash around to your place about six o'clock."

Is Bill legally bound to pay Sam the additional $50?

(A) Yes, because the original contract was not in writing.

(B) Yes, because the contract, as modified, does not exceed the minimum dollar amount required to invoke the Statute of Frauds.

(C) No, because no additional consideration was given for the oral modification.

(D) No, because neither Bill nor Sam is a merchant.

Questions 40-42 are based on the following fact situation:

Advanced Microelectronics Manufacturing ("AMM"), owned by Willard, manufactures electronic game cartridges and related devices for use with other manufacturers' electronic game systems. It advertised its products in an industry trade journal called *The Microchipper*. On July 1, AMM's regular monthly advertisement included the following: "For sale, 'Dunk the Gorilla' game cartridge plus adaptor, 100 unit lots, $2,500 each lot."

On July 15, AMM received the following letter from the owner of Leroy's Toy World Stores: "Please send me two 100-unit lots of 'Dunk the Gorilla' plus adaptors. Payment upon delivery. Adaptors must be compatible with Sega, Nintendo, and Sony systems. Agree to price of $2,500 per lot."

40. Assume for purposes of this question only that, shortly after receiving the letter from the owner of Leroy's Toy World Stores, AMM shipped two 100-unit lots of "Dunk the Gorilla" cartridges plus adaptors to Leroy's. Accompanying the invoice on the carton containing the cartridges and adaptors was a letter from Willard including the following: "The adaptors contained within are compatible with all Sega and Nintendo systems. I make no warranties as to the compatibility of the adaptors with any other game systems." An employee of Leroy's authorized to do so accepted shipment of the units without any other action. Shortly thereafter, store personnel learned that the adaptors would not permit the cartridges to be played on Sony systems. If Leroy's institutes an action against AMM, which of the following, if true, would be the strongest support in favor of Leroy's position?

(A) Leroy's letter was an offer, and shipment of the units was an acceptance.

(B) Leroy's letter was an offer, and Willard's letter accompanying the invoice was an acceptance.

(C) Willard's letter was an offer, and acceptance of the units by the Leroy's employee was an acceptance of the offer.

(D) Shipment of the units was a counteroffer, and acceptance of the units by the Leroy's employee was an acceptance of the counteroffer.

41. Assume for purposes of this question only that a valid contract existed between AMM and Leroy's for the sale of two 100-unit lots of game cartridges and adaptors that would be compatible with Sega, Nintendo and Sony systems. After an employee of Leroy's authorized to do so had accepted shipment of the units, store personnel learned that the adaptors would not work with Sony systems. Leroy's filed suit. Leroy's attorneys prove to the satisfaction of the court, who is the trier of fact, that the cartridges alone are worth $1,000 per lot of 100, and that the adaptors, compatible with only Sega and Nintendo systems, are worth $1,000 per lot of 100. Which of the following should be the measure of damages applied to determine Leroy's loss?

(A) The cost of purchasing adaptors compatible with Sony systems from another supplier.

(B) The contract price of $5,000, since Leroy's has not received the benefit of its bargain.

(C) The difference between the value of the adaptors as received and their value if they had been compatible with all three systems—$500 per lot of 100.

(D) Leroy's is not entitled to damages, because its employee accepted the adaptors in the condition shipped by AMM.

42. Assume for purposes of this question only that no warranties of any type regarding the compatibility of the adaptors with any game systems were made by AMM, but that both parties reasonably believed that the adaptors were compatible with all three game systems. Upon receiving the shipment, store personnel of Leroy's discover that the adaptors do not work with Sony systems. Which of the following is the most appropriate remedy for Leroy's?

(A) Specific performance of the contract, requiring AMM to ship two 100-unit lots of adaptors compatible with all three game systems.

(B) Rescission of the contract.

(C) Restitution by AMM of the purchase price of the two lots.

(D) Restitution by AMM of the value of adaptors.

Question 43

Downtown Department Store engaged Swift Service Company to service all electrical appliances sold by Downtown for a flat fee of $5,000 per month. Pick-up and delivery of the appliances to be repaired and the billing for the work was the responsibility of Downtown. The contract was in writing and was to continue until either party gave 180 days' written notice of its intent to terminate. Several months ago Swift informed Downtown that it was losing money on the deal and was in financial trouble. Swift requested that the fee for the next three months be increased by $1,000 and that this increase be paid to Uptown Bank to help pay off the loan that Uptown had made to Swift. Downtown orally agreed to so modify the original contract. However, Downtown did not pay Uptown and now Uptown is suing Downtown for $3,000.

How will the court rule in this case?

(A) For Downtown, because there was no consideration to support the promise to pay Uptown.

(B) For Downtown, because Uptown is only an incidental beneficiary of the Downtown/Swift modification.

(C) For Uptown, because Uptown is an intended creditor beneficiary of the Downtown/Swift modification.

(D) For Uptown, provided that the court finds that Swift exercised good faith in requesting the modification regarding the payment to Uptown.

Question 44

On June 1, Jacques, a resident of France, wrote the Detroit Bank Agency ("DBA") this letter: "If you people will sell a car costing not more than $10,000 to my daughter Francine, I will guarantee payment of the purchase price." After receiving Jacques's letter on June 15, DBA sold a $9,500 car to Francine for $2,000 down with the balance to be paid by the end of the year. Jacques died unexpectedly on June 17. DBA was unaware of Jacques's death and on June 19 mailed this letter to Jacques in France: "We are happy to accept your offer. You should know, however, that Francine is a good customer of ours and we had planned to extend her credit for the purchase before receiving your letter." In August, Francine was killed and her estate is bankrupt.

Can DBA succeed in an action against Jacques's estate for the balance of the price of the car when it becomes due?

(A) Yes, because DBA had accepted Jacques's offer before he died.

(B) Yes, because DBA reasonably, justifiably, and foreseeably relied on Jacques's promise.

(C) No, because DBA would have sold the car to Francine even without Jacques's promise.

(D) No, because Jacques died before DBA mailed the letter notifying him that DBA had accepted his offer.

Question 45

Jenny, a general contractor, advertised in a trade publication that she planned to bid on the construction of a new building to be located in the Civic Mall. The advertisement welcomed bids from subcontractors to perform various functions, such as plumbing, electrical work, and masonry. The lowest plumbing bid was from Plunger, who bid $10,000. Jenny used Plunger's bid in preparing her general bid. At 2 p.m. on June 22, Jenny submitted her general bid. At 3 p.m. Plunger called her and said, "I'm sorry, Jenny, but I made a mistake on that bid I submitted to you; I can't possibly do that plumbing work for a dime less than $12,000." Jenny told him, "Look, you've done a lot of good work for me in the past and we all make mistakes. I'll just forget you ever made that $10,000 bid." Plunger effusively thanked Jenny. Jenny then hired Flusher to do the plumbing work for $12,000. She then sued Plunger for damages. Jenny will:

(A) Win, because there was no additional consideration to support a release.

(B) Win, because the dollar amount of the agreement is large enough that the Statute of Frauds applies.

(C) Lose, because a rescission has taken place.

(D) Lose, because Jenny and Plunger mutually agreed to a release.

Question 46

Barte and Sarte entered into a written agreement, whereby Sarte, a wholesaler, would sell Barte 500 thingamabobs for a total price of $10,000. Prior to the date set for execution of the contract, Sarte discovered that the price of yttrium, a rare earth element essential to the manufacture of thingamabobs, had soared, because a civil war had broken out in Gonvaria, a third-world country that produces 80% of the world supply of yttrium. Sarte realized that he would have to pay at least $11,000 for 500 thingamabobs. Sarte called Barte and after explaining the general situation, Sarte asked Barte if he would be willing to pay $12,000 for the 500 thingamabobs. Sarte characterized this as "a *very* fair price, given the conditions in Gonvaria." Barte agreed orally to pay the $12,000, but no written confirmation was exchanged between the parties.

In the meantime, United Nations intervention halted the war in Gonvaria and yttrium production swiftly rose to prewar levels, while the price dropped accordingly. Sarte shipped 500 thingamabobs to Barte. Upon receipt of the thingamabobs, Barte sent Sarte a certified check in the amount of $10,000, marking it "payment in full." Sarte did not cash the check, but telephoned Barte demanding an additional $2,000. Barte refuses to pay the additional sum.

May Sarte enforce his demand for an additional $2,000 in a court of law?

(A) No, because of the parol evidence rule.

(B) No, because of the Statute of Frauds.

(C) Yes, because the parol evidence rule would allow evidence of a changed price term, as it is material to the contract.

(D) Yes, because a subsequent modification can also be a waiver after the initial agreement.

Question 47

Ironmongers, Inc. was a small processor of specialized steel. For many years, Ironmongers sold steel to Toyco, a small manufacturer of children's toys. Toyco contracted in writing with Ironmongers whereby Ironmongers agreed to supply all the specialized steel requirements of Toyco over a period of years at a certain price per ton of steel. Toyco's management found that intense competition in the toy market was hurting its sales. Although Toyco had a very good reputation for quality products, its products were also more expensive than those of many of its competitors. Thus, Toyco's managers decided to abandon their "Steeltoy" line (which used steel from Ironmongers) and to concentrate on plastic toys, which were more competitive. One of the actions taken by Toyco when the Steeltoy line was abandoned was the assignment of Toyco's rights and delegation of its duties under the contract with Ironmongers to Behemothtoy, a large toymaker that was dominant in the metal toy market.

Must Ironmonger supply the requirements of Behemothtoy?

(A) Yes, unless there was a nonassignment clause in the contract.

(B) Yes, because requirements contracts are assignable under the Uniform Commercial Code.

(C) No, unless Behemothtoy acts in good faith to assure Ironmongers that its requirements will approximate those of Toyco.

(D) No, because requirements contracts are not assignable.

Questions 48-49 are based on the following fact situation:

On February 1, Ridewell Rubber Co. telephoned Smithson Tire Shop and offered to sell to Smithson 500 series 4 Ridewell tires for $20,000. Smithson accepted immediately. On February 3, Smithson sent Ridewell a letter confirming the deal and stating that Smithson was counting on a 20% discount due to the size of the purchase. On February 20, Ridewell telephoned Smithson and stated that it could not afford to sell the 500 series 4 tires for less than $30,000.

48. If Smithson brings suit against Ridewell and Ridewell asserts the Statute of Frauds as a defense, will Smithson prevail?

(A) Yes, but only if its February 3 letter contained the quantity term.

(B) Yes, regardless of whether its February 3 letter contained the quantity term because the letter merely confirms a prior deal for 500 series 4 tires.

(C) No, because Smithson's February 3 letter varied the terms of Ridewell's offer.

(D) No, because Ridewell is the party to be charged and has signed nothing.

49. Assume for purposes of this question only that Smithson's February 3 letter created an enforceable contract between the parties. What is the price that Smithson must pay for the 500 series 4 tires?

(A) A reasonable price as fixed in good faith by Smithson.

(B) The reasonable value of the goods because the parties cannot agree on the price.

(C) $20,000, if the discount term is a material alteration of the original deal.

(D) $16,000, because Ridewell did not object to the discount term in Smithson's February 3 letter.

Question 50

Shirley had an opportunity to get in on the "ground floor" of a very promising new business venture. However, Shirley lacked the investment funds needed to take advantage of the opportunity. Therefore, she resolved to sell Plushacre, a piece of real estate that she owned. Because it was essential that Shirley raise the money quickly, she employed Royal, a real estate broker. Shirley and Royal entered into a written agreement whereby Royal would receive a commission of 10% of the sale price if he procured a "ready, willing, and able buyer" and if the sale actually proceeded through closing. Shirley told Royal that she wanted $100,000 for Plushacre.

Royal found Burton and told Shirley that Burton was an appropriate buyer. Burton agreed in writing to buy Plushacre from Shirley for $100,000, and Burton put up $6,000 as a down payment. The agreement between Shirley and Burton contained a liquidated damages clause providing that if Burton defaulted by failing to tender the balance due of $94,000 by July 1, the closing date, damages would be 10% of the purchase price. Although Shirley could not be positive how much she would lose if she were unable to raise the money to participate in the business venture, it appeared as if she could make at least $10,000 if she became a charter subscriber.

Burton became seriously ill and defaulted. When Burton recovered from his illness, he demanded that Shirley return his $6,000. Shirley told Burton that she was keeping the money. Royal also demanded the $6,000 from Shirley and was refused. Royal and Burton filed separate suits against Shirley, which were consolidated into a single case.

How should the court rule as to the disposition of the $6,000?

(A) Shirley keeps the entire $6,000 because the liquidated damages clause is reasonable.

(B) Burton gets the entire $6,000 if he pleads impossibility of performance as a defense.

(C) Royal gets the entire $6,000 because he substantially performed his part of the contract by producing a buyer and is entitled to 10% of the $100,000 purchase price.

(D) Royal gets $600 and Shirley gets $5,400 because the damages clause was reasonable and Royal is entitled to 10% of whatever Shirley realizes from the deal.

Questions 51-52 are based on the following fact situation:

Aunt Sheila told her niece, Sinead, "I'd like you to go to Tara Imports and select the $300 lace shawl of your choice and I'll buy it for you if you wear it to the ethnic festival. I want you to look as sweet and delicate as an Irish rose." Sinead, a modern 22-year-old, despised shawls because she thought they were "the sorts of things old ladies wear." Also, her taste in music

ran to heavy metal rock and roll, rather than the traditional Celtic bagpipe and fiddle music she would be subjected to if she went to the ethnic festival. However, Sinead really loved Aunt Sheila and did not want to hurt her feelings. She went to Tara Imports and purchased a $300 lace shawl imported from Ireland. Sinead accompanied Sheila to the ethnic festival wearing the shawl, and Sheila was very pleased.

51. Assume for purposes of this question only that Sheila died shortly after the festival and her estate refuses to reimburse Sinead for her purchase. Sinead filed suit. Her attorney advanced four legal theories on which he asserts that Sinead can collect the $300 from Sheila's estate. They are as follows:

I. Promissory estoppel.

II. Bargain and exchange.

III. Conditional gift.

IV. Account stated.

Which of the following represents the correct combination of legal theories that support Sinead's case against Sheila's estate?

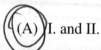

(A) I. and II.

(B) I. and III.

(C) II. and IV.

(D) I., II., III., and IV.

52. Assume for purposes of this question only that instead of being prompted by her aunt to purchase the shawl, Sinead herself decided that she wanted an imported lace shawl. She went to Tara Imports, and Erin, the proprietor, let her take the shawl of her choice on approval. No mention was made by Erin of the method of payment she expected. Sinead wore the shawl on a visit to Aunt Sheila. Sheila told Sinead, "That

shawl surely looks lovely on you, but it must have cost a pretty penny." Sinead told Sheila that the shawl cost $300, and that she had taken the shawl on approval. Sheila said, "Well, I think you should keep it, even if it is expensive. I'll tell you what. If you promise to give some of your old clothing to the poor through the St. Vincent DePaul Society at Christmastime, I'll pay Erin for the shawl." Sinead said, "Wow! That's great! I will absolutely give some of my old clothes to the Society at Christmas." This pleased Sheila a great deal. Sheila called Erin and told her that Sinead had decided to keep the shawl and to send the bill for the shawl to Sheila, which Erin did. Before the bill was paid and before the Christmas season arrived, Sheila died. Sheila's executor has refused to pay the bill. Sinead has not yet given any old clothing to the poor.

Will Erin prevail in a suit against the estate for the $300?

(A) Yes, because Erin was the intended beneficiary of the promise between Sheila and Sinead.

(B) Yes, because Sinead has no duty to give the clothing to the Society.

(C) No, because Sheila's implied promise to pay Erin arising from the phone call is unenforceable.

(D) No, because a condition has not yet occurred.

Questions 53-54 are based on the following fact situation:

Wendy, a wealthy widow, owned a prime piece of land in an exurban area populated by affluent residents. Wendy had a daughter, Dorothea, who was Wendy's only child and the "apple of her eye." Dorothea was 23 years of age and engaged to be married to Pemberton d'Argent, a rich, polo-playing investment banker. Wendy wanted to give Dorothea a very special wedding gift. Wendy therefore entered into a written agreement with contractor Brikk whereby Brikk would build

a house on the property for $300,000. The house was to be built to very exacting specifications that described in great detail the materials to be used, the exact shape of each room, etc. These specifications were included in the written agreement between Wendy and Brikk. The agreement provided that Wendy would pay Brikk $300,000 upon completion of the building according to specifications and that Brikk would turn the keys to the home over to Dorothea. After the agreement was signed by both Wendy and Brikk, Dorothea and Pemberton looked at some fine homes in the same general area. They had two opportunities to purchase suitable homes at good prices, but decided to turn them down. Since then, property values in the area have increased by approximately 30%. Just as Brikk was about to begin construction of the house, he discovered that an underground river bisected Wendy's property. This left insufficient subterranean support to construct the house as planned.

53. Assume for purposes of this question only that upon discovering the underground river, Brikk refused to try to build the house for $300,000. If Wendy files suit demanding specific performance or damages from Brikk, which of the following additional facts, if proven, would most favor Wendy's case?

(A) It is physically possible to build the house according to the original specifications by the sinking of many pilings deep into the ground for support, although it would add $1 million to Brikk's costs.

(B) The detailed specifications in the agreement had been drawn up by Brikk, as were other blueprints and plans for the house.

(C) Neither Wendy nor Brikk had reason to know of the underground river before the contract was signed.

(D) Dorothea knew of the contract between Wendy and Brikk, and her sole reason for turning down the opportunities to purchase suitable housing was reliance on the contract.

54. Assume for purposes of this question only that before Wendy contracted with Brikk, Dorothea had paid $5,000 for a 60-day option to purchase a lovely home at a good price. Immediately after Wendy and Brikk contracted for Brikk to build the home, Wendy showed the plans and specifications to Dorothea. Dorothea simply loved the concept and thought it would be a dream house. She allowed her option to purchase the other house to lapse. In the meantime, but prior to the lapse, Brikk discovered the underground river. He explained to Wendy that he could build a house on the property with all the same features of the original plan, but that it would have to be located on one side of the lot, rather than in its center. The house would, however, be a rather strange, long and narrow shape, unlike the almost square construction in the original plan. Without informing Dorothea, Wendy told Brikk to go ahead and build the house. He did so. When Dorothea saw the completed version she was outraged and cried, "That funny-shaped house would make me the laughing stock of the whole Junior League." Dorothea demanded that Brikk either build the house according to original specifications, as approved by Dorothea, or pay her damages. Brikk refused and Dorothea filed suit. Who is more likely to prevail?

    (A) Dorothea, because she was an intended beneficiary of the contract whose rights had vested.

    (B) Dorothea, because the subsequent agreement between Wendy and Brikk to modify the specification was unsupported by consideration.

    (C) Brikk, because Brikk may raise all defenses that he had against Wendy against Dorothea.

    (D) Brikk, because Dorothea is merely an incidental beneficiary of the contract between Wendy and Brikk and, as such, has no power to enforce the contract against Brikk.

Question 55

Which of the four following fact situations best describes a case where a court would be likely to determine that an implied-in-fact contract existed?

(A) Norm, who has just taken a CPR course, is dining at a restaurant with his friend, Ford. Ford, who has a tendency to talk while eating, begins to choke on a bit of food trapped in his windpipe. Norm promptly performs the Heimlich maneuver on Ford, causing the food to be expelled and Ford to resume normal breathing.

(B) Hugh is a wealthy attorney who normally charges $200 per hour for his services. Deborah is an old friend of Hugh's family who often sent him checks when he was an impoverished law student. Deborah, now 75 years old, needs a paper notarized to apply for a medicare benefit. Deborah takes the bus to Hugh's office. Hugh, who is also a notary public, witnesses Deborah's signature and puts his notary seal on the paper. State law allows a maximum charge of $5 per signature for notarization.

(C) There has been a three-year drought in the area. The water table has dropped substantially, and many homeowners and farmers need to have their water wells deepened. Charlotte, a contractor, has a contract to deepen the well on Pattie's property. Charlotte mistakenly enters the neighboring property of Mike. Charlotte proceeds to deepen Mike's well. Mike watches Charlotte at work and says nothing until after the job is completed.

(D) John Babbington received his monthly credit card bill from Golden Fleece Department Store. He promptly paid the bill. Due to a computer error, a week later Babbington received the bill for John Barrington from Golden Fleece. Thinking that he must owe the money, Babbington paid Barrington's credit card bill.

Question 56

Insco, a major insurance carrier, launched an experimental "Catastrophic Health Insurance Plan" ("CHIP"). CHIP differed from other plans designed to cover the costs of catastrophic illness in that premiums were not to be paid on a monthly or annual basis, but rather as a large one-time payment at the inception of coverage. Insco then was prepared to cover the insured for the remainder of his or her life. Because the program was experimental, Insco would only take applications during an "enrollment period" lasting from August 15 through August 30, and the number of participants was limited to 200. The one-time premium was set at $30,000, and those eligible for enrollment had to be between the ages of 57 and 63. After selection for the program, which was to be made by September 15, those selected had until October 1 to pay their premium, and coverage would begin at 12:01 a.m., October 2.

Harry was a 62-year-old male in apparently good health, but he was concerned that a catastrophic illness could destroy him and his family financially. He therefore filed an application for CHIP during the enrollment period. Insco selected Harry to be one of the 200 participants in CHIP. He paid his premium on October 1, and was issued a CHIP policy with coverage beginning October 2. On October 3, Harry was crossing the street when he was struck by a city bus. Harry died before reaching the hospital. Under the terms of Harry's will, his estate was to be divided equally among his three children. Harry's daughter, Daisy, was named executor. Upon discovering that Harry had just made a $30,000 payment to Insco, Daisy had Harry's bank stop payment on the check. Insco filed suit demanding payment of the premium.

Who will prevail?

(A) Insco, if it declined to take another applicant during the enrollment period because of Harry's promise to buy the CHIP policy.

(B) Insco, because the risk of the timing of Harry's death was assumed by both parties and built into the cost of the contract.

(C) Daisy, because the purpose of the contract between Harry and Insco had been frustrated.

(D) Daisy, because it is unconscionable for Insco to have charged Harry so much for so little value received.

Questions 57-58 are based on the following fact situation:

Lehman was a limited partner in Bountiful Homes, a partnership organized by Lehman's nephew, Sanders, which purchased land, subdivided it, then constructed and sold single-family residences on the lots thus created. Sanders was the sole general partner. During the construction of the only housing development undertaken by the partnership, Lehman discovered that Sanders had taken most of the money invested by the limited partners and all of the money paid to the partnership by purchasers of the homes in the development and lost it gambling in Las Vegas. When confronted by Lehman, Sanders admitted everything, then went to his apartment and committed suicide.

When news of Sanders's suicide was made public, Lehman was besieged by creditors of the partnership and by people who had purchased homes. The jurisdiction statutorily limited the liability of limited partners for debts of the partnership or acts of the general partner to the extent of their investment in the partnership, but being unaware of this, Lehman believed himself liable to all who had claims against Bountiful Homes. He told Wolcott, a single mother whose house was partly completed, that he would "make good any losses caused by my nephew's actions," and then orally agreed with Smith, a contractor, to pay for the completion of Wolcott's house. Lehman also told Brubaker, an unsecured creditor of Bountiful Homes, that if Brubaker would hold off filing an involuntary bankruptcy petition against the partnership, Lehman would pay the partnership debt.

In a bankruptcy action filed by secured creditors of the partnership, the assets of the partnership, which were very small, were consumed by the costs of the proceedings and no creditor received any payment. Sanders himself left no assets and was in fact heavily indebted on a personal basis due to his compulsive gambling.

57. If Brubaker brings an action against Lehman for the amount of the debt owed him by the partnership—an open account for $2,000—will he prevail?

   (A) No, because his claim against the partnership was worthless.

   (B) No, because Lehman's only obligation to pay the debts of the partnership was a moral one based upon his relationship with Sanders.

   (C) Yes, because Brubaker detrimentally relied upon Lehman's promise.

   (D) Yes, because Lehman's promise was supported by a bargained-for exchange.

58. If Smith did not complete construction of Wolcott's house and Wolcott brings an action against him for breach of contract, which of the following would be an effective defense for Smith?

   I.   Smith's contract was with Lehman.

   II.   Wolcott furnished no consideration.

   III. Any agreement between Wolcott and Smith was discharged by novation because of the agreement between Smith and Lehman.

   (A) I. only.

   (B) I. and II. only.

   (C) II. and III. only.

   (D) None of the above.

Questions 59-61 are based on the following fact situation:

The marketing surprise of the current Christmas season were the Onion Field dolls, graphic representations of the characters of the well known police murder, as made notorious by the book of the same name. On November 15, Weldon, owner of a toy shop, realized that his stock of 15 Onion Field dolls would not last until the first of the next month. Reading in his trade journal, *Doll World*, that the manufacturer of the Onion Field dolls advertised "One gross Onion Field dolls, twelve of each character, $3,000; delivery two weeks from order," Weldon sent a fax to the maker, Cuddly Toy Co., that read: "Rush me three gross Onion Field dolls at $3,000 per gross." There were no further communications between Weldon and Cuddly Toy.

By December 1, Weldon realized that Cuddly Toy was not going to deliver any dolls. Weldon thus was forced to obtain additional stock by purchasing from a middleman at a cost of $4,000 per gross.

59. If Weldon brings an action for breach of contract against Cuddly Toy Co., what will be the probable outcome?

   (A) Weldon will lose, because the communications between him and the manufacturer were not definite or certain enough to form a contract.

   (B) Weldon will lose, because Cuddly Toy never accepted the offer contained in Weldon's fax.

   (C) Weldon will win, because his fax was an acceptance of the offer contained in the trade journal.

   (D) Weldon will win, because he changed his position for the worse in reliance upon Cuddly Toy's offer to deliver dolls within two weeks.

60. Assume for purposes of this question only that the communications created a valid contract but that Cuddly Toy Co. refused to send any Onion Field dolls to Weldon. Weldon files an action to force Cuddly to send the dolls. What will the result most likely be?

(A) Cuddly will not be forced to send the dolls because a contract for the sale of goods is not subject to specific performance.

(B) Cuddly will not be forced to send the dolls if Weldon can buy them from another retailer.

(C) Cuddly will have to send the dolls because it is the only manufacturer of the dolls.

(D) Cuddly will have to send the dolls because time is of the essence.

61. Assume for purposes of this question only that Cuddly Toy tries to convince Weldon to buy its line of Famous Supreme Court Justices dolls. Weldon is understandably skeptical of the dolls' marketability, but he eventually agrees to try them out as long as he will not be stuck with them after the holiday season. Thus, the contract provides for the sale to Weldon of 100 Supreme Court dolls. Weldon is to pay "$1,500 for the dolls provided that they sell during the Christmas season." Some dolls did sell, but on February 12, Weldon has 80 of them in inventory. He sends Cuddly notice that he is returning the 80 dolls. Cuddly replies that it does not want the dolls back, that Weldon should continue to try to sell them. Despite this reply, Weldon sends Cuddly a check for $300 and tries to return the dolls to Cuddly. Cuddly refuses to accept the dolls, but does accept the check. Weldon stores the dolls at his warehouse. If Cuddly brings an action for $1,200, what will be the most likely result?

(A) Cuddly will recover the $1,200 because Weldon still has the dolls in his possession.

(B) Cuddly will recover the $1,200 because the phrase "during the Christmas season" was not a condition precedent but merely a convenient time for payment.

(C) Cuddly will not recover the $1,200 because sale during the Christmas season was a condition precedent to payment.

(D) Cuddly will not recover the $1,200 because accepting the $300 waived any rights Cuddly may have had to enforce the contract.

Question 62

Laurie owns Redwood, a one-acre tract of land with a small house on it. Laurie rented it to Tony at a monthly rental of $500. Several years later, Laurie and Tony orally agreed that Tony would purchase Redwood from Laurie for the sum of $60,000, payable at the rate of $500 a month for 10 years. The oral agreement provided that Laurie would give Tony a deed to Redwood after five years had passed and $30,000 had been paid toward the purchase price, and that Tony would execute a note secured by a mortgage for the balance. Tony continued in possession of Redwood and made all monthly payments in a timely fashion. When Tony had paid $30,000, he tendered a proper note and mortgage to Laurie and demanded delivery of the deed as agreed. Laurie told Tony that she had changed her mind and has refused to complete the transaction. Tony brought suit against Laurie for specific performance.

If Laurie wins it will be because:

(A) The transaction had not proceeded far enough to amount to an estoppel against enforcement of the Statute of Frauds.

(B) Nothing Tony could have done would have overcome the original absence of a written agreement.

(C) Oral agreements are generally revocable unless expressly made irrevocable.

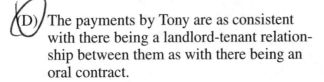

(D) The payments by Tony are as consistent with there being a landlord-tenant relationship between them as with there being an oral contract.

Question 63

Buffy grew tired of her Jet Ski after owning it one season and put an ad for its sale in the paper. Jody saw the ad and had wanted a personal watercraft. Therefore, he phoned Buffy and made arrangements to meet with her. Jody wanted to buy the Jet Ski, but had to arrange for financing. Buffy suggested that they write a contract for sale then and there so that they would not have to waste any time when Jody got his financing. They orally agreed that the contract would not become binding unless Jody obtained financing, but the written contract did not mention this and appeared to be a fully integrated document.

Assume that Jody could not obtain financing and Buffy brings suit to enforce the written contract. Who will prevail?

(A) Buffy, because the contract was a fully integrated writing.

(B) Buffy, because parol evidence is not allowed to contradict a writing.

(C) Jody, because the oral agreement that the contract would not be binding if Jody did not get financing was made contemporaneous with the writing.

(D) Jody, because obtaining financing was a condition precedent.

Questions 64-65 are based on the following fact situation:

Richard owned and operated "Richard's," a highly successful restaurant in Spakton that was described as "locally popular" in all the major travel guides. As soon as Richard's daughter, Rita, was born, Richard changed the name of the restaurant to "Richard's & Rita's." When Rita turned 18, she participated meaningfully in the operation of the restaurant. As she became more assured of her skills as a restaurateur, she pestered Richard with suggestions as to how Richard's & Rita's might be made to appeal to a "younger crowd." Richard always told her how he had successfully run the restaurant for 30 years and did not need some young kid to tell him how to run his business. When Rita reached her 24th birthday, she received the proceeds of a trust fund that Richard and his wife had established for her. Rita had been told once too often that her suggestions were unwelcome. She had a falling out with Richard and used most of the proceeds of her trust fund to establish a new restaurant, which she called "Richard's Rita." Although she feared she was undercapitalized, Rita was sure that her ideas would quickly produce a successful restaurant.

While setting up her business, Rita contacted a number of purveyors of foods and beverages to assure herself an adequate supply of provisions. She planned to use "Chateau Barre," produced by the CalVint Winery, for her house wine, as Richard's & Rita's had done for years. She wrote CalVint, "We are opening Richard's Rita, our new restaurant on Ross Boulevard in Spakton. We are planning to use 'Chateau Barre' as our house wine and would like to contract with you to supply our requirements of 'Chateau Barre' for the next year at $10 per bottle." Although he had not directly dealt with Rita before, the sales manager of CalVint recognized her name and believed, because of the similarity of the names of the two restaurants, that Richard's Rita was operated by Richard. The sales manager wrote back, "In light of our long-standing business relationship, we will ship, as you requested, your requirements of 'Chateau Barre' wine at $10 per bottle, payment due within 30 days of receipt." After receiving the letter, Rita placed an order for 500 bottles of "Chateau Barre." Shortly before CalVint shipped the wine to Rita, the sales manager discovered that Richard's Rita had no connection with Richard's & Rita's. He therefore sent an express mail letter to Rita stating: "It has come to our attention that your restaurant has no relationship with Richard's & Rita's. Therefore, we will require you to furnish us with indications that you have sufficient funds on hand to cover any future orders. For your first order, we require that you pay us, in cash or by certified check, in advance or we will not ship the wine. Furthermore, the price per bottle on this and any subsequent order is $12 per bottle. Under such circumstances, we are willing to fulfill your requirements for the next year as you requested."

64. If Rita seeks to enforce the original agreement to supply wine at $10 per bottle, which of the following would be CalVint's best defense to the action?

   (A) CalVint can establish that Rita is insolvent.

   (B) Rita intentionally misrepresented the identity of her business.

   (C) Rita should have known that there was a mistake because of the reference to "long-standing business relationship" in the letter.

   (D) Unilateral mistake is a basis for rescission by the mistaken party.

65. Assume for purposes of this question only that Rita, telling CalVint that she was anxious to see her restaurant open on time, sent $6,000 to CalVint and received 500 bottles of "Chateau Barre" in time for the grand opening of Richard's Rita. Immediately thereafter, Rita filed suit against CalVint for $1,000 (the difference in price between 500 bottles at $10 per bottle and 500 bottles at $12 per bottle) plus any consequential damages. In her pleadings, Rita asserts that CalVint violated its contract to sell wine to her for a year for $10 per bottle and that she never actually consented to pay $12 per bottle but was required to pay that price to get the wine in time for her restaurant to open. Will Rita prevail in her suit?

   (A) Yes, because there was no consideration to support the alleged agreement to change the price term to $12.

   (B) Yes, because CalVint, knowing the restaurant was to open very soon, took unfair advantage of a superior bargaining position to improperly increase the price.

   (C) No, because the change in the price term is a valid subsequent modification of the original agreement.

   (D) No, if $12 per bottle was a fair market price for the wine at the time of the contract.

Question 66

Hoping to gain a major position on a campaign staff, and perhaps a patronage job if the campaign was successful, Hack sent a large mailing envelope to Graft, a candidate for Congress in the third district of State Blue. Graft got the envelope and read its contents. It contained a detailed outline of a campaign strategy for Graft. Graft turned the materials over to Toady, Graft's campaign manager. While Toady thought the overall plan simplistic and amateurish, he told Graft that a few ideas were pretty good, and Graft adopted some of them in his television spot commercials. Graft wrote Hack, telling him: "Thank you for your interest in my campaign for Congress. Although I already have a campaign staff and strategy in place, some of your ideas are good and we'll be adopting them. However, to say 'thanks' to a future constituent, I'd like to offer to pay you for your expenses in developing the materials you sent me. Send the bill to my campaign headquarters." Graft lost the election. One week after election day, Hack's bill for $1,500 arrived at Graft's campaign headquarters. Graft's campaign debts were high, and Graft told Toady not to pay Hack's bill. Hack filed suit against Graft to obtain payment of the bill plus an additional $10,000 for his ideas.

What additional fact, if true, would most strengthen Graft's defense against Hack's suit?

(A) Graft lost the election by a close margin.

(B) Hack is a relative of Graft.

(C) Graft did nothing to solicit Hack's proposal.

(D) Hack sent a similar campaign strategy to Graft's opponent.

CONTRACTS ANSWERS

Answer to Question 1

(A) Wing gave up her legal right to smoke cigarettes, thus incurring detriment and fulfilling her agreement with Biddlebaum. As a result, Biddlebaum is obligated to pay Wing the $50. For a valid contract to exist, there must be (i) mutual assent, and (ii) consideration or an appropriate substitute. Consideration requires two elements: (i) there must be a bargained-for exchange between the parties; and (ii) that which is bargained for must be of legal value. Traditionally, "legal value" has meant that either some benefit passed to the promisor or some detriment was incurred by the promisee. Most courts today hold that detriment to the promisee is the exclusive test of consideration. There is a bargained-for exchange when the promise induces the detriment and the detriment induces the promise; *i.e.,* the detriment must be the price of the exchange, and the promisor's motive must be to induce the detriment. There is legal detriment if the promisee does something she is under no legal obligation to do or refrains from doing something that she has a legal right to do. There is no requirement that detriment entail any actual loss by the promisee. Here, Biddlebaum offered to pay Wing $50 if she did not smoke during Campout Weekend. Wing accepted this offer. Thus, there was mutual assent between the parties. There was bargained-for exchange, in that Biddlebaum's motive in offering to pay the money was to induce Wing not to smoke, and in turn the promise of receiving the money induced Wing to promise not to smoke for the weekend. Finally, Wing incurred legal detriment in promising to refrain, and in fact refraining, from smoking for the weekend. Although Wing had never smoked and probably had no intention of smoking that weekend, the fact remains that she had a legal right to smoke if she so chose. By giving up that right at the request of Biddlebaum, Wing is deemed in the eyes of the law to have incurred a detriment. Hence, Biddlebaum and Wing have entered into a legally enforceable contract. With Wing having performed her part of the agreement, Biddlebaum is obligated to pay as per his part of the agreement. (D) is incorrect because, as noted above, the fact that Wing would not have smoked anyway is not determinative of whether there is legal detriment. Detriment existed in the sense that Wing gave up her *right* to smoke, and was induced to do so by Biddlebaum's offer of money. (C) is incorrect because the detriment to Wing arose by virtue of her refraining from doing something that she was legally entitled to do. The fact that refraining from smoking was probably beneficial to Wing's health does not change the character of her actions as a legal detriment. (B) is incorrect because Biddlebaum could only be obligated to pay Wing pursuant to the bargained-for exchange between the parties; *i.e.,* payment would be due upon Wing's fulfillment of her promise not to smoke for the weekend. Had Wing failed to perform as promised, there is no principle of law that would impose on Biddlebaum a "moral" obligation arising from his anti-drug activities.

Answer to Question 2

(B) Ringo should recover $2,000 because that is the amount by which Cogburn would be unjustly enriched. In a proper tender of delivery under U.C.C. section 2-503, the seller must put and hold conforming goods at the buyer's disposition for a time sufficient for the buyer to take possession. The seller must give the buyer notice reasonably necessary to enable him to take possession of the goods. Proper tender of delivery entitles the seller to acceptance of the goods and to payment according to the contract. [U.C.C. §2-507] Having made a proper tender of delivery at the place designated by Ringo and having notified Ringo of Derby's nonacceptance, Cogburn has discharged his duty under the contract. When a party's duty of performance is discharged, the other party is entitled to restitution of any benefits that he has transferred to the discharged party in an attempt to perform on his side. With Cogburn's contractual duty to deliver Grit to Derby discharged, Cogburn would be unjustly enriched, to the detriment of Ringo, if he were permitted to keep the entire $5,000 paid to him by Ringo. Ringo conferred a benefit upon Cogburn by paying him $5,000 in exchange for two horses, one of which was to be delivered to Ringo, the other to Derby. Because delivery to Derby cannot be accomplished, Ringo finds himself in a position of having paid $5,000 for one horse, the fair market value of which is $3,000. Thus, if Cogburn is permitted to retain the sum of $5,000, he will be unjustly enriched by $2,000. Therefore, Ringo should recover restitution of $2,000. (A) is incorrect because $3,000 represents more than the amount by which Cogburn has been unjustly enriched. Although the value of Grit is $3,000, keep in mind that Cogburn's duty to deliver Grit to Derby has been discharged (and Cogburn still has title to the horse under the U.C.C. rule that title passes on delivery). Ringo received a discount of $1,000 off of the total fair market value of the two horses because he was buying both of them. Once Cogburn's duty under the contract is discharged, Ringo cannot recover the benefit of that bargain under the contract; he can only recover the benefit conferred upon Cogburn, the retention of which would unjustly enrich Cogburn. Because Cogburn has received $5,000 from Ringo for one horse worth $3,000, the amount of unjust enrichment is $2,000. (C) is incorrect because, if Ringo recovers nothing, he will have incurred financial harm by paying $5,000 for one horse worth $3,000. (D) is incorrect because the fact that Cogburn tendered performance but was unable to complete delivery of Grit to Derby, solely due to Derby's refusal to accept the horse, does not justify Cogburn's keeping the entire $5,000 paid by Ringo, because Cogburn would be unjustly enriched.

Answer to Question 3

(D) Dos Santos has either option available because Capistrano is in breach of the accord agreement. An accord is an agreement in which one party to an existing contract agrees to accept, in lieu of the performance that she is supposed to receive from the other party, some other, different performance. The accord must be supported by consideration, but the consideration is sufficient if it is of a different type than called for under the original contract, even if the substituted consideration is of less value. Performance of the accord cuts off the parties' rights to enforce the original contract. Here, the accord was supported by sufficient consideration since Dos Santos was giving a ring in lieu of some cash. As with any contract, Dos Santos's duties under the accord were discharged when he timely tendered delivery of the ring and cash. By refusing the ring and filing suit for the part of the original debt that has not been paid, Capistrano has breached the accord agreement. If a creditor breaches an accord agreement, the debtor has the option of either raising the accord agreement as an equitable defense in the creditor's action and asking that it be dismissed, or waiting until he is damaged (*i.e.,* until the creditor is successful in an action on the original contract) and then bringing an action at law for damages for breach of the *accord* contract. (A) is incorrect because the amount of the debt does not have to be in dispute to have an enforceable accord as long as there was some alteration in the debtor's consideration, as discussed above. (B) is incorrect because Capistrano would only have the right to enforce the original contract if Dos Santos had breached the accord agreement. Here, Dos Santos's tender of the ring discharged his duty under the accord agreement, precluding Capistrano from suing on the original contract. (C) is incorrect because Dos Santos has both a breach of contract remedy and an equitable defense option available to him. Also, whether the ring is unique does not affect his right to specific performance of the accord agreement; he is simply raising the agreement as an equitable defense to prevent Capistrano from continuing with his suit on the original contract.

Answer to Question 4

(C) Artemesia's employee sold the painting in good faith to a customer. Because Artemesia no longer actually has the painting, there is no way to specifically enforce her agreement to convey it to Crafty. Specific performance is granted when: (i) there is a valid contract; (ii) the legal remedy is inadequate; (iii) enforcement is feasible; and (iv) mutuality of remedy is present. Crafty and Artemesia had a contract, pursuant to which Artemesia promised to sell Crafty the painting for $2,700. Although this was an oral contract for the sale of goods for a price exceeding $500 and thus subject to the Statute of Frauds, the contract is removed from the Statute by the fact that Crafty tendered full payment for the painting. Thus, the oral nature of the agreement is no hindrance to its validity. A painting by a rising young artist is sufficiently unique as to render the legal remedy for breach of the contract inadequate. However, feasibility of specific performance against Artemesia is lacking here. Morton, Artemesia's gallery manager, sold the painting to a customer, who paid value for it and was unaware that Artemesia had already agreed to sell it to Crafty. Morton also was unaware of Artemesia's agreement with Crafty. With the subject matter of the contract having been transferred in good faith to a third party, there is no feasible means to enforce against Artemesia her agreement to sell the painting to Crafty. Thus, the right to specific performance is cut off. Regarding (A), it is true that there was a bargained-for exchange of promises between Crafty and Artemesia. Nevertheless, specific performance is unavailable because enforcement is not feasible. (B) is incorrect because Crafty's assistance to Artemesia during her illness does not form part of the basis of the consideration. The assistance given by Crafty occurred before Artemesia's promise to sell the painting, and thus was not given in exchange for the promise when made. Also, even if the assistance given did form part of the quantum of adequate consideration, specific performance would still be denied because enforcement is not feasible. (D) is incorrect because a gift is a voluntary transfer of property from one person to another without compensation or consideration. Artemesia clearly stated that she wanted Crafty to pay her $2,700 for the painting. Thus, the donative intent necessary for a gift was absent.

Answer to Question 5

(D) The language of the rubber stamp impression indicates that Plumboco did not give a definite expression of acceptance; rather, acceptance was conditioned upon assent to the new terms regarding a crating charge. Thus, this was a counteroffer, and there is at this time no contract between the parties. The circular sent by Plumboco was an announcement of prices at which Plumboco was willing to receive offers. Thus, the circular was a mere invitation for offers rather than an offer. Middlemaker's order that was faxed to Plumboco was an offer to purchase the designated number and type of plumb bobs at the specified price, with delivery to be made on the specified date. By referring to the circular, Middlemaker's offer also includes the item that the price was C.I.F., meaning that the price would include the cost of the goods, plus insurance and freight. Under U.C.C. section 2-207, a written confirmation is effective as an acceptance even though it states additional terms, unless the acceptance is expressly made conditional on assent to the additional terms. Plumboco's confirmation form, in stating that acceptance of the order was *conditioned on* an additional crating charge, not only states an additional term but indicates that Plumboco does not accept the offer unless Middlemaker agrees to this term (*i.e.,* agrees to pay a charge for crating in addition to the quoted price figure). Thus, Plumboco has not expressed a definite acceptance, but has communicated a counteroffer. Middlemaker is free to accept or reject this counteroffer, but until it does accept (if at all), there is no contract. Because there is no contract at this time (A) and (B) are both incorrect as stating that there is a contract. (B) is also incorrect because if Plumboco's response did constitute an acceptance, it probably would have included the crating fee. Between merchants, additional proposed terms in a valid acceptance automatically become part of the contract unless: (i) they materially alter the original contract; (ii) the offer expressly limits acceptance to its terms; or (iii) the offeror has already objected to the particular terms, or objects within a reasonable time after receiving notice of them. Had Plumboco definitely accepted, the additional term would have become part of the contract because the term probably is not a material alteration (as discussed below) and both parties are merchants. Although (C) correctly states that there is no contract, it reaches this result for the wrong reasons. First of all, it is doubtful whether the term regarding a crating charge materially alters the offer. The crating charge will add $300 ($150 times two lots) to an order that otherwise totals $7,000. This change would probably not be deemed material. Second, even if the alteration were material, its inclusion in the confirmation would mean that a contract was still created, but without this additional term (assuming that Plumboco had conveyed a definite acceptance rather than a counteroffer). The salient point in determining whether there was a contract is Plumboco's conveyance of a counteroffer, rather than the materiality of the proposed addition.

Answer to Question 6

(D) The agreement is not enforceable because Greengrocer's promise is illusory. For a contract to be enforceable, consideration must exist on both sides, *i.e.,* each party's promise must create a binding obligation. If one party has become bound but the other has not, the agreement lacks mutuality because one of the promises is illusory. Here, Pitt has promised to supply Greengrocer with fuzzy peaches at a fixed price. Greengrocer, however, has not promised to order any peaches from Pitt. Even if Greengrocer decides to sell fuzzy peaches, it has not bound itself to order them from that particular wholesaler. The illusory nature of Greengrocer's promise makes the agreement unenforceable on consideration grounds. (A) is incorrect because in a valid requirements contract both parties' promises create binding obligations. In a requirements contract the promisor is binding itself to buy all that it requires from that particular supplier. Consideration exists because the promisor is suffering a legal detriment; it has parted with the legal right to buy the goods it may need from another source. Under the U.C.C., which governs in this case because a contract for the sale of goods is involved, a good faith term is implied: the buyer's requirements means such actual requirements as may occur in good faith. Thus, if the provision had stated instead that "Greengrocer will buy as many standard crates of fuzzy peaches as Greengrocer shall require," it would be a valid requirements contract under the U.C.C. because it requires Greengrocer to buy fuzzy peaches only from Pitt and to act in good faith in setting its requirements. (B) is incorrect even though the U.C.C. will imply reasonable terms under certain circumstances. Such terms as price and time for performance need not be spelled out in the contract; the terms will be supplied by a "reasonableness" standard if that is otherwise consistent with the parties' intent. However, supplying reasonable terms will not change the express terms of the contract. The provision that Greengrocer will buy as many peaches as it chooses to order is not sufficiently obligatory to be saved by the court supplying reasonable terms. (C) is incorrect because if the agreement were otherwise a valid requirements contract, the absence of a total quantity term would not matter. As a general rule in sale of goods contracts, the quantity being offered must be certain or capable of being made certain. The U.C.C. provides that an agreement to buy all of one's requirements is sufficiently certain because requirements usually can be objectively determined. Furthermore, the quantity ultimately required in good faith must not be unreasonably disproportionate to (i) any stated estimate or (ii) any normal requirements (in the absence of a stated estimate). Hence, if Greengrocer had contracted to buy all of its requirements from Pitt, the absence of a term specifying total quantity would not have made the agreement unenforceable.

Answer to Question 7

(B) The communications between the parties establish an enforceable contract for 150 crates of peaches at $35 per unit. An enforceable contract requires mutual assent (offer and acceptance), consideration, and an absence of defenses. For a communication to be an offer, it must be an expression of promise, undertaking, or commitment, it must be certain and definite in its terms, and it must be communicated to the offeree. The written agreement between Pitt and Greengrocer, even though it was not sufficient as an enforceable contract, qualifies as a valid offer on Pitt's part. It was a promise to supply Greengrocer with a particular item at a definite per unit price, and both parties were familiar with the size of the unit referred to. The offer was a continuing offer, *i.e.,* an offer looking to a series of contracts, with each order by the buyer being a separate contract, and the offer had not been revoked before Greengrocer placed its order for 150 standard crates. Greengrocer's order is a valid acceptance of the offer (there is no indication that the payment term is inconsistent with the offer), and consideration exists on both sides of the contract because Pitt is obligated to supply the 150 crates of peaches and Greengrocer is obligated to pay $35 for each crate. Given that there appear to be no defenses to formation or enforcement of the contract, the court should find that an enforceable contract exists. (A) is incorrect because the fact that the original promises were unenforceable does not alter the status of Pitt's promise as an offer. While no valid requirements contract was created by Greengrocer's "promise" in the original agreement, his subsequent placement of an order created a contract for that amount. (C) is incorrect because the offer by Greengrocer to purchase the additional 150 crates was terminated by Pitt's express rejection. An offer can be terminated by an express rejection. Once it is terminated, it is no longer in existence and cannot be subsequently accepted by the offeree. Here, Pitt responded to Greengrocer's communications by stating that it was not going to ship Greengrocer any peaches. As to Greengrocer's offer to order the additional 150 crates, Pitt's response amounted to an express rejection, terminating the offer. (D) is incorrect because Greengrocer's proposal to order additional crates at a lower price was not an attempted acceptance of Pitt's original offer. Rather, it was a rejection of the price terms in the original offer and a counteroffer on different terms.

Answer to Question 8

(A) Patti's has no grounds for avoiding its obligations under the contract with Farm Fresh. In effect, Patti's is advancing the position that its duty to perform under the contract is discharged by impracticability. In contracts for the sale of goods under the U.C.C., a party's duty to perform may be discharged where performance would be impracticable. Impracticability exists where a party encounters extreme and unreasonable difficulty and/or expense, and such difficulty was not anticipated. Duties will not be discharged where performance is merely more difficult or expensive than anticipated. The facts giving rise to impracticability must be such that their nonoccurrence was a basic assumption on which the contract was made. Where, as here, parties enter into a contract for the sale of goods to be supplied to the public through a retail outlet, both parties must anticipate the possibility that there will be a change in market conditions, resulting in either an increased or decreased demand for the product. Although the decreased demand results in increased expense to Patti's in performing its contract because of waste, such difficulties arising from changing demand are to be anticipated. Under the U.C.C., a shutdown by a requirements buyer for lack of orders may be permissible if the buyer is acting in good faith. [U.C.C. §2-306, comment 2] Thus, Patti's does have the right to no longer buy any Farm Fresh ice cream, but this right would only arise if there were no longer a market for frozen desserts entirely. Here, Patti's simply wants to curtail its losses by selling a more popular type of frozen dessert, which is forbidden by the exclusivity provision. Thus, Patti's continues to be bound by its duties under the agreement with Farm Fresh. (B) is incorrect because, although a court will imply a promise on the part of Patti's to use its best efforts to sell Farm Fresh products, the facts do not indicate that Patti's did not use its best efforts. At issue here is whether, despite those efforts, circumstances exist that were unanticipated and now create extreme and unreasonable difficulty or expense for Patti's in the performance of its contractual duties. (C) is incorrect because Patti's relinquished its legal right to sell any frozen desserts other than those of Farm Fresh. This giving up of a legal right constitutes legal detriment to Patti's, so there is consideration. (D) is incorrect because an agreement to buy or sell all of one's requirements or output is capable of being made certain by reference to objective, extrinsic facts (*i.e.,* the buyer's actual requirements or the seller's actual output). There is an assumption that the parties will act in good faith; thus, there may not be a tender or demand for a quantity unreasonably disproportionate to a stated estimate or prior output or requirements. Here, the agreement by Farm Fresh to sell all of its output of Fancy Grade ice cream to Patti's can be made certain by referring to such factors as the normal output of such product by Farm Fresh. In addition, Patti's agreed to pay $25 for each container of ice cream, so the total price is also ascertainable. Thus, it is not grounds for avoiding enforcement that the total price and quantity were not established.

Answer to Question 9

(C)   Tarbel should be able to recover $250,000 in quasi-contract. Where a builder in a construction contract breaches during the construction, the owner of the building is entitled to the cost of completion plus compensation for any damages caused by the delay in completing the building. Most courts, however, at least where the breach is not willful, will allow the builder to offset or recover for work performed to date to avoid the unjust enrichment of the owner. This recovery, which would be based on quasi-contract, is usually measured by the benefit received by the unjustly enriched party. Here, Tarbel's duty to complete the project was not discharged by impossibility; he could have hired another contractor to take his place or yielded to his employees' demands. Hence, Tarbel's failure to complete the remodeling constituted a breach of contract and resulted in the college having to expend $150,000 to have the building completed in time. However, Tarbel did not receive any payments for the work that he did before breaching; the college would be unjustly enriched if it does not have to pay for any of this work. The benefit of the completed remodeling is measured by the contract price, $400,000, because a quasi-contract recovery here would be based on the failed contract between the parties. This amount is reduced by the $150,000 cost of completion that the college can recover from Tarbel, leaving a net recovery of $250,000 for Tarbel. (A) is incorrect. Because Tarbel's breach was not willful, most courts would permit him to recover in quasi-contract to prevent the college's unjust enrichment from the work that he did. (B) is incorrect because recovery measured by the claimant's detriment (*i.e.,* his reliance interest) is only an appropriate alternative where the standard "benefit" measure would achieve an unfair result; it is not applied where the party seeking quasi-contract recovery was the breaching party. (D) is incorrect because courts will always limit relief to the contract price where the claimant is the breaching party. Measuring the benefit to the college in terms of the value of the improvements rather than the contract price will deny to the college the benefit of the bargain that it became entitled to when Tarbel breached.

Answer to Question 10

(D)   Contractual terms that are set forth in a writing intended as a final expression of the parties' agreement cannot be contradicted by evidence of any prior agreement or contemporaneous oral agreement. Although this parol evidence rule prohibits contradicting the writing, the terms of the writing may be explained or supplemented by consistent additional terms, unless the court finds from all the circumstances that the writing was intended as a complete and exclusive statement of the parties' agreement. To determine whether the parties intended the writing to be the complete and exclusive statement of their agreement, it must be determined whether parties situated as were the parties to this contract would naturally and normally include the extrinsic matter in the writing. Here, the writing at issue states clearly that the painting subject to sale is "any painting by Bleu." Brandon's assertion of a prior agreement allowing him to buy a painting by Ruyter clearly contradicts the terms of the writing. Consequently, the parol evidence rule will render inadmissible testimony as to such an alleged agreement. Choices (A) and (C) are therefore incorrect. The assertion that the parties agreed prior to signing the writing that Brandon could have a $250 frame at no additional cost does not contradict any of the terms of the writing. However, it does supplement those terms. As noted above, such supplementation is permitted unless there is a finding that the writing was intended by Brandon and Marlowe as a complete and exclusive statement of the terms of their agreement. It is likely that a court would find that parties situated as were Brandon and Marlowe would normally and naturally include in their written agreement for the sale and purchase of a painting at a specified price the additional provision that the purchaser could also have a specifically priced frame at no extra cost. Such a finding would lead to the conclusion that the writing, standing as it is without any reference to the frame, constitutes a complete and exclusive statement of the agreement. Given this finding, evidence of the alleged agreement regarding the frame will not be admissible even for the purpose of supplementing the terms of the writing. Thus, choice (B) is incorrect. (D) is the only choice correctly stating that testimony as to neither agreement is admissible.

Answer to Question 11

(C) A contract was formed because Charles's acceptance was effective on dispatch. Under the "mailbox rule," acceptance by mail or similar means creates a contract at the moment of posting, properly addressed and stamped, unless: (i) the offer stipulates that acceptance is not effective until received; or (ii) an option contract is involved. The mailbox rule does not apply where an offeree sends a rejection but then sends an acceptance, and the rejection arrives before the acceptance (even if the acceptance was dispatched before the rejection was received). In such a case, there is no contract. However, the mailbox rule does apply if the acceptance is dispatched before the rejection. In such a case, there is a contract upon dispatch of the acceptance. Here, Charles dispatched first an acceptance and then a rejection of Ernest's offer. The mailbox rule applies because Ernest's offer did not specify that acceptance was not effective until receipt, nor is an option contract involved. Because Charles dispatched his acceptance before he called with his rejection, the mailbox rule applies. Thus, Charles's acceptance was effective, thereby creating a contract at the moment it was mailed, and his attempted rejection was ineffective. (B) is incorrect because once the acceptance was effective, the fact that Ernest received the "rejection" by telephone before he received the accepting letter has no effect on the formation of the contract. (A) is incorrect because the letter from Ernest indicates that the subject matter of the contract was Ernest's camera equipment that Charles had admired for some time. This description on its face appears to be sufficiently definite that a court would be able to determine with reasonable accuracy what equipment is subject to Ernest's offer to sell. (D) is incorrect even though it is true that, pursuant to the Statute of Frauds, a contract for the sale of goods of $500 or more is not enforceable unless evidenced by a writing. There is no requirement that a rejection of an offer to enter into such a contract must be in writing.

Answer to Question 12

(C) The fact that Ernest did not really need an answer within one week is not a material term of the contract, only a limitation on the offer, and thus would not be barred by the parol evidence rule. The parol evidence rule bars evidence of expressions of the parties' agreement, made prior to or contemporaneous with a writing that is the complete embodiment of that agreement, where such expressions vary the terms of the writing. Here, the terms of the agreement between Ernest and Charles are embodied in Ernest's letter—the sale of Ernest's camera equipment for $1,500. Ernest's statement in the letter that he needed an answer within a week is not a material term of the contract. Thus, the proffered evidence does not—and is not being offered to—contradict or vary the terms of the written agreement of the parties, and is therefore not barred by the parol evidence rule. (A) is incorrect because Ernest's time limit on his offer is not a material term of the contract, nor is it even part of the agreement; it is simply a recital of collateral facts. Thus, the proffered evidence does not contradict a material term of the contract. (B) is incorrect because Charles is not denying the truth of a contract that he has accepted, but is rather contradicting a statement of fact contained in the letter that embodies the agreement. (D) is incorrect. Although evidence of fraud can be admitted into evidence despite the parol evidence rule, the proffered evidence here does not establish a fraud. To constitute fraud, there must be an intentional mis-statement of a material fact. Here, although Ernest's statement that he needed an answer within one week might have been untrue, his reasons for limiting the validity of the offer to one week are irrelevant to the contract. Thus, the reasons for the one-week limit are not material and so could not be the basis for fraud.

Answer to Question 13

(C) Nicholas's silence while allowing Cisco to repave his driveway will be treated by the court as an acceptance by silence of an implied-in-fact contract. An implied-in-fact contract is a contract formed by manifestations of assent other than oral or written language, *i.e.,* by conduct. The manifestations of mutual assent are analyzed ***objectively*** under contract law. Even if there is no subjective "meeting of the minds," the parties will be bound if their conduct objectively appears to manifest a contractual intent. In this case, Cisco, by beginning to pave Nicholas's driveway, has made an offer by his conduct because a reasonable person would conclude that the services were offered with the expectation of compensation rather than gratuitously. Cisco's offer has been accepted by Nicholas even though he said nothing. While generally an acceptance must be communicated to the offeror to be effective, courts will often find an acceptance where an offeree silently accepts offered benefits, such as when the offeree receives the benefit of services and he (i) had a reasonable opportunity to reject them and (ii) knew or should have known that the provider of the services expected to be compensated for them. [Restatement (Second) of Con-tracts §69(1)(a)] Here, Nicholas has objectively manifested an acceptance of the offer by stand-ing by while Cisco was repaving his driveway even though he had a reasonable opportunity to stop him. Even if he believed that Cisco had made a mistake, Nicholas knew or should have known that Cisco was not providing the paving services gratuitously. Thus, the court will prob-ably find that an implied-in-fact contract existed between Cisco and Nicholas. (A) is incorrect because the pedestrian has not manifested assent to an implied-in-fact contract with Dr. Hacksaw (in contrast to a patient who goes to Dr. Hacksaw's office and submits to treatment by him). A court will not find an implied-in-fact contract unless the conduct of ***both*** parties objectively indicates assent to a contract. Dr. Hacksaw is not without a remedy, however, if he wants com-pensation for his services. The court may permit Dr. Hacksaw to recover the value of his services under a quasi-contract or implied-in-law contract theory. A quasi-contract is not really a contract at all; rather, it is a legal fiction designed to avoid injustice by preventing unjust enrichment of one party to the detriment of another. Here, Dr. Hacksaw conferred a benefit on the pedestrian and the law will presume that the pedestrian would have requested the emergency medical care had he been able to do so, and will allow Dr. Hacksaw to recover reasonable compensation for his services. (B) is incorrect. The conduct of Olivia and Nelda does not appear from an objective standard to manifest contractual intent because of the close family relationship of the parties and the minor burden on Nelda to render the services. Courts generally will not presume that a contractual relationship was intended under these circumstances. (D) is incorrect for the same reason as (A). Without some conduct on the part of Nils, such as knowingly accepting offered benefits in silence, a court will not find the manifestation of ***mutual*** assent necessary for an implied-in-fact contract.

Answer to Question 14

(C) The exoneration clause will be the clause most likely to bar Crane from assigning to Derrick, because as a result of the exoneration clause an assignment would substantially alter Girder's risks. Here we are dealing with both an assignment of rights (the right to receive compensation for installing the toll booths) and a delegation of duties (the duty to install the booths). The general rule is that most duties are delegable and most rights are assignable. However, assignment and delegation are prohibited where they would substantially alter the obligor's (Girder's) risks. An example of a situation where the obligor's risk will be changed occurs where the obligor extends any degree of trust or confidence to the particular obligee. The exoneration clause here amounts to such an extension—by agreeing to hold Crane harmless, Girder was acting as an insurer of Crane's performance. It would be unfair to force Girder to accept the risk of someone else's performance because the risk of faulty performance will be different from the risk assumed. It does not matter that Derrick is equally qualified. (A) is incorrect because the "time is of the essence" clause merely makes performance on the exact day agreed upon critical. Absent such a clause, a court might allow some damages for late performance, but could find late performance to be only a minor breach. The clause makes late performance a material breach. This would not affect an assignment in any way other than by requiring the assignee to perform in a timely matter. (B) is incorrect because it only requires written approval of modifications, and an assignment technically is not a modification—if it were there could never be unilateral assignment since modification requires mutual assent. Thus, while a contract clause providing that "any purported assignment by a party is void" may effectively prohibit assignment, the clause here requiring that modifications be approved in writing will not have the same effect. Moreover, a requirement that modifications be approved in writing generally is unenforceable (except under the U.C.C.) because the new (modified) contract implicitly includes a mutual agreement to abandon the writing requirement set out in the old contract. (D) is incorrect because a liquidated damages clause merely stipulates the damages to be paid in the event of breach. Assigning Crane's part of the contract to Derrick could mean that Derrick, instead of Crane, would be chargeable with $1,000 per day for failure to complete the job on time. Thus, the liquidated damages clause would not bar the assignment.

Answer to Question 15

(D) By assigning "his part of the contract" to Derrick, the majority rule would hold that Crane has not only assigned his rights under the contract, but also that Derrick has assumed Crane's duties under the contract. Generally, the delegator remains liable on the contract, even if the delegate has expressly assumed the duties. This is not always the case where the obligee expressly consents to such a transfer of duties. Such circumstances could be construed as presenting an offer of novation. A novation substitutes a new party for an original party to the contract, requires the assent of all parties, and completely releases the original party. Girder (the obligee) has expressly consented to the transfer of Crane's duties under the contract to Derrick. In so doing, Girder may be deemed to be offering to discharge Crane's duties in exchange for Derrick's assumption of the duties; i.e., an offer of novation. Consequently, a new party (Derrick) is substituted for Crane. Because this substitution has the assent of the new obligor (Derrick), Crane may be completely released from his duties under the original contract. (A) states correctly that an assignment by itself does not relieve Crane of liability under the original contract. As stated above, Crane, as delegator, would generally remain liable even if Derrick had expressly assumed the duties. However, Girder's approval of the transfer of duties from Crane to Derrick does operate to relieve Crane of his underlying liability. Therefore, (A) is incorrect. (C) is incorrect because it presumes, contrary to the general rule mentioned above, that a transfer of duties, without more, will relieve a delegator of liability. (B) focuses on an irrelevant issue. The question actually addresses Crane's potential liability as part of the underlying original contract. Since Crane is no longer liable on that contract, the fact that the job cannot be redone properly in a timely fashion will not impose liability on Crane. The responsibility for proper and timely performance now rests solely with Derrick.

Answer to Question 16

(D) Cedric can recover $2,000 as lost profits plus the $4,000 in costs he incurred before Mable breached the contract. The purpose of a damages remedy based on an affirmation of the contract is to give compensation for the breach; *i.e.,* to put the nonbreaching party where he would have been had the promise been performed. In most cases, the plaintiff's standard measure of damages will be based solely on an "expectation" measure, *i.e.,* sufficient damages for him to buy a substitute performance. A reliance measure of damages, on the other hand, awards the plaintiff the cost of his performance, *i.e.,* his expenditures in performing his duties under the contract. In certain situations, an award of compensatory damages will contain both an expectation and a reliance component. In a construction contract, if the owner breaches after the builder has already begun his performance, the builder will be entitled to any profit he would have derived from the contract *plus* any *costs* he has incurred to date. This formula contains an expectation component (the profit the builder would have made) and a reliance component (the cost incurred prior to the breach). This formula is applicable to the facts in this case. Cedric has begun performance by ordering and purchasing the custom-made fixtures at a cost of $4,000. Because they are usable only for Mable's purposes, their cost, which is treated just like any other expenditure of labor and material in a partially completed construction contract, can be recovered as reliance damages. The other element of his recovery is the $2,000 profit that he would have derived from the contract—his expectation damages. His total recovery will therefore be $6,000. (A) is incorrect because Cedric can do nothing further to mitigate his damages. The nonbreaching party is always under a duty to mitigate damages after learning of the other party's breach. In construction contracts, the builder's duty to mitigate generally dictates only that he not continue work after the breach and not incur further expenditures. While the builder would also have a duty to apply any usable materials that he purchased to other jobs or to attempt to resell them to another contractor, the facts specify that the custom-made fixtures here were not usable in other remodeling jobs. Hence, Cedric's failure to attempt to sell the fixtures did not amount to a failure to mitigate damages. (B) is incorrect because an award of $2,000 does not put Cedric in the position he would have been in had the contract been performed—the $4,000 that he spent on the fixtures would have been covered by part of the $10,000 that he was to receive as the contract price. Had Mable not breached, Cedric would have received the contract price of $10,000, and he would have spent an additional $4,000 in labor and materials to complete the job. The difference, $6,000, consists of the $4,000 that he already spent on materials and the $2,000 profit that he expected to make. (C) is incorrect. Instead of seeking a damages remedy based on an affirmance of the contract, the nonbreaching party may rescind and sue for restitution for any "benefit" that he has transferred to the breacher in an attempt to perform the contract. The restitution recovery is generally based on the fair market value of the benefit transferred. Here, Cedric can provide Mable with the fixtures and seek restitution, but there is nothing to indicate that their fair market value is $4,000. Even if that is the case, however, Cedric has a provable compensatory damages remedy on the contract of $6,000; he will elect that remedy rather than the lesser restitution remedy.

Answer to Question 17

(B) Retailer is entitled to recover $800. Wholesaler's notice that it would be unable to fill Retailer's order constituted an anticipatory repudiation, which Retailer was entitled to treat as a total breach. Under the U.C.C., the buyer's basic remedy where the seller breaches by refusing to deliver is the difference between the contract price and either the market price or the cost of buying replacement goods ("cover"). If the buyer intends to fix damages based on the latter measure, the buyer must make a reasonable contract for substitute goods in good faith and without unreasonable delay. Here, Retailer chose to make a contract for a higher quality of sunglasses at a higher price, even though the model that he had originally ordered was available from a supplier outside the area. While Retailer need not find the lowest available price in the country or make a contract for substitute goods with an unreliable supplier, he was aware that he could have obtained the "Red Star" sunglasses in plenty of time from the nonlocal supplier. Absent additional facts that would justify Retailer's decision, he can recover only the difference between the contract cost and a reasonable contract for substitute goods. Hence, (A) is wrong because Retailer's contract for cover probably would not be deemed to be commercially reasonable. (C) is wrong because Retailer's remedy based on market price would be determined at the time Retailer learned of the breach, not necessarily the time of performance. In the case of an anticipatory repudiation such as this, the buyer may either treat the anticipatory repudiation as a total breach and pursue his breach of contract remedies, or suspend his performance and await seller's performance for a commercially reasonable time. Retailer chose to treat Wholesaler's notice as a total repudiation and breach of contract. Hence, the market price remedy would be measured at that time because that is when Retailer "learned of the breach," rather than at the time of performance. (D) is wrong because the nonrepudiating party need not wait for the repudiating party to retract its repudiation. Retailer exercised its option to treat the repudiation as a total breach and buy substitute goods. Once that occurred, Wholesaler was not entitled to retract its repudiation and force Retailer to accept the sunglasses.

Answer to Question 18

(D) Although the crossing offers as to price were identical, there is no requisite mutual assent without an acceptance. If offers stating precisely the same terms cross in the mail, they do not give rise to a contract despite the apparent meeting of the minds. An offer cannot be accepted if there is no knowledge of it. Here, Chip and Dale each sent offers setting the price of the ensemble at $22,000. Despite the fact that these offers were identical, there is no mutual assent without at least one of the parties manifesting acceptance of the terms of the offer, and communicating that acceptance to the other. We are told that this has not yet happened even though Chip and Dale both have received the letters. Consequently, although there is an apparent meeting of the minds as to price, there has not been a sufficient objective manifestation of this agreement as to denote a mutual assent. (C) fails to account for the principle discussed above, that identical crossing offers do not give rise to a contract. Despite their receipt of identical offers before April 12, there is no agreement between the parties. (A) is incorrect because it misstates the mailbox rule. Acceptance by mail or similar means creates a contract at the moment of posting, properly addressed and stamped, unless the offer stipulates that acceptance is not effective until received, or unless an option contract is involved. This rule does not operate to create a contract from the moment an *offer* is mailed (or in this case, two identical offers are mailed). Thus, (A) is incorrect. Regarding (B), the fact that a merchant sends an offer in writing is significant because it will limit the offeror's power to revoke if it gives assurances that it will be held open for a stated time. Here, the written offer by Chip is irrevocable at least until April 12, but the issue in the question is whether it has been accepted rather than whether it has been revoked.

Answer to Question 19

(D) Despite her reliance, Priscilla has no recourse against Dale. A third-party donee beneficiary has no cause of action against the promisee, because the promisee's act is gratuitous and she may not be held to it (unless she has directly created the reliance by personally informing the beneficiary). This rule applies even if the third-party beneficiary has detrimentally relied on the contract. Priscilla is a third-party beneficiary of the contract between Chip and Dale because she is expressly designated in the contract and performance is to be made directly to her. Because the object was to arrange a gift for Priscilla rather than to bring about payment of a debt owed to her by Dale, Priscilla is a donee beneficiary. The rights of an intended beneficiary vest (thus allowing her to enforce the underlying contract) when she: (i) manifests assent to the promise in a manner invited or requested by the parties; (ii) brings suit to enforce the promise; or (iii) materially changes position in justifiable reliance on the promise. Priscilla materially changed her position in justifiable reliance on the promise by donating her new bedroom set upon learning that she was to receive an antique ensemble. However, as noted above, even such detrimental reliance will not create a cause of action in favor of Priscilla against the promisee, Dale. (Note that while Dale might have been liable to Priscilla directly under a promissory estoppel theory if Dale had personally promised the bedroom set to Priscilla, here Priscilla was informed of the agreement by Chip.) Dale's act in purportedly donating the ensemble to Priscilla was totally gratuitous and nonbinding on her. Thus, Priscilla cannot compel Dale to honor the original contract or pay damages. (A) is incorrect because, although Priscilla is an intended beneficiary of a valid contract, she is a *donee* beneficiary, and as such, has no claim against the promisee. (B) is incorrect because, as explained above, Priscilla's reasonable detrimental reliance does her no good because of her status as a donee beneficiary. (C) is incorrect because Priscilla was designated in the contract as the party to whom the ensemble was to be tendered. Thus, she was an intended, rather than incidental, beneficiary.

Answer to Question 20

(D) Approval of the modernization plans by Marina is a condition precedent because without such approval the parties have no agreement. Where there is an oral condition precedent, evidence of the condition falls outside the parol evidence rule. The parol evidence rule provides that where the parties to a contract express their agreement in a writing with the intent that it embody the full and final expression of their bargain, any other expressions, written or oral, made prior to the writing, as well as any oral expressions contemporaneous with the writing, are inadmissible to vary the terms of the writing. Certain forms of extrinsic evidence are deemed to fall outside the scope of the parol evidence rule. For instance, a party to a written contract can attack the validity of the agreement. One way of doing so is by asserting that there was an oral agreement that the written contract would not become effective until the occurrence of a condition. Such a condition would be deemed a condition precedent to the effectiveness of the agreement, and evidence of the condition will be freely offered and received. Here, Yott and Salty have entered into a written agreement that apparently embodies the full and final expression of their bargain. However, Yott's oral statement at the time of entering into the agreement indicates quite clearly that the parties had no agreement absent the approval of Marina, and Salty agreed with this statement. Thus, there is an oral agreement that the written contract would not become effective until the occurrence of a condition precedent. As discussed above, evidence of this oral condition does not come within the purview of the parol evidence rule and is therefore admissible. Consequently, Yott can assert the nonoccurrence of a condition precedent as a way to avoid liability on the contract. (B) is incorrect because, as explained above, the nature of the oral agreement takes it outside the scope of the parol evidence rule. Therefore, the rule will not be decisive in determining the outcome of this case. (A) is incorrect because the agreement at issue here is not of a type that is covered by the Statute of Frauds. The agreement does not involve: (i) a promise by an executor or administrator to pay the estate's debts out of her own funds; (ii) a promise to answer for the debt of another; (iii) a promise made in consideration of marriage; (iv) a promise creating an interest in land; (v) a promise that by its terms cannot be performed within one year; or (vi) a promise for the sale of goods at a price of $500 or more. Therefore, the Statute of Frauds is inapplicable to these facts. (C) is incorrect because the term "rules of construction" refers to rules used by courts when interpreting contracts; *e.g.*, contracts are to be construed as a whole, words are to be construed according to their ordinary meaning, or custom and usage in the particular business and locale should be considered. The facts and issues presented by this question do not call for the application of any such principles of contract interpretation.

Answer to Question 21

(B) By his statement to Salty, Yott waived the benefit of the condition requiring Counter's approval of the modernization plans, and Salty detrimentally relied on the statement by modernizing the boat. Thus, there is a binding waiver of the condition. A condition is an event, other than the passage of time, the occurrence or nonoccurrence of which creates, limits, or extinguishes the absolute duty to perform in the other contracting party. The occurrence of a condition may be excused under a number of different circumstances. One such circumstance is where the party having the benefit of the condition indicates by words or conduct that he will not insist upon it. If a party indicates that he is waiving a condition before it happens, and the person addressed detrimentally relies on it, a court will hold this to be a binding estoppel waiver. The promise to waive the condition may be retracted at any time before the other party has detrimentally changed his position. Here, the contract provided that Salty could not begin the work without Counter's prior approval. This approval was a condition that had to be met before Yott's duty to pay would arise. When Yott told Salty to commence his work on the boat, even though Counter had withheld his approval, Yott was telling Salty that he was waiving the condition of Counter's approval. Salty then acted in detrimental reliance on this statement by in fact starting and completing the modernization of the boat. While Yott could have retracted his statement and reinstated the condition prior to Salty's detrimental reliance, he did nothing when Salty began modernizing the boat. Under such circumstances, Yott has made a binding waiver of the condition and will be estopped from asserting it. Thus, Salty is entitled to recover the full contract price. (A) is incorrect because, as discussed above, Counter's approval was a condition precedent for the parties' contractual duties to arise. Salty's duty to modernize the boat and Yott's duty to pay for the modernization would not arise without the condition of Counter's approval either being satisfied or being excused. (C) is incorrect because unjust enrichment is a quasi-contract alternative that Salty could utilize if he did not have a contract remedy. Here, however, Salty can recover the full contract price because Yott waived the condition and is estopped from retracting the waiver. Regarding (D), the parol evidence rule does not prohibit evidence of a *subsequent* modification of a written contract; the rule applies only to prior or contemporaneous expressions. Consequently, it may be shown that the parties altered the integrated writing after its making. The oral agreement between Yott and Salty described in the facts was made subsequent to the writing. Therefore, the parol evidence rule is inapplicable to this agreement.

Answer to Question 22

(C) The court should rescind the contract for mutual mistake and order Beryl to return the ring to Sparkler. Mutual mistake of a material fact to a contract is a defense that allows the adversely affected party to rescind as long as that party did not assume the risk of mistake. Mutual mistake arises where both parties are mistaken as to a basic assumption of the contract and the mistake has a material effect on the agreed-upon exchange. Here, both parties were mistakenly operating under the assumption that the ring was worth only $4,800 when in fact it was worth $6,200. While generally courts will not allow mistakes in value to be the basis for rescission, because the courts will presume that both parties assumed the risk of mistake, the facts here are sufficient to take this case out of the general rule—it appears that neither party wanted to assume the risk of determining value, since both agreed to rely solely on the valuation by an independent expert. (A) is incorrect because it does not take into account that the facts here are sufficient to show that neither party assumed the risk of mistake, and so the general rule does not apply. (B) is incorrect because the statement by Marquis two years ago does not indicate the value of the ring today, both because market conditions could have changed in two years and because Marquis gave a fairly equivocal valuation ("it's probably worth about"). (D) is incorrect because the appraisal was not a condition precedent—an event creating, limiting, or extinguishing the absolute duty to perform—since when Beryl requested the appraisal, she did not obligate herself to buy the ring based on the appraisal. Beryl's promise at that time ("if the price isn't too high I'll buy it from you") was too illusory to form a contract, because what is "too high" is very subjective. Since there was no contract, the appraisal could not be a condition.

Answer to Question 23

(A) Tina has delegated to Gabrielle her duties under the agreement with Cordero, and Gabrielle has agreed to assume such duties by agreeing to make the 18 installment payments to Cordero. Where a delegate's promise to perform the delegated duty is supported by consideration, there results a third-party beneficiary situation, so that the nondelegating party to the contract can compel performance or bring suit for nonperformance. Gabrielle's promise to make the payments to Cordero, totaling $1,800, was given in exchange for Tina's promise to forgive the $2,000 debt owed to her by Gabrielle. Tina thus relinquished her right to take action against Gabrielle for the full amount owed, thereby incurring legal detriment. Consequently, the promise of Gabrielle was supported by consideration, and a situation arose in which Cordero became a third-party beneficiary of the agreement between Tina and Gabrielle, able to enforce performance of Gabrielle's promise to pay. (C) is incorrect because, as explained above, Gabrielle's promise to Tina *was* supported by consideration. (B) is incorrect because there was no assignment of Tina's rights to Cordero; *i.e.,* Tina did not manifest an intent to transfer to Cordero her rights against Gabrielle. Rather, Tina transferred to Gabrielle the duties that she owed to Cordero. (D) is incorrect because the surety provision of the Statute of Frauds requires only that a promise to answer for the debt or default of another must be in writing. Such a promise must be collateral to another person's promise to pay rather than a primary promise (a promise to pay directly for the benefits given to another). Here, Gabrielle did not promise Cordero that if he sold the entertainment system to Tina, and Tina did not pay, Gabrielle would pay. Instead, Gabrielle promised to Tina that she would directly perform Tina's obligation to pay Cordero. Thus, this is not the type of promise required by the Statute of Frauds to be in writing.

Answer to Question 24

(C) Tina will remain liable to Cordero for the debt unless the parties have agreed to a novation. When a party to a contract delegates her duties to another, the original party (the delegator) remains liable on her contract. This is so even if the delegate expressly assumes the delegator's duties. However, a different result would obtain if the obligee (the person to whom the duties are owed) expressly consents to this transfer of duties. This would constitute an offer of novation. A novation occurs when a new contract substitutes a new party to receive benefits and assume duties that had belonged to one of the original parties under the terms of the old contract. For a novation, all parties must agree that the contractual duties between the original contracting parties are extinguished; a valid and enforceable new contract takes the place of the previous contract. The effect of the novation is to discharge the old contract. Here, Gabrielle has expressly assumed Tina's duty to pay Cordero, but that does not discharge Tina's liability to Cordero. Cordero may still sue Tina on the existing obligation between them. However, if the parties expressly agree to the substitution of Gabrielle for Tina, a novation would occur and the original contract would be extinguished. In that case, Tina would be discharged of all of her duties to Cordero regardless of whether Gabrielle subsequently performs her duties. (A) is incorrect because Cordero, who is a third-party beneficiary of the assumption agreement between Tina and Gabrielle, does not need to elect between the third-party promisor (Gabrielle) and his own debtor (Tina). He may sue both of them (although he can recover only one satisfaction). Thus, whether Cordero has filed suit against Gabrielle is irrelevant to his right to recover the money from Tina. (B) is incorrect for the same reason. Tina cannot change her status to that of a guarantor simply by delegating her duties to Gabrielle. Cordero can choose to sue Tina on the existing obligation between them without first trying to recover from Gabrielle. (D) is incorrect because, as discussed above, the fact that the delegate (Gabrielle) expressly assumed the duties of the delegator (Tina) does not discharge the delegator's liability to the obligee (Cordero).

Answer to Question 25

(B) Because the subject matter of the contract became illegal after Flipper's offer but before Arcade's acceptance, the supervening illegality is deemed to revoke the offer. It will be a defense to enforcement of a contract if either the consideration or the subject matter is illegal. If the illegality is present at the time of the offer, there is no valid offer. If the illegality arises after the offer but before acceptance, the illegality operates to revoke the offer. If the illegality arises after formation of a valid contract, it discharges the contract because performance has become impossible. Here, Arcade received Flipper's offer to sell the games on August 5. Generally, an offer not supported by consideration can be revoked at will, even if the offeror has promised not to revoke for a certain period. However, an offer by a merchant to buy or sell goods in a signed writing that, by its terms, gives assurances that it will be held open is not revocable for lack of consideration during the time stated. Flipper is a merchant who deals in goods of the kind being sold. Its offer contained in the letter of August 3 assured Arcade that its terms would be open until September 2. Thus, the offer was not revocable until September 2, and Flipper's purported revocation of August 17 was ineffective. The legislation rendering illegal the sale of the type of machines to be sold by Flipper to Arcade took effect on August 28, two days prior to Arcade's acceptance. Thus, the illegality arose after Flipper's offer and before Arcade's acceptance. Hence, the state law serves to revoke the offer. (C) is incorrect because, as explained above, Flipper's attempted revocation was ineffective. (D) is incorrect because the state law would only create a condition of impossibility of performance if it became effective after formation of a valid contract. Here, the law was effective prior to Arcade's acceptance. (A) is incorrect because if the state law had not been enacted, Flipper would have been bound by the terms of its offer until September 2. The fact that Flipper was able to obtain a higher price for the machines would not permit it to revoke its offer prior to expiration of the specified period.

Answer to Question 26

(C) The original contract was modified by Vishun and Diggum, and this modification discharged the payment term of the original contract. If a contract is subsequently modified by the parties, this will serve to discharge those terms of the original contract that are the subject of the modification. A modifying agreement must be mutually assented to, and must be supported by consideration. In most cases, consideration is found to be present in that each party has limited her right to enforce the original contract as is. If a modification will benefit only one of the parties, it may be unenforceable without some consideration being given to the other party. Note, however, that if a promisee has given something in addition to what he already owes in return for the promise he now seeks to enforce, or has in some way agreed to vary his preexisting duty, there is consideration. Here, Vishun and Diggum agreed that Diggum would perform the additional work necessary to lay the cables in a timely manner for an additional $50,000. There was consideration in that this modification would benefit both parties (*i.e.,* Diggum would receive more money and Vishun would receive a guaranteed completion date). Each party has limited his or her right to enforce the original contract as is (*i.e.,* Vishun must now pay more money and Diggum must perform additional work in order to lay the conduit through the soggy soil and complete the job on time). Given all of these circumstances, there is consideration supporting the modification of the original contract. Thus, the modification is enforceable, and Diggum is entitled to the additional $50,000. (A) is wrong because neither the Statute of Frauds nor the parol evidence rule affects the validity of the oral modification. The Statute of Frauds does not require a writing for the contract involved here, and parol evidence can be offered to show subsequent modifications of a written contract, since the parol evidence rule applies only to prior or contemporaneous negotiations. (B) is incorrect because, as explained above, Diggum's agreement to vary his contractual duty by promising to perform all of the work by a certain date constitutes consideration for Vishun's agreement to pay the additional money. (D) is incorrect because it suggests that the court will evaluate the adequacy of consideration. A court of law will not concern itself with the relative values being exchanged. If Vishun has agreed to pay $3,050,000 for the job performed by Diggum, the court will not inquire as to whether this is a fair price or otherwise attempt to make a new agreement for the parties.

Answer to Question 27

(C) Diggum is entitled to collect $2,950,000 because his breach of contract entitled Vishun to offset the amount of money that will be needed to compensate her for the breach. A failure to perform in accordance with contractual terms constitutes a breach of the contract. A breach is minor if the obligee gains the substantial benefit of her bargain despite the defective performance. In the case of a minor breach, the aggrieved party is entitled to a remedy for such breach, such as damages. However, the aggrieved party is not relieved of her duty of performance under the contract. The purpose of contract damages based on affirmance of the contract is to put the nonbreaching party where she would have been had the promise been performed, *i.e.,* sufficient damages to allow her to buy a substitute performance. Because the nonbreaching party in a case involving a minor breach has a duty to tender counterperformance, her claim for damages is usually asserted as a setoff against her liability to the obligor. Here, the contract imposed on Diggum a duty to lay the conduit so as to avoid magnetized rock. By failing to do so, Diggum breached the contract. Despite this breach, Vishun received the substantial benefit of her bargain because the studio and broadcast transmitter have been built. Therefore, the breach is minor, entitling Vishun to a remedy but not relieving her of her duty to pay Diggum under the contract. Vishun has suffered damages of $50,000, because she will have to expend that amount to reroute the cable in order to put her in the position she would have been in had Diggum not breached. Thus, Vishun can assert the $50,000 claim as a setoff against the $3 million she is under a duty to pay Diggum, leaving $2,950,000. (A) is incorrect because a measure of damages based on the difference between the value of what the owner would have received if the builder had properly performed the contract and the value of what the owner actually received is appropriate only if having a third party properly complete the project would be wasteful. Here, correcting the breach will cost only $50,000. (B) is incorrect because the fact that the studio and transmitter are now worth more than the contract price does not put Vishun in the position she would have been in had Diggum not breached. The higher value of the property is part of Vishun's "benefit of the bargain" and does not reduce the damages that she is entitled to collect from Diggum. (D) is wrong because it states a reliance measure of damages that is inapplicable here. Had Diggum's breach been material, Vishun would not have been under a duty to pay him under contract, but Diggum could have recovered in quasi-contract for the benefits he conferred in partially performing. Here, however, because his breach was only minor, he can recover the amount he is owed under the contract minus the setoff for Vishun's damages.

Answer to Question 28

(A) Scratch may be able to rescind the contract on the grounds of unilateral mistake if Fang was aware that Scratch was mistaken about the identity of the artist. Where only one of the parties is mistaken about facts relating to the agreement, the mistake usually will not prevent formation of the contract. However, if the nonmistaken party is aware of the mistake made by the other party, he will not be permitted to snap up the offer; *i.e.*, the mistaken party will have the right to rescind the agreement. Under the facts in this choice, Fang knows that Scratch is mistaken about the identity of the artist, which is a basic assumption of the contract for the paintings. To obtain rescission, Scratch would also have to establish that the mistake creates a material imbalance in the exchange and that he did not assume the risk of that mistake. The facts in choice (A) give him the best grounds for doing so. (B) is incorrect because the fact that one of the parties to the contract has superior knowledge about the subject matter of the contract does not by itself justify rescission, even if the other party is unaware of that fact. Fang's knowledge or lack of it was not a basic assumption on which the contract was made and was not relied on by Scratch in making the sale. (C) is wrong because the fact that Scratch was angry when he agreed to the contract is not grounds for rescinding it. Regardless of Scratch's state of mind, there was an objective manifestation of mutual assent between the parties. (D) is incorrect because Fang's misrepresentation to Scratch as to how he will use the paintings does not appear to have been relied on by Scratch. Hence, the misrepresentation is not significant enough to serve as grounds for rescinding the contract.

Answer to Question 29

(C) The circumstances of (C) offer the best grounds for rescinding the contract based on mutual mistake. When both parties entering into a contract are mistaken about facts relating to the agreement, the contract may be voidable by the adversely affected party if (i) the mistake concerns a basic assumption on which the contract is made; (ii) the mistake has a material effect on the agreed-upon exchange; and (iii) the party seeking avoidance did not assume the risk of the mistake. Here, both parties believed that the paintings would be suitable for viewing and had no reason to suspect that their color would fade away when exposed to light. This occurrence probably rendered the paintings virtually worthless, creating a material imbalance in the exchange. Finally, despite Fang's superior knowledge of the subject matter, it is doubtful that he would be deemed to have assumed the risk of what occurred. In contrast to this situation, the circumstances in (A) are not as strong a basis for avoidance. Even assuming that both parties mistakenly believed that the paintings were not too fragile to be transported, that risk is more likely to be deemed assumed by Fang. The circumstances in (B) suggest only that Fang may have made a mistake as to the value of the paintings, but since Scratch knew nothing about the identity of the artist, the mistake is unilateral and Fang cannot rescind on this ground. Choice (D) is incorrect because the circumstances do not satisfy the requirements for discharge by frustration. Frustration will exist where the purpose of the contract has become valueless by virtue of some supervening event not the fault of the party seeking discharge. To establish frustration, the following elements must be shown: (i) there is some supervening act or event leading to the frustration; (ii) at the time of entering into the contract, the parties did not reasonably foresee the act or event occurring; (iii) the purpose of the contract has been completely or almost completely destroyed by this act or event; and (iv) the purpose of the contract was realized by both parties at the time of making the contract. Here, it is doubtful that the purpose for which Fang made the contract was destroyed by the destruction of that one gallery, and there is no indication at all that Scratch was aware of Fang's purpose in making the contract. Thus, Fang cannot raise frustration of purpose as a defense to the contract.

Answer to Question 30

(B) The written agreement between Chip and Data was not to take effect unless Data notified Chip in writing by October 7 that Data had obtained a buyer. This notification was a condition precedent to Chip's absolute duty of performance. Upon failure of this condition, Chip is discharged from his duties under the contract. A condition is an event, other than the passage of time, the occurrence or nonoccurrence of which will create, limit, or extinguish the absolute duty to perform in the other contracting party. A promisor may insert conditions on his promise to prevent his duty of immediate performance from arising until the conditions are met, so that failure of a condition discharges the liability of the promisor, whose obligations on the conditional promise never mature. A condition precedent is one that must occur before an absolute duty of immediate performance arises in the other party. Here, the oral agreement between Chip and Data quite clearly states that the written agreement will not take effect unless Data supplies the required notification by October 7. Data's timely, written notification constitutes a condition precedent, because it is an event that must occur before an absolute duty to deliver the computer arises in Chip. The failure of Data to supply the required notification by October 7 thus constitutes a failure of a condition precedent, so that Chip is discharged from any obligations on the contract. (Note that evidence of the oral agreement does not run afoul of the parol evidence rule because where a party asserts the existence of an oral agreement that a written contract would not become effective until the occurrence of a condition, evidence of the oral understanding may be offered and received. This is simply a way of showing that the agreement never came into being, rather than a means of altering the written agreement.) (D) is incorrect because a condition subsequent is an event the occurrence of which cuts off an already existing absolute duty of performance. Here, Chip was not under an absolute duty unless Data fulfilled the terms of the condition. Thus, the condition that failed was precedent rather than subsequent. (A) is incorrect because contractual duties will be discharged by frustration if a supervening event unforeseen by the parties renders valueless the purpose of the contract. Here, the purpose of the contract (the sale of the computer) has not at all been rendered valueless by a supervening act or event. All that has happened is that, due to the sudden increase in value of the computer, Chip is now faced with having to sell a computer for much less than he could now get on the open market. This in no way establishes a discharge by frustration. (C) is incorrect because the mistake regarding the delivery date is a mere clerical error, rather than a mistake of fact going to a point that is material to the transaction. As such, this is not the type of mistake that would relieve either or both of the parties of their obligations under the contract.

Answer to Question 31

(C) Data's best argument is that Chip's assurances that there was no problem with Data's failure to provide written notification by October 7 amounts to a waiver of the condition. As explained in the answer to the preceding question, Data's written notification by October 7 that he had obtained a buyer for the computer was a condition precedent to Chip's absolute duty to perform under the contract. It is clear that Data did not provide the required notification by October 7; thus, the condition was not fulfilled. However, one having the benefit of a condition may indicate by words or conduct that he will not insist upon it. When a condition is broken, the beneficiary of the condition has an election: (i) he may terminate his liability; or (ii) he may continue under the contract. If a choice is made to continue under the contract, the person is deemed to have waived the condition. Chip was fully aware that Data had not satisfied the condition, yet, when speaking with Data on October 8, he stated unequivocally that "this was no problem." This is a definite indication that Chip elected to continue under the contract. Having so elected, Chip is deemed to have waived the condition. Therefore, Chip's duty of performance under the contract became absolute. Regarding (A), the only way the Statute of Frauds could bolster Data's position would be if the original oral agreement setting forth the condition were required by the Statute to be in writing. Thus, Data could argue that the condition is unenforceable because it is not in writing. However, the oral agreement is not of a type that falls within the purview of the Statute of Frauds. Therefore, the Statute of Frauds will provide no basis for an argument in response to Chip. Similarly, regarding (B), the parol evidence rule could help Data only if it could be used to preclude admissibility of the original oral agreement. Under the parol evidence rule, where the parties to a contract express their agreement in a writing with the intent that it embody the full and final expression of their bargain, any expression made prior to the writing and any oral expression contemporaneous with the writing is inadmissible to vary the terms of the writing. However, as noted in the answer to the preceding question, where it is asserted that there was an oral agreement that the written contract would not become effective until the occurrence of a condition, evidence of the oral agreement may be offered and received. Because the original oral agreement between Chip and Data established a condition precedent to the effectiveness of the written agreement, Data will be unable to raise the parol evidence rule as a bar to the admissibility of evidence relating to the oral agreement. (D) is unsupported by the facts. If a party with a duty of performance that is subject to a condition prevents the condition from occurring, he no longer has the benefit of the condition. This is referred to as excuse of condition by hindrance. Chip did nothing to prevent the occurrence of the condition regarding written notification by October 7. Consequently, it cannot be said that the condition is excused by hindrance.

Answer to Question 32

(D) Of all the alternatives listed, (D) is the only one that presents any real basis for supporting Eider's case. One of the general rules of contract construction, including contracts for goods under the U.C.C., is that courts will look to see what custom and usage are in the particular business and in the particular locale where the contract is either made or to be performed. [*See* U.C.C. §1-205] If the premise contained in (D) is established, Eider could claim that when Eider and Furry entered into the distribution contract, both parties implicitly understood that the custom of distributing only one brand of outerwear would be followed in their transaction. Under such circumstances, Eider may be able to successfully assert that Furry's distribution of Nolyn's outerwear constitutes a breach of contract. The fact that Nolyn's advertising campaign at least impliedly denigrates the appearance of Eider's outerwear (as in choice (A)), or that Eider's sales have dropped since the introduction of Nolyn's products (as in choice (B)) establishes no cause of action against Furry. Absent some provision in the contract, or some reference to custom and usage as mentioned in (D), there is no basis for holding that Furry was prohibited from distributing other companies' products, or that Furry can be held liable for a decline in Eider's sales due to sales or advertisements made by a company whose products are being distributed by Furry. (C) is incorrect because the written agreement between Furry and Eider would probably be deemed to be a full and final expression of the bargain, so that evidence of Furry's prior expression would be inadmissible to vary or supplement the writing under the parol evidence rule. Under U.C.C. section 2-202, a party cannot offer consistent additional terms if the writing was intended as a complete statement of the terms of the agreement. (In contrast, evidence of custom in the trade can be offered regardless of the completeness of the written agreement.) Also, Furry's statement ("This is an exclusive deal") is not specific enough on its face to establish whether he meant that Furry would distribute only Eider's products, or that Eider would have its products distributed in the state only by Furry, or perhaps some other meaning. The statement, even if admissible, is not definite enough to form a basis for a cause of action against Furry.

Answer to Question 33

(B) Although Vixen is entitled to reject the coat for even a minor defect such as one button being missing, she is required to give the seller an opportunity to cure this defect. Because this is a contract for the sale of goods, the Uniform Commercial Code applies. Pursuant to the U.C.C., if goods or any tender fail in any respect to conform to the contract, the buyer may reject the goods. This rule of perfect tender allows rejection for *any* defect, and does not require material breach. However, the perfect tender rule is softened by the rules allowing the seller to cure the defect by giving reasonable notice of an intention to cure and making a new tender of conforming goods within the time originally provided for performance. Also, where the buyer rejects a tender that the seller reasonably believed would be acceptable with or without money allowance, the seller, upon reasonable notification to the buyer, has a further reasonable time beyond the original contract time within which to make a conforming tender. Here, one button missing on a $12,000 coat is a very minor defect. However, pursuant to the perfect tender rule, Vixen has the right to reject the coat even for this defect. In turn, Minx is entitled to cure the defect by notifying Vixen of his intention to do so and by making a conforming tender. Minx has told Vixen that the tailor will sew on the button, which will conform the coat to the contract. Although the tailor, due to the holiday, will not be able to sew on the button by the agreed-upon date of delivery, being able to do so early in the morning of the day after falls within a further reasonable time beyond the original contract time within which to make a conforming tender. In any event, at this point Vixen must give Minx an opportunity to cure. (A) is incorrect because it fails to add that Minx must be allowed an opportunity to cure, as discussed above. (C) and (D) are incorrect because with the failure of perfect tender, Vixen is not required to accept the coat. This right of rejection is not affected by the minor nature of the defect, as (C) suggests. Similarly, the buyer's right of rejection is not impaired by the fact that the defect is easily curable, as (D) states.

Answer to Question 34

(C) Choice (C) is correct because Triton extended a merchant's firm offer and the U.C.C. requires that such offers be held open for a reasonable time. Offers not supported by consideration generally can be revoked at will by the offeror, even if he has promised not to revoke for a certain period. However, an offer by a **merchant** to buy or sell goods in a signed writing that, by its terms, gives assurances that it will be held open is not revocable for lack of consideration during the time stated, or if no time is stated, for a reasonable time (not to exceed three months). [U.C.C. §2-205] Triton is a merchant as defined by the U.C.C. because it regularly deals in goods such as the drill bits. [U.C.C. §2-104(1)] Therefore, because the written offer by Triton contained assurances that it was a "firm offer," Banfield's acceptance resulted in an enforceable contract with Triton, unless the court determines that the March 11 telegram was not sent within a commercially reasonable time. (A) is incorrect because, as stated above, Triton could not revoke its offer at will, but instead had to hold the offer open for a reasonable time since this was a merchant's firm offer. (A) would be correct if a firm offer were not involved. (B) is incorrect because while Triton's firm offer must be held open for a reasonable time, this period may be less than the U.C.C.'s three-month limit. As discussed above, a merchant's firm offer is not revocable for lack of consideration during the time stated, or if no time is stated, for a reasonable time (but in no event may such period exceed three months).

Therefore, while three months is the *maximum* period a firm offer can be held open under the U.C.C., a "reasonable" period for Triton's offer might be less than three months. (D) is incorrect because, as discussed above, the U.C.C. abolishes the need for consideration to make a merchant's firm offer irrevocable. While offers not supported by consideration generally can be revoked at will by the offeror, the U.C.C. provides that a merchant's firm offer is not revocable for lack of consideration.

Answer to Question 35

(D) The court should admit parol evidence to construe the ambiguous terms of the contract. The terms of a contract that are set forth in a writing intended as a final expression of the parties' agreement cannot be contradicted by evidence of any prior agreement or contemporaneous oral agreement. However, the terms of a contract may be *explained* or *supplemented* by parol evidence. [U.C.C. §2-202] The offer does not indicate whether the drill bits are to be sold only as a single lot. Therefore, to clear up the ambiguity in Triton's offer, the court could consider trade practices, past course of dealing, etc., in determining whether Banfield had a reasonable expectation of being able to purchase the goods piecemeal. (A) is incorrect because such a narrow interpretation is not clear from the ambiguous language in Triton's offer. When a term of a contract is ambiguous in a writing, the term may be explained by course of dealing, usage of trade, or course of performance. Because it is unclear from the language whether Triton's offer contemplated sale of the bits as a single lot or piecemeal, the offer is not subject to partial acceptance at the buyer's option, and the court may consider parol evidence to clear up the ambiguity. (B) is incorrect because it is not clear from the language of Triton's offer whether the bits were being offered as a single lot only. As discussed above, because the language of Triton's offer is ambiguous as to whether sale of the bits as a single lot or piecemeal was contemplated, Triton is not entitled to judgment solely on the basis of the written offer. Instead, the court will admit parol evidence, such as trade practices and past course of dealing, to clear up the ambiguity. (C) is incorrect because the court may consider other evidence to clear up ambiguities. As discussed above, the U.C.C. provides that a written contract's terms may be explained or supplemented by (i) course of dealing or usage in the trade, or (ii) the course of performance to date, even if the terms appear to be unambiguous. Therefore, Triton's ambiguous offer to sell the bits, which comes under the U.C.C., is not fatal to the formation of the contract because parol evidence is admissible on the question of whether the offer contemplated a piecemeal sale of the bits.

Answer to Question 36

(D) Choice (D) properly states the U.C.C. position regarding the terms of the contract. Under the U.C.C., if both parties to a contract are merchants, additional terms in an acceptance will be included in the contract unless (i) they *materially alter* the original contract; (ii) the offer *expressly limits acceptance* to the terms of the offer; or (iii) the offeror has already objected to the particular terms, or objects within a reasonable time after notice of them is received. [U.C.C. §2-207(2)] Triton and Banfield are both merchants because they regularly deal in goods such as the drill bits. [U.C.C. §2-104(1)] Therefore, their contract for the sale of the bits comes under Article 2 and will include the term of Triton's offer plus those in Banfield's purported acceptance which do not amount to a material alteration of the offer or to which Triton did not object within a reasonable time. Note that Triton's offer did not expressly limit acceptance of its terms. (A) is incorrect because this was a contract between two merchants. Contract formation under the U.C.C. for contracts between merchants is governed by the rule stated above. If one of the parties were not a merchant, (A) would be correct—if one of the parties to a contract for sale of goods is not a merchant and the acceptance includes additional or different terms, such terms are considered to be mere proposals that do not become part of the contract unless the offeror accepts. [U.C.C. §2-207(1)] However, because this is a contract between merchants, Banfield's terms regarding mode of shipment will be included in the contract unless they materially alter the original contract, as discussed above. (B) is incorrect because it does not fully state the Code's "battle of the forms" provision. The choice fails to mention Triton's power to object within a reasonable time. (C) is incorrect because, like (B), it does not note Triton's power to object within a reasonable time.

Answer to Question 37

(C) If Hank refuses to pay, Leon will recover a reasonable price for his services as a contract remedy. Generally, an offer must be certain and definite in its terms. However, all terms do not have to be spelled out completely. Most courts today will supply reasonable terms if the terms are consistent with the parties' intent as otherwise expressed. Terms that can be supplied by a reasonableness standard include a price term. Unless the parties have shown at the time of contracting that they do not want a contract until they have agreed on a price, a reasonable price will be supplied by the court. [*See* Restatement (Second) of Contracts §33, comment e] Here, the parties evidenced an intent to enter into a contract: Hank agreed to pay Leon to make it rain and Leon undertook to perform by operating the machine. Nor does the absence of a duration term preclude enforcement by Leon. If the duration of a contract for employment or services is not specified, it is construed as a contract terminable at the will of either party. Here, however, Leon has fully performed prior to either party terminating, and can therefore enforce the contract. Hence, Leon can recover a reasonable price for his services. (A) is incorrect because under contract law, a party is entitled to the other party's performance as soon as all conditions precedent have been satisfied; the party need not prove that he caused the conditions to be satisfied, merely that they are in fact satisfied. (B) is incorrect because mere absence of the price term is not sufficient to prevent a contractual remedy; as discussed above, a court could find the offer certain enough and supply a reasonable price term. (D) is incorrect because the contract remedy would be a reasonable price; the court may take into account Leon's normal fee when it determines the reasonable price, but it will not be bound by it.

Answer to Question 38

(A) Leon will be able to enforce the contract with Will because it was supported by consideration. For a promise to be enforceable as a contract, there must be an offer, an acceptance, and consideration. There was an offer here made by Will ("If you [Leon] make it rain by tomorrow, I'll pay you $20,000."), Leon accepted the offer by performing, and the performance was valid consideration since Leon was not under a preexisting duty to make it rain by the next evening; Leon agreed with Hank to try to make it rain, but there was no time limitation and no specified consideration. Thus, Will's condition that Leon had to make it rain by the following day was new consideration and not a preexisting duty. Therefore, the contract is enforceable. (B) is incorrect because a contract is usually governed by the terms agreed upon by the parties, and Will and Leon agreed that if Leon made it rain by the next day, Will would pay Leon $20,000. Thus, Leon should be paid $20,000. (C) is incorrect because, as discussed above, Leon's making it rain *by the next day* was consideration sufficient to support Will's promise to Leon. Moreover, Leon probably did not owe any duty to Hank in the first place, since the offer appears to be for a unilateral contract—an offer looking for performance rather than a promise to perform, and which does not become binding until performance. Thus, even if there was a contract, Leon was not under a duty when he performed for Will. (D) is incorrect because a promise to pay $20,000 in exchange for performance is a legal detriment.

Answer to Question 39

(B) Bill must pay Sam the additional $50 because the parties have an enforceable contract. A contract for the sale of goods (the car) was formed when Bill said, "You've got a deal." The parties then orally agreed to a modification of the contract when Sam called Bill at work. Under the Statute of Frauds provision in the U.C.C., which applies to all contracts for the sale of goods, a promise requires a writing signed by the party to be charged to be enforceable if it is for the sale of goods of $500 or more. Here, the contract as modified is under $500, so it is enforceable even though it is not in writing. (A) is incorrect because the fact that the original contract was not in writing is irrelevant to the issue of whether the modified contract is enforceable. If the modification had caused the contract to reach or exceed $500, Sam could not have collected the additional $50 from Bill. (C) is incorrect because under U.C.C. section 2-209, no consideration is needed for a good faith modification of a contract for the sale of goods. (D) is incorrect because the U.C.C. rules on modifications and the Statute of Frauds apply to all contracts for the sale of goods, not just those between merchants.

Answer to Question 40

(A) If Leroy's letter was an offer, and shipment of the units was an acceptance, then the shipment of nonconforming goods both created a contract and breached that contract, affording Leroy's an immediate cause of action. The contract at issue involves the sale of goods, and is thus governed by Article 2 of the U.C.C. Under U.C.C. section 2-206, an offer to buy goods for current or prompt shipment is construed as inviting acceptance either by a promise to ship or by current or prompt shipment of conforming or nonconforming goods. The shipment of goods, even though they are nonconforming, is an acceptance creating a bilateral contract and a breach unless the seller reasonably notifies the buyer that the nonconforming goods are offered only as an accommodation to the buyer. Here, if Leroy's letter was an offer, then AMM was invited to accept by either a promise to ship or a prompt shipment.

If AMM's shipment of the units is held to be an acceptance of Leroy's offer, it will be because the court determined that Willard's letter accompanying the shipment was not sufficient as an accommodation notice (which would have made the shipment a counteroffer rather than an acceptance). The units contain nonconforming goods, because the adaptors are not compatible with Sony systems, as specified in Leroy's offer. The shipment of nonconforming goods as an acceptance both created a bilateral contract between the parties and constituted a breach of that contract by AMM, thus allowing Leroy's to sue for any appropriate damages for breach of contract. (B) is incorrect because, if Willard's letter was an acceptance, then there is a chance that Leroy's will be bound by the terms of the letter. Between merchants, additional proposed terms in an acceptance become part of the contract unless: (i) they materially alter the original contract; (ii) the offer expressly limits acceptance to its terms; or (iii) the offeror has already objected to the particular terms, or objects within a reasonable time after receiving notice of them. [U.C.C. §2-207] AMM and Leroy's are both merchants, in that they deal in goods of the kind involved in the contract. If Willard's letter is an acceptance of Leroy's offer, then the sentence disclaiming compatibility of the adaptors with other game systems is an additional proposed term. Leroy's offer did not expressly limit acceptance to its terms, nor did Leroy's object to the additional terms. Thus, the additional terms will become part of the contract unless the court finds that they materially alter the original contract. If these terms are held to be part of the contract, Leroy's will have no cause of action for the incompatibility of the adaptors with Sony systems. Because (B) creates a framework in which Leroy's might lose (*i.e.,* if it is found that the additional terms do not materially alter the original contract), (B) is not as good an answer as (A). (C) and (D) represent the worst scenarios for Leroy's. If Willard's letter was an offer as stated in (C) and acceptance of the units by the Leroy's employee was an acceptance of the offer, there is a contract based on the terms in Willard's letter; *i.e.,* no warranties as to the compatibility of the adaptors with any other game systems. In that event, Leroy's would have no cause of action against AMM based on the adaptors' incompatibility with Sony systems. The same result would arise if shipment of the units were treated as a counteroffer as stated in (D) (this would be the result if Willard's letter were held to be a sufficient accommodation notice under U.C.C. section 2-206(1)(b)). Acceptance of the units would be acceptance of the counteroffer according to the terms of the letter accompanying the shipment, so that Leroy's could not bring an action based on the adaptors' incompatibility with Sony systems.

Answer to Question 41

(C) Leroy's measure of loss should be the difference between the value of the goods as received and the value they would have had if they had conformed to the contract. When goods are delivered that do not conform to the parties' contract, the buyer has the option to accept all, reject all, or accept any commercial units and reject the rest. If the buyer chooses to accept the goods, as Leroy's did here, he has a right to recover damages for the nonconformity. The standard measure of damages as to accepted goods is the difference between the value of the goods as delivered and the value they would have had if they had been conforming (plus incidental and consequential damages). Here, the goods as delivered were worth $2,000 per lot ($1,000 for the cartridges and $1,000 for the adaptors) and they would have been worth $2,500 if they had been as the contract required. Thus, (C) is correct. (A) is incorrect because it describes the remedy of "cover," and cover is available only when the buyer rejects the goods. (If the buyer rejects the goods, he may either cancel the contract or buy substitute goods and charge the breaching seller for the substitutes.) (B) is incorrect because the buyer is entitled to return of the entire contract price only when he cancels the contract. Otherwise, the buyer would get a windfall based on the value of the goods received. (D) is incorrect because, as indicated above, a buyer who accepts nonconforming goods is still entitled to damages.

Answer to Question 42

(B) Leroy's is entitled to rescission on the ground of mutual mistake. Rescission is a remedy that discharges the contractual duties of the parties and puts an end to the transaction, leaving the parties as though the contract had never been made. Unilateral rescission results where one of the parties desires to rescind it but the other party refuses to agree to a rescission. For unilateral rescission to be granted, the party desiring rescission must have adequate legal grounds. One ground for unilateral rescission is mutual mistake of a material fact. If AMM reasonably believed that the adaptors were compatible with all game systems when shipped to Leroy's, then both parties were operating under a mistake of fact. This mistake concerns a basic assumption on which the contract is made, because the compatibility of the adaptors with all systems was a fact without which Leroy's would not have entered into the transaction. The mistake creates a material imbalance in the agreed exchange, and the party seeking avoidance (Leroy's) did not assume the risk of the mistake. Because of this mutual mistake of material fact, which existed at the time the contract was entered into, Leroy's is entitled to rescission of the contract. Choices (C) and (D) may look attractive because if a plaintiff is entitled to rescission and has paid money to the defendant in an attempt to perform his duties under the contract, he is entitled to restitution. Here, as part of its rescission remedy, Leroy's would be entitled to restitution of the purchase price if it has already paid AMM. However, it will also have to return the cartridges and adaptors to AMM before it will be granted restitution. [*See* Restatement (Second) of Contracts §384] (B) is a better choice than (C) because restitution of the purchase price is dependent on—and just one element of—the remedy of rescission. (D) is additionally incorrect because, if Leroy's is entitled to restitution, it will receive the entire amount it paid to AMM (*i.e.,* the purchase price of the two lots) rather than simply the value of adaptors. (A) is incorrect because AMM is not obligated to provide adaptors compatible with all three systems. Even if it were, this would not be an appropriate remedy because a buyer has a right to specific performance of a sales contract only where the goods are unique or in other proper circumstances. [U.C.C. §2-716] There is no indication that adaptors compatible with all game systems are unique. Thus, a contract for the sale of such goods is not an appropriate subject for specific performance.

Answer to Question 43

(A) Downtown will win because there was no consideration to support its promise to pay Uptown the additional $1,000 per month. This question looks like it concerns third-party beneficiaries, but it actually presents a consideration issue. Generally, there must be consideration for modification of a contract, and a promise to perform an act that a party is already obliged to do is not sufficient consideration (the "preexisting legal duty" rule). Here, Swift is promising to do exactly what it was obliged to do under its original contract with Downtown; thus, there is no consideration to support the promise to increase the fee. (B) is wrong because Uptown is an intended beneficiary, not an incidental beneficiary. An intended beneficiary is one who is clearly intended to benefit from the agreement. Hence, Uptown was named in the agreement and performance was to be made directly to it, and so it is clearly an intended beneficiary. (C) is wrong even though it is true that Uptown is an intended creditor beneficiary. Despite this status, Uptown will not recover because there was no consideration to support the modification of the contract. The status of creditor beneficiary does not give Uptown any more rights than Swift would have had to enforce the agreement, and Swift could not enforce the agreement for the additional money because there was no consideration. (D) is wrong because it is based on the rule of U.C.C. section 2-209, which states that an agreement subject to the U.C.C. does not need consideration to be binding. However, the U.C.C. governs only in cases of the sale of goods, and this question presents a contract for services. Thus, the U.C.C. does not apply and the common law rule requiring consideration controls.

Answer to Question 44

(A) Jacques made an offer, which was accepted by DBA by doing the requested act. Jacques's offer was to guarantee the purchase price, up to $10,000, of a car in exchange for DBA's selling a car to his daughter. This offer traditionally could be accepted by an act (the sale of the car), but today could also be accepted by a promise to sell the car to Jacques's daughter. Here, DBA accepted the offer by selling the car, and it then notified Jacques of the acceptance by mail. A contract was formed when DBA sold the car. Therefore, when Francine did not pay for it, DBA could collect from Jacques. (B) is wrong because it relies on a promissory estoppel theory, but here Jacques's promise is supported by a bargained-for exchange (his promise in exchange for DBA's sale); thus, there is no need to rely on promissory estoppel. (C) is wrong because DBA's *motive* in selling the car to Francine is not relevant. DBA did something it was not under a duty to do (sell the car to Francine) and that is sufficient consideration to support Jacques's promise to guarantee payment. (D) is wrong because the offer was accepted when DBA did the act, and Jacques was alive at that time.

Answer to Question 45

(C) The unilateral option contract between Plunger and Jenny to keep Plunger's offer open was effectively rescinded by Jenny's expressed intent to make a gift of the obligation owed her. The typical case of rescission involves a bilateral contract where neither party has yet performed; *i.e.,* the duties of both parties are still executory. However, no contract to do the plumbing work has been created yet, because Jenny has not communicated her acceptance of the bid to Plunger. Despite her use of Plunger's bid to prepare her own bid, she is free to award the plumbing work to someone else if she is awarded the general contract. Hence, the contract to do the plumbing cannot be rescinded because it has not been created. Another contract is present under this fact pattern, however. Under section 87 of the Restatement (Second) of Contracts, Plunger's offer is binding as an option contract because Jenny reasonably relied on it to submit her bid. The option contract here is unilateral: Jenny's acceptance of the option contract by using the bid also consti-tuted performance of her duties under the option contract. In a unilateral contract case, a rescis-sion promise must be supported by either (i) an offer of new consideration, (ii) elements of promissory estoppel (*i.e.,* detrimental reliance), or (iii) the offeree's manifestation of an intent to make a gift of the obligation owed her. The first two alternatives are absent in these facts, but the gift alternative is indicated by Jenny's statement that she will "forget" that Plunger ever made the bid. Jenny's response was an effective rescission of the option contract. (A) is an incorrect choice even though it is a true statement. A discharge of contractual duties by means of a release re-quires additional consideration or some substitute, such as a signed writing or reliance by the offeror on the discharge. Here there is no additional consideration to support a release, as choice (A) indicates, but Jenny will not win because a rescission has taken place. (B) is incorrect be-cause a large dollar amount for purposes of the Statute of Frauds is irrelevant unless there is a contract for the sale of goods, which must be in writing if the goods are priced at $500 or more. The agreement between Jenny and Plunger involved a contract for services, which is not within the $500 provision of the Statute. (D) is incorrect because, as discussed above, a release requires additional consideration, a signed writing, or detrimental reliance by the offeror. Since none of these is indicated by the facts, a release has not taken place.

Answer to Question 46

(B) Sarte will not be able to enforce his demand because the contract, as modified, is within the Statute of Frauds, and there is no writing evidencing the modification. Since the contract here is for the sale of goods, the Uniform Commercial Code will govern. Under the U.C.C., a modification of a con-tract is enforceable even though it is not supported by consideration (which is required under the common law), as long as the modification is sought in good faith. Here, the modification was sought in good faith (the civil war raised the price of yttrium, making the contract unprofitable). Thus, the modification may be enforceable despite the lack of consideration. However, the U.C.C. also provides that contract modifications must comply with the Statute of Frauds if the contract as modified is within the mandate of the Statute. Under the Statute, a contract for the sale of goods for $500 or more must be in writing and signed by the party to be charged to be enforceable. Here, the contract as modified is within the Statute and the modification is not in writing; thus it is unenforce-able. (A) is incorrect because the parol evidence rule does not prohibit introduction of the modifica-tion here. The rule provides that the terms of a contract set forth in a writing intended as a final expression of the parties' agreement cannot be contradicted by evidence of any prior or contempo-raneous oral statement. The agreement to modify the price to $12,000 is neither prior nor contem-poraneous, but rather was subsequent to the written contract. Thus, the parol evidence rule will not prevent admission of the modification. (C) is incorrect because even though the modification is admissible under the parol evidence rule, it is unenforceable under the Statute of Frauds. The parol evidence rule does not override the Statute; both hurdles must be overcome before a contract may be varied. (D) is incorrect because there was no reliance on the waiver. It is true that an attempted modification, invalid because it does not comply with the Statute of Frauds, may operate as a waiver of the right to enforce the contract as written. However, waivers may be withdrawn unless the retraction would be unjust because of a mat...

Here, with prices dropping to prewar levels, Sart...

anticipated and there is no other evidence that he...

waiver. Thus, (D) is incorrect.

Answer to Question 47

(C) If Behemothtoy acts in good faith in setting its requir...
contract may be assigned. This case is the rare exceptic...
of the right to receive goods under a requirements contr...
"requirements" contract: Ironmongers must sell Toyco a...
its toys. Generally, the right to receive goods under a requ...
because the obligor's duties could change significantly. In...
seem possible because Behemothtoy is a larger company tha... ...greater.
However, the U.C.C. would allow the assignment of requirem... *assignee acts in*
good faith not to alter the terms of the contract. [U.C.C. §2-30... ...C. applies here because
goods are involved.) Thus, if Behemothtoy demands double the ...ount of steel that Toyco usually
ordered, the action would not be in good faith and would not be enforced against Ironmongers.
However, if Behemothtoy's requirements remain about the same as Toyco's, Ironmongers could
be required to honor its contract, now assigned to Behemothtoy. (A) is wrong because requirements contracts may be nonassignable, even without a nonassignment clause. Thus, the clause
would be irrelevant. The only thing that could allow assignment of a requirements contract is a
good faith limitation, as in choice (C). (B) is wrong because it is overbroad. It is true that the
U.C.C. appears to allow requirements contracts to be assigned, *but* the good faith limitation is
crucial. As stated, if Behemothtoy requires twice the amount of steel as Toyco, the contract would
not be assigned. (D) is wrong because it is also too broad. Although many requirements contracts
are not assignable, as explained, the U.C.C. would allow assignment if there is a good faith
limitation on the requirements.

Answer to Question 48

(A) If the quantity was stated in the February 3 letter, the Statute of Frauds is satisfied and Smithson
may prevail. This contract is for the purchase and sale of goods; thus, the U.C.C. applies. The
Statute of Frauds requires that a contract for the sale of goods for $500 or more must be in writing.
However, U.C.C. section 2-201(2) provides that in a deal between merchants, a writing confirming
the deal sent by one party will bind *both* parties, unless the other party objects in writing within 10
days. Also, the U.C.C. requires that the quantity term be included in the writing for it to be sufficient under the Statute of Frauds. [U.C.C. §2-201(1)] Here, Ridewell's objection came after 10 days
and so Smithson's letter confirming the deal is sufficient for the Statute of Frauds if it lists the
quantity. (B) is wrong because the quantity term is the key to the sufficiency of a memorandum. All
other terms may be proved by parol evidence, but the quantity term must be in the writing. (C) is
wrong because it does not bear on the Statute of Frauds issue, but rather on the issue of the additional terms. (D) is wrong because of the rule stated above that in a contract between merchants a
written confirmation by one party binds both parties, unless objected to within 10 days. Thus,
Ridewell can be charged although it has not signed the memorandum.

Answer to Question 49

(C) Smithson must pay the original price if the discount submitted in the confirmation materially
alters the original deal. Under the U.C.C., in a deal between merchants, additional terms in the

acceptance or in the writte...
tional terms materially the off...
the offer, or the...
variation of the...
in the cont...
attempt...
Un...

confirmation will be included as part of the deal *unless* the addi-
alter the original deal, the offer expressly limits acceptance to the terms of
eror objects to the terms within a reasonable time. [U.C.C. §2-207(2)] If
price term by 20% is a material alteration, then the discount term is not included
act and Smithson must pay the original price. (A) and (B) are wrong because they
to use the U.C.C. rules regarding open price terms in a material alteration situation.
er the U.C.C., if the price is not stated in the contract but it appears that the parties intended
to form a contract, a reasonable price will be implied. For the price to be implied: (i) there must
be nothing about price in the contract; (ii) the price must have been left to be agreed upon later;
or (iii) the price was to be fixed by a third party or external factor. None of these situations
occurred here; thus, the open price term rules do not apply. (D) is wrong because only an additional term that is *not a material variation* becomes a part of the deal in the absence of an objection. Therefore, even without an objection by Ridewell, if the discount materially alters the deal,
it is not part of the contract.

Answer to Question 50

(A) Shirley may keep the $6,000 as liquidated damages. A liquidated damages clause is enforceable
if: (i) damages are difficult to ascertain at the time of the making of the contract, and (ii) the
damages are a reasonable forecast of compensatory damages. Here, Shirley was unsure what her
damages would be if she did not receive the sales proceeds from Plushacre, but $10,000 seemed
a reasonable amount. Thus, both criteria for valid liquidated damages clauses are met. (B) is incorrect because impossibility must be "objective"; *i.e.,* performance cannot be accomplished by
anyone. Physical incapacity of a person necessary to effectuate the contract may discharge
contractual duties *if* that person's performance is clearly impossible. (Usually this occurs in
personal services contracts, where only that one person can perform the required duty.) Although
Burton was seriously ill, it is not clear that this made it *impossible* for him to produce the $94,000.
Without more facts, it is reasonable to assume that someone else could have delivered the money
or that his mortgage would still have gone through, etc. (C) is incorrect because the conditions
for Royal's payment were not met: it is debatable whether he produced a "ready, willing, and
able" buyer, and in any event the sale did not actually proceed through closing. (D) is incorrect
because Royal was to receive proceeds from the sale of the property; the $6,000 was damages
and not sale proceeds.

Answer to Question 51

(A) Sinead can use both a promissory estoppel theory and a bargain and exchange theory to collect
from Sheila's estate. To be enforceable, a contract must be supported by consideration or there
must be a substitute for consideration. Generally, consideration requires a bargained-for exchange of something of legal value from each party. To be bargained-for, the promise must
induce the detriment and the detriment must induce the promise. Here, Sinead was induced to
purchase the shawl and incur a debt in exchange for Aunt Sheila's promise to pay, and Aunt
Sheila was induced to pay in exchange for Sinead's promise to purchase the shawl and attend the
festival. It does not matter that Aunt Sheila did not receive an economic benefit—influencing
Sinead's mind is sufficient to establish an exchange. Both parties gave something of legal value
since Aunt Sheila had no legal duty to pay for a shawl for Sinead and Sinead had no legal duty to
purchase a shawl and attend the festival. Therefore, there was a bargained-for exchange of
something of legal value and a contract was formed. Thus, II. states a theory that is helpful to
Sinead. Promissory estoppel (I.) is also helpful. Promissory estoppel is a substitute for consideration: A promise is enforceable to the extent necessary to prevent injustice if the promisor should

reasonably expect to induce action of a definite and substantial kind, and such action is induced. Here, Aunt Sheila's promise would reasonably induce Sinead to buy the shawl and she was in fact so induced. Thus, promissory estoppel would allow Sinead to recover. Neither of the other two theories will lead to enforcement of Aunt Sheila's promise. A promise to make a gift is unenforceable for lack of consideration, and this result is not changed where the promise to make the gift is conditional and the conditions have been fulfilled. In fact, an argument that there was a conditional gift would negate the bargain and exchange needed to establish an enforceable contract, since it would involve arguing that Aunt Sheila did not intend to induce Sinead's detriment (*i.e.,* Aunt Sheila was not seeking to trade her promise to pay in exchange for Sinead's promise to attend), but rather was merely stating upon what conditions Sinead could receive her gift. Therefore, III. is not helpful to Sinead. An argument that there was an account stated (IV.) is inappropriate because that is a contract where parties who have had a series of transactions agree to a final balance due from one to the other. Here, Sinead is seeking to enforce a single transaction. Therefore, (A) is correct, and (B), (C), and (D) are wrong.

Answer to Question 52

(A) Erin will prevail against Sheila's estate because Erin is an intended third-party beneficiary and her right to enforce the contract has vested. The rights of an intended third-party beneficiary vest when the beneficiary (i) manifests assent to the promise in a manner invited or requested by the parties; (ii) brings suit to enforce the promise; or (iii) materially changes her position in justifiable reliance on the promise. Here, Erin qualifies as an intended beneficiary of the agreement between Sheila and Sinead because Erin was expressly designated in the contract, she was to receive performance directly from Sheila, and she stood in an existing contractual relationship with Sinead that required Sinead to either pay for the shawl or return it, making it likely that Sinead's purpose in making the arrangement with Sheila was to satisfy the obligation to Erin. Erin can enforce the contract because her rights vested when she sent the bill to Sheila at Sheila's request. Thus, Erin will prevail against Sheila's estate. (B) is wrong because Sinead does have a duty to give the clothes to the charity; if she does not do so, she will be in breach of her contract with Sheila, and this would give Sheila a defense to payment. However, Sinead's time for performance (Christmastime) has not yet occurred and so Sinead is not in breach. Nevertheless, this fact is not the reason Erin will recover; she will recover due to her status as an intended beneficiary, not because this possible defense has been negated. (C) is wrong because both the result and the rationale are incorrect. Erin is not relying on Sheila's implied promise to her in the phone call; she is seeking to enforce her rights as a third-party beneficiary of the agreement between Sheila and Sinead. Even if Sheila had not called Erin, Erin could still have recovered against Sheila's estate because of her status as a third-party beneficiary. (D) is wrong because Sinead's giving the clothes to charity is not a condition that must be fulfilled before Sheila's estate must pay. Sheila promised to pay for the shawl if Sinead promised to donate the clothes; *i.e.,* the consideration for Sheila's promise was Sinead's promise, not her actually donating the clothes. As soon as Sinead made the promise, Sheila's duty to pay became absolute. (If Sinead does not donate the clothes, she will be in breach of her contract with Sheila, but Sheila's performance was not conditioned on Sinead's donating the clothes.)

Answer to Question 53

(B) Wendy's strongest argument is that Brikk had drawn up both the detailed specifications of the agreement and the plans for the house. When both parties entering into a contract are mistaken about facts relating to the agreement, the contract may be voidable by the adversely affected party if (i) the mistake concerns a basic assumption on which the contract is made; (ii) the mistake has a material effect on the agreed-upon exchange; and (iii) the party seeking avoidance did not assume the risk of the mistake. Here, it is likely that neither party knew that the soil conditions were unsuitable. But if Brikk had drawn up the specifications and plans for the house, it will be more likely that the court will conclude that he has assumed the risk of any mistake as to the sufficiency of the soil to support the house, and will not be able to avoid the contract. (A) might be helpful to Wendy, but it might also be harmful to her and so is not as good an answer as (B). The fact that it is physically possible to build the house at an increased cost negates the defense of impossibility (which is also unavailable because the impossibility existed at the time the contract was entered into). However, the argument may aid a defense of impracticability, which is available where the party to perform has encountered extreme and unreasonable difficulty in performing which was not anticipated by either party. While a moderate increase in the cost of building would not be sufficient for impracticability, the fact that performance here will cost over 300% more than the anticipated cost will support the impracticability defense. [*See* Restatement (Second) of Contracts §261, comment d] (C) would not be as helpful to Wendy's case as (A) because it only indicates that there was a mutual mistake, and a contract can be avoided for mutual mistake unless the adversely affected party bears the risk of the mistake, which the fact in (B) would establish. (D) is irrelevant because whether Dorothea, the third-party beneficiary, knew of the contract affects only her ability to enforce the contract. Wendy, as a party to the contract, may enforce regardless of whether Dorothea knew of it.

Answer to Question 54

(C) Brikk will prevail because he may raise all defenses that he had against Wendy against Dorothea. Dorothea is an intended third-party beneficiary of the contract between Brikk and Wendy, since the contract specifically indicated that the keys to the house were to be turned over to Dorothea. Generally, a third-party beneficiary has rights under the contract as soon as she does something to vest her rights (manifests assent to the promise, brings suit to enforce the promise, or materially changes position by justifiably relying on the promise). Here, Dorothea materially changed her position by justifiably allowing her option on the other house to lapse. Generally, once the third-party beneficiary's rights have vested, the original contracting parties may not modify the contract without the assent of the third-party beneficiary. However, the third-party beneficiary is subject to any defenses that the promisor could have used against the original promisee, and here Brikk could have used the defense of impracticability against the promisee, as indicated in the previous answer. Therefore, he could use that defense against Dorothea to avoid having to pay damages for not building the house as he originally agreed. (A) is incorrect because although it is true that Dorothea's rights had vested, the answer fails to take into account the defenses available to Brikk. (B) is incorrect because there was consideration for the modification. Since the original contract was impracticable to perform, Brikk would have been discharged. By agreeing to build the new house, he undertook something that he was not otherwise bound to do. Likewise, because of the impracticability, Wendy would have been discharged from her original contract to pay. (D) is incorrect because Dorothea is not an incidental beneficiary; rather she is an intended beneficiary since she was specifically mentioned in the contract as the recipient of the house.

Answer to Question 55

(C) Mike's silence while Charlotte deepened his well will be treated by the court as an acceptance by silence of an implied-in-fact contract. An implied-in-fact contract is formed by manifestations of assent other than oral or written language, *i.e.,* by conduct. Where a person knowingly accepts offered benefits, such conduct, viewed objectively, may be said to manifest an agreement to the conferral of such benefits, resulting in a contract implied in fact. While generally an acceptance must be communicated to an offeror to be effective, courts will often find an acceptance where an offeree silently accepts offered benefits. In (C), Charlotte (albeit mistakenly) conferred upon Mike a benefit by deepening the well on his property. Although there was no oral or written communication between Charlotte and Mike prior to Charlotte's deepening the well, Mike's conduct in standing by and doing or saying nothing while Charlotte performed the work will be taken as a manifestation of Mike's assent to the performance of this work. Thus, a court will be likely to find an implied-in-fact contract in this situation. In (B), while we are told that state law permits Hugh to charge as much as $5 for such notarization services, the conduct of the parties under the circumstances is as consistent with a conclusion that Hugh is now performing a small favor free of charge for an old friend as it is with a conclusion that Deborah is to pay for the notarization. Therefore, (B) is much less likely than (C) to be found to reflect an implied-in-fact contract. Regarding (A), Norm is simply performing a gratuitous humanitarian act by saving Ford's life. There is no conduct on the part of either party manifesting any assent to an agreement whereby Norm was to save Ford from choking in return for compensation from Ford. This was merely an emergency situation with no implications of mutual assent between Norm and Ford. (D) is incorrect for the same reason as (A). Although Barrington received a benefit by Babbington's payment of his credit card bill (for which Babbington might have a quasi-contract remedy against Barrington), Barrington did nothing to indicate assent to Babbington's conduct. Hence, mutual assent for purposes of an implied-in-fact contract is not present here.

Answer to Question 56

(B) In entering into the contract, the possibility that Harry would die shortly after paying the premium and therefore receive virtually nothing in return should have been apparent to both parties. Actually, both parties took risks in this regard, as Harry could have incurred medical expenses for a catastrophic illness during his lifetime that would have required Insco to make payments far exceeding the one-time $30,000 premium. Harry and Insco were equally aware of these various possibilities, yet they freely entered into an agreement with this knowledge and on terms that were apparently acceptable to each of them. Despite the apparent unfairness of the result, a court generally will not interfere with the parties' right to make their own deal. Thus, Insco is entitled to the premium. (D) is incorrect because the price paid by Harry was freely arrived at by the parties. There is no indication of any inequality in bargaining power or any other factors indicative of hardship or oppression exerted against Harry by Insco. Harry was free to enter into an agreement that turned out to be a bad one for him. Therefore, there are no factors pointing to the existence of unconscionability. (A) is incorrect because Insco prevails regardless of whether it declined to take another applicant. As detailed above, the possibility of Harry's death occurring in the time frame that it did was part of the risk voluntarily undertaken by the parties, and as such, will not afford a basis for preventing Insco from recovering the premium payment. The payment of $30,000 in return for Insco's promise of catastrophic insurance coverage was part of a bargained-for exchange. Regarding (C), discharge by frustration of contractual purpose requires that, at the time of entering into the contract, the parties did not reasonably foresee the occurrence of the act or event leading to the frustration. Here, the parties should have foreseen the possibility that Harry would die shortly after the policy took effect. Consequently, this is not a proper case for the application of frustration of purpose.

Answer to Question 57

(D) Brubaker will prevail because Lehman's promise was supported by a bargained-for exchange. Legal detriment will result if the promisee does something he was under no obligation to do or refrains from doing something that he has a legal right to do. The detriment to the promisee need not involve any actual loss to the promisee or benefit to the promisor. Here, there was a bargained-for exchange in Brubaker's forgoing of a claim in which he had a good faith belief, even though the claim might have been worthless. Thus, (D) is correct, and (A) is wrong. (C) is not a good answer because there is no need to rely on promissory estoppel when an enforceable agreement, which can be enforced according to its terms, is present. (B) is wrong because there was more than a moral obligation. Even though Lehman may have been motivated by a feeling of moral obligation, there was a bargained-for exchange between him and Brubaker.

Answer to Question 58

(D) None of the defenses would be effective for Smith. I. is not valid because it does not matter that Smith's contract was with Lehman; Wolcott was an intended third-party beneficiary of their contract. An intended beneficiary can enforce the contract once her rights have vested, such as by manifesting assent to the promise in a manner invited or requested by the parties. Here, Wolcott's rights would have vested when she assented to have Smith do the work. II. is not valid; the fact that Wolcott furnished no consideration is immaterial because consideration was furnished by Lehman. III. is not valid. A novation occurs when a new contract substitutes a new party to receive benefits and assume duties that had originally belonged to one of the original parties under the terms of the old contract. Here, the fact that Smith subsequently contracted with Lehman does not establish a novation; there was no agreement between all of the parties to discharge the existing contract. Thus, (D) is correct, and (A), (B), and (C) are incorrect.

Answer to Question 59

(B) Weldon will lose because Cuddly Toy never accepted the offer. For a communication to be an offer, it must contain a promise, undertaking, or commitment to enter into a contract, rather than a mere invitation to begin negotiations. The broader the communicating media, *e.g.*, publications, the more likely it is that the courts will view the communication as merely the solicitation of an offer. An advertisement in a trade journal generally is construed as an invitation to submit offers, not an offer itself. It is an announcement of the price at which the seller is willing to receive offers. Thus, Weldon's fax was an offer that was never accepted by Cuddly Toy Co. (A) is wrong because if the communication were otherwise a contract, the less formal requirements for certainty in contracts under the U.C.C. (which governs here because goods are involved) would not be a bar to enforcement. (C) is wrong because, as discussed above, the ad is not an offer. (D) is incorrect because the ad in the trade journal was not a promise; hence, Weldon cannot rely on promissory estoppel or detrimental reliance to recover.

Answer to Question 60

(B) If Weldon can cover (*i.e.*, buy the dolls from another source), then a court will not grant specific performance. If the seller fails to deliver goods under a valid contract, the buyer has a number of remedies available, including the right to cover and the right to obtain specific performance if appropriate. A buyer may obtain specific performance of a contract for the sale of goods if the goods are unique or in short supply, but that is not the case here if Weldon can buy them from another retailer. If he does so, he can get the difference between the cost of the substitute goods and the contract price. Thus, (B) is correct. (A) is incorrect because, as discussed above, under certain circumstances a seller of goods may be subject to specific performance. (C) is incorrect because even though Cuddly is the only manufacturer of the dolls, if Weldon can cover by buying them from another retailer, specific performance is not the appropriate remedy. (D) is irrelevant to whether specific performance is granted and is unsupported by the facts.

Answer to Question 61

(C) Cuddly will not recover because sale during the Christmas season was a condition precedent. A condition precedent is one that must occur before an absolute duty of immediate performance arises in the other party. Based on the facts here, the intent of the parties was that Weldon would have to pay for the dolls only if they sold during the Christmas season. Sale during that time was a condition precedent to payment. Thus, Weldon had no obligation to pay for the 80 dolls that had not sold by February 12 (well after the Christmas season). Thus, (C) is correct, and (B) is wrong. (A) is wrong because Cuddly refused Weldon's tender of the dolls, and Weldon is just holding them awaiting Cuddly's instructions. (D) is wrong because accepting the check did not result in a waiver of any rights Cuddly may have had. If a monetary claim is uncertain or subject to a bona fide dispute, an accord and satisfaction can be accomplished by a good faith tender and acceptance of a check when that check (or an accompanying document) conspicuously states that the check is tendered in full satisfaction of the debt. Here, there is no indication that Weldon stated that the check was payment in full.

Answer to Question 62

(D) If Laurie wins it will be because the payments by Tony may be based on a valid landlord-tenant relationship. A promise creating an interest in land must be in writing to be enforceable. This includes not only agreements for the sale of real property or an interest therein, but also leases for more than one year. However, under the part performance doctrine, conduct that unequivocally indicates that the parties have contracted for the sale of land will take the contract out of the Statute of Frauds. Here, the parties had originally created a landlord-tenant relationship, and the lease would be enforceable even without a writing as a month-to-month tenancy. The continuation of the monthly payments can as readily be explained by a continuation of the lease relationship as by an oral agreement for an installment land sale contract. Thus, because the conduct does not unequivocally indicate a contract for the sale of land, the Statute of Frauds requirements will not be excepted. (A) is wrong because while part performance may create an estoppel, Tony will have a hard time proving it because the parties' conduct is consistent with a lease relationship as well. (B) is wrong because if Tony's actions had clearly indicated a contract, the court would probably find the contract enforceable, despite the absence of a writing. (C) is wrong because it states an incorrect position of the law; other than Statute of Frauds requirements, oral agreements are no more revocable than written agreements.

Answer to Question 63

(D) Jody will prevail because obtaining financing was a condition precedent. When the parties to a contract express their agreement in a writing with the intent that the writing embody the full and final expression of their bargain, no other expression made prior to or contemporaneous with the writing is admissible to vary the terms of the writing. Nevertheless, a party can still attack the validity of the contract through parol evidence, and this includes an argument that the writing never became enforceable because a condition precedent to enforceability had not been fulfilled. In such a case, all evidence of the understanding may be offered and received. The rationale is that the written agreement is not being altered by means of parol evidence if the written agreement never came into being. While (A) and (B) are true statements, they are wrong because Jody will not try to vary the writing, but rather he will show that the writing never became effective. (C) is wrong; if Jody were seeking to vary the writing with the oral agreement, the fact that it was made contemporaneous with the writing would not make it admissible. Any oral expressions contemporaneous with the written agreement are inadmissible under the parol evidence rule.

Answer to Question 64

(C)   Because Rita should have known of CalVint's unilateral mistake as to the identity of her business, CalVint is entitled to rescind the original agreement. Unilateral mistake as to a material fact is generally not a basis for rescission by the mistaken party unless the nonmistaken party knew or should have known of the mistake. To use this defense, CalVint does not need to establish that Rita did in fact know of the mistake by its sales manager. CalVint need only show, based on an objective standard, that Rita should have known of the mistake. Here, the sales manager accepted Rita's offer "in light of our long-standing business relationship." In conjunction with the similarity in the names of the two restaurants, this statement should have alerted Rita to the mistake of identity. It also indicates that the presumed connection between Richard's restaurant and Rita's restaurant was a material factor in CalVint's acceptance of the terms of Rita's proposal. Thus, CalVint's rescission of the original agreement was justified. (A) is not as good a defense because CalVint's second letter to Rita sought to change two terms of the original agreement: the price per bottle and the manner of payment. Under section 2-702 of the U.C.C., which applies because the sale of goods is involved, Rita's insolvency would entitle CalVint to require cash before or upon delivery instead of allowing 30 days' credit, but it would not entitle CalVint to increase the price to $12 per bottle. Rita could, therefore, still enforce the original agreement at $10 per bottle if she were willing to pay cash. (B) is not as good a defense as (C) even though misrepresentation by one party does not allow the other party to rescind the contract. To use the defense of misrepresentation, CalVint would need to show, at a minimum, that Rita had *actual knowledge* that CalVint's sales manager agreed to the contract only because he believed the two restaurants were connected, creating a duty on her part to disclose the true facts. Because CalVint has a right to rescind based on unilateral mistake without having to establish Rita's state of mind, choice (C) offers a better defense than choice (B). (D) is incorrect because it is an incomplete statement of the law. Unilateral mistake is a basis for rescission by the mistaken party only if the other party knew or should have known of the mistake.

Answer to Question 65

(D)   The fact that $12 was a fair market price for the wine at the time of the contract suggests that the change in the price term was not extorted in bad faith. Because this is a contract for the sale of goods, it is controlled by U.C.C. Article 2. Section 2-209 provides that an existing contract may be modified without additional consideration, but this is subject to the general provision of section 1-203 that every U.C.C. contract imposes an obligation of good faith in its performance or enforcement. Comment 2 to section 2-209 specifically states that extortion of a "modification" without legitimate commercial reason is ineffective as a violation of good faith. Here, the facts in the question itself do not establish that CalVint extorted the modification in bad faith; CalVint might have agreed to the $10 per bottle price initially because that was the price it was charging Richard, even though it was lower than the price CalVint would charge new customers. If CalVint is only seeking to charge Rita what it would have charged her at the outset had it known of all the circumstances, its demand meets the test of good faith. (C) is not as good a choice as (D) because the additional fact in (D) creates a stronger case that the modification was made in good faith. Had the market price been only $10 per bottle, CalVint's demand for the higher price shortly before the restaurant was to open could be viewed as bad faith conduct. (A) is incorrect even though it is a true statement of fact. As noted above, U.C.C. section 2-209 explicitly authorized modification of contracts for the sale of goods without additional consideration. (B) is incorrect because the fact that CalVint knew the restaurant was opening soon does not establish bad faith on its part. CalVint made the demand for the modification as soon as it discovered that

Rita's restaurant was not associated with Richard's restaurant. As discussed above, CalVint would have been justified in trying to modify what was a year-long requirements contract if the price per bottle was $2 below what it would have charged Rita had all of the circumstances been known.

Answer to Question 66

(C) If true, the fact that Graft did nothing to solicit Hack's proposal would most strengthen Graft's defense. Since there is no consideration supporting Graft's promise to pay Hack, the only way Hack could recover is off contract; *i.e.,* by making out a case for quasi-contract. A quasi-contract is not really a contract, but rather it is a legal fiction imposed to avoid unjust enrichment. Where there is no existing contractual relationship between the parties, a quasi-contract remedy may be available where: (i) the plaintiff has conferred a benefit on the defendant by rendering services or expending property, reasonably expecting to be compensated therefor; (ii) the benefits were conferred at the express or implied request of the defendant; and (iii) if the defendant is allowed to keep the benefits, he will be unjustly enriched. Here, Hack conferred his services expecting to be compensated, or at least to obtain employment, and Graft received the benefit of using Hack's ideas. However, if Graft did nothing to request that Hack send him ideas, then the middle prong of the prima facie case cannot be established. (A) is incorrect because it is irrelevant whether Graft won or lost the election. The benefit conferred was the use of Hack's ideas, and their value cannot be measured by Graft's success (*e.g.,* perhaps the results would have been the same absent the suggestions or Graft would have won without the suggestions; it cannot be known). (B) might be helpful, because if Hack is Graft's relative there might be a presumption that the idea was a gift. However, the presumption would depend on the closeness of the relationship, and in any case it would be irrelevant if Graft had requested Hack's services and there was an understanding that Hack was to be paid. (D) is incorrect because even if Hack sent similar suggestions to Graft's opponent, it does not negate any element of the prima facie case for quasi-contract; *i.e.,* Graft still received the benefit of Hack's suggestions.

CRIMINAL LAW QUESTIONS

Question 1

Max was angry at Coach Timm for removing Max's son from a high school football game. Max consulted a book entitled *1001 Ways to Get Even*, which the dust jacket described as "a guide to revenge, ranging from practical jokes, through dirty tricks, to assassination." Max was intrigued by the book's "Recipe for an incendiary device." The last time Max visited Coach Timm's office in the school athletic department, he noted that the offices of Timm and the other coaches were thin plywood cubicles. Max surmised that planting an incendiary device behind Timm's office would start a fire that would destroy Timm's office and perhaps injure him as well.

While constructing the "incendiary device," Max mistakenly followed the instructions for making the "Handy-Dandy Stink Bomb," which was on the same page as the incendiary device "recipe." Max visited the school during Coach Timm's office hours and went into the empty corridor behind Timm's office. Max was surprised to discover that during the summer the school had rebuilt the offices in the athletic department. Instead of flimsy plywood, the offices were now surrounded by heavy cinder block walls. Max placed the device behind Timm's office after ascertaining that the coach was in his office as scheduled. Max placed a timing mechanism on the device and promptly left the school grounds. Five minutes later the device went off. It produced some foul-smelling gas but caused no injury to either Coach Timm or the school building.

If Max is charged with attempted murder and attempted arson, which of the following decisions is most likely to be reached by the court?

(A) Max is guilty of attempted murder if he did not know that the device could not harm Timm.

(B) Max is guilty of attempted murder if a reasonable person would not know that the device could not harm Timm.

(C) Max is not guilty of attempted murder, but Max is guilty of attempted arson because he thought an incendiary device was involved.

(D) Max is not guilty of attempted murder or attempted arson, because it was impossible for the device to harm Timm or burn the building.

Questions 2-3 are based on the following fact situation:

Josephine and Wanda both played backgammon regularly at the weekly meetings of the backgammon club, but were not close friends. Wanda intended to enter a big backgammon tournament in Las Vegas the next weekend, and so asked Josephine if she (Wanda) could borrow Josephine's attractive custom-made backgammon set. Josephine, who had heard that Wanda was very bad about returning borrowed items, agreed if Wanda would let her hold Wanda's expensive backgammon computer until the backgammon set was returned. Wanda agreed, and the exchange was made.

Wanda was very lucky at the tournament and played skillfully, winning several thousand dollars in the "open" division of the tourney. She decided to travel to the national championship tournament in Atlantic City the following weekend, but needed her backgammon computer to hone her game. Not wanting to go to the nationals with her own cheap set, Wanda told Phil, another weekly club player, that Josephine wanted to return the backgammon computer and asked him to get it from Josephine's car at the next meeting of the club. Wanda did not tell Phil about the agreement with Josephine, and Phil believed that Wanda was entitled to the computer. At the backgammon club meeting, he removed the computer from Josephine's car without telling her, and placed it in his backgammon set when he left the meeting.

The next day, while waiting to meet Wanda at the airport to give her the computer, Phil was playing a game on it when a stranger stopped to admire it and offered Phil $400 for the computer. Phil agreed, and used the $400 to buy a plane ticket to Hawaii.

2. If Phil is prosecuted for larceny of the backgammon computer when he took it from Josephine, he will be found:

    (A) Guilty, because Josephine was rightfully in possession of the computer when Phil took it.

    (B) Guilty, because he sold the computer to the stranger and pocketed the proceeds.

    (C) Not guilty, because Wanda was the rightful owner of the computer, and he was acting on Wanda's behalf.

    (D) Not guilty, because he thought Wanda was entitled to the computer when he took it from Josephine.

3. If Wanda is prosecuted for larceny of the backgammon computer from Josephine, she will be found:

    (A) Not guilty, because she did not personally take the computer from Josephine.

    (B) Not guilty, because she is the rightful owner of the computer.

    (C) Guilty, because Phil took the computer from Josephine without the latter's permission.

    (D) Guilty, because she did not tell Phil about the agreement regarding the backgammon set in exchange for the computer.

Question 4

Barlow was on probation after pleading guilty to possession of cocaine. Acting on a tip from a police officer that Barlow was selling cocaine out of his home, the probation officers came to his house and rang the bell. As soon as Barlow opened the door to see who was there, the officers entered the house despite his protests. After searching the house, they discovered several bags of marijuana in a drawer. Barlow was arrested and charged with possession of marijuana with intent to sell.

Barlow moves to have evidence of the marijuana suppressed by the court, claiming that the state statute that authorized the search was unconstitutional under the Fourth Amendment prohibition of unreasonable searches and seizures.

Will he prevail?

(A) Yes, unless probable cause was established by the officer's tip in conjunction with other circumstances.

(B) Yes, because a search warrant was not obtained and no exception to the warrant requirement applies.

(C) No, because reasonable grounds for the search existed.

(D) No, because the search was incident to a lawful arrest.

Question 5

Criminal statutes in the state of Leland define murder as "the unlawful killing of another human being with malice aforethought, either express or implied," and define voluntary manslaughter as "the unlawful killing of another human being under an extreme emotional disturbance for which there was reasonable explanation or excuse, without express or implied malice aforethought." Another statute provides that "it shall be an affirmative defense to the charge of murder if the defendant proves by clear and convincing evidence that defendant was unable to control his actions or conform his conduct to the law."

Dumont was charged with murder and tried in state court. At trial, Dumont introduced evidence regarding his state of mind at the time of the homicide, including testimony from a psychiatrist. At the conclusion of the case, the court instructed the jury as follows:

> Any homicide committed without justification or excuse is murder if the prosecution establishes beyond a reasonable doubt that the defendant intentionally and unlawfully killed another human being, and malice aforethought may be presumed from proof of the felonious homicide. However, if the defendant establishes by a preponderance of the evidence that he acted under extreme emotional disturbance for which there was reasonable explanation or excuse, he shall be liable only for voluntary manslaughter, because extreme emotional disturbance is inconsistent with, and negates the existence of, malice aforethought.

The judge further instructed the jury that it could return an acquittal by reason of insanity "if the defendant established by clear and convincing evidence that he was unable to control his actions or conform his conduct to the law."

The jury found Dumont guilty of murder. Dumont appealed, claiming that his constitutional rights were violated by the court's instruction as to voluntary manslaughter and by the requirement that he prove insanity by clear and convincing evidence.

Dumont's rights were violated by:

(A) The court's instruction as to voluntary manslaughter, but not the requirement of clear and convincing evidence for insanity.

(B) The requirement of clear and convincing evidence for insanity, but not the instruction as to voluntary manslaughter.

(C) Both the voluntary manslaughter instruction and the clear and convincing evidence requirement.

(D) Neither the voluntary manslaughter instruction nor the clear and convincing evidence requirement.

Question 6

Thugg and his friend Robby broke into the Gold Mansion one evening and took a number of valuable items from the home, including a television set and a number of pieces of jewelry. Acting on a tip that provided sufficient probable cause for the swearing out of a warrant, the police obtained one and went to Robby's house, where they found some of the items stolen from the mansion. Robby was taken into custody and given his *Miranda* warnings. Robby knowingly waived his *Miranda* rights and confessed to burglarizing the Gold Mansion. He signed a written confession that also implicated Thugg in the burglary. Acting under a proper warrant, the police arrested Thugg and duly gave Thugg *Miranda* warnings. Upon being told that Robby had confessed, Thugg waived his *Miranda* rights and signed a confession admitting the burglary and implicating Robby as well. Both Robby and Thugg were charged with burglary and theft and they were tried together.

At the trial Robby maintained that his confession had been obtained through improper coercion by the police. For the purpose of countering Robby's claim of coercion, the prosecution seeks to place Thugg's confession into evidence. The following conditions for admission of the confession are discussed between the judge and counsel.

I. All references to Robby will be removed from Thugg's confession.

II. Thugg will take the stand and subject himself to cross-examination regarding the confession.

III. The judge will issue a limiting instruction indicating that the confession is to be considered only with regard to the question of whether Robby's confession was coerced.

Which of these would be a valid basis for admitting Thugg's confession?

(A) I. only.

(B) II. only.

(C) I. or II., but not III.

(D) I., II., or III.

Question 7

Trent, who was mentally incompetent and a ward of the state, became a patient at Carter Convalescent Center to receive extensive rehabilitation for leg and back injuries she suffered in a fall at a state institution. After her rehabilitation was nearly completed, she became entitled to state payments as compensation for her injury, which the center began applying to her outstanding rehabilitation bill. At the same time, Boyce, a distant relative of Trent, obtained court appointment as Trent's legal guardian and sought to remove her from the center, although Trent had never shown any desire to leave. Carter, the director of the center, was aware that her departure would prevent the center from directly applying the state payments to her bill. He was erroneously advised by his attorney that judicial decisions would support his refusal of Boyce's request until the bill was paid. When Boyce arrived at the center, Carter refused to allow Boyce to remove Trent.

A criminal statute in the jurisdiction defines false imprisonment as knowingly confining a person without valid consent and without authority of law.

If Carter is arrested and charged with false imprisonment, can he be found guilty?

(A) Yes, if Carter's reliance on the advice of his attorney was not reasonable.

(B) Yes, because Carter kept Trent without lawful authority.

(C) No, because Trent was not held against her will and was not harmed by the confinement.

(D) No, because Carter's belief in the lawfulness of his conduct precluded him from having the mental state required for the offense.

Questions 8-9 are based on the following fact situation:

The statute books of State Blue contain the following provisions:

> Murder in the first degree is the killing of a human being without justification and with premeditation.
>
> Murder in the second degree is any murder which is neither a murder in the first degree nor a murder in the third degree.
>
> Murder in the third degree is any killing that occurs during and as a result of the commission of a felony.

The jurisdiction also provides that robbery is a felony for purposes of the felony murder rule. Using a realistic-looking toy pistol, Hammer held up a convenience store owned and operated by Nail. As soon as Nail handed over all the money in the store's two cash registers, he retrieved a pistol from a drawer behind the counter and when Hammer turned to leave, Nail pointed the gun at Hammer and shouted, "Stop or I'll shoot!" Hammer ducked behind a pillar and Nail discharged three shots in Hammer's direction. Because it was near closing time, Bystander was the only customer in the store. Although Bystander was crouched behind a counter and not in the line of Nail's fire, one of the three shots bounced off the pillar and struck Bystander in the neck, severing an artery. Bystander died a few minutes later from loss of blood.

8.   The most serious homicide crime of which Hammer can be convicted is:

(A) Murder in the second degree.

(B) Murder in the third degree.

(C) Manslaughter.

(D) No homicide crime.

9. The most serious homicide crime of which Nail can be convicted is:

(A) Murder in the second degree.

(B) Murder in the third degree.

(C) Manslaughter.

(D) No homicide crime.

Question 10

Esther's and Ned's Social Security retirement benefits came in a single check payable to both each month, two-thirds of which was Ned's retirement payment and one-third of which was Esther's spousal benefit. Each month when the check arrived in the mail, Esther would take it to their bank and cash it, receiving the entire proceeds in cash, which she and Ned would use for food, entertainment, and related purchases for the month.

After Ned died, the Social Security check continued to come in the same amount and made payable to both Esther and Ned. Esther knew that she was no longer entitled to Ned's benefit, but that her own spousal benefit would increase greatly as a widow's benefit. She also knew that she would receive a one-time "death benefit." She concluded that the continued receipt of the combined check reflected these increases, so for several months after Ned's death she continued to cash the combined check, signing both Ned's and her names when she negotiated it.

When the federal government eventually processed the notification of Ned's death provided by the funeral home, it discovered that Esther had negotiated checks containing $2,000 in benefits to which she was not entitled. Acting on new "get tough" orders from the highest levels of executive power, the Justice Department

prosecuted Esther for obtaining money by false pretenses.

Is she guilty?

(A) Yes, because her actions constituted a public welfare offense for which she is strictly liable.

(B) Yes, because she should have known that the combined check, payable in part to a deceased person, contained benefits to which she was not entitled.

(C) No, as long as she reasonably believed that she was entitled to the funds in the combined check.

(D) No, because she believed that she was entitled to the total amount of the combined check.

Question 11

The laws of the state of Blue provide that "any person who engages in sexual intercourse with a person under the age of 16 shall have committed the crime of statutory rape." The statute also provides for a prison sentence of one to five years for persons found guilty of the offense.

In which of the following situations is the defendant *least likely* to be found guilty of statutory rape?

(A) Don finds Traci, who works as a prostitute, sitting on the barstool next to him. Don finds Traci attractive and haggles with her over the price of her services. After reaching an agreement, Don takes Traci to a sleazy hotel down the street. Once in the room, he asks her, "How old are you, anyway?" Traci produces a cleverly forged driver's license indicating that she is 18 years old. He pays her $100 and they engage in intercourse. The next day Traci, who is actually only 15 years old, discovers that Don paid her in counterfeit money and reports him to the police. Don is charged with statutory rape.

(B) Seventeen-year-old Duffy Bob wants to have sex with his 15-year-old sweetheart, Karen Sue, but she tells him, "I'm saving myself for my husband." Duffy Bob talks Karen Sue into driving across the state line into Appalachian, which allows 15-year-olds to marry. After being married by a justice-of-the-peace in Appalachian, the newlyweds drive back into Blue and engage in sexual intercourse in a motel there. Upon discovering this, Karen Sue's parents report Duffy Bob to the police and he is charged with statutory rape.

(C) Sixty-year-old Doug became concerned about several recent occasions when he was unable to perform sexually with his wife. Doug reads an article in a tabloid newspaper stating that certain ancient Asian sages believed that sexual powers in older men could be restored by engaging in intercourse with young girls. On May 2, Doug enters into a conversation with Maxine, who works at a nearby fast food restaurant. She tells Doug that she will be 16 on May 15. Maxine is an adopted child whose adoptive parents, fearful of a search by Maxine's birth mother, always told her that her birthday was May 15, when her actual date of birth was April 15. Maxine, who has been sexually active in the past, thinks Doug is "a nice old guy" and agrees to meet him after work on May 3. He takes her to a motel where they engage in sexual intercourse. Doug's wife discovers the incident and reports him to the police. Doug is charged with statutory rape.

(D) Delia is a 28-year-old science teacher at a local high school. One Saturday evening, Scott, a 15-year-old student in one of Delia's classes, enters Delia's house through an open window. When Delia emerges from the shower she finds Scott sitting on her bed. He tells her that he is in love with her. Although Scott does not directly threaten her, she is concerned that he might get violent, so she agrees to have sex with him. The next day Scott brags that he is "going steady" with Delia. School authorities hear of this and report Delia to the police. She is charged with statutory rape.

Questions 12-13 are based on the following fact situation:

Mugg and Yegg decided to rob a grocery store. They entered the store just before closing time and locked the outside doors. While Mugg held a gun on Greengiant, the manager, and made him empty out the safe, Yegg directed Chiquita, the produce clerk, to the rear of the store. At the rear was a cold storage compartment designed to look like an ordinary storeroom from the outside. The compartment was not in use at the time and was no colder than the rest of the store. Yegg opened the door, dragged Chiquita into the compartment and raped her, after which he tied her up and left her in the compartment. Yegg returned to the front of the store, where Mugg had just finished putting the store's money in a large sack. Mugg asked Yegg, "Where's the girl?" Yegg said, "I tied her up and put her in the storeroom." Although Mugg knew that Yegg had served time in prison for a series of sex offenses, he never asked Yegg if anything else transpired. He did ask, "Where's that storeroom? I'll put this joker there, too." Yegg directed Mugg to the back of the store, where Mugg tied Greengiant and threw him into the compartment with Chiquita. Mugg closed the door and flipped a switch that he thought turned on the lights. In fact, the switch caused the cold storage unit to begin operating. Yegg and Mugg then made their escape. After 45 minutes, Chiquita was able to untie herself. She untied Greengiant, and they were able to use the emergency switch to open the compartment. Greengiant called the police, and Greengiant and Chiquita gave a full description of Mugg and Yegg. Unfortunately, Greengiant had a chronic lung condition, which the time in the cold storage compartment had aggravated to the point that Greengiant was hospitalized and soon after died of pneumonia.

12. Of which of the following crimes at common law is Yegg guilty?

   (A) Rape only.

   (B) Rape and robbery only.

   (C) Rape, robbery, and felony murder only.

   (D) Rape, robbery, burglary, and felony murder.

13. Of which of the following crimes at common law is Mugg guilty?

   (A) Robbery only.

   (B) Robbery and conspiracy to rape only.

   (C) Robbery and criminal homicide only.

   (D) Robbery, conspiracy to rape, and criminal homicide.

Questions 14-15 are based on the following fact situation:

A statute in the jurisdiction enacted with the express purpose of preventing public employees from taking advantage of the status of illegal aliens made it a felony to accept money or other benefits in exchange for issuing a state identification card. During an undercover investigation, Drell, an illegal alien, was recorded offering $500 to Keating, a public employee, in exchange for issuance of a card. Keating agreed to the deal and made an appointment for Drell for the next day.

14. Assume for purposes of this question only that Keating and Drell were arrested and charged under the statute after Drell returned the next day and exchanged the money for the card. In a jurisdiction following the common law approach to conspiracy, which of the following statements is correct?

   (A) Keating can be convicted of violating the statute and conspiracy to violate the statute, and Drell can be convicted of no crime.

   (B) Keating can be convicted only of violating the statute, and Drell can be convicted of no crime.

   (C) Keating can be convicted only of violating the statute, and Drell can be convicted as an accomplice to violation of the statute.

   (D) Keating can be convicted of violating the statute and conspiracy to violate the statute, and Drell can be convicted of conspiracy to violate the statute.

15. Assume for purposes of this question only that Keating and Drell were arrested after their first meeting. In a jurisdiction following the unilateral approach to conspiracy, which of the following statements is correct?

   (A) Drell can be convicted of solicitation and Keating can be convicted of conspiracy to violate the statute.

   (B) Both Drell and Keating can be convicted of conspiracy to violate the statute.

   (C) Drell cannot be convicted of either solicitation or conspiracy, but Keating can be convicted of conspiracy to violate the statute.

   (D) Drell cannot be convicted of either solicitation or conspiracy, and Keating cannot be convicted of conspiracy.

Question 16

The state of Meddle's legislature enacted a law totally revising the tax structure. While the legislation purported to abolish the unpopular "inheritance" tax, which was modeled on the federal gift and inheritance tax laws, it in fact amounted to a massive tax increase, because all inherited money now qualified as "income" and became subject to the state's high income tax. Because of the negative political consequences of voting for a tax increase, the legislators who drew up the bill made it exceedingly complicated and difficult for laypersons, or even trained professionals, to comprehend. Since tax forms were not to be mailed out until after the November elections, enough votes were found to pass the new tax law. One provision of the law stated: "Any person who knowingly fails to declare any income in excess of $500 received during a tax year shall be guilty of a Class 4 felony and be subject to incarceration in the state penitentiary for a period not to exceed 367 days and/or be subject to appropriate fines as listed in Schedule S of section 32.666 of the Meddle Statutes Annotated."

During the course of the first tax year in which the new tax law was in effect, Donna inherited $3,500 from her Uncle Enos. When Donna received her tax forms, she was rather confused because of all the complicated computation schedules and fine print. The State Department of Revenue had planned to include a supplemental booklet explaining the new law along with the tax forms. However, a computer glitch caused the booklet not to be included in the mailings to the "panhandle" area of the state, where Donna lived. Donna called Lem, her attorney, and asked him if the inherited money needed to be included on her income tax return. Lem assured her that the income tax applied only to earned income, interest, and dividends. Donna also called the regional branch of the State Department of Revenue. The telephone operator transferred her call to Michael, who was a law student at South Meddle University and a part-time intern in the revenue department. His work in the revenue department dealt mostly with state sales and use taxes, but he had recently completed law school courses on federal income and gift and estate taxes. Michael told Donna that inherited funds were not "income" for purposes of the income tax. Donna filed her state income tax return, but did not declare the $3,500 inherited from Enos.

If Donna is subsequently charged with a Class 4 felony pursuant to the statute quoted above, which of the following represents Donna's best defense?

(A) Donna's mistake regarding the law's coverage negates the state of mind required by the statute.

(B) Donna never received a booklet explaining the law from the Department of Revenue.

(C) Donna relied on Michael's advice.

(D) Donna relied on Lem's advice.

Question 17

Domby suffered from a rare allergic condition that only tended to occur during early spring. While suffering an allergic seizure, Domby would find himself completely debilitated and unable to work. Domby's physician, Dr. Hakkum, told Domby of a new experimental drug that a leading pharmaceutical manufacturer had developed for those suffering from Domby's allergic condition. Hakkum told Domby that the medication was experimental, but he failed to inform Domby that during the first 12 hours after the initial dose of the medication some patients had suffered severe hallucinations. After receiving the medicine from Hakkum, Domby drove home and took his first dose of the medicine after a meal, as Hakkum had directed. About two hours later, there was a knock on Domby's door. Chauncy, Domby's 12-year-old neighbor, had come by at his mother's request to borrow a cup of sugar from Domby. Chauncy had a large glass measuring cup in his hand. Domby opened the door. Under the influence of the medication, Chauncy appeared to Domby to be a Martian invader and the glass cup a "ray gun." Domby quickly seized a nearby paperweight and threw it at Chauncy, screaming, "You won't get me, you alien slime!" The paperweight struck the child in the head, injuring him. Chauncy's mother promptly called the police. Domby was arrested and charged with criminal battery. Assume that the jurisdiction in which these events took place applies the *M'Naghten* test for insanity. Domby's attorney considers the following defenses:

I. Voluntary intoxication.

II. Involuntary intoxication.

III. Insanity.

Which of these defenses would be likely to prove effective against the crime with which Domby is charged under the circumstances described in the facts?

(A) I. only.

(B) II. only.

(C) III. only.

(D) II. and III. only.

Question 18

In the final seconds of a crucial football game that would determine whether Illiana Tech or Dakota Central would receive a bid to the prestigious Raspberry Bowl, Dakota Central, behind by one point, was driving against Illiana, hoping to at least get within field goal range. On a critical fourth-down play, Central's quarterback threw the ball before he was tackled and then received a vicious hit from one of Illiana's blitzing linebackers. A penalty flag was thrown, which Central fans assumed would be a "roughing the passer" call that would have resulted in a 15-yard penalty, placing Central well within field goal range. Instead, the fans saw Riker, the referee, signal "intentional grounding" against Central, which resulted in both a loss of yardage and a loss of down. The ball went over to Illiana, which ran out the clock for a 15-14 victory and a trip to the Raspberry Bowl. The angry Dakota Central fans went wild with anger.

In which of the following cases that occurred as the game ended or shortly thereafter is the defendant *least likely* to be convicted of the crime with which he is charged?

(A) From the stands, Pinhead intends to hit Riker with a missile, although he has no intention of killing him. He throws a piece of cast iron pipe at Riker. The pipe misses Riker but strikes Ulrich, the umpire, in the back of the head. The blow kills Ulrich and Pinhead is charged with murder.

(B) Dolt does not intend to strike anyone, but wishes to register his displeasure. He throws a bottle in Riker's general direction, but clearly to Riker's right. The bottle strikes Leary, the line judge, but does not seriously injure him. Dolt is charged with battery.

(C) Micromind does not wish to strike anyone, but wishes to register his displeasure. He throws a bottle onto the field that just misses the head of Seidel, the side judge, who is looking in the other direction. Micromind is charged with assault.

(D) Shortly after the game, Kook, an angry fan, sets off an incendiary device in the alley behind Riker's house, intending to burn down the house. Although the device goes off as planned, wind currents carry the flames to the dwelling of Nixx, Riker's neighbor. Nixx's home suffers significant fire damage, but Riker's house is untouched. Kook is charged with arson.

Question 19

Acting pursuant to a valid search warrant, the police entered and searched Judd's garage and discovered a cardboard box containing cocaine in the rafters storage area. The box was securely taped and bore a freight label addressed to Carl, a friend of Judd's. At his trial for violation of the jurisdiction's statute making it a felony to knowingly possess cocaine, Judd testified that Carl had brought him the package a week before it was seized by the police, telling him that he needed to store it at Judd's for a while, and that he had not asked Carl what it contained.

What additional facts must the prosecution prove to establish Judd's liability for the charged felony?

(A) That Judd knew or believed that the box contained cocaine and had moved or handled the box.

(B) That Judd knew or believed that the box contained cocaine.

(C) That Judd should have known that the box contained cocaine and had moved or handled the box.

(D) No additional facts.

Question 20

Dumar planned to rob a liquor store. His idea was to arrive at 6:05 a.m., which was just after the store opened each morning. By observing the store over a period of time, he noted that there was only one clerk on duty until about 7 a.m., and that there were seldom any customers in the store before about 6:20 a.m. On the night before the planned robbery, Dumar discovered that his clock radio had stopped working. The clock radio was Dumar's only alarm clock and his plan for the next day would be foiled unless he awoke by 5 a.m. at the latest. He called his friend Korri and asked her if she would telephone him with a wake-up call at 5 a.m. She asked Dumar why he needed to get up so early, and he told her, "To rob the liquor store at Maple and Grand." Korri regularly awoke at about 4 a.m., because she started work at 5:30 a.m. The next morning, just before she left home to go to work, Korri called Dumar at 5 a.m., waking him from a sound sleep. She said, "Here's your wake-up call." He responded, "Thanks, gotta go now," and hung up. Dumar robbed the liquor store at 6:10 a.m., but was arrested less than an hour later. After being given proper *Miranda* warnings, Dumar confessed to the robbery and told the police of his conversations with Korri.

If Korri admits the conversations with Dumar, what is she likely to be convicted of?

(A) Robbery only.

(B) Conspiracy to commit robbery only.

(C) Robbery and conspiracy to commit robbery.

(D) Neither robbery nor conspiracy to commit robbery.

Question 21

In the dock area of Port Nasty, a number of taverns catered to stevedores and merchant seafarers. These taverns were regarded as "tough" places to be and were seldom patronized by local residents not involved in waterfront activities. One evening, however, during the course of a fraternity "beer blast" at a local college, a group of fraternity members drove to the waterfront area. They entered "The Anchor Inn," a typical waterfront tavern. Among the patrons was Karl-Heinz, a German merchant seaman, who was watching an international soccer match on television while seated at the bar. Hearing Karl-Heinz's accent while ordering a beer, Prepper, one of the college students, began making insulting remarks about foreigners in general and Germans in particular. Upon receiving no response from Karl-Heinz, who was fluent in English, Prepper plopped himself down on the barstool next to Karl-Heinz. He yelled in Karl-Heinz's ear, "You Nazis have got a lot of nerve coming over here and drinking foreign beer in an all-American bar." Karl-Heinz threw a punch that connected to Prepper's jaw and sent Prepper sprawling to the floor. He then returned to watching the soccer match and ordered another imported beer. Getting up off the floor, Prepper reached into his pocket, pulled out and opened a pocket knife, and charged at Karl-Heinz. The bartender shouted, "Look out!" Karl-Heinz tried to dodge, but was cut on the forearm by Prepper's knife. Karl-Heinz immediately drew a small caliber pistol and shot Prepper, killing him. Karl-Heinz was charged with murder.

Which of the following points raised in Karl-Heinz's defense will be *least* valuable in gaining him an acquittal?

(A) Prepper had no reason to fear serious bodily injury when he drew the knife.

(B) Prepper's drawing of the knife constituted an escalation of the fight.

(C) Three college students were standing between Karl-Heinz and the door, so there was no clear route of retreat.

(D) Prepper's comments were motivated by a desire to provoke Karl-Heinz.

Question 22

Paris is charged with the burglary of the home of Menelaus. Evidence presented at Paris's trial indicates that he talked Helen into assisting him. The jury is instructed on the provisions of the Criminal Code of New Hellas relating to burglary, solicitation, conspiracy, and attempt.

If Paris is found by the jury to be guilty of burglary:

(A) He also may be found guilty of conspiracy, but not of solicitation or attempt.

(B) He also may be found guilty of conspiracy and solicitation, but not of attempt.

(C) He also may be found guilty of conspiracy or solicitation but not both, and he may not be found guilty of attempt.

(D) He also may be found guilty of solicitation or attempt but not both, and he may not be found guilty of conspiracy.

Question 23

Charlotte and Dobie were good friends of long standing. Dobie knew that Charlotte was about to take a week-long business trip to New York City. Dobie told Charlotte that his sister was in the hospital with a serious illness, and that his automobile was undergoing repairs in a local body shop. He asked Charlotte if he could borrow her car when she was out of town, volunteering to drive Charlotte to the airport in it and to pick her up at the airport when she returned from New York. In fact, there was nothing wrong with either Dobie's car or Dobie's sister, but Charlotte believed Dobie's stories. On the day her trip was to begin, she drove her automobile to Dobie's house and gave Dobie the keys. He drove Charlotte to the airport, telling her, "See you in a week. I'll drive carefully." Two days later, Dobie drove Charlotte's car across the state line to Withrow, and entered the car in a "demolition derby." Dobie, who was heavily in debt, had seen an advertisement in the newspaper a month before announcing a $10,000 prize to the winner of the annual demolition derby at Withrow. He hoped to win by being the last car left running, but was fearful of entering his own vehicle. Dobie, who had never driven in a demolition derby before, wrecked the car in a matter of minutes as more experienced drivers rammed it repeatedly. Dobie took a bus back to Spooner, his own place of residence. When Charlotte returned, Dobie told her the car had been stolen. Charlotte filed an insurance claim. A computer check of engine block numbers showed that her car had been wrecked in the demolition derby. She pressed charges against Dobie, who was duly arrested.

If Dobie is convicted, he will most likely be found guilty of:

(A) Common law larceny.

(B) Embezzlement.

(C) False pretenses.

(D) Larceny by trick.

Questions 24-25 are based on the following fact situation:

After years of employment as a car salesman with Anderson Automotive, Duncan Farquhar had three sub-par months. His boss, Angus Anderson, told Farquhar, "I can see we need some new faces around this place," and summarily fired Farquhar. Pressed by an angry desire for revenge and a need to get some ready cash to appease the bill collectors, Farquhar decided that he would break into Anderson's house, steal some valuables that could be easily fenced, and then burn down the Anderson home. Farquhar knew that Anderson and his wife spent every Thursday night playing bridge at the Country Club. Therefore, Farquhar resolved to get even when the next Thursday arrived.

After dark on a Thursday evening, Farquhar arrived at the Anderson home. He broke in through a basement window and went upstairs to search for valuables. Unbeknownst to him, he had set off a silent alarm at the police station when he broke in. Officer DiNapoli was sent to investigate. She arrived just as Farquhar was carrying a blanket filled with jewelry and other valuables over to the side door of the house. When he saw the squad car, Farquhar dropped the blanket and bolted out of the side door. DiNapoli quickly caught up with him and seized him. Farquhar pulled out two $100 bills from his wallet, saying, "I didn't get anything from the house. Let's just forget the whole thing." DiNapoli took the money, saying, "I'll give you a break this time, but don't ever show your face in this part of town again." She then let Farquhar go.

24. Other than bribery, Farquhar has committed:

   (A) Burglary and attempted larceny.

   (B) Burglary, attempted larceny, and attempted arson.

   (C) Burglary and larceny.

   (D) Attempted burglary and attempted larceny.

25. Officer DiNapoli is:

   (A) An accessory after the fact to burglary and larceny.

   (B) An accomplice to the crimes of burglary and larceny.

   (C) An accessory after the fact to burglary.

   (D) Neither an accomplice nor an accessory after the fact.

Question 26

The criminal statutes of State Yellow contain the following provisions:

MURDER: Murder is an unlawful killing of a human being with malice aforethought.

VOLUNTARY MANSLAUGHTER: Voluntary manslaughter is an intentional killing distinguishable from murder by the existence of adequate provocation. Such provocation exists if: (i) the provocation is such that would arouse sudden and intense passion in the mind of an ordinary person such as to cause him or her to lose self-control; and (ii) the defendant must have in fact been provoked; and (iii) there must not have been a sufficient time between the provocation and the killing for the passions of a reasonable person to cool.

INSANITY: Under the defense of insanity a defendant may be entitled to acquittal if because of mental illness the defendant was unable to control his or her actions or to conform his or her conduct to the law.

In State Yellow, John Doe was put on trial for the murder of his wife, Jane Doe, and Jane's co-worker, Richard Roe. The evidence at trial established that Jane and Richard were having an affair and that John learned of it and slew the pair. John did not take the stand in his own defense. In his closing statement to the jury, John Doe's attorney made a statement, "Ladies and gentlemen, you must consider that there are some things that would provoke any one of us to kill, and there are things that make one unable to control one's actions." John Doe's attorney requested that the judge give the jury instructions on manslaughter and on insanity. The judge agreed and gave instructions that defined voluntary manslaughter and legal insanity as set forth in the State Yellow Criminal Code. The judge also issued the following instructions:

INSTRUCTION #6: In order to mitigate an intentional killing to voluntary manslaughter, the burden of proof is on the defendant to establish that adequate provocation existed.

INSTRUCTION #8: Insanity is an affirmative defense and the burden of proof is on the defendant to establish that such insanity existed at the time of the killing.

The jury found John Doe guilty of murder and he was sentenced to 40 years in the state penitentiary. Doe filed an appeal in federal court asserting that Jury Instructions #6 and #8 violated his rights under the federal Constitution.

The federal court should:

(A) Reverse Doe's conviction, because Instruction #6 was improper.

(B) Reverse Doe's conviction, because Instruction #8 was improper.

(C) Reverse Doe's conviction, because both Instructions #6 and #8 were improper.

(D) Refuse to order Doe's release, because neither Instruction #6 nor Instruction #8 was improper.

Question 27

Cary approached a clerk at a local Food and Gas Mini-Mart and offered to exchange a pair of sunglasses for $10 worth of gas. The clerk refused, saying he could only accept cash. Cary then pulled a knife out of his pocket and told the clerk he wanted a fillup. The clerk, who was quite a bit older than Cary, gave him some "fatherly advice" that crime does not pay. In response to the advice, Cary put the knife away. Feeling sorry for Cary, the clerk then agreed to give him $10 worth of gas for the sunglasses. Cary got the gas and then left. The clerk then discovered that Cary had taken the sunglasses from a display case in the store and clipped the tag off before offering them to the clerk. Cary was apprehended shortly thereafter.

Which of the following statements is correct regarding Cary's conduct?

(A) Cary can be convicted of larceny by trick and attempted robbery.

(B) Cary can be convicted of false pretenses and attempted robbery.

(C) Cary can be convicted of larceny by trick but not attempted robbery because he voluntarily abandoned the attempt.

(D) Cary can be convicted of false pretenses but not attempted robbery because he voluntarily abandoned the attempt.

Question 28

Darwin was the subject of an investigation pertaining to the robbery and murder of Vance Victim. The investigation continued for over two years, with Darwin frequently being called in for questioning. Finally, Darwin was indicted for the robbery and murder of Victim. Darwin's lawyer filed a motion to dismiss all charges against Darwin. The motion contained the argument that the excessively long investigatory period violated Darwin's constitutional right to a speedy trial.

Despite the pending motion, Darwin decided he wanted to "get it over with," and he told the judge assigned to his case that he wished to plead guilty to both of the charges against him. The judge then explained the charges to Darwin and asked Darwin if he understood them. Darwin replied, "Yes." The judge then asked Darwin if he understood that he was not required to plead guilty. Darwin responded in the affirmative. Finally, the judge described the maximum sentences possible for the crimes with which Darwin was charged, and asked if Darwin understood that he could receive the maximum sentence, which was life imprisonment. Darwin again responded, "Yes," and maintained that he still wished to plead guilty. The judge accepted Darwin's plea and sentenced him to 30 years' imprisonment in the state penitentiary. Six months later Darwin filed a motion to set aside the guilty plea.

Which of the following provides the best argument that Darwin has a constitutional basis for relief?

(A) The judge did not rule on the pending motion to dismiss before accepting Darwin's guilty plea.

(B) The judge did not attempt to determine if Darwin had actually robbed and killed Vance Victim.

(C) The judge did not determine whether the files in the prosecutor's office contained any undisclosed exculpatory evidence.

(D) The judge did not determine whether Darwin understood that he had a right to a trial by jury.

Question 29

Janusz and Mirko, a pair of very tall Danubians who recently immigrated to the United States, turned to a life of crime after failing in their quest to get on a professional basketball team. Mirko suggested that they hold up a nearby convenience store. Wearing ski masks, Janusz and Mirko entered the store at 1 a.m. Although they were unarmed, their sheer size intimidated the clerk, Kim-Sung, who was the only person in the store. Her fear increased when Janusz barked out in a loud, heavily accented voice, "Have gun! Will shoot! Give all money now!" Kim-Sung promptly complied with Janusz's demand. Janusz and Mirko grabbed the cash and ran out the door and across the store's parking lot. They were immediately spotted by police officer Harry Callaghan. Seeing two masked men running from the store, he immediately surmised that a robbery had taken place. Callaghan swiftly drew out a large caliber pistol and fired two shots, one of which shattered Janusz's kneecap and sent him tumbling to the ground. The other bullet struck Mirko in the head, killing him

instantly. After firing the shots, Callaghan muttered in a barely audible voice, "You guys had better stop or I might shoot you."

If Janusz is placed on trial for felony murder, which of the following is the best argument in Janusz's defense?

(A) Both Janusz and Mirko were unarmed.

(B) Callaghan failed to warn Janusz and Mirko before firing.

(C) The felony had already been completed when Mirko was killed.

(D) Mirko was a co-felon.

Questions 30-31 are based on the following fact pattern:

Officer Benson, a member of the police narcotics squad, was approached by a 16-year-old student from Central High named Kirby. "There's some blond guy who lives down at the trailer park," Kirby told Benson, "and he's been hanging around the school dealing drugs." Benson immediately drove to the nearby Shady Glen Trailer Park, and asked the manager how many blond men had trailers or mobile homes in the trailer park. The manager replied, "Gee, I don't know, let me think . . . ," and gave Benson the names of six persons and the location sites of their residences. The first name Benson jotted down was "Smith," whose mobile home was situated on lot G17. Benson knocked on the door of the mobile home, announcing that he was a police officer and wished to talk to Jack Smith. The door was opened by Jack's girl-friend, Margaret. Margaret did not live with Jack in the trailer, but she had been visiting when Jack told her he had to go out for a couple of hours. Margaret told Benson that Jack would not be back for some time. Benson told Margaret that he suspected that Jack was dealing drugs and asked her if she minded if he looked around a little. Margaret said, "Sure, why not?" and let Benson in. Benson did look around. Seeing nothing in the main living area, he went into the small back bedroom and opened several small storage compartments. In the corner of one of the compartments, he found an opaque bag. Upon opening it, he observed that it contained what appeared to be marijuana. Benson confiscated the bag. Shortly thereafter, Jack was arrested and charged with possession of narcotics with intent to distribute, a felony. After further investigation, Margaret was also arrested and charged with delivery of narcotics, a felony, for providing Jack with the marijuana.

30. At a preliminary hearing, Jack's attorney moved to suppress the introduction of the marijuana into evidence. How is the court likely to rule on the motion?

   (A) For Jack, because Margaret did not live in the trailer.

   (B) For Jack, because the search exceeded the scope of the consent.

   (C) Against Jack, because mobile homes fall within the automobile exception to the warrant requirement.

   (D) Against Jack, if Benson reasonably believed Margaret lived in the trailer.

31. Assume for purposes of this question only that Margaret's consent for the search of the trailer was invalid. May Margaret claim that her Fourth Amendment rights have been violated by the seizure of the marijuana from Jack's trailer?

   (A) Yes, because the marijuana will be used in evidence against her.

   (B) No, because she was not the owner or occupier of the trailer.

   (C) Yes, if she was an overnight guest of Jack.

   (D) No, unless she admits to ownership of the marijuana.

Question 32

Dan beat out Rick for the starting middle linebacker position on the Central City College football team. After practice, Rick came up behind Dan and shoved him in the back. When Dan turned around, Rick punched him in the jaw, knocking out a tooth and giving him a split lip. Before Dan could retaliate, the two were quickly separated by other players. Rick taunted him, "The next time I see you I won't go so easy on you." That night Dan was at a bar frequented by the football players, some of whom were teasing him about the altercation that afternoon. Dan was enraged but did not respond. He then saw Rick enter the room but kept his back to him. Suddenly he felt someone shove him in the back. Pulling out his pocketknife, he whirled and stabbed the person behind him, believing it to be Rick. In fact, it was Tom, who was intoxicated and had stumbled and fallen into Dan. The knife severed a major artery, and Tom died on the way to the hospital.

Dan is charged with murder for Tom's death. At trial, Dan's attorney requests the judge to instruct the jury on voluntary manslaughter. How should the judge respond?

   (A) Agree to give the instruction if Dan presents evidence that he honestly believed in the need to use deadly force in self-defense, even though his belief was unreasonable.

   (B) Agree to give the instruction because the jury may consider the altercation earlier in the day together with the shove at the bar.

   (C) Refuse to give the instruction because Tom was an innocent victim of Dan's mistake.

   (D) Refuse to give the instruction because, regardless of Dan's mistake, a shove is an inadequate provocation as a matter of law.

Question 33

The state of New Persia prohibited the sale of alcoholic beverages to minors. One statute provided criminal penalties for "knowingly selling alcoholic beverages in violation of the regulations of the State Liquor Commission to any person under the age of 18." One of the State Liquor Commission regulations provided that "before an alcoholic beverage is sold to any person between the ages of 17 and 24, the seller must demand some form of photo identification to determine the buyer's age."

Bibber, a 17-year-old recent high school graduate, walked into "The Bazaar," a popular tavern located in a suburban town within the borders of New Persia. Bibber asked Dribble, the bartender, for a draught beer. Dribble never asked Bibber for any form of identification. He drew the beer and sold it to Bibber, who consumed the drink on the premises. Dribble was subsequently arrested and charged under the state statute for selling the beer to Bibber.

If Dribble takes the stand and testifies, and is believed by the trier of fact, which of the following assertions constitutes Dribble's best defense?

(A) Bibber had on his person a driver's license showing him to be 21 years old.

(B) Dribble reasonably believed that Bibber was 25 years old.

(C) Dribble's employer never told Dribble about the state statute and regulations.

(D) Dribble did not know that beer was covered by the statute's definition of "alcoholic beverages."

Question 34

Daniel was infuriated because he found out that Wallace was having an affair with his wife. Daniel saw a person whom he believed to be Wallace walking down the street ahead of him. This person was actually Victor, a first cousin of Wallace, who strongly resembled Wallace. Daniel struck Victor with a staggering blow. Daniel was arrested and charged with battery upon Victor.

Which of the following best states the rule to be applied?

(A) Daniel is not guilty of battery if a reasonable person would have mistaken Victor for Wallace.

(B) Daniel is not guilty of battery if a reasonable person would have mistaken Victor for Wallace, and also would have been so provoked under the circumstances as to strike him.

(C) Daniel is guilty of battery even if he honestly and reasonably believed that Victor was Wallace.

(D) Daniel is guilty of battery only if he realized that it was Victor whom he was striking.

Question 35

Police Officer Smith saw a car containing three teenagers driving slowly down the street at 1 a.m. She waited for it to go by her and, after it was far enough ahead, started to follow it. Several blocks later, the car rolled through a stop sign. At that time, Smith pulled the car over and requested the driver's license. A check of the license showed that the driver of the car had five outstanding parking tickets. A statute in the jurisdiction permits an arrest to be made if a driver has four or more outstanding parking or traffic violations. Smith decided to take the driver in on the tickets. When he exited from the car, she gave him a pat-down and found a gun in his waistband. Calling for backup, she decided to haul all three teenagers to jail.

Subsequent testing showed that the gun had been used in a recent homicide during a store robbery by three young men. One of the passengers, Cliff, made a motion to prevent the introduction of the gun at his trial for murder and robbery.

The judge should:

(A) Deny the motion, because Smith was legitimately concerned for her own personal safety.

(B) Deny the motion, because the gun was found after the driver had been arrested.

(C) Grant the motion, because Smith had no valid reason to be following the automobile.

(D) Grant the motion, because Smith had not arrested the driver for suspicion of robbing the store or committing the homicide.

Question 36

Doran set out to rob Second National Bank and entered the establishment heavily armed with two handguns and an AK47 assault rifle. An alert bank employee pushed the silent alarm button to summon the police, and most of the employees and patrons were successful in fleeing the bank. However, when the police surrounded the bank, Doran was still inside with two hostages, Tonya, a teller, and Veep, a bank vice president. Doran made Veep open the vault and he filled a large bag with large-denomination bills. Meanwhile, the police obtained a description of Doran from persons who had been in the bank when Doran entered it. Unfortunately, the descriptions were generally vague in that he was described as a white male of average height. However, the witnesses were all in agreement that Doran entered the bank wearing a bright yellow scarf around his neck. The police surrounding the bank attempted to negotiate with Doran through bullhorns and by phoning the bank, but Doran refused to respond. As night fell, a standoff existed, with the police surrounding the bank and Doran inside with hostages Tonya and Veep.

Doran made Veep put on the bright yellow scarf that Doran had been wearing around his own neck and stand near a window. The lights were still on in the bank and a police sharpshooter, stationed on a nearby roof, saw a white male of average height, wearing a bright yellow scarf, standing with his back to the window. The sharpshooter fired and the bullet struck the man in the base of the skull, killing him instantly. Doran then pushed Tonya out of a small back door that did not appear to be closely monitored. He followed her through it with his bag of money. Tonya and Doran ran off in different directions. Doran was spotted immediately and captured a block away.

If Doran is prosecuted and found guilty of Veep's murder, it will be because:

(A) Doran was still in the building and had not yet run out at the time that Veep was killed.

(B) The police sharpshooter did not have legal justification to use deadly force under the circumstances.

(C) Doran caused the death of the victim during the course of a felony.

(D) Doran's putting the victim in a position of danger shows intent to kill.

Question 37

National Mining Company, Inc., whose state of incorporation is Delaware, owned the mineral rights to large portions of land in West Virginia that had been thought to have had all commercially producible coal extracted from them. National developed a new deep extraction process that enabled it to produce coal at marketable cost from the "worn out" mines, and began operating the mines using the new process. As a cost-cutting measure that increased profit by 5%, the corporate officers knowingly permitted the new process to be utilized in such a way that federally and state mandated methane gas detection measures were not complied with, and a consequent methane explosion severely injured several miners. The corporation and its officers were prosecuted for attempted murder.

What should be the outcome of this prosecution?

(A) Not guilty, because the corporate officers had not proceeded sufficiently beyond the planning stage for their actions to constitute an attempt.

(B) Not guilty, because the corporate officers did not possess the requisite intent to constitute the crime of attempted murder.

(C) Guilty, because the corporate officers' actions created a situation so dangerous to human life or safety that their mental state would be considered an abandoned and malignant heart.

(D) Guilty, if the violation of the federal and state methane detection statutes is a felony.

Question 38

Dawes was arrested outside Wade's house shortly after he had broken in and stolen some jewelry. Dawes was indicted for larceny and later for burglary. He was tried on the larceny indictment and convicted. Thereafter, Dawes was brought to trial on the burglary indictment. Relying on the Double Jeopardy Clause of the Constitution, Dawes moves to dismiss the indictment.

His motion should be:

(A) Granted, because the Double Jeopardy Clause requires that all offenses arising out of the same transaction be adjudicated in the same trial.

(B) Granted, because the Double Jeopardy Clause allows the imposition of separate sentences for separate offenses occurring during the same criminal episode only if the offenses are tried together.

(C) Denied, because larceny and burglary are offenses that may constitutionally be tried and punished separately, even if they arise out of the same transaction, since each requires proof of a fact that the other does not.

(D) Denied, because the only protection double jeopardy affords to a defendant charged with multiple counts is under the doctrine of collateral estoppel.

Question 39

The criminal law of the state of New Canada uses the common law elements to define the crime of burglary. There is also a state statute making "flashing" (exposing of sexual parts) a felony. One night Daniel broke into the home of

Vanessa, a young woman who lives in Daniel's neighborhood. He entered Vanessa's bedroom and opened his trenchcoat to "flash" at her. Vanessa screamed and Daniel fled, taking nothing with him from Vanessa's abode. At the time of the "flashing," Daniel was wearing "long john" underwear, which was extremely difficult to remove and which Daniel knew he would not have time to remove. Thus, he did not in fact actually expose his sexual organs to Vanessa. Daniel knew about the "flashing" statute, but did not know that actual exposure of sexual organs is an element of the crime of "flashing," as defined in the New Canada statutes.

Can Daniel be convicted of burglary?

(A) Yes, because he broke into Vanessa's dwelling place in the nighttime with the intent to commit a felony.

(B) Yes, unless Vanessa knew that Daniel's "flashing" was not a felony.

(C) No, because Daniel did not commit a felony.

(D) No, because Daniel could not have committed the felony while still wearing concealing underwear.

Questions 40-42 are based on the following fact situation:

Xaviera ran a watch repair shop. A customer brought her a very unusual and costly watch to repair. Xaviera knew that she could not fix the watch, but out of curiosity she wanted to inspect it. Therefore, she told the customer that she could do the job and took the watch.

Yuri rented the shop and also an apartment above the shop to Xaviera. That night as Yuri happened by, he saw a light on in the shop and finding the door unlocked, decided to investigate. While looking around the shop, Yuri spotted the watch. Supposing that the watch belonged to Xaviera, and recalling that she was much behind in her rent, Yuri decided to take the watch and keep it until Xaviera pays.

Just as Yuri was leaving the shop, Xaviera entered. Afraid of a fracas, Yuri tossed her the watch and ran out. He was already well beyond throwing distance when Xaviera, by now enraged, picked up a heavy pendulum weight and hurled it at Yuri. The weight fell harmlessly to the ground.

40. Yuri cannot be convicted of common law burglary because:

(A) The door was unlocked.

(B) A different part of the building was used as a dwelling.

(C) Yuri owns the building.

(D) He had no intent to commit any crime until he entered the shop.

41. If Yuri is accused of grand larceny, his most promising defense would be:

(A) He did not manage to carry off the watch.

(B) If Xaviera obtained the watch by false pretenses, Yuri cannot be convicted of stealing it, at least from Xaviera.

(C) Yuri honestly thought he was entitled to take the watch as security for payment of the rent.

(D) Since Yuri owned the building, his taking of the watch was not "by trespass."

42. If Xaviera is charged with assault, which of the following statements would be helpful for her defense?

I. Xaviera did not succeed in hitting Yuri with the weight.

II. Xaviera knew that it was impossible for her to hit Yuri with the weight.

III. Yuri did not see Xaviera throw the weight and so was not put in fear.

(A) I. and II. only.

(B) II. only

(C) II. and III. only.

(D) III. only.

Question 43

Dave Defendant, a college dropout, still hung around the campus of Ivy University. Dave had no visible means of support, yet he drove a large luxury car and wore flashy clothing and jewelry. The police were tipped off by a reliable informant that Dave could afford these luxuries because he was selling narcotics. The police picked up Dave the next time he showed up on campus, took him to the station, and questioned him all night long without a break and without letting him communicate with anyone else. When Dave tired from the interrogation, he admitted that he sold cocaine to his friend, Charles, a student at Ivy University. The police went to Charles's dormitory room. The door was open but no one was in the room. The police searched the room and discovered a vial of white powder, which laboratory tests later established to be cocaine. Dave was charged with the sale of narcotics. At his trial, the prosecution attempted to admit the cocaine discovered in the dormitory room into evidence.

What is Dave's best argument for preventing the cocaine from being admitted into evidence?

(A) The search of the dormitory room was conducted without a warrant and without consent.

(B) The police arrested Dave without a warrant.

(C) Dave's confession was not voluntary under the circumstances.

(D) The police failed to give Dave his *Miranda* warnings.

Question 44

Jake and Esau were arrested and charged by the police with a series of armed robberies. Each suspect was given a *Miranda* warning, and different police interrogation teams questioned Jake and Esau separately. Upon being questioned, Jake said to the police, "I'm not going to talk until I see a lawyer." One of the police officers said, "You might want to reconsider that, Jake, because Esau has already confessed, and he's implicated you in the crimes. You might want to talk to him about it and come clean yourself." Jake then told the police that he wanted to talk to Esau privately. The police escorted Jake to Esau's cell, locked him in with Esau, and then left. Unbeknownst to Jake and Esau, the police had "bugged" Esau's jail cell. During the course of their half-hour conversation, both Jake and Esau made self-incriminating statements. Jake made no further statements to the police upon advice of counsel, whom Jake called immediately after his conversation with Esau. Jake and Esau were scheduled to be tried separately.

Jake was tried first, and at his trial the prosecution sought to introduce into evidence tapes of the bugged conversation between Jake and Esau. The defense made a motion to suppress the evidence.

Should the court grant the motion to suppress?

(A) Yes, because the evidence is the fruit of a wiretap that violated the Fourth Amendment.

(B) Yes, because the police created a situation likely to induce the defendant to make an incriminating statement.

(C) No, because there is no expectation of privacy in a jail cell.

(D) No, because the conversation constituted a waiver of Jake's *Miranda* rights.

Question 45

Georgia owed Betsy $1,000. Georgia had promised to pay Betsy back in one week, but three months passed, and no money was forthcoming. In response to Betsy's phone calls, Georgia always said, "The check's in the mail," or some other lame excuse, and now Georgia has installed an answering machine rather than answering the phone herself. Betsy's anger steadily grew, and one evening, when she again heard a mechanical voice telling her, "I'm sorry, Georgia's not here to answer your call right now, but if you leave a message . . . ," Betsy could take no more. She hopped in her car and drove to Georgia's house, intending to demand repayment in person. She parked in front of the house and walked up the steps to Georgia's porch. Betsy rang the doorbell, knocked on the door, and loudly screamed, "I know you're in there, you deadbeat!" No one responded, so Betsy tried the doorknob on the closed front door. To her surprise the door was unlocked, and Betsy entered Georgia's house. After yelling, "Where are you, deadbeat?" several times, she concluded that Georgia was not at home. She looked in Georgia's sugarbowl on the off chance that it contained the money owed, but found only two losing $100 racetrack betting tickets. Convinced that Georgia had run out the back door to avoid her, Betsy went to Georgia's living room, grabbed an overstuffed chair worth about $750, and wrestled it out the door, down the steps, and onto Georgia's front lawn. Betsy doused the chair with lighter fluid and set it afire. Alarmed at the flaming chair, Jeff, one of Georgia's neighbors, called the police. The police found Betsy standing over the smoldering ruins of the chair.

Assuming that the jurisdiction has not statutorily amended the common law elements required to establish crimes, with which of the following may Betsy be properly charged?

(A) Arson only.

(B) Larceny only.

(C) Arson and burglary.

(D) Burglary and larceny.

(handwritten margin note: receiving stolen prop not needed)

Question 46

The state of Yellow has a modern theft statute that combines such common law crimes as larceny, embezzlement, and receiving stolen property into one comprehensive crime. Police in Primrose, a city located in Yellow, were attempting to halt the traffic in stolen vehicles by emphasizing an attack on the "demand side," apprehending persons who purchased stolen vehicles from car thieves or "middlemen." Police had enough evidence to send Hawker to jail for a long time. Hawker would buy cars from thieves and sell them to third parties. When the police confronted Hawker and suggested strongly that it might be in his best interests to cooperate with the police anti-car-theft operation, Hawker readily agreed. The police told Hawker to continue to purchase stolen autos from thieves, but to inform the police when a buyer was about to purchase a stolen car from Hawker. Primrose police would then arrest the buyer.

Dinty approached Hawker on Hawker's car lot, asking for a late-model used car at a good price. Hawker told Dinty that he had a two-year-old sedan that he was willing to sell for $2,500, although the "book value" of the car was double that amount. Hawker told Dinty, "You realize, of course, that the only reason you're getting this car so cheap is that it's 'hot.' " Dinty responded, "It's none of my business where you got the car; I just asked for a late-model car at a good price." Dinty gave Hawker $2,500. Hawker went into his office to "draw up the papers" and called the police. Just as Dinty put his keys into the ignition of the car, the police arrested him and charged him with theft.

You are an attorney assigned to the district attorney's felony review group, which decides whether cases should be pursued or dropped. You should advise your supervisor that the case against Dinty should be:

(A) Dropped, because Dinty was entrapped.

(B) Dropped, because Hawker was an agent of the police, and when the stolen car came into his hands it was as if it had been returned to the rightful owner.

(C) Pursued, because the police never recovered possession of the car, and it retained its character as stolen property when Dinty purchased it knowing it had been stolen.

(D) Pursued, because Dinty had the specific intent to purchase a stolen car.

Question 47

After careful detective work by the Midtown police force, Dang was arrested and charged with burglary. At the time of his apprehension he was given *Miranda* warnings in compliance with standard police department procedures. At the station house, Dang requested and was granted permission to make a phone call. He telephoned his mother and asked her to come to the station house and post bail. Instead, his mother immediately called Alice, the family attorney. In the meantime, the police had begun questioning Dang. Although he never told them to stop the questioning, his answers were at first vague or clearly unresponsive. During the course of the questioning, Alice phoned the station house and told the police, "I've been hired to represent Dang, and I'll be there in half an hour." The police did not inform Dang of Alice's call. Ten minutes after Alice's call, Dang told the police, "Okay, I committed the burglary; can I have a cup of coffee?" The police quickly brought Dang a cup of coffee and typed up a statement: "I admit to burglarizing a sporting goods store located at 2215 W. Daisy Lane on or about January 26." Dang signed the statement. Alice arrived a few minutes after Dang signed the confession and was allowed to see Dang immediately. She advised Dang to remain silent, but Dang told her he had already signed a confession.

At the preliminary hearing, Alice moves to exclude the confession as evidence at Dang's trial. Should the court rule favorably on Alice's motion?

(A) Yes, because the police had a duty to inform Dang that an attorney was coming to represent him.

(B) Yes, because Dang has been deprived of his Sixth Amendment right to counsel.

(C) No, because Dang's statement admitting the crime was voluntary.

(D) No, because Dang waived his *Miranda* rights.

Question 48

In a jurisdiction applying only the common law to a criminal prosecution, in which of the following situations would the defendant be most likely found guilty of manslaughter rather than murder?

(A) Defendant burns down his retail clothing store in order to defraud his insurance company. A transient who slipped in through the door left open by the defendant falls asleep in a back room and is killed in the fire.

(B) Defendant, using a high-power hunting rifle, aims and shoots at Victim, intending to kill him, but since Victim is several hundred yards away and he slips and falls just as the defendant pulls the trigger, Bystander, sitting several yards behind Victim, is killed.

(C) Defendant, seeking to stop all shipments of toxic materials by rail through his home town, dynamites the railroad track just as a freight train is passing. The train derails, killing the engineer.

(D) Defendant, the initial aggressor, severely beating his much smaller opponent in a fistfight, unreasonably mistakes the opponent's silver wristwatch for a chrome-plated revolver, and thinking that the opponent is about to shoot him, kills him with a nearby shovel.

Question 49

In which of the following situations should Defendant's motion to exclude his statements be granted by the court?

(A) Defendant was arrested, not given *Miranda* warnings, and questioned about an armed robbery. He remained silent and was put in a cell with Ivan, who unknown to Defendant was a police informant. After Ivan bragged about the armed robberies that he committed, Defendant made incriminating statements about the armed robbery.

(B) Defendant was arrested, given *Miranda* warnings, and questioned about an armed robbery. After he asked to speak with an attorney, the police stopped questioning him about the robbery. Several hours later, the police gave Defendant *Miranda* warnings again and questioned him again about the robbery. Defendant then made incriminating statements about the robbery.

(C) Defendant was arrested, given *Miranda* warnings, and charged with armed robbery. After he asked to speak with an attorney, the police stopped questioning him and put him in a cell with Ivan, who unknown to Defendant was a police informant. Ivan talked with him about an unrelated home invasion homicide, and Defendant then made incriminating statements about the homicide.

(D) Defendant was arrested, not given *Miranda* warnings, and charged with armed robbery. At a preliminary hearing before a magistrate, he asked for the assistance of an attorney. After the hearing, the police gave Defendant *Miranda* warnings and questioned him about an unrelated home invasion homicide. Defendant then made incriminating statements about the homicide.

Question 50

Daimler was arrested after the car he was driving struck and seriously injured Benz, a pedestrian, while Daimler was fleeing from an armed robbery that he had committed. Daimler was charged with armed robbery and reckless driving, both felonies. Just prior to trial, Benz died from his injuries. The trial on the robbery and driving charges proceeded, and Daimler was convicted of the armed robbery charge and acquitted of the reckless driving charge. Daimler was then indicted under the jurisdiction's felony murder statute for causing the death of Benz during the course of committing an armed robbery. Daimler moved to dismiss the indictment on the ground that a second trial would violate double jeopardy.

Daimler's claim is:

(A) Correct, because he was acquitted of the reckless driving charge.

(B) Correct, because Benz died before Daimler's first trial had begun.

(C) Incorrect, because he was convicted of the armed robbery charge.

(D) Incorrect, because felony murder requires proof of an additional element not required by the felony itself.

Question 51

Bruton and Cruz were arrested and charged with conspiring to blow up a federal government building. After being given *Miranda* warnings, they were questioned separately and each of them gave a written confession. The confessions interlocked with each other, implicating both of the defendants as being involved in every stage of the conspiracy. Subsequently, Bruton attempted to retract her confession, claiming that it was false. At a preliminary hearing, the judge rejected her claim.

Both defendants were tried together, and the prosecutor introduced both confessions into evidence. At trial, Bruton testified that she was not involved in any conspiracy and that her confession was fabricated. Both defendants were found guilty by the jury.

If Bruton challenges her conviction on appeal because of the admission of Cruz's confession, will she likely be successful?

(A) No, because Cruz's confession was no more incriminatory to Bruton than her own confession.

(B) No, if the jury was instructed to consider Cruz's confession as evidence only of his guilt and not of Bruton's.

(C) Yes, if Cruz refused to testify at trial and therefore was not subject to cross-examination regarding his confession.

(D) Yes, if Cruz testified and was subject to cross-examination but denied making the confession attributed to him.

Question 52

Acting on information from usually reliable informants and undercover officers that drugs were being sold by residents of the Phi Upsilon fraternity house on the campus of Brownbag College, the police obtained a search warrant from Judge Jason. The warrant entitled the police to search the entire premises of the Phi Upsilon house for illegal narcotics. The police arrived at the house when a party was in progress and were admitted to the house by fraternity president Oakin Dalles after showing the warrant. Officers proceeded to search the house. In an upstairs bedroom, they found Delia sleeping on the bed. No one else was in the room. Delia had been attending the party as a guest of a fraternity member. The police found a footlocker under the bed on which Delia had been sleeping. They opened up the footlocker and found a variety of drugs, including marijuana, cocaine, and amphetamines. The police then demanded that Delia give them her purse. They opened it up and found a small quantity of marijuana. Delia was charged with a drug possession offense. At Delia's trial, the prosecution seeks to admit the marijuana seized from Delia into evidence over the objection of Delia's attorney.

Should the court admit the marijuana?

(A) Yes, because the footlocker was within Delia's reach.

(B) Yes, because Delia was present in the room where drugs were found.

(C) No, because Delia had no possessory interest in the premises.

(D) No, because the police had no reason to believe that Delia had drugs on her person.

Question 53

Lee was very proud of his "Wasp Wing" motorcycle because it was manufactured in the United States in the 1950s, which Lee considered the "Golden Age" of motorcycles. When his friend Marlon called to ask him for a lift downtown because he did not have money for bus fare, Lee was happy to oblige. Lee drove his bike over to the home of Marlon, who hopped on the bike behind Lee. As they were riding along a city street, Marlon asked Lee, "Can we stop someplace for a soda pop?" Lee said, "I thought you didn't have any money." Marlon smiled and showed Lee a tire iron in his backpack, saying, "We don't need any money with this." Lee drove the motorcycle to the parking lot of a neighborhood convenience store. Marlon went inside and demanded money from the clerk, brandishing the tire iron. The clerk tried to grab a gun under the counter while he was filling a bag with money for Marlon. Marlon jumped across the counter and wrestled with the clerk for the gun. During the struggle, the gun discharged, killing the clerk. Lee heard the gunshot and raced off, leaving Marlon behind. Marlon ran in the other direction with the gun, but was quickly cornered in an alley by a police car. A gun battle ensued, and Marlon was shot and killed by a police officer. Another employee of the convenience store accurately described the motorcycle and driver who had taken Marlon to the scene of the crime. The police tracked down Lee and he was charged with robbery and felony murder. The jurisdiction's criminal code provides that a death caused during the commission of certain felonies, including robbery, is first degree felony murder, for which the death penalty is permitted. The code also permits cumulative penalties for first degree felony murder and for the underlying felony.

Lee was convicted of both robbery and felony murder. After appropriate consideration of all relevant circumstances, the jury imposed the death penalty. On appeal, Lee challenged both the convictions and the sentence.

Assuming that the above facts were properly admitted into evidence, how should the appellate court rule?

(A) Lee's conviction for both offenses should be upheld, but imposition of the death penalty was not proper.

(B) Lee's conviction for both offenses should be upheld, and imposition of the death penalty was proper.

(C) Lee's conviction should be overturned under double jeopardy principles because robbery is a lesser included offense of felony murder.

(D) Lee's conviction for felony murder should be overturned because the circumstances do not establish the necessary degree of culpability.

Question 54

Dolly, a middle-aged woman who loved children but had never been able to have any of her own, often gave candy and other treats to children outside the Tot Town Kindergarten and Preschool. She befriended a number of the children, but was particularly fond of four-year-old Jane, who always called her "Aunt Dolly" and greeted her with a cheerful smile. One Friday afternoon, the school bus was late and Dolly talked to Jane in front of the school. She told Jane, "Your Mommy has had to go out of town for the weekend and asked me to take care of you." Although Jane had been taught, "Never talk to strangers," she did not consider "Aunt Dolly" to be a stranger and readily believed her. Dolly took Jane home with her and proceeded to give Jane treats and toys. On Saturday Dolly took Jane to the zoo, which Jane thoroughly enjoyed. Dolly heard on the radio that a search was being conducted for Jane, whom Jane's mother had reported as missing to the police. Dolly made sure that Jane did not watch any television where Jane might see her picture on the screen. Jane had a fine weekend with Dolly, and then Dolly returned Jane to her own front porch on Monday morning. Jane had three new dresses, a stuffed animal, and other toys with her. Jane rang the doorbell shortly after Dolly drove off. Jane's mother asked Jane where she had been. Jane told her, "I was at the zoo with Aunt Dolly." A police investigation quickly located Dolly, who was placed under arrest. Assume that the jurisdiction where this occurred maintains a traditional, common law definition of criminal false imprisonment and has a typical, modern kidnapping statute.

Dolly can be properly convicted of:

(A) Kidnapping only.

(B) Either kidnapping or false imprisonment.

(C) Both kidnapping and false imprisonment.

(D) Neither kidnapping nor false imprisonment.

Question 55

Acting with probable cause, the police arrested Darnell in connection with the armed robbery of a liquor store. After being given *Miranda* warnings, Darnell confessed to the robbery but denied his involvement with several other recent armed robberies of businesses in the area. He was formally charged with the one robbery and put into a cell with Henry, who was a paid informant working undercover for the police. Henry had been instructed to find out what he could about the other robberies but not to ask any questions. Henry began talking about a convenience store robbery in which a bystander was shot and seriously injured by the robber, and he deliberately misstated how it happened. Darnell, unaware that Henry was an informant, interrupted to correct him, bragging that he knew what really happened because he was there, and proceeded to make incriminating statements about the robbery. Darnell was subsequently charged with armed robbery and attempted murder in the convenience store robbery.

At a motion to suppress hearing on that charge, Darnell's attorney moves to exclude the statements made to Henry. Should the motion be granted?

(A) Yes, because Henry deliberately elicited incriminating statements in violation of Darnell's Sixth Amendment right to counsel.

(B) Yes, because Henry's conduct constituted custodial interrogation in violation of Darnell's Fifth Amendment privilege against self-incrimination.

(C) No, because Darnell had not yet been charged with the robbery of the convenience store when he made the statements to Henry.

(D) No, because Henry's conduct did not constitute interrogation.

Question 56

Harmon P. Lautenschlager had recently moved to Charlestown, where he rented an apartment and took a job in the Charlestown Boiler Works. Harmon phoned Ed's Electronics and asked if they carried Ankomay products, a premium line of sound reproduction equipment. He identified himself as "Mr. Lautenschlager" on the phone, and the clerk who answered was almost effusive in telling Harmon that Ed's carried the Ankomay line. The next day, Harmon went to Ed's and told the clerk, "Hi, I'm Harmon P. Lautenschlager. I telephoned yesterday about your line of Ankomay equipment." The clerk responded in an obsequious manner, "OF COURSE, Mr. Lautenschlager, ANYTHING you want we have or we'll get!" The clerk's behavior made Harmon realize that he had been mistaken for Hermann T. Lautenschlager, a young Charlestown millionaire, who was not related to Harmon. Fellow workers at the boiler plant had already commented on the similarity of Harmon's name with that of the local celebrity. Enjoying being treated like a big shot, Harmon did nothing to disabuse the clerk of his error. The clerk immediately directed Harmon to the most expensive piece of Ankomay equipment in the store, a $4,000 super stereo. Harmon really liked it and told the clerk he would take it. Before Harmon could say anything else, the clerk told him, "Normally we require a down payment on an item this expensive, but not for you, sir. Just fill out this form and we'll bill you for the stereo. Harmon put his correct name and address on the form. The clerk did not even look at it, but properly forwarded it to the delivery and billing departments. The super stereo was delivered to Harmon's home the following day.

Thirty days after the stereo was delivered, Harmon received the bill for $4,000. In the meantime, Harmon had lost his job when the Charlestown Boiler Works suddenly laid off half of its workforce. Harmon did not pay the bill. The accounting department of Ed's Electronics asked the sales manager why Harmon made no down payment on the stereo when he bought it. At that time, the clerk's mistake regarding Harmon's identity was discovered. Harmon then received a notice to pay Ed's in full for the stereo within 14 days or it would be repossessed. A week after Harmon received the notice, an electrical fire broke out in Harmon's building. All of the personal property in Harmon's apartment was destroyed, including the stereo. Ed's Electronics filed a complaint with the police, claiming Harmon had cheated them.

Which of the following is the most likely conclusion prosecuting authorities should reach regarding the complaint against Harmon?

(A) Harmon has committed false pretenses, because he improperly gained title to the stereo.

(B) Harmon has committed larceny by trick, because he improperly gained possession of the stereo.

(C) Harmon has committed neither false pretenses nor larceny by trick, because he may have intended to pay for the stereo upon receipt of the bill.

(D) Harmon has committed neither false pretenses nor larceny by trick, because he was under no duty to disabuse the clerk of his mistake as to Harmon's identity.

Questions 57-58 are based on the following fact situation:

State Green has the following homicide statutes:

Murder is the unlawful killing of a human being with malice aforethought. Such malice may be express or implied. It is express when there is manifested a deliberate intention to unlawfully take away the life of a fellow creature. It is implied when no considerable provocation appears or when the circumstances attending the killing show an abandoned and malignant heart. All murder that is perpetrated by willful, deliberate, or premeditated killing or committed in the perpetration of or attempt to perpetrate arson, rape, robbery, or burglary is murder of the first degree. All other kinds of murders are of the second degree.

Manslaughter is the unlawful killing of a human being without malice. It is of two kinds:

1. Voluntary—upon a sudden quarrel or heat of passion.

2. Involuntary—in the commission of an unlawful act, not amounting to a felony; or in the commission of a lawful act that might produce death in an unlawful manner or without due caution and circumspection.

57. Roy held up Dave. Dave was shot and killed. Roy is charged with first degree murder in State Green. Assuming evidence to support, what is Roy's best theory to advance?

(A) Dave suddenly attacked him and knocked him down. Afraid that Dave was going to hit him again, Roy pulled the trigger.

(B) Roy had the gun for many years, it was old and rusty, and he did not think it would fire.

(C) Roy had taken "angel dust" before the incident and does not remember getting a gun or holding up Dave.

(D) When Roy tried to hold up Dave, Dave said, "Get out of here, you dirty bum, or I'll kill you." Roy became so upset, he did not know what he was doing.

58. Reba and Myrna were professional shoplifters. One day while they were in a jewelry store, Reba was to watch the employees while Myrna stole a diamond bracelet. Just as Myrna put the bracelet into her pocket, a salesman saw her and grabbed her by the wrist. Reba grabbed a knife from one of the silver displays, and as she lunged at the salesman, a store guard shot and killed her. Myrna is charged in State Green with the first degree murder of Reba. Which of the following is Myrna's strongest argument?

(A) Myrna cannot be convicted of murder because when they went into the store they were not carrying any weapons; therefore, there was no felony upon which the felony murder rule may arise.

(B) Myrna cannot be convicted of murder because Reba's death was not murder but justifiable homicide.

(C) Myrna cannot be convicted of murder because she and Reba had an agreement never to use violence when they stole anything.

(D) Reba did not intend to hurt the salesman, but just wanted to scare him so that Myrna could run.

Question 59

Officer Ollie learned from a reliable informant that a major drug deal was about to take place at a local restaurant. Officer Ollie obtained a search warrant for the restaurant and arrived with other uniformed officers to search the premises. While conducting the search, Officer Ollie searched several of the customers of the restaurant. While searching Phil, a regular customer of the restaurant, Officer Ollie felt something strange. He reached into Phil's pocket and pulled out a container filled with heroin. Phil was arrested and later convicted of possession of heroin. A state statute permits officers executing a search warrant to search persons on the premises if the officers reasonably expect danger to themselves or a risk of disposal or concealment of anything described in the warrant.

Phil appeals his conviction to the United States Supreme Court. The Court will most likely rule that:

(A) The conviction of Phil must be reversed because the statute is vague and overbroad.

(B) The conviction of Phil must be reversed because his presence in the place to be searched by the police does not negate the requirement of probable cause.

(C) The conviction of Phil must stand because the search was conducted pursuant to a valid search warrant.

(D) The conviction of Phil must stand because the search was authorized by statute.

Question 60

In which of the following situations is David *least* likely to be found guilty of the charge made?

(A) David, using a false identification card, attempted to buy a watch from Jewelry Store. The store's owner did not believe that David was the person whose picture was on the card, and he refused to sell David the watch. David is charged with an attempt to obtain property by false pretenses.

(B) Believing that it is a crime to purchase gunpowder without a state license, David purchased five pounds of gunpowder from a man who purchased some in another state. Actually, a state license is required only for the purchase of 10 pounds or more of gunpowder in one year. David is charged with attempting to purchase gunpowder without a state license.

(C) Thad was arrested by the police after he had stolen some television sets from Trucking Company. In an effort to avoid going to prison, he told the police that he would lead them to David, who was a fence. The police had him take the stolen goods, and when David purchased them believing they were stolen, the police arrested him. David is charged with an attempt to receive stolen property.

(D) David, intending to kill Vincent, set fire to Vincent's trailer while Vincent was inside. Unknown to David, Vincent had committed suicide by taking an overdose of sleeping pills. David is charged with attempted murder.

Questions 61-62 are based on the following fact situation:

When Dave, a prominent state official, divorced his wife Carla, he was ordered to pay $1,000 per month alimony until Carla remarried. A few months after the divorce, Carla met and started dating Brian, a Marine Corps officer recently returned from a tour of duty in Germany. On learning that Carla was seeing Brian, Dave called Carla and encouraged her to get married "for the sake of the children." Carla told Dave that she would consider marrying Brian, but he had not yet asked. She also expressed to Dave her fear that Brian might already be married because "he refuses to discuss anything about his life while he was stationed in Germany." Dave told Carla he would have a friend in the Marines run a computer check on Brian that would reveal Brian's current marital status. However, Dave did not bother with the computer check; instead he called Brian and offered him $5,000 if he would propose to Carla. Dave then told Carla that according to Marine records Brian was single. Brian and Carla went through a wedding ceremony shortly afterwards. Brian was already married to Jane, a fact that would have been disclosed by a routine check of Marine records.

61. If Dave is charged with being an accessory to bigamy, he should be found:

(A) Guilty, because he aided, abetted, and encouraged the marriage.

(B) Guilty, because even though Dave did not know that Brian was married, bigamy is a strict liability offense.

(C) Not guilty, unless Dave's action in failing to check the records was a breach of duty to Carla.

(D) Not guilty, because Dave did not have the mental state necessary for aiding and abetting.

62. Assume for the purposes of this question that the state supreme court has held that under state law strict liability is abolished and all crimes require a culpable mental state. If Carla is charged with bigamy, the best reason for finding her not guilty would be:

(A) She made an honest and reasonable mistake about the marital status of Brian.

(B) She did not know that Brian was married and therefore never intended to commit bigamy.

(C) She made a diligent effort to determine the marital status of Brian.

(D) She relied on the information supplied by a state official.

Question 63

A statute in the state of New Olka provides "any person who knowingly sells intoxicating liquor to a person under 21 years of age is guilty of a misdemeanor and may be fined $1,000 or sentenced to up to six months in jail, or both."

John Jones ordered a drink at the Pussycat Lounge. The bartender, Don, asked for some identification, and Jones produced a driver's license stating that he was 25 years old. In fact, Jones was only 19. While the bartender was inspecting the license, Jones said, "Give me a break—if the license says I'm 25, you can't get into any trouble." Don shrugged and sold Jones a scotch and soda.

A plainclothes police officer was sitting at the bar and heard the conversation. She demanded to see the driver's license, determined it to be false, and arrested Don for violation of the statute.

Don will be found:

(A) Guilty, because this type of statute is a strict liability statute and Don's knowledge of Jones's age is irrelevant.

(B) Guilty, because Don in fact knew Jones was under 21 years old.

(C) Not guilty, if Don made a reasonable mistake concerning the age of Jones.

(D) Not guilty, because Jones produced a driver's license that stated he was 25 years old.

Question 64

Victor Victim routinely left the keys in his car when he placed it for the night outside his fashionable condominium in the suburbs of Philadelphia. One evening Dave stole the car and headed for his favorite beach resort, Wildwood, New Jersey. Dave was arrested for speeding on the New Jersey Turnpike. A check of the car license showed that the car was owned by Victor; a further check indicated that the car had been reported stolen.

Dave was charged with common law larceny. At trial, his defense to the charge was that he intended to return the car to Victor's home the following morning before anyone realized it had been stolen. The trial judge instructed the jury that while the state must prove the case beyond a reasonable doubt, the defendant has the responsibility to prove his defense by a preponderance of

the evidence. The court further instructed the jury that if they found by a preponderance of the evidence that Dave intended to return the car, they should find him not guilty. Dave was convicted; he appealed on the ground that the jury instructions were erroneous.

Dave's conviction should be:

(A) Reversed, because in a criminal case the state must prove all disputed issues beyond a reasonable doubt.

(B) Reversed, because the instruction placed an improper burden of proof on the defendant.

(C) Affirmed, because intent to return is not a defense to the charge.

(D) Affirmed, because the jury instructions were correct.

Question 65

Doberman, an overnight guest of Vosburg's housemate, took Vosburg's car keys from the kitchen counter and drove off with Vosburg's car in the middle of the night. Later the next day, it was destroyed in a collision while Doberman was driving it. If Doberman is charged with larceny of the car, which of the following is *least* likely to provide him with a defense?

(A) Doberman did not intend to keep the car but only to use it for the day, despite the fact that he knew that Vosburg needed it to go to work that day.

(B) Doberman was intoxicated when he took the car and unreasonably believed that the keys and the car were his.

(C) Vosburg owed Doberman a substantial gambling debt and Doberman took the car intending to sell it and use the proceeds as a partial recovery on the debt.

(D) Although Vosburg had given Doberman permission to borrow the car to get cigarettes at the convenience store, Doberman took the car intending to keep it, but he later changed his mind and was on his way back to return it when the accident occurred.

Question 66

In which of the following fact patterns is defendant's conviction for larceny *least* likely to be upheld?

(A) After having her car repaired at the local automotive repair shop, Debbie takes a spare key and drives away with the car without paying the repair bill because she thinks the shop charged her too much.

(B) Don takes Vic's car without permission, intending to return it the next day, but after using it for awhile, Don decides to keep it.

(C) Dave is fired from his sales job while calling on customers in another city and fails to return the company car that he used for his sales visits.

(D) Donna rents a car from a rental agency using a phony driver's license, intending not to return it, and sells it to a used car dealer for cash.

CRIMINAL LAW ANSWERS

Answer to Question 1

(C) Max lacked the specific intent to kill that is required for attempted murder. However, the circumstances surrounding the "incendiary device" constitute factual impossibility, and will not afford Max a defense to attempted arson. Criminal attempt is an act that, although done with the intention of committing a crime, falls short of completing that crime. To be guilty of attempt, the defendant must have the intent to perform an act and obtain a result that, if achieved, would constitute a crime. Regardless of the intent that would suffice for the completed offense, attempt always requires a specific intent to commit the target offense. Also, the defendant must have committed an act beyond mere preparation for the offense. Here, to be guilty of attempted murder, Max must have had the specific intent to kill Timm, even though the intent to inflict great bodily injury would be sufficient mens rea for murder. However, the facts indicate that Max intended at most only to injure Timm rather than kill him. Thus, Max cannot be guilty of attempted murder. Max did intend to burn the part of the school building housing the athletic department. Therefore, Max had the specific intent to commit arson (which is no longer limited to dwellings in most jurisdictions today) by means of placing an incendiary device behind Timm's office. Unbeknownst to Max, he was actually placing a stink bomb behind the office rather than an incendiary device. However, it is no defense to attempt that it would have been impossible for the defendant to complete his plan. This is factual impossibility. Consequently, the fact that it would have been impossible for Max to burn the building with the device he placed there will not constitute a defense to attempted arson. Max intended to commit arson, and his placing the device was an act beyond mere preparation for this crime. Thus, Max is guilty of attempted arson. (A) is incorrect because Max did not have the specific intent to kill. Even if, as (A) states, Max did not know that the device could not harm Timm, Max cannot be guilty of attempted murder because he did not have the specific intent to kill Timm. (B) is incorrect because the knowledge of a reasonable person is irrelevant to Max's liability for attempted murder. What is important is whether Max intended to kill Timm, and whether Max knew that the device could not accomplish this objective, not what the reasonable person might know. (D) is incorrect because, as explained above, the impossibility that the device could kill Timm or burn the building is factual impossibility, which will not serve as a defense to attempt.

Answer to Question 2

(D) Because Phil believed at the time he took the computer that Josephine would have permitted him to take it to return it to Wanda, he lacked the intent to permanently deprive Josephine of her interest in the computer that is necessary for larceny. Common law larceny consists of a taking and carrying away of tangible personal property of another by trespass with intent to permanently (or for an unreasonable time) deprive the person of his interest in the property. Larceny is a crime against possession; thus, it is only necessary that the property be taken from someone who has a possessory interest superior to that of the defendant. At the moment of the taking, the defendant must have had the intent to permanently deprive the person from whom the property is taken of his interest in the property. Here, although Wanda owned the computer, Josephine had the right of possession of the computer until Wanda returned Josephine's backgammon set. Thus, when Phil took the computer from Josephine's car, he was taking and carrying away tangible personal property in which Josephine had a possessory interest. However, Phil believed at the time of the taking that he was merely returning the computer to Wanda, and that Josephine would want him to do so. Phil did not have the intent to deprive Josephine of her interest in the computer because he was unaware that Josephine had any such interest. Because the intent element of larceny is lacking, Phil cannot be convicted of larceny. Alternative (A) is incorrect because, although it correctly states that Josephine was rightfully in possession of the computer when Phil took it, Phil lacked the intent necessary for larceny (as explained above). (B) is incorrect because the intent to deprive another of her interest in the computer, demonstrated by Phil's sale of the computer to the stranger, did not exist at the time that Phil took the computer. The intent and the taking must coincide. Phil's intent at the airport does not change the earlier innocent taking into larceny (although Phil might be guilty of embezzlement for intentionally converting the computer while in lawful possession of it). (C) is incorrect because, despite Wanda's ownership of the computer, Josephine had a superior right to possession at the time that Phil took the computer (*i.e.,* she had the right to possess the computer, even as against Wanda, until Wanda returned Josephine's backgammon set). Thus, had Phil known at the time of the taking that Josephine's right to possess the computer was superior to Wanda's, Phil would have been guilty of larceny because he would have had the requisite intent.

Answer to Question 3

(C) Wanda is guilty because she caused Phil, her agent, to take and carry away the computer, to which Josephine had a superior right to possession, intending to permanently deprive Josephine of her interest in the property. As noted in the answer to the preceding question, larceny is a crime against possession rather than ownership, requiring only that the property be taken from someone who has a possessory interest superior to that of the defendant. Even the owner of property can be guilty of larceny, if she takes it from one who, at the time of the taking, has a superior possessory interest in it. Josephine had the right to possess the computer until Wanda returned Josephine's backgammon set. Thus, in taking the computer (through Phil), Wanda was taking property to which Josephine had a superior possessory interest. Because the rightful owner of property can be guilty of larceny with respect to that property, (B) is incorrect. (A) is incorrect because a taking essential to larceny occurs even if a defendant obtains control of the property through the act of an innocent agent. Wanda's removal of the computer from Josephine's possession through the acts of Phil constitutes a sufficient taking, so that Wanda is guilty despite not having personally taken the computer. (D) is incorrect because *Phil's* knowledge as to the true possessory interest in the computer, or lack thereof, is irrelevant to Wanda's guilt. With respect to Wanda's guilt, the important point is that she knew that Josephine had a superior possessory interest in the computer, and that, with intent to deprive Josephine of that interest, she persuaded Phil to take and carry away the computer. Even if Wanda had told Phil about the agreement between Josephine and herself, Wanda would still be guilty of larceny if Phil took the computer as her agent.

Answer to Question 4

(C) Barlow will not prevail in his motion to suppress. To be reasonable under the Fourth Amendment, most searches must be pursuant to a warrant. However, several types of inspections and searches do not require a warrant or even probable cause. The Fourth Amendment is not violated by a statute authorizing warrantless searches of a probationer's home when there are reasonable grounds to believe contraband is present. Probation systems present "special needs" that justify departures from the usual Fourth Amendment warrant requirement. [Griffin v. Wisconsin (1987)] Because Barlow is on probation, his limited expectation of privacy was not violated by the search and the evidence will not be suppressed. (A) is incorrect. While probable cause may be based on this type of tip under the "totality of the circumstances" test, probable cause is not necessary to establish the validity of the search; all that is needed is reasonable grounds, which was satisfied here by the tip from the police officer even without evidence of the basis for his information. (B) is incorrect because a search warrant is not required for a search of a probationer's home that otherwise complies with procedures. (D) is incorrect because this was not a search incident to a lawful arrest. There was no basis for an arrest until after the search occurred; if the search were not otherwise independently valid, the fact that Barlow was arrested after the search revealed the drugs would not make the search valid.

Answer to Question 5

(A) Dumont's rights were violated by the voluntary manslaughter instruction. The Due Process Clause requires in all criminal cases that the state prove guilt beyond a reasonable doubt. The prosecution must bear the burden of proving all of the elements of the crime charged. Thus, the Supreme Court has held that if "malice aforethought" is an element of murder, the state may not require the defendant to prove that he committed the homicide in the heat of passion, because heat of passion negates malice and in effect requires the defendant to disprove the element of malice aforethought. [Mullaney v. Wilbur (1975)] Here, the judge's instructions create the same result with "extreme emotional disturbance." By instructing the jury that extreme emotional disturbance negates the existence of malice aforethought, which otherwise may be presumed from proof of the unlawful killing, and that the defendant bears the burden of proof on that issue, the judge improperly imposed on Dumont the burden to disprove an element of murder. Here, Dumont came forward with some evidence on the issue of emotional disturbance, but the prosecution still bore the burden of proving that whatever emotional disturbance he had did not negate malice aforethought. Thus, (B) and (D) are incorrect. Insanity is another affirmative defense for which it is constitutional to impose the burden of proof on the defendant. While many jurisdictions require a defendant to prove his insanity by a preponderance of the evidence, federal courts require proof by clear and convincing evidence, and one Supreme Court case upheld requiring a defendant to prove insanity beyond a reasonable doubt. [See Leland v. Oregon (1952)] Thus, (B) and (C) are incorrect and (A) is correct.

Answer to Question 6

(D) Where two persons are tried together and one has given a confession implicating the other, the general rule is that the Sixth Amendment right to confront adverse witnesses prohibits the use of such statement. This problem arises because of the inability of the nonconfessing defendant to compel the confessing co-defendant to take the stand for cross-examination at their joint trial. As exceptions to the general rule, the statement may be admitted if: (i) all portions of the statement referring to the other defendant can be eliminated (so that there is no indication of that defendant's involvement); (ii) the confessing defendant takes the stand and subjects himself to cross-examination with respect to the truth or falsity of what the statement asserts; or (iii) the confession of the nontestifying co-defendant is being used to rebut the defendant's claim that his confession was obtained coercively, in which case the jury must be instructed as to the purpose of the admission. Thugg's confession, which the prosecution seeks to introduce into evidence, implicates Robby in the commission of the crimes charged. Consequently, introduction of this confession raises a problem based on the right of confrontation. However, the three conditions set forth as points of discussion between the judge and counsel correspond to the exceptions pursuant to which a confession such as Thugg's may be admitted. Thus, the conditions in I., II., or III. would constitute a basis for admitting Thugg's confession. (D) is therefore correct and (A), (B), and (C) are incorrect.

Answer to Question 7

(D) Carter cannot be found guilty under the false imprisonment statute. Despite the general rule that it is no defense to a crime that the defendant mistakenly believed that his conduct was not prohibited by the criminal law, a mistake regarding some aspect of law other than the existence of the statute making the act criminal may negate the state of mind required for the crime. When a culpable state of mind is specified by an offense without indicating to which element it applies, the state of mind applies to all material elements of the offense unless a contrary purpose appears in the statute. Thus, the state of mind required here, "knowingly," requires not only that Carter know of Trent's confinement but also that he know there is no valid consent and that he has no legal authority to confine her. His mistake as to his legal authority to confine her negates the state of mind required for that element of the false imprisonment statute. (A) is wrong because whether Carter's reliance on his attorney's advice was reasonable is irrelevant. As long as he believed that he had lawful authority to hold Trent, he did not have the state of mind required for the offense. (B) is wrong because, as stated above, Carter would have had to have knowledge of the absence of lawful authority before he could be found liable under the false imprisonment statute. (C) is incorrect because Trent's compliance with her confinement and her absence of harm are not relevant. Valid consent to negate a charge of false imprisonment cannot be obtained from one without capacity to give such consent, and Trent, being mentally incompetent, did not have the capacity to consent to the confinement. Absence of harm may be a defense to a tort action for false imprisonment where the victim is not aware of the confinement, but it is not a defense to the crime of false imprisonment.

Answer to Question 8

(B) Hammer can be convicted of third degree murder based on the felony murder statute. The State Blue statute defines murder in the third degree as any killing that occurs during and as a result of the commission of a felony. Hence, even an accidental killing committed during the course of a felony is murder. To be guilty of felony murder under the statute, the defendant must be guilty of the underlying felony and death must have been a foreseeable result of commission of the felony. Under such a statute, a defendant can be held liable for felony murder when resistance by the victim results in the death of a third-party bystander who is not a co-felon; there is no requirement in the statute that the killing be caused by the defendant or an accomplice of the defendant. Hammer committed robbery of the convenience store. Even though Hammer had only a toy pistol, a jury could find that it was foreseeable that death could result from commission of the robbery, such as by resistance from the store owner or police. The killing of Bystander resulted from the resistance of Nail, the robbery victim. Consequently, Hammer can be convicted of third degree murder because the killing occurred during the commission of the robbery. (A) is incorrect because, by implication, murder in the second degree consists of murder as known at common law. Thus, to be guilty of second degree murder, a defendant must have intended to kill or to inflict great bodily injury, or have been recklessly indifferent to an unjustifiably high risk to human life. The facts do not indicate that Hammer engaged in any action while intending to kill or seriously injure, or that he acted with the degree of reckless indifference required for murder. Note that Hammer did not initiate the shooting and was "armed" only with a toy pistol. Therefore, Hammer did not unlawfully kill with malice aforethought (other than intent to commit a felony). Consequently, Hammer cannot be convicted of the more serious crime of second degree murder. (C) is incorrect because murder in the third degree, of which Hammer can be convicted, is more serious than manslaughter. Also, the facts do not support conviction for manslaughter. Hammer did not intentionally kill anyone while under provocation (voluntary manslaughter), nor did he cause a death through criminal negligence (involuntary manslaughter). (D) is incorrect because, as discussed above, Hammer can be convicted of third degree murder.

Answer to Question 9

(D) Nail can be convicted of no homicide crime because shooting at Hammer was authorized by law. A private person has the right to use deadly force to effectuate an arrest when the felon appears to pose a threat to the person or to others and deadly force is necessary to prevent his escape, as long as the felon was actually guilty of the felony. Similarly, a person has the right to use deadly force in preventing the completion of a crime being committed if the crime is a "dangerous felony" involving risk to human life. Here, Nail had the right to use deadly force against Hammer, even though he was not directly threatened with imminent death or great bodily harm, because Hammer appeared to be armed with a deadly weapon in the commission of a robbery and appeared to pose a danger to anyone who might try to stop him. While this right to shoot at Hammer would not justify the killing of Bystander if Nail acted with malice aforethought as to Bystander, in this case the store was virtually empty and Bystander was not in the line of Nail's fire. Thus, Nail's conduct would not constitute reckless indifference to an unjustifiably high risk to human life or any other state of mind constituting malice aforethought. Nail therefore can be convicted of no homicide crime. (C) is incorrect because the facts do not support a conviction for manslaughter. Nail is not guilty of voluntary manslaughter because he did not intentionally kill anyone while under legally adequate provocation. He is not guilty of involuntary manslaughter because his shooting at Nail was authorized by law and, given the low probability of anyone else being hit, was not such a great deviation from the conduct of a reasonable person as to constitute criminal negligence. (A) is incorrect because, as discussed above, Nail did not act with reckless indifference to human life or any other state of mind constituting malice aforethought as to anyone other than Hammer. (B) is incorrect because Nail did not cause a death during the commission of a felony; he was trying to *stop* the commission of a felony when he shot the gun.

Answer to Question 10

(D) Esther is not guilty because she lacked the intent to defraud the government. False pretenses consists of obtaining title to the property of another by an intentional false statement of past or existing fact, with intent to defraud the other. This is a crime requiring specific intent, *i.e.,* intent to defraud. Esther believed that she was entitled to the total amount of the combined check, because she thought that the amount of the check equaled what she would have received as a death benefit and an increased spousal benefit. Because Esther believed that she was simply receiving money to which she was entitled, rather than money actually belonging to the government, she lacked the intent to defraud the government. Absent the requisite specific intent, Esther is not guilty of obtaining money by false pretenses. (B) is incorrect because it would hold Esther to a "reasonable person" standard; *i.e.,* imposing liability if she *should have known* that she was receiving benefits to which she was not entitled. Even if Esther should have known this, the fact remains that she sincerely believed that she was only receiving money to which she was entitled. This sincere belief, even if unreasonable, will negate the existence of intent to defraud the government. (C) is virtually identical to (B), stating in effect that Esther is guilty if her belief as to her entitlement to the money is unreasonable. As explained above, the reasonableness of Esther's belief is not significant. As long as Esther truly believed that she was entitled to all of the money, she did not intend to defraud the government. (A) is incorrect because the question asks about the offense of false pretenses. As noted above, this offense clearly requires specific intent, and is therefore not an offense to which strict liability would be properly applicable.

Answer to Question 11

(C) The state statute proscribes sexual intercourse with a person under the age of 16. In (C), Doug had sex with Maxine at a time when he thought she was still 12 days shy of being 16. Actually,

Maxine already was 16, a fact unknown even to her. Although Doug thought he was having sex with someone under the age of consent, the fact is that Maxine had attained the age of consent. Thus, Doug has not engaged in the conduct that is prohibited by the statute. In (A), Don will be found guilty despite the fact that Traci showed him an apparently authentic driver's license indicating that she was 18. A defendant's reasonable mistake as to the victim's age does not prevent liability for statutory rape in most jurisdictions because this is a strict liability crime. Although the facts at least imply that Don might not have had sex with Traci had he known her true age, and that he reasonably believed she was 18, this will not relieve him of liability for having had sex with a 15-year-old. In (B), Duffy Bob and Karen Sue were married according to Appalachian law at the time they had intercourse. Although ordinary rape at common law was often defined as requiring no marital relationship between the defendant and the victim, the Blue statutory rape law at issue here does not list the absence of a marital relationship between the parties as an element of the offense. There is simply a blanket proscription of sexual intercourse with a person under 16. Thus, the fact that Duffy Bob and Karen Sue were married under Appalachian law when they had intercourse might not serve as a defense to a charge of statutory rape (depending on how the Blue courts have interpreted the statute). Note also that the marriage may not be valid in Blue, because Duffy Bob and Karen Sue went to Appalachian to enter into a marriage that would not have been valid in Blue, intending to return and remain residents of Blue. Such a marriage might be regarded as void by Blue. (D) presents a somewhat close question. In effect, Delia will be asserting the defense that she had sex with a 15-year-old because of duress. A person is not guilty of an offense, other than homicide, if she performs an otherwise criminal act under the threat of imminent infliction of death or great bodily harm, provided that she reasonably believes death or great bodily harm will be inflicted on herself or on a member of her immediate family if she does not perform such conduct. Here, there is no strong factual indication that there was a threat of imminent death or great bodily harm that would befall Delia if she did not have sex with Scott. Although Delia was concerned that Scott might get violent, the facts are not strong enough to conclusively establish that Delia acted under duress. Thus, the situation in (D) is not as certain as the situation in (C) to absolve the defendant from liability for statutory rape.

Answer to Question 12

(B) Yegg is guilty of rape and robbery but not felony murder or burglary. The facts state that Yegg raped Chiquita; thus he is guilty of that crime. Robbery consists of a taking of the personal property of another from the other's person or presence by force or intimidation, with the intent to permanently deprive him of it. The property must be taken from some location reasonably close to the victim, but not necessarily from the victim's person. Here, Mugg used the threat of force posed by his gun to obtain the store's money from Greengiant, intending to permanently deprive Greengiant of the money. Thus, Mugg committed robbery. Although Yegg did not actually take the money, he is guilty of robbery as an accomplice. Mugg, who actually engaged in the act of robbery with the requisite mental state, is guilty as a principal. Yegg, who aided Mugg during the commission of the robbery, *with the intent* to aid Mugg in the commission of the robbery, is an accomplice to the robbery and is responsible for the crime. Thus, Yegg is guilty of both the rape that he personally committed and the robbery to which he was an accomplice. Therefore (B) is correct and (A) is incorrect. The common law elements of burglary are: (i) a breaking (ii) and entry (iii) of the dwelling (iv) of another (v) at nighttime (vi) with the intent of committing a felony therein. A structure is a dwelling if it is used with regularity for sleeping purposes, even if it is also used for other purposes, such as conducting a business. Modern statutes sometimes broaden the description of structures that can be burglarized beyond dwellings. Here, it seems that the grocery store is not used for any purpose other than conducting a business. Thus, the store is not a dwelling. Absent a statutory provision to the contrary, the store, not being a dwelling, cannot be burglarized. Thus, Yegg cannot be guilty of burglary for the events described in this question. Therefore, (D) is incorrect. Pursuant to the doctrine of felony murder, a killing committed during the course of a felony is murder. Death must have been a foreseeable result of commission of the felony. Here, Greengiant's death was caused during the commission of a felony (robbery). Although most deaths so occurring are found to be foreseeable, this death was probably not foreseeable. Yegg did not know that the "storage room" was actually a cold storage compartment. Consequently, the death of Greengiant, which resulted from having been locked in the cold compartment, likely will be deemed an unforeseeable consequence of Yegg's commission of a felony. Therefore, (C) and (D) are incorrect. Note that the simple fact that Yegg was unaware of Greengiant's preexisting lung condition would not, by itself, render the death unforeseeable. Had Yegg known that Greengiant was being placed in a cold storage compartment, Yegg would have been guilty of felony murder for Greengiant's death, even though he did not know about the chronic lung condition.

Answer to Question 13

(A) Mugg is guilty of robbery but is not guilty of conspiracy to commit rape or criminal homicide. Conspiracy consists of: (i) an agreement between two or more persons; (ii) an intent to enter into an agreement; and (iii) an intent to achieve the objective of the agreement. Here, Mugg and Yegg may have entered into an agreement to rob the grocery store, but there is no indication that Mugg and Yegg ever entered into an agreement to rape anyone. The mere fact that Mugg was aware that Yegg was a convicted sex offender does not establish any sort of agreement between the two to commit rape. Absent the necessary agreement, there is no basis upon which Mugg can be convicted of conspiracy to commit rape. Therefore, (B) and (D) are incorrect. Regarding Mugg's potential guilt for criminal homicide, it must be noted that, because Mugg did not know about Greengiant's lung condition or that the "storeroom" was really a cold storage compartment, Mugg did not have intent to kill Greengiant or to inflict great bodily injury on him, nor did he act with an awareness of an unjustifiably high risk to human life. Thus, Mugg lacked the intent for homicide. In addition, as explained in the answer to the preceding question, Mugg is not guilty of felony murder. The fact that neither Mugg nor Yegg knew that they were placing Greengiant in a cold storage compartment probably renders Greengiant's resulting death an unforeseeable consequence of their commission of the robbery, thus precluding guilt for felony murder. Also, Mugg is not guilty of involuntary manslaughter based on criminal negligence. Criminal negligence requires a greater deviation from the "reasonable person" standard than is required for civil negligence liability. Because Mugg was unaware of Greengiant's lung condition or of the true nature of the cold storage compartment, Mugg did not exhibit the sort of negligence needed to constitute criminal negligence. Consequently, Mugg is not guilty of involuntary manslaughter. Therefore, since Mugg cannot be convicted of criminal homicide, (C) and (D) are incorrect.

Answer to Question 14

(B) Drell cannot be convicted of a crime under the statute because it was enacted for his protection, and Keating cannot be convicted of conspiracy under the statute because, under some circumstances, a person who would otherwise be liable as an accomplice is not subject to conviction because of a legislative intent to exempt him. If a statute is intended to protect members of a limited class from exploitation or overbearing, members of that class are presumed to have been intended to be immune from liability, even if they participate in the crime in a manner that would otherwise make them liable. Because Drell is an illegal alien, he would not be liable as an accomplice under the statute, making (C) incorrect. Keating clearly can be convicted for the substantive offense but he cannot be convicted of conspiracy. One of the implications of the common law requirement that there be at least two guilty parties in a conspiracy arises when the crime involves members of a class protected by the statute. If members of a conspiracy agree to commit an act that violates a statute designed to protect persons within a given class, a person within that class not only cannot be guilty of the crime itself, as discussed above, but also cannot be guilty of a conspiracy to commit the crime. (D) is therefore incorrect. Because the member of the protected class cannot be guilty of conspiracy, if no other guilty party exists, the other member of the agreement cannot be guilty of criminal conspiracy because there were not two guilty parties to the agreement. Thus, since Drell cannot be convicted of conspiracy under the statute, neither can Keating. (A) is therefore incorrect and (B) is correct.

Answer to Question 15

(C) Keating can be convicted of conspiracy in a unilateral jurisdiction even though Drell can be convicted of neither solicitation nor conspiracy. Under the unilateral approach, the crime of conspiracy is shown by proof that the defendant agreed with another to commit a crime (even if that other person does not share the commitment), and does not require proof of an actual agreement between two or more persons. Thus, the fact that no other party to the conspiracy could be found guilty does not prevent the defendant from being convicted of conspiracy. Here, the fact that Drell is a member of the class that the statute was designed to protect prevents him from being found guilty of conspiracy; (B) is therefore incorrect. However, unlike under the common law approach in the previous question, under the unilateral approach this fact has no bearing on Keating's liability for conspiracy. Thus, (C) is correct and (D) is incorrect. (A) is wrong because the crime of solicitation is treated the same as conspiracy. If the solicitor could not be guilty of the completed crime because of legislative intent to exempt him, he cannot be found guilty of solicitation of the crime. Because Drell is a member of the class intended to be protected by the statute, he cannot be found guilty of soliciting Keating to commit it.

Answer to Question 16

(B) Donna's best defense is that the statute was not reasonably available because she did not receive the explanatory booklet. Generally, it is not a defense to a crime that the defendant was unaware that her acts were prohibited by the criminal law or that she mistakenly believed that her acts were not prohibited. However, the defendant has a defense if the statute proscribing her conduct was not published or made reasonably available prior to the conduct. The statute under which Donna is charged was presumably published prior to her filing her income tax return. However, the statute was exceedingly complicated, as were the computation schedules and other information accompanying the tax forms. Consequently, the failure of the state to include the explanatory booklet with the tax forms may amount to a situation in which the pertinent statute was not made reasonably available to Donna prior to filing her return. If this is the case, then Donna will have a defense. (C) is incorrect. At common law, it was no defense that the defendant relied upon an official interpretation of the law by the public officer or body responsible for its interpretation or administration. Under modern law, it is a defense if the defendant relies upon an erroneous official statement of the law by one charged by law with responsibility for the interpretation, administration, or enforcement of the law. However, even under this rule Donna would not have a strong defense because Michael, as a law student working at the revenue department part-time, is not the type of public officer charged by law with responsibility for interpreting or enforcing the statute, upon whose advice Donna would be entitled to rely. (D) is incorrect because generally it is no defense that a defendant simply relied on the erroneous advice of counsel. An emerging trend provides that if reasonable reliance on the advice of counsel negates the necessary state of mind for the crime, such reliance may be a defense. However, choice (D) focuses on Donna's reliance on Lem's advice rather than her lack of intent, so (B) is the better answer. (A) is incorrect because Donna's mistake as to the scope of the law does not negate the required state of mind. If the mental state for a crime requires a certain belief concerning a collateral aspect of law, ignorance or mistake as to that aspect of law will negate the requisite state of mind. Such a situation involves ignorance of some aspect of law *other than* the existence of the statute making the act criminal. The statute here simply penalizes one who knowingly fails to declare "any" income. Donna knew that she was not declaring certain income; her ignorance that the law applied to that income does not negate her state of mind and is not a defense.

Answer to Question 17

(D) Domby can raise the defenses of involuntary intoxication and insanity. The facts here indicate involuntary intoxication. Intoxication is involuntary if it results from the taking of an intoxicating substance without knowledge of its nature, under direct duress imposed by another, or pursuant to medical advice. Such intoxication may be treated as mental illness (in which case the defendant is entitled to acquittal) if, because of the intoxication, the defendant meets the applicable test for insanity. Here, Domby took the medicine without knowing of its hallucinatory properties and pursuant to the advice of his doctor. Thus, Domby's resulting state of hallucination will be considered to be involuntary intoxication. We are told that the applicable test for insanity is the *M'Naghten* Rule. Pursuant to this test, a defendant is entitled to acquittal if a disease of the mind caused a defect of reason such that the defendant lacked the ability at the time of his actions to either: (i) know the wrongfulness of his actions; or (ii) understand the nature and quality of his actions. If a defendant suffers from delusions (false beliefs), it must be determined whether his actions would have been criminal if the facts had been as he believed them to be. Domby falsely believed that he was being confronted by a Martian with a ray gun. Had this delusion been accurate, Domby would have been legally entitled to use force (such as throwing the paperweight at the "Martian") to defend himself from imminent death or great bodily harm. Because of the hallucination, Domby lacked the ability to know the wrongfulness of his conduct (*i.e.,* Domby believed that facts existed that justified throwing the paperweight at Chauncy). Therefore, the elements of the *M'Naghten* test are satisfied, and Domby is entitled to an acquittal on the basis of insanity at the time of the pertinent actions. Because Domby met the *M'Naghten* test as a result of his involunary intoxication (*i.e.,* the intoxication caused him to hallucinate that Chauncy was a Martian armed with a ray gun), involuntary intoxication also would be an effective defense. (B) and (C) are incorrect because each choice excludes one of these two defenses as an effective defense. (A) is incorrect for two reasons. First, Domby did not know that the medicine was intoxicating. Thus, this is not a case of voluntary intoxication. Second, voluntary intoxication is a defense only to a crime that requires intent or knowledge (where the intoxication prevents the defendant from formulating the intent or obtaining the knowledge). Domby is charged with battery, the definition of which does not require intent. Thus, battery is not a crime to which voluntary intoxication will be a defense.

Answer to Question 18

(C) Because Seidel did not see the flying bottle coming at him, there was no reasonable apprehension of imminent bodily harm. Thus, there cannot be a conviction for assault. Assault is either: (i) an attempt to commit a battery, or (ii) the intentional creation, other than by mere words, of a reasonable apprehension in the mind of the victim of imminent bodily harm. Micromind did not intend to hit anyone. Thus, Micromind's actions do not constitute an attempt to commit a battery, which would require a specific intent to bring about bodily injury or an offensive touching. In addition, the fact that Seidel did not see the bottle being thrown at him means that Micromind did not create in Seidel a reasonable apprehension of imminent bodily harm. Consequently, under the facts of (C), Micromind is not likely to be convicted of either type of assault. In (A), Pinhead intended to hit Riker with the pipe, so he could be found to have acted with intent to inflict great bodily injury or, at a minimum, with reckless indifference to an unjustifiably high risk to human life. Either of these states of mind constitutes malice aforethought for purposes of murder. Therefore, Pinhead acted with malice aforethought. Under the principle of transferred intent, if a defendant intends a harmful result to a particular person or object, and in trying to carry out that intent causes a similar harmful result to another person or object, his intent will be transferred from the intended person or object to the one actually harmed. Thus, although Pinhead did not intend to hit Ulrich, his intent to hit Riker will be transferred to Ulrich, so that Pinhead will be deemed to have caused the death of Ulrich with malice aforethought. Thus, Pinhead is likely to be convicted of murder. In (B), Dolt can be convicted of battery because a battery need not be intentional. It is sufficient that the defendant caused the application of force with criminal negligence. Although Dolt did not intend to strike anyone, his act of throwing a bottle onto an occupied football field exhibited at least criminal negligence, if not recklessness. Therefore, Dolt unlawfully applied force to Leary's person, causing bodily injury to him, with the requisite state of mind for battery. In (D), Kook, intending to burn down Riker's house, actually brought about the burning of Nixx's house. Under the principle of transferred intent discussed above, Kook's intent is transferred from Riker's house to Nixx's house. Therefore, Kook can be convicted of arson.

Answer to Question 19

(B) Judd should be found guilty of the charged felony if he knew or believed that the box contained cocaine. Judd is being tried for "knowingly" possessing cocaine. A person does not act knowingly unless he is aware that his conduct is of the proscribed nature or that the proscribed circumstances exist. Thus, Judd could not have acted knowingly unless he knew or believed that the box contained cocaine. (A) is incorrect because criminal statutes that penalize the possession of contraband generally require only that the defendant have *control* of the item for a long enough period to have had an opportunity to terminate the possession. Thus, Judd need not have moved or handled the box. (C) is wrong for the same reason as (A) and also because Judd's failure to know when he should have known would constitute negligence—failure to be aware of a substantial risk that prohibited results will follow or that circumstances exist—and negligence is not sufficient to establish knowledge. Note, however, that a deliberate failure to learn facts when it is readily possible to do so may be held to be knowledge. (D) is incorrect because, as discussed above, the statute requires that Judd knew or believed that the box contained cocaine.

Answer to Question 20

(D) Korri did not have the requisite intent to be convicted of either robbery or conspiracy to commit robbery. Because Korri did not actually engage in the act constituting the robbery, the only way she can be convicted of this crime is as an accomplice. An accomplice is one who aids, counsels, or encourages the principal before or during commission of the crime. To be convicted as an accomplice, a person must have given aid, counsel, or encouragement with the intent to aid or encourage the principal in the commission of the crime charged. Mere knowledge that a crime will result from the aid provided generally is insufficient for accomplice liability. Here, Korri did aid Dumar in the commission of the robbery prior to the crime by awakening him at the time he requested. However, the facts do not even establish that Korri believed Dumar's statement. Assuming that she did believe that Dumar was going to rob the store, there is no indication that she was interested in the outcome of the plan or had a stake in the robbery (*i.e.,* she did not have the intent to bring about the permanent deprivation of the money from the store). Such mere knowledge that Dumar intended to rob the store upon awakening, without a clear indication of an actual intent to aid in the commission of the robbery, will not suffice as the mental state required to be convicted as an accomplice. Therefore, Korri cannot be convicted of robbery. Thus, choices (A) and (C) are wrong. Choice (B) is wrong because Korri is not likely to be convicted of conspiracy to commit robbery. Conspiracy consists of: (i) an agreement between two or more persons; (ii) an intent to enter into an agreement; and (iii) an intent to achieve the objective of the agreement. Here, for much the same reasons as set forth above concerning accomplice liability, Korri probably will be found not to have intended to achieve the objective of robbing the store. Conspiracy is a specific intent crime that requires both an intent to agree and an intent to achieve the objective of the conspiracy. The intent to agree can be inferred from Korri's conduct of providing Dumar with the wake-up call. However, it cannot be said that Korri intended to bring about the robbery of the store. Such intent cannot be inferred from mere knowledge that Dumar planned to rob the store. As an apparently disinterested bystander, Korri probably will be found not to have the state of mind necessary to be convicted of conspiracy to commit robbery.

Answer to Question 21

(D) Even though Prepper's words may have been intended to provoke Karl-Heinz, this fact alone would not justify Karl-Heinz's use of deadly force. A person may use deadly force in self-defense if he is: (i) without fault; (ii) confronted with unlawful force; and (iii) threatened with imminent death or great bodily harm. Generally, one who begins a fight has no right to use force in his own defense during that fight. However, if the victim of the initial aggression suddenly escalates a relatively minor fight into one involving deadly force and does not give the aggressor a chance to withdraw, the aggressor may use force in his own defense. Here, although Prepper instigated the hostile situation by repeatedly insulting Karl-Heinz, Karl-Heinz's throwing of a punch probably calls for his being characterized as the aggressor. Prepper (as the victim of the initial aggression) escalated matters by using a knife, especially since Karl-Heinz had gone back to drinking and was not threatening him in any way. This escalation (which is the point stated in choice (B)) entitled Karl-Heinz to employ deadly force in his own defense against the imminent threat of death or great bodily harm posed by Prepper's use of the knife. Thus, (B) presents a point that will be helpful to Karl-Heinz. (A) is incorrect because, if Prepper had no reason to fear serious bodily injury when he drew the knife, Prepper's use of the knife constitutes unlawful force, in response to which Karl-Heinz was entitled to use deadly force of his own. Consequently, (A) will also be of value in gaining Karl-Heinz an acquittal. Regarding (C), many courts hold that a person is not under a duty to retreat before using deadly force. Thus, even if Karl-Heinz could have safely retreated, he was still entitled to use deadly force in self-defense, so that he is not required to show why he did not retreat. Other courts, however, do require retreat before the use of deadly force, but only if the retreat can be made in complete safety. The fact that Karl-Heinz's route of retreat was blocked by college students (apparently friends of Prepper) would indicate that a retreat could not be made in safety, and would be significant in a jurisdiction holding that there is a duty to retreat. Therefore, (C) also presents a point that can be helpful to Karl-Heinz. (D) is correct because the motive of Prepper in insulting Karl-Heinz is of no help to the defense. Even if the words did provoke him, Karl-Heinz would not be entitled to employ deadly force against Prepper on the basis of Prepper's desire for trouble. Use of such force would be justified only if Karl-Heinz held a reasonable belief that he was faced with imminent death or great bodily harm from one of the students if he did not respond with deadly force.

Answer to Question 22

(A) Paris may also be found guilty only of conspiracy if he is found guilty of burglary. One who solicits another to commit a crime cannot be convicted of both the solicitation and the completed crime. Likewise, one who completes a crime after attempting it may not be convicted of both the attempt and the completed crime. However, if conspirators are successful, they can be convicted of both criminal conspiracy and the crime they committed pursuant to the conspiracy (*i.e.,* conspiracy does not merge with the completed offense). Thus, if Paris is found guilty of burglary, he cannot also be convicted of either attempt or solicitation. Paris *can* be convicted of conspiracy in addition to burglary (with conspiracy liability being based on the apparent agreement between Paris and Helen to bring about the burglary of the home of Menelaus). (B) incorrectly states that Paris may be found guilty of solicitation as well as the principal offense of burglary. (C) and (D) make the same incorrect assertion. In addition, (D) incorrectly states that Paris may be found guilty of attempt as well as the completed crime, and that he may not be found guilty of conspiracy.

Answer to Question 23

(D) Dobie is guilty of larceny by trick because he obtained possession of Charlotte's car by means of misrepresentations. Larceny is the taking and carrying away of tangible personal property of another by trespass, with intent to permanently (or for an unreasonable time) deprive the person of her interest in the property. The taking must be without the consent of the person in possession of the property. If such consent is induced by a misrepresentation, the consent is not valid. The resulting larceny is called larceny by trick. Here, Dobie obtained possession of Charlotte's car with her consent. However, this consent was obtained by means of Dobie's statements concerning the illness of his sister and the unavailability of his own car. These were false statements as to present facts, made with the intent that Charlotte rely on them. Thus, these were misrepresentations that were used to induce Charlotte's consent. At the time of this taking Dobie intended to deal with the car in a manner that involved a substantial risk of loss. This suffices as intent to permanently deprive. Therefore, all the elements are in place for larceny by trick. (A) is not as good a choice as (D) because the taking in this case is better characterized as larceny by trick rather than larceny, given that Dobie induced Charlotte to consent to his taking possession of the car. (C) is incorrect because Dobie obtained only possession of the car, not title. False pretenses differs from larceny by trick in what is obtained. If the defendant obtains only possession of the property, the offense is larceny by trick, whereas obtaining of title means that false pretenses has been committed. What the victim intended to convey to the defendant is determinative. Charlotte intended only to let Dobie borrow her car for the week she was to be away, not to convey title to him. Consequently, the only thing Dobie obtained was possession of the car. Because title to the car was not obtained, there can be no conviction of false pretenses. Regarding (B), embezzlement is the fraudulent conversion of property of another by a person in lawful possession of that property. In embezzlement, misappropriation occurs while the defendant has lawful possession of the property, while in larceny, it occurs generally at the time the defendant obtains wrongful possession of the property. Here, as detailed above, Dobie's taking of possession of the car was trespassory due to the manner in which he obtained Charlotte's consent to such possession. The crime of larceny was complete upon Dobie's taking possession with the requisite intent to permanently deprive. Thus, at the time the car was wrecked, Dobie had already misappropriated the car and was not in lawful possession of it. As a result, there can be no conviction for embezzlement.

Answer to Question 24

(C) Farquhar has committed burglary and larceny. Burglary consists of a breaking and entry of the dwelling of another at nighttime, with the intent of committing a felony therein. It is not necessary that a felony actually be carried out, only that the defendant have the intent to commit a felony at the time of entry. After dark, Farquhar broke into and entered Anderson's house, with the intent to commit the felonies of larceny and arson. Regardless of whether Farquhar took anything or committed a burning, the burglary was complete upon Farquhar's breaking and entering Anderson's dwelling at nighttime with the requisite intent. Farquhar has also committed common law larceny. Larceny is the taking and carrying away of the personal property of another, by trespass, with the intent to permanently deprive the owner of his interest in the property. The element of carrying away, or asportation, is satisfied as long as there is some movement of the property as a step in carrying it away. The movement need only be slight as long as it was part of the carrying away process. Here, Farquhar piled valuables into a blanket and carried the blanket toward the side door, which he apparently was going to use as his exit. This movement was sufficient to constitute a carrying away. Having acted with the requisite intent to permanently deprive the Andersons of their property, Farquhar has committed larceny. (A) is incorrect because, as discussed above, Farquhar is liable for the completed crime of larceny rather than attempted larceny. (B) is incorrect for the same reason and also because Farquhar probably has not committed an act sufficiently close to success to be liable for attempted arson. An attempt requires an intent to commit the completed offense and an act beyond mere preparation for the offense. Traditionally, courts used the proximity test, requiring an act that is dangerously close to success. The Model Penal Code and most state criminal codes require that the act or omission constitute a "substantial step" towards commission of the crime. Here, although Farquhar was in the house and had the intent to burn it, he has done nothing else towards committing the arson and it is not clear that the items he needs to start the fire are in his possession yet. Hence, his acts probably are not so dangerously close to success or a substantial enough step towards committing the crime as to make him liable for attempted arson. (D) is wrong because, as discussed above, Farquhar is liable for the completed offenses of burglary and larceny.

Answer to Question 25

(C) Officer DiNapoli is an accessory after the fact to burglary. An accessory after the fact is one who receives, relieves, comforts, or assists another, knowing that he has committed a felony, in order to help the felon escape arrest, trial, or conviction. The crime committed by the principal must have been completed at the time aid is rendered. Here, DiNapoli had a duty to arrest Farquhar and failed to do so, instead letting him go. Her omission to act under these circumstances constituted sufficient assistance to Farquhar to make her liable as an accessory after the fact. She almost certainly knew that Farquhar had committed the felony of burglary because she was responding to a silent alarm at the house and Farquhar admitted that he was inside but had not gotten anything. Under these facts, she can be liable as an accessory after the fact to burglary. (A) is incorrect because the facts do not indicate that DiNapoli knew that Farquhar had committed larceny when she let him go. She had stopped him outside of the house, and since he apparently had nothing stolen on him, she had no reason to doubt his claim that he had not gotten anything from the house. Although she probably surmised that he had broken in with the intent to commit larceny, she had no way of knowing that he had completed the crime of larceny by carrying valuables in a blanket to the door (as discussed in the preceding question). (B) is incorrect because an accomplice is one who, with the intent that the crime be committed, aids, counsels, or encourages the principal before or during the commission of the crime. Because Farquhar had already completed his crimes when DiNapoli stopped him, her only liability will be as an accessory after the fact. (D) is incorrect because, as discussed above, DiNapoli can be held liable as an accessory after the fact to burglary.

Answer to Question 26

(A) The court should reverse Doe's conviction because Instruction #6 requires the defendant to disprove one of the elements of murder. Due process requires in criminal cases that the state prove guilt beyond a reasonable doubt. The prosecution has the burden of proving all of the elements of the crime charged. Thus, if malice aforethought is an element of murder and voluntary manslaughter is distinguished from murder by the existence of adequate provocation, the defendant cannot be required to prove that he committed the homicide in the heat of passion (*i.e.*, with adequate provocation). Such a requirement would impose on the defendant the burden of disproving the element of malice aforethought, since "heat of passion" negates malice. While the defendant can be given the burden of going forward with some evidence on the provocation issue, once he has done so, the prosecution bears the burden of proving that the killing was not done in the heat of passion. In the case at issue, Instruction #6 requires a defendant to prove that he committed the intentional killing under adequate provocation. In State Yellow, malice aforethought is an element of murder. Therefore, this instruction in effect requires the defendant to disprove the element of malice aforethought, thereby relieving the state of its burden of proving all elements of the crime. As discussed above, such an instruction cannot pass constitutional muster. On the other hand, for an affirmative defense such as insanity, it is permissible to impose the burden of proof on the defendant. Thus, Instruction #8 does not affect the state's obligation to prove all elements of the crime, and is permissible under the general principles mentioned above. Thus, (B) and (C) incorrectly state that this instruction is improper. (D) is incorrect because it states that Instruction #6 is proper. As explained above, this is not an accurate statement of the law.

Answer to Question 27

(B) Cary can be convicted of false pretenses and attempted robbery. False pretenses consists of obtaining title to the property of another by an intentional or knowing false statement of past or existing fact with intent to defraud another. With regard to the false representation, all that is required is that the defendant create a false impression as to a matter of fact, which is what happened here. Cary obtained title to the gasoline by creating a false impression that he owned the sunglasses that he was offering in exchange, and he had the requisite intent to be convicted of false pretenses. He can also be convicted of attempted robbery because he attempted a taking of the property of another in the presence of the victim by force and with the intent to permanently deprive the victim of it. The fact that he was persuaded not to carry out the robbery does not affect his liability for attempt; that crime was completed as soon as he pulled out a knife and demanded the gas. (A) and (C) are incorrect because larceny by trick occurs when *possession* of the property is obtained by the defendant's misrepresentations, whereas false pretenses is the appropriate offense when the misrepresentations have prompted the victim to convey *title* to the property to the defendant. Here, the clerk intended to convey title to the gas to Cary in exchange for the sunglasses. (C) and (D) are incorrect because the majority rule is that abandonment is not a defense to attempt. As discussed above, the crime of attempted robbery was completed as soon as Cary pulled the knife out of his pocket and demanded the gas.

Answer to Question 28

(D) The judge's failure to determine whether Darwin understood his right to trial by jury indicates that his guilty plea does not satisfy the constitutional requirement that it be "voluntary and intelligent." A guilty plea is a waiver of the Sixth Amendment right to a jury trial. To be a valid waiver, the judge must determine on the record that the guilty plea represents a voluntary and intelligent choice among the alternative courses of action open to the defendant. To ensure that this is the case, the judge should inform the defendant personally of the nature of the charge to which the plea is offered, of the maximum possible penalty, that he has a right not to plead guilty, and that by pleading guilty he waives his right to a trial. If the judge did not determine whether Darwin understood that he had a right to a trial by jury, Darwin's plea will not be a sufficiently intelligent choice to satisfy the constitutional standard, and therefore will not be immune from a post-sentence attack on it. (A) is incorrect because Darwin had no legitimate grounds for his motion to dismiss for violation of his right to a speedy trial. The Sixth Amendment right to a speedy trial does not attach until the defendant has been arrested or charged. Pre-arrest delays do not violate this standard, nor do they violate general due process requirements unless they were in bad faith and prejudice the defendant. Otherwise, the only limitation on pre-arrest delay would be the statute of limitations for the particular crime. Thus, the failure of the judge to rule on the motion to dismiss would not be a good argument for setting aside Darwin's guilty plea. (B) is incorrect because most jurisdictions do not require that the record contain evidence of the defendant's guilt or other factual basis for the plea. Unless the defendant protests his innocence while offering a guilty plea, the judge need not determine whether there is evidence to indicate that the defendant actually committed the crime. (C) is incorrect. While the prosecutor has a duty to disclose exculpatory evidence to the defendant, the judge may accept a guilty plea without determining whether the prosecutor has satisfied that duty.

Answer to Question 29

(D) Janusz's best argument is that under the majority view, a defendant is not liable for the death of a co-felon from resistance of the victim or police. A killing committed during the course of a felony is murder, with malice being implied from the intent to commit the underlying felony. Liability under the felony murder doctrine requires that death have been a foreseeable result of commission of the felony. Under the majority view, felony murder liability cannot be based upon the death of a co-felon from resistance by the victim or police pursuit. Mirko, a co-felon of Janusz, was killed by a pursuing police officer following commission of the robbery. Under the majority rule, Janusz is not guilty of felony murder for such a death. Thus, (D) represents his strongest defense. (A) is incorrect because, despite the fact that Janusz and Mirko were unarmed, they still committed robbery of the store, in that they took the money from the clerk by means of threats of immediate death or serious physical injury, with the intent to permanently deprive. Certainly, it was reasonable for the clerk to believe they had guns, as Janusz said they did, and in any case she was intimidated by their size. Thus, Janusz is guilty of the underlying felony of robbery. Armed resistance by the victim or police that results in death is a foreseeable result of robbery even where the robbers are not armed. Consequently, the fact that Janusz was unarmed at the time of committing the robbery will have no bearing on his guilt of felony murder. (B) is incorrect because Callaghan's failure to warn the fleeing felons before firing is irrelevant to Janusz's liability for felony murder. Even had Callaghan given a warning, Janusz would not be guilty of the felony murder of his co-felon killed by the police. The lack of a warning might go to the issue of whether Callaghan's shooting was justified, but it does not impact on Janusz's guilt of felony murder. (C) is incorrect because, although death must have been caused during the commission or attempted commission of a felony, the fact that the felony was technically completed before death was caused does not prevent the killing from being felony murder. Deaths caused while fleeing from the crime are felony murder. Although Mirko and Janusz had completed the robbery at the time Mirko was killed, the killing occurred while the felons were fleeing from the crime. Thus, if all other required factors were present, this would be felony murder.

Answer to Question 30

(D) The court should deny Jack's motion because if Benson reasonably believed Margaret lived in the trailer, the search would be valid. Under the exclusionary rule, evidence obtained from an unconstitutional search must be excluded from trial. To be valid, searches must be reasonable.

The Supreme Court has held that most searches are unreasonable unless the police obtain a warrant before searching. However, there are six categories of searches that the Court has held to be reasonable without a warrant. One such category is searches conducted pursuant to consent. To fall within this exception to the warrant requirement, consent must be given by one who appears to have an apparent right to use or occupy the premises and the search cannot go beyond the scope of the consent given. The consent is valid as long as the police reasonably believed that the person who gave the consent had the authority to do so, and the scope of the consent is limited only to areas to which a reasonable person under the circumstances would believe it extends. Here, Margaret's consent was valid if Benson reasonably believed that she lived there. (It was reasonable to believe that Margaret lived in the trailer, or at least had authority to be there, since she answered the door, knew of Jack's whereabouts, and readily consented to the search.) The search did not exceed the scope of the consent because a reasonable person would believe that Margaret's consent would extend to small storage compartments since Benson told her that he was looking for drugs. Therefore, the search was valid under the consent exception and the evidence should not be excluded. (A) is incorrect because consent is not invalid merely because the person who gave it did not actually have authority to do so; the police need only reasonably believe that the person had authority to consent, and as explained above, it was reasonable for Benson to believe that Margaret had authority here. (B) is incorrect because, as explained above, the scope of consent extends to any area where a reasonable person under the circumstances would assume it extends, and since Benson told Margaret that he suspected Jack of dealing drugs, it was reasonable to assume that he was looking for drugs and so would probably look in even small containers. (C) is incorrect because it appears that Jack's trailer would not fall within the automobile exception. Certain searches of automobiles are excluded from the requirement of a warrant because the Supreme Court has held that people have a lesser expectation of privacy in an automobile than in other areas and automobiles are likely to disappear before a warrant can be acquired. The automobile exception extends not only to cars, but also to other vehicles that are readily mobile and as to which there is a lesser expectation of privacy. However, nothing in the facts here indicates that Jack's mobile home may readily be moved, and since it appears to be Jack's regular home rather than a vehicle, it is doubtful that the Court would find the requisite lesser expectation of privacy. Therefore, the trailer would not fall within the automobile exception to the warrant requirement.

Answer to Question 31

(C) Margaret can claim a reasonable expectation of privacy for Fourth Amendment purposes if she was an overnight guest of the owner of the place searched. To raise a Fourth Amendment claim of an unreasonable search or seizure, a person must have a reasonable expectation of privacy with respect to the place searched or the item seized. It is not enough merely that *someone* has an expectation of privacy in the place searched. The Supreme Court has imposed a standing requirement so that a person can complain about an evidentiary search or seizure only if it violates her *own* reasonable expectations of privacy. The Court has held that a person has a legitimate expectation of privacy anytime (i) she owned or had a right to possession of the place searched, (ii) the place searched was in fact her own home, whether or not she owned or had a right to possession of it, or (iii) she was an overnight guest of the owner of the place searched. Thus, Margaret would have standing to challenge the search of Jack's trailer if she was an overnight guest of Jack. (A) is incorrect because standing to raise a Fourth Amendment claim does not exist merely because a person will be harmed by introduction of evidence seized during an illegal search of a third person's property. The person must establish that her own legitimate expectation of privacy has been violated. (B) is wrong because the fact that Margaret was not the owner or occupier of the trailer does not preclude her from challenging the search. As discussed above, an overnight guest may also have a reasonable expectation of privacy in the premises for purposes of the Fourth Amendment. (D) is incorrect. While Margaret may have standing to object to the seizure of the marijuana if she claims ownership of it, that is not the only basis for raising a Fourth Amendment claim; she will have standing to object to the search of the trailer under the circumstances in choice (C) regardless of whether she claims ownership of the marijuana.

Answer to Question 32

(B) The judge should give the manslaughter instruction and allow the jury to consider the earlier altercation. Provocation will reduce a killing to voluntary manslaughter only if four requirements are met: (i) the provocation was a type that would arouse sudden and intense passion that would cause a reasonable person to lose self-control, (ii) the defendant in fact was provoked, (iii) there was not sufficient time between the provocation and the killing for the passion of a reasonable person to cool, and (iv) the defendant in fact did not cool off between the provocation and the killing. While at common law some provocations were defined as inadequate as a matter of law, modern courts are more likely to submit to the jury the question of what constituted adequate provocation. Similarly, whether there has been a sufficient time for a reasonable person to cool off is a factual question that depends on the nature of the provocation and the attendant circumstances. Here, Dan's belief that he was being shoved again by Rick and set up for another punch in the face may have rekindled his rage at the earlier punch and taunting by Rick. The jury should be allowed to consider all of the circumstances, including the earlier altercation, to decide whether there was a sufficient provocation or a sufficient time for a reasonable person to cool off. Hence, the judge should agree to give the manslaughter instruction. (A) is incorrect. Some states recognize an "imperfect self-defense" doctrine under which a murder may be reduced to manslaughter even though the defendant unreasonably but honestly believed in the necessity of responding with deadly force. However, the doctrine is not necessary here; Dan should be entitled to a manslaughter instruction regardless of whether he shows that he believed in the need to use deadly force in self-defense. (C) is wrong because under the principle of transferred intent, which would transfer Dan's intent from the intended person to the person actually harmed, any mitigating circumstances that the defendant could have asserted against the intended victim (such as provocation) will also be transferred. While the jury could decide that Dan, even if adequately provoked, acted with reckless disregard by stabbing at a person before looking to see who it was and thus is guilty of murder, Dan is at least entitled to have the jury consider the manslaughter issue. (D) is incorrect because, as discussed above, the court would probably allow the jury to consider the earlier altercation as well as the later shove in deciding whether Dan was adequately provoked.

Answer to Question 33

(B) Dribble's reasonable belief that Bibber is 25 years old is a mistake of fact that negates the state of mind required by the statute. Ignorance or mistake as to a matter of fact will affect criminal guilt only if it shows that the defendant did not have the state of mind required for the crime. In addition, the mistake must be reasonable unless the offense is a specific intent crime. Here, the statute requires that the defendant have acted "knowingly" with respect to each of the material elements of the offense. A person acts knowingly with respect to the nature of his conduct when he is aware that his conduct is of that nature or that certain circumstances exist. At least one of the material elements of the offense here is that the sale be to a person under the age of 18. If Dribble reasonably believed that Bibber was 25 years old, Dribble has not acted knowingly with respect to the fact that the purchaser was under 18, and he cannot be convicted of violating the statute. (A) is not a good defense because it is irrelevant under these circumstances. Because Dribble never asked for any identification, Bibber's possession of the driver's license had no effect on Dribble's state of mind. (C) is incorrect because, as general rule, it is not a defense to a crime that the defendant was unaware that his acts were prohibited by the criminal law, even if such ignorance was reasonable. A narrow exception exists for crimes that require a certain belief concerning a collateral aspect of law—ignorance as to that aspect of law may negate the requisite state of mind. Such crimes involve ignorance of some aspect of law *other than* the existence of the statute making the act criminal. Here, Dribble could contend that the statute requires that he have acted "knowingly" as to whether his conduct is a violation of the regulations, and that his ignorance of the regulations negates that state of mind. It is not at all clear, however, that a court would accept this interpretation of the statute. A court could conclude that the reference to violation of the regulations was a shorthand designation for the specific conduct that would violate the statute rather than a material element of the statute itself, and that knowledge of the existence of the regulations was therefore not required to establish a violation of the statute. Thus, the assertion in (C) would not be as strong a defense as the statement in (B). (D) is wrong because Dribble's ignorance of the statutory definition of "alcoholic beverage" falls within the general rule that ignorance or mistake of law is not a defense. He is not claiming that he didn't know that beer is an alcoholic drink; rather, he is claiming that he didn't know that the statute applied to his act of selling the beer to Bibber. This would not be a defense.

Answer to Question 34

(C) Daniel is guilty of battery regardless of his belief. Battery is an unlawful application of force to the person of another resulting in either bodily injury or an offensive touching. Here, Daniel made a mistake as to the identity of the person whom he struck, but there was no mistake as to the intention of Daniel to strike this person. Mistake of fact affects criminal guilt only if it shows that the defendant did not have the state of mind required for the crime. Although battery need not be intentional (*i.e.,* it can result from criminal negligence), it is clear from the facts that Daniel intended to strike Victor. Thus, the mistake made by Daniel (who apparently believed that he was striking Wallace) does not show the absence of the state of mind required for battery, and will therefore not affect Daniel's guilt. (A) is incorrect because, even if a reasonable person would have mistaken Victor for Wallace, the fact remains that Daniel committed a battery against Victor. A case of mistaken identity provides no defense to the battery that was committed. (B) is incorrect for the same reason as (A), and also because it implies that a battery against Wallace would be excused by adequate provocation (presumably resulting from Wallace's affair with Daniel's wife). It is true that an intentional killing will be reduced from murder to voluntary manslaughter if the defendant acted under a legally adequate provocation, and finding one's spouse in the act of adultery is deemed to be adequate provocation. However, there is no rule of law that excuses a battery on the ground that the victim committed adultery with the defendant's wife. (D) is incorrect because it also is based on the premise that Daniel is not guilty if he thought that he was striking Wallace. As explained previously, regardless of who Daniel thought he was striking, the significant point is that he unlawfully struck Victor, and this constitutes a battery.

Answer to Question 35

(B) The judge should deny the motion. Smith had a valid reason under the statute for arresting the driver after she legally stopped the car for running the stop sign; thus, the search was incident to a lawful arrest. (A) is wrong because there is no indication that Smith had searched the driver because she was concerned with her personal safety. If she had searched him without having first arrested him under this factual situation, the search would have been unlawful. (C) is wrong because whatever the reason she first followed them, the fact remains that she had a valid reason for stopping them. Note that if an officer has probable cause to believe that a traffic law has been violated, she may stop the car even if her ulterior motive is to investigate whether some other law is being violated. (D) is wrong because the search, incident to a lawful arrest, need not have been based upon suspicion that the three had committed robbery and homicide.

Answer to Question 36

(C) If Doran is found guilty of murder, it will be through application of the felony murder rule as stated in choice (C). Under the felony murder doctrine, a killing—even an unintentional one—committed during the course of a felony is murder. Malice is implied from the intent to commit the underlying felony. For the doctrine to apply, the death must have been a foreseeable result of commission of the felony, but almost any death during an armed bank robbery would be deemed foreseeable by a court. Courts following the "proximate cause" theory of felony murder extend it to situations like the one in this fact pattern, where resistance by the victim or the police results in the death of a third party who is not a co-felon. While courts following the "agency theory" of felony murder would not apply it here, choice (C) states the only basis for Doran being guilty of murder because all of the other rationales are wrong. (A) is wrong because it is irrelevant that Doran had not yet run out of the building at the time Veep was killed; Doran would be liable even if he had already fled from the building. Only when the felon has reached a place of temporary safety after the felony has ended will the felony murder rule cease to apply. (B) is wrong because Doran's guilt under the felony murder rule is not dependent on whether the police were justified in using deadly force; it is Doran's commission of the robbery, rather than the response by the police, that establishes his liability for felony murder. (D) is wrong because Doran's putting Veep in a position of danger, while it might be sufficient to imply malice based on reckless indifference to human life, is not sufficient to establish an intent to kill (express malice). Here, malice is established by the felony murder doctrine.

Answer to Question 37

(B) The corporate officers cannot be guilty of attempted murder because criminal attempt requires a specific intent to commit a particular completed crime. A criminal attempt is an act that, although done with the intention of committing a crime, falls short of completing the crime. A defendant must have the intent to perform an act and obtain a result that, if achieved, would constitute a crime. Hence, attempt is a specific intent crime. Guilt of attempted murder requires that a defendant have the specific intent to commit the crime of murder. In contrast to the malice aforethought required for murder, which is satisfied not only by intent to kill but also by awareness of an unjustifiably high risk to human life, intent to inflict great bodily injury, or intent to commit a felony, *attempted* murder is satisfied only by intent to kill. Here, the corporate officers, in permitting the mining to proceed without compliance with methane detection measures, subjected the miners to an unjustifiably high risk to their lives. This "abandoned and malignant heart" demonstrated by the officers would suffice to convict the officers of murder if the miners had been killed. However, there were no deaths; the crime charged is attempted murder. Consequently, there must be a showing that the officers specifically intended to cause the deaths of the miners. Because the facts do not indicate such intent, the officers are not guilty of attempted murder. (C) is incorrect because, as explained above, the mental state of an abandoned and malignant heart will not satisfy the intent required for *attempted* murder. (D) is incorrect because, even if a felony was committed, the intent to commit a felony (although sufficient to constitute malice aforethought for a murder charge) will not satisfy the intent to kill that is necessary for a conviction of attempted murder. (A) is incorrect because the officers' actions had gone well beyond the planning stage; allowing the mining to proceed without compliance with methane detection measures satisfies the overt act requirement for attempt. Had the other requirements for attempt been satisfied, their actions would be sufficient to support a conviction.

Answer to Question 38

(C)   Dawes's motion should be denied because the Double Jeopardy Clause does not prohibit the second prosecution. The Double Jeopardy Clause of the Fifth Amendment provides criminal defendants with the right to be free of double jeopardy for the same offense. However, two crimes do not constitute the same offense if each crime requires proof of an additional element that the other crime does not require, even though some of the same facts may be necessary to prove both crimes. [Blockburger v. United States (1932)] Here, larceny requires a taking and carrying away of the property of another, which burglary does not require, and burglary requires a breaking and entry, which larceny does not require. Hence, they are distinct offenses for purposes of the Double Jeopardy Clause. (A) and (B) are incorrect because the Supreme Court does not use a "same transaction" or "same episode" test suggested by these answer choices; instead, the *Blockburger* test is used regardless of whether the two offenses were tried together at a single trial or at separate trials. (D) is incorrect because while double jeopardy also protects against inconsistent factual determinations at a subsequent trial, it protects against multiple prosecutions as well, as long as the crime is the "same offense."

Answer to Question 39

(D)   Daniel cannot be convicted of burglary because he lacked the requisite intent. At common law, burglary consists of a breaking and entry of the dwelling of another at nighttime, with the intent of committing a felony therein. Here, Daniel broke and entered Vanessa's home at night. However, at the time of entry, Daniel intended only to open his trenchcoat and expose his underwear to Vanessa, knowing that he would not have time to remove his underwear and expose his sexual organs. Although Daniel apparently believed that these actions would constitute the felony of "flashing," commission of this crime requires *actual exposure* of sexual organs. Thus, although Daniel was mistaken as to the felonious character of his actions, the fact remains that, at the time he entered Vanessa's home, he did not have the intent to commit the acts that would constitute the felony. Absent such intent, Daniel cannot be convicted of burglary. (A) incorrectly states that Daniel intended to commit a felony when he broke and entered Vanessa's dwelling place. As explained above, the act that Daniel intended to commit (opening his trenchcoat without exposing his sexual organs) is not a felony, despite Daniel's belief that it was (this is analogous to legal impossibility). Therefore, it cannot be said that Daniel acted with the intent to commit a felony. (B) is incorrect because the victim's knowledge concerning the status of a crime (felony or misdemeanor) is irrelevant to the issue of whether Daniel can be convicted of burglary. Daniel cannot be convicted of burglary unless, at the time of entry, he intended to commit acts constituting a felony. (B) implies that, if Vanessa did not know that Daniel's "flashing" was not a felony, then Daniel could be convicted of burglary. However, as long as Daniel intended to commit acts that were not felonious, he cannot be convicted of burglary, regardless of what Vanessa knew about the crime. (C) is incorrect because a conviction for burglary does not require that a felony actually be carried out. All that is required is that intent to commit a felony exist at the time of entry. Consequently, although Daniel did not actually commit a felony, he could be convicted of burglary if he had entered the home with the intent to commit acts constituting a felony.

Answer to Question 40

(D)   To be convicted of burglary, Yuri must have intended to commit a felony at the time of entry. The elements of common law burglary are: (i) a breaking; (ii) and entry; (iii) of the dwelling; (iv) of another; (v) at nighttime; (vi) with the intent of committing a felony therein. The intent to commit a felony must exist at the time of entry. If such intent is formed after the entry is completed, burglary has not been committed. At the time Yuri entered Xaviera's shop, he did not intend to commit any crime. Indeed, he probably intended to investigate to determine if a crime was being committed in the shop, because his suspicions had been aroused by seeing a light on in the shop at night. Because Yuri did not enter the shop with intent to commit a felony therein, one of the elements of burglary is missing. Consequently, he cannot be convicted of burglary. (A) is incorrect because opening a closed door, although it is unlocked, constitutes a breaking for purposes of burglary. A breaking requires some use of force to gain entry, but minimal force is sufficient. Even pushing open a door that is already partially open is considered a breaking under the better view, because some force was used to gain entry. Thus, the fact that the door was unlocked will not provide Yuri with a defense to burglary. (B) is incorrect because the entire premises rented to Xaviera includes a dwelling. As noted above, at common law the breaking and entry had to be of a dwelling. A structure is considered a dwelling if it is used regularly for sleeping. Such a structure remains a dwelling even if it is also used for other purposes, such as conducting a business. Xaviera is renting from Yuri an area that includes both an apartment and, directly underneath the apartment, space used as a watch repair shop. Assuming that Xaviera regularly uses the apartment for sleeping, this is a dwelling. The fact that Xaviera uses another part of the rented premises to conduct a business does not mean that the entirety of the area rented should not be considered a dwelling. Thus, (B) will not afford Yuri a defense to burglary. (C) is incorrect because burglary requires only that the structure be used as a dwelling by someone other than the defendant. Occupancy, rather than ownership, is material. Thus, an owner can commit burglary of his own structure if it is rented and used as a dwelling by others. Here, Xaviera has the right of occupancy. Consequently, Yuri's ownership of the building does not mean that he cannot be convicted of burglary with respect to the area rented and used as a dwelling by Xaviera.

Answer to Question 41

(C) If Yuri honestly thought he was entitled to take the watch as security for payment of the rent, then he lacked the requisite intent for larceny. Larceny consists of: (i) a taking (ii) and carrying away (iii) of tangible personal property (iv) of another (v) by trespass (vi) with the intent to permanently (or for an unreasonable time) deprive the person of her interest in the property. Taking property with the intent to hold it as security for a legitimate debt is not sufficient intent for larceny because the intent is *not* to permanently deprive the person of the property; rather the intent is to return the property when the debt is paid (or if it is not paid, to sell the property to satisfy the debt, with any excess proceeds going back to the debtor). Thus, if Yuri honestly intended to hold the watch as security for the back rent, he lacked the intent to permanently deprive Xaviera of the watch. (A) is wrong because Yuri's actions as to the watch constituted a sufficient carrying away. Larceny requires a "carrying away" (asportation), but that requirement is met by even a slight movement of the property. Here, Yuri took control of the watch and began to leave the shop with it. Although he did not actually leave the shop, he did apparently pick up the watch and move toward the door. This is sufficient movement for larceny. (B) is wrong because larceny can be committed against a thief. Because larceny is a crime against *possession,* all that is necessary is that the property be taken from someone who has a possessory interest superior to that of the defendant. Thus, even if Xaviera had obtained the watch by false pretenses, she had a possessory interest superior to that of Yuri. Therefore, Yuri could be convicted of larceny by taking the watch from Xaviera. (D) is wrong because the requirement for larceny of a taking "by trespass" means a wrongful taking (*i.e.,* one without consent). Here, Yuri took the watch without Xaviera's consent, and his status as the owner of the building does not save him. As the owner he did not have the right to take the property from his tenant. (Arguably, he did not even have the right to be in the shop.) Thus, the taking was wrongful, and Yuri could be convicted of larceny despite the fact that he owned the building.

Answer to Question 42

(C) Statements II. and III. are both helpful to Xaviera's defense. For purposes of the MBE, an assault is either (i) an attempt to commit a battery, or (ii) the intentional creation, other than by mere words, of a reasonable apprehension in the mind of the victim of imminent bodily harm. Statement II. negates the specific intent to commit a battery that is required for the first type of assault: If Xaviera knew when she threw the weight that it was impossible to hit Yuri, her conduct was not motivated by an intent to commit a battery against him. Statement III. negates the second type of assault because no apprehension of harm would have been created in Yuri if he did not see Xaviera throw the weight. Since the type of assault is not specified here, (C) is a better choice than (B) or (D) because both types of assaults are negated. Choice (A) is not correct because statement I. establishes only that there was a failure to commit a battery. It does nothing to negate Xaviera's potential liability for assault.

Answer to Question 43

(C) Dave's best argument for preventing the cocaine from being admitted into evidence is that his confession was not voluntary. This question is difficult because each of the choices appears to present a good argument for Dave. With regard to (A), the search of Charles's dorm room appears to be an unreasonable search under the Fourth Amendment. However, a person's Fourth Amendment rights against unreasonable search and seizure may be enforced by the exclusion of evidence only at the instance of someone whose own protection was infringed by the search and seizure. Here, Dave can assert no possessory interest or legitimate expectation of privacy in Charles's dorm room. Thus, Dave cannot successfully exclude the cocaine on the ground that it was seized in violation of the Fourth Amendment. (B) is incorrect because arrest warrants are usually required only for arrests made in the person's home. Police generally do not need to obtain a warrant before arresting a person in a public place, even if they have time to get a warrant, as long as the arrest is based on probable cause. Here the police had probable cause to arrest Dave, and because Dave was arrested on the grounds of the campus, the failure of the police to obtain an arrest warrant will be of no help to Dave. Choices (C) and (D) both focus on improper conduct during Dave's interrogation, but (C) is better because Dave will have a better chance of invoking the exclusionary rule if the confession is involuntary. For confessions to be admissible, the Due Process Clause of the Fourteenth Amendment requires that they be voluntary. While voluntariness is a fact question that is assessed by looking at the totality of the circumstances, the duration and manner of the police interrogation here indicate that Dave's confession probably was the result of actual coercion. If the confession is found to be involuntary, Dave can invoke the exclusionary rule to exclude the cocaine as "fruit of the poisonous tree." In contrast to an involuntary confession, a confession obtained without *Miranda* warnings, as long as there was no actual coercion involved, may not be sufficient to justify excluding the nontestimonial "fruits" of the confession. [*See* United States v. Patane (2004)] In *Patane*, although there was no majority opinion on this point, five Justices indicated that suppression was not necessary. Thus, the involuntariness of the confession, rather than the absence of *Miranda* warnings, is the best argument for excluding the cocaine.

Answer to Question 44

(B) The conversation should be suppressed because the police conduct violated Jake's Sixth Amendment right to counsel. The Sixth Amendment provides that in all criminal prosecutions a defendant has a right to the assistance of counsel at all critical stages. For Sixth Amendment purposes, a criminal prosecution begins when adversary judicial proceedings have commenced, such as the filing of formal charges in this case. Because interrogation is a critical stage of prosecution, the

Sixth Amendment is violated by post-charge interrogation unless the defendant has waived his right to counsel. Interrogation includes not only direct questioning, but also any other conduct by the police intended to elicit a response. The police conduct here (telling Jake that Esau had implicated Jake and then bugging the defendant's conversation) constitutes prohibited interrogation. [*See* Maine v. Moulton (1985)] (A) is incorrect because the wiretap was not an illegal search under the Fourth Amendment. Wiretapping and other forms of electronic surveillance are subject to the Fourth Amendment prohibition of unreasonable searches and seizures. However, to have a Fourth Amendment right, a person must have a legitimate expectation of privacy with respect to the place searched or the item seized. In a different context, the Supreme Court has held that prisoners have no legitimate expectation of privacy in their cells or in any personal property that they have in their cells. [Hudson v. Palmer (1984)] Hence, Jake probably cannot assert a Fourth Amendment claim based on the wiretap, because he had no legitimate expectation of privacy in the jail cell. The fact that he has no expectation of privacy does not make choice (C) correct, however. Even though he probably cannot claim that the bugging was an unreasonable search under the Fourth Amendment, he can claim that it was an interrogation in violation of his Sixth Amendment right to counsel, as discussed above. (D) is incorrect because it is irrelevant. The facts probably would not give rise to a *Miranda* violation in light of the Court's ruling in *Illinois v. Perkins* (1990) that *Miranda* does not apply unless interrogation is by someone known to be a police officer (on the rationale that *Miranda* is merely a prophylactic rule designed to offset the coercive nature of a custodial interrogation by a police officer). In any case, *Miranda* rights and Sixth Amendment rights to counsel can only be waived knowingly, and so Jake's ignorance of the fact that the cell was bugged precludes a finding of waiver here.

Answer to Question 45

(B)   Betsy can be charged with larceny, but not the other crimes. Larceny consists of a taking and carrying away of the tangible personal property of another by trespass, with the intent to permanently deprive the person of her interest in the property. Here, Betsy took and carried away Georgia's personal property (her chair). The taking was trespassory because it was without Georgia's consent. At the time of the taking, Betsy intended to deal with the chair in a manner that involved a substantial risk of loss (*i.e.,* burn it). Such intent is enough for larceny, as the "intent to permanently deprive" includes a substantial risk of loss. Thus, Betsy is guilty of larceny. (Note that if Betsy had simply taken the chair in the honest belief that she was entitled to it as **repayment** of the debt, there would be no larceny. However, setting the chair on fire indicates that Betsy intended to permanently deprive Georgia of the chair rather than take it as repayment.) (A) and (C) are wrong because common law arson has not occurred here. At common law, arson is the malicious burning of the **dwelling** of another. Here, the burning was of an item of personal property, not of the dwelling itself. (C) and (D) are wrong because Betsy did not commit common law burglary. Burglary consists of a breaking and entering of a dwelling of another at nighttime with the intent to commit a felony therein. Here, Betsy's unauthorized opening of the unlocked door is sufficient for a breaking, and the breaking and entering of Georgia's dwelling occurred at night. However, at the time Betsy entered, she did not intend to commit a felony; she simply wanted to confront Georgia and demand repayment of her money. Betsy did not decide to commit the larceny until **after** she was already in the house and found that Georgia was not at home. Since she did not have the requisite intent when she entered the house, she cannot be guilty of burglary.

Answer to Question 46

(C)   Dinty is liable for theft by receipt of stolen property because the car was still "stolen" when it was received by Dinty. At common law and under modern theft statutes such as the one in the state of Yellow, the crime of receiving stolen property requires (i) receiving possession and control (ii) of "stolen" personal property (iii) known to have been obtained in a manner constituting a criminal offense (iv) by another person, (v) with the intent to permanently deprive the owner of his interest in the property. Here, all of the elements of the prima facie offense have been established: Dinty "received" possession and control when he paid Hawker and received the keys (the fact that he was arrested before he drove away is irrelevant since there is no asportation requirement as there is for larceny); the car qualifies as personal property; Dinty knew that the car was stolen because Hawker informed him that it was "hot"; and Dinty intended to keep the car and not return it to the original owner. In a "sting" operation such as the one in this question, an attendant circumstance of the offense is that the property must still be "stolen" at the time it is received by the defendant. Once stolen property is recovered by the owner or by the police on the owner's behalf, it loses its "stolen" status. Even if the owner consents to the property's use for the purpose of trapping a suspected recipient of stolen goods, the property cannot be the basis of a receipt of stolen property charge because it is no longer "stolen." This situation is different, however. Here, neither the owner nor the police had recovered the stolen car before Dinty took possession of it. The police have permitted Hawker to continue to obtain stolen autos, but have not obtained the permission of the rightful owner of this car to use it in their operation, since neither they nor Hawker know to whom this particular car belongs. Therefore, the car retained its status as stolen property. [*See, e.g.,* United States v. Muzii, 676 F.2d 919 (2d Cir.), *cert. denied,* 459 U.S. 863 (1982)] Thus, Dinty is liable for receipt of stolen property under State Yellow's theft statute. (A) is incorrect because, under the majority rule, entrapment requires Dinty to prove that the criminal design originated with and was induced by the police and that he was not in any way predisposed to commit the crime. Here, the police merely offered the opportunity for Dinty to commit the crime. Dinty readily made the deal for the car even though he knew it was stolen. (B) is incorrect. Even though Hawker arguably may have been an agent of the police because he was cooperating with them, the police were not acting on behalf of, and with the permission of, the rightful owner of the car that Dinty purchased. Thus, that car never lost its status as stolen property even during Hawker's possession of it. (D) is wrong because intent is not required for the crime of receiving stolen property. While it is unclear whether Dinty "intended" to purchase a stolen car, it is clear that Dinty **knew** he was purchasing a stolen car, and knowledge satisfies the mens rea element of this offense.

Answer to Question 47

(D) Dang's confession should be admitted because he waived his Fifth Amendment privilege against compelled self-incrimination after receiving *Miranda* warnings. *Miranda v. Arizona* requires that a person in custody be informed of his right to remain silent and his right to the presence of an attorney during questioning. A suspect may subsequently waive his rights by making a confession, as long as the waiver was knowing, voluntary, and intelligent. In this case, Dang received proper *Miranda* warnings, and there is no indication that he did not understand what his rights were. Although his answers during questioning were initially unresponsive, he never asked for an attorney or indicated that he wished to remain silent, and he voluntarily confessed after a relatively short period of interrogation. Hence, he validly waived his *Miranda* rights. (A) is incorrect because the police have no duty to inform the defendant that an attorney is attempting to see him. Dang's ignorance of Alice's efforts has no bearing on whether he made a knowing waiver of his *Miranda* rights. (B) is incorrect because his right to counsel was not violated. Although Dang does have a separate Sixth Amendment right to counsel under *Escobedo v. Illinois* because he has already been arrested and charged with the crime, this right would only be violated if Dang, after being informed of his right to counsel, had requested an attorney or had been prevented from seeing his attorney. Here, Dang made no request to see an attorney—even when he called his mother—and his attorney was allowed to see him immediately upon her arrival. Thus, his Sixth

Amendment right to counsel has not been violated. (C) is incorrect even though it is true that Dang made a voluntary statement. Due process requires that for confessions to be admissible, they must be "voluntary," based on the totality of the circumstances, and here all of the circumstances indicate that Dang's confession was voluntary. However, even a voluntary confession will be inadmissible if it was obtained in violation of *Miranda* rights. (D) is therefore a better choice than (C).

Answer to Question 48

(A) In (A), Defendant is guilty of unlawful act manslaughter, but not of felony murder, because his burning of a building that was not the dwelling of another does not constitute arson at common law. Murder is the unlawful killing of a human being with malice aforethought. Malice aforethought exists if a defendant has: (i) intent to kill; (ii) intent to inflict great bodily injury; (iii) reckless indifference to an unjustifiably high risk to human life; or (iv) intent to commit a felony. A killing committed during the course of a felony is felony murder at common law, while a killing caused by an otherwise unlawful act is involuntary manslaughter. Thus, a killing in the course of commission of a misdemeanor is manslaughter if either (i) the misdemeanor is malum in se (inherently wrongful); or (ii) death is the natural consequence of the unlawful conduct. In (A), the only basis by which it might appear that Defendant has malice aforethought is intent to commit a felony (arson). However, the common law required arson to be a burning of the dwelling of another. While most jurisdictions now extend arson to structures other than dwellings and encompass arson with the intent to defraud an insurer, for felony murder you should assume that the common law version of the underlying felony is controlling, as the call of the question specifies. Thus, Defendant's burning down of a retail store is not arson, and he cannot be guilty of felony murder. Nevertheless, burning down the store is almost certainly an inherently wrongful misdemeanor, and the transient was killed during the commission of it. Thus, Defendant is guilty of unlawful act (misdemeanor) manslaughter. (B) is incorrect, because Defendant's intent to kill Victim is transferred to Bystander. If a defendant intends injury to a particular person and, in trying to carry out that intent, causes similar injury to another person, his intent will be transferred from the intended person to the one actually harmed. Thus, Defendant is deemed to have had the intent to kill Bystander, and is guilty of murder. (C) is incorrect because dynamiting a railroad track while a train is passing is an act undertaken with reckless indifference to an unjustifiably high risk to human life (an abandoned and malignant heart), thus constituting malice aforethought. Defendant's motivation (to stop shipments of toxic materials through his home town) will not reduce this killing to manslaughter. (D) is incorrect because it applies the "imperfect self-defense" doctrine to a common law jurisdiction. Pursuant to this doctrine, some states allow a murder to be reduced to manslaughter if the defendant unreasonably but honestly believed in the necessity of responding with deadly force. However, a jurisdiction applying only the common law would not recognize this doctrine. Thus, the killing in (D) would not be reduced to manslaughter.

Answer to Question 49

(B) Defendant's motion will be granted in this situation because his Fifth Amendment right to counsel has been violated by questioning him about the robbery. At any time prior to or during a custodial interrogation, the accused may invoke a *Miranda* (Fifth Amendment) right to counsel. If the accused invokes this right, ***all questioning must cease*** until the accused is provided with an attorney or initiates further questioning himself. Thus, the police questioning of Defendant about the robbery was improper, and he can have his statements excluded. (A) is incorrect because the conduct by the informant did not constitute a custodial interrogation. The Fifth Amendment requires that anyone in police custody and accused of a crime be given *Miranda* warnings prior to interrogation by the police. However, this rule does not apply where "interrogation" is by an informant who the defendant does not know is working for the police, because the coercive atmosphere of police-dominated interrogation is not present. (C) is incorrect because neither the Fifth nor Sixth Amendment rights of Defendant were violated. In contrast to the Fifth Amendment right to counsel, the Sixth Amendment right to counsel does not apply until adversary judicial proceedings have begun (*e.g.*, formal charges have been filed). On the other hand, the Sixth Amendment right to counsel would prohibit an informant from deliberately eliciting statements from the defendant about the crime for which he was charged (even though it would not be an "interrogation" under the Fifth Amendment). Here, however, the informant was talking with Defendant about a different crime. In contrast to the Fifth Amendment, the Sixth Amendment right to counsel is "offense specific," *i.e.*, it applies only to the charges that have been filed and not to other questioning. Thus, even though Defendant's Sixth Amendment right to counsel had attached regarding the armed robbery charge, he could be questioned without counsel concerning the unrelated homicide crime. Nor was Defendant's Fifth Amendment right to counsel violated because, as discussed above, the informant's conduct did not constitute an "interrogation" under the Fifth Amendment. (D) is wrong because Defendant did not invoke his Fifth Amendment right to counsel, and his Sixth Amendment right to counsel was not violated. A Fifth Amendment right to counsel can be invoked only by an unambiguous request for counsel *in dealing with the custodial interrogation*. Here, Defendant did not request counsel in dealing with the interrogation about the homicide, even after given *Miranda* warnings. His post-charge request for counsel at his initial appearance on the robbery charge was a Sixth Amendment request for counsel which, because it is offense specific, did not apply to the questioning about the homicide.

Answer to Question 50

(B) Daimler's claim is correct because the victim died before jeopardy attached for trial on the lesser included offense. The Fifth Amendment right to be free of double jeopardy provides that once jeopardy attaches for an offense, the defendant may not be retried for the same offense. Under the *Blockburger* test, two crimes do not constitute the same offense if *each* crime requires proof of an additional element that the other crime does not require. Under this test, a lesser included offense and the greater offense would be considered the "same offense," because the lesser included offense consists entirely of some, but not all, elements of the greater crime. Hence, under double jeopardy rules, attachment of jeopardy for the greater offense bars retrial for lesser included offenses, *and* attachment of jeopardy for a lesser included offense generally bars retrial for the greater offense. An exception to this latter rule exists if all of the elements for the greater offense had not occurred at the time of prosecution for the lesser offense, but in this case the final element for the felony murder charge—the death of the victim—occurred before jeopardy had attached in the first trial, so the prosecution could have added a charge of felony murder prior to proceeding with the first trial. Thus, the underlying felony of armed robbery was a lesser included offense of the felony murder and Daimler's being placed in jeopardy for it bars the subsequent trial for the felony murder. (A) is incorrect because the reckless driving charge was not the basis for the felony murder charge. Under principles of collateral estoppel embodied in the double jeopardy rule, a subsequent trial would be barred if it would require a factual determination inconsistent with the one in the prior prosecution. If the reckless driving charge were the underlying felony for the felony murder charge, Daimler could argue that proving felony murder based on reckless driving would require a determination that Daimler was guilty of the underlying felony, which would appear inconsistent with his acquittal. However, this principle is not applicable here because the armed robbery charge was the underlying felony for the felony murder charge. (C) is incorrect. As discussed above, double jeopardy applies regardless of the outcome of the trial on the robbery charge, because jeopardy attached for the robbery charge as soon as the trial started, barring a second trial for the greater offense of felony murder. (D) is incorrect because, as discussed above, two crimes are not the "same offense" for double jeopardy purposes only if *each* crime requires proof of an additional element that the other crime does not require. Because the underlying felony is a lesser included offense of the felony murder charge, *i.e.*, it has no other elements not required by the felony murder charge, it constitutes the "same offense" for purposes of double jeopardy.

Answer to Question 51

(C)   Bruton will prevail in her challenge to the admission of Cruz's confession if Cruz could not be cross-examined regarding his confession. Under the Sixth Amendment, a defendant in a criminal prosecution has the right to confront adverse witnesses at trial. If two persons are tried together and one has given a confession that implicates the other, the right of confrontation generally prohibits the use of that statement because the other defendant cannot compel the confessing co-defendant to take the stand for cross-examination. A co-defendant's confession is inadmissible even when it interlocks with the defendant's own confession, which is admitted. If Cruz refused to take the stand and subject himself to cross-examination, his confession was not properly admitted because it violated Bruton's Confrontation Clause rights. (A) is incorrect because the fact that Cruz's confession incriminates Bruton no further than her own confession is not relevant. The interlocking nature of Cruz's confession with Bruton's confession may make it more damaging by making it harder for Bruton to claim that her confession was false. (B) is incorrect because the Supreme Court has held that instructing the jury to consider the confession only as going to the guilt of the confessing defendant is inadequate to avoid Confrontation Clause problems, because the risk that the jury will not follow the limiting instructions is too great in this context. (D) is incorrect. Confessions of a co-defendant may be admitted if (i) all portions referring to the other defendant can be eliminated (so that there is no indication of that defendant's involvement), (ii) the confessing defendant takes the stand and subjects himself to cross-examination regarding the truth or falsity of the statement, or (iii) the confession of the nontestifying co-defendant is being used to rebut the defendant's claim that his confession was obtained coercively, and the jury is instructed as to that purpose. Even if the co-defendant denies ever having made the confession, as stated in choice (D), the opportunity at trial to cross-examine the co-defendant satisfies the Confrontation Clause.

Answer to Question 52

(D)   The court should not admit the marijuana into evidence because it was obtained as a result of an unreasonable search of Delia. Under the exclusionary rule, evidence obtained in violation of a defendant's Fourth Amendment rights is not admissible to establish the guilt of the defendant at trial. The Fourth Amendment protects against unreasonable searches and seizures by government agents. To have a protected Fourth Amendment right, a person must have a reasonable expectation of privacy with respect to the place searched or the item seized. For a search based on a search warrant to be valid, the warrant must be based upon probable cause and must describe with reasonable precision the place to be searched and the items to be seized. A search warrant does not authorize the police to search persons found on the premises who are not named in the warrant. However, if the police have probable cause to arrest a person discovered on the premises to be searched, they may conduct a warrantless search of her incident to the arrest. If a person is not named in the warrant and circumstances justifying an arrest of that person do not exist, the police may search her for the objects named in the search warrant only if they have probable cause to believe that she has the named objects on her person. Here, the search warrant was issued on the basis of information from reliable informants and undercover police officers, and it stated precisely the premises (the fraternity house) to be searched and the items (illegal narcotics) to be seized. Thus, the warrant is valid. However, the search warrant (which did not name Delia) did not authorize the police to search Delia's purse. The search cannot be justified as incident to a lawful arrest because: (i) the police searched the purse *before* they arrested Delia; and (ii) the police did not have sufficient probable cause to arrest Delia prior to searching the purse. Because the police had no reason to believe that Delia had drugs on her person, they cannot successfully claim that they were searching for the drugs mentioned in the warrant. Delia can challenge the search because she had a possessory interest and a legitimate expectation of privacy in her purse, which was the object of the search. Thus, because the marijuana was seized pursuant to an unreasonable search in violation of the Fourth Amendment, it must be excluded from evidence. (B) is incorrect because mere presence at a place for which the police have a search warrant does not authorize a search of a person not named in the warrant. Only if the police obtain probable cause to arrest a person on the premises may the person be searched (as incident to the arrest). (A) is incorrect. The footlocker was properly searched pursuant to the warrant, not because it was within Delia's reach. However, the marijuana at issue here was seized as a result of a search of Delia's purse. Thus, the proximity of Delia to the footlocker is of no consequence to the admissibility of the marijuana found in Delia's purse. (C) is incorrect because Delia's lack of a possessory interest in the premises does not invalidate a search of her purse. For example, if the police had probable cause to believe that Delia had drugs on her person, they could have searched her for the drugs, regardless of the fact that she had no possessory interest in the fraternity house.

Answer to Question 53

(A) Lee can be found guilty of robbery and felony murder, but the death penalty cannot be imposed. Lee can be found guilty of robbery as an accomplice to Marlon. The Supreme Court has held that, under the Eighth Amendment, the death penalty may not be imposed for felony murder where the defendant, as an accomplice, did not take or attempt or intend to take life, or intend that lethal force be employed. [Enmund v. Florida (1982)] Here, since Lee's involvement in the crime was only to provide transportation, it cannot be said that Lee participated in such a major way that he acted with reckless indifference to human life; hence, the death penalty cannot constitutionally be imposed against him. (B) is therefore incorrect. (C) is incorrect because Lee's conviction of both robbery and felony murder does not raise double jeopardy problems under these facts. Under the rule that lesser included offenses "merge" into greater offenses, a person may not be convicted of both the greater offense and a lesser included offense. While the Supreme Court has held that a subsequent prosecution for robbery is not permitted against a defendant who has been tried for felony murder where the robbery is the underlying felony, this situation is different. Imposition of cumulative punishments for two statutorily defined offenses arising from the same transaction and constituting the same crime does not violate double jeopardy when the punishments are imposed *at a single trial*, as long as the two offenses were specifically intended by the legislature to carry separate punishments. [Missouri v. Hunter (1983)] Here, the legislature did specifically provide for cumulative penalties for first degree felony murder and for the underlying felony. Thus, Lee can be convicted of both robbery and felony murder. (D) is incorrect because the jury could properly find Lee guilty of felony murder. When the felony murder rule is combined with accomplice liability rules, the scope of liability becomes very broad. The felony murder rule provides that a killing—even an accidental one—committed during the course of a felony is murder. All parties to the felony are liable for the murder as long as (i) it was committed during the commission of the felony or in fleeing from the scene, and (ii) it was a foreseeable result of commission of the felony. Courts have been willing to find most deaths committed during a felony to be foreseeable. Here, the jury could reasonably find the shooting death of a store clerk by Marlon during a struggle with a gun to be a foreseeable result of the commission of a robbery and impose felony murder liability on Lee as an accomplice.

Answer to Question 54

(B) Dolly can be convicted of either kidnapping or false imprisonment, but not both. False imprisonment consists of unlawful confinement of a person without her valid consent. Confinement requires that the victim either be compelled to go where she does not wish to go or to remain where she does not wish to remain. A confinement is unlawful unless specifically authorized by law or by the victim's consent. Any consent must be freely given by one with capacity to give such consent; *i.e.,* consent is invalidated if obtained by coercion, threats, deception, or incapacity arising from mental illness, retardation, or youth. Here, Dolly compelled Jane to go with her for the weekend by lying to her about her mother's having to go out of town and asking Dolly to care for Jane. This constitutes a confinement because, despite the fact that Jane enjoyed her time with Dolly, Jane was only four years old and incapable of validly consenting to go and remain with Dolly for the weekend. This confinement was not authorized by law. Consequently, Dolly can be convicted of false imprisonment. Kidnapping under modern statutes is confinement of a person that involves either some movement of the victim or concealment of the victim in a secret place. As with false imprisonment, consent freely given by a person competent to do so precludes a confinement or movement from being kidnapping. However, a young child is incapable of giving valid consent to her detention or movement. Dolly "moved" Jane by taking her home. This was a confinement because Jane was compelled to go where she did not wish to go. The fact that the experience apparently was totally enjoyable for Jane does not mean that there was a valid consent that would preclude a conviction of kidnapping. As explained above, Jane is incapacitated by her age from giving a valid consent to Dolly's actions. For the foregoing reasons, Dolly can be properly convicted of kidnapping. However, Dolly cannot be convicted of both kidnapping and false imprisonment, because false imprisonment is a lesser included offense of kidnapping (*i.e.,* kidnapping is a form of aggravated false imprisonment). A lesser included offense is one that consists entirely of some, but not all, elements of the greater crime. A person may not be convicted of both the greater offense and a lesser included offense. False imprisonment and kidnapping both consist of unlawfully confining a person against her will, with kidnapping containing the added elements of either moving or concealing the victim. Thus, false imprisonment is a lesser included offense of kidnapping. Consequently, Dolly may be convicted of *either* of these offenses, but *not both* of them. (A) is incorrect because kidnapping is not the only crime of which Dolly can be convicted. (C) is incorrect because, as discussed above, there can be a conviction for either of these crimes, but not for both of them. (D) is incorrect because these facts support a conviction for either of the crimes mentioned.

Answer to Question 55

(C) Darnell's motion should be denied because neither his Fifth nor Sixth Amendment rights were violated by Henry's conduct. The Sixth Amendment right to counsel applies to all critical stages of a criminal prosecution but does not apply in precharge custodial interrogations. Because this right is "offense specific," the fact that the right to counsel has attached for one charge does not bar questioning without counsel for an unrelated charge. Because Darnell has not been charged with the convenience store robbery, his Sixth Amendment right to counsel has not been violated. The Fifth Amendment privilege against self-incrimination requires *Miranda* warnings and a valid waiver before any statement made by the accused during custodial interrogation can be admitted. However, this requirement does not apply where interrogation is by an informant who the defendant does not know is working for the police, because the coercive atmosphere of police-dominated interrogation is not present. [Illinois v. Perkins (1990)] Because Darnell was not aware of Henry's status, Henry's conduct did not constitute a police interrogation. (A) is wrong despite the fact that Henry's conduct may have been deliberately designed to elicit incriminating remarks. As discussed above, Darnell's right to counsel did not attach for purposes of the convenience store robbery. (B) is incorrect because, as discussed above, the *Miranda* warnings need not be given before questioning by a cellmate working covertly for the police. (D) is incorrect because interrogation refers not only to express questioning, but also to any words or actions on the part of the police that the police should know are reasonably likely to elicit an incriminating response from the suspect. Here, Henry, working for the police, made statements about the convenience store robbery that were intended to, and reasonably likely to, prompt a response from Darnell. Hence, it is not the absence of "interrogation" that avoids the *Miranda* problem, but the fact that Darnell does not know that Henry is working for the police.

Answer to Question 56

(D) Harmon did not make a false representation for purposes of either false pretenses or larceny by trick. Both false pretenses and larceny by trick require a misrepresentation on the part of the defendant. In the case of false pretenses, the victim intends to convey *title* to the property, while in the case of larceny by trick, the victim intends to convey only *possession* of the property. For both crimes, the misrepresentation required is an intentional (or knowing) false statement of past or existing fact. The defendant must have created a false impression as to a matter of fact. There is no misrepresentation if the defendant merely fails to correct what is known to be a mistaken impression held by the victim, as long as the defendant is not responsible for creating the mistake or has no fiduciary duty to the victim. Here, while Harmon did not obtain unconditional title to the stereo because the seller could repossess it if payments were not made, he probably obtained enough of the title to qualify for the crime of false pretenses. However, Harmon did not create a false impression as to a matter of fact. Although Harmon was aware of the clerk's mistake regarding his identity, Harmon did not create this mistake, nor did he have a fiduciary duty to the clerk. Thus, Harmon had no duty to correct the false impression, and it cannot be said that there was a misrepresentation on the part of Harmon. Absent a misrepresentation, by means of which Harmon obtained either possession of or title to the stereo, he cannot be convicted of either larceny by trick or false pretenses. (C) is incorrect because, in the absence of a misrepresentation on the part of Harmon, his intent to pay for the stereo is not determinative of his guilt of either crime mentioned. Even if Harmon intended to pay at a later point, he would be guilty if he had obtained title to or possession of the stereo by a misrepresentation, with intent to defraud the store. Subjecting the store to a greater risk of loss as a result of the misrepresentation (because the store would otherwise have obtained a down payment) satisfies the intent to defraud element. (A) and (B) are incorrect because, as explained above, Harmon is guilty of neither crime due to the absence of misrepresentation. In addition, (B) is incorrect because most courts would find that title has been transferred under these circumstances, rather than merely possession, making the potential crime false pretenses rather than larceny by trick.

Answer to Question 57

(C) Since Roy was charged with first degree murder, the theory of the case is most likely felony murder. (C) is the only choice that sets out a theory to avoid a felony murder conviction. If Roy was so intoxicated that he could not form the intent to steal, then he is not guilty of robbery, and there would be no "felony" from which the felony murder rule is to arise. (A) is wrong because Roy would be guilty of first degree murder both under the felony murder rule and because he fired intentionally with no circumstances of justification, excuse, or mitigation present and with premeditation and deliberation. (B) is wrong. Although it is arguable that Roy did not intend to kill or injure anyone, it was wanton to point a loaded gun and to pull the trigger even though he may not have expected it to fire. In any event, he is still liable under the felony murder rule, and since the felony is robbery, it is first degree murder. (D) is wrong because insulting someone is not adequate provocation that would mitigate a homicide to voluntary manslaughter; neither would this "threat" in all likelihood. At most, the circumstances might produce the sort of unreasonable anger that would negate the premeditation and deliberation necessary for first degree murder. However, since Roy clearly caused the homicide during the felony of the robbery, his crime remains first degree murder.

Answer to Question 58

(B) Myrna's strongest argument is that Reba's death was justifiable homicide. Most courts today would not allow Myrna to be convicted on a felony murder theory when a co-felon is killed by a third party during the crime. Some courts base this result on the fact that the person who did the killing was justified in doing so. (A) is wrong. Aside from the fact that the attempt to steal from the jewelry store is probably statutory burglary, the fact that Reba attempted to aid Myrna in stealing the bracelet by attacking the clerk with a knife is probably robbery. When or how Reba came by the dangerous weapon is immaterial. (C) is wrong because the circumstances of one co-felon breaking an agreement not to commit violence would not prevent the application of the felony murder rule if it were otherwise applicable. (D) is wrong because if the felony murder rule is otherwise applicable, the fact that the person who killed the co-felon may have mistaken the co-felon's intentions does not prevent the operation of this rule.

Answer to Question 59

(B) To be reasonable under the Fourth Amendment, most searches must be pursuant to a warrant. The warrant must describe with reasonable precision the place to be searched and the items to be seized. A search warrant does not authorize the police to search persons found on the premises who are not named in the warrant. In *Ybarra v. Illinois* (1979), a case based on similar facts, the Supreme Court held that "each patron of the tavern had an individual right to be free of unreasonable searches, and presence at a location subject to search does not negate the requirement of probable cause to search the person present." (A) is incorrect because the validity of the statute is not the primary issue. Even in the absence of a statute, the search of Phil by Officer Ollie violated Phil's Fourth Amendment rights. (C) is incorrect because, as discussed above, the search warrant did not override Phil's Fourth Amendment rights. While the police would be able to search a person discovered on the premises for whom they had probable cause to arrest, because the search would be incident to a lawful arrest, here they searched Phil prior to an arrest and without probable cause. (D) is irrelevant; if a search is unconstitutional, it does not matter that it was authorized by statute. To the extent that the statute authorizes a search in violation of the Fourth Amendment, it is unconstitutional.

Answer to Question 60

(B) Since purchasing five pounds of gunpowder without a license is not a crime, the defendant cannot be convicted of purchasing gunpowder without a license, *or* of attempting to purchase gunpowder without a license, even if defendant believed he was committing a crime. Since there is no crime on the books to cover the defendant's behavior or his intended behavior, he cannot be found guilty of attempt. This is the doctrine of legal impossibility. In (A), the defendant might be found guilty of attempt. He intended to obtain the property by false pretenses, and the jury could find that he was close to completing the crime. In (C), the defendant could be found guilty of attempt. He intended to receive stolen property, and the jury could find that he was close to completing the crime. In (D), the defendant could be found guilty of attempt; he intended to kill Vincent and the jury could find that he was close to completing the crime. The fact that it was factually impossible for him to complete the crime is no defense to his liability for attempt.

Answer to Question 61

(D) While Dave might have been indifferent with respect to Brian's marital status, the facts do not show that Dave ***intended*** to see the offense of bigamy committed. To establish criminal liability under an accomplice theory, it must be established that the defendant helped with the commission of the crime ***and*** had the intent to see the crime committed. A mental state of recklessness would not justify a conviction as an accomplice, regardless of the mental state required by the definition of the principal crime. (A) is incorrect because although Dave did aid and encourage the marriage, he cannot be held as an accomplice without the necessary intent, which was lacking. (B) is incorrect. In some jurisdictions, bigamy is a strict liability offense when applied to the actual participants in the bigamous marriage. Thus, although Carla might be guilty under the theory of strict liability, Dave would not be. (C) is incorrect because even if Dave's actions amounted to a breach of duty, he still did not possess the mental state necessary for accomplice liability.

Answer to Question 62

(A) An honest and reasonable mistake as to a material element of the offense would negate criminal liability for all crimes except strict liability offenses. Thus, if the state had abolished strict liability crimes, Carla's mistake would be a defense regardless of the mental state required for the crime of bigamy. (B) is not as good an answer as (A). Carla's lack of intent to commit bigamy would negate criminal liability if bigamy was a specific intent crime requiring an actual intention to engage in the bigamous marriage. The question does not indicate the mental state required for the crime. Even though the state had abolished strict liability offenses, the state could punish a bigamous marriage entered into with a "reckless" or "should have known" state of mind. If so, Carla's lack of intent would not result in a not guilty verdict. (C) is not as good an answer as (A) because the fact that Carla made a diligent effort to determine the marital status of Brian would be an important consideration in deciding whether she made an honest and reasonable mistake, but it would not in and of itself automatically negate liability. The same analysis applies to (D). The fact that Carla relied on information supplied by a state official would be an important consideration in deciding the nature of her mistake; it would not by itself negate liability.

Answer to Question 63

(C) If Don made a reasonable mistake as to the age of Jones, he did not have the mental state necessary for the crime charged. In this question, the statute requires a mental state of ***knowingly*** selling to a person under age 21; therefore, a mistake concerning the age of the purchaser would negate criminal liability. (A) is wrong. In many jurisdictions, selling liquor to a minor is a strict liability offense. In such jurisdictions, a person would be guilty if he sold the liquor to a minor even if he made a reasonable mistake about age. The New Olka statute, however, is not a strict liability offense because it requires a ***knowing*** state of mind. (B) is wrong because it is simply an incorrect statement of the facts. There is nothing in the question that indicates that Don knew Jones was less than 21 years old. (D) is wrong because while the driver's license would be a consideration in deciding whether Don made a reasonable mistake, it would not of itself negate criminal liability: Don would be guilty if he knew Jones was underage even if Jones produced a driver's license stating otherwise.

Answer to Question 64

(B) Dave's conviction should be reversed because the court's charge to the jury required Dave to prove that he intended to return the car. In a criminal case, the state must prove beyond a reasonable doubt all "elements" of the crime. Elements include the behavior, result, and mental state found in the definition of the crime charged. Since common law larceny requires an "intent to permanently deprive," the state must prove beyond a reasonable doubt that mental state. In this question, the judge incorrectly placed the burden of proof on the defendant to prove an intent to return the car by a preponderance of the evidence. (A) is an incorrect statement of the law. The state is not required to prove *all* disputed issues beyond a reasonable doubt, only the basic elements of the crime charged. Many states require a defendant to prove a defense, such as entrapment or self-defense, by a preponderance of the evidence. (C) is wrong because an intent to return the car would show a lack of intent to permanently deprive, which would negate liability for common law larceny. (D) is wrong because the jury instructions were incorrect for the reasons stated above.

Answer to Question 65

(D) Doberman's change of heart after taking the car is least likely to provide him with a defense because it is irrelevant; the larceny was committed at the time he took Vosburg's car with the intent to permanently deprive him of possession. (Note that the taking was trespassory because Doberman obtained possession by misrepresentation—larceny by trick.) (A) is incorrect because Doberman intended to return the property at the time of the taking; thus, he can claim that he did not have the requisite intent for larceny. (B) is similarly wrong because Doberman can argue that he did not intend to permanently deprive Vosburg of possession when he took the car; because larceny is a specific intent crime, Doberman's intoxication can be introduced to negate the requisite intent. (C) is wrong because Doberman can argue that he honestly believed that he was entitled to the car as partial repayment of Vosburg's debt and that he therefore did not have the intent to deprive Vosburg of "his" property.

Answer to Question 66

(C) Dave's conviction for larceny will not likely be upheld because a court will probably find that he had "possession" of the car at the time he appropriated it, making him guilty of embezzlement rather than larceny. Larceny requires a taking from *another* person who is in possession of the property, and here Dave had lawful possession of the property at the time he converted it by failing to return it. (A) is not as good a choice as (C) because the court could find that, even though Debbie has title to her car, the repair shop has a superior claim to *possession* of the car because it has a mechanic's lien that entitles it to keep the car in its possession until the repairs are paid for. (B) is not correct because the "continuing trespass" doctrine applies to make Don's conduct larceny. Ordinarily, the intent for larceny must be concurrent with the trespassory taking. However, because Don took the car with a wrongful state of mind, the trespassory taking here "continued" until he formed the intent to commit larceny. (D) is incorrect because Donna committed larceny by trick; the rental agency's consent to her taking possession of the car was induced by a misrepresentation.

EVIDENCE QUESTIONS

Question 1

Ace Accountant and his sister, Alice, were arrested on the federal charge of tax evasion in connection with the family business. Perkins, the prosecutor, suspects that Ace is involved in many other such schemes and is a menace to the community. Prior to trial, Perkins tells Alice that he believes he can get her sentence reduced to probation if she pleads guilty to a lesser charge and agrees to testify against Ace. Alice reluctantly agrees for the sake of her three small children.

During Ace's jury trial, Alice is called by the prosecution. On cross-examination, Ace's attorney brings out the fact that Alice was arrested on the same charge. The attorney then asks Alice whether it is true that after her arrest, Perkins made the following statement to her: "If you agree to give us the dirt on Ace and testify at his trial, I can have your sentence reduced to probation and you can be home with your kids tonight." Perkins objects.

The objection should be:

(A) Sustained, because it is against public policy to reveal information about plea bargains to a jury.

(B) Sustained, because it calls for hearsay.

(C) Overruled, because the question goes to bias or interest.

(D) Overruled, because Alice waived the attorney-client privilege by testifying.

Question 2

Carl is on trial in Chicago for violating a statute forbidding possession of a concealed weapon within 100 yards of a government building. The prosecution presents evidence that Carl was arrested on the corner of Washington and LaSalle streets with a handgun in his pocket. The building housing the Chicago City Hall occupies the entire block on the north side of Washington Street and the east side of LaSalle Street.

Which of the following statements is most accurate regarding judicial notice of the location of the city hall?

(A) The judge may take judicial notice of this fact without resort to a map, and should instruct the jury that it may, but need not, accept this fact as evidence of an element of the offense.

(B) If the judge properly takes judicial notice of this fact, a presumption is created that shifts the burden of persuasion to the defendant to disprove this fact.

(C) The judge may not take judicial notice of this type of fact in a criminal case without a request by the prosecution.

(D) The judge may take judicial notice of this fact only upon reference to an official street map of the city.

Question 3

As the streets of her neighborhood have become more dangerous due to gang warfare, Tangerine has become very active and vocal in the anti-gang movement. One evening, a brick with Tangerine's name scrawled on it was thrown through Tangerine's bedroom window. The brick struck Tangerine, causing severe injuries. Tangerine believes that Dexter, who is both her former boyfriend and a gang member, threw the brick, but she did not actually see Dexter throw it.

If Dexter is arrested and put on trial for battery, which of the following items of Tangerine's proposed testimony is *least* likely to be admitted?

(A) Tangerine recently moved to a new apartment and only Dexter and a few family members knew its location.

(B) Tangerine had testified against a member of Dexter's gang last month in a drug case.

(C) On another occasion, Tangerine had seen Dexter throw a rock through the window of a rival street gang member.

(D) Immediately after the brick went through her window, Tangerine heard a voice she recognized as Dexter's yell, "If you don't start minding your own business, you'll get a lot worse than this next time!"

Question 4

Jane Doe, a resident of a large suburban apartment complex, reported to the police that she had been victimized by a masked rapist. Although the mask made it impossible for Jane to give the detectives a complete description of her attacker, the police did retrieve a pair of gloves from the apartment. After a thorough criminal investigation, the police concluded that Duncan had been given a key to Jane's apartment by Matthew, the manager of the apartment complex, and that Duncan used the key to facilitate the attack on Jane Doe. Warrants were issued to arrest Duncan on charges of rape and conspiracy to commit rape, and against Matthew for conspiracy to commit rape. Duncan was successfully apprehended, but Matthew got wind that "something was up" and disappeared. At the time of Duncan's trial, Matthew had not yet been apprehended. Duncan's defense is that he never had been in Jane Doe's apartment. The prosecution wishes to call Gina, who was Matthew's live-in girlfriend at the time of the rape. Gina is prepared to testify that, two days after the attack on Jane, Matthew told her, "I never should have given the key to Jane Doe's apartment to a bumbler like Duncan—not only did he not get the stereo like he was supposed to, he also said that he thinks he left his gloves in her apartment."

After appropriate objection by Duncan's attorney, the court should find the statement:

(A) Admissible, because it is a statement against interest.

(B) Admissible, because it is a statement by a co-conspirator.

(C) Inadmissible, because it is hearsay within hearsay.

(D) Inadmissible, because the statement does not indicate that Matthew knew of or agreed to a plan to rape Jane Doe.

Question 5

Don is charged with beating Vic to death with a set of brass knuckles during the course of a fight in a tavern. Vic was found to have a pistol on his person at the time of the fight. During the course of the trial, Don took the stand in his own defense and testified that Vic threatened him with a gun and Don had hit Vic with the brass knuckles in self-defense. To rebut Don's claim, the prosecution wishes to place Barmistress on the stand. Barmistress is prepared to testify that two years prior to the attack on Vic, she had seen Don approach a customer in her tavern from behind. Don then put on a pair of brass knuckles and, still standing behind the customer, struck the customer a severe blow on the side of the face with a brass-knuckled fist. The prosecutor, in accordance with local court rules, has apprised Don's defense attorney of the general tenor of Barmistress's proposed testimony. As soon as Barmistress is sworn in, Don's attorney raises an objection.

The court should rule that Barmistress's testimony is:

(A) Admissible, to establish Don's propensity for violence.

(B) Admissible, to attack Don's credibility.

(C) Inadmissible, because prior bad acts cannot be admitted to prove the defendant's propensity to commit the specific crime with which he is charged.

(D) Inadmissible, because Don has not put his character in issue in this case.

Question 6

Edison, who has an advanced degree in engineering, is testifying at trial as an expert to the possible causes for the failure of an enclosed pedestrian bridge in a shopping mall. If the following data that form the basis of his opinion are disclosed by him on direct examination, which may the jury consider as substantive evidence?

I.   His statements relating facts that he personally observed about the wreckage.

II. His repetition of statements told to him by witnesses to the collapse, as long as such statements are reasonably relied on by experts in his field.

III. Statements that he reads from a text on structural engineering that he has testified is authoritative.

(A) I. only.

(B) I. and II.

(C) I. and III.

(D) I., II., and III.

Question 7

Three masked men robbed a convenience store in Petersburgh, during the course of which a clerk was killed. An investigation led the police to believe Dearborn was one of the robbers and they placed him under arrest. Dearborn protested that he was innocent and volunteered to take a lie-detector test. The test was conducted by Belial, a qualified polygraph expert. According to Belial's analysis of the test, Dearborn lied about his participation in the armed robbery. Dearborn is placed on trial by a jury for the armed robbery. The prosecution calls Belial to the stand to testify as to his analysis of the results of Dearborn's polygraph test. The defense objects.

If the objection is sustained, it will most likely be because:

(A) Belial's testimony would violate Dearborn's right against self-incrimination if Dearborn elects not to take the stand in his own defense.

(B) Belial's testimony would violate Dearborn's right against self-incrimination, regardless of whether Dearborn elects to take the stand in his own defense.

(C) Polygraph evidence is considered to be unreliable and potentially confusing to jurors.

(D) The Federal Rules specifically classify polygraph evidence as irrelevant.

Question 8

Poyn sued Dexter for defamation, asserting in his complaint that Dexter had called Poyn "a thief" in front of a number of business associates. Poyn calls two witnesses to the stand, both of whom testify that they heard Dexter refer to Poyn as "a thief" in front of the business associates. Poyn does not take the stand himself. Dexter pleads truth of the statement as an affirmative defense and calls Wendy to the stand. Wendy is prepared to testify that she was a co-worker of Poyn when Poyn supplemented his income by tending bar three nights a week. Wendy will testify that she saw Poyn take a $20 bill from the tavern's cash register and secrete the money in his pocket. Poyn's attorney objects.

May Wendy's testimony be allowed?

(A) Yes, as substantive evidence that Poyn is, in fact, a thief.

(B) Yes, because theft is a crime indicating dishonesty.

(C) No, because specific bad acts may not be used to show bad character.

(D) No, because Poyn never took the stand.

Question 9

In a trial for bank robbery, a teller has identified the defendant as the robber. Defense counsel offers into evidence a still frame from a video taken by the bank security camera the day after the robbery to show that a column obstructed that teller's view of the defendant.

Such evidence is:

(A) Admissible upon testimony by the camera operator that the still frame was developed from film that was taken from that camera the day after the robbery.

(B) Admissible upon testimony by a bank employee that the photo accurately portrays the scene of the crime.

(C) Not admissible into evidence but usable by a witness for explanatory purposes.

(D) Not admissible if a still frame can be obtained from a video taken at the time of the robbery.

Question 10

Permian sued Devon over a claimed $1,000 debt. At the trial Permian established the existence of the debt and testified that he never received payment. In response, Devon presents evidence sufficient to establish that she took her check to the post office and sent it to Permian's proper address by certified mail. She offers a certified mail receipt with an illegible signature, which she claims is Permian's signature. Devon also presents evidence that her basement flooded on March 28, and she claims that she cannot produce a canceled check because her box of canceled checks was converted into an unrecognizable blob from the water damage. Evidence is also presented that due to a computer glitch Devon's bank cannot reproduce Devon's checking account records for the months of February and March.

After Devon's testimony:

(A) The burden of persuasion and the burden of going forward with the evidence are on Permian.

(B) The burden of persuasion is on Permian, but he has no burden of going forward with the evidence.

(C) Permian has satisfied his burden of persuasion, but he has a burden of going forward with the evidence.

(D) Permian has satisfied both his burden of persuasion and his burden of going forward with the evidence.

Question 11

Potter was injured in an automobile accident caused by Dawson. Potter sued Dawson for his injuries. The state recognizes only the common law privileges. In preparation for trial, Anson, Potter's attorney, hired Dr. Wand to examine Potter. At trial, Dawson's attorney attempts to call Dr. Wand as a witness to testify about statements Potter made in confidence to Dr. Wand about his injuries, and that Wand then communicated to Anson.

This testimony should be:

(A) Admitted, because Potter's statements are the statements of a party-opponent.

(B) Admitted, because Potter waived the physician-patient privilege by placing his physical condition in issue.

(C) Excluded, because Potter's statements are protected by the attorney-client privilege.

(D) Excluded, because Potter's statements are protected by the physician-patient privilege.

Question 12

While driving home late one night, Don struck Peter, a seven-year-old who was playing in the street near the curb. Peter was seriously injured, suffering permanent brain damage. After being questioned by the police and released,

Don went home and, while lying in bed that night, told his wife, Wilhelmina, what had happened. During this conversation, Don stated, "Between you and me, just before all this happened, I took a quick peek at the back seat to make sure I brought my briefcase home with me. If I had kept my eyes on the road, I never would've hit the kid." Unknown to either Don or Wilhelmina, Anastasia, their next-door neighbor, overheard this conversation through their open window. Although it was near midnight, Anastasia had gone onto her porch to get some air because it was a very warm night.

Peter's parents filed a lawsuit on his behalf against Don. Shortly before the trial, Don and Wilhelmina were divorced. Greatly embittered by the circumstances of the divorce, Wilhelmina agreed to testify to the statement made to her by Don on the night he struck Peter.

Assuming a proper objection by Don's attorney, will Wilhelmina be permitted to so testify?

(A) Yes, because Wilhelmina and Don were divorced during the time between the making of the statement and the trial.

(B) Yes, because the fact that Anastasia heard the statement removes the privileged status of the statement.

(C) No, because Don's statement was a confidential marital communication.

(D) No, because the privilege to foreclose such testimony belongs to the party-spouse.

Question 13

The guardian ad litem of Pulliam, a minor, filed an appropriate tort suit against Filet Memorial Hospital and Dr. S. L. Tipp, the resident physician attending Pulliam when Pulliam suffered irreversible brain damage. Both parties stipulated that such damage could be caused by an excessive fever. The plaintiff alleges that Dr. Tipp was negligent in not administering the fever-reduction drug Koollum when its use was

called for. Uncontroverted testimony at the trial indicates that the commonly accepted practice is to refrain from administering Koollum until the patient's temperature reaches 102 degrees Fahrenheit, because the drug causes dangerous side effects in about 10% of the population, and there is no test that accurately predicts such reactions to Koollum.

"Plaintiff's Exhibit F" has been introduced into evidence. The exhibit in question is the chart indicating that Pulliam's temperature reached 103.7 degrees at 3 p.m. on February 26. The chart is signed by the head nurse of the pediatric care division, and the signature has been properly authenticated. Other testimony indicates that it is standard procedure at Filet Memorial Hospital for the head nurse of each division to submit medical charts to resident physicians for additional notation before the charts are filed in the hospital's permanent records. The charts are not always signed by resident physicians, but any additional notations added by the physicians are usually initialed by the notating physician. Plaintiff's Exhibit F contains no notation, initial, or signature from Dr. Tipp.

When Dr. Tipp takes the stand he wishes to testify that he was in the room when Pulliam's temperature was taken at 2:30 p.m. on February 26, and at that time his temperature was 101.7 degrees.

Such testimony would be:

(A) Admissible, because Dr. Tipp has firsthand knowledge of the patient's condition at the time in question.

(B) Admissible, because the plaintiff "opened the door" to such testimony by introducing the chart into evidence.

(C) Inadmissible, because the chart is the best evidence of Pulliam's body temperature.

(D) Inadmissible, because Dr. Tipp had ample opportunity to correct the temperature record and his failure to do so constitutes an adoptive admission.

Question 14

Hudson and his wife Deirdre were arrested by federal agents and charged with distributing obscene materials through the United States mails. When called before a grand jury, Deirdre refused to say anything, invoking her Fifth Amendment right to be protected from compelled self-incrimination. Hudson was terrified of the grand jury and readily admitted under questioning that he sent obscene matter through the mail. He also incriminated Deirdre in the illegal activity. The thought of a trial and a prison term drove Hudson over the edge, and he committed suicide two days before his trial was to begin.

A month after Hudson's suicide, Deirdre was put on trial in federal district court. The federal prosecutor seeks to introduce a transcript of Hudson's grand jury testimony into evidence against Deirdre. Deirdre's attorney objects.

The court should rule that the grand jury transcript is:

(A) Admissible, as an admission.

(B) Admissible, as former testimony.

(C) Inadmissible, because Deirdre can invoke the spousal privilege, even though Hudson is now deceased.

(D) Inadmissible, because Hudson's testimony was not subject to cross-examination.

Question 15

Philip brought a suit against Wonderful Widget Company for breach of a contract for the sale of 1,000 widgets, alleging that the widgets failed to conform to contract specifications. Shortly before the trial of the case was to begin, Philip suffered a stroke that left him paralyzed and virtually unable to communicate. Greta was appointed as Philip's guardian and was properly substituted, in her capacity as guardian, as the plaintiff in the lawsuit.

At trial, following presentation of the plaintiff's case, the defendant calls as a witness Father Harrison, a Roman Catholic priest, to question him about a conversation he had several months ago with Philip at a church dinner-dance fundraiser. In this conversation, Philip told Father Harrison in confidence that the widgets he received from the defendant were actually quite functional, but that he had become aware of a lower price being offered by another company, and thus wanted to get out of his contract with Wonderful Widget Company. The plaintiff's attorney immediately objects on the basis of clergy-penitent privilege.

The objection should be:

(A) Sustained, because the statement of Philip was made to Father Harrison in confidence.

(B) Sustained, because this is not a criminal case.

(C) Overruled, because the privilege can be invoked only by the person who made the confidential statement.

(D) Overruled, because the circumstances under which Philip made the statement take it outside the scope of the privilege.

Question 16

Dimer's executor filed an appropriate suit against the Michiana Western Railway for the wrongful death of Dimer. Dimer was killed as a result of a collision between Dimer's automobile and a Michiana Western freight train, which occurred at the intersection of State Route 47 with the Michiana Western right-of-way. The grade crossing was equipped by the railroad with crossing gates that were designed to lower automatically when a train approached within 500 yards of the crossing. Flashing lights and ringing bells were designed to be triggered when a train approached within 800 yards of the crossing. After the accident it was impossible for experts to tell whether one of the crossing gates was broken because a vehicle drove through it or if it broke while being lowered suddenly on top of a vehicle entering the grade crossing. Buck, a motorist who did not see the accident, but who arrived on the scene just seconds later, heard Parkes, a pedestrian standing near the grade crossing, exclaim, "My God, that gate didn't come down on time!" Parkes collapsed after making his statement. A county paramedic unit that arrived shortly thereafter determined that Dimer was beyond help. Norma, a highly trained emergency medical technician, promptly tended to Parkes. She told Parkes that he had probably suffered a mild heart attack, but that he would be fine after a few days' rest. Parkes told Norma, "Well, I guess I'm a lot luckier than that poor fool who rammed his car right through that crossing barrier into the train." Two months later, Parkes suffered another heart attack and died.

Six months after the accident, the executor's suit came to trial. The plaintiff called Buck to the stand, and the court allowed Buck to testify to what he heard Parkes say after the accident. Mildew, the railroad's attorney, wishes to call Norma to the stand to testify as to Parkes's statement when Norma was treating him.

Norma's testimony should be ruled:

(A) Admissible, but solely for the purpose of impeachment.

(B) Admissible, both for impeachment purposes and as evidence of the positioning of the crossing gate at the time of the accident.

(C) Inadmissible, because Parkes is not available to be questioned about the inconsistent statements.

(D) Inadmissible, as hearsay not within any recognized exception to the hearsay rule.

Question 17

The best-known accredited graduate schools of agriculture entered into an agreement that persons seeking admission to their graduate programs would have to take a national exam designed strictly for agricultural students, similar to the GMAT for business and the LSAT for law. Testee's Buddy ("TB") was the dominant test preparation program for most of the specialized graduate school entrance exams, and TB quickly set up a division to deal with the AgTest, as the specialized agricultural test was known. The division was directed by Legree, who hired three clerks and entered into contracts with several noted professors of agriculture to conduct lectures. Two years later, about 85% of students taking the AgTest were also taking TB's preparation courses.

At that time, Deer decided to set up a rival course. Deer knew that the AgTest division at TB was woefully understaffed. He therefore visited various agricultural colleges and removed TB's business reply cards from the bulletin boards. He sent them to TB's AgTest division hoping to swamp the clerks with work and to cut into TB's AgTest profit margin. Deer also induced Mike Moo, an agriculture professor under contract with TB, to break his contract and lecture with Deer's course for a percentage of the profits. Legree caught on to what Deer was up to after Moo suddenly left TB. Legree ordered his clerks to log in, for a two-week period, any and all business reply requests from Deliberate Falls, Wisconsin, where Deer lived, or with return addresses at the Sodd Building, where Deer had his offices. When such reply cards were received, one of the clerks would enter it on a tally sheet posted in the office. Immediately after the tally was completed and a large number of cards had been received, TB filed suit against Deer for interference with business relations. TB's attorney offers the tally record into evidence. Deer's attorney objects.

The court should find the tally record:

(A) Admissible, as past recollection recorded.

(B) Admissible, as a business record.

(C) Inadmissible, because unless it is shown that the clerks are unavailable, their testimony is the best evidence.

(D) Inadmissible, because it is hearsay not within any exception.

Question 18

Senior was prosecuted for criminal violations of a hazardous waste disposal act and convicted, in part on the testimony of Wilma, who worked for him. After Senior's death, Porta, on whose property Senior dumped the hazardous waste, brought suit to recover the cleanup costs against Junior as executor of Senior's estate. Because Wilma is currently incarcerated in another state, Porta seeks to introduce the transcript of Wilma's testimony from Senior's criminal trial in the present action. Junior objects to its admission.

The court should rule that the transcript is:

(A) Admissible, because Wilma was subject to cross-examination in the previous action.

(B) Admissible, because the transcript of the criminal trial is a public record.

(C) Inadmissible, because Porta has not shown that Wilma is truly "unavailable."

(D) Inadmissible, because Junior was not a party to the previous action.

Question 19

The only eyewitness to a serious felony was Marieke, who witnessed the crime from the window of her apartment. Marieke is the key witness in the prosecution's case against Dawson, who has been accused of the crime in question. Marieke, a recent immigrant from Belgium, has had a total hearing impairment since birth and only speaks a few words of Flemish, her family's native language. In addition, the system of "signing" for the deaf is different in Belgium from the method used in the United States. The only person in the county conversant with both the Flemish language and the Belgian signing method is Astrid, who is employed as a clerk in the county prosecutor's office. Astrid had assisted the police in their questioning of Marieke prior to Dawson's arrest, and also assisted the police when Marieke identified Dawson in a lineup.

Should the court allow Marieke to testify using Astrid as an interpreter?

(A) Yes, because Astrid is qualified.

(B) Yes, if Astrid takes an oath to make a true translation.

(C) No, because as a result of her employment and previous activities, Astrid is inherently biased.

(D) No, unless Astrid discloses to the jury her employment and previous activities in this case.

Question 20

Dosch had recently been released from prison on parole from an armed robbery conviction. Police officer Margaret and her partner Roy were driving down Talbot Street in their squad car when they spotted Dosch, whom the officers knew because they had arrested Dosch for the armed robbery. They followed Dosch for awhile and noted that he kept looking nervously over his shoulder at the squad car and that he was carrying a brown paper bag in his hand. Suddenly, Dosch darted into an alley. A few moments later, he emerged from the alley and began running north along the sidewalk of Talbot Street. Still at a run, Dosch turned right onto Bowler Boulevard, a crowded shopping street. Margaret and Roy put on their siren and pursued Dosch. Dosch was unable to lose himself in the crowd and he was quickly cuffed and searched by the officers. About 15 minutes after they had seen Dosch emerge from the alley, the officers drove back to the alley entrance. Officer Margaret got out of the squad car and searched the alley. About six feet from the entrance to the alley, she found a paper bag against the wall of the back of a building. The brown paper bag contained a handgun. Officer Margaret copied the gun's serial number before taking the gun back to the police station. Dosch was charged with illegal possession of a handgun and carrying a concealed weapon. At Dosch's trial, while Officer Margaret is testifying, the prosecution seeks to admit the gun that Officer Margaret found into evidence against Dosch. The defense attorney objects on the grounds that the gun lacks proper identification.

The objection should be:

(A) Sustained, because the gun was not in Dosch's possession at the time of his arrest.

(B) Sustained, because there is insufficient proof that the gun belonged to Dosch.

(C) Overruled, because there is sufficient evidence that the gun belonged to Dosch.

(D) Overruled, because the objection should have been based on chain of custody.

Question 21

Reginald and Veronica were engaged to be married after a long courtship. About two months before the wedding date, Veronica fell in love with Archie and began having a clandestine affair with him. About two weeks before the wedding, Archie went to Veronica's apartment after work. The next morning Veronica's body was found in a forest preserve; she had been strangled to death. Veronica's best friend and confidante, Betty, told the police that Archie had been having an affair with Veronica. The police questioned Archie, who readily admitted visiting Veronica at 6 p.m., but he denied slaying her. The police believed that Archie was telling the truth. Reginald was subsequently arrested and charged with the murder of Veronica.

At Reginald's trial, the prosecution wants to call Archie to the stand to testify that he left Veronica's apartment at 9 p.m., after Veronica told him, "You'd better get out of here now, because I'm going over to Reginald's in a little while to tell him that the wedding is off." The defense objects.

Archie's testimony should be:

(A) Admissible, as a present sense impression.

(B) Admissible, to show Veronica's state of mind.

(C) Inadmissible, as more prejudicial than probative.

(D) Inadmissible, as hearsay not within any recognized exception.

Question 22

Several members of a small terrorist group are on trial in federal court for conspiring to bomb a military installation in Nevada. The prosecution would like to introduce the testimony of a military guard at one of the installation's gates. The guard had been present when a bomb that was being planted by Norton, a member of the group, had exploded prematurely. The guard will testify that he ran over to administer first aid to Norton, who had lost both legs in the explosion, and that Norton, in great pain, told him that his group was in the process of planting three other bombs in other areas of the military installation and was going to detonate them all at the same time to get publicity for their cause. The guard will also testify that Norton disclosed the locations of the other bombs and the names of two other members of the group. The authorities were able to prevent the other bombings and arrest the other members of the group. Norton died from his injuries.

What is the best basis for allowing the guard to testify as to Norton's statements?

(A) As a vicarious admission of a co-conspirator.

(B) As a statement against interest.

(C) As a statement of present state of mind.

(D) As a dying declaration.

Question 23

Hy retained the firm of Fleesum, Goode, and Klaw to represent him in a suit against several perfume companies, based on Hy's claim that exposure to the fragrances manufactured by the companies in question caused him to have severe allergic reactions. Fleesum, Goode, and Klaw had over 50 partners and associates and, during the course of his suit, Hy had contact with a number of them. After Greene, an associate with the firm, presented the plaintiff's case, the defendants moved for a directed verdict, which was granted. An angry Hy went to Luckett, another attorney, and filed a malpractice suit against the firm. Hy's pleading contends that the partnership was derelict in failing to interview, among others, one Dr. Bronson as a prospective expert witness. Hy had suggested that Bronson be used after reading *Odor of Doom,* a book written by Bronson on the dangerous health effects of inhaling perfume odors. The partnership's pleadings contend that Bronson was never brought to the attention of anyone at the firm and was never considered as a witness.

Hy wants to introduce a "proposed witness list" from his case file at Fleesum, Goode, and Klaw. After the name "Dr. H.R. Bronson" is the notation, "Hy wants us to check this guy out before trial." The notation is in the handwriting of John, a paralegal with Fleesum, Goode, who is responsible for updating various case files as part of his regular duties. John did no direct work on Hy's case and he cannot remember which lawyer in the firm asked him to make the notation after Bronson's name. The defendant's attorney objects to the introduction of the proposed witness list containing the notation.

The proposed witness list and notation is:

(A) Admissible, as past recollection recorded.

(B) Admissible, as a business record.

(C) Inadmissible, because it is hearsay not within any recognized exception.

(D) Inadmissible, as hearsay within hearsay, and one level is not within an exception.

Question 24

Nora hosted a garden party in honor of her nephew, Fingal, who was visiting her from Ireland. At the party Fingal got to meet many of Nora's friends, including Adam and Eve, a married couple living next door to Nora. A week later, Fingal went out to have a few beers with his new American friends at the neighborhood tavern. At 11 p.m. that night, Fingal appeared back at Nora's house, pounding loudly on the door. Nora let him in, and noted that Fingal was panting and out of breath. He immediately told her, "Aunt Nora, you won't believe what I just saw. I was walking past Adam and Eve's just now and Eve ran up to me with a gun in her hand. She looked me straight in the eyes and said, 'I killed the philandering fool' before running off down the street." Eve was put on trial for the murder of Adam. The prosecution wants to put Nora on the stand to testify regarding Fingal's statement to her. The defense objects.

Can Nora testify to Fingal's statement?

(A) Yes, because it qualifies as an excited utterance.

(B) Yes, but only if Fingal is not available to testify.

(C) No, because Eve did not make her admission to Nora.

(D) No, because Nora's testimony would constitute hearsay within hearsay.

Question 25

Mrs. Walton, an elderly woman living in a nursing home, was the only eyewitness, other than the parties, to an automobile accident that resulted in a lawsuit. Walton viewed the accident while on an outing about one block from her nursing home residence. During the course of the trial, the plaintiff calls Walton to the stand. After a few questions, it becomes clear that Walton remembers having seen the accident, but her memory of the details has grown fuzzy. The plaintiff's attorney wishes to introduce into evidence the contents of some handwritten notes made by Walton after she returned to her room after witnessing the accident.

Which of the following are true statements with respect to the admissibility of the contents of the notes?

I.   Walton must testify that the notes are accurate.

II. It must be shown that the notes were prepared at a time when Walton was under the stress of excitement of the event and had not had time to reflect on the accident.

III. Walton must be given the notes to examine to determine if she still has insufficient memory, after consulting the notes, to testify fully and accurately.

IV. The plaintiff's attorney may not introduce the notes into evidence as an exhibit under any circumstances.

(A) I. and II. only.

(B) II. and III. only.

(C) IV. only.

(D) I., III., and IV. only.

Question 26

Gladys was crossing the street at the intersection of Fourth Street and Wisconsin Avenue in Queen City when she was struck by a car driven by an uninsured driver. Gladys suffered a fractured skull and other injuries and had to be hospitalized. She subsequently filed an appropriate suit against Queen City, claiming that it was negligent in not marking the crossing as a pedestrian crossing and in not painting lines on the pavement indicating a crosswalk. This is a busy intersection through which many vehicles and pedestrians pass during weekday rush hours.

The city attorney is defending on the grounds that Gladys was contributorily negligent. The plaintiff's attorney wishes to introduce evidence showing that two weeks after Gladys was struck by the vehicle, a city street maintenance crew painted pedestrian crosswalks at the intersection of Fourth and Wisconsin where no such crosswalks existed before and placed pedestrian crossing signs on the two streets at appropriate distances from the intersection. The city's attorney objects.

The court is most likely to rule that evidence regarding the crosswalks is:

(A) Admissible to show that the intersection was within the city's ownership or control.

(B) Admissible to show that the city is attempting to conceal or distort evidence.

(C) Inadmissible, because subsequent repairs are deemed irrelevant under the Federal Rules.

(D) Inadmissible, because public policy favors the encouragement of safety improvements.

Question 27

Theodore was on trial for allegedly burning down his business establishment because it was losing money. The prosecution seeks to introduce testimony from an insurance agent that Theodore purchased two insurance policies for the building within a month before the fire. Each policy had been purchased from a different insurance carrier and each policy was in the amount of the full value of the business. Theodore's attorney objects to the introduction of this testimony.

The court should rule that the testimony is:

(A) Admissible only for purposes of impeachment if Theodore takes the stand in his own defense.

(B) Admissible as substantive evidence against Theodore.

(C) Inadmissible, because the Federal Rules ban using evidence that a party carried insurance to prove that the party acted wrongfully.

(D) Inadmissible, because the policies themselves are required to be introduced under the original document rule.

Question 28

Poston, the owner of a small manufacturing company, filed a trademark infringement suit against TransAmerica Industries. While Trans-America's director of marketing, Denton, was on the stand, TransAmerica's attorney produced a "product recognition survey," a document generated by TransAmerica's marketing division. Poston's attorney objects that the record is hearsay. TransAmerica's attorney responds, "Your Honor, this is a business record and, as such, can be admitted into evidence as an exception to the hearsay rule." Poston's attorney complains, "Your Honor, this so-called product recognition survey is some self-serving writing concocted for this litigation. The hearsay exception requires that business records be made in the ordinary course of business. I demand a hearing to determine whether this qualifies as a business record."

Which of the following is the most appropriate way for the issue to be decided?

(A) The issue should be decided by the judge after hearing evidence from TransAmerica's attorney outside the presence of the jury.

(B) The issue should be decided by the judge after hearing evidence from TransAmerica's attorney and Poston's attorney and may be conducted in the presence of the jury.

(C) The issue should be decided by the jury after hearing evidence from both sides.

(D) The issue should be decided by the judge after hearing evidence from both sides outside the presence of the jury, but if the document is admitted by the judge, Poston may present evidence challenging that finding while presenting his case, and the ultimate decision rests with the jury.

Question 29

After an accident in which a car driven by Delta struck pedestrian Phi, Officer Kopp, of the local police, was called to the scene. According to standard police department procedures, Kopp measured skid marks in the intersection and interviewed all eyewitnesses present on the scene. He then wrote out in longhand all the pertinent information on the standard "Police Accident Report" form. Officer Kopp turned the report in to the department, where a police typist, according to the prescribed procedure, transcribed Kopp's longhand record into a typed record which, after it was checked by the investigating officer, was then placed on file in the police department.

Phi sued Delta for his injuries and the case actually came to trial about two years after the accident occurred. Officer Kopp was called to the stand by Phi to testify regarding the skid marks. Kopp can remember nothing about the specific accident, as Kopp has made at least 200 accident reports since the accident in question. After looking at the report, Kopp can remember preparing the report but still cannot remember the accident scene. He wishes to read the information regarding the skid marks in the police report to the jury from the stand. Delta's attorney objects.

How should the court rule?

(A) Kopp may read from the report, because it is past recollection recorded.

(B) Kopp may read from the report, because it is a present sense impression.

(C) Kopp may not read from the report, because a police report does not qualify as a business record.

(D) The report should be given to the jury to read, but it should not be read to them by Kopp from the stand.

Question 30

James is suing several members of the police department of the city of Baconia for near-fatal injuries incurred as a result of a beating administered by the officers. The suit is brought in federal court for violation of federal civil rights laws. Which of the following items of relevant evidence is the court *least* likely to exclude?

(A) Counsel for James calls as a witness a person who was locked up in an adjoining cell, and who will testify that James was in fact beaten by the defendant police officers. Counsel for the police moves to exclude this testimony on the ground that calling this witness constitutes an unfair surprise.

(B) Counsel for the police, after having called a nationally recognized expert to testify that the injuries suffered by James were inconsistent with injuries likely to be inflicted by the alleged police beating, attempts to call another expert to testify similarly. James's attorney moves to exclude this testimony on the grounds that it will constitute a waste of time and will unnecessarily present cumulative evidence.

(C) Counsel for James attempts to introduce the bloodstained shirt that James wore on the night of the beating. Counsel for the police moves to exclude this evidence on the ground that it will create a danger of unfair prejudice.

(D) Counsel for the police calls as a witness Officer Batista for the purpose of testifying that, because James was arrested in a bar frequented by gay people, the officers feared he might have AIDS, and as a result they would not have beaten him for fear of being infected by any open wounds. James's attorney moves to exclude this testimony on the ground that it may confuse the issues or mislead the jury.

Question 31

During the trial of a personal injury case, Perry, the plaintiff, calls Warren to testify that he saw Dunderhead, the defendant, spill a slippery substance in the roadway. Following the testimony of Warren, Dunderhead calls Womack, who testifies that Warren has a poor reputation for truth in the community. Perry's attorney then cross-examines Womack, asking him, "Isn't it true that last year you committed the crime of false pretenses?" Last year, Womack had been arrested for and charged with the crime of false pretenses. Dunderhead's attorney objects to this question. The objection should be:

(A) Overruled, unless Womack was not convicted of the crime of false pretenses.

(B) Overruled, if Perry's attorney asked the question in good faith.

(C) Sustained, because an impeaching witness cannot be impeached on collateral matters.

(D) Sustained, because such an inquiry is not proper on cross-examination.

Question 32

Paar lived in Chartreuse, a city in the state of Yellow located about 20 miles south of the state line where Yellow abutted the state of Green. Green had a much lower state tax on liquor, so Paar drove across the state line into Green to stock up on alcoholic beverages for a forthcoming New Year's Eve party that Paar planned to host. Shortly after Paar crossed the state line, but before he reached his favorite liquor store, Paar's auto was struck in the rear by a vehicle driven by Grant, a Green resident. At the time the accident occurred, weather conditions had deteriorated badly, and an ice storm had made the pavement dangerously slick. Paar suffered personal injuries and damage to his vehicle amounting to approximately $60,000. Having managed to obtain proper service on Grant, Paar filed suit in the Federal District Court for the Northern District of Yellow. Under the laws of Yellow, the driver of a vehicle that strikes another vehicle in the rear is presumed to have acted negligently, regardless of the surrounding circumstances. Neither the law of Green, nor the federal statutes or case law, have adopted such a rule.

Regarding the presumption in question, the court should apply:

(A) The Yellow rules of procedure and the federal common law.

(B) The Federal Rules of Civil Procedure and the Yellow substantive law.

(C) The whole law of Yellow, because in a diversity case a federal court must always apply the law of the state in which the federal court sits.

(D) The whole law of Yellow, because the presumption at issue operates upon elements of the prima facie case.

Question 33

Bertha's husband Bill was murdered. Bertha told the police that a shot was fired through the undraped picture window of their home's living room, and that the bullet struck Bill, killing him. After questioning neighbors, the police learned that Bertha and Bill often had loud arguments and that the arguments had increased in frequency in recent months. Bertha immediately became a prime suspect. The police asked Bertha to undergo a polygraph examination, and she agreed to do so. The polygraph analyst, an experienced lie-detector operator, told the police that Bertha was telling the truth when she asserted that she had nothing to do with Bill's death. Two weeks later, the police arrested Bob, a former business partner of Bill's, who held a grudge against Bill because of the way assets were distributed after their business partnership was wound up. The police had circumstantial evidence linking Bob to the crime, but there were no eyewitnesses who could identify Bob as the killer.

During Bob's trial, the prosecution called Bertha to the stand to testify to the happenings on the night Bill was slain and to the "bad blood" that existed between Bob and Bill. Bob's defense attorney, without objection by the prosecutor, asked Bertha questions regarding her stormy marital relationship with Bill. Bertha was very nervous under cross-examination, and the obvious point of the defense attorney's questioning was to plant a seed of doubt in the mind of the jury, implying that the slayer of Bill might have been Bertha and not Bob. Having

seen one of her key witnesses' testimony weakened, the prosecutor on re-direct asked Bertha, "After Bill was killed, didn't the police have you take a lie detector test?" As soon as the question was asked the defense attorney leapt to her feet and shouted, "Your Honor, I object to this line of questioning!"

The objection is likely to be:

(A) Sustained, because the scientific reliability of the lie detector evidence is substantially outweighed by its confusing effect on the jury.

(B) Sustained, because Bertha is not on trial for murder.

(C) Overruled, because the prosecutor has the right to rehabilitate a witness whose credibility has been impeached.

(D) Overruled, because the defense attorney "opened the door" to the prosecutor's line of questioning by asking questions that implied that Bertha might have killed Bill.

Question 34

Dagwood was on trial for the murder of his business partner, Xavier. The prosecution offered testimony by Rachel, the telephone operator in Dagwood's office, that she had listened in without Dagwood's knowledge to a telephone call Dagwood had received the day before Xavier's death, in which an unidentified man said to Dagwood, "I heard talk in Al's Bar last night that your partner, Xavier, is going to spill the beans to the cops about the phony insurance claim that you two guys cooked up last month."

Dagwood's attorney objects to this testimony. The trial court should:

(A) Sustain the objection because Rachel was an eavesdropper.

(B) Sustain the objection because the testimony is hearsay not within any exception.

(C) Overrule the objection because the statement is relevant to show motive.

(D) Overrule the objection because the statement constitutes an admission by a co-conspirator.

Question 35

In a criminal battery case brought against Dixon, the prosecutor asked the court to take judicial notice of the fact that a car driven from Chicago to Detroit has to cross state lines. Dixon's attorney raised no objection, and the judge declared that she was taking judicial notice of the fact as requested by the prosecution.

The effect of such judicial notice is:

(A) To raise an irrebuttable presumption.

(B) To satisfy the prosecutor's burden of persuasion on that issue.

(C) To shift the burden of persuasion on that issue to the defendant.

(D) That the judge should instruct the jury that it may, but is not required to, accept the noticed fact as conclusively proven.

Question 36

While waiting for a flight to Oak Ridge, Tennessee, Webster heard a ticking sound emanating from one of his suitcases. Webster noticed that whenever a bearded man with a large valise passed close to where Webster was sitting, the ticking sound became both faster and louder. Webster's suitcase contained a very sensitive Geiger counter, designed to detect small amounts of radiation. Webster informed the airport police, who quickly accosted the bearded man, a medical technician named Durham. His suitcase contained some expensive radioactive isotopes used in treating certain forms of cancer. Durham was also found to have a one-way ticket to a Third World country in his coat pocket. The police were aware that the same type of isotopes had been reported missing from Spencer Memorial Hospital a few days

before. Durham was charged under a federal statute making it a crime to export radioactive materials without a license from the Nuclear Regulatory Commission. At a pretrial conference involving the federal charge, the federal prosecutor tells Judge Jones that she plans to call Webster to testify regarding the reaction of the Geiger counter to Durham's presence. Jones tells her that the Federal Rules of Evidence will allow the testimony only if the prosecution shows the following:

I. How the Geiger counter operates.

II. That the Geiger counter was in sound operating condition at the time of the airport incident.

III. That there was no other radioactive material in the area that could have set off the Geiger counter.

Judge Jones is correct as to:

(A) I. only.

(B) II. only.

(C) I. and II. only.

(D) I., II., and III.

Question 37

Distil has been placed on trial for the murder of Victor, who was found beaten to death in his home. Evidence already presented has shown that Victor was killed when no one was at home except for Victor and his dog, Spotty. The prosecution wishes to call Victor's neighbor Nancy to the stand. Nancy is prepared to testify that she went to Victor's home the day after his murder to help arrange things for Victor's family and that when Distil came by, Spotty ran to a corner, where he cringed and whimpered. Nancy is also prepared to testify that Spotty is normally a very friendly dog, usually greeting visitors to the house, including Distil, by approaching them with his tail wagging. The defense objects to Nancy's proposed testimony.

How should the court rule on Nancy's testimony regarding Spotty's behavior?

(A) Admissible, if Spotty can be brought into court for a demonstration of his reaction to Distil.

(B) Admissible, as circumstantial evidence against Distil.

(C) Inadmissible, for the dog may have been reacting as he did for reasons other than those implied by Nancy's testimony.

(D) Inadmissible, because even though the testimony has probative value, such value is outweighed by its prejudicial nature.

Question 38

Donnybrook was shot in the leg during a gun battle with police while holding up a jewelry store. After escaping and hiding out for a few days, he visited the office of Dr. Thomas to seek treatment for the wound. While he was treating the wound, Dr. Thomas asked Donnybrook how he was shot. Donnybrook replied that he was struck by a police officer's bullet while running away from a jewelry store he had robbed, but he implored Dr. Thomas not to tell this to anyone. Dr. Thomas promised that he would not. Acting on an informant's tip, the police arrested Donnybrook and charged him with armed robbery. At the trial, the prosecution calls Dr. Thomas to testify to the statement made to him by Donnybrook. Donnybrook's attorney objects on the ground that such testimony is barred by the physician-patient privilege.

The objection should be:

(A) Sustained, because Dr. Thomas acquired this information while attending Donnybrook in the course of treatment.

(B) Sustained, because Dr. Thomas agreed to Donnybrook's specific request that this information be kept confidential.

(C) Overruled, because the physician-patient privilege is inapplicable to Donnybrook's statement.

(D) Overruled, because Dr. Thomas is the one who is entitled to either claim this privilege or waive it.

Question 39

Effie has brought suit in federal district court against the Social Security Administration because it denied her retirement benefits on the asserted ground that she had not reached the requisite age to qualify. At trial, Effie introduced into evidence a family Bible in which is inscribed, "To my daughter Effie, with love, on the day of her birth, June 3, 1917, your father." The government introduced a certified copy of Effie's birth certificate on which the date of her birth is listed as June 3, 1927. The court admitted both items over objection of the nonpropounding party.

Was this error?

(A) Yes, as to the Bible only, because it contained inadmissible hearsay.

(B) Yes, as to the birth certificate only, because it was not authenticated by the custodian of records.

(C) Yes, as to both, for the reasons stated in the previous answers.

(D) No, both records were admissible.

Question 40

The largest employer in Gear City was Lemon Motors, a large auto manufacturer. On Christmas Eve, Peter Piston, the chairman of the board and chief operating officer of Lemon Motors, announced the immediate layoff of 30,000 Lemon Motors employees and the closure of Lemon's largest plant in Gear City. On the morning of December 26, editors of *The*

Gear City Liberty, Gear City's largest newspaper, decided to move columnist Rod Kikkum's daily article from its usual position on page 3 to the editorial page. The column took Peter Piston to task for announcing the layoffs on Christmas Eve. It also pointed out that the board of Lemon Motors had recently voted Piston an extraordinary $750,000 "performance bonus." Although Kikkum used strong adjectives, most of his column was strictly factual, but his final paragraph ended, "You've heard of Ebenezer Scrooge and the Grinch Who Stole Christmas, but these guys should step aside in the august presence of Peter Piston. If Piston was ever in the Boy Scouts, his good deed of the day was probably tripping an old lady and stealing her purse rather than helping her across the street. A nasty scoundrel like Piston no doubt never performed a real act of charity in his life." A livid Peter Piston filed a defamation suit, naming the *Liberty,* its editors, and Kikkum as defendants.

Piston's suit came to trial a few months later. During the presentation of the plaintiff's case, Piston wanted to put Nud, an agent of the Internal Revenue Service, on the stand. Nud is prepared to testify that Piston, on his own initiative, reimbursed the IRS for an erroneous overpayment of a tax refund. Counsel representing the *Liberty* objects.

The court is likely to rule Nud's testimony:

(A) Admissible, because Piston's character is at issue in the case.

(B) Admissible, because Piston has a right to defend his good character.

(C) Inadmissible, because Nud's testimony, in and of itself, is not probative of any material issue in the case.

(D) Inadmissible, because specific instances of conduct are not admissible to prove character.

Question 41

The Amalgamated Widgetworkers Union ("AWU") was involved in a bitter struggle over a period of years to organize plants operated by Consolidated Widgets Corporation ("CWC"). The management of CWC was vigorously antiunion. AWU noted that many of its most active members at CWC soon found themselves fired by the company. AWU filed suit against CWC asserting that its members were discharged in retaliation for membership in AWU rather than for any failure to perform their jobs properly. Under the pretrial discovery orders, Una, a clerk employed by AWU, was allowed to examine all of the records held in CWC files concerning discharge of employees for a seven-year period prior to the instigation of suit by AWU. Una sorted through this large volume of material and discovered that persons who were union activists usually had "lack of corporate spirit" listed as their reason for discharge, while other fired workers tended to have more specific grounds for discharge listed, *e.g.,* persistent lateness. Una developed a chart showing grounds for dismissal for AWU members and grounds for nonmembers based on the data in the CWC files. At the trial, AWU placed Una on the stand. Una testified in some detail regarding how she had conducted her research. Una brought out the chart and AWU's lawyer asked that the chart be admitted into evidence. CWC's attorney objected.

The court should rule that the chart is:

(A) Admissible, because copies of the original documents upon which the chart was based were available to CWC prior to trial.

(B) Admissible, because the chart is helpful to the trier of fact.

(C) Inadmissible, because it is hearsay not within any exception.

(D) Inadmissible, in the absence of the underlying CWC records' having been first introduced into evidence.

Question 42

Elliot was placed on trial for robbery. There was no accurate eyewitness identification of the perpetrator because the perpetrator had worn a nylon stocking over his head while committing the crime. However, certain circumstantial evidence pointed to Elliot; therefore, the prosecutor's office obtained an indictment against him. At the trial, Elliot took the stand in his own defense. He stated, "I didn't have anything to do with that robbery, but I know who did. The robber was Evans." The jury acquitted Elliot of the robbery charge.

The prosecutor became convinced that Evans had, in fact, committed the robbery in question, and successfully argued that the grand jury should indict Evans for the crime. At Evans's trial, the prosecution called Elliot to the stand, with the expectation that Elliot would incriminate Evans. Instead, to the prosecutor's surprise, Elliot testified, "Evans didn't have anything to do with that robbery, but I know who did, because I committed the robbery myself." When asked about his testimony at his own trial, Elliot refused to answer, claiming his privilege against self-incrimination. Finding her case in a shambles, the prosecutor wishes to call Janet to the stand as a witness. Janet was a juror in Elliot's robbery trial and is prepared to testify that Elliot said Evans committed the robbery.

If the defense objects, the court should rule that Janet's testimony is:

(A) Admissible to impeach Elliot's credibility, but not as substantive evidence of Evans's guilt.

(B) Admissible to impeach Elliot's credibility and as substantive evidence of Evans's guilt.

(C) Inadmissible, because former jurors are not competent to testify concerning cases upon which they served as jurors.

(D) Inadmissible, because a transcript of Elliot's testimony at his robbery trial is the best evidence.

Question 43

Drake was arrested and charged with the battery of Burns. At trial, Drake testified that he struck Burns only in self-defense because Burns had threatened to kill him. Drake further testified without objection that he had told Crane, the arresting officer, that he had acted in self-defense. In rebuttal, the prosecutor called Crane to testify that Drake made no such statement to him.

Officer Crane's testimony is:

(A) Admissible, as an admission by silence of a party-opponent.

(B) Admissible, because it contradicts Drake's assertion.

(C) Inadmissible, because it is extrinsic evidence on a collateral matter.

(D) Inadmissible, because Drake had a constitutional right to remain silent.

Question 44

Red Circle Stores, a retail department store chain, and Farnsworth, a former front-end manager of one of its stores, were being sued for false imprisonment arising from the detention of Penny by a security guard for suspected shoplifting. Penny's attorney wishes to introduce a report from a police officer who was brought back to the store by Penny after she was released. In the report, Farnsworth is quoted as saying, "I wasn't here when she was stopped, but the guard told me he stopped her because of her shifty eyes—if she didn't look so suspicious, she wouldn't have been stopped."

If the attorney for Red Circle Stores objects to the use against Red Circle of Farnsworth's statement in the police report, how should the court rule?

(A) Overrule the objection, because Farnsworth's statement in the police report was made while he was employed by Red Circle Stores.

(B) Overrule the objection, because Farnsworth is also a party to the lawsuit.

(C) Sustain the objection, because Farnsworth had neither the authority nor a business duty to relate that statement to the police officer.

(D) Sustain the objection, because Farnsworth's statement was based on hearsay of another person rather than personal knowledge.

Question 45

Diana was charged with the murder of Bernie, her former boyfriend, in his home. During the course of the criminal trial, Warren testified on behalf of the defense that, at the time the murder took place, he saw someone who looked like Diana dancing at a local nightclub. Diana is eventually acquitted of the charge. Following the acquittal, the appropriate survivors of Bernie bring a wrongful death action against Diana. As part of her defense, Diana wishes to introduce the testimony given at the criminal trial by Warren, who Diana shows is now incarcerated in a prison in another state.

The testimony of Warren is:

(A) Admissible because Warren testified under oath at another hearing related to the same subject matter.

(B) Admissible because Diana is a party to both proceedings.

(C) Inadmissible because the plaintiffs were not parties to the criminal proceeding.

(D) Inadmissible because Warren can be subpoenaed to testify.

Question 46

On a controversial sports talk show that appeared on local television, Howard Maul, the sportscaster, would interview various sporting figures, discussing subjects related to sports. On one edition of the "Howard Maul Show," the topic was "What's wrong with high school athletics?" One of Maul's interviewees was

Doter, parent of a child who had been relegated to the third string on the Owlton Hooters High School football team. Doter told Howard, "The three biggest problems in high school athletics today are drugs, drugs, and drugs. For example, Parslow, the head football coach, openly condones the use of steroids by team members. Do you think those first string 275-pound linemen got that big naturally? What 17-year-old weighs 275 pounds?" Parslow, who had always conducted a strong antidrug program for his football players, was outraged, and he filed suit for defamation against Doter, Maul, and the television station. At the trial of the suit, Parslow wishes to testify as to what Doter said on the television show. The defense objects.

Should such testimony by Parslow be admitted?

(A) Yes, if he saw the live television broadcast.

(B) Yes, because the matter goes to the ultimate issue of the case and is thus highly relevant.

(C) No, if a videotape of the broadcast is available.

(D) No, because such testimony would be hearsay, not within any recognized exception to the hearsay rule.

Question 47

Beth is suing the trustee of the trust to which she is the beneficiary for breach of fiduciary duty. At trial, Beth's counsel asks Tess, the trustee, during direct examination during Beth's case in chief, "Isn't it true that you embezzled $50,000 from the bank at which you were a trust officer?"

Must Tess answer this question?

(A) Yes, because by taking the stand she waived her privilege against self-incrimination.

(B) Yes, because the Fifth Amendment has no application to a civil trial.

(C) No, if she has not waived the privilege against self-incrimination.

(D) No, because a witness may always assert the privilege against self-incrimination.

Question 48

During the course of their marriage, Henry told his wife, Wallene, that he stole *American Trashic,* a famous painting, from the Federal Museum of Art. Six months after Henry's admission, Wallene divorced him. Shortly after the divorce, Henry was killed in an automobile accident. Later, Wallene read in the paper that Drifter had been charged with the theft of *American Trashic* and was about to be tried in federal district court. She told her friend Francesca, "I'll bet that Drifter guy is innocent because Henry told me that he'd stolen that picture himself." Francesca told several other people what Wallene had told her, and eventually the story got back to Drifter's attorney, Danielle. Danielle now wants Wallene to testify in court to Henry's statement.

Can Wallene be compelled to testify?

(A) Yes, but only because Henry is dead and cannot invoke his privilege.

(B) Yes, but only because she and Henry were divorced.

(C) Yes, because there is no privilege when the defendant is not a spouse.

(D) No, unless her testimony becomes essential to prevent a fraud on the court.

Question 49

Joyce is an independent contractor who specializes in operating jackhammers. She contracted with BuildCo to tear up a stretch of pavement. BuildCo provided her with a jackhammer and Joyce proceeded to attack the pavement. As she was working, a rock flew up and struck Pahlavi, a pedestrian, in the head, causing him to be hospitalized. Pahlavi consulted an attorney and asked him to file a lawsuit for his medical costs, lost work time, and

pain and suffering. In the meantime, BuildCo has become insolvent and the jackhammer manufacturer has been out of business for several years. Thus, Joyce is the sole defendant. At trial, Pahlavi's attorney calls Witness, who testifies that, at the time of the incident, Joyce stated, "It was my fault." Joyce's attorney objects, but the judge overrules the objection on the ground that this is a declaration against interest.

Are the grounds for the judge's decision correct?

(A) Yes, because the statement subjected Joyce to tort liability.

(B) Yes, because Joyce is a party to the litigation.

(C) No, because the statement is not against an important interest.

(D) No, because Joyce is available to testify.

Question 50

Proctor sued Dahl for injuries received in an automobile accident. Wandrus was the only neutral eyewitness to the accident, and the lawyers for Proctor and Dahl mutually agreed on a time and place to depose Wandrus. The attorneys and Wandrus appeared as scheduled, but the court reporter who had been ordered for the occasion failed to show up. Because rearranging the deposition would be time-consuming and difficult, the attorneys decided to go ahead with the deposition. Wandrus was not required to give oath or affirmation prior to his testimony, but neither attorney had any reason to believe that Wandrus had any motivation to lie. During the deposition, the attorneys tape recorded their questions and Wandrus's responses. Each attorney received a copy of the tape of the deposition. Wandrus suffered a heart attack and died two months after the deposition. Shortly thereafter, the case came to trial.

Assuming proper notice is given, what evidence of Wandrus's deposition is admissible at trial?

(A) An authenticated copy of the tape of the deposition only.

(B) The testimony of the lawyers who conducted the deposition regarding Wandrus's statement only.

(C) Either an authenticated copy of the tape or the testimony of the lawyers is admissible.

(D) Neither a copy of the tape nor the testimony of the lawyers is admissible.

Question 51

M.A.G.N.I.F.A. was the box-office hit of the summer movie season. "*M.A.G.N.I.F.A.*" stood for "Middle-Aged, Giant, Nuclear-Irradiated, Fascist Aardvarks." The popularity of the film among children between the ages of six and 15 was nothing less than phenomenal, with many in this age group viewing the picture more than once. The *M.A.G.N.I.F.A.* cartoon figures began appearing on T-shirts, soft-drink mugs, and other novelties. All in all, *M.A.G.N.I.F.A.* proved a bonanza for Dizzy Studios, the producer-distributor of *M.A.G.N.I.F.A.*

Papageno read of the success of *M.A.G.N.I.F.A.* in various entertainment journals. He then filed suit against Dizzy Studios alleging that the production company unlawfully used Papageno's ideas for the movie. Dizzy Studios admitted that it had received a clay model of a cartoon animal from Papageno, but denied that the model had had any substantial similarity to the now-famous aardvarks. Dizzy Studios had returned the model to Papageno, but Papageno had destroyed it.

For Papageno to testify at trial as to the appearance of the model, which of the following conditions must be fulfilled?

(A) Papageno must give advance notice to the opposing party that he plans to use such oral testimony in his case.

(B) Papageno must show that the destruction of the model was not committed in bad faith.

(C) Papageno must introduce a photograph of the model, if one exists.

(D) None of the above, because the model is not a document.

Question 52

Famous television and nightclub comedian Ron Tickles had been missing for years. Ron's son and only heir, Samuel, presumed that his father was dead. Ron had a large life insurance policy which named Samuel as beneficiary. Samuel wished to collect on the policy and filed appropriate papers with Insco, Ron's insurer. Insco refused to pay, because there had been no determination that Ron was deceased. Samuel brought suit against Insco to collect the benefit amount.

At trial, Samuel testifies that he has not heard from Ron Tickles since prior to New Year's Day seven years ago. On that date, a chartered sportfishing boat left Port Everglades, Florida, and has never returned. The ship was last seen near midday on that day sailing into the "Bahamas Pentagon" area, a notorious "graveyard of ships." No trace of the boat has ever been found. Samuel establishes that the charter operator filed a passenger list with the Coast Guard, and that one of the names on the list is "Madd Hatter." Samuel wishes to testify that on the day before the disappearance, Ron Tickles told Samuel that he planned to propose a television pilot for a situation comedy starring himself as "Madd Hatter," a madcap owner of a haberdashery.

If Insco's attorney objects, is Samuel's testimony as to Ron Tickles's alleged statement to him admissible?

(A) Yes, as circumstantial evidence that Ron Tickles was on the boat.

(B) Yes, to create a rebuttable presumption that Ron Tickles was on the boat.

(C) Yes, to create a conclusive presumption that Ron Tickles was on the boat.

(D) No, Samuel's testimony is not admissible.

Question 53

Peters was injured when a portion of a spiral stairway in a shopping mall collapsed. Peters has been hospitalized for a long time and will suffer serious personal disabilities resulting from his fall. In the subsequent lawsuit arising from the incident, Peters filed suit against both Malco, owners of the mall, and Structural Design, Inc. ("SDI"), the designers of the staircase. At the trial of the case, Peters wishes to call Cicero, a highly qualified civil engineer, to the stand to testify as an expert witness. Cicero is prepared to testify that the spiral staircase was improperly designed, and the design defect caused a portion of the staircase to collapse under Peters. Cicero's proposed testimony is based in part upon a series of photographs taken by Erecto, a structural engineer hired by Cicero immediately after Cicero was engaged by Peters's attorney, and the accompanying report by Erecto. The photographs are of the collapsed stairway and of an identical stairway located in another part of the mall. Cicero carefully studied both the photographs and Erecto's report prior to the trial. Neither the photographs nor Erecto's report have been admitted into evidence.

Cicero's testimony should be ruled:

(A) Admissible, provided that other civil engineers ordinarily reasonably rely on structural engineers' reports in forming professional opinions.

(B) Admissible, provided that Cicero discloses to the jury the facts on which he relied in forming his opinion.

(C) Inadmissible, unless Cicero also testifies that his opinion is based upon his study of the photographs and not on Erecto's opinion.

(D) Inadmissible, because the photographs and report were commissioned solely for the purpose of preparing for litigation and were not admitted into evidence.

Question 54

Victor and his business partner, David, recently had a bitter falling out, arising from Victor's suspicions that David has been embezzling company funds. Before storming out of the office, David screamed, "Mark my words, I'll get you for this!" Knowing David to be an extremely vindictive and violent person, Victor remained on the alert for any possible reprisals. Two weeks later, while driving on the expressway, a car swerved suddenly in front of Victor's car. Although Victor applied the brakes immediately, his car failed to stop. To avoid colliding with the car ahead of him, he swerved to the right and smashed into a concrete retaining wall. Wanda, a passing motorist, stopped and came to the aid of Victor. Bleeding profusely from a head wound, and rapidly losing consciousness, Victor said, "I don't think I'm going to make it. Tell them I tried to slow down, but my brakes didn't work. My former partner must have tampered with them to get back at me." With that, Victor lapsed into unconsciousness.

Victor has been in a coma and on life support since the accident. A personal injury suit has been filed on his behalf by a court-appointed guardian, with David as the defendant.

At trial, can Wanda testify as to the statement made by Victor?

(A) No, because Victor did not know that David tampered with the brakes.

(B) No, because Victor is still alive.

(C) Yes, because Victor thought he was about to die.

(D) Yes, because this is a civil case.

Question 55

Martha brought a conversion action against Beatrice, alleging that Beatrice had wrongfully taken a necklace owned by Martha's mother, Felicia, who had recently died intestate. Beatrice's defense is that Felicia, who had lived next door to her, had freely given her the necklace because she had often given rides to and run errands for Felicia, who did not drive and had trouble getting around. Beatrice is cross-examined by Martha's attorney, who challenges Beatrice's claim that Felicia had given her the necklace. Beatrice wishes to testify that, before handing her the necklace, Felicia told her, "You've always been so good to me that there's something I want you to have. This necklace has been in my family for years. I myself don't go in too much for jewelry, so you keep it."

Beatrice's proposed testimony is:

(A) Inadmissible as hearsay not within any exception.

(B) Inadmissible under the state's Dead Man Act.

(C) Admissible because it is nonhearsay.

(D) Admissible because Felicia is unavailable to testify.

Question 56

Drew is charged with trafficking in firearms, in violation of federal firearms control laws, as well as receiving stolen property. The charges arise from Drew's having attempted to sell a semi-automatic weapon identified as one of dozens that were stolen from a warehouse a year ago. Drew denies intending to sell the gun or knowing that it had been stolen.

At trial, which of the following would the court be *least* likely to allow the prosecution to introduce as evidence against Drew?

(A) Evidence that Drew was once convicted of armed robbery with a semi-automatic weapon.

(B) The testimony of Thomas that, the day before Drew's arrest, Drew asked Thomas how much he would be willing to pay for a semi-automatic weapon.

(C) The testimony of Ted, a member of a secret paramilitary group, that Drew had been supplying the group with weapons for several months.

(D) Evidence that Drew had been previously convicted of receipt of stolen weapons.

Question 57

WXYZ is a local cable television station. As part of its continuing effort to keep the public informed, WXYZ broadcasts a weekly program consisting of live interviews from different sites. On the particular day in question, WXYZ broadcast from the local shopping mall. Madlock, who was shopping in the mall at the time, was asked to state his views concerning the state of local education. He responded by saying that Bunker, the principal of the high school that his daughter was attending, had been embezzling school funds for years. Bunker saw the telecast and Madlock's interview. He sued the owner of WXYZ for defamation. At trial, Bunker sought to testify to the defamatory statement made in the interview.

Bunker's testimony will most likely be held to be:

(A) Inadmissible, because the testimony would be hearsay not within any exception.

(B) Inadmissible, if a videotape of the interview exists.

(C) Admissible, if the jury is instructed concerning Bunker's self-interest.

(D) Admissible, because Bunker personally saw the interview on television.

Question 58

In an action to recover for personal injuries arising out of an automobile accident, Plaintiff calls Bystander to testify. Claiming the privilege against self-incrimination, Bystander refuses to answer a question as to whether she was at the scene of the accident. Plaintiff moves that Bystander be ordered to answer the question.

The judge should allow Bystander to remain silent only if:

(A) The judge is convinced that she will incriminate herself.

(B) There is clear and convincing evidence that she will incriminate herself.

(C) There is a preponderance of evidence that she will incriminate herself.

(D) The judge believes that there is some reasonable possibility that she will incriminate herself.

Question 59

Assume that Walter is called as a witness in a contract action between Paul and Denver. Walter takes his oath and testifies. During cross-examination, Denver's attorney asked Walter this question: "Isn't it true that even though you took an oath to tell the truth so help you God, you are an atheist and don't even believe in God?"

Upon the proper objection, will the judge require Walter to answer this question?

(A) Yes, because the question is relevant to Walter's character for truthfulness.

(B) Yes, because instead of taking the oath, Walter could have requested to testify by affirmation without any reference to God.

(C) No, because evidence of the beliefs or opinions of a witness on matters of religion is not admissible to impair credibility.

(D) No, because an attack on the competency of a witness must be made at the time the witness is sworn.

Question 60

Oscar testified against Drew in a contract action. Drew then called Travis, who testified that Oscar had a bad reputation for truth and veracity. Drew then also called Watson to testify that Oscar once perpetrated a hoax on an insurance company.

Watson's testimony is:

(A) Inadmissible, because it is merely cumulative impeachment.

(B) Inadmissible, because it is extrinsic evidence of a specific instance of misconduct.

(C) Admissible, provided that the hoax resulted in a conviction of Oscar.

(D) Admissible, because a hoax involves untruthfulness.

Question 61

Pringle is suing the Dover Railroad for injuries sustained when his car was hit at a railroad crossing. Pringle testified that just before the accident, Baker (a bystander) had yelled, "My God, the crossing signal isn't working!" Dover wants to offer the testimony of Wilma that Baker, who is now dead, told her that the crossing signal was working.

Wilma's testimony is:

(A) Admissible, for the purpose of impeachment only.

(B) Admissible, for the purpose of impeachment and to show that the crossing signal was working.

(C) Inadmissible, because it is hearsay not within any exception.

(D) Inadmissible, because Baker is not available to explain or deny the contradiction.

Question 62

In Weustof's trial for first degree murder, the prosecution wishes to introduce a tape recording of a telephone call made by the victim to police just before she was killed. The victim was extremely distraught at the time of the call and failed to identify herself. Kerry is called to the witness stand to identify the voice on the recording as that of the victim.

Under which of the following circumstances would the trial court be *least* justified in admitting the tape recording into evidence?

(A) Kerry had spoken with the victim numerous times, but had never heard her speak over the telephone.

(B) Kerry had spoken with the victim over the telephone many times, but had never met her in person.

(C) Kerry had heard the victim's voice in several tape-recorded telephone conversations between the victim and Smith, and Smith, the victim's father, told Kerry that the person he was speaking with was his daughter.

(D) Kerry had been present with the victim when she made the call to the police, but had heard only the victim's half of the conversation.

Questions 63-65 are based on the following fact situation:

Able is charged with the criminal battery of Baker, a security guard at Clark's Drug Store. At the trial, the prosecution introduces evidence that while Baker was attempting to question Able about a suspected shoplifting incident, Able committed a battery on Baker. Able attempts to defend against the charge on the basis of self-defense, insisting that Baker used excessive force in attempting to stop him and question him. Able attempts to introduce into evidence an authenticated copy of the drugstore records that show that three customers had written complaints against Baker within the past six months for the use of excessive force.

63. The prosecution objects on the grounds that the drugstore records are inadmissible character evidence. The court should:

(A) Sustain the objection, because the character of a victim can be established only by reputation or opinion evidence.

(B) Sustain the objection, because there is no evidence that the incidents involving the three customers were based on the same facts as Able's claim.

(C) Overrule the objection, because the records were authenticated.

(D) Overrule the objection, because the character trait of a victim may be established by opinion evidence, reputation evidence, or by specific acts of misconduct.

64. The prosecution objects to the admission of the drugstore records on the basis of hearsay. The court should:

(A) Sustain the objection, because the records are hearsay not within any recognized exception.

(B) Overrule the objection, because the records qualify under the business records exception.

(C) Overrule the objection, because the records qualify as a statement against interest.

(D) Overrule the objection, because the records are not hearsay.

65. Assume that the three customers who had filed written complaints against Baker had also obtained judgment for damages against Baker, based on battery. Evidence of the judgment would be:

(A) Admissible only in a subsequent civil trial.

(B) Admissible for the purpose of establishing Baker's dangerous propensities.

(C) Inadmissible as hearsay not within any recognized exception.

(D) Inadmissible as irrelevant.

Question 66

Paul was a passenger on an airplane owned by Fairway Airlines. The Fairway airplane in which he was riding was involved in an accident that caused Paul serious injuries to his back. Paul has now filed an action against Fairway Airlines for negligence, seeking to recover damages for his personal injuries. Fairway has answered the complaint with a general denial of negligence as well as of personal injuries.

Immediately after the accident, Paul was examined and treated by Dr. Apple. Dr. Apple made an affidavit stating that he had examined Paul the day after the accident and found Paul to be suffering from a back injury. Dr. Apple is now dead. Paul's counsel seeks to introduce the affidavit he had obtained from Dr. Apple.

The judge should rule the affidavit:

(A) Inadmissible, because it is hearsay not within any exception.

(B) Inadmissible, because the affidavit does not state that the injury occurred from the accident.

(C) Admissible as the prior recorded testimony of Dr. Apple.

(D) Admissible as a statement of present bodily condition made to a physician.

EVIDENCE ANSWERS

Answer to Question 1

(C) Perkins's objection should be overruled because the question goes to the witness's bias or interest. Evidence that a witness is biased or has an interest in the outcome of the suit tends to show that the witness has a motive to lie. A witness may always be impeached by evidence of interest or bias, either on cross-examination or, if a proper foundation is laid, by extrinsic evidence. In a criminal case, it is proper for the defense to ask a prosecution witness whether she has been promised immunity from punishment or a reduction of punishment for testifying. This shows a motive for the witness to curry favor with the state. Here, the defense attorney is trying to impeach Alice by showing that because she was offered an attractive sentence, she has a motive to curry favor with the prosecution. This is perfectly proper. Note that there is no need for a foundation since the attorney is eliciting this evidence on cross-examination, rather than attempting to introduce extrinsic evidence of the deal. (A) is wrong because it misapplies and misstates the rule with regard to plea bargains. Under Federal Rule 410, withdrawn guilty pleas, pleas of nolo contendere, offers to plead guilty, and evidence of statements made in negotiating such pleas are inadmissible against the defendant who made the plea or was a participant in the plea discussions. This rule does not apply in this case because it does not apply to accepted guilty pleas, and Alice is not the defendant. The rule applies only to offers and withdrawn pleas. After the plea is accepted, it is admissible. (B) is wrong for two reasons: (i) the statement by the prosecutor is not hearsay because it is not being offered for the truth of the matter asserted, but rather to show its effect on the hearer; and (ii) even if the statement were hearsay, it would not make the question improper because evidence that is substantively inadmissible may be admitted for impeachment purposes if relevant to show bias or interest. (D) is wrong because no attorney-client privilege arises with respect to communications between Perkins and Alice. The attorney-client privilege requires that the attorney-client relationship exist at the time of the communication. To be covered, the client must be seeking the professional services of the attorney at the time of the communication. Alice was not seeking the services of Perkins. Perkins could not in any way be considered to be Alice's attorney; they are clearly adversaries. Furthermore, even if this were not the case, the client holds the privilege and may waive it. Thus, the question would be proper, and it would be up to the client-witness to decide whether to waive the privilege.

Answer to Question 2

(A) The judge may take judicial notice of this fact because it is a matter of common knowledge in the community, but the jury is not required to accept the fact as conclusive in a criminal case. Judicial notice may be taken of facts that are not subject to reasonable dispute because they are generally known within the territorial jurisdiction of the trial court. [Fed. R. Evid. 201(b)] The facts need not be known everywhere as long as they are known in the community where the court is sitting. The location of City Hall in Chicago is such a fact. As choice (A) also states, in a criminal case the jury should be instructed that it may, but is not required to, accept as conclusive any fact that is judicially noticed. [Fed. R. Evid. 201(g)] (B) is incorrect because a "presumption" in a criminal case is nothing more than a permissible inference that the jury may make. Because the accused in a criminal case is presumptively innocent until the prosecution proves every element of the offense beyond a reasonable doubt, the burden of persuasion is not shifted to the defendant by a "presumption" or by a fact that has been judicially noticed. (C) is incorrect because a judge can take judicial notice of matters of common knowledge at any time, whether or not requested by a party, regardless of whether a criminal or civil case is involved. (D) is incorrect. While facts that are not generally known and accepted may be a subject of judicial notice if they are easily verified by resorting to easily accessible, well-established sources (*i.e.,* facts capable of certain verification), facts that are matters of common knowledge in the community, such as the location of City Hall, may be judicially noticed without resort to reference materials.

Answer to Question 3

(C) Evidence of the defendant's other crimes or misconduct is admissible only if relevant to some issue other than the defendant's character or propensity to commit the crime charged. Such acts would be admissible to show motive, intent, absence of mistake, identity, or a common plan or scheme. Of these, the only one possibly relevant to these facts is identity. Evidence that the accused committed prior criminal acts that are so distinctive as to operate as a "signature" may be introduced to prove that the accused committed the act in question. Merely throwing an object, such as a brick, through a window could not be considered so distinctive as to operate as a signature. Thus, this evidence would not show identity. The only possible reason for offering the evidence is to show Dexter's propensity to commit the crime charged, in which case the testimony will be inadmissible. (A) is incorrect because it is circumstantial evidence that Dexter threw the brick. It is relevant because it tends to make it more probable that Dexter threw the brick than it would be without the evidence. (B) is wrong because it is relevant and goes to motive. It too makes it more probable that Dexter threw the brick than it would be if Tangerine had not testified against a member of his gang. (D) is wrong because Tangerine's identification of Dexter's voice places him at the scene and is thus relevant. It is more probable that Dexter threw the brick than it would be in the absence of this testimony. The identification of a voice is properly authenticated by the opinion of a person familiar with the alleged speaker's voice. As Dexter's former girlfriend, Tangerine would be sufficiently familiar with his voice to make a proper identification.

Answer to Question 4

(A) Matthew's statement is admissible under the hearsay exception for statements against interest. Statements of a person, now unavailable as a witness, against that person's pecuniary, propri- etary, or penal interest when made, as well as collateral facts contained in the statement, are admissible as an exception to the hearsay rule. [Fed. R. Evid. 804(b)(3)] The declarant must have personal knowledge of the facts, must have been aware that the statement was against his interest, and must have had no motive to misrepresent when he made the statement. In this case, since Matthew cannot be located, he is unavailable. The statement that he gave Duncan the key was against his interest when made (exposing him to possible criminal and civil liability), and he should have been aware of that fact. Since he was making the statement to his girlfriend, he had no motive to misrepresent the facts when he made the statement. Note that the fact that he is also repeating a statement by Duncan does not cause an admissibility problem. Since Duncan's statement is an admission by a party-opponent, it is not hearsay under the Federal Rules. An admission is a statement made or act done that amounts to a prior acknowledgment by one of the parties of one of the relevant facts. If the party said or did something that now turns out to be inconsistent with his contentions at trial, the law regards him as estopped from preventing its admission into evidence. Here, Duncan's statement that he left his gloves in the victim's apart- ment is an acknowledgment of the relevant facts that he was in Jane Doe's apartment and that the gloves could be his. Since this is inconsistent with his position at trial, he is estopped from preventing the admission of the statement. (B) is wrong because neither portion of the statement was made in furtherance of the conspiracy. Admissions of one conspirator, made to a third party in furtherance of a conspiracy to commit a crime or tort, at a time when the declarant was partici- pating in the conspiracy, are admissible against co-conspirators as a vicarious admission by a party-opponent. Both Duncan's statement to Matthew and Matthew's statement to Gina were made after the conspiracy had ended and in no way were made in furtherance of the conspiracy. (C) is wrong because, as discussed above, Matthew's statement to Gina is admissible under the exception to the hearsay rule for statements against interest. Furthermore, under the Federal Rules, admissions by a party are nonhearsay. Thus, technically, this would not be hearsay within hearsay. (D) is wrong because the statement is sufficiently against Matthew's interest to qualify under the exception for statements against interest. A full admission to the crime is not required.

Answer to Question 5

(C)   Barmistress's testimony is inadmissible because Don's prior fight in the tavern cannot be admitted to prove Don's propensity to beat someone to death. The basic rule is that when a person is charged with one crime, extrinsic evidence of his other crimes or misconduct is inadmissible if such evidence is offered solely to establish a criminal disposition. [Fed. R. Evid. 404(b)] The danger is that the jury may convict because of past conduct rather than because of guilt of the offense charged. While evidence of other crimes is admissible if it is independently relevant to some other issue (*e.g.,* motive, intent, or identity), Don's prior fight appears to have no relevance other than as evidence of his violent disposition. It is therefore inadmissible. (A) is incorrect because, as stated above, extrinsic evidence of Don's prior misconduct is inadmissible if offered solely to establish a criminal disposition. Evidence of specific acts of the person in question as demonstrating that person's character is permitted only in the few instances when character is itself one of the ultimate issues in the case. [Fed. R. Evid. 405(b)] Don's propensity for violence is not an ultimate issue in this case. (B) is incorrect because extrinsic evidence of Don's previous bad acts cannot be used to impeach him. A specific act of misconduct must be probative of truthfulness (*i.e.,* an act of deceit or lying) and can be elicited only on cross-examination of the witness. Extrinsic evidence is not permitted. Therefore, testimony concerning Don's prior incident is not admissible for impeachment. (D) is incorrect because it is irrelevant. It is true that Don has not put his character in issue in this case simply by pleading self-defense. Even if he had, however, the prosecutor could not rebut by having a witness testify as to prior instances of misconduct; only reputation or opinion evidence would be admissible.

Answer to Question 6

(C)   The jury may consider statements from personal observation and from an authoritative text as substantive evidence. Under Federal Rule 703, an expert may base his opinion on facts that the expert knows from personal observation (statement I.). If the expert has examined the person or thing about which he is testifying, he may relate those facts observed by him and upon which he bases his opinion. Because Edison's statements are based on first-hand knowledge and are otherwise relevant, the jury may consider them as substantive evidence. An expert may also base an opinion on facts supplied to him outside the courtroom. One such source is authoritative texts and treatises (statement III.). Statements from a treatise established as reliable (which may be done by the expert's own testimony) may be introduced on direct examination of the expert and read into the record as substantive evidence under an exception to the hearsay rule. [Fed. R. Evid. 803(18)] Hence, the jury may consider the testimony in statements I. and III. as substantive evidence, making (C) correct and (A) and (B) incorrect. Choice (D) is incorrect because the evidence in statement II. may not be considered by the jury as substantive evidence. Rule 703 provides that where an expert bases his opinion on facts made known to him outside the courtroom, the facts need not be of a type admissible in evidence as long as the facts are of a kind reasonably relied on by experts in the particular field. However, the expert will only be permitted to disclose such facts if the court determines that their probative value in assisting the jury to evaluate the expert's opinion substantially outweighs their prejudicial effect. The jury would only be permitted to consider them as the basis for his expert opinion; the jury could not consider the facts as substantive evidence unless they were independently admissible. Here, the statements made to Edison by witnesses are a proper basis of his opinion because they are of a kind reasonably relied on by experts in his field. However, they do not appear to be admissible under any exception to the hearsay rule and therefore could not be considered by the jury as substantive evidence.

Answer to Question 7

(C) Belial's testimony should not be permitted under Federal Rule 403 because the probative value of polygraph evidence is substantially outweighed by the tendency of its results to mislead and confuse the jury. Federal Rule 702 permits opinion testimony by a qualified expert where the subject matter is one where scientific, technical, or other specialized knowledge would assist the trier of fact in understanding the evidence or determining a fact in issue. However, the methodology underlying the opinion must be reliable (*i.e.,* the proponent must show that the opinion is based on sufficient facts or data, the opinion is the product of reliable principles and methods, and the expert has reliably applied the principles and methods to the facts of the case). Furthermore, Rule 403 gives a trial judge broad discretion to exclude relevant evidence if its probative value is substantially outweighed by the danger of unfair prejudice, confusion of the issues, or misleading the jury. Most jurisdictions have concluded that the probative value of a polygraph test is slight because of its significant rate of error. On the other side of the balancing test, the tendency of jurors to give too much weight to a polygraph test makes the danger of unfair prejudice high. Therefore, the test's unreliability and the risk of confusion from the test's results justify excluding Belial's testimony. (A) is incorrect because Dearborn volunteered to take the polygraph test. The Fifth Amendment right against self-incrimination applies only when the defendant is compelled to make the statements. The fact that Dearborn did not take the stand in his own defense would not change this result because once a voluntary statement is made, it cannot be kept out of the trial on self-incrimination grounds. (B) is also incorrect because, as discussed above, Dearborn volunteered to take the polygraph test. His right against self-incrimination is violated only if he is compelled to testify against himself. Just as a defendant's voluntary confession cannot be kept out of the trial on self-incrimination grounds, so Dearborn's voluntary statements during the polygraph test cannot be barred on those grounds. (D) is incorrect because the Federal Rules do not specifically classify polygraph tests as irrelevant; in fact, polygraph evidence *could* be relevant under the Federal Rules. Relevant evidence is evidence having any tendency to make the existence of any fact that is of consequence to the determination of an action more probable than it would be without the evidence. [Fed. R. Evid. 401] Polygraph evidence is relevant under this test because it does tend to make the existence of a fact of consequence whether the person is telling the truth more probable. However, as discussed above, this relevant evidence can still be excluded under Federal Rule 403 if the court decides its probative value is substantially outweighed by the danger of unfair prejudice.

Answer to Question 8

(A) Wendy's testimony is admissible character evidence because Poyn's character is directly in issue in the case. As a general rule, evidence of character to prove the conduct of a person in the litigated event is not admissible in a civil case. However, where a person's character itself is one of the issues in the case, character evidence is admissible because it is the best method of proving the issue. Under the Federal Rules, any of the types of evidence—reputation, opinion, or specific acts—may be used. Here, character is an issue in Poyn's defamation action because Dexter has pleaded as an affirmative defense that his statement claiming that Poyn is a "thief" is the truth.

Wendy's testimony that she saw Poyn take the money from the cash register is relevant because it tends to show that Dexter spoke the truth. Hence, it should be allowed. (B) is wrong because the fact that theft is a crime of dishonesty would be relevant only if Poyn's credibility were being impeached, and only then if proof of an actual conviction were provided. Here, the testimony is admissible because it is being offered as substantive evidence of an aspect of Poyn's character that is directly in issue in the case. (C) is incorrect. One of the few cases where testimony as to specific acts of a person may be used to show that person's character is when character itself is one of the ultimate issues in the case, as it is here. (D) is incorrect because the fact that Poyn never took the stand only means that he has not placed his *credibility* in issue and become subject to impeachment. Here, however, Poyn's *character* is in issue and the testimony is being offered as substantive evidence of his character rather than to impeach his credibility.

Answer to Question 9

(B)   The photo should be admitted into evidence upon testimony that it is an accurate representation of the location depicted. To be admissible, real or demonstrative evidence must not only be relevant but must also be authenticated, *i.e.,* identified as being what the proponent claims it to be. For a photograph that is used as demonstrative evidence, authentication is by testimony that the photo is a faithful reproduction of the object or scene depicted. Here, testimony by a bank employee that the still frame from the video accurately portrays the setting where the robbery took place is sufficient for admissibility. (A) is incorrect because the frame from the video is not being offered as original evidence that played an actual role in the robbery itself, such as a gun used by the robber, which would require the "chain of custody" type of authentication in (A). Here, the still frame is only being used for demonstrative purposes; hence, authentication focuses on whether it is an accurate representation rather than how it was handled. (C) is incorrect. Charts and diagrams that are used solely to help explain a witness's testimony may be permitted at trial but not admitted into evidence where they are not offered as representations of a real object or scene but only as aids to testimony. Here, however, the photo is being offered as a faithful representation of the scene of the crime and should therefore be admissible into evidence. (D) is incorrect because it is a misapplication of the best evidence rule. The best evidence or original document rule, which is made applicable to photographs by the Federal Rules, generally requires that in proving the terms of a writing the original writing must be produced where the terms are material. The terms are material and the rule applies only when (i) the document is a legally operative or dispositive instrument or (ii) the witness's knowledge results from having seen the fact in the document. Neither situation arises in this case. The location of the columns in the bank and the circumstances of the robbery are facts that exist independently of the document (the videotape on the day of the robbery), and thus may be proved by other evidence.

Answer to Question 10

(A)   The burden of persuasion and the burden of going forward with the evidence are on Permian because Devon's testimony raises a rebuttable presumption that the check had been delivered in the mail. The burden of persuasion is the burden of a party to persuade the jury to decide an issue in its favor. If, after all the proof is in, the issue is equally balanced in the mind of the jury, then the party with the burden of persuasion must lose. The burden of persuasion does not shift from party to party during the course of a trial. Because Permian sued Devon for the debt, he has the burden of persuasion when the time for the jury to make a decision arrives. The burden of going forward with the evidence is the burden of producing sufficient evidence to create a fact question of the issue involved. If a plaintiff makes out a prima facie case, he has met his burden of going forward with the evidence and the burden shifts to the defendant. When Permian made out a prima facie case of Devon's debt, the burden of going forward with the evidence shifted to

Devon. Devon met this burden through the use of a presumption. Federal Rule 301 provides that a presumption imposes on the party against whom it was directed the burden of going forward with the evidence to rebut or meet the presumption. Devon's evidence regarding the proper posting of the check raises a rebuttable presumption that the check was delivered to Permian because a letter shown to have been properly addressed, stamped, and mailed is presumed to have been delivered in the due course of mail. Therefore, the burden of going forward with the evidence has shifted back again to Permian, who must now produce evidence to rebut the presumption (*i.e.,* evidence that he did not receive the check). (B) is incorrect because, as discussed above, Devon's testimony raised a rebuttable presumption that the check was delivered in the mail, which shifted the burden of going forward with the evidence to Permian. The fact that Permian met his burden of going forward with the evidence of the debt once, when he made out his prima facie case, does not mean the burden cannot shift back to him. (C) is incorrect because Permian has not satisfied his burden of persuasion. As discussed above, the burden of persuasion does not shift from party to party and is only a crucial factor when all the evidence is in. This burden is satisfied when the jury finds a party has been more persuasive in arguing his side of the issue than the other party. Because Devon's testimony raises a rebuttable presumption that the check was delivered to Permian, Permian's burden of persuasion cannot be met until he offers evidence to prove that the check was not received (a necessary element of his case). (D) is incorrect because, as discussed above, Devon's testimony raised a rebuttable presumption of delivery of the check in the mail to Permian, which shifted the burden of going forward with evidence of nondelivery back to Permian. Permian's burden of persuasion cannot be satisfied until he comes forward with this evidence because a necessary element of his case is that Devon never paid him.

Answer to Question 11

(C) The testimony should be excluded because the attorney-client privilege applies to the examination done in preparation for trial. The communication between the doctor and the attorney's client is necessary to help the client convey his condition to the attorney. (B) is a true statement; the physician-patient privilege does not apply to any proceeding in which the condition of the patient has been put in issue by the patient. This is the case in Potter's suit, so (D) is incorrect. However, (B) is incorrect because the attorney-client privilege applies here. (A) is incorrect because admissions by party-opponents, while not hearsay under the Federal Rules, are still subject to potential privilege assertions.

Answer to Question 12

(C) Don's statement to Wilhelmina was made in reliance upon the intimacy of what was at that time their marital relationship. Thus, Don has a privilege to prevent Wilhelmina from disclosing the statement. Either spouse (whether or not a party) has a privilege to refuse to disclose, and to prevent another from disclosing, a confidential communication made between the spouses while they were husband and wife. Divorce does not terminate this privilege retroactively. At the time that Don made the subject statement to Wilhelmina, they were married. Given that the statement essentially constituted an admission of liability by Don, that he prefaced it with "between you and me," and that he made the statement in the privacy of the marital bedroom, it seems likely that the statement was made in confidentiality and in reliance upon the intimacy of the marital relationship. Thus, both Don and Wilhelmina may refuse to disclose, and may prevent the other from disclosing, the statement. Consequently, Don can prevent Wilhelmina from testifying to the statement. (A) is incorrect because the communication was made during the marriage, and the privilege is not abrogated by a later divorce. (B) is incorrect because the fact that Anastasia heard the statement was unknown to Don and Wilhelmina. If the communication is made in the *known* presence of a stranger, it is not privileged. However, if the statement was not made within the **known** hearing of a third party and it is overheard, absent a showing of negligence on the part of the speaker, it remains privileged. Nothing in these facts indicates negligence. Thus, Don can prevent Wilhelmina from testifying to the statement. (D) is incorrect because the privilege for confidential marital communications belongs to both spouses, rather than to just one. In cases involving spousal immunity (*i.e.,* the privilege not to testify against one's spouse in a criminal case), most state courts hold that the privilege belongs to the party-spouse only. However, the trial here is a civil case, so the spousal immunity is inapplicable; this question involves the privilege for confidential marital communications.

Answer to Question 13

(A) The testimony is admissible because Dr. Tipp has firsthand knowledge of Pulliam's temperature at the time in question. The best evidence rule requires that in proving the terms of a writing, where the terms are material, the original writing must be produced. [Fed. R. Evid. 1002] This rule applies only where the terms of a writing are at issue or the knowledge of a witness concerning a fact results from having read it in the document. Where the fact to be proved has an existence independent of any writing, the best evidence rule does not apply. Here, Dr. Tipp's knowledge of Pulliam's temperature at the time in question came from firsthand knowledge, not just from having read it in the chart. Pulliam's temperature on February 26, therefore, is a fact that has an existence independent of the chart and the best evidence rule does not apply. Dr. Tipp's firsthand knowledge of Pulliam's temperature is obviously relevant to the issue of whether his fever reached 102 degrees and should be admitted. (B) is incorrect because Dr. Tipp's testimony would have been admissible even if the chart were not in evidence. While the best evidence rule prohibits the material contents of a writing to be proved by oral testimony rather than by producing the original, the rule does not apply here because Dr. Tipp's testimony was based on firsthand knowledge instead of the chart, as discussed above. Therefore, whether the chart was in evidence is irrelevant to the admissibility of his testimony. (C) is an incorrect statement of the law. The best evidence rule, as discussed above, requires that original writings be produced to prove their material contents. It does not apply when a fact exists independent of a document. It does not require that the "best" evidence always be used to prove an issue. (D) is incorrect because a prior admission does not make the testimony of the person who made the admission inadmissible. A party may expressly or impliedly adopt someone else's statement as his own, thus giving rise to an "adoptive admission." [Fed. R. Evid. 801(d)(2)(B)] If a defendant makes such an admission, it will not be considered hearsay if offered into evidence. However, such an admission will not bar a defendant from testifying about the matter admitted. Therefore, even if Dr. Tipp's failure to correct the chart were considered an adoptive admission, his testimony would not be inadmissible as a result.

Answer to Question 14

(D) The grand jury transcript is not admissible because Hudson's testimony was not subject to cross-examination. Hudson's testimony was hearsay because it was an out-of-court statement offered to prove the truth of the matter asserted. [Fed. R. Evid. 801(c)] If a statement is hearsay, and no exception to the rule is applicable, the evidence is inadmissible. [Fed. R. Evid. 802] Under the former testimony exception to the hearsay rule, the testimony of a now unavailable witness given at another hearing is admissible in a subsequent trial as long as there is a sufficient similarity of parties and issues so that the opportunity to develop testimony or cross-examine at the prior hearing was meaningful. [Fed. R. Evid. 804(b)(1)] The party against whom the former testimony is offered must have had the opportunity to develop the testimony at the prior proceeding by direct, cross-, or redirect examination of the declarant. Thus, the grand jury testimony of an unavailable declarant is not admissible as former testimony against the accused at trial. This is because grand jury proceedings do not provide the opportunity for cross-examination. Therefore, because Hudson's testimony was in front of the grand jury and was not subject to cross-examination, it is inadmissible as hearsay. (A) is incorrect because Hudson's testimony cannot be considered a vicarious admission. An admission by a party-opponent is not hearsay under the Federal Rules. [Fed. R. Evid. 801(d)(2)] An admission is a statement made or act done that amounts to a prior acknowledgment by one of the parties to an action of one of the relevant facts. An admission does not have to be the statement of the party against whom the statement is being offered at trial if it qualifies as a vicarious admission. For example, admissions of one conspirator, made to a third party in furtherance of a conspiracy to commit a crime, may be admissible against co-conspirators. Here, however, Hudson's grand jury testimony was not made in furtherance of a conspiracy. Because Hudson was not a party here, and his testimony does not otherwise qualify as a vicarious admission of Deirdre, it cannot be considered an admission of a party-opponent. (B) is incorrect because Hudson's grand jury testimony was not subject to cross-examination. Federal Rule 804(b)(1) allows the former testimony of an unavailable witness to be admitted under circumstances where the opportunity to develop testimony or cross-examine at the prior hearing was meaningful. Hudson was an unavailable declarant because he was unable to testify because of death. [Fed. R. Evid. 804(a)(4)] However, as discussed above, his grand jury testimony is not admissible as former testimony because grand jury proceedings do not provide the opportunity for cross-examination. (C) is incorrect because the spousal privilege does not belong to Deirdre in federal court and because it may only be asserted while the marriage relationship exists. In federal courts, the spousal immunity privilege belongs to the witness-spouse. This means that one spouse may testify against the other in criminal cases, with or without the consent of the party-spouse. Thus, while Hudson could not have been compelled to testify against Deirdre, he could not be foreclosed by her from testifying (except as to confidential communications).

Answer to Question 15

(D) The plaintiff's objection on the basis of the clergy-penitent privilege should be overruled. Pursuant to the clergy-penitent privilege, a person has a privilege to refuse to disclose, and to prevent others from disclosing, a confidential communication by that person to a member of the clergy in the clergy member's capacity as a spiritual adviser. The operation of this privilege is very similar to that of the attorney-client privilege. Here, Philip made the statement to Father Harrison during a conversation at a social occasion. There is no indication that this was a communication made to the priest in his capacity as a spiritual adviser, as would be the case, for instance, with a statement made in the confessional or during a counseling session. Thus, the matters stated to Father Harrison by Philip do not come within the clergy-penitent privilege, and Father Harrison cannot be prevented from disclosing the contents of the conversation on the basis of this privilege. (A) is incorrect because, although Philip undoubtedly made the statement in confidence (*i.e.,* intending and expecting that it would not be disclosed to third persons), as explained above, it was not made to Father Harrison in his capacity as a spiritual adviser. Therefore, the clergy-penitent privilege is inapplicable. (B) is incorrect because it implies that the clergy-penitent privilege does not apply to civil cases. Actually, this privilege applies to both civil and criminal cases. (C) is incorrect because, where the privilege exists, it can be claimed by the person who made the confidential communication, his guardian or conservator, or his personal representative if he is deceased. Thus, if the privilege were applicable, Greta (through her attorney) would be able to invoke the protection of the privilege, as Philip's guardian, to prevent Father Harrison from disclosing the contents of the conversation with Philip.

Answer to Question 16

(A)   Norma's testimony is admissible, but solely for purposes of impeaching Parkes, a hearsay declarant. Parkes's statement to Buck, even though hearsay, was admissible as an excited utterance
or present sense impression because it was made immediately after the crash. Under Federal Rule
806, the credibility of a hearsay declarant may be attacked by evidence that would be admissible
if the declarant had testified as a witness. For the purpose of impeaching the credibility of a
witness, a party may show that the witness has, on another occasion, made statements that are
inconsistent with some material part of his present testimony. Parkes's statement to Buck may
therefore be impeached by proof that he made the inconsistent statement to Norma. (B) is incorrect. Parkes's statement to Norma is hearsay because it is an out-of-court statement offered to
prove the truth of the matter asserted, *i.e.,* that Dimer rammed the crossing barrier. [Fed. R. Evid.
801(c)] If a statement is hearsay, and no exception to the rule is applicable, the evidence is
inadmissible for substantive purposes. [Fed. R. Evid. 802] Parkes's statement does not come
within either the excited utterance exception or the present sense impression exception to the
hearsay rule because the statement to Norma was not made immediately after the accident. Nor
does his statement fall under Rule 801(d)(1)(A), which provides that where a prior inconsistent
statement was made under oath at a prior trial, hearing, other proceeding, or deposition, it is
admissible nonhearsay (*i.e.,* it may be considered as substantive proof of the facts stated). Because Parkes's statement to Norma was not made under oath, it is hearsay that may only be used
to impeach and not as evidence of the position of the crossing gate. (C) is incorrect because a
hearsay declarant, such as Parkes, does not have to be given an opportunity to explain or deny his
alleged prior inconsistent statement. Generally, extrinsic evidence of the prior inconsistent
statement of a witness is inadmissible unless the witness was examined so as to give him an
opportunity to explain or deny the alleged inconsistent statement, but this foundation requirement
may be dispensed with where "the interests of justice otherwise require." [Fed. R. Evid. 613(b)]
The courts generally agree that inconsistent statements by ***hearsay declarants*** may be used to
impeach despite the lack of foundation. [Fed. R. Evid. 806] Therefore, Norma's testimony may
be admitted even though Parkes is not available to be questioned about the inconsistent statements. (D) is incorrect because Parkes's statement to Norma, although hearsay, may be used for
impeachment purposes. As discussed above, a hearsay declarant may be impeached by evidence
of his prior inconsistent statements. Parkes's statement to Buck was properly admitted hearsay,
which can be impeached by evidence of his inconsistent statement to Norma. However, because
the statement to Norma is hearsay not within an exception to the hearsay rule, it may be used
only for impeachment purposes and not as evidence of the position of the crossing gate.

Answer to Question 17

(D)   The tally record should not be admitted because it is hearsay that does not fall within a recognized exception. The Federal Rules define hearsay as "a statement other than one made by the
declarant testifying at the trial or hearing, offered in evidence to prove the truth of the matter
asserted." [Fed. R. Evid. 801(c)] Any written document, such as the tally record, that is offered
into evidence constitutes a "statement" for hearsay purposes. The tally record was prepared out
of court by the clerks and is being offered to prove the truth of its assertion, *i.e.,* that Deer had
sent many reply cards. Because the tally record fits the definition of hearsay, and no exception to
the rule is applicable, as discussed below, it is inadmissible. [Fed. R. Evid. 802] (A) is incorrect
because the tally record is not being used to substitute for the forgotten memory of the clerks.
Where a witness states that she has insufficient recollection of an event to enable her to testify
fully and accurately, even after she has consulted a writing given to her on the stand, the writing
itself may be introduced into evidence if the proper foundation is laid for its admissibility. [Fed.

R. Evid. 803(5)] This is the past recollection recorded exception to the hearsay rule. Here, the tally record is not being used to substitute for the insufficient recollection of any witness. It is being offered to stand on its own as evidence, not in connection with a witness on the stand. Therefore, the tally record does not qualify as a past recollection recorded exception to the hearsay rule. (B) is incorrect because the tally record was recorded in preparation for litigation. Any writing or record, whether in the form of an entry in a book or otherwise, made as a memorandum or record of any act or event, is admissible in evidence as proof of that act or event if made in the regular course of a business, as long as it was the regular course of such business to make it at the time. Because the records must have been maintained in conjunction with a business activity to qualify for this exception to the hearsay rule, courts generally exclude reports prepared primarily for litigation. The Federal Rules deal with this problem by giving the trial court discretion to exclude any business record if circumstances indicate the record lacked trustworthiness. [Fed. R. Evid. 803(6)] Because the tally sheet was prepared only in anticipation of litigation instead of in conjunction with a business activity, it does not fall within the business record exception. (C) is an incorrect statement of law. The best evidence rule, also known as the "original document rule," may be stated as follows: In proving the terms of a writing, where the terms are material, the original writing must be produced. [Fed. R. Evid. 1002] The rule does not mean that the "best" evidence must be used to prove a fact. In this case, TB is not trying to prove the terms of a document. The fact to be proved (*i.e.,* that Deer was flooding the office with business reply requests) exists independently of any writing. Thus, the best evidence rule does not apply.

Answer to Question 18

(A) The transcript is admissible under the former testimony exception to the hearsay rule. Under this rule, the testimony of a now unavailable witness given under oath at another hearing is admissible in a subsequent trial as long as there is a sufficient similarity of parties and issues so that the opportunity to cross-examine at the prior hearing was meaningful. In a civil proceeding, the parties do not need to be identical, but the party against whom the testimony is being offered must be in privity with the party in the original action, so that a similar motive existed to develop or cross-examine the declarant's testimony. Here, Senior was a predecessor in interest of Junior in his capacity as executor of Senior's estate and had adequate opportunity and motive to cross-examine Wilma's testimony against him, which was given under oath at a criminal proceeding. Hence, the testimony is admissible under the former testimony exception. (B) is wrong because the transcript of Wilma's testimony, to the extent that it is being offered to prove the truth of her assertions, does not fall under the public records exception to the hearsay rule. While the Federal Rules also allow a judgment of a felony conviction to be used to prove any fact essential to the judgment, the transcript of a witness is not admissible for that purpose. (C) is incorrect because in civil cases, the unavailability requirement for the former testimony exception is satisfied if the declarant is beyond the reach of the court's subpoena and the statement's proponent is unable to procure her attendance or testimony by process or other reasonable means. (D) is incorrect because, as discussed above, the similarity of issues and parties is sufficient to permit the testimony to be admitted against Junior even though he was not a party to the original action.

Answer to Question 19

(B) The court should allow Marieke to testify if Astrid takes an oath to make a true translation. The services of an interpreter may be used where a witness, due to language problems or other reasons, would otherwise have difficulty communicating. Under Federal Rule 604, an interpreter must meet the qualifications required of an expert witness (*i.e.,* by reason of knowledge, skill, experience, training, or education, she is capable of providing a true translation). Also, an interpreter must take an oath or affirmation that she will make a true translation (*i.e.,* that she will communicate exactly what the witness is expressing in her testimony). Here, Marieke will have extreme difficulty communicating, due to the fact that she speaks only a few words of Flemish and uses a signing method different from that which is used in the United States. Thus, the circumstances allow the use of an interpreter to assist Marieke in communicating at the trial. Here, the facts establish that Astrid is the only person qualified to act as an interpreter for Marieke. If, as (B) states, Astrid takes an oath to communicate what Marieke expresses in her testimony, then the requirements of Rule 604 are met. (A) is incorrect because it omits the requirement of taking an oath or affirming to make a true translation. (C) is incorrect because there is no principle of law that renders Astrid "inherently biased" simply because she works for the prosecutor and has assisted the police in their communications with Marieke. If Astrid takes the required oath, she is bound to render a true translation, regardless of her affiliation with the prosecutor's office. (D) is incorrect because there is no requirement that Astrid disclose this information to the jury. Determining whether an interpreter is qualified is a matter within the judge's discretion.

Answer to Question 20

(C) The gun should be admitted into evidence. The gun is a form of real evidence, in that the object in issue is presented for inspection by the trier of fact. To be admissible, the object must be authenticated (*i.e.,* identified as being what the proponent claims it to be). One method of authentication is recognition testimony, in which a witness may authenticate the object by testifying that it is what the proponent claims it is. Here, Officer Margaret found the gun in a paper bag in the alley shortly after having seen Dosch run into the alley holding a paper bag and emerge from the alley without the bag. Officer Margaret could now be called to identify the gun being offered into evidence as the one she found in the alley. This should be particularly easy in this case since Officer Margaret noted the serial number of the gun when she found it. The fact that the gun was found in the alley is circumstantial evidence that the gun was carried by Dosch on the night of the arrest. The evidence here is sufficient to withstand an objection to its admissibility on the ground that the gun has not been properly identified. Thus, (B) is incorrect in concluding that there is insufficient proof that the gun belonged to Dosch. (A) is incorrect. Real evidence may be circumstantial; *i.e.,* facts about the object are proved as a basis for an inference that other facts are true. The circumstances surrounding the discovery of the gun support the inference that it had been in the bag carried by Dosch. It is not necessary for the gun to have been in Dosch's possession at the time of his arrest in order to admit the gun into evidence against Dosch. (D) is incorrect because chain of custody problems arise where the evidence is of a type that is likely to be confused or can be easily tampered with (*e.g.,* evidence of a blood alcohol test) after it is in custody. In such a case, the proponent of the evidence must show that the object has been held in a substantially unbroken chain of possession. Here, there is no evidence of a break in the chain of custody after the gun was taken by the police. Furthermore, a gun is generally not a type of evidence that is susceptible to confusion or tampering. Also, if need be, the serial number can be compared with that which was originally copied by Officer Margaret. Thus, there is no viable objection based on chain of custody.

Answer to Question 21

(B) The testimony of Archie is admissible to show Veronica's state of mind, which in turn is circumstantial evidence that Veronica in fact saw Reginald and told him that the wedding was off. Hearsay is a statement, other than one made by the declarant while testifying at the trial or hearing, offered in evidence to prove the truth of the matter asserted. Hearsay to which no exception is applicable is not admissible into evidence. One of the exceptions to the hearsay rule is the present state of mind exception, under which a statement of a declarant's then-existing state of mind, emotion, sensation, or physical condition is admissible. [Fed. R. Evid. 803(3)] Such a statement can be used not only when the declarant's state of mind is directly in issue, but also as a declaration of intent to do something in the future, offered as circumstantial evidence tending to show that the intent was carried out. The prosecution is offering Archie's testimony as to Veronica's statement to prove the truth of the matter asserted therein; *i.e.,* that Veronica was going to see Reginald and tell him that the wedding was off. Thus, Archie's testimony is hearsay. However, the statement regarding her intent is being offered as a basis for a circumstantial inference that Veronica carried out her intent to see Reginald (the prosecution's theory apparently being that Reginald became enraged and killed Veronica when he was told that the wedding was off). Consequently, Veronica's statement of her then-existing state of mind is admissible under the present state of mind exception. (A) is incorrect because a present sense impression relates to a person's perception of an event that is not particularly shocking or exciting, but which does move her to comment on what she perceived at the time she perceived it or immediately thereafter. Veronica's statement to Archie simply relates what she is going to tell Reginald, and does not convey a comment on some event then occurring in front of Veronica. Therefore, this is not a present sense impression. (C) is incorrect because, although the testimony will certainly be damaging to Reginald, it cannot be characterized as unfairly prejudicial. Exclusion of evidence on the ground of prejudice is a matter within the trial judge's broad discretion, and Federal Rule 403 requires that the evidence's probative value be **substantially** outweighed by the danger of unfair prejudice for it to be excluded. While all evidence is prejudicial to the adverse party, "unfair" prejudice refers to evidence that suggests a decision on an emotional or otherwise improper basis. Certainly, this testimony renders more probably true than would otherwise be the case that Reginald had a motive for killing Veronica and that he did kill her. Thus, the testimony has probative value that is not substantially outweighed by its prejudicial effect. (D) is incorrect because, as discussed above, the testimony is admissible under the present state of mind exception.

Answer to Question 22

(B) Norton's statements are admissible as a statement against interest. Under the Federal Rules, statements of a person, now unavailable as a witness, against that person's pecuniary, proprietary, or penal interest when made are admissible as an exception to the hearsay rule. Here, Norton's statements implicating himself in the bombing conspiracy were against his penal interest when he made them; hence, they are probably admissible under that exception. (A) is incorrect because for a statement to qualify under the Federal Rules as a vicarious party-admission of another member of the conspiracy, the admission must have been in furtherance of the conspiracy by a participant in it. Here, Norton's statements were not made in furtherance of the conspiracy but instead served to thwart its success. (C) is wrong because Norton's statement is not being used to show his then-existing state of mind but rather the scope of the conspiracy and the defendants' participation in it. (D) is wrong because, even assuming that Norton made the statement while believing his death was imminent (which the facts do not clearly establish), dying declarations are admissible under the Federal Rules only in a prosecution for homicide or in a civil action, and this case was neither of those.

Answer to Question 23

(B) The witness list should be admitted as a business record. A writing or record made as a memorandum or record of any act, transaction, occurrence, or event is admissible as proof of such act, transaction, occurrence, or event if it was made in the course of a regularly conducted business activity and if it was customary to make the type of entry involved (*i.e.*, the entrant must have had a duty to make the entry). The business record must consist of matters within the personal knowledge of the entrant or within the personal knowledge of someone with a business duty to transmit such matters to the entrant. The entry must have been made at or near the time of the transaction. The list of proposed witnesses and the notation constitute a statement that the law firm was alerted to the existence of Dr. Bronson as a potential expert witness. Hy wants to introduce these documents to prove the truth of this statement (*i.e.*, that he alerted the firm to the existence of Dr. Bronson). Thus, the documents present a hearsay problem. Making a list of proposed witnesses would be part of the regular course of business for a law firm, and it would be part of the duties of John, as a paralegal responsible for updating case files, to enter the handwritten notation regarding Dr. Bronson at the direction of one of the firm's lawyers. The matters contained in the list and notation would be within the personal knowledge of the lawyer, who was under a business duty to report the information accurately to John, who was under a business duty to properly record the information. Thus, all the requirements for a business record are present, and the list and notation, made as records of the firm's having been alerted to Dr. Bronson as a potential expert witness, are admissible as proof of that fact. (A) is incorrect because past recollection recorded comes into play when a witness's memory cannot be refreshed by looking at something. At that point, there may be an attempt to introduce a writing made by the witness or under his direction at or near the time of the event. The writing is characterized as past recollection recorded. Here, there is no indication that a witness who has an insufficient memory is testifying, and the list of proposed witnesses and notation are not being offered as a record of anyone's past recollection. Rather, the evidence is offered as a record of the firm's being informed of Dr. Bronson as a potential expert witness. Therefore, the evidence will not be admitted as past recollection recorded. (C) is incorrect because, as explained above, the proffered evidence does come within a recognized hearsay exception. (D) is incorrect because the facts do not present any problem of "levels" of hearsay. The list and notation are considered to be an out-of-court statement that the firm was alerted to Dr. Bronson as a potential expert witness, and are being offered as proof of that fact. If the notation had simply repeated an assertion made by one outside of the business (*e.g.*, "Dr. Bronson says that he will be available to testify on the date of the trial") and been offered to prove the truth of the assertion (that Dr. Bronson was available as a witness), a hearsay within hearsay problem would exist. Because the statement within the notation would be hearsay not within any exception, the notation itself, despite the fact that it is a business record, would not be admissible to prove Dr. Bronson's availability.

Answer to Question 24

(A) Nora can testify to Fingal's statement because it qualifies as an excited utterance. The statement of Eve that Fingal is relating is admissible as an admission of a party-opponent. The problem presented here is one of hearsay within hearsay. Hearsay is a statement, other than one made by the declarant while testifying at the trial or hearing, offered in evidence to prove the truth of the matter asserted. A hearsay statement to which no exception to the hearsay rule is applicable must be excluded upon appropriate objection. Hearsay included within hearsay is admissible only if each layer of hearsay falls within a hearsay exception. Here, two separate statements are really being offered for the truth of the matter asserted therein. First, Fingal's statement is being offered to prove that he actually said that Eve admitted killing Adam. Second, Eve's statement is being offered to prove that Eve killed Adam. However, Eve's statement is an admission by a party-opponent, which is traditionally treated as a hearsay exception and is treated as nonhearsay under the Federal Rules. In either case, this statement alone would be admissible. Fingal's statement relating Eve's admission is also admissible; it comes within the excited utterance exception to the hearsay rule. Under this exception, a declaration made during or soon after a startling event is admissible. There must have been an occurrence startling enough to produce a nervous excitement and thus render the declaration an unreflective expression of the declarant's impression of the event. Also, the statement must have been made while the declarant was under the stress of the excitement. Here, Fingal has witnessed Eve running with a gun in her hand and declaring that she had killed her husband. Fingal immediately ran back to Nora's house and told her, "You won't believe what I just saw!" The occurrence, including Eve's statement, was certainly a startling event, and Fingal seems to have made his statement to Nora while he was still under the stress of excitement caused by the occurrence. Thus, Nora can testify to Fingal's statement, including the part relating what Eve had told him. (B) is incorrect because the exception to the hearsay rule for excited utterances such as Fingal's statement does not require the declarant to be unavailable to testify. (C) is incorrect because it does not matter in this case that the party-opponent made her admission to someone other than the testifying witness. The testifying witness (Nora) can repeat what Fingal said—including Eve's admission—because it was an excited utterance. (D) is incorrect because, as discussed above, both parts of Fingal's statement are admissible.

Answer to Question 25

(D) Where a witness has insufficient recollection of an event to enable her to testify fully and accurately, even after she has consulted a writing given to her on the stand, the writing itself may be introduced into evidence if a proper foundation is laid for its admissibility. The foundation for receipt of the writing into evidence must include proof that: (i) the witness had personal knowledge of the facts in the writing; (ii) the writing was made by the witness or under her direction, or adopted by the witness; (iii) the writing was timely made when the matter was fresh in the mind of the witness; (iv) the writing is accurate (witness must vouch for accuracy); and (v) the witness has insufficient recollection to testify fully and accurately. Under the Federal Rules, if admitted, the writing may be *read* into evidence and heard by the jury, but the document itself is not received as an exhibit unless offered by the adverse party. Thus, Walton must vouch for the accuracy of her notes, making I a true statement. The notes must be given to Walton on the stand to prove that she still has insufficient memory to testify fully and accurately. Finally, the plaintiff's attorney, who is seeking introduction of this material, is limited to having the contents of the notes read to the jury. While the defendant (the adverse party) may have the notes introduced as an exhibit, the plaintiff's attorney in this case may not do so under any circumstances. (A) and (B) are wrong because in addition to being incomplete, they contain the statement that the writing must be made while the witness is under the stress of excitement of the event. That is a requirement for the excited utterance exception to the hearsay rule; it is not a requirement for the recorded recollection exception to the hearsay rule. Under the recorded recollection exception all that is required is that the writing be made in a timely fashion while the matter is still fresh in the witness's mind. (C) is wrong because it fails to include the correct statements of I. and III.

Answer to Question 26

(D) Evidence of repairs or other precautionary measures made following an injury is inadmissible to prove negligence, culpable conduct, a defect in a product or its design, or a need for a warning or instruction. [Fed. R. Evid. 407] The purpose of this rule is to encourage people to make such repairs. Such evidence is admissible for purposes other than to prove negligence. Among such permissible purposes are: (i) to prove ownership or control where that is at issue; (ii) to rebut a claim that the precaution was not feasible; and (iii) to prove that the opposing party has destroyed or concealed evidence. The painting of the pedestrian crosswalk at the intersection at which the accident occurred, and the posting of the signs, are subsequent remedial measures of the type contemplated by Rule 407. With none of the circumstances present that would render evidence of subsequent repairs admissible, (D) is the correct answer. (A) is incorrect because the city is not contesting ownership or control of the intersection; its defense is that Gladys was contributorily negligent. Hence, this evidence is not admissible for that purpose. (B) is incorrect because the city is not attempting to conceal or distort evidence. It is probably undisputed that there was no marked crosswalk or signs at the time of the accident. (C) is incorrect because subsequent repairs is a type of evidence that, while relevant, is excluded on the public policy ground that society wishes to encourage immediate repair of dangerous conditions. Therefore, it is incorrect to state that the Federal Rules deem subsequent repairs to be irrelevant.

Answer to Question 27

(B) The testimony is admissible to show that Theodore had a motive to destroy the building. Federal Rule 411, which prohibits the admission of evidence of liability insurance to show a person acted negligently or wrongfully, does not apply to these circumstances. The insurance at issue in this case is not liability insurance; it is casualty insurance. The rationale for the exclusion of evidence of liability insurance (*i.e.,* that a trier of fact might improperly infer that a person acted more carelessly because he knew he was insured) has no application here. Whether a person was negligent is not at issue. The insurance policies are relevant because they make a fact in issue, that Theodore set his building on fire, more likely than it would be without evidence of the policies. Since it is relevant and not subject to any exclusionary rule, the testimony regarding the insurance policies is admissible to show motive for the arson. (A) is wrong because evidence of the insurance policies is admissible as substantive evidence in the prosecution's case in chief; it is not limited to impeachment uses. The rule stated in (A) is the one applicable to character type evidence that may be brought in to impeach a criminal defendant's credibility if he takes the stand. The evidence of the insurance policies, apart from having substantive value in proving the case, is of no help in attacking Theodore's veracity should he take the stand. Thus, this rule is totally inapplicable to this evidence. (C) is wrong because, as noted above, Rule 411 bans the use of evidence of liability insurance only. Liability insurance is not at issue here. (D) is wrong because the admission of testimony regarding the insurance policies does not violate the original document rule (also known as the best evidence rule). The rule requires the original writing to be produced to prove the terms of the writing, where the terms are material. Here, the testimony is not being sought to prove the terms of the policies, but rather that Theodore obtained them. That fact can be established independent of the policy itself.

Answer to Question 28

(B) The question of the existence or nonexistence of preliminary facts other than those of conditional relevance is to be determined by the court. All preliminary fact questions involving the standards of trustworthiness of alleged exceptions to the hearsay rule are to be determined by the court. Thus, the court, not the jury, must decide whether a purported business record was made in the regular course of business. In the case at bar, the question to be decided is whether the "product recognition survey" was in fact made during the regular course of business. Thus, this issue must be decided by the judge. During the hearing at which the judge makes the preliminary fact determination, both parties must be given an opportunity to present evidence with regard to the fact to be determined. Also, it is within the judge's discretion whether the jury should be excused during the preliminary fact determination. (B) is correct because it calls for the determination as to whether the document is a business record to be made by the judge, it allows for the presentation of evidence by both sides, and holding the hearing in the presence of the jury is within the judge's discretion. (A) is incorrect because it precludes Poston's attorney from presenting evidence on the matter to be decided. (C) incorrectly calls for the jury to decide the issue. There is no question here of conditional relevance. The question is one of competency of the evidence. Therefore, this is not the type of preliminary fact to be decided by the jury. (D) also reaches the incorrect conclusion that the jury has the ultimate decision on this matter. Only the judge may decide whether the document in question qualifies as a business record. Once the decision has been made, this issue cannot be further pursued by the jury.

Answer to Question 29

(A) Because a proper foundation has been laid, Kopp may read from the report while on the witness stand. Past recollection recorded is an exception to the hearsay rule. When a witness, after consulting the writing while on the stand, still has insufficient recollection to testify, the writing itself may be introduced into evidence if a proper foundation is laid. The foundation must establish four elements: (i) The witness at one time must have had personal knowledge of the facts in the writing; (ii) the writing must have been made when the matter was fresh in the witness's mind; (iii) the writing must have been made by the witness or under his direction, or adopted by him; and (iv) the witness must be presently unable to remember the facts. [Fed. R. Evid. 803(5)] Kopp had personal knowledge of the skid marks. (Note that because of this personal knowledge requirement, any part of the report not relating to Kopp's personal observation of the skid marks, such as statements of eyewitnesses, would not be admissible under this exception.) Kopp also made the original writing when the facts were fresh in his mind, and he is presently unable to remember the facts. Thus, the record is admissible as a past recollection recorded. (B) is incorrect because a present sense impression is a statement describing or explaining an event made while perceiving the event or immediately thereafter. [Fed. R. Evid. 803(1)] Generally, a present sense impression is an oral statement made to another rather than a written report. Here, Kopp's statement was made in a report prepared some time after he first perceived the skid marks and after he had interviewed all of the witnesses. Thus, Kopp's report is not a present sense impression. (C) is incorrect. A police report may qualify as a business record under Federal Rule 803(6) because it was made in the course of a regularly conducted business activity (and "business" is defined very broadly), even though it also qualifies as a public record or report under Federal Rule 803(8) or as past recollection recorded under Federal Rule 803(5). (D) is incorrect because the procedure is exactly the opposite. Under Federal Rule 803(5), a recorded recollection that qualifies under the exception may be read into evidence (because it is a substitute for the witness's testimony) but may not be received as an exhibit for the jury to read unless offered by an adverse party.

Answer to Question 30

(A) Under Federal Rule 403, a trial judge has broad discretion to exclude relevant evidence if its probative value is substantially outweighed by the danger of unfair prejudice, confusion of the issues, or misleading the jury, or by considerations of undue delay, waste of time, or needless presentation of cumulative evidence. Although some states list unfair surprise as an additional basis for exclusion, the Federal Rules do not, reasoning that surprise can be prevented by discovery and pretrial conference, or mitigated by granting a continuance. From the foregoing principles, if the witness in (A) is in fact a surprise witness, this will not suffice as a basis to exclude this otherwise relevant evidence under the Federal Rules, which govern this action. At most, the court should grant a continuance. In all of the other situations, while the evidence is arguably admissible, the circumstances present the judge with a basis under the Federal Rules for exclusion.

The testimony in (B) may be excluded because the testimony of the second expert will not add anything to the testimony already given by the first expert. Thus, allowing this testimony will simply waste time and repeat evidence already presented. Pursuant to Rule 403, this constitutes a permissible ground of exclusion. Regarding (C), the bloodstained shirt might be deemed to be inflammatory and capable of producing an unfairly prejudicial effect on the jury. As such, it is within the realm of the judge's discretionary power of exclusion. Regarding (D), the testimony of Officer Batista is relevant because it tends to render more probably untrue the allegation of a police beating than it would have been without this testimony. However, James's alleged homosexuality and whether he has AIDS are not issues in the case, and the statement referring to them might well cause confusion of the issues or tend to mislead the jury. Thus, the testimony of Officer Batista is subject to exclusion under the Federal Rules.

Answer to Question 31

(B) The question by Perry's attorney should be allowed as long as he was acting in good faith. A witness may be impeached by means of being interrogated upon cross-examination, in the discretion of the court, with respect to any act of misconduct that is probative of truthfulness (*i.e.,* an act of deceit or lying). It is not required that the witness have been convicted of a crime. Also, the cross-examiner must act in good faith with some reasonable basis for believing that the witness may have committed the bad act inquired about. Here, Perry's attorney is attempting to cast an adverse reflection on the truthfulness of Womack. The commission of the crime of false pretenses would involve the making of a false representation and would therefore be an act of misconduct that would be probative of the actor's truthfulness. Thus, if (as is stated in (B)) Perry's attorney inquired as to this matter in good faith, his question is a permissible method of impeachment, and the objection of Dunderhead's attorney should be overruled. (A) is incorrect because, as noted above, such an inquiry can be conducted regardless of whether the witness was convicted. Therefore, the fact that Womack was not convicted of false pretenses would not be grounds for sustaining the objection. (C) is incorrect. Although impeaching witnesses who testify to a witness's reputation for truth and veracity are often impeached by asking the "Have you heard" and "Do you know" questions, that is not the only method of impeachment available. *Any* witness who takes the stand puts his character for honesty and veracity in issue and may be impeached by evidence that might show him to be unworthy of belief. Instances of misconduct may properly be inquired into only if they are probative of truthfulness. By taking the stand, Womack has put his character for honesty in issue. The crime of false pretenses is probative of truthfulness and is a proper subject for impeachment. (D) is incorrect because a specific act of misconduct offered to attack the witness's character for truthfulness can be elicited *only* on cross-examination of the witness. Extrinsic evidence is not permitted. Thus, (D) states the opposite of the correct rule.

Answer to Question 32

(D) The court should apply the law of Yellow with regard to the presumption. In a civil case, the effect of a presumption regarding a fact that is an element of a claim as to which state law supplies the rule of decision is determined in accordance with state law. [Fed. R. Evid. 302] Under the *Erie* doctrine, in a case based on diversity of citizenship, the federal court must apply the substantive law of the state in which the court sits, but usually applies federal law to procedural issues. State procedural law applies only if it would result in an important difference in the outcome of the litigation. With respect to presumptions, the Federal Rule, which follows the *Erie* doctrine, provides that application of state law is appropriate only when the presumption operates on a substantive element of a claim or defense. The presumption here at issue, by presuming negligence on the part of a driver who strikes another vehicle in the rear, impacts on the prima facie case elements of duty and breach of duty. Matters involving elements of a prima facie case are substantive in nature; thus, state law applies to such matters. Because the presumption regards a matter for which state law supplies the rule of decision, the effect of the presumption should be determined according to state law, pursuant to Rule 302. Consequently, both the substantive law of Yellow and the Yellow "procedural" law relative to the presumption of negligence should be applied by the court on this issue. (A) is incorrect because there is no general federal common law. The substantive law to be applied in a diversity case is that of the state. Furthermore, it would not be appropriate to apply all of Yellow's rules of procedure. Except in certain circumstances, such as when the rule applied would be outcome determinative, the Federal Rules of Civil Procedure apply in diversity cases. (B) is incorrect. Although it is true that the Yellow substantive law is to be applied, with respect to the procedural issue in question (the applicability of the state presumption), it is Yellow law, not the Federal Rules of Civil Procedure, that the court should apply. (C) is incorrect because it implies that it is the general rule to apply both the substantive and procedural law of the state in which the federal court sits. As detailed above, state procedural law is applied only in certain instances.

Answer to Question 33

(A) The objection is likely to be sustained under Federal Rule 403 because the scientific reliability of lie detector evidence is substantially outweighed by the tendency of its results to mislead and confuse the jury. Testimony concerning the lie detector test would be relevant because it would tend to make the existence of a fact of consequence, whether Bertha was telling the truth, more probable. However, Rule 403 gives a trial judge broad discretion to exclude relevant evidence if its probative value is substantially outweighed by the danger of unfair prejudice, confusion of the issues, or misleading the jury. The probative value of a lie detector test depends on its scientific reliability, and its reliability generally is deemed to be slight because of its significant rate of error. On the other side of the balancing test, the tendency of jurors to give too much weight to a polygraph test makes the danger of unfair prejudice high. Therefore, the test's unreliability and the risk of confusion from the test's results justify excluding the prosecutor's question. (B) is incorrect because the credibility of a witness may be attacked by any party and then rehabilitated, regardless of whether the witness is on trial. In terms of relevance, any matter that tends to prove or disprove the credibility of a witness should be admitted. Bob's defense attorney properly asked Bertha questions about her marriage because this line of questioning tended to discredit Bertha's testimony about what happened the night Bill was slain. A witness, like Bertha, who has been impeached may be rehabilitated on redirect by explaining or clarifying facts brought out on cross-examination. While the question about the lie detector test should be excluded under Rule 403, as discussed above, the question may not be barred just because Bertha is not on trial. (C) is incorrect because while the prosecutor has the right to rehabilitate Bertha's credibility, she may not do so with lie detector evidence. As discussed above, a witness who has been impeached may be rehabilitated on redirect by explaining or clarifying facts brought out on cross-examination. While prior consistent statements generally may not be used for rehabilitation, an exception exists if the opposing counsel has expressly or impliedly charged that the witness is lying or exaggerating because of some motive. Bertha can be rehabilitated because her credibility was impeached by the questions concerning her marriage. Because the defense attorney implied that Bertha's testimony was biased because she killed Bill, some prior consistent statements may possibly be used for rehabilitation. However, questions about the lie detector may not be used for this purpose in light of Rule 403, as discussed above. (D) is incorrect because, while the defense attorney's questions opened the door to explanation of her answers concerning her marriage, they do not justify testimony concerning the lie detector test. As discussed above, the defense attorney's questions impeaching Bertha by probing into her marriage opened the door to her rehabilitation by the prosecutor. While she may be rehabilitated on redirect by explaining facts brought out on cross-examination, and may even testify as to prior consistent statements if charged with lying or exaggerating because of some motive, she may not be asked questions about the lie detector test. This is because, as discussed above, the slight probative value of the test is substantially outweighed by its tendency to confuse and mislead the jury.

Answer to Question 34

(C) The court should overrule the objection because the testimony is relevant to the issue of motive and is not precluded by any exclusionary rule. Evidence is relevant if it tends to make the existence of any fact that is of consequence to the action more probable than it would be without the evidence. Here, motive is an important fact of consequence to the action; thus, it is relevant. Since no exclusionary rules apply, the statement should come in. (A) is wrong because Rachel's status as an eavesdropper has no effect on the admissibility of her testimony. Being an eavesdropper could have some effect if some sort of testimonial privilege (*e.g.,* attorney-client) were at issue, but nothing in the facts indicates such a relationship between the caller and Dagwood. (B) is wrong because the statement is being offered for its effect on the hearer, not for the truth of the matter asserted. It does not matter whether Xavier was really going to talk to the police. The statement is relevant on the issue of Dagwood's motive regardless of whether the statement is true. Therefore, even though the statement would be inadmissible hearsay if offered to prove that Xavier intended to talk to the police, it is admissible to show its effect on Dagwood, the hearer. (D) is wrong because there is no evidence of a conspiracy, and the caller's statement could not be construed as a statement made to a third party in furtherance of the conspiracy. Dagwood is not a third party.

Answer to Question 35

(D) The effect of the judge's noticing that a car driven from Chicago to Detroit must cross state lines is that the judge will now instruct the jury that it may, but is not required to, accept that fact as conclusively proven. Under the Federal Rules, in a civil case, the court must instruct the jury to accept the judicially noticed fact as conclusive. [Fed. R. Evid. 201(g)] Because this question deals with a prosecution for criminal battery, the applicable rule is that the jury be instructed that the fact that has been judicially noticed may be accepted by it as conclusive, but that the jury is not required to do so. (A) would be correct if this were a civil case. In such an instance, the jury would be instructed to accept as conclusive the judicially noticed fact. This would have the effect of raising an irrebuttable presumption. (B) is incorrect because, in a criminal case, the prosecution has the burden of proving every element of the crime beyond a reasonable doubt. Only the jury can decide, after all of the evidence is in, whether the burden of persuasion is satisfied. (C) is incorrect because the burden of persuasion does not shift from party to party during the course of the trial. The burden of persuasion is never on a criminal defendant.

Answer to Question 36

(C) The prosecution must show how the Geiger counter functions and that it was in good working condition at the time in question in order for evidence of its reaction to be admissible. Only relevant evidence is admissible. Relevant evidence is evidence having the tendency to make the existence of any fact that is of consequence to the determination of an action more probable than it would be without the evidence. [Fed. R. Evid. 401] Here, Webster's testimony is being offered to prove that the Geiger counter reacted to the substances in Durham's suitcase. The issue of the Geiger counter's reaction to the suitcase is material because the government is claiming that Durham had radioactive isotopes in his suitcase, to which the Geiger counter would have reacted. Webster's testimony of the reaction must be sufficiently probative of the proposition that the Geiger counter reacted to the isotopes in the suitcase. To be sufficiently probative, the evidence must show that the Geiger counter functions by reacting to radioactive material and that the reaction of the Geiger counter was authentic. To authenticate such a reaction, all that is necessary under the Federal Rules is proof sufficient to support a jury finding of genuineness. To establish that the reaction of the Geiger counter was authentic, it would be essential to show that it was in sound operating condition at the time in question. As discussed below, this proof is sufficient to support a jury finding that the machine's reaction was genuine. (A) is incorrect because, as discussed above, the prosecution must also establish that the Geiger counter was in sound operating condition. To be sufficiently probative, testimony about the machine's reaction must be authenticated by proof that the reaction was genuine. This proof must include evidence that the Geiger counter was in sound working condition at the time in question. (B) is incorrect because the prosecution must also show how the Geiger counter functioned; *i.e.,* that the noise made by the Geiger counter would be caused by radioactive material in the vicinity. (Note that the fact that a court may take judicial notice of how a Geiger counter operates does not relieve the prosecution from establishing that fact. A request for judicial notice is merely a method of proving that fact.) (D) is incorrect because Webster's testimony would be relevant without evidence that there was no other radioactive material in the area. To be relevant, evidence must have a tendency to prove or disprove a material issue. While the reaction of the Geiger counter must be shown to be genuine to be sufficiently probative, as discussed above, all that is necessary under the Federal Rules is proof sufficient to support a jury finding of genuineness. It is not required that the prosecution establish the genuineness of the reaction by a preponderance of the evidence as a condition to admissibility. Therefore, while the condition of the Geiger counter must be established, it is not necessary to establish that there was no other radioactive material in the area before Webster's testimony can be admitted.

Answer to Question 37

(B) The court should admit Nancy's testimony because it is relevant circumstantial evidence. The Federal Rules of Evidence define relevant evidence as evidence having any tendency to prove or disprove a fact that is of consequence to the action. [Fed. R. Evid. 401] Generally, all relevant evidence is admissible unless it is barred by a specific exclusionary rule or by the general balancing test of Rule 403, which permits exclusion of relevant evidence if its probative value is substantially outweighed by the danger of unfair prejudice, confusion of the issues, etc. Nancy's testimony is relevant because Spotty's behavior when Distil came by tends to prove circumstantially (*i.e.,* indirectly) the prosecution's contention that Distil beat Victor to death (in Spotty's presence). Nancy is competent to testify as to the dog's behavior toward Distil both before and after the murder, and no other competency rule warrants excluding the testimony; hence, it should be admitted. (A) is incorrect because the availability of other evidence that might demonstrate the dog's reaction more clearly does not preclude Nancy's testimony on that issue. As long as Nancy is competent to testify regarding Spotty's behavior, Spotty's availability is irrelevant. (C) is incorrect because it is up to the trier of fact to evaluate the inference for which the circumstantial evidence is being offered. The defense may attack Nancy's testimony on cross-examination by suggesting other reasons for the dog's reaction, but it cannot exclude Nancy's testimony on this basis. (D) is incorrect because the balancing test of Rule 403 provides only that a court may exclude relevant evidence if its probative value is **substantially** outweighed by the danger of **unfair** prejudice. While all evidence is prejudicial to the opposing party, "unfair" prejudice refers to suggesting a decision on an emotional or otherwise improper basis. There is nothing in Nancy's testimony to justify excluding it on unfair prejudice grounds.

Answer to Question 38

(C) The court should overrule the objection because the physician-patient privilege cannot be invoked for information dealing with a nonmedical matter. Under the physician-patient privilege, a physician is foreclosed from divulging in judicial proceedings information that he acquired while attending a patient in a professional capacity, which information was necessary to enable the physician to act in his professional capacity. Information given by a patient that deals with a nonmedical matter is not protected by the privilege. Hence, Donnybrook's admission that he was shot while running from a jewelry store that he robbed is not barred by the privilege. (A) is incorrect because, although it is true that Dr. Thomas acquired the information while attending Donnybrook in the course of treatment, the privilege is inapplicable because, as discussed above, the statement deals with a nonmedical matter. (B) is incorrect because a promise to comply with a request by the patient that information be kept confidential will not by itself render the information protectable under the physician-patient privilege. To qualify for such protection, the information must have been necessary for treatment, and there must be no applicable exceptions to the privilege. (D) is incorrect because this privilege belongs to the patient. Thus, Donnybrook is the one who is entitled to claim or waive the privilege, not Dr. Thomas.

Answer to Question 39

(D) It was not error to introduce either item of evidence, even though both contain hearsay. Hearsay is a statement, other than one made by the declarant while testifying at the trial or hearing, offered in evidence to prove the truth of the matter asserted. Here, both items of evidence are being offered to prove the truth of what they are asserting—the date of Effie's birth. However, they both fall within exceptions to the general rule that hearsay is not admissible at trial. Under Federal Rule 803(13), statements of fact concerning personal or family history contained in family Bibles, engravings on tombstones, etc., are admissible (regardless of whether the declarant is available). Effie's Bible is therefore admissible, and (A) and (C) are incorrect. The certified copy of the birth certificate is also admissible hearsay under Federal Rule 803(9), which admits official records of births, deaths, and marriages. (B) is incorrect because official records are self-authenticating when they are certified [Fed. R. Evid. 902]; the custodian need not authenticate them in court.

Answer to Question 40

(C) Nud's testimony is inadmissible because it is not probative of any material issue in the case. Relevant evidence tends to make the existence of any fact that is of consequence to the determination of an action more probable than it would be without the evidence. [Fed. R. Evid. 401] While evidence tending to prove Piston's charitable nature, which is a material issue in this case, would be relevant, the evidence here tends to prove only Piston's honesty, which is not at issue here. Therefore, it is not relevant and should not be admitted. (A) is incorrect because even though Piston's character has been called into question in this case, only evidence that is probative of the particular character trait in issue may be admitted. When a person's character itself is one of the issues in the case, evidence of specific facts may be used to prove character. [Fed. R. Evid. 405(b)] Because this is a defamation case, Piston's character as to generosity is directly in issue, and specific acts may be used to prove his generosity. However, as discussed above, Nud's testimony is not probative of Piston's generosity. (B) is similarly incorrect. Piston has a right to prove his good character, but only with regard to the particular character trait that has been defamed. (D) is incorrect because specific acts may be used to prove character when character is directly in issue, as discussed above. Piston's generosity is directly in issue in this case and specific acts of his may be used to prove his generosity. Therefore, Nud's testimony is not inadmissible on these grounds.

Answer to Question 41

(A) The chart is admissible because the original documents are in CWC's files. The original document or best evidence rule generally requires the original writing to be produced when the terms of the writing are sought to be proved and are material to the case. [Fed. R. Evid. 1002] However, under Federal Rule 1006, the contents of voluminous writings that are otherwise admissible may be presented in the form of a chart as long as the original documents are available to the other party for examination and copying. Here, the underlying documents belonged to the adverse party (CWC), and thus CWC had unlimited access to them. (B) is incorrect because the chart could be helpful to the trier of fact and still be inadmissible, such as if the underlying material were not available to CWC or the chart were based on inadmissible hearsay. Furthermore, (B) is not as good a choice as (A) because (B) states a generality (it basically states the relevance requirement) whereas (A) applies the law to the specific facts of this case. (C) is incorrect because the chart is admissible provided the underlying documents are admissible. Even if the documents in this case would be hearsay, they would be admissible under the business records exception to the hearsay rule because they are records of events made in the regular course of business. [Fed. R. Evid. 803(6)] (D) is incorrect because Rule 1006 is an exception to the best evidence rule designed to avoid the introduction of voluminous writings into evidence; therefore, it does not require their introduction as a prerequisite to introduction of a chart.

Answer to Question 42

(B) Janet's testimony is admissible to impeach Elliot's credibility and as substantive evidence of Evans's guilt. As long as the witness is given an opportunity to explain or deny the statement, extrinsic proof of a prior inconsistent statement is admissible to impeach the witness's testimony. If the prior inconsistent statement was made under oath at a prior trial, hearing, or other proceeding, it is admissible nonhearsay; i.e., it is admissible as substantive evidence. In this case, the prior inconsistent statement was made under oath at Elliot's trial and thus is admissible for its substance as well as for impeachment. (A) is incorrect because, as discussed above, Janet's testimony is admissible as substantive evidence of Evans's guilt. (C) is incorrect because jurors are incompetent to testify only (i) before the jury on which they are sitting, and (ii) in postverdict proceedings as to certain matters occurring during jury deliberations. Since Janet is not testifying before the jury on which she was sitting and is not testifying about jury deliberations, she is a competent witness. (D) is incorrect because the best evidence rule does not apply to this situation. Janet is not being called to prove the terms of a writing or to testify about knowledge she gained from reading a writing. The facts as to which she is testifying exist independently of any writing; thus, the best evidence rule does not apply.

Answer to Question 43

(C) Crane's testimony is not admissible because Drake's statement that he told Crane that he acted in self-defense is extrinsic evidence on a collateral matter. A witness's statement on a collateral matter may be impeached only by cross-examination. A collateral matter is one that is not directly relevant to the issues in the case. Here, Officer Crane's testimony is being offered to disprove Drake's claim that he told the officer that he acted in self-defense, which Drake related just to bolster his self-defense claim. While the ***circumstances*** of Drake's altercation itself are relevant to a self-defense claim and could be the proper subject of testimony, his ***statement*** to Officer Crane is just an assertion of his innocence and is not directly relevant to whether his self-defense claim was proper. (The prosecution could have objected to Drake's statement as irrelevant, and could have challenged it on cross-examination, but it cannot impeach the statement with extrinsic evidence.) (A) is incorrect because for silence to be an admission, the party must have remained silent when faced with an accusatory statement. Here, Drake was not confronted with an accusatory statement at his arrest. (B) is incorrect because, as discussed above, the testimony constitutes impeachment by extrinsic evidence on a collateral matter. While it may cast doubt on Drake's overall credibility, it is not directly relevant to the issue of self-defense in the case. (D) is incorrect. The Fifth Amendment privilege against self-incrimination would prevent the prosecution from using Drake's silence for substantive purposes as an admission. Here, however, Drake's silence is not being offered as an admission, but only for the limited purpose of impeaching his claim that he made a statement to Officer Crane.

Answer to Question 44

(A) The court should overrule the objection because Farnsworth's statement is a vicarious admission of Red Circle Stores. Under the Federal Rules, statements made by an agent concerning any matter within the scope of his agency, made during the existence of the employment relationship, are not hearsay and are admissible against the principal. Here, while the police report itself is admissible under the business records exception to the hearsay rule, Farnsworth's statement within the report is not admissible under that exception because he was under no business duty to convey such information to the police officer. However, because he was the front end manager of the store at the time he made the statement, his statement is admissible against his principal, Red Circle Stores, as a vicarious admission. Hence, the objection should be overruled. (B) is incorrect because admissions of a party are not receivable against his co-defendants merely because they happen to be joined as parties to the action. Here, the statement is admissible against Red Circle Stores because of the principal-agent relationship. (C) is incorrect because the Federal Rules have broadened the scope of vicarious admissions by an agent. The statements need not be within the scope of his authority to speak as long as they concerned any matter within the scope of his agency, and the court most likely would find that the reasons for detention of a suspected shoplifter is a matter within the scope of employment of the front end manager of a department store. (D) is wrong because the fact that an admission is predicated on hearsay rather than personal knowledge is not a ground for excluding it. Here, Farnsworth was adopting the guard's statement as his own when he related it to the police officer as the justification for stopping Penny; thus, it can be admitted against both him and his employer.

Answer to Question 45

(C) Warren's testimony is inadmissible. Under Federal Rule 804(b)(1), the testimony of a witness who is unavailable, given at another hearing, is admissible in a subsequent trial if there is sufficient similarity of parties and issues so that the opportunity to develop testimony or cross-examination at the prior hearing was meaningful. The former testimony is admissible upon any trial of the same subject matter. The party against whom the testimony is offered must have been a party, or in privity with a party, in the former action. Examples of parties in privity are grantor-grantee, testator-executor, life-tenant-remainderman, and joint tenants. These requirements are intended to ensure that the party against whom the testimony is offered (or a party in privity with her) had an adequate opportunity and motive to cross-examine the witness. In the civil suit here at issue, the survivors of Bernie were not parties to the criminal case, nor were they in privity with any such party. (The parties to that case were Diana and the government.) These survivors, who are plaintiffs in the instant litigation, are the parties against whom the testimony of Warren is being offered. Because they were not parties to the action in which Warren testified, they had no opportunity to cross-examine him. Consequently, the testimony of Warren does not come within the former testimony exception to the hearsay rule, and the testimony is inadmissible hearsay. (A) and (B) incorrectly conclude that the testimony is admissible. Although it is true that Warren testified at an earlier hearing related to the same subject matter, and that Diana is a party to both proceedings, what is missing is the requisite identity of parties against whom the testimony is being offered. (D) is incorrect because a witness incarcerated in another state is "unavailable" for purposes of civil proceedings. Under the Federal Rules, a witness is unavailable if he is absent from the hearing and the proponent of the statement is unable to procure the declarant's attendance by process or other reasonable means. The Supreme Court has held that the Confrontation Clause requires a greater showing of "unavailability" in criminal cases than in civil cases. Because all states permit extradition of witnesses against the accused in criminal cases, a mere showing that a witness is incarcerated in a prison outside the state is insufficient to establish "unavailability." In contrast, the reach of process in civil cases is more limited and the Confrontation Clause does not apply. A mere showing that the witness is incarcerated in a prison out of state will suffice to show unavailability in a civil case.

Answer to Question 46

(A) Parslow should be allowed to testify as to what Doter said if he observed Doter making the statements in the television broadcast. To be a competent witness, the witness must have personal knowledge of the matter and be willing and able to testify truthfully. The first requirement is satisfied if the witness observed the matter and has a present recollection of his observation. Thus, Parslow would be a competent witness if he observed the publication of the defamation, which occurred through the television broadcast. Even though (B) is a true statement, (A) is a better answer because there are many instances where relevant evidence going to the ultimate issue is excluded (*e.g.,* hearsay). Furthermore, (A) is a better answer because Parslow must have personal knowledge to testify, regardless of how relevant the subject matter of his testimony is to an ultimate issue in the case. (C) is incorrect because the availability of the videotape does not preclude independent oral testimony of the statements that Doter made. The best evidence rule does not apply here because the fact to be proved (the defamatory statement) exists independent of the recording and Parslow's knowledge of the fact was not derived from the recording. (D) is incorrect because the allegedly defamatory statement is not hearsay. Doter's out-of-court statement is a verbal act or legally operative fact. It is not being offered to prove the truth of the matter asserted (that Parslow condones steroid use by his players), but rather merely to show that the legally actionable statement was made.

Answer to Question 47

(C) Tess does not have to answer the question unless she has waived the privilege against self-incrimination. A person may assert the privilege against self-incrimination in *any* proceeding, civil or criminal, in which testimony that could incriminate the person (*i.e.,* expose her to criminal liability) is sought. Thus, Tess may raise the privilege unless she has waived it. (A) is incorrect because the privilege here cannot be waived merely by taking the stand. While a criminal defendant may refuse to take the witness stand at all, in a civil action, a witness is required to take the stand if called, but taking the stand is not a waiver of the privilege. The privilege must be raised as to each objectionable question asked and will be waived only if the witness discloses incriminating information. (B) is incorrect because the Fifth Amendment applies to all trials at which the witness's appearance and testimony are compelled. (D) is incorrect because it is too broad; if a witness waives the privilege by testifying as to the subject, and then attempts to raise the privilege later, it is too late. She can no longer assert the privilege.

Answer to Question 48

(A) Wallene can be compelled to testify because Henry is dead and cannot invoke the privilege. There are two separate spousal privileges. There is *spousal immunity*, under which: (i) a married person whose spouse is the defendant in a criminal case may not be called as a witness by the prosecution, and (ii) a married person may not be compelled to testify against her spouse in any criminal proceeding. In federal court, this privilege belongs to the witness-spouse so that she may not be compelled to testify, but neither may she be foreclosed from testifying. This privilege terminates upon divorce. There is also a privilege for *confidential marital communications*, under which either spouse, whether or not a party, has a privilege to refuse to disclose, and to prevent another from disclosing, a confidential communication made between the spouses while they were husband and wife. Both spouses jointly hold this privilege. Divorce does not terminate this privilege retroactively. Since the communication must be made in reliance upon the intimacy of the marital relationship, if the communication is made in the known presence of a stranger, it is not privileged. Similarly, if one spouse voluntarily reveals the contents of the communication to a stranger, that spouse waives the protection of the privilege as to herself (*i.e.*, she cannot use the privilege to refuse to disclose, or to prevent another from disclosing, the communication), but the other spouse (*i.e.*, the one who did not reveal the communication) retains this privilege. Here, the spousal immunity between Henry and Wallene terminated upon their divorce. Thus, the only consideration is the applicability of the privilege for confidential marital communications. Henry's statement to Wallene came during their marriage and was made in reliance upon the intimacy of their relationship (marital communications are presumed to be confidential). Thus, the statement was covered by the privilege for confidential marital communications. The subsequent divorce of Henry and Wallene did not terminate this privilege. However, when Wallene revealed to Francesca what Henry had told her concerning the theft of the painting, she lost her privilege to refuse to disclose the matter. If Henry were alive, he would retain the privilege despite Wallene's disclosure and could prevent Wallene from testifying to his statement concerning the theft of the painting. Because Henry is dead, he cannot invoke his privilege. Since Wallene has waived her privilege and Henry is unable to foreclose her testimony, she can be compelled to testify. (B) is incorrect because it implies that the divorce terminated the privilege. As explained, the divorce did terminate the spousal immunity, but did not terminate the privilege for confidential marital communications. Thus, the reason that Wallene can be compelled to testify is not because of the divorce; Wallene can be compelled to testify because her disclosure of the communication to Francesca waived her privilege. (C) is incorrect because the privilege for confidential marital communications applies to the disclosure of matters communicated during and in reliance on the intimacy of the marital relationship regardless of whether one of the spouses is a defendant in a criminal case. Even spousal immunity is deemed to preclude the compelled testimony of one spouse against the other in any criminal proceeding, regardless of whether the other spouse is a defendant. The difference when a spouse is a criminal defendant is that the other spouse may not even be compelled to take the stand. (D) incorrectly concludes that Wallene cannot be compelled to testify. Due to her knowing and voluntary revelation of Henry's statement to Francesca, Wallene has waived her privilege and may be compelled to testify. Note that, if the privilege were still applicable (*i.e.*, if Wallene had not waived it), Wallene could not be compelled to testify as to the contents of the privileged communication simply on the ground that such testimony would be essential to prevent a fraud on the court.

Answer to Question 49

(D) The ground for the judge's decision is incorrect because Joyce is available to testify. The statement against interest exception to the hearsay rule requires that the declarant be unavailable as a witness. A declarant is unavailable if: (i) she is exempted from testifying on the ground of privilege; (ii) she refuses to testify concerning the statement; (iii) she testifies to lack of memory of the subject matter of the statement; (iv) she cannot testify because she has died or is ill; or (v) she is absent and the statement's proponent is unable to procure her attendance or testimony by process. [Fed. R. Evid. 804(a)(1)-(5)] None of the bases for a finding of unavailability is present here. Joyce, the declarant whose statement is at issue, is available as a witness; thus, the judge was incorrect in basing his decision on this exception. (A) is incorrect because the fact that the statement subjected Joyce to tort liability, and thus was against her interest, is not enough; she must also be unavailable. Also, this choice implies that this exception would be available only if Joyce were subjected to tort liability, not criminal liability. Although some courts so limit the exception, the Federal Rules include statements against penal interest within the parameters of the statement against interest. (B) is incorrect because Joyce need not be a party to the litigation for her statement to qualify as a statement against interest. Thus, her status as a party would not be a basis for deciding that the statement against interest exception applies here. Of course, this choice is also incorrect because her availability to testify precludes application of this exception. (C) is incorrect because Joyce's statement, which effectively acknowledges liability for Pahlavi's injury, is most certainly against an important pecuniary interest; *i.e.*, it subjects Joyce to the possibility of being held financially liable for Pahlavi's damages. Note that the judge correctly overruled the objection by Joyce's attorney, but for the wrong reason. Joyce's statement constitutes an admission by a party-opponent, which is an act done or statement made that amounts to a prior acknowledgment by a party of one of the relevant facts. Such an admission is nonhearsay under the Federal Rules. [Fed. R. Evid. 801(d)(2)] Joyce is a party, and her statement is a prior acknowledgment of the highly relevant matter of fault. For an admission by a party-opponent, the declarant need not be unavailable. (Don't be confused by the fact that, although the judge was correct in allowing the testimony as to Joyce's statement, the call of the question pertains to the grounds for the ruling, which were incorrect.)

Answer to Question 50

(C) Either an authenticated copy of the tape or the testimony of the lawyers is admissible. Hearsay is a statement, other than one made by the declarant while testifying at the trial or hearing, offered to prove the truth of the matter asserted. Wandrus is obviously not testifying at the current trial, and his statements are being offered for their truth. Thus, his deposition testimony is hearsay. The next issue is whether it falls within an exception to the hearsay rule. Ordinarily, a now unavailable declarant's statements made in a deposition are admissible under the former testimony exception to the hearsay rule. That rule, however, requires that the statements be made under oath. Since Wandrus was not under oath when he testified, this exception would not apply. When a declarant is unavailable, a statement not specifically covered under the specific hearsay exceptions but having equivalent guarantees of trustworthiness is admissible if: (i) it is offered as evidence of a material fact; (ii) it is more probative of the issue than any other evidence the proponent can procure with reasonable efforts; (iii) the purposes of the rules of evidence and the interests of justice will best be served by admission of the statement; and (iv) the proponent gives the adverse party sufficient notice of his intention to use the statement and the statement's particulars. [Fed. R. Evid. 807—the "catch-all" exception] Here, Wandrus's statements are being offered as evidence of the material fact—the accident. Clearly, since Wandrus was the only neutral eyewitness, his statements are more probative of the issue than any other evidence that can be produced. Because Wandrus was the only neutral eyewitness and because the statement comes with guarantees of trustworthiness (*e.g.,* Wandrus was subject to cross-examination by the parties involved in this trial), the interests of justice would best be served by admission of the testimony. Since both sides agree that Wandrus had no motive to lie, the oath is a less important guarantee of trustworthiness, and the lack of an oath should not affect the admissibility of the statements. Since both parties were present (in the form of their attorneys) when the statements were made and knew that Wandrus was being questioned for the purpose of this suit, the notice requirement was probably satisfied. Therefore, Wandrus's deposition is admissible. Since Wandrus's statements exist independently of the recording, the best evidence rule, which requires that the original "document" be produced to prove its terms, does not apply, and either the authenticated recording *or* the lawyers' testimony would be admissible. Thus (A) and (B) are both true but not as good as (C) because (C) contains both options. (D) is incorrect because, as stated, the tape or the testimony is admissible. (D) would have been the correct choice were it not for the unusual set of circumstances making this declarant's statements extraordinarily useful and trustworthy.

Answer to Question 51

(D) None of the other choices is correct. (B) and (C) each state an element under the best evidence rule (also called the original document rule), and the model of the cartoon animal is not a document. (A) incorrectly assumes that notice must be given. The best evidence rule covers writings and recordings, which are defined as "letters, words, or numbers, or their equivalent, set down by handwriting, typewriting, printing, photostating, photographing, magnetic impulse, mechanical or electronic recording, or other form of data compilation." A clay model clearly does not fit within that definition. (A) is wrong because this type of notice is not a prerequisite for Papageno's testimony even had the best evidence rule been applicable. (B) is wrong because it states the foundation requirement for the admissibility of secondary evidence under the best evidence rule, and as discussed above, that rule does not apply under these circumstances. Similarly, (C) states an acceptable form of secondary evidence under the best evidence rule, which does not apply here. Note, however, that under the Federal Rules (unlike most states), there are no degrees of secondary evidence. Therefore, this choice would be wrong even if the best evidence rule were applicable, because Papageno would not be limited to photographic evidence.

Answer to Question 52

(A) Samuel's testimony about Tickles's statement is admissible as circumstantial evidence that Tickles was on the boat. The statement is hearsay, but is admissible under the state of mind exception to the hearsay rule. Hearsay is an out-of-court statement offered to prove the truth of the matter asserted. Upon objection, hearsay must be excluded unless it falls within an exception to the rule. Here, Tickles's out-of-court statement is being offered for its truth—*i.e.,* to prove that he planned to propose a television show starring himself as Madd Hatter. The statement is, therefore, hearsay. Declarations of a declarant's then-existing state of mind, however, are admissible if made under circumstances of apparent sincerity. This exception includes declarations of intent offered to show subsequent acts of the declarant. In this case, Tickles's statement to his son was made under circumstances of apparent sincerity and so may be admitted as circumstantial evidence that Tickles used the name Madd Hatter and was aboard the boat that vanished. (B) is wrong because this evidence would not create a rebuttable presumption that Tickles was on the boat. A presumption is a rule (established by statute or case law) that requires that a particular inference be drawn from a particular set of facts. There is no indication in the facts, nor is it likely, that such a rule exists in this jurisdiction with respect to the subject matter of Samuel's testimony. Note that Samuel may be offering this testimony as part of his attempt to establish the rebuttable presumption that Tickles is dead because he has not been heard from in seven years. However, that presumption is distinct from a presumption regarding his presence on the boat. At best, his testimony allows the jury to find that Tickles was on the boat; it does not require them to do so. (C) is incorrect. A conclusive presumption is a rule of substantive law rather than a true presumption because it cannot be rebutted. There is no conclusive presumption applicable here. (D) is wrong because, as discussed above, the testimony is admissible as circumstantial evidence that Tickles was on the boat.

Answer to Question 53

(A) Cicero's testimony is admissible, provided that other civil engineers ordinarily reasonably rely on structural engineers' reports in forming professional opinions. Expert testimony is admissible if the subject matter is one where scientific, technical, or other specialized knowledge would assist the jury in understanding the evidence or determining a fact in issue. [Fed. R. Evid. 702] The proper design of a spiral staircase would not be a matter of common knowledge and the testimony of an expert would be of assistance in determining whether the design was faulty. The expert's opinion may be based on facts not in evidence that were supplied to the expert out of court, and which facts are of a type reasonably relied upon by experts in the particular field in forming opinions on the subject. [Fed. R. Evid. 703] Cicero may therefore give an opinion based on the photographs and Erecto's report if such photographs and reports are of a type reasonably relied upon by civil engineers in forming opinions on structural design. Federal Rule 703 allows Cicero's testimony even though the photographs and report are not in evidence. (B) is incorrect because Federal Rule 703 does not require an expert to disclose the facts on which he relied in forming his opinion. In fact, the proponent of the expert opinion must not disclose those facts to the jury (since they may be of a type not admissible in evidence) unless the court determines that their probative value in assisting the jury to evaluate the expert's opinion substantially outweighs their prejudicial effect. (C) is incorrect because the Federal Rules allow Cicero to base his opinion on opinions in Erecto's report as long as such opinions in reports would be reasonably relied upon by civil engineers in forming opinions. An expert traditionally is not permitted to rely on the opinions of others as a predicate for his own opinion. However, Federal Rule 703 significantly expands the traditional rule and permits an expert to base his opinion on the opinion of others if they are of the type reasonably relied upon by experts in the field, as discussed above. Therefore, if civil engineers ordinarily reasonably rely on such opinions in reports from structural engineers, the Federal Rules allow Cicero to base his opinion on opinions in Erecto's report. (D) is incorrect because the fact that the report and photographs were commissioned solely for the purpose of litigation and were not admitted into evidence is irrelevant when an expert is basing an opinion on facts reasonably relied upon by experts in that field. When determining whether a report comes under the business records exception to the hearsay rule, the courts sometimes look at whether the report was prepared for litigation in determining if it was a record maintained in conjunction with a business activity. [Palmer v. Hoffman (1943)] Here, whether Erecto's report is hearsay is not at issue because an expert may base his opinion on facts reasonably relied upon by experts in that particular field even if those facts are inadmissible hearsay.

Answer to Question 54

(A) Testimony as to the statement made by Victor is inadmissible as a statement under belief of impending death, because Victor did not actually have firsthand knowledge that David was responsible for the collision. The statement of Victor is hearsay, because it is a statement made by the declarant (Victor), other than while testifying, offered to prove the truth of the matter asserted therein. Here, the plaintiff wants to present this testimony to prove the truth of the statement that David was responsible for the brake failure, and will argue that the statement falls under the hearsay exception for dying declarations. In a civil case or a homicide prosecution, a statement made by a now unavailable declarant while believing his death to be imminent, that concerns the cause or circumstances of what he believed to be his impending death, is admissible. [Fed. R. Evid. 804(b)(2)] For this exception to apply, the declarant need not actually die. Rather, the declarant must be "unavailable" when the statement is offered. A declarant is unavailable if he: (i) is exempted from testifying on the ground of privilege; (ii) refuses to testify despite a court order; (iii) testifies to lack of memory of the subject matter of the statement; (iv) cannot be present or testify because of death or physical or mental illness; or (v) is beyond the reach of the court's subpoena and the statement's proponent has been unable to procure his attendance or testimony by process or other reasonable means. Regarding the statement at issue here, Victor certainly thought he was about to die from his injuries. In addition, Victor is unavailable, as his physical condition prevents him from testifying. However, Victor's statement represents a mere suspicion that David tampered with the brakes. As well-founded as such a suspicion may be (given the history between Victor and David), a statement based on mere suspicion rather than actual knowledge does not constitute a statement concerning the cause or circumstances of an "impending death" for purposes of the dying declarations exception. Thus, (A) is the correct answer and (C) is incorrect. (D) is incorrect for the reasons stated above and also because it incorrectly implies that the dying declarations hearsay exception applies only in civil cases. As noted above, the exception also applies to homicide cases. (Note that the traditional view, still followed by some states, would only allow the declaration in a homicide prosecution.) (B) is incorrect because the declarant's death is no longer required; unavailability is sufficient. Thus, if Victor's statement otherwise qualified under the dying declarations exception, the fact that Victor is not dead would not render Wanda's testimony inadmissible.

Answer to Question 55

(C) The statement of Felicia is admissible as a legally operative fact. Hearsay is a statement, other than one made by the declarant while testifying at trial or a hearing, offered in evidence to prove the truth of the matter asserted therein. Where an out-of-court statement is introduced for any purpose other than to prove the truth of the matter asserted, the statement is not hearsay. One type of out-of-court statement that is not hearsay is evidence of legally operative facts. These are utterances to which legal significance is attached, such as words of contract, bribery, or cancellation. Evidence of such statements is not hearsay because the issue is only whether the statement was made. Beatrice is defending the lawsuit on the basis that she received the necklace as a gift, and the statement by Felicia contains words that constitute an expression of donative intent, which is essential to a finding of a gift having been made. Thus, (C) is correct and (A) is incorrect. (D) is incorrect because unavailability of a declarant controls whether certain kinds of hearsay are admissible as exceptions to the hearsay rule. Because the statement here at issue is not hearsay, the declarant's unavailability is irrelevant. (B) is incorrect because, assuming a Dead Man Act is applicable, its protection has been waived. Dead Man Acts provide that a person interested in an event is incompetent to testify to a personal transaction or communication with a deceased, when such testimony is offered against the representative or successors in interest of the decedent. One who claims under a decedent may waive the protection of the statute by cross-examining the interested person about the transaction. In such a case, the interested person may explain all matters about which she is examined. Here, because Martha's attorney is questioning Beatrice about her dealings with Felicia, the statute's protection has been waived.

Answer to Question 56

(A) Drew's armed robbery conviction is least likely to be admitted. In a criminal case, evidence of the defendant's other crimes or misconduct is inadmissible if offered solely to establish criminal disposition. A broad exception to the general rule permits evidence of other crimes or misconduct to be admitted if such acts are relevant to some issue other than the character of the defendant to commit the crime charged. Such evidence may be used to show motive, opportunity, intent, preparation, plan, knowledge, identity, or absence of mistake. Here, (A) is least likely to be admitted because evidence of Drew's previous conviction for armed robbery does not come within any permissible use of evidence of other crimes or bad acts. Since Drew apparently is not contesting the issue of whether he possessed the semi-automatic weapon, it is irrelevant that the robbery conviction shows possession of such a weapon at some earlier time. The only use to which evidence of this conviction can be put is to show Drew's bad character and disposition to commit the crimes with which he is presently charged. (B) is likely to be admitted because testimony that Drew apparently tried to interest Thomas in buying a semi-automatic weapon tends to show that Drew had the intent to engage in selling the weapon. For the same reason, (C) is also likely to be admitted. Supplying guns to a paramilitary group is certainly evidence of involvement in a plan of firearms trafficking. (D) is likely to be admitted as evidence of intent or knowledge. Because Drew has denied knowing that the weapon was stolen, evidence of his prior convictions for receipt of stolen weapons can be introduced to show the likelihood that he knew the weapon was stolen in the present case, negating his claim of good faith.

Answer to Question 57

(D) Since Bunker had firsthand knowledge that the statement was made, his testimony will be admissible unless there is a specific rule excluding the evidence. Witnesses are generally presumed competent to testify until the contrary is demonstrated. While a witness may not testify to a matter unless evidence is introduced to support a finding that the witness has personal knowledge of the matter, this evidence may consist of the witness's own testimony. (A) is incorrect. Hearsay is a statement, other than one made by the declarant while testifying at the trial or hearing, offered in evidence to prove the truth of the matter asserted. In a defamation action, evidence of the statement alleged to be defamatory is not hearsay because the evidence is by definition not offered to prove the truth of the matter asserted. It is offered only to show that the actionable statement was made. (B) is incorrect. Since Bunker had firsthand knowledge of the event he can testify about the event, even though there might exist a recording that would be better proof of the event. The "best evidence rule" does not apply when the witness is testifying on the basis of firsthand knowledge. (C) is wrong. The opposing party is free to attack the weight of Bunker's testimony on self-interest grounds, but there is no requirement that the judge charge the jury on the self-interest of a party.

Answer to Question 58

(D) The judge should allow Bystander to remain silent if there is some reasonable possibility of self-incrimination. Preliminary facts to establish the existence of a privilege must be determined by the court outside of the presence of the jury. Under the Fifth Amendment, a witness cannot be compelled to testify against herself. The privilege against self-incrimination can be raised by a witness to refuse to answer a question whose answer might incriminate him. Thus, there needs to be only some *reasonable possibility* of self-incrimination. (A) is wrong because the judge does not have to be certain that the witness will incriminate herself before granting the privilege. (B) is wrong because it states the standard for the burden of proof (*i.e.*, burden of persuasion) for certain disputed issues in civil cases, such as whether scienter existed in fraud cases or actual malice existed in defamation cases. (C) is incorrect because it states the general measure of proof in civil cases, and is defined as requiring the fact finder to be persuaded by the proponent that the fact is more probably true than not true. The standard for determining the application of the privilege against self-incrimination is a lesser standard.

Answer to Question 59

(C) The judge should not require Walter to answer the question because evidence of the religious beliefs of a witness is not admissible to challenge credibility. Lack of religious belief is no longer a basis for excluding a witness. Not only are a person's religious convictions irrelevant in determining the competence of a witness, Federal Rule 610 provides that a witness's religious beliefs or opinions are not admissible to show that the witness's credibility is thereby impaired or enhanced. Thus, (C) is correct and (A) is incorrect. (B) is wrong. While it is true that Walter could have requested a different type of oath, Rule 610 prohibits this type of question because it would have shown his lack of religious beliefs. (D) is incorrect because, as discussed above, lack of religious belief is no longer a basis for disqualification; thus, this would not constitute an attack on the witness's competency.

Answer to Question 60

(B) Watson's testimony is inadmissible because it is not a permitted way to impeach a witness. A witness may be impeached by ***cross-examining*** him about specific criminal or immoral acts, but extrinsic evidence is not permitted. A specific act of misconduct offered to attack the witness's character for truthfulness can be elicited only on cross-examination of the witness. If the witness denies it, the cross-examiner cannot refute the answer by calling other witnesses or producing other evidence. Thus, Oscar could be asked on cross-examination about the hoax, but Watson cannot properly be called to testify about it. (A) is incorrect because there is no specific rule limiting cumulative impeachment. (C) is incorrect. A witness may also be impeached by introducing evidence that the witness was convicted of a crime involving dishonesty or false statements. However, the prior conviction must be shown by cross-examination of the witness or by introducing the record of the judgment. It is not proper to bring in another witness to testify about the conviction. (D) is wrong because even though a hoax would impair a witness's credibility, it cannot be shown through testimony of specific acts, as discussed above.

Answer to Question 61

(A) Wilma's testimony is admissible for purposes of impeachment only. There are many occasions in which out-of-court statements are admitted into evidence by means of hearsay exceptions. These statements are frequently admitted into evidence even though the person who made the statement does not testify at trial. The party against whom the statement has been admitted may wish to impeach the credibility of the declarant so that the jury will discount the statement. Under Federal Rule 806, if hearsay statements are admitted, the person who made the out-of-court statements can be impeached the same way any in-court witness could be impeached. (B) is wrong. Prior inconsistent statements are admissible for impeachment only, unless they were given under oath at a trial or other proceeding. If they were given under oath at a trial or other proceeding, they can be used both to impeach and as evidence to prove the facts contained in the statement. (C) is incorrect; prior inconsistent statements offered to impeach are not hearsay because they are not being offered for the truth of the matter asserted, only that the declarant made inconsistent statements about the matter. (D) is incorrect. Since Baker is a hearsay declarant, the statement is admissible to impeach even if he does not have an opportunity to comment on the statement.

Even if Baker were a live witness, the Federal Rules do not always require that he be given an opportunity to comment.

Answer to Question 62

(C) The least likely circumstance for admitting the tape recording into evidence is when the authentication was based in part on hearsay. Before secondary evidence of statements may be received into evidence, it must be authenticated by some evidence showing that it is what its proponent claims it to be. A voice, whether heard first-hand or through a device (such as a tape recording) may be identified by the opinion of anyone who has heard the voice at any time. However, the identification must be based on the first-hand knowledge of the listener. In (C), Smith's statement to Kerry that the person who was on the telephone was his daughter is hearsay, because it is being offered to prove its truth. Thus, Kerry's knowledge of the victim's voice is based on hearsay and not personal experience, and this would not be sufficient to authenticate the tape recording. (A) and (B) are wrong because whether Kerry had heard the victim in person or over the phone goes to the weight rather than the admissibility of the evidence. She can still authenticate that the recording contains the voice of the victim. (D) is wrong because if Kerry had heard the conversation recorded, even if only the victim's half, she could obviously authenticate it.

Answer to Question 63

(A) The court should sustain the objection because the records are evidence of specific bad acts. The Federal Rules permit a defendant to introduce evidence of a bad character trait of the alleged victim if it is relevant to the charge or the defense, but limit it to reputation and opinion evidence. Evidence of specific acts of the person in question as demonstrating that person's character is only permitted in a few instances, such as where character itself is one of the ultimate issues in the case. Here, such evidence would not be admitted. (A) is therefore correct and (D) is wrong. (B) is wrong because the facts do not have to be identical. If evidence of bad acts were admissible, the conduct would be relevant as long as it involved the same bad character trait as the one at issue. (C) is wrong; documentary evidence, even if fully authenticated and relevant, may be excluded if it violates a rule of competency, such as the rule for character evidence. Here, the objection should be sustained because the document is improper evidence of a specific bad act.

Answer to Question 64

(A) The court should sustain the objection because the records are hearsay not within any recognized exception. Hearsay is a statement, other than one made by the declarant while testifying, offered into evidence to prove the truth of the matter asserted. Here, the records are being offered to prove that Baker had used excessive force against other customers, to support Able's contention that Baker used excessive force against him. Since the statements are offered to prove the truth of the matter asserted, they are hearsay, and since there is no recognized exception that would allow the records to be admitted, they must be excluded. Therefore, (D) is incorrect. (B) is incorrect. The business records exception applies to records or writings made in the course of a regularly conducted business activity by one who was under a duty to do so. Here, because the informants with personal knowledge (*i.e.*, the complaining customers) were not under a business duty to convey the information, the business records exception does not apply to their statements. (C) does not agree with the facts. A statement against interest is a hearsay exception allowed when a declarant is unavailable. Here there is no showing of unavailability, and also the declarants are the complaining customers and they said nothing against their interests.

Answer to Question 65

(C)   Evidence of the judgment would be inadmissible hearsay. Hearsay is a statement, other than one made by the declarant while testifying, offered into evidence to prove the truth of the matter asserted. While the Federal Rules create an exception to the hearsay rule for judgments of felony convictions used in any subsequent criminal or civil actions, it is not applicable for judgments in civil actions. The general rule is that a civil judgment is inadmissible in a subsequent criminal trial due to the differing standards of proof. Since the prior judgment in the civil case would be offered to prove the truth of the matters determined in the judgment (that Baker had previously committed batteries), it would be inadmissible hearsay. (A) is incorrect because, even in a subsequent civil trial, the evidence would still be hearsay that is not within the exceptions of Federal Rule 803(23). The narrow statutory exceptions to the rule of inadmissibility do not apply to these facts. (B) is wrong. Evidence of a criminal defendant's dangerous propensities would be inadmissible character evidence. (D) is wrong; the evidence is relevant but it would be inadmissible as hearsay.

Answer to Question 66

(A)   Dr. Apple's affidavit constitutes hearsay. Hearsay is a statement, other than one made by the declarant while testifying, offered into evidence to prove the truth of the matter asserted. Here, the affidavit is an out-of-court declaration offered to prove the truth of the assertion that Paul suffered a back injury. Because none of the listed exceptions is applicable, the affidavit should be excluded. (B) is incorrect because stating a conclusion as to causation is not a prerequisite for admissibility. If the affidavit were otherwise admissible, the fact that it did not address the cause of the back injury would only go to the weight of the evidence, not its admissibility. (C) is incorrect because an affidavit does not constitute former testimony; the party against whom it is offered did not have an opportunity to develop the testimony by direct or cross-examination. (D) is incorrect because the exception to the hearsay rule for declarations of physical condition applies to the **declarant's** own bodily condition. Dr. Apple's declaration of someone else's bodily condition does not fall under this exception.

REAL PROPERTY QUESTIONS

Question 1

Vendor owned Straightacre and Flushacre, two properties located in a scenic but arid region, which he offered for sale. Sutter purchased Straightacre. Prior to making the purchase, Sutter hired Dowser, a highly qualified engineer, to conduct a survey of Straightacre. Dowser was instructed to pay particular attention to the availability of subsurface water, because Sutter made it clear that he eventually wished to build a retirement home on the property, which he expected to supply with water from a well drilled on the property. If the water supply was the least bit questionable, Sutter would seek to purchase another piece of property in the same general area. Dowser conducted a thorough survey of Straightacre and assured Sutter that the underground aquifer was adequate to supply Sutter's needs for his proposed retirement home. After receiving Dowser's report, Sutter went ahead with his purchase of Straightacre. However, Sutter put off his plans to retire the next year. Therefore, Sutter delayed building his planned retirement home.

About a year after Sutter bought Straightacre, Mr. and Mrs. Mill purchased Flushacre, an adjoining but much larger parcel than Straightacre. They built a large house on Flushacre, as well as a swimming pool, and they and their four children took up residence there. Mrs. Mill was fond of beautiful flowers and natural food, so she set out a large garden area on the property, one-quarter of which was dedicated to decorative flowers, and three-quarters of which was devoted to vegetables, most of which were consumed by the Mill family. The house, the pool, and the garden were all supplied with water from a well the Mills had drilled on Flushacre. After becoming firmly established on Flushacre, they built two small houses on the property and rented them out to tenants, giving each tenant a one-year lease. The tenants' needs for water were supplied from the Mills' well.

Two years later, Sutter finally constructed his retirement home and drilled a well on Straightacre.

Sutter moved into the home during the winter and found the supply of water for his personal needs to be adequate. However, during the ensuing summer, when Mr. Mill filled the pool and Mrs. Mill irrigated her garden, the pressure dropped in Sutter's well, and many days only a trickle of water came out of Sutter's pipes. Sutter again called on Dowser. Dowser told Sutter that there would be plenty of water if the Mills were not "overusing" the common aquifer by providing water for the pool, the garden, and the rental houses, because a single family's normal usage of water from a well on Flushacre would not significantly affect Sutter's water supply of Straightacre.

In a jurisdiction applying the "reasonable use" doctrine in determining rights to underground water, which of the following is a suit that Sutter is likely to win?

(A) A suit against the Mills for monetary damages.

(B) A suit against the Mills for injunctive relief.

(C) A suit against Vendor for rescission.

(D) None of the above.

Question 2

Which of the following statements is most correct?

An easement appurtenant will be extinguished:

(A) If the owner of the dominant tenement attempts to convey the easement to a third party without conveyance of the dominant tenement itself.

(B) If the owner of the easement does not use the easement at all for a period of time exceeding the jurisdiction's statutory prescription period.

(C) By conveyance of the easement to the owner of the servient tenement.

(D) Only with the owner of the dominant tenement's express permission.

Question 3

Guy Verdant owned and lived on Greenacre. He worked for many years as an employee of Chem Corp., a company not noted for its concern for public health or the environment. After years of trying to justify his job to his ecology-minded friends, Guy decided to quit and open an environmentally correct business of his own. He discussed the matter with his friend, Cleveland Furban, a wealthy backer of environmental causes. Furban assured Guy that the era of the gas-guzzling automobile was over and that soon people would opt for more natural methods of transport. Guy considered the possibilities and then opened a business specializing in the sale of designer horseshoes and buggy whips. After using up most of his capital to purchase inventory, however, Guy was disappointed at the lack of public response. After six months in business, his gross receipts were insufficient to cover even the rent and utilities, and his tax and insurance bills were soon coming due. He told Furban of his difficulties, and Furban encouraged Guy to stick with the business for a while longer because soon people would "see the light." Convinced to give it another shot, Guy asked Furban for a $30,000 loan, to be secured by the business's inventory. Despite Furban's enthusiasm for equine transport, he declined the loan. A desperate Guy then told Furban he would convey Greenacre, which had a fair market value of $100,000, to Furban if Furban would give him the loan at the current market rate of interest. Furban agreed, and Guy conveyed Greenacre to Furban the next day. At that time, Furban gave Guy $30,000 in cash, and the parties orally agreed that Guy would pay Furban back at the rate of $1,000 per month, and that after the loan was paid in full, Furban would reconvey Greenacre to Guy. Furban immediately recorded his deed to Greenacre.

Three days after this transaction, the newspapers announced the discovery of an immense off-shore deposit, which the paper asserted would provide "cheap gasoline for the U.S.A.

for many years to come." What little business interest Guy had managed to generate dried up completely. Guy made three $1,000 payments to Furban and then paid no more. He continued to live on Greenacre, but being very much in debt, he told Furban he could not repay the loan. Furban, meanwhile, had received an offer to buy Greenacre for $100,000. Furban told Guy that he plans to sell the property within the month.

Which of the following most accurately states Furban's right to sell the property?

(A) Furban may sell Greenacre and keep the entire proceeds.

(B) Furban may sell Greenacre, but he must give $73,000 of the proceeds to Guy.

(C) Furban may sell Greenacre only after formally foreclosing on the property.

(D) Furban may not sell Greenacre.

Question 4

Otis conveys Staracre to the City of Spacely. The deed contains the following language: "I, Otis, hereby grant Staracre to the City of Spacely for the purpose of constructing a planetarium thereon." The city holds the property for a number of years, but decides on another site for the planetarium. When presented an offer to purchase the property by the Astronomers Guild, a private organization, the city accepted and conveyed Staracre to the Guild.

Which of the following statements about the title of Staracre is true?

I. Otis's conveyance to the city created a fee simple determinable in the city and a possibility of reverter in Otis.

II. Upon conveyance of Staracre to the Guild, the property reverted back to Otis.

III. The Guild owns Staracre, but it will revert to Otis or his successors in interest if the property is used for anything other than a planetarium.

IV. The Guild owns Staracre in fee simple absolute.

(A) I. and II. only.

(B) I. and III. only.

(C) IV. only.

(D) I. and IV. only.

Question 5

Baron and Earl had been in the real estate business in Buxton for many years. Although they were, in a sense, competitors, they made so many deals with each other over the years that a strong bond of mutual trust had developed between them. Although both realtors acted as agents for buyers and sellers of real property, they also each purchased properties for themselves for investment or speculative purposes. Because of their long-standing relationship, Baron and Earl, neither of whom was an attorney, often dispensed with certain legal formalities when dealing with each other, thus saving the costs of lawyers' fees and other attendant expenses. Earl owned a parcel of land known as Grayacre. Baron was interested in Grayacre and offered to buy it from Earl for $50,000. Baron had reason to believe that a new commercial-entertainment complex might be built near Grayacre, and that the property stood a chance to increase quickly in value. Earl thought that $50,000 was a good price for the undeveloped Grayacre and readily agreed to sell it to Baron at that price, which was significantly more than Earl had paid for the property three years before. Earl and Baron agreed on June 15 as the closing date. Baron handed Earl a check for $2,500 and said, "Here's your earnest money. I'll see you on June 15." Earl responded, "You betcha," and the men shook hands on their deal. On the memo part of the check, Baron had written "Earnest money—Grayacre."

On May 28, Baron learned that his "inside information" on the location of the complex was wrong and that the complex, if it was ever built, would be located on the north side of Buxton, rather than the west side, where Grayacre was located. Earl was out of town for the Memorial Day holiday, but when he returned on June 1, Earl found a number of messages to call Baron as soon as possible. Earl called Baron, and Baron told him, "I've changed my mind about buying Grayacre." To which Earl replied, "The heck you have. We've got a deal, and the closing is on June 15, in case you've forgotten." Earl appeared at Baron's office on June 15 with the deed to Grayacre in his hand. Baron refuses to tender the balance due, and Earl sues Baron for specific performance.

Will Earl prevail?

(A) No, because the agreement does not comply with the Statute of Frauds and is, therefore, unenforceable.

(B) No, but the court will allow Earl to keep the $2,500 earnest money as damages.

(C) No, because Baron's purpose for purchasing Grayacre was frustrated by the relocation of the entertainment complex site.

(D) Yes, because Baron and Earl had established a course of dealing.

Question 6

Professor Flunkum teaches a course to prepare aspiring real estate brokers for the state licensing exam. The jurisdiction has a standard race-notice recording statute and maintains the common law Rule Against Perpetuities without any modern statutory reformation. In his lecture on marketable title, Flunkum gives his students the following examples of when a seller of real estate cannot convey marketable title to the buyer:

I. The seller has a long-term lessee in possession of the land. There are 25 years left on the lease and the lease gives the lessee (and his heirs and assigns) an option to buy. The buyer is aware of the lease and has agreed to take title subject to it, but the buyer is not aware of the option.

II. The seller's land contains a large office building. The noses of two stone decorative gargoyles on the side of the building extend approximately one-half inch across the property line into the airspace of the adjoining property owner. The noses do not interfere with any current or future use of the adjoining lot.

III. The seller's home is subject to a $5,000 lien arising from a dispute involving some remodeling work. The seller says he will pay off the lien at closing with the proceeds from the $25,000 sale.

Courts would be likely to agree with Flunkum as to:

(A) I. only.

(B) II. only.

(C) I., II., and III.

(D) Neither I., II., nor III.

Question 7

Ann Tenna inherited a 30-acre tract of farmland from her parents. Tenna had no interest in farming and was pleased to learn that the property was rising rapidly in value because of the suburban development radiating outward from nearby Metro City. Tenna entered into a partnership with Bildem, a reputable local contractor, to develop the land. As required by law, Tenna and Bildem filed a plat with the County Planning Board, but did not record it. The plat divided the parcel into 87 residential lots of one-third acre each. A strip on the eastern edge of the parcel, totaling one acre in area and labeled parcel A, was set aside for commercial development, because it abutted a busy highway and was, therefore, less desirable for residential use. All of this complied with the rather loose county zoning and use restrictions. The plat carefully described the residential lots and numbered them 1 through 87. In addition, it listed various restrictions on use of the lots. Each lot was limited to a single residence set back a minimum

distance from the sidewalk. In addition, all "nonconforming detracting structures or appurtenances" were banned. Among the specific items listed under this category were "free-standing flagpoles more than six feet in height, television antennas and receiving equipment of excessive size and obtrusiveness, and windmills."

The restrictive clause was put into the deeds of all the residential lots in the subdivision, except for the deeds to lots 23, 24, and 25. This oversight was due to an error by a secretary in Bildem's offices. All the other lots had deeds stating that the restriction applied "to grantee and his or her heirs and assigns."

Alice purchased Lot Number 24, and duly recorded the deed in the office of the County Recorder of Deeds. Bildem's salesperson had orally informed Alice of the general restrictions applicable to lots in the subdivision. A year after Alice took possession of her residence on Lot Number 24, Champions Sports Bar opened on parcel A, the commercial strip at the eastern end of the original parcel. Champions installed a large satellite dish to obtain the maximum number of games for its patrons. Two years later, Alice's employer transferred her to another city. She sold the property to Fan. Alice never mentioned any of the restrictions to Fan. Fan loved all sports but, as a recovering alcoholic, he felt uncomfortable watching the games in a bar. He, therefore, put a satellite dish on top of his house to receive transmissions of the games. His dish was not as large as Champions's dish, but it was obviously bigger than any of his neighbors' modest antennas. The owners of 15 lots in the subdivision sued Fan, demanding that he remove the dish.

If the court finds for Fan, it will probably be because:

(A) Fan is not charged with record notice based on other deeds given by a common grantor.

(B) Fan's predecessor in interest, Alice, was not bound by the oral restriction told to her by Bildem's salesperson.

(C) The property owners suing Fan all purchased their lots prior to Alice's purchase
of Lot Number 24.

(D) The existence of a satellite dish on the
eastern end of the original parcel indicates
that neighborhood conditions have changed
to the point where it would be inequitable
to enforce the restrictions.

Question 8

A statute of the state of Zonarado states, in
relevant part:

> Any judgment against a person prop-
> erly filed in a county of Zonarado
> shall attach to all real property located
> in that county that is owned by that
> person or acquired by that person
> within 10 years following the filing of
> the judgment.

Mavis was involved in an automobile accident
with Pete. Pete received personal injuries and
filed suit in Jackson County Court in Zonarado
against Mavis. Pete was awarded a judgment in
the amount of $115,000. The limit of Mavis's
liability insurance was $100,000. Her insurance
carrier paid Pete the $100,000, which left a
$15,000 outstanding judgment, which Mavis
was unable to pay. Pete's attorney properly filed
the judgment with the Jackson County
Recorder's office.

Mavis owned an undeveloped Jackson County
lot in co-tenancy with her cousin, Charmaine,
each cousin holding an undivided one-half
interest. The cousins put the property up for sale
and conveyed it to Roy via quitclaim deed for
$20,000. Roy gave Mavis $10,000 and he gave
Charmaine $10,000. Mavis promptly applied her
$10,000 toward payment of the unsatisfied
judgment. Pete's attorney then brought an
appropriate action against Charmaine, demanding $5,000 from her share of the proceeds of the
sale of the Zonarado lot to satisfy the judgment
against Mavis.

Will Pete's attorney prevail?

(A) Yes, if Mavis and Charmaine held the lot as
joint tenants, but not if they were tenants in
common.

(B) Yes, if Mavis and Charmaine held the lot as
tenants in common, but not if they held it
in joint tenancy.

(C) No, because Pete's remedies are limited to
a personal action against Mavis and the
$5,000 lien on Roy's property.

(D) No, because Pete's sole remedy is against
Mavis.

Question 9

Paulina was injured in a car accident when
Dennis, the driver of the other car, ran a red
light. Paulina subsequently sued Dennis to
recover for her injuries, and obtained a money
judgment of $50,000. The state where Paulina
and Dennis reside has the following statute:

> Any judgment properly filed shall, for
> 10 years from filing, be a lien on the
> real property then owned or subse-
> quently acquired by any person
> against whom the judgment is ren-
> dered.

Paulina filed the judgment in Colfax County
where Dennis owned Ranchacre, a valuable
ranch consisting of several hundred acres.
Sometime later, Dennis, who was also injured in
the accident, undertook to remodel all the
buildings on the ranch to make them wheelchair
accessible. Dennis borrowed $30,000 from Atlas
Bank for the improvements, securing the loan
with a mortgage on Ranchacre. Atlas properly
recorded its mortgage. Before he paid any
principal on the Atlas loan, Dennis decided to
build a new barn. He borrowed $20,000 from
Big Bank for this purpose, also secured by a
mortgage on Ranchacre. Big Bank properly
recorded its mortgage. Dennis subsequently
defaulted on the Atlas mortgage, and Atlas
brought a foreclosure action, joining Big Bank
in the proceeding. The foreclosure sale resulted
in $90,000 in proceeds after all expenses and

fees were paid. Dennis still owes Paulina $50,000, Atlas Bank $30,000, and Big Bank $20,000.

Which of the following statements are true?

I. Paulina is entitled to $50,000 of the foreclosure proceeds, Atlas is entitled to $30,000 of the proceeds, and Big Bank is entitled to the remaining $10,000 in proceeds.

II. Big Bank is entitled to $10,000 of the proceeds, has a cause of action against Dennis for the deficiency, and its interest in Ranchacre is destroyed by the foreclosure.

III. Atlas is entitled to $30,000, Big Bank is entitled to $20,000, and Dennis is entitled to $40,000.

IV. The buyer at the foreclosure sale will take Ranchacre free of all liens and mortgages.

(A) I. and II. only.

(B) II. only.

(C) III. only.

(D) II. and IV. only.

Question 10

Orizaba, who lived in Eastmark County, owned Greatacre, a valuable undeveloped parcel of land in Westmark County. Orizaba had become wealthy running a successful construction business after emigrating to the United States from Guatemala. Over the years Orizaba had received much assistance from his best friend Gustav, who had emigrated to America from Sweden as a young man. Although Gustav had no children of his own, he doted on his nieces, Sigmar and Ingrid. After Gustav's death from a sudden heart attack, Orizaba decided the best way to honor his friend would be to do something for the people Gustav loved. Without telling anyone else, Orizaba instructed his lawyer, Lynette, to draw up an instrument

deeding Greatacre "to Gustav's nieces." Lynette brought the instrument to Orizaba. He acknowledged the deed and signed it. As directed by Orizaba, Lynette recorded the deed at the office of the Westmark County Recorder. Lynette then returned the deed to Orizaba. Orizaba put the deed in the drawer of his favorite rolltop desk, intending to present it to Gustav's nieces upon their return from visiting relatives in Sweden.

Before the nieces returned from Sweden, Orizaba became gravely ill and lapsed into a coma. He died two weeks after the women returned from Sweden. He had never regained consciousness. He left his daughter Juanita as his sole heir at law. Juanita was named executor of Orizaba's estate, and she discovered the deed to Greatacre in Orizaba's drawer. Juanita filed an appropriate action to quiet title in Greatacre, naming Sigmar and Ingrid as defendants. The only evidence presented at the trial was the deed itself, the evidence of recordation, and Lynette's testimony regarding Orizaba's intent.

The court should rule that Greatacre is owned by:

(A) Sigmar and Ingrid, because recordation is prima facie evidence of delivery.

(B) Sigmar and Ingrid, because a deed is prima facie valid absent evidence to the contrary.

(C) Juanita, because the evidence is insufficient to support a valid delivery.

(D) Juanita, because the grantees in the deed are too indefinite.

Question 11

Persia owned a strip mall and the buildings thereon, located in the suburban community of Calvista. Persia gave Toy a written lease to one of the stores. The lease was for a five-year period, with a monthly rent of $1,000, payable on or before the first day of each month. Toy opened "The Scent Center," a discount retail perfumery, in the store, and dutifully paid her rent on time for two years and three months. At that time, Toy got another business opportunity and, with the oral permission of Persia, transferred her interest in the remainder of the lease to Ayes in writing, and added a clause requiring Ayes to get permission from Toy for any subsequent assignments. Ayes promptly paid the $1,000 monthly rent to Persia for 14 months. Ayes was then approached by Dominique, who thought the store would be an ideal location for a video rental business. An economic downturn had been having a negative effect on Ayes's business, so Ayes asked Persia to approve a transfer of Ayes's interest in the lease to Dominique. Persia gave her oral assent. Ayes made no representations to Persia about Dominique's reliability or responsibility, but Toy was very concerned about it. To obtain Toy's approval of the transfer to Dominique, Ayes wrote a letter to Toy. The letter stated in relevant part: "I hope you'll approve the transfer of my interest in the store lease to Dominique. I consider you a good friend and I want you to know that if any problems arise and anyone tries to go after you for money, I'll make it good to you. However, I doubt it will be a problem because Dominique seems like a bright and responsible businesswoman." Ayes knew nothing substantial about the laws of the jurisdiction and did not consult with an attorney before sending the letter to Toy.

After Toy sent a letter back to Ayes agreeing to the transfer, Toy executed a written transfer of her interest to Dominique. Dominique promptly paid her $1,000 monthly rent for three months. Unfortunately, two weeks after she opened the video rental store, Bigfilm, a national video rental chain, opened up a large store right across the street from Dominique's location. The bulk of Dominique's clientele went to Bigfilm to rent movies. One night, Dominique drove a semi-trailer up to the store, removed her inventory, and disappeared. She ceased paying any rent to Persia and cannot be located. Persia has been unable to find anyone interested in the store because of the general economic distress in the area.

Given that any judgment against Dominique would be worthless, Persia can collect the unpaid rent owed on the lease from:

(A) Either Toy or Ayes.

(B) Toy only, but Toy may recover in turn from Ayes.

(C) Toy only, and Toy has no recourse against Ayes.

(D) Neither Toy nor Ayes.

Question 12

Thomas included the following provision in his will: "I hereby devise and bequeath all of my property, both real and personal, wherever situated, to my widow for life, and after her death to any of our children who may survive her."

The gift to the children is:

(A) A contingent remainder.

(B) A vested remainder.

(C) A shifting executory interest.

(D) Void, as violating the Rule Against Perpetuities.

Question 13

Longley leased residential property to Tamara. The written lease was for a period of one year, with the monthly rent of $1,000 payable on or before the first of each month. The termination date set out in the lease was October 1. On August 10 of the first year of her tenancy, Tamara received a letter from Longley along with a new lease form. The lease was for a period to terminate on October 1 of the following year, and the rent stated in the new lease was $1,200 per month. Both the rent increase and the notice given were in full compliance with relevant state statutes. An accompanying letter, signed by Longley, asked Tamara to sign the lease on the line marked "tenant." The letter also stated that the rent increase was due to increased taxes and utility rates. On September 15, Tamara sent the lease back to Longley unsigned. On

September 20, Tamara sent a letter to Longley by certified mail. Longley signed the "return receipt," which the post office duly sent to Tamara. Tamara's letter stated: "Twelve hundred bucks is way too much for this place. You'll find enclosed a check for $1,000 to cover next month's rent." Longley removed the check and deposited it into her bank account. With Longley's acquiescence, Tamara remained in possession after October 1.

Which of the following statements is most accurate?

(A) Tamara has a month-to-month tenancy at $1,000 monthly rent.

(B) Tamara has a month-to-month tenancy at $1,200 monthly rent.

(C) Tamara has an annual tenancy at $1,200 per month rent.

(D) Tamara has a tenancy at will.

Question 14

Michael, owner in fee simple absolute of Oyster House, a restaurant and inn on the Atlantic coastline of the United States, provided in his will that the property should go upon his death "in fee simple to my good friend George, but if during George's lifetime my son Jake has children and those children are alive when George dies, then to said living children."

When Michael dies, George takes over Oyster House. If Jake has children and one or more of them are alive when George dies, who will take title to Oyster House at that time?

(A) George's heirs, because the attempted gift to Jake's children is invalid under the Rule Against Perpetuities.

(B) Jake's children, because their interest is not contingent, being a possibility of reverter.

(C) Jake's children, because their interest is vested, subject to defeasance.

(D) Jake's children, because their interest will vest, if at all, within a life in being plus 21 years.

Question 15

Vittorio entered into a written contract with Piemonte on April 4, whereby Vittorio agreed to convey Tuscanacre to Piemonte for $100,000. The terms of the contract set the closing date as June 1. At the time Vittorio entered into the agreement with Piemonte, Vittorio had no interest in Tuscanacre. On April 15, Vittorio entered into a written agreement with Savoy, whom Vittorio believed to be the owner of Tuscanacre. According to the terms of the agreement, Savoy was to convey Tuscanacre to Vittorio on or before May 25. Another term of the agreement stated "time is of the essence." On May 24, Savoy conveyed his interest in Tuscanacre to Vittorio. When Vittorio went to record the deed, he discovered from records in the recorder's office that Savoy held clear title to only seven-eighths of Tuscanacre. It took some time for Vittorio to remove the cloud from the title and procure ownership in full of Tuscanacre. He finally did so on June 14, and on that day he tendered a warranty deed to Tuscanacre to Piemonte. Piemonte refused to tender $100,000 or any other sum to Vittorio, asserting that Vittorio had broken his agreement by failing to close on June 1. Vittorio then sued Piemonte for specific performance. At trial, Vittorio's attorney made the following statements:

I. Time was not of the essence in the Piemonte-Vittorio contract.

II. It is not necessary to hold title at the time a land sale contract is made.

III. Vittorio did not unreasonably delay the closing.

Which of the above statements must the court find to be true in order for Vittorio to prevail?

(A) I. only.

(B) II. only.

(C) I. and II. only.

(D) I., II., and III.

REAL PROPERTY ADVANCED DRILLS
ANSWER SHEET

1. Ⓐ Ⓑ Ⓒ Ⓓ	23. Ⓐ Ⓑ Ⓒ Ⓓ	45. Ⓐ Ⓑ Ⓒ Ⓓ
2. Ⓐ Ⓑ ● Ⓓ	24. Ⓐ Ⓑ Ⓒ Ⓓ	46. Ⓐ Ⓑ Ⓒ Ⓓ
3. Ⓐ Ⓑ Ⓒ Ⓓ	25. Ⓐ Ⓑ Ⓒ Ⓓ	47. Ⓐ Ⓑ Ⓒ Ⓓ
4. Ⓐ Ⓑ ● Ⓓ	26. Ⓐ ● Ⓒ Ⓓ	48. Ⓐ Ⓑ Ⓒ Ⓓ
5. Ⓐ Ⓑ Ⓒ Ⓓ	27. Ⓐ Ⓑ Ⓒ Ⓓ	49. Ⓐ Ⓑ Ⓒ Ⓓ
6. Ⓐ Ⓑ Ⓒ Ⓓ	28. Ⓐ Ⓑ Ⓒ Ⓓ	50. Ⓐ Ⓑ Ⓒ Ⓓ
7. Ⓐ Ⓑ Ⓒ Ⓓ	29. Ⓐ Ⓑ Ⓒ Ⓓ	51. Ⓐ Ⓑ Ⓒ Ⓓ
8. Ⓐ Ⓑ Ⓒ Ⓓ	30. Ⓐ Ⓑ Ⓒ Ⓓ	52. Ⓐ Ⓑ Ⓒ Ⓓ
9. Ⓐ Ⓑ Ⓒ Ⓓ	31. Ⓐ Ⓑ Ⓒ Ⓓ	53. Ⓐ Ⓑ Ⓒ Ⓓ
10. Ⓐ Ⓑ Ⓒ Ⓓ	32. Ⓐ Ⓑ Ⓒ Ⓓ	54. Ⓐ Ⓑ Ⓒ Ⓓ
11. Ⓐ Ⓑ Ⓒ Ⓓ	33. Ⓐ Ⓑ ● Ⓓ	55. Ⓐ Ⓑ Ⓒ Ⓓ
12. Ⓐ Ⓑ Ⓒ Ⓓ	34. Ⓐ Ⓑ Ⓒ ●	56. Ⓐ Ⓑ Ⓒ Ⓓ
13. Ⓐ Ⓑ Ⓒ Ⓓ	35. Ⓐ Ⓑ Ⓒ Ⓓ	57. Ⓐ Ⓑ Ⓒ Ⓓ
14. Ⓐ Ⓑ ● Ⓓ	36. Ⓐ Ⓑ Ⓒ Ⓓ	58. Ⓐ Ⓑ Ⓒ Ⓓ
15. Ⓐ Ⓑ Ⓒ Ⓓ	37. Ⓐ Ⓑ Ⓒ Ⓓ	59. Ⓐ ● Ⓒ Ⓓ
16. Ⓐ Ⓑ Ⓒ Ⓓ	38. Ⓐ Ⓑ Ⓒ Ⓓ	60. Ⓐ Ⓑ Ⓒ Ⓓ
17. Ⓐ Ⓑ Ⓒ Ⓓ	39. Ⓐ Ⓑ Ⓒ Ⓓ	61. Ⓐ Ⓑ Ⓒ Ⓓ
18. Ⓐ Ⓑ Ⓒ Ⓓ	40. Ⓐ Ⓑ Ⓒ Ⓓ	62. Ⓐ Ⓑ Ⓒ Ⓓ
19. Ⓐ Ⓑ Ⓒ Ⓓ	41. Ⓐ Ⓑ Ⓒ Ⓓ	63. Ⓐ Ⓑ Ⓒ Ⓓ
20. Ⓐ Ⓑ Ⓒ Ⓓ	42. Ⓐ Ⓑ Ⓒ Ⓓ	64. Ⓐ Ⓑ Ⓒ Ⓓ
21. Ⓐ Ⓑ Ⓒ Ⓓ	43. Ⓐ Ⓑ Ⓒ Ⓓ	65. Ⓐ Ⓑ Ⓒ Ⓓ
22. Ⓐ Ⓑ Ⓒ Ⓓ	44. Ⓐ Ⓑ Ⓒ Ⓓ	66. ● Ⓑ Ⓒ Ⓓ

Question 16

Olson, a newspaper reporter in a large city, was laid off indefinitely from his job. Seeing no other way out, he decided to sell Pine Knoll, a summer home that had been in his family for generations, to his former boss, White. Not wanting to lose control of the family property forever, Olson inserted a provision in the deed to White binding "White, his heirs, and assigns" to offer "Olson, his heirs, and assigns" the right of first refusal to purchase Pine Knoll when it was offered for sale. White was not happy with the provision, but Olson refused to sell the property without the covenant included. White reluctantly agreed. Pine Knoll was conveyed to White, and the deed containing the right of first refusal was duly recorded.

White lived on Pine Knoll for 25 years. When he learned that Olson, for whom he had an intense dislike, had become a successful author with several bestsellers, White decided to develop a strategem to get around the covenant. When informed that Lane was interested in buying the property, White decided to execute his plan. White's friend Kent agreed to act as a "straw man" to avoid the consequences of the covenant. White deeded Pine Knoll as a "gift" to Kent. Kent recorded the deed, which did not contain the right of first refusal covenant, and Kent then sold the land to Lane for $150,000, giving the proceeds of the sale to White. Lane knew nothing about the right of first refusal because she inspected only Kent's deed from White. When Olson learned of what had happened, he filed suit to compel conveyance of the land to him. To back up his words, Olson produced a $150,000 letter of credit. The jurisdiction in which the property is located has an unmodified common law Rule Against Perpetuities and the following recording statute:

> Any conveyance of an interest in land, other than a lease for less than one year, is not valid against any subsequent purchaser for value and without notice, whose conveyance is first recorded.

How will the court most likely rule in this case?

(A) Olson will prevail, because the deed with the covenant granting the right of first refusal was in Lane's chain of title.

(B) Olson will prevail, because White and Kent acted in bad faith.

(C) Olson will not prevail, because the covenant is not enforceable.

(D) Olson will not prevail, because the covenant, although enforceable against White personally, does not run with the land.

Questions 17-18 are based on the following fact situation:

Cassandra owned a fine apartment building in Beach City. Because a number of the apartments had a beautiful view of the ocean over the neighboring vacant lot, highway, and beach, Cassandra could charge premium rents. The vacant lot was owned by Lena, who assured Cassandra that she had no plans to develop it, because she held a number of pieces of property as investments that she planned to pass on to her children. Lena was only 52 years old and in good health, so Cassandra assumed there would be no problem for many years. However, Lena was killed in an automobile accident, and her will left the lot to Apollo, who wanted to make a quick profit. Over Cassandra's objections, Apollo began building an office structure that would abut the highway. Cassandra's building was only three stories tall and the office structure, at 10 stories, would dwarf it. Once the construction began, the contractor's workers continually swung large girders suspended from a crane over Cassandra's building. Cassandra complained incessantly because the tenants complained to her that the girders frightened them, but Apollo did nothing about it. Even when the building was only partially completed it put Cassandra's building in shadows for the greater part of the afternoon. Her apartments not only no longer had an ocean view, but were dark and devoid of sunlight. Cassandra slashed her rents by 40%, but still had difficulty keeping the building fully occupied.

17. If Cassandra brings a suit seeking all available relief, a court will most likely find that she has:

    (A) A cause of action for damages or an injunction against Apollo because the girders repeatedly pass over her air space.

    (B) A cause of action for damages against Apollo because of the loss of the ocean view.

    (C) A cause of action for damages or an injunction against Apollo because of the loss of sunlight.

    (D) No cause of action.

18. Assume for purposes of this question only that two months after Apollo's building was completed, Cassandra noticed that cracks were beginning to appear in the basement and along some of the walls of her apartment building. A city engineer inspected the premises and told Cassandra that the land under her building was subsiding. Cassandra consulted a contractor who told her it would cost $50,000 to repair the damage and that the damage would not have occurred but for Apollo's construction of a large building on the adjacent site. To collect damages for this damage to her property from Apollo, Cassandra must prove that Apollo's project caused the damage and that:

    I.   Apollo was negligent.

    II. Apollo's project would have damaged Cassandra's property even if her property was unimproved.

    III. The damage was intentional.

    (A) I. *or* II.

    (B) III. only.

    (C) I. *and* II.

    (D) None of the above; proof of causation alone is sufficient.

Question 19

Curtiss put his house and lot on the market for $200,000. The house was located in a splendid part of town where property values were rising rapidly. Curtiss received several offers within $5,000 of his asking price, but he rejected them all because he believed the house was worth more than his asking price. After telling all of her clients not to bother making a low bid, Rhonda the Realtor brought Curtiss a $200,000 bid from Wright. Curtiss readily accepted, and both parties signed a real estate contract drawn up by Curtiss's lawyer. The contract provided that Wright put up $4,000 in earnest money, which the seller could treat as liquidated damages "unless Curtiss fails to tender marketable title to the Buyer by the agreed-upon closing date, Curtiss commits a material breach of this contract, or Wright dies prior to the closing date, in which case the earnest money shall be reimbursed to Wright's estate." The contract was signed on July 24, and the closing date was set for September 12.

On August 5, Wright was seriously injured in a skydiving accident. Although the doctors told Wright that he would eventually be able to walk with a cane, he would have to use a wheelchair for quite some time. Even after his rehabilitation was complete, the doctors predicted that it would be difficult for Wright to negotiate stairs without pain and time-consuming methods. Curtiss's house was a two-story home, with stairways leading to both the bedrooms on the second floor and the basement. Wright determined that a ranch-style house would make his life much more bearable. On September 10, Wright was released from the hospital in a wheelchair. Wright told Curtiss that he has decided not to proceed with the purchase because his physical problems would be compounded if he tried to live in Curtiss's house. He asked Curtiss to cancel the contract and to refund the $4,000 earnest money. Curtiss refused. Wright did not appear on the closing date. On September 16, Curtiss contracted to sell the home to Martin for $198,000. The closing occurred as planned on October 20. Wright files suit against Curtiss, praying for a refund of the $4,000 earnest money.

Wright is likely to recover:

(A) The entire $4,000, because Wright had a justified medical reason for his failure to perform.

(B) $2,000, because the diminution in value of the property was only $2,000.

(C) $2,000 less any of Curtiss's out-of-pocket costs involved in remarketing the home.

(D) Nothing, because at the time the contract was entered into, $4,000 represented a reasonable estimate of damages in the event of breach.

Question 20

In the late 1930s, Orson, a well-known vintner, divided his massive vineyard into two parcels, Grapeacre and Vineacre. The vineyard had been irrigated with the water from a single well. When he subdivided the property he purposely drew the boundaries so that the well fell on the border of the two properties. Orson then conveyed Grapeacre to Masson by a deed that contained the following covenant: "If the well located on the boundary of Grapeacre and Vineacre continues to be used for irrigation purposes and becomes in need of repair or replacement, the grantee, his heirs, and assigns and the grantor, his heirs, and assigns each promise to pay one-half of the cost of such repair or replacement. This covenant shall run with the land." The deed from Orson to Masson was not recorded, and Orson did not record a copy with the records for Vineacre. Masson later sold Grapeacre to Sutter. Sutter's deed did not contain the covenant about the well. After many years of use by the owners of both Grapeacre and Vineacre, the well began to fail. Sutter took it upon himself to have the well repaired. He accepted the lowest bid on the job, which was $30,000. About two weeks later, he was rummaging through the

files at his winery and discovered the deed from Orson to Masson. By this time, Vineacre had passed to Orson's son Ernest by inheritance and again to Ernest's son Julio by inheritance from the now deceased Ernest. Julio knew nothing of the covenant concerning the well. Sutter presented Julio with the bill for the well repair with a copy of the Orson/Masson deed and a note that said he expected to be reimbursed for $15,000. Julio refuses to pay, and Sutter sues. The jurisdiction has a 10-year statute of limitations for acquiring property by adverse possession, and the following recording statute:

Any conveyance of interest in land shall not be valid against any subsequent purchaser for value, without notice thereof, unless the conveyance is recorded.

The court is most likely to rule in favor of:

(A) Julio, because the deed from Orson to Masson was never recorded.

(B) Julio, because Sutter has acquired the well by adverse possession.

(C) Sutter, because the covenant runs with the land.

(D) Sutter, because he is a bona fide purchaser.

Question 21

Lee owned a small commercial structure on Main Street, which he rented to Tan to use as an art studio. Under the terms of the signed, written, two-year lease, Tan agreed to pay Lee $1,000 per month and to assume responsibility for all necessary repairs. After the first year of the lease, Tan received a commission for a mural in Paris, and assigned the balance of his lease to Tracy, a sculptor. Lee had approved Tracy as a tenant and had accepted two rent payments from her, when he sold the building to Lucinda. Tracy had made two payments to Lucinda when an electrical fire broke out in the studio. Tracy suffered burns and smoke inhalation that required a lengthy and painful hospital stay. Fire investigators determined that the fire was caused by faulty wiring. Lee was aware that there was a dangerous wiring problem when he leased the property to Tan. Before selling the property to Lucinda, he had sought bids for the repair work. When he discovered how costly it would be, he decided it would be more profitable to sell the property than to repair it. The problem was not easily discoverable by anyone other than an expert electrician, and Lee did not tell Tan, Tracy, or Lucinda about the problem. Tracy consults an attorney about a suit to recover damages for her injuries.

If the attorney gives Tracy good advice, she will tell Tracy that she can recover from:

(A) Lucinda, because she breached the implied warranty of habitability.

(B) Lee, because he failed to disclose a latent defect.

(C) Tan, because Tan is considered Tracy's landlord.

(D) No one, because the covenant to repair runs with the land, and Tracy is bound by it.

Questions 22-24 are based on the following fact situation:

Clementine owned Argentacre, a working silver mine that had been in her family for three generations. When Clementine married Sebastian, they agreed that she would keep Argentacre as her separate property. After the birth of her third, and Clementine believed her last child, Clementine executed a will that provided: "Argentacre shall pass to my husband, Sebastian, for life or until he enters a religious order, then Argentacre shall pass to my children, with the issue of any pre-deceased child taking that child's share. All the rest, residue, and remainder of my estate I leave to my husband, Sebastian." Because she wanted to keep Argentacre in the family, Clementine added the following proviso: "Sebastian shall have no right to convey any interest in Argentacre.

Likewise, should any of my children attempt to convey any interest in Argentacre prior to the date that the children's interest becomes possessory, that child's interest shall pass to the other children." At that time, Clementine had three children, Alice, Ben, and Carl. Many years later, Clementine, Alice, and Alice's son Ed were involved in a freak mining accident. Alice was killed instantly. Clementine died a few days later. Ed lingered for two weeks before dying. They left the following survivors: Sebastian, Dan (Alice's son), Elsa (Ed's wife and sole heir), Ben, and Carl. The jurisdiction retains the Rule Against Perpetuities, unmodified by statute, and the common law destructibility rule.

22. Assume for purposes of this question only that, upon Clementine's death, Sebastian notifies her executor that he intends to enter the priesthood, and thus renounces any interest he may have in Clementine's estate. The executor noted that the disclaimer had been executed with the necessary formalities and was valid. Before the estate is distributed, Carl is killed in a car accident. Carl left his entire estate to his girlfriend, Fran. Who has an interest in Argentacre?

    (A) Ben, Dan, and Fran only.

    (B) Ben, Fran, Dan, and Elsa.

    (C) Ben and Dan only.

    (D) Ben, Dan, and Elsa only.

23. Assume for purposes of this question only that Alice survived the mining accident and that Sebastian took possession and control of Argentacre, which was very profitable. After a few years, Sebastian began to feel that his life lacked meaning, and so he joined the Brothers of Charity, a religious order. Instead of leaving Argentacre, however, he convinced the Brothers to open a monastery on Argentacre, which would be completely financed by the mining operation. Clementine's children are alarmed by this turn of events and seek a court order to remove Sebastian and the

Brothers from Argentacre, and to prevent Sebastian from taking any more profits from the mine. The court will most likely rule in favor of:

(A) Sebastian, because the gifts following Sebastian's life estate violate the Rule Against Perpetuities.

(B) Sebastian, because his life estate and reversion have destroyed the children's remainder.

(C) The children, because they are the fee simple owners of Argentacre.

(D) The children on the ejectment issue, but Sebastian can continue to take income from the mine for the rest of his life.

24. Assume for purposes of this question only that Alice survived the mining accident. Sebastian does not join a religious order, but instead marries a wealthy socialite. Having no need for money and believing the restriction on his transfer to be unenforceable, Sebastian transfers all of his interest in Argentacre to his brother, George. Several weeks after Sebastian's conveyance, Carl finds himself in need of cash and conveys his interest in Argentacre to Hal, a loan shark, in exchange for $20,000. Ben is outraged by the conduct of Sebastian and Carl. Ben brings a suit to quiet title to Argentacre. Who will the court find has title to Argentacre?

(A) Alice and Ben only.

(B) Alice, Ben, and Hal only.

(C) Alice, Ben, and Hal, subject to Sebastian's defeasible life estate.

(D) Alice and Ben, subject to George's defeasible life estate pur autre vie.

Question 25

Ollie owned a parcel of land in a rural area. Strapped for cash, Ollie decided to sell off some of his land. He divided the parcel into two halves, Frontacre and Backacre. One side of Frontacre abutted a public highway. The shortest route from Backacre to the highway was over a small private road that crossed Frontacre. There was another route from Backacre to the highway that did not involve crossing Frontacre. However, this route was a single-lane dirt and gravel thoroughfare that wound for over four miles through the woods. Ollie sold Backacre to Beverly, who planned to open an inn on the property. Ollie knew of Beverly's plans. Because of the access problem for Backacre, Ollie included an express easement in Beverly's deed allowing her to reach the highway from Backacre via the private road across Frontacre. Beverly built the inn but never opened it to the public since, soon after it was completed, she won a large sum in the state lottery and did not need the money or work.

Fifteen years after Beverly purchased Backacre from Ollie, she sold the land to Tera. Beverly had never properly recorded her deed to Backacre, but Tera promptly recorded her deed to the property from Beverly. Tera's deed made no mention of a right to cross Frontacre via the private road. Tera planned to open the inn to the public. About a week after Tera took possession of Backacre, she learned of the provision in Beverly's deed to the land. Tera told Ollie that she planned to use the road across his property to reach the highway. Ollie, who had not aged gracefully, snarled at her and said, "Not without my permission you won't, and I'm not about to give you permission!"

Does Tera have a right to cross Frontacre?

(A) No, because the easement is not mentioned in Tera's deed, and Beverly's deed containing the easement was not recorded.

(B) No, because Tera's opening of the inn would increase the use of the easement.

(C) Yes, but only if Beverly exercised her right to use the easement when she owned Backacre.

(D) Yes, even if Beverly never exercised her right to use the easement when she owned Backacre.

Question 26

Tyson agreed in writing to lease a retail site in a shopping mall from Lomax, the owner of the property. The term of the tenancy was two years, and rent was payable in monthly installments at the beginning of each month. At the end of the second year, there had been no discussions between Tyson and Lomax regarding renewal or termination. Tyson did not vacate the premises at the end of the term; instead, she sent a check for the next month's rent to Lomax. Lomax cashed the check and then informed Tyson that he was holding her to a new tenancy and a rent increase of 10%.

What is the status of the tenancy that Lomax created?

(A) A month-to-month tenancy for the original rent amount.

(B) A year-to-year tenancy for the original rent amount.

(C) A month-to-month tenancy for the increased rent amount.

(D) A tenancy at will, terminable at any time, for the increased rent amount.

Question 27

Upon his retirement, Arnie conveyed Goldacre, the large family estate, "to my son Grant for life, then to Grant's widow for her life, then to Grant's children." At the time of the conveyance, Grant was 20 years old and unmarried. Grant eventually married Wanda and had two children, Ann and Bradley. Many years later, while on a grandfather-grandson adventure for Bradley's 25th birthday, the train that Bradley and Arnie were taking to the mountains derailed. Arnie was killed instantly. Bradley died a short time later of his injuries. Arnie left his entire estate by will to his friend, Zeke. Bradley left a will devising his entire estate to the City Zoo. Wanda was so grief-stricken that she became ill and died the next year, leaving her entire estate to Grant.

Years later when Grant retired to another state, he met and married Wilma, a 21-year-old waitress. Despite the great age difference between Grant and Wilma, they lived happily for 10 years; then Grant died, leaving everything to Wilma. Wilma moved to Goldacre.

Ann, who had never approved of Wilma, does not want her living there. Ann brings suit to quiet title to Goldacre, joining all of the appropriate parties.

If the jurisdiction recognizes the common law Rule Against Perpetuities, unmodified by statute, the court will most likely find title to Goldacre is held:

(A) One-half in Ann and one-half in the City Zoo, subject to Wilma's life estate.

(B) One-half in Ann and one-half in Wilma, because Wilma took Grant's interest.

(C) The entire estate in Zeke, subject to Wilma's life estate, because the gift to the children violates the Rule Against Perpetuities.

(D) The entire estate in Ann, subject to Wilma's life estate, because Bradley did not survive Grant.

Question 28

Pamela wanted to purchase a quaint commercial property from which she intended to operate an upscale bath accessories boutique. Seth owned a small antique store in a section of town that attracted many shoppers. Pamela entered into a written contract with Seth, under which he agreed to convey the store and the land on which it is situated to Pamela for $100,000. The contract did not specify the quality of title to be conveyed, and made no mention of easements or reservations. The closing was set for November 25, three months from the signing of the contract.

Shortly after the contract was signed, Pamela obtained a survey and blueprints for the property so that she could plan her renovations. She noticed that the city had an easement for the public sidewalk that ran in front of the store. Since this actually enhanced the property for her purposes, she did not mention it to Seth. On October 30, Pamela learned that her bank was not willing to lend her as much money as she had hoped for, and so she would not be able to purchase as large an inventory as she had planned. Soon afterward, she learned that she needed major dental work which was going to be very costly. Her final bit of bad news was that her son lost his football scholarship at the state university and so was expecting her to help pay for his tuition. All of these problems gave Pamela "cold feet" about opening her business. Thus, on November 1, she notified Seth that she no longer intended to purchase the property. Seth told her that he intended to hold her to her contract. At closing, Pamela refused to tender the purchase price, claiming that Seth's title is unmarketable and citing the sidewalk easement as proof of that fact.

In a suit for specific performance, Seth will most likely:

(A) Prevail, because the contract did not specify the quality of title to be conveyed.

(B) Prevail, because Pamela was aware of the visible easement and it enhanced the value of the property.

(C) Not prevail, because an easement not provided for in the contract renders title unmarketable.

(D) Not prevail, because Pamela gave him sufficient notice of her change in plans and yet he made no effort to try to find another purchaser.

Question 29

In which of the following situations is the court most likely to grant reformation of the land sale contract?

(A) Bill agreed to purchase a portion of Sam's parcel, Purpleacre, for $25,000. Bill and Sam agreed that the property included in the purchase would be the westerly third of the property, with the eastern boundary to be a stone fence that runs from the northern border of Purpleacre to the southern boundary. Due to a clerical error by Sam's secretary, when the agreement is reduced to writing, the eastern boundary is stated to be the picket fence, which is 275 yards beyond the stone fence.

(B) Vanessa agreed to sell her rural property to her sister, Peggy. Peggy thought she was purchasing three acres. Vanessa believed that she was selling two acres. The writing states that two acres will be transferred.

(C) Betty agreed to buy Steve's farm for $300,000. The property, Farmacre, had two grain silos, a modern one and an old, dilapidated one. Betty felt the old silo was dangerous and thought they had agreed that Steve would demolish the old silo before Betty took possession at closing. Steve did not think they had agreed on the demolition of the silo as a condition of Betty's payment of the purchase price. The writing makes no mention of the silo.

(D) Victor agreed to sell a portion of his forested parcel, Timberacre, to his neighbor, Pete. Pete wanted to build a log cabin on a wooded lot. Pete and Victor walked out onto Timberacre and agreed that Pete's lot would be bounded by the fence on the north, the creek on the west, a stand of pines on the south, and the railroad track on the east. Pete thought the stand of pines was included in the parcel, and Victor thought the boundary was at the pines and the trees were not included in the conveyance. The writing states that the pines are included in the parcel.

Question 30

Peterson purchased Siltacre from Sedgwick for $500,000. She financed the purchase by obtaining a loan from Sedgwick for $300,000 in exchange for a mortgage on Siltacre. Sedgwick promptly and properly recorded his mortgage.

Shortly thereafter, Peterson gave a mortgage on Siltacre to Carter to satisfy a preexisting debt of $100,000 owed to Carter. Carter also promptly and properly recorded the mortgage. Within a year, Peterson stopped making payments on both mortgages, and Sedgwick brought an action to foreclose on his mortgage. Carter was not included as a party to the foreclosure action. Sedgwick purchased the property at a public foreclosure sale in satisfaction of the loan. Carter subsequently discovered the sale and informed Sedgwick that it was not valid.

Who has title to Siltacre?

(A) Sedgwick, because he gave a purchase money mortgage and Carter's mortgage was for a preexisting debt.

(B) Sedgwick, because the public foreclosure sale extinguished Carter's interest.

(C) Sedgwick, but he must redeem Carter's mortgage to avoid foreclosure.

(D) Peterson, because Sedgwick's foreclosure action was invalid without the inclusion of Carter as a necessary party.

Question 31

Dickens purchased an old house in a neighborhood undergoing gentrification. He planned to slowly fix up the house as his time and finances permitted. Dickens financed his purchase by taking out a mortgage on the property with Britannia Bank, which the bank recorded. Although the house needed a lot of work, for most purposes it was quite livable. However, the windows were very dilapidated, and it was clear that Dickens's winter heating bills would skyrocket because of the ineffective insulation provided by the windows. Therefore, Dickens purchased some custom-made windows from Fenster, a retail dealer specializing in windows, awnings, and gutters. The modern windows used three panes of glass for improved insulation and they were easily removable from the window frames to make cleaning them a less odious chore. Because Dickens had spent a lot of money on the house already, he lacked sufficient

funds to pay the $3,000 Fenster wanted for a complete set of new windows. Fenster agreed to sell the windows to Dickens on an installment payment plan with the windows as security. Dickens installed the windows himself and stored the old windows in the basement of the house. Dickens made three payments to Britannia Bank on the $30,000 mortgage and he made two payments to Fenster on the windows. Dickens then lost his job and ceased making payments to Britannia Bank and Fenster. Dickens has departed to parts unknown and Fenster wishes to remove the windows from the house. Britannia Bank objects. The matter winds up in court.

How should the court rule on Fenster's request to remove the windows?

(A) Fenster may remove the windows, because the old windows are available for the bank to restore the house to its original condition.

(B) Fenster may remove the windows, because the windows are designed to be removable.

(C) Fenster may not remove the windows, because regardless of their form, windows are an integral part of the house.

(D) Fenster may not remove the windows, because the bank's lien is senior to Fenster's.

Question 32

Alan and Bucky held Brubacre as joint tenants. Bucky was involved in an automobile accident and was sued by Prufrock, who had received serious bodily injuries. The jury ruled against Bucky and assessed a large damages award that Bucky was unable to pay in full. Therefore, Prufrock went back into court and secured a statutory lien on Brubacre. Shortly thereafter, a depressed Bucky committed suicide.

What are the respective interests of Alan and Prufrock in Brubacre?

(A) Alan is the sole owner of Brubacre, but the property is subject to Prufrock's statutory lien.

(B) Alan is the sole owner of Brubacre, and the property is not subject to Prufrock's statutory lien.

(C) Alan and Prufrock own Brubacre as tenants in common.

(D) Alan and Prufrock own Brubacre in joint tenancy.

Question 33

Bixby entered into a written contract to buy Appleacre, a farmhouse with a small orchard, from Seaver for $100,000. The contract stipulates that the closing is to be on September 30. In addition, the contract contains the following provision: "The taxes shall be prorated as agreed to by the parties at a later date." Upon the signing of the contract, Bixby gave Seaver a check for $10,000 as a down payment.

On September 28, Bixby notified Seaver that he would not be able to close on Appleacre until October 2, because the closing on his current home, the proceeds from which were to be applied to his purchase of Appleacre, was unavoidably delayed due to his buyer's illness. Meanwhile, Seaver had difficulty finding a home he liked as well as Appleacre. He decided that he would rather not sell Appleacre and wished to avoid the contract with Bixby. On October 2, Bixby showed up at the closing with the $90,000 to tender to Seaver. Seaver did not show up. Bixby sues for specific performance.

The court will most likely rule in favor of:

(A) Seaver, because the tax provision is an essential term of the contract, and it is not specific enough to satisfy the Statute of Frauds.

(B) Seaver, because Bixby is in material breach by not tendering performance on September 30.

(C) Bixby, because of the operation of the doctrine of equitable conversion.

(D) Bixby, because time was not of the essence.

Question 34

To satisfy a debt owing to Barb, Son executed and delivered to Barb a warranty deed to Desert Acres, a large tract of undeveloped land located 200 miles from City. Barb promptly recorded the deed. Shortly thereafter, her health failed and she decided to retire to Desert Acres; she built a house on the property and has lived there ever since.

Son never actually owned Desert Acres. It belonged to Father, but Father had promised to leave the property to Son.

Later, Father died and his will devised the property to Son. Pressed for money, Son then sold Desert Acres to Caleb by warranty deed, which Caleb promptly recorded. Although Caleb paid full value for the property, he purchased it strictly for investment and never visited the site. He therefore did not realize that Barb was living there, and knew nothing of Son's earlier deed to Barb.

The jurisdiction in which Desert Acres is located has the following statute:

> A conveyance of an estate in land (other than a lease for less than one year) shall not be valid against any subsequent purchaser for value without notice thereof unless the conveyance is recorded.

Which of the following is the most likely outcome of a quiet title action brought by Barb against Caleb?

(A) Barb prevails, because Son had no title to convey to Caleb.

(B) Barb prevails, because Caleb was not a purchaser for value without notice of Barb's interest.

(C) Caleb prevails, because under the doctrine of estoppel by deed, title inures to the benefit of the original grantee only as against the grantor.

(D) Caleb prevails, because under the recording acts, the deed from Son to Barb was not in the chain of title and hence did not constitute notice to Caleb.

Questions 35-36 are based on the following fact situation:

Larry owned an office building. He leased a portion of the lobby to Tom under a written lease that provided for a term of 10 years at $100 per month. The lease also provided: (i) the shop was to be used as a candy and cigarette counter, which would be the "exclusive" vending facility in the building; and (ii) the tenant is prohibited from assigning or subletting without the landlord's consent.

Later, Tom became ill and wished to sell his business and all his rights under the lease to Terry. Larry executed a signed writing stating: "I, Larry, consent to the assignment of Tom's interest to Terry." The deal went through. Terry ran the shop for a while, but found the business unprofitable. She transferred her interest to Tessie by a writing providing that Terry could reenter if Tessie failed to make rental payments to the landlord.

By the time of Terry's transfer to Tessie, Larry had sold the building. The new owner, Lorne, did not like Tessie and refused to consent to her becoming a tenant in the building. Lorne also installed several automatic candy and cigarette vending machines throughout the building. As a result, Tessie refused to pay any rent.

35. The transfer from Terry to Tessie was:

(A) Effective even though Lorne refused to consent.

(B) Effective, because Lorne had no reasonable basis to withhold consent.

(C) Effective, because the covenant against assignment is void as a restraint on alienation.

(D) Ineffective.

36. If Lorne files suit against Tessie for the rent due, a court following common law principles should rule that:

(A) Lorne has no direct claim against Tessie personally; his only remedy is to terminate the lease and sue Terry for the rent.

(B) Lorne can recover $100 per month rent from Tessie.

(C) Lorne can recover nothing from Tessie because his installation of the vending machines allowed her to immediately terminate her duties under the lease.

(D) Lorne can recover $100 per month rent from Tessie but only if the vending machines are removed.

Question 37

Tess owned a parcel of land in the mountains near White Pine National Forest that had been improved by the construction of a permanent campground, consisting of wooden floors and frames for tents, a wooden mess hall with kitchen, and wooden outhouses. Each year she allowed the Girl Scouts to use the parcel, Camp Humdinger, for their summer camp. The rest of the year Tess and her family and friends used the parcel for camping and other recreation.

Tess's will devised the parcel as follows: "Camp Humdinger to my niece Daphne, her heirs and assigns, so long as it is used for camping and recreational purposes; if used for any other purpose during her lifetime, then to the National Council of the Girl Scouts of America."

Tess died in 1986. The residuary clause of her will left all property not devised in the remainder of the will to her daughter Erma, who was also her sole heir. Erma died intestate in 1992, her only heir being her son Harold.

In 1993, Daphne entered into a contract to sell Camp Humdinger to Paul for its reasonable market value. After Paul received the title report called for in the contract, he refused to proceed with the purchase, claiming that Daphne could not convey good title. Daphne, the National Council of the Girl Scouts of America, and Paul executed a new contract calling for the former two parties to sell the property at the same price to the latter. Paul seeks legal advice from you as to whether to now proceed with the new purchase transaction.

The jurisdiction's decisional law follows the common law Rule Against Perpetuities, and a statute provides that future estates and interests are alienable, and may be devised or inherited, all in the same manner as possessory estates or interests.

What is your advice to Paul?

(A) Proceed, because good title can now be conveyed by the sellers.

(B) Proceed, if the National Council of the Girl Scouts of America promises never to use its right of entry should Paul use the property for other than camping and recreational purposes.

(C) Rescind, because Harold has not been included as a party selling the property.

(D) Rescind, because no one can convey good title to the property during Daphne's lifetime.

Question 38

To secure a loan of $100,000 from Bank, Sett, the owner in fee simple of Southacre, conveyed a deed of trust for Southacre to Trent, an attorney, on behalf of Bank, Trent's client. The deed of trust contained a "power of sale" clause, permitted by the jurisdiction, which allowed Trent to sell the property in the event of default without the necessity of a judicial foreclosure action. After several years, Sett defaulted on his loan payments to Bank. Bank informed Sett that it was instructing Trent to exercise his power of sale. After appropriate notices, Trent conducted a public sale of Southacre. Bank was the sole bidder and obtained the property for $80,000, which was $10,000 less than the outstanding balance on the loan plus the expenses of the sale. One month later, Sett notified Bank that he wanted to pay off the loan and extinguish the deed of trust, and was prepared to tender $80,000 to do so. Bank insisted that Sett must tender $90,000 to pay off the loan.

If a court in the jurisdiction will require Bank to accept only $80,000 under the circumstances above, it will be because:

(A) Sett had the power to revoke the trust as long as he was alive.

(B) Bank did not have the authority to bid on the property at other than a judicial foreclosure sale.

(C) Sett was exercising a statutory power rather than an equitable power.

(D) Bank does not have the power to clog the equity of redemption.

Question 39

Meredith owned a large home in which her family had lived for over 150 years. She wanted to ensure that her descendants would continue to live in the house for as long as possible, so she instructed her lawyer to draft her will so that the home passed upon her death to "my daughter Gretchen, for life, then to the eldest survivor of her three children, Jack, Robert, and Kimberly, for life, remainder to the eldest surviving offspring of the three grandchildren who is alive at the death of the last life tenant."

After Meredith's death, her daughter Gretchen lived in the family home for 15 years. Upon Gretchen's death, all three of her children were alive, so the home passed to Jack, the eldest. He lived in the house for three years, then conveyed it to the City Historical Society, which converted it into its headquarters and museum. Eight years later, Jack died. At the time of his death, he was survived by his sister Kimberly; his widow; his nephews Bob, Jr., Ken, and William, Robert's sons; and niece Sharon, Kimberly's daughter. Of the niece and nephews, Sharon was the eldest. Four years after Jack's death, Sharon brought an action for ejectment and to quiet title against the City Historical Society. The jurisdiction has a statutory period of adverse possession of 10 years, or five years if entry was made by the adverse possessor under color of title.

How should the court rule in Sharon's action?

(A) For the society, because it has occupied the home for the statutory period required for adverse possession.

(B) For the society, because it purchased the home in fee simple absolute from Jack.

(C) For Sharon, because the society has not been in adverse possession for the requisite period.

(D) For Sharon, because a purchaser of property from a life tenant cannot acquire a fee simple absolute through adverse possession.

Question 40

Leslie owned a beachfront lot and home in Lakeshore Estates, a subdivision occupying several hundred acres near Lake Pines. The recorded subdivision plan grants to each owner in Lakeshore Estates an easement to use the private roads therein for personal ingress and egress.

Following seismic activity in the area, the level of Lake Pines dropped substantially, exposing a considerable amount of land between the new shoreline and the old beachfront. It was judicially determined that this "new" land belonged to the county, which put portions of it up for sale. Leslie purchased the land extending from her old property line to the new shoreline,

and constructed a boat launching ramp on the new property. She then permitted persons who did not own land in Lakeshore Estates to drive through her old property to reach the boat launching ramp on her new property, and thus to utilize the lake, for a small fee. The land on either side of the new boat launching property was purchased by private citizens who use it for residential purposes.

The homeowners' association of Lakeshore Estates brings suit against Leslie seeking to enjoin her from using or permitting others not residents of Lakeshore Estates from traveling the streets of Lakeshore Estates to reach the boat launching ramp. How should the court rule?

(A) For the homeowners, since the scope of the easement granted to Leslie as an owner in Lakeshore Estates does not extend to the use that she is making of the new property.

(B) For Leslie, because she has an express easement over the streets of Lakeshore Estates.

(C) For Leslie, because she has an easement by necessity as to the new property over the streets of Lakeshore Estates.

(D) For Leslie, because she has an implied easement over the streets of Lakeshore Estates benefiting the new property since it abuts Leslie's old property.

Question 41

Wanda rented an apartment in a large multi-unit building. One day vandals broke into several of the building's apartments, including Wanda's, and smeared excrement into the carpets and on the walls, and broke out all of the windows. The jurisdiction provides by statute that if a tenant notifies her landlord in writing of a repair that is needed to keep the premises in a habitable condition and the landlord does not repair it within 15 days, the tenant may, at her option, either repair it herself and withhold the expenses from rent, or consider herself constructively evicted and terminate her tenancy. Wanda wrote a letter to the landlord of her building informing him that her walls, carpets, and windows had been damaged and needed repair, and after eight days she received a letter in reply stating that such damages to her apartment were her responsibility to repair.

After waiting another week, Wanda paid to have her carpets and walls cleaned and to have her windows replaced. She then withheld the entire next month's rent of $400, because the cleaning and repair bills had totaled $750. After sending her the required statutory notices, the landlord commenced unlawful detainer litigation, seeking to have Wanda evicted for nonpayment of rent.

How should the court rule?

(A) For Wanda, if she can show that the landlord was negligent in connection with the vandalism.

(B) For the landlord, because the damage was to a private apartment and not to the common areas of the apartment complex.

(C) For the landlord, because the damage was the result of the criminal acts of a third party.

(D) For Wanda, because she satisfied the requirements of the statute.

Question 42

Trout purchased Fishacre for $100,000, intending to operate a seafood restaurant on the site. As part of his financing, he obtained a purchase money mortgage from First Commercial Bank for $60,000. Due to a clerical error by the bank, the mortgage was not recorded in the county recorder's office. A statute in the jurisdiction provides:

> No conveyance of an interest in land, other than a lease for less than one year, shall be valid against any subsequent purchaser for value, without notice thereof, whose conveyance is first recorded.

After Trout's restaurant had been in operation for five years, a widely publicized case of food poisonings traced to the restaurant caused business to drop dramatically. To stay in business, Trout obtained a mortgage from Second Commercial Bank for $30,000. Second Bank was not informed by Trout of the mortgage held by First Bank. The next day, Trout contacted First Bank about renegotiating its mortgage. Checking its records, First Bank discovered that the original mortgage was not recorded and immediately recorded it. Later that day, Second Bank recorded its mortgage. A few days later, Trout and First Bank agreed to a modification of their mortgage agreement to allow Trout to make lower monthly payments in exchange for a higher interest rate and a longer period of repayment.

Despite this agreement, Trout was unable to make payments on the Second Bank mortgage. Second Bank instituted a foreclosure action six months later, but failed to include First Bank as a party to the foreclosure action.

If Second Bank takes title to Fishacre at the foreclosure sale, which of the following statements most correctly describes First Bank's interest?

(A) First Bank's mortgage on Fishacre survives under its original terms.

(B) First Bank's mortgage on Fishacre survives under its modified terms.

(C) First Bank's mortgage is extinguished because when it was modified it became junior to Second Bank's mortgage.

(D) First Bank's mortgage is extinguished regardless of the modification because it had not recorded before Second Bank obtained its mortgage interest.

Question 43

Ligget entered into a written lease of Greenacre for a term of 25 years with Tarr, who planned to open a bakery on the property. The parties also agreed to a right of first refusal if Greenacre was offered for sale during the term of the lease. Three years later, Tarr retired from the bakery business and, after notifying Liggett, transferred the lease to Ash. The lease permitted assignments and subleases upon notice to the landlord. Twenty-one years later, Liggett entered into a contract with Burns for the sale of Greenacre for $100,000. Liggett had informed Burns of the lease but had forgotten about the right of first refusal. When Ash learned of the sale to Burns, she informed both Liggett and Burns that she wanted to exercise her option and was prepared to purchase Greenacre for the contract price. The jurisdiction's Rule Against Perpetuities is unmodified by statute.

Can Ash enforce the option?

(A) Yes, because an option held by a tenant on leased property cannot be separated from the leasehold interest.

(B) Yes, because the option touches and concerns the leasehold estate.

(C) No, because the transfer to Ash made the option void under the Rule Against Perpetuities.

(D) No, because the option was not specifically included when the lease was transferred to Ash.

Question 44

Ohn was the owner of Brownacre, a 240-acre piece of agricultural land. Pick, Ohn's neighbor, wished to expand his own holdings by purchasing 20 acres of Brownacre that abutted Pick's own property. The land Pick wanted was located in the northwest quarter of Brownacre. Ohn wrote out the following statement:

> Ohn agrees to sell to Pick, for $5,000, 20 acres in the northwest quarter of Brownacre, Brownacre beginning at a point in the northeast quadrant of Grange County on the 16th Grange County survey line, six minutes west of the 98th Meridian, and then proceeding due east 1,320 yards and from

that point due south to Little Tuba Creek, and then westward along the creek to the point at which it intersects Bell Road, and then northward along the eastern edge of Bell Road until Bell Road ends, and then due northward from that point to the original starting point of the survey.

Ohn had copied the language describing Brownacre from his own deed to Brownacre. Ohn then signed the paper and gave it to Pick. It was also agreed in the writing that the sale would take place on April 16. On April 16, Pick tendered $5,000 to Ohn. Ohn refused to accept the money and refused to convey 20 acres to Pick.

If Pick sues Ohn for specific performance:

(A) Ohn will prevail, because the writing did not adequately describe which 20 acres were to be sold.

(B) Ohn will prevail, because the writing was not signed by both parties.

(C) Pick will prevail, because metes and bounds are a sufficient way to legally describe property.

(D) Pick will prevail, because the writing satisfies the Statute of Frauds.

Question 45

The state of New Hellas has the following statute: "Any conveyance of an estate in land, other than a lease for less than one year, shall not be valid against any subsequent purchaser whose conveyance is first recorded." Alpha inherited Wineacre, a residence in New Hellas, free of encumbrances. Alpha promptly recorded his deed. The property needed some fixing up, so Alpha took out a $100,000 mortgage on Wineacre with Athenian Bank. The instrument was promptly recorded. Alpha regularly made the scheduled payments on the mortgage. Alpha then decided he wanted to sell Wineacre and that he needed just a little more cash to fix it up to the point where he could get top price for the property. He took out another mortgage with Spartan Bank for $50,000, and the mortgage instrument was properly recorded. Alpha then put Wineacre up for sale. Theta purchased Wineacre from Alpha subject to both mortgages. Theta procured another loan of $100,000 secured by a mortgage on Wineacre from Omega. Omega knew about Athenian's mortgage, but Theta did not inform her of the Spartan Bank mortgage. Omega lent the money to Theta on the understanding that Theta would use the money to pay off the Athenian Bank mortgage, placing Omega in first priority. Theta promptly paid off Athenian Bank but made no further payments to Spartan Bank. Spartan Bank initiated steps to foreclose on Wineacre. Omega brings an appropriate action seeking to have her rights declared superior to those of Spartan Bank.

If the court rules in Omega's favor, it will be because:

(A) Omega could reactivate the first mortgage and step into the shoes of Athenian Bank.

(B) The balancing of equities clearly favors Omega.

(C) Omega lacked actual knowledge of the second mortgage.

(D) Omega received no benefit from Spartan Bank, and therefore cannot be burdened by the bank's demands.

Questions 46-47 are based on the following fact situation:

Arthur owned a tract of land that was newly incorporated into Sleepytown, a rapidly growing suburban community. Arthur discovered that the general scheme for development of the area in which his tract lay was primarily residential, with no building containing more than six residential units to be constructed on any standard lot. Arthur decided that he could get the most for his property by limiting use on each lot to single-family housing. Accordingly,

he divided the tract into four standard lots, which he conveyed to Bertha, Charles, Delia, and Edgar, respectively. Each deed granted by Arthur contained a covenant requiring that the property be used only for single-family housing. All deeds were duly recorded in the office of the County Recorder of Deeds. Bertha and Charles proceeded to build single-family houses on their lots. Delia and Edgar did not develop their properties immediately. Bertha later sold her property to Frank. Her deed to Frank included the covenant limiting use to single-family dwellings. Charles sold his property to Gertrude, but did not include the covenant in the deed. Delia sold her property to Howard. The deed to Howard contained the covenant, but the deed was not properly recorded. Edgar sold his property to Iris and the deed to Iris did not contain the restriction. Frank died and his property passed by will to his daughter, Judy. Gertrude gave her land to her son, Kurt, who had recently married. Howard sold his property for value to Lorelei. These last three transfers of title were all recorded, but none of the deeds mentioned the covenant.

46. Which of the following landowners would have a good argument for building a multi-family dwelling on his or her property?

(A) Judy, because she took title under a will.

(B) Kurt, because he received the property as an inter vivos gift.

(C) Lorelei, because she paid value for the property.

(D) None of the above.

47. Assume for purposes of this question only that Lorelei is aware that Arthur had included the single-family restriction in all of the deeds from his tract. May she sue to enforce the covenant against Iris to prevent her from building a multi-family dwelling on her property?

(A) No, because there is no privity with Iris.

(B) No, because the zoning laws have not been violated.

(C) No, because there was no restriction in Iris's deed.

(D) Yes, because Iris's building would alter Arthur's common scheme.

Question 48

Felipe conveyed Secoacre to his son, Sancho, by warranty deed. The deed stated that Sancho paid $125,000 for the land, but Sancho had not, in fact, paid Felipe the money for the land. However, Sancho and Felipe agreed orally that Sancho would not record the deed until he paid Felipe the $125,000. Sancho neither paid Felipe nor recorded the deed for three years, at which time the property values in the area began to climb rapidly. Wishing to turn a fast profit, Sancho recorded the deed from Felipe and one week later conveyed Secoacre to Gonzalez for $200,000. Gonzalez promptly recorded the deed. When Felipe discovered what had transpired, he filed a lawsuit, and the court determined that Sancho owed Felipe $125,000. Unfortunately, Sancho and his $200,000 from Gonzalez are nowhere to be found. Felipe asks the court to levy on Secoacre. Gonzalez, of course, challenges the attempt to levy.

The jurisdiction in which the parties reside and Secoacre is located has a recording statute that reads, in relevant part: "No interest in land shall be good against a subsequent purchaser for value, without notice, unless the interest is recorded."

If Felipe cannot levy on Secoacre, it will be because Gonzalez's best defense against the levy is based on:

(A) The Statute of Frauds.

(B) The rights of a bona fide purchaser.

(C) Gonzalez's recording of the deed, which gave him protection under the recording act.

(D) The parol evidence rule.

Question 49

Ash held good record title to Whiteacre. Ash conveyed Whiteacre to Bay for $90,000. Bay never recorded her deed. A year after Ash conveyed Whiteacre to Bay, Ash drew up a deed for conveyance of Whiteacre and gave it to Cedar as a gift. Cedar knew nothing of the prior conveyance to Bay, and Cedar recorded his deed. A year later, Cedar sold Whiteacre to Date via an installment land sale contract. The full purchase price was $100,000, and Date made his first installment payment of $40,000 to Cedar. Date received a deed from Cedar and promptly and properly recorded it. According to the terms of the installment agreement, Date was to make two further payments of $30,000 each. The first of these payments was due a year after the closing date and the second payment a year after that. Bay learned from a friend about Cedar's conveyance of Whiteacre to Date. Bay files suit against Date, seeking to oust Date from Whiteacre and to quiet title in Bay. The recording statute in State White, where Whiteacre is located and where all the parties reside, reads in relevant part: "No conveyance shall be good against a subsequent purchaser for value, without notice, unless it be recorded."

The court considers the following possible orders regarding ownership of Whiteacre:

I.   Partition of Whiteacre between Bay and Date.

II. Grant Whiteacre to Bay, but order Bay to pay Date $40,000.

III. Grant Whiteacre to Date, but order Date to pay Bay the remaining $60,000 in payments.

IV. Grant Whiteacre solely to Date, based upon the recording statute, without any compensation to Bay.

V.   Grant Whiteacre solely to Bay without any compensation to Date.

Which of the judicial orders would it be appropriate for the court to make?

(A) I. or II. only.

(B) III. or IV. only.

(C) V. only.

(D) I., II., or III. only.

Question 50

Arthur purchased Lot A, a large suburban lot. Arthur had a house built on the lot, which became Arthur's residence. Shortly thereafter, Ben purchased Lot B, a lot similar to Lot A and immediately adjacent to Lot A. Ben built a home on Lot B, which became Ben's family residence. Both Lot A and Lot B were undeveloped prior to their purchase by Arthur and Ben, and both owners drove over dirt paths to their respective garages. Arthur suggested to Ben that a common driveway be built where the two lots joined. Ben thought this was a great idea. Arthur and Ben split the cost of constructing the driveway and they afterwards entered into a written agreement whereby Arthur and Ben agreed to share the costs of upkeep and maintenance of the driveway on a 50-50 basis. Their agreement regarding the driveway was recorded in the county recorder's office.

Two years after the agreement was made, Ben built a new driveway, which was located entirely on Lot B. The common driveway, which Arthur continued to use but which Ben no longer used, began to deteriorate. Arthur asked Ben for money to maintain the common driveway, but Ben steadfastly refused to contribute, saying, "I've got my own driveway now. Why should I pay to maintain something I never use?" Three years after Ben built his own Lot B driveway, Ben conveyed Lot B to Callie. Callie entered into possession, used the home on Lot B as her residence, and used only the Lot B driveway built by Ben. By this time, the

common driveway had deteriorated badly and contained numerous potholes. Arthur asked Callie to pay half of what it would take to repair the common driveway. Callie refused. Arthur repaired the driveway and sued Callie for a contribution amounting to 50% of the cost of repairs.

Will Arthur prevail?

(A) Yes, because easements run with the land.

(B) Yes, because the agreement between Arthur and Ben was recorded.

(C) No, because Ben abandoned use of the easement.

(D) No, because Arthur is not in privity of contract with Callie.

Question 51

Oscar, the owner in fee simple of Maroonacre, sold it to Alvin for $850,000. To finance the purchase, Alvin obtained a mortgage loan from Sequoia Bank for $600,000. The deed from Oscar to Alvin was promptly and properly recorded, but due to an oversight the mortgage from Sequoia Bank was not immediately recorded. A few months later, Alvin's business was struggling and needed additional funds, so he approached Sequoia Bank about getting a second mortgage. Sequoia Bank turned him down, so he contacted Weeping Willow Bank. Not having knowledge of the previous mortgage on the property, Weeping Willow Bank agreed to loan Alvin $300,000 secured by a mortgage on Maroonacre, which it promptly and properly recorded. One day later, Sequoia Bank, having discovered that its original mortgage had not been recorded, properly recorded it in the appropriate recording office.

The jurisdiction's recording statute provides as follows:

> Any conveyance or mortgage of an interest in land, other than a lease for less than a year, shall not be valid against any subsequent purchaser for

value, without notice thereof, whose conveyance is first recorded.

Alvin struggled to keep up with his mortgage payments, but was unable to do so. He kept falling farther behind, and finally stopped making payments altogether on both mortgages. Weeping Willow Bank began foreclosure proceedings, but did not include Sequoia Bank as a party. At the foreclosure sale, Cornelius purchased Maroonacre, having no actual knowledge of the mortgage with Sequoia Bank. Soon after these events, Sequoia Bank declared its loan in default and sought to foreclose on Maroonacre.

Describe the rights of Sequoia Bank against Cornelius.

(A) Sequoia Bank may foreclose because the holder of a senior mortgage interest is unaffected by foreclosure of a junior interest.

(B) Sequoia Bank may foreclose because the holder of a junior mortgage interest is a necessary party that must be included in a foreclosure proceeding by the holder of a senior interest.

(C) Sequoia Bank may not foreclose because its failure to promptly record extinguished its rights against all parties except Alvin, the original mortgagor.

(D) Sequoia Bank may not foreclose because Cornelius succeeds to Alvin's right of redemption.

Question 52

Victoria conveyed Oakacre, a residential city property, to Percy. Upon taking possession of the property, Percy discovered that the garage of Niobe, a neighbor, encroached six inches onto Oakacre. Victoria's warranty deed to Percy included the following covenants for title:

I. Seisin.

II. Encumbrances.

III. Warranty.

IV. Further assurance.

If Percy wishes to compel Victoria to assist him in a suit against Niobe, which of the following covenants may he rely upon to do so?

(A) I. and II. only.

(B) III. and IV. only.

(C) I., II., and III. only.

(D) I., II., III., and IV.

Question 53

John's father had purchased 80 acres of desert land in the state of Arid over 30 years ago, but the family had never even visited the land. They had the deed by which the property was conveyed, which had been recorded in the appropriate county, and John's father had described the little two-room cabin that sat in the middle of the parcel near the dry streambed, but except for the father, no one had ever seen the place.

Ten years ago, John won the state lottery and was entitled to annual payments of $200,000 for 20 years. He quit his job and headed out west. John found what he was certain was the little cabin and over the next few years he built a barn, a greenhouse, and some corrals, all enclosed by a sturdy wire mesh fence. The area bounded by the fence, containing all John's structures, occupied about one and one-half acres of the 80 owned by his father.

When John's father died, the title to the property passed validly to John. When he attended his father's funeral back east, John met his high school sweetheart. Romance flowered anew, and they decided to get married. She had a prospering law practice in an eastern metropolis, so John decided to sell the ranch house and related structures because he would not be able to maintain them in absentia. With the aid of a local real estate agent, he entered into a contract for sale of the one and one-half acres, describing it in detail with reference to the structures and nearby landmarks.

The purchaser flew west to inspect the property, taking with him a surveyor. They discovered that John had settled onto a completely different parcel from the one owned by his father. The purchaser immediately announced that he would not proceed with the sale contract.

The state of Arid's statutory period for establishing adverse possession is five years. John occupied the land around his cabin for six and one-half years before his father died.

If John brings an action for specific performance of the sale contract, how should the court rule?

(A) For the purchaser, since John does not own the land he is purporting to sell.

(B) For the purchaser, because John does not have marketable title to the land he is purporting to sell.

(C) For John, if he conveys by quitclaim deed.

(D) For John, because the description in the contract of sale is sufficient to identify the property and need not be as accurate as one contained in a deed conveying land.

Question 54

As a result of a personal injury lawsuit, Len obtained a judgment against Deb, who had few assets, in the amount of $100,000. Deb did not pay the judgment. On April 1 of the following year, Deb inherited Brownacre from her great uncle Bjorn. On May 1, Deb entered into a contract with Bill to sell Brownacre for $120,000. The contract was not recorded. Bill immediately applied to FirstBank for a loan of $100,000. FirstBank approved Bill's loan, and on May 15, a closing was held. Deb deeded Brownacre to Bill, and Bill executed a mortgage for $100,000 to FirstBank. However, due to an error by the title company, the deed from Deb to Bill was not recorded, although the mortgage to FirstBank was recorded. Neither Bill nor FirstBank had any knowledge of Len's judgment. On May 20, Len recorded his judgment in the county recorder's

office where Brownacre was located. At that time he had no knowledge of Bill's rights or FirstBank's rights. When he learned about them, he immediately brought a proceeding to foreclose his judgment lien, naming Deb, Bill, and FirstBank as parties.

The jurisdiction has a typical grantor/grantee recording index, and has enacted the following pertinent statutes:

> Any judgment properly filed in the county recorder's office shall, for ten years from filing, be a lien on the real property then owned or subsequently acquired by any person against whom the judgment is rendered.

> No conveyance or mortgage of real property shall be good against subsequent bona fide purchasers for value and without notice unless the same be recorded according to law.

As between Len and FirstBank, which party's interest in Brownacre will be given priority?

(A) FirstBank, because FirstBank recorded its mortgage before Len recorded his judgment lien.

(B) FirstBank, because Len is not protected by the recording statute.

(C) Len, because Len's judgment was filed in the recorder's office before Bill's deed was recorded.

(D) Len, because the judgment lien extends to after-acquired property.

Question 55

Moore, the owner in fee simple of Blackacre, obtained a loan of $60,000 from Maple Savings and Loan, in exchange for a promissory note secured by a mortgage on Blackacre, which Maple promptly and properly recorded. A few months later, Moore obtained another loan of $60,000 from Oak Savings and Loan, in exchange for a promissory note secured by a mortgage on Blackacre, which Oak promptly and properly recorded. After his employer transferred him to another city, Moore sold Blackacre to Grant for $150,000 and conveyed a warranty deed. Neither mortgage agreement contained a due-on-sale clause or prohibited transfer of the property. Grant expressly agreed with Moore to assume both mortgages, with the consent of Maple and Oak. A few years later, Maple Savings loaned Grant an additional $50,000 in exchange for an increase in the interest rate and principal amount of its mortgage on Blackacre. At that time, the balance on the original loan from Maple was $50,000. Shortly thereafter, Grant stopped making payments on both mortgages and disappeared. After proper notice to all appropriate parties, Maple instituted a foreclosure action on the Blackacre mortgage, and purchased the property at the foreclosure sale. At that time the principal balance on the Oak mortgage loan was $50,000. After fees and expenses, the proceeds from the foreclosure sale totaled $80,000.

Assuming that the jurisdiction permits deficiency judgments, which of the following statements is most accurate?

(A) Maple keeps the entire $80,000 and can proceed personally against Moore for its deficiency, while the Oak mortgage remains on Blackacre.

(B) Maple keeps the entire $80,000, the Oak mortgage on Blackacre is extinguished, and both Maple and Oak can proceed personally against Moore for their deficiencies.

(C) Maple keeps $50,000, Oak is entitled to $30,000, and only Oak can proceed personally against Moore for its deficiency.

(D) Maple keeps $50,000, Oak is entitled to $30,000, and neither Maple nor Oak can proceed personally against Moore for their deficiencies.

Question 56

Lemmon owned a piece of property located on the corner of First Street and Park Avenue. In response to the development of the adjoining properties, Lemmon used his entire savings to build a shopping center on his land. He leased half of the units in the shopping center to various merchants. Desperately in need of money for his day-to-day living expenses, Lemmon borrowed $50,000 from Fry. Lemmon gave Fry a promissory note for $50,000, payable in five years, and secured by a mortgage on the shopping center. The note and mortgage contained an assignment of the rent and profits from the shopping center. Fry promptly and properly recorded the note and mortgage. Within one month, Lemmon leased the remainder of the units in the shopping center. At the end of five years, Lemmon defaulted on the note.

In the absence of an applicable statute, Fry is entitled to collect rents as they accrue from:

(A) All of the tenants.

(B) None of the tenants, unless their leases with Lemmon permitted assignment of the rent.

(C) Only those tenants whose leases became effective before Fry's mortgage was recorded.

(D) Only those tenants whose leases became effective after Fry's mortgage was recorded.

Question 57

Able owned Oilacre, a 100-acre parcel that contained several asphalt lakes. Conco was constructing highways for State Red in the vicinity of Oilacre and needed a supply of asphalt.

Able executed a document that, in return for a payment of $1 per barrel by Conco, gave Conco the right to enter on Oilacre and to take asphalt in whatever quantities Conco desired. Able reserved the right to remove asphalt himself and to grant this right to others.

Last year, State Red commenced an action in eminent domain to take Oilacre for a public park to display the fossils of animals that had been trapped in the asphalt lakes eons ago.

State Red denies that Conco is entitled to compensation. Is this position correct?

(A) Yes, because the nonexclusive nature of Conco's right makes it a license, which is not an interest in property.

(B) Yes, because a nonexclusive profit, although an interest in property, has no value separate and apart from the land itself.

(C) No, because Conco has a nonexclusive profit, which is a property right for which Conco is entitled to compensation.

(D) No, because Conco has a license coupled with an interest, which is a property right for which Conco is entitled to compensation.

Question 58

Oscar is the owner of Black Acre, a 10-acre tract of agricultural land used to grow corn. After negotiation with the Valley Cable Co., Oscar conveyed to Valley Cable the right to construct and use an overhead cable across Black Acre to deliver the cable television signal to adjoining properties. The conveyance was signed by both parties and was duly recorded. Valley Cable installed the poles and the cable line in a proper and workmanlike manner. The cable remained in place for several years. Over this period of time, the cable had fallen into a state of disrepair. Neither Oscar nor Valley Cable took any steps towards the maintenance or repair of the cable line, and neither party complained to the other about any failure to repair. Because of the failure to repair the cable line, it fell to the ground when struck by a sudden gust of wind and set fire to Oscar's corn crop. The crop was totally destroyed. Oscar brought suit against Valley Cable to recover for damages to the corn crop.

The decision should be for:

(A) Oscar, because the owner of an easement is absolutely liable for any damage caused to the servient estate by the exercise of the easement.

(B) Oscar, because the owner of an easement has a duty to so maintain the easement as to avoid unreasonable interference with the use of the servient estate by its lawful possessor.

(C) Valley Cable, because an easement holder's right to repair is a right for his own benefit and is therefore inconsistent with any duty to repair for the benefit of another.

(D) Valley Cable, because the possessor of the servient estate has a duty to give the easement holder notice of defective conditions.

Question 59

Venkman's will provided, among other things, that his home, Withering Heights, would pass upon his death as follows: "To Stantz, for life, remainder to Egon Spengler if Spengler survives Stantz. If Spengler predeceases Stantz, then to my grandchildren, share and share alike." Venkman's will contained a residuary clause providing that any of his property not specifically devised would pass to Dana Barrett. Upon Venkman's death, he was survived by two children (Rudy and Ross), Stantz, Spengler, and Barrett. Venkman had no grandchildren at the time of his death. The jurisdiction has not modified the common law with any relevant statutory rules.

Upon Stantz's death, predeceased by Spengler, if Venkman's children have still produced no issue, who has the right to possession of Withering Heights?

(A) Stantz's heirs.

(B) Dana Barrett.

(C) A trustee appointed by the court to hold Withering Heights for the benefit of any children born to Venkman's children.

(D) Rudy and Ross.

Questions 60-61 are based on the following fact situation:

Paul was the owner in fee simple of Redacre, a large tract of land. Redacre is located in an area that is nicknamed "Gold Country," because a large amount of gold ore has been mined in the area. Although no excavation had been done on Redacre, it was believed that there might be gold on the land. Paul therefore began to mine Redacre, looking for gold. To finance his mining operation, Paul mortgaged Redacre for $100,000 to Bank. Shortly thereafter, Paul became ill and abandoned his gold mine. He then sold all of the interest to gold on Redacre to Zim. Paul's health became worse, and he was advised by his doctor to move to a warmer climate and retire. Shortly before moving, Paul conveyed his ownership in Redacre to Mineco. When Zim, Bank, and Mineco discovered that Paul had moved from the area, they became concerned over their interests, and recorded them in the following order: Bank recorded its mortgage first; Zim recorded his deed second; and Mineco recorded its deed third. Zim's continuation of Paul's mine on Redacre proved to be unsuccessful, and the land was reduced in value to less than $100,000. None of the parties dealing with Paul had any knowledge of the others at the time of their transactions.

60.   Assume for purposes of this question only that the jurisdiction has the following statute:

   No conveyance or mortgage of an interest in land is valid against any subsequent purchaser for value without notice thereof, unless it is recorded.

   If Mineco brings an action to quiet title in Redacre, the most likely result is:

   (A)   Since the rights of Bank, Zim, and Mineco are different in nature, the court would most likely validate all of the interests with Mineco having the ownership subject to the payment of the mortgage to Bank.

   (B)   Mineco would be successful in quieting title to Redacre.

   (C)   Bank's mortgage would be declared valid because it is first in time to all of the grants by Paul concerning Redacre.

   (D)   Bank's mortgage would take priority over Zim and Mineco, because Bank had no notice at the time it recorded the mortgage.

61.   Assume for purposes of this question only that the jurisdiction has the following statute:

   No conveyance or mortgage of an interest in land is valid against any subsequent purchaser for value without notice thereof whose conveyance is first recorded.

   If Mineco brings an action to quiet title to Redacre, the most likely result would be:

   (A)   Mineco would have only a reversionary interest.

   (B)   Bank's mortgage would be valid and superior because it was first in time.

   (C)   Mineco would be deemed the owner in fee simple absolute and subject only to the payment of the mortgage held by Bank.

   (D)   Mineco would have a fee simple interest subject to the gold rights of Zim and the mortgage held by Bank.

Question 62

Avaricious Acquisition Corporation ("AAC") was in the business of purchasing real property at below-market prices at tax, probate, and foreclosure sales, and then reselling the properties through its own sales force to investors. The bylaws of the corporation authorized the chief executive officer and the director of the marketing division to enter into contracts on behalf of the corporation for purchase or sale of properties.

For several months, Hogan, the CEO, had been getting reports from the accounting department that LeBeau, director of the marketing division, had been selling AAC properties at less than market value in order to inflate the number of sales the division accomplished under her leadership. AAC had recently purchased a large parcel of Atlantic City beachfront from a hotel-casino operation that went bankrupt, and Hogan expected to be able to resell the property to developers for at least $40 million. Concerned that LeBeau would try to move the property for less so that she could claim another swift sale, Hogan secretly opened his own negotiations with Playland International, a company that built and operated amusement parks, for purchase of the beachfront land. He simultaneously approached members of the board of directors on an informal basis and proposed to each that the corporate bylaws be amended to require approval by the CEO for every sale of AAC property. Meanwhile, unknown to Hogan or anyone else in AAC, LeBeau reached agreement with representatives of the Hottentot Hotel chain for the sale of the Atlantic City property for $35 million. On April 23, LeBeau and an authorized representative of Hottentot signed a written contract providing for sale by AAC of the beachfront property to Hottentot Hotels for $35 million. On April 25, the board of directors of AAC amended its bylaws as Hogan had suggested, effectively depriving the director of the marketing division of authorization to bind the corporation in purchase or sale transactions. This action was immediately publicized and became known to both LeBeau and the Hottentot Hotel people. On April 26, pursuant to a state statute permitting the recordation of contracts for the sale of real property, Hottentot Hotels duly recorded the written agreement signed by LeBeau. On May 1, Hogan, still unaware of the LeBeau-Hottentot agreement, approved sale of the Atlantic City property to Playland International for $39 million. The necessary documents of title were prepared and properly recorded by Playland International on May 5. Playland International first learned of the LeBeau-Hottentot agreement on May 7, when the Playland purchase was announced to the press by Hogan, and Hottentot's lawyers informed

Playland of Hottentot's assertedly prior interests. On May 10, the date scheduled for closing of the Hottentot Hotels sale agreement, Hogan refused to accept Hottentot's tender of $35 million and refused its demand for a deed to the Atlantic City property.

In a subsequent action by Hottentot Hotels against AAC and Playland International for specific performance of the agreement signed by LeBeau and to quiet title to the Atlantic City property, the probable outcome will be:

(A) Judgment for defendants, since the board of AAC had deprived LeBeau of authority to bind the corporation in the sale of real property.

(B) Judgment for defendants, because Playland International is the only purchaser who properly recorded a deed to the subject property.

(C) Judgment for Hottentot, since Playland International had constructive notice of Hottentot's interests in the beachfront property when the agreement with Hogan was made.

(D) Judgment for Hottentot, because the attempt to divest LeBeau of authority to approve sales of AAC property was invalid.

Questions 63-64 are based on the following fact situation:

Elmo owns a large tract of undeveloped land near Mountainview. The jurisdiction in which the land is located has adopted the following statute:

> No conveyance or mortgage of an interest in land is valid against a subsequent purchaser for value without notice thereof whose conveyance is first recorded.

The following sequence of events occurred in the following order:

1990: Elmo owed money to Stanley, and in satisfaction of this debt, Elmo conveyed the Mountainview property to him. Although Stanley intended to have the deed recorded, he mistakenly failed to do so.

May 1992: Elmo borrowed $40,000 from First Central Bank and, to secure the loan, executed a mortgage deed on the Mountainview property. First Central promptly recorded this mortgage.

September 1992: Elmo, just before he died, donated the property to his son, Tom, who did not know about the prior events, by a general warranty deed. Tom recorded the deed and entered into a contract with Becky to sell her the Mountainview property.

November 1992: Stanley discovered that the deed in his safe was not recorded, and so without notice of any of the prior transactions, Stanley recorded the deed.

December 1992: Becky paid Tom full value for the property, and without actual knowledge of any of the other transactions regarding the Mountainview property, Becky had the deed duly recorded.

63. By late 1993, Becky had expended substantial sums of money to prepare for a subdivision she intended to build on the Mountainview property. However, when she put up the property as security for a loan from the bank for construction costs, she learned for the first time of Stanley's claim. In a suit between Becky and Stanley, which of the following statements most accurately describes the probable outcome?

(A) Becky would prevail, because the money she paid for the property and to prepare for its subdivision was far in excess of what Stanley paid, and under equity, Becky would be deemed

the owner; however, she would have to reimburse Stanley for what he paid for the property.

(B) Becky would prevail, because under the doctrine of equitable conversion, her "right" to the property preceded Stanley's recordation, and thus whatever right he may have had would have been terminated before he could record.

(C) Becky would prevail because she purchased from Tom, whose deed was recorded before Stanley's deed.

(D) Stanley would prevail, because he recorded first.

64. First Central Bank intervened in the suit between Stanley and Becky to assert its claim with regard to the $40,000 mortgage. With regard to Stanley's claim to the property, First Central Bank most likely will:

(A) Not prevail, because Elmo conveyed his entire interest to Stanley, and therefore, had no property left that he could have mortgaged.

(B) Not prevail, because to enforce First Central Bank's claim would aid Elmo to work a fraud on Stanley, and the law will not aid someone to commit an unlawful act.

(C) Prevail, because it loaned Elmo the money without notice of Stanley's interest, and it recorded first.

(D) Prevail, because the instrument that is recorded first under this type of statute always prevails over the unrecorded or subsequently recorded instrument.

Question 65

Ludwig owned the City Centre Building, a prestigious downtown office building. Tom leased the entire building from Ludwig for a term of 20 years. The lease included a provision that taxes on the building would be paid by "the lessee, his successors, and assigns."

Tom occupied the building and paid the rent and taxes for eight years. At the end of the eight-year period, Tom assigned the balance of the lease to Audrey and vacated the premises. The assignment was written, but there was no provision concerning Audrey's assumption of the duties under the lease.

Audrey occupied the building and paid the rent and taxes for five years. At the end of the five-year period, she subleased the building for five years to Sam and vacated the premises. The sublease was written, but there was no provision concerning Sam's assumption of the duties under the lease.

Sam now occupies the building and has paid the rent but not the taxes. Ludwig has sued all three (*i.e.*, Tom, Audrey, and Sam) for failure to pay the taxes.

Ludwig would prevail against whom?

I. Tom

II. Audrey

III. Sam

(A) I. only.

(B) I. and II., but not III.

(C) II. and III., but not I.

(D) I., II., and III.

Question 66

Oliver owned Redacre in fee simple. Oliver conveyed Redacre to "Abner and Boris jointly, with right of survivorship."

Shortly thereafter, Abner was in an automobile accident, which resulted in the death of three persons. Clark, the driver of the other vehicle, sued Abner on a theory of negligence. Clark obtained a judgment in the amount of $250,000 against Abner.

Abner had no insurance. Because Abner did not have enough cash to satisfy the judgment, Clark levied on Abner's interest in Redacre.

Clark will get:

(A) Nothing, because Abner's interest in Redacre cannot be partitioned.

(B) An undivided half interest, regardless of whether Abner and Boris's title to Redacre is construed as a joint tenancy or a tenancy in common.

(C) An undivided half interest, assuming Abner and Boris's interest is construed as a tenancy in common and not a joint tenancy.

(D) A contingent right of survivorship which will vest if Abner survives Boris.

REAL PROPERTY ANSWERS

Answer to Question 1

(D) Pursuant to both the absolute ownership doctrine and the reasonable use doctrine, which together comprise the majority view with regard to determining rights in underground water, the Mills are entitled to use the water from the well on their property in the manner described in the facts. Under the absolute ownership doctrine (followed by about 12 states and the common law rule), the overlying owner may extract as much water as he wishes and use it for whatever purpose he desires, including hauling or piping it to other properties. Thus, under the absolute ownership doctrine, the Mills are entitled to extract as much water from Flushacre as they wish for any purposes they desire. Under the reasonable use doctrine (followed by about 25 states), a land-owner is limited to reasonable use of the underground water for beneficial purposes on the overlying land. "Reasonable" use is just about any use on the land that is not merely malicious or a waste of water. Thus, the use of water for gardening, filling a pool, and for the needs of tenants will constitute a reasonable use for beneficial purposes on the Mills' overlying land. Thus, under the reasonable use doctrine, the use of the water by the Mills from their well is permissible. Consequently, the Mills will be allowed to continue using the water as they presently are doing. Sutter will have no right to control, modify, or otherwise affect their use of the water. Because the Mills are using the water in a manner permitted by law and are not infringing on any legally protectible right of Sutter, Sutter is not entitled to monetary damages or injunctive relief. There-fore, (A) and (B) are incorrect. (C) is incorrect because the facts do not indicate the existence of any grounds for rescission (*i.e.,* mistake or misrepresentation) as between Sutter and Vendor at the time they entered into the contract for the purchase of Straightacre.

Answer to Question 2

(C) An easement is extinguished when the easement is conveyed to the owner of the servient tene-ment. For an easement to exist, the ownership of the easement and the servient tenement must be in different persons. (By definition, an easement is the right to use the land of ***another*** for a special purpose.) If ownership of the two property interests comes together in one person, the easement is extinguished. (A) is wrong because, although an attempt to convey an easement appurtenant apart from the dominant tenement is ineffective, it does not extinguish the easement. The easement continues despite the attempted conveyance and will pass with the ownership of the dominant tenement. (B) is wrong because mere nonuse does not extinguish an easement. An easement may be extinguished by abandonment, but to constitute abandonment sufficient to extinguish an easement, the easement holder must demonstrate by physical ***action*** an intent to ***permanently*** abandon the easement. Nonuse of the easement is not enough to show the intent never to make use of the easement again. (D) is wrong because, under certain circumstances, an easement may be extinguished without the easement holder's permission. For example, easements may be terminated by prescription, or by condemnation or destruction of the servient estate.

Answer to Question 3

(C) Furban may sell Greenacre, but only after formally foreclosing on the property. If a deed is given for security purposes rather than as an outright transfer of the property, it will be treated as an "equitable" mortgage and the creditor will be required to foreclose it by judicial action like any other mortgage. In determining whether an absolute deed is really a mortgage, the court consid-ers the following factors: (i) the existence of a debt or promise of payment by the deed's grantor;

(ii) the grantee's promise to return the land if the debt is paid; (iii) the fact that the amount advanced to the grantor/debtor was much lower than the value of the property; (iv) the degree of the grantor's financial distress; and (v) the parties' prior negotiations. Here, Guy owed Furban a debt; Furban promised to return the property if the debt was paid; the amount advanced ($30,000) was much lower than the value of the property ($100,000); Guy was in great financial distress; and the parties' negotiations reveal that this transaction was intended as security for the loan. Thus, Furban must bring a judicial foreclosure proceeding before he can sell Greenacre. (A) is wrong because a foreclosure is required. Furthermore, even in a foreclosure sale, Furban is not entitled to all of the proceeds. The proceeds are used to first pay the expenses of the sale, attorneys' fees, and court costs; then to pay the principal and accrued interest on the loan that was foreclosed; then to pay off junior interests. Any remaining proceeds are returned to the mortgagor. Furban is entitled only to his expenses and the amount still owing on the $30,000 loan, including accrued interest. Since Furban has a buyer willing to pay $100,000, Verdant should get some money back. (B) is wrong for two reasons: (i) as explained above, Furban cannot sell the property without a judicial foreclosure; and (ii) Verdant would not be entitled to $73,000. Furban is entitled to his expenses of sale, the principal amount owing, plus accrued interest. (D) is wrong because Furban *can* sell Greenacre, provided he undertakes formal foreclosure proceedings.

Answer to Question 4

(C) The Guild owns Staracre in fee simple absolute because the city had a fee simple absolute, which it conveyed to the Guild. The language in the deed "for the purpose of constructing a planetarium" merely expresses the grantor's *motive* for conveying the property; the city received the estate that the grantor had, a fee simple absolute. Since the city held a fee simple absolute, that is what it conveyed to the Guild. Therefore, IV. is correct. I. is wrong because the grant does not create a fee simple determinable. A fee simple determinable is an estate that automatically terminates upon the happening of a stated event. To create a fee simple determinable, durational language (*e.g.,* "for so long as," "until") must be used. Here, the grant does not contain the durational language necessary to create a fee simple determinable. Since the interest is not a fee simple determinable, Otis cannot have a possibility of reverter. II. is wrong for two reasons: (i) as explained above, a fee simple determinable was not created by the grant; and (ii) even if a fee simple determinable had been created, the transfer of the property would not by itself cause it to revert back to Otis. Determinable estates are alienable; the successor merely takes subject to the condition. The conveyance of a fee simple determinable would not automatically result in the property reverting to the grantor (*i.e.,* the Guild could build a planetarium on the property and avoid the property reverting back to Otis). III. is wrong because the grant did not create a fee simple determinable. (Had the grant contained the proper durational language, rather than "for the purpose of," III. would have been correct. In that case the Guild would own Staracre subject to the estate being terminated if the land is not used for a planetarium.) Thus, since IV. is the only correct choice, (C) is correct and (A), (B), and (D) are wrong.

Answer to Question 5

(A) Earl will not succeed in a suit for specific performance because the agreement is unenforceable under the Statute of Frauds. Under the Statute of Frauds, a land sale contract is unenforceable unless it is in writing and signed by the party to be charged. The Statute of Frauds requires the writing to contain all essential terms of the contract, which are: (i) a description of the property; (ii) identification of the parties to the contract; (iii) the price and manner of payment; and (iv) the signature of the party to be charged. Here, the agreement between Earl and Baron concerns the sale of land; thus, the agreement must be in writing to comply with the Statute of Frauds. The only writing mentioned in the facts is the check given to Earl by Baron. This check contains neither a description of the property that is the subject of the agreement nor the price and manner of payment. Thus, the check is not a writing sufficient to satisfy the Statute of Frauds. Consequently, the agreement is unenforceable, and Earl will not prevail. (Note that, under the doctrine of part performance adopted by some states, a court may grant specific performance of a contract despite the absence of a writing if there has been payment of the purchase price. Even under this view, Baron's payment of $2,500 out of a total price of $50,000 will not constitute sufficient performance to remove this agreement from the purview of the Statute of Frauds.) (B) is incorrect because, if there is no enforceable agreement, there can be no "breach" of the agreement, for which breach Earl will be entitled to damages. Therefore, Earl may not keep the earnest money as damages. (C) is incorrect for two reasons: (i) there is no need to determine whether duties have been discharged by frustration of contractual purpose where the contract itself is unenforceable under the Statute of Frauds; and (ii) frustration of a contract's purpose exists where some supervening event destroys the purpose, which must have been realized by both parties at the time of making the contract. Here, Earl had no idea that Baron wished to purchase Grayacre because he believed a new commercial-entertainment complex was to be built nearby. Thus, both parties did not realize the purpose. Also, it cannot really be said that a superseding event destroyed the contract's purpose. Baron was simply proceeding on the basis of inaccurate information. Finding out that his sources were incorrect hardly constitutes a supervening event. (D) is incorrect because "course of dealing" (*i.e.,* a sequence of previous conduct between the parties that may be regarded as establishing a common basis of their understanding) may be used to explain or supplement the terms of a written contract under the Uniform Commercial Code (U.C.C.). This question does not involve the sale of goods, so the U.C.C. is inapplicable. Furthermore, here there is no written agreement, the terms of which can be explained or supplemented by showing a course of dealing between Baron and Earl. Although Baron and Earl often dispensed with legal formalities as a cost-saving measure, this "course of dealing" will not confer validity on their oral agreement for the sale of land.

Answer to Question 6

(A) The seller in I. is unable to convey marketable title because of the option to buy. Ordinarily, an option of this duration would violate the Rule Against Perpetuities and be stricken. An interest violates the Rule Against Perpetuities if there is any possibility, however remote, that it will vest more than 21 years after some life in being at the creation of the interest. Here, the relevant measuring life would be the lessee. The lessee could die within the next three years, and the option could be exercised by his successors more than 21 years after his death. There is a special exception to the Rule, however, for options to purchase attached to leaseholds. Since the one who holds the option in this case is the current lessee, the Rule does not apply. Thus, the option is valid, and it renders title unmarketable. Hence, (D) is incorrect. II. is wrong because only a *significant* encroachment will render title unmarketable. A one-half-inch encroachment on airspace would not be considered significant, particularly since it does not interfere with the use of the adjoining property. Thus, this encroachment will not affect marketability. III. is wrong because a lien on property will not render title unmarketable if the seller pays the lien at closing. Unless the contract provides otherwise, the seller need not provide marketable title *until closing*. A seller has the right to satisfy a lien at the closing with the proceeds of the sale. Therefore, as long as the purchase price is sufficient and the lien is satisfied simultaneously with the transfer of title (*e.g.,* by using escrows), the buyer cannot claim that the title is unmarketable. The closing will result in marketable title. In the example given, the $25,000 purchase price is clearly sufficient to satisfy the $5,000 lien. Thus, the seller may satisfy the lien at the closing and convey marketable title to the buyer. Therefore, (B) and (C) are incorrect.

Answer to Question 7

(A) The most likely reason to find for Fan is that the court is not charging Fan with record notice of deeds to other lots given by Tenna and Bildem. When a developer subdivides land into several parcels and some of the deeds contain negative covenants but some do not, negative covenants or equitable servitudes binding all the parcels in the subdivision may be implied under the doctrine of "reciprocal negative servitudes." Two requirements must be met before reciprocal negative covenants and servitudes will be implied: (i) a common scheme for development and (ii) notice of the covenants. The second requirement may be satisfied by actual notice, record notice, or inquiry notice. Here, Fan has not been given actual notice, and the antenna restriction is not so obvious that the appearance of the neighborhood would provide Fan with inquiry notice. Finally, Fan has no record of the restriction in his chain of title to establish record notice. If Fan had been the first purchaser of the lot, some courts might require him to read all deeds given by a common grantor, but the better view does not require such a search. In any case, Fan's grantor here is Alice, and the restriction was not contained in her deed; Fan thus does not have record notice of it and is not bound. (B) is incorrect because the restriction could have been enforced against Alice as an equitable servitude even in the absence of an express restriction (oral or written). A common scheme for development existed and Bildem's salesperson gave Alice actual notice of the restriction. (C) is incorrect because courts will allow prior purchasers to enforce the restriction against a subsequent purchaser even if the original grantor made no covenant in the deeds that all subsequent parcels would be subject to the restriction. One theory courts use is that an implied reciprocal servitude attached to the common grantor's retained land at the time the first lots were deeded to the prior purchasers, and the prior purchasers are merely enforcing this implied servitude against the purchaser of a subsequent lot. Hence, if Fan were deemed to have had notice of the restriction, a court would allow prior purchasers to enforce it. (D) is incorrect. While changed neighborhood conditions is an equitable defense to enforcement of a servitude, the strip on the eastern edge of the parcel was always earmarked for commercial uses; the presence of a satellite dish on that property is not sufficient to bar enforcement of the restriction against the residential parcels.

Answer to Question 8

(C) Pete's remedies are limited to a personal action against Mavis and the lien that remains on the property. A judgment lien runs with the land and thus is binding on subsequent owners who have notice of it. Since the lien was properly filed in the recording office, Roy had notice of it and took the lot subject to it. Of course, Mavis is still personally liable on the amount of the judgment against her until paid. Charmaine is not liable. A joint tenant or a tenant in common may encumber her own interest, but may not encumber the other co-tenant's interest. Thus, the lien attached only to Mavis's half of the property; it did not attach to Charmaine's interest. (A) and (B) are wrong because the form of co-tenancy is irrelevant with respect to whether Pete can reach Charmaine's proceeds. The lien would not attach to Charmaine's interest regardless of the form of co-tenancy. If it were a tenancy in common, Pete could have executed the lien on Mavis's one-half interest. If Charmaine and Mavis owned the property as joint tenants with the right of survivorship, execution of the lien would sever the joint tenancy, but would not affect Charmaine's one-half interest. Since Pete did not execute his lien, it remains on the land. (D) is wrong because, as stated above, Pete has the lien on Roy's property in addition to his personal action against Mavis.

Answer to Question 9

(C) After the foreclosure sale, Atlas is entitled to $30,000, Big Bank is entitled to $20,000, and the balance passes to Dennis. When an interest is foreclosed, after the expenses and fees are paid, the proceeds of the sale are first used to pay the principal and accrued interest on the loan that was foreclosed, next to pay off any junior liens, and finally any remaining proceeds are distributed to the mortgagor. (A) and (D) are wrong because Paulina's interest, an interest senior to Atlas's, is not affected by the foreclosure. Without Paulina foreclosing her lien, she is not entitled to a share of the proceeds, and her lien continues on the property in the buyer's hands. (B) and (D) are wrong because, contrary to the statement in II., Big Bank is entitled to have its mortgage fully discharged.

Answer to Question 10

(A) Sigmar and Ingrid own Greatacre because recordation is prima facie evidence of delivery. To be valid, a deed must be "delivered," which means that the grantor must have taken some action (not necessarily a manual handing over of the deed) with the intent that it operate to pass title immediately. Recording the deed is such an action and is presumed to carry with it the requisite intent. Even without the knowledge of the grantee, delivery to the recorder's office will satisfy the delivery requirement. If the grantor intends the recording of the document to be the final act in vesting title in the grantee, then such recording constitutes delivery. (B) is wrong because a deed alone is not prima facie valid absent delivery. There must be evidence of delivery. (C) is wrong because recordation can constitute valid delivery, and there is sufficient evidence that the deed was recorded. Note that a rebuttable presumption of no delivery may arise from the grantor's retention of the deed. However, this presumption is rebutted by the recording of the deed. (In contrast, there is no evidence that delivery was not intended to rebut the presumption of delivery that arises from recording.) (D) is wrong because a description of the grantees in a deed is sufficient if it describes the grantees with sufficient particularity that it can be determined who is to take the property. The grantee need not actually be named. Since Gustav has a finite number of nieces and they are easy to locate and identify, the deed from Orizaba satisfies this requirement.

Answer to Question 11

(A) Persia may collect the unpaid rent from either Toy or Ayes. A complete transfer of the tenant's entire remaining term is an assignment of the lease. However, the original tenant can still be held liable on his original contractual obligation in the lease to pay rent; *i.e.,* on privity of contract. (D) is therefore incorrect because Toy is liable for the rent. (B) and (C) are also incorrect. Since the covenant to pay rent touches and concerns, and hence runs with the tenant's leasehold estate, an assignee owes the rent directly to the landlord. If the assignee reassigns the leasehold interest, his privity of estate with the landlord ends, and he generally is not liable for the subsequent assignee's failure to pay rent in the absence of a specific promise to the landlord. However, even if the assignee made no promise to the landlord but did promise the original tenant that he would pay all future rent, the landlord may sue the assignee as a third-party beneficiary of the promise to the original tenant. Here, while Ayes made no promise to Persia, Ayes did make a promise to Toy regarding the obligation that Toy owed to Persia. Thus, Persia can sue either Toy or Ayes for the unpaid rent.

Answer to Question 12

(A) The children have a contingent remainder. A remainder is a future interest created in a transferee that is capable of taking in present possession upon the natural termination of the preceding estate created in the same disposition. Note that as a rule of thumb, remainders always follow life estates. A remainder will be classified as contingent if its taking is subject to a condition precedent, or it is created in favor of unborn or unascertained persons. Here, the interest in the children follows a life estate and is a remainder because it is capable of taking in possession upon natural termination of the preceding estate. It is subject to the condition precedent of surviving Thomas's widow, and additionally, is in favor of unascertained persons (the children who survive Thomas's widow will not be ascertained until her death). Thus, the interest is a contingent remainder. (B) is incorrect because a vested remainder can be created in and held only by ascertained persons in being, and cannot be subject to a condition precedent. As discussed above, the will provision clearly does not satisfy these requirements because the takers are not ascertained and their interest is subject to a condition of survival. (C) is incorrect because a shifting executory interest is one that divests the interest of another transferee; *i.e.*, it cuts short a prior estate created by the same conveyance. The gift to the children does not divest the interest of the widow; she retains a life estate in the property. The children's interest takes in possession only upon the natural termination of the widow's estate (*i.e.*, at her death). (D) is incorrect because the interest does not violate the Rule Against Perpetuities. The children's interest will vest, if at all, not later than 21 years after the lives in being. Thomas's widow and the children themselves are lives in being. There is no unborn widow problem because the instrument takes effect on Thomas's death and the gift is to his own widow. She must be in being at his death. Likewise, his children would be in being at his death. Thus, the vesting will be within the period of the Rule.

Answer to Question 13

(B) Tamara has a month-to-month tenancy at $1,200 per month. When a tenant continues in possession after termination of her right to possession, the landlord may bind the tenant to a new periodic tenancy. While the terms and conditions of the expired tenancy generally apply to the new tenancy, if the landlord notifies the tenant before termination that occupancy after the termination date will be at an increased rent, the tenant will be held to have acquiesced to the new terms if he does not surrender. This is so even if the tenant objects to the increased rent, as long as the rent increase is reasonable. (A) is therefore incorrect. (C) is also incorrect. In commercial leases, where the original lease term was for a year or more, a year-to-year tenancy results from holding over. In residential leases, however, most courts look instead to the period of the rental payment, and make that the period of the new periodic tenancy. Hence, the tenancy would be month-to-month rather than annual. (D) is incorrect because a tenancy at will generally arises from a specific understanding between the parties that either party may terminate the tenancy at any time. Unless the parties expressly agree to a tenancy at will, the payment of regular rent will cause a court to treat the tenancy as a periodic tenancy.

Answer to Question 14

(D) The interest given to Jake's children does not violate the Rule Against Perpetuities because the interest will vest, if at all, within 21 years after the life of George. Pursuant to the Rule Against Perpetuities, no interest in property is valid unless it must vest, if at all, not later than 21 years after one or more lives in being at the creation of the interest. In the case of a will, the perpetuities period begins to run on the date of the testator's death, and measuring lives used to show the validity of an interest must be in existence at that time. Here, the interest given to any of Jake's children who are born during George's lifetime and who survive George must vest, if at all, on the death of George (who is a life in being at the time of Michael's death). Thus, this interest will vest, if it does vest, within 21 years after George's life, and is therefore not in violation of the Rule Against Perpetuities. (A) is therefore incorrect; if one or more of Jake's children is alive at the time of George's death, George's heirs will get nothing because their fee simple will be divested. (B) incorrectly characterizes the interest of Jake's children as a possibility of reverter. A possibility of reverter is the future interest left in a grantor who conveys a fee simple determinable estate. Although under different circumstances Jake's children could acquire a possibility of reverter as heirs of the grantor (Michael), their interest in this case was conveyed directly to them in Michael's will. (C) is incorrect because the interest of Jake's children is not vested. Their interest is a shifting executory interest rather than a remainder because it divests the fee simple determinable estate of George and his heirs. George has a fee simple determinable because the estate will remain with his heirs if none of Jake's children are alive when George dies. George's death while Jake's children are alive divests the interest of George's heirs; it is therefore a shifting executory interest rather than a remainder.

Answer to Question 15

(D) The court must find all three of the statements by Vittorio's attorney to be true for Vittorio to prevail. Statement II. is true as a general rule; contracts for the sale of land do not require the seller to hold title at the time he enters into the contract. He is only required to have marketable title at the date of closing so that he can deliver it to the buyer. Hence, Vittorio did not breach his contract with Piemonte by not having an interest in Tuscanacre at the time of the contract. Statement I. is true because courts will assume that time is not "of the essence" in real estate contracts unless (i) the contract states otherwise, (ii) the circumstances indicate that the parties intended time to be of the essence, or (iii) one party notified the other, within a reasonable time prior to closing, that he wishes time to be of the essence. If time is of the essence in the land sale contract, a party who fails to tender performance on the date set for closing is in total breach and loses his right to enforce the contract. Here, nothing in the contract or the surrounding circumstances indicated that time was of the essence in the Piemonte-Vittorio contract. If the court were *not* to reach this conclusion, Vittorio's failure to tender performance on June 1 would be a total breach of the contract. Statement III. is true because even when time is not of the essence in the contract, a party must tender performance within a reasonable time after the date set for closing or he will be unable to obtain specific performance. A delay of one month after the closing date has been deemed reasonable by the courts where the buyer has been delayed in obtaining financing or the seller has been delayed in obtaining marketable title. Here, Vittorio tendered performance to Piemonte two weeks after the closing date because he was unable to obtain marketable title by June 1. Thus, the court will probably find that Vittorio did not unreasonably delay the closing, and must make this finding in order for Vittorio to prevail.

Answer to Question 16

(C) Olson will not prevail because the covenant will be rendered unenforceable by either: (i) the application of the Rule Against Perpetuities, or (ii) imposition of a reasonable time limit of less than 21 years to avoid application of the Rule Against Perpetuities. A majority of jurisdictions would probably hold that the covenant granting the right of first refusal is void because it violates the Rule Against Perpetuities. Under the Rule, no interest in property is valid unless it must vest, if at all, no later than 21 years after a life in being at the creation of the interest. If the right might be exercised later than the perpetuities period, it is void. In this case, since the interest ran to both parties' heirs and assigns, there was no limit on Olson's right of first refusal. The right clearly could be exercised beyond the perpetuities period and so violates the Rule. Note that there is mixed opinion as to whether a court will avoid a right of first refusal that has an unlimited life, as this one purportedly has. There is a substantial body of opinion to the effect that the court should treat the right as exercisable only for a reasonable time, which is less than 21 years.

Hence, under this analysis, the right is valid, but becomes unenforceable by the passage of time. In this case, the right has not been exercised in 25 years; therefore, even under this analysis, the right is no longer enforceable. (A) is incorrect. The recording statute quoted by the question is a race-notice statute. Under a race-notice statute, a subsequent bona fide purchaser, such as Lane, is protected if she records before the prior grantee. To qualify as a bona fide purchaser, a person must, at the time of conveyance, take without actual, constructive, or record notice of the prior interest. Since the deed to White was recorded, Lane had record notice of the right of first refusal because it was in her chain of title. Had the covenant been within the perpetuities period, Lane would not have been protected by the recording act. However, since the covenant is void, Olson has no right to the property. Similarly, (B) is incorrect. The bad faith transaction of White and Kent would not have overcome the covenant had the covenant not violated the Rule. In light of the fact that the covenant is void, however, their bad faith is irrelevant. (D) is incorrect because the covenant runs with the land. The requirements for the burden of the covenant to run are met in this case: The fact that the original covenanting parties intended the right of first refusal covenant to run to their successors is indicated by the use of the language "heirs and assigns." The notice requirement was fulfilled by recording the deed. The horizontal privity requirement is satisfied by the fact that Olson and White share an interest in the land independent of the covenant, *i.e.,* as grantor and grantee. The necessary vertical privity is also present since Kent and Lane held the entire durational interest held by Olson when the covenant was made. Last, the covenant runs with the land because it "touches and concerns" the land; *i.e.,* it diminishes the landowner's right with respect to Pine Knoll.

Answer to Question 17

(A) A court will most likely find that Cassandra has a cause of action for nuisance because of the girders passing over her property. If land is repeatedly invaded by someone without permission, the possessor has a choice: she may sue for trespass (the intentional invasion of a person's land, which includes the space above the land, by a physical object), or for nuisance (substantial and unreasonable interference with the use of property). Here, the continual swinging of the girders over Cassandra's land constitutes a repeated invasion by a physical object that interfered with Cassandra's right of exclusive possession of the space over her building and with her enjoyment and use of her land. The interference is shown by her tenant's complaints. Thus, Cassandra has the option of suing for trespass or nuisance to remedy this continuing invasion. Therefore, (A) would be a correct answer. (D) is incorrect because, as explained, Cassandra would have a cause of action for trespass and a cause of action for nuisance. (B) and (C) are incorrect because there is no generally recognized cause of action for loss of sunlight or loss of a particular view. Courts do recognize negative easements for light and air. However, the facts of this question do not indicate that any such easement arose. Easements are interests in land and generally must be in writing to be enforceable. Lena's oral statement that she would not develop her land would not give rise to an easement or to any other type of legally enforceable right on the part of Cassandra to prevent construction of the building or otherwise obtain redress for its construction. Note also that even if there were a negative easement, this would merely entitle Cassandra to compel Apollo to refrain from engaging in the construction on his property and would not necessarily entitle Cassandra to damages as called for by (B) and (C).

Answer to Question 18

(A) Cassandra may recover damages for the subsidence if she can prove that Apollo's project caused the subsidence and that Apollo was negligent *or* that even without the buildings the property would have been damaged. A landowner has a right to have her land supported in its natural state by adjoining land. If, however, the land has buildings on it, an excavating neighbor is liable for damage to the buildings caused by the excavation if: (i) the excavating landowner was negligent; or (ii) the excavation would have caused the land to subside even in its natural state (*i.e.,* without buildings). Thus, if Apollo's excavation caused the damage to Cassandra's building, Cassandra can recover if she also proves negligence by Apollo *or* that the subsidence would have occurred if her land had been unimproved. (B) is wrong because intentional damage (III.) is not a requirement for recovery. Even if the damage to the property is unintentional, a landowner may recover if she proves causation and one of the two requirements above. (C) is wrong because Cassandra does not need to prove **both** negligence and that damage would have occurred to the land in its natural state; one or the other would be sufficient. (D) is wrong because proof of damage to the property with nothing more would not be a basis for recovery in this case. If the land had been unimproved, then the excavating landowner would be strictly liable for injury to neighboring land, but since Cassandra's property was improved, to recover she must prove more than the fact that the damage was caused by Apollo.

Answer to Question 19

(D) Wright will most likely recover nothing because, at the time of the contract, $4,000 represented a reasonable estimate of damages in the event of breach. When a sales contract provides that a seller may retain the buyer's earnest money as liquidated damages, courts routinely uphold the seller's retention of the money upon breach if the amount appears reasonable in light of the seller's anticipated and actual damages. Many courts uphold retention of earnest money of up to 10% of the sales price without inquiry into its reasonableness. In this case, the earnest money represented 2% of the purchase price. Given the fact that Curtiss had received other offers within $5,000 of the price offered by Wright, $4,000 would be a reasonable estimate of damages if Curtiss were forced to accept another offer. (A) is wrong because the fact that Wright had a good reason for not performing does not change the fact that he is in breach. The contract is not impossible for Wright to perform; it is just not as attractive a purchase as it was before the accident. He cannot escape liability on this basis. (B) and (C) are wrong because if there is a valid liquidated damages clause, it will be enforced and actual damages are irrelevant. (If the liquidated damages clause were not enforceable, (C) would be a better choice than (B) because Curtiss would be entitled to his expenses in remarketing the property.) Thus, since the liquidated damages clause is enforceable, Wright will not be able to recover any of the $4,000 he paid as earnest money.

Answer to Question 20

(C) Sutter will most likely prevail in his suit for one-half the cost of the well repairs because the covenant runs with the land. When a covenant runs with the land, subsequent owners of the land may enforce or be burdened by the covenant. If all of the requirements for the burden to run are met, the successor in interest to the burdened estate will be bound by the arrangement as effectively as if he had himself expressly agreed to be bound. To be bound the parties must have intended that the covenant run with the land; the original parties must have been in horizontal privity; the succeeding party must be in vertical privity with the original promisor; the covenant must touch and concern the land; and generally, the burdened party must have actual or constructive notice of the covenant. Here, the intent is shown by the express language of the covenant, which says that it is intended to run with the land. Even without that language, the use of the words "heirs" and "assigns" would show the intent for the covenant to run. The original parties were in horizontal privity because at the time Orson entered into the covenant, he and Masson shared an interest in the land independent of the covenant—as grantor and grantee. Julio is in vertical privity with Orson because he holds the entire interest in Vineacre held by Orson. The covenant touches and concerns the land because promises to pay money to be used in a way connected with the land are held to touch and concern the property. Since Julio was unaware of the covenant, the required notice seems to be missing. While it is generally true that the owner of the burdened land must have notice, it should be remembered that the requirement is a function of the recording statute. (At common law, the covenant was enforceable in an action for damages regardless of notice; this was changed by the recording statutes.) However, since Julio is a donee (an heir) and not a bona fide purchaser, he is not protected by the recording statute and thus is subject to the covenant even without notice. For that reason, (A) is wrong. (B) is wrong because Sutter's possession does not satisfy several of the requirements for adverse possession. Since Sutter had a legal right to use the well, his use was not adverse or hostile to the rights of Ernest and Julio, but was rather permissive. Sutter's possession also fails the exclusivity requirement, since the facts state that the well was used to irrigate both parcels for most of the statutory period. (D) is wrong because Sutter's status as a bona fide purchaser has no effect on his ability to enforce the covenant. A successor in interest to the original promisee may enforce the covenant (enjoy the **benefit**) if there was intent and vertical privity, and the covenant touches and concerns the land. Notice is **not** required for the benefit to run. Thus, since the above requirements are met here, Sutter may enforce the covenant regardless of his status as a bona fide purchaser. Had Sutter taken the property as a donee, the above analysis would be the same.

Answer to Question 21

(B) Lee is liable for Tracy's injuries because he failed to disclose a latent defect. If, at the time the lease is entered into, the landlord knows of a dangerous condition that the tenant could not discover upon reasonable inspection, the landlord has a duty to disclose the dangerous condition. Failure to disclose the information about the condition results in liability for any injury resulting from the condition. Since Lee knew of the dangerous electrical problem at the time he leased the premises to Tan and did not disclose it to either Tan or Tracy, he is liable for any injuries resulting from that condition. (A) is wrong for two reasons: (i) the implied warranty of habitability does not apply to commercial leases; and (ii) even if this were a residential lease, it is doubtful that Lucinda would be liable for a condition of which she had no knowledge or notice. (C) is wrong because it describes the relationship between Tan and Tracy as though there had been a sublease, when the facts clearly state that Tan assigned the balance of the lease to Tracy. If a tenant sublets the premises (*i.e.,* tenant retains part of the remaining term), the tenant is the landlord of the sublessee. The sublessee cannot sue or be sued by the landlord. However, if there has been an assignment (*i.e.,* tenant makes a complete transfer of the entire term remaining), the assignee is substituted for the original tenant and can sue or be sued by the landlord. The original tenant's relationship to the assignee is at most that of a surety. Here, since Tan transferred the balance of his lease to Tracy, there was an assignment and thus Tan cannot be considered Tracy's landlord. (D) is wrong because, as stated above, Tracy can recover from Lee. The statement that the covenant to repair runs with the land and binds Tracy is true, but Lee's failure to disclose a dangerous preexisting condition renders Lee liable for Tracy's injuries despite the covenant; *i.e.,* Tracy's covenant does not relieve Lee of his tort liability.

Answer to Question 22

(B) Ben, Fran, Dan, and Elsa all have an interest in Argentacre. Clementine's will created a defeasible life estate in Sebastian, with a remainder in Clementine's children. The will further provided that if a child predeceased her, that child's issue would take the predeceased child's share. When a person renounces a gift in a will, he is treated as having predeceased the testator. Thus, in this case, since Sebastian renounced his gift, his life estate would be stricken, leaving the gift to Clementine's children, with the issue of any predeceased children taking in the stead of their parent. Since the gift of Argentacre was by will, it was of no effect until Clementine's death. At Clementine's death, her son Ben was still alive and so is clearly entitled to an interest in Argentacre. Clementine's son Carl also survived her and so is entitled to a share. There is no requirement that he survive until the administration of the estate is completed; thus, his share will go to his estate and pass by will to Fran. Clementine's daughter Alice did not survive Clementine but she did leave issue. Therefore, her issue will split her share. Alice's sons, Ed and Dan, were both alive at Clementine's death and so they are entitled to take Alice's share. When Ed died, his share passed through his estate to his widow, Elsa. Therefore, the interests in Argentacre are: one-third to Ben, one-third to Fran (taking through Carl), one-sixth to Dan, and one-sixth to Elsa (taking through Ed). (A) is wrong because, as explained above, Elsa is entitled to Ed's share. (C) is wrong because it omits Fran and Elsa, and as explained above, Fran takes Carl's share and Elsa takes Ed's share. Carl and Ed had to survive Clementine to take but they did not have to survive the administration of the estate. Therefore, Carl and Ed were entitled to shares in Argentacre and their shares passed through their estates to Fran and Elsa. (D) is wrong because it omits Fran, who is entitled to Carl's share.

Answer to Question 23

(C) The children are the owners of Argentacre in fee simple absolute. The grant here gave Sebastian a defeasible life estate, which would end at his death or when he entered a religious order. In this case, Sebastian's life estate ended upon his entry into the religious order, and at that time Clementine's children took Argentacre in fee simple. Since Sebastian no longer has any right to be on Argentacre, he became a trespasser and could be forcibly removed. Obviously, as a trespasser, he is not entitled to any money from the mining operation. (A) is wrong because none of the gifts violates the Rule Against Perpetuities. The Rule states that an interest is not valid unless it must vest, if at all, within a life in being at its creation plus 21 years. Since the grant to Sebastian and the children was made in Clementine's will, it did not take effect until Clementine's death. At that time, the gifts became vested. Sebastian takes a present possessory life estate upon Clementine's death (when the will speaks). It is not a future interest, and consequently, the Rule Against Perpetuities has no effect on it at all. The gift to the children will vest within the perpetuities period. The children have both a remainder following Sebastian's life estate and an executory interest (which will divest Sebastian's life estate if he joins a religious order). The remainder became vested at Clementine's death because at that time her children would be ascertainable (she can have no more children) and there was no condition attached to the grant. The executory interest would also be valid under the Rule because it will vest, if at all, within Sebastian's lifetime (*i.e.,* when he joins the religious order). Therefore, there is no question that the gifts are valid under the Rule. (B) is wrong because, as explained above, the children have both a vested remainder and an executory interest, neither of which is subject to the destructibility rule (which applies to contingent remainders) or to the related doctrine of merger (which takes effect when one person owns all interests in the land except perhaps for a contingent remainder). (D) is wrong because when Sebastian entered the religious order, his entire interest in Argentacre, not just his right to possession, ended. Thus, since he no longer has any interest in the property, he no longer has any right to the income from the mine.

Answer to Question 24

(D) Argentacre is owned by Alice and Ben, subject to George's estate for the life of Sebastian. Clementine's will attempted to restrain alienability of the interests in Argentacre. A disabling restraint is one that renders any attempted transfer ineffective. All disabling restraints on legal interests (*e.g.,* a fee simple or life estate) are void. Here, Sebastian's life estate, a legal interest, is subject to a disabling restraint. The restraint prohibiting him from transferring his interest is void; therefore, Sebastian's conveyance to George is valid. George takes what Sebastian had: a life estate for ***Sebastian's*** life ***or*** until Sebastian joins a religious order. In contrast to a disabling restraint, a forfeiture restraint on alienation, under which an attempted transfer forfeits the interest, is valid if placed on a future interest only for the period when the interest is a future interest. In this case, any attempt by Clementine's children to transfer their interest while the interest was still a remainder caused a forfeiture. Since the restraint ended when the interest became possessory (and thus a present interest), it is a valid restraint. Thus, Carl's attempted transfer to Hal was invalid and caused a forfeiture of Carl's remainder in favor of the other children. Consequently, Alice and Ben own Argentacre, subject to the defeasible life estate in George. (A) is wrong because it does not include George's life estate pur autre vie. (B) is wrong because, as noted above, the forfeiture restraint on the transfer of Carl's remainder was valid. Thus, the attempted transfer to Hal was void. (C) is wrong because as discussed above, the disabling restraint on the transfer of Sebastian's interest was void and therefore Sebastian's life estate was freely transferable. Since Sebastian conveyed his interest to George, he no longer has any interest in Argentacre.

Answer to Question 25

(D) Tera has an easement to cross Frontacre even if Beverly never exercised her right to use the easement. The original easement granted to Beverly was an easement appurtenant, the benefit of which passes with a transfer of the benefited land. An easement is deemed appurtenant when the right of special use benefits the easement holder in her physical use or enjoyment of another tract of land. The land subject to the easement is the servient tenement, while the land having the benefit of the easement is the dominant tenement. The benefit of an easement appurtenant passes with transfers of the benefited land, regardless of whether the easement is mentioned in the conveyance. All who possess or subsequently succeed to title to the dominant tenement are entitled to the benefit of the easement. The easement granted to Beverly was an easement appurtenant because the right to use the private road across Frontacre (the servient tenement) benefited Beverly in her use and enjoyment of Backacre (the dominant tenement) by providing her with the most convenient access to the public highway. Thus, when Beverly sold the benefited land to Tera, the benefit of the easement also passed to Tera as an incident of possession of Backacre. (A) is wrong because, as explained above, this benefit passed to Tera despite the fact that the deed to Tera made no mention of the easement. The failure to record does not affect the validity of the easement. Recordation is not essential to the validity of a deed, but only serves to protect the interests of a grantee against subsequent purchasers. Here, the dispute is between the original grantor and the successor of the original easement holder. The purpose of most recording statutes is to provide notice to a ***burdened*** party. The person who granted the easement is in no need of notice. The only relevance of recording in this situation is with respect to the servient tenement, Frontacre. The grant of easement should be recorded on Frontacre, or bona fide purchasers from Ollie will take free of it. However, no such purchasers are involved in this question. (B) is incorrect because Tera's use of the easement would not be a change in its use. This choice goes to the scope of the easement. The key for determining the scope is the reasonable intent of the original parties, including the reasonable present and future needs of the dominant tenement. Here since Ollie knew of Beverly's plans to open an inn, he knew that she and her guests would use the road across Frontacre. Tera's use of the easement would be the same—her use and that of her guests. This is not a change in intended use sufficient to allow Ollie to legally prevent Tera's use of the easement. (C) is incorrect because nonuse does not extinguish an easement. Abandonment, which does terminate an easement, requires a physical act by the easement holder that manifests an intent to permanently abandon the easement (*e.g.,* erecting a building that blocks access to an easement of way). Since there is no indication of such an act by Beverly, the easement continues to benefit Backacre even if Beverly never used it.

Answer to Question 26

(B) Lomax can hold Tyson to a year-to-year tenancy for the original amount. When a tenant continues in possession after the termination of her right to possession, the landlord has two choices of action: he may treat the hold-over tenant as a trespasser and evict her under an unlawful detainer statute, or he may, in his sole discretion, bind the tenant to a new periodic tenancy, in which case the terms and conditions of the expired tenancy apply to the new tenancy. Unless a residential lease is involved, a year-to-year tenancy results from holding over if the original lease term was for a year or more. The new tenancy has the same terms as the original tenancy unless the landlord notified the tenant before termination of the original tenancy that occupancy after termination will be at an increased rent. Here, the original lease was a commercial lease for a two-year term, so Lomax's decision to hold Tyson to a new tenancy makes it a year-to-year tenancy. However, since Lomax did not notify Tyson of the rent increase prior to the end of the term, the new tenancy is at the original amount of rent. (A) is wrong because the lease here is not a residential lease; thus, the periodic tenancy created is a year-to-year tenancy rather than a month-to-month tenancy. (C) is wrong for the same reason that (A) is wrong and also because the new tenancy is at the original amount of rent, as discussed above. (D) is incorrect because when a landlord elects to bind a hold-over tenant to a new tenancy, it will be a periodic tenancy rather than a tenancy at will.

Answer to Question 27

(A) Ann and the City Zoo each own one-half of Goldacre, subject to Wilma's life estate. At the time of the conveyance by Arnie, Grant had a life estate, Grant's widow had a contingent interest (because "Grant's widow" cannot be ascertained until Grant's death), and Grant's children had a contingent remainder (because they have not yet been born). When Ann and Bradley were born, however, their interests became vested subject to open (*i.e.,* if Grant had more children). Thus, when Bradley died, he had a vested remainder subject to open that he was free to devise by will. Thus, the City Zoo took his vested remainder subject to open. At Grant's death, the class of Grant's children closed (because Grant could not have any more children), and Ann's and the zoo's vested remainders subject to open became indefeasibly vested. Also at Grant's death, his widow was ascertained and her interest vested in possession. Since Wilma was Grant's widow, she is entitled to the valid life estate. Thus, Ann and the City Zoo hold one-half interests, subject to Wilma's life estate. (B) is wrong because Grant had no interest in Goldacre when he died. He merely had a life estate, which ended at his death. He did not inherit any interest in the property from anyone else. The only person he inherited from in these facts was Wanda, and she had no interest in Goldacre. Furthermore, this choice overlooks the City Zoo's interest, which was inherited from Bradley. (C) is wrong because the children's interest does not violate the Rule Against Perpetuities. To be valid under the Rule, an interest must vest if at all within a life in being at its creation plus 21 years. Grant is a life in being. At Grant's death, the children's interest is certain to vest or fail: If Grant had any children, at his death, the children's interest would become indefeasibly vested (*i.e.,* the class would close and the children's interest would no longer be subject to open). Note that the children need not come into possession within the perpetuities period; the only requirement is that their interests vest within the period. Likewise, if Grant had no children, the gift to them was certain to fail at his death. Thus, the children's interest does not violate the Rule. Since Grant had children and their interest was valid, there was no interest to revert to Arnie and to be devised to Zeke. Note that the unborn widow aspect of this question is a red herring. The fact would be relevant only if the children's gift were conditioned on their surviving the widow, in which case the takers would remain unascertained and their interest would remain contingent until that time. But since the children's interest vested at Grant's death, it is irrelevant that "Grant's widow" is not a life in being. (D) is wrong because the gift to Grant's children was not conditioned on their survival of Grant. The law does not imply such a condition. Bradley's interest was vested subject to open and could be disposed of by his will.

Answer to Question 28

(B) Seth will prevail in his suit for specific performance because the easement was visible, Pamela was aware of it at the time she entered into the contract (*i.e.*, she knew a public sidewalk ran in front of the store), and the easement enhanced the value of the property. There is an implied warranty in every land sale contract that, at closing, the seller will provide the buyer with marketable title. Marketable title is title reasonably free from doubt, which generally means free from encumbrances and with good record title. Easements are generally considered encumbrances that render title unmarketable; so if an easement is not provided for in the contract, it usually renders the seller's title unmarketable. There is an exception, however. A majority of courts have held that a *beneficial* easement that was *visible or known* to the buyer does not constitute an encumbrance. In this case, the sidewalk was visible, known to Pamela, and beneficial to the property. Thus, the sidewalk easement does not impair the marketability of Seth's title. Therefore, Pamela's excuse for her nonperformance is not valid, and since land is involved, Seth can get specific performance of the contract for purchase of the property. (A) is wrong because, as noted above, the warranty that the seller will convey marketable title is *implied* in *every* land sale contract. So the fact that the contract did not specify the quality of title does not relieve the seller, Seth, from providing marketable title. Thus, (A) reaches the correct result for the wrong reason. (C) is wrong because, as noted above, there is an exception to the general rule, stated in (C), for beneficial easements that are visible or known to the buyer. (D) is wrong because Pamela cannot escape the contract merely by giving notice of her intent to breach it. It apparently was a valid contract that can be enforced against her. Failure to mitigate damages might prevent Seth from recovering avoidable damages but would not negate the breach.

Answer to Question 29

(A) Reformation is the remedy whereby the writing setting forth the agreement between the parties is changed to make it conform to the original intent of the parties. Reformation may be available where there is a mutual mistake (*i.e.*, the writing does not conform to the original agreement and the parties are not aware of the discrepancy). As long as the parties were in agreement as to the terms before the contract was reduced to writing, reformation can be had regardless of whether both parties signed the contract without noticing the deviation from the oral agreement or one party knew of the deviation and the other did not. In (A), both parties believed the stone fence constituted the eastern boundary of Bill's parcel. There was no mistake in the oral agreement, merely in putting it in writing. Thus, the court will reform the contract so as to indicate the stone fence as the eastern boundary of Bill's parcel. (B), (C), and (D) are situations in which reformation is inappropriate. The mistake in all three cases is with the agreement itself, not merely with reducing the agreement to writing. In each case, one of the parties believes the agreement to be different from that which the other party believes to be the agreement. Thus, reformation is not available.

Answer to Question 30

(C) Sedgwick has title to Siltacre, but he must redeem Carter's mortgage to avoid foreclosure. As a general rule, the priority of a mortgage is determined by the time it was placed on the property. When a mortgage is foreclosed, the buyer at the sale will take title as it existed when the mortgage was placed on the property. Thus, foreclosure will terminate interests junior to the mortgage being foreclosed but will not affect senior interests. However, if a lien senior to that of a mortgagee is in default, the junior mortgagee has the right to pay it off (*i.e.*, redeem it) to avoid being wiped out by its foreclosure. Thus, those persons with interests subordinate to those of the foreclosing party are necessary parties to the foreclosure action. Failure to include a necessary party results in the preservation of that party's interest despite foreclosure and sale. Hence, Sedgwick's failure to include Carter as a party to the foreclosure action preserved Carter's mortgage on the property. Unless Sedgwick were to reforeclose his mortgage and make Carter a party, he will need to pay off Carter's mortgage to avoid Carter foreclosing (because Peterson was in default on Carter's mortgage as well). (A) is wrong because it is irrelevant. While a purchase money mortgage, given when the mortgagor buys the property, is considered to have priority over non-PMM mortgages executed at about the same time, even if the other mortgages are recorded first, that rule is not applicable here because the facts indicate that Sedgwick's purchase money mortgage was executed and recorded before Carter's mortgage came into existence. (B) is incorrect because Carter was not included as a party to the foreclosure action. Thus, as discussed above, his interest is not extinguished by Sedgwick's foreclosure action. (D) is wrong because the failure to include Carter in the foreclosure action does not invalidate the action, it just preserves Carter's junior mortgage on the property.

Answer to Question 31

(D) Fenster may not remove the windows because they are fixtures and the bank's mortgage on the real property takes priority. Under the concept of fixtures, a chattel that has been annexed to real property is converted from personalty to realty. As an accessory to the real property, it is subject to any mortgage on the real property. In all common ownership cases (*i.e.*, those in which the person who brings the chattel onto the land owns both the chattel and the realty), whether an item that is not incorporated into a structure is a "fixture" (*i.e.*, part of the realty) depends upon the objective intention of the party who made the "annexation." This intention is determined by considering: (i) the nature of the article; (ii) the manner in which it is attached to the realty; (iii) the amount of damage that would be caused by its removal; and (iv) the adaptation of the item to the use of the realty. Under this analysis the windows are fixtures. It should first be noted that Dickens is the fee simple owner of the house rather than a tenant and intended to make numerous permanent improvements to the house in future years; the state-of-the-art windows were simply the first step in what he believed would be a long-term process. The fact that the windows were easily removable (and therefore would cause minimal damage in the event of removal) would ordinarily indicate less of an intention to permanently improve the freehold, but here the facts indicate that they were easily removable to make it easier to clean them. Another important factor indicating that the windows are fixtures is that they cannot readily be used at any other house unless the window sizes happen to correspond to those at Dickens's house. They were custom-made specifically for that house and therefore they were specially adapted to the use of the realty. They serve both functional and aesthetic purposes, they are an integral part of the house, and are necessary and appropriate to the use of the premises. Thus, in view of factors (i) and (iv) above, and considering Dickens's fee simple ownership and long-term plans for the house, they should be deemed fixtures.

The fact that the windows are fixtures does not resolve the dispute between Fenster and the bank, however. Under Article 9 of the Uniform Commercial Code, a seller of a chattel that will become a fixture can grant a security interest in the chattel for a portion of the purchase price and protect his interest by making a "fixture filing" even though the real property has a mortgage. Under U.C.C. section 9-313(4), a seller who provides a purchase money security interest in an affixed chattel will prevail (to the extent of his claim) over a prior recorded mortgage on the land as long as the chattel interest is recorded within 20 days after the chattel is affixed to the land; this allows the seller to remove the chattel without having to reimburse the mortgagee for any diminution in the property's value. However, if this exception does not apply, the general rule that the first interest to be recorded prevails will be applied by the court. Here, while Fenster has a purchase money security interest in the windows, there is no indication that he made a fixture filing within 20 days of when the windows were installed. Thus, the bank's recorded mortgage interest is superior to Fenster's security interest, so Fenster will not be permitted to remove the windows. (A) is incorrect. In determining whether a chattel is a fixture in landlord-tenant cases, courts will generally allow the tenant to remove any chattel that he installed (*i.e.,* deem it not to be a fixture) if removal does not cause substantial damage to the premises or the virtual destruction of the chattel. However, that reflects the probable intent of the tenant who purchased the chattel, since he has no interest in permanently improving the freehold. Here, however, Dickens was the fee simple owner of the house. The fact that he saved the old windows does not negate his intent to permanently improve the real estate with the new ones. (B) is incorrect because, as discussed above, the ease of removing the windows was for purposes of cleaning and does not negate an intent to permanently improve the real estate. (C) is incorrect even though it states an important factor for concluding that the windows are fixtures. As discussed above, that fact would not have precluded Fenster from prevailing had he recorded his security interest in the windows.

Answer to Question 32

(B) Prufrock's lien was extinguished at Bucky's death, leaving Alan as the sole owner of Brubacre. The distinguishing characteristic of a joint tenancy, which is how Alan and Bucky held Brubacre, is the right of survivorship. When one joint tenant dies, the property is freed of his concurrent interest and the survivor continues to retain an undivided right in the property no longer subject to the interests of the deceased co-tenant. The survivor does not succeed to the decedent's interest; he holds free of it. Hence, as long as the joint tenancy is still intact, the decedent's devisees, heirs, and judgment creditors have no claim on the joint tenancy property that the decedent held. For the joint tenancy to remain intact, the unities of time, title, interest, and possession that were necessary to create the tenancy must be undisturbed. Any disturbance of the unities causes a severance of the joint tenancy, and thereafter the parties whose unities are disturbed hold as tenants in common. In most jurisdictions, however, the fact that a creditor has obtained a lien on one joint tenant's interest does not by itself result in severance; there must also be at least a judicial sale of the property. Thus, judgment and other lien creditors easily can lose their security interest by the death of the debtor. That is what happened to Prufrock in this case. He obtained a statutory lien on Brubacre through Bucky's interest as a joint tenant. This did not cause a severance of the joint tenancy; Alan and Bucky remain joint tenants. When Bucky died, Brubacre was freed of his concurrent interest and any claims arising through that interest. Prufrock, not having caused a judicial sale of the property, loses his security interest. Thus, Alan is the sole owner of Brubacre, and the property is not subject to Prufrock's statutory lien.

Answer to Question 33

(D) Bixby will prevail because there is no evidence that time was of the essence. In general, courts presume that time is not of the essence in real estate contracts. Thus, the closing date stated in the contract is not absolutely binding in equity, and a party, even though late in tendering his own performance, can still enforce the contract if he tenders within a reasonable time. (One to two months is usually considered reasonable.) Time will be considered of the essence only if: (i) the contract so states; (ii) the circumstances indicate it was the parties' intention; or (iii) one party gives the other notice that he desires to make time of the essence. The contract in this case made no mention that time was of the essence. The facts do not indicate any circumstances, such as rapidly fluctuating prices or the need for the money to close another critical transaction, that would indicate that Bixby and Seaver intended time to be of the essence. Seaver did not give Bixby reasonable notice before September 30 that he wanted to make time of the essence. Thus, the court will not find that time is of the essence here. Since time is not of the essence, Bixby is not in material breach and is entitled to specific performance. (A) is wrong because the Statute of Frauds is not violated here. Contracts for the sale of land must be in writing to be enforceable. The essential terms for purposes of the Statute of Frauds are: the description of the property, the identification of the parties, and the price. The tax provision is not an essential term. It is an incidental matter, which need not appear in writing or even be agreed upon. (B) is wrong, because as discussed above, Bixby is not in material breach. Time was not of the essence, so the fact that Bixby did not tender his performance on September 30 did not constitute a breach of the land sale contract. (C) is wrong because the doctrine of equitable conversion will not affect the rights of the parties in this situation. The doctrine of equitable conversion holds that once an enforceable contract of sale is signed, the purchaser's interest is real property, and the seller's interest (the right to proceeds) is personal property. This is important with respect to which party bears the risk of loss if the property is damaged before the date set for closing or if one of the parties dies prior to closing. It has no effect in situations like this one where the question in issue is the enforceability of the contract itself.

Answer to Question 34

(B) Barb will prevail in a suit to quiet title because Caleb had notice of Barb's interest in the property and, thus, is not a bona fide purchaser for value. When a grantor purports to convey property that he does not own, his subsequent acquisition of title to that property vests in the grantee under the doctrine of estoppel by deed. Most courts, however, hold that this is personal estoppel, which means that title inures to the grantee's benefit only as against the grantor, not a subsequent bona fide purchaser. If the grantor transfers his after-acquired title to an innocent purchaser for value, the bona fide purchaser gets good title. There is a split of authority as to whether the original grantee's recordation of the deed imparts sufficient notice to prevent a subsequent purchaser from being a bona fide purchaser, but the majority view is that it does not because it is not in his chain of title. Thus, it is not the fact that Barb recorded that prevents Caleb from being a bona fide purchaser. The fact that Barb built a home and was living on the property gave Caleb constructive notice of her interest. A title search is not complete without an examination of possession. If the possession is unexplained by the record, the subsequent purchaser is charged with knowledge of whatever an inspection of the property would have disclosed and anything that would have been disclosed by inquiring of the possessor. Therefore, Caleb is charged with knowledge of Barb's possession and with what Barb would have told him about her possession; *i.e.,* that the property was conveyed to her by Son prior to his conveyance to Caleb. Consequently, Caleb does not qualify as a bona fide purchaser, and (C) is an incorrect choice. (A) is wrong because, although Son is estopped to deny that he acquired title for the benefit of Barb, he could have conveyed valid title to a subsequent purchaser for value who had no notice of Barb's interest. Therefore, it is not exactly correct to say that Son had no title to convey. (D) is wrong because Caleb will not prevail. It is true that under the recording acts Barb's deed was not in the chain of title, but Caleb still does not qualify as a bona fide purchaser. Caleb is on inquiry notice arising from Barb's possession of the property.

Answer to Question 35

(A) The transfer from Terry to Tessie was effective even though Lorne refused to consent. If a landlord grants consent to one transfer, he waives his right to avoid future transfers unless he expressly reserves the right to do so. The reservation of this right must take place at the time of granting consent. Here, Larry consented to the transfer from Tom to Terry, without reserving his right to prohibit future transfers without his consent. Thus, the provision barring assignment and sublease is deemed waived, and cannot be enforced by Lorne. Furthermore, even if the provision were effective, it would not make the transfer from Terry to Tessie ineffective. The transfer itself is valid, but the landlord may usually terminate the lease under either the lease terms or a statute. Here, there is no mention of such lease terms or a statute that would permit Lorne to terminate the lease. He would be left with an action for damages (if he can prove any) for breach, but the transfer would be effective. Since the transfer is effective, (D) is wrong. (B) is wrong because it states the wrong reason that the transfer is effective. Even if the provision were not deemed waived, the reasonableness of Lorne's withholding of his consent would not affect the outcome. First, the limitation that a landlord may not unreasonably withhold consent is a minority position. Second, as discussed above, a transfer in violation of a lease provision prohibiting transfer is not void, but would affect only the landlord's remedies; therefore, defenses to compliance with the provision are not necessary to uphold the transfer's effectiveness. (C) is wrong because restrictions on the transferability of leaseholds are valid restraints on alienation. A provision in a lease prohibiting the lessee's assignment or sublease of her leasehold interest without the consent of the landlord is given effect in all jurisdictions.

Answer to Question 36

(B) Lorne can recover $100 per month rent from Tessie. Tessie is liable to Lorne for the rent because of her status as an assignee, and because at common law the rent and anti-competition covenants are independent. Tessie is an assignee of Terry's interest in the leasehold (in turn, Terry was an assignee of Tom's leasehold interest). To be an assignment, a transfer must be on the same terms as the original leasehold *except* that the transferring tenant may reserve a right of termination (reentry) for breach of the terms of the original lease that has been assigned. Because Terry transferred all of her interests to Tessie, this transfer will be given effect as an assignment rather than a sublease despite Terry's reservation of a right of reentry. An assignee takes the place of the original tenant in a direct relationship with the landlord. The assignee and landlord are in privity of estate, so that each is liable to the other on all lease covenants that run with the land. Covenants held to run with the land include covenants to pay money. Because a covenant to pay rent runs with the land, an assignee owes the rent directly to the landlord, for the time that they are in privity of estate. Lorne and Tessie are in privity of estate. The burden of Tom's original covenant to pay rent runs with the land and binds Tessie. (A) incorrectly states that Lorne has no direct claim against Tessie personally for payment of the rent. (C) and (D) are wrong because, at common law, a tenant's duty to pay rent is considered an obligation independent of the landlord's performance of his obligations. Larry's original agreement that the space leased to Tom would be the exclusive vending facility in the building ran with the land. The provision would certainly have been intended to run with the land (it is highly doubtful that Tom would have intended that a successor in interest to Larry could lease space for competing vending facilities). Also, this agreement touched and concerned the leased premises, because it benefited the tenant and burdened the landlord with respect to their interests in the property. Lorne has breached this covenant by installing the vending machines. This breach by the landlord will not, however, allow Tessie to terminate the lease or her obligation to pay rent under the lease. Regardless of Lorne's breach of his covenant, Tessie's obligation to pay rent remains fully enforceable. (C) and (D) are incorrect because they are based on the false premise that Tessie's duty to pay rent is dependent on Lorne's performance of his agreement that there would be no other vending facilities in the building. Lorne can recover the rent payments regardless of whether the vending machines are removed, and Tessie's remedy for Lorne's breach is to bring an action against Lorne for any damages resulting from his installation of the vending machines.

Answer to Question 37

(C) Good title cannot be obtained without Harold's inclusion in the conveyance. All contracts for the sale of land contain, unless the contract expressly provides otherwise, an implied warranty by the seller that he will deliver to the buyer a marketable title at the date of closing. Private restrictions or encumbrances, including executory interests and possibilities of reverter, will render title unmarketable unless the holders of those interests join in the transaction. Here, the Girl Scouts have a valid executory interest that does not violate the Rule Against Perpetuities because their interest must vest, if at all, during Daphne's lifetime. However, Daphne's fee simple determinable is not limited in duration like the interest of the Girl Scouts. Thus, Daphne's heirs will only have a fee simple determinable rather than a fee simple absolute. Because the Girl Scouts' interest vanishes on Daphne's death, and no other provision was made for the property if it should thereafter be used for noncamping or nonrecreational purposes, the transferor (Tess) retained a possibility of reverter. This interest passed to Erma and then to Harold, and so Harold's interest must be included in the conveyance. (A) is wrong because Paul has contracted to receive good title to a fee simple absolute without any restrictions on the use of the property. Unless Harold joins in the contract to convey his possibility of reverter, good title cannot be conveyed. (B) is wrong because Harold's interest is the one blocking good title; the Girl Scouts have already agreed to sell their interest. Furthermore, their interest is not a right of entry but a shifting executory interest that would automatically divest Paul's interest if he violated the use restriction, and so their promise would be meaningless. (D) is wrong because Daphne, the Girl Scouts, and Harold together can validly convey a fee simple absolute to Paul.

Answer to Question 38

(C) If Sett can compel Bank to accept his offer, it will be because he has a statutory power to redeem the property after the foreclosure sale has occurred. In all states, the equity of redemption provides the borrower with an equitable right, at any time *prior to* the foreclosure sale, to redeem the land or free it of the mortgage or lien by paying off the amount due or, if an acceleration clause applies, the full balance due. Only about half the states, however, give the borrower a statutory right to redeem for some fixed period *after* the foreclosure sale has occurred; the amount to be paid is generally the foreclosure sale price, rather than the amount of the original debt. Thus, if Sett can redeem Southacre for $80,000, it will be based on the jurisdiction's statutory power of redemption. (A) is wrong because the deed of trust is a security interest (similar to a mortgage) to which the revocation rules for trusts do not apply. The deed of trust was created in part to allow the lender to foreclose on the property without going through a judicial foreclosure proceeding. (B) is incorrect. In states that permit a nonjudicial sale with deeds of trust containing a power of sale, the lender may bid at the sale, and in many cases the lender is the sole bidder. (D) is wrong because the prohibition against "clogging the equity of redemption" refers to the rule that a borrower's right to redeem his own mortgage cannot be waived in the instrument itself. Here, there is nothing to indicate that Sett's deed of trust prohibited him from redeeming the property prior to foreclosure. However, it is only through a statutory right of redemption that Sett would be able to redeem the property for $80,000 after the foreclosure sale had occurred.

Answer to Question 39

(C) Sharon prevails, because the statutory period for adverse possession did not begin to run against her until Jack died. The doctrine of adverse possession provides that possession for a specified statutory period in the requisite manner will establish the possessor's title to the land. For possession to ripen into title, it must be: (i) actual; (ii) open and notorious (*i.e.,* such as the usual owner would make of the land and sufficient to put the true owner or the community on notice of the fact of possession); (iii) continuous; and (iv) hostile (*i.e.,* without the true owner's permission). The statute of limitations that determines the time period for adverse possession does not run against the holder of a future interest (*e.g.,* a remainder) until that interest becomes possessory, because the holder of the future interest has no right to possession (and thus no cause of action against a wrongful possessor) until the prior present estate terminates. Here, the society has possessed the home for eight years; however, as against Sharon, the holder of the remainder, the statute did not begin to run until the death of Jack. Prior to the termination of Jack's life estate, Sharon had no cause of action against the society because she had no right to possession. Upon Jack's death, when Sharon's interest became possessory, the statute began to run against her. Thus, as against Sharon, the society has not been in adverse possession for the requisite period. (A) is incorrect because it fails to account for that fact; as against Sharon, the applicable statute did not begin to run until her interest became possessory (on the termination of Jack's estate). (B) is incorrect because the society could not purchase from Jack a fee simple absolute; Jack was only a life tenant in the home. Consequently, when Jack conveyed the home to the society, the society received a life estate rather than a fee simple absolute—the society could not receive from Jack what he did not own. (D), on the other hand, is incorrect because the society could eventually obtain title in fee simple absolute by means of adverse possession, even though it could not receive a fee simple absolute by means of the conveyance from Jack. If, for example, the society had maintained its possession for the statutory period starting at Jack's death, such possession would have ripened into title against Sharon. Thus, (D) is not an accurate statement.

Answer to Question 40

(A) The express easement for Leslie's old property benefits that property only and cannot be used for Leslie's expanded access to the new property. An easement is a liberty, privilege, or advantage that one may hold in the lands of another. The holder of an easement has the right to use a tract of land (called the servient tenement) for a special purpose; *e.g.,* laying utility lines, or for ingress and egress. An easement can be created, as in this question, by express grant. If the parties to the original creation of the use specifically state the location of the easement, its dimensions, and the special use or limits to such use, the courts will honor this expression of specific intent. Absent specific limitations, it will be assumed that the parties intend that the easement meet both present and future ***reasonable*** needs of the dominant tenement. However, a basic change in the nature of the use is not allowed. Leslie's easement by express grant merely allows her to use the private roads in Lakeshore Estates for her personal ingress and egress to and from her beachfront property. The use of the easement for access to a new boat launching ramp for which a fee is charged goes beyond the specific language of the grant (and arguably beyond the reasonable needs of the dominant tenement). Therefore, the homeowners will be able to prevent use of the streets of Lakeshore Estates to reach the boat launching ramp. (B) is incorrect because even if Leslie's express easement over the streets of Lakeshore Estates is construed to benefit the property that was recently acquired as well as her old property, the scope of the easement will not be expanded beyond the language of the grant. (C) is incorrect because the elements of easement by necessity are missing. Where the owner of a tract of land sells a part of the tract and by this division deprives one parcel of access to a public road or utility line, a right-of-way by absolute necessity is created by implied grant over the parcel with access to the public road. Leslie has not purchased her new property from the owners of Lakeshore Estates. Thus, she has no implied right-of-way by necessity over the streets of Lakeshore Estates to reach her new property. (D) is incorrect because the elements of an easement by implied grant are missing. Where an owner sells a portion of his property, and prior to the conveyance a use had been made, the existence of the prior use may give rise to an easement by implication, even though no reference is made to a continuation of that use. Here, when Leslie purchased her original property from the original owner of the Lakeshore Estates subdivision, there was no prior use of the subdivision land to reach her new property (because it did not even exist at that time). Consequently, no such use can now be implied simply by virtue of the fact that Leslie's new property abuts her old property. The new property was purchased from a different owner, and there is no basis for implying a grant to use the land of Lakeshore Estates to benefit land purchased from the county.

Answer to Question 41

(D) Wanda will win because she had a right under the statute to withhold the rent. The general rule at common law was that the landlord was not liable to the tenant for damages caused by the landlord's failure to maintain the premises during the period of the leasehold. Today, however, a majority of jurisdictions, usually by statute, provide for an implied warranty of habitability for residential tenancies. The statute in this question allows the tenant to make the repairs and withhold the cost of the repairs 15 days after notifying the landlord in writing. The statute is applicable because the damage done by the vandals makes it unfit for habitation under whatever standard the court would apply. Wanda has complied with the terms of the statute; she therefore cannot be evicted for nonpayment of rent. (A) is incorrect because Wanda does not need to show that the landlord was negligent. (B) is incorrect because the statute has extended the common law duty of the landlord, which applied only to the common areas of a multi-unit building. (C) is incorrect. The fact that the damage was caused by a third party would be relevant only if Wanda were relying on the judicially developed remedy of constructive eviction, which requires that the damage making the premises uninhabitable have been caused by the landlord. The warranty of habitability is not limited in this way.

Answer to Question 42

(B) First Bank's mortgage survives under its modified terms because Second Bank did not include First Bank in the foreclosure action. The general rule is that when a mortgage is foreclosed, the buyer at the sale will take title as it existed when the mortgage was placed on the property. Thus, foreclosure generally will destroy all interests junior to the mortgage being foreclosed, but will not discharge senior interests. However, those with interests subordinate to those of the foreclosing party are necessary parties to the foreclosure action. Failure to include a necessary party results in the preservation of that party's interest despite foreclosure and sale. Here, First Bank's original mortgage was senior to Second Bank's mortgage. However, where the landowner enters into a modification agreement with the senior mortgagee, raising its interest rate or otherwise making it more burdensome, the junior mortgagee will be given priority over the modification. Thus, First Bank's modification would not have priority over Second Bank's mortgage. Nevertheless, because Second Bank failed to include First Bank in its foreclosure action, First Bank's mortgage interest survives under its modified terms, even though the modification did not have priority. (B) is therefore correct and (A) is incorrect. (C) is incorrect because the modification of a senior mortgage does not nullify its original senior status; it only means that the junior mortgage will be given priority over the *modification.* Because the buyer at the foreclosure sale ordinarily will take title as it existed when the mortgage was placed on the property, the senior mortgage ordinarily survives in its original form. (As noted above, here the mortgage survives in its modified form despite its junior status because of the failure to include First Bank in the foreclosure action.) (D) is wrong because the recording statute applicable here is a race-notice statute rather than a notice statute. Under a race-notice statute, a subsequent bona fide purchaser (including a mortgagee) is protected only if it records before the prior grantee or mortgagee. Here, First Bank recorded its mortgage before Second Bank recorded its mortgage. The fact that Second Bank had no notice of First Bank's interest at the time it granted the mortgage on Fishacre does not help Second Bank because it did not record first.

Answer to Question 43

(B) Ash can enforce the option to purchase because it is a covenant that runs with the land. When a tenant makes a complete transfer of the entire remaining term of his leasehold interest, it constitutes an assignment. The assignee and the landlord are then in privity of estate, and each is liable to the other on all covenants in the lease that run with the land. The covenant runs with the land if the original parties so intend and the covenant "touches and concerns" the leased land, *i.e.,* burdens the landlord and benefits the tenant with respect to their interests in the property. Here, the transfer of the lease to Ash was an assignment, making all covenants in the lease that run with the land enforceable by the assignee. The right of first refusal burdens Liggett's power of alienation over Greenacre, and there is nothing to indicate that the parties intended the option to be personal to Tarr. Hence, Ash can enforce the option and purchase the property. (A) is incorrect because most courts do not bar an option from being separated from the leasehold interest if that is the parties' intent. The tenant may transfer the leasehold interest while retaining the option to purchase, or vice versa. Whether the option in this case stayed with the leasehold interest depends on whether it was a covenant that runs with the land. (C) is wrong because options and rights of first refusal are not subject to the Rule Against Perpetuities when connected to leaseholds. If the option had been separated from the leasehold estate, so that it was no longer exercisable by the tenant, the Rule would have become applicable to the option (and it would have invalidated the option here because it could have been exercised more than 21 years after a life in being). Here, however, the option was not severed from the leasehold; the entire interest was transferred to Ash as the new tenant. Hence, the Rule Against Perpetuities is not applicable. (D) is incorrect because, as discussed above, the option is a covenant that runs with the land regardless of whether it was specified in the assignment to Ash. Ash, as the assignee of the leasehold, can enforce the option on privity of estate grounds.

Answer to Question 44

(A) Ohn will prevail because the writing did not adequately describe the 20 acres to be sold. For a court to grant specific performance, there must be a valid and enforceable contract. The Statute of Frauds requires that the writing contain a description of the land to be sold sufficient to identify it. If the description is too indefinite, the contract is not enforceable. In this case, the description given is 20 acres from the northwest quarter of Brownacre. Brownacre consists of 240 acres; therefore the northwest quarter of Brownacre contains 60 acres. Since there is no guidance as to which 20 acres were intended by the parties, the contract is not enforceable and Ohn will prevail. (B) is wrong because the writing need not be signed by both parties. To be enforceable under the Statute of Frauds, the writing need only be signed by the party to be charged. In this case, Ohn is the party to be charged, and the writing was signed by him. Thus, the Statute of Frauds was satisfied in this regard. (C) is wrong because the metes and bounds description here described the whole of Brownacre, rather than the property to be conveyed. It is true that metes and bounds is a sufficient way to describe property. In this instance, however, this method was used to describe the wrong property. (D) is wrong because, as discussed above, the description of the property does not satisfy the Statute of Frauds.

Answer to Question 45

(A) The only way that Omega could prevail would be to step into the shoes of a party with an interest senior to that of Spartan Bank. A second mortgagee's rights are subject to the rights of the first mortgagee. Thus, a foreclosure by the second mortgagee will not cut off the first mortgagee's rights. Omega's only way to win would be to acquire Athenian's rights. (B) is incorrect because the balance of equities does not clearly favor Omega. She had record notice of Spartan's mortgage (since it was properly recorded). Spartan Bank did nothing wrong. Furthermore, there is no legally recognized right being infringed by Spartan Bank. (C) is incorrect because, in a pure race recording jurisdiction, as here, notice is irrelevant; whoever records first has priority. (Note that even in a notice jurisdiction, record notice is sufficient—actual notice is not required.) (D) is incorrect because benefit to a subsequent purchaser or mortgagee is not a consideration in a foreclosure action.

Answer to Question 46

(D) None of these people has a good argument. (C) is wrong because merely paying value does not make one a bona fide purchaser. Lorelei is bound by the covenant restricting use to single-family housing because the covenant runs with the land. Also, since she had a duty to make a diligent title search, she should have found the covenant. If all requirements are met for the burden to run, Lorelei, as successor in interest to the burdened estate, will be bound by the arrangement entered into by her predecessor as effectively as if she had expressly agreed to be bound, and her neighbors, as successors of the original promisee, could enforce the covenant as an equitable servitude and enjoin the construction. The requirements are: (i) The covenanting parties must have intended that successors in interest to the covenantor be bound by the terms of the covenant. The requisite intent may be inferred from circumstances surrounding creation of the covenant. This requirement is satisfied since Arthur's deed to each of the grantees contained a covenant requiring that the property be used only for single-family housing. (ii) By virtue of the recording statutes, a subsequent purchaser of the promisor's land must have actual, inquiry, or constructive (record) notice of the arrangement at the time she purchased the land; otherwise, she is not bound. Lorelei bought her property from Howard under a recorded deed that did not contain the restriction. However, Lorelei is charged with constructive notice since the restriction was in her chain of title, and she had a duty to inquire of Howard where he obtained the property. (iii) The other requirements for the burden running with the land have also been satisfied. For successors in interest to enforce the covenant as an equitable servitude (*i.e.,* to obtain an injunction), the covenant must "touch and concern" the land; *i.e.,* the performance of the burden must diminish the landowner's rights, privileges, and powers in connection with her enjoyment of the land. Lorelei's rights as a landowner are diminished because she cannot use her land to construct a four-family building. Note that the covenant could also be enforced at law (if damages were sought) because the privity requirements for a covenant to run at law (which are not required for an equitable servitude) have been satisfied here. Horizontal privity requires that, at the time the promisor entered into the covenant with the promisee, the two shared some interest in the land independent of the covenant. Arthur and Delia, as grantor and grantee, shared an interest in the land independent of the covenant. Vertical privity, which means that the successor in interest to the covenanting party holds the entire interest that was held by the covenantor at the time she made the covenant, is also required. Lorelei possesses the entire interest (fee simple absolute) held by her predecessor in interest (Delia), who was one of the original parties to the covenant.

(A) and (B) are wrong because taking by will or inter vivos gift is irrelevant. In fact, taking in this manner increases the chances that they will be bound because it means they are not bona fide purchasers for value and thus not protected by the notice requirement of the recording act. The only way Judy and Kurt can escape from being bound by the covenant is by demonstrating that all of the requirements for the burden running at law have not been satisfied. Judy and Kurt will fail in this endeavor because, as noted above, the requisite intent is present, horizontal and vertical privity exist, and the covenant "touches and concerns" the land since a restriction against a multi-family dwelling diminishes the enjoyment of their land. Even if notice were required to bind Judy and Kurt, they would fail because they would be deemed to have constructive notice since the restriction is in their chain of title and a diligent search would have provided them with notice of the restriction. Thus, by exclusion of (A), (B), and (C), (D) is the only correct answer.

Answer to Question 47

(D) Lorelei may enforce the covenant as an equitable servitude against Iris because Iris's building would alter the common scheme Arthur created by using restrictive covenants in all of his deeds. For a successor of the original promisee to enforce a servitude against a successor of the original promisor, both the benefit and burden of the servitude must run with the land. For the burden to run and thus bind the successor of the promisor (Iris): (i) the covenanting parties must have intended that the servitude be enforceable by and against assignees; (ii) the covenant must touch and concern the land; and (iii) the party to be bound must have had actual, constructive (record), or inquiry notice. The common scheme is evidence that the original parties intended that the restriction be enforceable by assignees. The covenant touches and concerns Iris's property since it restricts her in her use of the property. Iris had constructive and inquiry notice because the restriction is in her chain of title. Therefore, the burden of the servitude runs with the land. The next issue is whether the benefit of the servitude runs with Lorelei's land. For a benefit to run, it must be so intended by the original parties and the covenant must touch and concern the land. As noted above, intent may be inferred from the common scheme. The benefit touches and concerns Lorelei's land because it benefits her in her use and enjoyment of the lot. Thus, Lorelei may enforce the covenant. (A) is incorrect for two reasons: (i) privity is not a requirement for the enforcement of equitable servitudes; and (ii) if privity were a requirement, both horizontal and vertical privity would be satisfied. (B) is incorrect because both zoning laws and restrictive covenants must be complied with. (C) is incorrect because, as discussed above, the restriction runs with the land and is enforceable against successors of the original parties. Actual notice is not required; constructive or inquiry notice is sufficient, and Iris had both.

Answer to Question 48

(B) Gonzalez's best defense against Felipe's attempt to levy on Secoacre is his bona fide purchaser status. By purchasing Secoacre for value and without notice of any prior claim or interest, Gonzalez cut off Felipe's interest in the property. Felipe's remedy is exclusively against Sancho. (A) is incorrect for two reasons: (i) If Felipe could enforce his claim for the money, the Statute of Frauds would not be a defense. The Statute would not apply to Sancho's subsequent promise not to record until he paid the money; since the property had already been conveyed, the promise no longer involved a conveyance of an interest in land. Therefore, the promise does not fall within the Statute. (ii) Any writing between Felipe and Sancho would have no effect on the rights of Gonzalez, a bona fide purchaser. (C) is not as good a choice as (B) because Gonzalez does not need the recording statute for protection. Felipe's interest in the property was cut off by Gonzalez's bona fide purchaser status even without resort to the recording act. The recording act, which is a pure notice statute, protects those who purchase property for value and without notice of prior claims against prior unrecorded conveyances. Felipe's lien against the property was not recorded so as to give Gonzalez notice at the time he purchased the property. Thus, Felipe could not win under the recording statute because Felipe's lien was never recorded at all. (B) is a better choice, however, because the mere fact that Gonzalez complied with the statute is not the basis of Gonzalez's rights in the property. Even under the statute, Gonzalez's recording would be irrelevant because his status as a bona fide purchaser allows him to prevail against Felipe. Thus, it is Gonzalez's status as a bona fide purchaser and full owner of Secoacre that prevents Felipe from levying on the property. (D) is wrong because the oral agreement between Felipe and Sancho is irrelevant for purposes of defending Gonzalez's rights in Secoacre. Even if the agreement could be proven, Felipe would not be able to levy on Secoacre, so the parol evidence rule does not matter.

Answer to Question 49

(D) When a purchaser has paid only part of the purchase price under an installment land contract, most courts hold that the purchaser is protected by the recording acts only to the extent of payment made. Depending on the equities involved in the case, the court has three options: (i) divide the property, with the contract purchaser receiving a portion of the property equal to the proportion of payments made; (ii) award the land to the prior claimant, but give the contract purchaser a right to recover the amount she paid (with interest), secured by a lien on the property; or (iii) award the land to the contract purchaser, but require the contract purchaser to make the remaining payments to the prior claimant. This last obligation is also secured by a lien on the property. Thus, I., II., and III. are all appropriate actions for the court. (A) is wrong because it does not include the remedy under which the property is awarded to Date and the remaining payments are made to Bay. (B) is wrong because IV. misstates the law. When only partial payment of the purchase price has been paid, the subsequent purchaser is protected only to the extent of payment. Thus, even if the equities favored Date and he were allowed to retain the property, Bay would be entitled to the remaining payments. (C) is wrong because the subsequent contract purchaser, Date, is protected by the recording act to the extent of his payment. Since Bay did not record, he will have to pay Date $40,000 if he is awarded Whiteacre.

Answer to Question 50

(B) Arthur will prevail because recording the agreement gave Callie constructive notice, thus preventing her from claiming the protection of the recording act as a defense to enforcement of the covenant. A covenant at law will run with the land and be enforceable against subsequent grantees if: (i) the contracting parties intended it to run; (ii) there is privity of estate between the original promisor and promisee (horizontal privity), as well as between the promisor and his successor (vertical privity); (iii) the covenant touches and concerns the property; and (iv) the recording statute requires that the burdened party have notice of the covenant. If common driveway owners agree to be mutually responsible for maintaining the driveway, the burdens and benefits of these covenants will run to successive owners of each parcel. The implied cross-easements for support satisfy the horizontal privity requirement because they are mutual interests in the same property. Each promise touches and concerns the adjoining parcel. So here, where Callie is in vertical privity with Ben (holding the same interest he held) and has notice, she will be bound by the agreement to maintain the driveway. Although easements appurtenant, such as those involved in these facts, pass with the transfer of the estates involved, (A) is wrong because the easements are not at issue here. The easements involved are implied cross-easements for support and the easements allowing each party the right to enter the other's property when using the driveway. The issue here is the accompanying covenant to pay for the maintenance of the driveway. (C) is wrong for the same reason. The fact that Ben abandoned the easement does not affect the enforceability of the separate covenant. (D) is wrong because privity of estate, not privity of contract, is required for the burden of the covenant to run.

Answer to Question 51

(B) Sequoia Bank may foreclose against Cornelius because it was not included as a party in the foreclosure proceeding brought by Weeping Willow Bank. Generally, the priority of a mortgage is determined by the time it was placed on the property. When a mortgage is foreclosed, the buyer at the sale will take title as it existed when the mortgage was placed on the property. Thus, foreclosure will terminate interests junior to the mortgage being foreclosed but will not affect senior interests. However, the junior mortgagee has the right to pay the senior interest off (*i.e.*, redeem it) in order to avoid being wiped out by its foreclosure. Thus, those with interests subordinate to those of the foreclosing party are necessary parties to the foreclosure action. Failure to include a necessary party results in the preservation of that party's interest despite foreclosure and sale. Here, even though Sequoia Bank created its mortgage first, its interest was junior to Weeping Willow's interest by virtue of the recording statute. Hence, when Weeping Willow brought its foreclosure action, it should have included Sequoia Bank as a necessary party. Because Sequoia was not included, its mortgage interest on Maroonacre is preserved and it may bring a foreclosure action. (A) is incorrect because Sequoia Bank did not hold the senior mortgage interest at the time of the foreclosure by Weeping Willow Bank. Mortgagees for value such as Weeping Willow Bank are treated as "purchasers" under recording statutes. By failing to record its mortgage before Weeping Willow executed and recorded its mortgage for value, Sequoia became the junior mortgagee under the jurisdiction's race-notice recording statute. Thus, had it been made a party to the foreclosure proceeding by Weeping Willow Bank, its interest would have been wiped out. (C) is incorrect because Sequoia Bank's delay in recording only affected its rights vis-a-vis Weeping Willow Bank. By the time of the foreclosure sale, Sequoia's mortgage interest was recorded; hence, Cornelius will take subject to it because he had constructive (record) notice of it. (D) is wrong because the fact that Cornelius obtained the right to redeem the property when he purchased it does not preclude Sequoia Bank from beginning foreclosure proceedings. To redeem the property, Cornelius must pay off the Sequoia Bank mortgage prior to the date set for the foreclosure sale.

Answer to Question 52

(B) Percy would rely on the covenants of warranty and further assurance to compel Victoria, the seller, to assist him in a suit against his encroaching neighbor. Under the covenant of warranty, the grantor agrees to defend, on behalf of the grantee, any lawful or reasonable claims of title by a third party, and to compensate the grantee for any loss sustained by the claim of superior title. The covenant for further assurance is a covenant to perform whatever acts are reasonably necessary to perfect the title conveyed if it turns out to be imperfect. These covenants are "continuous" (run with the land) and require the grantor to assist the grantee in establishing title. The covenants of seisin (in I.) and encumbrances (in II.) do not require such assistance. A covenant of seisin is a covenant that the grantor has the estate or interest that she purports to convey. Both title and possession at the time of the grant are necessary to satisfy this covenant. The covenant against encumbrances is a covenant assuring that there are neither visible encumbrances (easements, profits, etc.) nor invisible encumbrances (mortgages, etc.) against the title or interest conveyed. While Victoria may have violated these two covenants because of the garage encroachment, they do not provide the basis to compel her to assist Percy in a title suit. Instead, Percy merely has a cause of action against Victoria for their breach. Therefore, (A), (C), and (D) are wrong.

Answer to Question 53

(B) The purchaser prevails because John's acquisition of the land by adverse possession does not satisfy his implied warranty to deliver a marketable title. Unless expressly provided otherwise, all contracts for the sale of land contain an implied warranty by the seller that he will deliver to the buyer at closing a marketable title. Title is marketable if a reasonably prudent buyer, ready and able to purchase, would accept it in the exercise of ordinary prudence. Generally, inability to establish a record chain of title will render title unmarketable. If a seller attempts to rely on adverse possession to establish marketable title, many courts will hold that such title is not marketable until the adverse possessor has perfected it by a judgment quieting title. In other words, the purchaser is not required to "buy a lawsuit." Other states require only that the seller provide written evidence or some other proof that the buyer can use in court to defend any lawsuit challenging title. Even under the latter approach, it does not appear that John can provide enough evidence to make his title marketable. Thus, although John has acquired title to the land by occupying it in an open, notorious, hostile, and continuous manner, for a period exceeding that prescribed by statute, the fact that he has acquired title only by adverse possession renders his title unmarketable. Because John has thus breached his warranty of marketable title, implied in the sale contract, his action to specifically enforce that contract will fail. (A) is incorrect because John *does* own the one and one-half acres he is trying to sell. John's fencing of the land and building a structure on it qualifies as open and notorious possession because it is such as the usual owner would make of the land and puts the true owner or the community on notice of the fact of possession. His possession was continuous for more than the five-year statutory period, and it was hostile because it was without the permission of the true owner. Under the majority view, John's good faith belief that he was possessing the land described by his father's deed is irrelevant. Thus, John acquired title by adverse possession. However, as explained above, such title, as far as the purchaser is concerned, is not marketable. (C) is incorrect because the type of deed by which title is transferred does not affect the seller's warranty of marketable title, which is implied in the contract. It is true that the implied warranty of marketability is no longer assertable once a deed has been delivered (absent fraud or mistake), so that if John delivered a quitclaim deed (*i.e.,* without making any assertions relative to the title being transferred), the purchaser could no longer assert the implied contractual warranty of marketable title. However, no deed has yet been delivered; the warranties under the contract are still in effect. (D) is incorrect because the fact that a contract describes land with sufficient specificity does not establish the marketability of title to that land.

Answer to Question 54

(B) Len will not be likely to prevail against FirstBank because a majority of courts hold that the judgment lienor is not protected by the recording statute. If the statute here, which is a "notice" statute, were applicable to protect Len, Len would have priority over FirstBank because Len's judgment lien was recorded before Bill's deed was recorded. Under this view, FirstBank's mortgage would have been considered "wild" and would be deemed unrecorded because the preceding conveyance, Bill's deed, was actually unrecorded. A searcher in the public records would therefore have been unable to find the mortgage. Hence, if the statute were applicable to protect Len, he would have priority over FirstBank. However, most courts reason that either (i) a judgment creditor is not a bona fide purchaser, because he did not pay contemporaneous value for the judgment, or (ii) the judgment attaches only to property "owned" by the debtor, and not to property previously conveyed away, even if that conveyance was not recorded. Under the statute in the present question, a judgment does not attach until it is recorded. Here, Len's judgment did not attach to Brownacre until after FirstBank obtained a mortgage on it, and the recording statute does not change that result. The failure of Bill to record, and the resultant treatment of FirstBank as unrecorded, is irrelevant. Thus, FirstBank's mortgage is superior to Len's lien. (A) is incorrect because it does not matter whether FirstBank's mortgage was recorded, as against a subsequent judgment lien creditor. The judgment lien creditor is not protected by the recording statute, so FirstBank prevails even though its mortgage would be deemed unrecorded, as discussed above. (C) is wrong because, as discussed above, a majority of courts hold that the judgment lienor is not protected by the recording statute. (D) is wrong because Brownacre was not after-acquired property, since the judgment lien was not filed until Deb had obtained—and conveyed away—an interest in the property. However, if Len had in fact recorded his lien before Deb inherited Brownacre, the after-acquired property provision of the statute would have applied, Len would have had a recorded lien on Brownacre as soon as Deb acquired it, and Len would have gained priority over FirstBank.

Answer to Question 55

(C)   Maple's original mortgage has priority in the proceeds, followed by Oak's mortgage, and only Oak can proceed against Moore because Maple modified its mortgage after Moore had transferred to Grant. Generally, the priority of a mortgage is determined by the time it was placed on the property, and the proceeds of a foreclosure sale will be used to pay off the mortgages in the order of their priority. However, if the landowner enters into a modification agreement with the senior mortgagee, raising its interest rate or otherwise making the agreement more burdensome, the junior mortgage will be given priority over the modification. Thus, if the first mortgage debt is larger because of the modification, the second mortgage gains priority over the increase in the debt. Here, Maple and Grant modified the original mortgage by increasing the principal amount and the interest rate. This modification is not given priority over the Oak Savings mortgage, and foreclosure proceeds will not be applied against it because the senior Oak mortgage was not fully satisfied from the proceeds. With regard to the deficiency, Moore is liable to Oak because when a grantee signs an assumption agreement, becoming primarily liable to the lender, the original mortgagor remains secondarily liable on the promissory note as a surety. Here, Grant assumed the Oak mortgage but is no longer available to satisfy the deficiency; hence, Moore will be liable as surety to pay off the rest of the Oak mortgage loan. On the other hand, Moore will not be liable to pay off the balance of the Maple loan, because when a mortgagee and an assuming grantee subsequently modify the original obligation, the original mortgagor is completely discharged of liability. Moore had nothing to do with the modification agreed to by Maple and Grant that increased the amount of the mortgage debt, and will not be even secondarily liable for that amount. (A) and (B) are incorrect because Maple is not entitled to the entire $80,000 in proceeds from the sale and because Moore is not liable to Maple for more than the original loan amount. (D) is incorrect because, as discussed above, Moore is secondarily liable to Oak for the $20,000 deficiency on its mortgage.

Answer to Question 56

(A)   Fry can collect rents from all of the tenants. A landlord may assign the rents to a third party at any time. Unless required by the lease (which is very unlikely), consent of the tenants is not required. Assignment is usually done by an ordinary deed from the landlord to the new owner of the building, but it can also be accomplished as part of a security interest given for a loan, as in these facts. The assignment clause in the note and mortgage did not become effective until Lemmon defaulted on the note. At that time, Fry would be entitled to recover rent from all tenants. (B) is incorrect because, as discussed above, consent of the tenants is not required unless specifically stated in the lease. If assignment of leases is not addressed in the lease, it is presumed to be permitted. (C) and (D) are incorrect because the recording of Fry's mortgage does not affect which of the leases are subject to the assignment of rent. The date of recording would be relevant only if Lemmon had made another assignment of the rents from the shopping center.

Answer to Question 57

(C) Conco is entitled to compensation because it has a property right to enter and remove minerals. Like an easement, a profit is a nonpossessory interest in land. The holder of the profit is entitled to enter on the servient tenement and take the soil or the substance of the soil (*e.g.*, minerals, timber, oil, or game). When an owner grants the sole right to take a resource from her land, the grantee takes an exclusive profit and is solely entitled to the resources, even to the exclusion of the owner of the servient estate. By contrast, when a profit is nonexclusive, the owner of the servient estate may grant similar rights to others or take the resources himself. Although here the profit is nonexclusive, it is nevertheless an interest in property for which Conco is entitled to compensation in any condemnation proceeding. (B) is incorrect because a profit is the right to take something from another person's land; it has a value apart from the land itself and it is alienable. (A) is incorrect because a license is merely revocable permission to enter upon another's land. Unlike a profit, a license is not an interest in land; it is merely a privilege, ordinarily terminable at the will of the licensor. (D) is incorrect because a license coupled with an interest has the effect of making the license irrevocable, but it does not convert the license into an interest in land for which compensation is required.

Answer to Question 58

(B) Oscar will prevail because Valley Cable failed to maintain the easement. An easement in gross is created when the holder of the easement interest acquires a right of special use in the servient tenement independent of his ownership or possession of another tract of land. Absent an express restriction in the easement, the owner of the servient estate may use his land in any way he wishes so long as his conduct does not interfere with performance of the easement. Furthermore, the holder of the benefit of an easement has duty to make repairs to maintain the easement, so as to avoid unreasonable interference with the use of the servient estate by its owner, as (B) states. (A) is wrong because the liability is for negligence, such as the unreasonable failure to maintain the cable in these facts, and is not a type of strict or absolute liability. (C) is wrong because while the easement holder does have a right to repair for his own benefit, he also has a duty to make repairs reasonably necessary to prevent harm to the servient tenement. (D) is wrong because the law does not impose any general duty on either party to give notice of defective conditions to the other. As holder of the easement, Valley Cable had the right, and the duty, to enter onto Oscar's land at reasonable intervals to maintain the cable without waiting for notice from Oscar.

Answer to Question 59

(B) Dana Barrett has the right to possession of Withering Heights. A remainder is contingent if its taking in possession is subject to a condition precedent or if it is created in favor of unborn or unascertained persons. The gift to Venkman's grandchildren was a contingent remainder, since it followed a life estate and was conditioned on Spengler's not surviving Stantz. At common law under the doctrine of destructibility of contingent remainders, a contingent remainder had to vest prior to or on termination of the preceding estate or it was destroyed. In other words, termination of the estate preceding a contingent remainder prior to vesting destroyed the remainder. Here, the contingent remainder did not vest because no grandchildren of Venkman had been born when the life estate terminated (on Stantz's death). Thus, title to Withering Heights reverted to Venkman's estate and passed through the residuary clause to Barrett. (A) is wrong because Stantz had only a life estate—*i.e.*, nothing that could pass to his heirs. (C) is wrong because the court will not wait to see if grandchildren are born under the common law rule; if there is no grandchild at Stantz's death, the gift to the grandchildren fails. (D) is wrong; Ross and Rudy never received any interest under the will's provision, which had a valid residuary clause.

Answer to Question 60

(B) Mineco would likely be successful. Under a notice statute, which the jurisdiction in this question has, a subsequent bona fide purchaser prevails over a prior grantee who fails to record. The important fact under a notice statute is that the subsequent purchaser had no actual or constructive notice *at the time of the conveyance*, not at the time of recording. When the property was conveyed to Mineco, it had neither actual nor constructive notice of the conveyances to Zim or Bank, whose interests were not recorded at that time. Therefore, Mineco was a bona fide purchaser and would be entitled to protection under the statute. (A) is incorrect because the recording statute applies to all conveyances and mortgages of an interest in land, including a conveyance of the mineral interests. Thus, both Bank's and Zim's interests are not enforceable against Mineco. (C) is incorrect because that would be the result in the absence of a recording statute—priority is given to the grantee who was first in time. The recording statute changes this result. (D) is wrong because, as discussed above, Mineco did not have notice of Bank's interest at the time of its conveyance from Paul, so it takes free of that interest under the statute.

Answer to Question 61

(D) Mineco's fee simple ownership of Redacre would be subject to Bank's mortgage interest and Zim's mineral interest. Under a race-notice statute, which the jurisdiction in this question has, a subsequent bona fide purchaser is protected only if he records before the prior grantee. The rationale of this type of statute is that the best evidence of which interest was created first is to determine who recorded first. As an inducement to record promptly, race-notice statutes impose on the bona fide purchaser the additional requirement that he record first. Since Bank was the first to receive a conveyance, Bank could not be held to have knowledge of any other conveyance, and when Bank recorded its conveyance first, Bank won out over Zim and Mineco under the statute. (A) is incorrect because Mineco has a present ownership interest in Redacre, but it is subject to Bank's mortgage and Zim's mineral interest. (B) is incorrect because the jurisdiction has a race-notice statute. Thus, Bank's interest is superior only if it is first in time *and* without notice of all other interests. (C) is wrong because, as discussed above, Mineco does not have a fee simple absolute; Zim owns the mineral interest in gold on Redacre because Zim recorded before Mineco.

Answer to Question 62

(C) Judgment should be for Hottentot regardless of whether the jurisdiction has a notice statute or a race-notice statute. Under either type of recording statute, the only persons protected by the statute are bona fide purchasers. To attain this status, the person must take without notice—either actual, constructive, or inquiry—of the prior instrument. Since the LeBeau-Hottentot Hotels agreement was properly recorded under the statute, which permitted the recordation of contracts for the sale of real property, Playland International had constructive notice of Hottentot's interest in the beachfront property. Thus, it could not become a bona fide purchaser when it entered into its contract. (A) is wrong because LeBeau had not been deprived of authority to bind the corporation at the time she signed the agreement with Hottentot, and any subsequent change in her powers did not affect the validity of that agreement, nor Hottentot's power to subsequently record the agreement. (B) is wrong because the facts indicate that the jurisdiction permitted recordation of contracts of sale, and so Hottentot's failure to record a deed does not deprive it of protection of the recording statute. (D) is not correct because regardless of the validity of the board's attempt to divest LeBeau of authority, it is immaterial to Hottentot's rights; it came after the valid LeBeau-Hottentot contract was properly signed by LeBeau.

Answer to Question 63

(D) Stanley would prevail because he recorded his deed before Becky recorded her deed. The jurisdiction in this question has a race-notice statute, under which a subsequent bona fide purchaser is protected only if she records before the prior grantee. While Becky was a bona fide purchaser, she did not record her interest in the property before Stanley did; thus Stanley will prevail. (A) is incorrect because priority under a race-notice recording act, such as the one in this question, is determined by the subsequent purchaser's status as a bona fide purchaser and on the basis of who records first. Courts do not determine ownership by balancing the equities on the basis of who spent the most money. (B) is wrong because the doctrine of equitable conversion, wherein equity regards the purchaser in a land sale contract as the owner of the real property, does not change the result under the recording statute. Stanley will prevail because he recorded first. (C) is incorrect because Becky cannot rely on Tom's recording of his deed; Stanley recorded his interest before Becky recorded hers. Furthermore, even if the issue were whether Becky had actual notice of Stanley's interest, Becky could not rely on the "shelter rule" that protects transferees from a bona fide purchaser, because Tom was not a purchaser for value and therefore not protected by the recording statute.

Answer to Question 64

(C) First Central Bank will prevail under the recording statute. The jurisdiction in this question has a race-notice statute, under which a subsequent bona fide purchaser is protected only if she records before the prior grantee or mortgagee. Here, First Central Bank recorded its mortgage prior to Stanley's recording of his deed; thus, Stanley will take Mountainview subject to the bank's mortgage. (A) is incorrect because even though at common law Elmo would not have had any title to mortgage to the bank after the conveyance to Stanley, the race-notice statute nullifies that priority as to the subsequent bona fide purchaser who first records. (B) is wrong because the court is not aiding Elmo, but protecting his innocent creditor, First Central Bank. (D) is incorrect because it more accurately describes a pure race jurisdiction. In a race-notice jurisdiction, only the bona fide purchaser for value will prevail over a prior unrecorded deed or mortgage interest; hence, a purchaser who records first under this statute would not prevail if he had actual notice of a prior unrecorded interest.

Answer to Question 65

(B) Tom and Audrey are liable. After an assignment, the original tenant is no longer in privity of estate with the landlord. However, a tenant may still be held liable on his original contractual obligations to the landlord on privity of contract grounds. Here, Tom is liable because he made the original deal with Ludwig, which included the obligation to pay taxes on the building. He remains in privity of contract with Ludwig throughout the term of the lease unless he is otherwise discharged. Thus, I. is correct. In an assignment, the assignee stands in the shoes of the original tenant in a direct relationship with the landlord. Each is liable to the other on all covenants in the lease that run with the land, which would include the obligation of the lessee to pay taxes on the property. Here, Audrey is liable because as an assignee she is in privity of estate with Ludwig. She remains in privity of estate until she assigns to someone else. The sublease to Sam is not an assignment. Thus, II. is correct. A sublessee is not personally liable to the landlord for rent or for the performance of any other covenants made by the original lessee in the main lease (unless the covenants are expressly assumed) because the sublessee does not hold the tenant's full estate in the land (so no privity of estate). Here, Sam is not liable because, as a nonassuming sublessee, he is not in privity of contract or estate with Ludwig, and so III. is incorrect. Therefore, (B) is the correct choice, and (A), (C), and (D) are wrong.

Answer to Question 66

(B) Clark will get an undivided half-interest in Redacre regardless of the status of Abner and Boris's title. A joint tenancy is a concurrent estate with a right of survivorship, while a tenancy in common does not have a right of survivorship. At common law, the conveyance here would qualify as a joint tenancy because the unities of time, title, interest, and possession are present in the conveyance. Although under modern law a joint tenancy must be created with specific language or else it will be presumed to be a tenancy in common, the conveyance here still would probably qualify as a joint tenancy, even though it did not use the words "joint tenancy," because it contained the "right of survivorship" language. However, regardless of whether the estate is characterized as a joint tenancy or tenancy in common, one tenant's interest may be transferred without the consent of the other tenant, and a creditor may levy on the interest. In most jurisdictions a lien against one joint tenant's interest does not sever the joint tenancy until the lien holder proceeds to enforce it by foreclosure. At that point, the purchaser at the foreclosure sale will hold the property as a tenant in common with the other tenant, but will still have an undivided one-half interest in the property unless and until he brings an action to partition the estate. (A) is incorrect because both joint tenancies and tenancies in common may be subject to partition. (In contrast, tenancies by the entirety cannot be terminated by involuntary partition.) (C) is wrong because, as discussed above, a joint tenant may validly convey or encumber his interest in the property. (D) is incorrect because Clark does not have a contingent interest; he has a present lien on Abner's interest that can be enforced immediately by foreclosure, which would sever the joint tenancy.

TORTS QUESTIONS

Question 1

While shopping at the Everfresh Supermarket in Violettown, Purvis slipped and fell when he stepped in some water that had seeped out from a malfunctioning freezer case. The fall caused Purvis to break an ankle. He filed suit against Everfresh for his injuries. Violettown is located in State Purple, which assesses liability in tort actions on a "pure" comparative negligence basis.

Is Purvis likely to recover damages from Everfresh?

(A) Yes, if the floor in that aisle had not been swept or mopped in the last two hours.

(B) Yes, because he was injured after coming onto Everfresh's premises for a purpose connected with its business.

(C) No, unless Everfresh employees knew that the freezer case was leaking.

(D) No, if Purvis could have seen the water if he had been looking where he was walking.

Question 2

Pylon competed in the local stock car racing circuit. His customized yellow Volkswagen, known as "the Golden Bug" on the circuit, had brought him a number of victories in the last few seasons and a substantial amount of prize money. Before the first race of the new season, Pylon brought the car to Dexter's Body Shop to have some black trim added to specified areas of the body. When Pylon returned to pick up the car, he was horrified to discover that it was painted all black. Dexter apologized and offered to repaint the car, but Pylon refused because the first race was the next day. Pylon was greatly distressed when he brought the car to the track and was subjected to some ridicule from other drivers about the Golden Bug's new look. He felt better, however, after he drove the car to victory in the first race.

If Pylon sues Dexter's Body Shop for their treatment of his car, will he prevail?

(A) No, because Pylon won the race with the car.

(B) No, unless Pylon can prove that Dexter or his employees breached a duty of care owed to Pylon.

(C) Yes, if the value of Pylon's car was reduced.

(D) Yes, because Pylon suffered severe distress as a result of the conduct of Dexter's Body Shop.

Question 3

Pam and Dot were roommates in a dormitory at State University. After a morning of intense studying, they decided to reward themselves with an "everything but anchovies" pizza from Mario Brothers, their favorite pizzeria. Pam called in a carryout order and was told that the pizza would be ready in 45 minutes. Dot volunteered to fetch the pizza, and Pam gave Dot the keys to her car. Dot did not own an automobile. Dot drove Pam's car to a bookstore approximately two miles from Mario Brothers. She spent 10 minutes in the store finding and purchasing a book she needed for a class. She arrived at Mario Brothers 55 minutes after Pam had placed the order. Dot parked Pam's car on the street, which had parallel parking spaces marked. Dot's pizza was ready about seven minutes after she entered Mario Brothers. When Dot returned to the car, to her consternation, Pam's car had been struck by a hit-and-run driver, and there were a number of dents in the back of the car, amounting to $400 in damages.

If Pam sues Dot for the damage to her car, Pam will recover:

(A) Nothing, because Dot had to wait for the pizza even after her 10-minute detour.

(B) The value of the car before the accident, because Dot used the car for unauthorized purposes.

(C) $400, because the car was under Dot's control.

(D) $400, but only if Dot failed to use reasonable care in parking the car.

Question 4

After their marriage, Prudence and her husband went for genetic counseling because of a hereditary genetic disease in both of their families. When it was determined that their offspring were certain to inherit the disease, they decided not to have children of their own. Prudence then went to Dr. Desmond to have her fallopian tubes tied to ensure that she would not become pregnant; for religious reasons, abortion was not an option for her. Dr. Desmond did not properly perform the surgery. Tests taken after the surgery indicated that it was not successful, but Dr. Desmond failed to inform Prudence of that fact. Two years later, Prudence became pregnant and gave birth to a child, Charlotte, who was afflicted with the disease. Furthermore, the pregnancy left Prudence partially disabled because of an internal condition that could not have been foreseen by her or her doctor.

Prudence sues Dr. Desmond, seeking to recover the medical expenses of her pregnancy and her pain and suffering during labor, her lost future earnings because of her disability, the future costs of raising Charlotte, and the extraordinary medical expenses to treat Charlotte's disease.

Under current law, which element of damages is Prudence least certain to recover?

(A) Medical expenses and pain and suffering for her labor.

(B) The future costs of raising Charlotte.

(C) The additional medical expenses to treat Charlotte's disease.

(D) Lost future earnings because of her disability.

Question 5

An article in the *Tabloid Times* newspaper read as follows:

> The owners of the Flying Rainbows basketball franchise announced yesterday that financial difficulties have forced them to sell the franchise to a group of investors who will probably move the team to another state. Inside sources say that the main reason for the financial difficulties is that Paul Python, the Rainbows' general manager and chief operating officer, has been siphoning off the proceeds from ticket sales to support his gambling habits.

In fact, Python has never diverted any ticket sale proceeds. Python, who is well-known in the community, brings an action against the *Tabloid Times* for defamation. The parties will stipulate that the statement regarding Python is false.

What additional facts does Python have to prove to recover from the *Tabloid Times*?

(A) That the newspaper was at least negligent in verifying the story.

(B) That Python suffered pecuniary damages from publication of the story.

(C) That the newspaper acted with actual malice in publishing the story.

(D) That Python suffered actual injury as a result of the story.

Questions 6-7 are based on the following fact situation:

Westside Shopping Center contracted with Bill's Security Service to provide nighttime monitoring of mall property. Bill employed five security guards, two of whom were regularly assigned to the shopping center and three who had other assignments in town. Because a giant new shopping mall had recently opened in nearby Metropolis, business at the shopping center had been very bad, causing some stores to leave and others to demand reductions in rent. Wesley, the shopping center manager, informed Bill that the center could only afford to pay 60% of what it had been paying for security service, and if that rate was not acceptable, the center would make other arrangements.

One of Bill's employees had just reached retirement age, and when he left Bill's employment, he was not replaced. Bill transferred the other shopping center guard to other duties and took over the monitoring of the mall himself. He had heard about a store in another part of the country that used poisonous snakes as deterrents to burglars. Bill was something of an amateur herpetologist, and so, without the manager's permission, he began placing several of his pet rattlesnakes in the shopping center at night and posting signs at night saying, "Beware of poisonous snakes."

The shopping center was conducting a contest to attract shoppers in which a compact car was filled with jelly beans, and the contestant who came nearest to guessing the number of beans would win the car. John, a graduate student at the local liberal arts college, decided to break into the shopping center, take a sample of the jelly beans in a given volume of the car's interior, then, using the manufacturer's figures for interior volume, calculate the number of beans in the car. Sunday morning at 5 a.m., John used a crowbar to lever open a glass entryway and tiptoed toward the contest car. As he was carefully opening a vent window to take his sample of jelly beans, one of Bill's rattlers that had been lying under the car bit John on the ankle. Bill came running upon hearing John's screams and applied snakebite treatment. John was hospitalized for two weeks and had to miss a semester of school as a result of the snakebite.

6. If John brings an action against the shopping center, will he likely recover?

    (A) No, because he was a trespasser on shopping center property.

    (B) No, because he was guilty of breaking and entering.

    (C) Yes, because the use of poisonous snakes for security amounted to unreasonable force.

    (D) Yes, if he had not seen the signs warning of the poisonous snakes.

7. If John brings an action against Bill, will he likely recover?

    (A) No, because he was a trespasser.

    (B) No, because he was committing a crime at the time he was injured.

    (C) Yes, because Bill used unreasonable force to protect the property.

    (D) Yes, because Bill did not have the authorization of the property owner to use the poisonous snakes.

Question 8

Mountaineer, Inc., manufactured a variety of motorcycles, including the "Pinnacle." The Pinnacle was promoted as an all-terrain motorcycle in advertisements showing it going over very rugged terrain. However, the shock absorbers that were sold with the motorcycle as standard equipment were not designed for rough terrain and would not provide a safe ride under these conditions. The owner's manual specified that the motorcycle should not be driven over rough terrain without equipping it with heavy-duty shock absorbers designed for that purpose.

Harley was 19 and infatuated with motorcycles. He lived near a state wilderness area with rugged terrain and had always wanted to take a motorcycle through there. He saw the advertisement for the Pinnacle and decided that it was just what he needed. He obtained a loan and purchased a Pinnacle equipped with the standard shock absorbers from Capitol Cycle Sales, receiving a copy of the owner's manual at the time of the purchase. The next day, Harley took his motorcycle to the wilderness area. He drove off of the road, riding over the crest of a hill and landing hard when his shock absorbers failed. This caused Harley to lose control of the motorcycle, which landed on top of him. He suffered serious injuries that left him permanently disabled.

Harley brought a lawsuit against Mountaineer for his injuries in a jurisdiction that retains traditional contributory negligence. At trial, he presented evidence of the advertisements and the fact that the shock absorbers installed on the Pinnacle were dangerously inadequate under off-road conditions. Mountaineer presented evidence that Harley had received the owner's manual with the warning about the shock absorbers and had disobeyed a posted state statute in the wilderness area forbidding motorized vehicles from leaving the roadway.

Is Harley likely to recover damages from Mountaineer?

(A) Yes, if Harley's use of the motorcycle over rough terrain was foreseeable.

(B) No, because the owner's manual adequately warned of the unsuitability of the shock absorbers for off-road use.

(C) No, because Harley was in violation of the law when he drove off of the road.

(D) Yes, unless the shock absorbers conformed to all safety requirements for motorcycle shock absorbers.

Question 9

Alice loaned her car to her best friend Bob to use while Bob's car was in the shop for repairs. When Bob's car was repaired, Bob let Carol borrow Alice's car instead of returning it to Alice. Carol took it for several days on a 900-mile trip. While Carol was gone on the trip, Alice discovered that Bob had gotten his car repaired; Alice asked for her car back but was told that Bob had lent the car to Carol. Alice was furious that Bob had done this without consulting Alice. Carol eventually returned the car to

Bob and Bob then attempted to return the car to Alice. However, Alice refused to accept the car even though it was undamaged, and sued Bob for conversion of the car.

Which of the following would be the most likely result of this suit?

(A) Alice will not recover for conversion.

(B) Alice cannot recover for conversion, but can recover for trespass to chattel.

(C) Alice will recover the rental value of the car for the 900-mile trip.

(D) Alice will recover the fair market value of the car from Bob.

Question 10

Petunia was shopping in Duck's Department Store ("DDS") for a spring ensemble to match a scarf that she had received as a present. She brought the scarf with her in her purse and occasionally took it out to see how it went with an outfit. Not finding what she needed, she put the scarf back in her purse and headed toward the exit. She was stopped at the door by a plainclothes security guard, who requested her to accompany him to the manager's office, which had an interior window overlooking the sales floor. Because the blinds were up on the window, the occupants of the office could be seen from the sales floor. When she entered the office and the security guard left, the manager began to berate her for trying to steal the scarf and threatened to prosecute her as a shoplifter, saying, "It's thieves like you that force us to keep raising prices for our honest customers." Unknown to the manager, the public address system that he used to announce specials was still on, and his statements were broadcast to everyone in the store.

Petunia institutes an action against DDS for defamation. Can she recover?

(A) No, because the manager was speaking directly to Petunia.

(B) Yes, if the manager should have checked that the public address system was not on.

(C) No, because the manager did not intend for others to hear his statements.

(D) Yes, unless the manager's belief that Petunia had stolen the scarf was reasonable.

Question 11

Denville was the star center for the Whippanong Wildcats, a contending team in the Continental Hockey Association ("CHA"). In their final game of the season, the Wildcats needed a victory to get into the playoffs. The game was a seesaw battle, with the Wildcats down by a goal in the final seconds. Just before time expired, Denville had an open shot on the opposition's goal but he shot it wide and the horn sounded, ending the game. As the puck bounced back to him off the boards, he shot it in anger into the stands. Parsip, who was sitting in the stands, had been looking the other way and turned back toward the rink just in time to be struck in the face by the puck. He suffered a broken nose and a severe gash under his eye. After the game, the CHA commissioner fined Denville for violating league rules by directing the puck out of the playing area.

If Parsip sues Denville for battery, will Parsip prevail?

(A) No, because by attending a hockey game, Parsip assumed the risk of pucks being shot into the stands.

(B) No, unless Denville intended to cause the puck to strike a spectator or intended to cause apprehension on the part of a spectator of being struck by a puck.

(C) Yes, if Denville acted recklessly in shooting the puck into the stands.

(D) Yes, because Denville violated CHA rules by shooting the puck out of the playing area.

Question 12

Delbert owned a large tract of land on which was located a small lake. The lake had a sand beach and a boat launching area that Delbert opened to the public for a fee. He also rented canoes for use on the lake. Delbert was very safety-conscious, especially in his canoe rentals, requiring all canoe users to wear life vests and requiring anyone under 16 years old to be accompanied by an adult. He also inspected the canoes regularly.

When the summer season had come to an end, Delbert removed the canoes from the water and put them up on racks attached to a trailer. He arranged for them to be towed the next day to a storage shed for the winter. That evening, Curtis and Freddy, both age nine, came onto Delbert's property even though they knew that the lake was closed to the public for the season. Both of them had used the canoes (with an adult) several times during the past summer. They unhooked one of the canoes from the rack, lifted it down, and pushed it into the water. Although the life vests were sitting in an open bin nearby, neither boy put one on. When they were out in the middle of the lake with the canoe, they tried to switch seats and caused the canoe to capsize. They both tried to swim to shore. Freddy was able to make it, but unfortunately Curtis did not and drowned. Had he been wearing a life vest, he would have survived.

Curtis's parents bring a wrongful death action against Delbert. Who will likely prevail?

(A) Curtis's parents, if children of Curtis's age, intelligence, and education would be likely to take the canoe out without a life vest.

(B) Delbert, because he took reasonable precautions to make the canoes inaccessible.

(C) Delbert, if he can show that Curtis appreciated the risk of taking the canoe out onto the lake without a life vest.

(D) Curtis's parents, if they can show that Curtis was lured onto Delbert's property by the canoes.

Question 13

Sam Spangler, who was born on the fourth of July, loved to celebrate his birthday every year with fireworks. For his thirtieth birthday he purchased an assortment of Roman candles and skyrockets for a party in his backyard. Because the area where Sam lived had been in a severe drought for several months and a ban on watering lawns was in effect, the grass was extremely dry. Sam nevertheless proceeded with his party and lit off the fireworks at the end of the night. Most of them burned out before they hit the ground, but one went slightly off course and landed in a pile of dry grass clippings behind Sam's garage. Neither Sam nor any of his guests went behind the garage to check where it landed. A spark from the misdirected firework caused the grass clippings to ignite, and the fire eventually spread to the rear wall of the garage. By the time Sam discovered the fire and called the fire department, the flames were reaching as high as the vacant apartment on the second floor of the garage.

Lenny, one of the first firefighters to arrive, rushed with a hose to the back of the garage. As he went up the outside stairs leading to the back door of the apartment, one of the steps broke, causing him to fall to the ground and break his leg. Unbeknownst to Sam, the wood on the underside of the step had rotted away.

Lenny sued Sam for his injury. Is Sam liable?

(A) Yes, if Sam was negligent in allowing the fire to start.

(B) No, unless Sam could have discovered the condition of the step with a reasonable inspection.

(C) Yes, because it was foreseeable that Sam's shooting off the fireworks would necessitate the assistance of the fire department.

(D) No, because a firefighter cannot recover for negligent conduct of another that causes him to be injured while performing his duties.

Question 14

Demand Delivery Company employed several messengers to deliver packages by car to nearby towns. The company also allowed some employees to use company cars for personal use from time to time. Because her car was in the repair shop, Eileen had borrowed a Demand car for the weekend and was using it to do some grocery shopping. Because she was glancing at a newspaper on the seat next to her, she did not notice the traffic light at the upcoming intersection change to red. She proceeded into the intersection, crossing the path of a rented van driven by Billy. Billy swerved to avoid Eileen and struck a lightpost and several parked cars, severely damaging the van. At the time of the accident, Billy was exceeding the posted speed limit; he would have been able to avoid hitting the lightpost and the cars had he been going the proper speed. Precision Leasing, which rented the van to Billy, brings a lawsuit against Eileen and Demand. The jurisdiction retains traditional contributory negligence rules.

Will Precision be able to recover any damages from Demand?

(A) Yes, if Demand was aware that Eileen had a poor driving record.

(B) No, because Billy exceeded the posted speed limit.

(C) Yes, unless Billy had the last clear chance to avoid the accident.

(D) No, because Eileen was not acting within the scope of her employment when the accident occurred.

Question 15

When the family lawn mower began running poorly, Jimmy brought it to Dewey, who was the sole proprietor of a small lawn mower repair business. Dewey replaced some parts and reassembled the mower. When Jimmy started it up the next day in the backyard, a metal bracket that Dewey had negligently installed flew off, striking Jimmy in his eye and injuring him. Pat,

Jimmy's mother, was on the back porch and saw the piece of metal strike her son. She became greatly distressed as a result.

Pat sued Dewey for negligent infliction of emotional distress in a jurisdiction in which the "zone of danger" approach has been abandoned in favor of the "foreseeability" approach. Dewey moved for a directed verdict at the close of Pat's case.

Should the court grant the motion?

(A) Yes, because Pat was too far away from the accident to be a foreseeable plaintiff.

(B) Yes, unless Pat has also introduced evidence that she suffered physical injury.

(C) No, because the jury could find that severe distress to Pat was a foreseeable result of Dewey's negligence.

(D) No, because Pat was Jimmy's mother.

Question 16

When he was eight years old, Charlie went with his mother, Martha, to Dr. Dalton, the family dentist, for his annual checkup. Dr. Dalton discovered two cavities in Charlie's lower left molars. Since she had no more appointments that afternoon, she offered to fill them right away. Charlie became very upset because he had suffered a lot of discomfort the last time he had a cavity filled. Dr. Dalton assured Charlie and Martha that it would be painless because she was using a newly developed local anesthetic that was better than Novocain. In fact, while it was more effective than Novocain, it carried a 1% risk of causing a serious seizure when administered to children, which Dr. Dalton did not mention to Martha. Charlie's dental work was completed without any problem. A week later, Martha read an article in a magazine that discussed the risk of that anesthetic, and she called Dr. Dalton about it. Dr. Dalton said that she believed that using the new anesthetic was justified in Charlie's case because otherwise he would not have been willing to sit still for the dental work.

Does Martha have a cause of action on behalf of Charlie against Dr. Dalton?

(A) Yes, if a reasonable person would have considered information about the risk important.

(B) Yes, if Martha would not have consented to the use of the anesthetic if she had known of the risk of seizure.

(C) No, if Dr. Dalton used her best judgment in deciding that the benefits of using the anesthetic outweighed the risk.

(D) No, because Charlie suffered no harm from use of the anesthetic.

Question 17

Sherm owned and operated a large hunting lodge in the hills of an arid western state. Northwest of his property was a private lodge owned by Governor Grafton and used by his family. Southwest of Sherm's property was a lumber mill owned by the Redwood Pulp Company. After a particularly arid summer in that region, the danger of forest fires was acute. One evening, Governor Grafton's son was having a party at his family's lodge with some of his friends. At the end of the night he failed to properly extinguish a bonfire that he and his friends had built. Within a few hours, wind-blown cinders had spread the fire to the trees east of the lodge. At the same time several miles away, a Redwood worker was making emergency repairs to a pipe running between two mill buildings. He did not notice some of the sparks from his welding torch land in a pile of dried lumber and catch fire, and he failed to check the area after he was finished. By the time the fire was noticed by another employee, it was out of control. The wind blew both fires toward Sherm's hunting lodge. They merged a mile away and shortly thereafter totally consumed the lodge. Either fire alone would have destroyed the lodge as well.

Sherm, who had been engaging in some low-key lobbying of the governor to persuade him to sign a bill opening up a nearby state forest for hunting, did not bring a lawsuit against the governor or his son. He did, however, file a lawsuit against Redwood, alleging that its employee's negligence caused the destruction of his lodge. The state in which Sherm is located follows the traditional rules regarding joint tortfeasors.

Can Sherm recover from Redwood?

(A) No, because Sherm's lodge would have been destroyed regardless of the conduct of Redwood's employee.

(B) Yes, because the negligence of Redwood's employee was a cause of Sherm's injury.

(C) No, because the damage is indivisible and cannot be apportioned unless Sherm adds the other tortfeasor to the lawsuit.

(D) Yes, but Sherm can recover only 50% of his damages from Redwood.

Question 18

Bert had the area's finest collection of homing pigeons and often participated in races with them. He had trained them with great care and they unfailingly returned to their roosts by a direct route. One summer evening, he brought several of his pigeons for a practice session to a park that he often used for training. When they were released, one of the pigeons inexplicably turned in the opposite direction from home. Several blocks away at the other end of the park, it collided with a state-of-the-art radio-controlled model airplane that Mike had just purchased and was trying out for the first time. The collision sent the airplane out of control; it crashed on the highway and was run over by a truck.

Mike sued Bert for the destruction of his airplane. The parties stipulated to the above facts and Mike presented evidence of his damages. Bert then moved for a directed verdict.

Should it be granted?

(A) No, because Bert's pigeon caused the destruction of the airplane.

(B) No, because the jury could find negligence on Bert's part under the doctrine of res ipsa loquitur.

(C) Yes, because the truck, rather than Bert's pigeon, was the direct cause of the airplane's destruction.

(D) Yes, because Bert took reasonable care in training his pigeons.

Question 19

Southland International Airport was known by law enforcement officials to be one of the primary points of entry for illegal drugs smuggled into the country. However, as a result of a decision by the supreme court of the state in which Southland was located, local law officers were not permitted to detain any travelers unless there were reasonable grounds to arrest them. Not wanting federal agents to get credit for all of the drug seizures at the airport, local police arranged to have airport security officials make random searches of passenger luggage while it was being sent to the baggage claim area. The searches were conducted so that there was no delay in the luggage being released to those claiming it. Warren was passing through Southland on his way home from a Caribbean vacation. He went to the baggage claim area but his luggage, which contained a number of valuables but no contraband, did not appear. It had been selected for a search but the X-ray machine had malfunctioned and security officers were having difficulty getting it unlocked to search it by hand. When Warren inquired about the luggage, he was told that it was being inspected and that he would have to remain in the area if he wanted to claim it when it was released. About 15 minutes later, the luggage was returned to Warren with an apology for the delay.

Can Warren bring an action against the airport security officials for false imprisonment?

(A) Yes, if Warren suffered harm because of the delay in releasing his luggage.

(B) No, because Warren was not restrained from leaving the airport.

(C) Yes, if Warren reasonably believed that he would not get his luggage back if he left the airport.

(D) No, because the delay in releasing the luggage was not done for the purpose of restraining Warren.

Questions 20-21 are based on the following fact situation:

Mrs. Parker, troubled by an irritating skin rash, consulted Dr. Dennis, a dermatologist, for treatment. Dr. Dennis diagnosed the rash as an unusual strain of herpes transmitted by sexual contact. Mrs. Parker expressed doubt about the diagnosis, indicating that she had only had sexual contact with her husband. Dr. Dennis stated that he was certain of the diagnosis because he had just been alerted by the local board of health about this strain of herpes, which had only recently been introduced into the area through female prostitutes who had immigrated from another country. Mrs. Parker was very upset by the diagnosis and the statements by Dr. Dennis. She confronted her husband with the information and accused him of infidelity. Mr. Parker denied any wrongdoing and, after several days of strained communications, persuaded his wife to obtain a second opinion. Mrs. Parker, whose rash had shown no sign of improvement, consulted the second doctor a week later. That doctor immediately diagnosed her skin rash as a common bacterial infection and prescribed an ointment that cleared up the condition in a few days.

20. Can Mrs. Parker recover from Dr. Dennis for the distress caused by his erroneous diagnosis?

(A) No, because Dr. Dennis's conduct did not create a foreseeable risk of physical injury to Mrs. Parker.

(B) Yes, because the misdiagnosis by Dr. Dennis caused her actual harm.

(C) No, unless Mrs. Parker had to pay for the second doctor visit.

(D) Yes, if her distress caused her some physical injury.

21. Can Mr. Parker recover damages from Dr. Dennis for defamation?

(A) No, because Dr. Dennis made no defamatory statement about Mr. Parker.

(B) Yes, because Dr. Dennis's statements constituted slander per se.

(C) Yes, if Mr. Parker can show pecuniary harm to him from Dr. Dennis's statements.

(D) No, because Dr. Dennis made the statements for Mrs. Parker's benefit.

Question 22

Drayton was employed as a plumber by Drainwell Plumbing Services. Drainwell had contracts with a number of large office and condominium buildings to provide emergency plumbing services and repairs at any hour of the day or night. Drainwell also advertised in the telephone "yellow pages": "If it's a plumbing emergency, call Drainwell Plumbing Services—night or day." Although Drayton usually worked from 8 a.m. to 4 p.m. at Drainwell, the nature of Drainwell's emergency services required Drayton to be "on call" 24 hours a day. Therefore, Drainwell required Drayton to drive his company van to his home each night, so he would be in a position to speed off to an emergency with all of his tools and equipment at hand. One afternoon, Drayton left the Drainwell Plumbing offices at 4 p.m. as usual. However, when he left the main highway, he did not turn left toward his home but instead turned right toward the supermarket a few blocks away to pick up some items for dinner. While entering the supermarket parking lot, Drayton drove negligently and struck Peter, a pedestrian. Peter suffered serious injuries and required several operations and a lengthy hospital stay. Peter filed suit against Drainwell, and the jury awarded him $100,000 in damages, which Drainwell paid. Assume that the jurisdiction maintains traditional common law rules regarding contribution and indemnity.

If Drainwell sues Drayton to recoup its loss in the lawsuit, which party will prevail?

(A) Drainwell can recover 100% of the judgment as an indemnity, because Drayton was negligent, not Drainwell.

(B) Drainwell will prevail, if Drainwell had a rule against using company vehicles for personal errands.

(C) Drainwell will not prevail, because Drainwell has already been found liable under principles of vicarious liability in the lawsuit by Peter.

(D) Drainwell will not prevail, because Drainwell required Drayton to be "on call" 24 hours a day.

Question 23

Donald was not a very patient person and he hated having to drive in the city. In particular, he hated having to yield to pedestrians, who never paid any attention to their own safety and constantly jaywalked. One afternoon, he had to drive into the city during rush hour for an appointment with his therapist. After having to stop several times for pedestrians crossing against the traffic signal, Donald decided that he would teach a lesson to the next jaywalking pedestrian. A half a block away from him, Penn was crossing the street, oblivious to the "Don't Walk" signal and the traffic around him. Although there was room to pass behind Penn, Donald drove straight toward him, leaning on the horn and intending to make Penn jump. Penn, however, did not change his pace. He was listening through headphones to his favorite heavy metal tune on his portable CD player, which was turned up to full volume. Frank, who was standing on the corner, rushed out to pull Penn to safety. Donald steered around both of them safely, but Penn tripped when Frank pulled him to the curb and suffered a fractured kneecap.

If Penn sues Donald for assault, the likely result will be:

(A) Donald wins, because Penn did not know at the time that he was in danger from Donald.

(B) Donald loses, because his conduct was a substantial factor in causing Penn's injury.

(C) Penn wins, because Donald intended to create in Penn an apprehension of immediate harmful contact.

(D) Penn loses, because Donald did not intend for Penn to be injured by Donald's conduct.

Question 24

Jackie, who was 13 years old, lived on a farm with his parents. He had always helped out with chores on the farm and had learned how to drive the tractor when he was 11. One morning, as he had done several times before, Jackie took the tractor onto the public road to reach one of the outlying fields a few hundred yards away. A state statute permitted persons without a driver's license to temporarily operate farm vehicles on public highways. As he was turning off the road into the field, he saw a classmate riding her bicycle at a crossroads a short distance ahead of him. Jackie, who had a crush on her, decided to change course so he would have a chance to say hello to her. He pulled back onto the road right in front of a milk delivery truck driven by Putt. Putt, swerving to avoid Jackie, went off the road into a drainage ditch and sustained serious injuries.

Putt sued Jackie for his injuries. At trial, Jackie requested the judge to instruct the jury that he should be held to the standard of care of a child of the same age. Putt then requested the judge to submit the following instructions to the jury:

I. A higher standard of care is warranted for the particular activity in which the defendant was involved.

II. Persons 13 years of age or older are held to the same standard of care as adults.

III. It is appropriate to take into account the fact that the defendant was experienced at driving a tractor when considering the standard to be applied.

Which of the above numbered instructions would it be appropriate for the judge to submit to the jury?

(A) I. only.

(B) I. and III. only.

(C) III. only.

(D) I., II., and III.

Question 25

Olson owned and managed a small fleet of taxicabs. He had always had his cabs serviced by Vehicle Maintenance, Inc., a large auto service operation specializing in commercial vehicles. However, when Vehicle Maintenance doubled its charges for routine maintenance, Olson decided to look elsewhere. He noticed that Goodstone, a national chain of auto service centers, had just opened a branch in a new building a block away from his business. After a visit there and a discussion with the manager, Olson made a deal to bring all of his cabs there for repairs in exchange for a discount. Six months later, Penny was a passenger in one of Olson's cabs when the brakes failed without warning. Despite the driver's efforts, the cab went through a stop sign and was struck by a bus. Penny was seriously injured in the collision. An investigation revealed that brake repairs had been made on the cab a week before, but the Goodstone mechanic had used the wrong parts and had made numerous errors in reassembling the brakes.

If Penny sues Olson for her injuries:

(A) Penny should prevail, unless Olson exercised a high degree of care in selecting Goodstone for maintenance of his cabs.

(B) Olson should prevail, because he had no reason to know that Goodstone's mechanic would be negligent.

(C) Penny should prevail, because Olson breached his duty to her to provide a safe vehicle in which to ride.

(D) Olson should prevail, because he is not vicariously liable for the negligence of an independent contractor.

Question 26

Dobbins lived next door to Gretel's Day Care Center and Preschool. Because he had a large yard and there were no applicable zoning restrictions, Dobbins decided to install a kennel and train attack dogs to sell to businesses. As soon as he opened the business and posted signs in front advertising the exceptional ferocity of the dogs, some parents who had children enrolled in the day care center became alarmed at the prospect of the dogs right next to the yard where the children played, especially since the children could see the training area where the dogs were taught to attack people. Within a few months of the dogs' arrival next door, Gretel lost 10% of her enrollment.

If Gretel brings a nuisance action against Dobbins, what will be the most critical factual issue that the trier of fact must resolve to determine who should prevail?

(A) Whether Gretel suffered other damages in addition to her economic losses.

(B) Whether Dobbins conducted his business with reasonable care.

(C) Whether Gretel's use of her property makes her business abnormally sensitive to the presence of the dogs.

(D) Whether Dobbins was apprised of Gretel's concerns and did nothing to alleviate them.

Question 27

Picard, the owner of several thriving shopping malls, was negotiating with Trieste, the owner of the Waterloo Mall, to purchase it from him. Deneuve, who shopped at the mall regularly, was delighted when she learned of the negotiations.

The mall had deteriorated noticeably during the time that Trieste had owned it and Deneuve believed that Picard's ownership would revitalize the mall considerably. Deneuve contacted Picard and told him, "I heard that you were discussing the purchase of the Waterloo Mall with Trieste. I think this is the best acquisition that you could ever make. The state is planning to construct a new interchange for the turnpike only three blocks from the mall." Picard, who knew that Deneuve was a staff attorney for the state transportation department, decided to make the purchase in the hope that the new interchange would help reverse the steady decline in sales that the mall had been experiencing. In fact, no interchange was being considered by the state at that time, and nothing that Picard did after he purchased the mall could stem the decline in sales. He ended up selling the property at a substantial loss several years after the purchase.

Does Picard have a cause of action against Deneuve for his losses?

(A) Yes, for negligent misrepresentation, because Picard made a business transaction in reliance on Deneuve's statements.

(B) Yes, for intentional misrepresentation, if Deneuve was aware that she did not know whether the state was planning an interchange.

(C) No, because Deneuve's statement pertained to a future event that may not be justifiably relied upon.

(D) No, because Deneuve made her statement to Picard gratuitously.

Question 28

Ichabod was a cautious individual who did not like surprises. A week before Halloween, his girlfriend Katrina persuaded him to go with her to the Sleepy Hollow Haunted House, which was put on each year by a local theater group and was widely recognized as the most terrifying haunted house production in the state. Ichabod was not aware of its reputation but he noted with alarm the signs in front of the haunted house warning that this attraction has live "monsters" who will be trying to scare people and is not for the faint of heart. His alarm increased when he went up to the ticket booth and noticed the same warning printed on the tickets. Katrina, however, assured him that the haunted house was safe and that the warnings were just added "to keep the lawyers happy." Ichabod paid for his ticket and reluctantly went into the darkened house with Katrina. In the first room they were to enter, a headless Frankenstein monster was being played by Brom, a burly member of the theater group. He had overheard Ichabod expressing his apprehension to Katrina outside the door and decided to make an extra effort to play his part to the hilt. Waiting until they had passed, he came at them out of the shadows with a shriek and held the head of the monster in his hand as if to throw it at them. Although Brom stopped short of throwing the head, Ichabod had already turned and with an enormous leap dove out of the house through one of the plate glass windows, severely lacerating his arms and face in the process.

Ichabod brings an action against Brom for his injuries. The jurisdiction in which they are located has adopted a "pure" comparative negligence statute. Will Ichabod recover damages from Brom?

(A) No, because Ichabod expressly assumed the risk of injury.

(B) No, unless Brom acted negligently in trying to scare Ichabod.

(C) Yes, because Brom intended to cause apprehension on the part of Ichabod.

(D) Yes, but Ichabod's recovery will be reduced by a certain percentage if the trier of fact determines that he was also at fault.

Question 29

Delco was the owner and manager of a large office building. It contracted its elevator maintenance to Plastico, an elevator repair company that did not have a good reputation for safety. One of Plastico's employees incorrectly set a switch while repairing an elevator. As a result, the elevator dropped suddenly when Ira, an office worker in the building, used it the next day.

Ira sued Plastico in a jurisdiction that has adopted comparative contribution rules but has retained joint and several liability. The trier of fact determined that Plastico was 70% at fault and Delco was 30% at fault in causing Ira's damages. After Ira had obtained a full recovery of his damages from Plastico, Plastico sued Delco to obtain reimbursement for the damages it paid to Ira.

Plastico should recover from Delco:

(A) All of the damages through indemnity because Delco owed a nondelegable duty to occupants of its building.

(B) None of the damages because Plastico was more at fault for Ira's injury than Delco.

(C) 30% of the total damages because Delco is jointly liable for the injury to Ira.

(D) 50% of the total damages because joint tortfeasors are liable for contribution in equal shares.

Question 30

Denver owned a thriving honey farm with numerous hives for her honeybees that she carefully maintained. Denver's property was adjacent to a busy state highway. One day after a brief rain shower, Turner was driving his sports car on the highway at a high rate of speed when he lost control on the wet pavement. His car crossed in front of Perkins, who was going in the opposite direction on his motorcycle, causing Perkins to crash into a ditch on the side of the road. Turner's car continued off the road onto Denver's property. The car smashed into one of the beehives, driving an angry swarm of bees out of the hive. Perkins, who suffered only a few bruises when his motorcycle crashed, saw the swarm of bees

heading toward him and started to run across the road to get away from them. He stumbled and was struck by a truck driven by Wanda, causing him to suffer several broken bones and serious internal injuries.

Perkins filed suit against Denver, Turner, and Wanda for his injuries. Can Perkins recover any damages from Denver?

(A) Yes, because Denver is strictly liable for injury caused by the honeybees.

(B) No, because the honeybees did not directly inflict injury on Perkins.

(C) Yes, because Perkins was a traveler on a public road.

(D) No, unless Denver violated a state statute in placing the beehive adjacent to the public road.

Questions 31-32 are based on the following fact situation:

Carlyle had just purchased a powerboat from Aquapower Sales and Service. He filled up the gas tank and took it out on a large lake near his home. The gas tank, which was manufactured and assembled by Machinecorp, had a defect that caused it to spring a leak when he was several miles out on the water. The defect was not discoverable by an ordinary inspection. Before he was aware of the problem he had run out of gas. His frantic signaling alerted Rensler, who was passing by in his boat. Rensler pulled up alongside and offered his assistance. When Rensler attempted to start Carlyle's boat, a spark ignited a pool of gas that had leaked from the gas tank and collected in the lower part of the boat, causing an explosion and fire. Carlyle fell into Rensler's boat and was knocked unconscious. Rensler, who was closest to the explosion, was severely burned and fell into the water. Carlyle eventually was rescued, but Rensler died before the rescuers could reach him. The jurisdiction in which the events took place follows traditional contributory negligence rules.

31. Carlyle files a lawsuit against Aquapower, Machinecorp, and Rensler's estate seeking damages for the injuries he suffered in the explosion. Does Carlyle have a cause of action for damages against Rensler's estate?

    (A) No, because Rensler had no duty to come to Carlyle's aid.

    (B) No, because Rensler did not survive the explosion.

    (C) No, unless Rensler acted negligently in attempting to start the boat.

    (D) No, unless Rensler acted with gross negligence in his attempt to assist Carlyle.

32. Rensler's estate brings a wrongful death action based on strict liability against Aquapower and Machinecorp. Can the estate recover any damages from Aquapower?

    (A) Yes, unless Carlyle was negligent in failing to investigate where the gas had gone.

    (B) Yes, because harm to someone in Rensler's position was a foreseeable result of the gas leak.

    (C) No, if Aquapower had no reason to anticipate that Machinecorp assembled the gas tank improperly.

    (D) No, because Rensler did not have a sufficient relationship to Carlyle to make Aquapower liable for Rensler's death.

Question 33

Preston was spending the day with his friends at Deep Springs Resort, a privately owned lake for which a fee for admission was charged. The beach had a roped-in swimming area and large signs directing swimmers not to swim anywhere but within the ropes. The lifeguards strictly enforced this rule. The resort also rented canoes and rowboats to its patrons, who could take them anywhere on the lake. After swimming for a little while, Preston and two of his friends rented a canoe for an hour. They started to paddle out toward the other side of the lake when Preston saw a volleyball game starting on the beach. Not wanting to miss the opportunity to play his favorite game, he left his friends in the canoe and started swimming to shore. He was only a few yards outside of the roped-in swimming area when he started, but he angled away from the swimming area toward the area of the beach where the volleyball net was set up. When the depth of the water was about four feet, he put his foot down and was immediately cut by the jagged edge of a rusted metal stake protruding a few inches out of the bottom of the lake. Preston had not seen the stake because a recent rain had stirred up the sediment and made the water cloudier than usual. Preston suffered a torn tendon in his foot that required surgery to repair.

Can Preston recover against Deep Springs Resort for his injury?

    (A) No, unless the stake had been in the water for a long period of time.

    (B) No, because Preston was swimming outside of the roped-in area.

    (C) Yes, if the lifeguard on duty saw Preston and did not warn him to return to the swimming area.

    (D) Yes, because Preston is a public invitee of the resort.

Question 34

The *Daily Herald* printed in a news article that Doug Banks, a successful businessman running for the state legislature, had attempted suicide and had just been released from the hospital where he had undergone intensive psychotherapy. Actually, Banks had been hospitalized because he had contracted hepatitis. Banks's incumbent opponent, Lucy Arnold, read the story into the legislative record the next day.

If Banks sues Arnold for defamation, what is the result likely to be?

(A) Banks will recover if he establishes actual malice by Arnold.

(B) Banks will not recover if Arnold relied on the newspaper article.

(C) Banks will recover because the statement was slander per se.

(D) Banks will not recover because Arnold was privileged to make the defamatory statements.

Question 35

Dogalert Co. manufactured dog whistles. Its factory was located near a residential area of Catston, and it was at the factory that Dogalert tested its whistles. Dogalert used the most modern and effective testing methods. Although Dogalert attempted to shield the sound of the whistles from the neighborhood, it was impossible to completely soundproof the testing area. Doberman, a dog breeder, bought some property near Dogalert's factory and built a kennel on the property. Although the whistles were too high-pitched to be heard by human ears, they could be heard by Doberman's dogs. Consequently, the dogs were in a constant state of agitation. Doberman could not understand why her dogs were under such stress, but eventually she discovered the cause of her dogs' problems.

If Doberman brings suit against Dogalert, will she prevail?

(A) Yes, on a trespass theory, because the sound waves are entering onto Doberman's property.

(B) Yes, on a nuisance theory, because the sound of the whistles is a substantial interference with Doberman's use of her land.

(C) No, because the sound of the whistles is not a substantial interference with Doberman's use of her land.

(D) No, because Dogalert has acted reasonably in testing its whistles.

Question 36

A state statute requires that any pilot who flies passengers for hire must have a commercial pilot's license. Gremlin, an experienced pilot, sometimes flew a passenger or two to nearby cities. Gremlin never had a mishap, but he only had a private pilot's license and not the commercial license required by statute. Paulette, a successful salesperson who had the entire state for her territory, wanted to go to Alphaville to close a deal with a client. Alphaville is 150 miles away, and Paulette wanted to fly there to save the time involved in driving there and back, a six-hour round trip. However, Paulette discovered that there was only one commercial flight per day to Alphaville, and the flight was at an inconvenient time. Paulette's friend, Frieda, told her that perhaps Gremlin could fly her to Alphaville, but Frieda informed Paulette that Gremlin did not have a commercial license. She also told her, "That commercial license law is a bunch of regulatory baloney designed to put a few bucks in some bureaucrat's pocket; Gremlin is a darn good pilot, and you're as safe with him as with anybody."

Paulette went to the airfield and asked Gremlin if he would fly her to Alphaville and back. Gremlin agreed to do it, and charged her a reasonable fare. Gremlin took off with Paulette and flew toward Alphaville. The weather became a bit rough, but Gremlin did a fine job handling the small plane. However, as Gremlin prepared to land, he made a navigational error. He saw an airport through the clouds and assumed that it was the Alphaville airport. In fact, it was the Betaville airport, located three miles across the Alphabeta River from the Alphaville airport. Gremlin landed the plane safely on the proper runway. Just as Paulette was about to congratulate Gremlin on his excellent flying in the bad weather, a plane piloted by Dooley taxied down the wrong runway and struck Gremlin's aircraft. Dooley had disregarded directions from the control tower and entered the landing runway instead of the takeoff runway. Paulette was injured in the collision.

If Paulette sues Gremlin for her injuries, who will prevail?

(A) Gremlin, because Paulette knew he lacked a commercial license and she voluntarily assumed the risk of flying with him.

(B) Gremlin, because the injuries to Paulette were caused by Dooley's negligence.

(C) Paulette, because Gremlin violated a statute designed to prevent persons without commercial licenses from flying passengers for a fee, and such violation imposes liability per se.

(D) Paulette, because Gremlin landed at the wrong airport, and but for this mistake she could not have been injured by Dooley's aircraft.

Question 37

Dack was a patient in Gitwell Mental Hospital. Dack was known to have dangerous proclivities and was kept in the high security area of the hospital. The doors in that section had sophisticated double locks. Shrink, administrator of the hospital, had prepared a "Manual of Instruction for Staff," which included a provision that all doors in the hospital should be locked after 8 p.m. It was customary that the staff would be reminded of this rule in a general meeting held the Friday nearest the 15th of each month. Walder was a new employee of Gitwell, having worked there only two weeks. Walder had been given a copy of the "Manual of Instruction" a few days earlier but had not been instructed as to when he would be expected to know all of the provisions, and he had not yet been hired on the day of the last general meeting. One night, Walder was left in charge of the high security area. That night, Dack escaped from the hospital out the back door and without any provocation brutally beat Citizen, a resident of the town in which Gitwell is located. Dack was apprehended and returned to the hospital shortly after his attack on Citizen. Walder was subsequently fired and his whereabouts are unknown.

If Citizen sues Gitwell Hospital for his injuries, what is Citizen's best argument for a recovery?

(A) Gitwell is strictly liable for the actions of its abnormally dangerous patients.

(B) Negligence is presumed from the fact of Dack's escape.

(C) Gitwell is vicariously liable for the intentional torts of its patients.

(D) Walder acted negligently when he failed to lock the door.

Question 38

For many years, Priscilla Pompous was socially prominent in a city in the Pacific Northwest. She had served as chairperson of Communityfund, a major charitable agency, and was also elected to the school board. However, when Communityfund's board of directors declined to offer Priscilla the customary second term as chairperson of Communityfund, she withdrew in a huff from all her philanthropic activities, including her places on the boards of the Civic Symphony and Child Welfare Guild. She remained, however, as co-hostess of a weekly local television show concerned with antique collection and retained her position on the school board. A month after her resignations, Gilbert Gabb, society columnist of *The Salmonton Newsfisher,* the second largest newspaper in town, was talking to Roger NoseyParker, a neighbor of Priscilla. Roger told him, "It's really too bad about old Pris Pompous. You know she's not paying her bills, and her whole family is completely broke. That's the real reason that she wasn't offered another term as chairperson." Roger had supplied little tidbits like this to Gabb in the past, and he had always proven to be reliable. Without further investigation, Gabb printed in his column, "It's with sorrow that we report the hard times that have befallen Priscilla Pompous. Her family has lost all its money and she is unable to pay her bills." In fact, Priscilla's family was still very wealthy, and Priscilla had never failed to pay a bill on time. Priscilla sues *The Salmonton Newsfisher* for defamation.

Will Priscilla prevail?

(A) Yes, but only if she can prove special damages.

(B) Yes, because the newspaper displayed reckless disregard for the truth.

(C) No, if Gabb honestly believed he was printing the truth.

(D) No, unless Gabb was negligent.

Question 39

After a bitter custody battle, the court dissolving Mary and Jason's marriage ordered that Mary had sole custody of their three-year-old son, Mark. Jason was allowed to have Mark for visitation purposes for two weeks every summer, one weekend per month, and Christmas or Thanksgiving during alternate years. During the first summer visitation period, Jason took Mark to stay with Jason's parents (Mark's grandparents). When the two-week period ended, both Jason and Mark disappeared from sight. Under an assumed name, Jason leased a poultry farm 15 miles from his parents' home and kept Mark there. Mark enjoyed living on the farm and really enjoyed helping collect eggs and doing other activities with his dad.

Mary was distraught and frantic when Jason failed to return Mark. She tried to find Jason but was unable to learn of his whereabouts. Two years after Mark and Jason's disappearance, one of Jason's neighbors saw a program about missing children on television. The neighbor saw Mark's picture and notified local police. Mark and Mary were quickly reunited.

If Mary files suit on Mark's behalf seeking damages from Jason for false imprisonment, who will prevail?

(A) Mark, because Jason did not have legal custody of Mark.

(B) Mark, because Jason deprived Mark of his mother's care for two years.

(C) Jason, because Mark did not realize he was confined.

(D) Jason, because Mark enjoyed living on the farm.

Question 40

Dingo had taken his dog, Growler, to obedience training school. After Growler's graduation, Dingo wanted to see how well Growler would perform his lessons outside of the classroom situation. There was an open field across the road from Dingo's house, and Dingo took Growler there and started putting Growler through his paces. After 10 minutes of this, Growler grew bored and ran off into a flower bed belonging to Princess. Growler dug up many of the flowers.

If Princess sues Dingo for the damage to her flower bed, who will prevail?

(A) Dingo, because he never intended for Growler to run into Princess's flower bed.

(B) Dingo, unless he was negligent in training or supervising the dog.

(C) Princess, because Dingo owned the dog.

(D) Princess, because Growler's invasion of the flower bed constituted a trespass on the part of Dingo.

Question 41

Phil, an avid skier, was spending the day at Default Mountain Ski Resort. On his second ride up one of the chair lifts, both skiers on the chair in front of him fell while disembarking. The employee of Default who was operating the chair lift was not paying attention, however, and did not shut off the lift. When Phil came to the top, he tried to jump off to the side to avoid hitting the skiers on the ground in front of him. He was knocked off balance by the chair and fell off a ledge of icy snow, fracturing his leg in several places. Ski patrol personnel came to Phil's aid and carefully placed him on a stretcher, which they then hooked up to a snowmobile to bring him down the mountain along the edge of a ski trail. Midway down, Dan, a skier of moderate skill, decided to show off by seeing how close he could come to the stretcher without hitting it. He lost control, however, and landed on top of Phil's leg, damaging it further. As a result, Phil's leg was permanently disabled and he had to give up his career as a ballet dancer.

Phil filed a lawsuit against Dan and Default to recover damages for his disability and loss of future earnings. The jurisdiction has adopted a comparative contribution system in joint and several liability cases. At trial, Phil's physician testified that neither injury, by itself, would have left his leg permanently disabled but that it was impossible to quantify how much each injury contributed to the disability. The jury determined that the damages from Phil's permanent disability equaled $2 million, and that Dan and Default were each 50% at fault.

What amount of damages can Phil recover from Dan for his permanent disability?

(A) $1 million, because the jurisdiction follows comparative contribution rules.

(B) Nothing for his permanent disability, because Phil has not met his burden of proof as to the amount of damages that Dan caused.

(C) $2 million, because it was not possible to identify the portion of the injury that Dan caused.

(D) Nothing for his permanent disability, because the injury inflicted by Dan, by itself, would not have caused the disability.

Questions 42-44 are based on the following fact situation:

Assume that Kenbraska has maintained traditional common law tort defenses, Alasippi has adopted "partial" comparative negligence, and Illiana has adopted "pure" comparative negligence. Joint and several liability is retained in all of the jurisdictions.

Aiken failed to stop at a stop sign before he entered an intersection. Bacon, who had the right of way, saw Aiken but was unable to stop because he had neglected to get his brakes repaired even though he knew they were going bad. The two cars collided and then struck Cogg, who had ridden her motorcycle through the intersection from the other direction, also without stopping at a stop sign.

Aiken sued Bacon and Cogg, each of whom countersued Aiken and sued each other. At trial, it was determined by the trier of fact that Aiken suffered $10,000 in damages, Bacon suffered $1,000 in damages, and Cogg suffered $100,000 in damages. It was also determined that Aiken was 45% at fault, Bacon was 35% at fault, and Cogg was 20% at fault.

42. How would damages be assessed in Kenbraska?

(A) Aiken, Bacon, and Cogg all are awarded nothing.

(B) Bacon is liable to Aiken for $10,000, because Bacon had the last clear chance to avoid hitting him, and Bacon and Cogg are awarded nothing.

(C) Cogg is awarded $100,000 and Aiken and Bacon are awarded nothing, but one of them will have a claim against the other for contribution if he pays more than $50,000 of the award.

(D) Cogg is awarded $100,000 and Aiken and Bacon are awarded nothing, but one of them will have a claim against the other for contribution if he pays more than his proportionate share of the award.

43. How would damages be assessed in Alasippi?

(A) Cogg has a claim for $80,000, and Aiken and Bacon have no claims.

(B) Cogg has a claim for $80,000, which she can collect from either Aiken or Bacon, Bacon has a claim for $650, which he can collect only from Aiken, and Aiken has no claim.

(C) Aiken has a claim for $5,500, Bacon has a claim for $650, and Cogg has a claim for $80,000.

(D) Aiken has a claim for $10,000, Bacon has a claim for $1,000, and Cogg has a claim for $100,000.

44. Assume for purposes of this question only that Bacon suffered no damages, while Aiken suffered $10,000 in damages and Cogg $100,000. Assume also that it was determined that Aiken was 55% at fault, Bacon 45% at fault, and Cogg not at fault. After damages are assessed and judgment entered in Illiana, Aiken paid Cogg a total of $100,000, while Bacon has paid nothing. How much, if anything, can Aiken recover from Bacon if Illiana has adopted comparative contribution?

(A) $45,000, because Bacon was 45% at fault.

(B) $49,500, because Bacon was 45% at fault and Aiken suffered damages.

(C) $50,000, because Aiken and Bacon are jointly liable.

(D) Nothing, because Aiken was more at fault than Bacon.

Question 45

Prell was the driver of a tanker truck transporting radioactive waste from a nuclear power plant to a permanent storage facility in a remote western region of the United States. After driving all night, Prell fell asleep at the wheel and the truck crossed over the center line, off the road, and onto Dell's property, coming to rest after crashing into several glass cases containing Dell's collection of poisonous snakes, the keeping of which was permitted by local ordinance. When Prell exited from the truck, he was bitten on the leg by one of the poisonous snakes and became seriously ill.

Prell brought an action against Dell for his injuries in a jurisdiction following traditional contributory negligence rules. The parties stipulated to the above facts, and that Prell violated a state statute by driving off of the road. Both parties moved for judgment as a matter of law on the liability issue. How should the court rule?

(A) Grant Prell's motion and deny Dell's motion, because Dell is strictly liable for the injury caused by the snake.

(B) Deny Prell's motion and grant Dell's motion, because Prell was a trespasser on Dell's property.

(C) Deny Prell's motion and grant Dell's motion, because Prell's violation of the state statute establishes Prell's contributory negligence as a matter of law.

(D) Deny both parties' motions, because both parties were engaged in activity for which strict liability is imposed.

Question 46

Disasterco was engaged in the hauling of hazardous chemical waste by truck. After picking up a load of waste, Steve, the Disasterco truck driver, set out on the road to his next stop. However, Steve had failed to secure the latch on the back panel of the truck. Consequently, the panel opened while Steve was on the road, and a metal canister full of chemical waste fell onto the road. A car driven by Pat struck the canister, causing Pat to veer off the road, injuring him. Pat filed suit against Disasterco for his injuries.

The jurisdiction in which the above events took place has adopted a rule of partial comparative negligence. At trial, Pat admitted that he had momentarily taken his eyes off the road to look at his speedometer. When he had looked up again, the canister was there and he could not stop in time. The jury found that Disasterco acted willfully and wantonly and was 90% at fault, while Pat was 10% at fault. Pat filed a motion for judgment notwithstanding the verdict.

If the judge rules that Disasterco is liable for 100% of Pat's damages, it will most likely be because:

(A) Plaintiff's comparative negligence is not taken into account in cases of willful and wanton conduct by the defendant.

(B) A state ordinance mandating motorists to stay within the posted speed limit requires as a matter of law an occasional glance at the speedometer.

(C) Disasterco was more than 50% at fault.

(D) Disasterco was engaged in an ultrahazardous activity.

Question 47

A statute in State A required that any freight train operating within the city limits be able to stop within 200 yards of applying its brakes. No fixed speed limit was established or particular type of braking mechanism required, but through either lowered speed or braking power, the 200-yard limit was required of all trains. Another statute prohibited vehicles from being within the railroad crossing when the lights on the warning signs are flashing or when the gates are lowered. One day, as an Eastern Pacific freight train was entering the city limits of Metropolis, the engineer saw a car stalled at a street crossing ahead. He immediately applied full braking power, but was unable to stop the train before it had hit and demolished the car. Parnell, the driver of the car, had gotten clear before the impact, but brought suit against Eastern Pacific for property damage to the $25,000 car. At trial, the parties stipulated that Parnell's car was stalled within the crossing while the warning lights were flashing. Evidence at trial established that the distance from

the point at which the engineer applied the train's brakes to the point of impact was 150 yards, and from the braking point to the point at which the train finally stopped was 225 yards. No other evidence of negligence was presented by Parnell.

At the end of Parnell's case, Eastern Pacific moved for a directed verdict. Should the court grant the motion?

(A) No, because Eastern Pacific was negligent per se.

(B) No, because Eastern Pacific was strictly liable for its violation of the braking statute.

(C) Yes, because the plaintiff's car was on Eastern Pacific's tracks in violation of the crossing statute.

(D) Yes, because Eastern Pacific's violation of the braking statute was not the cause in fact of the accident.

Question 48

Phil Phossell owns Phil's Antiques, a small antique shop in an area of the country rife with Revolutionary War artifacts. On a visit to an estate sale, he purchased a 200-year-old powder horn inscribed with the name Stuart Harrison, a soldier in the Revolutionary War and a member of a family that was very prominent in the area at that time. Donna Director is the curator of the nearby Harrison Museum, which displays numerous artifacts owned by the family during that period. She approached Phil when she heard of his purchase and indicated that she wanted to acquire the powder horn for the museum. The price that she offered was slightly higher than what Phil had been planning to ask for it when he offered it for sale in his shop and was a very fair price for an item of that nature. Phil, however, refused to sell to her because he did not like the way she had done business with other antique dealers in the past. After her attempts at friendly persuasion had failed, Donna turned to threats. Saying that she had a power of attorney from the heirs of Stuart Harrison, she claimed that the law allowed her to bring a replevin action to seize it from Phil if he did not accept her offer. In fact, her statements were false and she had no power to obtain the powder horn. However, Phil believed her and grudgingly agreed to sell her the item for the price that she had offered. Several days later he learned that her statements were false and he became very distressed.

Can Phil recover damages in a misrepresentation suit against Donna?

(A) Yes, but only if Donna knew that her statements were false when she made them.

(B) No, because Phil suffered no pecuniary harm.

(C) Yes, because Phil would not have made the transaction with Donna if not for her false statements.

(D) No, because Phil had no right to rely on Donna's statements regarding the law.

Question 49

Hendrik was on his way to meet Vanya, his wife, for lunch at the restaurant in the lobby of the BanqueZero building, where she worked. He had just entered the building when he heard screams and the sound of breaking glass. He rounded the corner and saw the wreckage of a large piece of artwork made of stained glass that had fallen onto the seating area of the restaurant. Looking further, he saw several seriously injured persons lying in the wreckage. He fainted and hit his head on the marble floor, fracturing his skull. The artwork had collapsed because the pedestal that the building had provided for the artwork was not properly constructed.

Hendrik sues BanqueZero Corp., which owns and operates the building, for his injury in a jurisdiction following the "zone of danger" approach in bystander cases. Hendrik will:

(A) Prevail, because he suffered physical injury as a result of defendant's negligence.

(B) Not prevail, because Hendrik was not personally put at risk by defendant's negligence.

(C) Prevail, if one of the persons he saw lying in the wreckage was his wife.

(D) Not prevail, because he did not actually see the accident occur.

Question 50

Winthrop, the president of Mid-Valley Bank, told George, the head of maintenance for the bank, that the massive metal door that sealed off the bank's vault had been sticking and making grinding noises when it was shut the last few evenings. The next morning, George began inspecting the door mechanism in an attempt to find the problem. He disconnected the time lock devices and opened and shut the metal door a few times, listening to it and watching for it to stick. Believing that something was wrong with the electrical circuits that operated the door, George knew that the door would have to be in operation for him to effectively check those circuits. On the main control panel that operated the door was an emergency stop button that would instantly freeze the door if required. George activated the door closing circuits, then hit the emergency stop button, so that the door to the vault was frozen open but the circuits were live. He then went back to the door, which was several feet from the control panel, and began testing the circuits.

Leon was an auditor for the county government who had been called to the bank that morning to be present when a safe deposit box was opened by court order, so that he could inventory the contents of the box. Winthrop had told Leon to make himself comfortable in the employees' lounge until the sheriff arrived with the court order. After about 15 minutes, Leon decided to check the vault to see if there was a table or other surface there where he could set out his briefcase and inventorying materials, which consisted of an electronic printing calculator and numerous forms. At the same time Leon decided to inspect the vault, Sam, a loan officer, noticed that the emergency stop button was engaged on the vault door mechanism. George had gone to his office to obtain some additional tools, and Sam could see no reason for the button to be engaged, so he disengaged it. Freed of restraint, the massive vault door, its closing circuits on, began to swing shut. Leon had just entered the vault, where he dropped the pencil he had been carrying, and was bent over to pick it up, oblivious of the heavy metal door swinging towards him. Maurice, a security guard, saw Leon's danger and lunged toward him, hitting Leon with his shoulder and propelling both into the vault just as the door clanged shut. Leon was brought up short by the wall of safe deposit boxes, dislocating his shoulder and breaking two ribs. The jurisdiction follows traditional contributory negligence rules.

If Leon brings an action in negligence against George for personal injuries, will he likely prevail?

(A) No, because Leon was outside the zone of danger when George committed negligence.

(B) No, because Maurice was the direct and proximate cause of Leon's injuries.

(C) Yes, because George activated the vault door closing circuits and then left the vault door control panel unattended.

(D) Yes, unless the trier of fact determines that Winthrop instructed Leon to wait in the employee lounge.

Questions 51-52 are based on the following fact situation:

Harold purchased a home in a beautiful location in the foothills overlooking City. He moved into the home and frequently entertained his friends and associates at the large pool in the rear patio area. Harold gave a key to the house to his friend Ray, and told the latter that he could come over and use the pool any time.

The next year, Harold decided that he was ready to begin remodeling his home. He met with his architect and interior designer and worked out a complete set of plans for the remaking of his living space, including relandscaping the rear patio area and redoing the pool and related structures. Harold entered into an agreement with Carl, a general contractor, to make all the necessary changes during the six-week period that Harold would be out of the city and the house would be vacant. Carl subcontracted much of the work, including making arrangements with Skip, a local pool builder, to remove the existing pool and construct and install its replacement.

All of the work except that to be done by Skip was to commence the week after Harold left, but Skip was available to start the first day that Harold would be gone. Part of the preparation for removal of the existing pool and its surrounding components required that Skip spread a powdered substance that, when mixed with an alcohol-based solvent, would assist in dissolving the cement used in the construction of the materials in place. While applying the powder, Skip spilled some of it on a portion of wooden decking that was not to be removed. He then proceeded with removal of the existing structure, leaving the site at 4 p.m. after nine hours of work. When he left the house, all of the powdered substance had been removed from the rear patio area except the portion on the wooden deck, which had not been affected by the work done that day. Skip, knowing that no other workers would be at the house until the next week, planned to clean that up the next day.

At 5 p.m., Ray, who had been in Europe for several months and was unaware that Harold had left the city or that he was engaged in remodeling, arrived at the house and let himself in with his key. Since it was a warm summer day he decided to take a swim in the pool, but when he went outside to the rear patio area he saw that the pool was dry and much of the surrounding area was broken up. He decided to relax on the wooden decking and to douse himself with cool water from the garden hose. He noticed the powdery substance on the deck but thought that he would just hose it off before he set down his lawn chair. When he turned the water on the powdery substance, it exploded into flames, setting the deck on fire and severely burning Ray.

The powdery substance was a silicate of magnesium manufactured by Oxxon Petroleum Corporation. The label of the container, which Skip had read because he was using the substance for the first time, stated in part, "Danger. Extremely caustic. Do not use near any alcohol-based solvent except under professional supervision. Do not use near source of high heat or open flame." The manufacturer knew that the substance was volatile when exposed to water, but in the 15 years since the substance had been originally formulated, no one had ever been injured as a result of exposure of the substance to water.

51. Ray brings an action for personal injuries against Skip. What is the probable outcome of this litigation?

    (A) Ray will win, because Skip left the powder on the wooden deck.

    (B) Ray will win, because Skip is held to the same standard of liability as the manufacturer of the powder.

    (C) Skip will win, because he used the powder for the purpose for which it was designed.

    (D) Skip will win, because it was not reasonably foreseeable that the powder would cause injury to anyone.

52. Ray brings an action against Oxxon Petroleum on a theory of strict liability. Will Ray recover?

    (A) Yes, because the product was being used as intended and because he was injured thereby.

    (B) Yes, because the label on the container of powder did not warn of its volatility when exposed to water.

    (C) No, because the fact that no one had previously been injured demonstrated that the warning label on the powder was sufficient.

    (D) No, because his hosing of the powder was a negligent act relieving Oxxon of liability.

Question 53

Wallace owned a feed store in Decatur, Illinois. Industrial Farms, Inc., a large manufacturer of cattle feeds, recently sent a salesman to see Wallace, and as a result of the meeting, Wallace signed a contract in which he agreed to purchase several tons of grain products at a specified price. Industrial Farms later failed to deliver the promised grains, and Wallace was forced to cover by purchasing from local producers at a substantially higher price.

On the advice of a friend, Wallace contacted a large law firm headquartered in Chicago and obtained their agreement to represent him in connection with his possible claims against Industrial Farms. Due to error, the applicable statute of limitations period passed without the filing of any action on Wallace's behalf.

Wallace retained another lawyer, a sole practitioner in Decatur, and sued the large law firm for malpractice. The jurisdiction retains traditional contributory negligence.

In addition to the firm's negligence, Wallace will also have to establish, as part of his prima facie case, that:

    (A) He had a good faith claim against Industrial Farms that was lost by the law firm's dilatoriness.

    (B) He would have recovered from Industrial Farms if an action had been timely filed.

    (C) He did not contribute to the failure to timely file an action through his own negligence.

(D) The losses resulting from breach of the sales agreement by Industrial Farms severely harmed his financial situation.

Questions 54-55 are based on the following fact situation:

Rene and Leveque were both professional bicycle racers competing in cross-country races in the United States. Rene was also an amateur inventor, and for several years had been trying to develop a new kind of rear axle for racing bikes that would enable the rider to obtain greater speed with the same amount of leg effort. Finally, Rene succeeded and built a prototype racing bicycle on which a rider could achieve 20% greater speed than was possible with an unmodified bike. He started using it in his cross-country races in the United States and won the first three races he entered with the new device.

Rene had always had success in his racing but had never considered himself good enough to enter the very tough European road racing circuit. With his new axle permitting such increased speed, Rene knew he had a chance at the world championship and so prepared to travel to Europe to race, lining up sponsors and making other preparations. He also received several offers to purchase his new axle, and a few racers offered him as much as $30,000 for his modified bicycle, which, without the new axle, was worth about $1,500.

Because of the preparations for his European trip, Rene dropped out of the remainder of the United States racing circuit. Leveque asked if he could borrow Rene's modified bike while Rene was still in the United States to use in the United States races, and Rene agreed, on the condition that Leveque would return the bicycle no later than March 1. Leveque agreed and used the bike in his next two races, winning both. On March 1, Leveque had not returned the bike, and Rene learned that Leveque had arranged a match race with the current European champion, who was visiting the United States before the opening of the racing season in Europe. The winner of the match was to receive $10,000. Rene went to the site of the match and demanded the return of his bicycle. Leveque refused, and Rene grabbed the bike, trying to wrestle it away from Leveque. Although Rene elbowed Leveque in the mouth, he was unable to obtain control of the bike, and Leveque rode it away to begin the match. Leveque subsequently won the match and received $10,000.

Rene immediately contacted his lawyer, who filed suit on his client's behalf against Leveque for not returning the bicycle. At the trial several months later, Rene proved that on the day of the match race between Leveque and the European, the market value of the bicycle was $30,000. Leveque proved that the world bicycle racing authority had outlawed use of Rene's new axle in all sanctioned events shortly before Rene had filed his suit, and that the market value of the bicycle as of that date and continuing to the time of trial was $2,000.

54. What should be the outcome of Rene's claim for conversion against Leveque?

(A) He will recover $30,000, because Leveque refused to return the bicycle on Rene's demand.

(B) He will recover $10,000, because Leveque deprived Rene of an opportunity to win that money.

(C) He will recover $2,000, because Leveque refused to return the bicycle on Rene's demand.

(D) He will recover nothing, because he is entitled to damages for loss of use of the bicycle, and he had no opportunity to use it during the relevant period.

55. If Leveque files a counterclaim against Rene for battery, will Leveque recover on this claim?

(A) No, unless Rene used unreasonable force in attempting to seize the bicycle.

(B) No, unless Rene proves that Leveque's delay in the return of the bicycle was unreasonable.

(C) Yes, because Rene had originally agreed to lend him the bicycle.

(D) Yes, because Rene had to give him a reasonable period of time after demand in which to return the bicycle.

Question 56

Owner owned a piece of property located on the corner of a busy intersection. People walking past the intersection would often cut across Owner's property rather than walk along the sidewalk. Owner erected a sign asking people not to cut across his property, as it was ruining his lawn, but this did not stop the practice. Owner had captured a young bobcat several months earlier and had decided to keep him as a pet. In an effort to stop people from cutting across his yard, Owner erected a large sign which read, "Beware of Bobcat." Knowing that a bobcat attacks using its claws, he took it to Vet to have its claws removed. Vet failed to remove all of the bobcat's claws. Owner was not aware that Vet had not removed all of the bobcat's claws. Owner kept the bobcat on a leash in the front yard. The leash was long enough to allow the bobcat access to most of Owner's property; however, the bobcat could not reach the sidewalk which ran adjacent to Owner's property. The next day, Tina was walking home from the market. When she came to the intersection, she cut across Owner's property rather than staying on the sidewalk. The bobcat charged at Tina and slashed her legs severely with its one remaining claw.

If Tina brings suit against Owner for her injuries caused by the bobcat, Tina will:

(A) Recover, because the bobcat was not a domesticated animal.

(B) Recover, unless Tina was aware of the sign on Owner's property.

(C) Not recover, because Tina was a trespasser.

(D) Not recover, because Vet was the cause of the injury.

Question 57

Walker Printing operated a small printing shop on the second floor of an older two-story industrial building. The front entrance of the shop was located on Jones Street, but, for security reasons, the front door was always kept locked. Anyone seeking to do business with Walker Printing had to talk with an employee over an intercom system and then wait for that employee to come from the back of the building to open the front door. As a consequence, the majority of persons who did business with Walker Printing went to the parking lot in the alley behind the building and gained access to the shop by use of the shop's freight elevator. This elevator did not have a call-button for use by the public and anyone wanting to use it had to wait for one of Walker Printing's employees to send the elevator down.

Sterling was a city fire inspector and had to inspect the building in which Walker Printing was located for violations of the city fire code. Sterling first inspected the printing shop itself and then informed Norman, the foreman, that he was going to inspect the lower floor, the trash area, and the elevator shaft. Sterling told Norman that he would let him know when he was in the elevator shaft, and Norman said that he would turn the elevator off until Sterling called up from downstairs that he was finished with his inspection.

About 10 minutes later, as Sterling was under the elevator in the shaft, the freight elevator suddenly started descending. Sterling immediately started yelling that he was in the shaft, but, when the elevator did not stop, he tried to escape. As he was getting out of the shaft, he was unable to move his left leg in time and it was severed by the elevator.

Sterling brings suit against Walker Printing for the loss of his leg. At the time of the accident, there were three employees in the building, but all deny that they pushed the button that would send the elevator to the first floor. Evidence at trial indicated that Norman had turned the switch to "off" as he agreed to do. However, Sterling's expert testified that there was nothing wrong with the elevator that would cause it to malfunction and operate when it was turned off.

Sterling, in his claim for negligence against Walker Printing, most likely will:

(A) Not prevail, because the evidence indicated that Norman had turned the switch to "off."

(B) Not prevail, because, as a fire inspector, Sterling was merely a licensee and Norman took steps to protect him from injury.

(C) Prevail, because Norman must have forgotten to turn the switch to "off."

(D) Prevail, because Walker Printing's elevator could not be controlled from the first floor.

Questions 58-59 are based on the following fact situation:

Late one night, Leroy and Beau were walking up a narrow street in their city when they noticed that a large garbage truck parked near the top of the hill had begun to roll, driverless, down the street toward them. Seeing that if they turned and ran downhill, the quickly accelerating juggernaut would overtake and crush them in a few seconds, they smashed open a window in the apartment building they were passing and climbed inside, the truck narrowly missing them as it careened down the street. Menachem, an elderly tenant in the apartment, thought that they were some of the local gang members trying to burglarize his apartment.

58. Assume for purposes of this question only that Menachem grabbed the shotgun he kept near the bed. Pointing it in their direction in an attempt to frighten them away, Menachem shouted, "Get out or I'll shoot!" and fired what he thought was a warning shot into the ceiling. Unfortunately, Menachem's aim was bad and a bullet struck Leroy in the shoulder. If Leroy sues Menachem for battery, Menachem's best defense is:

(A) Leroy was a trespasser.

(B) Menachem used reasonable force to protect his property.

(C) Menachem did not intend to hit anyone.

(D) Menachem reasonably feared for his life.

59. Assume for purposes of this question only that Menachem has a serious heart condition. When Leroy and Beau burst into his apartment, Menachem suffered a major heart attack. If he sues Leroy and Beau, he can most likely:

(A) Recover damages because of their negligent infliction of his emotional distress.

(B) Recover damages because of their trespass on his property.

(C) Not recover, because Leroy and Beau had no alternative to avoid the garbage truck.

(D) Not recover, if a reasonable person would not have been frightened.

Questions 60-61 are based on the following fact situation:

Howard, a repairman employed by Acme Business Machines, was called to the premises of Fifth National Bank because their copy machine, purchased from Acme, had malfunctioned. Because it was Friday afternoon, and Howard's vacation started on the following Monday, he decided to try to complete the repairs on the spot even if it required working past the normal end of the work day at 5 p.m. Thus, after the bank closed, he continued to work without alerting anyone as to his presence.

At 5:30 p.m., when the repair job was almost complete, the bank's security guard activated its electronic security system, which automatically locked the solenoid locks in every door in the building. The guard then went home for the weekend. When Howard completed his work at 5:45 p.m., he attempted to leave the photocopy room, but discovered that the door was locked. There was no phone in the room. The prospect of spending the weekend and the first few days of his vacation in the little room made Howard extremely uneasy. He looked for a way to escape. He noticed a smoke detector on the ceiling and got an idea. Grabbing some papers nearby, he lit them with his lighter and waved them near the detector. Realizing that the papers did not provide enough combustion to set off the alarm, he emptied a complete file of papers into a waste basket and set them ablaze. Eventually, the detector picked up the smoke and burning particles from the fire and set off a fire alarm, as well as the building's sprinkler system. The fire department arrived soon after and eventually freed Howard.

60. If the bank sues Howard for damages for the destruction of the important documents he burned, and for the copier and other things that were damaged by the water from the sprinklers, what theory or theories of recovery could the bank assert?

   I.   Negligence.

   II. Trespass to land.

   III. Conversion of chattels.

   (A) I. only.

   (B) I. and II. only.

   (C) II. and III. only.

   (D) All of the above.

61. If Howard counterclaims against the bank for false imprisonment, he will most likely:

   (A) Win, because the guard failed to check if someone was inside the building before setting the security system.

   (B) Win, if the guard acted recklessly and Howard suffered severe distress.

   (C) Lose, because the guard did not know that Howard was still in the bank.

   (D) Lose, because he was a trespasser.

Question 62

Panda was riding his bicycle up Spruce Street, when a car negligently driven by Alma struck Panda's bike. Panda fell from the bike and broke his right ankle. Alma immediately stopped her car and went to Panda's assistance. Panda was lying in the middle of the street in intense pain. Alma got Panda to his feet. Because of the pain in his right ankle, he relieved the weight by putting his right arm around Alma's shoulder, and proceeded toward the curb using his left leg and the support provided by Alma. As they were moving toward the curb, a car negligently driven by Baker struck Panda in the left leg. Panda was hospitalized. The right ankle was splinted and eventually healed well. However, complications developed in his shattered left leg and it had to be amputated.

If Panda consults an attorney about suing Alma and/or Baker in a jurisdiction following the traditional rules for joint and several liability and contribution, which of the following statements would be correct statements of the law as applied to these facts?

I.   Panda can recover from either Alma or Baker for all of his injuries as they are jointly and severally liable.

II. Panda can recover from Alma for the injury to his right ankle only and can recover from Baker for injury to his left leg only.

III. Panda can recover from either Alma or Baker for injury to the left leg and can recover from Alma only for injury to the right ankle.

IV. If Panda recovers from Alma for all the injuries, Alma will have contribution rights against Baker.

   (A) I. and IV.

   (B) Only II.

   (C) III. and IV.

   (D) Only I.

Question 63

Clarence and Oglethorpe both owned identically sized, red backgammon boards. Clarence's was made of some synthetic material and contained plastic "stones"; Oglethorpe's was covered with leather and had stones surfaced with onyx and pearl. Clarence had purchased his board at a discount store for $15; Oglethorpe had been given his board by his wife, who paid $500 for it. After a lengthy series of matches at a club meeting one night, Clarence and Oglethorpe met in the final match, playing on a board borrowed from another club member. Despite Clarence's superior play, the dice were with Oglethorpe, who won the match and the first prize. Clarence, upset over the loss, inadvertently grabbed Oglethorpe's board—thinking it was his own—and rushed from the room. Clarence quickly drove home to his apartment and went to bed, leaving the backgammon board in the trunk of his car, as was his usual practice. Meanwhile, Oglethorpe had discovered the board switch and drove to Clarence's apartment to make an exchange. After Clarence was awakened, he led Oglethorpe to his parking place, where he saw that his car had been stolen. The police discovered Clarence's car several days later, stripped and abandoned in a vacant lot with no backgammon board in the trunk. Oglethorpe demanded that Clarence replace the expensive backgammon board, but Clarence refused.

In an action by Oglethorpe against Clarence to recover the value of the backgammon board, Oglethorpe will likely:

(A) Recover, because when Clarence took the backgammon board he committed a trespass to Oglethorpe's chattel.

(B) Recover, because when the backgammon board was stolen along with the car, Clarence became liable for conversion of Oglethorpe's chattel.

(C) Not recover, since Clarence believed in good faith that the board was his when he took it from the backgammon club.

(D) Not recover, since the backgammon board was lost through no fault of Clarence's.

Question 64

Carla was flying her small airplane to a business meeting in Metropolis when she realized that her plane was losing fuel at an alarming rate. Observing the fuel gauge for a few moments, she quickly calculated that she would not make it to the Metropolitan Airport several miles away. Looking down, she saw that she was flying over the densely populated suburbs of Metropolis, and could find no large open space on which to attempt a landing except for a highway a few hundred yards off to her left. Carla could also see glints of light from Lake Woeisme about a mile to the west, and briefly considered ditching the plane in the water, but decided against it.

As Carla maneuvered over the highway, the plane's engine quit for good. Holding the plane in a barely controlled glide, Carla plunged toward the ground. Because traffic on that late afternoon was at its usual heavy level, Carla was unable to make a safe landing on the highway. Her left wing sideswiped a tractor trailer rig as she set down, and her plane veered to the right, crashing into a car driven by Boole. Carla's plane and Boole's car catapulted together off the highway and into a chain-link fence, injuring both of them severely.

If Boole brings an action for personal injuries against Carla, what result?

(A) Judgment for Boole, if Carla's selection of the highway rather than Lake Woeisme was not a reasonable choice under the circumstances.

(B) Judgment for Boole, if his injuries were the result of Carla flying a plane with a dangerously defective fuel system.

(C) Judgment for Carla, if she was not negligent in failing to discover the defect in her fuel system.

(D) Judgment for Carla, because she made the decision to land on the highway rather than the lake under emergency conditions.

Question 65

Sassoon, whose deer hunting forays had been unsuccessful for the past four years running, resolved that this season he would get a deer. Sassoon constructed a hunting outfit which made him appear, from the waist up, to be a sixteen-point buck. Below the waist he wore camouflage pants and hiking boots. Opening day, he stationed himself in the midst of a thicket in what was reputedly the most heavily populated deer area in the state, doused himself with the odor of a doe in estrus, and awaited his prey.

Meanwhile, O'Shaunessy was also happily embarking upon opening day activities. After consuming several Bloody Marys and cans of beer while he waited for the deer to come to him in the field, he was barely able to distinguish flora from fauna. O'Shaunessy caught sight of Sassoon as the former staggered along a game trail. O'Shaunessy took one look at the rack (antlers) on the papier mache deerhead, and let loose with his rifle. One of the bullets grazed Sassoon's head, knocking him unconscious.

The jurisdiction in which Sassoon and O'Shaunessy hunt and live retains traditional contributory negligence. In an action by Sassoon for personal injuries against O'Shaunessy, what is the probable outcome of the litigation?

(A) O'Shaunessy will win, because he did not have the requisite intent to justify imposing liability.

(B) O'Shaunessy will win, if he can prove that he did not have the last clear chance to avoid injuring Sassoon.

(C) Sassoon will win, if he can establish that O'Shaunessy's act of hunting while intoxicated was willful and wanton.

(D) Sassoon will win, because he can show that O'Shaunessy was negligent in hunting while intoxicated.

Question 66

Doris, who enjoyed entertaining her friends, had a swimming pool and a dressing cabana constructed in her spacious backyard. The pool was entirely within the confines of Doris's property. However, one corner of the cabana extended a few inches onto a far corner of the land of Pat, Doris's next door neighbor. At the time of the construction, neither Pat nor Doris was aware that the cabana extended onto Pat's property. When Pat discovered the encroachment, she threatened to sue for trespass.

Will Pat prevail?

(A) Yes, because the cabana extends onto Pat's land.

(B) Yes, unless the presence of the cabana on Pat's land has caused no damage to her property.

(C) No, because Doris did not actually enter Pat's property.

(D) No, because Doris did not intend to have the cabana encroach on Pat's property.

TORTS ANSWERS

Answer to Question 1

(A) Purvis will likely recover damages from Everfresh if the water had been on the floor for a long enough time that Everfresh employees would have discovered it if they had been exercising reasonable care. Under the facts here, Purvis is an invitee as to Everfresh because he came onto the premises for a purpose connected with Everfresh's business. Everfresh therefore owes him the duty to warn of nonobvious dangerous conditions **and** to make reasonable inspections to discover dangerous conditions and make them safe. The fact that the floor where the water was had not been swept or mopped in the last two hours tends to indicate that Everfresh employees failed to make reasonable inspections of an area in which its invitees would walk, which would make Everfresh liable to Purvis. (B) is incorrect because it essentially imposes a strict liability standard on Everfresh towards its business invitees. While the duty of care owed by a possessor of land to an invitee is high, there must be some negligence on the part of the landowner before liability will be imposed. Purvis must show that Everfresh employees knew of or should have discovered the water on the floor; in the absence of that fact, Purvis cannot recover damages because Everfresh will not be deemed to be negligent. (C) is incorrect because Everfresh could be liable even if its employees did not know that water was leaking onto the floor. Because Purvis was an invitee, Everfresh owed a duty to make reasonable inspections to discover unsafe conditions. (D) is incorrect for two reasons: first, the fact that Purvis might have seen the water if he had been watching where he was walking does not mean that Everfresh owed no duty regarding it. While a duty to warn or make safe a dangerous condition does not exist if the condition is so obvious that an invitee should reasonably be aware of it, obviousness is determined by all of the surrounding circumstances. If a shopper's attention is likely to be diverted by displays of goods, a dangerous condition on the floor in front of him will not be considered obvious even if he could have seen it had he been watching where he was walking. Furthermore, even if Purvis was negligent in not paying attention to where he was going, he will still be able to recover damages from Everfresh because the jurisdiction has adopted "pure" comparative negligence, which allows recovery against a negligent defendant no matter how great plaintiff's negligence is. Because Everfresh would likely be found negligent if its floor had not been swept or mopped in the last two hours, Purvis's contributory negligence would only reduce his damage award rather than bar it entirely.

Answer to Question 2

(C) Pylon can recover for trespass to chattels if he can show that the value of his car has been reduced as a result of the conduct of Dexter's. Trespass to chattels requires (i) an act of defendant that interferes with plaintiff's right of possession in the chattel, (ii) intent to perform the act bringing about the interference with plaintiff's right of possession, (iii) causation, and (iv) damages. The act of interference may be either dispossession of or damage to the chattel. Here, Dexter's employees interfered with Pylon's possession of his car by painting it contrary to his instructions, and they intended to do the act (painting) that caused the interference. If Pylon suffered damage because their conduct reduced the value of his car, Pylon will be able to satisfy the prima facie case for trespass to chattels. (A) is wrong because the fact that Pylon won the race with the car does not establish absence of actual damages. Any loss in value of the chattels will suffice. (B) is wrong because it is not necessary for Pylon to show negligence on the part of Dexter's to recover. Pylon can recover damages for trespass to chattels without proof of breach of duty. (D) is incorrect because emotional distress alone is not sufficient to satisfy the actual damages requirement for the tort of trespass to chattels.

Answer to Question 3

(D) Because Dot borrowed Pam's car for the mutual benefit of Dot and Pam, Dot is liable only if she was negligent in her use of the car. Pam's loan of her car to Dot created a bailment situation. It was a bailment for the mutual benefit of the bailor and bailee, since the pizza was for both of them, and therefore the bailee is only required to exercise ordinary due care. (A) is not as good a choice as (D) because it addresses only Dot's liability for conversion and trespass to chattels, as discussed below. Dot may also be liable to Pam under negligence principles if she failed to use reasonable care when parking the car. (B) is wrong because it states a remedy for conversion. Conversion requires an act by defendant interfering with plaintiff's right of possession that is serious enough to require defendant to pay the full value of the chattel. In this case, Dot's unauthorized use of the car was not significant enough to constitute a serious interference with Pam's right to possession; it was a short detour that did not prolong Dot's use of the car beyond the time period for which Pam had lent it. (C) is wrong because it appears to impose liability on a bailee in the absence of fault. Liability under mutual benefit bailment requires that the bailee be negligent. Alternatively, (C) could be read as stating liability for trespass to chattels, since the appropriate measure of damages for this tort would be the actual amount of the damage, and the interference with Pam's right to possession does not need to be as serious as for conversion. However, no actual damages flowed from Dot's detour, even assuming that it exceeded the use to which Pam had consented. The $400 worth of damage occurred while Dot was using the car for the purpose for which Pam had lent it. Hence, a trespass to chattels action would not lie for this damage.

Answer to Question 4

(B) The element of damages that Prudence is least certain to recover is the future costs of raising her child. Prudence is suing Dr. Desmond for "wrongful pregnancy," which is a recognized basis for a negligence action in most states. Dr. Desmond owed a duty to Prudence to properly perform the contraceptive procedure. He breached that duty by improperly performing it and failing to inform Prudence that it was ineffective. This breach of duty was the actual and proximate cause of Prudence's pregnancy because it would not have happened but for Dr. Desmond's negligence and it was foreseeable that Prudence would become pregnant after being led to believe that the surgery was successful. While Prudence certainly suffered damages as a result of Dr. Desmond's breach of duty, completing the prima facie case, the law is unsettled as to the extent of damages recoverable, particularly over whether parents can recover future child-rearing expenses for the child. Some permit recovery of these expenses but offset them against the benefits of raising a child. Other courts deny recovery, reasoning that the intangible benefits of raising a child cannot be reduced to a monetary figure. Hence, Prudence is least certain to recover future child-rearing expenses. In contrast, most courts do permit recovery of the additional expenses of treating Charlotte's disease (choice (C)). These expenses were part of what Prudence was trying to avoid when she underwent the surgery, and are not offset by the benefit of having the child. (A) is also incorrect. All courts recognizing a wrongful pregnancy action permit the mother to recover the damages from the pregnancy itself. Similarly, (D) is incorrect because Prudence's impaired earning capacity is a direct result of her pregnancy. The fact that these damages were unforeseeable does not prevent their recovery (*i.e.*, the tortfeasor takes his victim as he finds her).

Answer to Question 5

(C) Python will have to prove that the newspaper acted with actual malice because he is a public figure. The facts indicate that all of the elements are present to establish a prima facie case of defamation at common law: a defamatory statement of or concerning Python was published to others by the newspaper. Because it is libel, damage to reputation, the final common law element, is presumed. However, Python is a public figure: he is the general manager of a professional basket-ball franchise and is well-known in the community. Thus, he has to prove two additional elements: falsity of the defamatory language and fault amounting to "actual malice" on the part of the newspaper. Given that the parties will stipulate that the statement regarding Python is false, the only fact not established is that the newspaper acted with actual malice. (A) is incorrect because negligence is the fault standard that private figures have to establish when suing on a matter of public concern. Python, as a public figure, has to prove a higher level of fault. (B) is wrong because pecuniary or special damages do not need to be established in a libel case; the common law presumes damages. (D) is incorrect because proof of actual injury is required by the Constitution only when a fault standard of negligence is applicable. If actual malice is established, the common law rules regarding presumed damages apply.

Answer to Question 6

(A) John's status as a trespasser on shopping center property precludes his recovery against the shopping center. This question does not identify the basis for John's action against the shopping center; therefore, you have to consider all of the shopping center's potential grounds for liability. Because Bill's Security Service is an independent contractor, something more than simple vicarious liability is needed to make the shopping center liable for Bill's torts. And because the shopping center did not authorize the use of snakes to guard the stores, it is not liable for an intentional tort, even though the use of poisonous snakes would otherwise be unreasonable force in defense of property. Another potential basis for liability is the shopping center's status as owner or occupier of the property. The general rule is that a landowner owes no duty to a trespasser whose presence is undiscovered to warn of or make safe concealed dangerous conditions or dangerous activities on the land. However, trespassers who are discovered or whom the landowners should anticipate because they habitually and routinely enter the land are owed a higher duty. The landowner will be liable for concealed, dangerous, artificial conditions known to the landowner and negligently conducted active operations, including those of third persons of whom the landowner has the ability and authority to control. Here, John was neither discovered nor anticipated. No one actually noticed him before his injury, and nothing in the facts indicates that people habitually broke into the mall—the mere fact that the shopping center had a security guard is not sufficient to make someone breaking in an anticipated trespasser. Thus, even if the shopping center should have supervised Bill more closely, it owed no duty to John because he was a trespasser. (B) is incorrect because the fact that John was guilty of breaking and entering is irrelevant. Had John been a discovered or anticipated trespasser, the shopping center might be liable to John for, *e.g.,* negligent supervision of the security service, even though John broke into the building. (C) is incorrect because the shopping center did not authorize use of the poisonous snakes. If it had, (C) would be correct because a landowner may only use reasonable force to defend his property, and may not use indirect force that will cause death or serious bodily harm, such as a spring gun or deadly animal, when he could not use such force directly, such as here. (D) is incorrect because it is irrelevant. Undiscovered trespassers need not be warned of the dangers on the land; the landowner owes no duty to them.

Answer to Question 7

(C) Bill is liable because the rattlesnakes constituted an unprivileged use of force likely to cause serious bodily harm. In the absence of any threat of harm to a person, only reasonable, nondeadly force may be used to defend property. Force that may cause death or serious bodily harm may not be used. Furthermore, one may not use indirect deadly force, such as a trap, spring gun, or deadly animal, when it would not be lawful for such force to be directly used, such as against a mere trespasser. In the absence of a privilege, a landowner (and one acting on behalf of the landowner) is liable on intentional tort grounds even to ordinary trespassers for injuries inflicted by vicious watchdogs or other animals likely to cause serious bodily harm. In contrast to dangerous animals that happen to be on the landowner's property, for which the landowner is not strictly liable for injuries to trespassers, dangerous animals put on the property for the purpose of defending the property are treated like dangerous mechanical devices: if they are likely to cause serious bodily harm and the landowner would not have been privileged to directly use force likely to cause such harm, the landowner will be liable. Here, because Bill has been hired by the shopping center to protect its property, he has the right to use reasonable force on behalf of the shopping center to prevent the commission of a tort against the property, and can use indirect force, such as a mechanical device or animal, in circumstances where he would have been privileged to use direct force. However, he may *not* use force, either directly or indirectly, that will cause death or serious bodily harm where property alone is being threatened. Because Bill's use of a rattlesnake constituted the use of force likely to cause serious bodily harm against someone who had broken into the mall for a nonthreatening purpose, Bill will be liable to John. (A) is incorrect because, as discussed above, John's status as a trespasser does not prevent Bill from being liable to him for defending property with an animal likely to cause serious bodily harm. (B) is incorrect because John's crime did not constitute the kind of threat that would have allowed Bill to use force against John likely to cause serious bodily harm. [*See* Restatement (Second) of Torts §§85, 516] (D) is incorrect because the property owner's authorization would have no effect on Bill's liability. The use of poisonous snakes by the shopping mall itself to defend its property would not be privileged because the force is unreasonable; hence, its authorization for Bill to do the same would not protect Bill.

Answer to Question 8

(A) Harley can recover damages from Mountaineer in a products liability action based on strict liability if Harley's misuse of the motorcycle was foreseeable. A strict products liability action requires plaintiff to establish: (i) a strict duty owed by a commercial supplier, (ii) breach of that duty, (iii) actual and proximate cause, and (iv) damages. A supplier has breached its duty when it supplies a product that is so defective as to be "unreasonably dangerous." If the product was dangerous beyond the expectation of the ordinary consumer *or* a less dangerous alternative or modification was economically feasible, the supplier has breached its duty. Furthermore, while some products may be safe if used as intended, they may involve serious dangers if used in other ways. Courts require suppliers to anticipate reasonably foreseeable uses even if they are misuses of the product. In this case, Mountaineer has supplied its Pinnacle motorcycle with standard shock absorbers that are probably safe for use on the road. However, the advertisements promoted use of the Pinnacle for off-road purposes and purchasers may not have taken note of the warning in the owner's manual. If Mountaineer should have foreseen that purchasers would use the motorcycle on rough terrain without buying different shock absorbers, it should have either dropped that type of advertising or provided appropriate shock absorbers as standard equipment for the Pinnacle. By not doing so, it supplied a product in a "defective condition unreasonably dangerous to users" and brought about Harley's injury. (B) is wrong because a simple warning of danger in an owner's manual is not sufficient under the "feasible alternative" approach if it would not be effective to deter users of the motorcycle from using it on rough terrain. Providing different shock absorbers or changing the way the motorcycle is advertised would be feasible ways of eliminating or greatly reducing the danger. (C) is incorrect. The fact that Harley was in violation of the law when he drove off of the road may establish that his conduct was negligent. However, ordinary contributory negligence such as failing to discover a defect or guard against its existence is not a defense to a products liability action based on strict liability in jurisdictions retaining traditional contributory negligence rules. The type of contributory negligence where one voluntarily and unreasonably encounters a known risk, which is essentially assumption of risk, would be a defense to strict liability, but there is no indication that Harley learned of the risk (such as by reading the owner's manual) and decided to take a chance anyway with the shock absorbers that he had. (D) is wrong because the fact that the shock absorbers conformed to all safety requirements does not establish that they were not "defective" for purposes of a products liability action. If the shock absorbers were not safe for a purpose that they would foreseeably be used for, they may be deemed unreasonably dangerous to users.

Answer to Question 9

(D) Alice most likely will recover the fair market value of the car. The tort of conversion does not require that the defendant damage or permanently deprive the owner of the chattel. All that is required is that defendant's volitional conduct result in a serious invasion of the chattel interest of another in some manner. In this case Bob could be considered the bailee of Alice's car. A bailee is liable to the owner for conversion if the bailee uses the chattel in such a manner as to constitute a material breach of the bailment agreement. A substantial interference with Alice's possession, such as shown by the facts in this question, would constitute a material breach. Hence (A) and (B) are wrong, because Alice could recover for conversion, and (D) is correct rather than (C) because (D) states the correct measure of damages.

Answer to Question 10

(B) Petunia can recover against DDS for defamation if the DDS manager negligently communicated his defamatory statements to third persons. A prima facie case for defamation at common law consists of (i) defamatory language by defendant (ii) of or concerning the plaintiff, (iii) publication of the defamatory language by the defendant to a third person, and (iv) damage to the reputation of the plaintiff. The publication requirement is satisfied when there is a communication of the defamatory statement to a third person who understood it. The communication to the third person may be made either intentionally or negligently. Here, the store manager's statements were defamatory, they were of or concerning Petunia since those hearing the statement could see that the manager was talking to her, and damage to Petunia's reputation is presumed by law because the allegation that she was a thief is slanderous per se. If the manager should have checked that the public address system was not on, his failure to do so, allowing his statements to be broadcast to third persons, was negligent. Hence, the publication requirement is satisfied. DDS, as the employer of the store manager, will be vicariously liable for the manager's defamation because it was committed within the scope of his employment. (A) and (C) are wrong because a publication may occur even when the defendant is not speaking to third persons or does not intend that third persons hear his statements, as long as he was negligent in letting third persons overhear him. (D) is wrong because the manager's reasonable belief in the truth of his statements is irrelevant in a common law defamation action. Because the statements here did not involve a matter of public concern, Petunia does not need to establish that the manager was negligent in his belief as to the truth or falsity of his statements.

Answer to Question 11

(B) Parsip will prevail in his battery action if Denville intended to commit a battery or an assault against Parsip. A prima facie case for battery requires plaintiff to prove (i) an act by defendant that brings about a harmful or offensive contact to the plaintiff's person, (ii) intent on defendant's part to bring about harmful or offensive contact, and (iii) causation. Denville's conduct in shooting the puck into the stands was a harmful contact to Parsip, because Denville set into motion the force that caused injury to Parsip. If Denville intended (or knew with substantial certainty) that the puck would strike a spectator, he would be liable even if he did not single out Parsip as the target. Even if he only intended to cause apprehension of contact (which is the intent for assault), this intent would suffice for liability for battery under the doctrine of transferred intent. Because Denville did strike Parsip, committing the act necessary for battery, his intent to commit an assault would be transferred to the tort of battery for purposes of completing the prima facie case. (A) is wrong because assumption of risk is not a defense to intentional torts. Parsip may have assumed a risk of injury from a hockey puck's being accidentally or even negligently shot into the stands, but he did not assume the risk of a player's intentionally shooting the puck at a spectator. (C) is incorrect because recklessness does not satisfy the intent requirement for battery. Intent requires, at a minimum, that the actor know with substantial certainty what the consequences of his conduct will be. Therefore, Parsip cannot recover if Denville acted recklessly rather than with intent. (D) is incorrect. The fact that Denville violated CHA rules when he shot the puck into the stands tends to establish only that a spectator does not impliedly consent to a puck's intentionally being shot at him, thus negating the defense of consent in a battery action. It does nothing to establish that Denville did have the intent to commit a battery.

Answer to Question 12

(C) Delbert will not be liable to Curtis's parents if he can show that Curtis appreciated the risk of using a canoe without a life vest. A landowner owes a higher duty of care to a child trespasser than to an adult trespasser. Under the "attractive nuisance" doctrine, a landowner has a duty to exercise ordinary care to avoid reasonably foreseeable risk of harm to children caused by artificial conditions on his property. To assess this special duty on the landowner, the following elements must be shown: (i) there is a dangerous condition on the land of which the owner is or should be aware; (ii) the owner knows or should know that young persons frequent the vicinity of this dangerous condition; (iii) the condition is dangerous because the child trespasser is unable to appreciate the risk; and (iv) the expense of remedying the situation is slight compared with the magnitude of the risk. The third element would not be established if it can be shown that Curtis appreciated the risk of taking the canoe out onto the lake without a life vest. In that case, the attractive nuisance doctrine would not apply and Curtis would be treated like an adult trespasser. Delbert would likely prevail because leaving the canoes out would not constitute a breach of his limited duties to adult trespassers. (A) is incorrect even though the fact that children of like age, etc., would do the same thing that Curtis did tends to indicate that the canoes potentially could be an attractive nuisance. However, if Curtis had sufficient familiarity with the canoes to appreciate the risk of not using a life vest, the condition would not be an attractive nuisance as to him; *i.e.*, it would not be foreseeable that he would subject himself to the risk of drowning had he appreciated that risk. Hence, despite what children of Curtis's age would be likely to do, Delbert will prevail if he can establish Curtis's appreciation of the risk. (B) is wrong because the precautions that Delbert took might not be sufficient to avoid liability under the attractive nuisance doctrine. Delbert would have to show that the expense of taking further precautions to remedy the situation was so great as to outweigh the magnitude of the risk. (D) is incorrect because most jurisdictions do not require a showing that the child was lured onto the property by the dangerous condition. Foreseeability of harm is the true basis of liability; the element of attraction is important only insofar as it indicates that the trespass should have been anticipated by the landowner.

Answer to Question 13

(D) Sam is not liable because the "firefighter's rule," based on assumption of risk or public policy grounds, generally will preclude a firefighter from recovering for injuries occurring on duty that are caused by another's negligence. One engaged in the activity of firefighting is deemed to know of the risks inherent in that activity, including the fact that a landowner may have failed to inspect or repair dangerous conditions on the land. (D) is therefore correct. (A) is incorrect because a common cause of fires is negligence by the property owner; that does not affect application of the rule. Thus, even if Sam acted negligently in allowing the fire to start, he is not liable. (B) is incorrect because Lenny would not be treated as an invitee under these circumstances. A landowner such as Sam owes a duty to invitees not only to warn of nonobvious dangerous conditions known to him but also to make reasonable inspections to discover and rectify dangerous conditions. However, under the "firefighter's rule," firefighters and police officers are generally treated as licensees because they are likely to enter the property at unforeseeable times and under emergency circumstances. As licensees, they cannot hold the landowner liable for failing to make reasonable inspections to discover a dangerous condition. (C) is incorrect because the fact that it was foreseeable that Sam's conduct would start a fire establishes only that Sam was negligent in setting off the fireworks. Despite his negligence, Sam has a complete defense because of the "firefighter's rule."

Answer to Question 14

(A) Demand will be liable if it entrusted its car to Eileen knowing that she had a poor driving record. In the absence of negligence on Demand's part, it will not be liable for Eileen's negligent driving either as Eileen's employer or as the owner of the automobile she was driving. An employer will be vicariously liable for tortious acts committed by its employee only if the tortious acts occur within the scope of the employment relationship. While Eileen was using Demand's car, she was not conducting any business for Demand. Her use of the car to go grocery shopping was a personal errand outside the scope of her employment for which Demand is not vicariously liable. Demand is also not vicariously liable for permitting Eileen to drive its car—the general rule in most jurisdictions is that an automobile owner is not vicariously liable for the tortious conduct of another driving the owner's automobile. However, the owner may be liable for its own negligence in entrusting the car to a particular driver. If Eileen had a poor driving record and Demand was aware of this fact, its furnishing Eileen with a car constituted a breach of its duty to other drivers. This breach was an actual and proximate cause of the damage to Precision's van, making Demand liable to Precision for damages. (B) is incorrect. Even though Billy's violation of the posted speed limit probably constituted contributory negligence, it will not be imputed to Precision. Just as an automobile owner generally would not be vicariously liable for the driver's negligence, a driver's *contributory* negligence will not be imputed to the automobile owner who is suing the other driver. Since there is no indication that Precision was itself negligent in leasing the van to Billy, Billy's conduct in exceeding the speed limit will not prevent Precision from recovering. (C) is incorrect because the fact that Billy had the last opportunity to avoid the accident is irrelevant to Precision's right to recover from Demand. The doctrine of last clear chance does not apply because it is essentially *plaintiff's rebuttal* against the defense of contributory negligence; it would not be raised by Demand as a defense (*i.e.,* if Demand asserted that Billy was contributorily negligent, Precision could rebut by asserting that *Eileen* had the last clear chance to avoid the accident). (D) is wrong because the fact that Eileen was on personal business only establishes that Demand is not vicariously liable in its status as Eileen's employer. It could be liable for its own negligence if it furnished her with a car knowing that she had a poor driving record.

Answer to Question 15

(B) The court should grant the motion unless Pat has offered some evidence of physical injury from her distress. In most jurisdictions, the duty to avoid negligent infliction of emotional distress is breached when defendant creates a foreseeable risk of physical injury to a plaintiff in the "zone of danger" from defendant's negligent conduct. A strong modern trend allows recovery even if plaintiff is outside the zone of danger as long as (i) plaintiff and the person injured by defendant are closely related, (ii) plaintiff was present at the scene of the injury, and (iii) plaintiff personally observed or perceived the event. Regardless of which approach is used to determine the scope of the duty, however, the bystander plaintiff can recover damages only if defendant's conduct resulted in some physical injury from the distress; emotional distress alone is insufficient in the usual case. Thus, despite the fact that Pat has satisfied all of the requirements for the modern "foreseeability" test, the court should grant the motion in the absence of evidence of physical injury to Pat. (A) is wrong because Pat does not need to be within the zone of danger to recover under the foreseeability approach, and whether Pat was a foreseeable plaintiff in the location she was in is a question of fact for the jury. (C) is wrong because even though it is a jury issue as to whether Pat's distress was foreseeable, Pat also has to show that her distress caused her physical injury. (D) is similarly incorrect; while Pat's close relationship with Jimmy is a necessary element of the foreseeability test, it does not substitute for the requirement of physical injury.

Answer to Question 16

(D) Martha has no cause of action because Charlie suffered no damages from Dr. Dalton's breach of duty. One of the duties that doctors, dentists, and other health professionals owe their patients is the duty to provide a patient with enough information about the risks of a proposed course of treatment or surgical procedure to enable the patient to make an "informed consent" to the treatment. If an undisclosed risk was serious enough that a reasonable person in the patient's position would have withheld consent to the treatment, the health care professional has breached this duty. However, breach of duty is only one element of a cause of action for negligence. The plaintiff must also establish actual and proximate cause and some damage to plaintiff's person or property. Damage means actual harm or injury. Unlike for some intentional torts, damage will not be presumed and nominal damages are not available. While a complete absence of consent to a medical or surgical procedure may in some cases constitute battery, which does not require damage as an element, a nondisclosure of the *risks* of the procedure is characterized instead as a breach of the duty of care. Here, Charlie's dental work was completed without any problem and no other injury is apparent from the facts; Martha's possible distress at not being informed of the risk is not, standing alone, a compensable injury. [Restatement (Second) of Torts §436A] Hence, Martha does not have a cause of action against Dr. Dalton. (A) is wrong even though it is the key factor for establishing that Dr. Dalton breached her duty by not disclosing the risk of seizure. As discussed above, breach of duty is just one element of the prima facie case. (B) is incorrect. If Charlie had suffered harm from the anesthetic, the element of actual cause would be established if Martha could show that she would not have consented to the use of the anesthetic had she known of the risk (*i.e.*, but for Dr. Dalton's nondisclosure, Charlie's injury would not have occurred). However, in the absence of the injury element, the prima facie case is not complete. (C) is incorrect because the fact that Dr. Dalton used her best judgment in deciding not to disclose the risk would not be a defense if Charlie had been harmed by the anesthetic.

Answer to Question 17

(B) Sherm can recover the full amount of his damages from Redwood because the negligence of its employee caused the destruction of the lodge. Before a defendant will be liable for a breach of duty to the plaintiff, it must be shown that the breach was the actual and proximate cause of the injury. The general test for determining whether an act or omission is the actual cause of the injury is the "but for" test, *i.e.*, whether the injury would not have occurred *but for* the act or omission. Under certain circumstances, however, the "but for" test is inadequate to determine actual cause. Where several causes combine to bring about an injury—and any one alone would have been sufficient to cause the injury—the actual cause requirement is satisfied if defendant's conduct was a substantial factor in causing the injury. Under this analysis, the fire started by the Redwood employee was an actual cause of the destruction of Sherm's lodge because it was a substantial factor in causing the harm. It was also a proximate cause of the harm because no intervening forces broke the causal connection between the act and the harm. Because its employee was acting within the scope of his employment when he caused the fire to start, Redwood is vicariously liable for the injury that resulted. (A) is incorrect because the "but for" test is not applicable to these facts. Under that test, neither fire would be the actual cause of the harm because, looking at either fire alone, the harm would have occurred even without it. However, under the substantial factor test, both fires are actual causes of the injury. (C) is incorrect even though it is true that the damage is indivisible. Sherm can still recover from Redwood even if he does not sue the other tortfeasor. (D) is incorrect because traditional joint and several liability rules allow Sherm to recover his full damages from Redwood. Where two or more tortious acts combine to proximately cause an indivisible injury to plaintiff, each tortfeasor will be jointly and severally liable for that injury, even though each defendant acted entirely independently. The effect of joint and several liability is that the plaintiff may recover the entire amount of the damages from any tortfeasor, who then may have a right of contribution from the other tortfeasor. Hence, even though the negligence of another tortfeasor was also an actual cause of the destruction of Sherm's lodge, Sherm is entitled to recover all of his damages from Redwood.

Answer to Question 18

(D) The court should grant a directed verdict for Bert because Mike has not shown that Bert breached any duty that he owed to Mike. A prima facie case of negligence requires plaintiff to show the following elements: (i) the existence of a duty on the part of the defendant to conform to a specific standard of conduct for the protection of the plaintiff against unreasonable risk of injury, (ii) breach of that duty by the defendant, (iii) that the breach of duty was the actual and proximate cause of plaintiff's injury, and (iv) damage to plaintiff's person or property. Here, it is doubtful that Bert's releasing his pigeons created any duty to other users of the park. To the extent that it did, the fact that he had taken great care to train them to return directly to their roosts indicates that he did not breach his duty to Mike. Because Mike has offered no other evidence of negligence nor any reason to impose strict liability on Bert (as discussed below), Bert's motion for a directed verdict should be granted. (A) is wrong because that choice indicates the imposition of a strict liability standard on Bert. The owner of a domestic or inherently non-dangerous animal is not strictly liable for the injuries it causes. The conduct of Bert's homing pigeon would not make Bert liable in the absence of some negligence on his part. (B) is incorrect because the doctrine of res ipsa loquitur applies only to situations where the fact that a particular injury occurred itself establishes that defendant breached a duty. If the doctrine is applicable, no directed verdict may be given for defendant because plaintiff has established a prima facie case. However, the accident must be the type that would not normally occur unless someone was negligent. The collision between Bert's homing pigeon and the model airplane is not that type of accident; by itself, it provides no suggestion that anyone was negligent. (C) is incorrect because the truck is not a superseding force that breaks "the causal connection" between the action of Bert's pigeon and the airplane's destruction. In indirect cause cases, where a force came into motion after defendant's act and combined with it to cause injury to plaintiff, defendant will still be potentially liable for foreseeable intervening forces that are within the increased risk caused by his acts. Even if the intervening force is independent (*i.e.,* not a natural response or reaction to the situation), it will be foreseeable where defendant's negligence increased the risk that the independent force would cause harm. Hence, if Bert were negligent in releasing his pigeon, the fact that the destruction of the airplane was directly caused by the truck would not relieve Bert from liability, because the initial collision with the pigeon caused the airplane to go out of control and created a substantial risk that it would be damaged by an intervening force.

Answer to Question 19

(C) Warren can bring an action for false imprisonment if the delay in releasing his luggage had the effect of confining him to the airport against his will. To establish a prima facie case for false imprisonment, a plaintiff must prove (i) an act or omission to act on defendant's part that confines or restrains plaintiff to a bounded area, (ii) intent on the part of defendant to confine or restrain plaintiff to a bounded area, and (iii) causation. The act or omission can be directed against plaintiff's property if its effect is to restrain plaintiff from leaving. Here, airport officials, who had no legal authority to conduct a search of Warren's luggage, were under a duty to release it to him when he requested it. Requiring him to remain in the area to claim it when it was released was a sufficient confinement or restraint for purposes of false imprisonment. (A) is incorrect because harm is not an element of the prima facie case for false imprisonment. Warren can recover at least nominal damages even if he suffered no harm from the delay in releasing his luggage. (B) is wrong because the seizure of Warren's luggage did have the effect of restraining him if he believed that he would not get it back if he left the airport. (D) is wrong because, for purposes of intentional torts, an actor "intends" the consequences of his conduct if he knows with substantial certainty that these consequences will result. Even if the delay in releasing the luggage was not done for the purpose of restraining Warren, it was substantially certain that he would remain in the area rather than risk losing his luggage. Hence, the security officials had a sufficient intent for false imprisonment liability.

Answer to Question 20

(B) Mrs. Parker's distress is a recoverable element of damages caused by Dr. Dennis's breach of duty to her. Dr. Dennis, as a professional, owed a duty to his patient, Mrs. Parker, to possess and exercise the degree of knowledge and skill of other doctors in similar localities. Furthermore, as a specialist, he owed a duty to exercise the superior knowledge and skill that he possessed in his area of specialty. He breached that duty by misdiagnosing a common skin infection that another doctor was able to diagnose immediately. His failure to properly diagnose the condition was the actual and proximate cause of injury to Mrs. Parker; but for the misdiagnosis, she would not have had to continue suffering from the rash until the other doctor properly treated it. The continuation of the rash and any pain and suffering from it are compensable damages that she can recover from Dr. Dennis. Also compensable is the emotional distress that she suffered because of the misdiagnosis. While recovery for emotional distress is restricted when there is no other injury caused by the breach, these restrictions do not apply when plaintiff is the victim of another tort that causes physical injury. Plaintiff can "tack on" damages for emotional distress because they are "parasitic"; *i.e.,* they attach to the physical injury damages. (A) is incorrect. Given Mrs. Parker's physical condition, a failure to make a proper diagnosis did create a foreseeable risk that she would continue to suffer from a condition that could otherwise have been alleviated. Thus, Dr. Dennis's conduct did constitute a breach of the duty he owed Mrs. Parker. (C) is incorrect because Mrs. Parker has suffered compensable injury regardless of whether she had to pay for the second doctor visit. The continuation of the skin rash until she saw the other doctor suffices as the damage element of the prima facie case. (D) is incorrect because it states a requirement for recovery in cases where the only harm caused was through the negligent infliction of emotional distress. Here, Dr. Dennis's negligent diagnosis directly caused Mrs. Parker physical injury in addition to emotional distress. Hence, the emotional distress is recoverable as a "parasitic" element of damages even if the distress itself did not cause physical injury.

Answer to Question 21

(D) Mr. Parker cannot recover damages for defamation because Dr. Dennis's statements were made under a qualified privilege. To prove defamation, Mr. Parker must show (i) defamatory language by the defendant (ii) of or concerning the plaintiff (iii) published to a third person (iv) that causes damage to reputation. Because a public figure or matter of public concern is not involved, falsity and fault are not part of the prima facie case. In this case, the defamatory element of Dr. Dennis's statement is that someone infected Mrs. Parker with a sexually transmitted disease acquired from sexual contact with a prostitute. The statement can be shown to be of or concerning Mr. Parker through pleading extrinsic facts, *i.e.*, colloquium. The extrinsic fact is Mrs. Parker's statement to Dr. Dennis that she had only had sex with her husband. The statement was published by communicating it to Mrs. Parker, and damage to reputation is presumed because the verbal allegation that Mr. Parker probably has a venereal disease falls under the loathsome disease category of slander per se, and the implicit allegation that he had sexual contact with a prostitute falls under the slander per se category for crimes involving moral turpitude. While this completes the prima facie case for defamation, Dr. Dennis has a qualified privilege that excuses his utterance of a defamatory statement. A qualified privilege is recognized when the recipient has an interest in the information and it is reasonable for the defendant to make the publication of the statement. Here, it was certainly in Mrs. Parker's interest to be informed that her husband may have given her a sexually transmitted disease. While the privilege does not encompass the publication of irrelevant defamatory matter that the speaker does not reasonably believe to be connected with the interest entitled to protection, here it was reasonable for Dr. Dennis to persuade a doubting Mrs. Parker why he was certain of the diagnosis and the source of the disease. Therefore, even though Dr. Dennis's statements defamed Mr. Parker, they are protected by a qualified privilege under the circumstances. (A) is wrong because, as discussed above, Dr. Dennis's statement would be perceived by a reasonable listener as referring to Mr. Parker when Mrs. Parker's statement that she did not have sexual contact with anyone else is pleaded as an extrinsic fact. (B) is wrong even though the statements are slander per se. Dr. Dennis is not liable because he has a qualified privilege. (C) is wrong because Mr. Parker does not need to show pecuniary harm (*i.e.*, special damages). Because the statements are slander per se, damage is presumed.

Answer to Question 22

(A) Drainwell can recover 100% of the judgment under common law indemnity rules. The principle of indemnity permits a shifting between the tortfeasors of the entire loss (*i.e.*, the payment made to satisfy plaintiff's judgment). This is in contrast to contribution, which apportions the loss among those who are at fault. Indemnity is available in vicarious liability situations, where one party is held liable for damages caused by another simply because of his relationship to that person. Hence, an employer such as Drainwell that has been held vicariously liable under the doctrine of respondeat superior can obtain indemnification from the employee (Drayton) whose conduct actually caused the damage. (B) is incorrect because Drainwell need not show that Drayton breached a company rule before it can obtain indemnity. The fact that Drayton's negligence caused the injury and that Drainwell was liable for the judgment solely because of its relationship to Drayton permits indemnification here. (C) is incorrect because vicarious liability is one of the most common areas where indemnity is available. (D) is incorrect because Drainwell's requirement that Drayton be on call 24 hours a day merely establishes that Drainwell will be vicariously liable for Drayton's negligence; it does not bar Drainwell from recovering from Drayton because Drayton's negligence actually caused the damage.

Answer to Question 23

(A) Donald is not liable for assault because he did not cause Penn to reasonably apprehend an immediate harmful contact. The prima facie case for assault requires (i) an act by defendant causing a reasonable apprehension in plaintiff of immediate harmful or offensive contact to plaintiff's person, (ii) intent by defendant to bring about in plaintiff apprehension of that contact, and (iii) causation. For there to be apprehension, plaintiff must be aware of defendant's act at the time that it is occurring. Here, because Penn was oblivious to Donald's attempt to scare him, Donald is not liable for assault. (B) is incorrect even though Donald's conduct was a substantial factor in causing Penn's injury (*i.e.*, the causation element would have been satisfied if damages were required for assault). Because Donald did not cause an apprehension of contact on Penn's part, Donald is not liable for assault. (C) is incorrect. While Donald did have the intent to commit an assault, his act does not meet the requirements for the prima facie case since his act did not cause reasonable apprehension. (D) is wrong because whether Donald had an intent to injure Penn is irrelevant for purposes of assault.

Answer to Question 24

(B) The judge should instruct the jury that an adult standard of care is warranted for operation of a tractor and that the defendant's experience in driving a tractor should be taken into account. Thus, instructions I. and III. are appropriate. The usual standard of conduct to which a child must conform is that of a child of like age, education, intelligence, and *experience*. This permits a subjective evaluation of these factors. Hence, instruction III. is appropriate because it permits the jury to take into account the fact that Jackie had driven a tractor since he was 11 years old. Instruction I. is appropriate because the modern rule is that when a child engages in an activity that is normally one in which only adults engage, he will be required to conform to the same standard of care as an adult in such an activity. Operating a motor vehicle such as a tractor on a public road is normally an adult activity requiring an adult standard of care. Thus, it was appropriate to instruct the jury that a higher standard of care is warranted for the particular activity in which the defendant was involved. Thus, (B) is correct, and (A) and (C) are incorrect. (D) is incorrect because instruction II. would not be appropriate. The fact that Jackie may be held to an adult standard of care in this case is not because he is 13 years old. There is no blanket rule that children 13 years of age or older are held to the same standard of care as adults. The standard of care depends not only on age but also on education, intelligence, and experience, as well as the type of activity in which the child is engaged.

Answer to Question 25

(C) Penny will recover against Olson for her injuries because Olson owed her a nondelegable duty to provide a safe vehicle in which to ride. The general rule is that a principal will not be liable for tortious acts of his agent if the latter is an independent contractor. However, a major exception to this rule applies when the duty, because of public policy considerations, is nondelegable. In these cases, the principal is vicariously liable for the agent's negligence despite the principal's own exercise of due care. Common examples of these types of duties are the duty of the owner of a vehicle to keep it in safe working order and the duty of a business to keep its premises and instrumentalities safe for its customers. The case here involves both of these duties. Thus, Olson's duty to Penny, a passenger in his cab, was nondelegable. The negligent conduct of the Goodstone mechanic is deemed to be that of Olson. The negligent conduct was the actual and proximate cause of Penny's injuries. Thus, Olson is vicariously liable to Penny for those injuries. (A) and (B) are wrong because Penny will prevail regardless of how careful Olson was in selecting Goodstone to maintain his cabs. As a common carrier, Olson owes his passenger, Penny, a very high degree of care; *i.e.*, he will be liable for slight negligence. However, because his duty to provide a safe taxicab is not delegable, the fact that he was careful in selecting the mechanic is irrelevant. Even though Olson had no reason to know that a Goodstone mechanic would be negligent, he is vicariously liable for that negligence because it caused injury to Penny. (D) is wrong because, as stated above, the situation here falls within an exception to the general rule of no liability for the torts of an independent contractor.

Answer to Question 26

(C) The determining factor for Gretel prevailing will be whether her use of the property is abnormally sensitive to the presence of the dogs. Nuisance is an invasion of private property rights by conduct that is either intentional, negligent, or subject to strict liability. Strict liability will be the basis for a nuisance action (sometimes called an "absolute" nuisance or a "nuisance per se") when wild animals or abnormally dangerous domestic animals are involved, or when defendant is engaged in an abnormally dangerous activity. Thus, dogs known by their owner to be vicious may create a private nuisance when they interfere with the use and enjoyment of the land next door, and the owner may be subject to strict liability because of his knowledge of the dogs' dangerous propensities. [*See* Restatement (Second) of Torts §822, comment j] For the presence of the dogs to be an actionable nuisance, however, they must result in a **substantial** interference with Gretel's use of her land. The interference will not be characterized as substantial if it is merely the result of plaintiff's specialized use of her own property. [*See* Foster v. Preston Mill Co., 268 P.2d 645 (1954)—D not strictly liable for blasting operations that caused female mink on P's ranch to kill their young in reaction to the vibrations] Hence, choice (C) states the most critical factual issue. (A) is incorrect because Gretel does not need to establish other types of damages to recover once she has established that Dobbins's activity is an actionable interference with the use and enjoyment of her land. (B) is incorrect because the exercise of reasonable care by Dobbins is irrelevant; Gretel's nuisance action arises from an activity for which Dobbins is strictly liable. (D) is incorrect because Dobbins's knowledge of his interference with Gretel's use of her property would only establish that his conduct might also be an intentional nuisance, which would require Gretel to show unreasonableness, *i.e.,* that her injury outweighs the utility of his conduct. She does not need to make that showing for a nuisance action based on strict liability.

Answer to Question 27

(B) Deneuve acted with scienter for purposes of an intentional misrepresentation action if she was aware that she did not know whether the state was planning an interchange. To establish a prima facie case of intentional misrepresentation or fraud, plaintiff must prove (i) misrepresentation by defendant, (ii) scienter, (iii) intent to induce plaintiff's reliance on the misrepresentation, (iv) causation (actual reliance on the misrepresentation), (v) justifiable reliance on the misrepresentation, and (vi) damages. The element of scienter, which involves defendant's state of mind, requires plaintiff to show that defendant made the statement knowing it to be false or made it with reckless disregard as to its truth or falsity. If Deneuve made her statement even though she was aware that she did not know whether the state was planning an interchange, she acted with scienter. The other elements of intentional misrepresentation are established by the facts. Thus, Picard has a cause of action against Deneuve under the condition stated in choice (B). (A) is wrong because an action for negligent misrepresentation is not supported by these facts. Negligent misrepresentation requires (i) a misrepresentation made by defendant in a business or professional capacity, (ii) breach of duty toward that particular plaintiff, (iii) causation, (iv) justifiable reliance, and (v) damages. Here, even though Picard was involved in a business transaction, Deneuve was not. She was not acting in a business capacity but rather for her own personal interests. Hence, she is not liable for negligent misrepresentation. (C) is incorrect because Deneuve's statement was a false representation of an existing fact—that an interchange was currently being planned. If Deneuve had instead assured Picard that the interchange would be built, Picard could not justifiably rely on the statement because it is a statement of a future event over which Deneuve did not have control. The statement here is actionable because an interchange was not even being planned. (D) is incorrect. The fact that Deneuve made the statement to Picard gratuitously rather than in a commercial transaction absolves her from liability for negligent misrepresentation, but it has no relevance to her liability for intentional misrepresentation.

Answer to Question 28

(A) Ichabod will not recover damages from Brom because Ichabod's express assumption of risk is a complete defense. A plaintiff in a negligence action may be denied recovery if he assumed the risk of any damage caused by defendant's acts. The risk may be assumed by express agreement. Exculpatory language in a consensual agreement between the parties that is intended to insulate one of the parties from liability resulting from his own negligence is closely scrutinized but generally enforceable as long as it is not an adhesion contract situation (*i.e.*, a situation where one party essentially had no choice but to accept the terms set by the other party). Here, the risks were clearly stated on the signs and on the ticket, and Ichabod was aware of them when he purchased the ticket. Because an entertainment rather than a necessity was involved, it was not an adhesion contract—Ichabod was free to decline to enter the haunted house. Even in comparative negligence jurisdictions, express assumption of risk is a complete defense. Thus, Ichabod will not recover damages from Brom. (B) is incorrect because any negligence on Brom's part in trying to scare Ichabod is one of the risks that Ichabod would be deemed to have assumed by purchasing the ticket and entering the haunted house. The disclaimer warned that the "monsters" would be trying to scare people who entered. A failure to predict what a person's reaction would be when scared, even if it amounted to negligence, was the type of risk that was expressly assumed by participants. (C) is incorrect because Brom's intent to cause apprehension does not make his conduct an assault or any other tort. An assault requires an intent to bring about in plaintiff apprehension of immediate harmful or offensive contact to plaintiff's person. Here, the conduct in which Brom engaged was impliedly consented to by Ichabod when he entered the haunted house. His attempt to scare Ichabod did not clearly go beyond the bounds of the implied consent inherent in that activity. (D) is wrong because most comparative negligence jurisdictions do not treat express assumption of risk like contributory negligence and apportion damages between the parties. As in contributory negligence jurisdictions, express assumption of risk is a complete defense.

Answer to Question 29

(C) Plastico can recover 30% of its damages from Delco under a comparative contribution system. Contribution rules allow any defendant required to pay more than his share of damages under joint and several liability to have a claim against the other jointly liable parties for the excess. In states with a comparative contribution system, the traditional method of equal apportionment of damages is rejected; nonpaying tortfeasors are required to contribute only in proportion to their relative fault. Thus, Plastico should be able to recover 30% of the total damages from Delco because Delco was 30% at fault. (A) is incorrect for several reasons. The fact that Delco may have had a nondelegable duty to occupants of its building would only establish that Delco would be vicariously liable to the plaintiff (Ira) for Plastico's conduct even if Delco were not at fault; that rule does not allow a defendant to recover indemnity from another defendant. Furthermore, if Delco were only vicariously liable here, Delco would have had a right of indemnity against Plastico if Delco had had to pay damages to Ira, but Plastico has no such right against Delco. (B) is incorrect because the fact that Plastico was more at fault would not preclude it from recovering contribution from Delco under a comparative contribution system, which replaces indemnification rules based on identifiable differences in degree of fault. (D) is incorrect because, as discussed above, traditional contribution rules based on equal shares are not applied in a comparative contribution system, which apportions contribution based on relative fault.

Answer to Question 30

(D) Denver will prevail unless she was negligent in positioning her beehive, which would be indicated by her violation of the statute. The appropriate standard of care in a common law negligence case may be established by proving the applicability of a statute providing for criminal penalties. If this is done, the statute's specific duty will replace the more general common law duty of care. To utilize the statutory standard, plaintiff must show (i) that he is within the class protected by the statute, (ii) that the statute was designed to prevent the type of harm that the plaintiff suffered, and (iii) that the standards of the statute are clearly defined. If a state statute prohibited placement of the beehive adjacent to the public road, it would apply in this case because its purpose would be to protect travelers on the public road, such as Perkins, from harm by bees living in the hive. Denver's violation of the statute is "negligence per se" (*i.e.*, it establishes a conclusive presumption of duty and breach of duty). The breach was the actual and proximate cause of the injury to Perkins because but for the position of the hive adjacent to the road Perkins would not have been hurt, and being struck by another vehicle on the road while fleeing the bees was a foreseeable consequence of the bees being released. Thus, if Denver violated a statute in her placement of the beehive adjacent to the public road, Perkins can recover damages from her. (A) is wrong because honeybees are domestic animals for which strict liability does not apply. In contrast to keepers of wild animals, the owner of a domestic animal is not strictly liable for the injuries it causes. Strict liability would only apply if the owner has knowledge of that particular animal's dangerous propensities (*i.e.*, propensities more dangerous than normal for that species). Here, while honeybees as a class can inflict harm by stinging, there is no indication that any of these particular honeybees were more aggressive or dangerous than normal. Hence, Denver would not be strictly liable for the injury to Perkins. (B) is incorrect because another vehicle on the highway striking Perkins was a foreseeable intervening force that did not break the causal connection between the release of the bees and Perkins's injury. If strict liability were applicable here, the duty owed would be limited to the "normally dangerous propensity" of the animal involved, but fleeing from the perceived danger is part of the risk that the dangerous propensity creates. Similarly, if Denver did violate a statute, the fact that the bees did not reach Perkins would not cut off Denver's liability to Perkins. (C) is incorrect because the fact that Perkins is a traveler on a public road establishes only that Denver, as the adjacent landowner, owes a duty of ordinary care as to dangerous conditions and active operations on her property. Here, in the absence of the statute in choice (D), the facts do not establish that Denver acted unreasonably in the placement of her beehives.

Answer to Question 31

(C) Rensler's estate may be liable against Carlyle if Rensler acted negligently when he came to Carlyle's aid. As a general rule, no legal duty is imposed upon any person to affirmatively act for the benefit of others. However, one who gratuitously acts for the benefit of another, although under no duty to do so in the first instance, is then under a duty to act like a reasonable person. Here, Rensler was under no duty to come to Carlyle's assistance. Having done so, however, he was under a duty to use reasonable care in attempting to start Carlyle's boat. If he acted negligently in doing so, he was in breach of his duty to Carlyle and Carlyle would have a cause of action against his estate. To prevail, Carlyle would also have to establish that the spark that occurred while Rensler was negligently starting the boat would not have occurred but for Rensler's negligence, and that Carlyle himself was not at fault. In any case, Carlyle has a cause of action stemming from Rensler's negligent conduct. Thus, (C) is correct and (A) is incorrect. (B) is incorrect. At common law, a tort action abated at the death of either the tortfeasor or the victim. However, most states have adopted survival statutes that change this result. Thus, the fact that the potential tortfeasor died would not preclude Carlyle from bringing an action against the tortfeasor's estate. (D) is incorrect because Carlyle would have a cause of action even for Rensler's *ordinary negligence*. Many states have "Good Samaritan" statutes that exempt those who gratuitously render emergency assistance from liability for other than gross negligence, but most of these statutes apply only to health care providers rendering emergency medical assistance. Therefore, Carlyle could recover even if Rensler's negligence was not gross negligence.

Answer to Question 32

(B) Rensler's estate can recover from Aquapower on a strict products liability ground because Rensler was a foreseeable bystander and Aquapower is a commercial supplier. Recovery in a wrongful death action is allowed only to the extent that the deceased could have recovered in a personal injury action had he lived. Rensler could have recovered from Aquapower in a products liability action based on strict liability because Aquapower is a commercial supplier of the boat and owes a duty not to sell a product that is so defective as to be unreasonably dangerous. The defect in the assembly of the gas tank was unreasonably dangerous because it allowed gas to leak out and collect where it could be ignited. The duty was owed to Rensler, despite the fact that he was not in privity with Aquacorp, because he was a foreseeable plaintiff. The disabling effect of the gas leak made it foreseeable that someone passing by would come to Carlyle's assistance and thereby come within the zone of danger from the leak (*i.e.*, danger invites rescue). The explosion that resulted from the leak was the actual and proximate cause of Rensler's death. Finally, nothing in the facts indicates that Rensler knew of a risk of explosion from the gas and proceeded negligently in the face of that risk. Therefore, Rensler's estate can recover damages from Aquapower. (A) is incorrect because, as with proximate cause analysis in ordinary negligence actions, the negligence of a subsequent actor is foreseeable and therefore not a superseding cause that would cut off the liability of the original tortfeasor. In any products liability case, the negligent failure of an intermediary to discover the defect or the danger does not void the commercial supplier's strict liability. Hence, Carlyle's negligence would be irrelevant. (C) is wrong because in products liability actions based on strict liability, the retailer may be liable even if it had no reason to anticipate that the product was dangerous or had no opportunity to inspect the product for defects. While Aquapower could assert that defense if the action were based on negligence, the call of the question indicates that the action is based on a strict liability theory. Under strict liability, Aquapower is liable simply because it is a commercial supplier of a product with a dangerous defect. (D) is wrong because the fact that Rensler was not in privity with Aquapower is irrelevant in a products liability action based on strict liability. The strict duty is owed not only to buyers, but also to the buyer's family, friends, and employees, and to foreseeable bystanders. As a rescuer, Rensler was a foreseeable bystander to whom Aquapower owed a duty.

Answer to Question 33

(B) Preston cannot recover from Deep Springs Resort because he did not have invitee status when he was injured. In most jurisdictions, the nature of a duty of an owner or occupier of land to those on the premises depends on the legal status of the plaintiff in regard to the property, *i.e.*, whether the plaintiff is a trespasser, licensee, or invitee. An invitee is a person who enters onto the premises in response to an express or implied invitation of the landowner. Those who enter as members of the public for a purpose for which the land is held open to the public and those who enter for a purpose connected with the business or other interests of the landowner are considered invitees. However, a person will lose his status as an invitee if he exceeds the scope of the invitation—if he goes onto a portion of the property where his invitation cannot reasonably be said to extend. Here, Preston was an invitee of Deep Springs Resort in the areas to which it allowed its patrons to go. However, the resort clearly identified the boundaries of the area held open to swimmers, and Preston could not reasonably have believed that he was invited to swim in the area where he was injured. Because Preston was at most a licensee when he was injured, the resort did not owe him a duty to make reasonable inspections of that area to discover dangerous conditions and make them safe. At most, the resort had a duty only to warn Preston of known dangerous conditions that create an unreasonable risk of harm to him and that he is unlikely to discover, and nothing in the facts indicates that any employees of the resort knew of the stake under the water. Preston therefore cannot recover against Deep Springs. (A) is incorrect. If Preston were an invitee when he was injured, the fact that the stake had been in the water for a long time could establish that the resort did not make a reasonable inspection to discover hidden dangers. However, Preston was at most a licensee when he was injured, and the length of time that the stake was in the water does not establish that anyone from the resort knew of it. (C) is incorrect because the lifeguard's failure to direct Preston to the swimming area would not constitute an invitation to swim in the restricted area; at most, it would establish only that Preston was a licensee rather than a trespasser when he swam in that area. A licensee is one who enters on land with the possessor's permission, express or implied, for his own purpose or business rather than for the possessor's benefit. The lifeguard's conduct may have constituted implied permission for Preston to exit the lake in a nonswimming area for his own benefit, but it does not establish that he reasonably believed that he was invited to swim in that area. (D) is incorrect because Preston lost his status as an invitee when he exceeded the scope of his invitation by swimming in an area where swimming was not permitted.

Answer to Question 34

(D) Banks will not recover against Arnold because, as a state legislator, Arnold was absolutely privileged to read the story into the record on the floor of the legislature. Under certain circumstances, a speaker will not be liable for defamatory statements because she is afforded an absolute privilege. Such a privilege is *not* affected by a showing of malice, abuse, or excessive provocation. Remarks made by either federal or state legislators in their official capacity in hearings or floor debates are absolutely privileged. There is no requirement of a reasonable relationship to any matter at hand. Arnold is a state legislator. When Arnold read the newspaper article into the legislative record, she was speaking in her official capacity as a legislator, on the floor of the legislature. Thus, Arnold's reading of the article is cloaked with absolute privilege, and she will be shielded from liability for defamation. (A) is incorrect because, even if Banks establishes actual malice by Arnold, he will not recover. Banks, as a candidate for public office, is a public figure, and information about his health is probably a matter of public concern. Thus, to recover, Banks must show actual malice (knowledge of falsity or reckless disregard for truth or falsity). However, this showing of malice still will not provide Banks a recovery because Arnold has an *absolute* privilege. If Arnold had only a qualified privilege, a showing of malice would defeat the privilege. (B) is incorrect for two reasons: (i) Even if Arnold did not rely on the newspaper article, her reading it in the legislature is protected by her absolute privilege. (ii) If Arnold were not protected by the absolute privilege, the mere fact that she relied on the article would not afford her a defense. A republisher (one who repeats a defamatory statement) is liable on the same general basis as a primary publisher. (C) is incorrect because slander per se will not provide Banks a recovery. Slander per se is a characterization applied to certain categories of spoken defamation. If defamation falls within one of these categories, injury to reputation is presumed without proof of special damages. One such category is a defamatory statement that adversely reflects on the plaintiff's abilities in his business, trade, or profession. Although statements to the effect that Banks suffered from severe psychological problems might adversely reflect on his fitness for public office, this would be significant only in terms of establishing that Banks need not prove special damages. However, proof of damages is of no importance here, because of the fact that Arnold is not liable due to her absolute privilege. If Arnold is shielded from liability, the possible existence of slander per se is of no use to Banks. Note also that, in any event, any defamation here would be characterized as libel, rather than slander. Libel is a defamatory statement recorded in writing or some other permanent form. Where the original defamation is libel, any repetition, even if oral, is also libel. Here, the original defamation was in a newspaper article and thus was libel. Consequently, Arnold's oral repetition of the article would also be libel, if Arnold was subject to defamation liability.

Answer to Question 35

(C) Doberman will not recover because there has been no substantial interference with her use or enjoyment of her land, nor has there been a trespass. A private nuisance is a substantial, unreasonable interference with another person's use or enjoyment of her property. The interference must be offensive, inconvenient, or annoying *to the average person in the community*. It is not a substantial interference if it merely interferes with a specialized use of the land. Here, the testing of the dog whistles did not bother humans, and so it did not disturb the average person in the community. It is disturbing to Doberman's dogs, but this affects only her specialized use of her land for dog breeding. Thus, Dogalert's actions do not constitute a private nuisance. (Nor do they constitute a public nuisance—an act that unreasonably interferes with the health, safety, or property rights of the community.) Therefore, (C) is correct, and (B) is incorrect. (A) is incorrect because the sounds reaching Doberman's property do not constitute a trespass. A trespass is an intentional *physical invasion* of another's land. Sound waves do not produce a physical invasion. Thus, the facts here do not support a basis for trespass. (D) is incorrect because Dogalert could be found liable to Doberman even if it acted reasonably. In determining whether there is a nuisance, a court would consider Dogalert's care in testing its whistles, but that factor alone would not be determinative. If the activities were offensive to the average person, the court might still find there is a nuisance—even if it is impossible to do a better job of soundproofing. The court would have to consider the "reasonableness" of the interference, *i.e.,* balance the injury against the utility of Dogalert's conduct.

Answer to Question 36

(B) Gremlin will prevail because Dooley's conduct constituted a superseding intervening force that relieves Gremlin from liability. To establish a prima facie case for negligence, Paulette must show that Gremlin's breach of his duty to her was the actual and proximate cause of her injury. Paulette can establish actual cause because but for Gremlin's error, she would not have been injured. However, not all injuries "actually" caused by a defendant will be deemed to have been proximately caused by his acts. The general rule of proximate cause is that the defendant is liable for all harmful results that are the normal incidents of and within the increased risk caused by his acts. This rule applies to cases such as this where an intervening force comes into motion after the defendant's negligent act and combines with it to cause plaintiff's injury (indirect cause cases). Here, Gremlin's navigational error did create a greater risk of collision with other planes in the process of landing, but it did not increase the risk of a plane using the landing runway to take off in disregard of the control tower's instructions once Gremlin was safely on the ground. Hence, Dooley's unforeseeable conduct was not within the increased risk created by Gremlin's negligence and constitutes a **superseding force** that breaks the causal connection between Gremlin's conduct and Paulette's injury, enabling Gremlin to avoid liability to Paulette. (A) is incorrect because assumption of the risk requires knowledge of the specific risk and the voluntary assumption of that risk. Although Paulette knew that Gremlin lacked a commercial license, she also was under the impression that he was a very good pilot. There is no indication that she knew of or voluntarily assumed any risk. Certainly, she did not assume the risk of the type of harm she suffered. (C) is incorrect because even though Gremlin may be negligent per se, he would not be liable per se. A specific duty imposed by a statute may replace the more general common law duty of due care when: (i) the plaintiff is within the class to be protected by the statute; (ii) the statute was designed to prevent the type of harm suffered; and (iii) the statutory standard of conduct is clearly defined. The statutory duty arguably applies here because Paulette, as Gremlin's paying passenger, is within the protected class, runway collisions and other pilot errors are what the license requirement is officially designed to prevent, and the statutory standard of conduct is clear. There are no grounds for excusing Gremlin's violation of the statute, so Gremlin's conduct could be seen as "negligence per se." This means that plaintiff will have established a conclusive presumption of **duty and breach of duty**. However, for Paulette to prevail, she must also establish actual and proximate causation. As explained above, Paulette will not be able to show that Gremlin's negligence was the proximate cause of her injuries. Thus, while she may be able to establish "negligence per se," she has not made a case for "liability per se." (D) is true as far as it goes. An act or omission to act is the cause in fact of an injury when the injury would not have occurred but for the act, and this injury would not have occurred but for Gremlin's landing at the wrong airport. However, Paulette must also be able to establish that Gremlin's conduct was a proximate cause of her injury. As noted above, Gremlin's conduct was not a proximate cause of her injury because Dooley's actions acted as a superseding intervening force.

Answer to Question 37

(B) Citizen's best argument is that negligence is presumed from the fact that Dack escaped. This choice raises the doctrine of res ipsa loquitur, which allows the trier of fact to infer negligence simply from the fact that a particular injury occurred. Res ipsa loquitur requires the plaintiff to establish that: the event causing the injury is of a type that would not normally occur unless someone was negligent; the negligence was attributable to the defendant; and plaintiff was not at fault regarding his injury. Here, the event causing injury is due to Dack's escape, and it seems that Dack would not have escaped unless someone was negligent (*e.g.,* Walder in not locking the door or the hospital in not making sure that Walder knew of his responsibility to lock the door). The fact that the hospital had sole control over Dack can be used to show that the negligence is attributable to the hospital (through its employees). Finally, Citizen was not at fault regarding his injury. Thus, res ipsa could be used to find negligence and allow Citizen to recover. (A) is wrong because the hospital is not strictly liable. Strict liability occurs only where there is an absolute duty on the defendant's part to make safe (*e.g.,* in ultrahazardous activity situations). Hospitals do not have an ***absolute*** duty to protect against dangerous acts of their patients. (C) is wrong because there is no basis for holding the hospital vicariously liable. A person or entity can be vicariously liable for the acts of others only if there is a relationship between them that gives rise to such liability (*e.g.,* master-servant). There is generally no such basis for holding a hospital liable for its patients' actions, nor is there any specific reason to do so here. (D) is wrong because it is not clear that Walder acted negligently even if he did fail to lock the door. Walder was under a duty to act reasonably under the circumstances. If he was unaware of the duty to lock the door, he was not negligent in failing to do so. Arguably Walder was negligent in not reading the entire manual, but if the hospital had not told him that it was important for him to read it immediately, he would not be negligent in not finishing the manual.

Answer to Question 38

(C) If Gabb honestly believed he was printing the truth, Priscilla will not prevail in a defamation action because Gabb's statement was not made with reckless disregard as to its truth or falsity. In order to establish a prima facie case for defamation of a public official or public figure, the following six elements must be proved: (i) defamatory language on the part of the defendant; (ii) the defamatory language must be "of or concerning" the plaintiff (*i.e.,* it must identify the plaintiff to a reasonable reader, listener, or viewer); (iii) publication of the defamatory language by the defendant to a third person; (iv) damage to the reputation of the plaintiff; (v) falsity of the defamatory language; and (vi) fault on defendant's part. Although Priscilla had resigned from some of her "public figure" positions, she still retains her status as a public official because of her position on the school board. Since Gabb's statement was in fact false, the issue under these facts is whether Gabb's statement was made with malice. A public official may not recover for defamatory words in the absence of clear and convincing proof that the statement was made with "malice." Malice was defined by the Supreme Court in *New York Times v. Sullivan* as: (i) knowledge that the statement was false, or (ii) reckless disregard as to its truth or falsity. Priscilla must show that Gabb was subjectively aware that the statement he published was false or that he was subjectively reckless in making the statement. "Reckless" conduct is not measured by a reasonable person standard or by whether a reasonable person would have investigated before publishing. There must be a showing that Gabb in fact (subjectively) entertained serious doubts as to the truthfulness of his publication. If Gabb honestly believed he was printing the truth, then he did not have knowledge of falsity or reckless disregard for truth or falsity. (B) is incorrect because Gabb's reasonable reliance and subjective belief in the accuracy of Roger's information does not suggest a display of reckless disregard for the truth. (A) is incorrect. Special damages in a defamation law context means that the plaintiff must specifically prove that he or she suffered pecuniary loss as a result of the defamatory statement's effect on his or her reputation, and are not proved merely by evidence of actual injury (such as the loss of friends, humiliation, or wounded feelings). While special damages are sometimes required for slander (*i.e.,* spoken defamation), they are not required for a written defamatory statement (libel). (D) is incorrect because reckless disregard (and not negligence) is the standard applied to public official cases.

Answer to Question 39

(B) Jason will be liable for false imprisonment because he deprived Mark of access to the person that the court had determined should be his primary caretaker. This fairly difficult question is testing your knowledge of the issue of awareness in a false imprisonment action. A prima facie case for false imprisonment consists of: (i) an act or omission to act by defendant that confines or restrains plaintiff; (ii) intent on the part of defendant to confine; and (iii) causation. Under the general rule, confinement is not present unless the plaintiff is aware of the confinement at the time. However, most courts recognize an exception to the awareness requirement if the plaintiff is actually injured by the confinement. Here, there is no indication that Mark was aware of any confinement. However, even though Mark enjoyed living on the farm, he has been deprived of his mother's custody and care for two years during a time in which the divorce court had decided that his best interests would be served by having his mother as the primary custodial parent. Even though Mark was not physically harmed, Mary would have little difficulty establishing that Mark's lengthy separation from his mother during his formative years constituted harm to Mark. [*See* Restatement (Second) of Torts, §42, illus. 4] (A) is wrong because it implies that a person with legal custody cannot be liable for false imprisonment. An intentional confinement of a child by his legal custodian could constitute false imprisonment if the other requirements for the tort are met. (C) is wrong because the fact that Mark was not aware of his confinement will not prevent recovery for false imprisonment if he was harmed by the confinement. (D) is wrong because the fact that Mark enjoyed living on the farm does not establish that he was not harmed by the confinement. As discussed above, the deprivation of contact with his mother for two years constituted harm to Mark.

Answer to Question 40

(B) Dingo is not liable for the damages to Princess's flower bed unless he is shown to have been negligent. The owner of a trespassing animal is strictly liable for damages done by the animal if it is foreseeable that the animal will trespass and cause that damage. Thus, if the animal involved is of a type likely to roam and do damage to another's property (*e.g.,* livestock such as cows or sheep), the owner is strictly liable. Here, it is not foreseeable that Dingo's dog would damage Princess's flower bed because the dog had been graduated from an obedience class, and therefore it was not foreseeable that Growler would disregard his training and run off for no apparent reason. Also, it was not foreseeable that the dog would do this type of damage. Generally, run-away dogs do not immediately head for the nearest flower bed and start digging. Thus, since Growler's actions and the type of damages caused by him are unforeseeable, Dingo is not strictly liable; any recovery for the damages must be based on a showing of fault (intentional tort or negligence) on the part of Dingo. Dingo did not act with the goal of having Growler destroy the flower bed, nor did he know with substantial certainty that this would happen. Therefore, Dingo did not commit an intentional tort; consequently, Dingo can be liable for the damage only if he was negligent in training or supervising the dog. (A) is wrong even though it is true that Dingo did not intend that Growler run into the flower bed. (A) ignores the possibility that Dingo might be liable for negligence. (C) is wrong because to impose liability on Dingo simply because he owned the dog would amount to strict liability, and as explained above, Dingo cannot be strictly liable here since it was not foreseeable that Growler would escape and do this type of damage. (D) is wrong. Dingo could not be liable for trespass because he lacked the intent for that tort. Trespass requires an intent to make an entry onto that particular parcel of land. Here, Dingo did not intend for Growler to go onto Princess's land, nor did he know with substantial certainty that that would happen. Thus, Dingo has not committed a trespass.

Answer to Question 41

(C) Phil can recover $2 million from Dan because Dan is jointly and severally liable for the injury. The doctrine of joint and several liability provides that when two or more tortious acts combine to proximately cause an indivisible injury to plaintiff, each tortfeasor will be jointly and severally liable for that injury. This means that plaintiff can recover the entire amount of his damages from any one defendant. The doctrine applies even though each tortfeasor acted entirely independently and at different times. Here, both Dan and the employee of the ski resort breached their duty to

Phil to act with reasonable care. Each tortfeasor's act was the actual cause of Phil's disability because but for either one of the acts, his leg would not have been permanently disabled. Dan's act was the proximate cause of Phil's disability because the disability was the direct result of Dan's act. The fact that the extent of the harm was unforeseeable is irrelevant; *i.e.,* the tortfeasor takes the victim as he finds him. Thus, Phil can recover the entire $2 million from Dan. (A) is incorrect because the contribution rules govern only whether a defendant required to pay more than his share of damages has a claim against the other jointly liable parties for the excess. Contribution does not involve the amount of damages that the plaintiff can collect in the first place. (B) is incorrect because Phil has met his burden of proof by establishing that Dan was an actual and proximate cause of his permanent disability. Since the injury caused by the tortfeasors was not divisible, under joint and several liability rules, Dan is liable for the full amount of the damages, including that attributable to the permanent disability. (D) is wrong because but for Dan's collision with Phil, Phil would not have been disabled. The "but for" test applies in concurrent cause situations—cases where several acts combine to cause the injury, but none of them standing alone would have been sufficient. The fact that Dan's act standing alone would not have caused the disability is irrelevant to Dan's liability.

Answer to Question 42

(A) None of the parties receive anything because Kenbraska is a contributory negligence jurisdiction. Under the traditional defense of contributory negligence, any negligence on the part of the plaintiff barred his recovery regardless of the fault of the defendant. Here, all of the parties were negligent and therefore cannot recover against any of the other parties in a state that retains the common law rules. Thus, (C) and (D) are wrong regardless of what contribution rule the jurisdiction follows. (B) is wrong because last clear chance applies only where defendant could have avoided the accident after the occurrence of plaintiff's negligence. Here, Bacon's negligence in not fixing his brakes, which prevented him from stopping in time, occurred before Aiken's negligence.

Answer to Question 43

(C) All of the parties would have a claim for a percentage of their damages, measured by their degree of fault. In a partial comparative negligence jurisdiction, a plaintiff can recover damages as long as her negligence was less serious than, or no more serious than, that of the defendant. When multiple defendants have contributed to plaintiff's injury, most of these jurisdictions use a "combined comparison" approach to determine the threshold level, whereby plaintiff's negligence is compared with the total negligence of all of the defendants combined. Here, each of the parties' negligence is less than the combined negligence of the other two parties. Hence, each of them will have a viable claim for damages, reduced by the percentage of their fault, as reflected in choice (C). (A) and (B) are wrong because they do not reflect the "combined comparison" approach, and (D) is wrong because it does not reflect the reduction in their damage claims due to their percentage of fault.

Answer to Question 44

(B) Aiken can recover $45,000 through comparative contribution for Cogg's claim and $4,500 on his own claim against Bacon. Most comparative negligence states have adopted a comparative contribution system based on the relative fault of the various tortfeasors. Nonpaying tortfeasors who are jointly and severally liable are required to contribute only in proportion to their relative fault. Here, because the jurisdiction retained joint and several liability, Aiken had to pay Cogg all of her damages. Under comparative contribution rules, Aiken can obtain contribution from Bacon for 45% of that amount, because Bacon was 45% at fault. In addition, Aiken has a direct claim against Bacon for his own damages of $10,000, reduced by 55%, the amount of his fault. Thus, the total amount that Aiken can recover from Bacon is $49,500, making (B) correct and (A) incorrect. (C) is incorrect because it reflects traditional contribution rules, in which all tortfeasors were required to pay equal shares regardless of their respective degrees of fault. (D) is wrong because a tortfeasor who was jointly and severally liable is not precluded from recovering contribution merely because he was more at fault than the other tortfeasors.

Answer to Question 45

(B) The court should grant Dell's motion for judgment as a matter of law because Prell has not established a prima facie case against Dell. An owner of wild (dangerous) animals is strictly liable for injuries caused by those animals as long as the person injured did nothing, voluntarily or consciously, to bring about the injury. However, strict liability generally is not imposed in favor of undiscovered trespassers against landowners in the absence of negligence, such as when the landowner knows that the trespassers are on the land and fails to warn them of the animal. Here, despite the fact that Prell did not intend to enter Dell's land (and thus would not be liable for the intentional tort of trespass), his status on Dell's land is that of a trespasser rather than a licensee or invitee. Prell has presented no evidence of negligence on Dell's part and therefore has not established a prima facie case against Dell. (A) is wrong because, as discussed above, Dell is not strictly liable to Prell because Prell was a trespasser. (C) is incorrect because Prell will not prevail regardless of whether he was contributorily negligent, because he cannot establish a prima facie case against Dell in either negligence or strict liability. (D) is incorrect for several reasons. While Prell's transport of radioactive waste may have been an abnormally dangerous activity, that danger had nothing to do with the accident that occurred. Further, the fact that Prell may have been engaged in an abnormally dangerous activity would not prevent him from recovering damages from another tortfeasor if he established the requisite prima facie case. Finally, the fact that the parties were engaged in activities potentially creating strict liability has nothing to do with whether issues of fact regarding liability still exist that would require denying both motions and going to trial.

Answer to Question 46

(B) If Pat was effectively required by statute to take an occasional quick look at his speedometer to make sure that he was complying with appropriate speed limits, then his momentary glance at the speedometer in the instant case would, as a matter of law, not constitute negligent conduct. Because this is a matter of law, the judge would be authorized to correct this aspect of the jury's verdict. If Pat is thus found to be not negligent in this matter, his recovery will not be reduced. (A) is incorrect because in most states that have adopted comparative negligence, the plaintiff's negligence will be considered even in cases where the defendant has acted willfully and wantonly. (C) is incorrect because the fact that the defendant is more than 50% at fault does not mean that the plaintiff is entitled to receive 100% of his damages from the defendant in a partial comparative negligence jurisdiction. It only means that the plaintiff's recovery is not totally defeated. (D) is incorrect because, although the transportation of chemical waste would probably be considered an ultrahazardous activity, liability for conducting an ultrahazardous activity attaches only if the harm results from the kind of danger to be anticipated from such activity, *i.e.*, the injury must flow from the normally dangerous propensity of the activity. The canister falling from the truck is not the "normally dangerous propensity" of transporting chemical waste.

Answer to Question 47

(D) The court should grant the motion because Parnell did not establish the cause-in-fact element of his prima facie case against Eastern Pacific. The primary test for cause in fact (actual cause) is the "but for" test: an act is the cause in fact of an injury when the injury would not have occurred ***but for*** the act. Even though Eastern Pacific had a duty created by the statute to be able to stop the train within 200 yards of first braking, and breached that duty (establishing the first two elements of Parnell's prima facie case), it must still be shown that the collision would not have occurred in the absence of the breach. Since the car was only 150 yards from the point of braking, even a train in compliance with the statute would have struck it. Since no other evidence of negligence has been presented, the motion should be granted. (A) is incorrect because establishing Eastern Pacific's "negligence per se" through violation of the statute only establishes a conclusive presumption of duty and breach of duty; plaintiff must still prove causation. (B) is incorrect because generally violation of a statute does not create strict liability; even if it did in this case, plaintiff would still have to prove causation as part of the prima facie case for strict liability. (C) is not correct because the court will not reach the issue of plaintiff's contributory negligence in this case because the prima facie case for defendant's negligence has not been established. Furthermore, establishing plaintiff's contributory negligence by violation of a statute uses the same rules that govern whether a statute can establish defendant's negligence. Hence, Parnell's violation of the crossing statute may be excused if the trier of fact determines that compliance was beyond his control because his car stalled.

Answer to Question 48

(B) Phil cannot recover damages in a misrepresentation action against Donna because he has suffered no pecuniary loss as a result of reliance on the false statement. An action for intentional misrepresentation requires plaintiff to show (i) a misrepresentation by defendant, (ii) scienter, (iii) an intent to induce plaintiff's reliance on the misrepresentation, (iv) causation (*i.e.*, actual reliance on the misrepresentation), (v) justifiable reliance by plaintiff on the misrepresentation, and (vi) damages. The damages element permits plaintiff to recover only if he has suffered actual pecuniary loss as a result of reliance on the false statement. Here, Phil received a fair price for the powder horn and would not have obtained a higher amount had he sold it to someone else. His distress over selling it to her because of her false statement does not satisfy the damages requirement for intentional misrepresentation. (A) is incorrect not only because Phil suffered no actionable damages but also because Donna need not ***know*** that her statements were false. The element of scienter also encompasses statements that were made with reckless disregard as to their truth or falsity. (C) is wrong even though it correctly states the causation element of intentional misrepresentation. Without the element of pecuniary harm, the prima facie case is not complete. (D) is wrong because statements of law are viewed as statements of opinion that cannot be justifiably relied upon only if they are merely predictions as to the legal consequences of facts. In contrast, a statement of law that includes an express or implied misrepresentation of fact is actionable. Here, Donna's assertions that she had a power of attorney and the legal right to seize the horn through a replevin action are fact-based assertions that Phil had the right to rely upon.

Answer to Question 49

(B) Hendrik will not recover for his injuries because he was not in the zone of danger created by BanqueZero Corp.'s negligence. The duty to avoid negligent infliction of emotional distress is breached when defendant creates a foreseeable risk of physical injury to plaintiff, either by (i) causing a threat of physical impact that leads to emotional distress or (ii) directly causing severe emotional distress that by itself is likely to result in physical symptoms, and plaintiff suffers some physical injury from distress rather than from physical contact. If plaintiff's distress is caused by threat of physical impact, courts require that plaintiff be within the "target zone" or "zone of danger" of physical harm from defendant's negligent conduct. Hence, a bystander can recover for physical harm caused by emotional distress from witnessing another person injured as long as the bystander was also in the zone of danger. Here, however, Hendrik was not in the zone of danger when the artwork collapsed. Merely witnessing someone else suffer injury from defendant's negligence, even though Hendrik suffered physical injury from his distress, is not sufficient for Hendrik to prevail. (B) is therefore correct and (A) is incorrect. (C) is also incorrect. A growing number of courts have allowed recovery based on foreseeability even if plaintiff is outside the zone of danger as long as (i) plaintiff and the person injured by defendant's negligence are closely related, (ii) plaintiff was present at the scene of the injury, and (iii) plaintiff personally observed or perceived the event. (Observation may be by sight, hearing, or other senses.) The court in this case, however, still imposes the zone of danger requirement in bystander cases. (D) is wrong because the fact that he did not see the accident occur is irrelevant in a "zone of danger" approach. Had he been in the zone of danger, he could have recovered even though he only heard the crash and did not see it (such as if he were looking the other way).

Answer to Question 50

(C) George probably is liable to Leon because his conduct with respect to the vault door created an unreasonable risk of injury to persons, such as Leon, who might enter the vault. The prima facie case for negligence requires that the defendant have a duty to conform to a standard of reasonable care for the protection of the plaintiff. Whether this particular plaintiff (Leon) is owed a duty of care by the defendant (George) depends on whether Leon is a *foreseeable* plaintiff. When George activated the closing circuits and left the control panel unattended, it was reasonably foreseeable that someone, unaware of what was happening, would disengage the stop button, thereby causing the door to close. This created a reasonably foreseeable risk of injury to anyone who might be in the vault at the time the door closed, such as Leon. Leon is therefore a foreseeable plaintiff to whom George owed a duty of care. By creating a risk of injury to Leon, George probably breached his duty of reasonable care, which caused Leon to incur personal injuries. While the question of whether George in fact breached his duty will ultimately be decided by the trier of fact, (C) is the best answer because (A), (B), and (D) are clearly incorrect. (A) is incorrect because, although Leon was not in the vault at the time that George activated the closing circuits, George's conduct created a reasonably foreseeable risk of injury to anyone who might enter the vault while the closing circuits were activated. Because Leon did in fact enter the vault during this time, he was, at the time of injury, located in a foreseeable zone of danger. (B) is incorrect because Maurice's action was a foreseeable intervening force that did not break the causal connection between George's conduct and Leon's injury. This is an indirect cause case, in that a force came into motion (Maurice's actions) after George's negligent conduct and combined with it to cause injury to the plaintiff. In cases where the intervening force is a normal response or reaction to the situation created by defendant's negligent act, it is a dependent intervening force and almost always *foreseeable*. Generally, rescuers are deemed to be foreseeable dependent intervening forces, and the original tortfeasor will be liable for their negligence. Here, Maurice's attempt to help Leon, even if performed negligently, was within the increased risk caused by George's negligent conduct. Thus, George will be liable for the consequences of any negligence on the part of Maurice. (D) is incorrect because Winthrop told Leon to wait in the employees' lounge to make him comfortable, not to protect him from the closing of the vault door. Thus, when Leon left the lounge, he was not disregarding any cautionary instructions or unreasonably creating for himself a foreseeable risk of injury. Consequently, Leon's action is not barred by virtue of his being contributorily negligent, as (D) implies.

Answer to Question 51

(D) Skip will win, because the facts indicate that he was unaware that anyone would be at the house or that the powder would react as it did when exposed to water. Because the call of the question does not identify the theory of liability that Ray is using, you have to consider all possible theories of liability. Skip did not commit an intentional tort against Ray and is not a commercial supplier of a product who would be liable under a strict products liability theory. Nor is he strictly liable for engaging in an ultrahazardous or abnormally dangerous activity, because the activity can be conducted safely if done carefully by professional users. Most likely, this suit is based on negligence. A prima facie case for negligence consists of: (i) a duty on the part of the defendant to conform to a specific standard of conduct for the protection of the plaintiff against an unreasonable risk of injury; (ii) breach of that duty by the defendant; (iii) the breach was the actual and proximate cause of the plaintiff's injury; and (iv) damage to the plaintiff's person or property. When a person engages in an activity, he is under a legal duty to take precautions against creating unreasonable risks of injury to other persons. However, a duty of care is owed only to foreseeable plaintiffs, and no duty is imposed to take precautions against events that cannot reasonably be foreseen. While courts usually conclude that the injured plaintiff in a negligence action was a foreseeable plaintiff, here, Skip was unaware that Ray had a key to Harold's house and might come over at any time. To the best of Skip's knowledge, no one was going to be at the house before he returned the next day because the other contractors were not starting until the next week and Harold was out of town for six weeks. In addition, Skip, who was using the product for the first time, evidently was unaware that the powder was volatile when exposed to water because the manufacturer did not include a warning to that effect. If Skip could not reasonably have foreseen that the powder would explode upon being sprayed with water, he would have had no duty to take precautions against such an explosion. Thus, Skip breached no duty to Ray by leaving the powder on the deck and will not be liable for Ray's injuries. (A) is incorrect because Skip did not know, nor did he have reason to know, of a foreseeable risk of injury to Ray by leaving the powder on the wooden deck. (B) is incorrect because Skip is not a commercial supplier of the powder. The manufacturer, as a commercial supplier of the powder, owes a strict duty to refrain from placing in commerce a product that is so defective as to be unreasonably dangerous. Skip is simply a user of the powder, not a commercial supplier. Thus, Skip is not held to the same standard of liability as the manufacturer; to recover, Ray must prove some fault on the part of Skip in leaving the powder on the deck. (C) is incorrect because using the powder for the purpose for which it was designed would not relieve Skip of liability if he were otherwise at fault. For example, if Skip knew that a person such as Ray might be harmed by leaving the powder on the deck, Skip would be liable for his failure to remove the powder despite the fact that he used the powder for its designed purpose.

Answer to Question 52

(B) Oxxon is strictly liable for Ray's injuries because its failure to warn of the powder's volatility when exposed to water caused the powder to be in a defective, unreasonably dangerous condition. A prima facie case for products liability based on strict tort liability consists of: (i) a strict duty owed by a commercial supplier; (ii) breach of that duty; (iii) actual and proximate cause; and (iv) damages. Breach is established by proving that the defendant placed in commerce a product that is so defective as to be unreasonably dangerous. A product may be defective if a less dangerous alternative or modification was economically feasible. Among factors to be considered are the obviousness of the danger and the avoidability of injury by care in the use of the product (including the role of instructions and warnings). Because the powder would explode upon contact with water, the powder was dangerous beyond the expectation of the ordinary person. Even though some professional users may have known of the danger, it was not obvious, and it could have been avoided at minimal cost by including a warning as to the danger. To prove actual cause where plaintiff's claim is that the product is defective because of lack of an adequate warning, plaintiff is entitled to a presumption that an adequate warning would have been read and heeded. Had there been such a warning, Ray could probably show that the danger to him would have been eliminated because Skip would have cleaned up the powder (if for no other reason than to reduce the risk of fire from a rain shower). Thus, Oxxon, a commercial supplier of the powder, breached its strict duty by manufacturing a product with hidden dangerous qualities and failing to include a proper warning as to the danger. The failure to include a warning most likely was an actual and proximate cause of Skip's failure to promptly remove the powder from the wooden deck, which in turn resulted in Ray's spraying the powder with water, igniting the powder and causing injury to Ray. Thus, Ray will recover against Oxxon based on strict liability. (C) is incorrect because, despite no previous injuries as a result of exposure of the powder to water, Oxxon did know of the danger. The absence of previous injuries merely indicates that the likelihood of injury was not that high, but it still outweighs the minimal cost of adding warnings. Thus, the product was defective because a less dangerous modification (adding a warning) was economically feasible. (A) is incorrect because Oxxon cannot be liable solely because its product, being used as intended, caused injury to Ray. It is Oxxon's failure to warn of the danger that makes its product defective. Had Oxxon included warnings with the powder, users of the powder would be on guard against exposing it to water. This would remove the unreasonably dangerous character of the powder and would allow Oxxon to avoid liability under a strict liability theory. (D) is incorrect because Ray had no way of knowing the danger involved in hosing the powder. Ray acted as a reasonable person would have and therefore was not negligent.

Answer to Question 53

(B) Wallace will have to show that he would have recovered damages in his lawsuit. The following elements must be proved for a prima facie case of negligence: (i) the existence of a duty on the part of the defendant to conform to a specific standard of conduct for the protection of the plaintiff against unreasonable risk of injury, (ii) breach of that duty by the defendant, (iii) that the breach of duty was the actual and proximate cause of the plaintiff's injury, and (iv) damage to the plaintiff's person or property. Here, Wallace can establish that the law firm breached its professional duty of care by failing to file a claim within the statute of limitations. He must also establish that this breach was an actual and proximate cause of him suffering damages, which here would be the loss of the contract damages that he could have recovered from the breach by Industrial Farms. (A) is incorrect because merely having a good faith claim that was lost because of the firm's negligence is not sufficient. Wallace has to show by a preponderance of the evidence that he suffered damages because of the firm's negligence. (C) is incorrect because it states a defense rather than part of the prima facie case; any contributory negligence on Wallace's part must be pleaded and proved by the law firm to either defeat or reduce his recovery. (D) is incorrect because it is irrelevant whether the breach by Industrial Farms severely harmed Wallace's financial situation. The only issue is whether he would have been able to recover any of his losses had he timely filed a breach of contract action. If he establishes that he would have recovered, then the law firm's negligence was an actual and proximate cause of his suffering damages.

Answer to Question 54

(A) Rene will recover $30,000. The prima facie case for conversion requires (i) an act by defendant interfering with plaintiff's right of possession in the chattel that is serious enough in nature or consequence to warrant that the defendant pay the full value of the chattel, (ii) intent to perform the act bringing about the interference with plaintiff's right of possession, and (iii) causation. If conversion is established, plaintiff is entitled to the fair market value of the chattel *as of the time and place of conversion.* Here, Leveque refused to return the bike despite a specific request and the use of physical force by Rene; this is deemed to be a conversion because it amounts to a claim of dominion and control by Leveque over Rene's property. At the time of the conversion, the market value of the bike was $30,000. Thus, this amount is what Rene should recover. (B) is wrong because, even assuming that the other contestant would have agreed to the substitution of racers, Rene may not be able to prove that he would have won the match and the $10,000. The more appropriate remedy is the conversion remedy of $30,000. (C) is incorrect because conversion damages based on fair market value are generally measured at the time and place of the conversion, which was when Leveque refused to return the bike, and not at the time of trial. (D) is wrong because it states a measure of damages more appropriate to trespass to chattels, which is a less serious interference with a plaintiff's right of possession in a chattel that requires proof of actual damages. Here, Leveque's refusal to return the bike despite Rene's attempts to get it back constitutes conversion rather than trespass to chattels.

Answer to Question 55

(C) Leveque will recover for battery because Rene did not have the right to use force. The defense of recapture of chattels is limited by the circumstances of the original dispossession. When another's possession of the owner's chattel began lawfully, the owner may use only peaceful means to recover the chattel. Force may be used to recapture a chattel only when in "hot pursuit" of one who has obtained possession wrongfully (*e.g.*, by theft). Here, Leveque's initial possession of the bike was a bailment, because Rene consented to his borrowing it. Thus, Rene is not entitled to use force to recover it, and his elbowing Leveque in the mouth constituted the requisite harmful or offensive contact to make Rene liable for battery. (A) is incorrect. One who is entitled to use force to recapture chattels is only permitted to use reasonable force, but here Rene is not entitled to use any force at all because Leveque's initial possession of the bike was lawful. (B) is incorrect because it is not relevant whether Leveque's delay in returning the bike was unreasonable; Rene is not entitled to use force because he lent the bike to Leveque originally. (D) is incorrect because the requirement that a timely demand to return the chattel must precede the use of force applies only if the owner of the chattel is entitled to use force. Here, as discussed above, Rene did not have the right to use force.

Answer to Question 56

(C) Tina will not recover because she was a trespasser on Owner's land. The general rule is that one who possesses an animal not customarily domesticated in that area is strictly liable for all harm done by the animal as a result of the harmful or dangerous characteristics of the animal. For trespassers, however, strict liability is not imposed against landowners. Trespassers cannot recover for injuries inflicted by the landowner's wild animals in the absence of negligence, such as where the landowner knows that trespassers are on the land and fails to warn them of the animal. Under this standard, even though Owner could anticipate that trespassers like Tina would cross his property, he will not be liable because he exercised reasonable care by posting a sign warning about the bobcat and by attempting to make the animal less dangerous. (A) is incorrect because, as discussed above, Owner is not strictly liable to Tina, a trespasser. (B) is incorrect because Tina cannot recover regardless of whether she saw the sign. Had strict liability applied, Tina's awareness of the sign may have allowed Owner to raise an assumption of risk defense. With regard to Owner's exercise of reasonable care, however, it does not matter that Tina did not see the sign as long as the sign was noticeable enough that it could have been seen. (D) is wrong because Vet's negligent conduct is the type of foreseeable intervening cause that would not supersede any fault on Owner's part. If Owner were negligent, he could be jointly liable with Vet for Tina's injuries.

Answer to Question 57

(D) Norman will likely prevail. Under the doctrine of res ipsa loquitur, the trier of fact is permitted to infer the defendant's breach of duty when the facts strongly indicate that the plaintiff's injuries resulted from the defendant's negligence. The facts here indicate that, because the elevator was not controllable from the first floor, the elevator would not have descended unless someone from the second floor changed it to "on" and pushed the down button. The fact that someone started the elevator while Sterling was in the shaft is circumstantial evidence that either Norman was negligent (*e.g.,* by failing to apprise his co-workers of Sterling's presence in the shaft) or one of his co-workers was negligent (*e.g.,* by forgetting Norman's warning and turning the elevator back on). Thus, under the doctrine of res ipsa loquitur, Sterling would be able to show that, through respondeat superior, Walker breached a duty owing to him. Thus, (A) is incorrect. (B) is wrong because Sterling's status is irrelevant. A possessor of land owes a duty of reasonable care in the exercise of all active operations on the property, regardless of whether the plaintiff was a licensee or invitee. Thus, regardless of Sterling's status, Walker Printing owed a duty of reasonable care in its employees' operation of the elevator. (C) is wrong because it may have been another employee who was negligent.

Answer to Question 58

(D) Menachem's best defense is that he reasonably feared for his life. When a person has reasonable grounds to believe that he is being, or is about to be, attacked, he may use such force as is reasonably necessary for protection against the potential injury; *i.e.,* reasonable mistake does not negate the defense. He may use force likely to cause death or serious bodily injury if he reasonably believes that he is in danger of serious bodily injury. If Menachem reasonably believed that his life was in danger or that serious bodily harm was likely, he had a right to use even deadly force to protect himself. Thus, (D) is his best defense. (A) is wrong because the fact that Leroy was a trespasser does not give Menachem the right to use deadly force against him. One may not use force likely to cause death or serious bodily harm against a trespasser who is not also threatening bodily harm to the owner. (B) is similarly incorrect; without being threatened with death or serious bodily harm, Menachem is not privileged to use deadly force to protect his property. (C) is wrong because Menachem intended to commit an assault (*i.e.,* create the apprehension of an immediate harmful contact) by threatening to shoot, and the doctrine of transferred intent will transfer this intent from the assault to the battery claim. Thus, he could still be liable for battery even though he had no intent to shoot anyone.

Answer to Question 59

(B) Menachem can recover damages because of their trespass. Under the defense of necessity, a person may interfere with the real or personal property of another when the interference is reasonably and apparently necessary to avoid threatened injury from another force and the threatened injury is substantially more serious than the invasion that is undertaken. However, when the act is done not for the general public good but to protect the actor or another person from injury, the defense is qualified; *i.e.*, the actor must pay for any injury he causes. Here, although Leroy and Beau were privileged to enter Menachem's apartment to prevent their injury or death (private necessity), the privilege does not extend to the infliction of damages. Thus, they must pay for any injury they caused, including Menachem's damages from his heart attack. (A) is wrong because negligent infliction of emotional distress requires that the distress be caused by negligent conduct by the defendant. These facts give no indication that Leroy and Beau acted negligently. (C) is wrong because, as stated above, their privilege is limited. While they cannot be forced off the premises as trespassers, they are liable for the injury they caused. (D) is wrong because it is irrelevant what a reasonable person would have felt. "A tortfeasor takes his victim as he finds him," and if Leroy and Beau's actions caused Menachem's injury, they are liable.

Answer to Question 60

(D) The bank may assert a cause of action based on all of these theories. A prima facie case of negligence requires proof of: (i) the existence of a duty on the part of the defendant to conform to a specific standard of conduct for the protection of the plaintiff against unreasonable risk of injury, (ii) breach of that duty by the defendant, (iii) that the breach of duty was the actual and proximate cause of the plaintiff's injury, and (iv) damage to the plaintiff's person or property. The bank can argue that Howard was negligent in burning the bank's papers to set off the alarm. While the trier of fact may ultimately find that his conduct was reasonable under the circumstances, a prima facie case of negligence can be made by the bank. Trespass to land requires (i) an act of physical invasion of plaintiff's real property by defendant, (ii) intent on the part of defendant to bring about a physical invasion of plaintiff's real property, and (iii) causation. A trespass to land may exist when defendant remains on plaintiff's land after an otherwise lawful right of entry has lapsed. Thus, since Howard intended to stay beyond the bank's normal hours and did so without permission, he has arguably committed a trespass. Conversion consists of (i) an act by defendant interfering with plaintiff's right of possession in the chattel that is serious enough in nature or consequence to warrant that the defendant pay the full value of the chattel, (ii) intent to perform the act bringing about the interference with plaintiff's right of possession, and (iii) causation. Although Howard did not intentionally cause the destruction of the copier and other items of property, he did intend to destroy the bank files that he burned. Thus, as to the files, he is liable for conversion. Thus, (D) is the correct choice, and (A), (B), and (C) are necessarily wrong.

Answer to Question 61

(C) Howard will lose because the guard did not know that he was still in the bank. For false imprisonment, the plaintiff must show (i) an act or omission on the part of the defendant that confines or restrains the plaintiff to a bounded area, (ii) intent on the part of the defendant to confine or restrain the plaintiff, and (iii) causation. Here, if the guard did not know of Howard's presence, there was no intent to confine him. (A) is incorrect because negligence is not enough; while Howard arguably has a cause of action for negligence against the guard, and through respondeat superior, the bank, his counterclaim is for false imprisonment. For liability for false imprisonment, there must be an intent to confine. (B) is incorrect because recklessness will not suffice for false imprisonment. Even if Howard could argue that his severe distress and the guard's recklessness would suffice for intentional infliction of emotional distress, it is doubtful that the guard's conduct in failing to check the bank before he locked up was extreme and outrageous conduct, as required by that tort, and in any case the doctrine of transferred intent does not apply from that tort to the tort of false imprisonment. (D) is incorrect because his status as a trespasser, while it may otherwise make him liable to the bank, does not preclude him from recovering for false imprisonment.

Answer to Question 62

(C) III. and IV. are correct. When two or more tortious acts combine to proximately cause an indivisible injury to a plaintiff, each tortfeasor is jointly and severally liable to the plaintiff for the entire damage incurred. Joint and several liability applies even though each tortfeasor acted entirely independently. However, if the actions are independent, plaintiff's injury is divisible, and it is possible to identify the portion of injuries caused by each defendant, then each will be liable only for the identifiable portion. Here, Baker would not be liable for the injury to the right ankle, because Baker did not cause the injury. Thus, I. is incorrect. With regard to the left leg, Baker was not the only cause of that injury. The original tortfeasor is liable for harm caused by the negligence of third persons when such negligence was a foreseeable risk created by the original tortfeasor's conduct. Here, as a result of Alma's original negligence, Panda was in a position of danger while she was still in the street. The negligence of Baker in striking Panda was a foreseeable risk while Panda was in the street; it is therefore a foreseeable intervening force that will not cut off Alma's liability. Hence, both Alma and Baker will be jointly and severally liable for that injury. Accordingly, III. is correct, and II. is wrong. IV. is correct because the rule of contribution allows any tortfeasor required under joint and several liability principles to pay more than his share of damages to have a claim against the other jointly liable parties for the excess. Thus, Alma will have contribution rights against Baker for damages Alma paid for the injury to the left leg. Consequently, choice (C) is correct, and (A), (B), and (D) are wrong.

Answer to Question 63

(B) Oglethorpe will recover from Clarence for conversion. Conversion consists of (i) an act by defendant interfering with plaintiff's right of possession in the chattel that is serious enough in nature or consequence to warrant that the defendant pay the full value of the chattel, (ii) intent to perform the act bringing about the interference with plaintiff's right of possession, and (iii) causation. Intent to trespass is not required; intent to do the act of interference with the chattel is sufficient for liability. Therefore, Clarence was guilty of conversion when he intentionally (*i.e.*, volitionally) took Oglethorpe's board, which resulted in its loss, even though Clarence did not intend to lose it or even realize that he had taken the property of another. (A) is not the best answer because complete loss of a chattel, permitting the plaintiff to recover its full value, is too serious an interference to be classified a mere trespass. Trespass to chattels consists of (i) an act by defendant that interferes with plaintiff's right of possession in the chattel, (ii) intent to perform the act bringing about the interference with the plaintiff's right of possession, (iii) causation, and (iv) damages. Had Oglethorpe been able to recover the board, and had he been able to show actual damages during the time of dispossession, he might have been able to recover for trespass to chattels. (C) is wrong because Clarence's good faith is irrelevant. Even if the conduct is wholly innocent, liability will attach when the interference with the chattel is serious in nature. (D) is wrong because the fact that Clarence's car was stolen does not relieve Clarence of liability. Clarence's initial trespassory interference with Oglethorpe's backgammon set was a substantial factor in its complete loss, because it would not have otherwise been in the trunk of his car. Thus, the causation element for conversion is satisfied.

Answer to Question 64

(A) Boole will recover from Carla if she acted unreasonably under the circumstances. A prima facie case of negligence requires proof of: (i) the existence of a duty on the part of the defendant to conform to a specific standard of conduct for the protection of the plaintiff against unreasonable risk of injury, (ii) breach of that duty by the defendant, (iii) that the breach of duty was the actual and proximate cause of the plaintiff's injury, and (iv) damage to the plaintiff's person or property. If Carla's selection of the landing site was unreasonable, then she has breached her duty of care to motorists on the highway, including Boole, and was the actual and proximate cause of his injuries. (B) would be correct if this were a products liability action based on strict liability. However, Carla is not a commercial supplier of a product and would not be liable without some evidence of negligence. (C) is incorrect because even if Carla was not negligent in failing to discover the defect in the fuel system, she could have been negligent in selecting the landing site, as (A) states. (D) is also incorrect. In selection of the landing site, Carla is held to the standard of care of a reasonable person in an emergency. If she acted unreasonably in selecting the landing site, she will be liable in negligence.

Answer to Question 65

(C)   Sassoon will win if O'Shaunessy acted willfully and wantonly. Because Sassoon was contributorily negligent in making himself appear to be a deer on opening day of deer hunting season, his recovery depends on the effect of his contributory negligence. Without comparative negligence principles, Sassoon's contributory negligence might bar his recovery unless he can show that O'Shaunessy's conduct was willful and wanton, as to which conduct contributory negligence is no defense. Thus, (C) is the correct pick. (A) is wrong because O'Shaunessy's liability is not dependent on intentional tort theories. He can be liable if he acted willfully or wantonly. (B) is not the best answer because even if O'Shaunessy did not have the last clear chance (the doctrine of last clear chance overcomes contributory negligence), he may still be liable if his actions are characterized as willful and wanton. (D) is wrong because, absent the factors discussed above, O'Shaunessy's negligence would be counterbalanced by Sassoon's contributory negligence.

Answer to Question 66

(A)   Pat will prevail because the cabana extends onto Pat's land. The tort of trespass to land requires an act of physical invasion of the plaintiff's real property by the defendant, intent by the defendant to bring about a physical invasion of the property, and causation. The intent required is the intent to enter on a particular piece of land, rather than intent to trespass. Also, it is not necessary that the defendant personally enter the land. It is sufficient if the defendant's act or something set in motion thereby causes a physical invasion of the property. By having the cabana constructed, Doris acted so as to bring about the physical invasion of Pat's land. (C) is incorrect because it makes no difference that Doris herself did not enter the property that was being violated. For this reason, (C) is incorrect. (D) is incorrect because Doris's intent to have the cabana built on its current site suffices for purposes of trespass liability. As noted above, the defendant need not have intended to commit a trespass. (B) is incorrect because actual injury to the violated property is not a prerequisite to sustain this cause of action. Damage is presumed.